MW00679740

A+ Certification and PC Repair Guide

Second Edition

ISBN 0-13-065203-2

9 790130 652033

90000

A+ Certification and PC Repair Guide

Second Edition

PETE MOULTON

Prentice Hall PTR
Upper Saddle River, NJ 07458
www.phptr.com

Library of Congress Cataloging-in-Publication Data

Moulton, Pete, 1944–
　　　A+ certification and PC repair guide / Pete Moulton.--2nd ed.
　　　　　p. cm.
　　　Includes index.
　　　ISBN 0-13-065203-2
　　　1. Microcomputers--Maintenance and repair--Examinations--Study guides. 2.
　　Computer technicians--Certification--Study guides. I. Title.

　　TK7887 .M68 2002
　　621.39'16'0288--dc21　　　　　　　　　　　　　　　　2001052077

Editorial/Production Supervision: *Vincent Janoski*
Acquisitions Editor: *Mary Franz*
Editorial Assistant: *Noreen Regina*
Marketing Manager: *Dan DePasquale*
Manufacturing Buyer: *Maura Zaldivar*
Cover Design: *Nina Scuderi*
Cover Design Director: *Jerry Votta*

© 2002 by Prentice Hall
Published by Prentice Hall PTR
Prentice-Hall, Inc.
Upper Saddle River, NJ 07458

Prentice Hall books are widely used by corporations and government agencies for training, marketing, and resale. The publisher offers discounts on this book when ordered in bulk quantities. For more information, contact Corporate Sales Department, phone: 800-382-3419; fax: 201-236-7141; email: corpsales@prenhall.com; or write Corporate Sales Department, Prentice Hall PTR, One Lake Street, Upper Saddle River, NJ 07458.

Printed in the United States of America

10　9　8　7　6　5　4　3　2　1

ISBN 0-13-065203-2

Pearson Education Ltd.
Pearson Education Australia PTY Ltd.
Pearson Education Singapore, Pte. Ltd.
Pearson Education North Asia Ltd.
Pearson Education Canada, Ltd.
Pearson Educación de Mexico, S.A. de C.V.
Pearson Education—Japan

CONTENTS

INTRODUCTION:
THE NEW A+ EXAMS

Chapter Syllabus

- A+ Exam Registration

- A+ Exams

- Using This Book to Pass the New A+ Exams

- New in This Revision

The Computing Technology Industry Association (CompTIA) A+ Certification is an entry-level certification for supporting and operating Personal Computers. A+ certification is accomplished by successfully passing an A+ Core Hardware Exam and an A+ Operating System Technologies Exam.

A+ Exam Registration

The worldwide networks of Prometric (Thomson Learning) and Virtual University Enterprises (VUE) administer the tests. Registering for the tests can be accomplished online or by calling Prometric or VUE.

Prometric can be contacted by calling:

- U.S. and Canada: 800-776-4276
- Europe and Africa: 31-320-239-800
  - English speaking countries: 31-320-239-895
  - French speaking countries outside of France: 31-320-239-892
- Australia: 61-2-9425-2300
- Japan: 813-5541-4700
- Latin America: 1-410-843-4300

The web sites for Prometric are:

- *http://www.prometric.com*—The main Prometric web site.
- *http://www.2test.com*—The online registration site for Prometric administered exams.

VUE can be contacted by calling:

- U.S. and Canada:
  877-551-PLUS (7587)
- Latin America:
  952-995-8758
- Europe/Middle East/Africa (EMEA):
  31-348-484-632
- Asia Pacific:
  61-2-9323-5586

The web sites for VUE are:

- *http://www.vue.com*—The main VUE web site.
- *http://www.vue.com/comptia/comptiaexam.html*—The online registration site for VUE administered exams.

Anyone can become A+ certified. The A+ exams are targeted for entry-level computer support personnel with 6 months' experience working with PCs. There are no restrictions to taking the A+ certification exams. The only requirement is that the A+ candidates pay the examination fee.

A+ exams are available worldwide in Spanish, French, German, and Japanese. CompTIA Certification Customer Service answers questions at (630) 268-1818.

A+ Exams

Both A+ exams test your knowledge of PC hardware and software. The A+ exams contain situation handling (about 25 percent), factual (about 50 percent), and component identification questions (about 25 percent). Situation handling questions ask things like, "If these were the sample directions, then you would do what?" Factual questions test on the facts, like identification of COM port IRQs, for example. Component identification questions ask the test-taker to identify what kind of a connection a 9-pin D-shaped male connector is, for example. All questions are multiple-choice with one correct answer. The test is not linked to any vendor-specific products but rather broadly covers PC hardware and software knowledge.

The exams provide four or more responses that best complete a statement or answer a specific question. The wrong answers are responses that someone with little knowledge or skill is likely to choose. The wrong answers are generally plausible responses to the questions.

Kinds of test questions used include:

- Multiple-choice—An option that best answers a question or completes a statement is selected. The option may be presented as part of a picture with a point and click option choice.

- Multiple-response—More than one option that best answers the question or completes a statement is selected.

- Sample directions—A statement or question is posed, and only the option(s) that represent the most correct or best answer(s) are selected from among the response options.

The A+ exams have been periodically revised and have recently been changed to an adaptive test format. They have also been updated to reflect new PC hardware and software.

Change to Adaptive Test Format

In July 2000 the A+ certification exam was changed to an adaptive test format. The adaptive format was first available worldwide in English. An adaptive format exam tailors itself to the test taker's ability. The testing results are as reliable and valid as a conventional exam. Adaptive tests have the advantage of testing knowledge by using fewer questions. With the Adaptive A+ exams, questions cannot be reviewed once you have completed answering them. There is no going back to review and/or change answers on previously answered questions.

Candidates who did not complete both portions of the A+ exam prior to the switch to the adaptive test could still become A+ certified by taking one conventional format exam and a second adaptive format exam.

The adaptive format exam highlights include the following:

- No new content was added to the exam. The same objectives in effect since July 1998 were used on the adaptive format.
- The customer service questions were eliminated from the CORE exam.
- Candidates answer approximately 20 to 30 questions.
- The passing scores are almost the same for the Core Hardware and OS Technologies adaptive format exam. The Core Hardware exam passing score is 445 out of 900 and the OS Technologies (A+ DOS/Microsoft® Windows® Service Technician Exam) passing score is 465 out of 900.

Exam Content Changes

CompTIA has revised the A+ exam objectives and content. The revised content exam was launched January 2001. This exam and A+ certification remains the same until the objectives and content are again revised. Since this is the first major content revision since 1998, it is likely that this exam and content will be used for the next few years. The code for the A+ Core Hardware exam is 220-201; the code for the A+ OS Technologies exam's code is 220-202.

The A+ Core Hardware exam measures basic Personal Computer (PC) or microcomputer systems knowledge and competencies, including:

- Installation, Configuration and Upgrading   – 30%
- Diagnosing, Troubleshooting, and Repairing   – 30%

- Preventative Maintenance — 5%
- Motherboard/Processors/Memory — 15%
- Printers — 10%
- Basic Networking — 10%

The A+ Operating System Technologies exam focuses on Windows 9x, Windows ME and Windows 2000 Professional Edition and covers:

- Operating System (OS) Fundamentals — 30%
- Installation, Configuring and Upgrading — 10%
- Diagnosing and Troubleshooting — 30%
- Networks — 10%

The original revision of this A+ book was developed around the 1998 A+ certification exams. Generally, the basic core hardware exam information for the January 2001 adaptive test was covered by the original version of this A+ certification book. Updates are needed to reflect the most current hardware components. This newly revised book updates the original A+ certification book version by including new information covered on the January 2001 revised A+ certification exams. This introduction highlights those changes and how they match up to the latest A+ certification exam.

This book is not like other A+ books that emphasize A+ exam questions and answers. There are more A+ sample questions and answers for each chapter, and explanations for some answers are provided to enhance reader comprehension. The original sample questions have been improved upon by adding questions that are derived from questions appearing in the new A+ exam. Consequently, the book may be used to study for the new A+ exams. However, the book goes beyond simple A+ test preparation. It is meant to be a general PC survival, operating, troubleshooting, repair, and maintenance reference book.

Some changes in PC and microcomputer systems are relentless. For example, CPU chips capabilities increase about every 4 months while their prices continue to decline. In the original version of this A+ certification book, copper technologies were just over the horizon. Today they are in full production with the new Intel Pentium 4 CPU chips. New technologies have greatly increased disk drive storage capacity while reducing disk drive prices.

In other cases changes are more measured. The Windows user interface has evolved significantly from Windows 95 into Windows ME with the most notable change made as Windows 98 SE (Second Edition) moved to Windows ME (Millennium Edition). However, the Windows ME user interface is very similar to the Windows 2000 Professional Edition interface. This interface and the movement to Windows 2000 and on to Windows XP are likely to remain stable for the next several years. The new exams no longer test on DOS and earlier operating system versions, but rather test on Windows 9x (this would include Windows ME), Windows 2000, and Windows XP.

Using This Book to Pass the New A+ Exams

This A+ certification book is structured like the A+ exams. Table A details the book and describes what areas it covers in preparation for the A+ Core Hardware Exam.

Table A   Core Hardware Exam Coverage

Chapter	Chapter Title	Exam Areas Covered
1	PC Components and Subsystems	Configuration as part of Installation, Configuration, and Upgrading
2	PC Installation and Upgrade	Installation and Upgrading as part of Installation, Configuration, and Upgrading
3	Troubleshooting and Problem Resolution	Diagnosing and Troubleshooting
4	Maintenance and Safety Practices	Preventative Maintenance
5	CPUs, RAM and Main Logic Boards	Motherboard/Processors/Memory
6	Printers	Printers
7	Laptop PCs	Configuration and Upgrading as part of Installation, Configuration, and Upgrading
8	LANs and Communications	Basic Networking

Similarly Table B identifies how the book covers the A+ Operating System Technologies Exam.

Table B   Operating System Technologies Exam Coverage

Chapter	Chapter Title	Exam Areas Covered
9	DOS Architecture	AUTOEXEC.BAT, CONFIG.SYS, and Command Prompt Procedures as part of Operating System Fundamentals
10	Windows 3.x Architecture	WIN.INI and SYSTEM.INI Reference parts of Operating System Fundamentals
11	Windows 9x/ME/2000 Architectures	Operating System Fundamentals
12	Disk Navigation and Management	Partitioning/Formatting/File System parts of Operating System Fundamentals
13	DOS and Memory Management	Memory Management parts of Operating System Fundamentals
14	Software Installation, Configuration and Upgrade	Installation, Configuration and Upgrade
15	DOS and Windows Software Problem Diagnosis and Resolution	Diagnosing and Troubleshooting
16	Windows Networking	Networks

Although knowledge of DOS and Windows 3.x are no longer part of the A+ exam objectives, the commands, disk preparation, and Windows program support structures (WIN.INI and SYSTEM.INI) are still used by Operating System software today. Some commands and functions have changed in minor ways, but basic functionality has largely remained the same.

Chapter 17, on Customer Satisfaction, is not tested as part of the newer A+ exams. They focus more on technical competence rather than people skills. We have retained Chapter 17 because we feel that handling the customer is part of every PC support person's job.

Chapter 18 has been modified to remove the Y2K materials that, as we thought, were largely over-hyped by the media. The other tales remain.

This book should provide a good foundation for any basic PC and A+ certification course. When combined with the study break exercises, it should provide sufficient knowledge and experience for anyone to pass the A+ exam. Included in this version is over two years of experience answering PC user questions from our radio and TV shows. This makes the revised book useful as a general PC hardware and software configuration, installation, troubleshooting, upgrading, and maintenance reference guide.

New in This Revision

Since we last worked on this A+ certification book many PC developments have reached the market. These developments are reaching the market at an increasingly rapid pace, transforming PCs again into general information, entertainment and control appliances for the home. These new developments are very exciting. The trend with all PC development is to make newer PCs easier to operate, maintain and configure. The newer Windows 2000 operating system is the easiest to operate and most reliable Windows operating system to date. The Windows XP operating system will reach the market by the time this book does, and is based upon Windows NT technology (just as is Windows 2000). It is targeted at more home entertainment multimedia and other home control functions than previous versions of the Windows operating system. Microsoft and the technical press tout Windows XP as a new and more fun operating system than previous Windows versions. It is difficult at this point to say whether this is true, or if it is merely an improved Windows 2000 operating system, like Windows ME was largely a few cosmetic and functional changes to Windows 98. Regardless, the configuration and troubleshooting Windows menus and Wizards outlined here for Windows 2000 are likely to be very similar to those used in Windows XP.

The new PC developments covered in this revision are:

- New Pentium 4 chips and the new Itanium chip from Intel. These chips are increasing PC operating speed for multimedia and video applications. We use a Windows 2000 PC to drive our television. Such developments are just the precursor of what is to come in home entertainment.
- New Universal Serial Bus (USB) and FireWire bus technologies are beginning to interconnect to a wider variety of PC components. In the next revision of this book we are likely to be discussing refrigerators that connect via wireless LANs to the kitchen PC.
- Flat panel monitors are becoming increasingly affordable. Even large 42" and 50" flat panel monitors will reach reasonable prices in the next year or two.
- The move away from Windows 95/98/ME and NT technology based Windows 2000 and Windows XP has begun. These operating systems

or Windows operating environments will reduce further software problems. The revision of this book was written on a Windows 2000 system that crashed about 100 times fewer than did the Windows 98 PC used to write the original version.

These developments are making it more exciting to be working with and writing about the PCs that serve us.

Acknowledgments

I would like to thank all of the people who have worked at The Moulton Company past and present and have helped me create this book. Special mention goes to Jeremy Moulton and Phil Crouse for helping with a couple of the chapters. Josh Moulton was the sacrificial nerd who took the A+ exams to see if the book content matched the new exam questions. Jason Moulton, Phil Lowry, and Ellen Mayes have taught many seminars so that I could focus my time on writing and revising this book. Melissa Clawson kept everything running smoothly. And finally, Cate, who knows that the answer to every question is "yes" or the multiple choice answer with the most words (or "c") and who has the patience to stick by me.

Chapter 1

PERSONAL COMPUTER (PC) COMPONENTS AND SUBSYSTEMS

Chapter Syllabus

- Hardware Components

- Software Components

- PC Boot Process

Several core components and ancillary subsystems comprise PCs. The core components provide the basic functionality of the PC. Ancillary subsystems enhance the basic functionality to support different applications, such as graphics imaging, multimedia applications, and more. PCs are a package of matched components. The components are matched for speed (somewhat tuned) to provide the best overall performance. It makes little sense to have a super fast Central Processing Unit (CPU) chip and a slow fixed disk drive or slow Random Access Memory (RAM). Such a combination produces a slow system. PCs are as fast as their most used and slowest component. Sometimes fixing PC problems is making sure that the PC components are properly matched for speed. However, the best PC is always the most reliable PC. Nerds may brag about their fast PCs, but their PCs rarely fail.

The PC core components ranked from fastest to slowest are:

- CPU chip—fastest
- RAM
- Display adapter
- Read-Only Memory (ROM)
- Fixed disk drive
- Universal Serial Bus (USB)
- Network adapter
- CD-ROM drive
- CD Rewriteable (CD-RW) drive
- Digital Versatile Disk (DVD) drive
- Floppy disk drive
- Parallel port
- Serial port
- Mouse
- Keyboard
- The nut behind the keyboard—slowest

Components and subsystems fall into three categories: hardware, software, and network. Hardware components are those components physically installed in the PC or connected to it. They are the core and ancillary subsystems examined in this chapter. Software components are covered in Chapter 9 through Chapter 16. Network connections are common components of most PC systems today.

Network connections are either dialup or Local Area Network (LAN). Cable modem and Digital Subscriber Line (DSL) connections are LAN connections as well. The network connections are attached to PC hardware components and work in conjunction with other computers and networking hardware residing somewhere on the attached network. I discuss networking as it impacts the PC hardware and software components and subsystems, but networks and external networking components are beyond the scope of this book.

Hardware Components

PC hardware is the focus of this section. PC hardware core components include the CPU chip, the ROM, the RAM, chip sets and buses, the power supply, serial and parallel Input/Output (I/O) ports, the floppy disk controller and drive, the fixed disk controller and drive, the CD-ROM drive, the DVD-ROM drive, the display adapter and monitor, the keyboard, and the mouse. See Figure 1–1. These components provide all basic PC functions. Ancillary subsystems are sound cards, LAN adapters, video cameras, and so forth.

The main PC chassis contains the central component for all PCs, the Main Logic Board (MLB). This is sometimes referred to as the system board or motherboard.

The MLB is based on a specific CPU and supporting chip set. It has a specific bus configuration and mounts the CPU, the ROM, and the RAM. Serial and parallel interfaces, as well as the keyboard interface, bus mouse interface, floppy disk controller, fixed disk Integrated Drive Electronics (IDE) con-

Figure 1–1
Typical PC system.

trollers, and USB ports are typically built into the MLB. Proprietary systems and laptop PCs have Video Graphics Array (VGA) display controllers incorporated into the MLB as well. Other controllers are bus-connected cards inserted into the bus of the MLB.

Main Chassis

The main chassis or case is the box containing most PC components. Components may be connected to the main chassis using USB connections. The main chassis would then contain the PC's core components, and the ancillary subsystems would occupy desktop space.

The main chassis for the PC Advanced Technology (AT) contained the MLB, its installed Intel 286 CPU chip, ROM, and RAM. The supporting chip sets provided Industry Standard Architecture (ISA) 8-bit and 16-bit connectors for installing adapter cards. Adapter cards typically installed in the AT were serial and parallel I/O controllers, display adapters, and disk controllers. The typical AT style PC chassis contained the floppy drive(s) and a fixed disk. The primary user input was by a keyboard. This was the typical 1985 PC.

In the early 1990s, PCs changed. At that time, Microsoft Windows made a successful entrance into the PC marketplace. It pressured PC manufacturers to change main chassis components more rapidly than before. Similar to the 1980s PCs, most MLBs had an installed Intel 386 or 486 CPU chip—although some supported Advanced Micro Devices (AMD) CPU chips—external CPU cache RAM, ROM, and RAM. The MLB also included the serial and parallel port I/O controllers and IDE fixed disk and floppy disk controllers. The bus connections were mainly ISA 8-bit and 16-bit connectors. Some systems had specialized connectors to speed up display and disk access. The Video Electronics Standards Association (VESA) bus and Extended Industry Standard Architecture (EISA) MLBs had connectors that supported higher speed transfers than the ISA bus connectors.

Now PCs incorporate both these evolutionary changes and revolutionary changes. Their MLB typically has Intel Pentium or AMD Athlon chips, RAM, ROM, built-in floppy disk, IDE fixed disk, USB, bus mouse, and keyboard controllers. PCs sometimes include a VGA controller and soundcard components as well. The chip sets and Basic Input/Output System (BIOS) support plug-and-play controller installation and sometimes a combination of ISA and Peripheral Component Interconnect (PCI) bus connectors. New MLBs are moving rapidly toward legacy-free configurations that support only plug-and-play PCI bus and USB components. This just means that it will not be your father's PC anymore. Also, maintenance and troubleshooting procedures change to accommodate new types of problems posed by these newer PC technologies.

System Board—MLB

The MLB, system board, or motherboard is the physical foundation of a computer. Baseboard, planar board, or main boards are other terms used to identify the MLB. It is the central PC building block because all other components must either plug into it or be physically mounted on it. Without a system board, no electrical interconnectivity is available to allow the PC's hardware components and subsystems to communicate.

System boards come in different configurations including:

- Extended Technology (XT) style
- AT style
- Baby AT style
- Advanced Technology Extensions (ATX) form factor and Mini ATX form factor
- Micro ATX form factor
- Flex ATX form factor
- NLX form factor

The early boards emulated an IBM PC XT configuration and then the IBM PC AT configuration. As chip sets incorporated greater functionality, MLBs shrank in size and, at the same time, incorporated more functions. The next generation of system boards had a standardized Baby AT form factor. This meant that they had one dimension that was from 8.6 to 8.8 inches and had specially placed mounting holes for plastic standoffs and bolts. Brand name PC manufacturers used proprietary system board configurations. Such proprietary configurations necessitated that replacement MLBs be provided from the PC manufacturer. These proprietary configurations limit the ability to upgrade PCs with faster CPU chips, RAM, and other capabilities. The ability to increase RAM, upgrade CPU chips, and swap adapter cards is designed into these proprietary MLBs, but such upgrade capabilities do not offer as many upgraded components as when an entire MLB is replaced. See Figure 1–2. For more detail on MLBs, see Chapter 5.

Today's PCs use MLBs that have ATX, Mini ATX, Micro ATX, Flex ATX, and NLX form factors. ATX form factor MLBs evolved from the Baby AT MLBs. Basically, the Baby AT MLB was rotated 90 degrees from its position facing the rear of a PC chassis, and a new power supply connection configuration was added. The longer ATX style boards permit relocation of the CPU and mounting of memory on the board. The longer ATX board also allows full-

Figure 1–2
Baby AT Slot 1 and Socket
7 (with AMD CPU) MLB.

length expansion card slots and permits more I/O functions installed as components on the MLB.

ATX form factor MLBs have up to seven expansion slots and external connectors for the PS/2-style keyboard and mouse, as well as serial, parallel, and USB connections installed directly on the MLB. Some ATX form factor MLBs also include a sound card and added USB connections. Figure 1–3 shows a dual Slot 1 ATX MLB with the PS/2-style keyboard and mouse connectors on the lower-left bottom of the figure. USB connectors are next to the keyboard and mouse connectors. Communication (COM) port and parallel port connectors are near the middle of the ATX-style MLB. ATX MLBs are 12 inches by 9.6 inches with specially placed mounting holes for standoffs and bolts. Mini ATX MLBs were the first variation of the ATX MLB form factor. The Mini ATX MLB was 11.2 inches by 8.2 inches.

Micro ATX MLBs followed the Mini ATX MLB and are smaller still with a 9.6 inch by 9.6 inch maximum size. Similar to the ATX MLB, the micro ATX MLB has built-in connections for mouse, keyboard, USB, serial, and parallel connectors. It supports up to four expansion card slots that may be a combination of ISA, PCI, ISA/PCI, and Accelerated Graphics Port (AGP) bus slots. The MLB-installed components may include standard connections, as well as Musical Instrument Digital Interface (MIDI)/game and audio output connections.

Figure 1–3
ATX Slot 1 MLB.

The Flex ATX MLB is also a smaller board. Its dimensions are 9.0 inches by 7.5 inches. It has the same mounting as the Micro ATX MLB and the same standard ATX rear I/O panel. The smaller packaging of the Flex ATX reduces the overall system manufacturing costs, resulting in lower total system cost to the PC user.

NLX MLBs are designed for low-profile PC systems. They support current and future processor technologies, AGP, tall Dual Inline Memory Modules (DIMMs), and flexible installation without screws. An AGP bus connector may be mounted on the MLB, but ISA and PCI bus expansion slots cannot. Thus, a distinguishing NLX motherboard characteristic is that the PCI and ISA bus card slots are implemented in a riser card into which the MLB inserts. The NLX riser card can support up to five PCI bus slots and an unspecified (but low, like one or two) number of ISA bus slots. The expansion cards are inserted parallel to the MLB and not vertically into the MLB. The NLX motherboard may be 8.0 inches or 9.0 inches wide and 10 inches, 11.2 inches, or 13.6 inches long.

One key area of evolution for the MLBs is in the power supply interface. The older boards used a power supply with a built-in power switch. In this case, the high-voltage (120 or 220 Volts Alternating Current [VAC]) wires were only exposed if the power supply case was opened. Other AT-style power supplies had an external front panel switch. This meant that the high-voltage wires ran from the power supply to the front panel switch, exposing them whenever the PC case was open. The ATX power supplies terminate the high-voltage wires in the power supply and control the PC power on/off function through a low-voltage MLB control circuit and internal power relay. The front panel power switch plugs into the ATX MLB using a low-voltage connection. Viewing any of the main boards, you see sockets for the CPU chip (or the Intel Slot 1 and AMD Slot A carriers) and sockets for RAM, PCI, AGP, and sometimes ISA 16-bit bus connectors. Plugs for the power supply cables are also on the main board.

To examine a system board, a PC's cover must be removed. After you get inside, the system board typically is the largest sheet of green or brown fiberglass mounted directly to the metal frame or chassis. In an older desktop chassis, the system board was typically mounted on the bottom. With the newer tower configuration chassis, the system board is mounted vertically. System boards are multilayer boards with four to seven or more layers of connections sandwiched between the layers of fiberglass. All layouts have keyboard and mouse connectors in the right rear corner of the board. (If you were facing a desktop PC, the connections would be in the rear on the right.) See Figure 1–4.

Figure 1–4
Mini-tower chassis with control, Light-Emitting Diode (LED), and speaker connection detail.

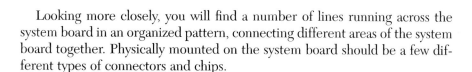

Looking more closely, you will find a number of lines running across the system board in an organized pattern, connecting different areas of the system board together. Physically mounted on the system board should be a few different types of connectors and chips.

CPU

The CPU is a computer on a chip. The CPU chip acts as the hands or heart of the computer. There are no brains here because computers are dumb. They only do what they are told. They are the hands that perform the work as directed and the heart that pumps the data to all PC components.

Processors are classified by their interface to the MBL and by processing horsepower. MLB interfaces are a socket interface or a slot interface. The socket interfaces are Socket 7 (Intel Pentium CPUs) and Socket 8 (Intel PentiumPro CPUs). Intel introduced the Single Edge Contact (SEC) or slot interfaces in 1998. Most slot interfaces are Slot 1, but some Intel chips may use the Slot 2 interface, and AMD Athlon chips use a Slot A interface. Newer chips have returned to socket mounting with Intel's Socket 370, Socket 423, and Socket 478 and AMD's Socket A (Socket 462) mounting. See Figure 1–5. Processing horsepower is mostly defined by clock speed. CPU purists would argue that point vigorously. However, general users would only notice performance improvements when clock speeds increase by greater than 50 percent.

Other components in the CPU also determine its performance, including the amount of Level 1 (L1) and Level 2 (L2) CPU cache incorporated into the chip configuration.

Figure 1–5
AMD Athlon Thunderbird CPU chip.

Starting with the 486 chips, CPUs had internal Level 1 CPU cache memory to speed up processing performance. Both Level 1 and Level 2 cache are a storage area used by processors to increase performance. Level 1 is a small, high-speed cache right on the chip, which holds recently used data and instructions from memory. Level 2 is larger in size and, until recent years, has been located outside the chip on the motherboard. PentiumPro chips were among the first to include the Level 2 CPU cache in the chip package. The latest Intel and AMD chips have both Level 1 and Level 2 CPU cache memory inside the chip to maximize performance.

Cache memory is a means of speeding up computer processing. Cache works on the 80/20 rule of computers. This is similar to the 80/20 rule of the Internal Revenue Service (IRS). They keep 80 percent of what you earn, and you get 20 percent of what you earn. In computers, 80 percent of the time, the next piece of information that you need is right next to the last piece of information that you used. This means that, if information is contained on a device, like a disk drive, that is slower than the component where the information is going to be used next, like RAM, it makes sense to bring the information into a temporary holding area—the cache—that is faster than the disk drive. In this case, 80 percent of the time the data is retrieved from the cache, and 20 percent of the time the data is received directly from the slower disk drive. This is disk cache operation.

To really envision cache operation, think of baking cookies. You go to the cupboard and get flour, then go back to get sugar, and go again to get chocolate chips, and finally go to get spices. Next, it is on to the refrigerator to get milk, then butter, and, finally, eggs. How much would it speed up cookie baking if you went to the cupboard and got the flour, sugar, chocolate chips, and spices all at once and put them on the countertop, the cookie baking cache? You could then get the milk, butter, and eggs and also place them on the countertop as well.

CPU cache performs similar functions between the faster CPU and the slower RAM. Level 1 cache inside the CPU chip runs at the same speed as the CPU chip, but RAM is from three to 10 times slower than the CPU and the Level 1 cache. Even Level 2 CPU cache external to the CPU chip is half the speed of the CPU. Anything external to the CPU chip requires a relatively long time for the electrical signals to travel from it into the chip; that makes it much slower than anything inside the chip. It is similar to communication by satellite versus terrestrial links. Electrical signals must travel 44,000 miles across some satellite links versus 3,000 miles across a terrestrial link. It means that the signals require approximately 11 times longer completing the trip by satellite.

Most PC chips today are based upon the x86 instruction set developed by Intel. Manufacturers like AMD and VIA Technology's Cyrix produce chips that emulate the instruction set of the Intel chip. This is possible because of

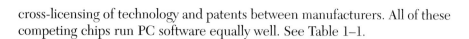

cross-licensing of technology and patents between manufacturers. All of these competing chips run PC software equally well. See Table 1–1.

Table 1–1   CPU Chip Summary

Chip	Multimedia Extensions (MMX)—Cache	Comment
Intel Pentium 4	Uses Intel Pentium III instructions with added multimedia instructions, has a special trace transfer cache, uses Rambus Dynamic RAM (DRAM), and is based upon copper technology	Intel's latest and greatest is no longer a Slot 1 cartridge. This chip is a Socket 423 or Socket 478 chip.
Intel Pentium III	MMX, Single Instruction-Stream, Multiple Data-Stream (SIMD) instructions, and internal Level 2 cache inside the cartridge	Best performance chip.
Intel Pentium II	MMX and external Level 2 cache inside the cartridge	Cheapest chip. This is a Socket 370 chip.
Intel Celeron 266/300	MMX, but no Level 2 cache	Cheap Intel. This is a slow performer.
Intel Celeron 300a/333/366/400/ 433/466/500/533/566/ 600/633/667/700/733/ 766/800	MMX and 128 kilobyte (KB) inside chip Level 2 cache	Cheap Intel. This is a competitive performer.
Pentium MMX	Initial MMX and external Level 2 cache	This is at the end of life.
Pentium Pro	No MMX and large internal Level 2 cache	This is a Windows NT server chip that is at the end of life.

Table 1-1   CPU Chip Summary (Continued)

Chip	Multimedia Extensions (MMX)—Cache	Comment
Xeon Pentium III	MMX, SIMD instructions, and large internal Level 2 cache	New Windows NT/Windows 2000 server chip.
Itanium	Explicitly Parallel Instruction Computing (EPIC) architecture and 64-bit CPU. Has Level 1, Level 2, and Level 3 internal cache	Server chip for Windows NT/Windows 2000, Linux, and NetWare.
AMD-K6	Initial MMX and external Level 2 cache	Good Pentium MMX competitor.
AMD-K6-2	3D; improved MMX and external Level 2 cache	Good Pentium II competitor.
AMD-K6-3	3D; improved MMX and internal Level 2 cache	Best Pentium II competitor.
AMD-K7	3D; improved MMX and inside the cartridge Level 2 cache Thunderbird chips have internal Level 2 cache	Slot A design competitor to Slot 1 Newer Thunderbird chips return to socket technology and use Socket A or Socket 462.
Cyrix® M II	MMX and external Level 2 cache	Good for business applications, but poor for imaging and Computer-Aided Design (CAD). Less widely sold than AMD and Intel CPU chips.
Cyrix® III	3D; improved MMX and internal 128 KB Level 1 cache	The VIA Cyrix® III processor is designed for cheap PCs and notebooks, as well as the new generation of information appliances.

ROM

ROM contains the start-up code and the 16-bit BIOS programs for the PC. ROM is divided into system ROM installed on the MLB and adapter ROM installed on adapter cards. See Figure 1–6.

System ROM is first accessed during the boot process. It performs the initial PC setup, loads the PC's cold boot loader program from the fixed disk Master Boot Record (MBR), and handles the PC's I/O operations under the Disk Operating System (DOS). Most PCs have 64 KB of ROM. The addresses are mapped into the last 64 KB memory page below the memory boundary. Some PCs have more system ROM. The most notable was the Micro Channel Architecture (MCA) IBM PS/2. To operate the MCA bus and its jumperless hardware installation, 128 KB of ROM was used. The MCA bus PC was the predecessor to the PCI bus plug-and-play designs that we have today. Plug-and-play PCs use special ROM code to implement plug-and-play. This ROM code does not, however, increase the system ROM size beyond 64 KB. Other PC cards also contain ROM. Adapter ROMs perform special adapter card operations. They handle I/O operation, or, in the case of some Small Computer System Interface (SCSI) adapters, they perform setup and diagnostic operations. Adaptec has ROM on its SCSI adapters; SCSI Select software configures the adapter, functions as a diagnostic program, and formats the SCSI drives attached. Virtually all display adapters have some type of video ROM. This ROM is about 32 KB in size. It is placed in the PC address range 832 KB to 864 KB (C000-C7FF). More details on memory addressing and ROM locations are provided in Chapter 9.

RAM

RAM is the working area of the PC. All data must flow into and out of RAM. It holds both programs and data. When a program is running (executing) and working on data, the program and most often the data reside in RAM. In a

Figure 1–6
Keyboard and main BIOS
ROM chips on MLB.

Windows environment, RAM is virtualized. The operating system has 4 gigabytes (GB) of virtual memory where components and applications can reside. Windows translates the virtual address space into a combination of disk accesses and memory paging and allocation, translating the virtual address space into real physical PC RAM and disk addresses. When any PC is running, most of its electronic activity involves swapping data between RAM and the CPU. When the PC is powered down, the data in RAM is lost. The PC's maximum RAM capacity has moved from 1 megabyte (MB) to 16 MB and up to 4 GB or more today for many servers. Most PC RAM is comprised of DRAM chips that must be continually refreshed. Thousands of capacitors acting like leaky buckets comprise DRAM. Static RAM (SRAM) acts like small switches that, after they are set, do not need to be refreshed. SRAM is very fast and more expensive than DRAM. SRAM is used for external CPU cache.

Older forms of RAM employed a parity chip for error checking. The parity chip created an extra bit depending upon just how many ones are in the byte or character stored. When the character is read from memory, the parity is recomputed and compared to the originally stored value. If they matched, everything was OK. If they did not match, older PCs signaled "201" or "Parity Check 2."

Newer memory chips are placed on modules that are minicircuit boards called Single Inline Memory Modules (SIMMs), DIMMs, or Rambus Inline Memory Modules (RIMMs). SIMMs, DIMMs, and RIMMs provide an entire bank of memory on the minicircuit board. Replacement involves replacing the entire minicircuit board instead of a single bad chip.

RAM is rated and classified by access time. The slowest RAM chips were 250 nanoseconds (ns), and the fastest is around 10 ns. Typically RAM chip speeds are about 50 to 70 ns. For more details on RAM, see Chapter 5.

Other types of RAM are Synchronous DRAM (SDRAM) and Extended Data Output (EDO) RAM. These are both DRAM that needs refreshing. They are, however, more tuned to the CPU chip's clocking and memory refresh operations and therefore speed up the PC by reducing CPU to memory transfer times.

Newer RAM types are Double Data Rate RAM (DDR RAM) and Rambus DRAM. DDR RAM moves data on every bus clock signal change, not just on leading edge changes. SDRAM operates at 100 megahertz (MHz), and the equivalent DDR RAM would then operate at 200 MHz. Rambus DRAM is a new RAM technology that increases RAM speed to 400 MHz or higher. The higher RAM operating speed does not necessarily mean that Rambus DRAM PCs are faster than DDR RAM PCs because the delay increases when accessing different parts of Rambus DRAM.

Nonvolatile RAM (NVRAM)

There is also NVRAM. This is similar to ROM in that it does not lose its contents when the PC is powered off. NVRAM is SRAM that retains its databits as long as power is supplied to the memory. NVRAM contents are saved when a computer is powered off or its external power is lost, and it is implemented using SRAM with battery power or by using an electrically Erasable Programmable ROM (EPROM).

Like RAM, NVRAM can also be written into. However, writing into NVRAM requires special software. Hence, NVRAM is used to hold ROM BIOS code that may need to be updated or changed. Flashing programs with names such as PHLASH and AWDFLASH update this information. Some modems store pre-set or user-specified phone numbers and modem profiles using NVRAM. They are specially designed to write the information into NVRAM without using a separate flashing program.

The BIOS is implemented in ROM or NVRAM. It is the code in the PC that boots the PC and controls I/O operations under DOS. Windows uses 32-bit driver software to perform the functions of ROM BIOS routines. The original PC BIOS had a built-in Basic interpreter program for the Basic programming language. Around 1990, that Basic interpreter code disappeared from even the IBM PC's BIOS. BIOS could be considered as only that part of ROM controlling I/O functions in the PC. However, a broader view would define BIOS functions as:

- Hardware setup—During boot, the PC allows you to enter hardware setup options and configure the PC's standard and advanced hardware options.

- Power-On Self-Test (POST) diagnostics—Performs cursory hardware testing to ensure that the PC hardware matches the setup parameters. These diagnostics are only effective in detecting major PC component malfunctions.

- Cold boot loading functions—Loads DOS from a diskette or loads the cold boot loader program from the fixed disk's MBR. It also loads the initial disk drive parameters from the fixed disk partition table.

- DOS I/O operations—Provides basic floppy disk, keyboard, display, and fixed disk I/O control operations.

With Windows, these BIOS functions are used during the initial system startup and then replaced by Windows 32-bit driver software.

Firmware

Firmware is PC component driver programs installed in ROM or NVRAM. Firmware was initially used to store hardware setup and BIOS routines because it was easier to update than hardware. In contrast, software stored on disk is the most flexible and easy to change. Firmware typically controls a PC when it is first switched on. Typical firmware would perform cold boot loading of the operating system from a fixed disk or from a network and then pass control to the operating system.

Complementary Metal Oxide Semiconductors (CMOS)

CMOS really describes a chip technology that uses low power. This technology was originally employed in the PC AT to store hardware configuration information in a nonvolatile battery-powered memory chip. A three- or six-volt lithium battery powered the CMOS memory chip. Today, CMOS technology is used in chips in almost all PCs to reduce power consumption. "CMOS" as a term is used to identify the PC's nonvolatile parameter storage memory, initially implemented with CMOS technology. See Figure 1–7.

When the PC is booted, the setup software implemented in ROM changes the PC operating parameters in CMOS memory. These parameters and the CMOS memory addresses are mapped into the first 64 KB memory bank. CMOS is much smaller than 64 KB. Most ROM BIOS setup programs automatically detect disk drive types and CPU speeds and set the PC up to run. CMOS setup parameters are not required for basic PC operation, but rather to tweak the PC for optimal performance. Be careful when changing any CMOS settings because, most often, what seems to be the best or fastest setting can cause the PC to go slower or to malfunction. Default CMOS operating parameters and automatically detected parameters are always the best bet when setting up a PC.

Figure 1-7
CMOS batteries.

Onboard Controllers

MLBs have built-in controllers for the keyboard, a bus mouse, serial ports, parallel ports, floppy disk drives, IDE fixed disk drives, CD-ROMs, and USB ports. Some servers have onboard SCSI controllers as well.

The first onboard controllers were for the keyboard and the serial and parallel ports. Next, systems incorporated bus mouse ports and floppy and fixed disk drive controllers. These ports were initially routed to outside the PC chassis by pigtail connectors that fit into the expansion slot card covers at the rear of the PC. Such pigtail connections were used on Baby AT system boards. Disk drive controllers had parallel cables attached directly to the stake pin connectors on the MLB. Today, these onboard controllers have their ports directly routed to a special connector area at the right rear of the MLB. This is an ATX MLB configuration.

MLBs typically had two Enhanced Integrated Drive Electronics (EIDE) controllers as shown in Figure 1–8. EIDE onboard controllers have increased transfer speed from 33 MHz Direct Memory Access (DMA) clock speed to 66 MHz DMA and 100 MHz DMA speeds. The number of MLB integral EIDE controllers has also doubled from two to four controllers on some MLBs. This permits those MLBs to support up to eight EIDE devices. The best performance is realized by assigning a single EIDE device to each controller. For example, two fixed disk drives, a DVD drive, and a CD-RW drive could be each connected to a separate EIDE controller to maximize performance because EIDE commands could be executed concurrently, which speeds up copying data from drive to drive.

Figure 1–8
MLB primary and secondary IDE bus connectors.

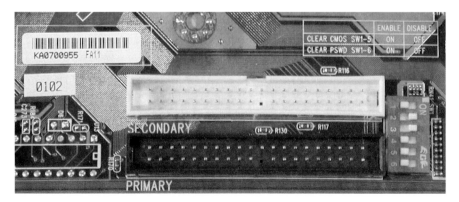

Expansion Slots

Expansion slots implement the PC's system bus. The system bus connectors allow other circuit cards to be plugged into them. Because they are card edge connectors, they are called expansion slots. The cards inserted in the edge-style bus connectors are referred to as daughter cards or expansion cards. The daughter card label was used because the cards were inserted into the motherboard.

The expansion slots had different configurations depending upon the bus supported by the system board. The simplest configuration was the 8-bit ISA bus used in the original PC. These bus expansion slots evolved to a 16-bit ISA bus and then on to a 32-bit EISA configuration. The physical size of the EISA slots was the same as the 16-bit ISA slots except the EISA slots permitted the expansion cards to plug deeper into the connector. Thus, EISA slots could support 8-bit, 16-bit, and 32-bit I/O transfers. Table 1–2 identifies expansion slots found in different PC systems.

Table 1–2 Expansion Slot versus PC System

Expansion Slot or Bus	PC System
ISA 8 bit	PCs and XTs
ISA 16 bit	ATs
EISA	386 and 486
ISA 16 bit + VESA Local (VL)-Bus	386, 486, and Pentium
EISA + VL-Bus	386, 486, and Pentium
ISA 16 bit + PCI	Pentium Class PCs built in 2000 and before 2000
PCI	Pentium Class PCs built after 2000
EISA + PCI	Pentium—Servers
Personal Computer Memory Card Industry Association (PCMCIA) or Card Bus	Laptops
MCA 16 bit	PS/2—old
MCA 32 bit	PS/2—new
AGP	Pentium class PCs built after the late 1990s

In early PCs, expansion slots were used for virtually all upgrades to the PC's basic capabilities, including RAM expansion. I had a PC AT that had 12 MB of RAM installed on several RAM expansion cards. The maximum RAM supported by the PC AT 80286 chip was 16 MB. This is not possible with today's PCs because RAM transfer to the CPU chip is at much higher speeds than the expansion slots and their buses can run. The top bus clock speed has increased from 8 MHz, to 33 MHz, to 66 MHz, and to 100 MHz. Front side bus (the CPU to RAM bus) speeds have increased from 66 MHz, to 100 MHz, to 133 MHz, to 200MHz, to 266 MHz, and to 400 MHz. This is slow when compared to the 1.5 gigahertz (GHz) and higher clock speeds of CPU chips.

Expansion slots are used to install disk controllers, display controllers, modems, video capture, and LAN adapter cards in the PC. Each type of adapter card enhances the functionality of the basic PC system. These adapters typically run at speeds that match the bus clock speed.

Typical PC expansion slots include ISA 16-bit, PCI, and AGP slots. See Figure 1–9.

Figure 1-9
PC MLB ISA 16-bit, PCI, and AGP expansion slots.

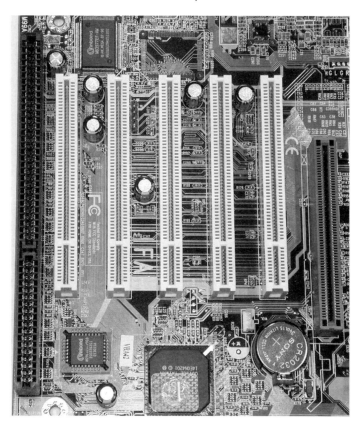

Power Supply

The PC power supply converts 120/240 volt Alternating Current (AC) into the 5- and 12-volt Direct Current (DC) used by the PC. Power supplies are rated by wattage. They range from 85 watts for the original PC to 300 watts for high-end PC power supplies. A watt is a power measurement that is voltage times the amperage delivered by the supply. Because voltage is the same for all supplies, a higher wattage translates into more current being delivered by the supply.

The original PC chips operated using Transistor-to-Transistor Logic (TTL) requiring 5-volt DC. The CPU chips of today's PCs can use lower voltage levels. Typically, these chips employ special voltage regulation incorporated into the MLB.

The original PC power supplies had built-in power on/off switches and power connectors for the MLB and the disk drives. As the PC changed, the power supplies did, too. Current power supplies are typically 230 to 250 watts. They have power connectors for either an AT-style or an ATX-style MLB. Additional power connectors support fixed disk drives, 3.5-inch floppy drives, and front panel lights. Each such connector has a different physical configuration. Furthermore, the power on/off switch is no longer on the side of the supply, but rather mounted on the front of the PC. See Figure 1–10. This

Figure 1–10
AT-style power supply with front panel switch.

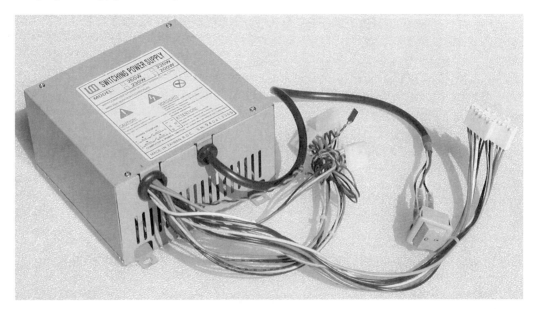

necessitates an insulated power connection to a front panel PC power switch. As discussed earlier in the System Board—MLB section of this chapter, newer ATX-style MLBs control the power on/off function by a low-power connection to the MLB. For further discussion on the types of connectors, see Chapter 5.

Fixed Disk Drives and Controllers

The fixed disk drive is the file cabinet of the PC. It is the device that holds all software and data while the PC is running and after the PC is powered down.

Fixed disks are described by their capacity, speed, physical size (form factor), and controller interface. Fixed disk capacities range from 8 GB to more than 80 GB. The largest IDE drives are over 80 GB in capacity. Fixed disk drives have Power-On Hour (POH) Mean Time Between Failure (MTBF) rates ranging from 150,000 POH to 1,000,000 POH.

Fixed disk speed is measured by the time it takes for the disk drive read-write heads to seek the data on the disk and the time it takes to transfer data from the disk to the PC's disk controller. Head seek times are influenced by the physical size of the drive, with smaller drives having better seek times because the read-write heads have shorter distances to travel. Typical seek times range from 8 milliseconds to just over 10 milliseconds. Fixed disk transfer rate is largely determined by the rotational speed of the disk. Disk drives originally rotated at 3,600 Revolutions Per Minute (RPM).

Today's disk drives range in rotational speed from 4,500 RPM to 15,000 RPM. The higher the rotational speed means the higher the disk drive transfer rate.

The physical size of the disk drives ranges from 1 to 2.5-inch quarter-height drives, to 3.5-inch third or half-height drives, and on to 5.25-inch full-height drives. Other form factor combinations exist as well. The form factor describes the size of the disk—1 inch, 2.5 inches, 3.5 inches, and 5.25 inches—and the height of the drive, with a full-height drive being 3.25 inches high.

Fixed disk drive interfaces are most often IDE, EIDE, or SCSI.

IDE and EIDE

Disk drive interfaces started with the Modified Frequency Modulation (MFM) interfaces that were standardized by the Seagate ST-402 and ST-512 specifications. These interfaces required two cables to the disk drive from the disk controller card. One cable (the wide one) handled 8 bits of data and the drive control signals, and the other (the narrow one) handled the second 8 bits of data. The data and control cable were an extension of the floppy disk interface. It was a 34-conductor cable. The second data-only cable was a 16-conductor cable.

Figure 1-11
IDE drive cable connection.

IDE interface disk drives having the drive controller built on the drive displaced MFM drives within a few years. This integration of controller and drive greatly simplified the control interface in the PC. The IDE interface is used today for both fixed disks and CD-ROM drives. It employs a single 40-conductor cable. See Figure 1–11. EIDE controllers provide improved transfer speeds and the ability to interface to four drives.

Today, IDE and EIDE interfaces can burst transfer data at 33, 66, or 100 MB per second. The largest IDE drives are around 80 GB, with their size expected to increase in the next few years. IDE and EIDE drives are the most commonly installed drives in PCs.

SCSI

Apple pioneered the SCSI. It was used to connect peripherals to Apple computers. This was the SCSI-I interface that transferred data at 5 MB per second. SCSI became the interface of preference for large-capacity drives. SCSI was relatively expensive because not only were the drives expensive, but they required the addition of a SCSI interface card.

The great advantage of the SCSI besides the increased drive capacity was the ability to connect up to seven drives on the same SCSI interface. This made it possible to build much larger disk volumes and to implement Redundant Array of Independent Disk (RAID) drives. The first CD-ROMs employed SCSI interfaces, but they have since migrated to the EIDE interface.

Many SCSI drives use a single 50-conductor parallel cable with terminating resistors at each end of the bus, which is often the end of the cable. This cable has changed as the SCSI interface speed increased. SCSI started with the Apple SCSI-I speed of 5 MB per second. Early PC SCSI drives operated at this speed. Because the SCSI bus was shared, the transfer speed increased rapidly to provide adequate PC performance. The SCSI bus was changed to fast operation, increasing the transfer speed to 10 MB per second. The fast SCSI set the basic clock rate for the SCSI interface at 10 MHz. The SCSI-II PC controllers operated at this speed. They transferred one byte at a time at 10 MHz, thus producing the 10 MB per second transfer rate.

The SCSI interface was upgraded to the fast wide SCSI that transferred 16 bits, increasing SCSI bus speed to 20 MB per second. The next enhancement was to improve the fast operating speed to 20 MHz with the 16-bit ultrawide SCSI bus, thus providing 40 MB per second transfers. Finally, we have Ultra-2 SCSI capable of 80 MB per second transfers, accomplished using a 40 MHz bus or a 32-bit bus operating at 20 MHz. The SCSI cables changed from the original 50-conductor cable to a 68-conductor cable and finally to fiber optic SCSI channels.

SCSI drives and interfaces are prevalent and preferred in high-end PC and network servers requiring RAID and high-capacity drives. Because the SCSI bus is shared, the transfer speeds of the fastest SCSI buses are divided among the drives attached to the controller. Depending upon the PC use, such a division might enhance overall PC performance. Such enhanced performance, while measurable, is not likely noticeable by most users.

Table 1–3 provides a summary of these interfaces, their characteristics, and their differences.

Table 1–3 Interface Types and Characteristics

SCSI Type	Bus Speed	Bus Width	Connector	Throughput	Distance of Cable Single Ended	Number of devices
Regular SCSI	5 MHz	8 bit	50 pin	5 MB/sec	6 meters	8
Wide SCSI	5 MHz	16 bit	68 pin	10 MB/sec	6 meters	16
Fast SCSI	10 MHz	8 bit	50 pin	10 MB/sec	3 meters	8
Fast wide SCSI	10 MHz	16 bit	68 pin	20 MB/sec	3 meters	16
Ultrawide SCSI	20 MHz	16 bit	68 pin	40 MB/sec	1.5 meters	16
Ultra-2 Wide SCSI	40 MHz	16 bit	68 pin	80 MB/sec	12 meters, but must be LVD cabling	16

Three types of cabling are most used with SCSI: single ended, differential, or Low Voltage Differential (LVD). Single ended has been the most commonly used through the years because of its low cost in comparison to differential. Now, with the higher speeds, single ended is very limited in the distance of cabling. Differential cabling is more expensive then single ended, but can do all speeds up to 25 meters, so it is used in long runs of external cabling. LVD is relatively new on the market and is supposed to have the best of both worlds because it can run all speeds of SCSI up to 12.5 meters at a much lower cost than differential. Remember, do not mix your SCSI cabling types; they are electrically incompatible.

Microdrives

New, very small fixed disk drives are being used in a variety of electronic equipment. Pioneered by IBM, microdrives provide 340 MB to 1 GB storage capacity for portable electronic devices in an industry-standard Compact Flash + (CF+) Type II form factor and an AT Attachment (ATA)/PCMCIA Type II interface support with appropriate adapter. The high-capacity microdrives enable digital cameras to capture more high-resolution photos, enable handheld PCs to access more applications and to maintain large databases, and permit notebook users to back up and to transport their data more quickly and conveniently. A single hard disk microdrive can provide 340 MB, 512 MB, or 1 GB storage capacity in about a 1.5-inch square 16-gram package. Microdrives support a maximum sustained data rate exceeding 4 MB per second.

JAZ and ORB

Iomega developed JAZ drive technology. JAZ drives are floppy disks that rotate at high speeds (5,394 RPM vs. 300 RPM for floppy disk drives). They employ the Bernoulli principle (fast moving air has less pressure than static air, which is what causes planes to fly) to permit the read-write heads to get very close to the floppy disk medium. As a result, they can store substantial amounts of data on 3.5-inch floppy disk cartridges. Because their rotational speed is high compared to floppy drives, they have performance that resembles fixed disks. The newer JAZ drives are capable of storing 2 GB of data on a single removable floppy disk cartridge. JAZ drives interface to the PC using SCSI. See Figure 1–12. JAZ drives can be installed internally or attached externally to the PC. External drives can be moved from PC to PC, using a USB or a FireWire (Institute of Electrical and Electronic Engineers [IEEE] 1394) interface to connect to the PCs. The older JAZ drives interfaced to the PC using the PC's parallel port, and the PC's parallel interface was trans-

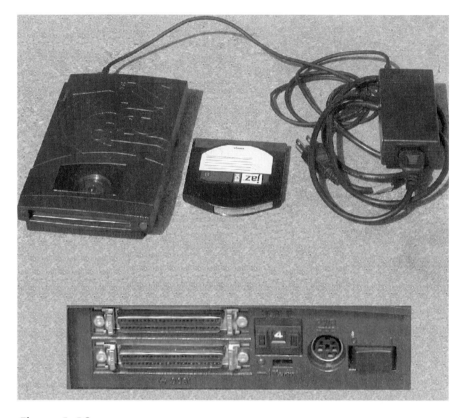

Figure 1–12
JAZ® drive, cartridge, and SCSI interface connectors.

formed into a SCSI interface using a special Trantor interface cable. JAZ drives have a MTBF of 250,000 POH.

JAZ drives provide removable media storage for PC backups. The benefit of such backup is that the JAZ drive's operation is similar to random access disks and not like linear access tape backups. Random access can make data accessibility faster than with tape. The limitation here is that each cartridge stores only a maximum of 2 GB of data. JAZ cartridges can be compressed, but this presents problems for the 2-GB capacity cartridges. Because JAZ drives look like older DOS fixed disks to the PC, they are limited to storing only a maximum of 2 GB of data effectively. Thus, when a 2-GB cartridge is compressed, it produces a 2-GB drive and 1-GB hidden drive. The 1-GB drive is usable, but not conveniently so. It is much more effective to compress a 1-GB JAZ cartridge to provide about 2 GB of storage. The 2-GB JAZ drive works with the 1-GB JAZ cartridges.

The ORB drives from Castlewood also store 2.2 GB of data. They perform similarly to the JAZ drives. ORB drives connect to PCs using EIDE and SCSI interfaces for internal drives and SCSI, USB, and FireWire for external drives.

Optical Rewriteable Drives and DVD-RAM Drives

Optical storage drives are similar to JAZ drives. They have an equivalent 2-GB capacity or greater, and they rotate at higher speeds than floppy drives, from 2,400 RPM to 3,755 RPM. (Sony's external optical drive runs at 3,600 RPM.) Rewriteable optical drives use a SCSI interface like the JAZ drives.

Optical rewriteable drives store data using a magneto-optical storage process. Magnetism is used to permit laser recording of data on the disk media. After it is recorded, the data is read using a laser. The main benefit here is that the recording medium is durable and lasts a long time. Where data in time can be corrupted on JAZ floppy media, it is good for 30 years on rewriteable optical media. The rewriteable optical cartridges use 5.25-inch media that may hold 650 MB, 1 GB, 1.3 GB, 2.6 GB, or 5.2 GB. This is physically larger than the JAZ 3.5-inch media.

The rewriteable optical technology has migrated from the original rewriteable optical drives to rewriteable CD drives (compact disc-erasable [CD-E]) and rewriteable DVD drives. The rewriteable CD drive provides more flexibility and storage capacity at a reduced cost than the original rewriteable optical drives, using a 5.25-inch media similar to a CD. It has the CD recording capacity of 600 to 700 MB. The media does not require a special carrier (container for the media), which the optical rewriteable drive does. Performance is similar to a slower CD-ROM.

Rewriteable DVD drives (also called DVD RAM drives) provide greater storage capacity than other rewriteable drives. Similar to a normal DVD drive, they use a blue laser to enhance storage capacity of the 5.25-inch media. The discs can store 2.6 GB on single-sided discs and 5.2 GB on double-sided discs. They can read and write DVD media and read CD-ROM media. Disc formats supported are DVD-RAM, DVD-R, DVD-ROM, CD-ROM, CD-RW, CD-Extra, and CD-Audio (CD-A). The interface to the PC is typically SCSI for these devices. DVD-RAM drives use rewriteable cartridges that are most commonly sold in a 5.2 GB, double-sided capacity. Some DVD RAM drives have a MTBF of 100,000 POH.

Floppy Disk Drives

Floppy disk drives were the original PC storage media. From 1981 through 1983, there were no PC fixed disk drives. The first fixed disk drive that we saw for a PC was a 5-MB drive that cost $5,000. Months later, IBM marketed the PC XT with its 10-MB fixed disk for $1,000. In the 1981 to 1983 timeframe, we first used single-sided and then double-sided floppy drives as the only permanent data storage for the PC. Of course, everything was smaller then. A large file was 30 KB because it contained ASCII text-only information.

5.25-Inch Floppy Drives

The original PC disk drives stored 160 KB of data on a single-sided 5.25-inch disk. They used 40 tracks with eight sectors per track with each sector storing 512 characters (bytes) of data. The total capacity then was (40 tracks) × (8 sectors) × (.5 KB), equaling 160 KB total capacity. At one time, we were so desperate for storage space that we attached four double-sided floppy disks to a PC. It was the ultimate machine at the time because of its active 1.44-MB storage capacity. See Figure 1–13.

These disks were soon replaced by double-sided drives, then nine sector-per-track drives, and, finally, by high-density 5.25-inch drives. Each disk drive enhancement increased the storage capacity. The high-density drives appeared with the PC AT. They stored data on 80 tracks with 15 sectors per track on two sides of the floppy. As always, the sectors contained 512 characters of data. Their capacity was (80 tracks) × (15 sectors per track) × (two sides) × (.5 KB), equaling 1.2 MB per disk.

The disks came in a plastic holder that provided the necessary mechanical support for inserting them into and removing them from the floppy disk drive. A paper sleeve protected the floppy media by covering the read-write window of the diskette.

Figure 1–13
5.25-inch floppy disk drive.

3.5-Inch Floppy Drives

The 3.5-inch floppy drives came out with the first IBM PS/2 PCs in 1987. They were about two-thirds the width and one-half the height of a 5.25-inch drive. They had new power connections requiring special power supply pigtail adapters to provide power to the drives. Today, all power supplies provide specific 3.5-inch disk drive power connections. The 5.25-inch drives used both 5-volt and 12-volt DC power, while the 3.5-inch drives used 5-volt DC power alone. See Figure 1–14. Some 3.5-inch drives were even smaller in height, and combination 3.5-inch and 5.25-inch drives were developed that fit into a single 5.25-inch half-height drive bay.

The 3.5-inch disk media is mounted in a permanent plastic sleeve with a special sliding door protecting the disk drive media. The sliding door is one of the greater hazards for 3.5-inch drives. The doors are typically made out of aluminum or plastic that is easily bent or broken. Any bending makes the aluminum door catch on the inside of the 3.5-inch drive, causing destruction of the disk and sometimes damage to the drive itself.

The 3.5-inch disk stores data on 80 tracks with 18 sectors per track. This gives a total capacity calculated by multiplying (80 tracks) × (18 sectors per track) × (two sides) × (.5 KB), equaling 1.44 MB per disk. These disks have become, in the late 1990s, the basic DOS boot and initial software installation mechanism for PCs. Their capacity today remains adequate for hardware diagnostics, but it has become insufficient for installing any software. Software installation is largely from CD-ROMs. Newer PCs can boot directly from the

Figure 1-14
3.5-inch floppy drive.

CD-ROM to facilitate direct software installation. Some of the latest floppy disk drives rotate at about twice the speed of older floppy drives. This significantly enhances their performance. Their capacity has not been increased, only their data transfer and seek time performance. Newer super disk drives, resembling floppy drives, do enhance both disk capacity and performance.

The typical mean time between failures for a floppy disk drive is 30,000 POH.

Super Disk or Laser Servo (LS) 120 Drives and High Floppy Disk (HiFD) Drives

The Imation, Inc. Super Disk or LS-120 drives stored 120 MB of data on special floppy disks, and Sony's HiFD can store 200 MB on its special floppy disk. These drives accomplish this by increasing the track density and the sectors-per-track storage density on the floppy media. A more precise LS head positioning mechanism makes this possible. The Super Disk 3.5-inch disks store data on 1,736 tracks with 69 sectors per track. This gives a total capacity calculated by multiplying (1,736 tracks) × (69 sectors per track) × (two sides) × (.5 KB), equaling 119.784 MB per disk.

Super disk drives interface to the PC using either the IDE/ATA Packet Interface (ATAPI), similar to CD-ROMs, or the parallel port, similar to Zip drives. Their performance is similar to parallel interface Zip drives. Super disk drives rotate at 720 RPM, about twice the speed of the older floppy disk drives. The higher rotational speed improves disk drive performance, making super disk drives faster than floppy drives, but somewhat slower than Zip or JAZ drives. Sony's HiFD drives connect to the PC using a parallel or USB interface.

In spite of their increased capacity, super drives still lack the storage space to act as an effective installation medium for most Windows application programs. Newer applications occupy several hundred MB of disk storage space, thus requiring the storage space on CD-ROMs or on DVD-ROMs to contain the software and supporting data being installed.

Because of the increasing need for storage capacity, Imation stopped selling super disk drives in 2000. Our guess is that these high-capacity, fast floppy disk drives that are backward compatible with 3.5-inch floppies are most likely to be relegated to a niche market in the long run.

Zip Drives

Zip drives, similar to super disk drives, originally stored 100 MB of data. Newer Zip drives store 250 MB in a 3.5-inch disk cartridge. There are Zip 250 drives that store either 100 MB or 250 MB of data. Zip drives interface to the

PC using either a parallel port or SCSI connection. A new USB 100 MB Zip drive is also offered. The Zip 250 drive operates using the original Zip SCSI or parallel port connection. The Zip drives, just like JAZ drives, work based upon the Bernoulli principle, permitting the read-write heads to move close to the floppy recording media and thus providing the ability to store more information and to provide high performance without damage to the media. Zip drives rotate at 2,945 RPM. Their performance is better than the super disk drives due largely to their rotational speed.

The PocketZip™ drives use smaller 2-inch by 2-inch disk cartridges that store 40 MB of data. Similar to microdrives, the PocketZip drives connect to PCs using USB interface.

CD-ROM

CD-ROMs have become a standard part of every PC. They are about to be displaced by the newer higher capacity DVD drives because of the growing need for more information storage capacity on PCs. Such increased information storage capacity will be used to store video (movies) and large databases. For example, the American Automobile Association (AAA) Map 'n Go software that stores road maps of the United States and Canada on a single CD-ROM is limited by the CD-ROM's capacity. Therefore, detailed street maps are only provided for specific areas surrounding major cities. The DVD version can have detailed street maps for virtually the entire United States.

Typical CD-ROMs store about 650 MB of data (or 74 minutes of audio recording in CD-A format) on a read-only 5.25-inch plastic media. CD-ROM drives read discs with CD-ROM, CD-RW, CD-Extra (a format supporting a mix of CD-A and CD-ROM information), Motion Picture Experts Group (MPEG) Audio Layer 3 (MP3), and CD-A.

CD-ROMs have become the primary distribution mechanism for virtually all PC software. With the advent of high-speed Internet connectivity, the software distribution and update methodology will change to an Internet focus because of the convenience. This will extend NVRAM upgrading for different hardware devices. For example, we recently upgraded a 3Com-USRobotics modem to the current firmware release by connecting to the 3Com site through the Internet and then dialup communications.

The 1X speed, 2X speed, and higher speed CD-ROM drives are measured relative to the original rotational speed of audio CDs. The 1X CD drives rotated from 210 RPM to 539 RPM, providing Constant Linear Velocity (CLV) as the CD was read from the outside to the inside tracks on the CD. Audio CD specifications are the basis for all CD standards. Higher X speeds mean faster writing speeds. When reading, access and seek times are often better for higher X speeds. Fixed disk drives behave differently. They rotate at one constant

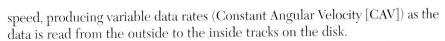

speed, producing variable data rates (Constant Angular Velocity [CAV]) as the data is read from the outside to the inside tracks on the disk.

CD-ROMs interface to the PC using the IDE/ATAPI interface. They occupy a single 5.25-inch half-height drive bay. CD-ROMs perform at different speeds and with different data-buffering capabilities. The top speed CD-ROM drives are 72X drives as compared to the original 1X and 2X speed drives. Some drives advertise higher speeds. They accomplish the higher speeds through buffering of data read from the CD-ROM drives. CD-ROMs rotate at variable speeds depending upon the track being read. The rotational speed varies from about 539 RPM to 210 RPM for a 1X drive, with the inside tracks being read at the higher rotational speed. This technique maintains a CLV of the data as it travels under the CD-ROM read heads because inside tracks have less data than outside tracks.

Different types of CD-ROMs have different CD storage formats. CD-ROM formats differ for CDs storing audio only, data, CD-R (Compact Disc-Recorders) data, and CD-RW data. There are also variations for storing photos (Kodak Photo CDs) and video.

CD-R (CD-RW/CD-R) Drives

CD-R drives write and read CD-ROMs. The original CD-R drives have been replaced by the CD-RW drives that can function as a CD-R drive, writing once on CD-R media, and, with the proper CD-RW media, they can write and rewrite recordable CDs. CD-RW drives read prerecorded CD-ROMs, both audio and data, and write and then read recordable CDs. The reading process is at a higher speed than the writing process. CD-RW drives operate at different speeds for reading CDs (up to 40X), writing CD-ROMs (up to 16X), and writing CD-RW media (up to 10X). The first CD-R drives interfaced to the PC using a SCSI bus connection. Most CD-RW drives use the IDE/ATAPI interface standard used by CD-ROM drives. Special software is required to perform the CD writing operation. This software writes data and audio CDs. CD-RW drives require a single half-height 5.25-inch drive bay for mounting in a PC. See Figure 1–15.

The major benefit of having CD-RW drives is that they can act as a backup for valuable data. In spite of their storage capacity being somewhat limited (650 MB), they are cheap (about $1 per disc) and very transportable. If properly cared for, the life expectancy can be as long as rewriteable optical drives.

There are different types of CD-R discs. Not every type of disc works with every CD-RW drive at the highest recording speed. To ensure that a disc works with a specific drive, you should perform a test of that manufacturer's media. Often, reducing the recording speed helps in recording the data. CD-RW drives have a MTBF of 30,000 to 60,000 POH.

Figure 1-15
CD-R drive.

DVD

DVD discs are similar in capabilities to CD-ROMs, but they are capable of storing significantly larger amounts of data. This is possible because they use a different color laser and because they can store data on both sides of the disc. This makes it possible to store 5.2 GB, 8.5 GB, 9.4 GB, or 17 GB of data on a single DVD disc. The single-sided DVD discs store 4.7 GB or 9.4 GB. When reading DVD discs, the drives run at slower speeds than when reading normal CD-ROMs. The DVD reading speeds are up to 16X, while CD-ROM speeds are as high as 72X.

DVD drives support a full variety of DVD and CD formats, including DVD-ROM (DVD-4.7, 8.5, 9.4, and 18), DVD-ROM book, DVD-Video book, CD-Digital Audio (CD-DA), CD-Graphics (CD-G), CD Text, CD-ROM, CD-ROM-Extended Architecture (CD-ROM-XA), CD-Interactive (CD-I), Photo CD, Video CD, CD-R, and CD-RW. This provides backward compatibility with older CD-ROMs and forward compatibility with the enhanced storage capabilities of the newer DVD CDs. Combination DVD and floppy drives are used in laptops. This dual DVD/floppy drive occupies a single laptop PC drive bay. Similar to CD-ROM drives, DVD drives have a MTBF of 100,000 POH.

Disk Drive Summary

Disk drive capabilities are summarized in Table 1–4.

Table 1–4   PC Disk Drives

Type of Drive	Media Size	Approximate Rotational Speed	Interfaces	Capacity	Physical Drive Size
5.25-inch floppy	5.25-inch disk	300 RPM	Floppy disk	160 KB to 1.2 MB	5.25-inch half-height drive; 5.25-inch quarter-height drive (combination units)
3.5-inch floppy	3.5-inch disk	300 RPM	Floppy disk	720 KB to 1.44 MB	3.5-inch half-height drive; 3.5-inch third-height drive; 3.5-inch quarter-height drive (combination units)
LS-120 Super Disk	3.5-inch disk; 3.5-inch Super Disk	300 RPM and 720 RPM	Parallel IDE	1.44 MB and 120 MB	3.5-inch half-height drive
Microdrives	CF+ Type II that fits a PCMCIA Type II slot with an adapter	3,600 RPM	PCMCIA Type II	340 MB to 1 GB	5 mm × 43 mm × 37 mm
Fixed disks	1-inch to 5.25-inch	3,600 RPM to 15,000 RPM	IDE EIDE SCSI	10 MB to 80 GB	5.25-inch full-height to 1-inch quarter-height

Table 1–4 PC Disk Drives (Continued)

Type of Drive	Media Size	Approximate Rotational Speed	Interfaces	Capacity	Physical Drive Size
CD-ROM	5.25-inch disk	210 to 539 RPM for 1X and 3,360 to 8,624 RPM for 16X	IDE SCSI	650 MB	5.25-inch half-height drive
CD-RW CD-R	5.25-inch disk	210 to 539 RPM for 1X and 3,360 to 8,624 RPM for 16X	IDE SCSI	650 MB	5.25-inch half-height drive
Optical CD-E	5.25-inch disk	2,400 to 3,755 RPM	IDE SCSI	2.3 GB per side or 4.6 GB total	5.25-inch half-height drive
DVD-RAM	5.25-inch disk	210 to 539 RPM for 1X and 1,100 to 9,200 RPM for 16X	IDE SCSI	2.6 GB one side 5.2 GB two sides or 4.7 GB one side 9.4 GB two sides	5.25-inch half-height drive
DVD-R	5.25-inch disk	210 to 539 RPM for 1X write and 420 to 1,078 RPM for 2X read	SCSI	3.95 GB and 4.7 GB	5.25-inch half-height drive
JAZ	3.5-inch cartridge	5,394 RPM	IDE SCSI	1 GB to 2 GB	5.25-inch half-height drive

Table 1–4 PC Disk Drives (Continued)

Type of Drive	Media Size	Approximate Rotational Speed	Interfaces	Capacity	Physical Drive Size
Zip Zip 250	3.5-inch cartridge	2,945 RPM	IDE SCSI USB	100 MB to 250 MB	3.5-inch half-height drive
DVD	5.25-inch disk	1,200 to 9,200 RPM as a DVD 9,500 RPM CD-ROM	IDE	4.7 GB (single layer, single side), 8.5 GB (dual layer, single side), 9.4 GB (single layer, double side) and 17 GB (double layer, double side)	5.25-inch half-height drive

Tape Drives

PCs sometimes come with tape drives for making backups of data on the fixed disk drives. Tape drives store data sequentially on Digital Audio Tape (DAT) tape cartridges. The DAT standard, created in 1987, is a digital recording format providing three hours of digital sound on a tape half the size of an analog cassette tape. The recording format uses a 44.1 kilohertz (KHz) sampling frequency; 16 bits is the same format used to record CD-ROMs.

Tape drives can store from 4 GB to 40 GB of data per cartridge. They use 4 mm DAT or 8 mm DAT tape cartridges, both of which can store up to 40 GB. Tape drives interface to the PC using SCSI interfaces or IDE interfaces.

Sound Cards

All PCs today have the capability to create and record sound. Sound cards installed in the PC provide this capability. Early sound cards were mainly used to produce sounds for Windows activities and to play CDs. Today's sound cards turn a PC into a programmable stereo system when it is connected to powered speakers. With the software and music data storage formats available, the PC becomes a programmable stereo system capable of producing three-dimensional sound. Sound stored in an MP3 format is greatly compressed. CD stereo music can be compressed by a factor of 12 compared to the files produced when sounds are directly recorded.

The original sound file format was a Windows Audio Volume (WAV) format used by the Creative Labs SoundBlaster sound cards. A more compressed format was a MIDI format. Some early music clips were recorded using that format. Most notably, Windows 95 and Windows 98 include several MIDI files useful in testing a PC's sound capabilities.

The original PC sound cards represented sounds with 8 bits of data. This did not give the best sound representation. Sound cards soon evolved to 16-bit, 32-bit, 64-bit, and 128-bit capabilities. CD quality sound requires a minimum of 16 bits. The 128-bit sound cards are capable of studio quality sound—three-dimensional sound, if used with four speakers—and can synthetically reproduce 128 different multitimbre sounds. Special sound effects, such as reverberation, are also possible.

The original sound cards were ISA bus cards, but newer cards use the PCI bus. Typically, they have input jacks for microphone input, auxiliary input, and audio input that permit recording sounds at sampling rates varying from 5 kHz to 48 kHz. Output jacks are provided for line output, rear speaker output (on three-dimensional soundcards), and amplified output. Often, these cards support joystick ports and MIDI ports for games. Newer sound cards support digital audio format encoding and playing MP3 files, providing 5.1-surround sound, and Dolby® Digital 5.1 audio supporting digitally mastered DVDs. These cards connect to two, four, and five speakers. They decode and play Dolby® Digital 5.1 audio to provide 5.1-surround sound in movies, games, and music without the need for a Dolby® Digital 5.1 receiver. See Figure 1–16.

Dolby® Digital 5.1 audio, which is also called AC-3, is an audio encoding technique that compresses as many as six channels of digital surround sound into a single bitstream, reducing CD storage space. When decoded, Dolby® Digital 5.1 audio produces a maximum of six separate, discrete audio outputs. These outputs are left, center, and right channels located in front, providing precise dialogue positioning; two separate rear channels located behind, delivering ambient sounds; and a subwoofer/effects channel, providing deep bass.

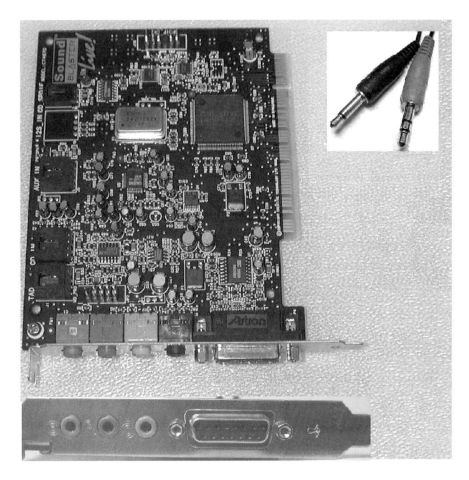

Figure 1–16
Digital sound card with stereo and mono sound plugs (in inset).

A combination of five discrete channels and one subwoofer is called a 5.1 speaker configuration.

LAN Adapters

Almost all business PCs are LAN connected. Many home PCs are networked as well using Ethernet, home wiring, or wireless LAN technologies. A LAN provides an easy mechanism for sharing disk drives and exchanging data between PCs. After people work with a LAN, they rarely want to go back to operating without the LAN. LAN connections bring high-speed Internet connectivity to the home. The bad news with LANs is that, when problems occur, the PC looks like it was frozen using liquid nitrogen. Because the PC's operating system gives high priority to communication activities, it can become locked when the communications software connections disappear. A LAN connection requires a LAN card in the PC, cabling to other PCs with LAN cards, and networking software installed in all interconnected PCs. LAN cards are referred to as Network Interface Cards (NICs). Cable modems and Digital Subscriber Lines (DSL) connect into PCs using Ethernet LAN adapter cards. There were three early PC LANs: Datapoint's ARCnet, the IBM token ring, and the Xerox-Intel-Digital Ethernet. Of these today, Ethernet is dominant and quickly evolving to meet the demand for increased transmission speeds that new applications place upon it. ARCnet has disappeared. A new LAN type, Asynchronous Transfer Mode (ATM), is also emerging for businesses. In the long run, it appears that Ethernet and ATM will become the dominant LAN types. LANs implement the electrical signaling on the LAN wiring and facilitate data transfer between equivalent NICs. Digital Equipment Corporation (now Compaq) marketed Ethernet LANs in 1982. It was one of the first LANs to interconnect PCs. In 1987, IBM delivered its token ring LAN. The first token rings were focused on IBM's mainframe computers and PCs. The token ring still holds a significant market niche today. It is moving to higher speeds, but may be displaced by newer technology LAN and telephony NICs in the next few years as ATM technology takes root. Ethernet dominates the PC LAN market and is likely to continue to dominate it. Ethernet uses Unshielded Twisted Pair (UTP) wiring to interconnect PCs. This wire is classified by its electrical characteristics, with different types of wire capable of higher transmission speeds. The initial Ethernet wiring was a coaxial cable bus, which is seldom used any more.

This was not the same coaxial cable used for television, but a version having different electrical characteristics. Television coaxial cable was 75-ohm cable while Ethernet cable was 50-ohm cable. PCs using coaxial cable were connected in a simple bus configuration with coaxial cable running from one PC to another.

UTP cable soon replaced coaxial cable. Twisted pair cable required that each network PC be wired into a hub. The hubs electrically isolated each individual LAN-attached PC from the others so that, if a PC malfunctioned electrically, it did not crash the remaining PCs and the LAN. This improved overall network reliability. Most Ethernet PCs today connect to a switch. Switches provide the same capabilities of a hub and more. They increase Ethernet performance by isolating traffic between PCs from PC traffic.

Ethernet uses a Carrier Sense Multiple Access with Collision Detection (CSMA-CD) media access protocol. Each PC connected to the Ethernet broadcasts as needed. When its broadcasts collide with broadcasts from other stations, the Ethernet NIC detects this by an excess voltage drop on the cable and then computes a new time to attempt a rebroadcast of the corrupted packet. The new time is based upon previous collisions and is randomized within the rebroadcast time window.

UTP wire is classified into categories, with ordinary twisted pair telephone wire being classified as Category-3 wire that is capable of transmission speeds of 10 MB per second. Most Ethernet wiring installations use Category-5 UTP wire, capable of speeds up to 100 MB per second. New Ethernet LAN installations use Category-5 data grade cable (Category 5e or Category 5+) or Category-6 cable, which supports higher speeds. Ethernet is designed to run up to 1 GB per second across Category-5, Category-5e, Category-5+, or Category-6 twisted pair wiring and across fiber optic cables. The general rule is that the higher the speed means the shorter the wires that run between the hub and the PC.

Ethernet PC NICs are ISA 8-bit, ISA 16-bit, and PCI bus cards. The newer Ethernet NIC cards are all PCI bus cards that operate at either 10 MB per second or 100 MB per second and in half-duplex (one way at one time) or full-duplex (two way simultaneous) transmission modes. The new Ethernet cards automatically sense transmission speed and half- or full-duplex transmission capabilities. The token ring network also uses hubs to interconnect the networked PCs.

Similar to Ethernet, the hub isolates each station from the other stations on the token ring network so that PC and NIC malfunctions do not impact the other network stations. The token ring is different from Ethernet and must have hubs to work normally while Ethernet works in a simple bus configuration or in a hub configuration. Furthermore, the token ring hubs must be configured as a closed loop to form a ring and function properly. In the token ring token-passing protocol or Medium Access Control (MAC) operation, a token frame circulates from station to station. When a station has data to transmit, it marks the token frame as busy and appends data to the frame. The frame then circulates around the token ring; the destination station copies the data from the frame as it passes. If the data is copied successfully, the receiving station signals success by setting bits at the end of the frame. As the frame again passes the transmitting station, the transmitting station removes it from the ring and then reissues a free token so that succeeding stations may use it to transmit data they have.

Token ring networks operate at 4, 16, or 100 MB per second and will operate soon at 155 MB per second. The NIC cards have ISA 8-bit, ISA 16-bit, and PCI bus interfaces. IBM specifies token ring cabling as types, with the preferred token ring cabling being Type-1 or Type-2. The data-carrying pairs in these cables are two shielded twisted pairs. IBM Type-3 is equivalent to

Category-3 UTP cable. Other token ring manufacturers use the Category-3 and Category-5 UTP cable equivalent to that used for Ethernet.

ATM NICs are beginning to emerge. The ATM technology promises to integrate LAN functionality and video telephony effectively into a single network connection. ATM has switches to switch data between interconnected PCs like a LAN, as well as between interconnected Wide Area Network (WAN) switches like telephony. ATM NICs transmit data at 25 MB per second, 155 MB per second, and 622 MB per second across Category-5, Category-5e, Category-5+, or Category-6 (when finalized) twisted pair wiring and fiber optic cable connections. ATM NICs interface to the PC through the PCI bus. Windows 98 comes with driver software and other software supporting ATM.

Modems

Dialup networking using modems provides Internet connectivity for many home PCs. A modem is basically a telephone for a computer. Modems modulate and demodulate digital data, converting it to analog voice-grade (0 Hz to 4,000 Hz) signals that travel across telephone channels. Modems are specified by their signaling technology, which in turn determines their maximum transmission speed. Table 1–5 lists the signaling specifications and related modem maximum transmission speed.

Table 1–5   Modem Transmission Speed versus Signaling Technology

Modem Transmission Speed	Signaling Specification
300 bits per second (bps)	WE 103/113 (WE—Western Electric)
1,200 bps	CCITT V.22; CCITT V.22bis; Bell 212A (most used in United States)
2,400 bps	CCITT V.22bis
4,800 bps	CCITT V.32
9,600 bps	CCITT V.32
7,200 bps to 14,400 bps	CCITT V.32bis
28,800 bps	CCITT V.FAST
33,600 bps	CCITT V.34; CCITT V.34 +
33,600 bps up and 56,000 (really about 53,000 bps) bps down	V.90 or K-Flex—USR-X2
56,000 bps both up and down	V.92

The speeds listed are the maximum theoretical speeds. Speeds of 28,800 bps and above are sometimes attained across telephone circuits. An excellent connection across a dialup circuit may reach a speed of 49,000 to 53,000 bps.

Modems can be internal or external. When a modem is an external device, it connects to the PC using a serial port conforming to the Electronic Industries Alliance (EIA) 232D specification (RS-232 interface) or through a USB port connection. Typical PCs have 9-pin connectors for their serial ports while modems use 25-pin connectors. This necessitates a 9-pin to 25-pin connector cable. Each wire in the cable has a specific function on controlling data transmission across the cable. For example, pin 2 transmits data while pin 3 receives data in the 25-pin modem connector. This is reversed for the 9-pin PC connector. Most all external modems now use the USB to connect into the PC. See Figure 1–17.

The modem behaves as though there were a cable when it is used. Modems are sophisticated microprocessor-controlled systems in themselves. They perform not only the modulation/demodulation of the data signal, but they also perform data compression and flow control handshaking with the PC and the remote modem. Data compression specifications for modems are listed in Table 1–6.

Figure 1–17
USB modem front and rear views.

Table 1-6 Modem Data Compression

Compression Specification	Error Detection Compression	Remarks
CCITT V.42bis	Error detection and correction Data compression up to 4:1	Little compression and speed increase for compressed files, such as ARC, ZIP, and LZH. Some compression and speed increase for binary files, such as EXE, COM, DLL, etc. Maximum compression and speed increase for text and tabular files. Transmission speed can increase as much as 400 percent above modem speed.
CCITT V.42	Error detection and correction	Error correction only. Uses synchronous transmission to increase effective data rate to as much as 120 percent of the rated modem speed.
MNP Class 5	Error detection and correction Data compression up to 2:1	Similar to V.42bis with less effective data compression. Transmission speed can increase as much as 200 percent above modem speed.
MNP Class 4	Error detection and correction	This protocol includes adaptive packet sizing and data optimization, producing improved data transfer speeds. Maximum improvement on clear telephone lines is 120 percent.
MNP Class 3	Error detection and correction	Uses full-duplex synchronous transmission to increase effective data rate. Maximum transmission speed increase is about 108 percent.
MNP Class 2	Error detection and correction	Uses full-duplex asynchronous transmission to increase data rate. Maximum transmission speed increase is about 84 percent of modem speed.

The flow control handshaking between modems and PCs should always be set to hardware handshaking or Request To Send/Clear To Send (RTS/CTS) handshaking. The modem-to-modem handshaking is software controlled. An example of software handshaking is XON/XOFF handshaking, which is not used for PC-to-modem flow control.

Modems interface to the telephone circuit using the standard Registered Jack (RJ)-11 telephone jack. Typically, each modem has two jacks, permitting the phone line to be connected to the modem and then a phone. One jack is marked line, and the other is marked phone for those connections, respectively. Bad things happen when the phone jack is connected into the line and the line jack is connected to the phone.

The modem card interface in the PC was typically an ISA bus connection, but plug-and-play internal modems plug into the PCI bus. ISA bus connections could be 8-bit or 16-bit connectors because modems are relatively slow devices compared to the other PC peripherals. Some ISA bus modems were plug-and-play compatible, but such ISA bus modems more often than not create installation and configuration problems.

Mouse

The mouse is the Windows pointing device of preference for most PCs. It is a rubber ball that rotates sensors on two right-angle axes. In this manner, the mouse movement is translated into vertical and horizontal pointer movement on the PC's display screen. A mouse is connected to the PC using a 9-pin serial port or through a PS/2 mouse port. Using a PS/2 interface with its small form factor for the mouse frees up the limited serial ports for other uses. Different driver software is required for each type of connection. Windows 9x and Windows NT come with all the needed serial and PS/2 mouse driver software.

A PC mouse has two or three buttons. The left mouse button is the most used. It performs all the selecting and dragging operations with a single click, click-hold, or double-click. The right mouse button expands the mouse functionality to perform specific operations. The middle button expands functionality in certain cases and can also accommodate left-handed usage.

The mouse has been revamped in several different configurations. There is the upside down mouse or trackball. In this case the user's thumb moves the ball and not the entire mouse. Trackballs are supposed to be more reliable because dirt from a mouse pad is not sucked into the movement-sensing mechanics. Of course, thumbs are greasy and sweaty, and dirt can fall down into the trackball mechanism. The trackball is formed to fit a hand. They have several strategically placed buttons to make clicking options easy. Some trackball buttons are configured to provide double-clicks automatically. This can be as troublesome as it can be helpful.

More interesting is the hand-held mouse. It can be used at a distance from the PC. It is held in the hand and not on any pad. Movement of the hand and arm is sensed by the mouse and translated into pointer movement on the PC's display screen. A simple flick of the wrist in this case moves the screen pointer. It also has buttons for selecting items and performing drag-and-drop operations.

Newer pointing devices include glide pads, wheel mice, cordless mice, and optical mice. Glide pads have a touch-sensitive pad area that serves as the mouse. By moving a finger across the pad, the PC's screen pointer moves. Tapping the pad serves as a right mouse button click, and double-tapping serves as a double-click. A tap and hold performs selecting and dragging an item. Touch pad mice are popular for laptop computers. They can be attached to desktop PCs as well. Several buttons are included on glide pad mice to perform both right and left mouse button functions. See Figure 1–18.

A wheel mouse is a traditional mouse with a wheel mechanism mounted between the right and left mouse buttons. The mouse operates normally until a page is selected using an Internet browser of some other desktop publishing application software. When pointing to the page, the wheel permits scrolling the text up and down the display screen. The wheel is rolled to scroll down or up pages of information displayed on the PC monitor. This is very convenient if you work with large text documents or surf the Internet. Wheel mice can be Microsoft compatible, or they can require added software to activate the

Figure 1–18
Glide pad, optical, cordless ergonomic wheel, standard ball, and original two-button mice (clockwise from top left).

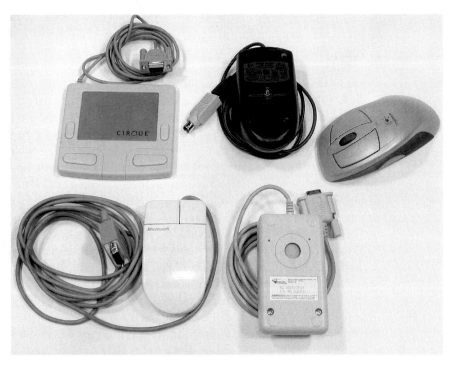

wheel scrolling function. Some wheel mice have an ergonomic shape that more precisely fits the hand with a fourth mouse button that is activated by the thumb. Most mice today have a wheel function.

Cordless mice carry the wheel function one step further. They transmit mouse movements and button clicks across a low power Radio Frequency (RF) connection to a base unit plugged into the PC. New optical mice have no mouse ball and require no special optical surface to function. They literally operate on any available surface (except water).

Mice connect to the PC using the PS/2 mini-DIN connector port, a USB connection, or through the tried-and-true 9-pin serial port.

Keyboard

The keyboard remains the primary input mechanism for the PC. In the not too distant future, direct voice input devices may displace it. This will not be a total replacement, however, for many more years. Many styles of keyboards are available. They can be broken down into 84-key keyboards like those delivered with the first PC or into 101-key keyboards like those delivered with the PC AT.

Most keyboards today have 104 keys. These are a variation on the 101-key keyboard with three special keys assigned to Windows functions. See Figure 1–19.

Figure 1–19
Wireless Windows 105-key ergonomic keyboard with 12 special function keys.

Important in keyboard layout is the placement and size of the ENTER and the BACKSPACE keys. In my case, these keys get the most use. A small backspace key means lots of mistakes because I tend to hit two keys at one time when they are small. The keys are laid out in a standard QWERTY arrangement with 12 function keys (F1 through F12) across the top of the keyboard. The cursor movement keys (this is somewhat different from the mouse pointer, even though in some cases they perform identical item selection functions) are an inverted "T" arrangement to the immediate right of the main typing area. Above that are the other cursor control keys, including INSERT, DELETE, HOME, END, PAGE UP, and PAGE DOWN. To the far right is a numeric keypad area that emulates an adding machine keyboard, but not a telephone keypad. Adding machines have the low numbers on the bottom of the numeric pad while telephones have them at the top. See Figure 1–20.

Many laptop keyboards have built-in touch pads to provide mouse functions. Other laptops use buttons (eraser heads) centered in the keyboard or trackballs for their mouse interface. These features, while convenient in a laptop, are really gimmicks that are of little effective use for other PC keyboards.

When a trackball or touch pad feature is installed in a keyboard, it is connected to the built-in keyboard connector and a serial connector on the PC. The keyboard connector can be the older PC/XT/AT style DIN plug or the newer and much smaller PS/2 plug.

If a keyboard breaks, there is no effective repair. In the best scenario, broken keys can be replaced with good keys from another broken keyboard.

Keyboards have evolved to an ergonomic layout with the keys split down the middle. The keys are sloped upward toward the split providing a more natural resting place for your hands. Some keyboards are wireless keyboards that connect to the PC in a fashion similar to wireless mice.

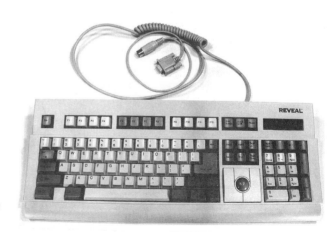

Figure 1–20
Keyboard with built-in trackball.

Video

Three components make up the display system: the monitor, the video cable, and a display controller. The video adapter card (display controller) and the monitor determine PC video capabilities. They work in conjunction with each other. The monitor must be capable of producing the image output of the PC video card. Monitors vary in capabilities as well as video cards. The trend is to produce higher resolution (more pixels—dots—spots) images that have more colors. These images then look closer to photographs and movies.

Monitor

The monitor or display is our window into the PC. Through it we see the information inside the PC. Displays have different resolutions or levels of visibility. This is expressed in the number of displayable dots (referred to as "pixels" for "picture elements"), dots per inch (DPI), or spots per inch (SPI). The more dots means the better the image. Displays vary from 320 by 200 resolution to 2,048 by 1,536 resolution and higher. Most monitors are multiscan or multi-synch monitors supporting a range of display resolutions. Display clarity also depends upon the dot pitch (from .21 mm to .31 mm) and the number of colors (or gray-scale levels) displayed.

The following is display terminology:

- Monochrome display—A one-color green, amber, or white-on-black background display.
- Monographic display—A single color that displays text and graphics.
- Display—The device producing the image. It may be a Cathode Ray Tube (CRT), Liquid Crystal Display (LCD), or gas plasma display.
- Refresh Rate—Measured in Hz. It is how frequently your monitor redraws its screen—the higher the refresh rate, the better.
- Interlaced—A technique used by monitors to produce higher resolution at lower costs. The actual monitor will only draw the odd horizontal lines on the screen in one cycle and then the even horizontal lines in the next cycle.
- Noninterlaced—A technique used by monitors where all the horizontal lines are redrawn every cycle.
- Monitor—The display and supporting electronics. Monitor and display are synonymous.
- Red, Green, Blue (RGB)—The primary colors forming a color dis-

play. This is used to identify the Color Graphics Adapter (CGA) monitor digital interface. Monochrome and monographic monitors used a TTL interface.

- Analog RGB—A VGA monitor interface producing an image with more colors and greater resolution.

Raster and vector graphics are display techniques for creating images. Vector displays draw the images on the screen while raster displays create the images from dots scanned on the display screen. PC displays are raster graphics displays. The original PC monitor was monochrome or CGA with at least 24 useable lines and 80 columns of text. The original PC display was either a monochrome display for text or a CGA display. Today, virtually all PCs use a VGA color display. Monochrome displays had a high persistence phosphor that left a bright green spot on the display after the monitor was turned off. The display resolution was 720 by 350 dots. They could not display graphics, only text characters. This was soon changed by an aftermarket product, the Hercules Graphics Adapter, often called the monographic adapter. This could display graphics and text on a monochrome monitor.

The CGA could display 320 by 200 dots. The resolution here was about half that of a monochrome display. The colors presented were limited to four colors. With the AT came the Enhanced Graphics Adapter (EGA). Color was now beginning to provide the resolution of a monochrome display. The EGA display could project 640 by 350 dots using 16 colors. The EGA's higher resolution permits it to display up to 43 lines of text on the screen.

With the announcement of the PS/2 in 1987 came the VGA display. It could display 640 by 480 dots in 64 colors. At first, these displays were expensive, but, by 1990, the price had dropped to a very competitive level. See Figure 1–21 and Figure 1–22 for display resolution comparisons.

Monitors are commonly CRT displays capable of displaying 2,048 by 1536 resolution with dot pitches around .22 mm to .28 mm. Very high-resolution monitors are made for CAD workstations and graphic designers.

PC CRT monitors vary in size from 14 inches diagonal to 29 inches diagonal.

At one time, Gateway made a combination TV and PC with a 35-inch monitor. The large monitor had low (800 by 600) resolution and a big dot pitch. Their interface to the video graphics card was a 9-pin analog RGB interface. Some monitors can connect to PCs using USB connections.

Images are constructed on the CRT screen by an electron beam that is scanned across the screen and switched on and off during the scanning. The electron beam is scanned across special color phosphors to create color images on the CRT screen.

Newer flat panel displays are becoming cost-effective. The new LCD or Thin Film Transistor (TFT) flat panels have a very crisp image because their pixels are

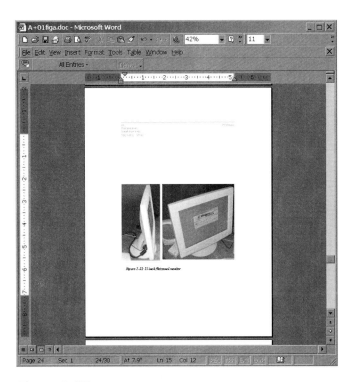

Figure 1-21
Display image with 1024 by 768 resolution.

Figure 1-22
Display image with 640 by 480 resolution.

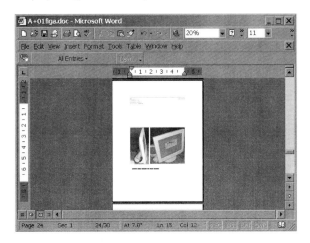

more precisely formed. They use horizontal and vertical connections to illuminate precisely a single pixel on the screen. They come in several sizes including:

15-inch	1,024 by 768 resolution	$400 to $600
17-inch	1,280 by 1,024 resolution	$900 to $1,500
18-inch	1,280 by 1,024 resolution	$1,300 to $3,400
20-inch	1,600 by 1,200 resolution	$2,500 to $3,900
21-inch	1,600 by 1,200 resolution	$5,500 and up

As you can see, flat panel prices vary dramatically depending upon size. The 15-inch flat panels can cost around $600 while a 21-inch model runs as much as $5,500 or more. See Figure 1–23. Within the next several years, virtually all monitors will be flat panel displays. Some flat panel monitors interface to the PC with the standard analog RGB 9-pin connector. Others require a digital display connection.

Flat panel displays use Cold Cathode Fluorescent (CCF) lamps for backlighting. These lamps lose brightness during their first few hundred hours of operation. After that, the rate of brightness loss tapers off. Lamp lifetime is

Figure 1-23
15-inch flat panel monitor.

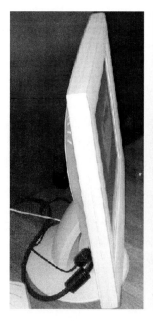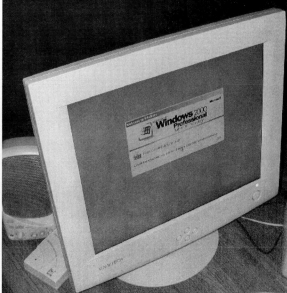

determined by lamp current, gas pressure, duty cycles, and other factors. A display is considered to be at end of life when the lamps produce only 50 percent of their original brightness. At end of life, a flat panel does not go dark. They remain about 50 percent brighter than conventional CRTs. The estimated time for a flat panel to reach 50 percent brightness is around 20,000 to 30,000 POH or 2 years and 3 months and 14 days if used 24 hours a day and 7 days a week. Dimming features and a power save shutdown after periods of inactivity extends flat panel end of life by several years.

Monitor safety is an important area. Monitors contain high voltages and consequently should be treated with respect. It is not a good idea to disassemble a monitor and power it on because of the danger of electrical shock. Monitors and water definitely do not mix. Some hospital employees playing with a Uzi water pistol one Friday accidentally squirted a monitor that promptly died in flames. It is a wonder that no one was electrically shocked.

Display Controller

The display controller drives the monitor. The display must be matched with the correct controller to produce the proper resolutions.

If we were to use a display that had only 320 by 200 resolution with a controller that was capable of 1,024 by 768 resolution, we could only display 320 by 200 resolution. Most display controllers today have onboard video coprocessors that speed up screen refreshes.

The industry moved from VGA display controllers to the next level called Super VGA (SVGA). SVGA provided a display of 800 by 600 dots and 64 colors. In 1990, IBM announced the next level display controller, the Extended Graphics Array (XGA). Its resolution was 1,024 by 768 dots and 256 colors. By 1992, most SVGA adapters provided a display mode with that resolution. This required so much processing to put information on the screen that the display was beginning to slow.

The speed up of the display comes with the latest VGA video coprocessor and a special AGP bus connection. This evolved from earlier VL-Bus cards. They perform the display processing and speed up the screen transfer rate.

All video cards have display RAM holding the video information we see on the screen. The video display information is first written to the card using a PC video memory-swapping area. The more memory on the display card means the more colors and dots it can display. SVGA and XGA displays require 512 KB video RAM. Newer three-dimensional AGP display cards use 4 MB RAM, but work much better with 8 MB or 16 MB. Most flat panel and laptop displays provide XGA resolution. See Table 1–7 for a monitor and controller feature comparison.

Table 1-7 Display Controller Summary

Display Controller Type	Resolution	Colors	Monitor Interface	Connector	Monitor Scan Rate
Monochrome	720 by 350	2	TTL	9-pin female	18.4 KHz
Monographic	720 by 350	2	TTL	9-pin female	18.4 KHz
CGA	320 by 200	4 from palette (choice) of 16 colors	RGB	9-pin female	15.7 KHz
EGA	640 by 350	16	RGB	9-pin female	21.8 KHz
VGA	320 by 200 640 by 480	256 (Standard VGA with 320 by 200 resolution) 16 (Standard VGA with 640 by 480 resolution)	Analog RGB	15-pin high-density female	35 KHz
SVGA	800 by 600	256	Analog RGB	15-pin high-density female	50 to 70+ KHz for non-interlaced
XGA	1,024 by 768	256	Analog RGB	15-pin high-density female	70+ KHz for non-interlaced
Super XGA (SXGA)	1,280 by 1,024 and higher	256 colors to 32-bit color (multimillions)	Analog RGB	15-pin high-density female	60 KHz and higher
AGP Adapters	1,280 by 1,024 to 2,560 by 1,024, and others	32-bit color (multimillions)	Analog RGB or Digital	15-pin high-density female or 28-pin DVI-I	60 KHz and higher

Display controllers are providing more onboard capabilities to enhance images. The movement is toward higher resolutions with more colors to produce three-dimensional visual effects. They employ onboard graphics processors (Graphics Processing Unit [GPU]) coupled with high-speed AGP bus transfers to speed up display refresh. Newer controllers provide a digital flat panel monitor output (Display Visual Interface [DVI-I]) connector. See Figure 1–24.

New display controllers provide support for two monitors or are aimed at video and other multimedia applications. The dual monitor displays make both displays into a single desktop operating area for Windows applications. This permits viewing several applications simultaneously, for example, writing this book on one monitor and browsing the Internet for information on the other monitor. Windows can support dual displays using two display cards or a single dual-head display card. Multimedia display cards support three-dimensional graphics and watching TV on your PC, capturing and editing MPEG-2 video, playing DVDs, and using big-screen TV monitors. The newest display controllers are fast becoming the heart of multimedia home entertainment systems. See Figure 1–25.

Figure 1–24
ATI dual monitor graphics card with VGA and DVI-I connectors and DVI-I to VGA adapter.

Figure 1-25
Multimedia PC home entertainment system with cable TV guide and CNN weather.

Printers

PCs today use several different printer technologies. These vary from impact printing, to color inkjet printers, to laser printers, to color laser printers. The market is moving to provide all PCs with high-speed affordable color printing capabilities.

The oldest printers were dot matrix impact printers. This type of printer formed images from small hammers hitting a printer ribbon to deposit ink on a piece of paper. These impact printers are now disappearing, but they remain the only printer type able to produce multipart forms. However, with laser printers becoming cheaper and faster, it is just as easy to print a form two or three times as it is to print on multiple forms simultaneously by impact. Dot matrix printers can produce color images by using multicolored ribbon. They do not effectively print transparency film.

Most low-cost printers are color inkjet printers. Normal inkjet printers use a black ink cartridge and a three-color ink cartridge. Higher quality ink jet printers use black and six colors of ink to produce images. They print by spitting drops of ink at the paper. The ink drops vary in size to produce images that vary from 120 by 120 dots per inch to 720 by 2,880 dots per inch. The ink deposited upon the paper dries to produce the printed image. Inkjet printers can print on plain paper, high-density paper for excellent image reproduction, and special transparency film for presentations.

Humans can discern a maximum resolution of 600 dots per inch. Anything more than that is not really distinguishable by the human eye. The goal for high-resolution printers is to print pictures with photographic quality. Having a relatively low 360 DPI resolution image print at a higher 2,880 DPI resolution does not noticeably improve image quality because your original image has only 360 dots per inch. However, printing a high-resolution image (600 DPI) at high-resolution print quality (720 by 720 DPI) provides an excellent printed image.

Laser printers use xerographic printing to produce black and white images on plain paper. Some laser printers print at high speed on both sides of the paper while others provide good high-resolution inexpensive black and white image printing. See Figure 1–26.

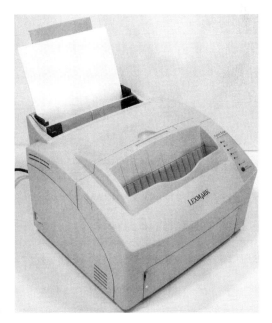

Figure 1–26
Inexpensive laser printer.

This process means that laser printers are page printers, not line printers. Dot matrix ribbon and inkjet printers are line printers that print a single line at a time. When printing to a laser printer, the printer does not start printing until an entire page of data has been sent to the printer. In contrast, dot matrix and inkjet printers print each line as it is received from the PC. To see this, just do Print Screen to a laser printer several times. Laser printer page printing often confuses people. They send a printout to the laser printer and nothing happens. They again send the printout to the laser printer, only to discover that they have printed it twice and run both printouts together.

Making sure that your software sends a Form Feed character to the laser printer at the end of each document printed solves this problem. The Form Feed character causes the laser printer to print all data it has in its buffer.

Color laser printers use multicolored dyes to produce color printouts on plain paper. They employ a variety of printing technologies to produce the images. Some color laser printers use xerographic toner, and others use thermal wax to produce images. See Figure 1–27. These printers are becoming much cheaper in price and consequently much more prevalent.

Printers interface to the PC using the parallel port. Some new printers are directly attached to a network to permit sharing between multiple workstations. Some printers use infrared links, and others use USB ports to connect to PCs.

Figure 1–27
Thermal wax laser color printer.

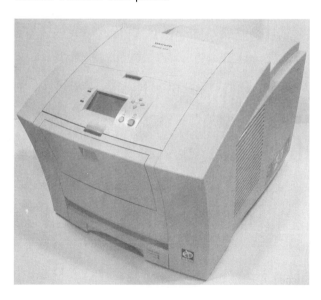

Scanners

Scanners scan paper and photographic images and convert them to digital images and text. Photos scanned in are processed by PC software to enhance image quality. Computer software can be sophisticated or relatively simple when handling images. Special optical character recognition software converts a scanned image into a formatted text file.

Several types of scanners are popular. These include:

- Flatbed scanners—These scanners operate like a standard copy machine. The document to be scanned is placed on a flat glass panel, and a light is run under it. They can scan single sheets, photos, or books. They're usually the most popular choice today. See Figure 1–28.

- Sheet-fed scanners—These scanners handle full-size paper fed through a slot. In this case, the paper moves and not the light. Until recently, sheet-fed scanners cost less than flatbed scanners, but prices are almost the same today.

- Specialty scanners—These scanners come in a variety of sizes and shapes. They can be handheld or sheet-fed models modified for a specific task or ease of use. Some are built into keyboards and others into PCs. This category includes dedicated devices designed to handle nothing but business cards or slides.

- Multifunction units—This is a combination scanner, printer, and fax in one space-saving unit.

Figure 1–28
Flat bed scanner with
automatic document feeder.

All scanners scan color images although some early scanners only scanned black and white images. They all have a set of specific scanning resolutions that they can produce. The specialty scanners and multifunction scanners are aimed at specific tasks, like scanning business cards or family photographs. These are typically sheet-fed scanners. Document scanners are mostly flatbed scanners. Some sheet-fed and flatbed scanners scan multiple sheets automatically. Hand-held scanners are best for mobile applications. A few scanners were even designed to scan multidimensional images. They used a camera mounted up away from the image placement area. Scanners most often attach to the PC using SCSI adapters or USB connections.

Web (Video) Camera

Video cameras are used to capture single frame images or continuous video streams for the PC. They help turn any PC into a video telephone with the appropriate communications and software. They are also capable of capturing single frame images for transmitting with email and other communications. See Figure 1–29 and Figure 1–30.

Figure 1-29
Pete from Web (video) camera.

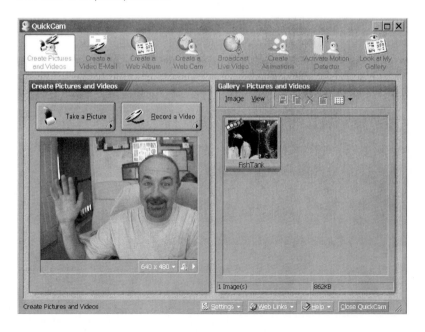

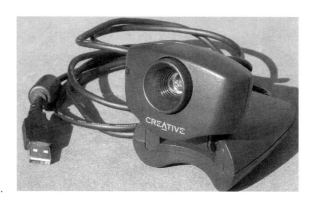

Figure 1–30
USB Web camera.

These are simple Charge-Coupled Device (CCD) imagers with varying resolution and color capabilities. The best Web cameras capture frames at 30 frames per second, but capture rate varies with resolution. Higher resolutions have slower video capture rates. Some Web cameras double as still-image cameras that go anywhere for snapshots. Older Web cameras connected to the PC through the parallel port or a special video capture card. Most current Web cameras connect through a USB connection. Web (video) cameras have become part of almost every PC system.

Still Cameras

PC systems have enhanced photography. Digital cameras are challenging film-based cameras as the most common household camera. A digital camera that produces a megapixel image provides all the capabilities needed to make acceptable pictures for the average photographer. The photographs in the first revision of this book were taken with a Sony Mavica camera that had a good lens and a maximum resolution of 1,024 by 768 XGA. They were OK pictures, but lacked some resolution. A Nikon CoolPix 990 camera with a maximum resolution of 2,048 by 1,536 (3.34 megapixels) shot the pictures for this revision. The new pictures contain much more detail than the original version pictures.

Most digital still-image cameras interface to the PC through the USB. Cameras use a variety of memory types as digital film. Sony cameras use Memory Sticks that are expensive. Other cameras use microdrives, CompactFlash (CF), Smart Media, Memory Stick, and floppy disk memory. See Figure 1–31.

Inexpensive USB devices connect the CF and Smart Media camera film directly into the PC using the USB. The pictures can be accessed and transferred to the PC as though they reside on a removable disk drive. The Windows Explorer program transfers images when they are dragged from the digital film-card and dropped into a folder on the PC's fixed disk drive. See Figure 1–32.

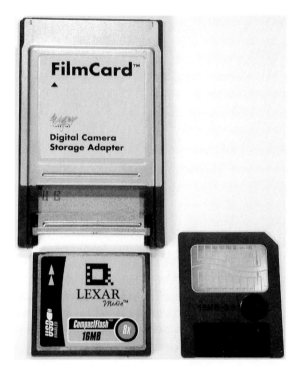

Figure 1- 31
CF and Smart Media digital
camera film.

Figure 1-32
Standard (left) and USB compliant (right) CF cards, USB interface devices, and PCMCIA
interface device (center).

Microphone and Speakers

Sound capabilities are an important part of every PC today. Soon, they will replace the audio systems used in most homes because the PC provides the capability to produce CD-quality surround sound with precise control of the music selections played. To provide these audio capabilities, the PC uses a good sound card attached to speakers. These speakers are stereo high-frequency speakers and a subwoofer speaker to produce the bass sounds. The PC speakers are self-powered. They do not get their power from the PC sound card, but rather from powered amplifiers built into the speakers themselves. Figure 1–33 shows powered PC speakers with the stereo minijack that connects into the soundcard. Figure 1–34 shows a PC powered subwoofer speaker that produces deep bass sounds. The speakers plug into the stereo outputs from the soundcard.

Some sound cards have a separate output for the subwoofer speaker while others have outputs for four-speaker surround sound, and still others support the new Dolby 5.1 surround sound. The audio quality rivals that of an expensive stereo system for most people. Only the most discerning audiophile would detect the difference between a PC-driven stereo system and a receiver-driven system. The only real advantage of a conventional system over a PC-driven sound system is that the conventional system connects to a tape deck, Frequency Modulation (FM) radio receivers, and a multitude of other audio components. PC systems can connect to such components as well, but they typically have limited output jacks on their sound card. It is almost easier to connect them to a conventional stereo receiver and connect that receiver to

Figure 1–33
Powered PC speakers with stereo minijack.

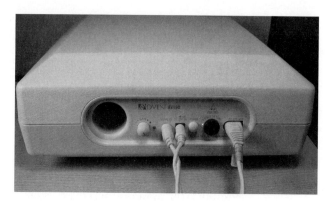

Figure 1–34
Powered PC subwoofer
speaker.

the other audio components than to attempt to connect the PC to the audio components directly.

Microphones permit sound input to the PC. The standard run-of-the-mill microphones provided with most soundcards do not provide sufficient quality for voice recognition and for broadcast audio use. Sound cards work with high-quality microphones. Such microphones reduce background noise and produce studio-quality sound. We used a high-quality microphone to record some audio material for our radio show that was stored in an MP3 compressed audio format, sent to a Diamond RIO MP3 player, and from there input to the radio station's control panel for broadcast. This worked quite well and provided near studio-quality sound. Other microphones are directional and use the USB to connect to the PC. See Figure 1–35.

MP3 is a sound file storage format. Music and sound files are stored on a computer disk in such a way that the file size is relatively small, but the recording sounds near perfect. MP3 files typically have file names with an MP3 extension.

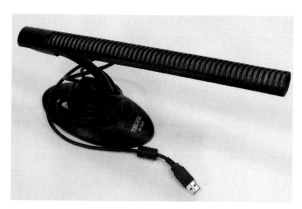

Figure 1–35
USB directional microphone.

Study Break: Adjusting Monitor Resolution

Let's try adjusting our current monitor resolution and color depth. Find the controls for your display inside your Control Panel in Windows. Click on the Settings tab of your display controls.

View your current color and screen area settings. The color setting could range from 16 colors to 32-bit True Color, and the screen area could range from 640 by 480 to 1600 by 1200 or as high as it will go.

Adjust your color settings to 16 colors, and save the settings. You may have to power off and then power on to display the color setting properly.

Adjust your screen area to the highest possible setting. This causes your icons and images on the screen to become smaller because the DPI is higher.

Software Components

PC software components depend upon the Operating System (OS) installed. The OS is a set of programs coordinating all work activity in the PC. Without it and other software, the PC does nothing but heat the room.

The most common PC operating systems are:

- DOS—The original PC operating system is used to set up and sometimes to troubleshoot PCs. DOS makes the functionality of the computer hardware accessible for running the Windows setup. DOS is the basic set of computer instructions that manages the flow of information in the PC.

- Windows—There are several major iterations of Windows: Windows 3.x, Windows 95, Windows 98, and Windows Millennium Edition (Me). Windows Me is the operating system that was delivered with most new PCs. It provides a graphical user interface (GUI) and multitasking capabilities. A version of Windows XP is now filling that role.

- Windows NT—This is the network server and industrial strength operating system for PCs. It provides a GUI similar to Windows 9x. Windows NT is a more robust operating system than Windows with better isolation of DOS, Windows, and Windows NT applications from each other. This makes for a more reliable operating environment.

- Windows 2000—This is the operating system that has evolved from Windows NT. The user interface is virtually identical to Windows Me. Underneath the user interface is an improved Windows operating system based upon the same core technology used in Windows NT servers. Windows 2000 supports a variety of CPU chips (Windows Me runs only on Pentium and Pentium-compatible CPU chips), runs on two CPUs simultaneously, and supports plug-and-play hardware components. In the long term, variations of Windows 2000, soon to be called Windows XP, will become the Microsoft operating system delivered with all Windows PCs. There are server and workstation versions of Windows 2000. The workstation version of Windows 2000 is called Windows 2000 Professional.

Each operating system has several major components.

DOS

DOS is not a knowledge objective of the current A+ certification. However, DOS is still an important operating system because hardware diagnostic and configuration programs use it. For example, a DOS program in most cases performs updating a PC BIOS by flashing NVRAM. Further, DOS commands are implemented in all Windows operating systems.

The PC DOS components are:

- COMMAND.COM—This is the command interpreter for DOS. Commands typed on the keyboard at the DOS user command prompt are processed first by COMMAND.COM. It interprets the command and initiates the other software activities to complete the command. COMMAND.COM interfaces to MSDOS.COM through the DOS Application Programming Interface (API).
- MSDOS.SYS—This performs the tasks and schedules the programs required to accomplish the DOS commands. This component is the heart and hands of DOS.
- IO.SYS—This DOS component handles the detailed I/O activities of DOS. It interfaces to device driver programs that perform the most detailed hardware operation and control activities. IO.SYS works in conjunction with device driver software for standard and special PC hardware.

- Device drivers—Device drivers tell DOS how to interface properly with an external device and are specified by DEVICE= statements in CONFIG.SYS. Some DOS device drivers are:
  - SMARTDRIVE.EXE—Manages the disk cache and double buffering for SCSI drives
  - HIMEM.SYS—Provides access to extended memory
  - EMM386.EXE—Manages the upper memory area and creates expanded memory from extended memory
- Application programs—Application program software interfaces with DOS to use the PC hardware to perform useful work for us. It is through the application program that we see the PC. Under DOS, the application program may have its own device drivers and command interpreter functions. Applications are typically a single large program loaded entirely into memory along with the data being worked upon.

DOS as an operating system runs one program at a time. It provides a command-line user interface. See Figure 1–36.

Figure 1–36
DOS architecture.

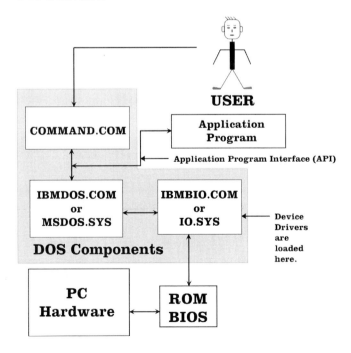

Windows Components

Similar to DOS, Windows 3.x knowledge is no longer an A+ certification objective. However, all Windows operating systems have evolved from the first Windows operating system. Windows 3.x best illustrates the evolution from DOS to Windows and helps us understand the further evolution of the current Windows operating systems.

Windows 3.x expanded upon DOS. It used the basic DOS disk and memory driver programs to perform I/O operations. Windows 3.x substitutes a multitasking KRNL.EXE program for MSDOS.SYS and adds to it GUI components, GDI.EXE and USER.EXE. In this manner, Windows 3.x expands on the foundation laid with DOS to provide the cooperative multitasking operating system with a GUI. See Figure 1–37.

Figure 1–37
Windows 3.x structure.

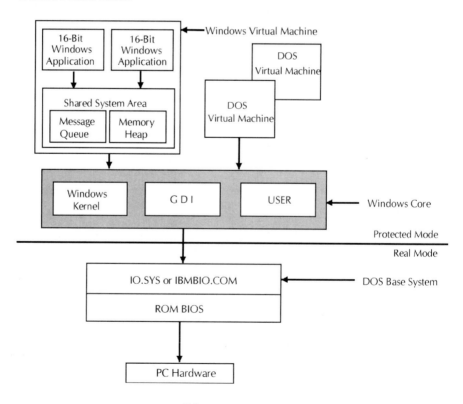

Windows 3.x components are:

- Windows Virtual Machine (VM)—The VM program manages the execution of all Windows applications, performing the cooperative multitasking between them.
- KRNL.EXE—The kernel is the scheduling program managing the DOS and Windows VMs.
- GDI.EXE—The GDI program is one half of the GUI. It handles the PC display and other graphical devices.
- USER.EXE—This is the user graphical interface program monitoring user mouse operations and similar tasks. This is the Windows equivalent to the DOS COMMAND.COM.

Windows 95, Windows 98, and Windows Me are referred to here collectively as Windows 9x. Windows 9x components are generally the same as those for Windows 3.x. However, they function differently to provide improved multitasking and GUI features. The improved features are due to Windows 9x incorporating improved file management, networking, Virtual Machine Manager (VMM), and device drivers as shown in Figure 1–38.

The Windows 9x overall architecture has the same basic components. These are:

- VM—Manages execution of both Windows 16-bit and 32-bit applications. Multitasking has been changed from cooperative multitasking to preemptive multitasking. In preemptive multitasking, no application program can dominate the VM as was possible with cooperative multitasking.
- API layer—Consists of the Windows kernel, the GDI, and user interface programs. The KRNL386.EXE still manages DOS and Windows VMs. The DOS VMs are not shown in Figure 1–38. The GDI.EXE program supports font scaling, color management, printing, and all the drawing on the screen. Finally, the USER.EXE program creates windows and controls mouse movement, dialogue boxes, and message handling and similar functions.
- Base system—Supports the system VM and the API layer. The base system is responsible for handling key functions implemented in the Windows 9x operating system.

A powerful feature of Windows 9x is its VMs. Under Windows 3.x, VMs used the 80386 CPU virtual 8086 operating mode. In virtual 8086 mode, a VM

Figure 1-38

General Windows 9x system structure.

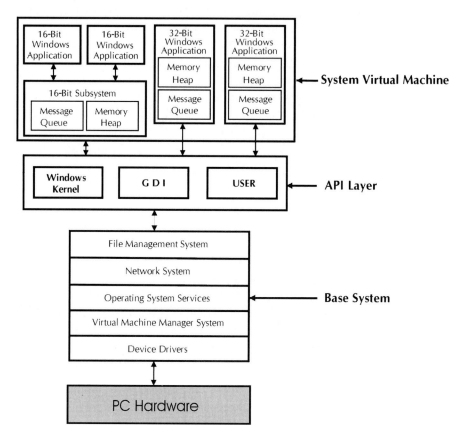

emulated an 8086 processor with 1 MB of RAM, I/O ports, and CPU registers. Windows 9x VMs are different. A Windows 9x VM contains a memory map of the memory allocated to the application program, identifies any Windows resources allotted to the application, and tracks hardware registers.

Under Windows 9x, there are the system VMs and DOS VMs. The system VM operates in the Pentium CPU's protected mode. All Windows programs, 16 bit or 32 bit, execute from this area and tie themselves into Windows through the API layer. This linkage between the application and the Windows subsystem is made during the program's load sequence. Within this VM, all 16-bit applications share a common address space, common message queue, and memory heaps. This means that, if one 16-bit application crashes, it often corrupts one of these shared areas.

Within this system VM, 16-bit Windows applications are cooperatively multitasked. Windows 32-bit applications do not use shared areas and resources. Each 32-bit application gets its own memory address space from the system VM. The application message queue and the memory heaps reside within its memory address space. The separate memory address spaces for 32-bit applications make them more reliable than 16-bit applications.

DOS VMs are very much like a PC running DOS with 1 MB of memory. The applications running in DOS VMs make service requests of the system, just like they would under DOS, through the Hexadecimal Interrupt 21 (INT21H). These requests, however, are intercepted and passed on to protected-mode code tying into system services. This is similar to the 32-bit file access function of Windows 3.11. Each DOS VM is formed from an invisible VM created during the Windows boot process. This VM contains the global environment for all DOS VMs, including information such as which Terminate-and-Stay-Resident (TSR) programs were loaded from the AUTOEXEC.BAT file. Similar to Windows 3.x, each DOS application runs in its own VM.

The Windows 9x API is designed to maintain backward compatibility to Windows 3.x. Most programs first used with Windows 9x were Windows 3.x applications (Windows 16-bit applications). Windows 9x is a 32-bit operating system, so it also has a 32-bit application API. This 32-bit API is compatible with the Win32 API of Windows NT and Windows 2000. Three main components, the GDI, the user graphical interface program, and the kernel, support the Windows 9x API. All Windows applications use these same modules. The modules additionally have been designed to handle both 32-bit and 16-bit operations.

The Windows 9x base system is comprised of several components including:

- Device Drivers—Windows 95 uses DOS device drivers as well as newer 32-bit device drivers. Some older DOS applications must have the older drivers loaded in order to function with the PC's hardware components. Windows 95 provides a number of these drivers in the 32-bit form, including those for PCMCIA cards, CD-ROMs, and the mouse.

- VMM System—This is likely the most important base system component, providing a central core of virtual services. Windows 95 has more than 700 services in the base system, and more than half of those are provided by the VMM. The VMM is a Virtual Device Driver (VxD) that resides in the file DOS386.EXE. It is responsible for handling event coordination (thread supervision), performing interrupt handling, managing memory (virtual and physical), scheduling (time slicing), and controlling the VMs.

- OS services—This area performs many of the miscellaneous functions of the OS, including fulfilling date and time requests and the plug-and-play configuration system.

- Network subsystem—The network subsystem is the latest version of the peer-to-peer network, released with Windows for Workgroups. This version uses the file management system as a way to coordinate file access across the network. Because of the Installable File System (IFS) manager, the network subsystem can also provide access to other network systems simultaneously. With the network subsystem comes support for Novell, Transmission Control Protocol/Internet Protocol (TCP/IP), and Server Message Block (SMB).

- File management system—In Windows 3.1, DOS performed the fixed disk file management functions. This caused most disk operations to be performed in real mode, not in protected mode. Such switching between real and protected mode was inefficient, but necessary, because DOS controlled disk operations. In Windows 9x, Windows controls disk operations with a new file system manager. The IFS manager provides interfaces for local fixed disks, CD-ROMs, and networks.

Windows NT Features and Components

Windows NT components carry the same nomenclature as Windows 3.x and Windows 9x components, but their functionality differs from Windows 9x. From a user perspective, the GUI appears nearly identical, but the VM, API, kernel, and driver programs provide capabilities beyond those of Windows 9x. The Windows NT functionality includes:

- Large platform support—Windows NT provided support for a wide array of CPU chip platforms, from Intel 386 to Reduced Instruction Set Computer (RISC) processors, like the Million Instructions Per Second (MIPS) R4000 and Digital's Alpha AXP.

- True 32-bit preemptive multitasking—Windows NT allows preemptive multitasking to DOS, Windows 16-bit, and Windows 32-bit, OS/2, and POSIX applications. The user only learns how to use another application, not another operating system.

- Easy networking—Windows NT comes with its own networking component built in. It comes with support for TCP/IP networking, Microsoft LAN Manager, Windows for Workgroups, Novell NetWare, Apple Talk, and more.

- Multiprotocol support—Windows NT supports all key network protocols including TCP/IP, Network Basic Input/Output (NetBIOS) Enhanced User Interface (NETBEUI), and Sequenced Packet Exchange/Internetwork Packet Exchange (SPX/IPX).

- Large capacities—Windows NT supports 4 GB of RAM and 16 exabytes of disk space. Disk drive capacity terminology is presented in detail in Chapter 14, but be assured an exabyte is much larger than a gigabyte.

- Broad file system support—Windows NT provides support for the DOS File Allocation Table (FAT), the OS/2 High Performance File System (HPFS), the Windows NT File System (NTFS), and the CD File System (CDFS).

The same basic architecture as Windows 9x provides these capabilities, including a system VM, an API, and base system functions supporting the system VM and the API. At this point, the similarity ends. Windows NT was written from the ground up to be both a client and a server OS. Its program code is not an improvement on existing Windows programs, but rather all new code designed to be run on high-end PCs and servers. Windows NT provides a user interface similar to Windows 95x.

Windows NT 4.0 lacks the plug-and-play capabilities of Windows 9x and is more limited in the PC hardware that it supports.

Finally, Windows NT was developed without regard for backward compatibility. This means that some Windows 16-bit applications do not run on Windows NT while they run just fine on Windows 9x. In contrast, Windows 9x is not designed to run as network server software. Windows 9x only supports peer-to-peer networking and is not robust enough to operate under heavy networking loads.

Windows NT additional server applications software augments Windows NT by design to customize its functionality to specific networking needs. Microsoft's Structured Query Language (SQL) and Exchange Server programs are examples of such server-centric applications.

Windows 2000

Some Windows 2000 software components have the same names as Windows 9x components. From a user perspective, the interface appears to be the same between Windows Me and Windows 2000. However, underneath, the operating system is very different. The similar Windows NT and Windows 2000 functionality includes:

- Multiple platform support—Windows 2000 provides support for several CPU chip platforms, from the Intel Pentium Complex Instruction Set Computer (CISC) chips to RISC processors.

- Robust OS—Windows 2000 provides Symmetric Multiprocessing (SMP); 32-bit preemptive multitasking; and the ability to run DOS, Windows 16-bit, Windows 32-bit, and POSIX applications.

- Network server capabilities—It has the ability to act as a network server, providing advanced networking controls, file system security, PC security, and networking security features not found in Windows 9x.

- Plug-and-play support—Windows 2000 supports a wide variety of multimedia plug-and-play hardware components unlike Windows NT.

- Reliable operating environment—It has fewer crashes than Windows 9x. Our experience is that Windows 2000 still vengefully crashes. Such crashes are caused most often by mismatched display driver software, bad network connections, and problematic USB devices. Windows 2000 is very reliable, however, once good drivers are installed.

Windows 2000 provides better memory management, reducing the conflicts between software applications, and provides automatic repair of errant applications. See Figure 1–39. The main reasons for moving to Windows 2000 include:

- Provides increased reliability and performance over Windows 95 and Windows 98
- Includes specific features for laptop computers
- Makes it easier to manage and support with the self-healing application features
- Includes comprehensive security features
- Supports USB and IEEE 1394 interfaces
- Provides an improved user interface over Windows 98

Windows XP is basically the same as Windows 2000 but, with a more modern look and feel.

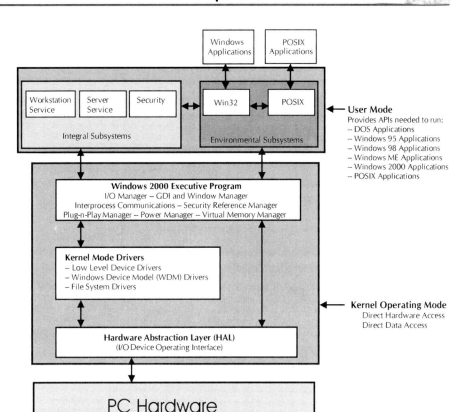

Figure 1–39
Windows 2000 architecture.

Study Break: Finding USER.EXE and GDI.EXE

It is time to find key components inside Windows. The two files that we are looking for are USER.EXE and GDI.EXE. These files should be locatable in Windows 95, Windows 98, Windows Me, Windows NT, and Windows 2000 by doing the following:

1. Click on the Start menu, drag to Find, and finally click on Find Files or Folders.
2. Type in "User*.*", and then click Find.
3. Next, type in "GDI*.*", and then click Find.

Both of these files should come right up because they are key components of the Windows operating systems.

PC Boot Process

The PC boot process varies depending on the OS being loaded. For DOS, Windows 3.x, and Windows 9x, booting requires some form of DOS. Windows 2000 loads differently using a separate NT Loader (NTLDR) program.

The DOS loading sequence is:

- POST in ROM
- BOOT program on fixed disk
- IO.SYS (or IBMBIO.COM)
- MSDOS.SYS (or IBMDOS.COM)
- CONFIG.SYS
- COMMAND.COM
- AUTOEXEC.BAT
- WIN.COM or DOS user application programs
- SYSTEM.INI
- WIN.INI
- Windows 9x registry

During a DOS/Windows boot, the PC first performs the POST procedure. This mainly determines which PC components are installed and quickly checks their basic operation. POST does not, however, perform a comprehensive system test.

The next step is either to load the cold boot loader program from the MBR of the fixed disk or to run the ROM cold boot loader to load DOS from a floppy disk. The cold boot loader program is a very simple program that loads the IO.SYS program from the disk or from the fixed disk. (Some viruses use this cold boot loader program to infect PCs.)

IO.SYS performs the main loading and I/O functions. It first loads MSDOS.SYS and then processes the CONFIG.SYS file commands. Device driver programs are loaded and matched to the PC hardware components. After the CONFIG.SYS file has been processed, IO.SYS loads the DOS command interpreter program. Control is turned over to COMMAND.COM, and it then processes the AUTOEXEC.BAT file. AUTOEXEC.BAT loads programs, establishing the DOS operating environment. TSR programs like DOSKEY.EXE are loaded in AUTOEXEC.BAT. After the commands in AUTOEXEC.BAT have been processed, applications programs are run.

When DOS is being used to boot into Windows, the first application run is

WIN.COM, the Windows loader program. WIN.COM processes the commands in the SYSTEM.INI file to load the hardware drivers for Windows. Finally, WIN.COM processes the commands from the WIN.INI file to load Windows TSR programs and to set up the Windows applications environment.

When loading Windows 3.x, all memory resident and network software are loaded first before starting Windows. It is the same with other hardware components used by a Windows PC workstation. For example, our PC workstation that is on a network and runs a scanner must have both the scanner and the network software started before Windows is initiated.

Windows 9x changes this because it loads the networking and other driver programs as part of Windows 9x. Windows 9x can use CONFIG.SYS and AUTOEXEC.BAT for backward compatibility with older DOS and Windows software. However, CONFIG.SYS and AUTOEXEC.BAT are not required for newer Windows 32-bit applications and often can be eliminated from the booting process. Similarly, WIN.INI and SYSTEM.INI provide backward compatibility for Windows 16-bit applications. They are still used to load and configure a small portion of the Windows 9x operating environment. The registry controls the main loading functions for Windows 9x. The registry loads device drivers and completes the Windows 9x operating environment configuration. It is responsible for configuring the user's desktop display, determining virtual memory configuration, allocating disk cache, and much more.

The Windows 2000 loading procedure differs from the DOS/Windows loading procedure because DOS is not required to load Windows 2000. This provides enhanced security for Windows 2000 because it is possible to better control and limit access to fixed disk drive files. The Windows 2000 loading sequence is comprised of seven steps or segments:

- POST in ROM, which is identical to Windows 9x boot process
- Boot initialization and operating system detection
- Boot strap loading, using the following root directory files:
    - NTLDR
    - BOOT.INI
    - NTDETECT.COM
    - CDLDR
  On a multiple operating system boot, PCs use:
    - BOOTSEC.DOS
  Large SCSI or EIDE drive systems also use:
    - NTBOOTDD.SYS

Some files may be in a WINNT directory on another drive. These files include:

– NTOSKRNL

– HAL.DLL

– SYSTEM KEY

– HYBERFILL.SYS

• NTLDR loads device drivers needed to launch the KRNL and does the following:

– Forces CPU into 32-flat memory (protected) mode

– Starts the file system (FAT or NTFS)

– Uses BOOT.INI to provide the OS load menu

• NTDETECT.COM finds hardware and determines configuration.

• NTLDR loads the NTOSKRNL and Hardware Abstraction Layer (HAL) software.

• User logon for security reasons requires users to press CTRL + ALT + DELETE and enter an authorized username and password either to log on to the local PC or to a network domain.

Similar to DOS and Windows 9x, Windows 2000 uses the cold boot loader program on fixed disk to load the NTLDR program. Windows 2000 uses its registry to perform the boot process.

The Role of CONFIG.SYS

The CONFIG.SYS file loads the basic hardware driver programs used by the PC. It tailors DOS to the specific hardware in the PC. It also is used to establish the memory management programs DOS and Windows use in accessing the HIMEM, upper memory blocks and extended/expanded memory areas of the PC. CONFIG.SYS can be used by Windows 9x to provide backward compatibility to earlier DOS and Windows programs.

The Role of AUTOEXEC.BAT

The AUTOEXEC.BAT file loads TSR programs and configures the operating environment for DOS and Windows software. It points to the subdirectories where temporary files are stored for both Windows and DOS. Windows uses temporary files for both programs and temporary data storage. Similarly,

AUTOEXEC.BAT can be used by Windows 9x to provide backward compatibility to earlier DOS and Windows programs. It is also helpful in loading some TSR programs, such as DOSKEY, globally for any command prompt windows that are opened when Windows is running.

Study Break: Stepping Through the AUTOEXEC.BAT

Here is a neat trick where you can step through each different component that loads from your AUTOEXEC.BAT.

Simply reboot your machine, and, as your machine is booting, hold down the F8 key.

If your machine has an AUTOEXEC.BAT, you will be able to choose if you would like to load the statement or not.

Summary

This chapter has identified a variety of PC components and subsystems. The PC hardware core components that were described in detail included the CPU chip, ROM, RAM, chip sets and buses, power supply, serial and parallel I/O ports, floppy disk controller and drive, fixed disk controller and drive, CD-ROM drive, display adapter and monitor, keyboard, and mouse.

We also briefly examined the various PC operating systems, including DOS; Windows 3.x; Windows 95, Windows 98, and Windows Me; Windows NT; and Windows 2000.

Software components that were covered included the common PC OS types, including DOS and the Windows family, their features, and key file components.

The final section covered the booting process for the DOS and Windows OSs, which perform similar boot functions, and Windows NT, which has a distinct boot process. This section discussed the role of key file components in booting these two types of systems.

Chapter Review Questions

1. *What disk is used to cold boot a PC?*

    A. Setup disk
    B. System disk
    C. Diagnostic disk
    D. Program disk

Answer: B. It is the system disk because the other disks may boot a PC, but they also perform added functions beyond booting the PC.

2. *What is not a typical PC system component?*

    A. Floppy drive
    B. Monitor
    C. Sound card
    D. SCSI disk
    E. IDE disk

Answer: D. A SCSI disk is found in servers and high-performance, expensive PCs.

3. *Fixed disk drives rotate at what speed?*

    A. 300 RPM
    B. 1,200 RPM
    C. 2,900 RPM
    D. 7,200 RPM
    E. 5,000 RPM

Answer: D. It is 7,200 RPM because floppy disks rotate at 300 RPM, CD-ROMs sometimes rotate at 1,200 and 2,900 RPM, and other fixed disk drives rotate at 5,400 RPM.

4. *CD-ROM drives connect to a PC using what?*

    A. Fiber cable
    B. IDE interface cable
    C. SCSI connector
    D. Floppy cable

Answer: B. It is IDE interface cable because it is the most common CD-ROM interface. Some older CD-ROMS used a SCSI interface. Some SCSI interfaces run across fiber cable, but this is not very common.

5. *IDE drives store a maximum of _____ GB.*

    A. 2
    B. 4
    C. 25
    D. 100
    E. 150

Answer: D. 100

6. *What file plays an important role in booting DOS?*

    A. DOSKEY.EXE
    B. MSCDEX.EXE
    C. CONFIG.SYS
    D. DRIVER.SYS

Answer: C. CONFIG.SYS loads the key memory management program and hardware driver programs. DOSKEY is a TSR program making the DOS command prompt easier to navigate. MSCDEX is the CD-ROM extension needed to operate CD-ROM drives. DRIVER.SYS helps resolve some disk drive incompatibilities with DOS.

7. *Multimedia PCs contain what?*

    A. Scanner
    B. Power supply
    C. LAN card
    D. Sound card

Answer: D. They contain the sound card because all PCs contain a power supply, and the scanner and LAN card are not absolutely required for multimedia applications.

8. *CD-ROM drives have a top speed of?*

    A.   72X
    B.   2X
    C.   4X
    D.   32X

Answer: A. 72X

9. *Top monitor resolution is?*

    A. 1,024 by 768
    B. 1,600 by 1,024
    C. 1,800 by 1,440
    D. 2048 by 1,536
    E. None of the above

Answer: D. 2,048 by 1,536 is the highest monitor resolution today, but that will change in time.

10. *Storage devices are?*

    A. LAN cards
    B. Monitors
    C. Sound cards
    D. RAM
    E. Disk drives

Answer: E. Disk drives store data and programs. LAN cards connect to a network and transfer information, but do not store it. Monitors display information, but store nothing. RAM only holds information when it is powered on, but stores nothing when the power is off.

11. *Which device stores the most data?*

    A. Floppy diskette
    B. Fixed disk
    C. CD-ROM
    D. DVD-ROM drive

Answer: B. Fixed disks store more than any other type of drive—80 GB. CD-ROMs store 650 MB, floppies store 1.44 MB, and DVD-ROMs store a maximum of 17 GB.

12. *The central component of a PC is?*

    A. Disk drive
    B. MLB
    C. LAN card
    D. CD-ROM

Answer: B. The MLB connects all key PC components. A PC can run, but not do much else, without a disk drive, LAN card, and CD-ROM.

13. *What is the fastest PC component?*

    A. Disk drive
    B. CPU chip
    C. Display controller
    D. RAM

Answer: B. The CPU chip rocks at speeds of 1.5 GHz and up. Fast RAM runs at 400 MHz, and the other components are slower.

14. *What is the first step in the boot process?*

    A. Run POST in ROM
    B. Test the floppy drive
    C. Test the fixed disk
    D. Load the OS

Answer: A. Run POST in ROM is always the first boot step. The lowest level of cold boot loader program is in the ROM. It in turn runs other software that may test the disk drives and load the OS.

15. *What does POST stand for?*

    A. A wooden pole
    B. Power-On Standard Test
    C. Power-up Original Self-Test
    D. Power-On Self-Test

Answer: D. Power-On Self-Test

16. *What does MLB stand for?*

    A. Major Logic Board
    B. Mother Logic Board
    C. Main Logic Board
    D. Motherboard

Answer: C. Main Logic Board

17. *A Pentium Pro processor has what type of cache built into the CPU chips?*

    A. L1 Cache
    B. L1 and L2
    C. L1, L2, L3
    D. L1, L2, L3, L4

Answer: B. L1 and L2 cache were built into the Pentium Pro CPU chip. Older Pentium chips have only a L1 cache, and newer chips may also have a L3 cache. No chips use L4 cache as yet.

18. *To speed up the use of frequently used programs?*

    A. Upgrade CMOS
    B. Phlash BIOS
    C. Increase RAM
    D. Install more L1 Cache

Answer: C. Increasing RAM reduces the need for the PC to swap files from RAM to slower fixed disk virtual RAM. There are no CMOS upgrades. Phlashing the BIOS cures hardware problems, but doesn't impact performance. Added L1 cache cannot be installed because it is built into the CPU chip.

19. *Software installed on a PC hardware component is known as:*

    A. BIOS
    B. RAM
    C. Firmware
    D. CMOS

Answer: C. Firmware is software encoded in ROM or NVRAM and installed on a hardware component. BIOS is a very specific type of firmware used to boot the PC. RAM is volatile memory and looses its contents when the PC is powered off. CMOS is a technology used to store the PC boot-up parameters.

20. *To manage expanded memory, a PC uses?*

    A. EMM386.EXE
    B. HIMEM.SYS
    C. LOADHIGH.EXE
    D. HIGHLOAD

Answer: A. The Expanded Memory Manager program is EMM386.EXE. HIMEM.SYS implements Extended Memory Specification (XMS), LOADHIGH.EXE loads programs into the upper memory blocks, and HIGHLOAD is not a program.

21. *Which OS first implemented plug-and-play installation features?*

    A. Windows 3.x
    B. Windows 3.11
    C. Windows 95
    D. Windows 98
    E. Windows Me
    F. Windows 2000

Answer: C. Windows 95 was the first OS to have significant plug-and-play hardware installation capabilities. Windows 3.x and 3.11 were not plug and play. They depended upon real mode DOS drivers to interface with PC hardware components. Windows 98, Windows Me, and Windows 2000 all followed Windows 95.

22. *All memory above the 1,024 KB boundary is called?*

    A. Reserved memory
    B. Extended memory
    C. Conventional memory
    D. Expanded memory

Answer: B. Extended memory is all memory above the 1,024 KB boundary. Any unused memory is labeled reserved memory. Conventional memory is below 1,204 KB. Expanded memory residing above the 1,024 KB boundary is created from extended memory, but extended memory is needed first or there is no expanded memory.

23. *Powering the PC off and then on constitutes a?*

    A. Hard boot
    B. Soft boot
    C. Warm boot
    D. Medium boot

Answer: A. Recycling power (off and then on) is called a hard boot because it kills all RAM contents. A warm boot is when CTRL + ALT + DELETE are pressed while the PC power remains on. This may be called a soft boot as well. There is no medium boot.

24. *The maximum MHz speed for a Pentium CPU chip is:*

    A. 66 MHz
    B. 366 MHz
    C. 800 MHz
    D. 1.5 GHz
    E. 2.0 GHz
    F. 10 GHz

Answer: D. This answer is good for 2001. However, in 2002, the answer may change to E. It is certain that, in time, answer F will become correct as well.

25. *The bus speed is the speed data on the system board is moving?*

    A. True
    B. False

Answer: B. The bus speed is measured as the clock speed of the bus. A bus may be 8 bits, 16 bits, 32 bits or 64 bits wide, so the data speed would be a 1X, 2X, 4X, or 8X multiplier of the bus speed.

26. *The common voltages found on system boards are?*

    A. +/- 5 volts
    B. +/- 10 volts
    C. +/- 12 volts
    D. +/- 110 volts
    E. +/- 120 volts

Answer: A and C. These are the voltages found on MLBs. The 10 volt and 110 volt amounts are not used in computers and are odd voltage levels. The AC line that powers a PC is 120 volts, but the power supply in the PC changes the 120 volts into 5 volts and 12 volts.

27. *VGA standard resolution is?*

    A. 1,600 by 1,200
    B. 1,280 by 1,024
    C. 800 by 600
    D. 640 by 480

Answer: D. Standard VGA resolution is 640 by 480. SVGA resolution is 800 by 600. The 17-inch, 18-inch, and 19-inch plasma panels have a resolution of 1,280 by 1,024. Most laptops and smaller flat panel displays support the XGA resolution of 1,204 by 768.

28. *How many devices can be connected to a single SCSI bus?*

    A. 2
    B. 4
    C. 5
    D. 7

Answer: D. Seven devices are most commonly connected to PC SCSI buses. The eighth connection is the SCSI controller board. Server SCSI buses can connect 15 devices.

29. *A serial mouse connector has how many pins?*

    A. 6
    B. 9
    C. 15
    D. 25

Answer: B. Serial mice connect into the 9-pin serial port on the rear of the PC. The PS/2 mouse connects into a 6-pin connector. The 15-pin connector is used to attach joystick controllers or monitors. Finally, the 25-pin connector is commonly the serial port on the rear of the PC.

30. *The PC parallel port D connector has how many pins?*

    A. 15
    B. 25
    C. 34
    D. 50

Answer: B. Parallel ports on the rear of a PC are 25-pin ports. Game controllers use 15-pin connectors, floppy disk drives use 34-wire cables, and SCSI connectors are 50-pin connectors.

Chapter 2

PC INSTALLATION AND UPGRADE

Chapter Syllabus

- PC Component Replacement Summary

- Removing and Adding FRUs

- Hardware Configuration Parameters

- I/O Cabling and Connectors

- Installing IDE/EIDE Fixed Disks and CD-ROMs

- Installing and Configuring SCSI Devices

- Installing Common Peripheral Devices

- Upgrading Your PC

Installing a PC can be as simple as plugging the monitor, keyboard, mouse, printer, and speakers into the main chassis; connecting the PC to AC power; and turning the power on. Yet, even in the simplest case, attention should be paid to providing adequate AC power; providing good ventilation and avoid-

87

ing direct sunlight for cooling; and proper user ergonomics. From a support and maintenance viewpoint, these considerations are important. However, equally or perhaps more important is PC component installation basics. This can vary significantly between PCs, depending on their mechanical configuration. Some components are very standardized, while others are not. In this chapter, we examine the procedures for removing and installing almost all PC components.

Before beginning, adequate grounding and static electricity discharge precautions should be taken. This means that both the PC and service person should both be attached to a common ground to minimize the chance of static electrical discharge into sensitive electronics. An assembled PC is relatively safe from damage from static discharge because most such discharges are conducted to a ground by the outside of the PC's case. There have been many times while traveling and carrying my portable PC on a metal cart with rubber wheels during the depths of winter that, upon reaching my hotel room after traveling across miles of wool carpets, I have shot blue sparks for several inches. Even when feeling the pain and hearing that audible snap of the static discharge, I felt secure in the knowledge that only I was mildly damaged and not my PC, because it was fully assembled and riding on the metal cart. In this case, the cart conducted the static charge to ground, bypassing the PC.

Some PCs, like many Compaq PCs, keep power applied to the Main Logic Board (MLB). In this case the AC power cord should not be considered as a grounding attachment for the PC. The AC power cord must be disconnected from the PC to assure that option cards and other internal components are not removed while power is applied to them, otherwise they could be damaged. In this case a separate grounding connection should be used to ground the PC and the service person. The safety practices in Chapter 4 should be reviewed if there are any questions on how to assure personal safety and prevent component damage from electrostatic discharge.

PC Component Replacement Summary

Over the last decade and a half, significant changes have occurred to the PC and to PC system troubleshooting and repair. The PC components have increased their reliability by placing more functions into custom chips, and manufacturing costs have been lowered by using surface mount technology.

Today repair of any PC board is not within the reach of the PC user because it requires special diagnostic equipment and repair tools. Furthermore, board repair is not cost effective when compared to the purchase cost of new components providing in most cases increased reliability and functionality. With the introduction of $500 PC systems, PC troubleshooting and repair now assumes another dimension. Whenever repair costs exceed half the cost of a new PC, the question, "Repair or replace?" must be asked.

Effective PC troubleshooting focuses on identification of a malfunctioning PC subsystem or software component, and reconfiguration or replacement of that component. PC hardware subsystems, their malfunction rate, the type of repair or upgrade, the tools required for the repair, and the approximate cost of the repair or upgrade are shown in Table 2–1. This table is based upon our experience with various PCs that we have purchased, resold, and repaired.

Table 2-1   PC Component Repair and Replacement Summary

PC Component or Subsystem	Repair	Tools	Cost	Failure Rate
System Board	RAM-ROM-CPU Replace or Upgrade	Screwdrivers	$50 to $250	Rarely—Obsolete in 12 Months
Display Controller	Replace	Screwdrivers	$50 to $300	Rarely—Obsolete in 12 Months
Video Monitor	Manufacturer Repair Replace or Upgrade	Screwdriver Shipping Box	$100 and up	Occasionally
Fixed Disk Controller	Replace System Board	Screwdriver	*See* System Board	Rarely
Fixed Disk Drive	Reformat Surface Scan Vendor Repair Replace or Upgrade	Software Software Hammer (satisfying temporary fix) Screwdriver	$100 to $1,000	About every 1 to 4 years
Floppy Disk Controller	Replace System Board	Screwdriver	*See* system board	Rarely
Floppy Disk Drive	Replace	Screwdriver	$15 up	Occasionally
RAM	Replace—Upgrade Capacity	Screwdriver	$0.70 to $2 per M	Occasionally

Table 2-1   PC Component Repair and Replacement Summary (Continued)

PC Component or Subsystem	Repair	Tools	Cost	Failure Rate
ROM	Flash the BIOS	Program on Diskette	$0	Obsolete
CPU	Replace	Screwdriver Special Tool	$70 to $700	Rarely or Never
Parallel Port	Replace System Board	Screwdriver	*See* system board	Rarely
Printer	Manufacturer Repair Vendor Repair Replace Upgrade	Shipping Box	$75 to $11,000	Somewhat Frequently
Serial Port	Replace System Board	Screwdriver	*See* system board	Rarely
Modem	Manufacturer Repair Replace Upgrade	Screwdriver	$20 to $70	Occasionally
Cable Modem	Manufacturer Repair Replace Upgrade	Screwdriver	$200 to $300	Occasionally
Power Supply	Replacement from Manufacturer Replace Fan	Screwdriver	$8 to $90	Infrequently Fan failure
Keyboard	Replace	None	$8 to $100	Rarely
Mouse	Replace	None	$5 to $60	Occasionally
Option Cards	Replace	Screwdriver	$20 to $200	Rarely

Study Break: Repair or Replace?

Try to answer the ultimate question when faced with PC repairs and compare it to Table 2–1. What is more cost effective, repairing the broken component or replacing the entire system? The following are three different scenarios with which you are confronted. Would you repair the component or replace the system?

1. Faulty power supply.
2. Upgrade motherboard, processor, and memory.
3. Faulty mouse.

Answers:

1. Replace power supply.
2. Buy a new system; more cost effective in the long run.
3. Repair by cleaning the rollers. If this does not fix it, jump up and down on it to relieve your frustration and just replace it.

Removing and Adding FRUs

Replaceable PC components are called field replaceable units (FRUs). FRUs are entire modules that are replaceable in the field that repair broken systems or subsystems on a PC. For example, a fixed disk drive is a FRU, while the circuit card on the fixed disk drive is not. FRUs can readily be removed and replaced as single components in the PC. Basic FRUs are the CPU chip, the main logic board, RAM SIMMs—DIMMs—RIMMs, the power supply, floppy and fixed disk drives, and the option cards. The components identified in Table 2–1 are FRUs. Almost all of these components are unbolt-and-unplug modules. Let's look in more detail at the procedures to remove and add FRUs.

Removing the Chassis Cover

The very first step is usually the most difficult; removing the PC's case. Each PC manufacturer has a different mechanism for securing the case. Generally, three to as many as six bolts hold it in place. These bolts can be hidden under the front bezel or exposed on the rear of the PC cabinet. Some cases have metal slots and tabs that hold them more closely to the chassis while others slide in a tray-like arrangement. Regardless, each PC is different depending upon the manufacturer.

All standard PCs look very similar. They first came apart just like the PC/XT/AT computers with bolts holding the cover at the rear of the PC. The front of the cover was fastened in proper position on the front of the PC by a slot into which slid a metal tab on the cover. These PCs were in a flat desktop configuration. Now, most standard PCs come in mini-tower, mid-tower, and full-size tower configurations. The case is sometimes bolted behind the front plastic bezel. In this case the front plastic bezel is snapped into place with plastic clips molded into the bezel. Pulling on the bottom of the bezel sometimes removes it, permitting access to the bolts holding the left chassis cover. Once unbolted, the cover slides forward to release it from its slot and tray-securing mechanisms. See Figure 2–1.

Figure 2–1
Front bezel removed.

Sometimes the case cover on one side is in an inverted "L" form. When it is removed, access to the top of the chassis and the right side of the chassis is permitted. On the left side, the PC option cards, disk drives, and memory slots are accessible. See Figure 2–1.

The side covers on other standard PCs are easy to remove, as shown in Figure 2–2. In the figure we see the cover behind the PC, and an exposed bottom slide that hooks over the bottom of the chassis. This piece slides so that the side-cover tabs engage the front of the chassis. Along the top of the side cover are notches that permit tabs along the top of the chassis to hold the cover. These top tabs engage the cover as it is slid forward. The two bolts on the top rear of the chassis secure the side cover.

Once the PC covers are removed, the remaining FRUs can be removed or added. Removing the cover is typically a very simple procedure. It requires keen observation and examination of the PC to ascertain how the cover is attached. If, when removing the cover, it gets very difficult to access a bolt, then the PC is probably being disassembled incorrectly. I tried to remove the

Figure 2–2
Standard PC chassis with side cover removed.

fixed disk on my first XT computer and it just would not slide out no matter what I did. I was almost to the point of prying it out with a screwdriver only to discover that there was the bottom bolt holding it into place. No amount of prying would release the disk drive. If you start to pry, then re-examine the case very closely for an alternate disassembly method.

The Pin One Rule

The next general rule for installing and replacing PC components is the data cable pin one rule. Every cable has numbered pins starting with pin one. When connecting data cables, pin one always connects to pin one. The only problem is in locating pin one on both the cables and the components. Some guidelines to follow are:

1. Pin one is the side of the cable with the colored wire. The color is a red or blue stripe down the side of the cable. On some cables the stripe is crosshatched. Figure 2–3 shows a cable with crosshatched coloring on the pin one wire. The figure also shows different types of ribbon cables with pin one designated by the colored wire on the upper edge of each ribbon cable. The uppermost right cable is a floppy disk cable with a twist at the end. Note the pin one side is nearest the twist. The next cable down as we move from upper right to lower left is an EIDE cable with a blue stripe on the pin one side. The following cable is an old ribbon cable with lots of red striped wires; the pin one wire is colored blue. The next cable is a new high-speed EIDE cable with pin one a very thin blue colored wire on the upper edge of the cable. The next cable is a high-speed SCSI cable with a bright red colored wire designating the pin one side. The final wire is a purple colored wire in an older 50-pin SCSI cable.

2. An offset notch marks pin one on cable connectors by an offset bar or by an arrow on the pin one side of the connector. Some connectors are keyed by a tab on the outside of the connector or by a blocked pin in the connector. See Figure 2–4. In the figure there are four connectors, and the top connector has an offset notch nearest pin one. The next connector is keyed and there is a triangular arrow on the (left) pin one side. The bottom two connectors both have an offset notch designating pin one. The bottom-most connector is also keyed with a tab in the center and also has a triangular arrow marking the pin one side.

Figure 2–3
PC ribbon cables with colored wire designating pin one.

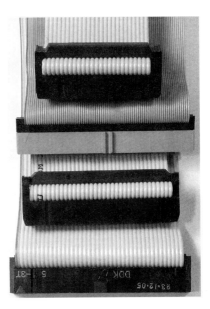

Figure 2–4
Ribbon cable connectors with pin one designation.

3. A square solder pad on the bottom side of the connector sometimes identifies pin one. The remaining pins have round solder
   pads. The five square solder pads are on the left side of Figure
   2–5. On the top two boards the square pad is on the left of the top
   row. On the bottom board the three square pads designating pin
   one are in the bottom rows.

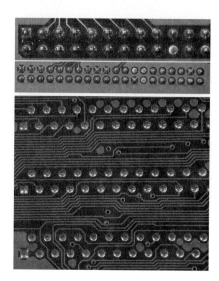

Figure 2-5
Pin one designated by square
solder pads.

4. Pin one on a board is often identified by a number label printed near the pin. It can be the number one, two, 34, or 50. One or two identifies the pin one side. Thirty-four or 50 identifies the opposite side of the cable. See Figure 2–6. The top board in the figure has pin one identified by a 1 next to the pins of both connectors. The bottom board in the figure also has pin one identified by the number 1 next to the pin, and a triangular arrow pointed at the number. If you look very closely, you might see that pin one also has a square solder pad.

5. Pin one is on the lower right side of the cable connector when the connector is horizontal. It is commonly nearest the power connector when the power connector is on the right of an EIDE disk

Figure 2-6
Numbers identifying pin one.

drive when facing the connectors at the rear of the drive. Figure 2–7 has pin one at the lower right of the power and control cable connector nearest the power connection. Note the tab at the top of the data and control cable connector slot and the broken pin at the center on the bottom of the connector. The broken pin is for a keyed connector.

6. "D"-shaped connectors are designed to mate pin one with pin one. See Figure 2–8. If you look closely, both "D"-shaped connectors have the pin numbers embossed next to the pins in the connector.

7. Connectors sometimes have the pin numbers written on them. Look for the number 1 on the cable connector. In Figure 2–9 the numbers are next to pins 1, 18, 19, and 36.

8. Edge connectors have a slot cut into the connector nearest pin one. Figure 2–10 shows two edge connectors with pins 10, 20, and 30 marked. Pins 2 and 34 are marked on the bottom connector.

Figure 2–7
A 3.5–inch fixed disk drive EIDE connector with pin one on the right next to the power connector.

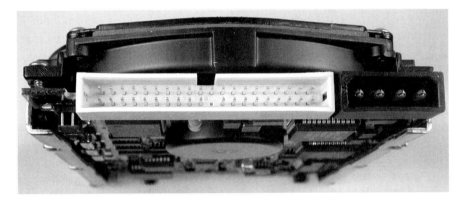

Figure 2–8
"D"-shaped connectors with pin one on the upper left.

Figure 2-9
SCSI Connector with pin numbers 1—upper left, 18—upper right, 19—lower left and 34—lower right.

Figure 2-10
Edge connectors with pins 10, 20, and 30 marked. Pins 2 and 34 are marked on the bottom connector.

If pin one is not connected to pin one, then the components do not work. They can, under some rare circumstances, cause electronic components to burn out. A common symptom of not properly connecting pin one on the data cable to pin one on the drive is that the drive light stays on.

Main Logic Board (MLB)

The system or main logic board (MLB) is typically set in the bottom of the chassis or on the rightmost side of tower-style chassis.

All option cards plug into it as well as the power supply and the front panel controls. Newer system boards also have the floppy and fixed disk drive cables, the option serial port cables, and the option parallel port cables connected into the board. These must all be removed in addition to the power supply in order to remove the system (main logic) board. Once these are disconnected, it is a matter of unbolting the board and sliding it out of its mounts. On older chassis the main logic boards were mounted on plastic standoffs that slide into bottle-shaped slots. They were then held in place by one or two bolts bolted into brass mounts. Figure 2–11 shows a plastic standoff inserted into the bottle-shaped opening in a chassis and a brass mounting bolt.

The most difficult part of this procedure was sliding the board out of the chassis. The newer ATX style boards mount differently. Figure 2–12 shows the mounting stanchions for an ATX board chassis. ATX MLBs have keyboard, mouse, and serial port connectors mounted on the rear of the main logic board. These slide into a bracket at the rear of the chassis. In some cases, they may be fastened to the rear of the chassis. If they are bolted to the rear of the chassis, they must be unbolted to remove the ATX style main logic board. NLX style MLBs may just slide into the chassis and the riser card. They can be unfastened and slid out of the chassis.

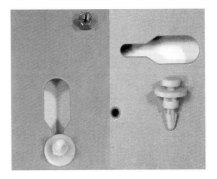

Figure 2–11
Plastic standoffs, brass mounting bolt, and bottle-shaped slots.

Figure 2–12
ATX chassis mounting stanchions.

Installing a main logic board is just the reverse process. The plastic standoffs are inserted into the main logic board holes corresponding to the bottle-shaped chassis slots. The board is slid into place so that the board mounting holes align with boltholes in the metal chassis. Sometimes small, male-female mounting bolts must be installed to provide the proper mechanism for securing the main logic board mounting bolts. ATX boards drop into place over the mounting stanchions. Once dropped or slid into place, the board is secured with one or two mounting bolts. These bolts ground the board to the chassis. On some AT-style chassis it was possible to short the MLB out if there were extra mounting boltholes that contacted the main logic board in the wrong area. Placing electrical tape over unused mounting boltholes averted such problems.

After the board is mounted, the power connections are put in place. Older style boards use power connections that are marked with the early PC, P8, and P9 connections. To assure that the P8 and P9 connectors are not reversed, the black (ground) wires on each connector are lined up with one another, as shown in Figure 2–13. The ATX power supplies generally use a single keyed connector for the main logic board. Newer ATX MLBs may use two power connections, an ATX style connector and a P9-like connector. Figure 2–14 shows a single ATX MLB power connection.

On ATX style boards, the P8 and P9 connectors are combined into a single power connector that cannot be misaligned easily. Power connectors plug into sockets generally at the right rear of the main logic board.

Once power is connected to the main logic board, the front panel control signal and switch connections are made. The basic connections may include the power LED, keyboard lock (KBLCK), the power button (PWR BTN), the reset button (RESET [RST BTN]), the speaker connection (SPEAKER –[SPKR]), the sleep button (SLP BTN), the sleep LED (SLP LED), and the fixed disk LED (HDD LED). Figure 2–15 illustrates the typical MLB con-

Figure 2–13
AT style power connector alignment.

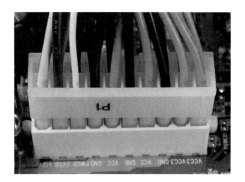

Figure 2–14
ATX P1 power connection.

Figure 2–15
ATX main logic board
control connections.

nections. On older PCs, sometimes a turbo switch connection (TBSW) and a turbo-operating mode LED (Turbo LED) was included.

Disk Drives

Both fixed disk and floppy disk drives can mount in 3.5-inch or 5.25-inch mounting slots in the main chassis. Figure 2–16 shows both 5.25-inch and 3.5-inch drive mounting bays. The 3.5-inch drive bay contains a 3.5-inch half height fixed disk drive. This chassis can hold three 3.5-inch drives and five 5.25-inch CD-ROM drives. The floppy disk is mounted on the topmost position in the chassis above the drive bays. Some chassis have removable 3.5-inch drive bays. They unbolt or have a release lever that permits them to slide from their mounts and be removed entirely from their chassis.

Disk drives are typically mounted so that the drive circuit board is on the bottom or tilted on the side. Some Compaq PCs had Quantum disk drives mounted upside down—the circuit board was on the top of the drive. Certain fixed disk drives cannot be mounted in this fashion.

When drives are mounted in larger slots, a mounting kit that adapts the smaller drive to the larger slot is used. These are simple mechanical spacers. The spacers are bolted to the drive and then the drive is bolted into the chas-

Figure 2-16
Full-height tower chassis drive mounting bays and slots.

sis. There are four bolt holes on the sides as well as on the bottom of each drive. These holes sometimes take fine thread bolts or coarse thread bolts depending on the drive manufacturer. Many manufacturers provide the bolts for mounting the drive in the chassis. Once a drive is bolted into place, the data cable and power cable connections are plugged into the drive.

Fixed Disk Drives

Today, most internal fixed disk drives are 3.5-inch drives. In some cases, larger 5.25-inch drives and in others, smaller 2.5-inch drives can be used in desktop PCs, but more frequently are found in laptops or network hubs.

All PC chassis have both 3.5-inch and 5.25-inch mounting slots for these disk drives. The 5.25-inch slots can accommodate a 3.5-inch drive with the proper mounting brackets. A 3.5-inch slot can accommodate a 2.5-inch drive again with proper mounting brackets. No 2.5-inch disk drive mounting brackets for 5.25-inch slots exist to our knowledge. However, because the 2.5-inch drives are so small and light it is possible to mount them with just two bolts into some 5.25-inch slots.

Fixed disk drives are EIDE or SCSI drives. The most common 3.5-inch drives use a standard disk drive power cable providing 5-volt and 12-volt power to the drive. The 2.5-inch drives use only 5-volt power. The data cables are parallel conductor flat ribbon cables that have 40 pins for EIDE drives and 50 pins for SCSI drives. See Figure 2–17.

In Figure 2–17, the power connector carries 12-volt power in the yellow conductor and 5-volt power in the red conductor. The black center conductors are the ground or return lines for the 5-volt and 12-volt power leads. The data cable pin one is on the left side, as indicated by the crosshatched red colored wire in the cable. Newer SCSI drives have different data cables that are described in more detail later. The 2.5-inch drives have a special drive connector combining the data and power cables together. This necessitates a special adapter on the rear of the drive to adapt the 2.5-inch drive to standard EIDE data and power cables. See Figure 2–18.

Special mechanical mounting brackets for the 2.5-inch drive enable it to mount in a 3.5-inch chassis slot. The drive is attached to a special 2.5-inch

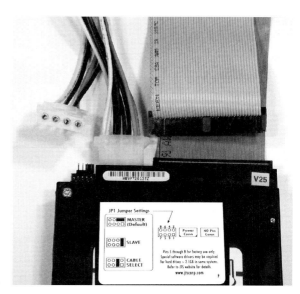

Figure 2-17
3.5-inch EIDE drive cabling.

Figure 2–18
2.5-inch drive top and bottom.

adapter that connects to both the standard 40-pin EIDE cable and the power cable at the same time. Note the power connection uses only red (5-volt) and black (ground) power connections.

Most EIDE controllers can handle two EIDE drives if the cable has two connectors. In this configuration, one drive must be designated as the primary or master drive and the other drive as the secondary or slave drive. A jumper on the drive changes the designation from master to slave drive. The data and control cable connects from the rear of the drive to the main logic board or to an EIDE drive controller board. Pin one connects to pin one precisely following the pin one rule. Most EIDE drives have a slotted connector that mates with a 40-pin data cable connector with a protruding tab to assure that pin one connects to pin one. Otherwise, the pin one connector pin is on the lower right hand side nearest the power connector on the right.

SCSI disk drive installation and removal is similar to EIDE drives. With SCSI drives, the physical drive mounting is the same as any EIDE drive. The power connection is also identical. The data and control cable connections differ. SCSI drives typically use a 50-pin cable to connect to a drive controller that is not built-in to the main logic board. The faster SCSI drives use a 68-

Figure 2–19
High-speed 68-wire SCSI cable with "D"-shaped connector.

wire cable with a push style pin connector or "D"-shaped connector on the end, as shown in Figure 2–19. The SCSI drive controller can control both the SCSI drive and floppy disk drives. The SCSI bus must be electrically terminated on both ends of the bus. With some controllers and devices, the termination can be automatic. Controller cards are usually terminated because they are at the end of the internal SCSI bus. When the SCSI bus must connect to external disk drives, the terminators on the controller card are disabled or removed. The last disk drive on each end of the SCSI bus (often the cable) must have termination enabled. If it is not enabled, you commonly have input/output errors. A quick test of proper SCSI bus and drive operation is to perform a verification of the drive using the SCSI controller card diagnostics.

One trick to use when disassembling and reassembling PCs is to use a magic marker and write everything about a component on the component in an inconspicuous spot. For example, on disk drives we write the number of cylinders, number of heads, number of sectors per track, and the total capacity. We also make notes for EIDE drives of master or slave status, and for SCSI drives of the SCSI address encoded in the switches. Sometimes it is good to mark pin one's position. This is especially true if it is not obviously marked on the component or cable itself. When we have bad components, we write BAD on the component in big, "slap you in the face" letters. This can save a lot of time later when sorting frantically through old components while trying to salvage a system.

Floppy Drives

Floppy drives mount in a 5.25-inch or a 3.5-inch drive bay slot in the same way fixed disk drives do. They also bolt in from the side. They can be mounted flat or vertical but not upside down. (See Table 2–2.)

Table 2–2   Floppy Drive Characteristics and Capacities

Type of Density	Double Density –DD	High Density –HD	Double Density –DD	High Density –HD	Extra-High Density –ED
Tracks Per Inch	48	96	135	135	135
Bits Per Inch	5,876	9,869	8,717	17,434	34,868
Disk Size and Capacity	5.25" 360 KB	5.25" 1.2 MB	3.5" 720 MB	3.5" 1.44 MB	3.5" 2.88 MB

Floppy drives are connected through a 34-pin cable to the floppy drive controller on the main logic board or the disk controller board. The 34-pin cable carries both 8 bits of data and the control signals for the floppy drive. One key control signal is the drive select signal. There are four drive select lines in the 34-pin cable, making it possible to attach four floppy disk drives to a PC. (In the early days of PCs, I had the ultimate disk storage with four 360-KB diskette drives running off a single floppy controller. Two were internal drives and two were external drives.) The diskette drives use only drive select line 1 to activate operation while the PC signals the drives using drive select lines 1 or 2. Originally this configuration was chosen to ensure that every floppy disk drive could be plugged into any PC without performing a special jumper configuration. To make this work, the floppy disk drive control cable was twisted between the first and second drive connector. In this manner floppy drive Ai at the end of the cable was activated by the PC's drive select 1 signal coming into its drive select 1 signal line. Floppy drive Bi in the middle of the cable was activated by the PC's drive select 2 signal that also came into its drive select 1 signal line. The twist permitted the floppy drives to use drive select signal line 1 while the PC used drive select signal line 1 to activate floppy Ai and drive select signal line 2 to activate floppy drive Bi (see Figure 2–20).

The floppy drive signal and control cable connects to the floppy drive using either an edge connector or a push style pin, or pushpin (you push the connector on the board pins) connector. Pin one on the edge connector is near a slot cut into the edge connector on the pin one side. This slot fit a cable key in the early floppy drive cables, ensuring pin-one-to-pin-one connection. Floppy cables installed backwards (that is, pin one to pin 34) cause the floppy drive light to come on and stay on when the PC is first powered on. Any floppy in the drive has all of its data corrupted and is not fixable.

The 5.25-inch floppy drives use the edge connector for the data and control cables, while the 3.5-inch drives use pushpin cables. The 5.25-inch drives also use the standard 5-volt and 12-volt disk drive power connector. The 3.5-inch

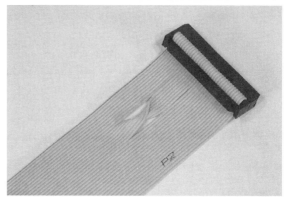

Figure 2–20
Floppy drive twisted cable
and connector configuration.

floppy drives use a special four-pin power connector to provide the drive with
5-volt power, as shown in Figure 2–21.

This connector makes it easy to plug in one pin to the left or right, shorting
the 5-volt power lead directly to the chassis ground. In this case the PC cannot power up, or the power cable catches fire. In either event, you know
immediately that something is wrong.

Figure 2–21
Floppy power connector.

CD-ROM Drives

CD-ROM drives are EIDE or SCSI drives. Most commonly, CD-ROMs are EIDE drives that install and uninstall like EIDE fixed disk drives. They have a 5.25-inch form factor and fit neatly into a half-height 5.25 drive bay slot. CD-ROMs are set typically as slave drives. In most cases they can be installed on the same EIDE interface as an EIDE fixed disk drive. But there has been at least one occasion where the fixed disk drive did not work in that configuration. When two EIDE controllers are available on the PC's main logic board, typically the fixed disk drives are on one EIDE interface and the CD-ROM is installed on the other EIDE interface.

In addition to the standard power connector and the EIDE data and control signal cable, CD-ROMS have an audio output cable that is tied directly to the PC's sound card. This audio cable permits playing music CDs just as with any music CD player.

Other high-density storage drives, such as Jaz and Zip drives, are installed in a fashion similar to the CD-ROM drive: they bolt into a 3.5-inch drive bay slot or a 5.25-inch drive bay slot. The power connection is a standard 5-volt and 12-volt power connector. Data and control functions run through an EIDE interface. It is possible to have in any PC more than two EIDE controllers, and thus it is possible to support more than eight EIDE devices. In some cases it is possible to add an EIDE expansion card, but in others a second set of EIDE ports are built into the MLB.

Power Supply

The power supply must sometimes be removed to detach the main logic board. It may be in the way, or it may simply provide more maneuvering room during main logic board removal. Typically, four bolts on the rear of the supply are bolted through the chasses to hold the power supply in place. Sometimes two slots on the bottom of the supply slide into slots on the chassis to further secure the supply. See Figure 2–22. The ATX style power supply shown in Figure 2–22 has P1 and P2 connectors as well as six fixed disk/CD-ROM power connectors and two floppy disk drive power connectors.

Once unbolted, the power supply slides out of the chassis. To finish the removal, unplug the wires connecting the supply to the main logic board, the disk drives, the PC's front panel, and the AC Power switch, as shown in Figure 2–23. The front panel power switch connections in the figure are at the end of the large black wire to the left of the P8 and P9 connectors (the rightmost con-

Figure 2-22
ATX style power supply with P1, P2, two floppy and six 3.5-inch drive power connections.

Figure 2-23
AT style power supply with front panel switch, two floppy connectors, and four 3.5-inch drive connectors.

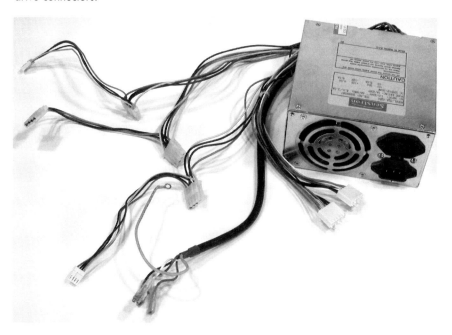

nectors). This AT style power supply has four fixed disk/CD-ROM power connectors and two floppy disk drive power connectors.

Reinstallation of the power supply is performed after the main logic board has been installed.

Brand name PC manufacturers have custom-built power supplies. These supplies are designed to fit into the brand name designer chassis enclosures. Such power supplies fasten into the PC in lots of different ways. Removing them is quite challenging. However, remember when you feel the need to get out the big screwdriver and begin prying, re-examine the chassis more closely to find that hidden bolt. We promise it is there somewhere.

CPU Chip

The Central Processing Unit (CPU) chip is typically mounted on the main logic board. It is inserted into a zero insertion force (ZIF) socket. Sockets are identified according to the number of pins they have. Older sockets are Socket-5 and Socket-7. The Pentium 4 chips fit into a socket 423 or a socket 478 and the AMD socketed processors chips fit into a Socket 462. See Figure 2–24. Note that the Pentium 4 CPU chip and the Socket 423 are irregular in shape. This prevents the chip from being inserted into the socket incorrectly.

Figure 2–24
Socket 7 and AMK K6 CPU Chip compared to Intel Socket 423 and Pentium 4 CPU chip.

Some Intel and AMD chips were installed using a special circuit card technology called a Slot-1 or Slot-A cartridge. However, the more recent chips have returned to the ZIP socket mounting technology with Celeron chips using the Socket 370, Pentium 4 Chips using Socket 423 or a Socket 478, and AMD Athlon chips using Socket 462, also known as Socket A.

The Slot cartridges contained the CPU chip, Level-2 cache, and power regulation components matching the chassis power to the power used by the CPU chip.

CPU chips are matched to the main logic board by the type of socket, the power regulation provided, and the clocking speed the main logic board provides. Chips are inserted into the ZIF socket with the chip's pin one matched to the socket's pin one. In Figure 2–25 the Celeron chip has beveled corners and staggered pins that match beveled corners and staggered pins of the Pin Grid Array (PGA) 370 socket. Notice the upper and lower left corners have the pin holes beveled across the corner in comparison to the remaining corners. In most sockets like the one used by our Celeron chip in Figure 2–25, the pins are offset (staggered) so that misinsertion is not possible. With some older sockets it was possible to insert the CPU chip incorrectly. If inserted incorrectly and powered on, very bad things happen necessitating almost certain chip replacement. See Figure 2–25.

Pin one of the chip was usually marked by a dot on the chip or a beveled corner on an otherwise very square or rectangular chip. There are similar markings around the socket on most main logic boards. Also, the socket pin one is on the same side as the ZIF lever. In Figure 2–25, it is opposite the hinged part of the lever.

Slot-1 Intel chips are easier to install because they ride on a cartridge-enclosed circuit board. The board is keyed to the Slot-1 socket so that it cannot be installed incorrectly. The AMD Slot A CPUs use the same physical connector as an Intel Slot 1 CPU. However, the CPU fan of the AMD chips mounts on the opposite side from the CPU fan mounting of the Intel chips. This often

Figure 2–25
Intel PGA 370 Socket-and
Celeron CPU chip.

prevents an AMD slot A CPU from being inserted into an Intel Slot 1 MLB because there are mechanical conflicts with the fan that prevent full insertion of the CPU chip. The electrical signals for Slot A and Slot 1 are different.

All CPU chips require cooling. This is accomplished by an oversized heat sink resembling the twin towers of the World Trade Center in New York City or by some kind of cooling fan that fastens to the CPU chip or Slot-1 cartridge. If an oversized heat sink is used to cool the chip, a fan usually blows air constantly across the heat sink, as shown in Figure 2–26.

CPU fans fail often and are one of the most frequently replaced PC components. They are clipped on, screw mounted, or sometimes glued to the chip. The CPU fan is a heat sink and fan combination. The fan uses screws to attach to the heat sink so it may be possible to leave the heat sink and just replace the CPU fan itself. The CPU fans have a power jumper cable that permits them to vampire tap into a disk drive power cable and use part of its 5-volt power to run the fan. Failing CPU fans make lots of noise. When you find a noisy PC it is most likely a CPU fan failing.

Figure 2–26
Celeron CPU and CPU Fan.

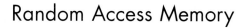

Random Access Memory

Random Access Memory (RAM) is installed in sockets on the main logic board. RAM comes in a variety of electronic types and mechanical mounting styles. These are summarized in Table 2–3.

Table 2–3   Common RAM Types

RAM Type	Number of Pins	Single In-line Memory Module (SIMM) or Dual In-line Memory Module (DIMM)
Static RAM – Level-2 Cache	NA	Chip Packages
Dynamic RAM	30	SIMM
Fast Page Mode RAM	72	SIMM
Extended Data Out (EDO) RAM	72	SIMM
Synchronous Dynamic RAM	168	DIMM
Rambus DRAM	184	RIMM

RAM must be matched to the main logic board. Main logic boards support specific types of RAM. If the correct RAM is not used, the PC doesn't see the RAM and it cannot be used. RAM is installed to increase the RAM capacity of the PC. RAM modules come in different capacities and speeds. The typical speeds of RAM range from 60 nanoseconds to 80 nanoseconds. They are slower than the static RAM chips used in Level-2 CPU cache. The Level-2 CPU cache static RAM chip speeds vary from 10 nanoseconds to 20 nanoseconds. See Figure 2–27. The Level-2 CPU cache makes it possible to use the slower dynamic RAM for main memory because it acts as an intelligent cache buffer between the slow RAM and the hyper-fast CPU.

In Figure 2–27, the top module is a 184-pin RIMM package, the next-to-top module is a 168-pin DIMM package, the next-to-bottom module is a 72-pin SIMM package, and the bottom module is a 30-pin SIMM package. These plug into specific slots on the main logic board. Sometimes the order that the packages are plugged in determines whether the CPU chip can see the RAM. These topics will be discussed further in Chapter 5.

RIMMs, DIMMs, and SIMMs are keyed so that they cannot be inserted into the main logic board sockets or clips incorrectly. If inserted incorrectly, the clips would likely break, necessitating a main logic board replacement or a chewing gum or super glue fix. Yes, I did say chewing gum. It is nonconductive and sets into a hardened, non-removable (but dissolvable) patch.

Figure 2-27
RAM SIMM, DIMM and
RIMM modules.

Device Controllers and I/O Cards

PCs interface to peripherals today using option cards. These cards plug into bus connectors on the main logic board. The main logic board commonly supports a combination of an Industry Standard Architecture (ISA) 16-bit bus, a Peripheral Component Interconnect (PCI) bus, and an Accelerated Graphics Port (AGP) bus. Option cards installed in the ISA bus usually have hardwired interrupts (Interrupt ReQuest [IRQ]) and input/output port addresses. PCI cards are plug-and-play with interrupts (IRQs) assigned when the PC first starts. Input/output controller cards can share IRQs. Installing such controller cards can be as simple as inserting the card into the appropriate bus connector, attaching external cables, and restarting the PC. If resource conflicts develop in the PC, the installation process can become quite time-consuming. When replacing device controllers and I/O cards, it is a good policy to first document the existing hardware configuration and make note of any special hardware driver programs used. This can help you get back to an operating configuration in the event that the component replacement changes resource allocations for the worse. The AGP bus is for high-performance graphics cards. In the new Windows machines, the control panel permits printing out all system settings for specific hardware configurations. For further detail on ISA and PCI cards, see Chapter 5.

Modems

Modems are installed on serial communications ports. While it is possible to have more than four COM ports in a single PC, most modems are installed on COM1, COM2, COM3, or COM4. Typically the main logic board has both COM 1 and COM 2 hardware incorporated into it. Thus, internal modem cards should be installed on COM 3 or COM 4. COM 3 shares IRQ 4 with COM 1 and COM 4 shares IRQ 3 with COM 2. The I/O port addresses differentiate COM 1 from COM 3 and COM 2 from COM 4. When installing a modem, make sure that it does not conflict with any of the main logic board serial ports. Modems most often plug into the ISA bus slots. Some modems are plug-and-play even when they plug into ISA bus slots. It is easier to disable their plug-and-play capabilities than to install them as plug-and-play devices. Once the physical installation is complete, the operating system must have drivers and software to complete the process. Windows 95 sometimes automatically found new hardware, but was not always reliable. Windows 98/Me/2000 are much more effective at finding plug-and-play hardware components. New USB modems are very easy to install because of the more effective USB plug-and-play operation.

Typical COM port settings are:

COM1 — IRQ 4 and PORT — 3F8
COM2 — IRQ 3 and PORT — 2F8
COM3 — IRQ 4 and PORT — 3E8
COM4 — IRQ 3 and PORT — 2E8

Uninstalling modem cards requires disconnecting phone and line cables, removing drivers and software, unbolting the cards, and pulling them out of their bus slot. Installation is the reverse process. Be sure that the cables to the phone and line are plugged into the correct modem ports. If not, the modem fails to work correctly.

Sound Cards

PCs today have a sound card installed. These cards often emulate a SoundBlaster sound card because SoundBlaster dominated the PC sound card market in its infancy, making the SoundBlaster card a defacto industry standard. Sound cards are ISA or PCI bus cards. They require several I/O port addresses, a Direct Memory Access (DMA) channel setting, and sometimes more than a single IRQ setting. Ensuring there are no conflicts with other devices is the most difficult problem with installing sound cards. The sound cards provide high-quality output and permit both microphone and line inputs. New sound cards have added outputs to support playing DVDs with 5.1 surround sound, as shown in Figure 2–28. The inputs permit creation of sound files on the PC from speaking or other sound sources. Microphone input is becoming increasingly important as better speech-to-text software comes to market. Sound cards also support game controller or joystick hardware. Some cards have connectors for CD drives and these are usually found when purchasing a multimedia kit.

Typical sound card external connections are a 15-pin "D"-shaped connector for the joystick, and mini-jack connectors for sound output (2 channel stereo, or more recently 4-channel surround sound, and 5.1 channel digital surround sound), microphone input and line input. See Figure 2–28. Some types of cards also have connectors for other devices, like CD drives. Uninstalling a sound card is as simple as disconnecting the external cables, unbolting it from the PC chassis, and removing it from its bus slot. Installation is the reverse process.

During installation be sure that the correct mini-jack is plugged into the socket. There has been more than one occasion when we have repaired a sound card by just moving mini-jack plugs.

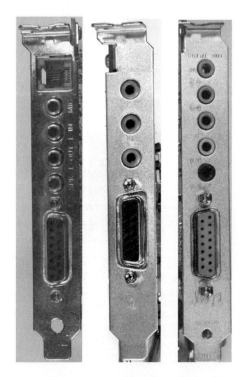

Figure 2–28
Combined modem sound card, analog sound card and 5.1 digital surround sound card.

LAN Cards

Home PCs generally do not have Local Area Network (LAN) cards as of yet. However, with peer-to-peer networking built into Windows software, more wireless and home LAN connectivity solutions, higher speed DSL and Cable Modem Internet access, lower LAN component prices, and multiple PCs in a single household, households will have a LAN in the very near future. Business PCs are largely LAN attached. There is nothing special about LAN cards from a PC hardware viewpoint. They act like any other I/O controller card. From a PC software viewpoint, they are quite problematic. Once a LAN card is installed, the PC can grind to a halt while talking with other network devices. It is best in this case to keep active logical network connections or drive letter mappings for any single PC to a minimum (i.e., very, very few).

Most LAN cards are Ethernet LAN cards. Some new cards will be Asynchronous Transfer Mode (ATM) cards. There remains a niche token ring LAN market as well.

The external connection for a LAN card is generally a MOD-8 (sometimes called an RJ-45) connector with unshielded twisted-pair wiring running into a wiring hub. The MOD-8 connectors can have special mechanical configurations to differentiate them from RJ-45 telephone connectors.

Uninstalling requires disconnecting the external cable to the LAN wiring hub, unbolting the board, and removing it from its main logic board bus slot. The reverse process physically installs the board. Once installed, the fun begins. Now the LAN software must be configured so that the LAN board talks to the other devices on the network. We discuss this more later. LAN cards are discussed in more detail in Chapter 8.

SCSI Controllers

Small Computer System Interface (SCSI) controllers are used to connect high-capacity fixed disk drives, Zip drives, tape drives, some JAZ drives, some rewritable Digital Versatile Disk (DVD) drives, some rewritable CD-ROM drives, and some scanners to the PC.

The disk controllers are commonly used to implement Redundant Arrays of Independent Disk (RAID) drives configurations. Some SCSI controllers provide hardware RAID support, while others let Windows NT software provide the RAID capabilities for the disks attached. SCSI controller cards have both internal and external ports. They can provide single or multiple SCSI bus connections. Each separate bus must be electrically terminated at each end of the bus. The controller boards usually have terminations installed because the most common configurations involve only internal SCSI drives.

Each device on the SCSI bus is assigned a unique SCSI Target ID from 0 to 7 or 0 to 15. ID seven has the highest SCSI bus priority. As a result, it is typically assigned to the SCSI bus controller card. ID six is the second highest priority. If two SCSI bus controller cards are on the same SCSI bus, then the second card uses ID six. Disk drives are installed starting at ID 0. CD-ROM drives can be installed at ID 3. Depending on the bus, more than eight IDs can be used. For a review of the types of SCSI devices, refer back to Chapter 1.

Uninstalling a SCSI card requires disconnecting both internal and external SCSI cables (and, when appropriate, the floppy disk cables), unbolting the card from the chassis, and removing it from its main logic board bus connector slot. Early SCSI controller boards were ISA bus boards. Newer boards are PCI slot boards. The SCSI boards have onboard ROM that sets up the attached fixed disk drives. This ROM configures the SCSI bus operation by setting parameters like transfer speed and synchronous transfer operation. It also contains programs for low-level formatting of the SCSI disk drives and for verifying the surface integrity of the drive, making it an excellent diagnostic tool. The ROM occupies an upper memory block address range and can have no conflicts with other devices installed in the upper memory area.

Reinstallation is the reverse process. Particular attention should be paid to SCSI bus terminations during installation to ensure that the SCSI controller operates smoothly once installed.

Video Capture Cards

Increasingly, PCs are capturing and displaying video information, whether it is a video feed off the Internet or video camera input to still pictures for video telephony. Video capture cards provide inputs for video feeds off of small CCD video cameras or from normal VCR and camcorder inputs. They have software that translates the raw video input into compressed video or still picture files for storage on the PC's fixed disks. Video capture capability may be incorporated into the display controller card. ATI produces these cards, such as their ATI All-In-Wonder display controllers.

New video capture devices connect through the USB bus or through an IEEE 1394 Fire Wire bus. In the longer term, the Fire Wire bus is likely to become the preferred means of connecting video capture devices into the PC. Such video capture devices can turn a high-end PC system into an amateur video editing facility.

Video capture cards share IRQs with other I/O devices. Uninstalling them requires disconnecting them from an external camera connection, unbolting them from the chassis, and removing them from their PCI bus slot. Installation is the reverse process. It is difficult to sometimes find an IRQ to share with other devices installed in the PC. A good one to choose is IRQ 9. Most plug-and-play PCs running Windows 98/Me/2000 resolve IRQ conflicts with little difficulty.

Common PC Reassembly Mistakes

When reconnecting cables, how must each connector with pins numbered from 1 to 9, 1 to 25, etc., be mated with the opposite gender connector? To which pin does pin one on the first connector match-up to on the second connector? You remembered—pin one connects to pin one. Now it is a simple matter of finding which pin is number one. Let's review the ways for identifying pin one. They are:

1. Check for the colored wire on each cable. Pin one is on the end with the colored wire. Refer back to Figure 2–3.

2. Often there is an arrow, notch, or bar on the connector. This connector mark is on the pin one end of the connector. Check Figure 2–4 to see what the notch or arrow looks like.

3. Pushpin connectors on disk controller boards have a single pin with a square solder pad. The other pins have round pads. The square-pad pushpin is pin one. See Figure 2–5.

4. The boards also identify pin one by having the pin number etched or painted on the board. The number is near the connector on the board. Refer back to Figure 2–6.

5. Cables with "D"-shaped connectors can only mate with pin one going into pin one. A "D"-shaped connector is shown in Figure 2–8.

6. Many connectors have the pin numbers written on them. Look for the pin number on the cable connector. In Figure 2–9 some pin numbers are written near the pins in the connector.

7. The boards with edge connectors have a slot cut into the edge connector nearest the pin one end. Figure 2–10 shows edge connectors.

After installing the power supply, did you remember to reconnect the ATX MLB P1 and P2 connectors or the AT MLB P8 and P9 connectors? Did the black (ground) wires on the P8 and P9 connector install next to each other? Refer back to Figure 2–13. Did you remember to attach the key lock, turbo LED (light-emitting diode), speaker, and turbo switch wires to the motherboard?

Did you connect the disk drive LED cable to the LED connector on the fixed and floppy disk controller board?

Did you remember to connect the power lines to the disk drives?

As you connected the fixed and floppy cables to the stake connections on the disk controller board, did you match pin one to pin one, or did you reverse the cables?

When you installed the motherboard, did it mount flush with the chassis, or was it higher on one end than on the other? Did you run a finger down the outside edge to determine if the main logic board mount is flush? If you have a hard time installing your boards in the PC bus (that is, they are difficult to bolt into the PC because they stick up too high), then probably the main logic board did not properly seat.

Study Break: Finding Pin One

Let's try finding the elusive pin one. This is the pin that must match when connecting cables.

1. Dig around your computer workshop to find any extra cables used for connecting hard drives or floppies; just about any cable will do. Looking closely at the outside edge of the ribbon cable you will find red or blue, usually red, running the full length of the cable. The red edge of the cable means that pin one is located on that side of the connector. This means that side of the connector must match up with pin one on the device. Next, examine the cable connector to see if the pin one side is marked with an offset slot, arrow, or a number 1.
2. Dig around your computer workshop to find any extra floppy drives, CD drives, or hard drives lying around. If you turn them over, printed on the circuit board next to the connector should be a 1 or possibly a square pin. These both mean that pin one is located here. Now all that needs to be done is to connect pin one of the cable to pin one of the device.

Hardware Configuration Parameters

In the controller installation discussion, we alluded to the hardware configuration parameters that are used to install various PC hardware components. It is time to examine these in detail. While these hardware parameters are important today and into the near future, in the long term, hardware installation has become easier. PC hardware components may not reside in a single chassis, but are rather connected through USB hubs to the PC. As more devices become USB connected and the ISA bus connections disappear from PCs, the problems of finding free hardware resources are replaced by problems like tuning the USB for high performance. There are always problems for us nerds to solve. PC hardware resources are:

1. Input/output ports
2. IRQ lines
3. Upper (reserved) memory areas
4. DMA channels

The most critical resource is the device's input/output port assignment. This cannot be shared between devices. Next comes the IRQ line. IRQs can be shared. Virtually all PC hardware components have an I/O port and an IRQ assignment.

Some devices use the upper memory area for ROM or RAM swapping. Video display adapters are prime examples of such devices. Finally, a few devices use DMA channels for I/O transfers as well. Similar to IRQs, DMA channels can be shared. DMA channel sharing is rare.

PC resource assignments can be viewed in any Windows 95/98 PC using the control panel. By selecting control panel–system–device manager–computer–properties, Windows displays the PC's resource assignments by IRQ, I/O port, memory address, and DMA channel assignment. Similar information is displayed for DOS PCs using the Microsoft Diagnostic program (MSD).

Common I/O Port Addresses

Each PC disk controller card requires an I/O address to exchange data with the CPU. The I/O address acts like a mailbox for the board. These I/O addresses look like standard RAM addresses in lower memory, but they are not. Intel chips perform I/O operations using special I/O instructions. The I/O port addresses only function with the special Intel chip I/O instructions. The I/O address locations are duplicated by lower memory locations. Those lower memory locations store DOS and Windows software environment and other parameters but perform no I/O functions.

In contrast, Motorola CPU chips (used in some Apple Computers) perform I/O operations using normal memory instructions and specially assigned memory locations. This is called memory mapped I/O.

The common I/O port addresses used in the PC are listed in Table 2–4.

Table 2–4 Typical PC I/O Port Assignments

I/O Port Address	Assignment
000-00F 081-09F	Direct Memory Access Controller
010-01F 0A0-0A1	Programmable Interrupt Controller
040-043 060-060	System Timer
064-064	Keyboard
061-061	Speaker
070-071	CMOS/Real Time Clock
0F0 – 0FF	Math Coprocessor
170-1F7	IDE Controllers
1F0 – 1F8	AT Hard Disk Controller
200 – 207	Gameport-Joystick Controller
208-20F	System Board Resources
210 – 217	Expansion Chassis
220-22F	Sound Blaster Card
274-277	I/O Read for Plug-and-Play Enumerator
294-297	PCI Bus
2A0—2A4	IBM Token Ring Network
2E8—2EF	COM4 Serial Port
2F8 – 2FF	COM2 Serial Port
300 – 301	Sound Card MPU401 Emulation

Table 2–4   Typical PC I/O Port Assignments (Continued)

I/O Port Address	Assignment
320 – 32F	Hard Disk Controller—PC and XT
330 – 337	Bernoulli Box Controller (historic)
376-376	PCI EIDE Controller
378 – 37F	LPT1 Printer Port
380 – 388	VGA Cards or old IBM SDLC Card
3A0—3AF	IBM—BSC Card (historic)
3B0—3BF	Monochrome Adapter—PC and XT
3C0—3CF	VGA Cards or old EGA Adapter
3D0—3DF	Color/Graphics Adapter—PC and XT
3E8—3EF	COM3 Serial Port
3F2 – 3F5	Floppy Disk Controller
3F6-3F6	PCI Primary EIDE Controller
3F8 – 3FF	COM1 Serial Port
480-48F 4D0-4D1	PCI Bus
570-57F 5F0-5F7	Primary EIDE Controller Alias
620-623 A20-A23 E20-E23	Sound card MIDI Port
776-776	Secondary EIDE Controller Alias
778-77A	ECP Printer Port
CF8-CFF	PCI Bus
4000-403F 5000-501F	PCI Bus
D000-D0FF	VGA Board
E000-E01F	USB Host Controller
E400-E4FF	Adaptec SCSI Controller
E800-E87F	Fast Ethernet Adapter
F000-F00F	EIDE Controllers

This table is not meant to be a comprehensive listing of all possible I/O port assignments. It is representative of a single PC system and some of the older IBM port assignments. It is interesting to note that available I/O addresses span the entire real mode address range of Intel CPU chips. This means that there is about 1 MB of available I/O addresses. Do you ever wonder when these will run out? Like maybe in 50 years.

Standard IRQ Settings

The main logic board uses IRQ lines to get the CPU chip's attention. Every board must have an IRQ assignment. Some conflicts can cause boards to not operate properly. On early PCs and XTs there are eight lines (0 through 7) but on AT class machines there are 16 (0 through 15). Typically, ISA bus boards require you to choose IRQs 2, 3, 4, 5, 7, 9, 10, 11, or 12. PCI bus boards can share IRQs. Furthermore, plug-and-play PCI and ISA bus boards permit Windows to assign IRQs and automatically resolve IRQ conflicts.

IRQ 2 and IRQ 9 are linked to permit cascading interrupts from the secondary IRQ controller to the primary IRQ controller. The primary controller handles IRQs 0 through 7 and the secondary controller handles IRQs 8 through 15. Table 2–5 lists common IRQ settings.

Table 2–5 Common PC IRQ Assignments

Device	Interrupt Line
System Timer	0
Keyboard	1
Programmable Interrupt Controller	2 (Used to cascade IRQs 8 through 15)
COM2 and COM4	3
COM1 and COM3	4
Hard Disk on PCs and XTs and LPT2 on AT Class Systems Modems	5
Floppy Disk Controller	6
LPT1—ECP Port Sound Card (shared)	7
System CMOS—Real Time Clock	8
Networking, Video, Sound (shared)	9

Table 2-5   Common PC IRQ Assignments (Continued)

Device	Interrupt Line
IRQ Holder for PCI Steering SCSI Controller (shared)	10 or (A)
IRQ Holder for PCI Steering USB Host Controller (shared)	11 or (B)
IRQ Holder for PCI Steering Video Input Controller (shared)	12 or (C)
Numeric Processor	13 or (D)
Primary EIDE Fixed Disk or CD-ROM	14 or (E)
Secondary EIDE Fixed Disk or CD-ROM	15 or (F)

As more devices are installed into PCs, IRQ sharing has become a necessity. The new PCI bus PCs can share IRQs. USB connections can also alleviate the shortage of IRQs. However, performance-related problems are surfacing with USB bus devices. This continues the PC configuration challenge but with a new set of problems to solve.

Upper Memory Used by PC Hardware

Some PC controller cards require space set aside in the upper memory area (UMA) for buffering and ROM. Aside from video boards, which have always used the upper memory area for buffering and ROM as well, the two types of boards that are most likely to use the upper memory areas are LAN boards and fixed disk controller boards. The IBM token ring LAN adapter cards use an upper memory area for RAM buffering and another for ROM. The RAM buffering area can vary in size from 8 KB to 64 KB. The upper memory block locations used vary depending upon whether the token ring adapter card is set up as the primary token ring adapter or the secondary token ring adapter. The primary adapter uses address CC000 for ROM and D800 for RAM. Figure 2–29 illustrates common ROM and RAM swapping area assignments.

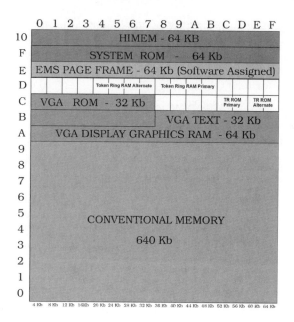

Figure 2-29
Upper Memory Area.

In the PC being used to write this book, some additional upper memory area assignments are:

1. C800-CA7F—Adaptec SCSI Controller—Windows displays this address as 000C8000-000CA7FF.

2. 10000-5FFFF—System Board Extension for the plug-and-play BIOS — This address is way off the scale in Figure 2–29. Windows displays this address as 00100000-05FFFFFF.

3. D0000000-DFFFFFFF—Pentium Processor to PCI bridge—This RAM is now way at the top of the memory address range of the memory installed in this PC system.

4. E8000000-E8FFFFFF—ATI 3D Rage Pro and Pentium CPU to AGP controller.

5. E9000000-E901FFFF—ATI 3D Rage Pro.

6. EA000000-EA000FFF—ATI 3D Rage Pro.

7. EE000000-EE000FFF—Video Capture Board Buffer.

8. EE001000-EE00107F—Fast Ethernet Card.

9. EE002000-EE002FFF—Adaptec SCSI controller.

10. FFFE0000-FFFFFFFF—System Board Extension for the plug-and-play BIOS.

Interestingly enough, these upper memory addresses span the entire memory range in the PC. They are not restricted to the real mode memory addressing area.

PC Direct Memory Access Channels

DMA channels transfer data between a controller board and the PC's RAM by stealing memory cycles away from the CPU to perform the transfer. The value here is that the CPU can start an I/O operation, assign it to DMA (which does not disturb the CPU until it is finished), and then perform other tasks while the DMA channel handles the data transfer. Chips on the PC system board implement direct Memory Access channels. These chips were fast for the original PC. Today they are slow compared to Pentium CPU chips operating at 1.5 to over 2.0 GHz. A Pentium CPU running at 1.5 to over 2.0 GHz can have the controller board buffering input/output data, interrupt the CPU, and tell it to transfer the data to RAM. It then transfers the data using software I/O instructions, and resumes what it was doing in less time than the data transfer could be performed by DMA. Sound cards, UDMA (Ultra-DMA) hard disk drives, CD-ROM, CD-RW, and DVD components benefit from using DMA channels.

Table 2–6 lists the PC's DMA channels and their use.

Table 2-6   DMA Assignments

DMA	Channel Assignment
00	RAM Refresh Sound Card
01	Available
02	Floppy Controller
03	ECP Printer port Bernoulli Box
04	Direct Memory Access (DMA) Controller
05	Sound Card
06	Available
07	Available

When lots of I/O activity takes place, the CPU load skyrockets. Consequently, we find that slower devices use DMA channels to reduce overall CPU load.

Study Break: IRQs

Now it is time to view some of your IRQs. We are going to view the IRQ settings inside Windows 95/98/Me/2000 system information.

1. Click on the Start Button and drag up to settings. Then click on control panel. Inside the control panel you find a system icon. Double-click on the system icon and a window will appear with four tabs. Then click on the tab Device Manager, or Hardware then Device Manager (Windows Me/2000).
2. Device Manager will display all the basic information on the devices inside or connected to your PC. Expand one of the options, such as System Devices. One of the devices inside there is the System Timer. If you double-click System Timer, it usually displays three tabs: General, Driver, and Resources. If you click on the Resources Tab it shows the Interrupt Request 00. This corresponds to Table 2–5.

I/O Cabling and Connectors

An important part of installing PC systems is the cabling. PCs use a variety of cables to connect to the peripheral components they support. These cables differ in the type of wire and the connectors used. Each cable is designed for a specific purpose. Over the next several years this will change. USB and other similar high-speed connections provide the capability to connect all PC peripheral components using one or two common wiring schemes. To achieve this, all communications to peripheral devices must be in digital form with the devices containing the electronics to convert the digital transmissions into the subsequent analog outputs. For example, there are USB speakers that receive sound information from the PC in digital form across the USB bus. They in turn transform that into amplified sound that plays over the speakers. The benefit here is that special speaker wiring is eliminated in favor of two or three digital USB connections.

USB ports were widely implemented on PCs beginning in 1998. Today, many USB PC components are available for purchase. These components range from mice, keyboards, and speakers to monitors and CD drives. The USB is PC technology for the new millennium.

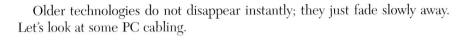
Older technologies do not disappear instantly; they just fade slowly away. Let's look at some PC cabling.

Peripheral Port Connector Types and Cabling

Peripheral port connectors and cables are summarized in Table 2–7.

Table 2–7 PC Peripheral Component Connectors and Cables

Component	Connector Description	Cable Description
VGA Display	Male 15-pin high-density "D"-shaped connector	Shielded 12 to 15-wire round cable with a ferrite yoke. Length is about four feet.
Flat Panel Display	Male 15-pin high-density "D"-shaped connector or Male 28-pin "D"-shaped digital display connector	Shielded 12 to 15-wire round cable with a ferrite yoke. Length is about four feet. or A four foot, 28-wire digital display cable.
Mouse	Male 9-pin "D"-shaped connector or Male 6-pin Mini DIN connector	Unshielded 4-wire round cable about four to eight feet long.
Keyboard	Male 5-pin DIN connector or Male 6-pin Mini DIN connector	Unshielded 4-wire round cable about four to eight feet long.
Serial Port	Male 9-pin "D"-shaped connector or Male 25-pin "D"-shaped connector	Unshielded 9-wire or 25-wire round cable up to 50 feet long.
Parallel Port	Male 25-pin connector plugs into PC and Centronics style 36-pin connector plugging into printer.	Shielded 25-wire round cable up to 15 feet long.
Game or joystick port	Male 15-pin low-density connector	Unshielded 4-wire round cable about four to eight feet long.

Table 2–7 PC Peripheral Component Connectors and Cables (Continued)

Component	Connector Description	Cable Description
Speakers	Male Mini-stereo audio plug	Shielded 2-wire round cable.
Ear Phones	Male Mini-stereo audio plug	Shielded 2-wire round cable.
Microphone	Male Mini-stereo audio plug	Shielded 2-wire round cable.
Modem	RJ-11 plug	Unshielded 4-wire "silver satin" or Category-3 twisted-pair cable.
Ethernet LAN card	Male Mod-8 plug Or RJ-45 plug Or BNC male "T" connector	Unshielded 8-wire twisted-pair Category-5 or Category-6 cable Or RG58—50 ohm coaxial cable.
Token Ring LAN card	Male 9-pin connector into the PC and IBM hermaphroditic connector or Mod-8 plug	Four wire IBM Type-1 or Type-2 shielded twisted-pair cable IBM Type-3 unshielded twisted-pair cable.
Video Camera	Male RCA plug or S-Type video connector	Shielded 2-wire round cable or S-Type connector cable.
USB Port	USB Connector	Unshielded 4-wire USB cable for 1.5 Mbps Shielded 4-wire USB cable for 12 Mbps From 2.5 to 9 feet long.
IEEE-1394 or FireWire Port	FireWire Connector	Unshielded 4-wire or 6-wire FireWire Cable.
External Drives SCSI-I	Male 25-pin connector plugs into PC and Centronics style 50-pin connector plugging into CD-ROM	Shielded or unshielded twisted-pair 50-wire up to 3.0 meters long.
External Drives SCSI-II Fast SCSI	Male Mini-Sub-D 50-pin (miniature) connector	Shielded or unshielded 50-wire twisted-pair round cable from 1.5 to 3.0 meters long.

Table 2-7 PC Peripheral Component Connectors and Cables (Continued)

Component	Connector Description	Cable Description
Internal Drives SCSI-I SCSI-II Fast SCSI	Male Pushpin 50-wire Ribbon cable connector	Unshielded 50-conductor ribbon cable from 1.5 to 3 meters long.
External Drives Fast-Wide SCSI Ultra SCSI Ultra-2 SCSI	Male Mini-Sub-D 68-pin high-density (subminiature) connector	Shielded or unshielded 68-conductor round cable 1.5 meters long.
Internal Drives Fast-Wide SCSI Ultra SCSI Ultra-2 SCSI	Male Mini-Sub-D 68-pin high-density (subminiature) connector	Unshielded 68-conductor high-density ribbon cable 1.5 meters long.
EIDE Drives AT-Attachment (ATA) Female	Pushpin 40-wire connector	Unshielded 40-conductor ribbon cable about 18 inches long.
Floppy Drive	Edge connector or female pushpin 34-wire connector	34-conductor ribbon cable about 18 inches long.

Each cable and connector type is designed to have specific electrical characteristics tailored to the type of electrical signals carried.

Using good cables can reduce PC problems. Some quality cable features are:

1. Molded ends provide the best end connections. There are no screws, nuts, rivets, or plastic tabs to hold the hood pieces together. These pieces can become loose and lost, causing the connector hood to fall off. Molded cables have the molding material injected directly into a mold surrounding the solder joints between the cable wires, connector pins, and the strain relief plug. This forms a single solid piece locking all components together. This prevents

failure when a cable is repeatedly flexed. Assembled cables permit the solder joints to strain under continued flexing, sometimes resulting in cable failure.

2. Gold-plated contacts provide the best connections because gold is an excellent electrical conductor. Gold also prevents pins from oxidizing forming a resistive coating, and is soft and malleable, making better connections when cables are joined together.

3. End-to-end shielding protects the cable from external electrical signals. Such shielding should be tied to the ground wire at one end to prevent voltage from building up in the cable. Grounding both ends is not good because that permits signal (ground) loops to occur. Unused wires should be grounded as well.

4. The number of wires in the cable is often important. Parallel printer cables need all 25 wires. Some modems require more wires than others. Asynchronous modems use nine wires. Some direct connections from PC to PC can use as few as three wires.

5. Thumbscrews make it easy to tighten the cable to the PC. This ensures that a cable does not fall off a connector.

6. Wire gauge (or diameter) determines the ease with which electrical signals travel through the wire. The larger the diameter (smaller gauge number 22–24 versus 26–28), the better the electrical signal at the other end. Cables longer than 15 feet should have 26 gauge or better (22–24 gauge) wire.

Follow cable length specifications given by the device manufacturer. Staying within the given distances ensures that the signal quality is not degraded. Cables longer than the recommended lengths can be flaky and cause errors in data transmissions.

Serial versus Parallel Cables

Printers can be connected to the PC using serial, parallel, or USB cables. Serial cables transfer data to the printer more slowly than parallel cables. Typical printing transfer speeds are 9,600 bits per second to 19,200 bits per second. The maximum transfer rate for any standard PC serial interface is 115,200 bits per second. The advantage of serial cables over parallel cables is that serial cables can run up to 50 feet or more to connect into the printer. Parallel cables are only good for much shorter distances, around a maximum of 15 feet. USB cables provide faster data transfer than serial cables but at relatively short distances from the PC.

Some of the distance advantage is lost today because printers are attached directly to a Local Area Network (LAN). Because LAN-attached printers can be located anywhere on the LAN, it is easy to lose your output. Data is sent to LAN-attached printers for printing via the LAN. In this case, the PC requires only the LAN connection to send data to the printer. LAN-attached printers can print data from any PC attached to the LAN.

Selected Cable Pin Connections

PCs signal over cables in one of two fashions. They either activate individual wires by placing voltages on them or they send messages across a single wire. Let me illustrate with two simple hypothetical cable configurations: a single-wire cable between two devices and a three-wire cable between two devices.

For the single-wire interface devices to communicate, they must send messages down the wire. A typical conversation could be:

Hello, anyone there?

Yep, you got me!

Great, I have data to send.

OK, send it.

Here it is—data.

The data was received OK.

Fine, that's all I have, goodbye.

OK, goodbye until next time we send data.

With such a conversation there needs to be only a single wire carrying the control messages and data transfer messages. Ethernet, USB, and FireWire work in this fashion. Their cables have eight, four, or six wires that form a bus similar to the single wire above.

More common PC cables have multiple wires with some wires assigned to specific functions. This would be like our second example, the three-wire cable between the two devices. In this cable, the sending device controls wire number 1, the receiving device controls wire number 2, and wire number 3 carries the data. The device conversation would be almost identical to the previous conversation, except that some messages would be communicated by pulling on wire number 1 or wire number 2. Let me illustrate:

Sending device pulls wire number 1—*Hello, anyone there?*

Receiving device pulls wire number 2—*Yep, you got me!*

Sending device pulls wire number 1—*Great, I have data to send.*

Receiving device pulls wire number 2 —*OK, send it.*

Sending device places data on wire number 3, while pulling on wire number 1. As transmission finishes, sending device stops pulling on wire number 1—*Here it is—data.*

Receiving device pulls wire number 2—*Data was received OK.*

Sending device pulls wire number 1—*Fine, that's all I have, goodbye.*

Receiving device pulls wire number 2—*OK, goodbye.*

In this case, each wire fulfills a different communications function. Serial or COM, mouse, keyboard, parallel, IDE, and SCSI interfaces behave in this fashion. These interfaces also have message exchanges controlling data transfers as well.

Keep in mind these types of operation as we examine some PC cable interfaces. It helps us understand their function, operation, and how to troubleshoot and repair them.

DB-25 and DB-9 for Serial COM interfaces (RS-232)

The DB connector notation identifies a "D"-shaped connector. Twenty-five or nine is the number of wires in the cable. PC serial ports use male connectors, making the serial cables use female connectors. PC serial ports use these cables to communicate with modems, mice, or other devices such as PDAs. Their use with mice has dropped since the PS/2 connector came on the scene. PDA devices use Infra Red (IR) wireless connections, while the newest devices are beginning to use Bluetooth wireless technology to connect into PCs. Most modems are now either internal or USB connected.

The original serial interface was the RS-232 interface. RS stands for Recommended Specification. The latest revision of this serial specification changed the designation to EIA-232. EIA represents the Electronics Industries Association, the group that developed and maintains the standard. This designation is a little self-promotion.

RS-232 serial interfaces have physical, electrical, and logical properties. Physically they use a 25-pin or a 9-pin connector. Electrically they use voltage signaling with voltages ranging between plus and minus 15 volts. Logically, each wire in the interface is assigned specific functions, as identified in Figure 2–30. The interface has specific operating characteristics. These characteristics are:

1. Software transparent—it does not care about what software drivers use it.

2. Cable length—it was designed and specified to work over 50 foot cables.

3. Low-speed data transmission—it was designed to transmit data at 20,000 BPS or lower. Speeds up to 115,200 BPS are common over short (4-foot) cables.

In one case data was transmitted at 56 KBPS for 114 feet and 6 inches over a standard RS-232 interface. I believed that they must have performed some detailed electrical engineering design to calculate that distance. When asked how they precisely determined the speed to operate over the 114-foot and 6-inch distance, they replied that they just kept shortening the cable until it started working.

The serial connector most commonly employed today is a DB-9 connector. This is a 9-pin "D"-shaped connector. It operates like our 3-wire interface above, with specific pins having specific functions. These functions were developed with the intent of communicating between a computer and a modem. The signal lines have their functionality described in that context. Figure 2–31 identifies the pins and pin assignments for both the 25-pin and 9-pin connectors. The DB-9 connector pin designations are on the inside of the diagram. The arrow indicates the direction of the signal. For example Request to Send (RTS) goes from the PC (Data Terminal Equipment [DTE]) to the modem (Data Circuit-terminating Equipment [DCE]).

Figure 2–30
RS-232 interface.

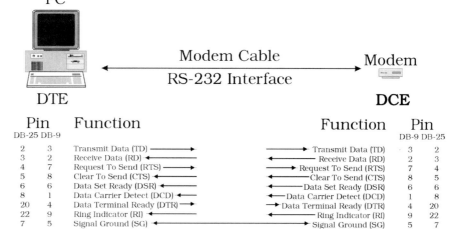

135

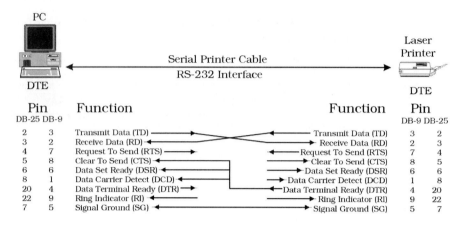

Figure 2-31
Serial printer cable configuration.

The pin 2 and pin 3 functions are reversed between the original 25-pin interface and the more popular 9-pin interface. The 9-pin interface was first produced on PCs with the introduction of the PC-AT in 1985. It was necessary to preserve space on the rear panel bracket of the AT.

There are a number of alternative serial cable configurations used to interface serial printers to the PC. Figure 2–31 illustrates one possible configuration. This cable connects a PC to a printer. Both devices act as DTE. Thus, pin 2 and pin 3 must be crossed so that transmit data on one side goes into receive data on the other side and vice versa. Printers know they are printers and thus do not need to think that they are talking to a modem. However, PCs always believe that the serial interface connects to a modem. Consequently, they look for approvals to transmit by signals on Data Set Ready (DSR) pin 6, Data Carrier Detect (DCD) pin 8 (or pin 1), and Clear To Send (CTS) pin 5 (or pin 8). Of these approval lines, CTS is the most important.

Printer cables make the PC think it has the requisite approvals to communicate by connecting the printer's Data Terminal Ready (DTR) pin 20 (or pin 4 on the 9-pin connector) to the PC's pin 5 (or pin 8 on the 9-pin connector), pin 6 (remains pin 6 on the 9-pin connector), and pin 8 (or pin 1 on the 9-pin connector). This is illustrated in Figure 2–31.

Null modem or modem eliminator cables are used to connect PC to PC. In this instance, the PCs both need approval to communicate. One possible cable configuration is to mirror the pin 20 to pin 5, pin 6, and pin 8 connections in the serial printer cable. In this fashion, when a PC is powered on, it pulls on its pin 20 and signals approval to the PC on the other end of the cable.

LapLink and the DOS Interlink/Interserv programs use null modem cable configurations to communicate between two PCs at high speeds using the PCs' serial ports. EIA-232 pin functions are listed in Table 2–8.

Table 2–8   Pin Functions

Data Leads	DTE PIN # for 25-Pin Connector	DTE PIN # for 9-Pin Connector	Abbreviation
Transmit Data	2 →	3 →	TD
Receive Data	3 ←	2 ←	RD
TIMING (CLOCK) LEADS			
Transmitter Signal Element Timing (DCE Source)	15 ←		TC
Transmitter Signal Element Timing (DTE Source)	24 →		TC
Receiver Signal Element Timing (DCE Source)	17 ←		RC
CONTROL LEADS			
Request to Send	4 →	7 →	RTS
Clear to Send	5 ←	8 ←	CTS
Data Set Ready (DCE Ready)	6 ←	6 ←	DSR
Data Terminal Ready (DTE Ready)	20 →	4 →	DTR
Data Carrier Detect (Received Line Signal Detector)	8 ←	1 ←	CD
Ring Indicator	22 ←	9 ←	RI
GROUND			
Signal Ground	7 ↔	5 ↔	SG
Protective Ground (Shield)	1 ↔		FG

Parallel Port Cables

Parallel port cables use a 25-pin standard "D"-shaped connector to connect into the PC. The PC port is a female port, making the cable connector a male connector. On the printer side of the cable, the connector is a Centronics style 36-pin male connector. The parallel port cables sometimes meet the IEEE-1284 specification. The pin specifications for this connector are shown in Table 2–9.

Table 2-9   Centronics Parallel Connector

DB-25 Pin Number	Printer Centronics Pin Number	Signal	Source	Comment
1	1	Strobe	PC	Valid Data on Pins 1 through 8
2	2	Data-1	PC	Data Bit – 0
3	3	Data-2	PC	Data Bit – 1
4	4	Data-3	PC	Data Bit – 2
5	5	Data-4	PC	Data Bit – 3
6	6	Data-5	PC	Data Bit – 4
7	7	Data-6	PC	Data Bit – 5
8	8	Data-7	PC	Data Bit – 6
9	9	Data-8	PC	Data Bit – 7
10	10	Acknlg	Printer	Data accepted by printer
11	11	Busy	Printer	Printer not ready
12	12	PE	Printer	Paper Error
13	13	Select	Printer	Printer on-line
14	14	AutoFeed	PC	Add carriage feed to each line
15	32	Error	Printer	Unspecified error
16	31	INIT	PC	Initialize Printer
17	36	SLCT IN	PC	Select printer
18-25	19-30	Signal Ground		Grounds signals
	16	Signal Ground		Grounds signals
	17	Chassis Ground		Grounds to chassis
	18	+5 Volts	Printer	5-volt power

BNC LAN Cable

The first Ethernet PC connections used coaxial cable. Similar but not identical coaxial cable is used for TV connections. The LAN coaxial cable was attached to the PC LAN card using push and twist BNC (Bayonet Neill Concelman or British Naval Connectors—we prefer Barrel Neutral Connectors, our invention) connectors. The coaxial cable was attached to the top part of a BNC "T"-shaped connector while the base of the "T" connected directly into the Ethernet LAN card. At each end of the coaxial cable bus was a 50-ohm terminating connector. The Ethernet coaxial cable bus was good for 187 meters (about 200 meters) with standard electrical signaling permitting multiple segments using repeaters, or for 300 meters for boosted electrical signaling and a single segment. Such BNC cabling is designated as 10Base2 cabling. This is 10 million bits per second baseband (digital) transmission over a 200-meter cable segment. 10Base2 cabling carried the informal identification of cheaper net.

This cabling easily implemented small Ethernet networks. Its primary drawback was that any break in the cable caused the entire network to fail. In larger networks, this happened quite frequently, necessitating the move to the 10BaseT unshielded twisted-pair wiring and wiring hubs. Most all networks today use Category 5 (CAT-5) or higher unshielded twisted pair wiring. Coaxial cable has all but disappeared from LANs.

RJ-45 or MOD-8 for LAN Cable

Twisted-pair wiring currently dominates wiring used in facilities for both LAN and telephone wiring. Unshielded twisted-pair (UTP) wire in wide use is typically 19- to 26-gauge. Premise wire is 24 to 26 American Wiring Gauge (AWG) with two twists per foot. This wiring is designated as 10BaseT wiring—10 million bits per second baseband transmission over unshielded twisted-pair wiring. The unshielded twisted-pair wiring used can be traditional telephone wiring (Category-3 wire) or specially designed wire for higher transmission speeds (Category-5, Category-5e, and Category-6 for 100 Mbps to 1 Gbps).

Twisting of the wire pairs cancels out radiated energy from current flowing in any one wire by the radiated energy from the same current flowing back in the return wire of the same pair. Radiated energy is called electromagnetic radiation (EMR). Twisting effectively and inexpensively minimizes crosstalk between adjacent pairs in a multi-pair cable. Twisting also makes wire pairs less susceptible to external electrical noise (that is, EMR). The noise is coupled equally into each wire in the pair, causing the noise to be cancelled out when the wires are properly terminated. At voice frequencies, each pair appears to be balanced—that is, equal electrical energy is emitted from each wire within the pair to any point outside the pair of wires.

Wire can be either plenum or non-plenum cabling. Plenum cabling has Teflon insulation outside to prevent its catching fire at low temperatures and producing noxious and deadly fumes in the air plenums.

Unshielded twisted-pair LAN cables use special Mod-8 or normal RJ-45 connectors. They require two of the four pairs for communications. Most cables have all four pairs wired.

Unshielded twisted-pair cabling (UTP) is tricky to use because Ethernet and Token Ring use different hub-to-Network Interface Card cable configurations and different schemes to cross-connect cables. Token ring and Ethernet use four wires, each of which has a different set of four wires in the hub-to-NIC cable. Low-priced NIC and hub concentrators or Multi-station Access Units (MAU) use RJ-45 connectors for UTP connections. This standardization allows a common cable pin configuration that works with Ethernet and token ring networks.

To determine the pin configuration for UTP, hold the RJ-45 connector by the wire with the clip down and the insertion end pointing away from you. The pin on the left is pin one. A standard RJ-45 connector has eight pins. Most UTP cable uses a solid and striped wire color scheme. The wire pairs are colored: orange and orange/white; blue and blue/white; green and green/white; brown and brown/white. This solid/striped combination identifies pairs of wires that must be twisted together in a specific sequence providing clean electrical signals. The pairs must match at the remote end of the cable to transfer the signal. Common cabling pin assignments or pin outs are:

1. Ethernet 10BaseT connections use pins 1 and 2 and 3 and 6

2. Token Ring UTP connection uses pins 4 and 5 and 3 and 6.

3. Creating a cable that works with NICs requires the following pin outs:

    a. Pin 1—Orange/White

    b. Pin 2—Orange

    c. Pin 3—Green/White

    d. Pin 4—Blue

    e. Pin 5—Blue/White

    f. Pin 6—Green

    g. Pin 7—Brown/White

    h. Pin 8—Brown

Cables with these pin outs are generally interchangeable between Ethernet and Token Ring networks. See Figure 2–32 for typical cable configuration.

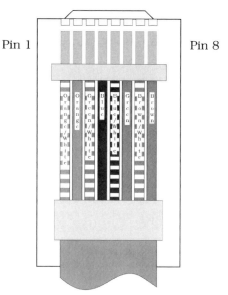

Pin 1   Pin 8

Figure 2-32
Mod-8 connector.   Bottom View of The Connector

One last word—there are two wiring schemes, an Integrated Services Digital Network (ISDN) T568A scheme or an AT&T T568B scheme. These T568A and T568B wiring specifications are used for cross-connect cables. T568A specifications use pair 3 and then 2, while T568B uses the same pairs but in the reverse order—2 and then 3. Both T568A and T568B wiring standards are compatible with 10BaseT and require no special configurations to work. As long as pin 1 connects to pin 1, pin 2 to pin 2, and so on, there should be no problems. To avoid facility wide wiring problems, pick a single facility wide wiring convention, T568A or T568B, and stick with it. If a building is wired to T568A, any moves, adds, or changes should be done with the T568A wiring. When T568A and T568B are mixed, wiring problems occur because they cross the signal pathways.

RJ-11 for Modems

Modems use RJ-11 modular telephone plugs connected to "Silver Satin" type telephone cable. "Silver Satin" cable runs two or four wires in parallel down a flat cable. It got its name from the silver color of the original cables produced for the telephone companies. Similar to RJ-45 connectors, RJ-11 connectors have pin 1 on the left side when viewed from the bottom of the connector. They have four wires that are often color-coded yellow, green, red, and black. Typical RJ-11 pin assignments are:

1. Pin 1—Yellow
2. Pin 2—Green—Tip
3. Pin 3—Red—Ring
4. Pin 4—Black

These wires can implement two analog phone line connections because each analog phone line uses only two wires. The center wires in the connector are red and green for the primary phone line and the outside wires are yellow and black for the secondary phone line. Modems expect to use only the center two pins, pin 2 and pin 3.

PS/2 Mini-DIN—Mouse and Keyboard

The DIN connector designation comes from the Deutsche Industrie Normenauschuss (German Industry Standard, loosely translated) or Deutsche Institut fuer Normung, a German standardization body. The DIN and mini-DIN connectors are used to connect keyboards into the PC. The mini-DIN connector also connects PS/2-style mice to the PC. The original keyboard DIN connector was a 5-pin male connector. The mini-DIN connectors are 6-pin male connectors. They are round and keyed to prevent misinsertion. See Figure 2–33.

Figure 2–33
Pin out of a PS 2 Keyboard and Mouse sockets.

The pin assignments are:

1. Pin 1—Clock
2. Pin 2—Ground
3. Pin 3—Data
4. Pin 4—Unused
5. Pin 5—+5 volts
6. Pin 6—Unused

EIDE—Enhanced Integrated Drive Electronics

Enhanced IDE (Integrated Drive Electronics or, alternatively, Integrated Disk Electronics) cables are parallel 40-conductor cables with pushpin connectors. They can run a maximum length of about 18 inches. EIDE cables have connectors for the EIDE disk controller and one or two connectors for the disk drives. EIDE cables are also identified as AT-Attachment or ATA cables. The AT designates the original IBM PC AT (Advanced Technology, for its time) introduced in 1985.

SCSI—Small Computer System Interface

Small Computer System Interface (SCSI) controller cards employ a wider variety of cables. The latest SCSI high-speed devices are beginning to use fiber optic connections. Such fiber connections are not discussed here beyond mentioning them at this point. The original external SCSI cables used an Apple-developed interface that connected to the SCSI PC controller using a DB-25 connector. The disk drive cables had a 50-pin Centronics-style connector. The external SCSI bus terminator was a similar 50-pin Centronics-style connector.

Internally, the SCSI cards used a 50-pin parallel cable with pushpin connectors. These cables could be quite long and could connect up to seven internal SCSI drives. We have some systems using these eight connector (one for the controller and seven for the drives) cables. The SCSI bus speed was 5 million bytes per second and the length was 3 meters, or about 9 feet. PC products often identified these SCSI components as SCSI-I.

SCSI controllers were soon upgraded to higher transfer speeds. The bus clock speed was increased to 10 MHz. The resulting data rate was 10 million bytes per second because each clock cycle transferred a single byte of data. SCSI-II designated these PC SCSI components. Internal cables remained the 50-wire pushpin cables with 3-meter length. External cables changed to a high-density 50-pin "D"-shaped mini-connector. Cables providing SCSI-II to SCSI-II and SCSI-II to SCSI-I connections were used to connect newer and older external disks and CD-ROMs to the newer SCSI-II controller cards. See Figure 2–34.

These cables transferred one byte of data every clock cycle. They are also identified as "A cables". The next cable designation was a wide SCSI. Wide SCSI increased the SCSI transfer speed to 20 million bytes per second. This was accomplished using the same cables at a higher clock speed, so the wide designation only described the SCSI operating speed and not the actual cabling.

In some cases a new 16-bit cable was used. This cable is identified as the "P cable." Internally, this cable used 68-pin high-density "D"-shaped connectors. The cable itself was a high-density ribbon cable. Externally, the same 68-pin "D"-shaped high-density connector was used. The external cable was not a ribbon cable, but rather a round twisted-pair cable.

The next iteration moved the SCSI speed up to 40 million bytes per second. This was sold as fast and wide SCSI. Here the 16-bit interface cables were used with a higher bus speed to achieve the 40 M per second transfer speed. The bus speed was increased to 20 MHz with each clock cycle transferring two bytes of data. Provided there were proper terminations, it was possible to configure cables that were a combination of the 8-bit and 16-bit cables. The fast and wide SCSI cables were restricted to a shorter 1.5-meter (about 5-foot) length.

SCSI transfer speed is 80 million bytes per second. This is sold as Ultra-2-SCSI, as if there would be no higher speeds. This is not very likely. A new Q cable that transfers 4 bytes of data per 20 MHz clock cycle provides this higher speed. Alternatively, the existing 16-bit P cable can be operated at 40 MHz clock speeds to provide equivalent SCSI transfer performance. For a review of the SCSI types and characteristics, see Chapter 1.

SCSI cables also vary depending upon the electrical signaling used. Most SCSI buses are single ended. This means that the electrical signaling is measured relative to the ground potential at each end of the SCSI bus. It is much more limited in the distance the electrical signals can travel, particularly at the higher SCSI clocking rates. Differential SCSI interfaces are not compatible

Figure 2–34
SCSI 50-pin connector.

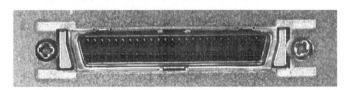

with single-ended interfaces. A differential interface measures the voltage difference between two signals in the cable. Consequently, differential cables at low speeds can run at distances up to 25 meters (about 75 feet). The SCSI differential interfaces used high power and were expensive to implement. They were used for special configurations.

The newest SCSI electrical interface is the low voltage differential interface. The interface is integrated into SCSI chip sets. It supports high-speed operation with bus lengths up to 12 meters.

Study Break: Identifying Connectors

Lets try to identify classic connectors found on the PC. Below is the list of devices found in and around your PC. Find the connector that corresponds to the device using Table 2–7 (page 129).

1. Ultra SCSI internal hard drive
2. Serial mouse
3. Ethernet LAN card

Answers:

1. Male Mini-Sub-D 68-pin high-density
2. Male 9-pin "D"-shaped connector
3. RJ-45 plug or BNC connector

Installing IDE/EIDE Fixed Disks and CD-ROMs

IDE and EIDE fixed disk drives—sometimes referred to as Ultra ATA drives—and CD-ROMs are easy to install. They bolt into a 3.5-inch or a 5.25-inch drive bay. Smaller drives require brackets to fit into larger bays. The brackets bolt to the drive and then are bolted to the PC chassis. CD-ROMs are 5.25-inch devices, so they must be installed in a larger bay. Fixed disks are mounted horizontally or vertically on one side. Once bolted into position, the EIDE drives have the data and control cable and the power cable attached. CD-ROMs have an additional audio cable that runs to the PC's sound card.

IDE drives are preformatted. All that remains to bring the new EIDE fixed disk on-line is to run the FDISK program and then the FORMAT program. Once completed, data and programs can be placed on the fixed disk.

Master versus Slave Designation

Some EIDE data and control permit installing two drives on the same cable. In this instance, one drive is designated as the master drive and one drive is designated as the slave drive. A jumper block on the rear of the drive has the master and slave jumper settings. When the settings are not clear, contact the drive manufacturer's web site to obtain the appropriate documentation.

A good strategy is to keep CD-ROM drives and fixed disk drives on separate controllers. While it is possible to install fixed disks and CD-ROMs on the same controller, such configurations have on occasion not worked and could slightly degrade the PC's performance.

IDE Devices per Channel

IDE controllers support two devices on each channel. A PC having four EIDE devices would then require master and slave devices installed on both its primary and secondary EIDE controllers. If additional EIDE devices were installed in a PC, additional EIDE controllers would need to be installed.

Study Break: Master-Slave Relationship

Let's try some basic EIDE configurations. In this instance we have a EIDE fixed disk drive and an EIDE CD drive that we would like to install. Our PC has two EIDE controllers, labeled controller A and controller B. Here are three different configuration possibilities; you must choose the correct ones:

1. Controller A EIDE fixed disk drive is set to master and controller B EIDE CD drive is set to master.
2. Controller A EIDE fixed disk drive is set to master and controller A EIDE CD drive is set to master.

3. Controller A EIDE fixed disk drive is set to master and controller B EIDE CD drive is set to slave.

Answers: Choice 1 and 3 will both work. Choice 2 is not properly configured, causing the drives to conflict.

Installing and Configuring SCSI Devices

SCSI fixed disks are more tricky to install. The basics are similar to those for EIDE drives. They are bolted into the PC chassis, and the cables are connected. There are both power and data/control cables to connect. In the process of cabling, the SCSI bus termination and device addressing must be set up. Each SCSI device must be assigned a unique SCSI ID from the 0 to 15 (excluding 7 because 7 is assigned to the SCSI controller board) SCSI IDs supported by each SCSI bus. See device addresses below. Similar to EIDE drives, SCSI fixed disks come preformatted. This means that low-level formatting does not need to be performed. Once installed, the FDISK and FORMAT programs are all that is needed to prepare the SCSI fixed disk drive to accept data.

Low-level formatting of a SCSI drive is a way to fix corrupted drives. This low-level format is performed using the SCSI BIOS ROM on the SCSI controller board or SCSI diagnostic software provided with the SCSI controller.

Other SCSI devices, like CD-RW drives and CD-ROM drives, install similarly to SCSI fixed disks. They attach to the SCSI bus like any other internal or external device but with an added audio connection to the PC sound card. See Figure 2–35.

The only difference from fixed disk installation is that SCSI CD devices may require added driver programs for proper operation. These software driver programs are special DOS drivers or Windows drivers. SCSI scanners are similar to CD devices. They also require special driver software to operate. Scanners always install using external SCSI cables.

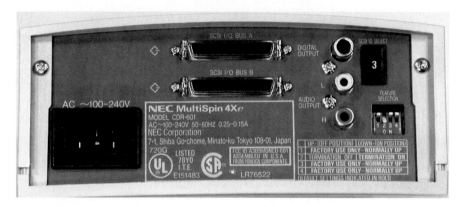

Figure 2–35
SCSI CD-ROM connections.

Bus Termination Basics

SCSI buses must be terminated at each end. Terminating resistor packs tie the bus signals to ground so their levels do not float and cause data and control errors. SCSI controller cards are typically terminated because they expect to be the last device on the bus. SCSI drives are terminated as well because they expect that they are the only device attached to the bus. This is not always the case. If the SCSI controller services both internal and external SCSI drives, then it is in the middle of the SCSI bus and needs to have the terminating resistors removed. When more than one internal or external SCSI device is chained together, the devices at the end of the SCSI bus are the only devices terminated. The remaining SCSI devices must have their terminating resistors bypassed or removed.

SCSI terminations are typically connectors with internal resistor packs. Some terminators are active components while others are strictly passive. Both terminators dampen signal reflections on the SCSI bus. Active terminators are more resistant to noise, making the SCSI bus operation more stable. Active terminations are preferred.

SCSI Types

There are several types of SCSI buses. They vary in data transfer capabilities. The number of bits transferred and the clock rate of the bus determines SCSI data transfer speeds. These are the characteristics of each type of SCSI bus.

Narrow

The narrow SCSI bus transfers one byte of data per clock cycle. These early SCSI buses ran at 5 M per second. SCSI buses increased the clock rate to 10 MHz, improving transfer speed to 10 M per second.

Wide

Fast SCSI was implemented first by increasing the bus clock rate from 5 MHz to 10 MHz. This increased data transfer speed to 20 M per second. Doubling the bus width caused the development of 68-pin wide SCSI connectors.

Wide SCSI bus operation was accomplished by increasing the width of the data transfer from one byte to two bytes. Fast wide SCSI doubled the SCSI bus clock speed to 10 MHz and transferred two data bytes per clock cycle. Fast wide SCSI provided 20 M per second operation.

Ultra Wide

Similar to both fast and wide SCSI, Ultra SCSI achieved its 40 M per second transfer speed by either increasing the clock speed to 20 MHz or by increasing the bus transfers to 4 bytes. The advantage of a higher bus speed was its backwards compatibility with existing SCSI cabling and connectors. The drawback is that higher clock speeds shortened the SCSI overall bus length to 1.5 meters. To extend such SCSI buses, repeater devices were sometimes installed.

Device Addresses

SCSI devices must be assigned unique SCSI target IDs. The ID is the address of the SCSI device on the SCSI bus. The narrow SCSI buses can have seven devices and one controller attached. Wide SCSI buses can have 15 devices and a controller attached. It is also possible to have multiple controllers on a single SCSI bus. With all SCSI buses, the highest priority ID is ID-7, with ID-6 being the next highest. Thus, the SCSI controllers are assigned ID-7. Table 2–10 lists the SCSI IDs in descending priority order.

Table 2–10 SCSI IDs Priorities

Priority Level	SCSI ID Number	Device Assignment
Highest	7	SCSI Controller
	6	Second SCSI Controller
	5	DVD
	4	CD-RW
	3	CD-ROM
	2	Third Fixed Disk
	1	Second Fixed Disk
	0	Bootable Fixed Disk
	15	
	14	
	13	
	12	
	11	
	10	
	9	
Lowest	8	Scanner

The table lists some of the common ID device assignments. In multiple fixed disk installations, the additional IDs are assigned to each fixed disk drive. The fixed disk and CD-ROM devices have either switches or jumpers on them that determine their ID. These selections are made during device installation. ID conflicts cause error messages and cause the devices with conflicting IDs to not work properly. Each SCSI ID also has a subset of addresses called Logical Unit Numbers (LUNs). Every SCSI device has a unique SCSI ID plus a LUN. The LUNs range from 0 to 7. LUN 0 is the highest priority and for the most part LUN configuration is not necessary.

Cabling

SCSI cables are selected depending upon the type of SCSI controller and the SCSI fixed disk drives being attached. The biggest source of SCSI device problems is the cabling. The newer high-speed SCSI devices are particularly sensitive. Care should be exercised when removing and installing SCSI cables to assure that no pins are bent and that no cable is loosened from its connector. Cable testing is accomplished by using the SCSI controller disk software to verify all device connections and proper cable termination. Generally, high-density cables often look fine but they have poor electrical connections, causing unpredictable drive errors. Furthermore, these errors indicate that the SCSI disk drives had failed and that the cable was fine. We have seen experienced service personnel work for hours fixing bad SCSI disk drive problems that were really caused by faulty cables and had nothing to do with the drives at all.

Typical Switches and Jumpers

SCSI device switches and jumpers control the ID assignment for the device and whether the device terminates the bus. ID is often set by a push-up or push-down switch with numbers in the center (see Figure 2–36). Alternatively, a twist style selector with a pointing arrow may also be used to set the unique SCSI ID.

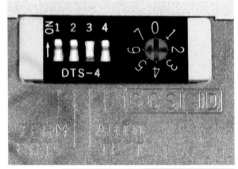

Figure 2–36
SCSI twist style selector and
push style switch.

On the push style switch, pushing up makes the ID number increase and pushing down does the reverse. Some fixed disks have jumper blocks that determine the ID number. Since the default for most fixed disks is set at 0, there are usually no jumpers installed in the fixed disk ID block. When two disks are installed, the jumper needs only to be set on position one. In this case it is relatively easy to guess the proper jumper setting.

Termination is set on by default. When a device is not at the end of the SCSI bus, the termination must be removed or bypassed. Here you are removing resistor packs or jumpers. Often, the no termination setting is readily apparent without documentation. Note that on device boot up, the SCSI BIOS lists the devices and their IDs.

Study Break: SCSI IDs

A unique SCSI ID is a vital part of SCSI bus configuration and can cause many installation and troubleshooting headaches. In the previous section we described the common SCSI ID given to certain devices in the SCSI. Now you are given a list of devices that all must be on the same narrow SCSI bus. Your task is to give them their proper SCSI ID. Refer to Table 2–10.

1. CD drive
2. Bootable fixed disk drive
3. Second fixed disk drive
4. Third fixed disk drive
5. SCSI controller

Answers:

1. ID 3, 4, or 5
2. ID 0
3. ID 1
4. ID 2
5. ID 7

Remember, you cannot have duplicate IDs on the same SCSI bus.

Installing Common Peripheral Devices

Other PC peripheral devices are relatively easy to physically install. Most problems arise when trying to make them operate with Windows 95/98/Me/2000 software. This most often is a driver program issue. Obtaining the latest drivers from a manufacturer's web site resolves most problems. The *http://www.DRIVERSHQ.com* web site is a quick reference to many hardware drivers for different PC components. On a few occasions a search is required to find the appropriate driver software because an older version is needed.

One strange behavior that has been observed is that some EIDE drives must be installed as SCSI devices. In fact, some Zip drives may require this configuration.

Keyboards and Mice

Keyboards just plug right in and work. Only when the keyboard has a built-in mouse would special drives be required. The mouse is different. Because of the variety of mouse types and manufacturers, driver software can be required to make a mouse fully functional. Logitech™ mouse drivers work with most all mice. So do the standard Windows mouse drivers. The Windows drivers do not provide any exciting mouse features like those provided by the Logitech mouse driver software. The wheel mouse being used on this PC works with both Logitech and Microsoft drivers, but the wheel function only works with its special driver software.

Video Card and Monitor

Video cards plug into the main logic board similar to other option cards. Newer video cards are Advanced Graphics Port (AGP) cards that must use a special AGP bus slot. This is similar to the old Video Electronics Standards Association (VESA) local bus slot. AGP slots transfer data at very high speeds. AGP boards use video memory differently from the older PCI bus graphics cards. All graphics cards require special driver software to utilize all their capabilities. When installed they start up in standard Video Graphics Array (VGA). This permits them to be used while installing their special Windows driver programs. See Figure 2–37.

153

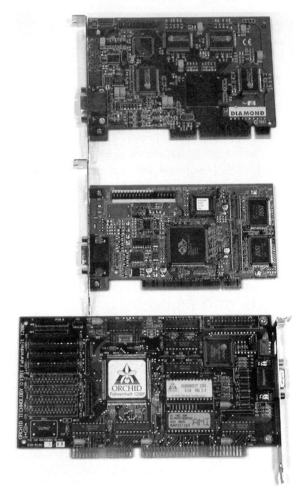

Figure 2–37
ISA, PCI and AGP
video cards.

Windows NT boots to a screen that permits booting into Windows NT in VGA mode as a diagnostic and recovery option in the event that the display controller drivers become corrupted. Windows 95/98/Me/2000 all have a safe mode operation that performs a similar VGA boot option, enabling restitution of malfunctioning display adapter driver programs. Striking the F8 key during the boot process enters the Windows 2000 safe operation mode.

Monitors must match the display adapter refresh rate. Without a good match the display does not fill the screen properly. Displays can be too short or narrow, they can have a keystone (trapezoidal) shape, or they can have a tight girdle look (shrunk in the middle). Adjustments on the monitor can change the display scanning to make the screen fill out squarely and clearly.

When the graphics board does not match the display's scanning rate, no amount of adjustment makes the display behave properly. When this happens, a monitor replacement or a display adapter downgrade usually resolves the problem.

Flat panel displays have few refresh rate problems. If the rate does not match, there is no display. They are adjusted up/down and right/left so that the image centers in the display area. To get the best image the VGA board output must match precisely the flat panel native resolution. For example, my displays have a native resolution of 1,280 by 1,024. If I set the PC for a 640 by 480 display, the flat panel gives me an ugly display! It works, but it is not pretty.

Modems

Modems can be internal or external devices. Most modems are internal because they save desk space. Installing an internal modem is as simple as plugging it into the main logic board bus. If a modem is a plug-and-play modem, it may be best to disable the plug-and-play feature (if possible) and set it to either a COM3 or a COM4 port. Newer PCI bus plug-and-play modems install easily with Windows 98/Me/2000. Modems installed on COM ports 1–4 work with virtually all communications software. If by chance the modem turns out to be on COM ports 5–8, AOL software doesn't see the modem. When the modem is on COM port 3 or 4, Windows software should install it automatically. This applies to Windows versions 95 and 98, but not on current versions of NT.

The modem then needs to be plugged into the phone line jack (and optionally a phone). Driver software, recognizing the modem manufacturer and sending setup commands to the modem, determines the transmission speed at which the modem connects. All modem setup commands contain the initial set of modem commands defined by the Hayes brand modems. These basic commands form the core of the modem command language. From there, two separate extensions to the modem command language have evolved. One followed the US Robotics (now 3Com) design and Practical Peripherals and Cardinal modems (both are now defunct) used the other. These command language variations cover the commands used to establish high-speed connectivity, error checking, and data compression functions. Fortunately, each manufacturer has default settings that make their modems perform optimally. These default settings are set into every modem using a standard Hayes &F (that restores factory defaults) command. Sometimes adding a standard Hayes command s9=1 (that sets the carrier detect time to 1 millisecond) improves the ability of the modem to connect at high speeds. Also, remember to always get the latest drivers possible.

155

Study Break: Modem Ports

The DOS mode command can be used to determine the COM port assignments in a PC. Open a DOS Windows in Windows 95/98 and try:

1. MODE COM1
2. MODE COM2
3. MODE COM3
4. MODE COM4

The COM ports that are not installed should return "Illegal device name" or other similar error messages. The error messages vary with DOS and Windows versions.

Upgrading Your PC

Upgrading PCs is limited to a few basic component areas. Furthermore, the money spent to upgrade any one area should be less than $200. When the $200 figure is exceeded, it may be more practical to purchase a new PC than to perform the upgrade because a new PC would have all its components configured and tuned for optimal performance. An upgrade may only produce a minimal performance increase in a single area. The most beneficial upgrade to an old PC is increasing the RAM capacity and increasing the disk drive capacity. CPU upgrades are expensive and provide a marginal performance enhancement.

RAM

PCs today are sold with adequate RAM. Windows can run with little RAM, but when this happens it swaps data heavily between RAM and the fixed disk. There have been some Windows 95 systems sold with only 8 MB of RAM. This killed performance. It was easy to tell because the display screen refreshed slowly to the sound of the disk drive flogging itself to death.

Windows 95/98 requires a minimum of 32 MB of RAM for simple operation. Windows NT needs 32 MB and Windows 2000 needs 64 MB of RAM as a minimum. If images and graphics applications are installed, more RAM is recommended. Many PC configurations find 64 MB of RAM sufficient, but 128 MB or 256 MB would be better today.

Upgrading RAM capacity is as simple as snapping in some new SIMMs or DIMMs. To upgrade RAM, first check the PC manual to determine the type of memory and the number of modules to install. Select the module capacity that, when installed, meets your minimum upgrade requirement—for instance, two 16 MB modules for a minimum of 32 MB. Selecting modules that meet your minimum capacity requirement ensures that if you must remove some RAM modules to install the upgrade, you still achieve your minimum RAM capacity. Note that SIMMs snap in at an angle while DIMMs push straight down. Similar to DIMMs, RIMMs push straight down into the RAM slots. However, RIMMs must be installed in pairs and each memory slot must have a RIMM or a terminating board installed. There can be no empty RIMM slots.

Open the case and install the RAM modules in any open RAM SIMM, DIMM, or RIMM socket. Power up the PC. During the Power On Self Test (POST), the PC should sense the added RAM capacity and display an error message stating "memory size mismatch." This is good because the PC found the added RAM. It then updates the memory size in the Complementary Metal Oxide Silicon (CMOS) setup memory and reboots. At this point no error message is displayed and your system RAM is upgraded.

If the RAM is not found, then install the SIMMs, DIMMs, or RIMMs in the other main logic board sockets until the PC recognizes them.

Upgrading RAM is the most cost-effective upgrade for any PC. With the lower RAM prices we have today, it is a good policy to have at least 64 MB and better to have 256 MB of RAM in any PC.

Fixed Disk

When thinking disk upgrades, most people think of replacing their existing disk drive. This is more difficult than just adding a second drive to an existing system. Most PCs have data and program files splattered across their fixed disk in a pseudorandom order. There is little thought given to organizing the data on the disk drive. This results in the disk drive becoming filled to capacity, eventually causing Windows to malfunction because there is no space for swapping data to the disk drive.

A good strategy is to place all data in a special, distinct data folder. In this manner, when a second disk drive is added to the PC, the data folder can be moved to it and immediately free up space on the primary disk drive. Another strategy to use on particularly troublesome PCs is to install all the software and drivers in a "C:" partition and then use GHOST.EXE (from Symantec) to image that partition to a "D:" partition. When Windows becomes belligerent and fails to start, use GHOST.EXE to return back to the previously good configuration and wipe all traces of the corrupted Windows configuration from the "C:" partition. If restoring the old Windows configuration does not fix the problem, at least you feel good because you performed the equivalent of a full frontal lobotomy on Windows.

A really good strategy is to install Windows, Windows Applications, and Windows utility programs on the primary disk drive or disk drive partition. This partition size should be about 10 GB to 20 GB. The data should be installed in a second partition. In this manner, Windows should have adequate disk space in its partition for swapping data from RAM to disk. This makes the system easy to upgrade because the data could be reinstalled or moved to another disk drive.

Most users would find a 40 GB disk drive adequate for their Windows needs. Of course, disk drive capacity today is plentiful, like beer in a bar, and not scarce, like water in a desert. A disk drive upgrade is a worthwhile expenditure. Besides adding capacity, a disk drive upgrade can make migration to a new PC easy by providing a mechanism for moving the data files used from one PC to another. It can be particularly satisfying when a disk drive containing data is reinstalled into a new PC minimizing data transfer hassles.

Display

Display capabilities continue to evolve rapidly. A good display with 3D capabilities is important for image manipulation and games. Display upgrades are relatively painless when the correct driver programs are installed. Display upgrades are about the third most cost-effective upgrade to a PC that enhances performance.

Some graphics card upgrades support integrated 3D functionality, because new 2D/3D chip sets permit a single graphics card to create both types of displays. In this instance, upgrades would require replacing one graphics card with another. For PC users that love video games, graphics card upgrades are incessant. The most powerful graphics cards generally only make an impact on display speed when 3D resolution is greater than 1,024 by 768.

Windows 98/Me/2000 permit installation of multiple graphics cards to drive multiple monitors. In this instance, the drivers make the monitors act like one super-wide display. Few PCs have such an upgrade because of the expense of the added monitor.

It reminds me of the days when I operated my PC XT with both monographic and CGA displays. Boy, was I cutting edge.

BIOS Upgrades

BIOS upgrades can be the cheapest to perform. Updating the BIOS software installed in nonvolatile RAM (NVRAM) completes the upgrade. BIOS and other NVRAM upgrades can update the PC to more current plug-and-play operations. BIOS upgrades are not made to increase PC performance, but rather to solve hardware problems like making added EIDE ports work with your operating system. Such upgrades are necessities and not niceties.

Determining When to Upgrade BIOS

When upgrading from one version of Windows to another (for instance, moving from Windows 98 to Windows 2000), a BIOS upgrade may be required. We had a laptop that just would not run and recognize all of its components under Windows 98 until the BIOS was upgraded. Determining if a BIOS upgrade is needed depends on exhaustion of other software upgrade alternatives. If all drivers are up to their latest revision, and the software still works improperly, then a BIOS upgrade is likely in order.

Procedures for Upgrading BIOS

BIOS upgrades are simple to perform. In the instance above, the PHLASH program and the new BIOS DAT file was downloaded from the PC manufacturer's web site. The PC was booted into DOS using a bootable floppy and the PHLASH program was run. It found the DAT file on the floppy, determined the BIOS revision installed was older than the DAT file BIOS code, and updated the BIOS code in NVRAM. Once complete, Windows 98 installed without a hitch.

CPU

CPU upgrades are the least cost-effective upgrades. Because CPU upgrade chips cost so much relative to their impact on actual PC performance, these upgrades are really make-you-feel-good upgrades. Because the main logic board support chips limit the CPU, installing a faster CPU may have a 10 percent or 20 percent impact on PC performance. Such an increase is barely noticeable to humans.

CPU upgrades must be specifically matched to the PC's main logic board. Zero Insertion Force (ZIF) makes popping out an old CPU a snap. Putting in the new CPU chip is equally easy, provided that no pins are bent in the process. A bent pin means no upgrade.

Slot 1 and Slot A CPU cartridges are easy to replace. They are keyed and just slide on and off the Slot 1 connector.

In some cases the MLB must support the CPU clock speeds. For example, we installed an AMD K6 in an old Socket 7 MLB that had a 133 MHz Pentium chip. The AMD chip could run at 466 MHz, but the MLB clock settings permitted us to get it to run at only 413 MHz. Quite an improvement, but the MLB prevented us from getting to the CPUs designated operating speed. In other cases no clocking adjustments are needed. The chip has different internal clock multipliers that function with current clock settings. In other cases, the system board base clock may have to be reset to match the multipliers of the new higher performance CPU chip.

CPU chip upgrades do not necessarily mean that the BIOS must be upgraded as well. Generally, popping in the new chip, adjusting the clock, and matching CPU chip voltages are all that is needed to complete a CPU chip upgrade, but it is always a good habit to check the manual to see if the MLB supports the new chip. Because CPU upgrades are not particularly cost-effective, in most cases it is better to purchase a whole new PC.

CPU Cache Memory (No Upgrade)

CPU cache memory can sometimes be increased on older PCs. Newer CPU chips have both Level-1 and Level-2 CPU caches built into the CPU chip so that it cannot be upgraded.

Upgrading Level-2 CPU cache is of marginal value because it has little impact on PC performance. CPU cache memory upgrade can only be performed on older Pentium and AMD chip systems with external Level-2 CPU cache memory. Furthermore, cache memory operates with diminishing returns as the cache memory size gets larger. This means that a small amount of cache memory produces the greatest performance impact. Larger and larger amounts of cache memory provide much less performance improvement.

External CPU cache memory uses static RAM chips. These are especially sensitive to static electricity. Special attention should be paid to static when upgrading the Level-2 CPU cache memory.

CPU cache memory upgrade requires adding or replacing static RAM chips on the main logic board. If chips are replaced, faster, higher capacity chips replace the older chips. Otherwise, more static RAM is added to empty sockets on the main logic board. Jumpers on the main logic board would then be changed to activate the additional Level-2 CPU cache memory capacity. No special software driver or CMOS configuration changes are required.

Summary

This chapter described how to remove and reinstall PC components including disk drives, display cards, LAN cards, and more. The first section covered the parameters and replacement costs for typical PC components. The next section discussed in detail the procedures for adding and/or removing FRUs.

Hardware configuration parameters needed for installing a diverse set of PC components were covered in detail in the next section. Following the hardware configuration section, cabling and connectors for I/O devices were discussed. PCs use a variety of cables to connect to the peripheral components they support. The purpose and functions of these cables and differences in the types of wire and the connectors used was covered in detail.

Installation of IDE and EIDE fixed disk drives and CD-ROMs followed the cabling section. Installing and configuring SCSI devices was detailed in the following section.

Section 2.7 covered the installation of common peripheral components such as keyboards, mice, video cards, and modems, which provided a good segue into the final section that covered upgrading your PC.

Chapter Review Questions

1. *What is the COM1 IRQ?*

    A. IRQ 4
    B. IRQ 2
    C. IRQ 3
    D. IRQ 7

Answer: A, IRQ 4. IRQ 2 is assigned to the programmable interrupt controller, IRQ 3 is COM2 or COM4, and IRQ 7 is LPT1.

2. *What is the COM2 IRQ?*

    A. IRQ 4
    B. IRQ 3
    C. IRQ 2
    D. IRQ 7

Answer: B, IRQ 3. IRQ 2 is assigned to the programmable interrupt controller, IRQ 4 is COM1 or COM3, and IRQ 7 is LPT1.

3. *What is the LPT1 IRQ?*

      A. IRQ 4
      B. IRQ 3
      C. IRQ 5
      D. IRQ 7

Answer: D, IRQ 7 or none. IRQ 4 is COM1 or COM3, IRQ 3 is COM2 or COM4, and IRQ 5 is LPT2.

4. *Identify the following connectors.*

      9-pin male
      Answer: serial port

      25-pin female
      Answer: parallel port

      50-pin Centronics style
      Answer: SCSI connector

      6-pin DIN
      Answer: mouse or keyboard

      BNC
      Answer: LAN

      MOD 8
      Answer: LAN

      RJ-11
      Answer: Modem

      RJ-45
      Answer: LAN

5. *How is the SCSI ID set on a fixed disk drive?*

Answer: Jumpers set the ID to SCSI ID 0, SCSI ID 1, or SCSI ID 2.

6. *Which ports on a PC should connect to a modem?*

Answers: Serial Ports, COM ports, COM 3, or COM 4.

7. *Identify in Figure 2–38:*

    A. a mouse
    B. a monitor
    C. a system unit
    D. a printer
    E. a keyboard
    F. a scanner

Answers: Figure 2–38 Question PC Components.

8. *You are using a modem. What two signals are required to accept information?*

Answers: CTS and DSR or DCD and Receive Data.

9. *You power on your PC, and the memory test runs displaying the amount of memory on the screen. What does this mean?*

Answer: It identifies the physical RAM present in the PC.

10. *How many SCSI devices can be on a PC?*

Answer: Seven for narrow SCSI buses or 15 for wide SCSI buses including the SCSI controller that is installed on device ID 7.

11. *When selecting SCSI IDs, what must be considered?*

    A. Each ID must be unique.
    B. Doesn't matter.
    C. All SCSI IDs should be the same.
    D. The SCSI controller should be on ID 0.

Answer: A, each SCSI ID should be unique. No SCSI IDs can be identical. SCSI controllers are installed on SCSI ID 7 that has the highest bus priority.

12. *Which pin is most important to remember when installing PC components?*

Answer: Pin one—it must connect to pin one.

13. *IDE devices use a _____ -pin cable.*

    A. 50
    B. 34
    C. 20
    D. 40

Answer: D, 40-pin cable for IDE and EIDE devices. A 34-pin cable connects floppy disk drives, a 50-pin cable connects SCSI devices, and 20-pin cables are not commonly used on a PC.

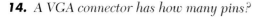
14. *A VGA connector has how many pins?*

    A. 20
    B. 15
    C. 9
    D. 25

Answer: B. 15 in three staggered rows. The 9-pin connector would be a serial or COM port, the 25-pin would be a parallel or LPT port connector (or a serial port connector—an uncommon implementation on PCs), and a 15-pin connector would connect to a midi/game port. The 20-pin connector is not commonly found on PCs.

15. *The most cost-effective PC performance upgrade is what?*

    A. Adding a new disk drive.
    B. Adding a new display monitor.
    C. Increasing floppy disk capacity.
    D. Adding RAM to increase size to a minimum of 64 MB.

Answer: D, adding RAM. The other selections increase capacity and add features, but do not increase performance.

16. *SDRAM comes in what packaging?*

    A. 30-pin SIMM
    B. 72-pin SIMM
    C. 168-pin DIMM
    D. 20-pin chips

Answer: C, 168-pin DIMM. 30-pin and 72-pin SIMMs are DRAM or EDO RAM. 20-pin chips are static RAM chips.

17. *What connection does a docking station use to connect to a laptop?*

    A. Serial
    B. Parallel
    C. FireWire
    D. USB
    E. None of these

Answer: E. Serial ports connect modems and PDAs, parallel ports connect printers, FireWire connects video equipment, and USB connects scanners, printers, and more.

18. *What device uses I/O Port 2F8-2FF?*

    A. COM1
    B. COM2
    C. COM3
    D. LPT1

Answer: B, COM2. COM1 is port 3F8, COM3 is 3E8, and LPT1 is 378.

19. *What network uses a single continuous cable?*

    A. Token Ring
    B. Star
    C. Bus
    D. Ethernet
    E. Ring

Answer: C, bus. Token Ring is a ring, most networks are wired as stars from wiring hubs, not all Ethernets are bus wired, and ring networks are not buses but rings.

20. *What FCC EMI certification classification must be met by home PCs?*

    A. A
    B. B
    C. C
    D. None

Answer: B, FCC class B certification is required for manufactured computers.

21. *A Bus carries data between the CPU and what?*

    A. RAM
    B. Modems
    C. EIDE drives
    D. None of the above

Answer: A, RAM because it is the only component always installed on the MLB and connected to the CPU through the front side bus. Modems can be internal (bus attached) or external, and EIDE drives connect to controllers plugged into the PCI bus.

22. *What IRQ do sound cards use?*

    A. 3
    B. 4
    C. 5
    D. 6

Answer: C, IRQ 5. COM ports use IRQ 3 and IRQ 4, and the floppy drive controller uses IRQ 6.

23. *The lightest, but most expensive laptop rechargeable battery is?*

    A. Li-Ion
    B. Alkaline
    C. NiMH
    D. Ni-Cd

Answer: A. Lithium Ion batteries are the lightest and most expensive. The other are older and heavier technologies.

24. *A type III PCMCIA card is_____ thick.*

    A. 3.3 mm
    B. 5.0 mm
    C. 10.5 mm
    D. None of the above

Answer: C. PCMCIA cards are 3.3 mm Type I, 5 mm Type II, and 10.5 mm Type III cards.

25. *Which added components are needed to install a CPU on an MLB?*

    A. ZIF Socket
    B. Co-processor
    C. BIOS Chip
    D. Heat sink with fan
    E. Level-2 Cache

Answer: D. The MLB already has a ZIF socket for the CPU, the numeric coprocessor is built into the CPU chip, BIOS makes the PC boot and run but does not install the CPU, and finally Level-2 cache is built into most CPUs.

26. *Extremely short over-voltage is called*

    A. Brownout
    B. Sag
    C. Voltage Surge
    D. Spike

Answer: D, Spike. Brownouts and sags describe low-voltage situations and a surge is a relatively long duration over-voltage situation.

27. *A CPU is:*

> A. An Integrated Circuit
> B. A big chip
> C. A SIMM
> D. Transistors
> E. A DIP chip

Answer: A. A CPU is an integrated circuit. New CPUs are not big chips; to be fast they get smaller and smaller. A SIMM is a memory expansion package. A CPU is comprised of transistors but has increased functionality from transistors, and a CPU is a Pin Grid Array (PGA) chip not a Dual Inline Package (DIP) chip.

28. *The size of conventional memory is:*

> A. 32 MB
> B. 640 KB
> C. 64 MB
> D. 320 KB
> E. None of the above

Answer: B, 640 KB. Some versions of Windows need a minimum of 32 MB or 64 MB of RAM to run. 320 KB means nothing.

29. *What is not an FRU?*

> A. Fixed Disk Drive
> B. Power Supply
> C. Motherboard
> D. Graphics Card
> E. MLB IDE controller

Answer: E. The MLB IDE controller is a chip on the main logic board and is not replaced in the field. All other components are FRUs.

30. *What does CMOS mean?*

> A. Cadmium Metallic Oxide Semiconductor
> B. Complementary Metal Oxide Semiconductor
> C. Compound Metal Oxide Semi Conductor
> D. Cadmium Metal Oxide Semi Conductor
> E. Complementary Metallic Oxide Semiconductor

Answer: E, Complementary Metallic Oxide Semiconductor. Cadmium is used in batteries (Ni Cad) and not chips.

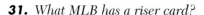

31. *What MLB has a riser card?*

    A. ATX
    B. Flex-ATX
    C. NLX
    D. Micro ATX
    E. LNX

Answer: E. The NLX form factor boards have a riser card. There is no LNX form factor. All ATX style boards have no riser cards.

32. *To display the contents of a TXT file, you use the DOS command:*

    A. ATTRIB
    B. DIR
    C. TYPE
    D. MORE
    E. FDISK

Answer: C. TYPE or EDIT displays text file (TXT) contents. ATTRIB displays file attributes (System, Read-Only, or Hidden), DIR lists all files, MORE creates secondary displays, and FDISK partitions disk drives.

33. *Each SCSI device requires:*

    A. A termination
    B. A Logical Unit Number
    C. A unique SCSI bus ID
    D. A LUN
    E. A 68-pin cable connector

Answer: C, a unique SCSI bus ID. The SCSI bus must be terminated at each end but not the SCSI devices. A LUN is a secondary addressing scheme within each SCSI ID. Only the Ultra SCSI drives use 68-pin cables.

34. *When upgrading or replacing a fixed disk drive, to remove all data, possible viruses, and Windows from a hard drive you would use the DOS _____ command.*

    A. FORMAT
    B. FDISK
    C. DELTREE
    D. DEL
    E. GHOST

Answer: B. FDISK kills all data and rewrites the partition table helping to remove data, viruses, and Windows. Format does not alter the partition table but does remove data and Windows. DELTREE deletes data in folders and folder trees. DEL deletes data in a folder but does not delete Hidden, Read-Only, or System files. GHOST is not a DOS command but it would wipe an entire partition or disk drive.

Chapter 3

TROUBLESHOOTING AND PROBLEM RESOLUTION

Chapter Syllabus

- Determining the Source of Problems

- Troubleshooting PC Hardware

- Diagnosing Error Symptoms and Problems by Subsystem

- Troubleshooting Tools

- Troubleshooting Procedures and Practices

This chapter describes how to diagnose and identify basic PC Field Replaceable Unit (FRU) problems. For definitions and characteristics of common FRUs, see Chapter 2.

Troubleshooting procedures using the system malfunction symptoms to identify common PC component failures are presented. PC troubleshooting requires identifying problems that fall into three key areas: PC hardware, Windows and applications software, and networks. Isolating the problem into one of these three areas is the first step in resolving PC malfunctions. After this is accomplished, more precise troubleshooting procedures can be applied.

This chapter discusses identifying the general malfunction area and then provides more detail on troubleshooting PC hardware problems.

Windows and application software and networking problems are discussed in subsequent chapters. Some fundamental guidelines for troubleshooting PCs follow.

1. First of all, remember that every PC problem can be solved. The worst-case scenario is to replace the PC. This guideline I learned from my ex-wife. Whenever we would argue, she would say, "I will win!" and she always did.

2. Make sure everything is plugged in and nothing has come loose. Check the power, display, phone lines, printer, network, and modem connections.

3. Check external signs. Are the power lights on, do fixed and floppy disk drive lights flash, does the monitor come on, does the monitor display the boot program displays, is the PC making normal or strange sounds, do you smell something? Make notes of any special signs.

4. Observe the POST diagnostics. Do they report any failures?

5. Boot using a DOS floppy. Can you run DIR commands on all disk drives? Does FDISK indicate fixed disk errors? Can you run DOS network software?

6. Check PC setup files. Are parameters correct? Have paths changed?

7. Ask, "Has anything changed?"

8. Copy key data to backup diskettes, network, or tape.

9. Disassemble the PC, clean it, reseat chips, and reassemble the PC.

10. Check the nut behind the keyboard.

11. Draw a picture of what connects to what. Write everything down. Try zeroing in on malfunctioning components.

12. Verify working components.

13. Reboot the PC by powering it off. Then, start again.

14. Use any available test equipment to test components. Test equipment with identical working components, anything to verify power, or software diagnostic programs.

15. Never guess. Just one setting out of thousands of possibilities is

correct. The chance of hitting the exact correct setting is about the same as winning the lottery.

16. Trust no one. You must fix the problem and no one will help you. Remember all PC error messages are lies.

17. Observe like Sherlock Holmes. Which light comes on first, the fixed disk drive light or the floppy disk drive light? It is the fixed disk drive light.

18. Wish for luck. You may need all the help you can get.

Determining the Source of Problems

How can a PC malfunction be quickly identified as a hardware, software, or network problem? It is quite straightforward. Typically, key hardware component malfunctions are identified during the boot process by power on self-test (POST). The PC refuses to run in this case. The error messages produced are simple and obvious. At this stage, less debilitating hardware failures rarely occur. These types of failures can be spotted by simple diagnostics, programs that test the malfunctioning component, or by swapping the component with an equivalent component—the "swap until you drop" diagnostic approach. For example, FDISK reports that a fixed disk is unreadable, indicating that the disk itself is bad.

Windows 95/98/Me software and hardware problems manifest themselves as missing VxDs and DLLs or as memory protection faults. With Windows 2000, most software problems have minimal impact; the application just crashes or quits, and Windows recovers and continues to run. However, incorrect hardware driver programs cause bad problems with Windows 2000. In this case Windows 2000 can inexplicably quit. The key root source of such problems is bad display drivers or outdated BIOS. Many malfunctions are caused by incorrect driver programs for the installed hardware, or from Windows 95/98/Me users corrupting the software by making mistakes while using the PC. Often times users will install software that kills the correct Windows 95/98/Me components, replacing them with bad software modules.

Network problems are the toughest; they can bring a PC to a grinding halt. Because networked PCs continually communicate with other networked PCs, and because the network software and disk I/O software components run at a higher priority than other Windows components, they tend to stop the PC dead when a network fails. This is often hard to recognize.

Furthermore, Windows can recover from these network failures, but the time-out values are set very high so minutes may literally pass before the PC can be shut down and restarted. Sometimes the PC cannot be started because network connections cannot be made or network address conflicts exist.

Let's look in detail at the troubleshooting procedures for PC hardware components.

Study Break: Network Failure Impact

To see the impact of network failures on PC performance, map a network drive to a drive letter and disconnect the LAN cable. This is done using the Windows Explorer.

1. Open the Explorer, expand the Network Neighborhood, find a server or a shared PC that permits you to map a drive letter to its shared drive, and map the drive letter. A drive letter should soon appear under the My Computer icon in the Windows Explorer saying something like, "DRD on Sam's PC."
2. Now click on the network drive icon to view the drive contents. How long did it take? Next click on a local drive icon. Disconnect the LAN cable from the LAN board in the PC. Now click on the network drive icon again to view the contents. This time how long did it take? Big difference.

Troubleshooting PC Hardware

Key PC components are those required for the PC to operate. They include the fixed and floppy disk drives, the main logic board with RAM, ROM, and CPU, power supply, keyboard, mouse, display adapter, and monitor. Without these components, the PC simply does not run in a useable fashion. Other components are nearly as important today, including CD-ROM devices, modems, and network interface cards.

A PC can run without these, but without them the PC is less useable.

When troubleshooting these components, we are looking for a chain of components, starting with the power at the wall outlet: no power, no PC. Next we check the power cord and then the power supply.

Finally, we move to the main logic board and the CPU, ROM, and RAM. If these components malfunction, you see nothing. We recently worked on a system with a bad AMD Athlon CPU. We installed the basic CPU, RAM, display controller, display, and MLB components and powered them up. Nothing happened. We had to replace each component to eventually narrow it down to the bad CPU. In this case everything was dead, and POST diagnostics did not run. This is like having a person with a body but no arms, legs, and head. They are able to, in some way, breathe and circulate blood, but they cannot do much else.

Power On Self-Test (POST)

The PC's power-on self-test (POST) is your primary PC hardware component-troubleshooting tool. The PC's ROM stores the POST diagnostics. They are the first programs that run when the PC boots. The POST diagnostics are loaded into the first bank of RAM to run. Without some functioning RAM, the only error indications from the POST diagnostics are beeps which output to the PC's speaker. These are the audio error codes described below.

When there is a functioning CPU and functioning RAM, the POST proceeds to run. It displays an opening screen identifying the PC components it detected and permits entering the CMOS setup program by striking the keys displayed. In Figure 3–1, the F2 key enters the setup program. POST tests the basic functioning of the key PC components—the CPU, RAM, floppy and

Figure 3–1
CMOS Boot Display.

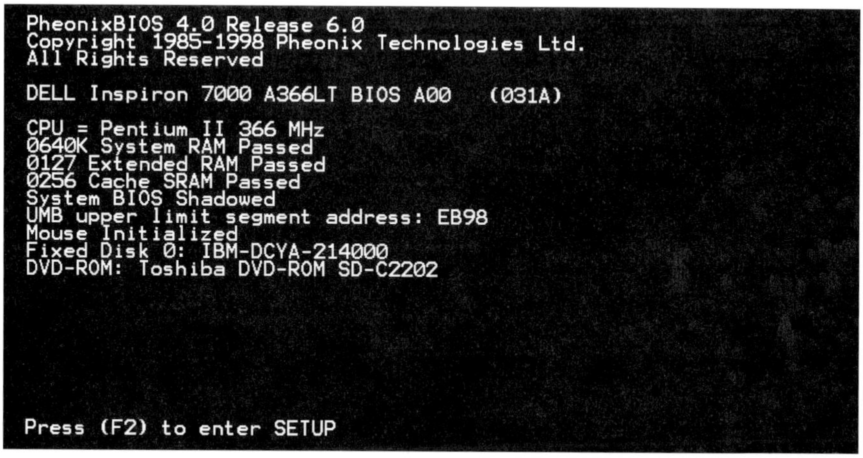

```
PheonixBIOS 4.0 Release 6.0
Copyright 1985-1998 Pheonix Technologies Ltd.
All Rights Reserved

DELL Inspiron 7000 A366LT BIOS A00    (031A)

CPU = Pentium II 366 MHz
0640K System RAM Passed
0127 Extended RAM Passed
0256 Cache SRAM Passed
System BIOS Shadowed
UMB upper limit segment address: EB98
Mouse Initialized
Fixed Disk 0: IBM-DCYA-214000
DVD-ROM: Toshiba DVD-ROM SD-C2202




Press (F2) to enter SETUP
```

fixed disk drives, the keyboard, and the display controller. The results of these tests are displayed on the PC's monitor in text format. Errors reported here identify a serious hardware problem because these tests are not comprehensive tests of any component.

For example, the POST RAM test verifies the amount of RAM installed in the PC and stored as a parameter in the NVRAM setup parameters. When there is a RAM mismatch, POST reports that the RAM size is incorrect, adjusts the size to the new size, and causes the PC to reboot. Sometimes, RAM can be malfunctioning and pass the POST RAM test. HIMEM.SYS performs a much more thorough test. It fails the RAM test when there are memory speed and other timing mismatches that often pass the POST RAM test.

Audio Beep Error Codes

Audio beep error codes are used to signal critical system errors when the PC's system board cannot display them. The actual audio beeps vary depending upon the BIOS used on the system board. The manual accompanying the board or the PC lists the beep codes and their meaning. Some of the original IBM PC beep codes are still used by system boards. These codes are:

No beep, nothing	Power supply failure or not plugged in
Continuous beep	Power supply failure
Repeating short beep	System board failure
1 long beep, 1 short beep	System board failure
1 long, 2 short beeps	Failure or lack of display adapter
1 short beep, blank screen	Missing or failed display adapter/cable
1 short beep, no boot	Floppy drive adapter failure

Because each PC BIOS is different these days, there is no guarantee that any particular system implements its beep in the same way as the original IBM PC implemented them.

Some AMI and Phoenix BIOS beep codes are:

Single beep	DRAM failure
Two beeps	Parity failure
Three beeps	Base 64 KB or CMOS Memory failure
Four beeps	System timer failure

Five beeps	CPU failure
Six beeps	Keyboard controller or A20 failure
Seven beeps	Virtual mode exception error
Eight beeps	Display controller read/write test failure
Nine beeps	ROM BIOS checksum failure
Ten beeps	CMOS RAM shutdown register failure
One long and three short beeps	Memory failure
One long and eight short beeps	Display failure

Other plug-and-play BIOS beep codes are:

Single short beep	Normal no problem boot
Two beeps	ROM option search failed
Three beeps	ROM BIOS checksum failure
Four beeps	DRAM failure
Five beeps	Keyboard failure
Six beeps	Unexpected interrupts found
Seven beeps	Problem configuring IRQs and I/O addresses
Eight beeps	Display controller failure
Nine beeps	Memory Failure

However, all beep codes are similar. You can infer that the most probable cause of a beep code is bad RAM, because the system board has power (enough to beep the speaker and run the ROM POST program), but the POST program cannot be run. Because it must run from RAM, the RAM is most likely bad. The beep code signals this. It is rare to encounter a system that halts and beeps. RAM today is very reliable, so the POST typically runs to completion.

Video Error Messages

POST displays video error messages. These messages are text error messages identifying the specific hardware component error. The components are those that are needed by DOS to boot the PC. Such components include:

- RAM
- Serial ports on the main logic board
- Parallel ports on the main logic board
- IDE controllers on the main logic board
- Keyboard
- Floppy disk controller

Commonly, there are no error messages for failure of the CPU or the cache memories. The rationale here is direct; when they malfunction, no programs run. The system is dead.

Video errors are in simple English indicating the error message rather than some cryptic code. A keyboard error states, "Keyboard missing or keyboard failure" as an example. Unlike on early PCs, error codes today are more self-descriptive.

IBM Numeric Error Codes

In 1981, the original IBM PC provided numeric error codes to identify component malfunctions. These error codes were a holdover from the "close to the vest" operation of IBM mainframe computers. They made knowledge of such numeric error codes essential for troubleshooting and repairing PCs. These are unnecessary today but are provided here for reference purposes. Some original IBM PC error codes are:

101—Motherboard Failure

109—Direct Memory Access Test Error

121—Unexpected Hardware Interrupt

163—Date and Time Not Set => change battery

161, 2, or 4—PS/2 Re-run configuration => change battery

199—User Response to Configuration Not Correct

201—Memory

301—Keyboard=>Heavy Fingers or Stuck Key

301 8602—PS -2 Power Off-On =>Mouse Failure

401— Monochrome Adapter or Display Failure

432—Parallel Printer Not Powered Up

501—CGA Adapter or Display Failure

601—Floppy Disk Drive or Adapter Failure

701— Math Co-processor Test Failure

901—Parallel Printer Adapter Test Failure

1101—Serial Port Test Failure

1301—Game-Control Adapter Test Failure

1302— Joystick Test Failure

1401— Printer Test Failure

1701— Fixed DISK Drive or Adapter Failure

1702— Controller Failure

1703— Disk Drive Failure

1704—Undetermined Failure—Drive or Controller

1780— Disk Drive 0: Failure

1781—Disk Drive 1: Failure

1782— Controller Failure on PC AT

1790— Disk Drive 0: Failure—Cannot read—Incorrect type

1791— Disk Drive 1: Failure—Cannot read—Incorrect type

2401— EGA Adapter or Display Failure

2501—EGA Adapter or Display Failure

There are many PC error codes, but generally the most frequently seen are **those in bold type**. They are more than sufficient to zero in on the malfunctioning component. Furthermore, standardized PCs do not necessarily implement any of these error codes in their ROMs. You might get "Stuck key failure" on a clone rather than the "301" that you would see on a IBM PC. Some manufacturers attempt to maintain user dependence on their maintenance and technical support by implementing proprietary error codes. This is self-serving, designed to promote their revenue-generating technical support function.

Study Break: Error Messages

In order to see PC component error messages, shut down the PC and disconnect in sequence the keyboard, the fixed disk drive cable, and the floppy disk drive cable.

1. Exit all software and turn off the PC. Disconnect the keyboard cable. Restart the PC. What error message appears? Write it down here:

2. Now Exit all software and turn off the PC. Reconnect the keyboard cable and disconnect the fixed disk power cable. Restart the PC. What error message appears? Write it down here:

3. Now turn off the PC. Reconnect the fixed disk power cable. Disconnect the fixed disk data cable. Restart the PC. What error message appears? Write it down here:

4. Now turn off the PC. Reconnect the fixed disk data cable. Disconnect all floppy drives from the floppy data cable. Restart the PC. What error message appears? Write it down here:

5. Now turn off the PC. Reconnect all floppy drives to the floppy data cable. Restart the PC. No error messages should appear.

Diagnosing Error Symptoms and Problems by Subsystem

PC hardware error symptoms are described in these subsections. They range from the PC acting like a rock and doing nothing to almost starting OK. Each indicates a specific type of malfunction. The key here is to think of how electrical power flows into the PC. It starts at the wall outlet. If there is no power, that must first be rectified before we can proceed further. Next is the PC's power cord. This is highly reliable, but not without an occasional failure. These failures are often caused by poor connector contacts. When these check out OK, we move on to the power supply.

Power Supply

The power supply converts 115-volts or 220-volts AC into 5-volts and 12-volts DC. Without this low voltage power, the PC does nothing. When some but not enough power is provided to the main logic board, the PC can beep to signal failure. Otherwise it is silent.

When nothing leaves the power supply, the PC is really dead on arrival (DOA). Some tests for the power supply are very simple, like listening for the fan to start. Others can require using a voltmeter to test output voltages on the power supply connectors. See Figure 3–2. Testing output voltages is great, but replacing the supply performs an equivalent test and repairs the problem in a single step. When the supply replacement does not fix the problem, the removed supply is probably good. The removed supply can act as future power supply test equipment. It is much more elegant to test with a multi-meter, but

Figure 3–2
Digital multi-meter that tests voltage.

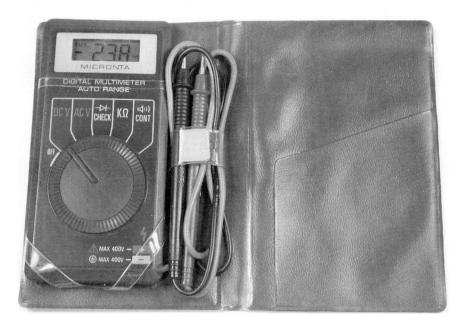

much quicker to test with a power supply. When you have lots of service calls to close in a day, the power supply test always wins. On the A+ test, the multi-meter test is likely a better answer.

Multi-meters are good for testing cable continuity. Using the K-ohm test on a multi-meter is an effective way to determine which pins are connected to which pins at the opposite end of any cable.

Main Logic Board

The next thing the power hits is the main logic board. This means that the PC begins to function if the CPU chip is working. At least there are beep codes when the CPU functions and the RAM fails. Once we have power to the main logic board, then we can verify the proper operation of the key PC components installed on the main logic board.

The key components on the main logic board are the BIOS in ROM, the CMOS or NVRAM, the battery, the on-board serial and parallel ports, the CPU, the RAM, the video controller, and the keyboard. A PC can function without a mouse, even within Windows. This makes the mouse an important component, but not a key component.

BIOS

The Basic Input Output System (BIOS) is software in ROM chips on the main logic board. The BIOS software performs 8-bit and 16-bit input/output functions. Chip failure here is extremely rare. A typical failure message states that there was a ROM checksum failure. BIOS upgrades were discussed in Chapter 2.

CMOS or NVRAM

The Complementary Metal Oxide Semiconductor (CMOS) or NVRAM stores system setup and operating parameters. Also, BIOS and the initial program load setup program can be stored in the CMOS or NVRAM. A failure here would cause the setup program not to run, resulting in a blank PC display or possibly a checksum error message.

The CMOS setup program permits changing the PC's basic hardware settings. Entering the setup program by striking a key—commonly F1, F2, or Delete—brings up a main system setup screen. See Figure 3–3. This menu permits setting the time and specifying the fixed and floppy disk drives.

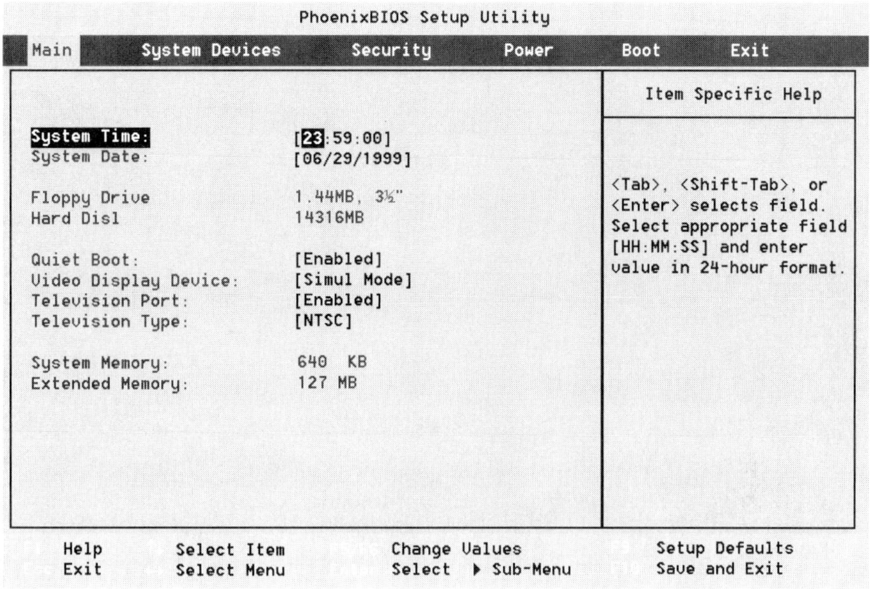

```
                          PhoenixBIOS Setup Utility
   Main      System Devices      Security      Power      Boot      Exit

                                                     Item Specific Help

     System Time:            [23:59:00]
     System Date:            [06/29/1999]
                                                  <Tab>, <Shift-Tab>, or
     Floppy Drive            1.44MB, 3½"          <Enter> selects field.
     Hard Dis1               14316MB              Select appropriate field
                                                  [HH:MM:SS] and enter
     Quiet Boot:             [Enabled]            value in 24-hour format.
     Video Display Device:   [Simul Mode]
     Television Port:        [Enabled]
     Television Type:        [NTSC]

     System Memory:          640  KB
     Extended Memory:        127 MB




     Help      Select Item        Change Values       Setup Defaults
     Exit      Select Menu        Select  ▶ Sub-Menu  Save and Exit
```

Figure 3–3
CMOS setup main menu.

Moving one tab to the right using the right arrow key provides a system devices setup menu screen. See Figure 3–4. Here, the main logic board built-in controllers are configured. This sets the IDE, serial, and parallel interfaces as well as ancillary options like infrared communications and MPEG operation. Each option is a simple menu selection. The arrow keys move up and down and across the menu selections. Striking the Enter key permits changing the option selection, with the selections often presented in a drop down menu.

The last tab sets the power management options that are incorporated into both the PC hardware and Windows software. See Figure 3–5. Conflicting power management settings cause many PC problems. Disabling hardware power management is one way to avoid such problems.

Battery

On newer PCs, the NVRAM or CMOS setup parameters are stored in a Dallas real-time clock chip. This Dallas real-time clock chip is installed in a main logic board socket and often secured with a tie-wrap. The fix for a faulty chip is a replacement of the entire Dallas chip. See Figure 3–6. This replaces both the battery and the CMOS memory.

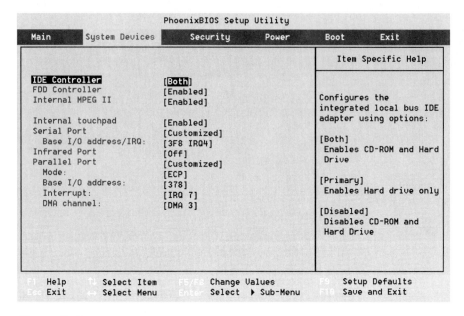

Figure 3–4

CMOS setup system device menu.

Figure 3–5

CMOS setup power management menu.

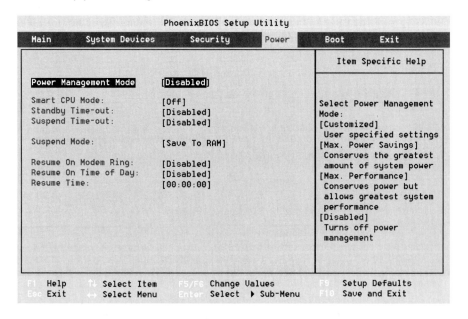

Figure 3–6
Dallas chip on MLB.

Older PCs used a separate 3-volt or 6-volt lithium battery to power the CMOS memory. When the lithium battery failed, there were no system signs to warn the user. The system functioned normally until it was physically powered off. Once the PC was powered down, the CMOS, without its functioning battery, would loose all of its setup parameters. Most importantly, the fixed disk parameters would be lost. This would cause the PC to fail to recognize the fixed disk, and consequently not boot. When booted from floppy diskette, the PC would appear to have lost every stitch of data on the fixed disk. Fortunately, this was not the case. To fix the problem, the setup program had to be run to restore the old fixed disk setup parameters. Once restored, the PC would be warm-booted to return to normal operation. As long as the power was not removed from the PC, it could be rebooted (using CTRL-ALT-DEL) without loosing the setup parameters. Most new plug-and-play BIOS have automatic settings for detecting the fixed disk operating parameters. They default to automatic detection that permits the PC to boot even if the fixed disk CMOS settings are lost.

Parallel Port

The parallel port is not considered a critical PC operating component and does not affect the PC boot process. During the boot process the PC would display the operating main logic board components. This display would include operating parallel ports and their I/O address (378 for LPT1, 278 for LPT2, or 3BC). If the parallel port was not operating or was turned off, it would not appear in the boot display. Since the display flashes briefly during the boot process, parallel port failure is only noticed when the PC fails to print to the printer. Sometimes a pause command is placed in the AUTOEXEC.BAT or CONFIG.SYS files to halt the display until the user presses a key to continue, in which case the message can be more easily seen or captured. Failure to print a document is not necessarily caused by a failure of the parallel port.

For example, when running Windows 98, the PC may become unable to print to its printer. The Windows PC displays an error message: "There was an error writing to LPT1: for TEST printer. There was a problem writing to the port. Check to make sure your printer is configured to use a valid port." This message does not necessarily indicate a printer port hardware failure, but more likely bad Windows printer drivers.

A simple test of the parallel port hardware is performed by connecting the printer to the LPT1 port, booting into DOS, and entering DIR>LPT1. This can also work from the Windows Command prompt without rebooting into DOS.

This sends the DIR command output to the parallel port and should print on any printer. To test LPT2, enter DIR>LPT2. If both ports print in the above test, the PC's port hardware is working fine. The problem is then with the driver program for the printer and how it interacts with Windows. To solve this problem, use the very latest driver programs downloaded from a support web site for the printer.

Serial Ports

Similar to parallel ports, a serial port is not a critical PC operating component. PCs boot without them operating. During the boot process, PCs display serial ports as operating main logic board components. The display includes operating serial ports and their I/O address (3F8 for COM1, 2F8 for COM2, 3E8 for COM3, and 2E8 for COM4). When a COM port is not operating or is disabled, it is not shown in the boot display. This display flashes briefly during the boot process, so serial port failure is only noticed if a serial device—for instance, a mouse—is attached to a serial port and that device fails to operate.

The MODE command provides a simple diagnostic capability. The MODE command has options to set up and redirect the printer and COM ports. See Figure 3–7. Other options permit setting the keyboard typematic rate, the basic display mode, and code pages for foreign language operation. We are interested in the capabilities of the MODE command to test for the presence and well being of serial and parallel ports.

The presence or absence of serial ports can be tested using the DOS MODE command. This is not a comprehensive test. Results vary depending upon the version of DOS. The MODE command test is:

```
MODE COM1 300
MODE COM2 300
MODE COM3 300
MODE COM4 300
```

```
Microsoft(R) Windows 98
   (C)Copyright Microsoft Corp 1981-1998.

C:\WINDOWS>mode /?
Configures system devices.

Printer port:        MODE LPTn[:] [COLS=c] [LINES=l] [RETRY=r]
Serial port:         MODE COMm[:] [BAUD=b] [PARITY=p] [DATA=d] [STOP=s] [RETRY=r]
Device Status:       MODE [device] [/STATUS]
Redirect printing:   MODE LPTn[:]=COMm[:]
Prepare code page:   MODE device CP PREPARE=((yyy[...]) [drive:][path]filename)
Select code page:    MODE device CP SELECT=yyy
Refresh code page:   MODE device CP REFRESH
Code page status:    MODE device CP [/STATUS]
Display mode:        MODE [display-adapter][,n]
                     MODE CON[:] [COLS=c] [LINES=n]
Typematic rate:      MODE CON[:] [RATE=r DELAY=d]

C:\WINDOWS>
```

```
Microsoft Windows 2000 [Version 5.00.2195]
(C) Copyright 1985-2000 Microsoft Corp.

C:\>mode /?
Configures system devices.

Serial port:         MODE COMm[:] [BAUD=b] [PARITY=p] [DATA=d] [STOP=s]
                               [to=on|off] [xon=on|off] [odsr=on|off]
                               [octs=on|off] [dtr=on|off|hs]
                               [rts=on|off|hs|tg] [idsr=on|off]

Device Status:       MODE [device] [/STATUS]

Redirect printing:   MODE LPTn[:]=COMm[:]

Select code page:    MODE CON[:] CP SELECT=yyy

Code page status:    MODE CON[:] CP [/STATUS]

Display mode:        MODE CON[:] [COLS=c] [LINES=n]

Typematic rate:      MODE CON[:] [RATE=r DELAY=d]

C:\>
```

Figure 3–7
Mode command options.

This sets up the serial ports to a speed of 300 bits per second. The speed setting is not critical here. Any speed can be used, but a speed must be specified. When a serial port is present, DOS responds with messages like:

```
"COM1: 300,e,7,1,-
 COM1: 300,e,7,1,- "
```

Any response here means that the serial port is present. The 300, e, 7, 1, etc., indicate that the port speed was set to 300 bits per second, the parity detection was set to even parity, there are seven data bits, one stop bit is used, and the retry status is not set. When testing a serial port, setting the speed to a slow speed, e.g., 300 bits per second, permits port testers with LEDs to flash when data is sent across the transmit or receive lines (pin 2 and pin 3).

If no serial port is present, the following error message is displayed:

```
"Illegal device name
COM3 "
```

This is not a complete test of the serial port. The next step would be to provide a Clear to Send (CTS on DB-25 is pin 5) signal from Data Terminal Ready (DTR on DB-25 is pin 20) to the port and perform the DIR>COM1, etc. When the serial ports are working, the PC just does nothing while the directory characters are sent out the port. If an external modem with lights is attached to the port, the Transmit Data (TD on DB25 is pin 2) flickers.

Another useful and inexpensive test tool is a "mini-tester" that uses light signals for each of the different tests.

Once finished, the PC returns to the DOS prompt. When the port malfunctions or does not have the CTS signal, the following error message is displayed:

```
"Write fault error writing device COM1
Abort, Retry, Ignore, Fail?"
```

CPU

CPU malfunctions typically result in the system lights coming on and the user being able to hear the fan turning on, but nothing is displayed on the screen. When the CPU does not work, there is no processor to perform the POST or to produce any system or error displays. Without the CPU running well, a PC cannot even beep.

It is possible to have the PC boot and not have the CPU chip operating reliably or properly. This can be the result of a clock mismatch or bad CPU Level-1 or Level-2 caches. It is possible to diagnose these error conditions.

One possible cause of clock mismatches is increasing the clock rate of the CPU chip. This is called overclocking. Overclocking is a popular way to boost PC performance without paying the price for a higher speed CPU chip. Since most CPU chips are underrated in clock speed, this often works fine—but not always. Sometimes overclocking does not work. In this case, the PC may pass the POST just fine, but it will not run any software application. As soon as Windows or applications are loaded, the PC crashes. All error messages in this instance are misleading and do not point to the root problem—the CPU chip clock mismatch.

Sometimes the overclocking failure happens well after the PC is started. When the clock frequency of the CPU is increased, it makes the CPU chip work harder and produce more heat. When insufficient cooling is provided, the CPU chip does not fail immediately but when the CPU chip overheats. This situation is bad and can cause the CPU chip to burn out and fail completely. Since overclocking stresses the CPU chip and diminishes its reliability, it is never recommended by any PC manufacturer or maintenance organization. Any PC warranty is voided when overclocking is detected.

It is possible to have a CPU with a bad Level-1 or Level-2 cache.

These CPUs may pass POST and may load and run software. However, they are hidden landmines waiting to explode. The errors manifest themselves during I/O operations, particularly network or fixed disk I/O. Error messages will indicate a fixed disk-read or a disk-write error. The message is misleading and does not point at the root of the problem, a bad cache.

To test the cache, it must be disabled. The CMOS setup program may permit the disabling of both Level-1 and Level-2 cache. There is no guarantee here that any specific PC is capable of disabling its cache. Once the faulty cache is disabled, the error disappears, but the PC runs very slow. Disabling the Level-1 or the Level-2 cache would determine which cache is the culprit. A PC will run with Level-1 and Level-2 cache disabled. When a cache failure happened to me, there was a bad chip in the external Level-2 CPU cache.

Random Access Memory (RAM)

Memory errors may be detected by running a memory test program (that is, HIMEM.SYS—this sometimes detects a problem), getting a memory error message from POST on power-up, or having an application crash continually. When applications crash, the error message or behavior rarely looks like an obvious memory or hardware problem, however.

The early PCs employed parity to check for memory errors. An extra bit (the parity bit) was added to each 8-bit byte stored in RAM. The parity bit value was set to one or zero, depending upon the number of ones in the remaining eight bits in the byte. Parity works like a dryer; you put in an even number of socks, and inevitably end up with an odd number of socks. The ones in our memory bytes are the socks. So as data is stored away the parity bit is set to assure that an odd (or even) number of ones are stored with each byte. Upon data retrieval, the parity is recalculated and compared to the parity bit stored. A mismatch is identified as an error. Today, error-correcting codes use the parity bits to detect and correct single bit errors in memory.

Early PCs would display "Parity Check 1", indicating a motherboard memory problem, or "Parity Check 2", indicating an expansion card memory error.

Some memory error messages allowed you to narrow the problem down to a single chip. Such detailed memory error isolation is not practical now that PCs have megabytes of RAM installed using SIMMs and DIMMs. For a review of SIMMs and their characteristics, see Chapter 2.

PCs have also stopped using parity as a memory-checking mechanism. A SIMM with parity is referred to as a 9x36 SIMM as opposed to a SIMM with no parity bits, which is an 8x32 SIMM. Common SIMM sizes and descriptions were briefly presented in Chapter 2, Table 2.3; common RAM types are covered in more detail in Chapter 5.

Older PCs have 640 Kb conventional main memory. This conventional memory was divided into 10 64 Kb logical banks. The logical banks are numbered 00 through 09. DOS and DOS-based application programs use conventional memory. All memory today is located on the main logic board. Each byte of memory holds one character. The PC uses hexadecimal addresses to indicate locations of memory areas or the logical banks. Portions of the memory are used as RAM and other portions are reserved for ROM or have the ROM contents copied into them (this is the shadow BIOS concept).

The original IBM PC, XT, and AT memory errors could be traced to an individual memory chip. Our worst memory error nightmare was finding a single bad RAM chip in 72 RAM chips. Needless to say this required several hours of effort because we had to swap banks of chips until the bad chip was precisely identified.

Once memory moved to SIMMs and away from chips, memory addresses were used to identify a bad SIMM. The movement to SIMMs came with the first 486 CPU PCs. SIMMs made it easier and less costly to manufacture PCs and increased the reliability of RAM. Socketed chips were a significant memory failure point.

To locate memory errors, you moved SIMMs. When a memory error address changed, the SIMM moved caused the memory error. Depending on how the address changed (it moved to higher address ranges or to lower address ranges), the bad SIMM could be precisely identified.

Because today's PCs have megabytes of RAM, because the RAM is typically non-parity RAM, because there are so few SIMMs, DIMMs, or RIMMs in a PC, and because RAM is inexpensive, in new PCs it is easiest to swap SIMMs, DIMMs, or RIMMs to find memory errors. The trick is determining if the error is a hardware memory error or just something caused by Windows software. Bad memory only fails when it is used. So PCs could have bad memory installed and conceivably never have a memory failure because the bad memory was never used. The chances of this are nil—today's programs are memory hogs. Furthermore, the program just crashes when bad memory is encountered, which is very misleading as to the cause of the error. The POST does catch memory errors and sometimes PCs are configured so that the better test performed by HIMEM.SYS is not run. If the HIMEM.SYS command parameter /TESTMEM:ON|OFF is set to OFF, HIMEM.SYS does not perform its memory test.

HIMEM.SYS has several option switches, including:

- **/A20CONTROL:ON|OFF**

  Specifies to HIMEM whether to control the A20 line. The A20 handler supports access to the High Memory Area (HMA). When /A20CONTROL:OFF is specified, HIMEM controls the A20 line only if A20 was off when HIMEM loaded. The default setting is /A20CONTROL:ON.

- **/CPUCLOCK:ON|OFF**

  Specifies whether HIMEM can affect the CPU chip clock speed. If a PC's clock speed changed when HIMEM was installed, specifying /CPUCLOCK:ON may correct the problem. Enabling this option slows down HIMEM. The default setting is /CPUCLOCK:OFF.

- **/EISA**

  Specifies allocation of all available extended memory. This switch is needed only on EISA (Extended Industry Standard Architecture) computers with more than 16 MB of memory. HIMEM automatically allocates all available extended memory on other computers.

- **/HMAMIN=m**

  Specifies how much memory in kilobytes an application must request from HIMEM for HIMEM to give that application use of the HMA. In DOS, only one application can use the HMA at a time; HIMEM allocates the HMA to the first application that meets the memory-use requirements set by this option. When the /HMAMIN option is not required, the default value is zero. Omitting this option or setting it to zero causes HIMEM to allocate the HMA to the first DOS application that requests it, regardless of how much of the HMA the application is going to use. The /HMAMIN option has no effect when Windows is running in 386 enhanced mode.

- **/INT15=xxxx**

  Allocates extended memory in kilobytes reserved for the Interrupt 15h interface. Some DOS applications use the Interrupt 15h interface to allocate extended memory rather than using the XMS (eXtended-Memory Specification) provided by HIMEM. Values from 64 to 65535 can be specified; however, you cannot specify more memory than your system has available. A value less than 64 is interpreted as a value of 0. The default value is 0.

- **/NUMHANDLES=n**

  Specifies the maximum extended-memory block (EMB) handles that are simultaneously used. Values from 1 to 128 can be specified with a default value of 32. Each handle requires 6 bytes of memory. /NUMHANDLES has no effect when Windows is running in 386 enhanced mode.

- **/MACHINE:xxxx**

  Specifies computer type. Usually, HIMEM can detect the PC type successfully; however, there are a few computers that HIMEM does not detect. HIMEM uses the default system type of IBM AT or compatible. Include the /MACHINE option if a PC is a type that HIMEM cannot detect. This is indicated when HIMEM does not work properly on a PC using the default system type.

- **/SHADOWRAM:ON|OFF**

  Disables shadow RAM (SHADOWRAM:OFF) or leaves the ROM code running from RAM (SHADOWRAM:ON). Some computers make ROM code run faster by "shadowing" or copying it into RAM which uses some extended memory. Computers that use shadow RAM and have less than 2 MB of RAM cause HIMEM to disable shadow RAM and thus recover additional extended memory for Windows to use. When HIMEM disables shadow RAM, the ROM code runs in the slower ROM instead of RAM.

- **/TESTMEM:ON|OFF**

  Determines whether HIMEM performs a memory test when a PC starts. By default, HIMEM tests the reliability of a computer's extended memory each time a computer starts. This test identifies memory that is not reliable. HIMEM's memory test is more thorough than the standard power-up memory test performed by most computers. To prevent HIMEM from performing the memory test, specify /TESTMEM:OFF. Disabling the memory test shortens the PC boot time. (The default setting is /TESTMEM:ON.)

- **/VERBOSE**

  Directs HIMEM to display status and error messages while loading. By default, HIMEM does not display any messages unless an error is encountered. /VERBOSE is abbreviated as /V. Status messages are displayed without adding the /VERBOSE switch by pressing and holding the ALT key when HIMEM starts and loads.

The PC needs the first bank of RAM operational to run the POST and the NVRAM setup program. Without that first bank of RAM, a PC just beeps. One problem is determining which is the first bank of RAM, and determining the number of SIMMs, DIMMs, or RIMMs required for the RAM. Some general rules are shown in Table 3–1.

Table 3–1   Types and Numbers of Chips Needed

RAM SIMM, DIMM or RIMM	CPU Chip	Number required for a bank
30-pin SIMM	386	2 or 4 SIMMs per bank
30-pin SIMM	486	2 or 4 SIMMs per bank
72-pin SIMM	386	1 or 2 SIMMs per bank
72-pin SIMM	486	1 or 2 SIMMs per bank
72-pin SIMM	Pentium	2 or 4 SIMMs per bank
168-pin DIMM	Pentium	1 or 2 DIMMs per bank
184-pin RIMM	Pentium (Pentium 4)	2 RIMMs per bank

When multiple SIMMs, DIMMs, or RIMMs are used in a bank, they should match exactly. In many new MLBs, the bank that the RAM is inserted into does not matter. In older PCs the RAM in some cases had to be installed in specific RAM slots and in a specific order. When installing RAM and having problems, it is a good idea to check the documentation to see in which RAM slots the first RAM SIMMs, DIMMs, or RIMMs should be installed. If there is no documentation, try one set of RAM slots and then the other.

Malfunctioning RAM is simply replaced to correct the problem.

Video and Monitor

Display problems are caused by the video controller, the cable, or the monitor. Of these components, the monitor is the most fragile. Monitors are cathode ray tubes (CRTs) or flat panel displays. The CRTs tend to fail after several years of use. Flat panel displays can also fail, but they should last longer.

Display problems are typically signaled by no display. There could be several reasons that nothing is visible. First, check the power to the display. While this may seem to be an obvious check, it can be more difficult because of the power management functions built into the monitor, the main logic board, and Windows software. Any or all of them stop the power from going to the monitor when the PC is inactive. This means that the monitor is powered off. It does not lack power, but the power management functions have shut power off to the display. Lack of power to the display and power shut off by power management look the same to the PC troubleshooter.

When power management has powered down the display, hitting a keyboard key or moving the mouse sometimes brings the PC back from its sleep state and causes it to power up the monitor. In this event, the power light on the monitor lights up green. If there is power and the monitor is sleeping, the power light on the monitor is some times yellow or amber. Other times, there is just no light, period. When the power light changes to green, within several seconds (which always seems like an eternity) a display usually appears.

In some cases, when the hardware power management function is in control, the PC can be in sleep mode (think deep sleep or hibernation). Here the power switch must sometimes (particularly on laptops) be switched on to awaken the PC and have the monitor display something.

The next thing to do is check the display brightness setting. If it has been turned all the way down, nothing is visible on the display. This is a favorite A+ question.

When there is power to the monitor and no display, check the monitor cable. The easiest test is to plug in another monitor. If it works and the monitor cable is swappable, then swap the cable to determine if the failure is the cable or the monitor. Most likely it is the monitor, but you never know.

Monitor failures are also indicated by visible display problems. We have seen vertical bars (like automobile racing stripes) down the middle of the display, a loss of colors, shaking displays, and others. Bars and loss of color require a monitor repair to correct. Shaking displays could require monitor repair or repositioning of other electrical equipment farther away from the monitor. Electrical equipment that can cause a monitor to shake are fans, fluorescent lights, other monitors, electric pencil sharpeners, televisions, and more. Influence from magnets can also affect monitor performance, as can electromagnetic interference. Spacing these three or more feet away from the monitor fixes this type of shaking.

It might also be a good idea to check the monitor type and display settings in the control panel before sending the monitor out for repair.

Other monitor shimmying may indicate failing components. For example, one time there was a lightning strike that destroyed a fuse inside a Samsung 17" monitor. After the fuse was replaced, the monitor had apparently become paranoid of another lightning strike because it just shimmied all the time until finally a year later it failed. In this instance, more component replacement was needed beyond the fuse replacement.

Controller failures show themselves as weird-looking displays. Either the monitor cannot display a nice straight rectangular picture that fully fills the screen, or spots are just dropped from the display. The former signals a controller scanning rate mismatch with the monitor. Reducing the display resolution down to standard VGA (640 by 480) can sometimes correct an unstraight display.

Otherwise, a monitor better tuned to the display controller is required. When spots or characters are dropped from the display, it indicates bad display controller RAM. A new display controller is typically in order when this happens.

Flat panel displays may have bad pixels. They are always set to an annoying color and appear (so it seems) right smack dab in the middle of the display screen and not near the edges where they would be much less annoying.

With our flat panel displays we have had virtually no problems. However, flat panels use fluorescent lighting to provide the display back light. Fluorescent lights have a definite life. They lose brightness over time. The loss is greater at first and then declines much more slowly until they reach half-brightness and are deemed unusable. The expected half-life is in the range of 20,000 power on hours (POH). This adds up to 2 years, 3 months, and 11 days if the display is on 24 hours a day 7 days a week. All flat panel displays power off during periods of inactivity to extend this half-brightness life span period. Of course, at half-brightness the display is still usable. The dimming changes over time are not noticeable to humans and must be measured by instrumentation.

Keyboard and Mouse

The keyboard and mouse are tested during POST. If they are found, keyboard- and mouse-detected messages are displayed.

Keyboard errors are the most critical. If during POST, the PC finds no keyboard, it displays a missing keyboard message with the strike F1 to continue. This seems dumb because there is no keyboard on which to strike F1, but it does provide an opportunity to plug in a keyboard if it was forgotten.

Sometimes the PC can just lose the keyboard. This happens when a keyboard is moved between PCs. To determine if a keyboard is not working with a PC, toggle the "Num Lock", "Caps Lock", or the "Scroll Lock" keys and observe the keyboard light emitting diodes (LEDs). When the keyboard LEDs turn off and on in response to toggling the keys, all is fine. When toggling the keys has no effect on the LEDs, the PC is not seeing the keyboard.

Mouse problems are obvious because the mouse produces no Windows or DOS pointer movement, or the movement is erratic. Sometimes AUTOEXEC.BAT loads DOS mouse driver programs. When these programs are loaded and no mouse is found, they state "mouse not found" or similar error messages. You may want to check the cable connections first to make sure they are firmly seated.

When Windows loads, it also loads its mouse drivers. If there is a serious mouse driver versus mouse mismatch, Windows does not display a mouse pointer. When Windows senses a mouse, it displays a pointer. This is no guarantee that the Windows drivers match the mouse. Only if the mouse pointer moves as expected is the mouse OK. If there remains a mismatch, the mouse pointer jumps erratically. Erratic mouse pointer movement can be due to a dirty mouse or bad driver software. Cleaning the mouse is the easiest to check. The mouse ball is removed and cleaned and the inside of the mouse is blown out to assure no dirt remains inside. If mouse movement is still erratic, it is likely the driver software.

Sometimes mice have a switch on the bottom that changes them from a Microsoft-compatible mouse to a MouseSystems-compatible mouse. This may cause the mouse to match the driver software and fix the problem. Other mice can switch when they first get electrical power, and a mouse button (generally the right one) is depressed. The button must be held down while the PC is powered up, or held down while the mouse is unplugged from the PC and then replugged into the PC. Again, if the movement stops being erratic, the problem is fixed. Otherwise call for the replacement mouse.

Serial mice connect to the serial port on the rear of the PC, while PS/2 mice connect to a special Mini-DIN connector. This means that the serial mice operate with standard COM port settings. The PS/2 mice generally use the bus mouse PC resources (IRQ, I/O port, etc.).

Floppy Drives

The most common problem floppy disk drives have is not being recognized when the PC boots. During POST, the PC can perform a floppy disk seek test. It tests for floppy drive A, but not floppy drive B. If floppy drive B is installed and set in the NVRAM, the PC can indicate a drive mismatch when the setting is for a 1.44 MB disk drive and a 1.2 MB disk drive is installed. However, the key diskette drive is drive A: because it is a potential boot drive.

NVRAM permits specifying a disk drive boot sequence. The sequence is set in the system setup area, normally entered by pressing DEL before the POST test and before Windows boots. There are several options, including:

- Floppy drive A; then drive C
- Drive C; then floppy drive A
- CD-ROM drive; then drive C; then floppy drive A
- CD-ROM drive; then floppy drive A; then drive C
- Floppy drive A; then drive C; then CD-ROM

This can help speed up the booting process and assist when there is only a CD-ROM for installing software and no floppy diskettes. It does present a potential problem when the fixed disk fails. The PC doesn't boot and cannot be booted without changing the NVRAM boot option specifications.

When a floppy disk drive is not connected to the PC, misconnected to the PC, or malfunctioning, it is not seen by the POST. This means that it is not available to DOS and Windows as well. Misconnected floppy drives often have their drive light come on and stay on when the PC is started. Normally, the floppy drive light flashes briefly after the fixed disk drive is tested. The fixed disk drive light is turned on before the floppy drive light. When the floppy drive light stays lighted, the floppy cable is reversed or is not connected properly. When a bootable floppy is present in a drive with a misconnected cable, the data on the diskette is destroyed. The data cannot be recovered. The diskette is rendered useless and nonbootable.

Leaving a data diskette in the floppy drive during the boot process when the NVRAM directs the PC to boot from the floppy drive first causes nonbootable disk errors. Removing the data floppy and striking any key to continue booting the PC from the fixed disk easily corrects this problem.

Sometimes floppy diskettes cannot be read. This is caused by a wide variety of circumstances. In such cases, the DOS COPY command should be used to copy the diskette files to the fixed disk. When read failures occur, an "Abort, Retry or Ignore" error message is displayed. When the data is important, the retry option should be used repeatedly in an attempt to recover the data. When this copies the file, the data copied is good. If this does not work, the "ignore" option can be used. It typically produces a bad file, but one time in a thousand good data can result. The DOS COPY command is used as opposed to the Windows copy command or the DOS COPY command in a DOS Window because DOS commands directly manipulate the PC's hardware. Windows commands and DOS commands in a DOS Window do not. They are much less likely to recover the data. However, if the data is really important, there are a number of recovery programs commercially available that can assist with this process.

Fixed Disk Drives

Fixed disk drives can have lost files or hardware failures. Both types of problems are covered in this section, with disk failures discussed first, followed by file loss.

Sometimes what appears to be a disk drive failure problem is a problem caused by bad memory, bad driver programs, or a bad BIOS in the PC itself. If DOS FDISK, as discussed later in this section, reveals no disk problems, it is good to check the memory, check for better driver programs, or perform a BIOS upgrade.

Fixed disks fail for a few simple reasons. The primary sources of failure are:

- **Manufacturer Design Defects**—The original IBM PC AT fixed disk drive was designed by CMI. It had defective head mechanisms that shortened its effective life considerably. The old Seagate ST-225 drives had batches of drives that failed after about one year of operation. They would get seek errors when positioning the heads to read data. Common defects include bad sectors, irregular surface flaws, etc. A few disk drive designs and manufactured batches are just plain bad. The majority of disk drives, however, are well designed and ruggedly built.

- **Vibration**—This is one killer of fixed disks. The greatest risk comes when they are in operation. On older disk drives, the fixed disk drive heads were parked when the drive was powered off. This did not protect from head crashes caused by vibration when the disk is operating. Fixed disk drives today lock the heads off the surface of the disk drive unless they are actually reading data from the drive. This makes them much less susceptible to vibration damage. The disks and the heads themselves are more resistant to head crash damage because the heads are smaller and lighter and the disk drive surface materials are more durable.

- **Temperature Shock**—Computers are designed to operate in average room temperature environments. Disk drives are vulnerable to both cold and hot extremes in temperature. As an example, leaving the computer off overnight and over weekends can cause it to be chilled in winter months. When the computer is restarted in the morning, the internal temperature can climb from 40 to 60 degrees Fahrenheit to 80 to 100 degrees Fahrenheit or more within the brief period of 20 minutes. This causes internal stress and strain on fixed disk components that have very narrow tolerances (fixed disk heads fly closer to the fixed disk surface than half the diameter of a human hair). Severe strain can cause head crashes or worse. Leaving the computer on all the time helps alleviate temperature shock problems.

  After exposing the computer to any temperature extremes, it is advisable to let it come back to ordinary room temperature before turning the system on. This minimizes potential shock to the components and, consequently, damage to them. Portable and laptop computers with fixed disks should always be kept warm. Never leave them overnight in an automobile. I lent one of my laptops to a friend who left it overnight in his truck, only to have it fail the next day when it was powered on. He swears to this day that he did nothing to make the fixed disk fail. But it failed nonetheless because the cool temperature caused moisture inside the drive to condense. This slight condensation crashed the disk drive heads when the laptop was started the next day.

- **Age**—Fixed disks have a life span. The early disks were designed to operate for 10,000 power-on hours. That is five years operating eight hours per day, five days per week and 50 weeks per year. Fixed disk life now runs from 100,000 to 1,000,000 power-on hours. After a while, all fixed disks can fail. All my first fixed disks have been replaced because they failed from old age. None of the recent disks have had aging problems in spite of being run 24 hours a day seven days a week (24x7 operation). They were replaced for lack of capacity. If you think about it, 1,000,000 power-on-hours (POH) are equal to over 114 years of operation before the disk drive quits. Disk drives could live longer than any of us! A well-made disk should never have an aging problem, but the difficulty arises with poorly made disks. Defects may shorten their lifespan significantly.

The irony is that new disks are more at risk of failing than older ones. A pilot once said to me that he would rather be flying a five-year old jet than a brand new one because the maintenance and testing was so thorough on the older jet; it is the same way with fixed disk drives. Recently, we had a new IBM 75 GB drive fail soon after it was installed. Data could not be written to it. It kind of worked, but under heavy use it would just blow up. The Windows 2000 event log was full of disk failure messages. This is sometimes referred to as infantile mortality. Once a PC component is burned in for several weeks or several months, they tend to work properly for years.

Because the directory and the FAT areas on the disk are used the most, they are likely to be the ones that lose data first. Once they are gone, the disk is unusable. Some fixed disk preparation programs allow you to move the directory and FAT to cylinders other than the beginning cylinders on the disk. This may extend the life of some disks.

Other factors that affect the life span of a disk drive are the degree of care when moving them, conscientious preventive maintenance, and exposure to magnets (which may also include exposure of laptops to airport security equipment). No matter what the situation, the best way to protect against possible disk drive failure is to make and protect regular system backups. Then, when the inevitable occurs, there is always a solid point for recovery.

Troubleshooting the disk drives is the last key area before the PC boots. Separate problems are encountered by floppy, fixed, and CD-ROM drives.

Lost files

Sometimes it looks like a disk is failing when files are lost. This is not representative of a hardware failure but more likely some software operation gone awry. Recovering from lost files depends on the software being used. Windows has the Recycle Bin that holds erased files until they are emptied from the recycle bin. Files mistakenly erased can recovered from the Recycle Bin. Some programs do not place the files they remove into the Recycle Bin. Those files cannot be recovered.

DOS also provides some file recovery capabilities. Have you been in a hurry and entered del c:*.*, thinking that you were killing the files in c:\temp? Or have you ever run format thinking that your PC is a mind reader and knows that you wish to format drive A:? Before you can think to strike CTRL BREAK, it has finished formatting and rewritten the directory and the fat on drive C: instead. Oops!

DOS provides help. It has UNDELETE and UNFORMAT commands. These commands can, within limits, restore deleted data from your fixed disk drive.

UNDELETE can be run at any time because a deleted file just has a special character placed in the first location in the file name. It also means that the chain of clusters forming the file has been released from the directory entry so that they may be reused to store new files.

This means that if you want to be sure to recover a deleted file, DO NOT WRITE ANY MORE DATA TO THE FIXED DISK UNTIL THE FILE HAS BEEN RECOVERED.

After deleting a file, immediately run UNDELETE for the best chance of recovering the total file. UNDELETE is menu-driven and relatively simple to run. UNDELETE is equivalent to the Windows recycle bin.

Similar to UNDELETE is UNFORMAT. UNFORMAT recovers data from recently formatted fixed disk drives. Similarly to UNDELETE, it is best to use UNFORMAT immediately to recover the drive, before any new data is written to the drive. Formatting a fixed disk drive does not destroy the data on the drive but merely rewrites the directory and the FAT. Data is no longer available because, in spite of the data physically being on the disk, there is no way for DOS to tell how to retrieve the clusters that form the files. UNFORMAT relies on a copy of the directory and the FAT being placed on the disk by the FORMAT program. These are then used to replace the erased directory and the FAT.

The UNFORMAT command restores a disk erased by the FORMAT command or restructured by the RECOVER command. To run UNFORMAT you enter:

```
UNFORMAT drive: [/J]
UNFORMAT drive: [/U] [/L] [/TEST] [/P]
UNFORMAT /PARTN [/L]
```

The UNFORMAT options are given in Table 3–2.

Table 3-2   UNFORMAT Command Options and Actions

Command Option	Definition
drive:	Specifies the drive to unformat.
/J	Verifies that the mirror files agree with the system information on the disk.
/U	Unformats without using mirror files.
/L	Lists all file and directory names found, or, when used with the /PARTN switch, displays current partition tables.
/TEST	Displays information but does not write changes to disk.
/P	Sends output messages to printer connected to LPT1.
/PARTN	Restores disk partition tables.

Both UNFORMAT and UNDELETE are useful DOS commands, when used within their capabilities. However, users misunderstand the limits of what these commands can do in recovering lost data and most often they write additional data to their fixed disk, making it impossible to fully recover their lost files. As mentioned earlier, if recovering files is crucial, there are options such as commercial data recovery programs or companies that specialize in data recovery that may help.

Hardware failures

There are some common failure symptoms between both EIDE (IDE) and SCSI fixed disk drives. The common failure symptoms and resolutions have to do with the drive failing, rather than the drive controller. When a drive fails, the disk becomes unreadable in one or many spots on its surface. This is not necessarily a catastrophic event. The disk can still be used to store data, but should probably be replaced as soon as it is practical to do so. However, surface failures in the master boot record, the root directory, or the FAT areas of the disk can quickly render the drive useless. Other areas on the disk cannot be substituted for these areas. Errors in data areas on the disk can be marked as bad and bypassed when storing and retrieving new data on the disk. The SCANDISK.EXE program can perform a thorough disk surface test, moving data from bad areas to good areas as it determines if a surface area is bad. It cannot recover a disk with a bad master boot record, root directory, or FAT. These problems are the same for either EIDE or SCSI drives.

Defragmenting a drive using DEFRAG.EXE on a regular basis reveals disk surface failures.

SCANDISK.EXE repairs failures in the data areas. It is possible to fix a bad disk drive with many surface failures. All disk drives use Error Correcting Code (ECC) to store and retrieve data from the disk drive. The ECC can sometimes become corrupted by bunches of errors. Returning the disk surface to its original all-zeros state can reset the ECC and make the drive appear error free. Because new data patterns are stored in the bad areas, the ECC now works, effectively making the disk appear error free. On SCSI drives, this is accomplished by performing a low-level format and surface verification on the disk drive. The SCSI adapter card typically contains the programs needed to perform the low-level format and disk surface scan. This wipes all data from the disk drive.

The drive must then be partitioned using FDISK and formatted using FORMAT. EIDE drives cannot be low-level formatted without voiding their warranty. In this case, a program like the old Norton Utilities WIPEINFO.EXE program that writes zeros all over the disk can be used to prepare the disk surface. Similarly to SCSI drives, the EIDE drive then needs to be partitioned using FDISK and formatted using FORMAT.

Sometimes the fixed disk heads get stuck on the drive surface. This causes the disk not to rotate.

Fixed disk controller and fixed disk drive problems can be diagnosed using the DOS FDISK program. When it is run, it provides the option to display partition information. See Figure 3–8.

When FDISK cannot read the drive, it displays an "Error reading fixed disk" message. If the fixed disk controller is bad, FDISK displays a fixed disk controller failure message. The "Error reading fixed disk" message suggests that the problem could be the cables or the fixed disk drive. Most likely it is the fixed disk drive, unless the drive is just being installed and the cables are put on incorrectly.

IDE/EIDE

Some problems unique to EIDE/IDE drives stem from the characteristics of the EIDE/IDE interface. For an EIDE/IDE drive to operate properly, its drive geometry parameters must be specified in the PC's NVRAM. These drive geometry parameters determine how the EIDE controller and the dri-

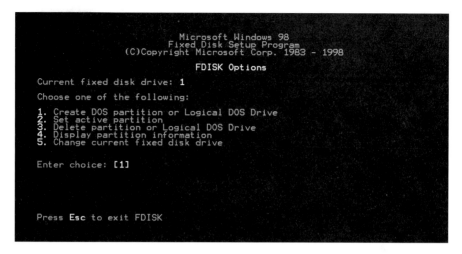

Figure 3-8
FDISK program.

ver software work with the drive to utilize its full capacity for storing data. The drive capacity is determined by the following equation:

```
(Cylinders) X (Heads) X (Sectors per Track) X (1/2 K) = Drive Capacity
(310) X (4) X (17) X (1/2 K) = 10,540 KB or 10 MB drive.
(620) X (4) X (17) X (1/2 K) = 21,080 KB or 20 MB drive.
```

This equation is referred to as the drive geometry.

A wide variety of drive geometry configurations have been employed from simple small-capacity drives defined in the ROM BIOS to drives limited to 1,204 cylinders and drives addressed using Logical Block Addressing (LBA). As drive capacities have increased, drive geometry descriptions have evolved to accommodate these larger drive capacities.

During the power-on and POST, when the drive geometry descriptions in NVRAM do not match the EIDE drive, the PC cannot read the drive. If for some reason the drive geometry descriptions are altered in NVRAM, the drive looks unusable. Windows has crashed and in the process corrupted NVRAM. This happened with the early versions of Windows but not with Windows 95/98/Me or Windows NT/2000. The problem is easily fixed by re-entering the correct drive geometry or by having the NVRAM setup program auto-detect the correct drive geometry by reading it off the EIDE drive.

PCs running earlier versions of DOS and Windows 95 could use large drives by subdividing them into 2 GB partitions. This 2 GB partition size limitation was due to software, and not the PC's hardware. In this instance, the bootable partition had to be marked active. If the disk was partitioned and formatted with the operating system installed, it still would not boot unless the primary partition was set as active. FDISK establishes a primary partition and a secondary partition with logical drives. The primary partition and the logical drives were limited to 2 GB in size under DOS, Windows 3.x, and Windows 95 version A. Windows 95 version B and Windows 98 both supported the 32-bit FAT, permitting them to break the 2 GB partition size limitation. See Figure 3–9.

Booting from a floppy that has DOS and no large disk support causes disk errors when trying to read or write to a 32-bit FAT drive.

Some PC manufacturers place configuration and diagnostic programs on the EIDE drive in a maintenance partition. The maintenance partition contains setup information and manufacturer identification that makes automatic drive setup in CMOS possible.

This partition can be the first or last partition on the disk drive. It is not marked as active and thus is not the bootable partition. It does however reduce the useable disk space on the drive. FDISK reveals these partitions and can be used to remove them. They are usually shown under FDISK as non-DOS partitions. This makes them invisible under DOS and Windows. They may only be accessible when the PC is booted using a special diagnostic diskette.

IDE and EIDE drive controllers have few electronics so there is little to fail. They are installed on the main logic board and can be installed as added controllers in the PC's bus. As long as there are no IRQ and I/O port conflicts, these controllers work reliably. They support EIDE fixed disks, CD-ROMs, CD-RW drives, Zip drives, Super Disk drives, and DVD drives. Our focus

Figure 3–9
FDISK large disk support.

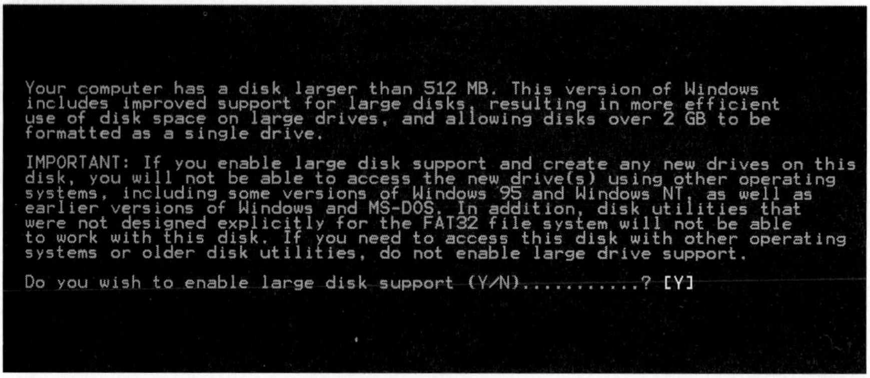

```
Your computer has a disk larger than 512 MB. This version of Windows
includes improved support for large disks, resulting in more efficient
use of disk space on large drives, and allowing disks over 2 GB to be
formatted as a single drive.

IMPORTANT: If you enable large disk support and create any new drives on this
disk, you will not be able to access the new drive(s) using other operating
systems, including some versions of Windows 95 and Windows NT, as well as
earlier versions of Windows and MS-DOS. In addition, disk utilities that
were not designed explicitly for the FAT32 file system will not be able
to work with this disk. If you need to access this disk with other operating
systems or older disk utilities, do not enable large drive support.

Do you wish to enable large disk support (Y/N)...........? [Y]
```

here is on EIDE fixed disk drives. Each EIDE controller can support two drives. There is a primary and a secondary EIDE controller on most PCs. When a controller connects to two drives, the drives must be identified to the controller as the master (primary) or slave (secondary) drive. From a boot disk perspective, it does not matter whether the primary or secondary is the bootable drive. However, when two EIDE drives are marked as the master drive, disk I/O errors occur.

Generally, CD-ROM drives can be mixed with EIDE fixed disk drives on the same controller, provided one is set as the master device and the other set as the slave device. However, this can also cause fixed disk I/O problems. This could be caused by DMA channel configuration, synchronous transfers for the CD-ROM drive, or other EIDE configuration mismatches. When this happens, it is easier to place the CD-ROM on the second EIDE controller than it is to figure out the exact cause of the incompatibility.

With MLBs that have four EIDE controllers, driver programs from the MLB manufacturer are needed to have the second set of EIDE controllers work properly with the fixed disks, CD-ROM, CD-RW, or DVD drives attached. These driver programs are sometimes provided by HighPoint Technologies (*http://www.highpoint-tech.com*) because they provide the chip sets for the second set of EIDE controllers.

EIDE cables must be connected pin one to pin one. It is possible to misconnect the cables, reversing the pin connections. When this happens, the fixed disk drive light comes on and stays on during the boot process. All of the times this has happened to us, no data on the EIDE drive has been destroyed. However, there is the potential for this to happen on some drives. Consequently, if, during the initial PC power-on and POST, the fixed disk light comes on and stays on, power the PC off immediately and check the cable connections at both the disk drive end and at the controller end to ensure pin one connects to pin one.

SCSI

SCSI drives require a separate controller from the EIDE drive controller. This controller has ROM BIOS for operating the SCSI drives under DOS and Windows. It also contains configuration management and control, surface verification, and low-level format programs. The SCSI controller BIOS routines are entered during the boot process by striking a key combination prompted on the display screen. For Adaptec controllers this combination is CTRL A. The next menu permits working with the adapter settings or running diagnostics. See Figure 3–10.

Adapter settings are used to set up SCSI bus operation, matching transfer speed and bus operation to the controller. If the devices attached to the SCSI

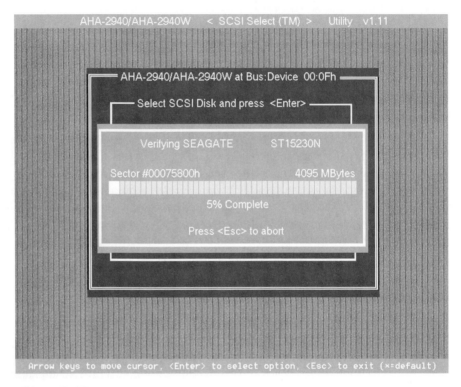

Figure 3-10
SCSI select verifying a SCSI disk drive.

bus are not matched to the controller transfer speed, the disk drives have I/O errors. This causes the PC to not run. The SCSI controller should be set at the highest priority (SCSI ID), which is 7. If it is set at a lower number, I/O errors could result. Parity checking for data transfers and host adapter termination should be enabled.

Each device must have a unique SCSI ID on the SCSI bus. Duplicate SCSI IDs cause devices to malfunction. The failure symptoms here are quite obvious. The operation of each SCSI ID is determined by the SCSI controller configuration. Parameters set include:

- Sync negotiation—to establish and perform synchronous data transfers.
- Transfer rate—the transfer speed must match here or the device fails.
- Send Start Unit command—a critical command for the SCSI IDs to initialize and run.

206

- Include in BIOS scan—makes the drive available to DOS and Windows.

The SCSI controller also provides drive geometry configuration translation for large SCSI drives. Since most SCSI drives are large drives, this is a vital feature.

When these parameters are not set properly, fixed disk I/O errors occur. These I/O errors look like the drive has failed when the problem can be corrected simply by changing to the correct parameter. Sometimes it is possible to test different SCSI bus transfer speeds with the drives attached. When the speed is set too fast, the drive has I/O errors. The PC may boot, but it doesn't run very long before failing.

The key area for SCSI disk and controller troubleshooting is the SCSI bus itself. The SCSI bus must be terminated at each end. That usually means that the controller card should have termination enabled and the last drive on the cable should also have termination set on or have a terminator attached. Any intermediate drives and devices cannot be terminated. When intermediate devices are terminated, the bus is overloaded electrically and I/O transfer errors occur. This makes the SCSI devices look like they have failed. The BIOS disk surface verification utility makes an excellent test of the SCSI bus. It shows I/O verification errors when the transfer speed and the termination are not correct on a SCSI bus. These verification errors happen almost immediately.

SCSI ID and SCSI termination are not related at all. The only concern for SCSI ID assignment is the priority assigned to the SCSI ID. The SCSI controller needs to have a SCSI ID of 7. So a SCSI device could be SCSI ID 3 and be installed at the end of the bus, thus requiring termination.

If a SCSI controller is attached to external devices, that most often means that it is installed in the middle of the SCSI bus and must not have termination enabled.

This may mean physically removing terminating resistor packs, or just setting a controller configuration parameter with the setup program. In this event, the SCSI devices at the end of the external cable and at the end of the internal cable must be terminated. Many SCSI devices can be configured to terminate the SCSI bus. This is not the best configuration because they might be inadvertently moved. Consequently, it is best to terminate a SCSI bus with a terminating resistor pack.

Active terminations support higher transfer speeds. Terminations at each end of the bus should be active or passive, but not mixed.

The 50-pin SCSI cables are quite reliable. The high-density 68-pin cables and connectors are much more prone to failure. Pins can be easily bent, causing some devices attached to the SCSI bus to fail and others to work properly. Usually this type of failure always happens to devices attached to a specific connector or assigned a specific SCSI ID on the SCSI bus. Bad pins in a connector may always cause the SCSI ID 5 device to fail, and no others. The failure looks to be caused by the device when it is really caused by a bad cable. One of the first troubleshooting steps for any SCSI chain, and especially for high-density 68-pin SCSI buses, is to carefully examine the cables and connectors.

Any cables and connectors that are the least bit suspect should be replaced to ensure that the SCSI bus is operating properly. When cables are not available, the bus termination can be moved up and down the bus as a means of testing the cable. While this is not the most effective test procedure, it does work.

No discussion of SCSI would be complete without some words on Redundant Array of Independent Disks (or Drives), or RAID. RAID uses SCSI almost exclusively. It is used mostly to provide redundancy to assure data recoverability in the event of a disk drive failure. The most commonly implemented types of RAID that provide redundancy are:

- RAID 1—mirroring data
- RAID 5—data striping with parity.

Several other types of RAID are defined and implemented, each with their own unique performance and reliability characteristics. Our discussion here focuses on RAID 1 and RAID 5. With RAID 1, mirroring, the same data is stored on two identical drives. When one fails, the other still has good data. With RAID 5, striping and parity, data and parity are stored on three or more drives. The data and parity information is spread more or less evenly across all drives. When one drive fails, the binary information on the remaining drives is used to rebuild the data on the failed drive. In this manner no data is lost. RAID can be implemented with disk controller hardware or with Windows NT or Novell Server software.

Troubleshooting RAID begins with the basic SCSI problems described above. Once SCSI bus issues are resolved, it is a matter of working with the particular RAID controller or software. Hardware RAID drives are often called hot swappable. This really means that they are warm swappable. All activity on a SCSI bus must be halted to swap a drive with the power on.

The SCSI bus must be shut down to swap a failed RAID drive. If not, corruption of the data on the remaining drives is possible. Similarly with software RAID, the PC should be shut down before a failed drive is swapped. Swapped RAID drives are rebuilt automatically, and the rebuilding is done at a binary level. Consequently, 1–12 hours may be needed to rebuild a single drive. Software RAID rebuilds drives much more slowly than does hardware RAID. As drives are being rebuilt, overall system performance is diminished because of the resources devoted to rebuilding the data on the replacement drive.

CD-ROM/CD-RW/DVD

The most common problem with CD-ROM/CD-RW/DVD drives is their tendency to elude DOS or Windows. CD-ROMs/CD-RWs/DVDs themselves are generally reliable. Other CD read/write devices are less reliable. Most CD-ROMs/CD-RWs/DVDs are EIDE devices which depend upon device drivers and the MSCDEX (Microsoft CD-ROM Extension) program to function with DOS. The device driver is loaded by CONFIG.SYS and linked to the MSCDEX.EXE program loaded by AUTOEXEC.BAT through a logical identifier. Typical CONFIG.SYS and AUTOEXEC.BAT file command lines for loading CD-ROM/CD-RW/DVD drivers are:

```
CONFIG.SYS
device=oakcdrom.sys /D:mscd001
AUTOEXEC.BAT
MSCDEX.EXE /D:mscd001
```

The logical identifier tying these command lines together is /D:mscd001. The MSCDEX command has several command line options including:

- /D:driver1 [/D:driver2...]
  Sets the driver identifier for the CD-ROM device driver. The driver 1 identifier must match the identifier specified by the /D switch on the CONFIG.SYS command that starts the corresponding CD-ROM/CD-RW/DVD device driver. The MSCDEX command includes at least one /D switch. Additional CD-ROM/CD-RW/DVD device drivers require specification of additional /D switches for each device driver.
- /E
  Permits the CD-ROM/CD-RW/DVD driver to use expanded memory, if available, to store sector buffers.
- /K
  Permits MS-DOS to recognize CD-ROM/CD-RW/DVD volumes encoded in Kanji. By default, MS-DOS does not recognize Kanji CD-ROM volumes.
- /S
  Enables CD-ROM/CD-RW/DVD drive sharing on MS-NET or Windows for Workgroups servers.
- /V
  Causes MSCDEX to display memory statistics when starting.

- /L:letter
  Assigns the specified letter to the first CD-ROM/CD-RW/DVD drive. When there is more than one CD-ROM/CD-RW/DVD drive, MS-DOS assigns additional CD-ROM/CD-RW/DVD drives the remaining available drive letters.

- /M:number
  Specifies the number of sector buffers MSCDEX can use.

If a CD-ROM/CD-RW/DVD drive is not accessible under Windows, the DOS commands can get the CD-ROM/CD-RW/DVD to work but using only the DOS mode compatibility drivers. Once this is done, forcing Windows to find new hardware or installing CD-ROM/CD-RW/DVD drivers can have Windows revert back to 32-bit drivers for the fixed disk drives and the CD-ROM/CD-RW/DVD drive. If this does not work, reinstalling Windows right over the existing Windows installation usually allows it to find the CD-ROM/CD-RW/DVD drive while preserving all of Windows' software settings. However, before resorting to a reinstallation of the OS, it might be worth trying the install program that comes with most CD drives or getting new updated drivers off the Internet.

Sometimes CDs are unreadable because they are not formatted correctly, their media is not compatible with the CD drive's laser, the CD drive's lens is dirty, or the CD's themselves are dirty. There are several storage formats for placing music and data on CD drives. When your CD-ROM/CD-RW/DVD drive cannot understand the specific CD format, the CD is unreadable. The solution here is to try a different CD-ROM/CD-RW/DVD drive to read the CD. You also may want to verify that the correct software or drivers are installed. As an example, if you try to play a music CD but you don't have a player installed, you experience problems.

Different CDs work with different CD drive lasers. This problem occurs with CD-RW burners and the burnable media that they use. Some CDs created on these burners could not be read by other CD-ROM/CD-RW/DVD drives. This is not a formatting problem, but rather a media compatibility problem. Changing the media solves this problem and makes the CD readable.

CD-RW media can be read by CD-ROM drives when the proper driver program is loaded into the Windows PC. When the CD-RW media cannot be read in a CD-ROM or DVD drive, the driver program is most likely not present.

Sometimes CD-RW drives cannot burn the CD media at the highest speed. This can be caused by poor media, or by using the CD-ROM and DVD drive on the same cable while copying a CD from the DVD drive. It is also problematic when EIDE does not use DMA, or when the CD-RW drive connects to the EIDE controller using a low-speed 40-wire cable rather than the high-speed 80-wire cable.

Dirt can cause CD-ROM/CD-RW/DVD drives to malfunction. CD-ROM/CD-RW/DVD drive lens-cleaning CDs that have small brushes can clean the CD drive lens. CD cleaning kits are also available to remove surface dirt from a CD. However, CDs that are scratched may not be recoverable. Smoky environments would most likely have problems with dirty CD-ROM/CD-RW/DVD drive lenses.

Sound Cards

One very obvious symptom for sound card malfunctions is a quiet PC. Several simple problems can cause silences, like having the speakers plugged into the wrong jack. Sound cards have jacks for speaker output, microphone input, and sometimes line input. Plugging the speakers into the microphone jack and vice versa is a common error.

Another common error causing no sound is a lack of power to the speakers. Most speakers are powered. They must have either battery power or power from a low-wattage transformer plugged into AC power. Without power, speakers make no sound. Not only must power be provided to the speakers, but they must also be turned on. The volume on the speakers must be turned up as well. There are several speaker volume controls. The most obvious are on the speakers themselves. The less obvious are the Windows software volume controls. These are available through the speaker Icon in the task bar (system tray) or through the sound-playing application program. When the PC sound card volume is set down in software, the PC is silent. Testing the sound can be performed using the Windows control panel sounds function or using multimedia programs. The control panel functions in Windows 2000 set the sound volume, sound recording and playback devices, and the type of speakers attached to the PC. See Figure 3–11.

Alternatively, in the Windows media folder are several MID or RMI files that play using the Windows media player. We prefer the Bach's Brandenburg Concerto No. 3.RMI file. This is an excellent sound test because it runs several minutes, permitting testing of jack connections, volume settings, and speaker power. Playing this in repeat mode provides continuous sound output to the speakers for longer periods when more thorough testing is required.

Sound cards need driver programs to operate. Installing the board in a PC is no guarantee that the driver programs are installed as well. Not only must the drivers be installed, but there can be no resource conflicts with other devices. To provide compatibility with others like them, sound cards use several I/O port addresses, a DMA channel, and sometimes more than a single IRQ. If these settings are not conflict free, then the PC produces no sound.

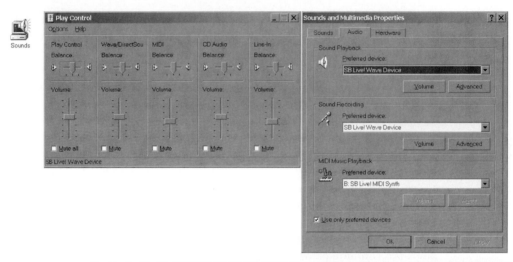

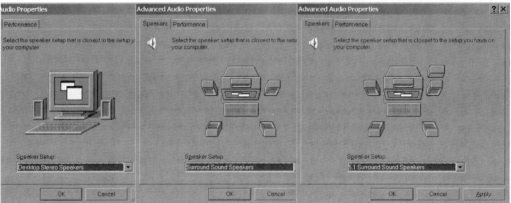

Figure 3–11
Control panel sounds Icon and sound controls.

Communications

The main communications devices are modems for Wide Area Networking (WAN) and Network Interface Cards (NICs) for LANs. Each PC component has its own unique problems. Most communications problems for LANs and modems are related to the communications channel. When a channel is bad, Windows becomes unstable and unpredictable.

Modems

Modems modulate digital data from the PC converting it into analog tones that travel through the telephone network. They convert four bits at a time into a unique token (combination) of signal phase and amplitude. Sixteen tokens are used to encode the incoming digital stream into a voice-like analog signal.

Bad telephone lines cause most common modem problems. The modem is installed in the PC and really working properly until it is time to place a phone call. The first thing that can go wrong is a miswiring of the phone jack so that the phone line is on the yellow and black wires on the outside of the RJ-11 jack. Modems expect the red and green wires in the center of the RJ-11 jack to be the active phone line. When the line is not connected, the modem displays a "no dial tone" message. A simple test is to plug any analog phone into the phone jack to verify dial tone.

Sometimes the modem can dial the target number but has difficulty making a connection. This is due to poor line quality. Both sending and receiving modems try to match up at the top signaling rate for the given analog line quality. They dynamically adjust their signaling to compensate for changing electrical characteristics of the telephone line. Unfortunately, there are some telephone lines that are so poor the modems just cannot communicate. The resolution here is to try different target numbers. If all the different numbers tried produce similar poor transmission quality results, then perhaps the line between your facility and the telephone company facility is at fault. Connecting an analog telephone in the line and dialing "1" can test its quality. This connects the phone to the long distance channel bank in the telephone company central office. When listening to this connection, the phone line should be perfectly silent. Any pops heard indicate impulse noise. A short circuit or current loss in the line causes a loud hum. These noises indicate poor line quality. Be sure that no wiring inside your facility is responsible for the poor transmission quality; otherwise it is an expensive telephone company line repair. Each telephone line has surge suppressors installed on them. Sometimes lightning destroys the surge suppressors, causing line corruption. The telephone company replaces faulty surge suppressors.

Another common problem is dialing a non-operating number or a long distance number requiring a full 11 digits to complete the call. In this case, the telephone company plays an error message that is audible to a caller, however, the caller cannot hear the message because its speaker volume is too low. Some programs provide a menu item for modem control. See Figure 3–12.

Using an analog phone to call the target number to verify it is a viable number identifies and helps solve this type of malfunction. When calling the target number, you should hear the modem at the remote end answer the phone. Of

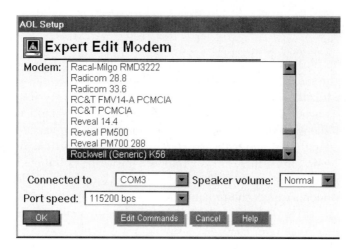

Figure 3–12
AOL program modem volume control.

course, calling people with your modem can really freak them out because you can hear them but they can only hear your modem. Dialing the correct number with the proper dialing digits solves this problem.

Some modem problems are caused by serial port conflicts. Common symptoms of this problem are the inability to talk to the modem. The software cannot communicate with the modem so it issues an error message.

In this case, the PC cannot talk to the modem at all. Adjusting the modem or serial port settings so that one or the other resides on COM3 or COM4 fixes this problem. Generally, the serial port setting adjustment involves pointing the software to the correct serial port. In some cases it may require that PC hardware be reconfigured to COM3 or COM4. This may be done using a PC's CMOS setup program.

When your PC displays a "no dial tone message" there are no serial port conflicts and the modem is working with the PC properly. The control panel modem settings permit testing the modem. See Figure 3–13.

Test the modem by selecting diagnostics, then more info. When the modem responds, the port settings don't conflict and the modem works. Resource conflicts are resolved by using the POST setup program to change the main logic board's serial port settings or by changing the jumpers of NVRAM settings on the modem card.

Most often, the cause of the conflict is the Windows 95/98 plug-and-play software's inability to find conflicts between modem option cards and the main logic board's built-in serial ports. Plug-and-play conflicts are better resolved by

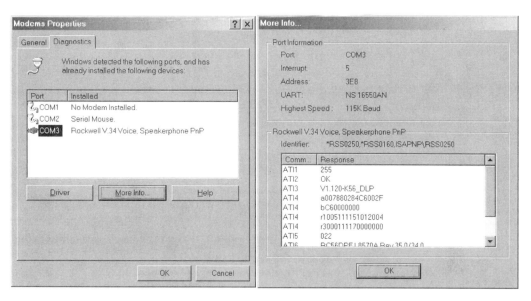

Figure 3–13
Control panel modem test.

Windows 98/Me/2000. This simply means that Windows cannot solve the problem without someone adjusting the PC hardware.

Win modems perform some of the modem functions with software modules that run under Windows. These modems seem to have lots of problems when the proper modem driver programs are not installed. Furthermore, if the drivers become corrupted for any reason, the modem and the driver software must be completely uninstalled and reinstalled to return the modem to proper operation. Installing the driver software without uninstalling it first typically will not fix the problem. There may be special uninstallation software needed to completely uninstall all the Win modem driver software. If the modem is uninstalled without using this software, the modem continues to malfunction. Win modems can be very frustrating.

LAN Boards

Somewhat similar to modems, Local Area Network (LAN) boards may have problems with LAN cabling. The PC displays error messages like "Unable to browse network" if the cable does not connect it to the LAN. Observing the lights on the wiring hub into which the LAN board is plugged is sufficient to perform simple cable verification. Bad cable connections do not light the lights.

Software conflicts or bad LAN board drivers in the PC cause the wiring hub lights to be out. In this instance, it is not a hardware problem, but a software conflict that is the culprit. Powering off the PC and restarting it generally identifies hardware or software problems. Bad LAN wiring can be identified by the collision light on a wiring hub remaining constantly lit. Broken or bad wiring causes hubs to think that there are excessive LAN collisions. If software is causing the problem, the wiring hub lights should light and stay lit until the LAN software deactivates the LAN board. When it is a hardware problem, the wiring hub lights never light. When installing a new PC, a good hardware test is to swap cables. If the light now lights, there is a cable or a hub problem on the old port. Otherwise the LAN board is probably defective or improperly installed.

Finally, the load on a LAN may cause things to be slow. If the transmission light on a LAN hub is constantly on, identify the PC sending all the data. Identification is easy; simply disconnect each wire from the hub until the activity light goes out. Recently on our cable modem there was excessive LAN traffic. This was killing the cable modem performance for all PCs. I disconnected each PC from the LAN hub until the light went out. In this manner I discovered that someone was running Napster software and creating a huge amount of data traffic.

Other LAN board problems are caused by resource conflicts with other PC components. LAN boards can sometimes share IRQ resources. Good settings are IRQ 5 and I/O port address 300, 320, or 340. IRQ 9 is also a good choice. Resource conflicts are resolved using the Windows control panel. The conflicting devices are removed and Windows restarted. Its plug-and-play capability can then resolve the resource conflicts. See Figure 3–14.

PCI bus devices may sometimes be moved into different slots to fix resource conflicts. The PC has a specific resource assignment scan order. Typically, main logic board resources are assigned first, then ISA bus devices, and finally PCI bus devices according to a specific PCI bus scan order. Changing the position of the LAN board in the PCI bus can change a LAN board's resource assignments.

The final network malfunction area is caused by network software. Unless the network software is configured precisely, network communications can fail. Key network software parameters for Transmission Control Protocol/Internet Protocol (or Internet Packet protocol), that is, TCP/IP, are:

- Dynamic Host Configuration Protocol (DHCP) enabled—specified obtain an IP address automatically.
- Windows Internet Naming Service (WINS) enabled and server specified—this points to a specific server which tracks all the other devices on the network. It is like an Internet Domain Name Server (DNS).
- Default Gateway—points to a system linking networks and routing data between them.

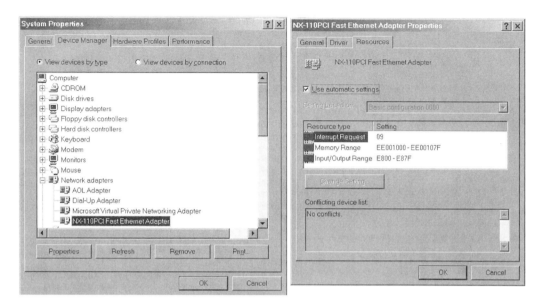

Figure 3–14
LAN board resources.

Other settings like IP address and subnet mask settings may also be important in assuring proper network software operation. These are discussed later in Chapter 8 and Chapter 16.

When the network software is not properly configured, the PC appears frozen while it attempts to communicate with other network components.

Other network software implements Network BIOS Extended User Interface (NetBEUI) protocol and Sequenced Packet Exchange/Internet Packet Exchange (SPX/IPX or, more commonly, IPX/SPX) protocol. This software, while more automatic than Windows' TCP/IP software, also has some configuration parameters that must be properly set for reliable network operation.

Whenever the network software is not configured accurately, the PC slows way down because it is looking for responses to broadcast messages from other stations on the network. The broadcast messages are network overhead identifying network devices and coordinating activity between devices attached to the network.

Slot Covers

PC boards are inserted in the bus connectors and bolted into the rear of the PC's chassis. When boards are not installed in the bus and bolted to the chassis, PC's have "L"-shaped covers for the bus connector slots. These slot covers should be installed when there are no boards in a connector slot. They assure that the cooling air is circulated around the components to provide proper cooling.

Each PC is designed to have the majority of the cooling air enter at the front of the PC, flow across the CPU and the option cards, then exit the rear assisted by the power supply fan blowing it out the rear of the PC. When this airflow is disrupted, the PC components can overheat. For example, one of the people working on this book installed a second fan in their personal PC. They had the second fan blowing air out of the PC's chassis, thinking this would increase the airflow inside the PC. It did not. What happened is that the flow of air across the CPU chip and other heat sensitive components was disrupted and reduced, causing them to overheat. The second fan should have blown air into the PC, enhancing the flow of air through the chassis, thus assisting in cooling. Slot covers keep the airflow across critical components smooth and in the flow pattern that promotes cooling. Removing them breaks up this smooth airflow, making it hotter inside the PC.

The slot covers also help reduce RF emissions from the PC. Every PC emits RF signals. The slot covers help reduce these RF emissions by covering the expansion card slot openings with chassis grounded metal covers.

Study Break: Disk Drive Geometry

To understand disk drive geometry we can use the CMOS setup to determine different disk drive capacities. Using the PC CMOS setup program:

1. Reboot the PC and hit the key (generally F1, F2 or Delete) that enters the CMOS setup program. In the main menu options, select a disk drive (first or second drive on primary EIDE controller or first or second drive on secondary EIDE controller). Use a drive location that does not have a physical drive installed. Cycle through the configuration options until user-defined or manual appears. Enter a cylinder—head—sector combination and record for that combination setting the disk drive capacity CMOS calculates. Try 1,024 cylinders—16 heads—63 sectors to get 504 MB. Try 1,024 cylinders—64 heads—128 sectors to get a 4 GB disk drive. Try 3,893 cylinders—16 heads—63 sectors. Are any of these configurations prohibited? If they are, the PC may have an older BIOS. Return the drive selection to its original configuration.

2. Go to the Advanced options and peripheral configuration. Select the serial ports and cycle through the addresses. Which options are possible? Which conform to standard COM1, COM2, COM3, and COM4 settings? Do any settings permit using COM1 on the serial ports?

Return the PC to the original settings.

Troubleshooting Tools

Almost anything is a troubleshooting tool. In the sections above, we suggest using an analog telephone to verify telephone line operation. Stereo headphones can be used as speaker test equipment because they do not require power to produce sound and they are easy to carry. A light that works is a tool that can verify AC power to a wall outlet.

These tools seem less than professional. After all, shouldn't an official service person walk in wearing a white jump suit and pulling a big chest of tools? Shouldn't there be soldering irons, chip extractors, etc. Well, no, not really. If this were the case, service personnel would be quite muscle bound. Also, with the low cost of PC components, by the time a chip is replaced on a defective component, the cost of that repaired component would be three times the cost of a brand new replacement component.

An effective PC troubleshooting tool kit contains both hardware and software components. Some recommended hardware parts, tools, and accessories are:

- A small flash light
- Battery packs and batteries
- A multimeter (See Figure 3–15)
- A standardized PC tool kit
- A hex-key set
- An antistatic mat
- An antistatic strap
- Compressed air
- Small vacuum cleaner
- SIMMs, DIMMs, and RIMMs—that have been tested—30-pin, 72-pin, 168-pin, and 184-pin configurations

- Ribbon cables for floppy, older fixed disk, EIDE, and SCSI controllers (both 50-pin and 68-pin high-density SCSI cables)
- Parallel cable 25-pin female to 25-pin female connectors
- Parallel cable 25-pin female to Centronics connectors
- Serial cable adapters 9-pin female to 25-pin male and 25-pin female to 9-pin male
- Power supply splitter cables that add connectors for 5.25-inch and 3.5-inch disk drives
- Power cords
- Keyboard DIN-to-IBM adapter and IBM-to-DIN adapter
- VGA extension cable
- Keyboard extension cable
- Cable ties
- Labels for I/O ports, cables, etc.
- Plastic mounts for PC MLBs
- Large and small cooling fans for power supplies
- Heat sinks and cooling fans for both socket style and slot 1 CPU chips
- Assorted screws for attaching miscellaneous hardware (i.e., mounting brackets)
- A small pen magnet for retrieving dropped hardware (caution around disks!)

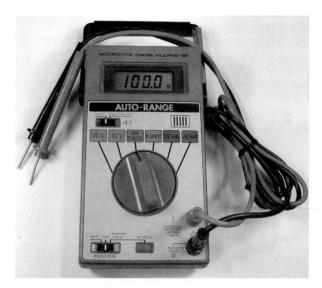

Figure 3–15
Typical digital multimeter.

The most effective troubleshooting tool is careful thinking and the ability to use what is at hand to verify proper PC operation—for instance, the analog telephone.

There are a few useful tools that a service person should have on hand. Most of this is software. A virus-free DOS bootable diskette is a key tool. There should be both DOS 6.2x and Windows 98/Me DOS bootable diskettes. Other software tools are important as well.

Troubleshooting Diskettes

One procedure to use in isolating malfunctions of PC hardware or software is to use a bootable diskette.

Study Break: Creating a Bootable Diskette

Create a bootable diskette using FORMAT and SYS programs. Then use the Windows 95/98/Me startup diskette feature to create a bootable diskette to start Windows.

1. Place a diskette in drive A: and then enter FORMAT A:/S. Once formatted, enter DIR A: /Ogn /A to see what files are installed. Is DBLSPACE.BIN or DRVSPACE.BIN installed?
2. Using the same diskette, enter SYS A:. Next enter DIR A:/Ogn /A to see the files installed. Have they changed at all?
3. Use the Windows control panel—add/remove programs—start up disk to create a bootable diskette. Has Windows placed any other programs on the diskette?

The user needs to copy several key DOS programs onto the floppy, including:

- HIMEM.SYS—Boots using memory management but no UMB space.
- EMM386.EXE—The DOS upper memory area and Expanded Memory Specification (EMS) manager program.
- FDISK—Tests fixed disk drive and controller.
- FORMAT—Formats (creates the directory and FAT) fixed and floppy disks.

- ATTRIB—This program changes the attributes of files. They can be set or reset as Hidden, System, or Read only.
- SMARTDRV—The DOS disk cache program.
- DOSKEY—The up arrow repeats command line.
- EDIT—Any good American Standard Code for Information Interchange (ASCII) text editor is fine here.
- MODE—Used to test serial and parallel ports (helpful)
- COMP—Compares files (helpful)
- FC—Compares files line-by-line and shows differences (helpful)
- MSAV—The MS DOS virus scanning program (optional)
- DEFRAG—The DOS disk defragmentation program (optional)
- MEM—The DOS memory viewing program (optional)
- UNDELETE and UNFORMAT programs to recover lost data (optional). A bootable diskette should include all files and programs referenced in CONFIG.SYS and AUTOEXEC.BAT. This would mean any drivers for the CD-ROM as well as MSCDEX.EXE. All these programs may not fit on just one diskette, so several bootable diskettes may need to be prepared.
- DEBUG—Sometimes used to setup fixed disk (optional)
- MSD—The DOS diagnostic program (optional)

Study Break: Bootable Virus Scanning Diskette

As an exercise, create a bootable diskette using drive A: and then place virus-scanning software on it. Next, power off the PC and restart booting from the diskette and scan your PC for viruses.

Other diskettes to have handy and clearly labeled are:

- Driver program diskettes for all hardware installed in the PCs supported. This would include SCSI disk drivers, sound card drivers, video drivers, RAID configuration software, and other special hardware drivers.
- A virus scanning program diskette.

- A diagnostic program diskette for special boards—for instance, LAN boards, mainframe communication boards, and scanner interfaces.

- A diskette containing standard CONFIG.SYS and AUTOEXEC.BAT files, standard Windows WIN.INI and SYSTEM.INI files, and standard Windows for Workgroups WIN.INI and SYSTEM.INI files.

- Novell DOS LAN programs for Ethernet and token ring adapters. These can provide a handy and quick way to test adapter settings.

- A TweakUI diskette to install and then remove the Windows user interface control program.

- An ERU program diskette to make Windows Registry backups.

- A diskette with a clean and simple SYSTEM.DAT registry file. Several different SYSTEM.DAT diskettes could be created each for a specific PC hardware/software configuration supported. Because the SYSTEM.DAT file is larger than 1.44 MB, it will need to be compressed.

- A CD with the service packs for Windows 95, Windows 98, Windows Me, Windows NT 3.51, Windows NT 4.0, Windows 2000, Microsoft Office, etc.

- Some performance and PC testing software like the DOS MSD program or Norton System Works 2001. Chapter 15 covers MSD and other programs in more detail.

These diskettes provide essential diagnostic and troubleshooting tools. The most important troubleshooting tool is a good, virus-free bootable DOS diskette and the PC's POST in ROM.

Multimeter

Multimeters test voltages and resistance. They are digital or analog. They can test for Alternating Current (AC) voltage, Direct Current (DC) voltage, and resistance.

The AC voltage test is useful in determining whether the PC has power. It is similar to plugging a lamp into a socket to determine that power is present. The multimeter can be used to trace power to and from the PC's front panel switch, making it more useful than the lamp.

DC voltage tests determine whether power is being provided to both the PC's main logic board and the disk drives. The tests also show whether 5-volt and 12-volt power is being delivered where needed. While the multimeter can provide detailed testing inside the PC for DC power, most times a lack of power is very obvious and multimeter testing is not needed.

The resistance test determines whether there is an electrical connection or pathway between components. Often wires in cables are broken or connected to the wrong pins. The multimeter resistance check quickly verifies electrical connections and cable configurations. This type of testing is very helpful when troubleshooting PCs.

Spare Parts or "Swap Until You Drop"

The objective here is to use a duplicate system to locate the malfunctioning component. You take an identical PC and swap the malfunctioning component. The goal is to have the good PC turn bad and the bad PC to turn good. This verifies that indeed the component has failed. See Figure 3–16. However, other scenarios might occur.

You swap the component and then both PCs turn into bad PCs. Bummer! This is probably caused by a setup problem in both PCs (let's hope). This is almost your worst nightmare.

Next you swap the components back and find that both PCs remain bad. Real bummer—this is your worst nightmare (kind of like realizing that you purchased the $100 million power ball lottery ticket and it was run through the wash in your shirt pocket). Fortunately, this rarely happens. In this case you cannot tell which is the killer (if there is any killer), because it could be the component or the original PC. The only way to know for sure is to use another PC to test the component again. If it were to then turn bad, you have the killer component. Should you perform this test? No way!

You could have things really go your way, and when the components are swapped both PC systems turn into good PCs. Should you swap back to see if they return to their old state of bad PC and good PC? If it ain't broke, then don't fix it.

Once a PC begins working fine, quit right there. Clean up the computer and leave. There have been several occasions where I thought that just one more step would make things better only to find myself sucked into a larger PC problem that I had just created.

Study Break: PC Resources

Using the Windows 95/98 control panel, view the PC resource allocations. Print a summary of the PCs configuration.

1. Open the Windows control panel and choose the system icon. Open it by double clicking and then select the device manager tab.

While computer is highlighted, click the properties button. A display of all the assigned IRQs should appear.

2. Select the Input/Output option and the assigned I/O ports are displayed.
3. Select the DMA and Memory buttons and review their assignments.
4. Exit the device manager properties and return to the main menu display. Select print for a detailed configuration for the PC.

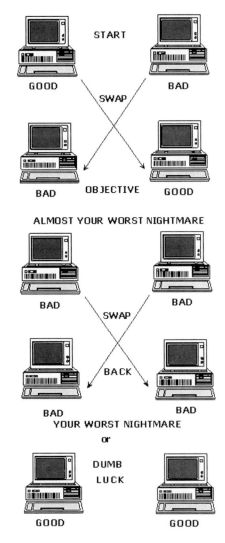

Figure 3-16
Swap until you drop.

225

Troubleshooting Procedures and Practices

Often times PC problems are obvious. If you cannot read from a fixed disk drive and the drive is making strange noises, chances are the drive has failed. I had a PRIAM drive that was squeaky. I fixed the squeak by periodically spraying WD-40 on the static electricity drain bearing. One day after returning from a trip, I performed a directory on my drive C: only to have my PC respond with "Failure reading fixed disk." I immediately rebooted and got the message "Boot drive not found." I then powered the PC off, then on. When it powered up, I could plainly hear the disk drive trying to reach its operating speed of 3,600 RPM, but it just could not quite get there. It would then fall back to a lower speed and try again.

What had happened was the WD-40 I had used to quiet the drive had gotten small particles of dust sucked up into the bearing. Those dust particles wore out the bearing so the drive could not spin at the correct speed. One dead drive and all its data lost. Oops!

As mentioned in the section under disk drive failure, your best insurance policy against system failures is a good and frequent set of backups. Your system is only as safe as the quality and reliability of your last backup, so the importance of making and storing regular backups cannot be overemphasized. It is also a good idea to keep some old backups. Being too zealous at making backups can leave you with all bad data as well.

Problem Isolation and Determination Procedures

Problem isolation and determination procedures are focused on isolating problems to a malfunctioning PC subsystem. When troubleshooting, always try to break down the problem at the highest level of subsystem. Major PC subsystems are:

- The fixed disk—the cable—the controller
- The floppy disk—the cable—the controller
- The display (monitor)—the cable—the controller
- The serial and parallel ports
- The battery
- The power supply and its fan

- The system board—RAM—ROM (BIOS and keyboard)
- Other installed boards (LANs—host connections—scanners)

For example, is the problem in the floppy or hard disk subsystem? Is it the cable? Or is it the controller? Use FDISK as a diagnostic and repair tool. Does FDISK say the controller is not working? Is it the drive? Does FDISK report that it cannot find a disk drive? In this case we are looking for the failed subsystem: fixed disk, fixed disk controller, cable.

FDISK /MBR (/Master Boot Record) rewrites the disk boot record without destroying all data on the drive. This is a mechanism for fixing nonbootable fixed disks and removing viruses from the boot record. A general problem isolation procedure is:

1. Start from ground zero by powering off the PC.
2. Power up the PC and observe System Operation and any error messages or signals. Typical signals and problems are:
   - No display, no fan running—power okay?
   - No display, fan running—bad power supply, bad memory in first bank, bad CPU, bad motherboard or bad display.
   - Basic or failure to boot message—bad fixed disk, lost boot sector or COMMAND.COM on fixed disk.
   - Boots and hangs—bad set up with memory, bad memory, memory speed mismatch, or incorrect LAN board setup.
3. Identify the Options in the PC—RAM, VGA, disk, sound card, CD-ROM, etc. Most PC hardware malfunctions are nonfatal. The truly fatal system errors are failure of:
   - The power cord
   - The power supply
   - The main logic board
   - The CPU chip
   - The system ROMs
   - The first bank of RAM
4. Isolate the failing or conflicting subsystem and remove it from the PC. Does the PC reboot?
5. Try a different configuration for the failed component.
6. Try a different PC.
7. Ask yourself, did it work before? Then what changed? Change it

back. Modifications in driver software can often be the culprit.

8. Review the component's documentation for any known problems.

9. Try an exact replacement component. Does it work?

The most logical troubleshooting thinking traces the power flow to the PC components that are malfunctioning. Where are the electrical power and data signals stopped or being corrupted? Answering this question usually determines the malfunctioning PC hardware.

DOS Boot Errors

Some problems are simple to solve; many DOS boot problems fall under this category. When DOS boots, it first loads IO.SYS and MSDOS.SYS, then the drivers specified by CONFIG.SYS. It then loads COMMAND.COM, and finally the programs specified in AUTOEXEC.BAT. When files are missing or corrupted, DOS displays boot error messages. Some common DOS booting problems are:

- Cannot find COMMAND.COM—The COMMAND.COM file was erased from the root directory or the DOS directory of the PC. Copy the correct COMMAND.COM file to the PC's root directory to fix this problem. It is also a good precaution to use the ATTRIB command to mark the COMMAND.COM file as read only. This prevents accidental erasure.

- Invalid COMMAND.COM—The COMMAND.COM file did not match the IO.SYS and MSDOS.SYS files on the fixed disk. Replace with the COMMAND.COM that matches. COMMAND.COM files can sometimes be found in \DOS and \WINDOWS\COMMAND subdirectories (folders). The date/time stamp identifies the COM-MAND.COM file. A time of 6:22 signifies DOS 6.22 COMMAND.COM. The following times and dates are generally accurate for different DOS releases.

```
DOS 3.1— 3/7/85 2:43 PM
DOS 3.3—9/16/87 1:00 PM
DOS 5.0—4/9/91 6:00 AM
DOS 6.0—3/10/93 6:00 AM
DOS 6.2—9/30/93 6:20 AM
DOS 6.22—5/31/94 6:22 AM
```

```
Windows 95a—7/11/95 8:50 AM

Windows 95b—8/24/96 11:11 AM

Windows 98—5/11/98 8:01 PM

Windows 98 SP#1—10/14/98 4:59 PM

Windows 98 SE—4/23/99 10:22 PM

Windows ME—6/8/2000 5:00 PM

Windows 2000 Professional—12/6/1999 4:00 PM
```

Occasionally, times are registered as 7:22 AM instead of 6:22 AM when DOS is installed. But overall, these dates and times should assist in matching COMMAND.COM to IO.SYS and MSDOS.SYS. When in doubt, match the dates and times on those files.

- Nonbootable disk—Sometimes DOS cannot boot because the IO.SYS and MSDOS.SYS files have been lost. Using a good bootable diskette and running the SYS C: command to reinstall IO.SYS, MSDOS.SYS, and COMMAND.COM on the fixed disk can correct this error.

- Nonbootable disk or suspected virus infection—Erratic behavior or boot problems can sometimes be corrected using the command FDISK /MBR to rewrite the fixed disk master boot record. However, if you really need this to work, the law of 'The Way Things Really Go' says it will probably not work for you.

- Lost CD-ROM drive—In this case, the CONFIG.SYS CD_ROM driver program and the AUTOEXEC.BAT MSCDEX program are not loaded or not logically linked together. Check to see that the driver program is referenced in CONFIG.SYS and is installed on the fixed disk where referenced. MSCDEX should be also present and loaded by AUTOEXEC.BAT. Furthermore, the logical identifier must correctly link the driver program to MSCDEX.

Errors Writing and Reading from a Fixed Disk Drive

Under DOS the disk cache program was SMARTDRV.EXE. Some SCSI and EIDE drives had problems working with SMARTDRV. To avoid trashing data on the fixed disk drive, they required double buffering of the data to help them resolve the differences between the virtual data address provided by SMARTDRV and the actual address used on the disk drive. The "Device=\...\SMARTDRV.EXE /double_buffer" entered in the CONFIG.SYS file installs double buffering for SCSI disk drives.

The double_buffer SMARTDRV option prevents some SCSI disk drive controllers from trashing the data they store on the fixed disk drive. It slightly diminishes (about a 4 percent reduction) the PC's disk performance. Double buffering ensures that the SCSI disk controller correctly translates the data address to the correct physical allocation unit (groups of sectors) address. To determine whether double buffering is required, first install SMARTDRV with double_buffer, then run SMARTDRV /S at the DOS prompt. If double buffering is not required, the buffering column states no. When double buffering may be required, a "-" is displayed. A "yes" indicates that double buffering should be used. See Figure 3–17.

Windows Boot Problems

The most common Windows boot error is when Windows has just been shut down without exiting gracefully. Windows has log files and registry settings

Figure 3–17
SMARTDRV status display.

```
Microsoft SMARTDrive Disk Cache version 5.0
Copyright 1991,1993 Microsoft Corp.
    Room for  2,048 elements of  8,192 bytes each
There have been  24,535 cache hits  and  2,208 cache misses
Cache size:  16,777,216 bytes
Cache size while running Windows:  16,777,216 bytes
        Disk Caching Status
drive  read cache  write cache  buffering
---------------------------------------------
  A:     yes         no           no
  B:     yes         no           no
  C:     yes         yes          yes <== Required
  D:     yes         yes          yes <== Required
  E:     yes         yes          -   <== Possibly Required
Write behind data will be committed before command prompt returns.
For help, type "SMARTDRV /?".
```

that it reads during system reboot. These files permit Windows to see that it has been shut down without closing everything properly; it then runs SCANDISK to verify that the directory, FAT, and file structure are intact and not damaged. Once complete, Windows starts normally. (Windows troubleshooting procedures are covered in more detail in Chapter 15.) When the Windows boot process is interrupted before it finishes, Windows displays a "boot process failure" message and indicates that it is booting with default values. Generally, the boot process completes normally in this instance as well.

Windows 95/98/Me has boot problems arising from plug-and-play hardware conflicts, lost DLL and VxD files, and corrupted registries. The error indications vary from starting directly into safe mode, to a variety of error messages. Windows 2000 does not boot into safe mode directly when problems are encountered, but rather the user must strike the F8 key during the boot process. Windows 2000's self-healing design makes it a much more robust OS than other Windows operating systems. With bad driver programs (especially bad display drivers) Windows 2000 can refuse to start necessitating an F8 boot into safe mode.

When the Windows registry is corrupted, Windows cannot start normally. In some instances it completely locks up. In others, error messages indicating lost or corrupted files are displayed. Sometimes lost files are referenced not by the registry, but rather by the WIN.INI or SYSTEM.INI files. Missing file messages typically identify the missing file by name and suggest searching through the Windows system files (WIN.INI and SYSTEM.INI) or the registry to remove references to the files. Actually, two solutions to this problem exist. First, you can remove the references to the missing files. They can be removed from the registry by scanning for the file names or by using an uninstaller program. Directly removing the file references from the registry is not recommended because it can create new problems while not fixing the old problems. Second, you can find copies of the missing files on other Windows PCs and copy them to the \WINDOWS\SYSTEM FOLDER. Once the missing files are replaced, the error messages disappear. Some new ones appear in their place, necessitating copying more files. Such is the nature of PC troubleshooting.

When a troublesome program is launched at Windows startup, the Windows "startup" folder can start it, the registry, or sometimes the WIN.INI file "run" or "load" commands. Removing the reference from the Windows "startup" folder and the Windows WIN.INI file is uncomplicated. Removing references from the registry is more difficult and an uninstaller program should be employed to accomplish this. Windows 2000 can have similar programs launched during startup, and they require removal from the registry. To spot them, use the Windows 2000 System Information utility program to identify them. They are listed under the Start Up folder. See Figure 3–18.

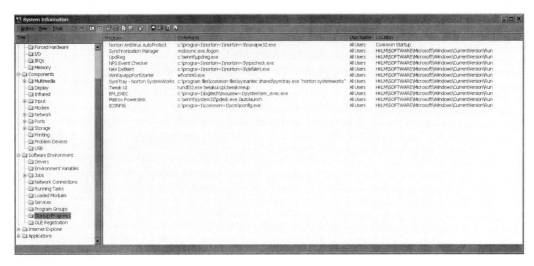

Figure 3–18
Windows 2000 System Information utility.

Corrupted registry files cause Windows to boot and display error messages like, "Windows memory protection fault" or "corrupted registry." The protection fault message is particularly nasty, because Windows just dies and offers no chance of recovery. The error is caused by a problem in the SYSTEM.DAT file. Replacing the SYSTEM.DAT file fixes the problem. To have a good copy of the SYSTEM.DAT file, use the Emergency Recovery Utility (ERU.EXE) program and save the backup files into a fixed disk folder and not to floppy diskette. A complete backup is only made when the files are saved to fixed disk. Booting into DOS and running the ERD program to replace all the key Windows system files can then restore the old registry.

Hardware conflicts and corrupted registry files cause Windows 95/98/Me to boot into "safe mode." Windows 2000 enters safe mode when the F8 key is struck during the boot process. Safe mode runs Windows with a minimal set of standard drivers as a means to fix plug-and-play hardware and other resource conflicts. Safe mode does not automatically assign hardware resources to any component or permit viewing resource assignments, but rather permits the operator to specify manual resource assignments for troublesome hardware devices. The intent is to define manual settings for conflicting components first, then have plug-and-play resolve the remaining resource allocations. Once all hardware resource conflicts are resolved, Windows boots normally. Sometimes when manually setting resources, it appears that there are no conflicts. But Windows still has the device conflicting or not working properly. In this instance, other I/O port and memory address settings should be tried, one at a time.

The real key in safe mode is to use it to load the proper device drivers. With the hardware plug-and-play features operating better in the newer Windows versions, hardware conflicts are much less irksome today provided the correct drivers are loaded for the devices having problems. Such devices can be identified by warning messages displayed by the Device Manager found in the Windows Control Panel System applet.

Application Errors

Similarly to Windows, application programs can have errors caused by missing components (DLL and EXE files mostly), a bad blend of old and new components that do not work together properly, and Windows garbage accumulation. These errors can result in obvious error messages like "DLL is missing" or "system resources low" to the blue death screen and memory protection fault messages. These errors are almost nonexistent with Windows 2000. If there is a software problem, Windows 2000 kills the offending application and provides somewhat instructive diagnostic error messages.

Missing file messages are caused when DLL and other key files are removed from the PC. This can happen when an unrelated application is uninstalled that has files used in common with an application remaining on the PC. Reinstalling the application can replace the missing files while retaining the configuration settings already in place for the misbehaving application. Windows 2000's self-healing features tend to mitigate caused by missing DLLs.

A bad blend of software mixing old and new EXEs and DLLs causes a variety of error conditions in Windows but most commonly a "memory protection fault" message. To fix these problems, reinstall the software that consistently causes the error messages; apply the current published patches or service packs to the software; or restore previous registry settings.

Out-of-resource messages are caused by Windows garbage accumulation. PCs that only run a few Windows applications rarely have such problems. We have some Windows PCs that have run for months without ever having such errors and shutting down. On other PCs that run lots of different applications (many of them at the same time), resource exhaustion and garbage accumulation problems force us to periodically restart the PC. See Figure 3–19.

Figure 3–19
Windows 95/98/Me System
resource meter.

The system resource meter program provides a means of continually monitoring Windows 95/98/Me resource levels. Such resource levels have no impact on Windows NT/2000. Windows NT and Windows 2000 use the task manager to observe the active programs and system resources available to support them. See Figure 3–20.

Out-of-memory errors are caused by lack of disk cache memory. When disk space runs low, the Windows 95/98/Me cache memory is reduced in size to fit into the available free disk space. When Windows needs more than is available, out-of-memory errors happen. Freeing disk space by removing junk data and programs corrects this problem. Sometimes it is just necessary to shut down Windows gracefully and restart it. Whenever there have been many Windows applications run and closed, or there are lots of them open simultaneously and a memory protection error pops up, it is best to shut down the PC and restart to fix the problem. Windows 95/98/Me applications are loaded like building a stack of pancakes or flapjacks. One is placed on top of the other. Of course, what happens when you eat a flapjack off the bottom of the stack? It surely creates a mess. Similarly with Windows 95/98/Me applications, those started last should be closed first, and those started first should be closed last to avoid Windows 95/98/Me garbage accumulation and memory allocation problems. If Windows 95/98/Me applications launched first are closed first, Windows 95/98/Me does not perform a memory and resource clean up as well as it does when those are closed last. A consistent pattern of applications usage makes Windows 95/98/Me more reliable. Windows NT and Windows 2000 behave differently because they allocate and manage memory resources differently. When programs have memory problems, usually closing the pro-

Figure 3–20
Windows NT/2000 Task Manager.

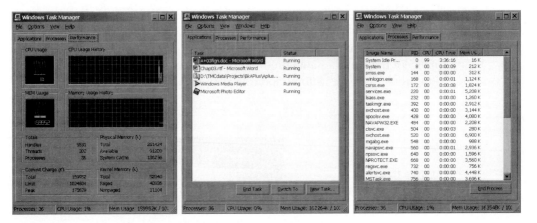

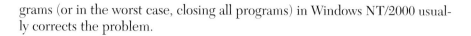

grams (or in the worst case, closing all programs) in Windows NT/2000 usually corrects the problem.

Viruses

When weird errors occur in a PC, one should always think of viruses as a possible cause. There are three types of viruses:

- Boot-sector-infecting viruses
- Program-file-infecting viruses
- Macro viruses and Trojan horse programs

The boot-sector-infecting viruses install themselves in the boot sector and partition table of any fixed and floppy disks. They are the most commonly encountered viruses. The Stoned virus, Form-B virus, Stealth-B virus, and GenB virus have been found on rental PCs and on PCs at client sites. The most famous boot-sector-infecting virus was the Michelangelo virus. Boot-sector-infecting viruses are not spread across a network because the network software prevents them from infecting boot sectors of network drives.

Program-file-infecting viruses infect programs and other files. They may be spread across networks. Some program-infecting viruses are very clever. They encrypt their code to hide from virus detection programs.

Macro viruses are dependent on the application programs supporting the macro commands. Microsoft Word was the first program to have a macro virus targeted at its macro language. The macro-language viruses have been the most prolific viruses because they were spread by Microsoft Office software. The Melissa virus was the first to bring this new terror to Internet-connected PCs. As Microsoft and other software developers use macro languages in more applications, additional macro viruses will appear. Microsoft Word had over 70 macro viruses targeted at it at one time. There is no doubt many more exist today.

Trojan horse programs look like legitimate programs, but they gather information about your PC and send it elsewhere. One recent program gathered AOL passwords and other information and forwarded these to an Internet site in China. This is really twenty-first century spying. See Figure 3–21.

Service personnel play a vital role in virus prevention. It is especially important for service personnel to rigorously check for viruses because their diagnostic diskettes are used in many computers. If the service diskettes become infected with a virus, that virus can easily spread to many computers in an organization. The first step in servicing any PC system should be scanning for viruses.

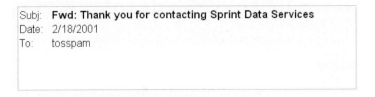

Subj: Fwd: Thank you for contacting Sprint Data Services
Date: 2/18/2001
To: tosspam

This message contained a Trojan horse.

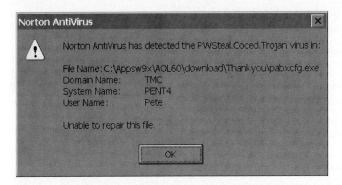

Subj: **Thank you for contacting Sprint Data Services**
Date: 2/16/2001 7:28:32 PM Eastern Standard Time
From: rosie.maggio@mail.sprint.com (Rosie Maggio)
Reply-to: rosie.maggio@mail.sprint.com (Rosie Maggio)
To: dialanerd@aol.com

File: **Thankyou.zip** (20662 bytes) DL Time (32000 bps): < 1 minute

Figure 3–21
Trojan horse delivered by AOL email.

The F-PROT virus-detecting program is shareware and must be licensed (see Figure 3–22). Many virus programs and new definitions are available from a variety of sites on the Internet.

Effective virus detection is now built into Windows and other operating environments. It is most important with all virus detection software to constantly maintain the virus signature file identifying the virus strains to the program. See Figure 3–23.

Only in this manner can the virus detection software detect and remove newly created viruses. See Figure 3–24.

Often virus detection software places a virus detection check code in software programs as a mechanism for discovering new viruses not listed in its virus signature file.

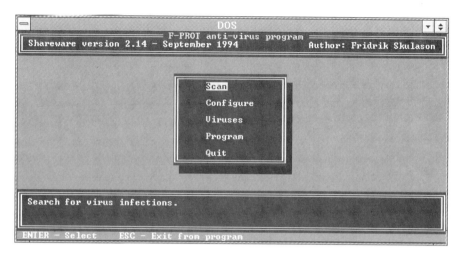

Figure 3–22
FPROT.

Figure 3–23
Norton Anti-Virus live update.

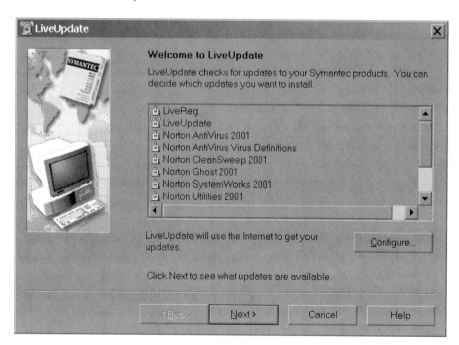

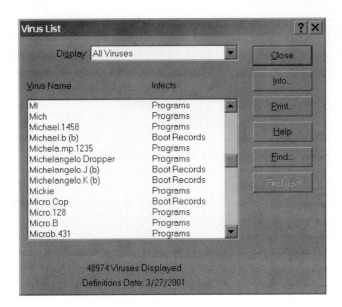

Figure 3–24
Norton Anti-Virus virus strains.

Most virus programs run under Windows are updated monthly via virus description files obtained from the web sites of the program developers. Because new virus variants emerge frequently, such updates and constant vigilance have become a part of everyday PC support. Not only should the virus-scanning programs be updated periodically, but the PC should be scanned regularly. See Figure 3–25.

If a virus is detected on a PC, it must be removed using a virus-free bootable floppy diskette and DOS-based virus detection and cleaning software. The PC must be completely powered off to remove the virus from memory. The bootable DOS diskette should have its write protection tab set on to prohibit writing to the diskette. This is to prevent further spreading of the virus. Once the PC has been cleaned and the virus removed, all the diskettes touched by the PC should be destroyed. It is easier to destroy them than to try to clean them while not reinfecting the PC with the same virus.

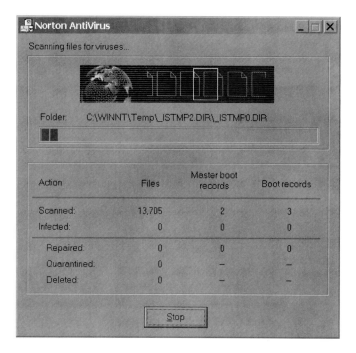

Figure 3–25
Running Norton Anti-Virus scan.

User Questions

A key part of troubleshooting PCs is having the problem described accurately by the PC user. Often times they have no clue as to how to describe the nature of the problem. In part, this is because all error messages are lies, akin to the promises from politicians. The error messages mislead because they often describe a problem symptom that is several steps removed from the root source of the problem. Observing the PC's behavior and all different signs first hand is often needed to determine the true nature of a PC problem. The PC user performs such first-hand observation.

Symptoms Observed and Error Codes

The PC user can observe some simple PC problem symptoms. If possible, they should write down any error messages displayed. Other simple symptoms to check for include:

- **Lights**—Are the LED's lit? Do they light when accessing the disk drive? Are they always on when they should not be?
- **Display**—Is it getting some kind of video signal? What does the screen look like? Are the colors correct?
- **Heat**—Does it feel very hot? Failed components give off lots of extra heat.
- **Smell**—Does it smell like Polyvinyl hot dogs cooking on the barbie? Does it have that distinctive burnt plastic electronic component smell? Where is the smell strongest?

Asking the PC user these and similar questions can help focus in on the source of the PC malfunction.

What Was Going on as the Problem Happened?

Problems are often related directly to the PC operations being performed. Knowing what happened the first time an error was observed can help identify the root source of the problem. Particularly, when an error is reproducible with a specific set of conditions, it can help troubleshoot the problem. Having a PC user describe what was happening when the error first occurred or when it repeatedly occurs can provide valuable troubleshooting clues. It's also important to ask the user what about the system may have changed—for example, was new software installed or has the computer been recently moved?

PC Operating Physical Environment

One key to problem-free PC operation is the physical environment. There are three major sources of potential PC environmental problems. These environmental problems can cause PC malfunctions. Checking out the PC's environment helps determine what caused a specific malfunction, what may have failed, and what must be done to correct the problem.

Power Problems

The first things to check for are power problems. Make sure that every PC is isolated from the power source. Trace the power line to determine if there is any heavy-duty electrical equipment on it. If there is, remove the equipment or change power lines. This is particularly important in old buildings where one power line often carries more than its rated load. At a minimum, the PC should be installed on a surge suppressor. If it is not isolated from the power source, the PC's internal components could be damaged. This would cause PC hardware component failures. It is not sufficient to just isolate the PC's power from external surges. Everything must be isolated, including printers, modems, and LAN connections.

PC Cooling

Heat is the enemy of every chip in the PC. When chips get hot working, they draw more power. When chips draw more power, they create more heat. At some point they stabilize, but the heat shortens the life of every chip. It can break down the electrical and chemical composition of the chip, eventually causing failures. This is like leaving a lawn chair in the sun all summer to find in the fall that the plastic is rotted and needs to be repaired. High heat shortens the life of your chips.

The best way to keep the PC cool is to provide plenty of space around it for air to circulate. When the office is comfortable for you, the temperature is good for the PC. The operating range for chips is from 50 degrees Fahrenheit to 140 degrees Fahrenheit. You're saying, 140 degrees? It never reaches 140 degrees. Not necessarily true. The temperature inside the PC is from 20 to 30 degrees higher than the outside temperature. As I write this, the room temperature is about 70 degrees, and the temperature inside my PC is around 95 degrees. PC cooling and CPU cooling are especially critical with high-clock speed CPU chips. Chips running at a GHz and above need excellent cooling or they literally burn up.

Dirt

If an environment is particularly dirty, then PC components could have heat failures, and CD-ROMs and diskettes could be dirty and unreadable.

Radio Frequency (RF) and Electromagnetic Interference

All electrical devices radiate electromagnetic signals. Some devices radiate many more signals than others. Radiating signals means electrical and magnetic fields radiate from every wire carrying an electrical current. It is like making a magnet from a wire wrapped around a nail and a battery. The electricity passing through the wire turns the nail into a magnet.

High frequency electromagnetic signals can disrupt the PC if they get onto the signal wires traveling around inside the PC. This doesn't happen often because it takes quite a strong signal to be picked up by the wiring inside the PC. Things to watch for are lamps next to the PC, power distribution lines in building walls, electrical transformers outside buildings, and electric pencil sharpeners.

PC's are supposed to meet FCC Class B specifications for radio emissions. To meet these RF emission requirements, all open spaces in the PC should be filled, specifically all open or unused bus slots; these should have a metal cover plate installed in the external board opening.

RF interference can cause monitors to misbehave, erase diskettes, and cause other PC malfunctions.

Static Electricity: PC Shock Therapy?

One culprit of static electricity in the cold dry winter months is static electricity. An assembled PC is reasonably safe from static discharge damage because the PC is attached to an earth-ground and there are many electrical pathways to dissipate the charge. The static charge heads for the ground rather than the chips. In the case of the cart with the PC, the static charge heads down the cart to the carpet and not into the PC on the cart.

A good preventive measure for static electricity is to make the air humid. Add a humidifier to the room. The high humidity helps drain the static charge from objects before they reach a really shocking level. There are other devices that can help, like antistatic mats and straps that tie you to your PC (as if you weren't already tied to it enough). But the easiest solution is higher humidity.

Static discharge, sometimes referred to as Electro Static Discharge (ESD), damages PC components and erases data from magnetic media. A more detailed discussion of EDS is in Chapter 4, Temperature Shock or Overcoming Monday Morning PC BLUES.

You thought that you were the only one with the Monday morning syndrome? Think of your PC. What happens to make Monday morning the prime failure time for PCs. The answer is simple—thermal shock. When you leave Friday, what do you do last to your PC? Turn it off. What happens to the building heat over the weekend? It is turned off as well. The building and the PC cool down to a chilly 50 degrees Fahrenheit over the weekend. Then Monday morning, you flick on your PC first thing. The internal temperature rises from 50 degrees to 95 degrees. All the PC components huddled tightly together to get warmth suddenly are transported to Miami Beach. They expand, and when they expand too much we get failures. Just think, some disk drives take a while to begin operation (they refuse to boot until warm).

How can you avoid thermal shock? Leave the PCs on. This presents a security problem (like the college student janitor playing Doom on your system with a virus-infected diskette). Is it better to just leave them on, or power on and off daily? The answer is that for most PC's in the office it does not matter because they are neither seldom used nor heavily used. For heavily used PCs, it is best to leave them on. For seldom-used PCs, it is best to power on and off every day. When you have recurring problems with thermal shock, it is prob-

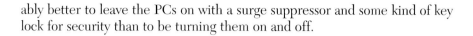
ably better to leave the PCs on with a surge suppressor and some kind of key lock for security than to be turning them on and off.

Vibration

Vibration is an enemy of PC components and fixed disks. The greatest risk of damage comes when the PC is being used (data is being saved on it, for example) and there is some harsh vibration. When moving your computer, the heads on the fixed disk vibrate because of the jostling received during the move. If the heads can receive a significant shock between 40 to 80 times the force of gravity (40 to 80 Gs), the heads could hit the disk surface hard enough to damage a disk rotating at high speed and cause data loss. All fixed disks have heads that automatically retract to a locked position when they are not being used to read and write data to the drive. Many disk drives now can withstand shocks in excess of 80 Gs.

Liquids—Are They Certain Disaster?

Can liquids harm your PC? What would happen if the office terrorist attacked you, you know, the one with the Uzi water pistol? They sprayed water inside your PC. Would it live?

The electronic components inside the PC are general hermetically sealed, so that water cannot get inside and hurt them. If the PC is dried out thoroughly it should easily survive being hit with water. Mechanical components are less hardy. If water gets inside them, they may be finished for life.

I had a keyboard that got coffee spilled on it. It cleaned up OK, but was still somewhat dirty from the coffee on the inside. This bugged me so I cleaned it with water. Then some keys wouldn't work. So I dried it with a hair dryer. More keys began to work, but still not all keys. I dried those keys more and melted the key caps. Oops! It cost me $120 for a new keyboard. In that case, water got into the mechanical components of the keyboard and killed them. By the way, I never was able to get all the keys to operate properly even with the key caps melted.

Water is very hazardous around high power devices like monitors and power supplies. High voltages and water do not mix: one shot of water and disaster. Recall earlier in Chapter 1 the PC monitor that had been squirted by a water pistol. Needless to say, the high voltages blew the monitor. More liquid experiences are described in Chapter 18.

Magnetism

Magnets destroy magnetically encoded information. They are a danger to all disk drives and diskettes. Once in class someone asked if magnets would harm the PC. So I took out my trusty magnetic screwdriver and waved it over the chips to illustrate that the PC would be unaffected. This went OK, but when I waved it over the fixed disk drive and then tried a DIR command, I got "Sector not found." Oops! Good thing it was a rental computer. The metal housing of the fixed disk is aluminum. This provides no protection from magnetism. So I scrambled up all the data on the disk.

If you really hate someone in the office and want to get even with them, here are some hints:

- Get a magnetic paper clip holder for them
- Get them an electric pencil sharpener
- Provide refrigerator magnets to hold their floppy disks to metal file cabinets
- Get them a high intensity lamp for their desk
- Get them a document holder with a magnetic highlighter on the side.
- Go to their office and place their phone on top of a stack of floppy disks on their desk, then run back to your office and call them on the phone to tell them what you have just done.

Magnets, regardless of size, are a danger to your data. Observing the user environment for PC hazards is an important troubleshooting step and a means of preventing future PC malfunctions.

Study Break: Disk Destruction

1. Format a floppy diskette and copy some data onto it. Get it about half full of data. Use the COPY/V option to assure that the data is properly copied to the diskette. Put a label on it and write Mr. Bob or Super Dave after the famous TV stunt men. Now test to see what destroys the data on the floppy. Place the floppy on a florescent desk lamp. Try several spots around the bulbs and the base. Place it in drive A and run a thorough SCANDISK test. Did it survive? If not, reformat it and copy the data to the drive again.
2. Place the floppy under an electric pencil sharpener. Oh Nooo! Now sharpen several pencils. Test it again with SCANDISK. Did it survive? If not, we can reformat and copy the data to it again. Remember to use the COPY/V option. The /V option has the copy process verify the data copied.

3. Now hold the floppy against a metal filing cabinet. Get one of those refrigerator magnets and Oh Nooo! hold it in place. Test it again with SCANDISK. Did any of the tests render the floppy total useless? This means that it could not be formatted and used to store data again.

The goal here is to see just what lies around the office that can destroy data on a floppy.

Summary

This chapter described how to find the sources of PC hardware and software problems and presented the solutions for these problems. A proactive approach of preventing problems by creating a PC-friendly environment was also covered. The first section covered how to determine whether a failure might likely involve hardware, software or network components. The next section on troubleshooting discussed various methods, including the PC's POST, audible beep error codes, and visual and numeric error codes. The PC hardware subsystem (which include components like the power supply, BIOS, and RAM), disk drives, and their respective error symptoms were described in detail in the following section. We also covered many various types of tools needed for troubleshooting the different types of PC problems, and provided a handy list of items that should be included in every PC "first-aid kit." The final section of this chapter discussed a method for troubleshooting procedures and practices. We covered problem isolation and determination procedures for identifying problems to a malfunctioning PC subsystem and methods for eliciting behavior information from users. We also briefly discussed viruses and gave other valuable tips to help determine the source and nature of a PC's malfunction.

Chapter Review Questions

1. *UPS means*

    A. Uninterruptible Power Source
    B. Uninterruptible Power Supply
    C. Usual Power Supply
    D. Unusual Power Source

Answer: B, Uninterruptible Power Supply. There is nothing unusual here. The device is a supply not a source of electricity. The electric company is a source of electricity.

2. *When a floppy drive light comes on and stays on, what is the problem?*

    A. It has no power.
    B. There is no floppy diskette in it.
    C. The cable is improperly connected.
    D. The sound cable is missing.

Answer: C, the cable is improperly connected. The light lights so there must be power, and the light is not dependent upon a diskette being in the drive or not. A sound cable has nothing to do with a floppy disk.

3. *Pentium is a _____ microprocessor.*

    A. x586
    B. superconductor
    C. superscaler
    D. super486

Answer: C, superscaler. Intel dispensed with the numbering scheme with the Pentium chip so there is no Intel 586. A superconductor is an electrical conductor with very low resistance, and there is also no super 486 chip.

4. *How much conventional memory do DOS diagnostics have to use?*

    A. 320K
    B. 640K
    C. 1024K
    D. 896K

Answer : B, 640K. Conventional memory always maxes at 640 K. Extended memory begins at 1,024 K and 896 K is a boundary in the upper memory blocks that is beyond the conventional memory limit.

5. *What PC component contains diagnostic programs?*

    A. The display controller
    B. RAM
    C. CPU
    D. ROM

Answer: D, ROM. The display controller drives the monitor but does not perform the initial PC diagnostics. It may have some display tests in its ROM, but they only test the display. RAM is the active PC memory but has no fixed diagnostics in it. The contents of RAM continually vary. The CPU executes the diagnostics but contains no diagnostic programs.

6. *Windows boot problems involve what?*

    A. The fixed disk
    B. The registry and plug-and-play components
    C. DOS
    D. SCSI devices and the registry

Answer: B. The registry and plug-and-play components often cause Windows 95/98/Me boot problems. Fixed disk problems occur before Windows boots, DOS is used as an OS for many diagnostic programs but runs before Windows boots, and SCSI devices are not necessarily installed on a Windows PC.

7. *A PCI bus does not have a specific scan order.*

    A. TRUE
    B. FALSE

Answer: B, FALSE. The PCI bus is scanned in a specific order when plug-and-play components are begun by the PC.

8. *SCSI drives are an older version of EIDE drives.*

    A. TRUE
    B. FALSE

Answer: B, FALSE. SCSI devices are a separate design from EIDE fixed disk drives. Some SCSI devices are fixed disk drives, but others may be scanners.

9. *CD-ROMs install on what?*

    A. EIDE Controllers
    B. SCSI Controllers
    C. MFM Controllers
    D. EIDE and SCSI Buses

Answer: D, EIDE and SCSI Buses. CD-ROM drives are not SCSI or EIDE devices alone. The best answer is both EIDE and SCSI devices. Most home PCs have EIDE CD-ROM, CD-RW, or DVD drives. MFM was the fixed disk interface that preceded the EIDE interface.

10. *Modems connect to:*

    A. The telephone
    B. The serial port and the phone
    C. The line and the phone
    D. None of the above

Answer: C, the line and the phone. The modem is not connected to the phone alone. External modems could be plugged into a serial port, but most modems are installed internally in PCs. So the best answer is C.

11. *An apparent modem malfunction is caused by:*

    A. Calling the wrong number
    B. Using bad modem cable
    C. Conflicting I/O port selection
    D. All of the above

Answer: D, all of the above. This says it all.

12. *CD-ROM speeds are typically:*

    A. Faster than fixed disk access times
    B. Slower than fixed disk drives
    C. Equivalent to fixed disk drive access times
    D. Measured in nanoseconds

Answer: B, slower than fixed disk drives. CD-ROMs, CD-RW, and DVD drives are all slower than fixed disks. They may rotate at a maximum speed of about 9,000 RPM, where fixed disk drives can rotate as fast as 15,000 RPM. The rotational speed of the fixed disk drive is constant while that of CD-ROM, CD-RW, and DVD drives varies depending upon the track being accessed.

13. *The first 32-bit bus was:*

    A. The PCI bus
    B. The EISA bus
    C. The MCA bus
    D. The VESA bus
    E. The AGP bus

Answer: C, the MCA bus. While all are 32-bit buses, the Micro Channel Architecture bus was the first 32-bit bus. It appeared on the IBM PS-2 PC.

14. *MMX means what?*

    A. Multimegahertz
    B. Multimedia extension
    C. Maximum megahertz
    D. Multisession extension

Answer: B, multimedia extension. Intel Pentium CPU chips have had several instruction set augmentations. The first was the MMX or multimedia extension augmentation aimed at enabling the Intel chips to better handle multimedia (sound and video) functions. None of the other terms are real PC terms.

15. *PCs can boot from what?*

    A. The fixed disk
    B. The floppy disk
    C. A CD-ROM
    D. All of the above

Answer: D, all of the above. Depending on how the setup program configures the PC BIOS, the PC can boot from the floppy, fixed disk, CD-ROM drive, or a LAN.

16. *Key PC environmental concerns are:*

    A. Heat, light, operator, and water
    B. Power, cooling, dirt, and RFI
    C. Magnets, dust, LAN boards, and temperature change
    D. Vibration, liquids, modems, and temperature shock
    E. None of the above

Answer: B, Power, cooling, dirt, and RFI. Operators are not an environmental concern, although they can be dangerous to the PC. LAN boards and modems are not part of the PC's environment. They are components that may be installed in the PC.

17. *What program detects and corrects (when possible) fixed disk problems?*

> A. DEFRAG
> B. SCANDISK
> C. FDISK
> D. FORMAT

Answer: B, SCANDISK. The SCANDISK program evaluates the fixed disk data structures and can physically scan the disk drive surface searching for errors. It recovers data and flags bad parts of the disk so that they will not be used again. DEFRAG improves PC performance but does not detect and fix disk problems. FDISK partitions the disk and FORMAT lays out the directory and FATs. Neither FDISK or FORMAT fix disk problems.

18. *What program optimizes the data layout on a fixed disk to improve performance?*

> A. DEFRAG
> B. SCANDISK
> C. FDISK
> D. FORMAT

Answer: A, DEFRAG. DEFRAG improves PC performance by optimizing the data layout. The SCANDISK program evaluates the fixed disk data structures and can physically scan the disk drive surface searching for errors. It recovers data and flags bad parts of the disk so that they will not be used again. FDISK partitions the disk and FORMAT lays out the directory and FATs. Neither FDISK nor FORMAT improve PC performance.

19. *Your motherboard is not working. What is affected first?*

> A. CPU
> B. HDD
> C. POST
> D. Fixed Disk

Answer: A, the CPU. The CPU must be running before POST is performed. Fixed disk drives are tested in the POST process.

20. *When you have a fixed disk error, what is the problem?*

> A. Loose CPU
> B. Memory
> C. Hard Drive
> D. Motherboard

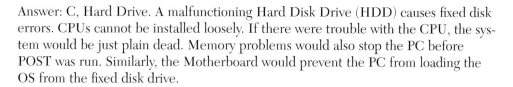
Answer: C, Hard Drive. A malfunctioning Hard Disk Drive (HDD) causes fixed disk errors. CPUs cannot be installed loosely. If there were trouble with the CPU, the system would be just plain dead. Memory problems would also stop the PC before POST was run. Similarly, the Motherboard would prevent the PC from loading the OS from the fixed disk drive.

21. *When there is a parity error, what is wrong?*

    A. RAM
    B. CPU
    C. Motherboard
    D. Disconnected cable

Answer: A, RAM. Parity errors are reported from I/O errors or RAM errors. No parity errors are reported for the motherboard, CPU, or disconnected cables.

22. *If a DOS program won't run within a window on Windows 95, you should try:*

    A. Real mode
    B. DOS mode
    C. Resting your computer
    D. Safe mode

Answer: B. Exit Windows to DOS mode. This shuts down all Windows drivers and runs DOS alone in the PC. Resting a computer is not a viable answer because computers do not rest. Safe mode is a diagnostic mode in which booting and other hardware conflict problems can be resolved by reconfiguring hardware or loading device drivers. Real mode is the CPU operating mode when DOS is the operating system.

23. *If an application won't run and an incorrect DOS version error message appears, you can solve this with what program?*

    A. DOSKEY
    B. VER
    C. TYPE
    D. SETVER

Answer: A, SETVER. The SETVER program permits DOS programs to run with different versions of DOS. DOSKEY is a TSR program that makes the keyboard easy to use. TYPE displays the contents of TXT files. VER displays version information but does not fix problems.

24. *When your system is booting just before the Starting Windows 95 message appears, an error message is displayed that says, "No operating system found". What file is missing?*

    A. CONFIG.SYS
    B. AUTOEXEC.BAT
    C. COMMAND.COM
    D. HIMEM.SYS

Answer: A, COMMAND.COM. A Windows 95/98/Me PC will boot without CONFIG.SYS and AUTOEXEC.BAT. HIMEM.SYS activates extended memory (XMS) but is not needed to boot into DOS.

Chapter 4

MAINTENANCE AND SAFETY PRACTICES

Chapter Syllabus

- Preventive Maintenance Products and Procedures

- PC Power and Other PC Operating Environment Hazards

- Safety Procedures for High Voltage and Laser Equipment

- Hazardous Waste Disposal

- Electrostatic Discharge (ESD) Procedures

This chapter presents preventive maintenance and safety procedures for working on PCs. Preventive maintenance covers cleaning products and procedures, precautions and environmental hazard considerations. Safety practices cover safety procedures when working with lasers, high voltages, electrostatic discharge, and hazardous materials. Cleaning PCs is an important maintenance function although not quite as critical as the maintenance cleaning letter we received in 1995 suggests (Figure 4–1). While cleaning is an

COMPUTER SERVICES, INC.

SUITE
SNOWDEN RIVER PKWY.
COLUMBIA, MARYLAND 21045
PHONE/FAX 410 NNN-NNNN

April 5, 1999

Dear Friend,

SAVE YOUR PERSONAL COMPUTER

from an early grave. Save yourself the hassle of down computers. Prevent data loss and sleep easier knowing your computer is not about to mess up your business.

We are currently offering a very special program and I wanted to be sure you knew about it.

PC Preventative Maintenance Program, this thing really works. Electro - Mechanical energy in your computer acts like a magnet attracting dust and dirt from the environment. This dirt builds up on the circuit boards in your computer and causes all kinds of problems, heat build up, short circuits, and component failure, We will come to your office and throroughly clean the interior and exterior of your computer.

Computers in this area should be cleaned at least once a year, if your computer is in an especially dry or dusty area, cleaning should be done twice a year. This can double the trouble free life of your computer.

We have reduced our normal rate of one hundred twenty-five dollars to only $75.00 for orders taken now. Call us today to get on the list.

Computer Services can also offer you complete repair and upgrading of your existing PC system. Remember, we come to you. You don't have to come to us.

Sincerely,

Laurel E.

Laurel E.
President

P.S. Call now before you forget.

(410)   or (310)   (Pager)

Figure 4–1
Maintenance cleaning letter.

important part of PC maintenance, it is not actually part of the A+ exam, but is presented here in this book as a supplemental and, hopefully, valuable feature for the reader.

Cleaning should be performed periodically in dirty and dusty environments. A dirty environment is that of a coal mine. A dusty environment is that of a wood shop. While we have talked and worked on PCs in such environments, most PCs in offices are not in such severe environments; an annual cleaning may be all that is required. The exception might be PCs installed in offices of smokers. Smoke particles, like dust, are naturally attracted to the PC because of the electrical charges present there. In this instance, more frequent cleaning could help maintain the PC and prevent some heat and dust related failures.

There are exceptions—for example, a digital server in my office kept shutting down at random times over a period of several months. When the service engineer came out to investigate and resolve the problem, he opened the server and found it full of half cockroaches. The cockroaches had been attracted to the server by the warmth and food inside. (They eat grease, plastic, and paper.) To get to this warmth and food, they entered the server through the power supply fan opening and were cut in half by the spinning fan. This slowed the fan down, which in turn caused the server to shut down because it sensed a cooling problem due to the slow fan. Of course, the fan speeded up again and the server automatically restarted when it sensed that the problem had passed. This was an unusual case, but you can see how cleaning PCs is an important part of maintenance.

Preventive Maintenance Products and Procedures

The primary objective in cleaning a PC is to reduce heat build-up. There are two impacts from heat: (1) The PC's electrical components can suffer from high temperatures, and (2) its mechanical components can suffer from rapid temperature changes. High heat can destroy the electronics inside a PC. High temperatures cause the components to draw more power, creating more heat. In most cases, this process stabilizes at some reasonable operating level. Sometimes components fail. Rapid temperature changes cause the mechanical parts to contract and expand dramatically, resulting in mismatched tolerances and component failures. Keeping the temperature stable in the PC's room prolongs the life of the PC. If the temperature varies significantly, leave the computer turned on to minimize its internal temperature fluctuations. If you leave the computer on, it must be connected to a good surge suppressor to prevent electrical damage from power surges due to storms, and so on.

Radiant energy, like sunlight, can cause significant temperature variations inside a PC. It may seem cool in a room, but if the sun is beaming in from a window on the PC, you can bet that its temperature is soaring, just as if it were sitting on a hot sunny beach.

Even though the temperature outside may be cool, the PC's temperature has moved from cool to very hot due to radiant energy from the sun. Keeping a PC clean helps mitigate heat-related problems. Regular cleaning can prevent unnecessary heat build-up inside the PC, which ultimately may lengthen its life. As dust and other pollutants collect on surfaces on and within the PC, normal and necessary airflow around components can become restricted. Also, dust and lint can serve as an insulator, trapping heat on or near components. It also makes the PC more pleasant to work on.

Cleaning Compounds

Table 4–1 summarizes the various compounds that have been used to clean PCs, what they can clean, and how they should be stored.

Table 4–1   Cleaning Compounds and Agents

Cleaning Compound	Use	Source and Storage	Disposal
Water—sprayed on a cloth first.	Almost all PC surfaces except electronic circuitry, especially high voltage equipment.	Tap water or distilled water.	Down the drain.
Water with fabric softener (antistatic chemicals)—sprayed on a cloth first—leaves antistatic film.	Almost all PC surfaces except electronic circuitry, especially high-voltage equipment.	Tap water or distilled water. Fabric softener can be stored in almost any storage area while kept in closed container.	Biodegradable; can be washed out of cloth down any drain. Empty fabric softener containers must be disposed of in appropriate recycling container.
Spit—yes, it's here, but it is not sanitary until the equipment has sat exposed to air for several hours! We have all used this at one time or another.	Almost all PC surfaces except electronic circuitry, especially high-voltage equipment.	The mouth.	Biodegradable; can be washed out of cloth down any drain.

Table 4–1 Cleaning Compounds and Agents (Continued)

Cleaning Compound	Use	Source and Storage	Disposal
Alcohol (denatured isopropyl 91% or greater)—sprayed on a cloth. **Caution—highly flammable, use in static free environment.**	Limited to disk drive and CD cleaning.	Temperature-controlled and fire safe room.	Evaporates. Empty containers must be disposed of in appropriate recycling container.
Glass and general purpose cleaner with ammonia—sprayed on cloth first.	Almost all PC surfaces except electronics.	Almost any storage area while kept in closed container.	Biodegradable; can be washed out of cloth down any drain. Empty containers must be disposed of in appropriate recycling container.
Detergent cleaners	Almost all PC surfaces except electronics.	Almost any storage area while kept in closed container.	Biodegradable; can be washed out of cloth down any drain. Empty containers must be disposed of in appropriate recycling container.
Antistatic sprays. **Caution—use in well ventilated areas**	Almost all PC surfaces—must be sprayed on cloth first to coat CRTs.	Temperature-controlled room.	Air, water and antistatic compound with a carrier that evaporates, coating surface. Empty spray cans must be disposed of in appropriate recycling container.

Table 4–1 Cleaning Compounds and Agents (Continued)

Cleaning Compound	Use	Source and Storage	Disposal
Electric circuit degreaser (hydrocarbon). **Caution—highly flammable, hazardous to breathe—high-heat produces toxic fumes.**	Cleans circuit boards and electronics.	Temperature-controlled and fire safe room.	Evaporates but must be vented to outdoors for very small quantities or into an air scrubber when used in volume. Empty spray cans must be disposed of in appropriate hazardous waste container.
Electronic contact enhancer—for instance, long polymer compounds like Tweak.	Circuit card contacts to improve electrical connectivity.	Almost any storage area while kept in closed container.	Carrier evaporates. Used in very small quantities.
High-abrasion chlorine bleach scrubbing compounds	Highly stained plastic surfaces.	Almost any storage area while kept in closed container.	Small quantities can be washed out of cloth down any drain.
Soft scrubbing chlorine bleach compounds	Stained plastic and painted surfaces and caked glass surfaces.	Almost any storage area while kept in closed container.	Small quantities can be washed out of cloth down any drain. Empty containers must be disposed of in appropriate recycling container.

Cleaning Agent or Device	Use	Storage	Disposal
Mouse Pad	Keeps grit and dirt out of mouse.	Almost any storage area	Can be placed in the trash.

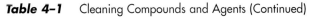

Table 4-1 Cleaning Compounds and Agents (Continued)

Cleaning Agent or Device	Use	Storage	Disposal
Paper tissues and towels	Wipes almost any surface—both can scratch plastic surfaces, for instance, CDs.	Almost any storage area but in large quantities they are a fire hazard.	Biodegradable. Can be placed in the paper recycle trash.
Laser printer cleaning paper	Run through laser printer to clean mechanism.	Almost any storage area but in large quantities they are a fire hazard.	Biodegradable. Can be placed in the trash.
Lint-free cloth	Wipes almost any surface but can scratch plastic surfaces, e.g., CDs.	Almost any storage area but in large quantities they are a fire hazard.	Biodegradable. Can be placed in the trash.
Wipes for screen and equipment containing detergent and antistatic agents.	Most all PC surfaces except electronics.	Temperature-controlled room.	Biodegradable. Can be placed in the trash.
Tweezers	Pull loose bolts, dirt, and dust from hard to reach areas.	Almost any storage area.	Dust can be placed in the trash. Metal should be recycled.
High-pressure air	Blows dust from inside PC.	Temperature-controlled room.	It is just air—no disposal necessary. Empty containers must be disposed of in appropriate recycling container.

Table 4-1   Cleaning Compounds and Agents (Continued)

Cleaning Agent or Device	Use	Storage	Disposal
Floppy disk drive cleaning disk—contains alcohol. Caution—highly flammable.	Limited to floppy disk drive cleaning (rarely needed).	Temperature-controlled and fire safe room.	Evaporates.
CD-ROM cleaning kit	CD-disk brush to clean CD lens.	Almost any storage area.	Can be placed in the trash.
CD cleaning kits—contains alcohol. Caution—highly flammable.	Limited to CD cleaning.	Temperature-controlled and fire safe room.	Evaporates.
Magnetic tape cleaning kit—contains alcohol. Caution—highly flammable.	Limited to cleaning and lubricating magnetic tape drives.	Temperature Controlled and fire safe room.	Evaporates.
Pink pencil eraser—acid content—not recommended as a cleaning agent.	Cleans circuit board contacts temporarily but boards become addicted to periodic erasures because of the acid in the eraser.	Almost any storage area.	Can be placed in the trash.
Plastic pencil eraser—recommended as a cleaning agent.	Cleans circuit board contacts and other surface marks where a mild abrasive is needed.	Almost any storage area.	Can be placed in the trash.
Brushes—Static discharge caution.	Loosens dust adhered to PC components for subsequent vacuuming.	Almost any storage area.	Can be placed in the trash.

Table 4–1   Cleaning Compounds and Agents (Continued)

Cleaning Agent or Device	Use	Storage	Disposal
Mini-vacuum cleaner	Sucks dust out of small areas.	Almost any storage area.	Dust can be emptied into the trash.
Vacuum cleaner	Sucks dust out of PC.	Almost any storage area.	Dust can be emptied into the trash.

Special Cleaning Compounds and Devices

There are a variety of antistatic and other special cleaning compounds and cleaning kits sold. See Figure 4–2 for compressed gas and other dusting devices and Figure 4–3 for special cleaning wipes, papers and Qtips™. Antistatic cleaners contain detergents and antistatic compounds in a water or volatile chemical solution. Some are sprayed on while others are wiped on. Antistatic cleaning compounds coat the surface of a component with chemicals that drain off the static charge. They leave an oily conductive residue that sometimes clouds monitor screens and makes other components feel sticky.

Figure 4–2
Compressed gas and other antistatic dusting devices.

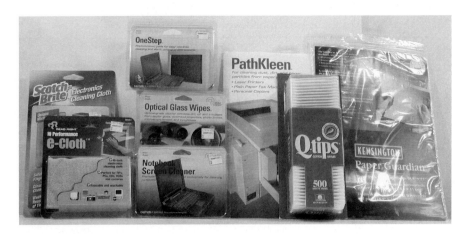

Figure 4–3
Special cleaning wipes, papers, and Qtips.

Dust sprays just blow the dust from specific areas within the PC. They are good at getting into tight spots. They are bad in that they do not remove any dust, only rearrange it. Nonetheless, this is often helpful in making fans spin freely again and removing heavy dust from areas that restrict airflow. A risk with compressed air dust removers is that the cans cannot be heated or they might explode (as is the potential with any compressed gas cleaner) and they can potentially increase the static charge of electronic components.

A better approach to removing dust is to vacuum it. Sometimes dust adheres tightly to electronic components and cannot be lifted by vacuuming. In this instance, blowing the dust sometimes dislodges it. However, using a small brush to mechanically loosen the dust is a better approach. Caution must be exercised to ensure that static discharge does not damage any sensitive components. Once the dust is loosened, it is then removed by vacuuming.

When vacuuming, the chance of static damage to components is increased. There is no chance that components can be sucked off a board (although in one PC troubleshooting seminar a student swore that they did just that). However, the flow of dry air through a vacuum can increase static potential, so care should be exercised.

Special cleaning wipes also deliver antistatic compounds in water to PC surfaces. They may have special anti-abrasion qualities or special surfaces designed to trap dirt and dust. Laser printer path cleaning paper is designed to trap dirt and dust and be exposed to the heat of the laser printer fuser. Qtips or any cotton swab on a stick can deliver cleaning compounds into and remove dirt and dust from hard to reach places.

Water-Based Cleaning Compounds

Water and water-based compounds (including spit, and my bet is that we have all used it at one time or another) can be used to clean a PC. Water-based detergents that are not biodegradable should not be purchased and used to clean PCs.

The hazard with water-based cleaners is contact with high voltage components like the monitor and the power supply. High voltages and water do not mix and electrical shock or worse could result. Given enough time, water can dissolve almost anything. However, we are rushed and do not have the time for water to work on most occasions. It is possible to wash some electronic components and cards in water and have them survive. In one of my first PC classes in 1981, a student swore that he washed the boards of his computer in Woolite® to remove accumulated metallic foundry dust. Sometimes dust (especially that with metallic content) and humidity can short out PC boards. There were no sparks generated here, only PC logic failures and resultant program crashes.

There are times when you certainly would wash PC boards off in water or in a water-and-detergent solution. The only time to use water directly is when the PC has been in a flood or a fire. The PC electronics are already wet anyway. The trick is making sure that the boards are completely dry before using them. We had wet memory SIMMs and immediately used them in a PC, as well as some other boards, on our first TV appearance. In both cases, they worked without incident. In another attempt, a VGA video card was wet and placed in a PC to operate. There was no video, but the PC did boot. It required several hours of drying before the video board resumed working. The key here is ensuring that any components are thoroughly dry before applying power to them.

Water and water-based compounds are good for cleaning PC surfaces. Water-based compounds contain water and some detergent additives—for instance, glass cleaner, as shown in Figure 4–4. The recommended procedure is to spray them on a cloth and then use the wet cloth to clean the component's surface. Spraying the compound on the component directly can result in dribbles into cracks and crevices, potentially damaging sensitive electronics.

Water and water-based compounds are good for cleaning stains caused by accidental spillage on PC components or by grease and oil from handling PC components. They break down and dissolve the compounds in these stains.

Water cannot be used in every situation. Recall the example in Chapter 3 where coffee was spilled on the keyboard of a PC, and we ran it under a water faucet to dissolve and remove all the last stubborn coffee stains. The running water cleaned all the stains, but caused some keys to fail, necessitating the purchase of a new keyboard.

Figure 4–4
Water-based compounds,
e.g., glass cleaner.

Abrasive Compounds

To remove stubborn stains on plastic and metal PC surfaces, chlorine abrasive compounds are sometimes used to augment water-based compounds, as shown in Figure 4–5. They scrub out ground-in dirt and stains on both plastic and painted surfaces. Lightly abrasive compounds should be used on painted surfaces so as not to damage the paint. They remove some paint regardless, but not so much as to severely damage the surface. Stronger abrasives are sometimes needed on plastic surfaces when they have been scraped or heavily soiled.

Alcohol and Volatile Compounds

Alcohol has been used to clean disk, tape, and disk drive read/write heads. It dissolves the magnetic dust and grit that accumulates on those components. There are two important things to remember about using alcohol: first, it is flammable. There was a case of a service engineer getting severely burned when using alcohol to clean a CRT screen and a static discharge ignited it. Since alcohol burns with a colorless flame, it is extremely dangerous and should not be used for casual cleaning. Second, when cleaning PC disk and tape drive components with alcohol, a compound solution with a small per-

Figure 4–5
Chlorine abrasive compounds.

centage of water should be used. See Figure 4–6. The alcohol on the left in the figure has too much water for cleaning disk components, while the alcohol on the right has less water content and is better for electronics cleaning.

CD cleaners use alcohol to clean the surfaces of CDs. They provide special tools for wiping the CD surface without scratching it. There are also CD scratch repair kits that repair scratched CDs using a special resurfacing compound. See Figure 4–7. The CD cleaning compound is primarily alcohol. CDs should not be cleaned with other compounds because they can damage the plastic CD surface. Once we tried acetone (nail polish remover) to remove a particularly stubborn smudge from the surface of a CD. This only made the smudge larger, rendering the CD unreadable.

CDs get dirty quickly when handled frequently. Surface scratches and dirt can make them easily unreadable. Often times it is not readily obvious that a CD has become damaged. Only when the dirty area is read does the CD fail. When having difficulty reading a CD, the first thing to do is examine the surface closely for scratches and dirt and then try cleaning the CD.

Since frequent handling damages CDs, it is a good policy to handle them as little as possible. Although they only cost pennies to manufacture, CDs contain software worth hundreds of dollars. Proper storage in jewel cases or special CD traveling cases preserves CDs.

Figure 4–6
Common denatured alcohol.

Figure 4–7
CD cleaning and repairing kits.

Storing data CDs is more critical than music CDs because the impact of dirt or a scratch on a data CD makes some data unreadable, thus effectively destroying it. Scratches on music CDs result in skips in some music, but most of the CD is still useable. We have not yet tried to repair a data CD with a CD repair kit. If you are desperate to recover data from a CD, then as a last resort, why not try repairing the CD?

Other volatile chemical cleaners and degreasers are designed to specifically clean electronic components, and do not harm sensitive electronics. Because they are volatile chemicals and often toxic in very large quantities, they must be handled and used with care, as shown in Figure 4–8.

When there are electrical connection problems, volatile chemical cleaners can make sure that the electrical contacts are free of grease and dirt. They work best for cleaning the specific types of dirt found that are a result of PC card manufacturing.

They also work best cleaning hard to reach or hard to clean electrical connections. Volatile cleaners are not general-purpose cleaners and so do not dissolve all kinds of dirt and grime. They should be used sparingly because of their toxicity and their limited cleaning capabilities.

Figure 4–8
Volatile compounds.

Some electrical contacts are best cleaned mechanically. Rubbing an eraser across them buffs them, removing residue that reduces electrical connectivity. Plastic erasers used by draftsmen are the best for this kind of abrasive cleaning. The normal pencil erasers have an acid chemical content that tends to etch pits into electrical contacts. These pits can make the electrical contacts addicted to periodic erasure.

Most PCs do not require chemical cleaning; they only require periodic dust removal. There are from time to time situations that arise requiring the use of special cleaning tools. In these cases, cleaning compounds beyond those used in cleaning dust from PCs are employed.

The PC Cleaning Process

Thoroughly cleaning a PC requires an organized approach as we have outlined in the following:

1. **Setup**—Pick a cleaning area and collect all of your cleaning supplies. The most common supplies used in thorough cleaning are water-based detergent compounds, abrasive scrubbing compounds for plastic surfaces, brushes, vacuum cleaners, special disk and CD-ROM drive cleaners, lint-free cloths, plastic contact erasers, and possible volatile contact cleaners for special contact cleaning problems. See Figure 4–9. The cleaning area should have a working area of about the size of a folding table (30 inches by 72 inches). Be sure appropriate static discharge precautions are in place. Since thorough cleaning requires disassembling and cleaning the machine's insides, paper to take notes, markers to document the configuration, and strips of masking tape or a bolt holder are needed. Use paper to diagram exactly where all the cards and cables are connected so the PC can be reassembled exactly as it was disassembled. Markers are used to write critical configuration and assembly information on components. Masking tape strips hold the bolts for the PC components. Alternatively, a bolt holder can be fashioned from egg-carton foam, which conveniently holds the bolts in an organized fashion. See Figure 4–10. Each time a group of bolts is removed, stick them with tape to the component they are used to fasten into the PC or place them in one area of egg-carton bolt holder and label exactly where they were used. It is also a good idea to back up the PC before cleaning and document the IRQs and system configurations. For an NT system, you might

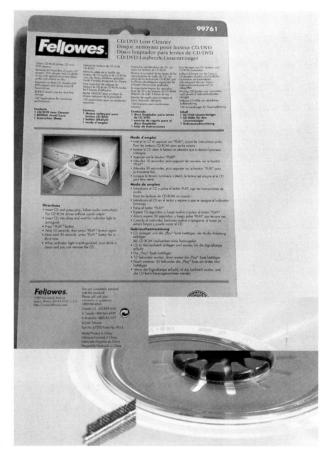

Figure 4-9
CD-ROM lens cleaners.

also want to create a repair disk. These are all good preventive measures that serve as an "insurance policy" in case something unexpected occurs during the dis- and reassembly of the PC during the cleaning process.

2. **Disassembly**—Completely disassemble the PC. Remove all cards, the main logic board, the power supply and disk drives. In this manner you start from the inside and work your way out. Diagram where everything connects and is installed. Place the cards and motherboard to the side in a static-safe location.

3. **Clean the chassis**—First clean the empty chassis. Vacuum out all dust and use water-based detergent cleaners to remove stains. Wipe down all surfaces with a lint free cloth.

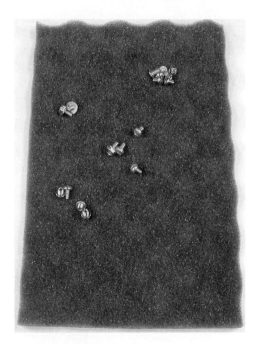

Figure 4–10
Egg-carton foam bolt holder.

4. **Clean the power supply**—The first component to clean is the power supply. It is usually the dustiest. Be sure it is unplugged. If it is really dirty, you will need to open it, brush it and vacuum it out. Blow the remaining dust out with compressed air when it cannot be dislodged with a brush. Examine the fan. If the bearings are bad or the fan blades do not rotate freely, consider replacing the fan with a new one exactly the same size using equivalent DC power. Once the power supply is thoroughly cleaned, reinstall it into the chassis.

5. **Clean the disk drives**—This means the fixed disk drives, CD-ROM drive, and the floppy disk drives. Vacuum them, taking the necessary static discharge precautions. When the dust is caked on, use a soft brush to dislodge it. The front panel and CD-ROM enclosure surfaces can be wiped with water-based detergent cleaner if there are stains. Blow out the slot in the floppy drive and the CD-ROM drive. If the drives are extremely dirty, consider cleaning the inside with a floppy disk and a CD-ROM lens cleaner once the PC is completely reassembled. See Figure 4–11 for an example of a floppy drive cleaning kit. After they are cleaned, reassemble them back into the chassis.

Figure 4–11
Mouse and floppy disk drive cleaning kits.

6. **Clean the boards**—Vacuum all cards and the main logic board while observing static discharge precautions. Resocket all socketed chips by placing the board on a flat static-free surface and pushing the chips back into their sockets. Remove SIMMs and DIMMs from the main logic board. Wipe them with a lint-free cloth, again observing static discharge precautions, and reseat them into their sockets. You also should verify that jumpers on the board are firmly in place. This is especially important for older boards. Reinstall the main logic board, then the option cards. Wipe all edge connectors with a lint-free cloth. When there is heavy dirt that is not removed from an edge connector by wiping with a lint free cloth, consider using an abrasive plastic eraser to remove it. Check all of the contacts and connectors to be sure they are clean.

7. **Complete reassembly**—Connect all cables. Inspect each cable connector for dirt and broken contacts. Replace bad and marginal cables as needed. Examine all push-pin connectors for broken and bent pins. Install cables without straightening pins when possible. Straightening pins can over stress the point of contact between the

pin and the circuit card, causing the pin to break off. Minimizing mechanical movement by leaving pins bent somewhat reduces the chance of breaking a pin.

8. **Clean the keyboard and mouse**—Detach both the mouse and the keyboard from the system before beginning the cleaning. Brush off the keyboard and vacuum. Use a lint-free cloth or cotton swabs dipped in water-based detergent to wipe down the keys and to swab between the keys as needed. Remove the mouse ball from the under side and clean the ball and rollers with cotton swabs, making sure to get all extra lint build-up off the rollers. See Figure 4–11 for special mouse cleaning kit. Blow out any dust with compressed air. A brush can be used to clean the lenses for the optical sensors. Do not use lubricants or antistatic wipes in the mouse because any oily residue can coat the optical sensor lenses, causing the mouse to malfunction. The ball itself can be cleaned with water to remove dirt and grime buildup. Dry thoroughly before reassembling.

9. **Power up**—Without replacing the outside cover, plug the machine back in and power up. Ensure that the PC boots as before and that the power supply fan is operating properly, creating airflow within the PC.

10. **Reinstall the chassis cover**—Now power down and replace the final chassis cover. If you have not already done so, wipe it down with a lint-free cloth. Use water-based detergent to remove any stubborn stains. Remember to spray the water-based detergent on the cloth first before wiping off the chassis cover stain.

11. **Clean the cable connections**—Prior to powering up the computer, clean and check the cables and their connection points using a damp cloth. Be careful as you do this as some of the connectors, especially RJ-45 connectors commonly used with networks, can be easily damaged over time.

12. **Power up and clean the disk and CD-ROM drives**—Test the floppy and CD-ROM drives to see if they can read disks and CDs OK. Use a cleaning disk to remove any stubborn dirt from floppy drive read/write heads or from the CD-ROM drive lens.

13. **Clean the monitor**—Vacuum out the rear and top of the monitor to ensure that there is clear airflow through the vent slots in the monitor case. Use a water-based detergent compound sprayed on a lint-free cloth to wipe down and clean all surfaces. Scratches and

stubborn stains on the plastic surfaces can be cleaned with a mild chlorine abrasive compound. The abrasive should be applied to a lint-free cloth and then wiped on the scratch or scuff mark. The monitor screen should be cleaned using a water-based glass cleaner sprayed on a lint-free cloth.

14. **Clean speakers and other external devices**—Power off each external device that needs cleaning. Remove dust by vacuuming the device's vents. As with cleaning a monitor, a water-based detergent compound sprayed on a lint-free cloth is used to wipe down and clean all surfaces. Scratches and stubborn stains on the plastic surfaces may be cleaned with a mild chlorine abrasive compound. Apply the abrasive to a lint-free cloth and then wipe it on the scratch or scuff mark.

Once these steps are completed, the PC is clean and ready to return to service.

Contact and Connector Cleaning

Sometimes special cleaning must be performed on electrical connectors and contacts. This was especially true of early PCs. Connectors can be cleaned by using volatile cleaning compounds specifically designed to clean electronic components and electrical contacts. These compounds dissolve greasy residues and wash them away, drying quickly without leaving a greasy residue. In rare instances, contact-enhancing compounds can be used to make better electrical connections, as shown in Figure 4–12. We cannot definitively say that contact enhancers have solved a specific PC cleaning problem. We have tried using them to improve SIMM electrical connections; they did no harm, but their beneficial effect could not be decidedly documented either. This makes their use a last resort.

Electrical contacts should not normally need cleaning. Only in especially dirty and humid environments is there a need to clean electrical contacts. Electrical contacts may need cleaning if they have not been cleaned for several years. Over a long period of time, they can build up resistive residue that necessitates cleaning.

Removing Dust—Chassis, Power Supplies, Fans

Dust inside the PC retains heat in the chips because it acts like an insulating blanket blocking conductive airflow, thus holding onto the heat generated by the chip inside of it. Hot chips draw more current and consequently create

Figure 4-12
Contact enhancer.

more heat. That heat is retained in the chip, causing it to draw more power. This vicious cycle either eventually stabilizes or the chip fails. As mentioned earlier, the frequency of cleaning varies depending upon how dirty and dusty the PC's environment. PCs in coal mines need frequent and regular cleaning because coal dust invades and adheres to everything. To complicate matters, coal dust is conductive because it is composed largely of carbon. In offices with smokers, there are very fine dust particles from smoke. This dust can shorten the life of disk drives and other PC components.

A rule of thumb is that a PC should have an annual inspection and clean up. Our servers run 24 hours a day, seven days a week (24x7) for months and months without cleaning. They are cleaned about once a year or when upgrades are performed, but anytime the computer is opened up—such as for installation of a new component—is a good time for a brief hose-out with a vacuum.

For PCs that require industrial-strength operation, some power supplies provide superior power output and cooling for them. These can be installed in place of the standard power supplies. Most desktop PCs do not need industrial-strength power supplies, but if a PC is being used as a network server, a power supply upgrade may be in order to support the added disk drive power requirements. Generally, servers operate with more than two disk drives; several of ours have seven.

Brushes are used to loosen dust adhering to PC components. The dust adheres because the PC components are electrically charged, attracting the oppositely charged dust particles. Once loosened by a brush, it can be vacuumed out of the PC. See Figure 4–13. When using brushes, care must be taken not to build up static charges that can harm PC components.

Keeping dust out of a PC is impossible because the principal cooling mechanism for PC components is the air flowing across the surface of the components. Each PC is designed with a specific airflow pathway through it. Disruption of that airflow pathway causes the PC to overheat. Recall the case where a second fan was installed in a PC to improve airflow. However, it blew air out of the PC rather than sucking air in. This disrupted the airflow and caused the PC to overheat. Another factor that can affect airflow is uncovered expansion card slots. Make sure that each expansion slot has a cover so there are no empty open slots that change the airflow.

The best cleaning mechanism is to keep the PC's environment free and clear of dust. When the PC is in a dirty and dusty environment, components have a shortened life. We have worked on PCs in an office where there were dogs. The dog hairs and associated dirt shortened the life of several PC components, especially disk drives. Moving the PCs from the floor to a desktop improved the reliability, but did not totally solve the problem.

Figure 4–13
Brushes.

Study Break: Cleaning Your PC

Open your PC to see how dirty it is inside.

1. Remove the cover from your PC and examine the interior for dust and dirt. Look at the power supply fan to determine the build-up of dust and other contaminants. Clean the PC interior as required.
2. Examine the monitor and other peripheral components for dust accumulation. Are there any areas with extraordinary dust accumulation? Make note of them. Clean the monitor and peripheral components as required.

PC Power and Other PC Operating Environment Hazards

A primary cause of PC and PC component failure is bad power. Power spikes and surges tend to shorten component and PC life dramatically. At a minimum, a surge suppressor should protect all PCs, as shown in Figure 4–14. A more detailed discussion of PC power follows.

Figure 4–14
Laptop PC surge suppressor.

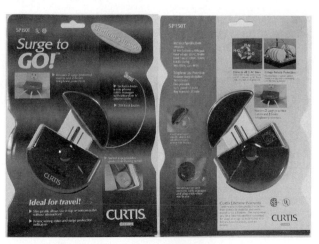

Power Problems and How to Spot Them

Electrical power is one of the most important things influencing the health of a PC. PCs like a stable electrical environment with no power surprises. Electrical surges and spikes can potentially harm the chips in the PC. Typical power problems are:

- **Power spikes**—short duration, very high voltages caused by lightning hitting the electrical power grid at some point. Turning off an electrical appliance may also cause spikes. Voltage spikes might get through the power supply and into the PC's chips, sometimes burning them out. You would not see fire and smoke (in rare cases that is possible), but the high voltage would burn out some part of a chip just the same. The result again would be some type of PC failure.

- **Surges**—like a spike, but of longer duration. A surge is a higher than normal voltage for a noticeable period of time. It can, if high enough, cause the DC voltages inside the PC to increase beyond specifications. This stresses the chips in the same way a 20-volt bulb would be stressed if it were plugged into a 120-volt line. In the case of the bulb, we would see it burn brightly for an instant before blackening out. In the case of our PC, we do not see it glow or anything, but we may have a memory chip failure just when the PC was cranking away on the month-end spread sheet.

- **Voltage sags**—the opposite of surges. They are low voltage for a significant period of time. They are caused by equipment that uses lots of electrical power being on the same power line as your PC. A simple radiant foot heater plugged into the wall outlet along with the PC can cause some terrible voltage sags (and surges) as it turns on and then later goes off again. The damage to the PC can be twofold here. If the sag is severe and long enough, it could cause the PC's power supply to deny the proper voltage level to the PC logic and memory, immediately causing an error. If it does not cause an immediate failure, it may cause the PC to draw more current through its components. This is like trying to cram size nine feet into size four shoes. When the foot gets into the shoe, the shoe never returns to its original shape. In a similar fashion, chips can be destroyed by the high current load they experience in a voltage sag.

- **Brownout**—a long-term sag caused by the inability of the local power company to provide sufficient power for the demands of all users. The voltage in a brownout can drop below 90 volts. Brownouts occur from 7 to 9 a.m. and 6 to 8 p.m., the peak power demand periods.

- **Blackout**—total loss of power caused by damaged power distribution systems, power generating equipment, or downed power lines.

Surge suppressors, uninterruptible power supplies, or stand-by power supplies solve power problems. All PCs must, at a minimum, have a surge suppressor in their power line. Voltage sags can be avoided by giving each PC its own power line to the power distribution box. When nothing else (like coffee makers, heaters, etc.) is on the same line, your PC should be relatively protected from voltage sags. If there is a severe thunderstorm overhead, that is the time you could experience a lightning strike. The surge from lightning strikes can go right past the surge suppressor and into the PC's logic destroying it. In that case, it may be best to unplug the PC and disconnect every electrical connection into the PC. Turning off the wall switch offers some protection, but a high voltage lightning spike can still jump across the contacts in the wall switch.

Surge Suppression

Surge suppressors reroute voltage spikes and surges back into the power line or to the ground. This stops these spikes and surges from reaching the PC and causing damage.

Surge Suppressor Specifications and Terminology

The electrical rating describes the power handling ability of the surge suppressor. Typical specification is: 120 VAC; 15A; 60 Hz; 1,800 Watts. This unit operates on a standard North American 115-120 volt Alternating Current line—a standard wall outlet. The "15A" states that it can draw up to 15 Amps of current before overloading the internal fuse or circuit breaker. The Watts defines the maximum power (volts times amps or $120 \times 15 = 1,800$ Watts). Here are some terms you should know:

- MOV—Metal Oxide Variable-resistor (or Varistor) is the principal protector against surge and spike damage. Most surge suppressors use a single MOV between the hot and return line, and better surge suppressors use three MOVs. This is referred to as three-mode protection.
- The clamping voltage is the minimum voltage that activates the MOV. Any voltage above this level crosses the MOV and returns to the source, bypassing the PC. The lowest clamping voltage measured by Underwriters Laboratories is 330 volts; lower levels are better.

Clamping voltages 50% higher than the electrical rating of 120 volts (around 180 volts) are typical.

- The clamping time is the time delay before the MOV activates. A lower time means better protection because quick reaction to the surge lowers the time that high voltage can damage the PC. MOVs react typically in nanoseconds.

- Maximum surge voltage describes the maximum voltage the MOV can absorb without damage. The higher the voltage, the better the MOV can absorb the surge without damaging itself.

- Maximum surge current specifies the maximum current the MOV can pass without damage. The higher the current passed, the better.

- Maximum energy dissipation describes the amount of energy that a MOV can pass before it is worn out; more joules means that the MOV will last longer. Generally, the bigger the MOV, the more energy it can absorb. In Figure 4–15 the smaller MOV on the left absorbs much less energy than the large MOV on the right.

- Voice rejection and/or noise attenuation describes the amount of noise or electrical interference that can be removed from the input power by Electromagnetic Interference (EMI) and Radio Frequency Interference (RFI) filters in the surge suppressor. See Figure 4–16.

Figure 4–15
Metal Oxide Variable-resistors (Varistors).

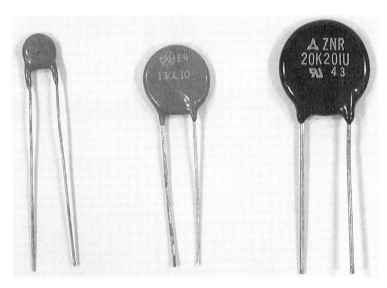

Figure 4–16
Surge suppressor with EMI/RFI filtering.

Surge suppressors are the first defense for power problems. They require periodic replacement because their MOVs degrade as they absorb power hits. The more hits they absorb, the more they need to be replaced. See Figure 4–17 for surge suppressor MOV configuration. Better overall protection is provided by stand-by power supplies and uninterruptible power supplies.

Personal Computer

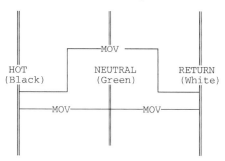

Wall Socket Connection

Figure 4–17
Surge suppressor MOV configuration.

Uninterruptible Power Supplies (UPS)

Alternatives to a surge suppressor or protector are devices such as uninterruptible power supplies (UPS) or stand-by power supplies (SPS). See Figure 4–18. Both SPS and UPS devices basically perform the same function, but UPS performs better than an SPS. A UPS is similar to a bathtub with water running into it: When the water stops running into the tub, it keeps draining until the bathtub is empty. No tub stopper must be removed to empty the bathtub into the drain. UPS power continues directly from the battery, just as the water would continue running out of a bathtub when the input spigot is turned off.

With a stand-by power supply, the tub fills somewhat more slowly and the drain has a stopper. The stopper must be removed to have the bathtub water continue down the drain. Similarly with an SPS, the battery must be switched

Stand-By Power System (SPS)

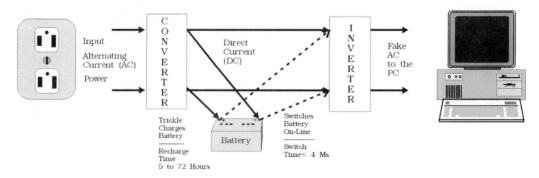

Un-interruptable Power System (UPS)

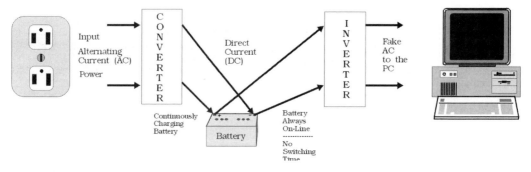

Figure 4–18
SPS versus UPS operation.

into providing electrical power for the PC. With a UPS, no switching is required. Most PC power systems are SPSs.

The cost of an SPS or UPS is about $.40 to $1.00 per Watt. A PC requires a 200 to 650 Watt SPS or UPS depending upon the options installed. The greater the wattage of the UPS or SPS unit, the longer the PC operates without power. A 200-Watt unit may run for as long as 10 minutes, while a 650-Watt unit may run for 30 minutes or longer. See Figure 4–19.

Both SPS and UPS units require periodic battery replacement. Their batteries degrade over a period of several years until they no longer hold a charge.

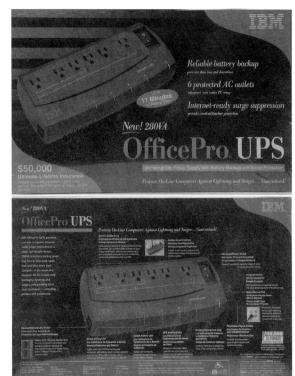

Figure 4-19
IBM 280VA/11 Minute UPS.

Furthermore, SPS and UPS surge suppression capabilities diminish as their MOVs and other components age. The major benefit of using an SPS or UPS over an ordinary surge suppressor is that when power fails and you are working on a PC, the SPS and UPS provide the opportunity to save your work in progress. They also permit a graceful PC shutdown, which can avert some Windows problems from occurring.

Radio Frequency Interference (RFI)

RFI noise is everywhere. It is radiated in the air and is caused by other electrical equipment on the same power line. Electric motors and fluorescent lights produce lots of RF noise. The risk here is that the noise can enter the PCs logic and cause it to make errors.

RFI noise visibly affects monitors. Once a PC's monochrome monitor started breathing (making a shimmering display) on me. The image on the monitor moved in and out as though the monitor was taking shallow breaths. It

283

looked like the monitor was defective, so I returned it on those grounds. Through a lot of convincing, IBM gave me a new monitor, which was installed immediately upon returning to the office. After a short time, the new monitor also began breathing. PC components were powered off to determine when the power drain on the circuit would stop and the breathing would cease. As the PC was about to be turned off, the breathing stopped. So the PC components were turned on one at a time, only to discover that the breathing started when a high intensity lamp next to the monitor was turned on. When the lamp was moved around the outside of the monitor, the breathing followed it. Oops! It looked like a new monitor was not needed after all.

A simple test for the presence of RF signals and noise can be performed using a cheap AM radio. Tuning the radio into the lowest or highest AM frequency normally produces no sound output because there are no stations broadcasting at those frequencies. However, when that same radio is moved close to a PC, static noise is present due to the RF generated by the PC. Moving the radio two feet from the PC eliminates most of the noise. Physical separation of the RF source from the PC is the most effective way to eliminate RFI problems.

Storing Electronic Components

Electronic components have both an operating physical environment and a storage physical environment. The temperature ranges and humidity for an operating PC is a narrower range than is the storage environment, as shown in Table 4–2.

Table 4–2 Operating versus Storage Environment

Parameter	Operating Range	Storage Range
Temperature	10 to 35 degrees Centigrade or 50 to 95 degrees Fahrenheit	–20 to 60 degrees Centigrade or –4 to 140 degrees Fahrenheit
Humidity	15% to 80% relative humidity with no condensation	10% to 90% relative humidity with no condensation

Electronic components should be stored in containers or bags designed to prevent damage from static discharge. This is particularly true of RAM memory SIMMs and DIMMs, RIMMs, and CPUs. Furthermore, since CPU chips can be very expensive and are small enough to be hidden in a pocket, they should be stored in a locked access-controlled area.

The storage area can be exposed to sunlight and does not need to be heated. However, when removing and installing disk drives from a cold environment, they should be given sufficient time to warm up prior to use. Rapid temperature changes are not good for the internal mechanical components of fixed disk drives, where tolerances are very tight. Minimizing temperature shock on a fixed disk drive is best to assure reliable operation.

Study Break: Radio Frequency Interference Sources

Check out the sources of RFI using a battery-powered AM radio.

1. Get a small battery-powered AM radio with good batteries. Tune it to the top or bottom of the AM dial where there are no stations. Hold it up in the middle of the room. It should be perfectly silent.
2. Next, move it over the top of the PC monitor. What happens? Move it slowly away from the monitor. How far away must it be to become quiet again?
3. Test the power cord going into the PC in a similar fashion.
4. Test the desk lamp.
5. Try testing an electric pencil sharpener.

The goal here is to develop a feeling for the presence and impact of radio frequency emissions.

Safety Procedures for High Voltage and Laser Equipment

Some safety precautions are required when servicing and working on PC components. Generally, a malfunctioning component is replaced in its entirety and not repaired—for instance, a bad CD-ROM/CD-RW/DVD drive is replaced by a newer faster CD-ROM/CD-RW/DVD drive for less than the original CD-ROM/CD-RW/DVD drive cost. Components in the CD-ROM/CD-RW/DVD drive are not replaced and thus there is no reason to open it and expose yourself to the laser inside the drive.

Being aware of potential dangers is the first step in preventing serious injury. For example, neckwear can become caught in fans and other moving components. While the motors here are not so powerful as to represent a potential death threat, they can easily strain sensitive neck muscles. Furthermore, they represent a static discharge danger to the PC components. Consequently, it is prudent to ensure that any neckwear does not hang into the components being worked upon. Lasers and high voltages are the primary cause of more serious injury when working on PCs, but other causes of injury are baggy sleeves, long hair, and neckties.

Laser Safety

A laser (Light Amplification by Stimulated Emission of Radiation) is a device producing a monochromatic light beam in which all the waves are in phase or are coherent. All lasers contain four primary components, regardless of use:

- An active medium—This can be solid crystals such as ruby or Nd:YAG, liquid dyes, gases like CO_2 or helium/neon, or semiconductors such as GaAs. The active medium atoms have electrons that can be energized to a meta-stable level by an energy source.

- An excitation mechanism—This pumps energy into the active medium by optical, electrical, or chemical stimulation.

- A high reflectance mirror—This reflects 100 percent of the laser light.

- A partially reflective/transmissive mirror—This mirror reflects less than 100 percent of the laser light and passes (or transmits) the remainder on to the desired destination.

Most laser injuries are eye injuries. They represent about 70 percent of the injuries from exposed lasers. The potential for laser-induced injury varies for different parts of the eye. The cornea, lens, or retina can all be affected depending on the type of laser (that is, the wavelength of the light emitted by the laser), the intensity of the light beam, and how the different parts of the eye absorb the laser energy.

Laser light beams between 400 nanometers (nm) and 1400 nm can be focused by the cornea and lens on the retina. When the beam forms a point of light on the retina, it focuses the power and increases the potential for damage. Diffused laser light beams have a large angle. They are labeled as an extended source and produce a large image on the retina. With a large image, energy is not concentrated in a small area.

Nonetheless, both point source and diffuse laser light can injure the eye.

Potential laser injuries to the eye include temporary welder's flash of the cornea, formation of cataracts, and burning of the retina from light absorption and conversion to heat.

Lasers may also injure the skin, but are of much less concern unless they are high power infrared lasers. Lasers creating ultraviolet light can cause sunburn, skin cancer, and accelerated aging. High power and prolonged exposure are required to produce skin injuries.

Warning labels identify the manufacturer's classification of the lasers used in the PC component they manufacture. Laser classification is based on the following:

- Emitted light wavelength—When a laser emits multiple wavelengths, the most hazardous wavelength determines the classification.

- Average power and limiting exposure time—Continuous wave (CW) or repetitively pulsed lasers are classified using the average power output wattage and the limiting exposure time designed into the laser component.

- Total energy in Joules per pulse, pulse duration, pulse frequency, and beam exposure—Pulsed lasers are classified using the total energy per pulse output, the duration of the pulse, the repetition rate of the pulses and radiant energy of the pulse beam.

Laser classifications are:

- Class 1 lasers—Are not hazardous for continuous viewing and are designed to prevent human access to laser radiation. These can be low-power lasers or higher-power embedded lasers, such as the kind in laser printers. CD-ROM, CD-RW, and DVD drives use Class 1 lasers.

- Class 2 visible lasers—Emit 400 to 700 nm visible light. Because of normal human aversion responses, this class does not normally present a hazard unless viewed directly for an extended time period.

- Class 2A visible lasers—Emit 400 to 700 nm visible light that is not intended for direct viewing. During normal operation, they do not produce eye injury if accidentally viewed directly for less than 1,000 seconds. Bar code scanners use Class 2A lasers.

- Class 3A lasers—Do not normally cause eye injury when viewed momentarily. However, they present a hazard when viewed using lenses like a loupe or a telescope.

- Class 3B lasers—Present both eye and skin hazards when viewed directly. Class 3B lasers are not hazardous when diffusely reflected unless viewed at close proximity.

- Class 4 lasers—Are eye and skin hazards. Eye injury can result from both direct and reflected beam exposures. They are capable of producing skin burns and also starting fires.

Lasers are used in CD-ROMs, CD-RWs, DVDs, and printers. See Figure 4–20. They can potentially blind a person when pointed directly into their eye. Even when not permanently blinded, a person can suffer some retinal damage from exposure to laser light.

Laser safety measures include keeping the laser in its protective covering, power interlocks preventing inadvertent exposure, disconnecting power, covering the laser with shrouds to prevent exposure, and wearing eye protection. As a fundamental safety measure, access to the work area where lasers are exposed should be restricted so that someone does not walk into the service area and become accidentally injured by a laser beam.

Whenever working on laser equipment, safety dictates that the laser should be covered so that if it is inadvertently powered on, people are not exposed to damaging laser light. This means that CD-ROMs and DVDs should not be opened where the laser can be exposed. Interlocks that prevent an exposed laser from powering on should not be bypassed during service. Laser protective eyewear is available and can be worn to protect from inadvertent laser exposure; most protective eyewear is designed to be used with Class 3B and Class 4 lasers.

Figure 4–20
CD Drive Laser Labels.

High Voltage Components and Safety Procedures

Voltage or Electromotive Force (EMF) is related to Current (C), Intensity (I), and Resistance (R). EMF is measured in volts, Current (Intensity) is measured in amperes, and Resistance is measured in Ohms. The relationship between EMF (Volts), Intensity (current in amperes), and Resistance (R in ohms) is:

EMF (Volts) = Intensity (current in amperes) times Resistance (ohms)
or (E=I*R)
Intensity (current in amperes) = EMF (Volts) divided by Resistance (ohms)
or (I=E/R)
Resistance (ohms) = EMF (Volts) divided by Intensity (current in amperes)
or (R=E/I)

The power output or consumption is measured in Watts. Watts (W) are:

Watts = EMF (Volts) times Intensity (current in amperes) or (W=E*I)

These basic electrical equations are helpful in understanding PC power and safety. Two last concepts are Direct Current (DC) and Alternating Current (AC) power. DC comes from batteries or devices that convert AC power to DC power. DC operates as it is named, the current flows directly (in one direction only) from positive to negative or from the power source to ground. PCs operate mainly on DC. DC voltage levels are generally low (12-volts, 5-volts, and lower). AC constantly changes direction so that electrons and power are constantly reversing direction. Generally these reversals are expressed as cycles or Hertz. Our home power here in North America is 60 Cycle or 60 Hz, 120 volt AC power. Power Companies use power generating equipment produce AC power. Transformers take advantage of these AC power reversals to break down the high voltage power delivered by the Power Company to lower voltage power we use in homes and businesses. The PC power supply takes the high power AC feed from a wall socket and further breaks it down into lower power DC for use in the PC.

After protection from lasers, the second safety area is protection from exposure to electrical power. PCs convert 120 AC 60 Hz or 240 AC 50 Hz power into 5-volts and 12-volts DC power. The 5-volt and 12-volt DC power is low voltage and not directly hazardous to humans, while 240-volt AC power is potentially lethal for humans. However, both low 12-volt and 5-volt DC power and high 120-volt and 240-volt AC power can be dangerous. The basic safety principal for handling high voltages is to have a ground that bypasses the person servicing the high voltage component. The ground must route the high voltage directly to earth ground for the facility. Each facility and work area should have an earth ground that is directly wired to a metal stake driven into the earth outside the building. The earth ground for the PC (the green lead) should be connected to the earth ground for the work area and the facility.

All tools should provide adequate insulation to prevent shock from AC power. Power tools should be grounded, insulated, or battery-powered for optimal safety. When working on or around electrically charged equipment, conductors, or circuits, OSHA's "Safety Related Work Practices" require using insulated tools. The sidebar provides excerpts from the OSHA regulations pertaining to working on electrically charged equipment.

CFR 1910.269, APPENDIX B

NOTE: ...When any object is said to be insulated, it is understood to be insulated for the conditions to which it is normally subjected...

...Installations energized at 50 to 300 volts: the hazards posed by installations energized at 50 to 300 volts are the same as those found in many other work places ... the employee must avoid contact with the exposed parts, and the protective equipment used (such as rubber insulating gloves) must provide insulation for the voltages involved.

CFR 1910.335, Safeguards for Personnel Protection

...When working near exposed energized conductors or circuit parts, each employee shall use insulated tools or handling equipment if the tools or handling equipment might make contact with such conductors or parts. If the insulated tools or handling equipment are subject to damage, the insulated material shall be protected...

...Protective equipment shall be maintained in a safe, reliable condition and shall be periodically inspected or tested, as required by 1910.137...

CFR 1910.137, Insulating Equipment

...Insulating equipment shall be inspected for damage before each day's use and immediately following any incident that can reasonably be suspected of having caused damage ... Insulating equipment with any of the following defects may not be used: a hole, tear, puncture or cut... Repaired insulating equipment shall be retested before it may be used by employees...

The power supply, the power supply switch, the power cord, and the monitor all have high voltages. The high voltage from the wall outlet enters the PC from the rear and is commonly routed to an AC power switch on the PC's front panel. Newer PCs have the high voltage controlled by relays inside the power supply so that no dangerous voltages are exposed to humans. Generally, hazardous voltages are kept inside the power supply.

Since power switches on PC front panels have potential high-voltage power running to them, all leads must be covered by electrical insulation that insulates both 120-volt and 240-volt power. When the switch is being worked on, the PC should be unplugged from its AC power source.

When working on other PC components that are not high-powered, the PC should be grounded via the power cord or a separate ground connection from the chassis to the facility earth ground. Optimal safety would employ both the power cord and the separate earth ground.

All power circuits should be on circuit breakers. For servicing, 15-ampere circuits are sufficient. Operating circuits may have higher amperage.

Low-voltage power can be hazardous when it is shorted to ground and produces high current flow and high heat in the shorted circuit. When handling and working with 12-volt and 5-volt DC power, the key safety precaution is to remove all metal that may contact power leads. The risk here is not from electrical shock, but rather from a burn that can easily happen as the metal rapidly heats up from a high current flow. In our equations above, we show that Amperes equals Volts divided by Resistance. High resistance causes few amperes to flow, but gold and silver in jewelry are excellent conductors (better than copper) that have little resistance. That means if they connect power to ground, a high current flow results producing heat. This heat can easily produce a severe burn. Working around a powered on PC with tools or even jewelry could cause this type of situation, so always unplug the PC before beginning to work on or with it.

The heat from a low-voltage short can easily and seriously burn a person's finger, neck, or wrist. To be absolutely safe, service personnel should remove jewelry such as rings and bracelets from their hands and wrists. Metallic neckwear also presents a potential safety hazard if it shorts a low-voltage circuit.

PC Power Supply Safety

When work is done inside a PC power supply, such as replacing a failed fan, the power supply should be unplugged from its AC power source. Special attention must be paid to the high-voltage connections inside the supply to ensure that they do not become shorted during any repairs performed inside the power supply.

Some PC power supplies have safety circuits built in that shut them down in the event of a DC short. Older power supplies incorporated such a crowbar circuit, but some of the newer, cheaper supplies do not. Supplies without such protection just keep supplying DC power to the shorted connection, causing heat and potential fire damage. If a PC powers up and fails to boot, carefully check all power connections, especially those into 3.5-inch floppy drives. Feel the power lines to determine if any are warm or hot. This is a certain indication of a power short.

Liquids are hazardous inside power supplies. Water causes high-voltage shorts, and volatile compounds can catch fire, resulting in serious burns. Power supplies should not be cleaned using liquid cleaners. In a seminar, we tried replacing a burnt-out fuse in a power supply that was in a PC that had had water sprayed into it during a fire. The PC was fine, but the power supply fuse was burned out. We replaced the fuse and went to demonstrate that the power supply had been returned to service by powering it on. When we did, blue flames shot out the rear through the fan. Liquids should never be used in a power supply.

Monitor Voltages and Safety

Monitors use a high-voltage transformer to provide voltage to the picture tube screen, making electrons emitted at the rear of the picture tube fly into it. The voltage levels generated are in the 10,000s of volts. When a monitor is powered down, this high-voltage is still retained by the picture tube. It can eventually drain off, but this can take days or weeks. Such high voltage is potentially lethal to humans. Also, AC power flows directly into the monitor, exposing that high voltage any time the monitor is worked on.

Since monitors are typically not serviceable in the field, there is little need to open them and expose these high voltages. However, in the rare instance when monitor adjustments or repairs are performed, the monitor should be disconnected from AC power, have its chassis grounded to the facility earth ground (not the power cord ground) and the picture tube high-voltage drained to ground. A screwdriver attached to the facility earth ground and inserted into the picture tube feed from the high-voltage transformer dissipates the high-voltage charge, reducing the potential shock hazard.

Warning

All tools used to adjust and work on a monitor must be insulated. They should be able to insulate the service person from a 100,000-volt electrical charge. Only trained technicians should undertake this type of work.

Study Break: CD-Cleaning and Maintenance

Clean a CD-ROM drive using cleaning supplies obtained at a local audio or electronics department store.

1. Get a CD-ROM lens cleaning kit from a local audio store or an electronics department store.
2. Use the lens cleaner to clean the lens of a CD-ROM drive by inserting the cleaning disk and performing the DIR command several times.
3. Find a CD-ROM drive that is behaving badly. Clean the lens of this drive. Does it improve its behavior? If not, examine the CD-ROMs that are being read by the drive. Are they dirty or badly scratched?
4. Try an XCOPY command to see if the CD-ROM drive can read the CD-ROM after cleaning. Remember to remove all data from the target drive using a DELTREE after you are finished testing the CD-ROM drive.

Hazardous Waste Disposal

The PC contains some items that use hazardous materials. The most common are batteries used in the PC and in the PC's SPS or UPS. Other items requiring hazardous waste or recycled waste disposal include the monitor, laser toner cartridges, chemical cleaning compounds and solvents, and paper.

Batteries

Lithium batteries are used to power the CMOS memory in PCs. Lead Acid batteries are used to provide backup power in SPS and UPS units. NiMH and Li-Ion batteries are used in laptop PCs for mobile power. These batteries all contain toxic materials and compounds such as lead and mercury. If a battery is leaking, make sure you are wearing gloves before you touch it, and make sure you thoroughly clean the area around it to ensure there are no residual chemicals present. The batteries do wear out over time, requiring replacement. When the old batteries are disposed of, they should be set aside and sent to the special battery disposal section of the local municipalities' waste disposal facility. These battery disposal sections recycle some battery components for raw materials (like the lead) and dispose of others in an environmentally safe fashion.

CRTs

Cathode Ray Tubes (CRTs) are a potential hazard because of the picture tube. They also have transformers that may contain toxic chemicals. The picture tube contains lots of glass and a high vacuum inside. If it is cracked or broken, it could implode (the opposite of explode) and spray glass shards in its immediate vicinity. As a result, old CRTs should be sent to an appropriate office equipment recycling facility where their picture tube and other internal components are safely recycled.

Laser Toner Cartridges

Laser toner cartridges contain plastic parts and some toxic materials so they should not just be thrown away. It is a good idea to wear gloves when you change the cartridges, and occasionally you should vacuum the particles out of the printer. Toner cartridge manufacturers provide recycling mailers with the toner cartridges when they are sold. These should be saved in a safe place along with the toner cartridge box. Once the cartridge is expended and can no longer be used, it should be shipped back to the manufacturer's recycling facility.

Recycled cartridges are often sold with the provision that the expended cartridge is returned to reduce the price of the replacement cartridge. Cartridge recyclers provide mailing labels that can be attached to the recycled cartridge box to send back to the facility.

In both instances, the boxes and packing materials should be saved to facilitate shipment of the expended laser cartridge to a laser cartridge recycling facility.

Solvents

Alcohol and volatile solvents are sometimes used in small quantities to clean PC components. They are quickly vaporized in the atmosphere. When large quantities are used, they must be applied in a room that vents their fumes through an air scrubber to the outside. The best approach for disposing of volatile solvents is to minimize their use.

Other

Water-based detergents and other cleaning supplies should be biodegradable, or else they should not be used. Biodegradable supplies can be disposed of by pouring into a building drain that runs into a sewage treatment facility. Pouring these chemicals down a storm drain or any other untreated drain is not an acceptable disposal procedure. Only drains running into sewage treatment facilities provide acceptable disposal for these biodegradable chemicals.

Study Break: Checking Batteries

Use a multimeter to check the voltage levels of batteries used in any PC equipment such as speakers, MP3 players, and dictation devices.

1. Get a multimeter and test the voltages in PC devices using batteries. The batteries should be at or above their specified voltage. Any batteries below their designated voltage level are suspect and should be replaced.
2. Power off the PC and unplug the UPS. Open the battery compartment and test the battery voltage level. If it is below the specified voltage level, consider replacing the battery.

Electrostatic Discharge (ESD) Procedures

Static electricity, most commonly created by friction and separation, is an electrical charge at rest. Friction causes heat that excites the molecular particles in a material. When two materials are later separated, electrons transfer from one material to the other, creating an absence or surplus of electrons in the materials. This absence or surplus produces an electrical field known as static electricity.

Simply separating materials always generates static electrical fields. The intensity of the static electricity generated depends upon the materials separated, the amount of friction between the materials, and the relative humidity at the time of separation. Common plastic typically creates an intense static charge. Low humidity (such as is present when air is heated during the winter) also promotes generation of intense static electrical charges.

A material like copper that easily transfers electrons between atoms is called a conductor. Copper has "free" electrons. Other conductors are metals, carbon, and human sweat. Insulators are materials that do not readily transfer electrons. Well-known insulators are common plastics, glass, and air. Conductors and insulators may become charged with static electricity. Because of their free electrons, charged conductors discharge rapidly when they come close to another conductor with a different potential.

Typical electrostatic voltages generated by common daily activities are shown in Table 4–3.

Table 4–3   Activities and ESD

Activity	Static electricity produced 10% relative humidity	Static electricity produced 55% relative humidity
Walking across carpet	35,000 volts	7,500 volts
Walking across untreated vinyl floor	12,000 volts	3,000 volts
Working at a bench	6,000 volts	400 volts
Opening a plastic envelope	26,000 volts	7,000 volts
Picking up a plastic bag	20,000 volts	1,200 volts
Removing chips from plastic tube	2,000 volts	400 volts

Electrostatic discharge or static discharge is a very high voltage spark with almost no current. ESD can last from a few nanoseconds to microseconds.

Static discharge can give both you and a PC a very nasty shock. Remember to try this for fun: Carry your PC on a rubber wheeled cart across wool hotel carpet on a cold dry winter day, then touch the door handle to a hotel room. Zappo! Static discharge shoots several inches. The PC should be fine because the cart and the human carry the static charge to ground.

Static discharge poses the most damage to the PC's chips, particularly the newer high-density CPU, logic and memory chips. When the chips receive a more or less direct static discharge in one pin, the chip can be damaged or destroyed. A charge that can destroy chips may not be noticed or felt by a human.

ESD Damage

Static electricity or electrostatic discharge can cause circuits in chips to have breakdowns in the gate oxide, shorting the circuit, spiking junctions, or latching the logic to a fixed state, often rendering the chips unusable. This shorting by static electricity is possible because circuit components in chips are only a few atoms wide. Even the small current produced in a static discharge looms large to such circuit components. ESD at relatively low voltage levels (between 200 to 2,000 volts) is dangerous to the most densely packed chips. These chips are CPU, Application Specific Integrated Circuits (ASICs), and RAM chips.

As chips get smaller and more powerful, the risk and cost of ESD damage increases. ESD damage can remain hidden for days, weeks, or even months after the ESD shock occurs. ESD is as short as one billionth of a second, and its most visible and dangerous form is lightning in thunderstorms. Voltages as low as 200 volts can damage devices; ESD is felt at around 3,000 volts and heard at around 6,000 volts. Visible sparks occur at levels of about 8,000 volts or more. At low voltage levels, ESD is not harmful to human beings, and cannot be felt, heard, or seen, even though it still damages or destroys electronic components.

Because high-voltage ESD tends to travel over the surface of the PC or component when neutralizing the charge, assembled PCs are less susceptible to damage than are disassembled PCs. Our portable PCs have withstood without incident many ESD events because they were fully assembled so that the chassis provided a pathway for the discharge to follow. Some keyboards and other devices are designed to absorb and conduct a static discharge of as high as 17 KVA to ground.

Protecting from ESD

Eliminating static charge generation and transfer are primarily accomplished by grounding service personnel and PCs. Some prevention techniques are as follows:

- Service personnel grounding—Static wrist straps drain off a service person's static charge. The wrist strap or ESD cuff must stay in constant contact with bare skin. It has a cable connecting it to a ground. Wrist straps have a current-limiting resistor for personnel safety. Wrist straps are tested frequently to ensure that they operate correctly. If attaching a wrist strap is impractical, special heel straps or shoes can be used to ground service personnel. Heel straps and shoes must be used in conjunction with a dissipating floor to be effective.

- Protective ESD clothing/smocks—Even though a wrist strap is used, clothing must not come in close contact with components or computer boards because the material in clothing generates high static charges. Protective ESD coveralls or smocks serve as a barrier/shield between an electrostatic field on clothing and the sensitive components.

- Antistatic or static dissipating mats—Mats provide a controlled discharge of static voltages when grounded. Surface resistance is designed to generate no more than 100 volts when sliding computer boards across the mat's surface.

- Antistatic or static dissipating chairs—Physical movement of the chair and your feet on the floor charge chairs. An antistatic chair is conductive with conductive wheels, and/or the frame grounded by a drag chain to the floor.

- Antistatic or static dissipating floor or floor mat—Floor mats dissipate static charges from personnel moving in a room. Conductive tile or floor treatments are used to dissipate static charges if mats are not practical or cause a safety hazard. Floor mats prevent accumulation of static electricity by quickly draining it from workers. They protect potentially volatile areas from dangerous sparks. Floor mats should be made of resilient sponge base material designed to reduce standing worker fatigue. Mats must have a grounding strap. Maximum effectiveness requires grounding the mat using the strap and keeping its surface clean. Industry specifications for smooth surface mats have a surface-to-surface resistance of 4×10^4 ohms and a surface-to-ground resistance of 4×10^4 ohms. Specifications for diamond plate surface mats have a surface-to-surface resistance of 10^5 ohms and a surface-to-ground resistance of 10^5 ohms.

- Air ionizers—Air ionizers provide some protection when all static electricity generators cannot be removed from an area. An air ionizer creates a stream of ionized air that neutralizes static charges for a short period of time.

- Electrostatic field meters—These meters measure the electrostatic voltage in a given area.

- Charge plate analyzer—These analyzers evaluate ionization systems by how quickly applied charges are neutralized.

- Static awareness labels—ESD-sensitive PC components and cards must be labeled to warn that they must be opened only in ESD-controlled environments. ESD damage to PC cards or components occurs most often when they are disassembled and are improperly handled. Damage is manifested in complete or intermittent failures. The following procedures prevent ESD damage:

- Use an ESD-preventive wrist or ankle strap to ground you to the component being worked upon. Ensure that the wrist or ankle strap has good skin contact.
- When handling PC components or touching any internal PC components, always use a wrist strap connected to one of the following:
  - Installation screws on the installed module or power supply,
  - Special ESD wrist strap connectors built into the PC (if present), or
  - Any unpainted chassis surface to make good electrical contact with the chassis.
- Handle PC cards by their edges only.
- Avoid contact between the PC cards, components, and clothing. A wrist strap protects only the card from ESD voltages on the body. ESD voltages on clothing may still cause damage.
- After removing any PC card or component, place it on an anti-static surface or in a static-shielding bag. PC cards or components that are being shipped should be immediately placed in a static-shielding bag.
- Periodically check the resistance value of antistatic straps to ensure they are between 1 and 10 million ohms (mega ohms).
- Humidity reduces the potential for static discharge. During cold dry winter months, increasing the humidity in a facility reduces the incidence of ESD. Aquariums throughout the office add humidity in addition to a pleasant and soothing view. Alternately, humidifiers also provide the required humidity without the aesthetic view. Both are excellent mechanisms for increasing humidity and reducing the potential for ESD. Fabric softener in a water solution can be sprayed around a room to temporarily reduce the potential for ESD.

Common ESD Environments

Virtually all environments develop static charges when materials are separated. The amount of static build up depends on the materials, the humidity and the duration of the separation process; for instance, opening a bag versus sliding or rolling a PC across a desktop. Environments that have lots of plastic compounds tend to have a greater propensity to build static charges than environments that do not.

Environments with insulators like plastics generate a surface resistance ranging from 10^{12} to 10^{20} ohms; these environments build large static charges, hold them for several hours, and attract conductive dirt, producing conductive paths dangerous to electronic semiconductor components. Conductive materials with surface resistances ranging from 10^4 to 10^{12} ohms do not hold static charges unless they are isolated (insulated) from a grounding path. Once connected to a grounding path, they discharge their static charges in nanoseconds. Ideally, static-free environments should be based on dissipative materials. Dissipative materials have a surface resistance ranging from 10^4 to 10^{12} ohms, and permit lessening of static charges at controlled rates, not in sudden damaging discharges. Common ESD environments where PCs and components are susceptible to ESD damage include when PCs are disassembled and their components and circuit boards are moved, i.e., when they are shipped to and moved around various facilities. This is particularly true in cold dry environments. Table coverings, flooring, and carpets can contribute significantly to the buildup of static charges. Nonconductive plastic and vinyl flooring create unwanted static charges, while conductive, static dissipative flooring minimizes static charge build up.

Study Break: ESD Inventory

Make an inventory of the measures in place in your facility to prevent or reduce ESD.

1. Are there specific times each year when there is low humidity? Are special static discharge precautions taken at those times?
2. What measures are generally in place to reduce ESD in the general office environment? Are antistatic carpets and mats used? Are PCs, desks, and carpets grounded so static charges can drain away? Is the air humidified?
3. What measures are used in PC service areas? Are there antistatic mats and straps available and used when equipment is disassembled? This is especially important when working on CPUs and memory. Are there standard ESD practices and procedures for your organization?

Summary

This chapter covered PC maintenance, cleaning, and safety procedures. These are an important part of everyday PC operation but often times ignored. The first section involved proactive measures to be taken around regular preventive maintenance of the PC and its individual components. This was followed by a detailed discussion of power-related issues and the types of hazards that can affect the PC's operating environment, such as power surges and brownouts, along with some safeguards against these hazards.

The next section covered safety procedures specific to high- and low-voltage power components and laser equipment that is commonly found in CD-ROMs/CD-RWs/DVDs. The types of technologies used in these products can cause damage or injury if not used wisely, and the PC technician is at risk without sufficient knowledge of potential dangers and diligent practice of safeguards.

The section on hazardous waste focused on the types of waste material generated by common PC components such as batteries, toner cartridges, video displays, and even the products used to clean the systems. For each of these topics, proper handling and disposal procedures were covered.

The last section of this chapter detailed the issue of electrostatic discharge (ESD). It discussed the causes of this hazard and the effects it has on PCs and their components; we also covered prevention methods. Following proper safety, cleaning, and ESD procedures and precautions prolong the useful life of PCs and PC components. More importantly, they help avert unanticipated hardware failures causing serious work delays and disruptions.

Chapter Review Questions

1. *What does SPS mean?*

    A. Stand-by Power Source
    B. Stand-by Power Supply
    C. Static Power Supply
    D. Static Power Source

Answer: B, Stand-by Power Supply. Although it is a source of power for the PC, the device is really a power supply and not one that is static.

2. *A principal enemy of most PCs is:*

    A. Grease
    B. Soot
    C. Dust
    D. Sand

Answer: C, dust. While grease, soot, and sand all make the PC dirty and cause heat build up, they are not as prevalent and as insulating a material as is dust.

3. *Water must never be used directly to clean PCs.*

    A. True
    B. False

Answer: B, false. Water-based cleaning compounds should not be used in electronic and electrical components, but they can clean various PC surfaces.

4. *Special cleaning compounds are used to clean* _____.

    A. The outside of the PC chassis
    B. Electrical contacts and connectors
    C. The PC case
    D. The monitor
    E. The keyboard

Answer: B, electrical contacts and connectors. The PC chassis, case, monitor and keyboard are cleaned be a variety of common and special cleaning compounds and devices. Only special cleaning compounds should be used on electrical components.

5. *What PC component collects the most dust?*

    A. The display controller
    B. RAM
    C. The keyboard
    D. The power supply

Answer: D, the power supply. The RAM, keyboard, and display controller (card inside the PC) all collect some dust, but the power supply collects the most dust because almost all of the PC cooling air flows through it. The charged dust particles in the air tend to adhere themselves to the electrically charged power supply components.

6. *Dust causes* _____.

    A. Fixed disk motor failures
    B. Heat to build up in PC components
    C. Monitor flickering
    D. Sticky keyboard keys

Answer: B, heat to build up in PC components. Dust insulates all PC components causing heat build-up. Disk motors fail because of mechanical impairment or bearing seizure, monitor flickering is caused by RF interference, and sticky keyboards are caused by soda or coffee spills.

7. *Water-based cleaners are dangerous* _____.

    A. When cleaning monitors
    B. Around high-voltage components
    C. On RAM
    D. Near option cards

Answer: B, around high-voltage components. Anything with high voltages (a high-voltage is any voltage over 24-volts, but generally 120-volts and higher) is dangerous to clean with water. This would include the monitor if the water were to drip inside it. RAM and other option cards use 5-volt power, so there is little danger with water in these parts.

8. *All PCs should have* _____.

    A. A 20-amphere circuit supplying power
    B. A surge suppressor in the input power line
    C. A UPS
    D. An SPS
    E. All of the above

Answer: B, a surge suppressor in the input power line. While a 20-ampere circuit, an SPS and a UPS are all desirable for every PC, the most basic need is a surge suppressor.

9. *A surge is:*

    A. A loss of power
    B. A change in power
    C. An instantaneous increase in voltage
    D. A short duration increase in voltage
    E. A static discharge

Answer: D, a short duration increase in voltage. Surge is a short duration increase in power from the AC power line, like a storm surge increases water inland from the ocean. A change in power could be an increase or decrease, an instant increase is too fast to be a surge, and a static discharge is caused by ESD and not by the power line.

10. *What does MOV mean?*

    A. Metal On Varistor
    B. Metallic Oxygen Variable Resistor
    C. Metal Oxide Resistor
    D. Metal On Resistor
    E. Metal Oxide Variable-resistor

Answer: C, Metal Oxide Variable-resistor. Metal is always the first word, the main component is chemically an oxide, and the function is that of a variable-resistor. With increased voltage, the MOV resistance drops to short the spike to ground.

11. *A power line spike is commonly caused by what?*

    A. Coffee makers on the PC power line
    B. The power company transformers
    C. Lightning hitting a phone line
    D. Thunderstorms

Answer: D, thunderstorms. Certainly lightning is the source of spikes, but they must hit the power line and not the phone line to be power line spikes. Coffee makers cause voltage sags, and transformers convert from high voltage to lower, more usable voltage levels.

12. *To absolutely ensure that lightning does not damage a PC, you must:*

    A. Turn off the power to the PC
    B. Install a surge suppressor
    C. Disconnect all cables from the PC
    D. Unplug the PC

Answer: C, disconnect all cables from the PC. Every switch has three wires (hot, return and ground), so turning off a power switch leaves two wires (return and ground) for spikes to travel into the PC. Unplugging the PC does not prevent surges from traveling into the PC from the LAN, monitor, modem and any other electrical connection to the PC.

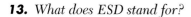

13. *What does ESD stand for?*

    A. Electro Sensitive Device
    B. Electrostatic Device
    C. Static Electricity
    D. Electrostatic Discharge
    E. Electronic Sensitive Discharge

Answer: D, Electrostatic Discharge. There are no devices in a discharge, and static electricity may be the high-voltage source of the discharge but not our answer. While electronics are sensitive to ESD they are not part of the name.

14. *What materials generate static charges?*

    A. Steel
    B. Plastics
    C. Water
    D. Carbon

Answer: B, plastics. Steel, water, and carbon tend to conduct away static charges, but those darn plastics used in keyboards, front panels, tables, etc. do not dissipate static charges.

15. *Abrasive compounds are helpful in cleaning what?*

    A. Plastic surfaces
    B. Semiconductor chip surfaces
    C. SIMM sockets
    D. Rubber cable stains

Answer: A, plastic surfaces. Chips, sockets and rubber cable are not good candidates for cleaning with abrasive compounds because the abrasive residue may damage them. Further, SIMMs and chips are not generally cleaned unless you plan to take pictures of them for a book. Plastic surfaces can become marked or scuffed so that cleaning with a mild abrasive compound may be required.

16. *To prevent damage from static discharge, what should you do?*

    A. Wear a wrist strap touching your skin and grounded to a common earth ground
    B. Increase humidity in dry environments
    C. Wear antistatic smocks or coveralls
    D. Install static dissipative floor mats
    E. Test and inspect static dissipative components regularly
    F. None of A through E above
    G. All of A through E above

Answer: G, all of A through E above. The answer says it all.

17. *PC CD-ROM drives, DVD drives and CD-RW drives use* _____.

    A. Class 3 lasers
    B. Class 4 lasers
    C. Class 2A lasers
    D. Class 1 lasers

Answer: D, class 1 lasers. The other laser classes are higher-powered lasers used in other devices and applications.

18. *When working with lasers, the greatest danger is what?*

    A. Blowing the CPU chip
    B. Burning the skin burn
    C. Erasing nonvolatile RAM
    D. Losing hair
    E. None of the above

Answer: E, none of the above. Working on a CD drive does not in any way impact the CPU unless the CD drive is dropped on the CPU chip, in which case the chip is crushed not blown. CD lasers are low power enough that they do not erase non-volatile memory and don't burn the skin. Losing hair is caused by aging and genetic factors, of which I am well aware.

19. *What do static wrist straps contain?*

    A. Plastic
    B. A resistor
    C. A transistor
    D. A watch

Answer: B, a resistor. Wrist straps have a resistive component in them, but no watch, transistor or plastic.

Chapter 5

CPUs, RAM, AND MAIN LOGIC BOARDS

Chapter Syllabus

- CPU Chips and Their Operating Characteristics

- Random Access Memory (RAM)

- Main Logic Boards (MLBs)

- PC Bus Architectures

- CMOS Setup

This chapter covers the specific terminology and specifications describing CPU chips, random access memory, main logic boards, PC buses, and CMOS setup. A detailed understanding of these parts helps in determining which PC core components can be replaced and upgraded.

The key components of a PC system lie in the PC chassis. These components, Central Processing Unit (CPU), Random Access Memory (RAM), and Main Logic Board (MLB) form the heart of any PC system. They are the pri-

307

mary determinants of PC performance and provide the ability to add the ancillary components that tailor each PC system to the tasks that it is to perform—running games, preparing documents, surfing the Web, and more.

The CPU is the component that performs all the work. We think of it as the hands of the PC. There are no brains in the CPU, but very fast hands. The CPU swaps data with the RAM across a CPU bus. The RAM provides the workspace for the software running in the PC. It is volatile, which means that it loses its contents when electrical power is turned off. The MLB provides the mechanical mounting for the CPU, RAM, and option boards. It is designed with a hierarchical structure of buses to support option cards with different bus interfaces—Industry Standard Architecture (ISA), Peripheral Component Interconnect (PCI), and Advanced Graphics Port (AGP) interfaces. This chapter examines these components in detail.

CPU Chips and Their Operating Characteristics

Intel is the largest manufacturer of PC Central Processing Unit (CPU) chips. American Micro Devices (AMD) and others manufacture CPU chips (like the Cyrix and Alpha chips) competing with the Intel CPU chip functionality. These chips provide performance equivalent to some Intel chips at substantially lower prices. Apple computers use chips manufactured by Motorola and some servers use Alpha chips manufactured originally by Digital Equipment Corporation that are not exact functional duplicates of the Intel chips. These chips run other operating systems like Apple Mac OS or UNIX or they run Intel chip emulation programs permitting Windows to run on them at lower performance levels. Windows NT/2000 has been adapted to run directly on Alpha chip computers. Regardless of the CPU chip features, the main difference between chips boils down to better performance. What really matters is how the CPU chip design delivers faster software execution. Chip features are nice, but the bottom line is execution speed. Let's examine these chips in greater detail.

The core or heart of a PC is the CPU chip. It is a complete computer on a single chip. By "complete computer," we mean that this chip has everything needed to execute program instructions performing data manipulation: a control unit, an Arithmetic Logic Unit (ALU), data registers, cache memory, and more. These microprocessor CPU chip internal units are driven by a raw PC clock signal external to the CPU itself. How effectively and efficiently the CPU runs software depends on its design or architecture. The CPU's architecture describes the internal way it processes data, which is one of the most important factors in determining overall PC performance. Another significant performance factor is raw external clock signal speed, or the megahertz (MHz) speed at which the CPU processes data. The CPU's external interfaces describe how it transfers data to and from the memory, the supporting chip set, and other devices in the PC.

Intel CPU Chips

Intel was, among others, a pioneer in developing a microprocessor CPU chip. As mentioned above, microprocessor CPU chips have a complete computer on a single chip. CPU chip or microprocessor CPU chip capabilities have increased at an exponential rate in the 30 years since they were originally developed. This increase in capability is largely due to the ability to fabricate and produce more powerful semiconductor CPU chips in larger quantities. Intel produces the largest number of microprocessor CPU chips used in PCs today. The Intel microprocessor PC CPU chip architecture evolved from the design of Intel's 8088 CPU chip introduced in April 1979. This CPU chip was used in the original IBM PC marketed in 1981. See Table 5–1. The latest Intel CPU chips are the Pentium 4 and the Itanium. Both are based upon the 0.18-micron (and soon on the 0.13-micron) technology that increases CPU speeds. The Pentium 4 is a continuation of the existing 32-bit or IA-32 chip architecture. It has been enhanced with added instructions, new instruction cache operation, and other features to improve performance. The Pentium 4 will be used in PCs and servers over the next several years. The Itanium chip is the first 64-bit chip using the new IA-64 chip architecture. It was developed by Intel and other chip manufacturers, including HP. It's first implementation will be in high-end Internet servers, but we can expect the technology to slowly migrate to desktop workstations and eventually to PCs.

CPU chips perform three basic functions within the PC: data input/output (I/O), CPU control functions, and arithmetic logical operations. Separate components in the CPU chip perform these functions. The CPU passes software commands and data to other parts of the PC requesting them, and back to the CPU through the I/O unit. Data from the I/O unit is translated into a useable form for the ALU by the control unit. ALU performs arithmetic and logical operations on the data, as directed by the control unit. Arithmetic operations are addition, subtraction, multiplication and division. Logical operations are "and," "or," "not," and "exclusive or." The ALU hands the results of its arithmetic and logical operations back to the I/O unit, which in turn transfers the results to CPU registers, PC RAM, or elsewhere. These functions are identified in how the CPU chip interfaces to the other components in the PC. See Figure 5–1.

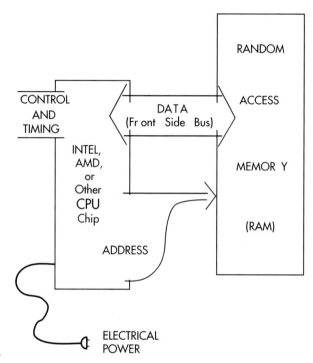

Figure 5-1
CPU chip PC interfaces.

Instruction Sets

CPUs are designed as Complex Instruction Set Computers (CISC) or as Reduced Instruction Set Computers (RISC). A single CISC instruction can be designed to perform a complex operation, while RISC CPU's contain a smaller set of basic instructions that can be combined to create complex instructions. Consequently, a CISC instruction needs a long time to finish because the electrical signals used to perform the work must flow through many logic gates. RISC instructions finish quickly compared to CISC instructions because they use few logic gates. A RISC instruction completes in about one fifth the time required to complete a CISC instruction. However, generally four RISC instructions are needed to perform the work of a single CISC instruction, making a RISC CPU faster than a CISC CPU. In reality, the equation is more complex but the end result is accurate. An offsetting factor is that if the software is optimized for a CISC CPU, the RISC CPU may need to complete more instructions to run the software, equalizing the CISC and RISC performance. Intel CPU chips are generally CISC chips.

Table 5-1 Intel CPU Chip Summary

CPU Chip	Internal Word Size	Data Bus	Addressable RAM	Clock Speed	Internal Cache	Math Co-CPU Chip	Operating Systems
8088	16 bit	8 bit	1 MB	4.77 MHz to 10 MHz	None	External	DOS
8086	16 bit	16 bit	1 MB	4.77 MHz to 10 MHz	None	External	DOS
80286	16 bit	16 bit	16 MB	6 MHz to 20 MHz	None	External	DOS
80386 DX	32 bit	32 bit	4,096 MB	16 MHz, 20 MHz, 25 MHz, 33 MHz, and 40 MHz	None	External	Windows
80386 SX	32 bit	16 bit	16 MB	16 MHz, 20 MHz, and 25 MHz	None	External	Windows
80486 DX	32 bit	32 bit	4,096 MB	25 MHz, 33 MHz, and 50 MHz	8 KB	Internal	Windows 3.x
80486 SX	32 bit	32 bit	4,096 MB	16 MHz, 20 MHz, and 25 MHz	8 KB	Disabled External	Windows 3.x
80486 DX	32 bit	32 bit	4,096 MB	20/40 MHz, 25/50 MHz and 33/66 MHz	8 KB	Internal	Windows 3.x
Pentium 80586 DX	32 bit	64 bit	4,096 MB	60 MHz, 90 MHz, 120 MHz, 133 MHz, 166 MHz, 200 MHz and higher	8 KB instruction 8 KB data	Internal	Windows & Windows NT/2000
Pentium MMX	32 bit	64 bit	4 GB	166 MHz, 200 MHz and higher	16 KB instruction 16 KB data	Internal	Windows

Table 5–1 Intel CPU Chip Summary (Continued)

CPU Chip	Internal Word Size	Data Bus	Addressable RAM	Clock Speed	Internal Cache	Math Co-CPU Chip	Operating Systems
Pentium II	32 bit	64 bit	4 GB	200 MHz, 233 MHz, 266 MHz, 300 MHz, 400 MHz, 450 MHz, and higher	16 KB instruction 16 KB data and 256KB L2 Cache	Internal	Windows
Celeron	32 bit	64 bit	4 GB	266, 300, 333, 366, 400, 433, 466, 500, 533, 566, 600, 633, 667, 700, 733, 766, 800, 850, 900 MHz and higher	16 KB instruction 16 KB data and 128 KB L2 cache on 300a and 333 MHz and higher Celerons		Windows
Pentium III	32 bit	64 bit	4 GB	450, 500, 533, 550, 600, 650, 667, 700, 733, 750, 800, 850, 866, 933, 1,000 and 1,100 MHz	16 KB Instruction 16 KB data and 512 KB L2 cache	Internal	PCs running Windows & Windows NT/2000
Pentium 4	32 bit	64 bit	4 GB	1.3, 1.4, 1.5, 1.6, 1.7, 1.8, 1.9, 2.0 GHz, and higher	12 KB Instruction and 8 KB data and 256 KB L2 cache	Internal	PCs running Windows & Windows 2000

Table 5-1 Intel CPU Chip Summary (Continued)

CPU Chip	Internal Word Size	Data Bus	Addressable RAM	Clock Speed	Internal Cache	Math Co-CPU Chip	Operating Systems
Pentium Pro	32 bit	64 bit	4 GB	166 MHz, 200 MHz and higher	8 KB instruction 8 KB data and 256/512KB and 1 Mb L2 cache	Internal	Multiple CPU Servers running Windows NT/2000, Netware, and UNIX
Pentium II Xeon	32 bit	64 bit	64 GB	400, and 450 MHz	16 KB Instruction and 16 KB data and 512 KB, 1 MB or 2 MB L2 cache	Internal	Multiple CPU Servers running Windows NT/2000, Netware, UNIX
Pentium III Xeon	32 bit	64 bit	64 GB	600, 667, 733, 800, 866, 933, 1,000, and 1,130 MHz	16 KB Instruction and 16 KB data and 512 KB, 1 MB or 2 MB L2 cache	Internal	Multiple CPU Servers running Windows NT/2000, Netware, UNIX
Itanium	64 bit	64 bit	6 TB	733 and 800 MHz	32 K L1, 96K L2 and 2MB or 4MB L3 cache	Internal	Multiple CPU Servers running Windows NT/2000, Netware, UNIX

Intel CPUs are CISC CPUs. Manufacturers such as Motorola and Compaq produce the RISC CPU chips found in Macintosh computers and high-end PC servers. They comprise a very small percentage of the CPU chip market. AMD and Cyrix Intel-compatible CPU chips are CISC CPU chips like Intel's CPU chips. Intel, AMD, and Cyrix chips use the x86 instruction set, which gets its name from the Intel CPU chips with 86 in their product name. This set of CPU chip instructions has evolved with the introduction of the 80386 CPU chips, the MMX extensions, and the Pentium III 3-D instructions. The Pentium 4 has streaming Single Instruction Multiple Data (SIMD) instruction set and the Intel Itanium CPU implements Explicitly Parallel Instruction Computing (EPIC) architecture. Each of these changes is aimed at tailoring the CPU chip to graphics, multimedia, and Internet processing tasks.

The 8088/8086 and 80286 CPU chips had fewer instructions and operating modes. This means that programs written for 80386, 80486, and Pentium CPU chips cannot run on 8086/8088 and 80286 CPU chips. Since 8088/8086 and 80286 CPU chips are obsolete, programs that do not run on them are not much of an issue. The 8086/8088 and 80286 CPU chips worked on 16 bits internally, while 80386, 80486, and Pentium CPU chips work on 32 bits. The Itanium chip is a 64-bit architecture CPU that works on 64 bits internally.

The 32-bit 80386 class CPU chip instruction sets are all compatible. Intel had to introduce the 80486 CPU chip without changing the instruction set because so many programs ran on the 80386 CPU chips. More compatible programs were written, increasing the importance of keeping the core instruction set compatible in future CPU chips.

MMX defined 57 new instructions. It was the first significant instruction set change since the introduction of the 80386 a decade ago. All CPU chips from Intel, AMD, and Cyrix support MMX or Multimedia Extensions. The MMX instructions provide a performance increase for multimedia programming. MMX instructions process large amounts of similar data at the same time with a single instruction. They are especially useful in processing graphics, video and audio data. MMX is an extension of the x86 instruction set. CPU chips supporting MMX instructions run all software that ran on non-MMX CPU chips. However, programs designed for MMX CPU chips are not backward compatible unless the program determines a non-MMX CPU chip and different coding is used where MMX instructions are employed as a result. The Pentium III CPU chip added another instruction set extension aimed at improving three-dimensional graphics performance. This is above and beyond the MMX instruction set extension. The Pentium 4 has the SIMD instructions aimed at multimedia and processing streaming data from the Internet. Pentium CPU chips follow the "IA-32" or "P6"architecture.

The extensions to the x86 architecture will eventually be abandoned in favor of a new CPU chip architecture designed from scratch. Intel and Hewlett-

Packard are designing a new CPU chip architecture, IA-64. The Itanium chip is the first Intel IA-64 architecture CPU chip. These CPU chips will be 64-bit CPU chips using a new instruction set specifically designed to raise CPU chip performance to a new level. The new Intel CPU chip is code-named Merced. It is also designated as the "P7" because it is the seventh generation of PC CPU chips. The new CPU chip must perform the x86 instructions because backward compatibility remains a dominant factor in PC hardware and software products.

CPU Mounting

CPU chip packaging has evolved dramatically over the last 18 or more years. The early CPU chips used a Dual In-line Pin (DIP) package. This evolved within about four years to a Pin Grid Arrays (PGA) package. PGAs (which we think of as the golfing package) come in several different sizes. There are PGA variations including a Plastic Pin Grid Array (PPGA) and a Flip Chip Pin Grid Array (FC-PGA). All PGAs fit into zero insertion force sockets. Intel's Pentium II and Pentium III CPU chips come on a Single-Edge Contact (SEC or SECC) cartridge. The SEC cartridge contains more than just the CPU chip. See Figure 5–2.

The socket mating the CPU to the MLB has evolved along with the chip packaging. The first socket for PGA chips was Socket 0. Socket 0 had fewer pins, a different mechanical CPU chip insertion and a different pin layout from the Socket 7, Socket 8, Socket 370, Socket 423, Socket 462, and Socket 478 used in PCs.

Socket 370, Socket 423, Socket 462, and Socket 478 are the most common sockets used today. Socket 370 mates Intel Celeron and Pentium II CPU chips, Socket 423 and Socket 478 mates Pentium 4 CPU chips, and Socket 462 (or Socket A) mates AMD Athlon CPU chips to MLBs. Socket 7 is used for older Pentium and AMD CPU chips. Socket 8 only mates Pentium Pro chips to MLBs at this time.

When installing any PGA CPU chip in a socket, the pin one rule applies—"Always connect pin one to pin one." Some PGA chips are designed so that it is impossible not to connect pin one to pin one in the socket, but in other cases it is possible. When pin one is not connected to pin one, our experience is that the CPU chip is rendered inoperative when power is applied to the MLB. Pin one on the CPU chip is generally identified by a square solder pad around the pin, a notch on the chip, a white dot on the chip's surface, or in some position relative to the label of the chip. See Figure 5–3.

Current Intel Pentium CPU chips cannot be inserted incorrectly into the socket. The arrangement of the pins on the CPU chip forms a specific pattern that fits into a socket in only one position. The pins may be specially staggered, or the socket may be designed with one narrow side, or have pins forming a

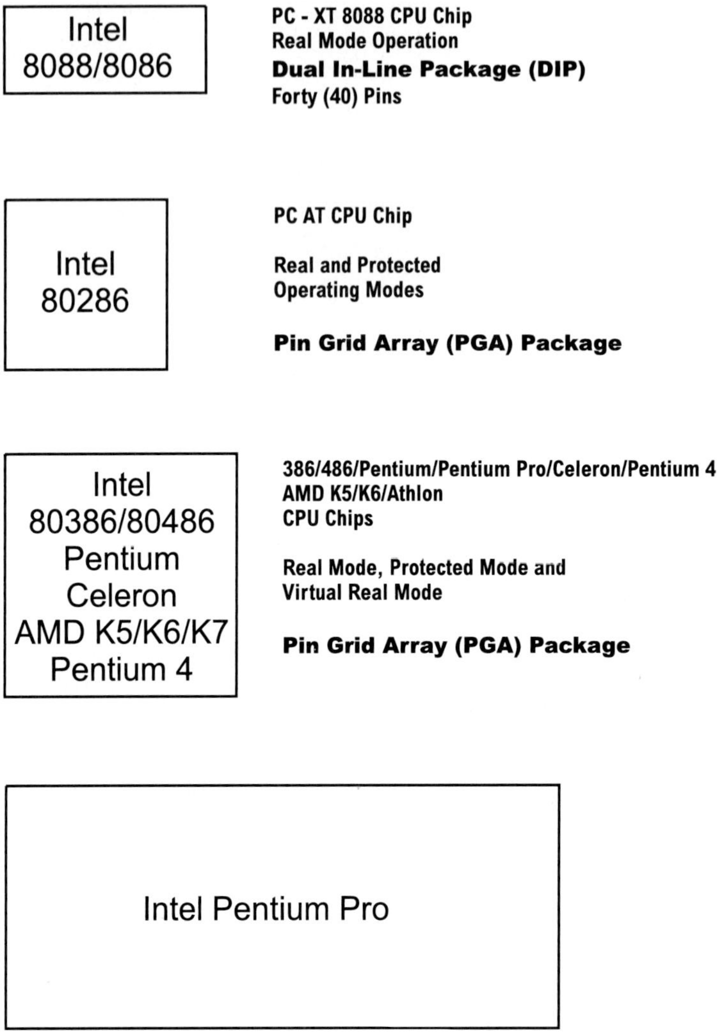

Intel 8088/8086	PC - XT 8088 CPU Chip Real Mode Operation **Dual In-Line Package (DIP)** Forty (40) Pins

Intel 80286	PC AT CPU Chip Real and Protected Operating Modes **Pin Grid Array (PGA) Package**

Intel 80386/80486 Pentium Celeron AMD K5/K6/K7 Pentium 4	386/486/Pentium/Pentium Pro/Celeron/Pentium 4 AMD K5/K6/Athlon CPU Chips Real Mode, Protected Mode and Virtual Real Mode **Pin Grid Array (PGA) Package**

Intel Pentium Pro

Figure 5–2
Some CPU chip packages.

beveled corner. When the CPU chip is placed on the socket, it only drops into the pin holes when the pins exactly match the socket pin holes. Some older Intel 386 and 486 CPU chips could be inserted incorrectly into sockets, resulting in PC malfunction and CPU chip destruction.

SEC cartridges use a connector slot rather than a socket. SEC cartridges insert into a Slot-1 connector, a Slot-A connector or a Slot-2 connector, similar-

Figure 5-3
Intel Pentium PRO CPU
PGA chip top and bottom.

ly to other PC cards. SEC cartridges are also keyed so that they cannot be inserted incorrectly. The AMD and Intel SEC cartridge share the same mechanical layout, but different electrical signal connections. In Figure 5–4, the Intel Slot-1 and the AMD Slot-A cartridges are side by side at the top of the figure. Note that the notch is offset on the opposite side of the CPU fan for each cartridge. When the Intel Slot-1 cartridge and the AMD Slot-A cartridge are placed on top of one another and the insertion notch matches up (as in the bottom of the figure), the CPU fans are on opposite sides of the CPU. This assures that Slot-1 and Slot-A cartridges do not insert into the wrong SEC connector.

CPU Modes

The CPU operating mode controls how the CPU chip views memory and manages the programs using memory. Intel CPU chips operate in real, protected, and virtual real or virtual 8086 modes.

Real Mode

The original 8088 CPU chip PC only addressed 1 MB of memory. DOS ran programs that worked within this memory limitation. DOS was a one task at one time operating system; it only permitted one program to run at any given time. This type of DOS operation has been carried forward with each new CPU chip. DOS one-task-at-a-time operation is still especially important for PC diagnostic programs that directly manipulate the PC hardware. One good example is programs that flash the BIOS of the PC and PC components. When a PC CPU chip emulates the operation of the 8088 CPU chip, it is operating in real mode. All PCs boot in real mode.

In real mode, DOS and standard DOS applications run in 640 KB of the 1 MB of available DOS RAM. Adding extended and expanded memory increases the DOS memory. Extended memory is memory over 1 MB. Programs like

Figure 5–4
Single-Edge Contact (SEC) Pentium II CPU.

HIMEM.SYS and EMM386.EXE permitted DOS to work in protected mode. The DOS Protected Mode Interface, or DPMI, specified how DOS was to operate in protected mode and access CPU chip memory over 1 MB. Because of an Intel chip design anomaly, the first 64 KB of extended memory is accessed in real mode. This real-mode accessible region is called the High Memory Area (HMA).

Protected Mode

The 80286 CPU chip operated in real mode and in protected mode. Protected mode is used by multitasking operating systems. In protected mode, the CPU chip can access all PC memory and the 1 MB limit is eliminated. The CPU runs multiple tasks, permitting the operating system to manage execution of several programs concurrently. Protected mode also supports virtual memory, which uses hard disk space to emulate RAM memory as needed. Protected mode has 32-bit access to memory, and supports 32-bit I/O drivers.

In protected mode, each program runs in its own assigned memory locations. The CPU protects the assigned memory locations from conflicting with other programs. When programs try to access protected memory addresses, the CPU chip generates a protection fault. This was displayed as the famous Windows 3.1 General Protection Fault message.

Windows 3.x/95/98/Me/NT/2000/XP run predominately in protected mode. DOS can use protected mode by running software that complies with the DOS protected mode interface specifications.

CPU chips from 80286 on have protected mode. The 32-bit 80386, 80486, and all Pentium CPU chips switch on the fly from real to protected mode and vice versa. The 80286 CPU chips must reboot to switch from protected mode to real mode. The 386 Enhanced Mode is protected mode.

Super-scalar Architecture

Super-scalar architecture CPU chips have multiple execution units that support execution of more than one software instruction at a time. Intel 80486 and Pentium CPU chips are super-scalar with two execution units operating in parallel. This side-by-side multiple parallel execution unit operation can be thought of as a form of internal CPU chip multiprocessing. Almost all modern CPU chips employ super-scalar architecture and are set up so that two processors in each CPU chip share internal L1 cache. How effectively these two CPU chip processors work together determines the CPU chip's power.

Super-pipelining

Super-pipelining CPU chips overlap instruction execution steps to accelerate software operations.

Pipelining is a computer design technique used to increase the processing speed of a CPU. Normally, the electrical signals implementing an instruction must flow through several logic gates to perform the function desired. This takes time. Each gate often requires clock timing to move an instruction's electrical signal to the next gate. Consequently, instructions could require several clock cycles to finish execution. These clock cycles were broken down into stages—fetch, decode, execute, and write. An instruction with these stages would require four clock cycles to execute. By overlapping four instructions (pipelining), the CPU could be writing the results of instruction 1, while executing instruction 2, while also decoding instruction 3, and at the same time fetching instruction 4. These overlapped instruction steps, called a pipeline, permit our hypothetical CPU to effectively execute one instruction per clock cycle. Normal pipelining requires several clock cycles to execute a single instruction, unlike the hypothetical CPU in our example.

In contrast, super-pipelining uses a longer pipeline with more stages than normal pipelining. This means that, for a given clock speed, the CPU chip could in theory achieve a one-instruction-per-clock-cycle execution rate. Most CISC Intel CPU chips employ super-pipelining. The 80486 chip increased instruction pipelining to achieve one instruction execution for a single clock cycle. Earlier CPU chips required multiple clock cycles per instruction. When the 486 chip pipelining was not fast enough, Intel produced Pentium chips incorporating two CPUs to increase the instruction rate per clock cycle to two. The Pentium 4 has an execution pipeline that is 20 stages long. More stages result in the use of fewer gates and, thus, the CPU runs stages faster and can operate at higher clock speeds.

Speculative Execution and Branch Prediction

Super-scalar CPU chips execute multiple instructions at once. However, the results of instruction execution are sometimes discarded because the program flow is directed to a different part of the program. The instruction should not have been executed in the first place. This happens when a program branches to a different part of the program based on a test of data results, for example, an answer to an IF/THEN question. The program execution path changes depending on the IF/THEN answers.

Branches are very common in programs. They impact the desired effect of pipelining because instructions not in a linear sequence disrupt the pipeline flow and slow down the CPU chip. Pipelining requires starting the next program instruction before the last program instruction has completed. A conditional test instruction (the IF/THEN question) determines the next instruction to execute based on the results of the test. Only after the test has been executed can the next instruction be determined, so what instruction is the CPU chip going to place in the pipeline?

Less sophisticated CPU chips wait and hold up the pipeline until the results are known, which degrades CPU chip performance. The new Pentium CPU chips are more advanced. They guess at the next instruction and hope that the branch goes the way they have guessed. More advanced CPU chips combine speculative execution (instruction guessing) with branch prediction, based on

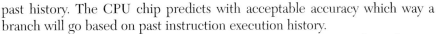

past history. The CPU chip predicts with acceptable accuracy which way a branch will go based on past instruction execution history.

For example, the following is a representative IF/THEN conditional test:

```
IF X = Y THEN
S = C + 1
ELSE
S = C - 1
END IF
```

Until the **IF X = Y THEN** instruction has executed, the CPU chip doesn't know which instruction is next. It could be the S = C+1 addition instruction or the S = C–1 subtraction instruction. CPU chips with speculate execution may start both the addition and subtraction instructions at the same time, and then simply throw out the results that are not needed. Alternately, the CPU chip could use branch prediction to guess, and as a result, start either the addition or subtraction instruction.

Branch prediction improves CPU chip branch guessing by using a special small Branch Target Buffer (BTB) cache. Whenever a CPU chip performs a branch, it stores information about it in the branch target buffer cache. If the CPU chip encounters the same branch, it makes an informed guess about the branch result using the branch target buffer cache. This keeps the CPU chip's pipeline flowing smoothly, improving CPU chip performance.

Other CPU Chip Features

Other CPU chip features include out-of-order execution, register renaming, and write buffers.

Out-of-order execution—Super-scalar CPU chips with multiple execution units can theoretically complete instructions in the wrong order. For example, instruction 9 can be executed before instruction 8 is completed. Such flexibility improves CPU chip performance by reducing waiting time. However, the results of out-of-order execution must be reassembled into the correct order, ensuring that programs run as designed. Logic is built into the chip to track instruction execution and resolve out-of-order execution issues. This increases the sophistication of the CPU chip design.

Register renaming—Register renaming allows for multiple execution paths without different execution units contending for the same registers. Multiple sets of registers are put into the CPU chip to allow different execution units to work simultaneously.

Write buffers—Write buffers hold the instruction execution results until they can be written back to registers or memory locations. The greater the write buffers, the greater the number of instructions that can be executed without stalling the CPU chip pipelines.

These other CPU chip features all contribute to increased instruction execution speed and thus to CPU chip performance.

Size

CPU chips vary in size, which impacts their packaging. Opposing design goals pull at CPU chip development. Small circuit size is one design goal because it speeds electrical signals between different CPU internal components—for example, L1 cache and the Arithmetic and Logic Unit (ALU). In contrast large die sizes allowing more components (ALU, L1 cache, L2 cache, etc.) to be crammed into a single chip is an opposing design goal. Small circuit size and bigger die size both improve CPU performance. The problem is now connecting this wonderful chip to the big electrical connections in the PC. A CPU chip package must contain the chip and provide sufficient electrical connections to permit the chip to communicate with RAM, the display controller, the disk drives, and so on.

Table 5–2 summarizes the physical CPU chip characteristics for common CPU chips.

Table 5–2 CPU Chip Size and Voltage

CPU Chip	CPU Chip Clock Speed	Circuit Process Technology (in microns)	Transistors (millions)	Voltages External/ Core	Power Management
8088/8086	All	3.0	0.029	5 V	None
80286	All	1.5	0.134	5 V	None
80386	All	1.5 to 1.0	0.275	5 V	None or System Management Module (SMM) on SL Chips
80486	All	1.0 to .5	1.2 to 1.6	5 V or (DX4 = 3.3 V but 5 V tolerant)	None or SMM on SL, DX2, and DX4 Chips

Table 5-2   CPU Chip Size and Voltage (Continued)

CPU Chip	CPU Chip Clock Speed	Circuit Process Technology (in microns)	Transistors (millions)	Voltages External/ Core	Power Management
AMD 5x86	All	0.35	2.0	3.45V	SMM
Cyrix 5x86	All	0.65	2.0	3.45 V	SMM
Pentium	66 to 200	0.8 to 0.35	3.1 to 3.3	5 V 3.3 V 3.52 V Voltage reduced	SMM
Pentium with MMX	All	0.35	4.5	3.3 V/2.8 V	SMM
Cyrix 6x86	All	0.6 to 0.35	3.0	3.3 V/2.8 V	SMM
AMD K5	All	0.35	4.3	3.52 V	SMM
Pentium II	233 to 450	0.35 to 0.25	7.5	3.3 V/2.8 V	SMM
Pentium III	450 MHz to 1.13 GHz	0.25 to 0.18	9.5+	3.3 V/2.8 V	SMM
Pentium 4	1.3 to 1.5 GHz	0.18 to 0.13	42+	1.7 V to 1.8 V core	SMM and Advanced Configuration and Power Interface (ACPI)
AMD K6	166 to 400	0.35 to 0.25	8.8	3.3 V/2.9 V or 3.3 V/3.2 V	SMM
AMD K7 (Athlon)	All	0.18	30 Million (my estimate)	1.2 V to 1.85 V core	APCI
Cyrix 6x86MX	All	0.35	6.0	3.3 V/2.9 V	SMM
Pentium Pro	150 to 200	0.6 to 0.35	5.5 (up to 36.5 including cache)	3.1 V or 3.3 V	SMM and APCI
Xeon	400 MHz to 1 GHz	0.25 to 0.18	7.5+	2.0 V CPU Core 2.5/2.7 V L2 cache	SMM and APCI

Table 5-2 CPU Chip Size and Voltage (Continued)

CPU Chip	CPU Chip Clock Speed	Circuit Process Technology (in microns)	Transistors (millions)	Voltages External/ Core	Power Management
Itanium	733, and 900 MHz	0.18 to 0.13	140+	1.7 core	SMM and APCI
Alpha 21164	500 MHz, 533 MHz, 600 MHz, 633 MHz, and 667 MHz	0.35	15.2	3.3 V/ 2.5V (2.0 V core)	Yes
Alpha 21264	500 MHz to 1.25 GHz	0.18	15.2	1.5 V	Yes

The table illustrates that advancing CPU chip-manufacturing technologies as indicated by decreasing circuit process technology sizes makes it possible to pack more components (transistors) into smaller die and package sizes. Now CPU chips use 0.13 micron circuit process technology, reducing chip size by 25 percent.

Voltages

The first CPU chips all used Transistor-to-Transistor Logic (TTL) circuitry, which operated on 5 volts DC. The components installed into a PC increased and the power consumption rose accordingly. PC power consumption soon became an issue. As a result, voltage specifications for CPU chips vary today. CPU chip power consumption relates directly to the heat generated by the CPU chip. Because newer CPU chips are larger and faster, keeping them cool is very important. Reducing CPU voltage levels reduces CPU power consumption and the heat generated by the CPU; lower voltages help reduce the heat given off by the CPU, and make it capable of being air-cooled. Because millions of PCs are in continuous use (a single company can have thousands), lower CPU voltage results in energy conservation that may represent a significant savings in power costs. Reduced power consumption began with notebook computers, since they ran on batteries with a highly limited operating life. Laptops were also more sensitive to heat because their CPU chips and other components were sandwiched into a small flat package.

New CPU chips add additional internal components and run at faster speeds, which increase the power consumption and the amount of heat generated by the CPU chip. CPU chips compensate for the added power consumption and heat generation by using low-power CMOS semiconductor technologies and by shrinking the CPU chip circuit size.

Lower CPU voltage levels translate into less power consumption and heat generation. The voltage level was reduced to 3.3 volts. CPU chips reduce voltage levels even more by using a dual voltage or split rail design. CPU chips with these designs use two different voltages, a higher external or I/O voltage (typically 3.3 volts to ensure compatibility with other chips on the MLB) and a lower internal or core voltage (usually 2.5 volts to 2.9 volts or in newer chips around 1.2 volts to 1.85 volts). Such a dual voltage design permits lower-voltage CPU chips to be used on MLBs without requiring design and chip set changes. Chips using less than 3 volts are still changing, while 2.8 or 2.9 volts are common core voltages for Intel Pentium with MMX, the Cyrix 6x86L and the AMD K6 chips. The 0.18 micron technology CPU chips (e.g., Pentium 4) use core voltage ranging from 1.2 volts for suspend mode operation and 1.85 volts for normal operation. Socket 7 MLBs provide 2.5 volts, 2.7 volts, 2.8 volts and 2.9 volts for CPU chip power to be compatible with future CPU chips. Correct voltages are supplied to the CPU chip on the MLB by a voltage regulator on the MLB. The newer MLBs and the CPU chips automatically regulate the power to the CPU chip using built-in power management features.

Pentium II CPU chips are designed to allow Intel to change the internal voltage required by the CPU without changing the voltages on the MLB. Intel created power management circuitry, enabling CPU chips to conserve energy use and to extend battery life in laptop PCs. Such power management features have been implemented universally. They are incorporated into all Pentium (and later CPU chips) as a System Management Mode (SMM) feature. SMM circuitry is integrated into the CPU chip and operates independently to manage the CPU chip's power consumption based on its processing activity. SMM permits specifying time intervals after which the CPU chip is powered down partially or fully. The SMM implements suspend/resume instant power on and power off, used mostly with laptop PCs to conserve battery life. These power management features are set up in the PC BIOS. A newer more general industry standard power management interface for Windows PCs is the Advanced Configuration and Power Interface (ACPI).

Speeds

Today's PCs have multiple system clocks. Clocks electrically oscillate at a unique designated frequency measured in megahertz (or millions of cycles per second). A clock cycle or tick is the smallest time unit in which processing happens. Some work can be done in a single cycle while other work consumes several cycles. The MLB clocks drive the CPU chip and other circuits in the PC. The higher the megahertz, the better the PC's performance.

Originally PCs used a single clock that provided clocking for the CPU chip, the RAM memory and I/O bus. As PCs evolved, the CPU chips ran faster than the RAM or the I/O bus, and the RAM was faster than the I/O bus. Multiple clocks provided these differing speeds. A typical PC has four or more different clocks, each running at a different speed. The system clock describes the memory bus speed on the MLB. It does not usually designate the clock speed of the CPU chip. The clocks in a PC are created from a single clock generator circuit on the MLB, which produces the system clock. Other clocks are produced by multiplying the system clock signal to get more clock cycles, or by dividing the system clock signal to get fewer clock cycles.

The clock multiplier and divider circuits create the other clock signals needed in a PC. Table 5–3 shows the typical clocks in a 333 MHz Celeron PC as an example. Most PCs today run at much higher clock rates. In addition PC bus clock rates have increased as well.

The PC's speed is determined by the system clock rate. Increasing a system clock speed provides better performance than increasing the CPU chip speed alone because it speeds up data movement throughout the PC, not just in the CPU chip.

Table 5–3 Some Typical PC Clocks

PC Component	Clock Rate (MHz)	Multiplier or Divider
CPU chip	800	System clock × 6
Level 2 cache	400	System clock × 3 (or CPU chip / 2)
System (memory) bus	133	The PC's basic clock rate for SDRAM
PCI bus	33	System clock / 4
ISA bus	8.3	PCI bus / 4

Thus, the MLB system clock provides the central clocking for the CPU chip, the memory bus, and the I/O bus. The base clock rate from a MLB was typically 66 MHz. The 133 MHz clocking is on newer PCs with SDRAM memory. A 6x multiplier is used to boost the CPU chip clock rate to 800 MHz for a 133 MHz MLB system clock. Different multipliers applied to the 66 MHz, 100 MHz or 133MHz basic clock rate produce higher or lower CPU clock speeds.

CPU chips work at the PCI bus clock speed to transfer data into and out of the chip and at the CPU clock speed to process the data inside the chip. Data

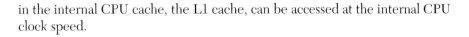

in the internal CPU cache, the L1 cache, can be accessed at the internal CPU clock speed.

L1 and L2 Cache

The CPU chip is the fastest component in the PC; it is faster than RAM and much faster than the disk drives. To handle the speed mismatches, CPU chips work off both an internal and external cache memory. The external cache (level 2) cache is a buffer between the CPU chip and the RAM, while the internal cache (level 1) is between the L2 cache and the CPU chip. The L1 cache is internal to the CPU chip. L2 cache can be internal or external, depending on the CPU chip. Xeon, Pentium Pro, high-speed Celeron, Pentium III, AMD K7, and Pentium 4 chips have an internal L2 cache. Pentium II chips have an external L2 cache that is designed to operate at half the CPU clock speed because it is mounted on the slot 1 CPU chip card. See Figure 5–5. Itanium chips have an L1, L2 and L3 cache in the chip.

Figure 5–5
PC CPU and disk cache.

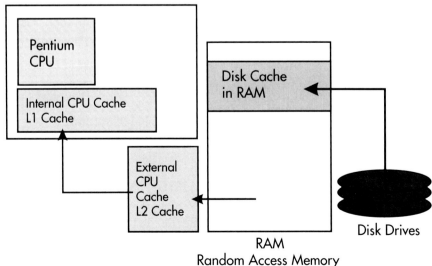

The L2 cache is external to the CPU chip on the MLB of older PCs. These are PCs with CPU chips installed in PGA sockets. The L2 cache is static RAM with cycle times of 8 ns to 15 ns, or operating speeds from 66 MHz to 125 MHz.

The L1 cache first appeared in the Intel 80486 CPU chip. It had 8 KB of L1 cache internally in the chip. This internal L1 CPU cache increased CPU performance more than a much larger L2 external CPU cache. Pentium chips typically have 16 KB of internal L1 cache with 8 KB dedicated to instructions and 8 KB dedicated to data. This has increased to 32 KB of internal non-blocking L1 cache in the Xeon and Pentium III CPU chip. Nonblocking means that the cache is structured so that each processor in the CPU chip has access to the data in the cache without impacting the other processor in the CPU chip. As with other Pentium L1 cache, the 32 KB cache is divided into 16 KB instruction and 16 KB data segments. The Pentium 4 CPU chip has an 8 KB data cache and a 12 KB execution trace cache for instructions. The execution trace cache provides much higher performance through more efficient cache memory use. The interfaces a CPU has to the rest of the PC's components are as important in determining PC performance as how well the CPU chip works internally. A very fast and powerful engine in a car goes nowhere without a good transmission and tires.

CPU Buses and Memory Addressing

The CPU chip uses buses to handle and control signals to send information between itself and L2 cache memory, RAM memory and other PC components. These CPU chip external interfaces can be different in seemingly similar CPU chips. PC buses are arranged in a hierarchy, carrying data into and out of the CPU chip. For the CPU chip, the important buses are the CPU chip I/O and memory buses. The CPU chip I/O bus carries information to and from the CPU chip and is controlled by the system chip set. The memory bus connects the CPU chip I/O bus to the PC RAM and cache. Older CPU chips use Level 2 cache on the MLB and pass data to it using a standard memory bus arrangement. We define two types of buses below.

Dedicated cache bus, or Dual Independent Bus (DIB)—CPU chips achieve better performance by using a dedicated high-speed bus to connect the CPU chip to the L2 external CPU cache. A Pentium 200 runs the system bus and the system cache runs at 66 MHz. In contrast, a Pentium Pro 200 has an internal L2 cache running at a full 200 MHz. A dedicated cache bus provides the high-speed data link between the CPU chip and the L2 cache. The Pentium Pro chip package contains the CPU chip, the dedicated cache bus, and L2 cache.

The Pentium II CPU chip has a combined bus arrangement. Its cache bus runs at half CPU chip speed. A 350 MHz Pentium II has a cache bus running at 175 MHz. This is slower than a Pentium Pro but faster than a normal Pentium. The L2 cache buses are nonblocking, which means they support concurrent data requests to the system cache. Also, separate caches and buses provide better multiprocessing support because each CPU chip processor has its own cache with a separate bus. Similarly, the internal L1 and L2 CPU caches of the Pentium III, AMD K7, and Pentium 4 use nonblocking cache buses in the chip.

Memory data bus or front side bus—Every bus is composed of data lines and address lines. The data bus carries the data being transferred, and the more bits in the data bus, the more bytes of information transferred in one cycle. Wider (32-bit versus 16-bit) data buses generally provide higher performance. The data bus bandwidth is how much information can flow across it in megabytes per second. The bus width in bytes and its speed in MHz determine the bandwidth of the bus. Memory bus bandwidth is extremely important in PC performance because it is a key bottleneck. Because CPU chips run so much faster than other parts of a PC, increasing the data speed to the CPU chip usually increases performance more than speeding up the CPU chip alone. Table 5–4 summarizes the bandwidth of common CPU chips. MHz is 1,000,000 cycles per second, but MB/second is 1,048,576 bytes per second. To calculate the bandwidth the formula is:

[Bus Width (64-bit)/8 bits per byte] × [clock speed in MHz]/[1,048,576 bytes per megabyte]

For example: 64/8 × 100 × (1,000,000/1,048,576 or 0.9536743) = 762.9 M/second.

Memory addressing is carried through address lines that point to the RAM location either from which data is read or to which data is written. The speed of the address bus is the same as the data bus it is matched to. The number of memory address lines controls the maximum RAM addressable by the CPU chip. This is the maximum RAM the CPU chip can read or write to. CPU chips usually can address far more physical memory than most people can ever afford to purchase. For example, the 8088 CPU chip could address only 1 MB of RAM, the 80286 CPU chip could address 16 MB of RAM, and some Pentium chips can address up to 64 GB of RAM. At $0.50 per MB, a GB of RAM would run $512 and 64 GB would cost $32,768.

The MLB usually restricts the maximum RAM more tightly than the CPU chip does.

Table 5–4   CPU Chip Bandwidth

CPU Chip	Bus Width in Bits	Bandwidth (MHz/Mbytes per second)
8088	8-bit	4.77 MHz / 4.5 Mbytes/second 8 MHz / 7.6 Mbytes/second
8086	16-bit	4.77 MHz / 9.1 Mbytes/second 8 MHz / 15.3 Mbytes/second
80286	16-bit	6 MHz / 11.4 Mbytes/second 8 MHz / 15.3 Mbytes/second
80386 DX	32-bit	16 MHz / 63.6 Mbytes/second 40 MHz / 152.6 Mbytes/second
80386 SX	16-bit	16 MHz / 31.8 Mbytes/second 25 MHz / 47.7 Mbytes/second
80486 DX/SX	32-bit	16 MHz / 63.6 Mbytes/second 25 MHz / 95.4 Mbytes/second 33 MHz / 127.2 Mbytes/second 40 MHz / 152.6 Mbytes/second
Pentium AMD K6 II/III	64-bit	60 MHz / 457.8 Mbytes/second 66 MHz / 508.6 Mbytes/second 100 MHz / 762.9 Mbytes/second
AMD K7	64-bit	133 MHz Double Pumped/ 2,133 Mbytes/second
Pentium 4	64-bit	100 MHz Quad Pumped/3.2 Mbytes/second

Table 5–5 shows the address bus width and maximum system memory for various CPU chips. A 32-bit address bus and 5-GB maximum addressable RAM are the most common.

Table 5–5   CPU Chip Maximum RAM

CPU Chip(s)	Address Bus Width (bits)	Maximum System RAM
8088, 8086	20	1 MB
80286, 80386SX	24	16 MB
80386, 80486, AMD K5, AMD K6, Cyrix 5x86, Pentium, Pentium with MMX, Cyrix 6x86	32	4 GB
Pentium Pro, Pentium II, Pentium III, Pentium 4	36	64 GB
Itanium	44	16+ TB

Multiprocessing

Windows NT/2000 uses multiprocessing in a workstation or server with more than one Pentium Pro, Pentium II-Xeon, Pentium III, Pentium III-Xeon, or Itanium CPU chip. Only specific CPU chips support multiprocessing with Windows NT/2000. In theory, using two CPU chips doubles performance. In reality, performance is increased and reliability is enhanced, but not always by a factor of two. Increasing reliability is the key reason for using multiple CPU chips. Typically, servers have two CPU chips, but some run with four and others can have as many as eight.

To support multiple CPU chips, a server must have:

- MLB enhancements—The MLB must have additional sockets or slots for extra CPU chips and a chip set capable of performing multiprocessing.

- Multiprocessing CPU chips—CPU chips must be capable of multiprocessing. Not all CPU chips are capable. The Pentium III can seamlessly support multiprocessing of two CPUs and the Xeon can support up to eight CPUs. Some versions of the same CPU chip can support multiprocessing while other versions cannot.

- A multiprocessing operating system—Windows NT/2000 and some versions of UNIX support multiprocessing.

Multiprocessing is most effective with application software designed to be broken into small routines that run independently. These small independent tasks are called threads. The operating system runs the threads (tasks) on more than one CPU chip simultaneously, improving performance.

Multiprocessing is asymmetric or symmetric. In asymmetric multiprocessing, some CPU chips are allocated to only perform system tasks, while other CPU chips only run application tasks. Asymmetric multiprocessing does not work well when a server needs to run many system tasks and few application tasks. Symmetric Multiprocessing (SMP) systems allow user tasks to run on any CPU chip. This is more flexible and provides better performance. Virtually all server MLBs use SMP.

Intel Pentium Pro, Pentium II-Xeon, Pentium III, Pentium III-Xeon, and Itanium are currently used for multiprocessing because each chip has a self-contained L2 CPU cache. In servers with external L2 caches, several CPU chips would share the L2 cache on the MLB. In this case, adding CPU chips without increasing the L2 cache gives each CPU chip less of the cache to use, since each chip must share. Furthermore, because the cache is shared, special non-blocking associations are required for the cache to fully support each CPU chip. This

331

can be done, but it makes for an expensive board design. Pentium Pro, Pentium II-Xeon, Pentium III, Pentium III-Xeon, and Itanium CPU chips come with their own internal L2 cache. This makes server MLB design less complex and less costly. Two Pentium III CPUs can be used for basic multiprocessor configurations. For up to four CPUs, the Pentium Pro, Pentium II-Xeon, Pentium III-Xeon, and Itanium CPU chips can be used. For eight CPUs, the Pentium III-Xeon and Itanium are the CPU chips designed for that level of multiprocessing. The Itanium CPU chip is designed to scale up to 32 CPUs and beyond, but no servers are yet designed to support that number of CPUs.

CPU Packaging

CPU packaging refers to how the silicon wafer (that is, the CPU) is encased for mounting on the MLB. CPU chips, like all chips, are packaged in materials that protect them from physical damage, dissipate heat properly, and have connectors of a standard size and shape. MLBs can be standardized without having to worry about the physical structure of any specific CPU chip. The CPU chip packaging is designed for a specific socket or slot that interfaces the CPU chip to the MLB. CPU chip packaging has evolved as CPU chips become larger and more complex.

Dual Inline Package (DIP)—The first PC and XT CPU chips used standard DIP packaging. The term "dual inline" describes two parallel rows of pins down each side of a plastic package. DIP packaging was the standard packaging for most regular integrated circuits. DIP packaging is disappearing today because of new automated manufacturing techniques, and the need to cram more components on a single board. The increasing number of signals used by CPU chips quickly made DIP packaging for CPU chips impractical.

Pin Grid Array (PGA)—Pin Grid Array packaging was first used on the Intel 80286 CPU chip introduced in 1985. PGA packages are square or rectangular. They have several rows of pins around their perimeter and are inserted into a special MLB socket. Common PGA packaging is made from ceramic materials, and is called Ceramic PGA (CPGA). Newer CPU chips use plastic packaging referred to as Plastic PGA (PPGA). Plastic packaging is less expensive and transfers heat away from the chip better than CPGA. As the number of CPU chip connections went from 200 to around 300, Intel had to pack even more pins into the same physical PGA space. A staggered pin layout was developed to tightly pack the pins. This is the Staggered PGA (SPGA) used by Pentium CPU chips. Pentium Pro CPU chips use a special dual pattern PGA because the Pentium Pro dual-chip package contains both the CPU chip and a secondary L2 CPU cache. Socket technology has again increased the number of pins in the PGA packaging to over 400.

Single-Edge Contact (SEC)—Intel's latest packaging design is the SEC cartridge. The SEC moves the L2 CPU cache out of the chip while maintaining a special high-speed bus connection between it and the CPU chip. An SEC is actually a daughterboard and not an actual chip package. The CPU chip itself is packaged using something like a regular PGA that is mounted onto a small circuit board with a proprietary edge connector. The L2 CPU cache also mounts onto this daughterboard, which mounts into a special slot on the MLB. This approach permits a high-speed interface between the CPU chip and the L2 cache.

Mobile Module (MMO)—Notebook PCs, because of their size, weight, and cooling requirements, represent the greatest design challenges. To meet these challenges, Intel increased component miniaturization by producing mobile module packaging incorporating CPU chip, L2 cache, and supporting chip set into a small module. From this design comes tighter integration of the interface between the chip set and CPU chip.

Tape Carrier Packaging (TCP)—Raw chips come taped to a plastic roll without any external packaging. These chips are soldered directly onto a special MLB designed specifically for them. This approach is more complicated than using a socket. It has the advantage of using much less space and as a result is found in some notebook PCs.

These chip packages are then mounted on the MLB using sockets or slots.

Sockets and Number of Pins

MLB sockets provide a place to install a CPU chip onto the MLB, and are similar to other sockets on the MLB used to install different PC components, such as ROM chips.

As PC CPU chips increased in sophistication, Intel defined interface standards for PC MLBs. These standards are implemented as socket and slot specifications for different Intel CPU chips specifically designed to mechanically and electrically use these standard sockets.

AMD and Cyrix are able to use these standards to provide Intel-compatible CPU chips. The CPU chip packages and sockets/slots evolved over time as systems became more sophisticated. The standard sockets and slots allow MLB manufacturers to produce MLBs that support several future CPU chips rather than tailoring each MLB to a specific CPU chip.

Up until about 1990, consumers believed that in order to upgrade to a faster PC they had to purchase a new one. This changed with Intel's overdrive CPU chips, when the company promised to upgrade CPU chips to improve performance on PCs by simply swapping the CPU chip. Defining standardized sockets allowed current systems to use future CPU chips that Intel designed for those sockets. An additional bonus for consumers was that these standards permitted AMD and Cyrix to create chips swappable with Intel's, provided they conformed to the socket standard. Standardized sockets also made it much easier for users to determine what CPU chips their MLB supported by knowing what socket their MLB used.

In the last two years however, we have come full circle back to the idea that replacement is cheaper than to upgrade. When our editor was working on the chapter covering disk drive failure, the disk drive he was working from ironically failed. We suspect an emotional tie between the disk drive and the book or hara-kiri. A swift consideration of options, their relative costs, and their time to obsolescence caused the editor to acquire a new computer to continue the job.

As mentioned in an earlier section in this chapter, sockets differ in keying and orientation. Most CPU chip packages and sockets are square. Thus, a concern when inserting CPU chips is to correctly insert them into a socket. Accidentally rotating the CPU chip 90 or 180 degrees can be fatal to the CPU chip because input power to the CPU chip would be on the wrong pin. The pin one rule applies to ensure that the socket and the CPU chip are correctly aligned. CPU chips are often marked with a dot or a notch in the corner that has pin one. This mates with the pin one corner of the socket. Most sockets today are keyed using asymmetrical pin layouts. Thus a CPU chip cannot be incorrectly inserted into the socket.

Early sockets had the chip inserted without the thought of removal. When Intel provided replacement chips for the 80486 that miscalculated some mathematical operations, they had to provide special tools to pry the old chips from the PGA sockets. Overdrive CPU chips were designed to replace installed CPU chips. This meant that consumers were pulling CPU chips out of sockets and inserting new ones. To facilitate overdrive chip upgrades, the Zero Insertion Force (ZIF) socket was developed. The ZIF socket was designed to either tighten or loosen the socket's connectors by moving a lever. Lifting the lever loosened the pin connections, allowing CPU chip insertion or removal with zero (or no) force. Lowering the lever tightened the socket's grip on the pins, ensuring good electrical contact for the CPU chip pins. See Figure 5–6.

Overdrive CPU chips are designed for upgrading older MLBs. As a result, they insert into sockets that do not accommodate regular versions of the same CPU chip. Some Pentium CPU chips fit into a Socket 5 or Socket 7 MLB. Pentium overdrive chips fit into Socket 2 through Socket 7. Because different overdrive CPU chips fit into different sockets, the overdrive CPU chip purchased must precisely match the socket on the MLB. Finally, overdrive CPU chips also regulate voltage differences between the MLB and the CPU chip. The 486DX4 CPU chip uses 3.3-volt power, but a 486DX4 overdrive chip uses 5-volt power because it incorporates a voltage regulator.

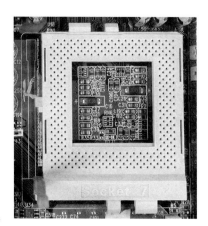

Figure 5–6
ZIF Socket 7 opened.

Table 5–6 summarizes characteristics of Intel socket and slot standards along with the CPU chips used with each socket.

Table 5–6   Some CPU Chip Sockets

Socket	Pins	Layout	Voltage	CPU Chips
0	168	In-Line	5 V	80486DX
1	169	In-Line	5 V	80486DX,SX
2	238	In-Line	5 V	80486DX, SX, DX2
3	237	In-Line	3 V or 5 V	80486DX, SX, DX2, DX4
4	273	In-Line	5 V	Pentium 60 or 66
5	320	Staggered	3 V	Pentium
6	235	In-Line	3 V	80486 DX4
7	321	Staggered	3 V	Pentium, Cyrix, AMD K6
8	387	Staggered	3 V	Pentium Pro
Slot 1/Slot A	242	Edge connector	3 V	Pentium II, Celeron, Pentium III, AMD K7 (*with different electronics*)
Slot 2	330	Edge connector	3 V	Xeon
Socket 370	370	Staggered	2.1 V	Celeron and Pentium III
Socket 423	423	Staggered	2.1 V	Pentium 4, 1.3 to 2.0 GHz
Socket 462	462	Staggered	2.5 V	AMD K7
Socket 478	478	Staggered	2.1 V	Pentium 4, 2.0 GHz and up

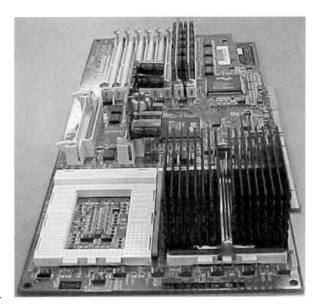

Figure 5-7
Pentium PRO ZIF Socket 8.

The top socket is the Socket 8 used by the Pentium Pro CPU chip. As described in the table it has the most pins. See Figure 5–7.

Cooling

The specialized cooling systems for CPU chips became of serious concern with 80486 and Pentium chips. The 80386 and earlier CPU chips ran at slow speeds and contained relatively few transistors. These CPU chips needed no specialized cooling. Airflow through the PC from the power supply fan was sufficient to cool the CPU chip.

The 80486 CPU chips were the first CPU chips that needed specialized cooling. Newer CPU chips require high performance specialized cooling, which varies depending on the CPU chip, the system in which it is installed, and the cooling ability of the device being used.

CPU chips must operate within a specific temperature range. When a CPU chip overheats, it causes problems and can self-destruct. Problems manifest themselves with different symptoms. An overheating CPU chip causes system crashes, lockups, and random reboots. An overheating CPU chip can also cause memory errors, application errors, disk problems, and more. These symptoms can be caused by other problems as well, making the overheating problem difficult to diagnose. Furthermore, overheating only occurs after the

PC has run properly for a time while warming up to the overheating condition. Severely overheated CPU chips are easy to permanently damage as well.

The old PC MLB design did not provide adequate cooling for CPU chips. Specialized cooling was needed because the CPU chip is located far from the power supply fan, and the fan itself is blowing out from the case. Airflow directly over the surface of the CPU chip is needed in most cases to provide adequate cooling.

Passive Heat Sinks

Passive heat sinks that had aluminum fins were the first devices used to cool CPU chips. A passive heat sink has no moving parts. Heat sink operation cools the CPU chip using thermal conduction and radiation. An aluminum extrusion creates fins. These extrusions are cut off and attached to the surface of the CPU chip. The heat sink draws heat from the CPU chip, and air crossing through the fins on the heat sink cools it. The larger the heat sink and its fins, the better the cooling. Heat sinks are fastened to the CPU chip using glue or, more commonly, clips pressing the heat sink to the CPU chip surface. A heat sink compound is used to improve the thermal transfer for heat sinks attached using clips. See Figure 5–8.

Figure 5–8
Server CPU board with passive heat sink.

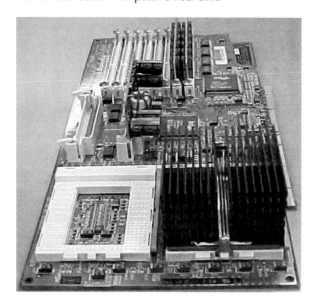

Active Heat Sinks

Active heat sinks with fans are an enhancement to the passive heat sink. Active heat sinks add a small fan that blows directly onto the heat sink metal to ensure direct airflow. Unfortunately, the typical CPU fan is made using a cheap sleeve-bearing motor having a short life span. It is the first thing to fail in most PCs. CPU fans using a ball-bearing motor with a multi-year warranty should be used to ensure that there is no fan failure, causing the CPU chip to overheat.

In theory, an active heat sink cools better than a passive one because it forces air to circulate across the heat sink, rather than relying on the heat from the heat sink making the air hotter so it circulates by convection. However, passive heat sinks have certain advantages over CPU fans—mainly, they are not prone to failure. Failed active heat sinks allow the CPU chip to overheat quickly. But where there is no fan, there is nothing to stop working. Passive heat sinks can be made larger than the heat sinks used with fans, and are less expensive to make. Heat sinks conduct heat from the CPU chip to the heat sink and then radiate it to the air. Good cooling depends on the transfer of heat between the CPU chip and the heat sink metal. Pockets of air between the heat sink and the CPU chip surface make the heat transfer much less effective because they tend to insulate the heat sink from the CPU chip. CPU chips with heat sinks directly glued to them have good heat transfer because the glue eliminates air pockets. Heat sinks attached to the CPU chip using clips

Figure 5–9
Clip-on active heat sinks.

use a special heat sink compound to eliminate air pockets. Heat sink compound is a white paste made from zinc oxide in a silicone base. Very little is needed—only enough to eliminate air pockets between the CPU chip and the heat sink (Radio Shack sells it). See Figure 5–9. The older Pentium chips used the smaller heat sink in the bottom of the figure. As speed increased, the heat sinks became larger like the heat sink at the top of the figure. The thermal transfer compound is in the packet on the right side of the figure. Figure 5–10 compares the heat sink fin size. The older Pentium heat sink is on top while a newer heat sink is on the bottom. The larger the heat sink fins, the more easily they dissipate the heat. The newest heat sinks are four or five times the size of the oldest heat sinks, illustrating how much more important dissipating heat from the CPU is today. High clock speed CPUs are easily destroyed if heat is permitted to build up in them: They cannot be run without a heat sink. Cartridge CPU heat sinks are shown in Figure 5–11. The three-fan heat sink is for an early 266 MHz Pentium II and the two-fan heat sink is for a 1 GHz AMD Athlon.

Figure 5–10
Socket Chip clip-on active heat sinks side view (oldest on top).

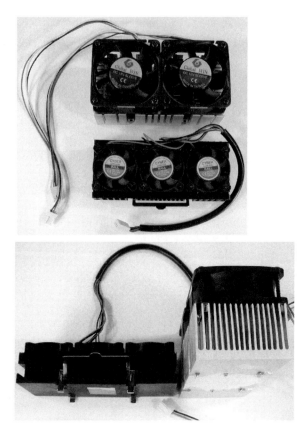

Figure 5-11
Single Edge Cartridge
clip-on active heat sinks.

Peltier Coolers

Peltier coolers are solid-state devices that pump heat from one surface to another. One becomes cool and the other becomes warm. Obviously, the cool side attaches to the CPU chip and the warm side attaches to the heat sink. The Peltier cooler constantly pumps heat away from the surface of the CPU chip to the surface of the heat sink. A Peltier cooler is the best form of CPU chip cooling since the Peltier cooler does not use moving parts to move the heat from the CPU chip to the heat sink.

Servers in particular have fan failure or high temperature alarms because heat sink failure or CPU chip fan failure leads rapidly to overheating the CPU chip. Fan failure devices monitor the electrical level on the power line that supplies the CPU chip and the PC chassis fans. Excessive current flow or no current flow detects when the fan fails, causing the device to sound an audible alarm and display an error message on an operator control panel. High temperature monitors use a thermometer to monitor the temperature of the CPU chip. When the temperature crosses a threshold, an audible alarm sounds or the PC is shut down. Most laptops use some kind of CPU temperature monitoring.

Other CPU Chips—AMD, Cyrix, Motorola, and Alpha

Other CPU chips are either Intel-compatible ones that mimic Intel chip features or are designed to be chips with superior performance. The AMD and Cyrix chips are Intel-compatible CPU chips. Their features have been included in the Intel chip section above. The Motorola and Alpha CPU chips (developed by Digital and now manufactured by Compaq) are RISC chips that run Apple Operating Systems or Windows NT. This section focuses on the Motorola and Alpha chips, as shown in Table 5–7.

Motorola CPU chips are used in Apple Macintosh and UNIX PCs. Alpha CPU chips are used in Windows NT and UNIX PCs. They are RISC-based CPU chips based on CMOS technology. They have L1 and L2 cache structures similar to Intel CPU chips. They employ super-scalar design technology with more than one processing unit inside each CPU chip. The highest clock rate chips today are the Alpha chips. They have been built into Windows NT servers and Windows NT workstations. The servers support multiple Alpha CPU chips running symmetric multiprocessing under Windows NT.

Table 5-7 Motorola and Alpha Chip Features

CPU Chip	Internal Word Size	Data Bus	Address Bus	Clock Speed	Internal Cache	Math Co-processor	Operating Systems	Mac Model
M68000	32 bit	16 bit	24 bit 16 MB	6 MHz–16 MHz	None	External 68881	Xenix, CP/M 68K, Mac OS	128K, 512K, 512Ke, PLUS, and SE
MC68000	32 bit	16 bit	24 bit 16 MB	6 MHz–16 MHz	None	External 68881	Mac OS	Mac Classic
MC68HC000 Low Power	32 bit	16 bit	24 bit 16 MB	6 MHz–16 MHz	None	External 68881	Mac OS	Mac Portable
MC6020	32 bit	32 bit	32 bit 4 GB	12Mhz–33 MHz	None	68881 or 68882	Mac OS A/UX	Mac LC and Mac II
MC6030	32 bit	32 bit	32 bit 4 GB	16Mhz–50 MHz	2KB Data & 2KB Instruction	68882	Mac OS, A/UX	SE/30, IIx, IIcx, IIci, IIsi, and IIfx
MC68040	32 bit	32 bit	32 bit 4 GB	16/32MHz to 50/100 MHz	4KB Data & 4KB Instruction	Internal	Mac OS, A/UX	Mac Quadras and many others
MC68LC040 "a 640SX"	32 bit	32 bit	32 bit 4 GB	16/32MHz to 50/100 MHz	4KB Data & 4KB Instruction	68040	Mac OS, A/UX	Mac Quadra 605 and others
MC68040V	32 bit	32 bit	32 bit 4 GB	16/32MHz to 50/100 MHz	4KB Data & 4KB Instruction	Internal	Mac OS, A/UX	Low Power 68040

Table 5-7 Motorola and Alpha Chip Features (Continued)

CPU Chip	Internal Word Size	Data Bus	Address Bus	Clock Speed	Internal Cache	Math Co-processor	Operating Systems	Mac Model
Power PC 601	64 bit	32 bit	32 bit 4 GB	50MHz–120 MHz	32KB Unified 8-way Associative	Internal	Mac OS, A/IX, Power Open NT, WARP	Macs and IBM RS6000's
Power PC 603	64 bit	32 bit	32 bit 4 GB	50MHz–120 MHz	8KB Data & 8KB Instruction	Internal	Mac OS– through WARP	Low 3.3 Volt Power
Power PC 603+	64 bit	32 bit	32 bit 4 GB	50MHz–120 MHz	16KB Data & 16KB Instruction	Internal	Mac OS– through WARP	A 603 with more cache
Power PC 603e	64 bit	64 bit	32 bit 4 GB	100MHz–300MHz	16KB Data & 16KB Instruction	Internal	Mac OS	
MPC 8240	64 bit	64 bit	32 bit 1 GB	100MHz–266MHz	16KB Data & 16KB Instruction	Internal	Mac OS	A 603 e with PCI interface
Power PC 740	64 bit	64 bit	32 bit 4 GB	200MHz–300MHz	32KB Data & 32KB Instruction	Internal	Mac OS UNIX Windows NT	Mac G3
Power PC 750	64 bit	64 bit	32 bit 4 GB	200MHz–400 MHz	32KB Data & 32KB Instruction	Internal	Mac OS UNIX Windows NT	Mac G3

Table 5-7 Motorola and Alpha Chip Features

CPU Chip	Internal Word Size	Data Bus	Address Bus	Clock Speed	Internal Cache	Math Co-processor	Operating Systems	Mac Model
Power PC G4 7410	64 bit	64 bit	32 bit 4 GB	400 MHz, 500 MHz, and 533 MHz	L1—32KB Data & 32KB Instruction, and L2—512 KB to 2 MB	Internal	Mac OS UNIX	Mac G4
Power PC G4 7450	64 bit	64 bit	36 bit 64 GB	533 MHz, 667 MHz, and 733 MHz	L1—32KB Data & 32KB Instruction, L2—256 KB, and L3—1MB or 2 MB	Internal	Mac OS UNIX	Mac G4
Alpha 21164	64 bit	64 bit	40 bit More than you can buy	500 MHz, 533 MHz, 600 MHz, 633 MHz, and 667 MHz	64KB Data & 64KB Instruction	Internal	Windows NT Linux	Not Applicable Internal 96 KB L2 Cache
Alpha 21264	64 bit	64 bit	40 bit More than you can buy	500 MHz to 1.25 GHz	8 KB Data & 8 KB Instruction	Internal	Windows NT Linux	Not Applicable 2 MB/4MB External L2 Cache

Size and Voltages

The physical size of the Motorola and Alpha CPU chips is similar to the size of Intel CPU chips. See Table 5–8.

Table 5–8 Motorola and Alpha Chips Size and Voltages

CPU Chip	CPU Chip Clock Speed	Process Technology	Circuit Size (microns)	Transistors (millions)	Voltage External/ Core	Power Management
Power PC 603e	100MHz– 300MHz	CMOS	0.5–0.29	2.6	3.3 V/2.5 V	Yes
MPC 8240	100 MHz– 266 MHz	CMOS	0.29	6.5	3.3 V/2.5 V	Yes
Power PC 740	200 MHz– 300 MHz	CMOS	0.29–0.22	6.5	3.3 V/2.5 V	Yes
Power PC 750	200 MHz– 400 MHz	CMOS	0.29–0.19	6.5	3.3 V/2.6 V 3.3 V/1.9 V	Yes (and thermal sensing)
Power PC 7410	400 MHz, 500 MHz, 533 MHz,	CMOS	0.15	My best guess is 20 Million	2.5V/1.8 V	Yes
Power PC 7450	533 MHz, 667 MHz, 733 MHz	CMOS	0.13	My best guess is 20 Million	2.5V/1.8 V	Yes
Alpha 21164	500 MHz– 667 MHz	CMOS	0.35	7	2.5 V	No
Alpha 21264	500 MHz to 1.25 GHz	CMOS	0.18	15	1.5 V	Yes
Alpha 21364	1 GHz and up	CMOS	0.18	100	1.5 V	Yes

The Motorola and Alpha chips run with voltages in the 1.5-volt to 1.8-volt ranges. These are high-speed chips that need low-voltage operation to keep heat generation within acceptable ranges. The Motorola Power PC CPU chips have thermal sensing capability built in as well.

Speeds and Cache

The Motorola and Alpha CPU chips operate at speeds of 100 MHz to 1.2 GHz. This is similar to Intel chips that run from 200 MHz to 1.5 GHz. The internal structure of the Motorola and Alpha CPU chips is a super-scalar structure with multiple processors per CPU chip. The L1 cache is generally split between data and instructions and is built into the CPU chip. CPU chips now have internal L2 cache, and some even have an L3 CPU cache.

Sockets and Pins

The Motorola chip uses Ceramic Ball Grid Array (CBGA) while Alpha CPU chips use a Ceramic Pin Grid Array (CPGA) mounting sockets. In addition, the Alpha CPU used the open industry standard AMD support chips for Socket 7 mounting. Motorola uses a similar (but not an industry standard) Socket 7 mounting. The Motorola CPU chips have their own proprietary CBGA socket layout. Consequently, MLBs are designed specifically for Motorola CPU chips. The Motorola CBGA sockets use 255 to 360 pins, depending on the CPU chip. The Motorola 8240 uses a Tape Ball Grid Array (TBGA) 352-pin linear pin socket.

The Alpha 21264 CPU chip CPGA has 587 pins in a staggered (compact) arrangement. This is not a Socket 7, which has only 321 pins. Although the physical socket does not match, the Socket 7 open standard chips manufactured by AMD provide the electronic support. The Alpha 21164 CPU chip employs a 499-pin socket mounting.

Study Break: What CPU Mount Does Your PC Use?

Open the case of your PC. Locate the CPU chip and examine the mounting.

Does the chip lay flat on the MLB? If so, it is most likely a socket mount. Can you read any information on the socket identifying the socket number? Refer back to Figure 5–6.

Does the chip mount vertically? This is then most likely a Slot 1, or less likely a Slot 2 Pentium chip.

Find the documentation on the MLB and look for references to the master system clock. Is more than one setting supported? Is the clock changed through jumpers or through CMOS settings? Sometimes this is not obvious from the manual. Check Tom's hardware guide on the Web for current MLB clock settings. (*http://sysdoc.pair.com/* or *http://www.tomshardware.com/*)

The goal here is to identify the type of CPU mounting and assess the feasibility of upgrading to a higher speed CPU.

Random Access Memory

Random Access Memory (RAM) is the working memory of the PC. Next to the CPU chip, it is the second fastest component in a PC. To match CPU speed with RAM speed, CPU caches are used. Most PCs use an L1 internal CPU cache and an L2 external (or internal) CPU cache. Newer chips use an L2 internal cache and an L3 cache as well. Each type of cache (L1, L2, and L3) is close to the CPU where the data in the cache is used to minimize the distance the electrical signals must travel. Keeping electrical signal distances short increases CPU speed. The function of these caches is to match the RAM speed to the CPU speed. RAM is also changing to increase its speed to come closer to that of the CPU chip. Matching CPU chip speed is only possible if all RAM is inside the CPU chip, making the distance that electrical signals must travel very short. Even then, some cache must still be strategically placed to ensure the desired CPU chip performance. This means miniaturizing the chip well beyond the capabilities of today's technology. Such miniaturization will be possible in the not-too-distant future. Chip fabrication technology has moved from 0.30-micron technology to 0.18-micron, and is moving to 0.13-micron It is expected to achieve 0.08-microns in the near future.

The most active components in a PC system are the CPU chip and the RAM. Different types of RAM have different operating speeds and are suited to specific tasks.

Types of RAM

The basic types of RAM sold are:

- Fast Page Mode SIMMs
- Extended Data Out (EDO) SIMMs
- PC-66 SDRAM DIMMs

347

- PC-100 SDRAM DIMMs

- PC-133 SDRAM DIMMs

- PC-150 SDRAM DIMMs

- PC-1600 Double Data Rate (DDR) SDRAM DIMMs

- PC-2100 DDR SDRAM DIMMs

- PC-400 RAMBUS RIMMs

- PC-800 RAMBUS RIMMs

A main difference in RAM is static versus dynamic RAM. Most types of RAM are dynamic RAM, designed to improve performance with special features. Fast page mode RAM, EDO RAM, SDRAM, DDR, and Rambus Direct RAM (RDRAM) are different RAM designs that improve performance over older DRAM. Some RAM is also designed to support special functions, such as video. Figure 5–12 conceptually presents the differences between these types of RAM. This section explores these different types of RAM.

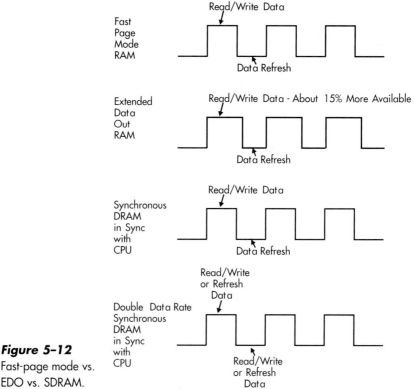

Figure 5–12

Fast-page mode vs. EDO vs. SDRAM.

Static versus Dynamic RAM

The first difference in RAM is static versus dynamic RAM. All RAM acts like buckets. When information is stored in RAM, it is like pouring water into some buckets and not others. The buckets containing the water represent the ones and the empty buckets represent the zeros. Dynamic RAM is leaky buckets and static RAM is non-leaky buckets. The water poured into the dynamic RAM buckets leaks out and must be replenished constantly. This means that some RAM cycles are needed to refresh the memory contents. The refresh cycles slow down the memory which means that static RAM is faster then dynamic RAM. However, dynamic RAM (DRAM) is cheaper to manufacture than is static (SRAM).

Typical DRAM cycle times are specified as 60 ns to 80 ns. This is half the effective cycle time, because full cycles are needed to refresh the RAM contents. Static RAM cycle times are around 10 ns to 20 ns. The most common type of RAM is some form of DRAM. Typically the SIMMs or DIMMs come in what are referred to as sticks, with capacities varying from 8 MB to 128 MB and cycle times of around 70 ns. Static RAM is used for external CPU chip cache (L2 or L3 cache). The total static RAM cache ranges from 512 KB to 2 MB, and will eventually reach 4 MB in the future.

Fast Page Mode

Page mode and fast page mode DRAM are types of DRAM that are organized into rows and columns of pigeonholes containing one or more bits of data. The pigeonholes are addressed and accessed by using row and column addressing. Page mode and fast page mode DRAM provide faster sequential access to DRAM by allowing the CPU chip to make many DRAM accesses to an open row after supplying a row address just once. This means that once a row address is activated, just changing the column address can repeatedly retrieve the data. In page mode, the Row Address Strobe (RAS) line is held active while a new column address is supplied upon a drop of the Column Address Strobe (CAS) signal, permitting the column bits to be accessed.

Since the row address setup and hold times are eliminated, this is faster than the full Row Address Strobe-Column Address Strobe (RAS-CAS) memory cycle used by older memory. Fast page mode improved upon the original page mode by eliminating the column address setup time during the page cycle. Fast page mode DRAM quickly replaced page mode DRAM. Most PCs today use fast page mode DRAM or other types of faster DRAM. See Figure 5–13.

Figure 5-13
Laptop Small Outline DIMM
(SO DIMM) RAM modules.

Extended Data Out (EDO) RAM

Extended Data Out (EDO) RAM is designed to access nearby memory locations faster than fast page mode RAM. EDO RAM keeps the RAM data outputs active after the Column Address Strobe (CAS) goes inactive by using an additional Output Extension (OE) signal line to keep data output enabled.

Pipelined CPU chip systems can overlap EDO RAM data accesses, where the next cycle is started before the data from the last cycle is removed from the bus. Intel Pentium CPU chips used EDO RAM because there was a small performance gain with slower CPU chips. The Intel Triton support chip set was needed for CPU chips to take advantage of advanced EDO RAM capabilities. EDO RAM was used in PCs in early 1995. EDO RAM is sometimes called standard EDO RAM.

Burst EDO (BEDO) RAM came out in early 1995. Burst EDO RAM batches read or write cycles in groups (or bursts) of four. The read or write cycle bursts wrap around on a four-byte boundary. This means that only the two least significant bits of the CAS address are modified internally (that is, 00, 01, 10, 11) to produce the addresses in the burst. This makes burst EDO RAM bus speeds range from 40 MHz to 66 MHz. These speeds are higher than a 33 MHz-bus speed produced using fast page mode or EDO RAM.

EDO RAM generally increases PC speed by extending the time that the CPU chip can access data versus the time that is needed to refresh the DRAM.

SDRAM

As memory bus speeds increased beyond 66 MHz to 100 MHz (and soon faster), DRAM was designed to operate with a synchronous interface to further reduce delays in accessing RAM by the CPU chip. An asynchronous DRAM interface causes the CPU chip to wait for the DRAM to complete internal operations. These operations use several different timing or strobe signals and consume about 60 ns.

A Synchronous DRAM (SDRAM) interface transfers data from the processor under control of the system clock. These transfers store the addresses, data, and control signals. The CPU chip is then free to perform other tasks. After several clock cycles, the requested data is produced and can be read from the output lines by the CPU chip. A second synchronous RAM interface advantage is that the only timing provided to the DRAM is the system clock, eliminating multiple RAM timing strobes and simplifying RAM control circuitry. Other inputs/outputs are simplified because control, address, and data signals can all be transferred to RAM without monitoring setup and hold timings.

SDRAM chips are specified in MHz, not the traditional nanoseconds of other DRAM chips. This directly matches the memory bus speed to the SDRAM speed. To calculate the SDRAM chip speed in ns, divide 1 second (1 billion ns) by the SDRAM MHz speed. For example, 67 MHz SDRAM has a 15 ns chip speed (1/67=0.0149 or 15 ns). This is not the equivalent to the nanosecond speed of fast page mode DRAM, EDO RAM or BEDO RAM because those DRAM chips have hidden internal operations incorporated into their timing specifications.

SDRAM modules were initially targeted at 66 MHz bus systems. These were 83 MHz (12 ns) or 100 MHz (10 ns) SDRAM chips. SDRAM 100 MHz bus chips operate reliably at about 83 MHz because of timing signal delays. Better bus design should increase the SDRAM speed to the advertised 100 MHz bus speed. The PC100 is an Intel specification for SDRAM that runs at 100 MHz, as shown in Figure 5–14. Higher-speed PC100 SDRAM works with lower-speed 66 MHz memory buses. SDRAM runs at 133 MHz bus speeds and may increase speed to 150 MHz bus speeds.

Double Data Rate RAM (DDR RAM)

Double Data Rate RAM is another form of SDRAM. The DDR RAM uses both the rising and falling clock signals to move information into and out of the RAM. This essentially changes PC-100 RAM operating at 100 MHz into RAM operating at 200 MHz.RAM. However, the RAM chips and MLB must be designed specifically to operate at the double data rate so PC-100 is not mag-

351

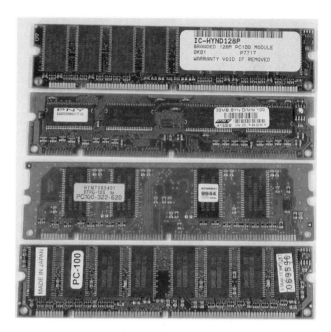

Figure 5-14
Labeled PC100 SDRAM
amodules.

ically changed into PC-200 RAM. The AMD Athlon CPUs are beginning to use DDR RAM.

Rambus Direct RAM (RDRAM)

Rambus Direct RAM connects the RAM to the CPU through a new high performance Rambus channel, which permits running multiple channels in parallel to increase memory speed to the CPU. RDRAM is implemented in RDRAM In-line Memory Modules (RIMMs). RDRAM operates at 400 MHz bus speeds and higher. The Pentium 4 uses RDRAM.

Video RAM (VRAM)

Video RAM (VRAM) is fast RAM on the video card used to store the image displayed on a PC's monitor. VRAM must supply data to the display electronics at the speed at which the screen is scanned. For example, a monitor with a resolution of 1,024 by 768 8-bit picture elements (pixels) refreshed at 70 Hz requires the VRAM to handle $1024 \times 768 \times 70 = 55$ M/sec or one byte every 18 ns.

VRAM can be dual-ported, permitting both the video processor chip and the CPU chip to access it simultaneously, thereby speeding up display operations. Typically, the video processor chip access to VRAM is through a wider data bus than that used by the CPU chip. Since it is performing most of the work producing the display, giving it a wider bus access to VRAM speeds up sending display data to the monitor. Hence, video processor chips access video display memory in 64-bit, 128-bit or 192-bit wide data chunks. Most VRAM is located on the video card. The amount varies from 4 MB to 64 MB and more. See Figure 5–15.

Accelerated Graphics Port (AGP) cards provide a faster way for main system memory (RAM) to update VRAM. AGP is a bus specification developed by Intel. It gives low-cost 3-D cards faster access to system RAM than can be provided by the PCI bus. AGP cards dynamically allocate PC RAM to store

Figure 5–15
PCI video board with 40 ns VRAM.

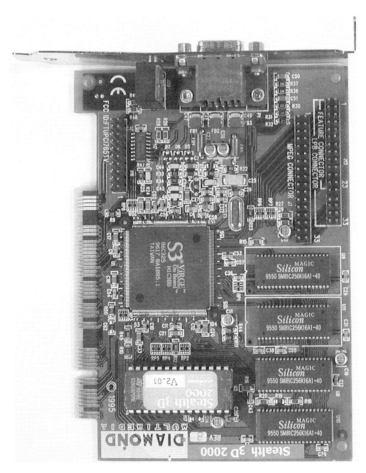

screen images and to support 3-D graphics features like texture mapping, z-buffering and alpha blending. The AGP card bus transfers data at 66 MHz doubled to 133 MHz. The PCI bus only operates at 33 MHz. The AGP design and specification provides coherent memory management and supports the CPU chip reading scattered data in the PC's RAM in rapid bursts. The AGP design and specification reduces the cost of high-end graphics subsystems by using existing system RAM for graphics storage. With AGP cards, the greater the amount of VRAM, the faster the transfers between VRAM and system RAM; this explains why an 8 MB AGP video card is faster than a 2 MB AGP video card.

To determine the VRAM needed to store a monitor image, multiply the horizontal resolution by the vertical resolution. Then multiply this result by 1 for 8-bit color (256 color), by 2 for 16-bit color (65,000 colors), by 3 for 25-bit color (16.7 million colors), or by 4 for 32-bit color (4 billion colors). For example, a 640-by-480 pixel resolution display with 8-bit color (256 colors) requires $640 \times 480 \times 1 = 307.2$ KB VRAM on the board. Increasing the color depth to 16.7 million colors (25-bit color) requires 921.6 KB VRAM, or about 1 MB VRAM. Most PCs use a 800-by-600 (SVGA) or a 1,025-by-768 (XGA) resolution on a 15-inch or a 17-inch monitor. Thus $1024 \times 768 \times 2 = 1.6$ MB. A graphics board would need at least 2 MB of VRAM to provide 16-bit color at 1,025-by-768 resolution. AGP 3-D graphics boards deliver 1,600-by-1,200 32-bit color images requiring about 8 MB of VRAM or more for fast display operation. High performance 3-D and dual monitor video cards use 32 MB or 64 MB of VRAM.

Windows RAM (WRAM)

Windows RAM (WRAM) is a special type of dual-ported VRAM that is used on Matrox video cards and developed by Samsung Electronics. WRAM is fast, dual-ported video RAM that has special features, such as dual-color block-write mode for fast text and color fill acceleration in Windows applications. A WRAM video adapter can fetch the contents of video memory for display at the same time that the PC is writing new information into the video memory. This produces faster image display than single-port video RAM.

Although similar to VRAM, WRAM performs faster at less cost because it addresses large blocks of Windows video memory. WRAM memory provides about a 50 percent performance increase at about 20 percent lower cost per bit compared to VRAM memory. These features and the dual ports provide high-speed video performance at all resolutions and color depths. The performance of dual-ported WRAM compared to single-ported memories increases with higher resolutions, color depths, and refresh rates.

RAM Operating Characteristics and Parameters

RAM has different operating characteristics and parameters. We have already discussed some of these. This section looks at some additional RAM parameters.

Memory Banks and Interleaving

DRAM memory chips are slower than CPUs. They require charging time equivalent to their access time. Table 5–9 illustrates the concept of interleaving. The RAM speed in the table must be faster than the 1 or 2 wait states determined by the computer clock rate. Today's CPU chip clock speeds of 400 MHz and 500 MHz easily outstrip memory speeds. As a result, memory must interface through both an L2 and an L1 cache to the CPU chip. SDRAM is not interleaved but is still slower than the CPU chip. SDRAM speeds are presented in the table for comparison purposes.

Matching CPU chip speed or CPU L2 cache speed to memory chip speed is accomplished by interleaving memory banks. When CPU chip speed is roughly twice as fast as the memory chip speed, the PC charges (prepares) a location in one bank for use, while during the same clock cycle it retrieves the contents of another location in a twin sister (or brother) bank. It then switches banks. It retrieves from the second bank and charges the first. It then retrieves from the first while again charging the second. This is called memory interleaving, as shown in Figure 5–16.

Figure 5–16
Memory bank interleaving.

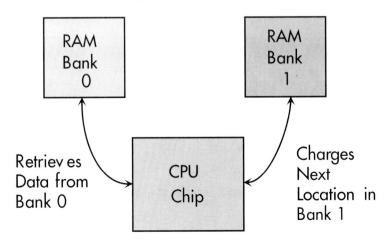

Table 5-9 RAM vs. CPU Clock Speeds

Clock Speed/Duration		Computer Clock Cycle Time in Nanoseconds			Minimum RAM Speed		
Clock Speed MHz	Clock Tick Duration Nanoseconds	0 Wait State 2 Clock Cycles	1 Wait State 3 Clock Cycles	2 Wait States 4 Clock Cycles	Minimum 0 Wait State 2 Clock Cycles	1 Wait State 3 Clock Cycles	2 Wait States 4 Clock Cycles
6	166.667	333.333	500	668	150	200	300
8	125	250	375	500	120	150	200
12	83.333	166.667	250	332	80	120	150
16	62.5	125	187.5	252	80 (Interleave)	100	120
20	50	100	150	200	80 (Interleave)	80	100
25	40	80	120	160	80 (Interleave)	80	80
33	30.303	60.606	90.909	120	70 (Interleave & Cache)	70	70
50	20	40	60	80	70 (Interleave & Cache)	70	70
100	10	20	30	40	60 (Interleave & Cache)	60	60
400	2.5	5	7.5	10	PC66 SDRAM	15 ns	15 ns
500	2	4	6	8	PC100 SDRAM	10 ns	10 ns
1 GHz	1	2	3	4	PC133 SDRAM/ DDR RAM/Rambus Direct RAM	7.5 ns/ 3.75 ns/ 2.5 ns	7.5 ns/ 3.75 ns/ 2.5 ns

Memory interleaving was evident in older 386 and 486 PCs. Memory expansion was performed using specific SIMM configurations because of the memory bank interleaving. For example some typical allowable memory sizes were:

Four banks of 256-KB chips for 1 MB total RAM

Two banks of 1-MB chips for 2 MB total RAM

Four banks of 1-MB chips for 4 MB total RAM

Two banks of 5-MB chips for 8 MB total RAM

Two banks of 5-MB chips and two banks of 1 MB chips for 10 MB total RAM

Four banks of 5-MB chips for 16 MB total RAM

Figure 5–17 shows two SIMM banks each with two SIMMS. The top two SIMMs are labeled Bank1 and the bottom two SIMMs are labeled Bank2.

With DIMMs, a single DIMM could provide two memory banks for interleaving by 486 CPU chips. Since Pentium CPU chips had 64-bit data paths, two DIMMs were required to permit memory bank interleaving. Since SDRAM did not require bank interleaving, as PCs moved to the faster SDRAM, single DIMMs provided the RAM required without bank interleaving.

Memory Bus (8 bit, 16 bit, 32 bit, and 64 bit)

The pathway between the PC's system RAM and the CPU chip has changed significantly since the introduction of the PC in 1981. Early PCs were so slow that memory was accessed through the normal ISA bus. In these PCs, memory expansion was accomplished by installing memory expansion cards in Industry Standard Architecture (ISA) bus slots. The first memory transfers to

Figure 5–17
SIMM memory banks.

the CPU chip were over an 8-bit bus. The 8088 chip was a 16-bit chip with an 8-bit data pathway into and out of the CPU chip. The 80286 chip moved to a 16-bit bus. Memory and CPU chips were still so slow that installing memory expansion cards into the ISA 16-bit bus provided RAM expansion. In this case the transfers between RAM and the CPU chip were 16-bit transfers.

The emergence of 32-bit 80386 and 80486 chips began to change the system RAM bus connection to the CPU chip. These changes were necessitated by higher CPU chip speeds and faster memory speeds that both exceeded the capabilities of the ISA bus. A special memory bus was required because the ISA bus couldn't meet the transfer speed requirements of the CPU chips. The bus data width changed to a 32-bit width and then on to a 64-bit width with the introduction of Intel Pentium chips around 1990. Today, system RAM and Video RAM both operate with high-speed 64-bit buses connected to the CPU chip.

Parity versus Nonparity

Parity is an error-checking mechanism employed in memory design to detect hardware memory errors. Parity provides an extra parity bit (memory test bit) for every 8-bit memory byte. Single In-line Memory Modules (SIMMs) are specified as 8 by 32 for nonparity memory and as 9 by 36 for parity-protected memory. This means that 8 by 32 memory stored 8 bits per byte for a total of $8 \times 4 = 32$ bits. It had no parity checking. In contrast, parity memory stored 9 bits per byte or $9 \times 4 = 36$ bits. This provided 4 extra parity bits on each SIMM.

Parity would be set as odd or, more likely, even depending on the number of 1s stored in each byte. Even parity added an extra 1 bit when the 8 bits in a byte contained an odd number of 1s. If a single bit changes from 1 to 0 or from 0 to 1, the parity would not match when it was recomputed as the byte was retrieved from memory.

Parity is best described as a dryer. When you put in an even number of socks to dry (the socks being equivalent to our ones), the dryer always returns an odd number of socks (ones). The data is stored in bytes and the parity computed and stored with each byte. Upon retrieval, it must match or there is a memory error.

Parity is only mathematically about 95 percent effective in detecting errors. If an even number of bits change, parity fails to detect the error. While missing even the smallest error is intolerable in PCs, parity is highly effective because double-bit memory errors are extremely rare (one stands a better chance of hitting a $100 million lottery jackpot than getting a double-bit memory error).

Most PCs do not use memory parity as a memory error checking mechanism because all SIMMs are tested quite thoroughly for errors. If a memory error happens, the PC behaves badly and crashes almost immediately after it is started. Servers are a different story. They must operate reliably without memory errors. This means that they use 9 by 36 SIMMs or DIMMs and error-correction circuitry to correct single-bit errors and detect double-bit errors. This is discussed in more detail in later sections.

Single In-line Memory Modules (SIMMs)

A SIMM is a single in-line memory module. It has from six to nine RAM chips mounted on one side or both sides of a small circuit board. SIMMs come in 30-pin and 72-pin sizes. SIMM only specifies the RAM packaging and not the type of RAM. Any RAM type—fast page mode, EDO, or SDRAM—can be found in each module configuration. Normally, two SIMMs are required to expand Pentium memory due to bank interleaving. In Figure 5–18, the SIMM expander at the bottom converts 30-pin SIMMs into 72-pin SIMMs.

Figure 5–18
30-pin and 72-pin SIMMs.

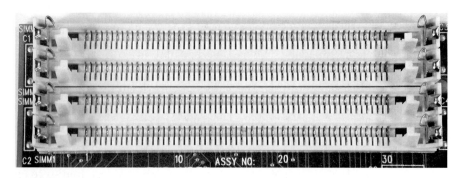

Figure 5–19
SIMM sockets.

Both 30-pin and 72-pin SIMMs are notched on one side so that they cannot be incorrectly installed. The 72-pin SIMMs are also notched in the middle. They are placed in the SIMM socket and rolled or rocked back into place. See Figure 5–19.

Clips on either side of the SIMM socket mounts hold the SIMM firmly in place. SIMM removal is accomplished by moving the metal (or plastic) tabs in the SIMM socket to the side, releasing the SIMM from the socket.

Dual In-line Memory Modules (DIMMs)

DIMMs are used for SDRAM and DDR SDRAM. DIMMs provide a 64-bit (72-bit with parity) wide data path. As a result, they can be used one at a time on Pentium boards. DIMMs of different capacities can be mixed unless there is associative memory interleaving. Such interleaving makes memory expansion in some PCs and servers much more structured than in any old desktop PC. Figure 5–20 shows a 168-pin DIMM and a 184-pin RIMM.

DIMMs are inserted by pushing them straight down into the DIMM socket. When inserted properly, plastic retainer clips at each end of the socket snap into place, securing the DIMM. Most PCs use synchronous DRAM in DIMMs, but soon DDR SDRAM will be common.

Rambus In-Line Memory Modules (RIMMs)

Rambus RIMM modules are general purpose high-performance memory suitable for applications where high bandwidth and low latency are required. The Rambus RIMM module consists of Rambus Direct RAM chips. These chips are high-speed CMOS DRAMs organized as 8 M words by 16 or 18 bits.

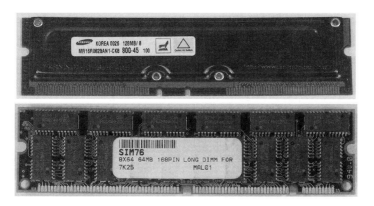

Figure 5–20
168-pin DIM and 184-pin RIMM modules.

RDRAM devices transfer data at rates of 1.25 ns per two bytes (or 10 ns per 16 bytes). RDRAM architecture enables sustained high data transfer rates for multiple, simultaneous, randomly addressed, memory transactions. Separate control and data buses with independent row and column control provide 95 percent or higher bus efficiency. RDRAM's bank architecture permits simultaneous memory transfers for each RIMM.

RIMMs are installed in pairs, and all RIMM sockets must be filled with RIMMs or with terminators. Similar to DIMMs, RIMMs are inserted by pushing them straight down into the RIMM socket. Pentium 4 PCs use RIMMs.

ECC RAM

Error-correcting codes are used to correct single and multiple bit errors in server disk and memory operations. They employ multiple bits to detect and correct errors.

In network servers and some PCs, RAM uses the 4 extra parity bits found in 9 by 36 bit SIMMs or DIMMs, combined with more sophisticated Error-Correcting Code (ECC) circuitry, to detect and correct single bit memory errors. The next study break exercise illustrates how error correcting codes work.

In one of my 80286 PCs, we installed an Orchid Technology memory board that used three extra bits of RAM to detect and correct memory errors. ECC memory is used routinely in network servers, and may be used in PCs. Similar error-correcting code circuitry is used to detect and correct errors on data stored on disk drives. In this case, several extra bytes of information are stored on the disk to perform error correction.

Study Break: ECC Operation

The operation of error-correcting codes is illustrated using a simple example. By adding three extra bits, single-bit errors in four bits can be detected and corrected.

Using Figure 5–21, write down any four bits in positions one through four.

Next write these bits down in the circle areas number one through four.

Then using even parity to always have an even number of ones, create the bits encompassed by circle 5, circle 6, and circle 7. Write these bit values in positions 5, 6, and 7.

Now alter a bit position (any bit position will do). Using the altered bit value, recalculate bits 5, 6, and 7.

Determine bits that do not match the originally created bits. The circled area unique only to those mismatched bits is the bit that is in error.

This is the simplest illustration of the operation of error-correcting codes.

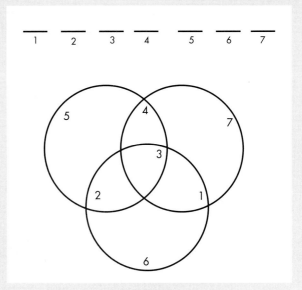

Figure 5–21
ECC operation.

Main Logic Boards

The primary function of the MLB is to provide a mechanism for interfacing ROM, RAM, cache RAM, and PC cards to the CPU chip. MLBs generally provide mounting for RAM SIMMs/DIMMs/RIMMs, ROMs, PC card bus connections, L2 cache memory, and power supply connections. The newer MLBs have serial, parallel, IDE, floppy controllers, and more integrated into their design. They come in different form factors and layouts that are all based on the original IBM PC AT form factor.

System boards fall into two general categories, either integrated or nonintegrated. An integrated system board has most of its components, such as video and mass storage interfaces, physically mounted on the circuit board. You typically find integrated system boards today in lower-end bundled systems (from manufacturers such as Compaq, IBM, and HP, to name a few) because they are cheaper to manufacture. The drawback to integrated system boards is that if an integrated component fails, the entire system board may need to be replaced. Some components on the system may not be easily upgraded. This can make upgrading a PC expensive because the upgrade requires purchasing a new system board.

The other category is a nonintegrated system board. This system board is unique because most of its components, such as video and storage, are not mounted physically on the system board. In this case, video and storage physically sit in the expansion slots. Today, nonintegrated system boards have the disadvantage of bus transfer limitations impacting system speed. Servers use special nonintegrated system boards to facilitate easy CPU chip replacement in the event of failure and to provide the ability to have multiple CPU chips in the same server.

Types of MLBs

MLBs are further classified by their form factor, which is determined by the board's mechanical size, how the integrated controllers attach to external devices, and the mounting hole layout.

The first clone MLBs duplicated the mechanical layout of the original PC and PC XT MLBs. They then moved to a PC AT form factor when the PC AT came out in 1985. Today's MLBs are derived from the AT form factor. They evolved through the baby AT form factor, the ATX and Mini-ATX form factors, the Micro ATX form factor, the Flex ATX form factor and the NLX form factor. Table 5–10 summarizes form factor features for different MLB styles.

Table 5-10 MLB Form Factor Features

MLB Form Factor	CPU Chip Mounting	RAM Mounting	Power Connector	External Connectors	Other Component Connectors
PC XT Style	DIP Socket	DRAM sockets	P8 and P9	Keyboard DIN	ISA 8-bit Bus
AT Style	PGA Socket	DRAM sockets	P8 and P9	Keyboard DIN	ISA 16-bit Bus
Baby AT Style	Typically ZIF PGA Socket 5 or ZIF PGA Socket 7	DRAM Sockets and/or SIMM sockets	P8 and P9	Keyboard DIN	ISA 16-bit Bus VESA Bus PCI Bus Dual IDE Floppy Serial Parallel
New AT Style	ZIF PGA Socket 7	SIMM sockets and /or DIMM sockets	P8 and P9 or ATX style	Keyboard and mouse, mini-DIN	ISA 16-bit Bus AGP Bus PCI Bus Dual IDE Floppy Serial Parallel
ATX Style and Mini-ATX Style	ZIF PGA Socket or SEC Slot	SIMM sockets, DIMM sockets, or RIMM sockets	ATX style	Keyboard and mouse, mini-DIN, VGA, Parallel Port, Dual Serial Ports, two USB Ports. Optional sound and game ports.	ISA 16-bit Bus AGP Bus PCI Bus Dual IDE SCSI (a few) Floppy Serial Parallel

Table 5-10 MLB Form Factor Features (Continued)

MLB Form Factor	CPU Chip Mounting	RAM Mounting	Power Connector	External Connectors	Other Component Connectors
Micro ATX	ZIF PGA Socket or SEC Slot	SIMM sockets, DIMM sockets, or RIMM sockets	ATX style	Keyboard and mouse, mini-DIN, VGA, Parallel Port, Dual Serial Ports, two USB Ports. Optional sound and game ports.	ISA 16-bit Bus AGP Bus PCI Bus Dual IDE SCSI (a few) Floppy Serial Parallel
Flex ATX	ZIF PGA Socket or SEC Slot	SIMM sockets, DIMM sockets, or RIMM sockets	ATX style	Keyboard and mouse, mini-DIN, VGA, Parallel Port, Dual Serial Ports, two USB Ports. Optional sound and game ports.	ISA 16-bit Bus AGP Bus PCI Bus Dual IDE SCSI (a few) Floppy Serial Parallel
NLX	ZIF PGA Socket or SEC Slot	SIMM sockets, DIMM sockets, or RIMM sockets	ATX style	Keyboard and mouse, mini-DIN, VGA, Parallel Port, Dual Serial Ports, two USB Ports. Optional sound and game ports.	ISA 16-bit Bus AGP Bus PCI Bus Dual IDE SCSI (a few) Floppy Serial Parallel

The key element driving the design of MLBs is the bus structure feeding the CPU chip. This structure is arranged in a hierarchical fashion, depending on the supporting chip set. The CPU chip connects to the host bus, which connects to the L2 (or L3) CPU cache and the host bus bridge chip (known as the "North" bridge). Next, the PC's main SDRAM and VRAM connect to the host bus through the host bus (North) bridge chip. The front side bus (FSB) is the bus connecting RAM into the "North" bridge. A bridge chip translates the electrical signals and timing from one bus to another. It may contain some data buffering to support speed-matching functions.

The VRAM connection flows across AGP bus connections for most MLBs produced today. The host bus bridge also connects to the much slower (33 or 66 MHz) PCI bus. Moving down the hierarchy, the next bridge chip bridges the ISA 16-bit bus to the PCI bus. This is regarded as the "South" bridge. Connected into the bridge are IDE and USB ports. Supporting chips may also connect in the slower serial and parallel port connections as well. Data flows from the slower devices and buses at the bottom of the hierarchy to the higher speed PCI bus in the middle of the hierarchy to finally the fastest devices and the CPU chip at the top of the hierarchy, as illustrated in Figure 5–22.

Buses are used to connect PC peripheral components and devices. The host bus is at the top end of the bus hierarchy and operates directly with the CPU chip, RAM, and AGP port through the "North" bridge Integrated Circuit (IC). The bridge integrated circuit matches the speed, electrical load, and voltage levels of the host bus to the other buses it services. Similarly, the main PCI bus is limited in terms of the devices that can connect to it. The "South" PCI-bus-to-ISA-bus and PCI-bus-to-PCI-bus bridge ICs support expansion of the primary PCI system bus into other ISA and PCI buses into which PC cards connect. The connection to the host bus for these other buses is a bridged connection, not a direct connection. Bridged connections have added delays or latencies in their data transfers. As a result, bridged buses are slower than direct buses when it comes to transferring data to the CPU chip. Because some buses have electrical load limits, they are bridged into a primary PCI bus that then passes their data via a host bus bridge to the host bus and RAM. PC MLBs with more than 4 PCI slots are likely to be bridged in this fashion.

Some brand name manufacturers such as Compaq built their own MLB designs that did not conform to the standardized MLB styles discussed here. These proprietary boards used Intel and competing chip sets to provide the bus and data hierarchy feeding into the CPU chip. Their ability to accept upgraded components or to be replaced by standardized MLBs was limited.

Now that we have examined MLBs in general, let's discuss the standardized MLB styles in more detail.

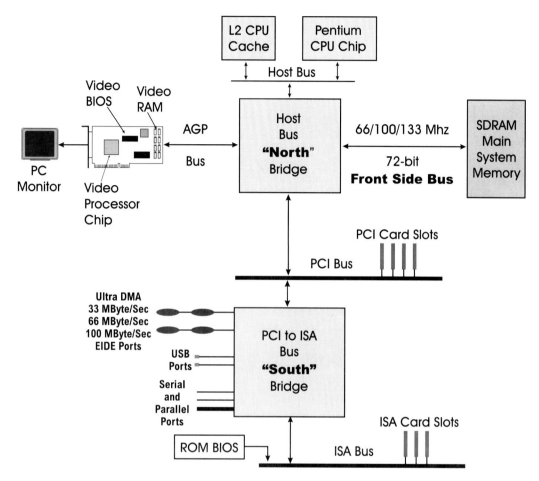

Figure 5–22
CPU board general structure showing "North" bridge, "South" bridge and Front Side Bus (FSB).

PC/XT Style

PC/XT style was the simplest MLB design. The ISA 8-bit bus connected directly to the CPU chip. Memory and all I/O flowed across the bus. This was possible because of the slow CPU chip speeds. RAM was installed in DRAM sockets for individual chips, and the power connectors were the old P8 and P9 style connectors. There was a single DIN connector at the rear of the MLB to connect in the keyboard. All display, disk drive, serial port and parallel port connections were made with ISA bus PC cards. This board may be found at

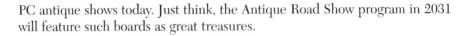

PC antique shows today. Just think, the Antique Road Show program in 2031 will feature such boards as great treasures.

AT Style

The AT-style board form factor started in 1985 with the IBM PC AT. It laid the foundation for almost all MLBs for the next 15 years. The original AT MLB was not that much different from the XT-style MLB. Basically, the ISA bus connected directly to the CPU chip. The difference here was that the ISA bus was now a 16-bit bus. Memory and all I/O flowed through this 16-bit ISA bus. Slow 80286 CPU chip speeds made this possible. With the AT, the ISA bus approached its top clock rate of 8 MHz. RAM was installed in DRAM sockets for individual chips or in DRAM add-on PC cards, while the old P8- and P9-style power connectors attached the power supply. The P8 and P9 designations came from the original IBM PC; the power connectors on it were labeled P8 and P9. Power supply manufacturers adopted these designations as a de facto industry standard. They are now being replaced with industry standard ATX-style connectors.

A single DIN connector at the rear of the MLB connected in the keyboard. All display, disk drive, serial port, and parallel port connections were made using 8-bit or now 16-bit ISA bus PC cards. One added feature was that the PC setup was now performed using a CMOS setup and diagnostic program on floppy disk. This was the first PC that permitted changing setup parameters without opening the PC, as shown in Figure 5–23.

As the 80386 and 80486 CPU chips appeared, the AT style of MLB changed to meet new PC hardware and configuration needs. The 80386 chip PC had external L2 CPU cache and the 80486 chip PCs had both internal L1 and external L2 CPU cache. This necessitated a host bus structure that connected the L2 cache, the system RAM and the CPU, separate from the 16-bit ISA bus structure. See Figure 5–24.

The VESA local bus that speeded data transfers to the display controller card VRAM provided faster graphic displays than graphics cards with slower bus transfer rates. Soon other faster devices like fixed disk drives were connected to the PC using the VESA bus. See Figure 5–25.

Around 1990, the Extended Industry Standard Architecture (EISA) bus was introduced to compete with IBM's Micro Channel Architecture (MCA) bus. The EISA is fading out of existence because the boards were expensive to purchase and the added performance was not more than Intel's PCI bus performance. In the 90s Intel's PCI bus and plug-and-play PC cards arrived. Each of these steps changed the architecture of the AT-style MLB.

As Pentium CPU chip PCs began to dominate the market, the AT-style

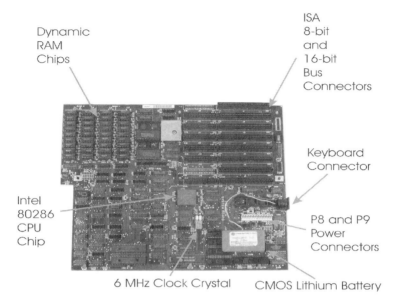

Dynamic
RAM
Chips

ISA
8-bit
and
16-bit
Bus
Connectors

Keyboard
Connector

Intel
80286
CPU
Chip

P8 and P9
Power
Connectors

6 MHz Clock Crystal   CMOS Lithium Battery

Figure 5–23
Original PC AT 80286 MLB.

Figure 5–24
Early Baby AT MLB.

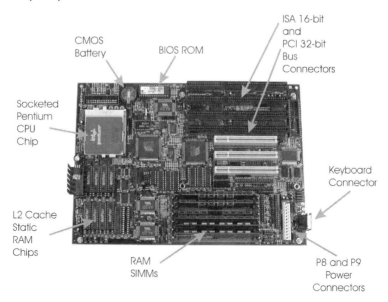

CMOS
Battery

BIOS ROM

ISA 16-bit
and
PCI 32-bit
Bus
Connectors

Socketed
Pentium
CPU
Chip

Keyboard
Connector

L2 Cache
Static
RAM
Chips

RAM
SIMMs

P8 and P9
Power
Connectors

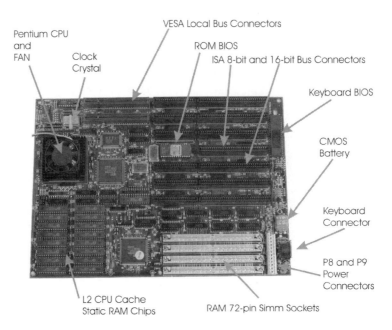

Pentium CPU
and
FAN   Clock
             Crystal

VESA Local Bus Connectors

ROM BIOS

ISA 8-bit and 16-bit Bus Connectors

Keyboard BIOS

CMOS
Battery

Keyboard
Connector

P8 and P9
Power
Connectors

L2 CPU Cache
Static RAM Chips

RAM 72-pin Simm Sockets

Figure 5–25
Baby AT Vesa Local Bus MLB.

MLB evolved to its present configuration. It implemented a hierarchical structure with host bus that connected the CPU chip to L2 cache and also bridged it to memory, AGP buses, and PCI buses. The physical connections supported the standard keyboard DIN connector, P8 and P9 power connectors, 16-bit ISA bus card slots, and PCI bus card slots. Recently, AGP graphics card bus slots have emerged to again speed up graphics data transfers.

Baby AT Style

The baby AT-style boards had all the same features as the AT-style boards except that they were smaller. Chassis mounting for baby AT-style boards and AT-style boards varied slightly. Virtually all PC chassis accommodated these variations. As chip sets required less MLB space, the baby AT-style board form factor became more prevalent. As seen in Figure 5–26, the board has a Socket 7 AMD K5 CPU chip mount, P8 /P9 power connectors, two ISA 16-bit bus connectors, three PCI bus connectors, and one shared (PCI or ISA) connector slot.

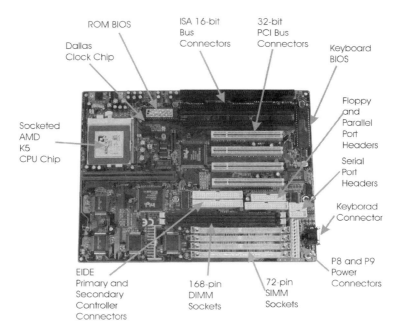

ROM BIOS

Dallas
Clock Chip

ISA 16-bit
Bus
Connectors

32-bit
PCI Bus
Connectors

Keyboard
BIOS

Socketed
AMD
K5
CPU Chip

Floppy
and
Parallel
Port
Headers

Serial
Port
Headers

Keyborad
Connector

EIDE
Primary and
Secondary
Controller
Connectors

168-pin
DIMM
Sockets

72-pin
SIMM
Sockets

P8 and P9
Power
Connectors

Figure 5–26
Baby AT Style Socket 7 MLB.

ATX Style

Many Pentium PC systems use an ATX-style MLB. This board differs from the AT and baby AT styles in that it has more PC subsystems built onto the board. ATX-style boards provide a home for the CPU chip, system RAM, BIOS ROM, ISA bus card slots, and PCI bus card slots. In addition, they incorporate serial port, parallel port, mini-DIN keyboard, mini-DIN mouse connections, Universal Serial Bus (USB), and IDE controller connections. The device connectors for the serial, parallel, mini-DIN, and USB ports are routed to a special connector bracket on the rear of the ATX-style MLBs. Power supply connections also differ from the P8 and P9 connectors on the older AT-style and baby AT-style MLBs. The big difference between ATX-style and AT-style boards is that the ATX-style boards have either SEC or Socketed CPU connections while baby AT-style boards are mostly Socket 7 boards. The ATX SEC Slot 1 MLB in Figure 5–27 has on the top an ISA 16-bit bus connector, a combined ISA 16-bit/PCI bus connector, and four PCI bus connectors. The SEC Slot 1 CPU connector is on the left side next to the DIMM sockets. The serial, parallel, USB, mouse and keyboard connections are on the right. To the left of the Slot 1 are

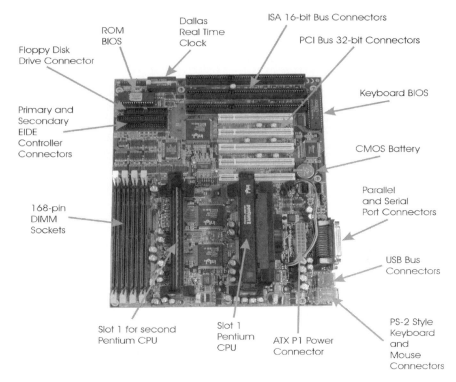

ROM BIOS

Dallas Real Time Clock

ISA 16-bit Bus Connectors

PCI Bus 32-bit Connectors

Floppy Disk Drive Connector

Keyboard BIOS

Primary and Secondary EIDE Controller Connectors

CMOS Battery

168-pin DIMM Sockets

Parallel and Serial Port Connectors

USB Bus Connectors

Slot 1 for second Pentium CPU

Slot 1 Pentium CPU

ATX P1 Power Connector

PS-2 Style Keyboard and Mouse Connectors

Figure 5–27
ATX style dual Slot 1 MLB.

sockets for four DIMMs. Directly above the DIMM sockets are the floppy disk connector, and the IDE interface connectors. The ATX power supply connector is on the lower right of the MLB. The ROM BIOS chip is mounted at the upper left of the MLB.

The ATX-style Socket 370 MLB is shown in Figure 5-28. It differs from the SEC Slot 1 MLB in the number of PCI and ISA bus connectors. Only one ISA bus connector is provided. As with the SEC Slot 1 ATX-style board, the ISA connector is a combined 16-bit ISA/PCI bus connector. The serial, parallel, USB, mouse, and keyboard connections are at the right side bottom of the board. Just to the left is the ATX-style power connector. The CPU and 370 PGA socket are in the lower center of the MLB next to the DIMM sockets. The floppy disk and IDE connectors are on the left side of the keyboard. Directly in the middle of the board is the AGP connector for the video card. The ROM BIOS chip is mounted to the left of the PCI bus connectors.

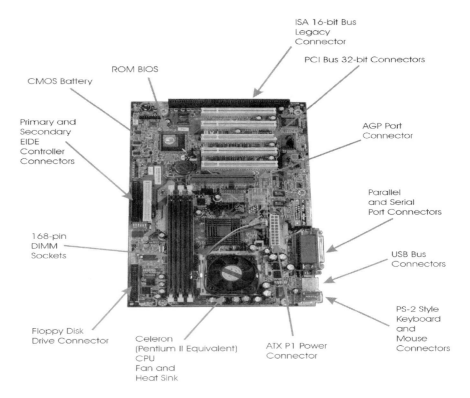

ISA 16-bit Bus
Legacy
Connector

PCI Bus 32-bit Connectors

ROM BIOS

CMOS Battery

Primary and
Secondary
EIDE
Controller
Connectors

AGP Port
Connector

Parallel
and Serial
Port Connectors

168-pin
DIMM
Sockets

USB Bus
Connectors

PS-2 Style
Keyboard
and
Mouse
Connectors

Floppy Disk
Drive Connector

Celeron
(Pentium II Equivalent)
CPU
Fan and
Heat Sink

ATX P1 Power
Connector

Figure 5–28
ATX Style Socket 370 MLB.

Mini ATX, Micro ATX, and Flex ATX Styles

These styles have basically the same features as the ATX style MLB. The major
difference between them and the ATX style is the size of the board. These
ATX style derivatives are smaller than the ATX style board. Each of these
styles uses a different size board with some, if not all, mounting holes that are
compatible with ATX style MLBs. In some cases they may support the standard rear ATX connections for keyboard, mouse, parallel port, serial ports, and
USB connections. Some may also provide the ATX optional sound and game
port connections. Plugs on the MLB allow floppy and IDE disk drives to connect directly to the MLB, and PCI and AGP bus connections are supported
for option cards.

373

NLX Style

This style has the distinguishing characteristic of providing a riser card that permits mounting option cards parallel to the MLB. This style is a derivative of the Western Digital LPX MLB style that also supported a riser card for option card installation. Similar to the ATX styles the NLX style MLBs support standard rear ATX connections for keyboard, mouse, parallel port, serial ports, and USB connections. Optional sound and game port connections are also supported. Floppy and IDE disk drives connect directly to the riser card. PCI and AGP bus connections are provided on the riser card for option cards. One unique characteristic of the NLX system boards is that they can be replaced without using bolts. The NLX board is designed to plug directly into the riser card, as are the option cards. Tall components such as the CPU with heat sink and the memory DIMMs are placed away from the option card installation area. This accommodates those components that are tall, and does not interfere with full-length option cards.

Now that we have toured some MLB styles, we should briefly examine each component. In determining MLB suitability for a PC, several factors are important. These factors are CPU chip socket or slot, board style, number of ISA slots, and number of PCI slots. Differences in CPU chip mounting and numbers of slots are the greatest areas of variability in board design.

MLB Components

The components installed on MLBs are serial communications ports, a parallel port, IDE or EIDE disk controllers, RAM, CPU chip, ROM BIOS, and external L2 CPU cache. Newer boards also incorporate USB ports. Some of these components are replaceable or upgradable while others are not. These integral MLB components reduce the need for expansion cards in the PC. Expansion cards are still used for modems, LAN, sound cards, and video controller cards. Additionally, other peripheral devices may require other controllers (for instance, SCSI controller cards).

Communication Ports

Most MLBs come with two serial ports built into the board. These are COM1 and COM2 serial ports. They can be configured through the CMOS setup program to COM3 or COM4 settings or can be entirely disabled. ATX boards route these serial ports to 9-pin "D"-shaped connectors on the rear of the ATX board. The AT-style (AT style and baby AT style) boards have 10-pin connector blocks that run through ribbon cables to 9-pin "D"-shaped connectors that fit into card slot mounting brackets or mounting holes in the rear of the chassis. The 10-pin connector blocks have the pins arranged in either one of two configurations. See Figure 5–29.

The headers are wired with two distinct types of pin outs, one which connects the pins down one side to the ten-pin connector, and one which crisscrosses the connector. Pin outs for both 9-pin serial connectors and 25-pin serial connectors are shown in Figure 5–30.

ATX MLBs route serial port connections to 9-pin "D"-shaped male connectors on the rear of the chassis. The serial ports are used to connect a mouse or palmtop PC to the MLB.

Figure 5–29
AT MLB serial connectors.

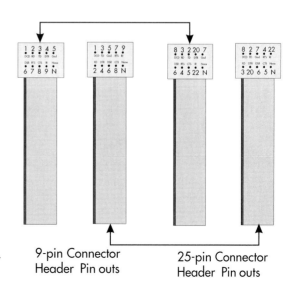

Figure 5–30
AT MLB serial port header pin outs.

9-pin Connector Header Pin outs

25-pin Connector Header Pin outs

Parallel Port

MLBs generally provide a single parallel port connection. This port can be set as compatible, bi-directional, EPP, or ECP. The configuration is set using the CMOS setup program. The parallel port connection is made using a 25-pin "D"-shaped female connector. ATX-style MLBs have this connector routed to the rear of the chassis. The parallel port connector is located over both serial port connectors in an ATX-style MLB.

USB Ports

Newer MLBs provide USB connections, which provide an easy way to expand the peripheral devices attached to the PC. It configures itself automatically (provided the correct drivers are loaded) and transfers data between the peripheral device and the PC at high speeds. In theory, a USB bus can support 128 devices, but our guess is that 10 devices is a more realistic upper limit. USB connections run out of the rear of ATX-style chassis. The USB is a 1.5 MBPS or 12 MBPS serial port for connecting a variety of peripherals to the PC, including scanners, printers, mice, keyboards, CCD cameras, palmtop PCs, and more. The USB devices either run into hubs or are daisy-chained to allow several devices access to the same USB port. Windows 98 has built-in software support for USB devices, but this must often be augmented by driver software provided by the USB device manufacturer. USB devices are plug-and-play devices.

IDE/EIDE and Floppy Controllers

The connectors for cabling to IDE or EIDE fixed disk drives are built into the MLB. These component connectors on ATX-style boards do not route to the outside because the fixed and floppy drives are installed internally. The IDE/EIDE controllers on newer MLBs are Ultra Direct Memory Access (UDMA) controllers, capable of transferring data between the disk drive and the MLB in bursts of 33/66/100 M per second. Each EIDE controller is capable of supporting two IDE devices, so the MLB can support four EIDE devices total. This permits installation of two fixed disk drives, a CD-ROM drive, and a high capacity Zip or Super Disk drive in a single PC. When there are more EIDE devices to install, an additional EIDE controller board must be installed in a PCI bus slot. Windows 95/98/Me must be configured to use the MLB UDMA capabilities because its default settings are not to use DMA disk access. Some MLBs have a second set of EIDE controllers. These controllers require special driver programs to function with Windows. The

IDE/EIDE headers on the MLB are 40-pin headers, and the floppy disk drive header is a 34-pin header.

SIMM, DIMM, and RIMM Sockets

SIMMs, DIMMs, and RIMMs were mentioned earlier in this chapter, but this section provides more detail about their functionality and use.

MLBs have provided many different combinations of SIMM, DIMM, and RIMM sockets to accommodate changing RAM configurations. The earliest MLBs had sockets for DRAM chips, which gave way to the first 30-pin SIMMs. These were the mainstay of memory chips for many 80386 CPU chip and 80486 CPU chip PCs. As PCs moved to Pentium CPU chips, the MLB RAM sockets moved to 72-pin SIMMs. Many MLBs provided combinations of 30-pin and 72-pin SIMM sockets. As Pentium CPU chip speeds increased and SDRAM became the predominant type of system memory, DIMM 168-pin sockets were installed on MLBs. Most MLBs use SDRAM and DIMMs. Pentium 4 MLBs use RIMMs. The RAM capacity is determined by the total capacity of the DIMMs/RIMMs installed in the MLB sockets. In our MLB figures, there are three or four DIMM sockets.

CPU Sockets

CPU chips are attached to MLBs using PGA sockets or SEC CPU daughter-boards. MLBs support PGA CPU chip mounting, Slot 1, or Slot A CPU daughterboard installations. The PGA CPU chip mounting uses socket 370, socket 423, socket 462, or socket 478 most often on newer MLBs. This is used to install Intel Pentium or AMD chips. Older MLBs used Socket 5, or Socket 7 mounts for Pentium CPU chips. The Slot 1 mount is used for new Pentium II, Celeron, and Pentium III CPU chip systems and the Slot A mount is for AMD Athlon chip systems. The CPU daughterboard and active heat sink fan assembly mount directly on the MLB as a unit.

External CPU Cache—L2 Cache

The L2 CPU cache for Socket 7 CPU chips was installed on the MLB. Several static RAM chips comprised L2 CPU cache. It was possible in this case to upgrade or, if needed, repair the L2 CPU cache because the static RAM chips were installed in DIP sockets on the MLB. Today L2 CPU cache is usually in the CPU chip and is no longer repairable or upgradable. Replacing the MLB or the CPU chip daughterboard performs upgrades or repairs. Figure 5–31 shows 15 ns static RAM chips on an 80486 MLB.

Figure 5–31
L2 MLB CPU cache.

Study Break: Motherboard Style

Go to the rear of the PC and examine the serial port, parallel port, and the keyboard and mouse ports. This indicates the style of motherboard used in the PC.

ATX-style and proprietary MLBs have the serial, parallel, keyboard, and mouse connectors clustered together on the left side of the MLB. AT-style may have the serial and parallel port connectors mounted in the metal card slot covers.

Open the PC case and find the power connections to the MLB. Are there two separate connectors labeled P8 and P9, or is there a single unified connector? The separate connectors are used on AT-style motherboards. Replace the power connector.

Do ribbon cables run from the serial port connectors to the MLB? AT-style MLBs connect to these ports with ribbon cables.

Brand name systems have some ATX-like features but also employ proprietary mounting features to make MLB replacement require an MLB from that manufacturer. Of course, in most cases it is cheaper to replace both the MLB and the chassis rather than pay for a proprietary MLB from a brand name manufacturer.

PC Bus Architectures

The rows for the connectors into which circuit cards are plugged are called expansion slots. These cards are expansion cards because they often expand the basic PC capabilities. Daughterboards are also plugged into the MLB. A daughterboard typically contains a CPU chip and is the core of the system, as opposed to expanding the PC's capabilities. Today, MLBs contain two general-purpose buses and some special-purpose buses. The general-purpose buses include the ISA 16-bit bus, which maintains backward compatibility with older PC expansion cards, and the PCI bus for newer expansion cards. Specialized buses are the AGP bus and the VESA bus which provide high-speed data transfer between the CPU chip and graphics memory. See Figure 5–32. The USB interfaces devices to the PC MLB. It is a specialized bus not targeted at PC expansion cards.

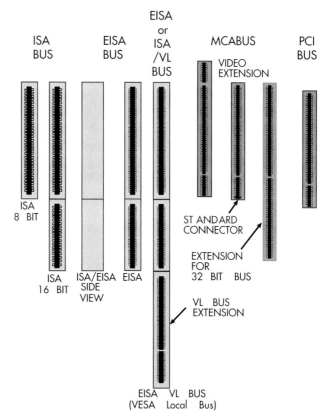

Figure 5–32
Bus Connectors.

These buses transferred one, two or four bytes at different clock speeds. Table 5–11 summarizes the data transfer rates and clock speeds of different buses.

Table 5–11 Bus Clock Speeds and Approximate Throughput

Bus Type	Speed—Bits Transferred	Approximate Bus Throughput in Megabytes per second
ISA – 8 Bit	8 MHz – 8 bits	8 MB/Second
ISA – 16-bit	8 MHz – 16 bits	16 MB/Second
MCA – 16-bit	24 MHz – 16 bits	48 MB/Second
MCA – 32-bit	24 MHz – 32 bits	96 MB/Second
EISA	33 MHz – 32 bits	132 MB/Second
Local Bus – 32-bit (VESA Standard)	33 MHz (System Clock Speed) – 32 Bits	132 MB/Second
PCI		
Peripheral Component Interconnect Bus (Intel)	33 MHz – 32 bits	132 MB/Second
	66 MHz – 32 bits	264 MB/Second
	66 MHz – 64 bits	528 MB/Second
Advanced Graphics Port (AGP)		
1X	66 MHz – 32 bits	264 MB/Second
2X	133 MHz – 32 bits	1,064 MB/Second
4X	264 MHz – 32 bits	2,112 MB/Second
PCMCIA (Personal Computer Memory Card International Association) Laptop PCs	8 MHz – 16 bits (asynchronous)	16 MB/Second
Card Bus Laptop PCs	33 MHz – 32 bits (synchronous and asynchronous)	132 MB/Second
USB 1.0	1.5 Megabits per second	0.1875 MB/Second
	12 Megabits per second	1.5 MB/Second
USB 2.0	480 Megabits per second	60 MB/Second
IEEE 1394	400 Megabits per second	50 MB/Second
	600 Megabits per second	75 MB/Second

Table 5-11   Bus Clock Speeds and Approximate Throughput (Continued)

Bus Type	Speed—Bits Transferred	Approximate Bus Throughput in Megabytes per second
Front Side Bus or Host Bus	66 MHz – 32 bits	264 MB/Second
	100 MHz – 32 bits	400 MB/Second
	133 MHz – 32 bits	532 MB/Second
	150 MHz – 32 bits	600 MB/Second
	133 MHz – 32 bits for DDR	1,064 MB/Second

Because of bus overhead, the actual bus throughput is lower than the throughput column in the table. Nonetheless, the approximate throughputs give us a good perspective on the evolution of PC bus speeds.

The MLB buses have evolved from the 1981 PC's Industry Standard Architecture (ISA) 8-bit bus to meet the increased performance demands placed on PCs while preserving compatibility with PC expansion cards sold in the market.

Buses are targeted at either general purpose or specialized applications. Specialized buses focus mainly on speeding up video operations. Most buses transfer all bits of a byte in parallel. The USB and IEEE 1394 buses are serial buses. Bus mastering permits peripheral controllers to take control of the bus and transfer data faster than if the CPU chip exclusively controlled the bus. Buses can connect directly to the CPU chip/memory bus, or they can be bridged into that bus through a PCI bus. Hot swappable buses permit changing expansion cards after bus I/O activity quiets down. Data transfers can be asynchronous, transferring one, two or four bytes at irregular intervals, or isochronous, transferring bursts of data at irregular intervals. Finally, precise internal PC clocks control some buses while others operate independently of internal PC clocks. These buses play a major role in PC peripheral component expansion and configuration. Table 5–12 summarizes bus features.

Table 5-12 MLB Buses

Bus Type	General Purpose vs. Specialized	Parallel vs. Serial	Bus Master	CPU/Memory Bus Connection Bridged via PCI bus vs. Direct Connection	Hot Swap	Data Transfers Asynchronous vs. Isochronous	Control Clock
ISA	General Purpose	Parallel	No	Bridged	No	No	Yes
EISA	General Purpose	Parallel	Yes	Bridged	No	Yes	Yes
VESA LB	Specialized	Parallel	Yes	Bridged	No	NA	System Clock
PCI	General Purpose	Parallel	Yes	Direct	No	Yes	Yes
SPCI	General Purpose	Parallel	Yes	Direct	No	Yes	Yes
Hot-pluggable PCI	General Purpose	Parallel	Yes	Direct	Yes	Yes	Yes
AGP	Specialized	Parallel	Yes	Direct	No	NA	Yes
CardBus	General Purpose	Parallel	Yes	Bridged	Yes	Yes	Yes
Zoomed Video	Specialized	Parallel	Yes	Bridged	Yes	NA	No
USB	General Purpose	Serial	No	Bridged	Yes	Yes	No
IEEE 1394	General Purpose	Serial	Yes	Bridged	Yes	Yes	No

ISA

The Industry Standard Architecture (ISA) bus began as an 8-bit expansion bus in 1981 that permitted the PC to address 8 MB of RAM. This one-byte-wide 4.77 MHz IBM PC bus had a theoretical bandwidth of about 4.5 MB per second. Increasing the bus clock speed to 8 MHz increased the theoretical bandwidth to 7.5 MB per second. Eight data lines were added, changing it to a 16-bit bus with the introduction of the PC AT in 1985. This 8-bit expansion increased the theoretical throughput to 15 MB per second and permitted the PC to address 16 MB of RAM. However, memory access operations above the first megabyte required two steps, limiting the effective data rate to about 8 MB per second. This speed is adequate for mouse controllers, modems, and similar low-speed devices. Disk drives and LAN boards need higher transfer rates to provide acceptable PC performance.

As CPU chips used faster and wider data paths, the basic ISA bus design did not keep pace. Many ISA expansion cards remain 8-bit wide bus cards. The few cards with 16-bit data paths, such as older SCSI fixed disk controllers, graphics adapters, and LAN network cards, remain constricted by the low bandwidth of the ISA bus. Newer buses provide the bandwidth required by higher-speed PC expansion cards. Figure 5–33 illustrates ISA 8-bit and 16-bit bus connections.

Figure 5–33
ISA PC card 8-bit and 16-bit
edge connectors.

The 16-bit AT bus is implemented on most MLBs to provide compatibility with thousands of ISA bus cards sold and installed in PCs. These cards are low-end performance cards. Most MLBs have some type of ISA bus expansion card slots. However, ISA expansion slots are coming to an end. The low-speed parallel and serial ports that resided on ISA cards are now integrated into most MLBs. Both Intel and Microsoft support legacy free PCs with no ISA slots starting with the PC 99 System Design Guide, a specification for PC hardware design and configuration.

EISA

As mentioned earlier in this chapter, the ISA MLB buses evolved to the Extended Industry Standard Architecture (EISA) bus around 1990, in response to IBM's introduction of the PS/2 and the Micro-Channel Architecture (MCA) Bus. The EISA bus was compatible with all ISA 8-bit and 16-bit PC expansion cards. It also supported newer 32-bit EISA cards. The EISA bus was cleverly conceived. To accommodate all card types, the connector slots were made to permit deeper insertion of EISA cards while supporting the standard insertion depth of the ISA 8-bit and 16-bit cards. See Figure 5–34. Furthermore, EISA was an early step toward plug-and-play PC expansion card configuration, and was meant to respond to IBM's MCA bus software configuration and PC card setup. The EISA bus used a special configuration program and parameter files set for each software configurable PC card. The MLB BIOS had to support the EISA bus software configuration.

Figure 5–34
EISA bus card edge connector.

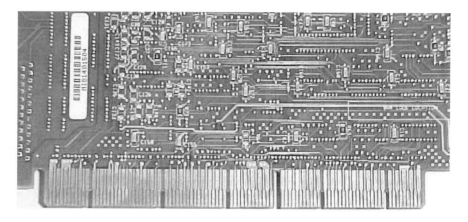

The EISA bus succeeded in getting PC buyers to think of an alternative PC design from IBM's PS/2 featuring the MCA bus, but failed as a major bus alternative because it was used mostly with ISA cards. Plus, the expensive EISA cards did not increase performance that much over cards in an ISA bus. The ISA bus met most PC card expansion needs. Over-priced EISA 32-bit SCSI controller cards and LAN cards did not sell well either.

The EISA bus laid the foundation for Intel to produce chip sets that made PC design and manufacturing easier. The PCI bus supports such chip sets. Before the PCI bus replaced the EISA bus, the VESA standardized a separate video bus that sped up video operations called the VESA local bus.

VESA Local Bus or VL-Bus

The VESA local bus was used on 80486 systems to improve both display and disk drive performance. The VESA bus operated at system clock speed. Since most 80486 systems operated at speeds that were less than 33 MHz (the 80486 chips became clock-doubling chips—for instance, 80486 33/66 MHz chips), matching the VESA local bus to system clock speed was not a problem. The VESA bus speed increased the display refresh performance and was also used to increase disk drive performance. This is similar to the data transfer speed enhancement provided by AGP port systems operating at a speed of 133 MHz. See Figure 5–35.

Figure 5–35
VESA bus card edge connector.

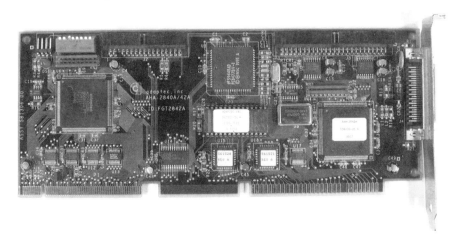

The VESA bus extended the capabilities of ordinary ISA bus slots by adding an extra extension connector to the MLB. This connector extension carried the VESA bus data at system clock speed. Sometimes the VESA bus was called the VL-bus. In this case it was used for both video and disk I/O data transfers.

Micro-Channel Architecture Bus

IBM developed the Micro-Channel Architecture bus (MCA), which first appeared on the IBM PS/2 PCs in 1987. It supported 8-bit, 16-bit, and 32-bit data transfers at 24 MHz. The MCA bus competed with the EISA bus but it had one serious marketing failure—it was not backward compatible with the ISA bus cards on the market. To expand a PS/2 system, a PC owner had to purchase new and expensive MCA bus PC cards. The MCA bus has all but disappeared today. It is difficult to find any information on it even at IBM's Web site.

PCI

The Peripheral Component Interconnect (PCI) has become the main bus used in PCs today. It started by performing 32-bit transfers at 33 MHz but is moving to support 66 MHz 64-bit data transfers. The PCI bus supports PC plug-and-play configuration capabilities.

Pentium processors with higher MHz speeds made the slow and narrow ISA bus a bottleneck between the processor and PC card expansion components. Intel created the PCI bus to alleviate this bottleneck, as shown in Figure 5–36.

The PCI bus runs at its own clock speed, separate from the system clock speed. The original 32-bit-wide bus running at 33 MHz with a maximum speed of 132 M/second is widely implemented in PC systems. PCI has simplified PC hardware configuration by supporting plug-and-play and by supporting shared IRQ assignments.

The PCI bus supports 125-pins per card slot. Added 64-bit extension connectors similar to the 16-bit extension connector to the ISA bus somewhat doubles the bus bandwidth. A further increase to a 66 MHz clock speed increases the maximum potential bandwidth to 264 MB per second. PCI cards run on either 5 volts or 3.3 volts. A notch cut into the edge connector toward the computer chassis's front mates with a corresponding key in a 5-volt connector slot to designate the 5-volt cards. The 3.3-volt cards have their designating notch cut toward the rear of the PC chassis. This 3.3-volt card notch corresponds with a key in a 3.3-volt connector slot. Universal cards fit either slot and run on either 5 volts or 3.3 volts. The cards shown in Figure 5–36 are universal cards.

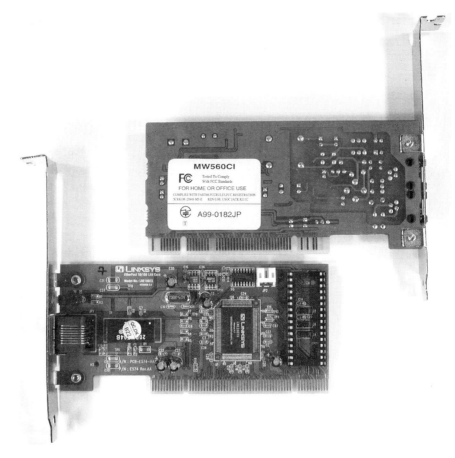

Figure 3–36
PCI bus universal card edge connectors.

The PCI bus is limited to ten electrical loads. Since most cards are more than one load, a practical limit to expansion cards inserted into a PCI bus is three or four cards. Using more than one PCI bus in a system mitigates this card limitation. In most PCs, bridge chips connect multiple PCI buses. The bridge chips install between one PCI bus and another.

Small Form-Factor PCI

Small form-factor PCI (SPCI) is a miniaturized PCI card format designed for space-constrained applications like laptop PCs. SPCI is designed to be a compact and inexpensive means to install add-in peripherals, such as LAN adapters, permanently or semi-permanently into a PC. Similar to full-size PCI cards, SPCI cards connect directly to a PCI bus. Direct attachment reduces card cost and complexity as compared to cards using bridges. SPCI cards cannot be hot-plugged (inserted into a running PC). SPCI cards are installed by removing chassis covers and rather than plugging into a conveniently accessible slot.

Hot-Pluggable PCI

Hot-pluggable PCI enhances standard PCI with hot-plug capability, permitting the PCI bus to be used in nonstop applications. The hot-plug capability lets the PCI bus compete with other hot-pluggable buses in applications, like telephone switching, that cannot tolerate brief lapses of operation. Similar to SPCI, hot-pluggable PCI connects to a PCI bus without bridging. Isolation buffers on the card are needed to keep card-generated signals from corrupting traffic on an operating bus during card insertion and removal, increasing the cost of hot-pluggable PCI cards.

Advanced Graphics Port Bus

The graphics display consumes more bandwidth than a PCI bus delivers. An XGA 1,204 by 768 pixel image with 16-bit color depth uses about 1.5 MB of data. Refreshing this at 75 Hz requires a bandwidth of 75 times 1.5 MB, or over 100 MB per second. In contrast, the ancient Color Graphics Array (CGA) cards with four colors or two bits of data at 320 by 200 pixel resolution per image required 128,000 bits of data refreshed at 60 Hz or over 900 kilobytes per second. Some displays provide a 1,600 by 1,200 pixel image with 32-bit color refreshed at 60 Hz. They need about 460 megabytes per second data rate to refresh the entire screen.

Three-dimensional graphics make possible modeling texture mapping and object hiding. These features used in creating detailed 3-D images require enormous amounts of data; 3-D graphics adapters also need fast access to the data.

The AGP bus solves this problem. AGP ports appeared with Pentium II motherboards; they are less like a bus and more like a point-to-point connection, dedicated to connecting graphics adapters directly to MLB RAM memory. The AGP port's focused work streamlines its design to achieve maximum speed, which gives AGP graphics adapters fast access to texture and buffer data. AGP cards access data directly from the PC's RAM system memory without using the CPU chip, reducing the need to store the data in special graphics card memory.

AGP is much faster than PCI. A 33-MHz 32-bit PCI bus provides roughly 132 MB per second bandwidth. The AGP 32-bit bus runs at clock speeds from

66 MHz to 264 MHz, producing a maximum bandwidth ranging from roughly 264 megabytes second to 2,112 megabytes per second. AGP graphics cards do not have to share this bandwidth with other devices, making the maximum bandwidth available to them at any time.

An AGP drawback is only one AGP device can be installed in a PC. In the event that a system has two displays (as supported by Windows 98), a second PCI bus graphics adapter is needed for the second monitor. Similar to the PCI bus, there are two different voltage designs for the AGP bus: 3.3-volt design (most common), and 1.5-volt design. As demand for increased bandwidth will certainly continue, higher AGP bus clock speeds and wider data paths are likely to meet such demands.

PC Card or PC-MCIA Bus

Around 1990, rapid growth in sales of laptop PCs inspired development of smaller, lighter, and more portable PC devices. PC card versatility and power made these portable devices common equipment on almost all laptop PCs. PC card technology has been standardized by the Personal Computer Memory Card International Association (PCMCIA). New PC card applications include smart cards, TV set-top boxes, automobile electronics, and more. PC card compact size and ruggedness make them an ideal solution in such applications.

The PC card standard specifies three physical types of PC cards; each use the same length and width and 68-pin connector. The single difference between Type I, Type II, and Type III cards is heights of 3.3 mm, 5.0 mm, and 10.5 mm, respectively. This means that thinner cards can be used in thicker slots, but thicker cards cannot be inserted into thinner slots.

Type I PC cards are typically memory devices such as RAM, flash, OTP, and SRAM cards. Type II PC cards are often I/O devices, such as data/fax modems, and LAN cards. Type III PC cards could be micro disk drives, but IBM's micro drive is only 5 mm high, making it a Type II PC card form factor. There are extended cards for components that must remain outside the laptop PC, such as wireless communication antennas.

PCMCIA Standard Release 1.0/JEIDA 4.0 of June 1990 defined a 68-pin interface, Type I and Type II PC card form factors, electrical requirements for memory cards alone, and the Card Information Structure (CIS) critical to interoperability and PC card plug-and-play capabilities. PCMCIA Standard Releases 2.0, 2.01 and 2.1 from 1991 to 1994 added an I/O interface to the 1990 standard. Release 2.0 included dual-voltage memory cards and card environmental requirements. Release 2.1 added the ATA specification, the Type III card, and the Auto-Indexing Mass Storage (AIMS) specification. Also included was the initial Card Services Specification. Release 2.1 enhanced the

Card and Socket Services Specification, and improved the Card Information Structure. In February 1995, the PC Card Standard was again revised to improve compatibility and add 3.3-volt cards, DMA, and 32-bit CardBus bus mastering.

CardBus implementations increase the speed and performance of the PC cards from something resembling that of an ISA bus adapter card to that of a PCI bus adapter card. This makes implementation of high-speed LAN and SCSI I/O PC cards effective.

Zoomed Video

Zoomed Video (ZV) is either 16-bit or 32-bit CardBus PC card technology to connect video data streams from a PC card source directly to a PC's video adapter. Zoomed video uses a dedicated data path from a PC card socket to the video adapter's feature port. This path either skirts the CardBus bridge by connecting from the card socket to the video controller, or connects through the controller with the card video data traversing the CardBus bridge en route to the video controller. Zoomed video cards have bus mastering capability that permit them to perform data transfers without using the laptop CPU chip or DMA, thus avoiding transfer of high-bandwidth video data over the PC's PCI bus. This leaves the PCI bus available for CPU traffic to and from system memory, etc. Zoomed video uses a standard PC card form factor and eliminates the need for a second dedicated PCI bus supporting video data. Zoomed video and audio data travel directly from the PC card socket to the video controller and audio coder/decoder (or codec), respectively. Consequently, this data cannot be modified by the laptop's CPU chip in real time. Zoomed video is a special-purpose interconnection providing a fixed video/audio pipe into a laptop PC.

USB

The USB is broadly implemented in both desktop and mobile computers. USB 1.1 operates at speeds of 1.5 or 12 Mbps. The USB 2.0 devices operate at 480 Mbps. USB interfaces are backwards compatible, so that USB 2.0 interfaces will support USB 1.1 devices running at 1.5 Mbps or 12Mbps.

The 1.5 Mbps USB speed adequately services mice, pointing devices, and keyboards; monitors and cameras require a 12 Mbps or higher speed. The slowest device on the USB bus determines the speed of the bus, for example, one 1.5 Mbps device on a USB bus limits the speed of the bus to 1.5 Mbps. USB devices are connected to ports on a hub device linked in a tree-wiring topology. Each device tree connects to a PC USB root-hub port through which the PC communicates with the tree's USB devices. USB devices attach to all

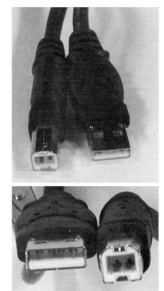

Figure 5–37
USB Connectors A and B.

ports with 4-conductor cables. There are two USB connectors, the USB A or flat connector and the USB B or narrow connector, as shown in Figure 5-37. In the top of the figure, the A connector is on the left and in the bottom it is on the right.

Most MLBs include USB ports, while IEEE 1394 FireWire bus connections are provided using add-on PC adapter cards. The rapid increase in USB and in IEEE 1394 serial bus is happening because:

1. They have simpler and user-friendly connectors and cables for these serial buses.
2. They connect multiple devices to a bus using hubs or chaining to form a tree structure.
3. They have bandwidths that match or exceed parallel buses.
4. They operate with low power consumption.
5. They provide plug-and-play self-configuration for connected devices.
6. They provide the capability to hot-swap devices.
7. They employ protocols supporting a broad range of transport services, including isochronous (guaranteed transmission bandwidth) service to multimedia applications.

These are compelling reasons for serial buses to replace the ISA and potentially the PCI parallel buses for many low speed devices. USB root-hub ports provide some 5-volt power for low-power devices. The root-hub ports support high-powered device attachment when they provide their own power from an AC source or from batteries. USB permits easy attachment and detachment of devices through plug-and-play software that finds devices, assigns addresses to them, and sets them up. USB software communication sends data packets from a source to a destination using logical pipes designed to perform specific functions. There are separate packet types for data and for control information. USB supports asynchronous communication for simple devices like mice and keyboards and isochronous communication guaranteeing a set portion of the available bus bandwidth for more demanding multimedia applications that have stringent latency limits.

USB devices may control their power consumption rather than letting the PC control power consumption. USB devices can automatically enter a suspended low-power consumption state if the bus to which they connect becomes inactive. The suspended devices can resume operation at their pre-suspend consumption level when they awaken.

These features make USB a cost-effective and user-friendly general-purpose attachment mechanism for many PC peripherals.

IEEE 1394 or FireWire

Apple Computer's FireWire bus has evolved into the IEEE 1394 high-speed serial bus. The IEEE 1394 specification covers several buses ranging in performance from about 25 MBPS, to 400 MBPS, to 800 Mbps and beyond. This will likely be increased to 1.2 GBPS and higher speeds. IEEE 1394 specifications are:

A.	IEEE 1394-1995	- 400 Mbps	– Twisted Pair Wire
B.	IEEE 1394a (IEEE 1394-2000)	- 400 Mbps	– Twisted Pair Wire
C.	IEEE 1394b	- 800 Mbps	– Twisted Pair Wire – Glass Optical Fiber (GOF) – Plastic Optical Fiber (POF)

IEEE 1394 is a general-purpose serial bus for connecting high-speed peripherals to PCs. IEEE 1394 bus connections includes connections between consumer Audio/Video (AV) and other Consumer Electronics (CE) electronics made possible by the peer-to-peer communication supported by IEEE 1394 bus-mastering features. Similar to the USB bus, the IEEE 1394 bus attaches multiple devices to a PC, as well as supporting peer-to-peer device connection like directly connecting a scanner to a printer. The IEEE 1394 buses can connect multiple devices through a hub or can connect a hierarchy of serial buses, each supporting up to 63 device attachments. Bridges transfer data between buses in the hierarchical IEEE 1394 bus configuration.

Like USB, IEEE 1394 bus communication uses packet transmission between devices. IEEE 1394 transaction software services present application software with read, write, and lock services. Each service translates into packet sequences in a link software layer that are transmitted over copper wires or fiber-optic cable. The IEEE 1394 provides both asynchronous and isochronous communication.

The IEEE 1394 bus has plug-and-play capability. When IEEE 1394 devices are added or removed from a bus, all devices connected to the IEEE 1394 bus reset and then perform a self-identification and enumeration process. Unique addresses are then assigned to all devices and normal bus operation resumes. A single device functions as bus manager, and performs bus power management, optimizes performance, maintains bus-connection information, and manages isochronous bandwidth allocation.

IEEE 1394 costs somewhat more than USB. IEEE 1394 bus power management depends on the power consumption of the IEEE 1394 Physical (PHY) layer. The IEEE 1394 standard requires a device's physical layer to be powered on whenever the device is connected to the IEEE 1394 bus. Devices that are not powered on can split an IEEE 1394 bus into two separate segments. IEEE 1394 devices can draw up to 1 Watt of power when attached to an IEEE 1394 bus. This presents problems in lower power consumption applications, such as those of laptop PCs. Both bus-powered and self-powered devices can attach to an IEEE 1394 bus. The bus manager reads the power source for each node and each node's power requirements. Using that information, the bus manager node sends power enabling or disabling packets to individual nodes to budget IEEE 1394 bus power. IEEE 1394-2000 provides advanced power management capabilities that resolve the IEEE 1394 power difficulties.

Study Break: PC Buses

Examine your PC to determine what bus connections it supports. Examine the outside of the chassis of a PC. Are there any ports labeled USB or IEEE 1394? If so, the PC supports both buses. None labeled? Are there any small rectangular ports? USB ports are usually placed together with one over the top of the other. Some Compaq PCs have both USB and IEEE 1394 ports in the front, hidden by a sliding panel.

Open the chassis and examine the card slots. Are they ISA, PCI, AGP or something else? Use Figures 5–24, 5–26, 5–27, 5–28, 5–32, 5–33, 5–34, and 5–36 to help identify the different bus connectors. What colors are the different connectors in the PC?

The goal here is to determine for a specific PC what option card expandability is supported.

Complementary Metal Oxide Silicon (CMOS) Setup

Complementary Metal Oxide Silicon (CMOS) refers to a semiconductor fabrication technology that produces low-power chips. In PCs, CMOS chips were first used in the PC AT to store configuration and date information. The setup memory based on complementary metal oxide silicon technology became known as CMOS setup memory. The more proper and accurate terminology is nonvolatile memory or nonvolatile RAM (NVRAM). In PCs, NVRAM stores basic configuration information in addition to the Basic Input/Output System (BIOS)—a recent addition. The BIOS comprises programs that perform power on self-test (POST), CMOS setup functions, and real mode input/output data operations. Setup information is changed by BIOS routines (the CMOS setup) entered as the PC boots or by diagnostic programs. This section examines the PC setup and control parameters that are changed by the BIOS CMOS setup program.

Depending upon the PC BIOS, usually striking a specific key enters the BIOS setup program. Some commonly used keys are DEL, F1, F2 or F10. Once the key is struck during system boot, the CMOS setup program in BIOS is started; the menu that controls the basic system settings is shown in Figure 5–38.

Basic Settings

Basic CMOS system settings generally establish the following:

- The system date and time
- The type of floppy disk
- The MLB IDE controller connections

```
Main   Advanced   Security   Exit


              System Date   March 08, 1999
              System Time   22:19:33                  F1    Help
                                                      ESC   Back
                                                      Enter Select

          Floppy Options   Press Enter
                                                       ^    Previous Item
        Primary IDE Master  Maxtor 72004 AP            v    Next Item
        Primary IDE Slave   Mashita CR-585           < >    Select Menu
      Secondary IDE Master  Not Installed
      Secondary IDE Slave   Not Installed              F5   Setup Defaults
                                                       F6   Previous Values
                 Language   English                   F10   Save & Exit
              Boot Options  Press Enter

               Video Mode   EGA / VGA
                    Mouse   Installed

              Base Memory   640 KB
          Extended Memory   64525 KB

              BIOS Version  1.00.05.CS1
```

Figure 5–38
CMOS setup initial menu.

- The language for the setup program menus
- How the system boots
- The initial video-operating mode
- Whether a mouse is detected
- The RAM detected
- The revision version of the BIOS

The basic settings vary from PC to PC and depend on the MLB, CPU chip, and RAM. Some options are simple, while the importance of others is much less evident. Some settings are for informational purposes and are not configurable. Many new PCs automatically determine the optimal CMOS settings and do not permit operator changes to those settings. These are displayed differently from the settings that can be changed. For example, some Dell Inspiron laptops do not permit disabling L2 cache. Some older PC BIOS support enabling/disabling L2 cache.

395

Date/Time Settings

This simply sets the date and time used by the PC to date- and time-stamp all events. The time settings use a 24-hour clock. Other software, like the date and time commands in DOS, changes these settings.

Floppy Drive Types

These settings control the floppy disk drives. They work with the two drives A and B and are supported by the single floppy disk interface on the MLB. Each floppy drive can be set to:

- Disabled—Prohibits access to the floppy drive. This acts as a security measure, thwarting use of floppy drives for booting the PC and bypassing the operating system security.
- 360 KB—This sets the designated floppy drive to support the original XT 5.25-inch double sided nine sector per track floppy drive.
- 1.2 MB—Drive A or drive B is set to support the AT 5.25-inch double-sided fifteen sector-per-track floppy drive.
- 720 KB—This sets a floppy drive to support the original PS/2 3.5-inch double density nine sector-per-track and 80-track floppy drive.
- 1.44/1.25 MB—This is the most common drive setting, and is intended for 3.5-inch 80-track floppy drives with 18 sectors per track.
- 2.88 MB—This sets the designated floppy drive to support 160 track 3.5-inch floppy drives with 18 sectors per track.

Floppy drives must match the CMOS settings. Mismatches cause the floppy to malfunction by being unreadable, but can also trash a disk's contents.

IDE Controller Settings

The IDE controller settings match the IDE disk or CD-ROM to the system. IDE fixed disks must have the system recognize the correct drive geometry—cylinders, heads, and sectors per track—to read and write data to the fixed disk drive. IDE device configuration options are:

- Auto Configured—In this setting, the MLB reads the configuration settings from the IDE drive itself. It uses the settings read to determine the read/write addressing it uses to access data on the fixed disk drive.

- User Definable—This setting permits manual control of the configuration. When the IDE drive does not contain the setup information (a real rarity today) or does not perform best with the automatic information, using manual settings will configure the MLB to work with the fixed disk drive. The manual settings require entering the number of cylinders, the number of heads, and the number of sectors per track. The setup then program computes and displays the maximum capacity available on the IDE disk drive.

- Disabled—This setting is for unused IDE ports, permitting reassignment of their resources to other peripheral devices.

With large (over 2 GB capacity) IDE drives, there is a problem working with a BIOS that was originally targeted at disk drives under 100 MB. The limitation is not in terms of total capacity, but rather in terms of the maximum addressable cylinders and how the maximum addressable cylinders are translated into sector addressing that the operating system can use. The IDE translation mode determines how this is accomplished. Translation mode options are:

- Auto detected—Let the disk drive tell if translation is required and how the translation is to be accomplished.

- Extended cylinders-heads-sectors—In this case, the number of cylinders is greater than 1024 cylinders and translation must be performed.

- Standard cylinders-heads-sectors—In this case the number of cylinders is less than 1024 cylinders and translation is not required. This translation is sometimes identified as Cylinders-Heads-Sectors (CHS) translation.

- Logical block—This is the Logical Block Addressing (LBA) supported by some IDE disk drives.

In cases where LBA translation mode or an extended translation mode is required and cannot be provided, the disk drive capacity is limited to the maximum capacity realized using 1024 cylinders alone. On an old MLB we got only 512 MB out of a 1.2 GB disk drive when the BIOS did not support LBA translation.

A Multiple Sector Setting permits the MLB to transfer data from the disk drive to the RAM, transferring several sectors with single interrupt. The settings are:

- Auto Detected—Lets the MLB detect the optimal setting.

- 8 Sectors/Block—This setting manually sets the number of sectors at eight sectors per block for each interrupt.

397

- 4 Sectors/Block—This setting manually sets the number of sectors at four sectors per block for each interrupt.

- Disabled—This uses whatever setting the software comes up with, most likely one sector per interrupt.

This setting is like the sector-interleave setting in reverse. It is asking, how fast is your CPU and how much buffering is available? Can the CPU chip run off and do lots of work before needing to service the fixed disk, or must it constantly watch it? The faster the CPU chip and the more buffering, the more sectors per interrupt.

The fast-programmed I/O mode determines how the MLB behaves with disk I/O operations. Typically, disk I/O is performed using program steps to transfer the data to RAM. There are different protocols used by different IDE drives to accomplish these transfers. The MLB queries the IDE drive and uses fastest-programmed I/O protocol to transfer data to and from RAM. The settings are Auto Detected and Disabled.

Boot Settings

The boot settings determine the device from which to boot as well as the initial operating states of the MLB and CPU chip.

Most PCs permit booting from several devices. This is sometimes specified as first boot device, second boot device, third boot device, and fourth boot device. These boot devices are selected in sequence from first to fourth. If a device is not found or does not work, then the next device is selected. The boot device settings are:

- Disabled—This inhibits booting from this boot device setting.

- Floppy—The boot device is specified as floppy drive A.

- Hard Disk—The PC boots from the active partition drive, typically assigned to drive letter C.

- CD-ROM—The boot device is the CD-ROM drive. Special bootable diagnostic and installation CD-ROMs are required. As the old floppies fade into the sunset, this will become the primary system-software installation device. At that time, booting from the CD-ROM will be critical.

- Network—This is for corporate environments where tight control of PC configurations is necessary. In this case, the OS boot programs are loaded from a special network server.

The System Cache setting enables or disables the L2 cache on the MLB.

The Boot Speed selects the system speed. In the old dual-speed CPU chips, the CPU chip speed could be set to MLB clock speed (nonturbo) or maximum CPU chip clock speed (turbo). The word turbo crept into PC jargon based upon its use in the Battle Star Galactica television program. Their rockets had a turbo setting that was no doubt inspired by turbo-supercharged cars in manufacture at that time.

The Num Lock setting just puts the keyboard into numeric Lock State upon booting.

The Speaker setting permits the speaker to beep and emit the audio diagnostic sounds. Disabling it just makes booting quieter.

Setup Prompt causes the message identifying the key (in my case here F1) that enters the CMOS setup BIOS program.

A Hard Disk Pre-delay setting is used to permit a hard disk to initialize itself fully before being accessed by the MLB and the operating system. It can be set to disabled or individual times ranging from 3 to 30 Seconds.

The typematic programming settings determine the keyboard auto-repeat behavior. Setting Typematic Rate Programming enables typematic operation. The Typematic Rate Delay is the amount of time before the keyboard automatically repeats an individual keystroke. The Typematic Rate is how many keystrokes per second is the typematic repetition rate. The smallest delay is a quarter (0.25) second and the fastest repetition rate is 30 keystrokes per second. Most people can adapt easily to these rates.

Advanced Settings

The advanced system settings cover:

- peripheral configuration
- advanced chip set configuration
- power management configuration
- plug-and-play configuration
- Event logging configuration

Event-logging configurations are specific in some newer BIOSs or a network server BIOS. Event logging would likely be supported by the BIOS for a Pentium Pro CPU chip PC because these chips were designed specifically for network servers demanding reliability. It is much less likely that this would be a feature in a desktop PC.

Peripheral Configuration

The peripheral configuration sets up the peripheral components built into the MLB. These peripheral components are serial and parallel ports.

The IDE and floppy interfaces are also enabled or disabled here, allowing their IRQ and I/O address resources to be used by other peripherals in the event they are not needed. The settings are described below in more detail.

IDE Interfaces

This setting controls the MLB built-in IDE interfaces. The settings are:

- Auto—automatically detect the interface.
- Disabled—disable the interface, freeing its resources.

Floppy Interfaces

This setting controls the MLB built-in floppy disk controller. The settings are:

- Auto—automatically detect the presence of a floppy drive.
- Enabled—enable permanently the floppy drive interface.
- Disabled—disable the interface, freeing the resources. This setting can also be used as a security setting. If the interface is disabled, any floppy drives in the system will not work. Combine this with the security features and it removes the ability to put information into a PC, or to boot a PC from a floppy disk drive. Disabling is more secure than making sure the system is only bootable from the fixed disk because you can prevent any viruses from entering a system through a floppy diskette. Because the PC cannot read floppy disk drives, viruses have one less pathway to enter your PC.

Serial Ports

Serial port configurations are set here. Each MLB has two built-in serial ports which can be set up as COM1, COM2, COM3, COM4, or disabled. The basic settings are Auto or Disabled; they either disable the port (freeing the resources for other peripheral components), or automatically assign them to COM1 or COM2.

The serial ports can be manually set to the COM1, COM2, COM3, or COM4 I/O address and IRQ settings. Standard PC settings for COM1-4 are:

COM Port	I/O Address	IRQ
COM1	3F8	IRQ4
COM2	2F8	IRQ3
COM3	3E8	IRQ4
COM4	2E8	IRQ3

When choosing these settings, it is best to not disable a COM port on the MLB, but rather assign it to an unused COM port setting. For example, if a mouse using COM1 and COM2 is used by an internal modem, then set the MLB's second COM port to COM3. This sometimes works better than disabling the COM port. Other COM port settings are:

COM Port	I/O Address	IRQ
COM1	3F8	IRQ3
COM2	2F8	IRQ4
COM3	3E8	IRQ3
COM4	2E8	IRQ4

These settings flip the IRQ lines but retain the same COM port I/O addresses.

Printer Port

Printer ports can be set to Auto or Disabled. The Auto setting has the MLB use default settings for the built-in parallel port. Otherwise, manual settings for the parallel port can be selected from the following:

LPT Port	I/O Address	IRQ
LPT1	378	IRQ7
LPT2	278	IRQ7
LPT1	378	IRQ5
LPT2	278	IRQ5

The original PC/XT used IRQ 7 for the parallel Line PrinTer (LPT) port. The AT assigned IRQ 5 to a second parallel port. The MLB has only a single parallel port built into it, but it can have either LPT1 or LPT2 settings.

The Port Mode setting is most critical for proper device operation. The compatible mode provides output only, and operates like an old PC AT parallel port. Bi-directional mode is an AT port that, using the control lines, permits both output and input operation. This is a two-way interface, but a very slow one because input data is received a half-byte (nibble) at a time. The Enhanced Parallel Port (EPP) mode is a high-speed bi-directional port whose operation specification supports Revision 1.7. The Extended Capabilities Port (ECP) conforms to the IEEE 1284 parallel port specification. Specific peripheral devices attached to the parallel port require a matching setting. Sometimes what appears to be a better setting for a device is not really better. Worst-case scenario is that all four settings must be tested to determine what the correct or optimal setting is for a specific peripheral.

Advanced Chip Set Configuration

On older PCs, this configuration option controlled a variety of detailed MLB operating parameters dealing with RAM, video, and CPU chip functions. These option configuration selections have been reduced today to very few because the BIOS is designed to self-configure most options based on the installed components. For example, on older systems there were several configuration settings for CPU chip clock ticks per memory cycle. Today the BIOS determines the type of RAM—for instance, fast page mode or EDO RAM—and automatically adjusts to the optimal timing for that type of RAM.

The one rule to remember here is that if a PC does not work, always choose the default settings. Several times we have tried choosing settings that make a PC run faster by tweaking up the CPU-chip-to-RAM interface, only to discover that the PC performed even poorer than before. In virtually every instance, choosing the BIOS defaults not only made a nonoperational system operate, but improved the performance overall.

Base Memory Size

This sets the real memory in the PC to 512 KB or 640 KB. Most systems have sufficient RAM today, so setting it to the traditional 640 KB is best. Some diagnostics and games that require more conventional RAM to run may not operate if 512 KB is chosen.

ISA LFB Size

This is an ISA bus parameter that sets a buffer size. In most new PC systems, this setting would be disabled, otherwise the setting is 1 M. ISA bus parameters are largely ignored or disabled in most new PCs. This is because the ISA bus is playing an increasingly minor role in peripheral component connection to the PC.

Video Palette Snoop

The video palette snoop feature permits sharing a common palette between ISA add-on cards and a built-in graphics controller. This feature is usually not required in new PCs, so it can be disabled.

Latency Timer (PCI Clocks)

Latency Timers is the maximum number of clock ticks that a PCI card must wait before it can access the PCI bus. The access in a Pentium Pro chip PC might be guaranteed to PCI bus cards after 66 clock ticks. Sometimes there are no menu options to select for this configuration option. Whenever there are no menu selections, it is best to not change the number. Changes are more likely to degrade than improve performance.

SIMM Detected

This option was automatically determined by the BIOS upon memory installation and power up operation. The PC CMOS setup displayed:

```
Bank 0 SIMM Detected    EDO mode
Bank 1 SIMM Detected    None Installed
```

Power Management Configuration

Power management is a real anathema to Windows 95/98/Me because they have power management functionality built in that often conflicts with the BIOS power management features. In the case of Windows PCs, it is best to disable the power management features in CMOS setup and let Windows control the power-saving features. The BIOS power management features are:

- Enabled—Disabled—turns on or off the power management functions.
- IDE Power Down—Enabled—When power management is enabled, this function controls power to the fixed disk drive. Power is removed after a designated interval.
- Video Power Down—Sleep—This feature controls power to the monitor. It shuts off display output after a specific interval.
- Inactivity Timer—10 minutes—This sets the interval duration before the power down state for the monitor and disk drive are entered.
- Laptop PCs a have much more extensive power management setup because they are designed to squeeze as much capacity out of internal battery power as possible.

Power control saves energy. It is not a factor in extending the life of PC components, because most components are designed to operate without failure for five or more years. Given the low cost of PCs (and how quickly they advance technologically) they are more likely to become obsolete well before any components wear out from being powered on constantly.

Plug-and-Play Configuration

These configuration settings are required to effectively work with the plug-and-play features of Windows. The Internal Configuration Utility (ICU) works with Windows to perform plug-and-play PC card configuration. The ICU installs the BIOS plug-and-play software and then relies on booting with a plug-and-play OS, namely Windows 95/98/Me or perhaps the new Windows 2000. Otherwise, a setup utility assigns system resources to bus slots and peripheral components. The IRQs that can be assigned in this case are IRQ 5, 9, 10, 11, and 15. IRQ 5 is typically the LPT2 IRQ. IRQ 9 is linked to IRQ 2 that also cascades IRQs 8 through 15, but can be assigned to a peripheral component. Typically, LAN cards have used this interrupt. IRQs 10 and 11 are generally unassigned in most systems, and the secondary IDE controller or SCSI controller cards use IRQ 15.

Event Logging Configuration

Event logging is not a typical BIOS configuration option. In some PCs, it is predominately used to track memory errors, and specifically logs single- and multiple-bit ECC errors to indicate memory problems. In network servers, it may be used to track other failures (e.g., cooling fan failures) as well.

Memory parity may be set using advanced setup options. This setting is not under the logging area but rather in the Advanced Chip Set Configuration settings. Memory parity settings can be parity or no parity, meaning that an extra bit must be provided for each 8-bit byte to maintain an even (or odd) number of ones in each byte stored. Nonparity SIMMs or DIMMs have 32 bits, while parity SIMMs or DIMMs use 36 bits (or one extra bit per each memory byte on the SIMM or DIMM). The Error-Correcting Code (ECC) circuitry uses these four extra parity bits to perform single-bit error correction and double-bit error detection.

Passwords and Security

The CMOS setup permits assignment of administrative and user passwords to provide system security. This prevents anyone from starting and using the PC without knowing the user password. Furthermore, BIOS settings cannot be altered without using the administrative password. These security settings cannot be bypassed easily by software, and can make a Windows 95/98 system quite secure. However, they CMOS passwords do not protect a system that is powered on in Windows; they only protect the system when it is first powered on. This means leaving your PC running while you go eat lunch will make it nonsecure.

Exit

The Exit setting exits the setup with an option to Exit Save or Exit Discard the configuration changes made.

The CMOS setup options presented in this book were for a specific system. They are typical of the settings found on many PCs. CMOS setup is becoming more automatic and less complex. Systems automatically match themselves to the hardware component parameters installed. For example, CMOS setup can automatically detect the CPU operating speed and the fixed disk geometry parameters. This makes setup much simpler than before. However, if there is any doubt about CMOS setup parameters, it is always best to choose and install the default settings.

Study Break: CMOS Setup

Shut down a PC and restart. Enter the CMOS setup program to determine what options can be set.

Shut down your PC and then reboot. Watch the screen to determine when and how the CMOS setup program is entered. Strike the key that starts the CMOS setup program (F1, F2, or Delete).

Check the main menu selections. Are the date and time correct? Reset them as needed.

Look at the floppy and fixed disk specifications. Make a note of the fixed disk type and geometry. Is LBA mode used to access the drive?

Find the chip set and integrated peripherals (the built-in serial, parallel, and IDE controllers) options. What settings can be changed?

Find (if you can) an option that enables/disables the L2 cache. This is usually not supported on newer PCs.

The goal here is to familiarize yourself with the different setup options and features controlled by the CMOS setup program.

Summary

This chapter has covered the MLB in extensive detail. The many types of PC CPU chips, characteristics such as size, speed, and their relative performance metrics, were covered in the first section, and the second section went into further detail about RAM and its evolution, covering operating characteristics, and parameters.

The primary purpose for the MLB is to provide a mechanism for interfacing ROM, RAM, cache RAM, and PC cards to the CPU chip. The third section provided a review of material presented in an earlier chapter, as well as new details on the types of MLBs and their functionality.

The fourth section, on PC bus architectures, provided details about the various types of buses and connectors used. Separate comments on well-known architectures such as ISA, PCI, AGP, USB, IEEE-1394 and PCMCIA (Card Bus) were presented. Additionally, some of the lesser-known buses such as MCA, EISA, and VESA were covered, providing a well-rounded view of the types of buses the reader might encounter.

The final section, CMOS setup, provided information on the purpose and functionality of the CMOS semiconductor. CMOS settings and setup options were discussed, as well as the relationship between this chip and the PC BIOS.

Chapter Review Questions

1. What does PCI mean?

>   A. Peripheral CPU Interconnect
>   B. PC Component Interconnect
>   C. Peripheral Component Interconnect
>   D. Peripheral Component Interconnection

Answer: C, Peripheral Component Interconnect. There is no PC or CPU on PCI bus because the PC and CPU do not connect directly to the PCI bus. The bus is not an interconnection but an interconnect.

2. What is the fastest Pentium CPU chip?

>   A. Pentium MMX
>   B. Celeron
>   C. Pentium III
>   D. Pentium II MMX

Answer: C, Pentium III. The highest number is usually the fastest. The Pentium 4 is even faster.

3. *Pentium is what type of microprocessor?*

    A. CMOS technology
    B. CISC
    C. superscalar
    D. 80386 32-bit based
    E. All of the above

Answer: E. All of the above All fast CPUs use CMOS technology to reduce power consumption and heat. Pentium CPUs are complex instruction set computers that have a super scalar architecture based on the original 32-bit 80386.

4. *Which CPU chips do Macintosh computers use?*

    A. AMD
    B. Cyrix
    C. Intel
    D. Motorola

Answer: D, Motorola The AMD and Cyrix chips emulate the Intel Pentium IA-32 architecture CPUs. Macintosh computers use the Motorola 74xx G4 CPU chip.

5. *Which CPU chips contain internal L2 cache?*

    A. Pentium Pro
    B. Xeon
    C. Celeron
    D. Pentium III
    E. None of the above
    F. All of the above

Answer: F, all of the above The give away here is "chips" plural. Hence all chips have internal L2 cache. Only older 386, 486, Celeron, and Pentium chips use external L2 cache.

6. *What buses are most commonly found on MLBs?*

    A. ISA, PCI, FireWire, USB
    B. ISA, PCI, AGP, USB
    C. ISA, PCI, VESA, USB
    D. EISA, PCI, AGP, USB

Answer: B, ISA, PCI, AGP, USB. This is changing and soon there will be no ISA bus connections on MLBs. VESA and EISA have come and gone; FireWire is implemented in some laptop computers and as an add-in card in desktop PCs, but not directly on the MLB.

7. *A PCI bus does not have a standard clock speed.*

    A. TRUE
    B. FALSE

Answer: B, FALSE. The standard clock speed of the PCI bus is 33 MHz or 66MHz.

8. *A VESA bus does not have a standard clock speed?*

    A. TRUE
    B. FALSE

Answer: A, TRUE.It runs at the speed of the MLB core clock or a 2X or 4X multiple of the clock.

9. *MLBs have a built in what?*

    A. IDE controllers, a floppy controller, serial ports, parallel ports
    B. IDE controllers, a floppy controller, serial ports, a SCSI controller
    C. IDE controllers, a floppy controller, serial ports, mouse ports
    D. IDE controllers, a floppy controller, serial ports, a parallel port

Answer: D, IDE controllers, a floppy controller, serial ports, a parallel port. MLBs do not typically have multiple parallel or mouse ports. SCSI controllers are typically installed as option cards.

10. *EISA buses accept _____.*

    A. ISA cards
    B. EISA cards only
    C. PCI cards and EISA Cards
    D. VESA and EISA cards

Answer: A, ISA cards. Both VESA and PCI cards do not fit into the EISA connectors because they are quite different mechanically. EISA (E ISA is the clue) and ISA cards share the same mechanical layout because EISA was designed to be backward compatible with ISA cards.

11. *The ISA bus is bridged into the _____ on MLBs.*

    A. EISA
    B. ESA
    C. USB
    D. PCI

Answer D, PCI. MLBs have a PCI bus that is a parallel bus like the ISA bus. Since the PCI bus is faster than the ISA bus, the ISA bus is bridged into the PCI bus. USB is a serial bus and not a candidate. EISA is no longer used in PCs, and there is no ESA bus.

12. *What does the CMOS setup control?*

    A. Floppy drive speed
    B. Keyboard typematic speed
    C. Disk drive capacity
    D. Floppy drive B booting

Answer: B, keyboard typematic speed. The floppy drive speed is controlled by the floppy drive and not the CMOS. Fixed disk capacity is determined by the design of the fixed disk and detected by the CMOS setup, but not controlled by the CMOS setup. Booting is done from floppy drive A: and not floppy drive B:. Alternate boot up drives are fixed disk C: or CD-ROM drives. The typematic speed is controlled by CMOS and can be set to as high as 30 cps.

13. *The first 16-bit bus was what?*

    A. The PCI bus
    B. The EISA bus
    C. The MCA bus
    D. The ISA bus
    E. The AGP bus

Answer: D, The ISA bus. PCI, EISA, MCA, and AGP buses are all 32-bit buses.

14. *What is L2 cache?*

    A. Secondary disk cache
    B. External CPU cache
    C. Faster than L3 and L1 cache
    D. Level 2 memory

Answer: B, external CPU cache. There is no secondary disk cache or Level 2 memory. L2 cache would be slower than either a L1 or a L3 cache because 2 is between 1 and 3. L1 is the fastest and smallest cache, L2 is the next fastest and somewhat larger cache, and L3 cache is the slowest and largest cache. Not all PCs have a L3 cache.

15. *CMOS sets PCs to boot from what?*

    A. The fixed disk
    B. The floppy disk
    C. The CD-ROM
    D. A network
    E. All of the above

Answer: E, all of the above. The CMOS setup can cause the PC to boot from first the floppy, then the fixed disk, then a CD-ROM and finally a network connection. This order may be changed by the CMOS setup.

16. *Pentium II and Pentium III CPUs install in MLBs using what?*

    A. Socket 7
    B. PGA
    C. Slot 1
    D. Slot 2
    E. None of the above

Answer: C, Slot 1. The Socket 7 is used for older Pentium chips but not Pentium II and Pentium III chips. The PGA mounting is used for Celeron, AMD Athlon, and Pentium 4 chips. They mount in socket 370, socket 462, and socket 423 respectively. Slot 2 is used for Pentium II Xeon and Pentium III Xeon CPUs. Pentium II and Pentium III used Slot 1 mounting.

Chapter 6

PRINTERS

Chapter Syllabus

- Printing Concepts, Components, and Operation

- Printer Connections and Configurations

- Resolving Common Printer Problems

- Printer Servicing and Preventative Maintenance

This chapter describes the operation of the major types of printers, their components, description and resolution of common printing problems, and preventative maintenance.

Printing Concepts, Components, and Operation

A prevalent PC problem area is printing. Most printer problems are caused by mismatches in printer driver programs and fonts used by application programs.

When a program like Microsoft Word formats a document, it formats it for a specific type of printer. If the printer at the other end of the parallel port is not the printer specified in the application that does the formatting, bad things happen.

Resolving printer problems requires determining whether DOS, the application, or Windows controls the printer. In the old DOS world, the application program was responsible for the printer and print formatting. It was a simpler world back then; there were few fonts with which to contend, and sharing data between PCs was limited because it was all transferred using floppy disks.

Things have changed dramatically since then; it's a real jungle out there! LANs make file sharing, printer sharing, and font sharing between PCs an every-minute occurrence. Users have access to several different printers. Printers are controlled by Windows and the network print server, and not by the applications, which format and display a document according to the printer on which they expect it to print. If you change the printer specification, the document display changes as well. DOS only transfers data to a designated printer port.

Windows printing is a multiple-step process. The application program stores a document in a special storage format that is editable (Microsoft Word uses a DOC format). Universal storage formats used by Windows desktop publishing programs are Rich Text Format (RTF), Hypertext Mark Up Language (HTML or HTM) format, and, less commonly, Standard Generalized Markup Language (SGML) or eXtended Markup Language (XML). The desktop publishing application opens these files and processes them to produce a display output that we view. Windows has helped install an appropriate printer driver that controls the printer.

Documents may now use Windows True Type fonts, Adobe Type 1 Fonts and the universal OpenType fonts. These fonts may be unique to Windows or universally transferable between Windows and Macintosh PCs. Adobe Type 1 Postscript fonts and OpenType fonts are used for document publishing more than are TrueType fonts. When creating and printing documents not only do document formats have to match, but the fonts must also match up in order for the document to print exactly as intended.

When a user requests a printout of a document through the application program, the program prepares the print data stream according to the printer and printer driver being used, as specified on the PC. When printing to a laser printer, the format used is typically Hewlett Packard Page Composition Language (HP-PCL or PCL) or PostScript. The formatted file is transmitted through the printer cable or a network connection to the printer. The printer processes PCL or PostScript commands to format the data for printing. In a laser printer, the document is printed one page at a time.

For an inkjet printer or dot matrix printer, the document is printed a line at a time. The printer driver sets up printing pages and lines, and the actual printout formatting is done by the laser printer. In the case of inkjet or dot matrix printers, the PC performs printout formatting. Generally, there are several reasons for a printout to be different than expected:

- Talking to the wrong printer—Your application is set for printing on an IBM Graphics Printer when you are attached to an HP Laser printer. Check the application carefully to determine what printer expectations it has. Some older applications assigned a printer to each document; even if one document printed successfully, another might not because an application program assigned it to a different printer.

- Fonts change—When special fonts are used, they may not be imbedded in the document; thus, the PC printing the document may not have the fonts installed. This results in the printing PC substituting a replacement font for the special font which may print differently than the original special font. For example, a document might be set in CG Times font, and you only have fixed spacing Courier font. This will make a big difference in the printout.

- Page setup—The document was set for a page with 0.5-inch margins on each side and 0.75-inch margins at the top and bottom. Your PC has the margins set at 0.75-inch on each side and at 1-inch on top and bottom. This makes for lots of fun; you end up with more pages and less per page. Printers can control margins independent of the PC. Document settings in PCs today generally override or reset the printer internal settings to those used by desktop publishing software. At one time this was not necessarily the case.

- Slow printing—Printers print slower under Windows applications than under DOS applications because Windows prints graphically instead of using fonts built into the printer. Thus, Windows applications can print fancy TrueType characters. On inkjet and dot matrix printers, graphics must be printed in unidirectional mode for proper print head alignment. However, some printers can print with their internal scalable fonts under Windows using a scalable font driver. Such a driver uses the printer's internal printer fonts for draft mode printing and for faster bidirectional printing. Many things cause slow printing, such as:
  - The printer CPU is slow—16 MHz vs. 35 MHz vs. 300 MHz.
  - The printer has a slow print engine (that is, a slower paper feeding and imaging system).
  - Your printer has only 2 MB RAM. If you print graphics, pictures, images, or many different special fonts, the PC must prepare the data for printing and cannot offload any work to the printer.

- You are using a slow PC. Someone once told me that creating the Bitstream fonts on their XT required a mere 17 hours of continuous processing. Today PCs use mostly True Type, Adobe Type 1, and Open Type scalable fonts. Nonetheless, the PC preprocesses a document to prepare it for the printer. A slow PC means slow printing.

- Your PC has only 8 MB RAM and only 40 MB of free disk space. This may not be enough working space for printout preparation.

- Your serial port connected to the printer is running at 9,600 BPS and not the 19,200 BPS expected by the settings specified for the printer. For data to be received properly across a serial port connection, both devices have to use the same speed (data clocking). Otherwise they cannot clock in the bits accurately. The PC's serial port settings must exactly match the settings expected by the printer (that is, baud rate or speed, data bits, parity type, and stop bits). For example, HP laser printers commonly use 9600 BPS, 8 data bits, none or no parity, and 1 stop bit. If there are any mismatches there will be no communications.

The quickest way to solve printer problems is to check everything from the PC to the printer to assure that they are all set up consistently.

Laser Printers (Page Printers)

Laser printers are page printers. They must receive an entire page of data before they print anything. Partial pages are printed only when there is a form-feed character at the end of the data sent to the printer. See Figure 6–1.

Laser printers process data received in HP-PCL (or PCL) format or in Adobe PostScript (PS) format. There are several versions of each format. The latest PCL format is HP-PCL-6. A printer that is capable of HP-PCL-6 can also print HP-PCL-5 and earlier versions. The latest HP-PCL version has more capabilities than earlier versions. Therefore, printing HP-PCL-5 on an HP-PCL-6 capable printer just means that the document being printed does not take full advantage of the printer's capabilities.

Translating this into simpler terms, it means that an HP LaserJet 8000 printer supporting HP-PCL-6 can print output destined for an HP LaserJet-4 printer supporting HP-PCL-5. This has specific advantages when it comes to producing specific quality printout, as we will soon discuss.

Most laser printers support PCL. The latest printers can process both PostScript and PCL output. Inkjet and other printers have output formats that are aimed at line printing rather than page printing. For example, ESC/P and

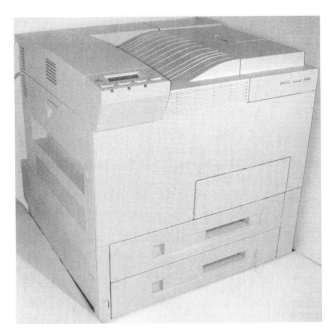

Figure 6–1
HP 8000 Laser Printer.

ESC/P2 are printer control languages used to control printer fonts and other printer functions like line spacing, bold, etc., on Epson inkjet and 9-pin dot matrix printers. Other 24-pin and inkjet printers also use the ESC/P2 control codes. A major difference between these printer control languages is that the ESC/P2 models are capable of printing internal fonts programmed into the printer in scalable sizes, from 8 point up to 72 point. The ESC/P models can print limited font sizes. A second difference is under Windows, the ESC/P2 printers can use a special scalable font driver to print internal scalable fonts in more sizes and print draft mode fonts. Printing with these fonts is much faster than with the fonts generated by Windows. The ESC/P printers only print using Windows graphical fonts, which are much slower.

Early printing used fixed-size fonts. These were precise bit maps (dot configurations and spacing) for each size character. They were wasteful of PC disk drive space and very inflexible. Scalable fonts reign today. These fonts are constructed using vectors (drawn by lines and curves). The drawing can be scaled to any size, meaning that one font specification can fit any printing requirement. Scalable fonts are Microsoft's True Type fonts and PostScript fonts. The True Type scalable fonts are the ones most generally used today, although PostScript dominates the publishing industry. See Figure 6–2.

Laser printers have a CPU and RAM to process the PC output and transform it into a page print image for printing. Fonts require some processing.

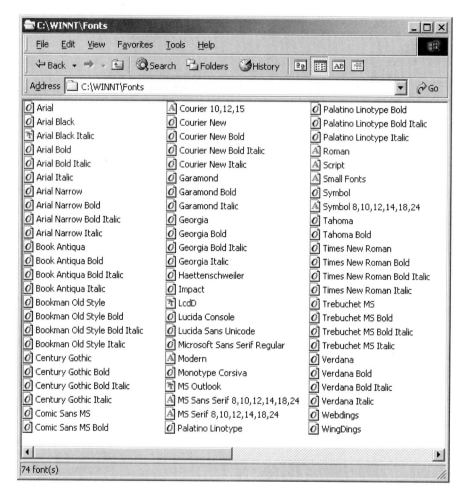

Figure 6–2
Windows 2000 standard fonts.

They can be processed once and then stored in the printer's RAM while the entire document is printed. Graphics and images require more processing. This is where a printer with a faster CPU outperforms one with a slower CPU. See Figure 6–3.

The large majority of laser printers produce black-and-white images. However, affordable color printers have arrived that use dye sublimation, thermal dot, thermal wax, and thermal resin technologies to produce color images. Cyan, magenta, yellow, and black colored toners are fused to paper using a heat-driven printing process. Color printers employ several techniques to produce color images.

Figure 6–3
Laser printer RAM modules.

Thermal dye transfer or dye sublimation printers heat dye-containing ribbons and transfer the dyes to specially coated paper or transparencies. Thermal dye transfer or dye sublimation printers are expensive and slow. They can produce continuous-tone photographic quality images. These printers require special costly paper and cannot be used with cheap xerographic paper.

Thermal wax transfer printers melt wax-based inks and print them as dots on regular paper or transparencies. Images printed as dots must be dithered to produce a full range of colors. As a result, images comprised of dots are not of photographic quality but can still be very good. The big advantage of thermal wax transfer printers is that they do not need special paper and print faster than dye sublimation printers.

Wax jet, solid inkjet or phase change printers melt dyed wax and spray it on paper similar to inkjet printers spraying ink on paper. The sprayed wax produces bright colors on virtually any type of paper. Wax jet printers print with acceptable speed and produce excellent images on paper, but wax transparen-

417

cies easily scratch. Solid inkjet or phase change printers are slow and somewhat expensive to operate.

Black-and-white laser printers are heat process printers that fuse the ink to the paper using a heated roller fuser unit. Color lasers are similar to black-and-white laser printers, but use three to four different colored toners to produce the image. They print at acceptable speeds and produce images that are quite lasting.

Laser printers are the fastest style of printer. Their speed ranges from about 4 pages per minute to 32 pages per minute, depending on the printing engine, the CPU processing speed and the amount of RAM in the printer. Laser printing CPUs are Reduced Instruction Set Computers (RISC) that range in speed from 16 MHz to 300 MHz. Printing graphics slows down the page per minute printing speed.

Laser printers feed from paper trays that hold from 100 sheets to a full ream of paper, as shown in Figure 6–4. They come with either single bin or dual bin feeders. They also perform duplex printing, i.e., printing both sides of a piece of paper without requiring the operator to remove the paper refeed it. See Figure 6–5. The sheet feeders can handle envelopes, but the printer must

Figure 6–4
Laser printer paper trays.

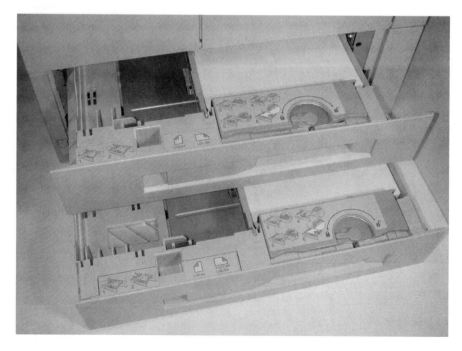

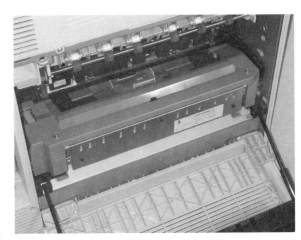

Figure 6–5
Laser printer duplexing unit.

often reorient the printing to ensure the address prints properly on the envelope. They can also print on overhead transparencies using a special transparency film designed to handle the heat fusing process.

Laser printers print using a six-step process:

1. Cleaning the printer drum—A soft plastic cleaning blade scrapes loose toner from the drum to prepare it for the next image. New laser printer engines eliminate the transfer corona assembly. By eliminating the high-voltage corona wires used for preconditioning exposure, ozone gas (O3) emissions are eliminated. The reduction of colorless and odorless ozone gas improves workplace environmental quality and lengthens printer life. A charging roller in the toner cartridge and a charging transfer roller in the printer replace the high-voltage corona wires. Unlike past transfer corona assemblies, the black foam-like charging transfer roller is replaced as part of periodic maintenance procedures.

2. Charging or conditioning the printer drum—A high-voltage negative charge placed on the corona wire is transferred to the drum by rotating the drum under the wire. This may be called preconditioning exposure.

3. Writing or forming the image—The previously charged drum is exposed to a scanning laser beam to form an uncharged image on the surface of the drum. This is sometimes referred to as scanning exposure.

4. Development—Charged toner sticks to the uncharged image area on the drum and is repelled by the charged non-image area of the drum.

This develops the invisible noncharged area into a visible image.

5. Transferring the image to paper—The drum rotates, permitting the paper and the drum to move together. As the paper and the drum contact each other, the toner is attracted from the drum to the paper. This is possible because a second corona wire charges the paper. This may also be called transfer and separation.

6. Fusing or fixing the image onto the paper—The paper (with its charged toner image) is passed through heated rollers that apply both heat and pressure to fuse the toner onto the paper.

Understanding the steps in this printing process is important for the A+ certification test. This printing technology uses electrostatic charges to form the image on the drum and transfer it to the paper. A heat-fusing process is then employed to fuse the ink to the paper. See Figure 6–6. The drum and

Figure 6–6
Laser printer components.

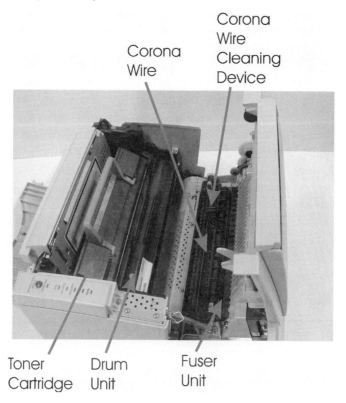

Figure 6–7
Laser printer drum and
toner cartridge.

toner cartridge are replaceable components in most laser printers. Figure 6–7
shows the replaceable drum and toner cartridges from a laser printer.

Inkjet Printers

The most inexpensive color printers are inkjet printers. They print both black-
and-white and color images by using two ink cartridges, one black cartridge
and one color cartridge with three heads (for cyan, magenta, and yellow). In
some cases, the cartridge contains the ink and the electronics to control how
it is deposited on the paper. For other inkjet printers, the cartridge only holds
the ink for printing. Inkjet printers spit the ink at the paper to form an image
on the paper from ink dots. See Figure 6–8. The inkjet printer in the figure
has a sheet paper feed in the rear, black and 3-color (yellow-red-green) ink
cartridges, and paper output tray in the front.

The resolution varies from 360 by 180 dots to 1440 by 720 dots. The images
formed are of very crisp quality even though they are printed one line at a time.
Paper feeding and movement are critical to producing a high-quality inkjet
image. Any shifting during the printing process tends to blur the image. A second key factor is the paper itself. Paper that absorbs too much ink tends to produce a washed-out image. Higher density paper produces a better printout.

Inkjet printers use sheet-fed paper. A hopper holds the paper or envelopes

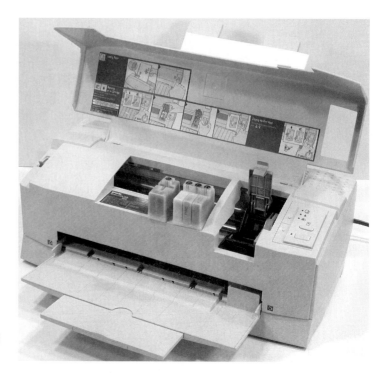

Figure 6–8
Inkjet printer.

that are fed through one sheet at a time. Printing orientation is changed electronically to print envelopes. The printing speed of inkjet printers is suitable for home use and as an auxiliary office color printer. They print slower in color than when printing black-and-white images alone. Color printing speed ranges from about two pages per minute to seven pages per minute. Inkjet printers print on both paper and transparency film, but they must use special inkjet transparencies to assure that the ink is held in place and does not smear before it dries.

Dot Matrix Printers

The oldest PC printing technology is dot matrix printing, a form of impact printing where print head pins hit an inked ribbon to produce an image on paper. Dot matrix printers are useful in situations where multipart forms need to be produced. The common 9-pin print head pins impact the ribbon to produce an image on the top form. The impact also produces images on the remaining forms.

Color ribbons are used to print color images. The colors are in bands on the ribbon. The print head moves between bands to print each color. Multiple passes are required to produce the color image. Inkjet printers are more efficient because they can print multiple colors in one pass. This reduces the number of passes needed to create the color image, making the inkjet printer faster.

The ink in the dot matrix printer ribbon lubricates the pins in the print head, and poor lubrication can cause the pins to freeze. This often overloads the printer's electronics, causing expensive repairs or printer replacement. Frequent ribbon replacement with certified ribbons is important for extending printer life.

Dot matrix printers can use sheet-fed paper, but more often use pin-fed paper. Multipart forms are typically designed to be pin-fed, meaning that the paper has strips on each side extending beyond the common 8.5-inch width. These strips have pin-feed holes punched in them, and are fed into pin rollers on each side of the printer. When a dot matrix printer uses sheet-fed paper, pressure sensitive rollers feed the printer a sheet of paper, in the same way paper is inserted into an ancient typewriter. Dot matrix printers can be adjusted for form thickness, paper type (sheet- or pin-fed), and paper width.

Paper Feeders

Paper-feeding mechanisms are built into most printers, and sheet-feeding is the most common type of paper-feeding mechanism. Single sheets are fed from a paper tray built into the printer: Inkjet printers have a hopper that holds up to 50 sheets of paper, and laser printers have trays that hold from 100 sheets to a ream of paper.

Envelopes can be fed lengthwise into printers from paper trays or hoppers. Printing is reoriented electronically so that it appears normal on each envelope. Both inkjet and laser printers can print envelopes directly, or they can print envelope labels when a larger mailing is performed. Dot matrix printers that worked with pin-feed paper required attachment of special sheet-feeding mechanisms to feed in sheet paper stock or envelopes. These never worked with any exceptional reliability. Most all printers now work with sheet feed paper.

Laser and inkjet printers do not print on multipart forms. Because they print faster than dot matrix printers, they print multiple copies of the same form in cases where more than a single copy is required. Multipart forms require a pin-feed paper handling mechanism to precisely position the form for printing.

Both laser and inkjet printers print transparency film. Transparency film is fed through normal sheet-feeding mechanism on both printers. Laser printers often have a side feed tray that can be used for special printing, as shown in Figure 6–9. The tray is opened and several sheets of transparency film are placed into it for printing. Once printing is complete, the extra transparency

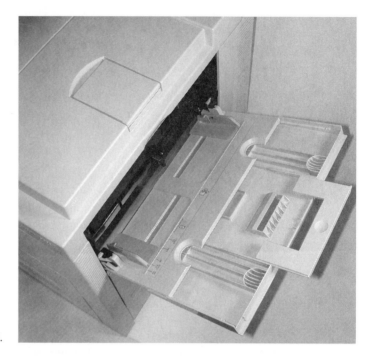

Figure 6-9
Laser Side Feed.

film is removed and the tray is closed up. Printing then resumes using the normal paper trays.

Transparency film must be designed for use with laser printers because of the heat fusing process. Using the wrong transparency film can have disastrous consequences for a laser printer. For example, using the wrong transparency film on an old Panasonic laser printer caused the film to disappear into the printer. The printer ate the transparency; it was nowhere to be found when the printer was opened. So a second sheet was fed into the printer with the same result. Finally, when a third sheet was also entirely eaten by the printer, a more detailed examination revealed that the three sheets of transparency film had wrapped tightly around the fuser's idle roller. Similarly, using the wrong transparency film in an HP LaserJet 4 printer caused the film to melt inside the printer. It gummed up the fuser unit, necessitating an expensive replacement.

Study Break: Laser Printer Operation

Find a laser printer and identify the different components.

Determine the paper's path through the printer.

Open the printer and remove the printing cartridge. Can you see the components that scrape the cartridge? They may not be visible because they can be inside the cartridge.

Are any corona wires visible? Similarly to the scrapers, these could also be located inside the drum/toner cartridge.

Can you locate the fuser unit? It should be quite warm to the touch.

The goal here is to visualize the laser printing process to better understand how an image is formed and fused to paper.

Printer Connections and Configurations

Several printer connections are used to connect printers to PCs. These connections have different operating characteristics and speeds, and include wired media as well as infrared wireless links, as shown in Figure 6–10. Figure 6–11 shows the printers installed on a Windows 2000 system.

Figure 6–10
Windows 98 printers.

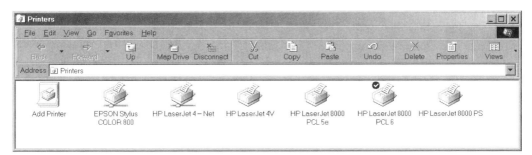

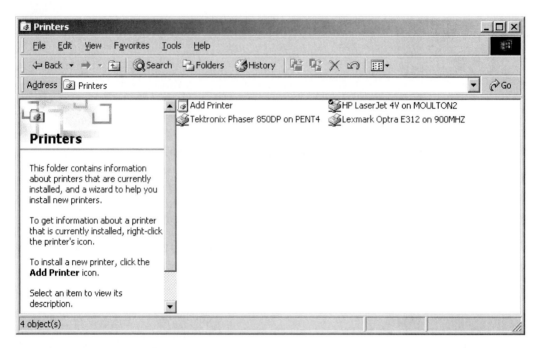

Figure 6–11
Windows 2000 printers.

Parallel Port

The parallel printer port is the most common connection. It transmits data to the printer from the PC one byte at a time. The fastest printer data transfers use the parallel port, although serial and infrared ports are sufficient to drive printers at their maximum speed. Parallel ports operate over 26-conductor cables that have a 26-pin male connector at one end and a 34-conductor Centronics connector at the opposite end. Newer printers use a high-density connector (see Figure 6–12) in place of the bulky Centronics connector (see Figure 6–13). These cables typically vary from 6 to 15 feet in length. Special cables can extend the distance a parallel interface can cover to some 30 or 40 feet. Overall, though, parallel cables run short distances at higher speeds.

The PC's parallel interface can be set up to operate in several different modes. These include a compatible mode that emulates the old PC-printer interface providing output-only mode, a bidirectional mode providing input and output capabilities, an Enhanced Parallel Port (EPP), and an Enhanced Capabilities Port (ECP) conforming to IEEE-1284 specifications. The ECP

Figure 6–12
Laser parallel port connection.

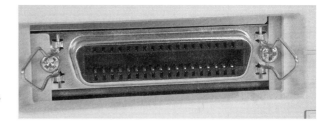

Figure 6–13
Inkjet printer Centronics connector.

and EPP modes sometimes do not work with older printers. In these instances, downgrading to bidirectional or compatible mode may resolve the printing problem. Bidirectional, EPP, and ECP modes may require IRQ and DMA channel resource assignments in addition to the standard LPT1 port I/O address resource assignment.

Serial Port

Serial ports are used to send data to printers as well. They need a special printer cable because they are not talking to a modem but rather talking to a printer. Modems are Data Circuit-Terminating Equipment (DCE) while printers and PCs are Data Terminal Equipment (DTE). This means that for the 26-pin serial cable, transmit data leaves the PC and printer on pin 2 and receive data enters on pin 3. If a standard serial cable were used to connect the printer to the PC, the parallel connections in the cable would connect pin 2 on the printer to pin 2 on the PC. Pin 2 to pin 2 would make transmit-data from the PC and the printer collide in the cable. In this instance, pin 2 transmit-data on the PC must be connected to pin 3 receive-data on the printer and vice versa. See Figure 6–14.

Serial communications to the printer operate at 9,600 bits per second or 19,200 bits per second. The speed the printer is using must exactly match the speed the PC is using. At 9,600 bits per second, the character-per-second rate is about 960 characters per second. Similarly, 19,200 BPS is about 1,920 characters per second. One printed page of characters alone has about 1,500 characters. Because text is printed as graphics, that number is much larger today. Each page is described using PCL or PostScript commands that are processed by the printer to create the image. However, if it took 15,000 characters to describe a page, this would at 19,200 BPS require about 8 seconds to transmit the page to the printer (this is about an 8 page-per-minute rate). This means that a serial connection can probably outpace any inkjet or dot matrix printer, but it may not be fast enough for the latest 32 page-per-minute laser printer. The benefit of having a serial port for printer connections is that they can connect over a longer cable than a parallel port. However, serial printer connections operate at slower speeds than do parallel port connections.

Serial communications require you to define the character setup. Each character is transmitted across the serial port beginning with a start bit and ending with a stop bit, making each character 10 bits long. The data inside the

Figure 6–14
Serial printer cable configuration.

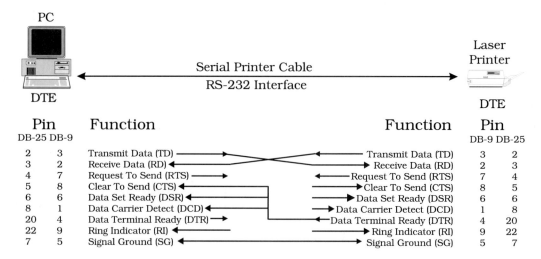

10 bits (start–8 data bits–stop) is 8 data bits. These bits are sent in ASCII code. As a standard, ASCII code has seven information bits; the eighth bit can be used to signal parity. However, since most data contains images and other binary information, it would require translation to an ASCII form and then translation back to a binary form for final printing. Transmitting 8 bits with parity requires unnecessary translations. Consequently, printer serial ports are set to 8 data bits with no parity and one stop bit.

LAN

LAN connections for printers are very common. Printers can be directly attached to a server through its parallel port or directly attached to the LAN using their own internal Network Interface Card (NIC). Data is routed to them directly or via a printer queue on a server in the network. When a printer is set up, it is configured for local print processing with the necessary drivers. The data is then routed to a printing queue on the network, as shown in Figure 6–15 for Windows 98.

Figure 6–15
Windows 98 network printers.

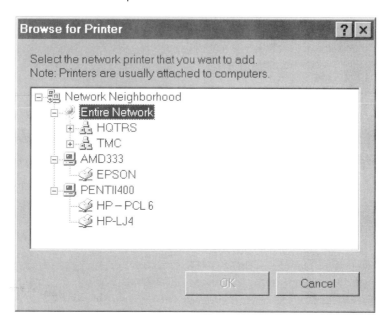

Browsing the network servers under Windows locates network printers, and they are then added as ports in the properties setup for the printer. Network printers are referred to using a network universal naming convention that identifies the server first and the printer second. Figure 6–16 identifies the server \\MOULTON2 and the port \HP4NTRAID.

Adding a printer port permits browsing the network to find other active printer ports.

Windows uses a universal printer driver that works with several page composition languages and mini-drivers that work directly with the printer hardware. The PC client universal driver communicates across the network to the printer server and the mini-drivers in the server directly control the printer. Typical network printer errors include failure to find the printer on the network (because it is powered off or has been changed in some fashion) or a mismatch between the PC printer definition and the network printer. Failure to

Figure 6–16
Windows 2000 network printer.

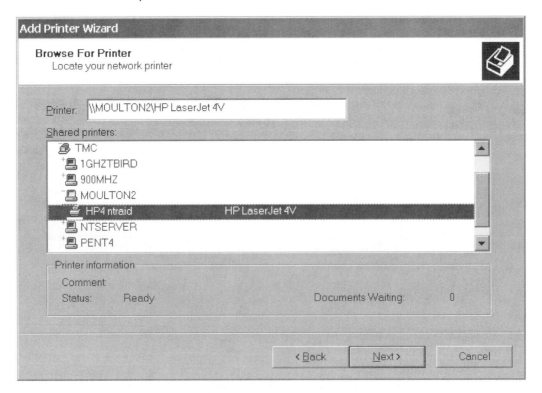

find the printer errors are easy to identify and resolve. Misconfigured printers can result in printing junk and wasting paper on a remote network printer.

Infrared Link

An easy means to link PCs to printers is across an infrared radiation (IR) connection. In this case, there is no physical connection between the printer and the PC. Both PC and printer must have IR ports that are in direct line of sight, and the distance between them must be short, several feet maximum. The PC must have the IR software link installed, as shown in Figure 6–17. Windows 98/Me and Windows 2000 have IR link software built-in. See Figure 6–18 for Windows 2000 IR software.

IR links are great for connecting printers to palmtop and laptop PCs for printing. Printing without cables makes the printing process very easy as long as there is a direct line of sight between the laptop IR port and the printer IR port (see Figure 6–19).

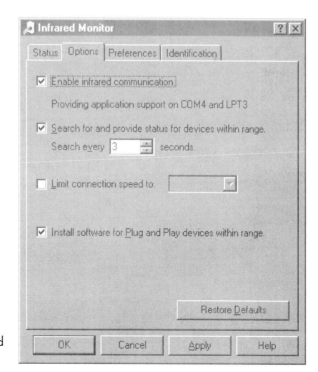

Figure 6–17
Windows 98 Infrared
software setup.

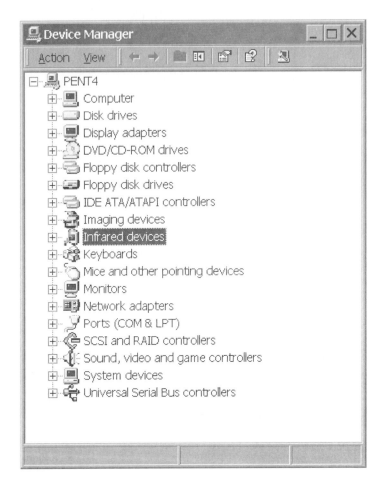

Figure 6–18
Windows 2000 IR device support.

The IR port can be assigned to either a virtual serial or a virtual parallel port, as shown in Figure 6–20. Regardless of its assignment, it acts much like a serial port.

Data is sent in bit-serial fashion over the IR link to the printer at speeds ranging from 9,600 BPS to 15,200 BPS. Faster IR speeds will soon be available that will boost the transfer rate up to 4 million bits per second. These high-speed IR ports are emerging on some laptop and palmtop PCs as well as newer printers.

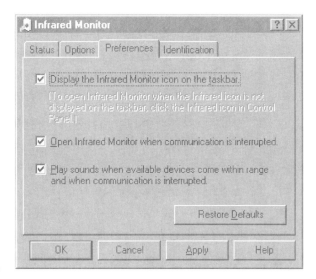

Figure 6–19
IR port preferences.

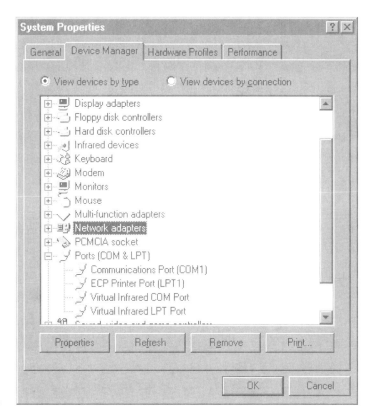

Figure 6–20
IR virtual ports.

Out of range ports and bad driver software cause problems with IR ports. In some cases, there is no way to connect devices using the IR ports because the driver software does not match. Troubleshooting indications point to no physical or IR link connection. As a result, it is easy to mistake this for a hardware problem when it is really the driver program's problem. If the IR port spots another IR device, it signals that a device is in range. When this happens, it usually indicates the IR hardware is operating properly. If communications still do not work, adjust the IR port speed downward until the speeds match and communication works. Otherwise, search for better driver programs.

Study Break: Setting Up A Printer

Let's define a new printer for Windows 95, Windows 98, Windows Me, Windows NT, or Windows 2000.

Open My Computer and then Printers.

Click on Add Printer to start the Add Printer Wizard.

Click on Next, select Local Printer and click Next again. Windows builds a driver data base to facilitate adding the new printer.

From the list of printers, select HP by pressing H two or three times. Next, press Tab to change panes in the Add Printer Wizard box. Scroll down until you can select HP LaserJet 4. Then click Next. Keep the existing printer driver, and move on to the next wizard box to select the printer port.

Pick the LPT1 port. Click Next and select a name like HP L J4 Test. Click Next.

Skip printing the test page unless there is a real printer attached to the port. Click Finish to have the new printer appear with your printers. To clean up, just delete the printer you created.

The objective of this exercise is to practice adding a printer. Not all printers are set up using the Add Printer Wizard; some come with a setup program that performs all the necessary steps to install the printer and its drivers into Windows 95/98/Me/NT/2000.

Resolving Common Printer Problems

Laser printer service typically requires you to examine print quality, check a printer's display panel for error codes or messages, determine a probable source of the problem, and swap the part that solves the problem. See Figure 6–21. The repair process requires printer disassembly to make the repair, and then reassembly and testing to determine whether the problem was solved. Unfortunately, laser printers are advanced electromechanical devices where any single problem may have several possible causes. As laser printers have become more complex, trial-and-error troubleshooting has become less efficient. However, built-in diagnostics and plain language control panel error messages make troubleshooting printer problems more manageable.

In the past, in order to exactly determine the correct cause of a laser printer problem it was necessary to test sensors, switches, and voltage levels while the printer ran, in addition to observing relevant mechanical operations. Since printers were generally not designed to operate with the covers open or any parts removed, such tests were almost impossible.

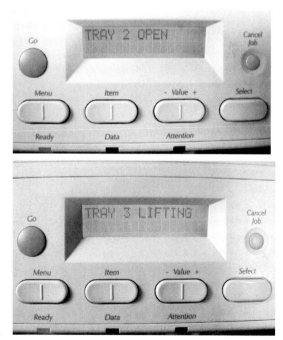

Figure 6–21
Laser printer display panel.

Laser printer troubleshooting decisions can be based on print quality and control panel error messages. Using these criteria alone, printer problems can be correctly identified.

Laser printers come in a wide variety of shapes and sizes. Their repair is limited to parts that are easily replaceable. In most cases, this is the printer toner cartridge and drum unit. Some printers may have replaceable fuser units and other small components. We have had laser units that have had drums, fuser units, fuser heating elements, cooling fans, ozone filters, and memory replaced.

Table 6–1 provides a summary of simple laser printer problems and possible solutions.

Table 6–1 Laser Printer Problem Resolution Summary

Laser Symptom	Probable Cause	Repair	Approximate Cost	Failure Rate
Pages run together	Need form-feed between pages	Add form-feed characters or page breaks to document	$0	Frequently
Memory overrun errors	Not enough RAM	Add RAM	$50 or more	Once
Prints bad pages	Wrong print driver or Corrupted or incorrect fonts	Replace Windows print driver Reconfigure Windows application Reset printer, then download fonts to printer	$0	Occasionally
Print pages are not the same or prints wrong fonts	Wrong fonts	Install fonts on PC Reset printer, then download fonts to printer Add RAM to printer to hold soft fonts	$50 and up	Occasionally
Lines in printout	Old drum Dirty printer	Replace drum unit Vacuum printer	$50 to $200	About every one to six months

Table 6-1 Laser Printer Problem Resolution Summary (Continued)

Laser Symptom	Probable Cause	Repair	Approximate Cost	Failure Rate
Faded printout	Old drum unit Low on toner	Replace drum Refill toner	$50 to $200	About every 1 to 3 months
Frequent jams	Dirty printer	Clean printer or reduce printing volume	$0	About every 2 to 4 years
	Bad paper	Replace paper	$20	
	Bad transparency film	Replace transparency film	$25 per box	
Failure to print	No power	Power on—check lights	$0	Rarely
	Bad or disconnected cable	Replace cable	$15	
Slow printing	Slow printer CPU	Upgrade printer	$500 to $6,000	All the time
	Fast RISC CPU 200 MHz or more needed for high speed printing today	Add after-market CPU cartridge		

Simple laser printer problems have required replacement of fusing units, paper rollers, and fans. These were all modular components that were easy to identify and replace.

Paper Feed and Output

Modern printers handle paper very well. The most that may need to be done in high static-charge situations is fluff the paper to reduce the charge (by holding the sheets together). Fluffing is separating the paper by running your thumb across each end of the ream of paper. Paper should be loaded with one specific side up in the laser printer, because the paper tends to curl slightly in one direction during manufacturing. The paper manufacturer usually indicates on the paper ream cover which side should be up with a message like "Image This Side First." Often this is the side that is considered the bottom of the ream because there is little advertising or descriptive material is printed on that side. High humidity can also impact paper feeding adversely, making sheets stick together and become limp. In this event, it may be necessary to replace the paper with new, dry paper for printing to resume normally.

Paper Jams

A main reason for paper jams is old or low-quality paper. This frequently results in paper that sticks together from retained static charges or that is too wet due to high humidity in the environment. Replacing the paper with fresh paper is the best cure for this problem.

Other paper jam problems are caused by the paper feeding and control rollers in the printer. When these get worn or dusty they do not feed the paper properly. We had an HP LaserJet 4 printer that was exposed to dust from a construction project. The dust affected the paper feeding rollers to the point that there was a paper jam every few pages. Replacing the rollers with new ones cured the problem.

The same printer had some problems printing from an add-on 500-sheet paper tray. This was caused by improper tension adjustment in the tray. Adjusting the paper tray tension cured this problem.

On an older Canon printer, the ozone inside the printer corroded all the rubber rollers, causing constant paper jams. In this instance as well, replacement of the rubber rollers solved the paper jam problem. Because new printers do not create ozone, this is not likely to happen with them.

When paper jams occur, it is important to be sure you get all the paper out, as little bits of paper left in the printer can cause additional paper jams.

Error Indications

Printers have warning lights, display and status panels, and self-test diagnostics. When errors occur, the lights may flash and a diagnostic message can appear. These messages are helpful in finding the most common errors. Sometimes problems can be obvious, like a printer power supply failure. In that event, a printer replacement is most likely in order.

In other cases, bad printing signifies a failure. We had a dot matrix printer that started printing erratically. In this case, the printer's self-test diagnostics ran fine. The problem was a failure of the printer's PC parallel interface. Fortunately for us, the printer had a serial interface that worked. This corrected the problem for about a year, then the printer quit altogether, necessitating replacement.

Printing to the Wrong Printer

A common printing failure with laser printers is misprinting, where the printer prints a page with several characters, then ejects the page, only to print another page with several characters and then eject that page, and so on until the paper supply is exhausted or the printer is reset.

Sending graphics to the printer and resetting the printer midstream causes this problem. Since the printer lost its downloaded fonts and graphics setup, it does not know how to handle the subsequent data stream sent by the PC. This causes the print-eject cycle as the printer interprets the graphics characters as text data for printing. Resetting the printer and dumping the print job from the PC or network-printing queue solves this problem.

Corrupted Print Files

Some print files are corrupted. When these are printed, they cause a printer error message. The message is caused by the printer acting on the data to be printed as though it were control commands to the printer. The problem is sometimes resolved by restarting both the PC and the printer from a power-off state or by fixing the offending data file. To fix a file, open a new data file window in the program that was used to create the original file. Then, cut and paste the contents of the old file into the new file.

Printer Timeout

Another common PC printer error message is the Windows timeout message. In this instance, the printer has not responded to a Windows printing request in the time expected by Windows, so Windows displays the error message. Timeout messages could be lessened if a printer had additional RAM installed to provide increased data buffering. Since Windows automatically retries the printout, typically printing is resumed without incident.

Network Printer Offline

When a printer or network server is offline, printing to the network printer results in network error messages. Network software is designed to send error indications to network administrators in the event of paper outages and similar malfunctions at network printers.

Many printers are directly network attached with specifically assigned IP addresses, as shown in Figure 6–22.

Figure 6–22
Network attached printer properties.

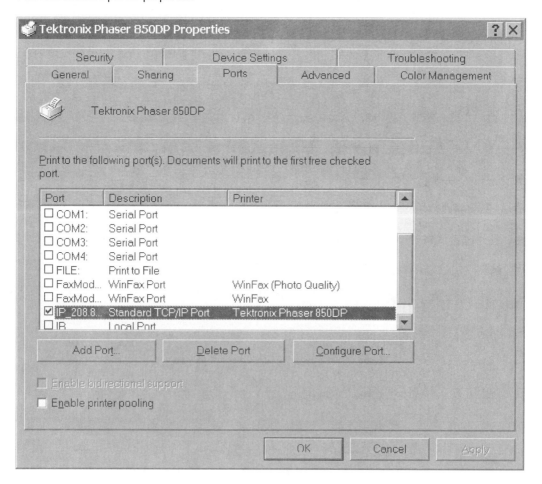

When printers are directly network attached, there may be no network administrator watching the printer. In that case printer troubleshooting must be performed across the network. The printer driver software includes troubleshooting utility programs that can detect and display common printer problems to any PC using the printer. See Figures 6–23 and 6–24.

Figure 6–23
Network attached printer troubleshooting.

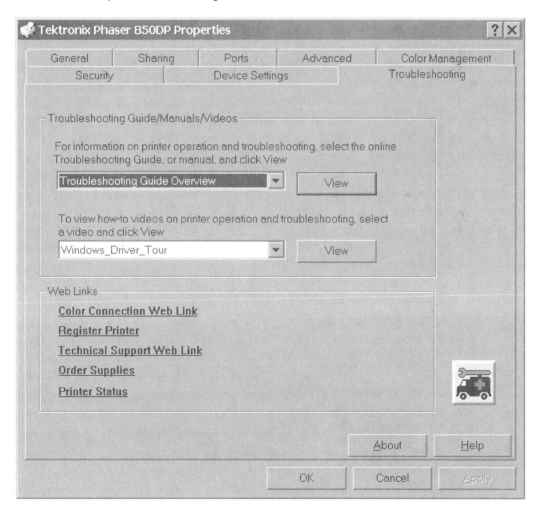

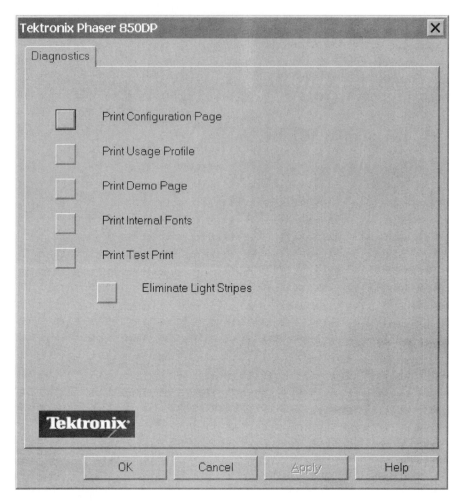

Figure 6–24
Network attached printer diagnostics.

Failed Printer Electronic Components

More difficult laser printer problems may have different indications. Fortunately, problems with printer electronics are rare. Nonetheless, some older laser printers, for example, would have horizontal black lines on printouts. This has several causes, including defective laser assembly, improperly seated fiber optic cable, or DC controller problems. Inspecting the laser assembly and laser diode, the fiber optic cable, the DC controller, and other parts for damage identifies these problems. When no damage is apparent, an Original Equipment Manufacturer (OEM) repair manual is consulted to determine the most likely cause of the problem.

These older printers sometimes print a black page with white bars. The likeliest cause for this problem is a bad scanner assembly. But is the scanner assembly really bad or did the laser contrast go out of calibration? The laser assembly is mounted in the scanner, and it is the laser's job to expose the drum. A look at a test print verifies that the drum was exposed because the entire page is black. The scanner assembly then sweeps the laser beam across the page using the scanner motor. This function must also have occurred because the page is black from left to right.

This print error occurs when a laser printer cannot detect the laser beam. In this case, the printer turns the laser on and off several times, attempting to detect a change in the output level. The white bars are printed when the laser is turned off. With time, a variable resistor found on the laser printer's MLB can fall out of calibration. This causes the intensity of the laser to be lower than the DC controller can detect.

These printers sometimes produce a laser-beam-detect malfunction error message whenever the laser beam goes undetected for more than two seconds. There are several electrical causes and solutions to this error message. The DC power supply could have malfunctioned; in which case a multimeter check for 6-volt DC output verifies a failed DC power supply. When 6-volts DC is not present, the DC power supply is replaced and the laser printer retested. The laser scanner unit might also be defective; replacing it and retesting solves this problem. Finally, the problem could be a defective DC controller board; replacing it and retesting corrects this.

This error message could be caused by mechanical problems, including:

- Malfunctioning laser shutter—To prevent a user or technician from becoming exposed to the laser beam, a laser shutter is built into the scanner unit. The shutter is opened when the printer cover is closed and a toner cartridge is in place. On the rear of the toner cartridge is a tab that opens the shutter. When this tab is missing on the toner cartridge, the shutter cannot be opened.

- Loose fiber optic cable—A fiber optic cable often runs from the scanner unit to the DC controller. This fiber optic cable can become loosened or damaged, not permitting the laser to travel to the DC controller to register. This problem commonly occurs due to mishandling.

- Bad scanner cables—Cable assembly connectors and crimps develop open and shorted connections from vibration, use, or mishandling (which occurs when you disconnect cables by pulling on the cable, not the connector). Most laser printer cables use Insulation Displacement Contact (IDC) connectors. IDC connectors act like a knife to the wire with which they make contact. Over time, such contacts can cut the wire in half, leaving nothing but the insulation holding the wire in the connector. When this is suspected, tugging lightly on an individual wire will cause it to break free from the connector.

Printer Fuser Problems

Other laser printer problem symptoms, like ghosting print, fuser assembly wear, toner buildup on the fuser roller, and void printing occur when the fuser assembly is not running at the correct temperature. Over time, a thermal resistor (thermistor) controlling the fuser assembly collects dirt, dust, and toner, causing the fuser's heat roller to wear out faster than it should. More importantly, it causes the fuser assembly to run both hotter and colder than it is designed to.

Build up of dust, dirt, and toner on the thermistor insulates it and retains heat in the heat roller. When a laser printer with dust, dirt, and toner build up is first turned on, extra heat is needed to get past the dust, dirt, and toner on the thermistor. Such extra heat causes toner to build up even more on the heat roller, exacerbating the problem. As the printer is used, this dust, dirt and toner become nice and hot, retaining heat as the fuser assembly cools. This hot material makes the printer think that the fuser is at the proper temperature.

These are representative of the types of problem symptoms found with printers. Printers have built-in sensors that detect many of these error conditions and produce a control panel error display message identifying the malfunction.

Print Quality

Since human eyes can only distinguish a resolution quality up to 600 dots per inch (DPI), it is difficult to observe that a higher DPI resolution constitutes better print quality.

Each printer has a built-in self-test function that prints a test pattern. This test pattern tests alignment of the dots that compose images from the printer. Poor dot alignment results in a blurry image and poor print quality, usually due to dirty electrical contacts. When the contacts are not clean, the ink doesn't print correctly from all nozzles. Also, a damaged interface between the printer and the PC can cause blurred or corrupted printing as well.

Higher-resolution printing from laser printers does not reproduce on copying machines correctly. The graphics images tend to fade out, and areas that have gray scale fill copy unevenly, because the copying machines cannot focus on the image. They get false readings of gray scale intensity from high-resolution (600 DPI or higher) graphics images. In this instance, lower resolution (300 DPI) and coarse graphics reproduce better on copying machines. Setting the printout for 300 DPI and coarse graphics causes the laser printer to print the image as dots, which a copying machine can focus on and accurately copy. On new printers, there may be no driver setting that directly controls the resolution and graphics printing. In this instance, using a different printer driver

Figure 6–25
Laser printer device setup under printer properties.

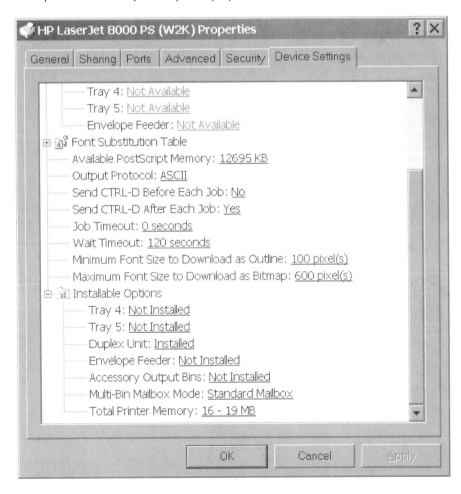

may be required to achieve the desired results. For example, on our HP LaserJet 8000 printer, we set the printer driver to be that of a LaserJet 4 printer, providing the requisite resolution and graphics printing settings. Since the HP LaserJet 8000 is compatible with the LaserJet 4 printer, everything prints as expected. See Figure 6–25.

Sometimes laser printers experience memory overruns, in addition to the incompatibilities that may occur. In this case, setting a printer as LaserJet II-compatible may resolve any problems. The LaserJet II became a de facto industry standard because its PCL printer language was implemented in printers made by many different manufacturers. Most new printers also emulate the HP LaserJet II printer. Since it had relatively simple features, most documents print just fine on any printer supporting that de facto printer standard.

Safety Considerations

There are several safety considerations when working with printers. The first is the most obvious (and the most neglected): size and weight. Lifting a heavy laser printer can cause serious back injury. High-end laser printers are both bulky and heavy and really require more than one person to lift them.

The laser can also cause ocular damage if activated and shines into an eye. Laser printers have interlocks to prevent this. Safety precautions outlined in the OEM maintenance manual should be followed to prevent eye injury from the printer's laser.

The fuser unit in laser printers is heated enough so that it is possible to be seriously burned by touching it. Just as there are safety precautions recommended by the OEM that should be followed for the laser, there are other recommendations for handling the fuser unit. These should be followed.

Also be wary of electrical power. Most printers operate their logic with low-voltage circuits, but there are high-power areas in laser printers. In older printers, the corona-charging wires carried high voltages while the printer was operating. The OEM recommendations for power protection should be followed when servicing any printer. Most simple maintenance functions like toner cartridge replacement may only require powering down the printer. Others, like adding paper can be done at any time. However, when clearing paper jams on some printers, make sure the power is off. Generally, these printers have a power interlock switch that kills the power to the printer when the printer is opened. To be safe, this switch should not be bypassed.

Study Break: Laser Printer Page Printing

Laser printers print one page at a time. It does not print until the laser printer buffer is full.

With a laser printer directly attached to LPT1 port on your PC, open a DOS Window.

Enter the command in the root directory DIR>LPT. This routes the directory display to the printer rather than to the screen. It performs a simple and effective test of the printer's operational status.

The printer may not print, or print some but not all, of the directory information. A difference in the page size of the data may cause some pages to be left in the printer's buffers and not printed.

On the printer control panel, press the form-feed button. The last printer data should print and the final page should eject.

Perform the DIR>LPT1 command again and again. Notice that the second directory printout begins in the middle of a page and not at the top of its own page. Clean up the printer by form-feed on the control panel.

This exercise illustrates the page printing operation of laser printers.

Printer Servicing and Preventive Maintenance

Most printer preventive maintenance involves cleaning and parts replacement. When replacing ribbons, ink cartridges, or toner cartridges, the printer should be cleaned to remove accumulated paper dust. Furthermore, it is good policy to periodically vacuum paper and other dust from within the accessible areas of the printer. Fans should be checked for noise indicating bearing wear. They should be cleaned as well because they tend to accumulate significant amounts of dirt.

Dusty environments are hard on printers. Dust puts an added burden on sensitive mechanical components, especially those that handle the paper moving through the printer. Sometimes cleaning the components to remove the dust may not be enough to ensure the printer operates as expected.

Replacing toner cartridges in laser printers and ink cartridges in inkjet printers is a constant maintenance task (Figure 6–26). Using certified or recycled laser printer toner cartridges have been debated as both good cost-savings or bad life-shortening approaches for printers. With the first laser printers, there was no choice—replacement toner cartridges were purchased from the OEM. This was great for the laser printer manufacturer because they could make lots of money on the cartridges. These cartridges delivered excellent print quality and high-speed printing. Whatever price the OEM supplies sold for, you paid.

Is a new toner cartridge really new? They are not totally new anymore. Parts of new toner cartridges have been used before. On the side of new Hewlett-Packard toner cartridge boxes, the phrase, "May contain material collected in the HP Toner Cartridge Recycling Program" is found. A toner cartridge's plastic must be recycled. Billions of toner cartridges are used each year; without some recycling program, we would be inundated with old toner cartridges.

An OEM toner cartridge produces consistent quality, but is more expensive. Remanufactured cartridges start with an empty toner cartridge that is disassembled, cleaned, and charged with new toner, resulting in a refilled toner cartridge for about half the price of a new one.

While this sounds great, quality control problems, scam artists, misconceptions, and new toner cartridge designs have greatly impacted toner cartridge remanufacturing.

Figure 6–26
Laser cartridge bay.

A recharged toner cartridge is as good as the company performing the cartridge recharging. Cost is the main reason for using recharged toner cartridges; you can save up to 50 percent. Inconsistency is the greatest pitfall of using recharged cartridges. Recharging a toner cartridge requires skill; it is not a cut-and-dried process. Also contributing to this problem is the inconsistency of the manufacturer who produces the toner and other materials for this industry. As if these obstacles were not enough to overcome, laser printer manufacturers at one time designed toner cartridges that were very difficult, if not impossible, to recharge. Today, most laser cartridges are rechargeable. The biggest risk of using a recharged cartridge is that it may mechanically jam and destroy the gears in the laser printer, resulting in costly printer repair or replacement.

Inkjet cartridges can be refilled as well. There are kits that provide color and black-and-white ink for refilling inkjet cartridges. The problem here is getting ink with the correct flow properties. If the ink flows improperly, the image produced by the refilled cartridge will be poor. Unlike replacement laser toner cartridges, refilled inkjet cartridges cannot damage the printer.

Study Break: Removing Laser Printer Toner Cartridges

Remove and reinsert laser printer toner cartridges.

Use several different laser printers, and for each printer remove the toner cartridge. Note that each manufacturer and model of printer is somewhat different.

Do some printers use the same cartridges? They may be because the actual print engine is manufactured by Canon. Our Canon and HP Laser printers share many of the same components.

Once the laser cartridge is removed, note the paper dust and dirt buildup in the printer. This should be vacuumed or wiped out of the printer.

Replace the cartridge to return the printer to its former operating state.

This exercise illustrates the most common maintenance procedures performed on printers.

Summary

This chapter has presented information on troubleshooting and maintaining printers. It has described how printers work, the source and resolution of common printer problems, servicing and preventive maintenance procedures, and printer-to-PC connections and configurations.

In the first section, basic printer concepts were presented along with common reasons for printer problems, such as inconsistency in fonts specifications, printer versus port speed, and similar issues. This led directly into a discussion on how to resolve these types of problems. The next section focused on avoiding problems by performing regular service and maintenance functions on printer components. The final section in the chapter discussed the types and configurations for printer port connections and how they operate.

Chapter Review Questions

1. *Non-impact printers are the same as laser printers.*

    A. TRUE
    B. FALSE

Answer: B, FALSE. Both inkjet and laser are non-impact. The impact printers are dot matrix and older daisy wheel printers. There were other impact printer technologies as well, but these are rarely found today.

2. *Negative charges attract toner during what?*

    A. Inkjet printing
    B. Laser printing
    C. Dot matrix printing

Answer: B, laser printing. Dot matrix printing uses a ribbon and no toner. Similarly, there is ink spit at the paper with inkjet printers but no toner.

3. *The IRQ of a printer port can be set at different levels.*

    A. TRUE
    B. FALSE

Answer: A, TRUE. Printers can use IRQ 7 or IRQ 5. LPT1 uses IRQ 7 and LPT2 can use IRQ 5.

4. *Which is the correct sequence for the laser printing process?*

    A. Cleaning, conditioning, writing, developing, transferring, fusing
    B. Conditioning, cleaning, writing, developing, fusing, transferring
    C. Conditioning, cleaning, writing, developing, transferring, fusing
    D. Cleaning, conditioning, writing, developing, fusing, transferring

Answer: A, cleaning, conditioning, writing, developing, transferring, fusing. The laser printer first cleans the drum, places a conditioning charge on the drum, writes the image on the drum, develops the image, transfers the developed image to the paper and then finally fuses the toner to the paper to produce the printout.

5. *During printing, an error message is displayed. The PC has printed recently and no changes have been made to the PC software or hardware. You check to see if the printer is turned on. Where do you look next?*

    A. To see if the correct printer driver is installed
    B. To see if the printer will print attached to a different PC
    C. To see if the printer is online
    D. To see if the printer is selected as default

Answer: C, to see if the printer is online. If it has printed recently and no changes have been made, the printer drivers should be OK. It was possibly set as the selected printer (but could be different from the default printer), and attaching it to a different PC is a lot of work. Looking at the printer control panel lights should quickly verify that the printer is online and ready to print.

6. *Discharging the negative charge on the drum that represents the printed image is which step of the laser printing process?*

    A. Transferring
    B. Conditioning
    C. Fusing
    D. Writing

Answer: D, writing. Transferring transfers the charged image to the paper for fusing or bonding the toner to the paper using heat. Conditioning places an initial charge on the drum.

7. *Positively charging the paper to pull the toner from the drum is performed during which phase of the laser printing process?*

    A. Writing
    B. Transferring
    C. Conditioning
    D. Fusing

Answer: B, transferring. Writing is discharging the charge on the drum to create the image. Conditioning places an initial charge on the drum. Fusing bonds the toner to the paper using heat.

8. *When attempting to print to a laser printer, the printer stops, freezes or hangs with "warming up" on its display panel. What should be checked first?*

    A. The PC is setup to print to the correct port
    B. The cable is plugged in
    C. The correct driver is installed
    D. The printer is powered on

Answer: A, the PC is setup to print to the correct port. (Always try the easiest thing first, then more difficult things.) The printer must be powered on to display anything. Driver programs should not affect the warming up display. Similarly, the printer should warm up even if the printer cable is not plugged in.

9. *In what laser printing step places a large negative charge on the drum?*

    A. Fusing
    B. Transferring
    C. Conditioning
    D. Cleaning

Answer: C, conditioning. Fusing bonds the toner to the paper using heat. Transferring transfers the charged image to the paper. Cleaning scrapes the toner from the drum so that it is clean for the next printing cycle.

10. *Toner is deposited onto the drum surface in which laser printing step?*

    A. Writing
    B. Conditioning
    C. Developing
    D. Transferring

Answer: C, developing. Writing is discharging the charge on the drum to create the image. Conditioning places an initial charge on the drum. Transferring transfers the charged image to the paper for fusing or bonding the toner to the paper using heat.

11. *Toner is bonded to the paper during the _____ step of the laser-printing process.*

    A. Writing
    B. Transferring
    C. Conditioning
    D. Fusing

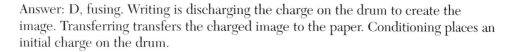

Answer: D, fusing. Writing is discharging the charge on the drum to create the image. Transferring transfers the charged image to the paper. Conditioning places an initial charge on the drum.

12. *What are the six (xerographic printing) steps in laser printing?*

    A. Charge drum—expose image—form image—copy image—fix image—clean drum

    B. Charge drum—expose image—develop image—copy image—fix image—clean drum

    C. Charge drum—form image—develop image—transfer image—fix image—clean drum

    D. Charge drum—expose image—form image—transfer image—fix image—clean drum

    E. Charge drum—expose image—copy image—transfer image—fix image—clean drum

Answer: C, charge drum—form image—develop image—transfer image—fix image—clean drum. This is similar to Question 4, but the process is started with charging the drum rather than cleaning the drum. Those steps used a slightly different terminology: conditioning, writing, developing, transferring, fusing, and cleaning.

13. *What adjustments can be made to dot-matrix impact printers?*

    A. Paper thickness, paper type

    B. Ink color, paper type

    C. Paper thickness, ink color

    D. Ink speed (impact strength), ink color

Answer: A, paper thickness, paper type (pin- or sheet-feed). Ink color cannot be adjusted on any printer.

14. *What is not important to consider when storing in laser printer paper?*

    A. Ream size

    B. Humidity

    C. Temperature

    D. Storage location

Answer: A, ream size. The size of the paper should be more or less standard: 8.5" × 11" in North America.

15. *Which part of a printer cannot cause a paper jam?*

    A. Fuser unit
    B. Scanning or registration guide
    C. Paper tray
    D. Developer unit

Answer: B, scanning or registration guide. The paper traveling through a printer does not touch the scanner or registration guide. The paper passes through the paper tray, the fuser unit, and the developer unit.

16. *If a laser printer does not feed paper what is the first thing you do?*

    A. Remove options
    B. Remove accessories
    C. Examine paper trays
    D. Examine toner cartridge

Answer: C, examine paper trays. The paper starts into the printer from the paper tray so check it first. Options and accessories may or may not affect paper feeding. The toner cartridge is most likely to impact print quality, not paper feeding.

Chapter 7

LAPTOP PCS AND PERSONAL DIGITAL ASSISTANTS (PDAS)

Chapter Syllabus

- Laptop Configurations and Components

- Personal Digital Assistants

- Common Laptop Problems

Laptop computers have special problems due to their integrated design and portability. This chapter examines the unique components of laptop computers, the problems associated with them, and some solutions to those problems.

Laptop Configurations and Components

Laptop computers come in a variety of forms. Some are small hand-held (palm-size) pocket organizer replacements. Others are highly portable, mini-laptops that are cut-down versions of laptop PCs, aimed at email and writing. Still others are high-end laptop systems that can rival the performance of low-end desktop PCs. (The palmtop and high-end laptop have built-in and replaceable components. The pocket organizer in the top left of Figure 7–1 is the size of a PC card and only uses replaceable batteries.

The hand-held pocket organizer PCs are mostly fixed in configuration and function. The memory is the single component that can be enhanced. The input/output options on hand-held PC CPUs are fixed, in addition to the CPU itself. Similarly, the options on the mini-laptop PCs are limited. Their input/output capabilities are greater than Personal Digital Assistants (PDAs) or palm-size PCs, but more limited than the high-end laptops. The mini-laptop PCs have different memory and disk drive options, USB and FireWire connections, internal modems, and the capability to use PC card bus (formerly the Personal Computer Memory Card International Association—PCMCIA Bus) cards.

Laptop PCs may have more capabilities and features like an integral Ethernet connection. Some laptop features are built in, like the sound card, while others are configured and may be upgraded at a later time, like memory or disk drive options. Laptops can plug into docking bays or port replicators, making it easy to use them as both a portable and a desktop PC. Figure 7–2

Figure 7–1
Pocket organizer, palmtop and high-end desktop replacement laptop PCs (counter clockwise from top left).

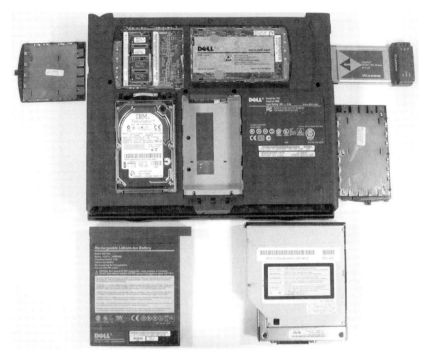

Figure 7-2
Laptop components.

shows some removable laptop components including (counter clockwise from bottom left) battery, combined floppy disk and DVD drive, Card Bus Card, Display Adapter, RAM Memory and fixed disk drive. Table 7–1 compares the features of different laptops.

Laptop expandability comes from adding in components that are compatible with the MLB and the chassis design. For example, some laptop MLBs accept Pentium CPUs that range from 200 MHz to 300 MHz, while others are designed to work with a variety of AMD K6 CPU chips set at varying speeds. As a result, upgrading the CPU chip in a laptop is possible, but not a recommended field upgrade. Although CPU chips are socketed, you must get the precise low-power CPU chip and fan that will fit the mechanical form factor and MLB CPU-supporting chip set to upgrade laptop CPUs. See Figure 7–3. Note the foam rubber spacer that directs airflow into the fan from outside. This foam rubber spacer caught the fan blades because it was crushed by the housing and stopped the fan. Repositioning the foam rubber spacer solved the problem. The fan sucks air in from the bottom of the PC and blows it across the CPU heat sink, then out the side channel.

Table 7-1   Portable PC Components

Type	Size/Weight & Batteries	Technical Features	Comments
Palmtop or Hand-held (PDA devices)	Palm Size Thickness—0.5 to 1.1 inches Width—3.1 to 7.8 inches Height—2.1 to 4.7 inches and 1.5 to 20 Oz. Two AAA Type, AA Type, NiMH, Li-Ion, or Li-polymer batteries	Display —Gray scale 160 by 160 —Gray scale 480 by 160 —65K color 160 by 160 —Gray scale 320 by 240 —4K color 320 by 240 —4K color 320 by 320 —2 to 6 inch diagonal Pen Input—Big time Keyboard—none, mini-sized, or folding VGA Port—None CPU—RISC from 16MHz to 206 MHz ROM—2 to 16 MB Contains Windows CE or Palm OS RAM—1 to 64 MB Disk Drives—None Secure Digital and Multimedia Cards Flash Memory Card—One Compact Flash Type I or Type II PC Card Slots—None or one PC Type II CD-ROM Drive—None Sound—Single speaker/Headphones (MP3) Serial port—Yes USB port—Yes	Palm OS, Windows CE (MS Windows for Pocket PC)

Table 7.1 Portable PC Components (Continued)

Type	Size/Weight & Batteries	Technical Features	Comments
		Infrared Port—Yes and Fast IR (4Mbps)	Windows Me
		Parallel Port—None	
		Wireless Communications Cards—Modem and LAN	
Mini-Laptop Sony Vaio C1 Picture Book and Vaio SR	Lap Size to File Folder Size	Display	
	Thickness—1.1 to 1.3 inches	—16 million color UWVGA 1,024 by 480	
	Width—1.4 to 10.2 inches	—16 million color XGA 1,024 by 768	
	Height—3.7 to 8.9 inches and 2 to 3 lbs.	—8.9 to 10.4 inch diagonal	
	One NiMH or Li-Ion battery	Pen Input—Maybe	
		Keyboard—Good-sized	
		VGA Port—None to one	
		CPU—Pentium or RISC from 600 MHz to 850 MHz	
		ROM—64KB to 128 KB Boot and BIOS	
		RAM—128 MB to 192 MB	
		Disk Drives—12 to 20 GB	
		Flash Memory Card—One Compact Flash Type II	
		PC Card Slots—None or one PC Type II CardBus	
		CD-ROM Drive – None	
		Sound – Stereo Speaker Output	
		Serial Port – None	

459

Table 7.1 Portable PC Components (Continued)

Type	Size/Weight & Batteries	Technical Features	Comments
		Infrared Port—None or One	
		Parallel Port—None	
		USB—None or one	
		Built-in Modem—Yes	
		IEEE 1394 Connection—Yes	
Full Size Laptop	Lap Size	Display	Windows Me
	Thickness—1.6 to 2.3 inches	—12-bit (16 million) color XGA 1,024 by 768	Windows 2000
	Width—12.5 to 14.1 inches	—32-bit color XGA 1,024 by 768	
	Height—8.8 to 10.8 inches	—32-bit color SXGA 1,400 by 1,050	
	and from 6 to 10 lbs.	—32-bit color UXGA 1,600 by 1,200	
		—13.3 inch to 15+ inch	
	One, two, or three NiMH or Li-Ion batteries	—2X or 4X AGP VGA with 8 MB Video RAM	
		Pen Input—No	
		Keyboard—87 Key To W95 Key Near Full-Size	
		VGA Port—One with up to 1,600 by 1,200 resolution	
		CPU—Pentium III 800 MHz to 1.3 GHz or AMD-Duron to 850 MHz to 900 MHz AMD-Athlon 4 at 1 GHz	
		ROM—64 KB to 128 KB—Boot and BIOS	
		RAM—64 MB to 512 MB—SDRAM	
		Disk Drives—Floppy, ZIP, and up to 30+ GB IDE	

Table 7.1 Portable PC Components (Continued)

Type	Size/Weight & Batteries	Technical Features	Comments
		Flash Memory Card—PC Card Type II	
		PC Card Slots—One to Three PC Type II or Type III	
		CD-ROM Drive—24x, CD-RW, DVD, or CD-RW/DVD combo (and Smart Bay for exchanging drives)	
		Sound—Stereo with Multimedia Sound Line-in, Microphone-in and Headphone-out Jacks	
		Serial Ports—Two	
		Infrared Port—Yes and Fast IR (FIR) 4Mbps	
		Parallel Port—One	
		USB—One or Two	
		Wireless Communications Cards—Modem and LAN (PC Bus cards)	
		Game Port—None or One	
		Expansion Chassis Port—One	
		PS2 Keyboard/Mouse Port—None or One	
		Built-in Modem—Yes	
		IEEE 1394 Connection—Yes	

Figure 7–3
Laptop CPU and fan.

Typical laptop CPU and supporting chip set combinations are shown in Table 7–2. Each chip set varies in operating speed and L2 CPU cache. Laptops all use SDRAM. The laptop manufacturer adds video, disk drive, and other components as their board design and form factor permits.

Table 7–2   Laptops and Common Supporting Chip Sets

Laptop CPU	Supporting MLB Chip sets
Pentium MMX 200–266 MHz Tillamook	Intel 430TX Mobile
Pentium II 200–233 MHz Deschutes	Intel 430TX Mobile
Pentium II 266 to 366 MHz Deschutes	Intel 440BX Mobile
Celeron 400 to 700 MHz Speed Step Technology Dixon	Intel 440BX Mobile AGP
Pentium III 400 MHz to 1GHz Speed Step Technology Geyserville	Intel 440BX Mobile AGP
Mobile AMD K6-2+ 500 MHz to 550 MHz	Super 7 Mobile
Mobile K6 III + 450 to 500 MHz	Super 7 Mobile
Mobile Duron 800 to 900 MHz	AMD-7xx and VIA
Mobile Athlon 4 1 to 1.4 GHz	AMD-7xx and VIA

Liquid Crystal Display (LCD)

The most prominent LCD display feature is size. They vary from 12.1-inch display to 15-inch diagonal display (see Figure 7–4). This is an improvement on 11-inch and smaller LCD sizes used in earlier models. Displays support varying resolution and colors on the LCD and higher resolutions with more colors on the external monitor port. The resolution varies from UWGA (1,024 by 480 resolution) to VXGA (1,600 by 1,200 resolution) for the LCD panel and up to 1600 by 1200 for the external display port. Colors range from 256 color displays to 32-bit true color display. Some laptop LCD panels do not display

Figure 7–4
Laptops (counter clockwise from bottom left) with 10-inch, 12-inch, 14-inch and 15.1-inch displays.

the high-color images as well as external monitors display them, because of the way those LCDs produce the colors.

Although they are all labeled LCDs because of the base technology used in their design, there are variations that can make the display more visible from an angle and in brighter lighting conditions. In bright sunlight, virtually all LCD displays are not visible. Today, most portables use the Thin Film Transistor (TFT) LCD flat-panel display active-matrix display.

A TFT screen has each pixel (dot or illuminated spot) controlled by from one to four transistors. TFT technology provides the best resolution of all the current flat-panel display technologies and is the most widely used. TFT screens are often referred to as active-matrix LCD displays.

DSTN, or Double-Layer Super-Twist Nematic, is a passive-matrix LCD technology using two display layers to counteract color shifting that is produced by other super-twist LCD displays. DSTN displays are labeled dual-scan LCD displays. CSTN, or Color Super-Twist Nematic, is an LCD technology developed by Sharp Electronics Corporation. Unlike TFT, CSTN is based on a passive matrix and consequently is less expensive to produce. Original CSTN displays produced in the early 90s suffered from slow response times and image ghosting, when image remnants remain in one spot on the screen when the image moves to another spot on the screen. In Windows, setting mouse tails on helps track the mouse position on screens that have slow responses to image movement and image ghosting. Advances in the technology are making CSTN a viable alternative to active-matrix displays. CSTN displays can provide 100 ms response times, a 140-degree viewing angle, and high-quality color rivaling TFT displays at about half the cost.

Both DSTN and CSTN displays may be backlit (having a light source behind the display) for optimal viewing. TFT are also backlit. See Figure 7–5.

High Performance Addressing (HPA) is a passive-matrix display technology that provides better image response rates and contrast than conventional LCD displays. HPA displays do not produce as crisp an image and are not as fast as active-matrix (TFT) displays; however, they are considerably less expensive to manufacture. Some computer manufacturers use HPA LCD displays in low-cost notebook computers.

All LCD displays are sensitive to heat. High heat and direct sunlight darken them, hampering their ability to display any image. The high heat and direct sunlight can destroy the display if the exposure is of sufficient duration. No matter what technology is used, the displays do not provide good image visibility in direct sunlight. Some shade or reduced lighting is needed for best visibility. The recommendation here is to never use a laptop in direct sunlight, like Sandra Bullock did in the movie "The Net" in the beach scene. Hollywood knows little about laptop PCs.

The surface of the displays is made of soft, nonreflective plastic that can

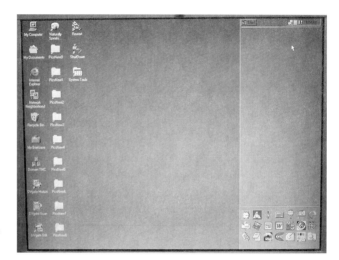

Figure 7-5
TFT polysilicon laptop display.

become scratched by small amounts of abrasive material. Laptop LCD screens require periodic cleaning and dust removal. This should be performed using a nonabrasive lint-free cloth. Gunk on the screen should be removed using a wet lint-free cloth. The water dissolves the gunk while the lint-free cloth does not scratch the LCD surface. It is possible to use cleaning chemicals on the LCD screen. However, a cloth dampened with plain water should remove all but the most stubborn gunk from the LCD screen.

Similarly to Cathode Ray Tube (CRT) displays, LCD displays can etch an image if the same image is left displayed for a long time. This happened on one of our laptops that had the same image displayed for three consecutive days. The image light areas remained bright after the image was moved. The good news is that over time (about a week or more) the display returned to normal operation and was not damaged. To avoid such problems, a Windows screen saver or the power management function that turns off the monitor should be activated. On back-lit displays, the LCD should be powered down during periods of inactivity to prevent burning out the back-light lamp.

On some of our older laptops a bad LCD display sometimes pops up. These bad displays have lines running through them. The colors in those lines generally are not visible and leave a blank line in the display. In these instances, the source of the problem is the connection between the LCD and the PC. Changing the angle of the LCD panel or moving it down toward the keyboard and then immediately back into operating position often fixes the electrical connection between the laptop PC and its LCD, correcting the problem.

The visibility of an LCD depends on the viewing angle. Most displays provide a 180-degree viewing angle, and all displays are most visible when viewed straight-on. Viewing at an angle can cause them to darken. This is great on airplanes when one desires privacy for playing strip poker on their laptop, but not good when viewing results with the boss or a group is important. Viewing many LCD displays from the far right side to far left side greatly degrades LCD display visibility. TFT displays provide the widest viewing angle.

Battery

Nickel-cadmium (NiCad) batteries powered early laptop computers. These had a short operating duty cycle and quickly developed a charging memory effect, preventing them from being fully recharged after several uses. This was especially true when the batteries were not fully discharged with each use.

My first laptop was a 386 DX 20 MHz system with 4 MB RAM and a 500 MB disk drive. The NiCad batteries were not removable but an integral part of the PC. I purchased it because I was scheduled to travel to Australia and New Zealand and I wanted to play solitaire electronically while on the 20+ hour flight. I fired up the laptop on the plane after we were about an hour out of San Francisco only to discover that the batteries lasted 20 minutes (386 DX 20 MHz, 4 MB RAM, and 500 MB disk drive ate copious amounts of power). I had about 18.5 hours of flying time left where I could no longer play solitaire.

Newer laptops use Nickel Metal Hydride (NiMH), Lithium Ion (Li-Ion), or Lithium polymer (Li-polymer) batteries. They provide superior performance to NiCad batteries, and Li-Ion or Li-Polymer batteries perform the best. All batteries develop a charging memory, preventing full recharge of the battery over time. With NiMH batteries, this can be from six months to a year of proper use (i.e., full discharge before recharge). With Lithium batteries this is about a year. Lithium batteries last longer than NiMh batteries under use; they can have about a 20 percent or longer operating cycle. Most laptops today use power management functions and Lithium batteries to produce operating times of up to 8 hours or more. See Figure 7–6.

Smart batteries change the charging cycle so they are discharged before charging, thus reducing the effect of charging memory. Batteries are also removable and used in combinations of two or sometimes three batteries to extend the operating cycle life.

Laptops that are inactive for some time or sense battery failure enter suspend mode, where almost all activity is stopped. The display is inactive, the disk drive ceases rotating, peripherals are not powered, and the CPU enters a lower power and slower operating speed state, looking only for power switch or keyboard activity. This keeps battery power drain to a minimum. The operating state of the laptop prior to entering suspend mode is stored in a special

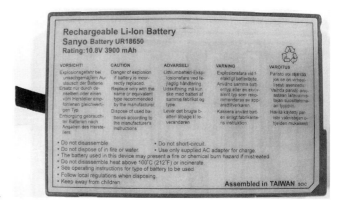

Figure 7–6
Laptop Li-Ion battery.

partition on the disk of the laptop so that it can be restored when the power switch is activated.

Batteries are recharged in the laptop. Some laptop PCs recharge the battery while they are operating, and others require that the battery be in the laptop while it is off for them to recharge. Generally, on each laptop there is software that shows the battery-charging status; external battery chargers are also available. Figure 7–7 shows a laptop status panel running on battery power and booting from floppy drive A:. The power switch and the display panel power-off switch are on the lower right. When the display panel is closed, the display panel power switch cuts power to the panel, blanking the display.

Laptops can be run without their batteries when plugged in to an external AC power source. Generally, hitting the power-off switch on the laptop removes power to the computer only under normal operation power-off scenarios. Because of suspend mode operation and Windows power management, it is possible for a laptop to enter an operating state where the power off/on switch is ignored totally. In this case removing both the AC power and the battery resets the laptop. By removing the battery and the AC power, all electrical energy is removed from the laptop computer, resetting it to a power-off state.

Figure 7–7
Laptop status panel.

AC Adapter

Laptop AC adapters are "ball and chain" adapters. They contain a transformer that converts AC power to DC power for either 120-volt 60-cycle or 240-volt 50-cycle AC power. The power adapters automatically sense the 120-volt or 240-volt input power and produce the required DC output. Typical output voltage and current vary for different laptops. Clone laptops use AC power adapters that produce a 19-volt DC output, with the amperage varying from 2 to 3 amps. The adapter plug into the laptop is a female connector whose center post is positive and outside conductor is negative, as shown in Figure 7–8.

Palmtop and other laptop PCs require different voltage and amperage output levels. The critical output parameter here is less voltage and more amperage (see Figure 7–9).

Mixing AC adapters on laptops is not recommended, but we have used different adapters between different laptop PCs. When the adapter did not provide sufficient amperage, the PC ran but did not maintain its internal battery.

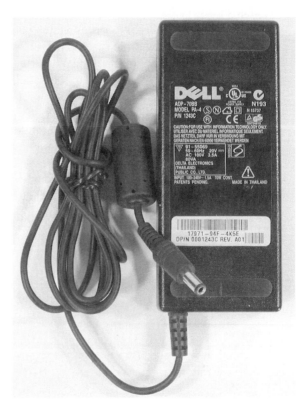

Figure 7–8
Laptop AC adapter.

Figure 7–9
Palmtop AC adapter.

If anything caused the battery to discharge, the PC would not run. In other cases, we have run laptops with the 13-volt DC output from an automobile cigarette lighter jack. It ran fine on the lower voltage. We used it to power the laptop while performing GPS navigation in the car. This is the best use for an automobile cigarette lighter we can think of.

PC Card Bus—Type I, II, and III Cards

Add-in components for laptop PCs use the PC card bus connectors. Most laptops provide both Type II and Type III slots for PC cards. The PC card (PCM-CIA card) adapters are 17-bit adapters with 68 pins in two rows.

Type I, Type II, and Type III cards have the same electrical interface, but their thickness is different. All PC cards are 85.6 mm long by 54 mm wide. Type I cards are 3.3 mm thick, Type II cards are 5 mm thick, and Type III cards are 10.5 mm thick. The Type III PC bus cards take up the mechanical space of two Type II cards, meaning that the PC card bus connections on a typical laptop PC can handle one PC card bus Type III card, or two PC card bus Type I or II cards. A single Type III and a single Type II card configuration is generally not supported unless a special extension adapter is used to unblock access to the second Type II card slot. Figure 7–10 shows two Type II or one Type III card slot in the same laptop PC.

Add-in components for laptops that come in PC card bus form are LAN adapters, modems (both wired and wireless), SCSI adapters for external SCSI

Figure 7-10
Laptop PC card slots.

devices like JAZ drives, IEEE 1394 Adapters for video input and editing, some hard drives, and multifunction adapters that are both LAN and modem.

These PC card bus adapters use plug-and-play installation under Windows. Windows works best with PC card bus adapters, although there can still be problems. One of our laptops had both a multifunction and a SCSI Type II PC card bus adapter installed. The SCSI adapter had to be installed after the multifunction adapter for the plug-and-play installation to work properly. Furthermore, the laptop must have the proper BIOS to support Windows installation and the PC card bus plug-and-play function. One of our laptop PCs would not function under Windows. It could not find the PC card bus plug-and-play devices until the laptop BIOS was flash upgraded to the latest release.

The PC cards use socket service drivers to detect insertion and removal of PC card devices. This permits warm removal and insertion of the PC card. A second level of card services drivers understands the function of the card—LAN, modem, or combo—and provides the drivers enabling it to work with Windows. Under DOS, several specialized drivers had to be loaded to enable socket services. Often times these were specific to the laptop and the PCMCIA cards being used. Making PC cards work under DOS and Windows 3.1 was a daunting task. Windows 95 improved this; Windows 98 improved this even more. Both Windows Me and Windows 2000 work best with PC cards. When installing PC cards in a Windows PC, they should be installed last after the PC is completely configured and operating without them. Once the PC is running, the PC cards can be installed by inserting them into the PC card bus socket. Socket services recognize that the PC card is installed and initiates the software driver installation process. As stated earlier, the sequence of insertion is important, and certain cards need to be installed prior to inserting other cards.

The most common problems with PC cards, aside from plug-and-play installation problems, are problems with the pigtail connections to LANs, phone lines, etc. These pigtail connections tend to break or the connector pins become bent, rendering them nonfunctional. Connecting and disconnecting the pigtail connectors is done constantly, providing countless opportunities to break the wiring in them or bend one of their connector pins (see Figure 7–11). When a specific PC card adapter malfunctions, it is easy to spot a software problem by examining the PC card icon in the Systray (Systray is a Microsoft Windows term). See Figure 7–12.

To remove a PC card, just double-click on the Systray icon and double-click on the card to remove when it displays the stop card panel. Figure 7–13 illustrates the socket services sequence of removing a PC card. The laptop PC then replies that it is okay to remove this card. After acknowledging removal, the card is no longer shown as an active PC card.

Figure 7–11
PC card pigtail connectors.

Figure 7–12
PC card Systray icon.

Right-clicking on the Systray icon provides a direct unplug or eject hardware display. When removing a PC card, the control panel PC card function can also be used.

Expanding the Systray icon by double-clicking on it identifies the operating PC cards. Cards not identified have software driver problems. Cards identified as nonfunctional usually have pigtail connector problems. See Figure 7–14.

Figure 7–13
Socket services PC card removal.

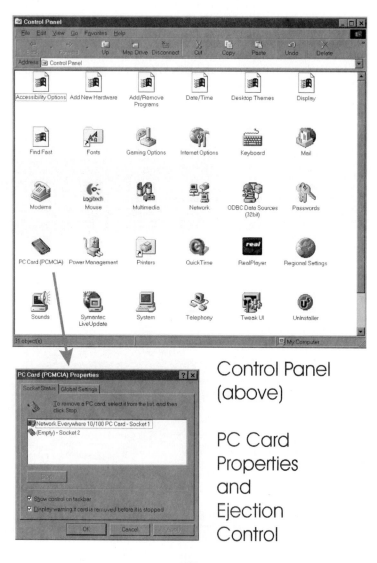

Control Panel
(above)

PC Card
Properties
and
Ejection
Control

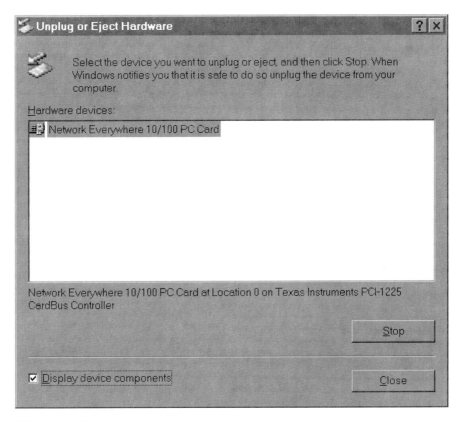

Figure 7–14
PC card Systray icon expanded.

The last PC card problem area is heat. Airflow across the cards drawn by the laptop CPU cooling fan is the principal cooling mechanism for these cards. If there is any blockage of airflow, both the CPU and the PC cards can easily overheat. The laptop should always be set on something providing sufficient airflow.

CD-ROM, CD-RW, and DVD Drives

CD-ROM, CD-RW and DVD drives are a key laptop component. They are used to install software and to hold data for some laptop applications, like GPS mapping programs. The CD-ROMs, CD-RWs and DVDs are removable units that fit in a bay that can hold a CD-ROM, CD-RW, DVD or battery. The extra battery extends the laptop operating time when not on AC power.

473

New CD-ROM, CD-RW and DVD units have both the CD-ROM, CD-RW or DVD and floppy disk drive in the same unit. This conserves space and increases the functionality of the laptop. DVD drives can hold lots of data, making mapping programs and other graphics programs useful on the road away from the office. See Figure 7–15.

CD-ROM, CD-RW and DVD units are 5.25-inch IDE drives mated to special carriers and docking connectors. Similar to laptop fixed disk drives, they can be removed from and reinserted into the laptop as needed. They should not be removed or inserted while the laptop is powered up and in operation. If this is done, the laptop can lock up Windows, requiring a power-off and reboot to restore it to normal operation.

Figure 7–15
Laptop DVD/CD-ROM drive.

Docking Stations and Port Replicators

Docking stations provide an added convenience for laptop PCs that are used both as a mobile unit and as an office PC. The laptop can be connected to the docking station through its expansion port, as shown in Figure 7–16. This single connection then makes connections to the other peripherals used by the laptop PC, including the monitor, speakers, keyboard, mouse, printer, floppy disk, and more. Typically, a lever assists in disconnecting the docking station from the laptop PC. Also, guides help align the expansion port connectors in the docking station and the laptop.

Docking stations are more than port replicators, permitting installation of ISA bus and PCI bus option cards and added disk drives. Most laptops do not require such expansion because they get the added disk drive space from network server drives. Port replicators do not support disk drive and LAN connections, but do provide keyboard, mouse, serial, parallel, microphone, and speaker connections.

Figure 7–16
Port replicator front and rear.

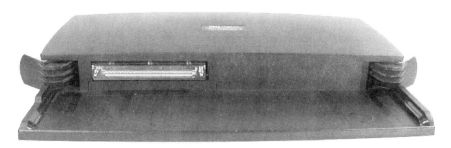

Fixed Disk Drive

Most laptop fixed disk drives are removable units. They are 2.5-inch IDE drives mounted in a carrier specific to each style of laptop. Laptop drives range in capacity from 0.5 GB to 48+ GB. Figure 7–17 shows a laptop IDE drive removed from its mounting slot. A special IDE connector mates to the laptop PC, making the drive removable.

Figure 7–18 shows an empty laptop drive carrier on the right, a 2.5-inch IDE drive used on a laptop with an IDE adapter in the center, and a 2.5-inch drive bottom view on the left. The push-pin connector on the 2.5-inch IDE drive connects to a small ribbon cable that runs to the mating connector on the 2.5-inch laptop drive carrier. The laptop 2.5-inch drive is connected to the ribbon cable and bolted into the carrier. Mounting the drive in a 3.5-inch drive bay requires attaching mounting brackets to the drive and a special 2.5-inch to 40-pin IDE cable connector.

Notice how the figure illustrates how power is provided to the 2.5-inch drive in the center through a power connector connected to the rightmost connector pins. Power is supplied to the 2.5-inch drive through the single connector on the end of the drive. Drive failures are easily fixed by replacing the

Figure 7–17
Laptop IDE drive.

Figure 7–18
2.5-inch drives.

faulty drive with a known good drive. The problem with this approach is that all data on the old disk drive is typically lost, thrilling all involved with the replacement.

Networking Cards

Laptops are generally connected to a network when in the office. This is essential to back up critical data on servers and to exchange files and email with other PCs. The PC cards connecting to a LAN are generally Type II PC cards with a pigtail connection supporting usually twisted-pair wiring, but sometimes both coaxial cable wiring and twisted-pair wiring. The pigtail connection to the network is through a standard Mod-8 (RJ-45) unshielded twisted-pair connector or through a coaxial cable BNC (push and turn) connector.

Laptop networking PC cards support 10 Mbps and 100 Mbps Ethernet. Figure 7–19 shows a combination modem/Ethernet PC card (top), a single 10 Mbps coaxial cable or twisted-pair wiring PC card (middle) and a 10/100 Mbps Ethernet PC card (bottom). The combo card (top) supports both unshielded twisted-pair Ethernet and coaxial cable Ethernet, while the 10 Mbps/100 Mbps Ethernet-only card (bottom) provides only a Mod-8 connector.

477

Figure 7-19
Laptop LAN PC cards.

These LAN PC cards are plug-and-play in laptop PC card slots under Windows 95/98/Me and Windows 2000. The top and middle cards in Figure 7–19 support Ethernet at 10 Mbps speeds. Other cards provide Ethernet support for both 10 Mbps and 100 Mbps Ethernet. Combo cards are installed as multifunction parent devices under socket services. Card services then installs the Ethernet network and modem drivers. Failed LAN cards are not repairable and are replaced. Pigtails can be replaced unless the connector in the PC card is broken. If the modem component of a combo card fails, then the card could be used as a LAN-only card. The modem part is not repairable.

RAM

RAM can be upgraded or replaced in laptop PCs. Often times access to RAM is through the laptop keyboard, but sometimes it is through a panel on the bottom of the PC. Typically the RAM is installed as SO DIMMs in sockets in the laptop. The trick is finding the sockets or determining how to remove the keyboard. In clone laptops, the plastic cover over the LCD status panel and the stereo speakers is typically removed first. It is usually pried open on the LCD panel side exposing the speakers and the status panel. See Figure 7–20.

Figure 7–20
Status panel plastic cover removed.

Lifting the keyboard reveals the RAM Small Outline DIMM (SODIMMs). Laptop keyboards are attached to the chassis electronics by one or two ribbon cables. These cables permit moving the keyboard aside to replace the RAM SODIMMs.

RAM expandability is determined by the MLB and supporting chip set. The RAM sockets fit specific RAM chips. RAM for laptop PCs is sold in specific chip configurations for a specific laptop manufacturer and model computer. The RAM is typically SDRAM in a SODIMM in a 72-pin or 144-pin configuration. Figure 7–21 shows 72-pin SODIMM RAM installed in a laptop PC.

Laptop memory is often memory without parity, which works fine until there is a memory error. In that case, the software just dies when it hits the memory location that is bad. In one case, this meant that Windows final installation quit in exactly the same procedure each time during installation. Good memory was used up to the point where the Windows product code was entered, then the laptop died. It appeared to be a software problem or a configuration problem, but it was not either. Bad memory caused the failure. A

479

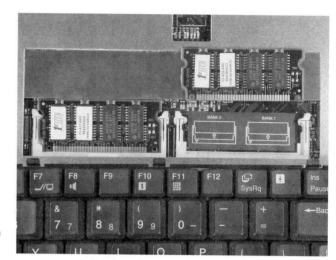

Figure 7-21
Two 72-pin DIMMs in laptop sockets.

simple replacement fixed the problem. Most laptops are burned in for 24 to 48 hours before being delivered to the customer. When this burn-in is performed properly, bad components are caught and replaced before the laptop leaves the factory.

Study Break: Laptop Components

Let's find a hapless laptop and examine its components.

Get hold of a laptop computer. Examine its underside and locate the bays for the RAM, fixed disk and CPU. Some simple printed icon should identify them.

Examine the bays to determine if a locking bolt secures them. This is usually located near the bay release slider.

Remove the locking bolt for the fixed disk drive. Release the locking slider tab and remove the fixed disk. Examine the mechanical mounting bracket to determine how to remove the fixed disk from it. Replace the fixed disk, the fixed disk bay cover, and the locking bolt.

Similarly, remove the locking bolt for the RAM bay. On some laptops, unlocking and lifting the keyboard accesses the RAM bay. Examine the

RAM. Are there any free slots for adding additional RAM? Replace the RAM bay cover and locking bolt.

In a similar fashion, remove the locking bolt and cover for access to the CPU. Is the CPU fan readily accessible and removable? Can it be cleaned of dust easily? Replace the CPU cover and locking bolt.

These procedures would be used to replace or clean the key components of a laptop PC.

Personal Digital Assistants

Personal Digital Assistants (PDAs) are small mobile hand-held devices providing limited computing along with information storage/retrieval for personal or business use. The information stored and retrieved is often calendar schedules, meeting and appointment details and alarms, and lists to telephone numbers and addresses. These devices are highly portable or hand-held, making them smaller and more accessible than laptop PCs. Sometimes the trademarked name of a popular PDA product is used generically, for example Hewlett-Packard's Palmtop and Palm's PalmPilot.

PDAs may permit use of a foldable small keyboard or a direct keypad for email. Most PDAs provide an electronically sensitive pad on which handwriting graffiti can be input to the PDA. Typical PDA applications include schedule, address book, and personal note storage/retrieval. The PDA applications synchronize their data with popular PC organizer applications such as MS Outlook. The synchronization is performed using a serial, USB or IR link connecting the PDA to a PC running the application program.

Applications are now written specifically for PDAs that include mapping and GPS locator, special wireless email, wireless Web surfing, and soon, Bluetooth Radio Frequency (RF) technology for close proximity financial transactions. PDAs functions are merging with cell phone and paging applications. See Figure 7–22.

Some PDAs use *Windows CE* a reduced function version of Micorsoft's Windows operating system with special Word Processing and Spreadsheet applets. Other PDAs have their own operating system, like the Palm OS.

PDA components and expandability are limited. Typically, adding memory modules and Type II CF cards may increase RAM and storage. Special wireless modems, GPS units, digital Web camera units, and card scanners may also be added.

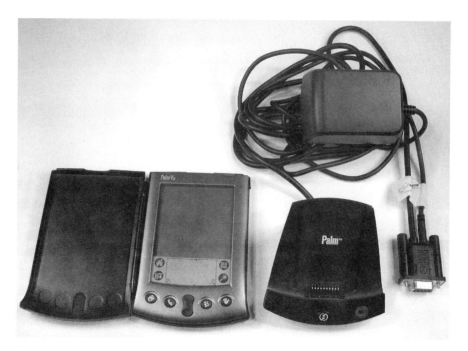

Figure 7–22
Palm PDA.

PDAs require similar maintenance and care to laptop PCs, and they have some similar hardware problems. Software problems are much less frequent with PDAs because their applications and operating environment is much more tightly controlled and standardized than it was with laptop PCs.

Common Laptop Problems

There are many laptop problems. The simplest come from plain physical abuse, while more complex problems are caused by the interaction of PCM-CIA cards with other laptop components. Many problems are solved simply, while a few require more hardware and software configuration work.

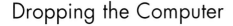

Dropping the Computer

The most common and preventable of the many types of problems seen with laptops comes from dropping the computer itself. Laptop cases should have a velcro strap that secures the laptop inside the case. It is easy to remember to fasten the strap. Often, if only the case's zipper secures the laptop, the zipper is left unzipped. This results in the laptop falling out of the case the second it is picked up for travel. Most laptops can survive a fall, but battery interlocks and other plastic components can be broken. The most critical part subject to breakage is the LCD panel. In this case, data can be removed from the laptop using an external monitor or by simply swapping removable fixed disk drives with a replacement laptop.

Significant physical damage to the laptop case and LCD screen necessitate factory repair. We have repaired plasma panels on some early Toshiba portable computers, and it was ugly. When repairing laptops, there is always the moment of truth or point of no return where some plastic case components must be pried apart. It is easiest to have factory repair personnel with plenty of spare chassis parts on hand perform these repairs.

Temperature Extremes

Another common problem area specific to laptop PCs is temperature shock. When traveling with a laptop PC, you should never leave it in the cold for an extended time period. The laptop should be kept as warm as a human. This means that those laptops left overnight in the car during the dead of winter or in the summer heat are candidates for potential disk failures, because cold causes condensation inside the disk drive. Just a small amount of moisture inside a drive can make them fail. One of our early Toshiba laptop computers was left overnight in a car in early November, and when it was powered on the next day it failed. If a laptop is left outside in freezing temperatures overnight or for an extended period of time, warm it up slowly over several days before attempting to power it up. The long warm up period gives any condensation inside the computer an opportunity to return to water vapor without causing damage to the laptop when it is powered on.

Heat is also a great enemy of laptops and PC cards. There needs to be adequate air circulation around the laptop to ensure that everything inside stays cool. Do not run a laptop on carpet because the laptop can sink into the carpet, preventing air from flowing into the CPU cooling fan intake. At least once or twice we have had laptops quit because they had inadequate airflow. Fortunately, no damage was done because the internal heat sensor powered off the laptop when it detected overheating. The CPU cooling fan should be checked and cleaned of debris when overheating is suspected.

Laptop overheating is avoided by providing adequate space around the laptop for air circulation. Cleaning the laptop fan exhaust should be performed periodically to ensure adequate airflow through the laptop chassis.

Exposure to X-rays

One question many laptop travelers have is, "Can I pass my laptop through the x-ray machine at airports without harm?" We used to always pass them around the x-ray machines at airports until one of our students (a West Point graduate in the military) told us that he always ran his disk drives through the x-ray machines without incident. Since then, for over ten years and hundreds of flights, our laptops have always passed right through the x-ray machines without a problem.

Unexpected Configuration Problems

The PCMCIA bus and DOS laptops were very tricky machines to configure. Socket services had to be run under DOS. Laptop and PC card manufacturers failed to uniformly implement PCMCIA bus standards. This forced laptop manufacturers to certify specific PC cards for their machines. Windows 95/98/Me and Windows 2000 changed this, and today, PC cards fulfill the plug-and-play promise.

A common problem is "losing" the laptop CD-ROM, CD-RW, or DVD drive, meaning that the CD ROM, CD-RW, or DVD becomes unexpectedly "invisible" to the computer when looking for files, directories or devices—it's there at one time only to be lost later. Reinstalling the CD-ROM drivers or installing DOS 16-bit CD-ROM drivers in CONFIG.SYS and AUTOEXEC.BAT can correct the problem. Sometimes on older laptops Windows must be reinstalled for it to pick up the CD-ROM, CD-RW, or DVD drive correctly. In one old laptop, it required specific IDE disk drivers for the CD-ROM drive to be found. Once they were installed, the CD-ROM reappeared.

Keeping the driver programs and the BIOS of the laptop up to the latest release levels is a good way to prevent unexpected configuration problems. The manufacturer's Web site should be checked for software driver and laptop BIOS updates about every six months. Migrating a laptop to Windows 98/Me/2000 (if it has the resources) with a fresh software install is a means of resolving some laptop plug-and-play problems.

Windows Configuration Problems

Often installing Windows on a laptop was a daunting task. This is especially true when network and other types of PC cards were required. USB bus connections can also cause installation problems. The best installation strategy with a laptop is to install Windows on a clean system with no PC cards inserted or USB devices connected. Once this clean Windows installation is complete, then the PC card devices can be inserted one at a time. Install LAN cards and modems first, and SCSI and strange devices last. Finally, USB devices are connected, usually to one of two USB ports. When a USB device is not working in one port, try the other port. Sometimes IRQ steering adjustments are required to make PC cards work.

In some Windows 95/98 systems, IRQ steering reroutes hardware IRQs for the PCI bus. IRQ steering loads the interrupt vector table. Interrupt vectors are software pointers to small programs called interrupt routines that perform the functions needed to satisfy the interrupt. On PCs the interrupt vector table is 256 4-byte pointers residing in the first 1,024 bytes of RAM. Each interrupt number is assigned to a specific task. The 16 IRQ lines are assigned to 16 of the interrupt vectors or pointers. See Figure 7–23.

Figure 7–23
Windows IRQ steering.

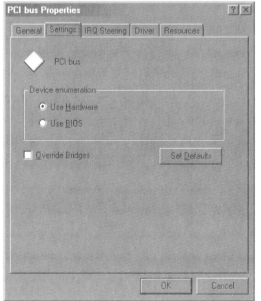
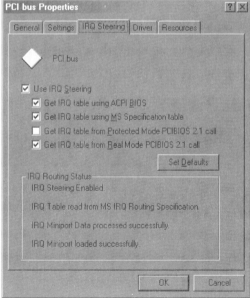

The IRQ steering settings are in the Control Panel ➤ System ➤ Device Manager ➤ System Devices ➤ PCI Bus menu selection. In laptops, PC card bus components and other laptop components are tied together using the PCI bus. The PC card socket services must be tied to the PCI bus to function properly. This can require steering PCI bus IRQs to the PC cards.

Windows 98/Me and Windows 2000 laptops do not use IRQ steering. Plug-and-play and IRQ issues that troubled earlier laptops have been resolved by more standardized laptop hardware and software.

Power Management Problems

Laptops have hardware power management functions that can often interfere with Windows power management software. Suspend-to-disk features automatically activate when low power is detected. This often confuses laptop users into believing that their laptop has malfunctioned when it is merely in power-saving hibernation. Proper configuration of power management options in Windows and in laptop hardware is essential for trouble-free operation. To provide the longest battery life, laptop power management must be properly configured. The Window's Advanced Configuration and Power Interface (ACPI) software shuts down the display, fixed disk, and CPU during periods of inactivity to reduce power consumption and extend battery life.

Damage to Connectors

Plugging and unplugging pigtail connectors from PC cards can cause the connector pins to bend, resulting in card failure. Pigtail connectors from other PC cards will not necessarily work with certain cards because each card manufacturer has their own pigtail connector design.

Pigtail connectors should be periodically checked for bent or damaged pins to prevent them from causing problems. Having spare pigtail connectors can resolve some problems. However, if the pins in the PCMCIA card get damaged, then replacing the card is the necessary repair step.

Display Problems

When operating a laptop with an external video display, the display resolution is often increased beyond an XGA 1024 by 768 resolution of many laptop LCD panels. This works fine until the laptop is returned to LCD panel operation, which cannot provide the high resolution of the external monitor. Two things can happen in this case. The LCD can fail to display anything at all (either black or diagonal lines) or it can display only a portion of the high-resolution display. This problem is easily fixed by returning the display to the VGA or XGA resolution supported by the LCD panel.

Some laptops permit simultaneous use of both the LCP panel and an external monitor, or use of just the external monitor. This dual screen capability is controlled from the Window's display driver and control software.

Laptop LCD displays can have an image burned into them by leaving the image on the screen for several days. Screen savers or power management functions prevent this problem. When LCDs do retain an image, it can gradually return to normal operation over several days; we have seen images be completely erased. Since most laptops have a top panel switch that turns off the LCD panel when it is folded down, it is a good idea to fold the laptop display down, thus turning off the display.

A more common LCD problem is bad pixels. LCD panels in clone PCs can have up to 10 bad pixels—ones that remain lighted all the time. Manufacturers are reluctant to replace them with good LCDs, and this can be one drawback to purchasing low-priced nonbrand name computers.

Clocking Problems

It is possible to overclock PC CPUs. Overclocking is running the CPU at a MHz clock rate that exceeds the manufacturer's specified clock rate. For example, 200 MHz Pentium Pro CPU chips run fine at 233 MHz. However, CPU overclocking in laptop PCs is dangerous because an overclocked CPU produces more heat than one running at the specified clock speed. It is possible to damage the CPU in a laptop with overclocking. Other components could potentially be damaged.

Study Break: PCMCIA Card Installation

Installing PCMCIA cards in a laptop is a common procedure, performed most often by laptop owners. They usually install a modem card or a LAN card or both.

Get a laptop that has no PCMCIA cards installed.

Find a modem card with the driver software from the manufacturer. If there is no modem card, a LAN card will work as well. Be sure to have the latest driver software from the manufacturer on floppy disk.

Also make sure you have a Windows CD or that the Windows CAB files are located in the laptop fixed disk in a Windows\options\cabs directory.

Power up the PC and be sure Windows is completely booted. Now insert the PCMCIA card in a PCMCIA socket on the laptop. Windows should beep and announce that new hardware has been found. Windows should now proceed to load the software for the PCMCIA bus and the driver programs for the PCMCIA adapter card.

If requested, use the disk of driver programs for the card to complete the installation.

Restart the laptop as Windows requests.

Go to Control Panel, click on modems, click on the diagnostics tab, highlight the port that has the modem icon, and click on more information. Does the modem return some diagnostic messages? If so, it is installed correctly. With a LAN board, click on system, then device manager, and expand the network adapters icon. If the LAN board is listed and there are no red or yellow icons, it is installed correctly.

Summary

This chapter has described common laptop PC components. It has illustrated which components are field replaceable and which require factory repair. The first section was dedicated to a detailed discussion on portable system components and their configuration. Components covered included:

CPUs and their associated chip sets

LCD displays

Batteries

Power adapters

PC and networking cards

CD ROMs and fixed disks

Docking Stations

RAM

The next section covered common problems associated with portable computers and suggested solutions and/or preventive measures. Our discussion addressed concerns about environmental factors such as damage from impact, temperature extremes, and x-ray machines; display problems; difficulties with the operating system; and device drivers. The solutions suggested were as simple as using cases with an extra velcro strap to fasten the laptop into the case and keeping the laptop warm, to keeping laptop driver programs and BIOS revisions current.

Chapter Review Questions

1. *What disk is used to COLD boot a PC?*

    A. Setup disk
    B. System disk
    C. Diagnostic disk
    D. Program disk

Answer: B, system disk. The setup disk can be used to install software and diagnostic disks may boot the system or may only contain the diagnostic programs. Program disks do not really exist because programs are so large.

2. *Laptops use what type of batteries?*

    A. Alkaline
    B. Nickel
    C. Lithium
    D. NiMH

Answer: D, NiMH. The other laptop battery types are Li-ion and Li-polymer. Alkaline batteries are used in MP3 players but not laptops.

3. *Which LCDs are typically backlit?*

    A. None
    B. TFT
    C. DSTN
    D. Super-Twist
    E. All of the above
    F. B and C
    G. C and D

Answer: F, DSTN and TFT may both be backlit to increase visibility. Most laptop panels are backlit TFT displays.

4. *Pentium CPUs are the only CPUs used in laptops.*

      A. TRUE
      B. FALSE

Answer: B, FALSE. There are several other CPUs used in laptops especially in Apple Macintosh laptops. See Figure 7–24.

5. *What are standard components on all laptops?*

      A. RAM, CPU, CD-ROM, floppy, modem
      B. CD-ROM, ZIP, floppy, SCSI drive
      C. LCD, CPU, RAM, floppy, PCMCIA bus
      D. LCD, CPU, LAN, floppy, fixed disk

Figure 7–24
Macintosh iBook revealed.

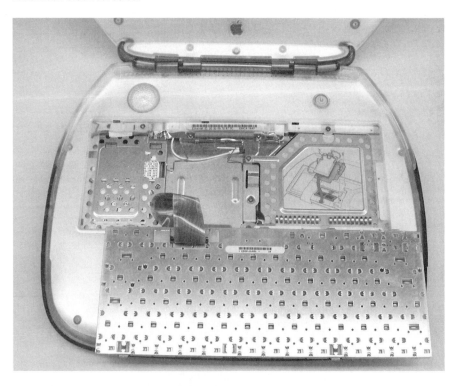

Answer: C, LCD, CPU, RAM, floppy, PCMCIA bus, but A and D might also be correct. Laptops do not typically contain SCSI drives and modems and LAN connections are extra cost add-on options.

6. *What is the greatest danger to laptop LCD displays?*

    A. Dust
    B. Driver programs
    C. Etching
    D. Direct sunlight

Answer: D, direct sunlight. Dust and etching can hurt a laptop display, but direct sunlight and excess heat cause more damage. Driver programs are easily updated.

7. *What is the difference between Type I, Type II, and Type III PC cards?*

    A. The number of pins in the connector
    B. The length and width
    C. Color
    D. Thickness
    E. Data transfer speed

Answer: D, thickness. While PC cards can vary in the length, color, and data transfer speed, the thickness is the determining factor for the Type I, Type II or Type III designation.

8. *A laptop CD-ROM drive and the fixed disk drive are what kinds of drives?*

    A. SCSI
    B. IDE
    C. PCMCIA
    D. MFM

Answer: B, IDE. SCSI and MFM drives could be found in some desktop PCs but not in laptops. IBM makes a micro-drive that can, with an adapter, fit into a PCMCIA Type II socket, but this is the exception, not the rule.

9. *Laptop computers cannot use SCSI*

    A. TRUE
    B. FALSE

Answer: B, FALSE. There are PC cards that provide SCSI interfaces for laptops. After all, they are PC and PCs sometimes use SCSI.

10. *Laptop field replaceable units include what?*

    A. Fixed disk drive
    B. Floppy disk drive
    C. CD-ROM drive
    D. LAN card
    E. Modem card
    F. All of the above
    G. None of the above

Answer: F, all of the above. There are replaceable modules for each of these laptop components.

11. *Modems use pigtail connections to connect to what?*

    A. The telephone line
    B. The serial port and the telephone line
    C. The PC card bus and the phone line
    D. None of the above

Answer: A, the telephone line. The PC card plugs into the PC card bus directly so that the pigtail connector only connects to the telephone line.

12. *Laptop disk drives are what type and size?*

    A. IDE 1-inch drives
    B. SCSI 2.5 inch drives
    C. Removable 3.5-inch disk drives
    D. IDE 2.5-inch drives

Answer: D, IDE 2.5-inch drives. While there are smaller IDE drives than 2.5-inch drives, the majority of laptop drives are 2.5 inch IDE drives. SCSI and 3.5-inch drives are used in desktop and server PCs.

13. *Most laptop PC cards are what type?*

    A. Type I
    B. Type II
    C. Type III
    D. None of the above

Answer: B, Type II. The majority of PC cards are Type II or 5 mm thick cards.

14. *Laptop computers have no USB ports.*

    A. TRUE
    B. FALSE

Answer: B, FALSE. Most laptops and smaller computers provide one or two USB ports. Some laptops also have IEEE 1394 FireWire ports.

15. *Which laptop battery lasts longest?*

    A. Alkaline
    B. NiCad
    C. NiMH
    D. Lithium
    E. Li-Ion

Answer: E, Li-Ion. Lithium is an element not a battery—Li-Ion is the battery that lasts longest. The newest long-lasting battery is Li-polymer.

16. *A big source of laptop destruction is what?*

    A. Heat
    B. Dust
    C. Water
    D. Dropping

Answer: D, dropping. Water also destroys laptops, but who uses them under water? Lack of heat can destroy them as well as excess temperatures. Of course, we would die of heat exhaustion at the same time.

17. *The most visible display used with a laptop computer is what?*

    A. TFT
    B. CRT
    C. DSTN
    D. CSTN
    E. None of the above

Answer: B, CRT Since laptops can be connected to an external CRT monitor, that is the most visible. Otherwise it would be a backlit TFT.

Chapter 8

LANs AND COMMUNICATIONS

Chapter Syllabus

- LAN Concepts

- Internet Access

- Installing and Configuring Network Interface Cards

- Network Problem Manifestations

Today, most computers are networked; this has significant implications for identifying and resolving PC problems. This chapter describes basic networking concepts and terminology, and covers LAN and Internet communications. Once a PC is network-connected, maintenance and troubleshooting take on new and more complex dimensions because when network connections fail, the entire PC often freezes.

LAN Concepts

The original concept of networking involved dumb terminals and mainframe systems. Today, most networks consist of personal computers and specialized PC servers. These are called Local Area Networks (LANs) because they connect the PC and servers in a single building and facility. Specialized PC servers are based on the technologies found on every desktop. They enhance and augment these technologies, focusing them on the LAN server function to create specialized PCs to act as network servers. However, it is easiest to think of servers as PCs on steroids.

An understanding of networking concepts is necessary to troubleshoot and fix PC problems, because almost all business and many home PCs are now networked. In this section we look at the basics of networking PCs.

The most fundamental networking concept is that networks are implemented in hardware, software, and channels. The hardware is the PC networking components needed to implement a network, mostly NICs which are added to a PC. Software is the program, or Network Operating System (NOS) that operates the LAN and transfers data from PC to PC. Channels are the wiring, hubs, bridges, routers, etc., that interconnect PCs to form a network. These hardware, software, and channel components are conceptually combined together in a layered model to perform the functions necessary to transfer data between PCs.

The next fundamental concept is that network functions and the PC hardware, software and channel components that perform them can be divided into seven logical layers. This is called the ISO seven-layer model. It is described in detail in networking specifications that every manufacturer of network components follows. Each manufacturer implements the layers in a standardized fashion, but not in perfect accordance to the specification. However, since Windows software dominates the PC marketplace, most manufacturers of PC products follow the Windows seven-layer model implementation. The ISO seven-layer model is a networking functionality yardstick that explains networking hardware, software, and channel functions. See Figure 8–1.

Before walking through the ISO reference model, we need to examine what is required to establish compatible communications between a PC and a server. There are two sides to compatibility: data format compatibility and networking compatibility, as shown in Figure 8–2.

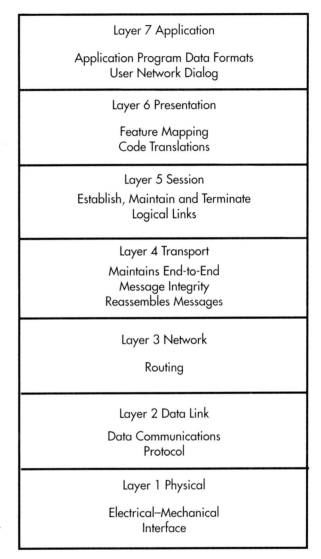

Figure 8–1
ISO seven-layer network-
ing model.

Data Format Compatibility

Data format compatibility begins with simple data transmission speed compatibility. Both the PC and the server (which might be another PC, or could
be a mainframe computer, often referred to as a "host") must communicate at
the same speed or bits-per-second transmission rate. The modems and the
LAN boards (NICs) in use determine speed compatibility.

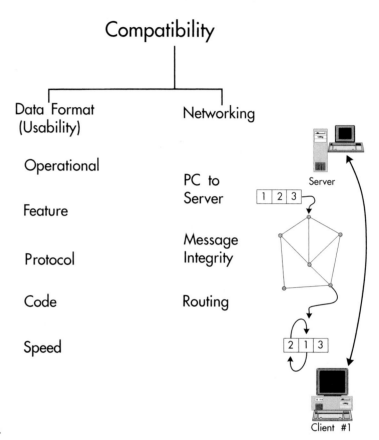

Figure 8–2
Compatibility.

Code Compatibility

Code compatibility is simple to solve because almost all computers today use either the underlying ASCII code or extended binary coded decimal interchange code (EBCDIC). IBM mainframe computers use primarily EBCDIC code, while all other computers in the world use ASCII. What is the maximum number of characters or bit combinations that must be handled with code compatibility? There are 256 possible combinations of eight bits.

Protocol Compatibility

Protocol compatibility is more difficult than code compatibility because we must account for every protocol handshaking scenario. Protocols are similar to a language in that there are specific handshake messages that coordinate information exchange between sending and receiving devices. Visualize, if you can, the equivalent English language handshake messages for a local phone call.

Caller: Dials number.
Answerer: Hears call; Hello?
    C: Hello.
    A: This is Pete, can I help you?
    C: Is Cate there?
    A: No, she is teaching today.

Each phone call scenario must be covered to achieve protocol compatibility.

Feature Compatibility

Feature compatibility requires matching the keyboard keys and the display size to what the communicating software expects. How many of you have worked with a PC as a VTxxx terminal on a VAX or used a PC as a 3270 terminal on an IBM host? How well did you like the keyboard mapping and display layout? What happened when it came time to display 132 characters on the PC's 80-character-wide screen?

Operational Compatibility

Operational compatibility is the final requirement to get useable data from a server into a client computer. Operational compatibility is determined by the data formats used by the application program. Lotus spreadsheets use WKS or WK1, etc., files while Excel Spreadsheets use XLS files. Some different image-file formats include JPG, TIF, PCX, BMP, RLE, AVI, CDR, and more. Terminal emulation requires speed-code-protocol-and-feature compatibility. Because PCs ran programs that manipulated data, they caused us to be concerned with operational compatibility.

Networking Compatibility

Networking compatibility is concerned with sending data across complex networks, which are comprised of nodes and links. They usually form a mesh- or Web-like arrangement. The goal of a complex network is to ensure that data stuffed in at the network's source end will pop out at the destination end. . The network transfer of data from source to destination across a complex network requires performing three functions.

- Data must be routed between source and destination. Which way does it travel through a network? Does it go down the right-hand pathway, the left-hand pathway or the straight-through pathway?

- Next, data must be sent through the network in small chunks rather than in larger blocks, because you are more likely to end up with an error in a large block of data. When an error occurs, the entire block must be retransmitted. With smaller chunks, the chance of error is much less and only the small chunk must be retransmitted. The problem of message integrity arises with the small chunks. If we chop up a message into chunk 1, 2, and 3, when it is received it must be reassembled as 1, 2, and 3. We have to be sure that chunk 2 belongs to us and does not belong to someone else.

- Third, we must establish and maintain a one-to-one or end-to-end connection between the client and the server. This logical link must be maintained for the duration of the communications activity. In LANs, this end-to-end connection is visible on the PC client as extra disk drives.

Understanding how to make a terminal compatible with a host computer lays the foundation for understanding the seven-layer ISO networking model. Now you are ready to understand the seven-layer model layers and their functions.

The ISO Seven-Layer Model

The ISO was the focal point for development of the Open System Interconnection-networking (OSI) model. This model divides up the functions necessary for communication between a client and a server into seven layers. (Yes, you might think of this as the ISO/OSI networking model. Confused? Keep in mind that the "S" is always in the correct spot.)

This seven-layer networking model divides up the communications in an arbitrary (but logical) fashion amonge the layers. In the real world, hardware and software communication products must work reliably first, and then perform the ISO layer functions. Consequently, these products did not precisely follow the hierarchical structure defined by the ISO model.

Let us match compatibility to the seven layers. First the seven layers and their associated compatibility functions are:

1. Application (Layer 7)—Operational Compatibility

2. Presentation (Layer 6)—Feature Compatibility

3. Session (Layer 5)—End-to-End or Logical Link Compatibility

4.   Transport (Layer 4)—Message Integrity Compatibility

5.   Network (Layer 3)—Routing Compatibility

6.   Data Link (Layer 2)—Protocol Compatibility

7.   Physical (Layer 1)—Speed Compatibility

Most communications and LAN products today are described and discussed using the ISO seven-layer networking model. This model is a set of general specifications for describing how communications products should be constructed so that they can communicate with each other and thus be interconnected. Figure 8–3 shows how the layers are implemented in PC products.

Which layer does speed compatibility fall into? Layer 1 covers speed compatibility. The physical layer wiring and electrical transmission can be summarized into two simple data communications parameters: speed and distance. The LAN card in the PC and the network wiring components implement this.

Figure 8–3
ISO Layers vs. compatibility vs. PC components.

ISO (International Standards Organization)
or
OSI (Open Systems Interconnection Model)

Seven Layers

ISO Layer	Compatibility	PC Component
7 - Application	- Operational	Application
6 - Presentation	- Feature/Code	Windows
5 - Session	- PC to Server	TCP
4 - Transport	- Message Integrity	TCP
3 - Network	- Routing	IP
2 - Data Link	- Protocol	LAN Board
1 - Physical	- Speed	LAN Board Wiring

Layer 2, the data link layer, handles protocol compatibility. The function of a data link protocol is to get information from point A to point B without any errors. It uses message handshakes to perform its function. The LAN card in the PC implements the protocols, which distinguish Ethernet networks from token ring networks.

The network layer performs routing compatibility, sending data from source to destination. It is implemented by the IP portion of the Windows TCP/IP protocol software.

The transport layer provides end-to-end message integrity by ensuring that entire messages are moved through a network from source to destination. The TCP portion of the Windows TCP/IP protocol software implements this.

The session layer provides a logical one-to-one or end-to-end connection. This layer, Layer 5, provides the entry point to the network. This is also implemented by TCP portion of the Windows TCP/IP protocol software.

The presentation layer provides feature compatibility and is performed by the PC's operating system, that is (in most cases) by Windows (95/98 or NT).

The application layer covers operational compatibility. It is largely the function of the application program to solve operational compatibility. Almost all programs accept data files in different operational formats.

The PC's NIC and the network wiring implement ISO seven-layer model Layers 1 and 2. ISO Layers 3, 4, and 5 are implemented by Window's TCP/IP protocol software. Finally, both Windows and the application software implement Layers 6 and 7. All networking hardware, software, and channels can be fit into this seven-layer networking model.

Types of LANs

A LAN allows PCs in a certain facility to communice with central servers or each other by connecting them with a communication channel that is most often copper wiring. The most popular type of wiring is telephone wire, or unshielded twisted-pair (UTP) wiring. This wiring comes in different categories or grades, the most popular of which is Category-5, rated at speeds up to 100 Mbps. Category-5+, Category-5e, and Category-6 wires are now being implemented. Category-6 wire is rated at speeds over 155 Mbps. Other types of wiring have been used in LANs but are found less frequently than UTP wiring. Fiber optic cable is also used in LANs. It is used to provide high-speed connections between network components and to provide electrical isolation between different parts of a network.

For a PC to be connected to a LAN, it must contain a LAN card (NIC) and LAN card driver software that integrates the LAN card into the operating system in each computer. Furthermore, the operating system LAN components must be installed as well. Chapter 16 contains more information on this subject.

The servers run a NOS, which is usually a Windows NT Server, Windows 2000 server, or Novell NetWare program. Thus, servers are typically NetWare-based, Windows-based, or UNIX-based. Clients connect to different types of servers using different communications software. See Figure 8–4.

Users view the LAN as an extension of their PCs. It appears to them as though there are now extra disk drives and printers attached to their PC. To transfer data from their system to the server, the user merely copies the file from a local disk drive C: to a server disk drive F:. See Figure 8–5.

Figure 8–4
Typical LAN.

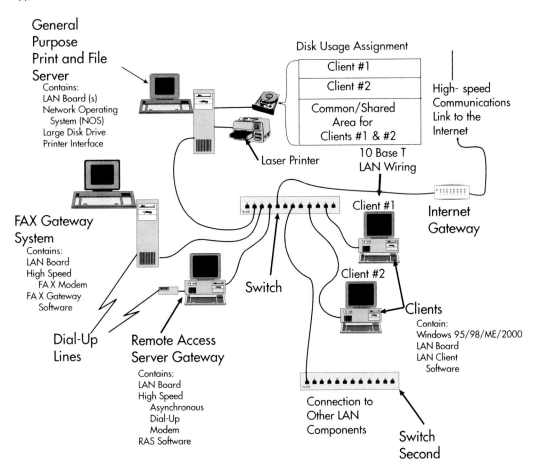

General Purpose Print and File Server
Contains:
LAN Board (s)
Network Operating System (NOS)
Large Disk Drive
Printer Interface

Disk Usage Assignment

| Client #1 |
| Client #2 |
| Common/Shared Area for Clients #1 & #2 |

High- speed Communications Link to the Internet

Laser Printer

10 Base T LAN Wiring

Client #1

Internet Gateway

FAX Gateway System
Contains:
LAN Board
High Speed
FA X Modem
FA X Gateway Software

Switch

Client #2

Clients
Contain:
Windows 95/98/ME/2000
LAN Board
LAN Client Software

Dial-Up Lines

Remote Access Server Gateway
Contains:
LAN Board
High Speed
Asynchronous
Dial-Up
Modem
RAS Software

Connection to Other LAN Components

Switch Second

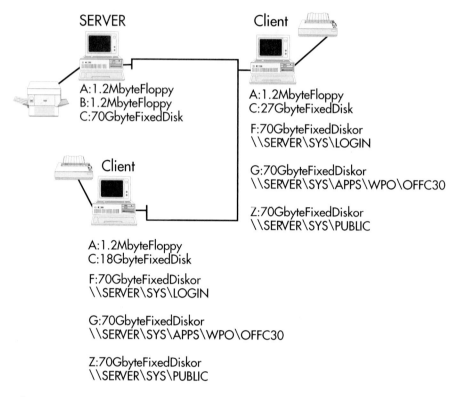

SERVER

Client

A:1.2MbyteFloppy
B:1.2MbyteFloppy
C:70GbyteFixedDisk

A:1.2MbyteFloppy
C:27GbyteFixedDisk

F:70GbyteFixedDiskor
\\SERVER\SYS\LOGIN

G:70GbyteFixedDiskor
\\SERVER\SYS\APPS\WPO\OFFC30

Z:70GbyteFixedDiskor
\\SERVER\SYS\PUBLIC

Client

A:1.2MbyteFloppy
C:18GbyteFixedDisk

F:70GbyteFixedDiskor
\\SERVER\SYS\LOGIN

G:70GbyteFixedDiskor
\\SERVER\SYS\APPS\WPO\OFFC30

Z:70GbyteFixedDiskor
\\SERVER\SYS\PUBLIC

Figure 8–5
LAN from client PC viewpoint.

Most people think that "type of network" means Ethernet or token ring. Others believe that their network is a Novell NetWare or Windows NT/2000 Server network, or they may say they have a twisted-pair network. These are all characteristics of their network, but do not define the network type. A network type is defined by how people actually use the it.

Actually, LANs share PC resources among multiple PCs connected to the LAN. Disk drives and printers are shared among all LAN-connected PCs, but how they are shared, controlled, and managed is what determines the type of network. Network types are either client-server or peer-to-peer. Client-server LANs are centrally managed. Typically large LANs or combinations of LANs with WAN or Internet communications serve big organizations. In contrast, peer-to-peer LANs are small LANs serving fewer than 10 PCs, where management of access to resources is decentralized. Each PC controls access to its disk drives and printers. In reality, virtually all LANs today have a combination of client-server and peer-to-peer operations. See Figure 8–6.

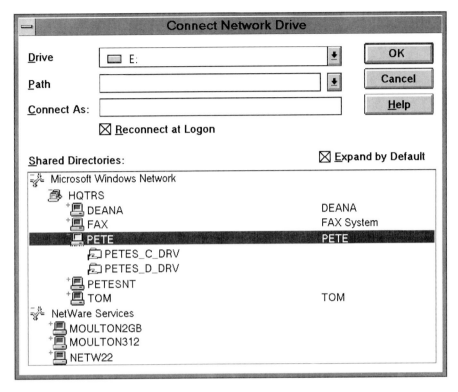

Figure 8–6
Windows NT peer-to-peer and Novell client-server connections.

Either type of network can be implemented with Ethernet or token ring technologies, different wiring, and Windows NT/2000 and Novell NetWare. Ethernet and token ring are the types of NICs used to communicate between PCs on a LAN. Wiring physically connects the devices on the LAN, and Windows NT/2000, Linux, and Novell NetWare are the software platforms for implementing client-server networks. Any combination of these LAN components can be used to implement peer-to-peer or client-server networks.

The key issues in determining the type of LAN is the number of PCs to be attached to the network and how the resources are going to be managed. Other considerations involve what the key networking applications for the organization are, what software products are used to implement these applications, and the location of each to another.

505

NICs

Different types of networks are implemented using specialized NICs. There are NICs for Ethernet, the token ring, Asynchronous Transfer Mode (ATM) networks, and more. Most LANs focus on two popular NICs, Ethernet and token ring.

Ethernet is the most widely installed LAN technology today. Ethernet is a standard specified by IEEE 802.3. Its original architecture for was developed by Xerox and marketed by Xerox, DEC, and Intel. Ethernet uses the Carrier Sense Multiple Access/Collision Detection (CSMA/CD) communications protocol and operates at speeds of 10 Mbps, 100 Mbps, and 1 Gbps. In the future, Ethernet will operate at 10 Gbps. This protocol is discussed further in the section "Ethernet CSMA/CD" later in this chapter.

The Ethernet standard allows for the use of coaxial cable, fiber, and specific categories of unshielded twisted pair cable. Ethernet networks are wired using hubs that act as wiring concentrators, network bridges, or high-performance switches.

A token ring network is another type of LAN. All the workstations in a token ring network are connected in a ring or star topology. Information circulates around this ring using a token-passing scheme to prevent workstation signals from colliding when they try to send a message simultaneously. The standard for the token ring protocol is IEEE 802.5. The most widely recognized implementation of token ring networking would be the IBM token ring network. Although not as popular as Ethernet, it is an effective and reliable networking scheme.

Table 8–1 summarizes differences between Ethernet and token ring networks.

Table 8–1 LAN Technology Comparison

	Ethernet	**Token Ring**
Number of nodes	1,024 per segment	255 per ring
Speeds	10 Mbps, 100 Mbps, 1 Gbps, and 10 Gbps	4 Mbps, 16 Mbps, 100 Mbps, and 155 Mbps
Cable	Unshielded twisted-pair (UTP) Category 3, 5, 5+, 5e and up.	IBM Type 1 and Type 2 shielded twisted-pair.
	Fiber optic cable—multi-mode and single mode	Unshielded twisted-pair (UTP) Category 3, 5 and up.
		Fiber optic cable—multi-mode and single mode

Table 8–1 LAN Technology Comparison (Continued)

	Ethernet	**Token Ring**
Protocol	Carrier Sense Multiple Access with Collision Detection (CSMA/CD)	Token passing
Networking components	Active wiring hubs Bridges Switches Routers	Active wiring hubs Bridges Switches (rare) Routers
Transport protocols Supported ISO Layers 3, 4, and 5	TCP/IP SPX/IPX NetBEUI	TCP/IP SPX/IPX NetBEUI
Transmission	Half duplex or full duplex	Half duplex
Data Encoding	Digital transmission using Manchester encoding	Digital transmission using differential Manchester encoding

An emerging LAN technology is ATM. It uses a cell relay protocol at transmission speeds of 25 Mbps, 155 Mbps, and 622 Mbps. An ATM NIC connects to ATM switching hubs to perform both LAN functions and multimedia telephony. Windows 98 software supports LAN functions and Internet communications using ATM NICs. ATM is a technology that can implement both LAN communications and WAN communications, versus Ethernet, which is a LAN technology alone. Furthermore, ATM's cell relay protocol can easily allocate communications channel capacity among voice, video, and data traffic as demanded. Ethernet performs this traffic balancing act less effectively. ATM was developed to provide desktop PCs the ability to perform a variety of communications tasks, including acting like a TV, video telephone, and an Internet access terminal simultaneously.

Network Protocols

Protocols are the languages of data communications. The primary objective of a protocol is error-free transfer of data from one end of an electrical communications channel to another.

There are protocols at different levels in a network. The lower-layer protocols we are focusing on here are implemented in the NIC hardware. Higher-layer protocols are implemented in software. The principal software protocols that permit PCs to exchange data across a LAN are TCP/IP, SPX/IPX, and NetBEUI. TCP/IP is the software protocols used for Internet communications, SPI/IPX are the software protocols supporting Novell NetWare client-server networks, and NetBEUI is the Windows protocol used for simple PC LANs.

In general, all protocols are thought of as the rules of communication. For example, think about how people communicate in a classroom. While the instructor is talking, everyone is quiet. They are quiet because they know that if they all talk at the same time, they disrupt what the instructor is trying to tell everyone.

If someone needs to speak, they raise their hand so that the instructor stops speaking and allows them to communicate their thoughts. When they are done speaking, the instructor waits an appropriate amount of time before responding. If the instructor did not wait, he or she would talk over the student and make their communication misunderstood. This is nothing more than a set of rules instructors and students follow to communicate effectively. Data communications protocols work in the same fashion.

Understanding hardware protocols is important for network troubleshooting and design. These protocols are less visible to us because they are embedded in the products and services we purchase. Furthermore, for products from one vendor to talk with the products of another vendor, these protocols must interoperate. They must work exactly the same way in both vendors' equipment. Let's take a look at two of these protocols.

Ethernet CSMA/CD

Ethernet uses the hardware communications protocol CSMA/CD to facilitate the communications from point A to point B. This makes Ethernet, regardless of how it is constructed, operate as a bus network. See Figure 8–7. The CSMA/CD is a simple protocol and is statistical in nature. It responds well to bursts of activity.

CSMA/CD protocol operation is similar to Citizens Band radios. Each station bids for access. Sometimes collisions happen. In that case, the stations back off and retry at a later time, as determined by the "automobile theory of insurance" algorithm. In the automobile theory of insurance, a person having a collision is prevented from getting back on the road again right away because the automobile repair, as determined by the insurance company, varies unpredictably from a short to a long time. Furthermore, people with a second automobile collision must wait even longer before getting their insurance reinstated, keeping them off the road for quite some time.

In the CSMA/CD protocol, the back-off algorithm is called binary exponential back off. Each station determines a random interval of time that must elapse before it can again attempt communication. Those stations with one collision must multiply their delay time by a factor of, say, two before attempting to communicate again. This means that stations with one collision must wait even longer before attempting to communicate on an Ethernet.

The benefit of CSMA/CD protocol is that devices can be added to or removed from the network at any time without disrupting the network. However, some network servers and PCs constantly send diagnostic frames to assure that connections across an Ethernet are still valid. When the server dies or that connection is lost, this can easily cause these PCs to crash.

The component that sets all of these parameters is the NIC. That is to say, buying an Ethernet card means you will be using CSMA/CD, and the connectors on the card determine the cabling used and the speed of data transfer.

Token-Passing Ring

The token-passing ring protocol is a sophisticated protocol. It is deterministic, that is, each and every station gets its turn on the ring. It operates like a train running around a track with one boxcar carrying all the packets from PC to PC. The train runs at either 4 Mbps (20 miles an hour) or 16 Mbps (80 miles

Figure 8–7
CSMA/CD protocol bus network.

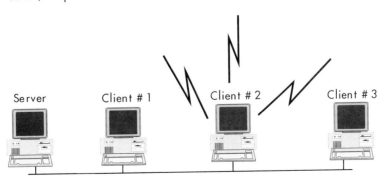

Server   Client # 1   Client # 2   Client # 3

an hour), and never stops. The token is a flag on the engine of the train. The token ring's greater sophistication (demanded by the requirement to keep the ring operating regardless of hardware failures) causes more operating overhead. Diagnostic messages constantly flow on the ring. See Figure 8–8.

Similar to Ethernet networks, token ring networks are hub-wired. This is absolutely necessary to assure reliable operation. If the ring were to break at any point, the entire network of stations would be inoperative and unable to communicate.

The token ring employs wiring hubs called Multistation Access Units (MAU). Although the token ring is a ring of wire, wiring topology does not physically look a ring but rather a star. Each point is wired from the MAU, as shown in Figure 8–9. Wiring topology for LANs today is star wiring from network hubs. This star wiring prevents common Ethernet and token ring PC wiring glitches from disabling the entire network, because a single break in the token ring wire would halt all traffic from circulating around the ring. Similarly, no electrical signals can traverse a broken Ethernet bus. Hubs prevent breaks in both token ring and Ethernet wiring from shutting them down.

To run at 16 MBPS over UTP wire, active hubs that perform signal retiming are required. IBM's active hubs have two components: a Controlled Access Unit (CAU), which is the intelligent part of the hub, and a Lobe Access Module (LAM). In token ring wiring involving both CAUs and LAMs, each LAM connects up to 20 devices (PC clients or servers), and each CAU supports up to four LAMs. You must use a CAU/LAM combination for the token ring to work. A single CAU with fully populated LAMs supports 80 devices. Maximum token ring size is 255 devices. The 255-device maximum is a token ring design limitation as specified by IEEE and IBM. The maximum length of the wire in any token ring network and the electrical signal propagation delay (the time it takes the token to electrically travel around the ring) determines this.

Figure 8–8
Token-ring token passing.

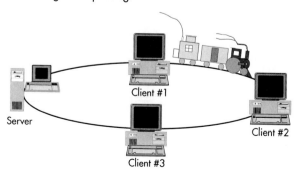

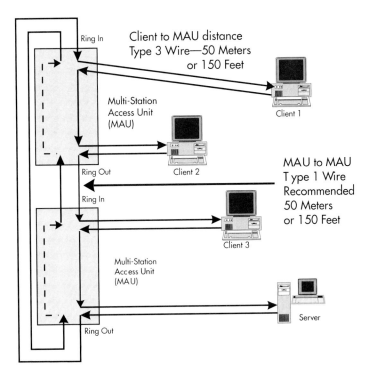

Figure 8–9
Token-ring wiring topology.

Network Types and Collisions

In the token ring network, devices take turns speaking to each other. Devices using Ethernet can speak at the same time. Where two devices transmit at the same time, there is a collision. Most LAN technologies can only have a single transmission down a cable at any given time.

Full vs. Half Duplex

Full-duplex data transmission means that data can be transmitted in both directions on a signal carrier at the same time. For example, on your LAN, if you had full-duplex transmission one workstation could send data and at the same time receive data from another machine. Full-duplex transmission implies a bidirectional line (one that can move data in both directions simultaneously).

Half-duplex data transmission means that data can be transmitted in both directions on a signal carrier, but not at the same time. So if your LAN uses a technology that has half-duplex transmission, one workstation can send data on the line and, when the transmission is done, receive data on the same line. Like full-duplex transmission, half-duplex transmission implies a bidirectional line (one that can carry data in both directions, but not at the same time).

Ethernet was designed to work on a single line with half-duplex transmission and collisions. Newer Ethernet networks support point-to-point full-duplex transmission.

CSMA/CD protocol is the basic Ethernet protocol used by 10 MBPS, 100 MBPS, and gigabit Ethernet. However, with higher-speed Ethernet implementations, the protocol has an additional full duplex (two-way simultaneous transmission) version. This eliminates any collisions on the full duplex links. When upgrading from 10 MBPS to 100 MBPS to full GBPS operation, system architectures remain the same. Both CSMA/CD mode for shared media applications and full-duplex mode for inter-switch and high-performance server connections are retained. To support these various modes, a new gigabit NIC architecture using existing fiber channel components to perform low-level optical and data encoding functions are married to the CSMA/CD or Medium Access Control (MAC) data link control level. By combining Ethernet MAC with selected fiber channel physical layer components that are familiar to users, all existing operational modes and system architectures can be retained while using fiber channels for gigabit data transmission. Gigabit Ethernet speeds are also achieved using half duplex transmission over Category 5 UTP wire by transmitting four separate 250 Mbps data streams. These separate data streams are recombined by the receiving NIC into a single Gigabit Ethernet data stream. See Figure 8–10.

Understanding the protocols that LANs use helps to understand how devices on a network communicate. Now let's take a look at the different types of cabling that we can use to link the devices together.

Network Cabling

The network cable is what binds the LAN in your office physically. How this cable connects all the devices in your office together is referred to as the physical topology of your network. There are two types of topologies that refer to your network; the logical topology and the physical topology.

A good example of the difference in topologies is the token ring network, which operates by circulating a token around a ring that all devices attach to. Drawing a circle and then drawing each device attached to that circle illustrates this nicely. This is logically how the token ring network is designed, but

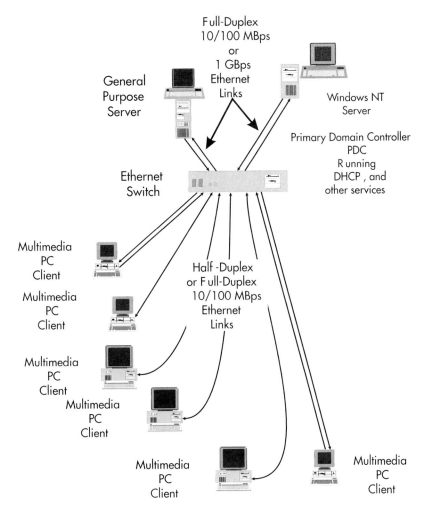

Figure 8-10
Ethernet switch.

it is not exactly how it is physically wired together. Token ring networks are wired together in what we call a star topology, meaning that there is a wiring hub or some other wire-concentrating device centrally located, and that device on a separate piece of twisted-pair wire connects to this hub. If you were to illustrate, this you would draw a box representing the hub, and from the box draw lines to each of the devices representing each device's independent connection to the hub. Even though the physical topology is a star-like design, token ring networks still operate logically as a ring, as shown in Figure 8–11.

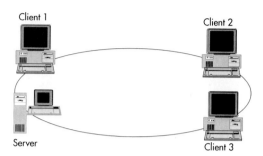

Token Ring Operating Topology

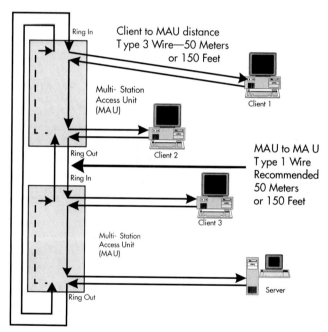

Figure 8-11
Ring vs. star topologies.

Token Ring Wiring Topology

There are three main types of topologies you may encounter: star, bus, and ring.
Star topology is the most common type of wiring topology today. Although not as expensive as a bus topology, it is not costly to set up yet is designed to be fairly fault tolerant. In a star topology, each device in the network is branched off of a central hub unit, which performs a signal regeneration (or repeater) function. It takes an attenuated (soaked up) digital pulse and recreates it back into its original form. The star topology design is very simple to set

up and adding new devices to the network is easy if you have a free connector on the hub. If a wire gets damaged, the machine connected to that wire is the only one affected because the electronics performing the repeater function (signal regeneration) electrically isolate the machine from the other machines attached to the same hub. If the hub goes down, then all machines are affected. This makes it very easy to troubleshoot problems on a star topology. Both token ring and Ethernet networks use star topologies. Star topologies can also use all cable types—coaxial, twisted pair, and fiber. See Figure 8–12.

Bus topology is the easiest of the three topologies to set up and the one that uses the least amount of cable. It consists of a single (usually coaxial) cable that is simply strung from one device to the next. At either end of this cable is a terminating resistor that makes the wire a closed electrical circuit. All devices share this communication path by taking turns sending and receiving information on the single wire. This means all devices hear all transmission being sent, but they ignore all transmissions not addressed to them. The simplicity of this design makes it ideal for use in small LAN environments; it is also a cost-effective solution. The disadvantage of bus topology, however, is in the lack of fault tolerance in the design. If there is a break anywhere along the wire, the whole network goes down. If this wire runs through the walls, it can be rather frustrating to find the break and repair it. Additionally, if terminating resistors go bad or one is removed, the whole network is shut down. Originally, early PC LANs were wired with 50-ohm coaxial cable using this topology. The Ethernet design permits a maximum of 1,024 machines per Ethernet, comprising five segments and four repeaters. A more practical limit is about 20 to 50 per Ethernet. With bridged or switched Ethernet networks, hundreds to thousands of PCs can be interconnected.

Ring topology is designed exactly as it is named. In a physical ring topology, all devices are connected to one another by tapping into or by facilitating a wire ring connection. Information in this topology then flows around the ring

Figure 8–12
Twelve-port Ethernet wiring hub.

in a single direction. This design is like the bus topology, in that it is also not very fault tolerant. If the ring is broken at any point or if a device linking the segments of the ring together is removed, the ring goes down completely. In practice, the LANs that use this topology have devices attached to them that compensate for this occurrence. Additionally most ring topologies use redundant ring paths to keep the network up in the event a single ring goes down. Fiber Distributed Data Interface (FDDI) is an example of a network that uses ring topology.

There is also what some people refer to as mesh topology, but you are very unlikely to encounter this type in LANs because the added reliability provided by mesh network links is offset by added wiring costs. An example of mesh network is the Internet. In the Internet, redundant links and alternate paths provide increased network reliability and capacity.

Now that you understand the different topology types, let's look at the cables that make up the physical connection of the networks.

Coaxial

The first widely accepted commercial uses of LANs were as broadband (analog transmission method) networks built in the early 1980s. These networks used 75-ohm coaxial cable, the cable used in cable TV today. In 1982, the first Ethernet products were developed by an alliance of Xerox, Intel, and Digital, who eventually marketed them. These early Ethernet LANs used a 50-ohm coaxial cable as opposed to the previous broadband use of 75-ohm coaxial cable. In this design, all devices communicated and were attached across a single strand of coaxial cable (bus topology). The primary drawback of this LAN wire design is that if the cable breaks at any single spot, the entire LAN fails to operate. Coaxial can also be used in a star topology, but today this is very uncommon.

Coaxial cable is composed of one physical channel that carries the signal. Surrounding this physical channel is a layer of insulation followed by another concentric physical channel. This outer channel serves as a ground. Many of these cables or pairs of coaxial tubes can be placed in a single outer sheathing and, with repeaters, can carry information for quite a distance. Depending on the technology used and other factors, twisted-pair and optical fiber are alternatives to coaxial cable. See Figure 8–13. Early PC LANs using the thin coaxial cable could be configured for a standard segment of 185 meters or an extended segment of 300 meters. Five short or standard segments could be connected using repeaters, with each active segment containing 30 PCs. PCs could not communicate with PCs that were separated by more than two repeaters. When configured as an extended segment, the coaxial cable Ethernet could not be

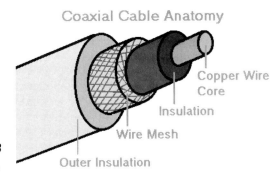

Coaxial Cable Anatomy

Copper Wire Core

Insulation

Wire Mesh

Figure 8-13
Coaxial cable.

Outer Insulation

extended using repeaters. There were electrical limitations on the number of devices connected so that the extended segment Ethernet could only support 100 PCs. Coaxial cable Ethernets have largely disappeared because twisted-pair Ethernet components has become so inexpensive.

Twisted Pair

To overcome the problems associated with coaxial cabling, twisted-pair cable and wiring hubs were used. All clients and servers are wired to hubs using UTP wire. In this case, if one cable broke, only that link to the hub was impacted. The demand for higher LAN transmission speeds required reduced signal crosstalk (signal crossover interference) from the cable. A cable grading scheme or category level was developed. The highest level is soon to be Category-6, rated to support transmission at speeds up to about 155 MBPS. Higher category UTP wire specifications supporting higher transmission speeds are under development. The original telephone wire is Category-3, rated at speeds up to 10 MBPS. Category-5 wire is rated at speeds up to 100 MBPS, and is the most widely used cable for telephony and LAN wiring today. The distance between the PC and the wiring hub is similar for all cable types, about 100 meters or 330 feet maximum.

Twisted pair is a set of ordinary copper wires that connects home and many business computers to the telephone company, or to a LAN. Electrical signaling is sent back and forth across this pair of wires. Since electrical signals travel across both wires, electromagnetic induction between pairs of wires may occur (This is known as crosstalk and can interfere with transmissions). To reduce crosstalk between pairs of wires, the two insulated copper wires are twisted around each other (thus becoming a twisted pair). Each signal on twisted pair requires both wires. Most twisted-pair cable contains multiple pairs. In some cases, the twisted pairs are enclosed in a foil shielding that functions as a ground. This is known as shielded twisted pair (STP). More commonly, when the pairs are simply wrapped in a vinyl insulatorthey are described as unshielded. Token ring networks use shielded twisted pair primarily. It initially operated at speeds up to 16 MBPS over IBM's Type-1 shielded cable and runs today at 100 MBPS over STP Type 1a cable and UTP Category-5 cable. Ethernet uses UTP. It began operating at 10 MBPS over Category-3 cable but has evolved to fast Ethernet at 100 MBPS over Category-5 UTP cable.

Twisted pair is now frequently installed with two pairs to the home; the extra pair makes it possible for you to add another line (perhaps for modem use) when you need it. Twisted pair comes with each pair uniquely color-coded (that is, blue/blue white, green/green white, brown/brown white, and orange/orange white color-coded pairs) when it is packaged in multiple pairs. Different uses such as analog, digital, and LAN Ethernet require different pair multiples. Although it is often associated with home use, a higher grade of twisted pair is often used for horizontal wiring in LAN installations because it is less expensive than coaxial cable.

The wire you buy at a local hardware store for extensions from your phone or computer modem to a wall jack is not twisted pair, but rather a side-by-side wire known as silver satin. The wall jack can have several configurations (for instance, RJ-1, RJ-45, Mod-8 offset) and pinouts (for instance, 2-wire, 4-wire, or 8-wire), depending on the kinds of wire the installation expects will be plugged in (for example, digital, analog, or LAN). (That's why you may sometimes find when you carry your notebook computer to another location that the wall jack connections won't match your plug.) See Figure 8–14.

Unshielded Twisted Pair Anatomy

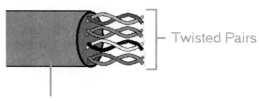

Twisted Pairs

Figure 8–14
Twisted-pair cable   Outer Insulation

Fiber

Fiber-optic cable refers to the technology of transmitting information as light impulses along a glass or plastic fiber, as shown in Figure 8–15. The fiber-optic cable used in LANs is usually multimode with a graded index of refraction. Refraction bends the light so much as it travels though the glass fiber that the light cannot escape the fiber during its journey.

Multimode cable has a core diameter of 62.5 microns and a cladding diameter of 125 microns. The amount that light is bent increases as the light moves to the outside of the core near the cladding. In the center of the cladding, the bending ratio is 1 to 1; at the outside, it is 1 to 1000. In this manner, light traveling down the core is bent back inward toward the center of the core until it emerges at the opposite end of the fiber cable.

The single mode fiber cable is used in telecommunications for telephony transmission and works on reflection. The core size is so small (8.3 microns) that the boundary between the core and the cladding forms a mirror-like surface, similar to the reflection that causes mirages in the desert. The light traveling through the core is reflected off this surface until it emerges at the other end of the fiber cable. Single mode cable is capable of longer runs and higher transmission speeds than is multimode cable. Multimode cable can run up to 6,000 feet before requiring a repeater, and operates at speeds up to 1 Gbps. In contrast, single mode cable can run about 20 miles before requiring a repeater, and operates at speeds up to 40 Gbps. As LANs move to higher speeds, more single mode cable will be employed to interconnect LAN components.

Fiber-optic cable carries much more information than conventional copper wire and is far less subject to electromagnetic interference. Most telephone company long-distance lines are now fiber optic. Transmission on fiber-optic cable requires repeating (signal regeneration), like digital transmission over copper wire does, but the distance between repeaters is significantly longer.

The glass fiber requires more protection within an outer cable than copper. This helps protect it from impact and other possible destructive occurrences.

Fiber-optic transmission passes an optical signal (flash of light) over an optical link using an electrical data signal and a modulated light signal.

The electrical data signal enters a driver that turns on and off (modulates) a source of light to produce a modulated light signal. The modulated light signal then travels through the fiber-optic cable until it reaches a light sensor (photoreceptor diode) at the far end. This sensor, sometimes called a detector, converts (demodulates) the light signal into a small electrical signal which passes through an amplifier that transforms it into a detectable electrical signal. The driver and the light source together are the transmitter. The detector and amplifier make up the receiver. The principle benefits of fiber-optic transmission are:

1. Fiber is capable of very high speeds—there is no electrical interaction at higher speeds as there is in twisted-pair wiring.

2. Fiber is good for harsh physical environments—strong electrical fields or water does not disrupt transmission.

3. Fiber isolates electrically one site from another site—this eliminates problems caused by ground loops and electrical storms.

In spite of the benefits of fiber-optic cabling, we are not likely to be running fiber-optic cable to each desktop. Wiring from wiring closets and the repeaters therein to the desktop remains UTP. To support the high transmission speeds required (more than 10 or 16 Mbps) for video, the UTP wiring needs to be UL Level V (or Electronic Industries Association/Telecommunications Industries Association Category-5) wiring.

For these reasons, and because the installation of any new wiring is labor-intensive, few communities have fiber optic wires or cables from the phone company's branch office to local customers.

Figure 8–15
Fiber cable operation.

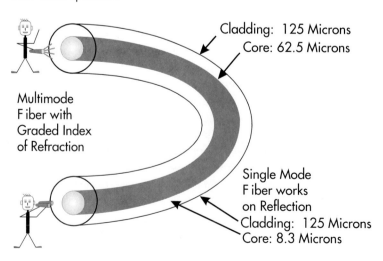

Cladding: 125 Microns
Core: 62.5 Microns

Multimode
Fiber with
Graded Index
of Refraction

Single Mode
Fiber works
on Reflection
Cladding: 125 Microns
Core: 8.3 Microns

Peer-to-Peer versus Client-Server Networks

Now it is time to examine the software used to bind the network together. The software chosen for a network determines how a network communicates and how you administer users and nodes.

Peer-to-peer and client-server are the two main types of network software operations, as discussed earlier. Most software today offers the ability to choose either a type or a combination of both types of networking. As an example, a Windows-based PC can be a peer in a peer-to-peer solution as well as a client in a client-server network on a single network or on an extended network. Before we look into the various software options, perhaps we should define peer-to-peer and client-server.

A peer-to-peer network is one in which all the devices on the network are considered equals. This means that each machine is responsible for maintaining its own users, resources, and security permissions for others accessing those resources on the network. This is a network that is easy to set up and maintain since logging on to a server is not required.

Client-server describes the relationship between two computers in which one acts like a client, making a service request to the server, which responds to the request. The client-server model has become one of the central ideas of network computing. Most applications written today use the client-server model. In this model, the application runs on two systems, with the client portion focusing most commonly on the resource-minimal tasks like data presentation and lighter processing, allowing the server to focus on the resource-intensive tasks it is geared for, such as data storage and retrieval. Using this scenario, the clients—usually PCs—can be smaller, less powerful, and therefore less expensive systems that share the resources of a server for large data manipulation tasks (jobs?).

In the past, the term has been used to distinguish distributed computing by smaller dispersed computers from the centralized computing of mainframe computers. But this distinction has for the most part disappeared, since mainframes and their applications now function using the client-server model.

In the usual client-server model, at least one computer is always active and awaiting requests from the clients. This computer runs special operating system software called the NOS. This software allows the server to create and administer users, monitor and control security, and provide shared resources to clients. Examples of NOSs would be Windows NT Server, Windows 2000 Server, Linux, and Novell NetWare. The other computers attached to the network act as clients, making requests of the server. These requests may be for shared information on the server, to log on and secure access to the network, or for the use of shared peripherals, like printers. In order for the client to be able to make these requests, the client must be running special software called the client software. This software allows the client to communicate with the server in a way that the server understands. TCP/IP is an example of this software. If the server uses TCP/IP to communicate with clients, then the client must also load TCP/IP. Today, Windows 95/98 comes with the client's software as part of the complete operating system. Earlier systems like Windows 3.x need separate software drivers provided by the NOS manufacturer.

Table 8–2 summarizes the conditions that influence the choice between peer-to-peer and client-server approaches.

Table 8–2 Peer-to-peer vs. Client-server

Peer-to-peer	Client-server
Few machines to connect together	A large number of computers and users to setup and administer
Lower cost, NOS purchase unnecessary	Centralized control over shared resources is needed
Setup is easier, complex user and groups are not required	Support for distributed applications that require a client-server NOS
Network security is not a concern	Security is a concern

Windows 3.11

We examine Windows 3.11 software here because it is the starting point for Windows networking software. The basic networking capabilities for peer-to-peer, client/server and TCP/IP networks were implemented in Windows 3.11, also known as "Windows for Workgroups." It was not Microsoft's first attempt at networking software; Microsoft had been in the networking arena for many years, selling a client-server product called LAN Manager. The trouble with LAN Manager was that it had to compete with the then market-dominant Novell NetWare. However, most networks using this LAN Manager software were relatively large PC networks.

There were a large number of computers that were not networked because the cost of networking them using client-server software was prohibitive. Also, client-server software required trained staff to administer it. Most nonnetworked users, however, could see the benefit of having network capabilities. What they needed was a software package that allowed them to do many of the same things as client-server software did but was inexpensive and required no specialized staff. This was the reason for the explosion of peer-to-peer packages in the early 90s. The two dominant products were LANtastic by Artisoft and Microsoft Windows for Workgroups 3.11.

The biggest advantage Windows for Workgroups had over LANtastic was due to networking software built into the operating system itself. In other words, there were very few things you had to load in the CONFIG.SYS or the AUTOEXEC.BAT in order to get the network running. Second, these drivers were included with the disks that came with the Windows for Workgroups product.

The following is the only driver that had to be loaded in the CONFIG.SYS file for Windows 3.11 to provide network capabilities.

```
DEVICE=C:\WINDOWS\IFSHLP.SYS
```

The IFSHLP.SYS file is used to provide real-mode support for the IFS Manager. The IFS Manager is a software component for Windows 3.11 responsible for passing information to the appropriate device, including networked devices.

The following is the only line required by Windows 3.11 for the AUTOEXEC.BAT file.

```
C:\WINDOWS\NET START
```

This line is used to initialize the programs used by Windows 3.11 and bind them to the network adapter.

When a Windows for Workgroups computer is not seeing the network, these two files are a good place to start troubleshooting. If there is a problem with either, error messages indicating that the network adapter is not functioning or that a server cannot be found are flashed on the screen. These screens scroll by quickly, so be sure to use the F8 key to see a line-by-line execution of both the CONFIG.SYS and AUTOEXEC.BAT file.

PROTOCOL.INI File

When Windows for Workgroups is installed, the setup program creates a file called PROTOCOL.INI. This file is used to define network parameters used by Windows for Workgroups networking. There is little need to examine and modify this file. Using the network icon under the control panel changes all the settings in it. The only exception is if more than one network card is used in the machine. In this case, settings such as the IRQ and the I/O address must be set on the boards so they do not conflict with each other. Generally, setting IRQ and I/O addresses is a function of setting up the LAN hardware. The best way to view and edit the PROTOCOL.INI file is to use the program SYSEDIT. Below is an example of a PROTOCOL.INI file.

523

```
[network.setup]
version=0x3110
netcard=ms$ne2clone,1,MS$NE2CLONE,4
transport=tcpip-32n,MSTCP32
transport=ms$netbeui,NETBEUI
lana0=ms$ne2clone,1,tcpip-32n
lana1=ms$ne2clone,1,ms$netbeui
[net.cfg]
PATH=C:\NET\NET.CFG
[MS$NE2CLONE]
[Link Driver NE2000]
[MSTCP32]
BINDINGS=NE2000
LANABASE=0
[NETBEUI]
BINDINGS=NE2000
LANABASE=1
SESSIONS=10
NCBS=12
```

Network Setup

To change and configure the network setting under Windows 3.11, you must use two different programs. The first is the Window's setup, found in the MAIN window group under the program manager. The second item is the network control panel, which we examine after going through the network setup program.

When entering the MAIN group, locate and double-click on the WINDOWS SETUP icon. A window opens that allows you to configure many areas of Windows networking. Point to the word OPTIONS on the Windows menu bar, then click and select CHANGE NETWORK SETTINGS. The Window in Figure 8–16 appears.

From here, many PROTOCOL.INI file settings can be modified You can choose which networks your machine participates in by selecting Networks. The Microsoft Windows Network is the peer-to-peer choice. If this machine is also going to work on a client-server network, then select an additional network from those listed in the drop-down box. If another network is chosen, add the programs for that network to the computer as well as any configuration parameters that may be required in the CONFIG.SYS and AUTOEXEC.BAT files. In Figure 8–17, a Novell NetWare network has been chosen along with the Microsoft Windows Network.

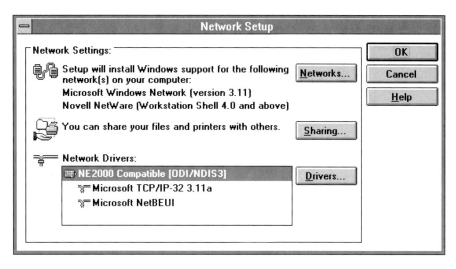

Figure 8–16
Windows 3.1 network setup.

Figure 8–17
Windows 3.1 networks.

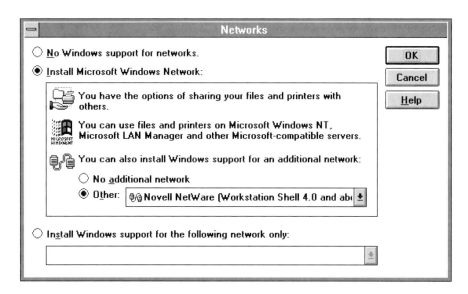

Sharing allows setup for sharing devices across the network. Selecting this option here allows others to access and use disks and printers attached to this PC. Enabling this does not mean, however, that existing disks and printers are shared automatically. In order to share a disk (and files on that disk), a share must be set up, by using the File Manager once sharing is enabled. Likewise, the Print Manager is used to set up printer sharing. See Figure 8–18.

The Network Drivers menu selection allows you to select and configure the network communication software. Specifically, this refersto the driver used by Windows 3.11 to communicate to the PC's network adapter and the transport

Figure 8–18
Windows 3.1 sharing.

Figure 8–19
Windows 3.1 network drivers.

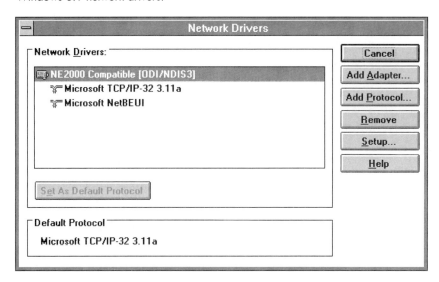

protocol. Both items must be selected correctly or the PC cannot talk with view the network. See Figure 8–19.

The PROTOCOL.INI file binds the network adapter driver to the Windows transport protocol when the transport protocol is selected. The PC uses a command in the AUTOEXEC.BAT file to load the actual driver file. The references here specify the type of NIC and the specific setting for the card, i.e., the IRQ and the I/O address. These would then be displayed in the [netcard] section of the PROTOCOL.INI file. The word NETCARD in the brackets would be replaced with the name of the actual card type displayed in the netcard= line. So, in the example of this file displayed earlier in this section, the [netcard] section is the [MS$NE2CLONE]. This section then has several lines of text which reflect the parameters set for the card. Since the card is using all automatic settings, the section is left empty. If they were not, then a list of the parameters displayed would be seen. See Figure 8–20.

A transport protocol must be selected for a network. Transport protocols perform the functions assigned to Layer 3, Layer 4, and Layer 5 of the ISO seven-layer model. The same transport protocol must be used on all machines for the network; if needed, multiple protocols can be used in a network. However, networks tend to be more reliable if only a single transport protocol is used. In this example, the client is using both NetBEUI and TCP/IP. Once these are set, Windows loads this during the Windows start-up sequence. If a network other than a Windows network like NetWare is selected, then additional transport protocol drivers may need to be loaded in the AUTOEXEC.BAT file.

Figure 8–20
NE2000 compatible card software setup.

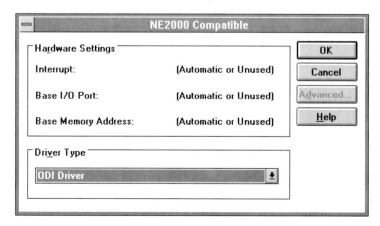

Like choosing an adapter, choosing a transport protocol requires setting certain parameters for each protocol selected. These parameters are different for each protocol. For example, Figure 8–21 shows TCP/IP settings for Windows for Workgroups. There are a number of settings that must be supplied to Windows in order for it to use TCP/IP. These settings would be available through a network administrator. If a Windows server using DHCP (Dynamic Host Configuration Protocol) is available, simply select it to have the Windows server configure these settings automatically for you during the log on. More detail is provided in Chapter 16. As with the adapter, choosing the protocol and the settings for that protocol writes that information to the PROTOCOL.INI file, specifically to the [protocol] section. Multiple [protocol] sections are created when more than one protocol is used under Windows. The section name is based on the names found in the transport= line of the [network.setup] section. In the earlier example of the PROTOCOL.INI file, there is a section [MSTCP32] for TCP/IP and a section [NETBEUI] for NetBEUI.

Figure 8–21
Windows 3.1 TCP/IP configuration.

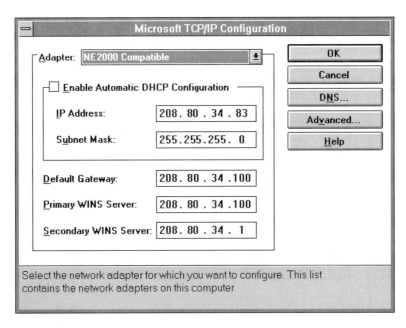

The Network Control Panel

The network control panel is used to configure the connection of the computer and user to the network. It is entered through the Windows 3.1 control panel. Connecting to the network implies the log-on process of supplying a password and a user name. Depending on what type of network the PC is connecting to, there can be individual settings that need to be configured. The key setting is the workgroup identification. If it is not set to the correct workgroup name, it becomes more difficult to find other peer-to-peer networked PCs on the LAN because only your workgroup is easily visible. Double-click on the network control panel to see the window in Figure 8–22.

This window controls the peer-to-peer network settings used by Windows for Workgroups. The network is organized as workgroups. Each machine belongs to a workgroup, and the workgroups that the machine belongs to can be switched. From here, passwords can be changed as needed.

Figure 8–22
Windows 3.1 Microsoft Windows Network.

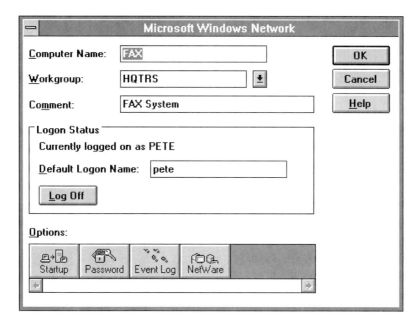

Windows 95/98/Me

Windows 95/98/Me, like Windows 3.11 for Workgroups, can provide peer-to-peer connectivity. Unlike Windows for Workgroups, Windows 95/98/Me both come with client software to allow them to behave as a client on multiple kinds of networks. This makes Windows 95/98/Me very flexible, regardless of what networks they are integrated into. To configure Windows 95/98/Me for networking, open the network control panel. The easiest way to do this is to point to the network neighborhood icon on the desktop and click the right mouse button. The only difference between Windows 95/98 and Windows Me is Windows Me has a My Network Places icon rather than a Network Neighborhood icon. Once the icon is selected and the right mouse button clicked, select properties from the adjacent pop-up menu, as shown in Figure 8–23.

Selecting properties leads to the networking control window as shown in Figure 8–24. This window controls all aspects of networking with a Windows 95/98/Me client. Notice the tabs across the top of the window; each one controls a different aspect of networking.

The first tab, Configuration, sets the client type, adapter cards, protocols used, and services loaded. An example of these would be Client for Microsoft Network, NE2000 adapter, TCP/IP, and File and Print sharing.

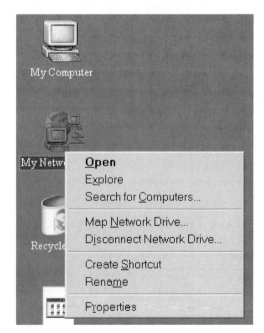

Figure 8-23
Windows Me My Network Places Menu.

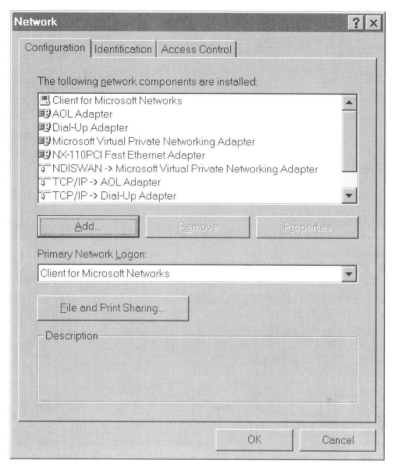

Figure 8–24
Windows 95/98/Me networking control window.

These choices can be added or removed from this screen, or if they have any defining properties, those can be set from here as well. An example of this would be the necessary TCP/IP settings required for this computer to talk across the network, or the properties for the client type. Client for Microsoft Networks has within its properties the ability to have this machine behave in a peer-to-peer fashion, or as a Windows 95/98 client on a Windows NT Server or Windows 2000 Server client-server network. To set up a peer-to-peer network under Windows 95/98, the service file and print sharing for Microsoft networks must be loaded.

One of each of these items must be selected for the PC to communicate across the network. Not all of them are set automatically when the plug-and-play system picks up the NIC. The Identification tab is shown in Figure 8–25. It is responsible for setting the identification and the name of the peer-to-peer workgroup. The name used is the name that appears to other users of the network neighborhood; it is also the name used by other users creating shares on this machine.

The Access tab sets the access level for this computer, as shown in Figure 8–26. The two choices reflect the different types of networks in which this client participates. User level security indicates that security is based on a user's name

Figure 8–25
Workgroup identification.

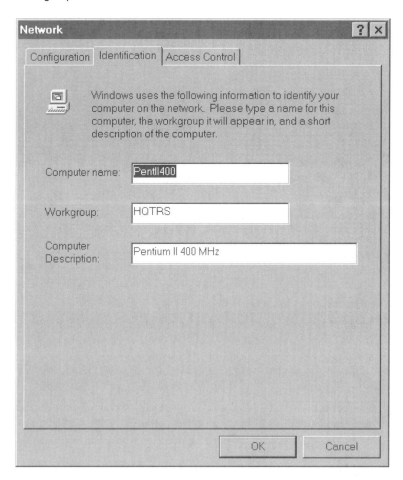

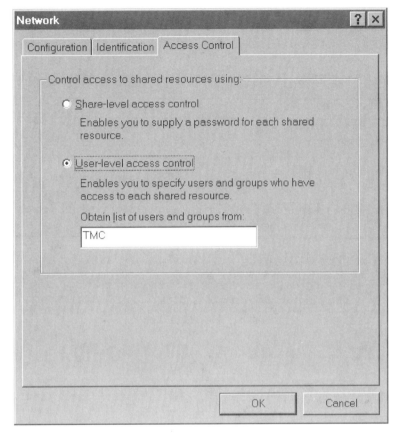

Figure 8-26
Windows 95/98/Me access control.

and password. In order for this to work, there has to be a centralized security provider, like an NT server, a Windows 2000 server, or a NetWare server.

Share-level security is security that is set for each resource share the machine has. A share represents a resource that the user of the machine allows other users to use. The user creating the share then chooses what level of use the other users have with this share. For example, a user may set one of his shared disk drives as read-only and the other as full access.

Any user on the network has that assigned level of access when using the share. The level of access has nothing to do with the user logging into the network with a specific name and password. Thus, share level access is designed for a peer-to-peer network.

Windows NT

Windows NT differs from the other systems in that Windows NT Server can be configured to be a server operating system or a client operating system. These are known as Windows NT server and Windows NT workstation, respectively. When installing Windows server software, make sure to install the server version for client-server networking.

If you install Windows NT workstation, you can participate in Windows peer-to-peer networks. This allows up to ten active connections to by supported by your PC. Servers, in contrast, can support hundreds of active connections. The advantage of using Windows NT is that the settings that are used to set up and configure the machines are almost identical. Let's look at the configuration screens for NT.

After installing NT, view the control panel for the networking by pointing at the network neighborhood and clicking the right mouse button. Then choose properties from the pop-up menu. The panel in Figure 8–27 appears. Much like Windows 95/98/Me, the different tabs control different aspects of networking, and each has specific settings that must be there in order for your network to work.

Figure 8–27
NT networking panel.

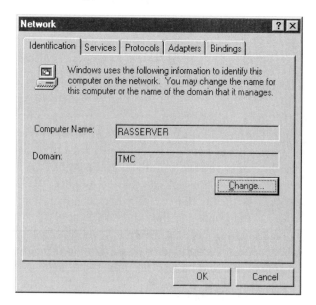

The Identification section is used to define the machine's network name and workgroup on the peer-to-peer network. On a client-server network, this is used to select a domain.

Windows NT uses domains as a way of creating a single administrative unit. All machines that are part of the domain are subject to domain control and rights. The machine that controls the domain is known as the Primary Domain Controller (PDC), and each domain has a single PDC. A domain may also have Backup Domain Controllers (BDC). A domain can have more than one BDC. If a PDC or a BDC cannot be found during the log-on process to verify a name and password, the user is not able to access and log on to the domain. The Services section controls the services running on the NT computer. Both servers and workstations use services. Services are used by the machine to provide certain functions to users that connect to it, or for users using it. An example of this would be Remote Access Service (RAS). RAS allows the machine to act as a dial-in or dial-out computer, thus providing remote access to another network or to the network to which the machine is currently attached. See Figure 8–28.

Figure 8-28
Windows NT services configuration.

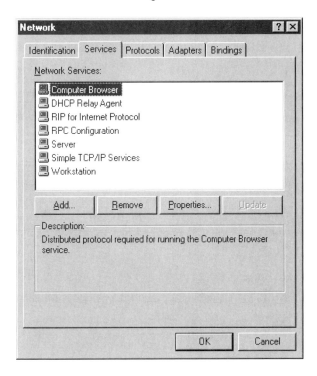

To add a service, click the "add" button to get a list of services not already installed. It is important to note that services take vital memory resources, so the more services loaded, the slower and less efficiently the Windows NT machine runs. It is a good habit to always remove services that are not being used. Additionally, each service may have properties that must be set in order for it to perform as expected. Some services have no properties to set.

Some basic NT services are:

1. Computer browser—finds shared PCs and servers on a Windows network.

2. DHCP relay agent—permits forwarding of DHCP broadcasts across a router to a remote DHCP server in order to assign IP addresses to the broadcasting PC.

3. RIP for Internet Protocol—enables IP routers to exchange routing information.

4. RPC Service—permits programs with Remote Procedure Calls (RPC) to run procedures on other PCs.

5. Server— sets up the server side of client-server networking; this is the server message block protocol.

6. Simple TCP/IP services—provides simple client-side TCP/IP network functions like Daytime and Quote of the Day.

7. Workstation—this is the client service for the server message block client-server network.

The Protocols section is used to install and configure any of the protocols NT can use. Like Windows 95/98/Me, NT can use multiple protocols, allowing NT to participate on almost all networks types. If a machine cannot see other machines on the network, make sure the right protocol is being used and that it is configured properly. See Figure 8–29.

As with services, it is best to limit the number of protocols used with Windows NT. Not only do protocols require precious memory resources, but they may also slow down the performance of Windows NT machines on the network. Common protocols that may be implemented on NT machines are:

1. Data Link Control (DLC) protocol—this is used to access IBM mainframe computers.

2. NetBEUI protocol—this is the original Windows peer-to-peer networking protocol.

3. NWLink IPX/SPX compatible transport protocol—this is used to

communicate with Novell NetWare servers.

4. Point-to-Point Tunneling Protocol (PPTP)— this is used to tunnel through TCP/IP networks and securely access resources on remote servers. The RAS software uses this protocol. PPTP encapsulates NetBEUI protocol and other communications and transmits them securely to a remote server over an IP network.

5. Streams environment—this is a client server protocol used in Windows and NetWare environments to support continuous data streams (for instance, MPEG video) between multimedia devices.

6. TCP/IP Protocol—this is the most commonly used suite of protocols today. TCP/IP supports both LAN and Internet communications.

When installing a protocol, make sure you know all the settings that are required for configuring it. For example, when using TCP/IP always know the

Figure 8–29
Windows NT Protocols section.

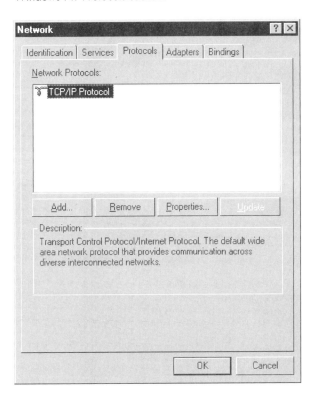

IP address, DNS server, and routers. Without these, loading the protocol is not enough to make the network function. Select protocol and then use the properties button to configure.

The Adapters section, like protocols, is used to add, remove, and configure any hardware network adapter in the machine. NT can have multiple adapters installed in it, meaning an Ethernet network card and a Ring token ring network card could be installed in the machine at the same time. Doing this enables the machine to route network traffic from one side of the network to another. See Figure 8–30.

During the installation of Windows NT, the setup program was given information about the NICs that are installed in it. It needs to know this because it has to load the correct drivers for each NIC. Additionally, the operating system needs to know certain hardware parameters that are specific to each card. From this screen, parameters for any of the installed adapters can be added, removed, or changed.

Figure 8–30
Windows NT adapters section.

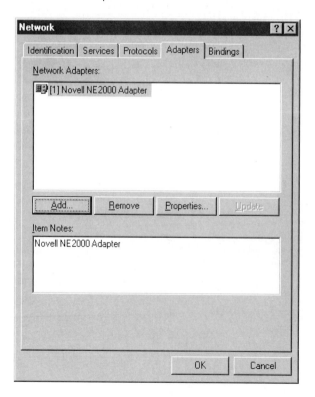

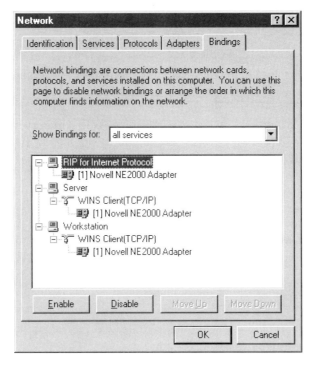

Figure 8–31
Windows NT binding section.

The Bindings section is used to show how the various services, protocols, and adapters are bound together as well as the order within which each is bound. See Figure 8–31. This means that not all services and protocols have to be bound to every adapter in the machine. Often times, network performance can be improved by changing the binding order. For example, TCP/IP and NetBEUI run on a Windows NT machine. If NetBEUI is used to communicate to all the machines on the network and TCP/IP is used to communicate only on the Internet, binding NetBEUI higher in the binding order means that the Windows NT machine uses NetBEUI first when any network request is sent. Since users communicate more often across their network than the Internet, placing TCP/IP higher than NetBEUI would enhance performance.

The bindings are displayed graphically so the order is easily visible. Clicking on the plus sign next to a service, protocol, or adapter allows the orders of bindings to be viewed. These graphical binding displays can be used with the up or down buttons to change the bindings order. Notice also that bindings can be enabled or disabled as well.

Windows 2000

Windows 2000 surpasses Windows NT. Similar to NT it comes both server and client versions. The client version is Windows 2000 Professional and the standard (not specialized) server configurations are Windows 2000 Server and Windows 2000 Advanced Server.

Similar to Windows 95/98/Me and Windows NT, Windows 2000 has a networking control window that is opened just like the control window for Windows 95/98/Me; simply right-click on the My Network Places icon on the desktop. Similar to other versions of Windows, it can also be entered through the Control Panel. The Networking control window for Windows 2000 presents a different view than that of other windows versions. See Figure 8–32.

This window shows the networking connections for the Windows 2000 PChe LAN Connection 4 is for the local LAN and the LAN Connection 5 permits connecting to AOL through the local TCP/IP LAN. Selecting one connection or the other connection, right-clicking and selecting properties permits configuring the network connection. The network control window for

Figure 8–32
Networking Control window for Windows 2000 Professional.

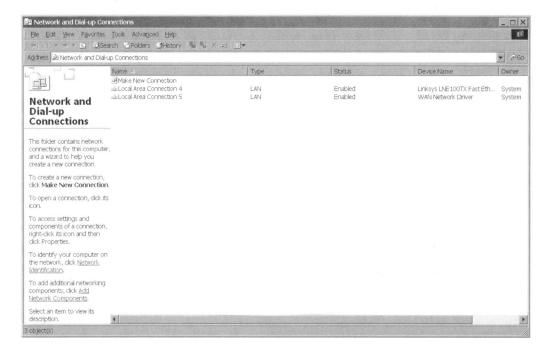

each connection permits configuring the network adapter as well as the services and protocols that operate over that adapter. See Figure 8–33.

Selecting the adapter configure button brings up a hardware configuration window that is also accessed through the control panel's device manager tab. The hardware configuration window has General, Advanced, Driver, Resources, and Power Management tabs. The General tab confirms the adapter is working properly. The Advanced tab permits configuring special network adapter functions such as Wakeup. The Driver tab lets you install updated NIC drivers. The Resources tab identifies the IRQ, I/O port and other system resources used by the network adapter. Since most adapters are plug-and-play, and since Windows 2000 plug–and-play works very well, the Resources tab is rarely used. The

Figure 8–33
Windows 2000 network connection window.

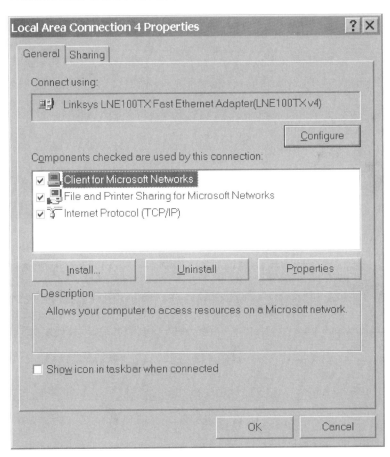

Power Management tab permits the NIC to wake the PC up from standby mode and permits the PC to turn off the NIC to save power.

The services and protocols are configured from the bottom window panel. There are few configuration options for the Microsoft Networks Client and File and Print Sharing. The protocol configuration has similar selections to the Windows 95/98/Me protocol configuration windows. For TCP/IP DHCP assigns IP addresses automatically and provides clients with other network information. Windows 2000 supports DHCP. Domain Name Service and Windows Internet Name service as well as some network security services may also be configured using the advanced protocol properties.

Although the network control windows presented by Windows 2000 look different than those of Windows 95/98/Me, the overall network configuration is very similar. The Windows 2000 network configuration is conceptually the same as Windows 95/98/Me network configuration. Similarly, Windows XP uses the same networking configuration as Windows 2000 but, the GUI looks quite different.

NetWare

NetWare is client-server network software. It is provided with a server NOS and client software for both Windows and DOS. See Figure 8–34.

The NetWare client programs for DOS and Windows 3.11 were originally IPX.COM and NETX.EXE. The IPX.COM program was tailored during installation to a specific LAN board. This tailoring involved setting IRQ and I/O port settings into the IPX.COM file. NetWare client software became more generalized with Open Data link Interface (ODI) software, which employed a base driver program LSL.COM that permitted up to four protocol stacks (like SPX/IPX and TCP/IP) to use the same LAN board. The board driver program, TOKEN for IBM token ring cards used a general NET.CFG file to get the board IRQ and I/O address parameters. The NET.CFG file was a text file easily edited using any text editor. This made adapting to different board configurations relatively easy.

Novell's transport protocol stack, the Sequenced Packet Exchange/Internet Packet Exchange (SPX/IPX), was loaded using IPXODI.COM and the NETX.EXE programs. This software was provided with NetWare version 3.xx. Version 4.xx of NetWare replaced the NETX.EXE program with Virtual Loadable Modules (VLMs) that were loaded using the VLM manager program VLM.EXE.

Today the Novell NetWare client is built into Windows 95/98/Me, Windows NT and Windows 2000. Novell provides special client software that enhances the security and performance of the basic Windows NetWare clients as well. Accessing Novell NetWare servers is done with TCP/IP for NetWare 5.xx or by SPX/IPX for Novell 3.xx and 4.xx servers.

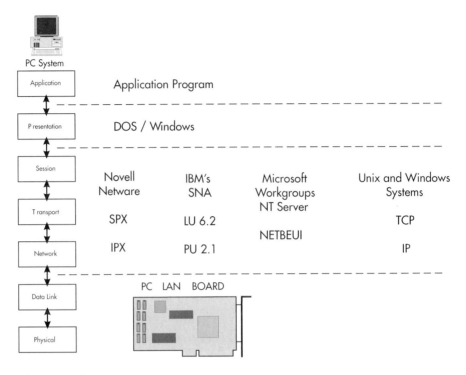

PC System

Application	Application Program
Presentation	DOS / Windows
Session	
Transport	
Network	
Data Link	PC LAN BOARD
Physical	

Novell	IBM's	Microsoft	Unix and Windows
Netware	SNA	Workgroups	Systems
		NT Server	
SPX	LU 6.2		TCP
		NETBEUI	
IPX	PU 2.1		IP

Figure 8–34
NetWare DOS client programs.

NetWare servers serve as a good diagnostic tool because they are easily accessible using NetWare drivers on a bootable DOS disk. Installing NetWare server software requires setting up a small DOS partition on the fixed disk drive, then running the NetWare installation disk to copy the software and configure the server's fixed disk drives and LAN boards for network operation. See Figure 8–35.

Server software installation and configuration starts with installing and configuring the LAN board drivers, where the disk drives have volumes installed and formatted for use. The format is a Novell NetWare format and not a DOS or Windows format. Software is then copied to the disk drives and the server is set to administer. In the final steps, an administrator must log on to the NetWare server and configure users, file access permissions, disk compression, printer sharing, and the other common tasks associated with configuring a network server.

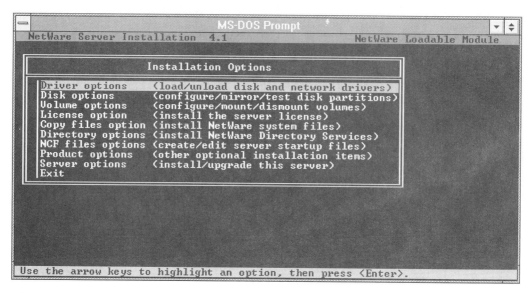

Figure 8–35
NetWare server installation menu.

Study Break: Windows 98/Me Network Options

Let's set up Windows 98/Me peer-to-peer networking. Find a PC with a network adapter installed. It can be a working PC on an existing LAN as long as you remember to cancel the changes to the network setup we are making.

Get to a PC that has Windows 98/Me networking software installed. Open the networking configuration window by going to the control panel and clicking on the network icon; you can also open in by highlighting the network neighborhood on the desktop, clicking the right mouse button and selecting properties. The window that appears should look like Figure 8–24. Remove all existing network setup by highlighting each item and selecting remove. Be careful here to not click on the access control tab because it changes the existing network configuration. We do not want to do that. Follow the steps below carefully to avoid changing the existing configuration.

Click on the add button, select service, and click on the new add button.

Select file and printer sharing for Microsoft Networks and click OK.

Client for Microsoft Networks, Dial-up Adapter, TCP/IP (or NetBEUI), and File and printer sharing for Microsoft networks should appear in the panel.

Select Add, pick Protocol, Microsoft, NetBEUI (or TCP/IP), and click OK. The NetBEUI protocol should appear in your list.

Select Add, pick Adapter, Novell/Anthem, NE2000 Compatible, and click OK. The NE2000 should be linked to the NetBEUI (and TCP/IP) protocols. The Dial-Up adapter is linked to these protocols as well.

Click on Client for Microsoft Networks and then click properties. Make sure the quick logon menu selection is checked. Click OK.

Click on file and print sharing and verify both file and printer sharing options are checked.

Click on the Identification tab, enter a computer name, workgroup name (for example, our favorite HQTRS), and enter a computer description— i.e., Pentium 4, 1.7 GHz screamer.

Click on the Access control tab and select share level access control.

This completes the peer-to-peer network setup. Clicking OK causes the computer to reboot and implement the changes you specified. So if the computer is on an existing network, click cancel to avoid changing the existing network settings.

Internet Access

Almost all PCs are configured to access the Internet. It is probably the most common use of home PCs today. Typically, the Internet is accessed using cable modems, dial-up networking into a local ISP, or through subscription-based software such as AOL or similar services provided by ISPs. AOL software can also be used with LAN connections and high-speed cable modems.

Internet communications use TCP/IP software, which is built into Windows 95/98/Me, Windows NT, Windows 2000, and it can be added to Windows 3.11. As an example, AOL software supports TCP/IP communication to AOL via the Internet. Web browser software and AOL software are the applications that are used to surf the Internet. See Figure 8–36.

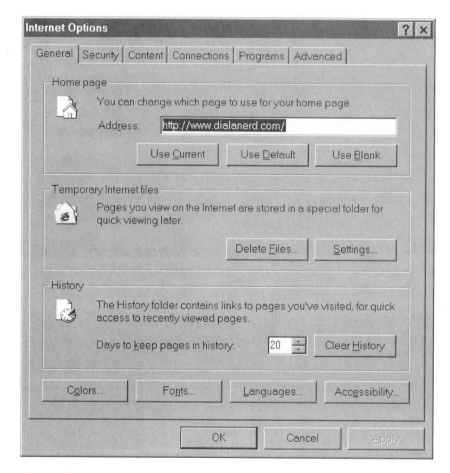

Figure 8–36
Internet Explorer network setup.

Dial-up and AOL connections require no special IP address assignment for access to the Internet. When logging on to AOL or an ISP, they automatically assign an IP address to your connection using DHCP. This is the same as DHCP in Windows networking that dynamically assigns IP addresses as users require them.

Cable modems are set up like any LAN configuration. They often require a fixed IP address assignment for the PC to precisely identify their subscribers. This fixed IP address is unique to the cable modem system, in which cable modem connection functions like a gigantic LAN and the IP address assigned is not a direct Internet IP address. In the cable modem, network routers reassign this internal cable modem IP address to an official working Internet IP address. Cable modem access is high speed and available 24 hours a day, 7 days a week, and is simple to operate because it makes your PC act like it has a direct LAN connection to the Internet.

Figure 8–36 shows a PC set up to access the Internet using a LAN. As long as the LAN TCP/IP is set up properly, the PC can use it to access the Internet. Setting the LAN connections properly requires that domain name servers, routers, and high-speed links into ISPs must all be configured to pass TCP/IP packets from the PC to the Internet and vice versa.

Similarly, AOL software can be configured for access to AOL using a LAN and the Internet. See Figure 8–37.

Figure 8–37
AOL TCP/IP LAN configuration.

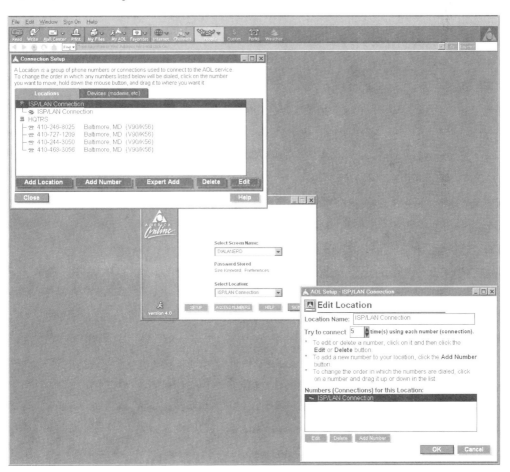

With AOL, the LAN and modem configurations are set up using the setup button on the sign-on screen shown in the middle of the figure. Expert add menu selection displays both the LAN and dial-up connections defined for this AOL installation. The LAN connection figures out the TCP/IP details automatically. It can also be manually configured.

The modem configuration for AOL is set up automatically by selecting menu options using the AOL software. Windows dial-up connections to the Internet are similarly set up automatically with a Windows Internet connection Wizard.

There is more discussion on Windows dial-up networking in Chapter 16. If these connections are not configured properly, or if there are problems on the Internet when accessing Web sites, the PC can easily lock up or crash. PCs are highly sensitive to communication problems. When troubleshooting any PC performance or lock up problems, one of the first questions should be, "Were you connected to a LAN or the Internet?"

Study Break: Testing an Internet Connection

This exercise sets up an AOL connection and tests access to the Internet via AOL.

Get a PC with installed modem and AOL software. Use this to set up and verify connection to AOL.

Open the Control Panel and select modems. Test the modem installation by selecting Diagnostics, the COM port with the modem board icon next to it and the modem description beside it. Click more information to display the modem commands, responses and the highest modem transmission speed (it should be 115,200 bps). When this response is received, the modem is working properly. If not, there is likely to be either bad driver software or hardware configuration conflicts that must be resolved for the modem to operate properly. Write down the COM port number to which the modem is assigned.

Install the AOL software using its installation Wizard. AOL software does not use Windows dial-up networking to operate; it contains its own modem control software. The AOL installation process guides you through modem selection and assigns phone numbers for accessing AOL. Let AOL complete the automatic installation process.

If the AOL software cannot detect a modem during installation, the modem may not be responding appropriately. Select a Hayes compatible modem and use the COM port setting of our working modem (or, if the modem manufacturer and description matches any of those on the list, pick it or one that is close to it).

Try to connect. If the AOL software cannot talk to the modem (that is, cannot initialize the modem) we have not reached first base. Go to the AOL setup menu, pick expert setup (it is not for experts but just quicker), select Devices (modems, etc.), choose the modem and select edit. The modem should appear highlighted in a panel. Verify the correct COM port is selected, the speed is set for 115,200 bps, and the speaker volume is loud.

Edit commands and enter in the modem setup string line: AT &F s9=1 ^M. AT means Attention modem, s9=1 means modem detect carrier signal in one millisecond, and ^M means send a carriage return character to the modem. Hit OK and close. Try reconnecting. If the modem does not initialize, we have a hardware or driver configuration error in the PC or a bad modem. If the modem dials the line and connects, we are fine. If the modem tries to dial the line and there is a phone problem, it is likely to return a message of no dial tone. The worst scenario is where the modem dials the number and nothing happens.

If the modem dials the number and nothing happens, pick up the phone and call the AOL access number to verify that a computer is answering that phone and not the telephone recording stating that it is a long distance call.

The goal of this study break was to set up and troubleshoot a dial-up connection to AOL. Similar steps would be followed to test any dial-up connection.

Installing and Configuring Network Interface Cards

The NIC is the interface between the PC and the network cabling. The job of the NIC is to prepare, send, receive, and control the flow of data from the machine. So far the software side of the network has been examined, but without NICs the network does not work. There are many different types of NICs, and only those of a particular type can communicate with one another. This is because they use different languages, called data communications protocols, as mentioned earlier. So an Ethernet card using CSMA/CD cannot talk directly to a token ring card using token-passing ring protocol.

Installing a NIC is like installing any other adapter into a PC. Basically, the PC case is opened and the NIC card is installed in an open bus slot for the type of bus it uses, that is, ISA bus slot or PCI bus slot. It is then bolted into place and the case is closed. Now the fun part begins. Like all adapters, LAN adapters must have a unique IRQ, I/O, DMA, and shared memory areas. Setting these parameters varies from NIC manufacturer to NIC manufacturer. Older cards used jumpers to set the parameters, while others used an EPROM that can be configured using special configuration programs. Most of today's cards are Windows 95/98/Me and Windows 2000 plug-and-play cards.

Jumpers

Some NICs have special jumpers in addition to those that set IRQ and I/O port address. These jumpers tell the NIC which cable type to use and how to configure its driver circuits to operate on that cable. For example, early Ethernet NICs used coaxial cable. They could be configured for a standard cable segment length of 185 meters or an extended cable segment of 300 meters. The 185-meter configuration permitted repeaters while the 300-meter configuration did not. Jumpers on the Ethernet NIC determined the cable configuration.

Some NICs have more than one port that they use to connect to different cable types. As an example, Ethernet cards use three different cable types, each of which has a different type of connector. In some NICs, jumpers determine which cable connector is active. This also can be done using the configuration software that may come with your card. Newer cards use twisted-pair cable and automatically adjust to the cable type and configuration (i.e., 10 Mbps half or 100 Mbps full).

Software Setup

Most LAN NICs today are configured using the Windows plug-and-play configuration software and driver programs that come with Windows 95/98/Me, Windows NT or Windows 2000 Some boards were configured using special configuration software to change IRQ settings and I/O port address settings. These boards were manufactured around the time that the IBM MCA bus was sold in PS/2 systems. Western Digital manufactured several Ethernet boards that were configured in this manner.

Software setup enables the PC's operating system to communicate and control access to the NIC. For the operating system to do this it must recognize and install driver software that communicates with the NIC. Similar to other installed adapters, a software driver program makes the operating system recognize and work with the NIC. Software driver programs must precisely match the NIC installed; the only exceptions are NE1000 and NE2000 NICs. These NICs became the standard to which clone NIC cards were designed and manufactured. These clone boards use generic Novell /Anthem-compatible drivers. See Figure 8–38. Most NICs are now plug-and-play that readily install with Windows 98/Me and Windows 2000.

Windows 3.X Setup

With Windows 3.X Setup for the NICs, the key file is the AUTOEXEC.BAT. In this file, you load the DOS real mode driver that allows DOS to interface with the NIC. A typical statement would be the following:

```
LH C:\NET\NE2000.COM
```

This statement only loads the board driver, not any of the supporting drivers. With NetWare, for example, you must load supporting software as well as the board driver. Additionally, this software must be loaded in a specific order if it is to interface properly.

```
LH C:\NET\LSL
LH C:\NET\NE2000.COM
LH C:\NET\IPXODI.COM
LH C:\NET\VLM.EXE
```

The commands above are used to load the LAN software for Novell NetWare in a DOS or Windows 3.1x client PC. The software loaded is the link support layer (LSL.COM), the Novell NE2000 NIC driver (NE2000.COM), the Internet Packet Exchange open data link interface protocol software (IPX-ODI.COM), and the Virtual Loadable Module (VLM.EXE DOS) client software control program.

An easy and common mistake made when networking with Windows 3.x and DOS is mixing up the loading order of the above LAN driver softwares. When these drivers load they display a message that can help you determine what may be wrong. The only trouble is that these messages display quickly and then disappear. To aid in troubleshooting, put a pause line between each.

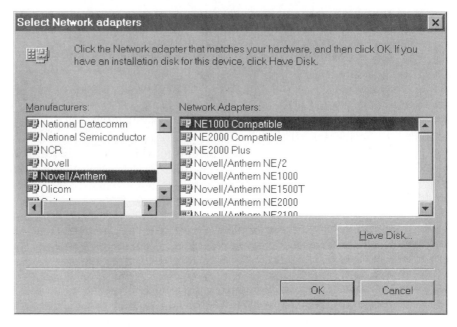

Figure 8–38
Windows 98 Novell/Anthem drivers.

```
LH C:\NET\LSL
pause
LH C:\NET\NE2000.COM
pause
LH C:\NET\IPXODI.COM
pause
LH C:\NET\VLM.EXE
pause
```

When each command is successful the following messages are displayed:

```
LSL.COM:
NetWare Link Support Layer v2.14 (941011)
(C) Copyright 1990-1994 Novell, Inc. All Rights Reserved.

The configuration file used was "C:\NET\NET.CFG"
Max Boards 4, Max Stacks 4

NE2000.COM
Novell NE2000 Ethernet MLID v2.02 (941014)
```

```
(C) Copyright 1991 - 1994 Novell, Inc. All Rights Reserved.

IRQ 11, Port 240, Node Address C07C0017CB L
Max Frame 1514 bytes, Line Speed 10 Mbps, Bus ID 0
Board 1, Frame ETHERNET_802.3, LSB Mode
Board 2, Frame ETHERNET_802.2, LSB Mode
Board 3, Frame ETHERNET_II, LSB Mode
Board 4, Frame ETHERNET_SNAP, LSB Mode

IPXODI.COM
NetWare IPX/SPX Protocol v3.01 (941031)
(C) Copyright 1990-1993 Novell, Inc. All Rights Reserved.

SPX CONNECTIONS 60
IPX PACKET SIZE LIMIT 1500
Bound to logical board 1 (NE2000) : Protocol ID 0

VLM.EXE
VLM.EXE - NetWare virtual loadable module manager v1.20 (941108)
(C) Copyright 1994 Novell, Inc. All Rights Reserved.
Patent pending.

The VLM.EXE file is preinitializing the VLMs.............
The VLM.EXE file is using extended memory (XMS).
You are attached to server MOULTON3
```

These messages indicate that the networking software loaded into DOS and set the PC up as a NetWare client successfully.

Windows 95/98/Me and Windows 2000 installation

Installing adapters under Windows 95/98/Me and Windows 2000 is somewhat easier because it is all done within the operating system, not in configuration files. There are three ways to add an adapter under Windows 95/98/Me and Windows 2000. First, it can be added during installation or by being recognized by the plug-and-play configuration feature (a good reason to use new plug-and-play compatible cards). Second, the add new hardware Wizard can be used to recognize the card and install it (this approach uses plug-and-play technology). Information can still be entered manually, but if it is plug-and-play compatible, it reduces the information that must be provided. Finally, open the network control panel and use the "add adapter" function. See Figure 8–39.

553

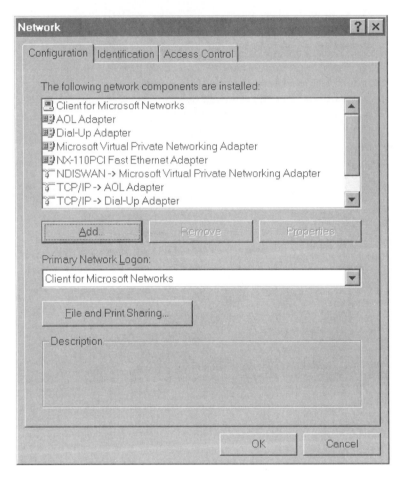

Figure 8–39
Windows 98 network setup.

In all these examples, be sure to have the driver file from the manufacturer. The driver file may not actually be a driver; in fact, many times it is nothing more than an INF file. This information file is used by Windows 95/98/Me and Windows 2000 to determine how to configure the existing drivers to work with the card.

Windows NT Installation

Windows NT is a lot like Windows 95/98/Me and Windows 2000 in that NICs can be installed during Windows NT installation, or by using the network control panel to select the adapter tab, and then the add button. Also, like 95/98/Me and Windows 2000, a driver file and an INF file are needed to complete the installation. Some adapters have software drivers that come with NT. A good thing to note is that a Windows 95/98/Me and Windows 2000 driver can rarely replace an NT driver. It is critical to have the correct driver for the operating system.

Figure 8–40 shows the Add Adapter screen for Windows NT 4.0. Again, be sure to have all the correct settings in addtion to the drivers.

Figure 8–40
Windows NT adapter setup.

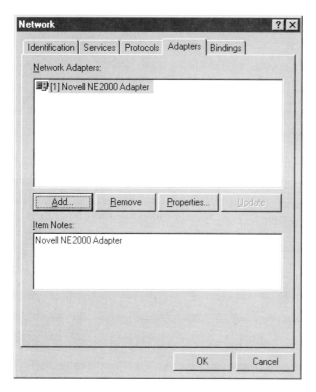

Board vs. IP Address

In PC networks using TCP/IP, there are two addresses that impact the network: the board address and the IP address. The board address is the six character 48-bit universal address encoded on the board by a manufacturer. IEEE issues this Medium Access Control (MAC) address to PC card manufacturers in blocks. The manufacturers encode ROM chips, or Programmable Array Logic (PAL) chips installed on the NIC. The MAC Address allows each board from a manufacturer to have a unique address at the data link layer (Layer 2) of the OSI model.

Network addressing refers to the way the network identifies the node (workstation, server, etc.) as a unique entity. This is the IP address assigned by software as part of configuring the network, i.e., the IP address given a PC by an ISP when it accesses the Internet. A typical IP address would be 208.80.68.70. This IP address is married to the MAC address by TCP/IP software modules. The IP address is assigned at the network layer (Layer 3) of the ISO seven-layer model.

IP addresses are like street addresses. Think of an IP address as "State ID. City ID. Street ID. House number." The four numbers are a similar means to specifically identify each PC attached to the Internet. An IP address identifies something like: "A corporate or regional network. A subnetwork. A server host network. A PC."

Whenever there are duplicate MAC or IP addresses, the cards with those duplicate addressees have problems using a network. MAC addresses only work on narrow segments broken up by bridges or switches, and bridges only work in Layers 1 and 2 of the ISO model. IP addresses work in sections of a network divided by routers. A router functions in ISO model Layers 1, 2, and 3. Each address plays a specific role in networking. The potential problem with networking and both MAC and IP addresses is again, conflicting addresses. MAC address conflicts are more serious than IP address conflicts because the MAC address is burnt into the LAN card hardware and consequently cannot be easily changed. On each segment of a network the MAC address must be unique to the node. It is possible to get two cards from a manufacturer that have the same MAC address. In this case, neither card works properly on the network. Since the MAC address is designed into a physical component, the solution usually is to swap out one of the conflicting boards Token ring cards can use the universally administered address (the hardwired MAC address) or a software-assigned address (a MAC address loaded by configuration software into the token ring board). With such software-assigned addresses, the board would be reconfigured by software. In the early days of the token ring (1987), delivery of token ring adapters stopped for about a month or so because it was said that IBM had manufactured an entire semi-trailer load of token ring boards with the same MAC address.

Network or IP addresses can also conflict. Only one machine is allowed to have a specific IP address; if two machines have the same address, they both have troubles communicating. Getting a new address from a network administrator easily solves this. DHCP resolves this problem by leasing IP addresses to active PCs on a network. This is similar to the IP address assignment performed when accessing the Internet.

Network address conflicts are easier to diagnose, since Windows usually displays a message indicating the conflict. MAC address conflicts are not so forthcoming.

Study Break: Viewing Windows 98/Me Network Configuration

Examine the Windows network configuration to determine the assigned IP address on a Windows 98/Me TCP/IP networked PC.

Find a TCP/IP networked Windows 98/Me PC. Open the control panel and then open networks.

Select the TCP/IP linked to the LAN adapter card. Select properties and record the following:

1. Fixed IP address or Obtained Automatically
2. DNS Configuration—server IP Address
3. WINS Configuration—WINS server IP addresses
4. Gateway configuration—Gateway IP address

Exit the network setup. Go to the START button and select RUN. Enter WINIPCFG and hit Enter. Use the list arrow to the right or the adapter display entry to select the LAN adapter from the drop-down list. Does the IP address and Default Gateway match what you found?

Click on More Info >> Does the WINS server match?

If DHCP is functioning properly and there are free addresses, you should be able to renew all IP address leases. Click on Renew All to see if the lease start time is reset to the current date and time.

This exercise illustrates Windows TCP/IP networking setup and the WINIPCFG simple diagnostic and reporting tool.

Network Problem Manifestations

Networks cause many types of problems, and although PC technical support personnel are not usually expected to solve all of them, it is helpful to understand what problems could arise and how they might be solved. This helps to enhance relationships with clients by providing a broader perspective from which to troubleshoot PC problems. Oftentimes what appears to be a PC hardware problem is really caused by difficulties in the network the PC is attached to. Users have no idea why their machine is saving files slowly when saving them to N: drive. Understanding that it is a slow network may help explain to them what the source of the problem may be.

Reduced Capacity—Bandwidth Loss

The maximum amount of data that can be sent across a network cabling per second is referred to as "bandwidth." This is an indication of the total capacity of the wire and network. Imagine the network as a pipe. The pipe at its best can pass 10 million gallons of water per second. This means that the sources of water all combined cannot send in total any more than 10 million gallons in one second. Networks allow all nodes access to this capacity, but just like the pipe, all of the devices share the total capacity and cannot exceed it. In effect, this total capacity is divided or shared among all devices attached to the network.

When a loss of capacity on the network occurs, PCs usually experience a slowdown in all operations, especially disk drive operations. Disk operations usually have some software looking at the network all the time. Whenever that software looks at a network connection and there is a heavy network load, it experiences long delays; this causes the software to freeze. In the example above, if one of the sources of water uses 5 million gallons per second of the total capacity of 10 million gallons per second, then all other sources now only have a total of 5 million gallons per second to divide up. This hampers their performance and delays all operations requiring water. This capacity tapping can occur on a network, for example, when a bad NIC continuously transmits diagnostic messages or error signals.

Most networks have a network analyzer or some software that can be used to identify where a loss of capacity is occurring. Windows NT has the System Management Server Software, that, when installed and properly configured, can display utilization of the network links connected to the SMS server and other reporting servers. This reports a percent utilization of the LAN. When the utilization of an Ethernet is constantly above 40 percent or a token ring above 70 percent, there are probably congestion problems. Protocol analyzers used by network service personnel also record similar utilization statistics and more. To resolve load problems, bridges or switches are used. These isolate loads to specific segments of a LAN and thus can reduce overall network load.

Data Loss

Another networking problem can be data loss. Since capacity has been limited, it is possible to have your communication time out, resulting in a full to partial data loss during the transmission. It is vital that the offending source be removed from the network, or else many of the users you support could suffer the same fate.

Another cause of potential data loss is from the collision of signals. On a digital network, there can be only one single carrier signal. If two signals exist, they collide, resulting in potential data loss. An occasional collision is nothing to worry about, but consistent collisions can result in a more serious problem.

Ethernet uses repeaters to extend network distances, a function that active hubs perform. Repeaters, while boosting the electrical signal, cause a small delay in the signal propagation across the network. Ethernet nodes must see collisions to know that data has been corrupted. To ensure the Ethernet NICs see collisions, there are minimum and maximum Ethernet packet sizes. When the repeater delays cascade, it is possible with both the minimum and maximum Ethernet frame sizes to have collisions go undetected. It is not easy to configure an Ethernet so that it has undetected collisions, but it happens. Only a few distant nodes in such a misconfigured Ethernet network suffer from undetected collisions. PC users would see these undetected collisions as data loss.

On wiring hubs, there is usually a collision light that indicates collision occurrences. Generally, a red or amber light indicates collisions; if the collision light is on continuously, it usually means there is a cable fault, or another problem. Sometimes it could indicate a network misconfiguration resulting in excessive collisions. A network analyzer can be used to find the potential problem machine. Cable faults are resolved by replacing bad cable with good cable. Other excessive collision problems are resolved by installing bridges or switches in the network. The bridges and switches in essence create multiple networks, isolating collisions to each network on opposing sides of the bridge or switch. When bridges or switches break a network down into sufficiently small network chunks, collisions problems should subside.

Reduced Performance—Slow Networks

Reduced network capacity results in loss of performance. This is, however, not the only reason for loss of performance. What servers are used and how often they are accessed can contribute to slow network response and performance loss. For example, if a company had one server that provided file sharing, email, faxing, and administrative functions, it would be a very busy (heavily loaded) server. The greatest performance loss and longest network delays would be experienced when the server was busiest. To solve these problems, distribute these functions over several servers to improve traffic.

A PC using Windows 95/98/Me Explorer that is connected to a network and has a network drive opened grinds to an inexplicable halt whenever there are significant network delays. Explorer accessing a network connection and waiting for a response from that connection before continuing a requested operation causes this. Furthermore, Explorer or other application software in the PC may have open network connections and may be sending idle or data messages across the network. Network delays caused by performance loss slows down these applications, which in turn cause all of Windows to operate more slowly.

Windows NT and Windows 2000 provide a performance monitor function that records CPU utilization and other performance parameters in a graphical display form. There is similar performance monitoring software for Windows 95/98/Me. With Windows NT and Windows 2000, simply activating the NT task manager and selecting Task Manager provides a graphic display of the Windows NT or Windows 2000 PC's CPU utilization and memory usage. Both of these can help to identify an overworked server or client PC.

Additionally, servers need to be run from the highest performance machines in the office. Slower performance machines can be used, but expect to experience performance loss. By giving the server the most RAM, the fastest CPU, and the Redundant Array of Independent Disks (RAID) fixed disk hardware technology, the server's ability to service network requests is significantly increased.

S u m m a r y

This chapter has described PC networking concepts and some networking software. The key to troubleshooting and understanding PC networking is knowing that all networks are comprised of hardware, wiring, and software components. When a PC is network connected, the connection can make it seem like other PC components have failed, when in fact the problem may reside in the network and not in the PC at all. PC problems in this case must be isolated to the PC hardware, the PC software, or the network.

Chapter Review Questions

1. *What disk is used to COLD boot a PC?*

    A. Setup disk
    B. System disk
    C. Diagnostic disk
    D. Program disk

Answer: B, system disk. While setup disks and diagnostic disks may boot a PC, they are not guaranteed to do so. Program disks permit running application programs.

2. *OSI means what?*

    A. Open System Interconnect
    B. Open System Interconnection
    C. Operating System Interconnection
    D. Open Service Interconnection

Answer: B, Open System Interconnection. OS in OSI is not Operating System or Open Service, but two answers with Open System should give you the clue there. Interconnections exist but not interconnects.

3. *The OSI model has how many layers?*

    A. Three
    B. Five
    C. Seven
    D. Six

Answer: C, seven. Early networking models had three layers. We generally map the seven layers into software, hardware, and channels (wire), but the official number of layers is seven.

4. *A LAN is what?*

      A. Limited area network
      B. PCs and servers
      C. A network operating system
      D. PCs wired together
      E. A local area network
      F. All of the above

Answer: E, a local area network. While a LAN is comprised of PCs wired together (two of the three things needed for a network – hardware and wire) that answer lacks software so it is not LAN. The software alone is not a network without the PCs and the channels (wire). PCs and servers cannot talk to each other without some wire connecting them together.

5. *What are two types of LANs?*

      A. Ethernet and token ring
      B. Local and wide area
      C. Novell and Microsoft
      D. Peer-to-peer and client-server

Answer: D, peer-to-peer and client-server. While a LAN may run Microsoft or Novell NOS over token ring and Ethernet NICs, they are not types of LANS. Wide area networks are not a type of LAN, either.

6. *What type of wiring is found in LANs?*

      A. Twisted pair
      B. Coaxial cable
      C. Fiber optic cable
      D. Unshielded twisted pair cable
      E. None of the above
      F. All of the above

Answer: F, all of the above. LANS use them all but the most popular wiring by far is Cat-5 Unshielded Twisted Pair.

7. *Ethernet operates like a what?*

      A. Star
      B. Bus
      C. Ring
      D. Train with one boxcar

Answer: B, Bus. Ethernet is wired like a star but operates like a bus. The ring and train with a boxcar is the token ring network.

8. *Ethernet is faster than the token ring.*

    A. TRUE
    B. FALSE

Answer: A, TRUE. Ethernet runs at 1 Gbps and soon at 10 Gbps. The token ring is slower.

9. *ATM is a new LAN and networking technology used with PCs.*

    A. TRUE
    B. FALSE

Answer: A, TRUE. ATM and Ethernet are likely to be head to head competitors in the LAN market.

10. *Windows provides what type of software for NICs?*

    A. TCP/IP software
    B. SPX/IPX software
    C. NetBEUI software
    D. Driver software

Answer: D, driver software. Driver software is the software directly interfacing with NICs. The other software provides functions unrelated to the NIC.

11. *IBM developed Ethernet.*

    A. TRUE
    B. FALSE

Answer: B, FALSE. IBM developed the token ring network.

12. *All NICs are what?*

    A. Are PCI plug-and-play cards
    B. Ethernet or token ring cards
    C. Connect to twisted-pair network wiring
    D. Work with TCP/IP software
    E. All of the above

Answer: D, work with TCP/IP software because there are ISA NICs, ATM NICs, and fiber cabling in LANs.

13. *NIC stands for what?*

    A. Network InterConnection
    B. Network Interface Card
    C. Network Interconnection Card
    D. Network Interface Connection

Answer: B, Network Interface Card. Because all answers had network and two (the majority) had Interface and card, the answer (by majority vote) is Network Interface Card.

14. *Windows network protocol software covers which ISO Layers?*

    A. Layer 6, Layer 5, and Layer 4
    B. Layer 5, Layer 4, and Layer 3
    C. Layer 1, Layer 2, and Layer 3
    D. Layer 2, Layer 3, and Layer 4
    E. Layer 3, Layer 4, and Layer 6

Answer: B, Layer 5, Layer 4, and Layer 3. NICs cover Layers 1 and 2 and the layers are covered and continuous (no jumps).

15. *TCP/IP stands for what?*

    A. Transmission Control Protocol/Interconnection Protocol
    B. Transmission Control Protocol/Internet Packet
    C. Transmission Control Protocol/Internet Protocol
    D. Transmission Control Packet/Internet Protocol

Answer: C, Transmission Control Protocol/Internet Protocol. A majority vote says Transmission Control Protocol is correct along with Internet Protocol.

16. *The most popular type of LAN wiring is what?*

    A. Radio frequency connections
    B. Coaxial cable
    C. Fiber-optic cable
    D. Twisted-pair cable
    E. All of the above

Answer: D, Twisted-pair cable. Coaxial cable has all but disappeared and fiber is used for network backbone connections.

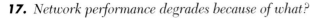

17. *Network performance degrades because of what?*

    A. Servers are under-powered

    B. Excessive or peak traffic on the network

    C. Unusually high collisions

    D. Large file transfers

    E. All of the above

Answer: E, all of the above. All of these use significant network capacity and consequently reduce performance.

Chapter 9

DOS ARCHITECTURE

Chapter Syllabus

- DOS Functions

- DOS Components

- Key System Files

DOS (Disk Operating System) has been the core operating system on personal computers for many years. DOS remains a key PC operating system because it is used to run diagnostic programs, set up fixed disk drives, and provide a means to start the installation of Windows operating systems. Knowledge of some DOS commands and the Windows Startup Disk that boots DOS and facilitates installation and PC hardware troubleshooting is important for supporting PC systems. For example, DOS's 32-bit File Allocation Table (FAT32) can be used by Windows 98/Me and Windows 2000 operating systems to store and retrieve files on very large disk drives. Although less secure than the NT File System (NTFS), FAT32 permits access to disk drives under DOS, enabling DOS diagnostic programs to work on files and troubleshoot PC disk hardware.

The original version of DOS used about 14 KB of RAM in a 1981 PC, and was originally written by Tim Patterson in the late 70s. It was adapted from Control Program for Microcomputers (CPM) and called QDOS, the quick and dirty operating system. To Microsoft and IBM, it became PC DOS 1.0. The most visible difference between the two operating systems was the floppy disk drive A: in PC DOS and C: in CPM. Microsoft bought QDOS from Seattle Computer Products for $50,000 and then licensed it to IBM and the world for up to fifty dollars per PC. PC DOS was released in August of 1981. The three key programs were COMMAND.COM (3,231 bytes), IBMBIO.COM (1,920 bytes), and IBMDOS.COM (6,400 bytes), for a total size of 11,551 bytes. With buffering, it consumed about 14,000 bytes of RAM. DOS 2.0 arrived in March of 1983. Its size had increased to 39,552 bytes. DOS 3.0 followed in August of 1984, just prior to the launch of the 80286 PC AT. DOS had now become bloated at 58,926 bytes. Along with the AT in 1985, PC DOS 3.1 arrived at 60,534 bytes. Other ignominious versions of DOS included DOS 4.0 (not noteworthy), DOS 5.0 (had good memory management), and DOS 6.0. DOS 6.22 was released in May of 1994 and was 133,557 bytes. The last official standalone DOS release was DOS 7.0 in December of 1995 (this was Windows 95 DOS). In contrast, the Windows 98 DOS of today is 317,957 bytes. The size of DOS has increased about as fast as has Microsoft's sales.

DOS is very simple, yet capable of running important diagnostic and hardware configuration programs on today's Pentium-based PCs. It provides not only a platform with which a user can access hardware, manage disk space, and launch applications, but is also very useful as a quick, simple operating system for a technician to load to troubleshoot a system. You cannot run a full version of Windows 95 from a single floppy disk, but you can run DOS and several diagnostics utilities from a single floppy.

DOS has internal commands and functions built into COMMAND.COM, IO.SYS, MSDOS.SYS, and external commands and functions like FDISK and FORMAT. The external commands are separate programs, which accompany DOS and installed in a DOS directory on the fixed disk. Windows builds upon this base by providing a GUI with point-and-click menus and programs. In contrast, entering commands typed on a command entry line operates DOS.

DOS Functions

DOS has evolved over the years, culminating in the current Windows 98 version. The significant (and good) versions are outlined below.

1. **PC DOS 1.0** was the original PC DOS released in 1981. A classic comprised of COMMAND.COM, IBMBIO.COM and IBM-DOS.COM, it supported single-sided floppy disk drives of 160KB capacity.

2. **PC DOS 1.1** was the first revision, issued in 1982, of PC DOS. It supported the much-needed double-sided 320KB floppies. We ran four floppy disk drives on a single PC with this DOS for a grand storage total of 1.44MB. Awesome!

3. **PC DOS 2.0** was the PC DOS for the PC XT released in 1983 that supported the first 10 MB fixed disk and 360 KB floppy disks. We really began to cook then.

4. **PC DOS 2.11** released in 1984 was a revised and cleaned up PC DOS 2.0. We created our first LAN using DOS 2.11.

5. **PC DOS 3.0** released in 1984 supported the first 1.2 MB floppy drives.

6. **PC DOS 3.1** was the PC AT DOS released in 1985. It supported CMI boat anchor 30 MB fixed disk drives in the PC AT. Most CMI drives were defective and failed just after the one year warranty period expired. They made really good boat anchors.

7. **PC DOS 3.2** and **PC DOS 3.3** were basically improvements on PC DOS 3.1. They did begin providing more real mode memory for use by applications by incorporating HIMEM.SYS. HIMEM.SYS probably first came with DOS 3.0 or 3.1, but we really did not begin to use it until DOS 3.2 and 3.3. It was used with disk drive cache and RAMDRIVE. DOS 3.3 was the first DOS sold separately from a PC.

8. **DOS 4.0** was released in 1988. It started the 1.44 MB floppy disk drive support. We think of it as the Joan Rivers (a very yucky yucky DOS) version of DOS. Microsoft began seriously selling DOS separate from PCs with the release of DOS 4.0. In this case, the COMMAND.COM was retained, but IO.SYS and MSDOS.SYS replaced IBMBIO.SOM and IBMDOS.COM, respectively.

9. **DOS 4.01** in 1989 is the PS/2 (Pretty Stupid Computer #2—oops, sorry IBM) DOS.

10. **DOS 5.0** saved us in 1991 and began the serious DOS support of Windows 3.xx. Memory management was a key feature here.

11. **DOS 5.01a** and **DOS 5.02** improved upon a good product and enhanced memory management features for Windows.

12. **DOS 6.0** and **DOS 6.1** were the last great DOS that could be purchased separately from Windows. It provided improved memory management and good disk compression, both of which were sorely needed at the time. DOS 6.0 was released in 1993.

13. **DOS 6.22** was Microsoft's last independent DOS product. After DOS 6.22, all DOS was incorporated into or paired with Windows 95/98.

14. **Windows 95 DOS** is incorporated into Windows to perform part of the boot up process for Windows. It also supports a DOS command prompt operation with the external DOS commands stored in the \windows\command directory. Sometimes this DOS is referred to as DOS 7.0. It retains COMMAND.COM and IO.SYS but MSDOS.COM becomes a text file helpful in the booting process. IO.SYS incorporates many DOS features including HIMEM.SYS functions, SMARTDRV functions and more. Windows 98 DOS came out in 1995 with Windows 95.

15. **Windows 98 DOS** is placed on the Windows 98 Startup Disk. The COMMAND.COM displays Microsoft Windows 98 as the version of DOS.

16. **Windows Millennium DOS** is the current DOS version installed by Windows Millennium on the Startup Disk. The COMMAND.COM displays Microsoft Millennium as the DOS version. Running this COMMAND.COM in Windows 98 or Windows 2000 results in an incorrect DOS version message.

The DOS operating environment handles one program at a time, and DOS performs one function at a time. Its applications can multitask, i.e., print and continue working data simultaneously. The multitasking is built into the application program, not DOS. Windows is a multitasking operating system (or environment). Windows 3.xx performed cooperative multitasking, requiring the operational control of the multitasking to be controlled by both Windows and the Windows applications. Windows 95/98/Me, Windows NT and Windows 2000 perform pre-emptive multitasking; they control the multitasking environment exclusively. While writing this book, we would upload files to the Internet while at the same time continue writing in MS Word.

DOS is a very simple operating environment that requires the application software to perform all special data formatting and input/output operations, meaning that the application programs must provide any special drivers or other software enhancements to use the components attached to the PC. The applications become responsible for a large part of the operating environment of the PC under DOSBecause DOS works on one task or program at a time, it provides an excellent troubleshooting environment for PCs.

DOS can directly manipulate the PC hardware, and this is why it is often used to load and run hardware diagnostic programs. In contrast, Windows programs' direct hardware manipulation is much more restricted and in some cases prohibited entirely. Direct hardware manipulation is limited by the capabilities of the DOS release. For example, DOS 6.2x can only work with FAT-16 disk drives. In order to work with FAT-32 disk drives, Windows 95/98/Me DOS must be used.

FAT is the physical structure that DOS uses to access the data stored on the fixed and floppy disk drives. The entire data access structure is comprised of the directory of files on the fixed disk and the FAT, which points at the allocation units containing the actual data and chains them together to form a series of allocation units (containers) for a file's data.

DOS provides the user and the computer with several key functions. These functions include managing the PC system, managing the disk drive, managing files stored on the disk drive, and launching applications.

PC System Management

DOS is a key tool for managing your system. It comes with a host of small programs, the external DOS commands that control important system functions. For example, MEM is a DOS command that displays a PC's current memory configuration. This is crucial when trying to maximize a PC's memory resources so application programs run more efficiently. It is also used to optimize DOS for running Windows 3.x. Another important DOS utility is the Microsoft Diagnostics Program (MSD). This is very helpful in displaying a PC's current system configuration.

The fact that such utilities are included with DOS, and that it requires little disk storage space, means that most DOS diagnostics tools and DOS itself can be saved on a single bootable floppy disk. This bootable floppy disk itself becomes an important PC troubleshooting tool.

Disk Management

Not only does DOS manage your system resources, but it also has utilities to manage your PC's fixed disk drive. One of the more important and useful utilities is FDISK. FDISK is a utility that you use to create and remove partitions on your fixed disk. The different versions of DOS provide different FDISK capabilities and functionality. Partitioning is only one of the disk management operations that DOS has to handle; there is also formatting, compressing, backing up, and restoring files as well.

The central function of disk management is to subdivide the disk's capacity into manageable chunks that can store the data placed on the disk drive. All disk drives are basically formatted into sectors. Each sector holds 512 characters (or bytes) of data. This sector size is used almost universally on all disks regardless of their total capacity. Sectors are not, however, the basic unit of storage capacity used by DOS and Windows. The disk drive sectors are used in chunks called clusters or allocation units, which may be comprised of 4, 8, 16, or more sectors.

Allocation units are managed using a FAT. Originally, DOS used FAT with 16,000 entries, which is referred to as FAT-16. The diagram below illustrates how the DOS directory and the FAT work together. When files of data are stored on a disk drive, a directory entry and a FAT chain are created, as shown in Figure 9–1. The directory entry contains the number of the beginning allocation unit (or cluster) of the chain of allocation units containing the data comprising the file. The FAT is just a table of numbers in sequence. So location, say, 0025 contains a number pointing to the next allocation unit in the chain. In the figure the file entry points to FAT entry number 102 for beginning cluster (or allocation unit) 102. The 102nd entry in the FAT table contains the number 103 pointing to the next FAT entry and identifying the next allocation unit in the chain of allocation units containing the data on the disk drive. The 103rd entry points to FAT entry 125, FAT entry 125 points to 126, FAT entry 126 points to entry 127 and 127 contains all ones, signaling the end of the FAT chain. The file is comprised of Allocation units 101, 102, 103, 125, 126, and 127.

Actual directory and FAT displays from an old version of Norton utilities are shown in Figure 9–2. The directory entry for IO.SYS points to the FAT table entry of 002, and the directory entry for MSDOS.SYS points to the FAT entry of 019. Following the IO.SYS chain links us from allocation unit 002, to 003, 004, 005, 006, 007, 008, 009, 010, 011, 012, 013, 014, 015, 016, 017, and finally 018. The EOF mark is in FAT location 18 in the FAT table. The next location is location 19, the starting point for the MSDOS.SYS file.

Data is stored on the fixed disk in chains that are one allocation unit right after another. However, as files are modified they grow or shrink. To save them, DOS needs additional clusters. It cannot get them exactly following the original clusters so it just grabs the next available allocation unit to place at the end of the chain. This means that the chains become broken into chunks called blocks. Noncontiguous blocks mean that DOS has the file stored in clusters (or allocation units) that are not next to each other on the disk.

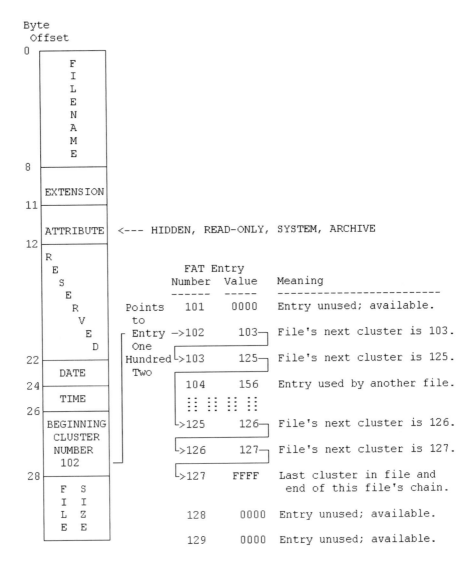

Figure 9–1
Directory and FAT entries.

The 16-bit FAT permitted DOS to store data on fixed disks that had a maximum capacity of around 30 MB. To increase the useable disk size, DOS permitted varying the sectors per allocation unit, which enabled FAT-16 to expand the maximum addressable drive capacity to 2 GB. Thus with FAT-16, DOS and Windows could divide a large disk up into 2 GB partitions and then

573

```
Boot sector and master boot record use allocation units 0 and 1.
Name      .Ext    Size     Date     Time    Cluster  Arc R/O Sys Hid Dir Vol

IO        SYS     33430   4-09-91   5:00 am       2   Arc R/O Sys Hid
MSDOS     SYS     37394   4-09-91   5:00 am      19   Arc R/O Sys Hid
PETE486P 1            0   9-12-91  11:28 pm       0   Arc                     Vol
BAT                   0   9-12-91  11:38 pm      62                    Dir
DISKFIX               0  11-23-91   7:05 am    1583                    Dir
DOS50                 0   9-12-91  11:38 pm      63                    Dir
NOVELL                0   9-12-91  11:38 pm      73                    Dir
PCKWIK                0   9-12-91  11:38 pm    1585                    Dir
PDOX35                0   9-12-91  11:38 pm      70                    Dir
PE                    0   9-12-91  11:38 pm      71                    Dir
QEMM                  0  11-27-91   3:21 pm      72                    Dir
TEMP                  0  11-27-91   3:17 pm      74                    Dir
UTIL                  0   9-12-91  11:39 pm      75                    Dir
WINDOWS               0  12-09-91   9:02 pm     988                    Dir
124       BAT        51  12-16-91   4:40 pm     356   Arc
386SPART PAR   12288000   1-20-92   2:39 am    8145   Arc       Sys Hid
Sector 130
64        BAT        48  12-12-91   7:18 am     561   Arc
80                   48  12-12-91   5:55 pm     562   Arc
```

FIXED DISK DIRECTORY (*OLD* NORTON UTILITIES)

```
Object    Edit    Lin:    View    Info    Tools    Quit                 F1=Help
Sector 1
   --       --       3       4       5       6       7       8
    9       10      11      12      13      14      15      16
   17       18   <EOF>      20      21      22      23      24
   25       26      27      28      29      30      31      32
   33       34      35      36      37   <EOF>      39      40
   41       42      43      44      45      46      47      48
   49       50      51      52      53      54      55      56
   57       58      59      60      61   <EOF>   <EOF>      64
<EOF>        0       0       0       0       0   <EOF>   <EOF>
<EOF>    <EOF>   <EOF>      76   <EOF>   <EOF>   <EOF>      80
   81       82      83      84      85      86      87      88
   89       90      91      92      93      94      95      96
   97       98      99     100     101     102     103     104
  105      106     107     108     109     110     111     112
  113      114     115     116     117     118     119     120
  121      122     123     124     125     126     127     128
  129      130     131     132     133     134     135     136
  137      138     139     140     141     142     143     144
  145      146     147     148     149     150     151     152
  153      154   <EOF>     156     157     158     159     160
FAT (1st Copy)                                          Sector 1
```

FIXED DISK FILE ALLOCATION TABLE (*OLD* NORTON UTILITIES)

Figure 9–2
Norton Utility Directory and FAT display.

store data in those partitions. In the case of 2 GB partitions, 64 sectors of data (32 KB) were assigned to each allocation unit. Such a breakdown was efficient for storing large files, but not small ones. A small file of a few characters (or bytes) would use a single 32-KB allocation unit. Most of the 32-KB allocation unit was wasted space.

The FAT-16 structure is now being replaced by a FAT-32 structure, which more efficiently stores data on the fixed disk. Similar to FAT-16, FAT-32 also varies the sectors per allocation unit. However, because it subdivides the disk into a different overall structure, the sectors per allocation unit increase more slowly than they do with FAT-16. With small improvements, the allocation in unit size can be one sector, or 512 bytes. With larger drives, it increases to four sectors per allocation unit. This is much more efficient use of the disk drive space than seen with FAT-16.

File Management

File management and disk management may seem like the same category, however, they are quite different. DOS provides you with a host of commands and utilities that you can use to manipulate and manage the files on your drive. These commands are discussed later on in this chapter.

The objective of file management is to be able to read and write files in an organized and efficient fashion to and from the disk. To fulfill this objective, there must be a management structure allowing those files to be tracked. This can be a daunting task when thousands of files are stored on a disk drive. DOS organizes your files by creating a hierarchy of directories (or folders). Files are stored in these directories that consist of a list of logical locations mapped to a set of physical locations. This mapping allows DOS to locate, delete, rename, and fix problems with stored files. This hierarchical structure has not changed significantly even in Windows 95/98, which uses an almost identical file storage structure.

This same hierarchical file management structure is employed with Windows NT's NTFS. The major difference between the NTFS and the DOS/Windows file management is that NTFS provides additional management attributes for the directories and files so that they can be shared across networks. However, the hierarchical file structure remains basically the same.

As with any good organizational structure, there are rules as to how those files are stored. For example, the number of characters in a file name and what characters can be used in file names are part of such rules.

For DOS, files are named using the following standard format: The first "NNN" pattern is any combination of up to eight letters and numbers, and the "XXX" designates a file extension of up to three letters. The extension is frequently used to indicate what type of file it is. For example, in the case of AUTOEXEC.BAT, the file name is "AUTOEXEC" and the ".BAT" extension is a standard DOS designation for a batch file.

Besides BAT files, some other common extensions found in DOS and their file types are:

- EXE: executable files, typically programs
- COM: command files
- SYS: system files
- DAT: data files

Managing Applications

The DOS applications architecture is shown in Figure 9–3. Applications communicate with DOS directly through the DOS API. DOS comprises programs that perform system configuration and data management functions, and applications are programs that produce useful information for PC users. For example, XCOPY is a DOS program for copying files, while MSWord is an application for writing books and seminar notes.

This API interfaces to the COMMAND.COM for internal DOS commands and to the external DOS command programs like FDISK, MEM, MSD, etc.The application is responsible for the details of using the video card, printer, and other PC hardware and peripherals.Game programs come with extensive driver software to maximize their use of the PC's display. DOS does provide rudimentary memory management functions (for instance, the ability to load programs into different memory areas to maximize conventional memory) and limited multitasking for terminate-and-stay resident (TSR) programs such as DOSKEY.

DOS facilitates installing and launching applications on PC systems. It is designed to load and execute programs in conventional memory (the lower 640 KB) from a PC disk drive. PC RAM under DOS can be classified as either real mode memory or extended memory. Real mode memory is the first megabyte (plus 64 KB of HIMEM) of RAM addressable when the CPU chip is operating in real mode emulating an old 8088 CPU chip. Extended memory is addressed in protected and other modes; it is all the memory available above 1 MB in the PC. DOS real mode memory is conventional memory (the first 640KB), HIMEM (the first 64 KB over the 1 MB boundary that is real-mode-addressable due to a design flaw in Intel CPU chips—oops, it's not a

Figure 9–3
DOS applications architecture.

DOS Application	COMMAND.COM Internal DOS Commands	External DOS Commands
Circa 1981-1995	**DOS**	

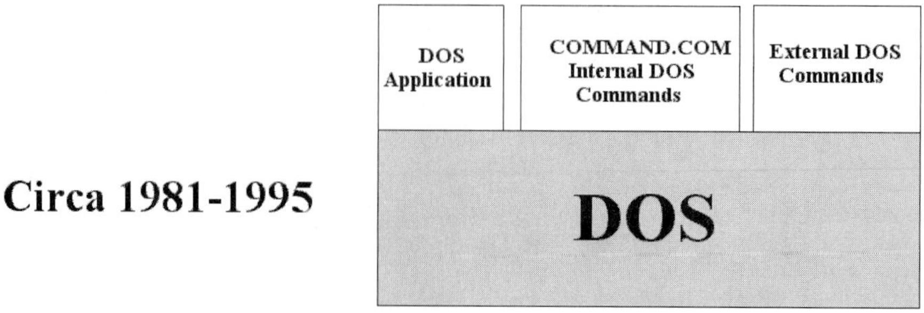

flaw but rather a feature), and finally the upper memory area (UMA). The UMA maps BIOS, VGA BIOS ROM, video paging RAM segments, expanded memory paging RAM segments, I/O card RAM swap areas, and more.

A typical DOS program loads the entire application program into the computer's conventional memory as well as all or some of the data it uses. Depending on the type of program, it may need to access several different memory areas, like extended memory or conventional memory (the lower 640 KB). PC memory management under DOS and the PC memory areas are discussed in more detail in Chapter 13.

Additionally, DOS is the common interface that most of the application programs use to interact with your computer's hardware. For example, a computer game that uses a CD-ROM drive does not communicate directly with the CD-ROM drive whenever it needs to access the data stored on the CD. The game actually passes a request to DOS, which then schedules the processes that have to occur in order to access the CD-ROM drive and transfer data to the application.

Study Break: DOS CHKDSK

Run the CHKDSK command from DOS on a PC with a **16-bit FAT** partition to see what messages you get.

1. Run CHKDSK *.* /V to check the directory and FAT structure of a 16-bit FAT disk drive. It should run through a listing of the files on the drive and finish with a display similar to the following:
    C:\ USER.NEW
    C:\ SYSTEM.NEW
    C:\ DETLOG.TXT
    C:\ NETLOG.TXT
    C:\ NOVLOG.TXT

    2,146,631,680 bytes total disk space
    56,852,480 bytes in 3 hidden files
    6,914,048 bytes in 211 directories
    568,950,784 bytes in 7,074 user files
    1,513,914,368 bytes available on disk

    32,768 bytes in each allocation unit
    65,510 total allocation units on disk
    46,201 available allocation units on disk

> 655,360 total bytes memory
> 505,424 bytes free

Examine the messages displayed.

2. Did you see 655,360 total bytes memory? This is the first 640 KB used by DOS. If the number is lower, the PC possibly has a virus infection.
3. What is the total disk capacity and allocation unit size? For 2 GB drives and FAT-16, the allocation unit size is 32 KB or 64 sectors.
4. Were any error messages displayed?
   > Errors found, F parameter not specified.
   > Corrections will not be written to disk.

This message indicates that there are conflicts between the directory and the FAT. Since we have not yet used the /F parameter, DOS does not resolve those conflicts, it only displays where they are on this fixed disk. After you recover as many files as you choose, you can then run CHKDSK with the /F parameter. It corrects the discrepancies between the FAT and the directory. When this is done, some data on the fixed disk is lost.

5. Did you see a message like:
   > A:\FASTCOPY.ARC
   > Allocation error, size adjusted.
   > No chain for this entry, size will be set to 0?
   This message says that the directory entry size did not match with the FAT size so the size will be set to zero. Helpful, isn't it?
6. Was a message similar to this message displayed?
   > 29 lost clusters found in 7 chains.
   > Convert lost chains to files (Y/N)? n
   > 29696 bytes disk space
   >   would be freed.

This message means that several chains of clusters discovered in the FAT have no corresponding directory entry. These chains are converted to files when CHKDSK /F is run. The files are placed in the root directory with the name FILE0000.CHK, FILE0001.CHK, etc. The FILE00xx.CHK files may contain salvageable data.

7. Did a message similar to this appear?
   > A:\FASTCOPY.ARC
   >   Is cross linked on cluster 255

A:\HDAT.ARC
   Is cross linked on cluster 255
A:\MIPS.ARC
   Is cross linked on cluster 255

This message shows three files all sharing the same cluster. Files are not sharing or caring things. Can this be true? No! What is true here? Two files are bad and one file might be good.

8. Our last potential CHKDSK message is:
A:\FASTCOPY.ARC
   Contains 2 noncontiguous blocks.
A:\HDAT.ARC
   Contains 2 noncontiguous blocks.

This message is innocuous. It shows that files are stored in noncontiguous allocation units. It might mean that we are having reduced performance from our fixed disk drive. This problem pales in comparison to the problems indicated by the proceeding error messages.

9. Find a disk that has been corrupted by a magnet like our Mr. Bill or Super Dave labeled disk. Run CHKDSK /V against it to see some real error messages. Can it recover the errors?

Whenever a DOS or Windows program is exited abruptly, allocation unit (or cluster) chains with no corresponding directory entry may be left on your fixed disk. These chains with no directory entry can eventually congest the disk, reducing space for additional files. It is a good policy to once a week or more perform a CHKDSK /F test for DOS or a SCAN-DISK for Windows of each fixed disk drive or partition on your PCs. When any lost chains are found, they should be converted to files and then erased from the fixed disk.

DOS Components

The architecture of DOS is best understood by examining its key software components. DOS is a software package comprising of several programs. These programs provide services to the user, hardware, and applications.

The user interacts with DOS using the command prompt. The default command prompt is the C:\> with the blinking cursor that appears when you first boot your computer using DOS. Note that you can change the command prompt, but the standard prompt is as described above. We call this the command prompt because it is here where the user can enter DOS commands like MEM or DIR. The command prompt is created by the COMMAND.COM DOS component. COMMAND.COM is loaded as part of the DOS boot sequence, and can be found in the root directory of any bootable disk. The commands that you type in at the command prompt are interpreted by COMMAND.COM and then passed on to the core files of the DOS operating system.

With Windows 95/98, you can open a DOS command prompt in Windows. Similarly, in Windows NT, a DOS prompt window can be opened. These windows are not DOS but rather an emulation of DOS using a COMMAND.COM program. Windows NT does not come with any DOS at all. If problems develop with Windows NT, Windows NT has a special recovery disk that permits booting and repairing an NT installation. Windows 95 and 98 do come with a Windows DOS. Exiting Windows 95/98 and restarting in MS DOS mode enters this DOS.

COMMAND.COM is generally found in the root directory of a bootable disk. This means floppy disks as well as fixed disks. Additionally, COMMAND.COM can often be found in the C:\DOS directory on a hard disk that has the full DOS operating system installed on it. More recent versions of DOS (6.0 and above are a kinder and gentler DOS) permit booting without having COMMAND.COM in the root directory.

The core system files provide the application and hardware interaction of DOS. They are also found in the root directory of your disk drive if it is bootable. Microsoft DOS core system files are MSDOS.SYS, COMMAND.COM, and IO.SYS.

IBM DOS core system files are IBMDOS.COM and IBMBIO.COM. These files receive the commands from either the user or the application and translate them into requests for the computer's ROM BIOS (read-only memory basic input/output system) interface. So when a user types in DIR at the command prompt, the following occurs:

1. The command is interpreted by COMMAND.COM and translated into a form that is useable by the DOS core system files.

2. The core system files in turn translate the request into more detailed BIOS commands.

3. BIOS then executes these detailed commands, activating the various hardware components needed to fulfill the user's DIR request.

4. The hardware, upon completing the requested task, produces the data desired or generates an error message code that is returned to BIOS. BIOS returns the data or error message code to DOS.

5. DOS hands the output results or error message code to COM-MAND.COM for it to display for the user.

6. COMMAND.COM then determines what to display for the user and hands the request back to DOS, which passes it to BIOS, which creates the actual video image displayed on the PC's monitor.

Figure 9–4 shows the interaction between the DOS system components. Applications follow a nearly identical procedure, except that application requests bypass COMMAND.COM and communicate directly with the DOS core system files. DOS then hands the results to the applications program, which creates a display for the user. It is then handed back to DOS and then to BIOS for it to create and display the actual image. In some rare cases applications may talk directly to hardware bypassing DOS altogether, but this is not common.

Figure 9–4
DOS Components and architecture.

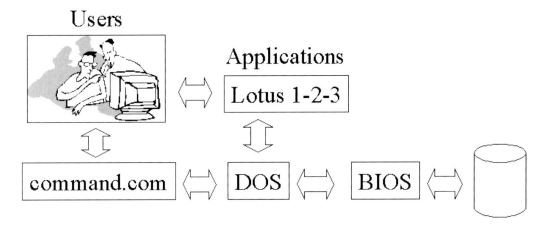

Study Break: Changing COMMAND.COM Locations

This exercise creates a bootable disk with COMMAND.COM on it, then boots from the disk and switches the location of COMMAND.COM.

1. Use FORMAT /S In Windows 95/98/Me to create a bootable floppy disk. Copy the EDIT.COM program to the disk. EDIT.COM can be found in the \windows\command directory.
2. Shut down Windows and reboot into DOS by using the disk. Run EDIT from the disk. Now remove the disk from the disk drive and exit EDIT using ALT-F-X keys. An error message "Not ready reading drive A:" should appear when DOS tries to read COMMAND.COM from the disk. Select the option "Fail" and Windows DOS (the kinder and gentler DOS) should respond "Current drive is no longer valid>." This permits you to specify C: as a valid drive, which should return you to the C:> prompt.
3. Run a DIR command. The directory should display.
4. Run a DIR COMMAND.COM /S command to see where DOS is locating COMAND.COM. It should be found in the root directory and in \windows\command directory.
5. Enter the command SET to display the environment space. This should display the COMSPEC=a:\command.com from where dos tried to reload COMMAND.COM.

This exercise illustrates how DOS searches for COMMAND.COM when an application program throws it out of memory and then, upon exiting, reloads COMMAND.COM.

Key System Files

To better understand the DOS operating structure; let's examine the key files that make up DOS as well as the files used to configure DOS on a personal computer. This goes beyond the three key DOS files COMMAND.COM, IO.SYS, and MSDOS.SYS and covers the function of other key files like HIMEM.SYS and SMARTDRV.EXE. Additionally, you can examine the DOS boot process and how these files work together to create the working environment for DOS application programs. DOS examines those key system files loaded in CONFIG.SYS and in AUTOEXEC.BAT. The commands and examples here generally represent DOS operations. However, different versions of DOS respond differently to these commands, meaning the examples represented here may not work exactly as explained depending upon the DOS version being used, for instance, DOS 5.0, DOS 6.22 or Windows 95/98/Me DOS. More details on DOS commands and memory management are covered in Chapter 13.

IO.SYS

IO.SYS (originally IBMBIO.COM) is one of the three files that make up the core system files of DOS. "IO" stands for input/output. It is a read-only hidden system file, and is located in the root directory of a bootable disk.

During the PC boot process, the cold boot loader program in the fixed disk master boot record or in the floppy boot record loads IO.SYS. It then proceeds to load the remainder of DOS. After DOS has been loaded, the primary job of the IO.SYS is to handle the input/output functions for the PC. It handles the communications needed between the various devices in the PC to perform functions, such as moving data between a PC's fixed disk drive and video card.

MSDOS.SYS

MSDOS.SYS (originally IBMSYS.COM) is the second of the core system files. Like the IO.SYS, it is a read-only hidden system file. Its main job is to break the DOS user and application commands into smaller tasks and schedule them for completion by IO.SYS and a PC's BIOS. For example, a DIR command may be broken down into components that find the directory on the designated disk drive, read the directory information, format it so humans can understand it, and send the output to the video display card and monitor. In this manner, it performs application and file management functions for the PC.MSDOS.SYS provides the API for PC applications and for COMMAND.COM.

COMMAND.COM

COMMAND.COM functions primarily as the command interpreter for user commands. Unlike the first two DOS components, COMMAND.COM interacts directly with user inputs, breaking them down into system commands that are then passed down to MSDOS.SYS and finally IO.SYS. COMMAND.COM also is responsible for the display of the command prompt when the computer is booted under DOS. COMMAND.COM also incorporates many of the DOS commands we use. These commands are what we term "internal commands," since they are part of COMMAND.COM. Below is a list of some of the internal DOS commands that reside in COMMAND.COM. Table 9–1 identifies internal DOS commands.

This is not an exhaustive list of internal DOS commands, just the most frequently used and helpful commands. In addition to internal commands, COMMAND.COM runs external commands, which differ from internal commands in that they are separate program files; internal commands, in contrast, are part of COMMAND.COM. For example, the FORMAT command is a program file called FORMAT.COM. These programs are typically found in the DOS directory of a PC's C: drive. If you are using Windows 95, external DOS commands are found in the C:\WINDOWS\COMMAND subdirectory. Table 9–2 lists some of the DOS external commands. This list is not an exhaustive list, but describes some of the most useful external DOS commands.

Table 9–1 Some Internal DOS Commands

CALL	CD (Change Directory)	CLS (Clear Screen)
COPY	DEL (Delete)	DIR (Directory)
ECHO	LH (Load High)	MD (Make Directory)
PATH	PAUSE	PROMPT
REM (Remark)	REN (Rename)	RMDIR (Remove Directory)
SET	TYPE	VER (Version)

Table 9–2 Some External DOS Commands

ATTRIB (Attribute)	CHKDSK (Check Disk)	DELTREE (Delete Tree)
EDIT	FDISK (Fixed Disk)	FORMAT
MODE	MEM (Memory)	MSCDEX (Microsoft CD ROM Extension)
SCANDISK	SMARTDRIVE	XCOPY

CONFIG.SYS

The CONFIG.SYS file is a system file. Its main purpose is to load drivers used by other devices or applications.

It differs from other system files because it is not a program itself, but rather a list of commands that are executed when DOS is loaded during the PC boot process. CONFIG.SYS does not automatically have read-only, hidden, or system attributes like IO.SYS and MSDOS.SYS do. However, it is possible to assign a read-only attribute to prevent accidental damage to it. In fact, this file was designed as a control structure intended to be altered or customized to suit a particular computer configuration. It can be easily edited using the edit command, the notepad utility, or any other text editor. Although it can be edited or even deleted, this does not make CONFIG.SYS unimportant. This file may be the most important file under DOS. DOS uses the CONFIG.SYS to load hardware driver programs and configure parameters used by applications that run on the computer. A driver program talks directly to the PC hardware. It forms a bridge between DOS (or Windows) and the hardware component. Driver programs know how much buffering a card has, its I/O port address, which IRQs it can use, and more.

The CONFIG.SYS file is only important on disks that are bootable, so you are not likely to find this file on floppies and additional fixed disk partitions. These parameters used by CONFIG.SYS include memory management, environment variables, and special system drivers for services like disk compression under DOS. The CONFIG.SYS should be found in the root directory of the floppy or bootable portion of the fixed disk you are currently using.

If you are curious about the CONFIG.SYS, now is a good time to look at it. Do this by typing at the C:\> prompt: EDIT CONFIG.SYS. The DOS Editor should open and display a file that looks something like the one below. Another way to produce the same result is to enter: TYPE CONFIG.SYS.

```
Device c:\dos\himem.sys
REM Loads HIMEM from C:\dos
Device c:\dos\emm386.exe NOEMS x=a000-c7ff
REM Loads EMM386.EXE from C:\dos
REM Sets type of memory requested to XMS only
REM Excludes UMA Video display area from use
DOS       = HIGH,UMB
Device        = oakcdrom.sys /D:mscd001
REM Loads a CD-ROM device driver and identifies it as MSCD001
Devicehigh    = c:\dos50\smartdrv.sys 2048 2048
REM Loads SMARTDRV and allocates 2MB for disk cache
Device        = c:\dos50\ANSI.SYS
```

```
FILES           = 30
BUFFERS    = 10
Stacks          = 9,256
Lastdrive           = e
REM Sets last DOS drive to E— not networked
```

Okay, this is more organized than most CONFIG.SYS files you find. When performing PC service, it is a good idea to create CONFIG.SYS files that are well organized and that contain documentation on the commands appearing in the file. This way, other service personnel examining the CONFIG.SYS file understand exactly how it has been configured for this specific PC system. Furthermore, they need not search for some long lost DOS manual to be able to properly modify the CONFIG.SYS file. This makes CONFIG.SYS much easier to troubleshoot and read. Neat or sloppy CONFIG.SYS files work just fine with DOS because DOS is not picky about their appearance, only about the structure of the commands within the file.

The job of this file is to load before COMMAND.COM and to configure memory, environment variables, and load any special device drivers. Let's break this file down into its various parameters.

Files, Buffers, Stacks, and Lastdrive

Files, buffers, stacks, and lastdrive are parameters that configure some fairly important areas of your computer. None of these parameters are necessary in a CONFIG.SYS file because there are default values for each if they are missing. Assigning these, however, can have a profound effect on whether certain components may function under DOS.

```
FILES = 30
```

The files parameter indicates to DOS how many file handles it is to keep track of simultaneously. A file handle is nothing more than a pointer to an open file. This affects the system when you are using applications and you attempt to open more files than DOS is set to keep track of. In such a case, DOS would respond with an error indicating you have too many files open. The files setting can range from 0-255. The default value for files is 8, but a recommended value is 60 for Windows. Each file handle uses about 64 characters of RAM.

Logically, you may think that it is best to set this to 255 and avoid such an error. This is, however, a bad practice, because the higher you set this, the more conventional memory is used to track them. This is a problem when you need as much free conventional memory as possible to run a particular application. The approximate 15 KB reduction in conventional memory may be sorely needed. A good range for the files parameter is between 30 and 90.

586

```
BUFFERS = 10
```

The "buffers" parameter, like files, indicates the number of disk buffers to set. Buffers act as a temporary holding place for data as opposed to placing it on the disk. Using buffers accelerates accessing information, since it is found now in RAM instead of on the disk. These buffers are similar to a disk cache program like SMARTDRV, only with far less sophistication and efficiency. For that reason, if you are running a disk cache, your buffers should be set to a number between 10 and 48 because the SMARTDRV and the buffers then all fit into the HIMEM area. If a higher value is set, then the buffers load into conventional memory. Each buffer uses about 532 bytes of RAM. When you are not running a disk cache, set buffers higher, toward 50. Buffers permit setting a secondary buffer cache that can speed up disk I/O for 8086 (antique) CPU chip computers. The syntax for specifying secondary buffer cache is BUFFERS = 30, 6. The number 6 specifies the secondary buffer cache. Windows 95/98 PCs automatically load the SMARTDRV disk cache, so a secondary buffer cache setting is rarely used.

```
STACKS = 9,256
```

Stacks are designed to handle hardware interrupts while an application program is active. Think of them as bookmarks. If you are reading a book and your dog whines at the back door, you get a bookmark and mark your page so that when you return to your reading after letting the dog out, you can pick up where you left off. Programs work the same way when a hardware interrupt is issued. Once answered, the application must pick up where it left off. The stack is used in this case as the bookmark. Most software does not require the stacks; they have their own stack set designed into them. If, however, you get an "Exception Error 12" or a "Stack Overflow" error, you can compensate for this by increasing the stacks variable.

The first variable in the stacks line is for the number of stacks. This can be a number from 0 through 64. Setting it to 0 means no stacks are to be used. The second number sets the size of the stacks. Valid ranges for stack size are 0 through 512 bytes. Again, 0 here would indicate no stacks are being used. As with files and buffers, more and larger stacks use more conventional memory, which may cause problems for programs that require large amounts of conventional memory.

```
LASTDRIVE = E
```

"Lastdrive" tells DOS what the last valid drive letter is. This saves memory so that the "lastdrive" letter is not by default set to Z. On standalone older DOS PCs, the "lastdrive" letter typically defaulted to E. However, if this computer is connected to a network you may have to set it to a higher letter. For example, if you are on a NetWare Network using the VLM shell, or on a Microsoft Windows

Network, the last drive parameter must be set to Z (valid settings range from A to Z). Windows DOS automatically sets the "lastdrive" letter to Z.

"Device =" and "Devicehigh=" Parameters

You may have noticed there are several of these types of parameters in the sample CONFIG.SYS file. The device line indicates that there is a device driver or service-specific driver that needs to be loaded during the boot process. Let's examine more closely the device lines of this CONFIG.SYS file.

The basic DEVICE parameter syntax is:

DEVICE[HIGH]=[Drive Letter - C:][Directory Path] driver-file-name [Parameters for that driver]. This is illustrated in the text on the next line below by pointing to HIMEM.SYS in the C:\DOS\ directory.

```
DEVICE = C:\DOS\HIMEM.SYS
```

This statement is designed to load the memory manager HIMEM.SYS. There is a more detailed discussion of HIMEM.SYS later in this chapter.

If you use extended memory (XMS) for applications, this HIMEM.SYS must be loaded. Windows 3.x always uses extended memory and consequently requires loading this driver. In order to load DOS into upper memory, HIMEM.SYS must first be loaded to activate XMS operation in the PC, then DOS=HIGH must unlock access to the HIMEM area.

```
DEVICE = C:\DOS\EMM386.EXE AUTO RAM X=A000-C7ff M9
```

This statement loads the second DOS memory manger, EMM386. This memory manager is required if you need to have expanded memory (EMS) for an application or if you wish to make the UMA available to device drivers and some terminate-and-stay-resident applications. The parameters that follow the loading of the memory manager specify how it should configure the memory of the computer. We examine these parameters in more detail later.

```
DEVICEHIGH = C:\DOS50\SMARTDRV.SYS 2048 2048
```

This statement loads the disk-caching driver for SMARTDRV. This is actually the device driver for DOS version 5.0. In DOS 6.0 and later, the device driver for SMARTDRV was only loaded from the CONFIG.SYS file to use double buffering for SCSI drives. Caching was initiated by loading SMARTDRV from the AUTOEXEC.BAT file.

You may have also noticed that this statement starts with DEVICEHIGH instead of just DEVICE. This designation is used to load the driver into the upper memory blocks as opposed to the conventional memory DEVICE uses.

If there is no space in the upper memory blocks for the driver, then it is loaded into conventional memory.

```
DEVICE = C:\DOS50\ANSI.SYS
```

This statement loads the ANSI enhancement driver. This driver can be used to define functions that change display graphics, control cursor movement, and reassign keys. The ANSI.SYS device driver supports ANSI terminal emulation of escape sequences to control your system's screen and keyboard. This device driver is rarely used except in a few cases when some applications require it, and can be loaded into the upper memory as well by using DEVICEHIGH.

DOS=HIGH, UMB

This line plays two roles in the CONFIG.SYS file. First, it tells DOS if the HIMEM.SYS driver is loaded into memory it should then load a portion of DOS into the HIMEM area of memory. This can help free up conventional memory for your DOS applications. Second, when using the EMM386 memory manager, it opens the upper memory blocks for the device drivers to use.

This statement can be written in another fashion in the CONFIG.SYS file. In the later versions of DOS, the line would look like this:

```
DOS = HIGH
DOS = UMB
```

Either way is equally effective. We prefer to have fewer lines in our CONFIG.SYS file, so we use the first style of DOS statement. It is possible to force DOS to remain in conventional memory with the DOS=LOW. The DOS=NOUMB parameter can also unlink conventional memory and the UMA. However, there are few benefits to DOS users for doing this so these commands are rarely used.DOS commands and memory management under DOS are covered in more detail in Chapter 13.

SHARE

Share supports file sharing and locking on the PC's disk drives. This is required by some applications that can open many files (and possibly the same file twice) and for network operation. The installation parameter is:

```
INSTALL=C:\DOS\SHARE.EXE /L:25
```

In this example, the /L parameter sets the number of locked files at 25.

AUTOEXEC.BAT

The AUTOEXEC.BAT is a batch file. Batch files contain a list of user commands that are executed when the user types in the name of that batch file. In essence, it is an executable file like a program. The commands contained in it are executed in a line-by-line order, starting with the first noncomment line at the top of the file and moving to the line displayed at the bottom of the display file.

This type of execution can make the running of many DOS commands much easier. What makes the AUTOEXEC.BAT different is that, by virtue of its name, it runs automatically at the end of the boot process. This can be very helpful, since there are many DOS commands you may need to run in order to set your machine up correctly. Just imagine how cumbersome it would be to have to type each DOS command with its accompanying switches and parameters.

To better understand the AUTOEXEC.BAT file, let's dissect a good example of one.

```
PATH C:\DOS;C:\WIN;C:\;C:\PE;C:\UTIL;C:\NET
REM Sets path
set TEMP=d:\temp
REM Sets Temporary storage directory to D: drive
prompt $p $g
REM creates my type of prompt
LH C:\DOS\MSCDEX.EXE /D:CD01 /M:10
REM loads the CD-ROM extension program with 10 buffers
C:\DOS\SMARTDRV.EXE
REM loads disk cache with default values
LH C:\DOS\doskey
REM loads everybody's favorite memory resident program DOSKEY
```

This AUTOEXEC.BAT may look simple, but it contains most of the key commands needed in an average AUTOEXEC.BAT file. If a typical AUTOEXEC.BAT is a bit messier it may be because this file was dressed up for publication in this book. Whenever you install new software, that software may alter a line, add a line, or remove a line from the AUTOEXEC.BAT file. Like the CONFIG.SYS, you should organize it so it makes more sense and is easier to troubleshoot. The other thing to keep in mind is that each of these lines is just a written DOS command. That means you could type each line in at the DOS prompt as you see them here and they would do the same thing. Let's examine the lines of this file.

PATH C:\DOS;C:\WIN;C:\;C:\PE;C:\UTIL;C:\NET

The PATH statement is common in most AUTOEXEC.BAT files. It sets the search path that is used to locate a COM, EXE, or BAT file when it is typed in at the command line. So let's say you wanted to run a small batch file called TEST.BAT; you type that file name in at the DOS prompt and immediately DOS would begin looking for the file. First DOS looks for the file in the directory you happen to be in when you typed in the command. If it is not found there, DOS begins to systematically look for the file in the directories that are specified by the PATH statement. Many times when stymied by an application not running, an investigation will reveal that the application would not run from the DOS prompt because the PATH statement did not specify the directory where the program resided. This being the case, putting every directory in the PATH statement seems like a good idea. One can certainly try, but the number of characters in a PATH statement is limited to 127 characters.

You may see in an AUTOEXEC.BAT file a line that looks like this:

```
PATH=%PATH%;C:\DOOM
```

This is a way to add to your existing PATH statement without rewriting it. The %PATH% is a special batch file variable that represents the entire first PATH statement plus any additional directories that need to be added. The C:\DOOM is the addition to the line. Most installation programs create AUTOEXEC.BAT lines using the %PATH% variable. Virus scanning programs in Windows create an AUTOEXEC.BAT command line that uses the %PATH% variable so they only add to the existing path without altering it.

Normal batch file variables are %1, %2, %3, etc. These are used to enter variable data into batch files. For example, copying data from drive C: to drive D: or E:, could be done by a batch file statement COPY C:\path\filename %1\path\filename. The %1 would be the placeholder for either D: or E:, depending on the designated target drive.

Another way to extend the path would be to use an APPEND command in this file. The APPEND command permits programs to open data files in directories that are different from the directory containing program files. An example of the APPEND command is:

```
APPEND C:\MYDATA;C:\WKSDATA;
```

SET TEMP=d:\temp

The SET command is used to place text string variables in the PC's environment space. The environment space is an area in the conventional memory that is used to store common and frequently used text string variables. It is fast and east for applications to access these variables. Think of it as the 7-11 of PC memory. By typing set and a parameter, you place that parameter into the environment space. Let's take a look at the DOS prompt. Type in "set" and hit the enter key. You should see a display similar to Figure 9–5.

The list that appears contains the user-settable environment variables. Notice that PATH is in there. Okay, let's set another variable. At the DOS prompt, type SET PCID = <YOUR NAME>. When this is complete, type SET again at the DOS prompt and see what happens. You should see the change illustrated in Figure 9–6.

So a variable was added to the environment space; in this case the variable is PCID and its value is Jeremy. The SET TEMP=C:\TEMP specifies to DOS that the directory where it should store its temporary files is C:\TEMP.

PROMPT $p $g

This command is used to set the prompt as it appears on the screen. By default, that prompt is set to the PG parameters. The $P is necessary so the PATH of

Figure 9–5
DOS SET command display.

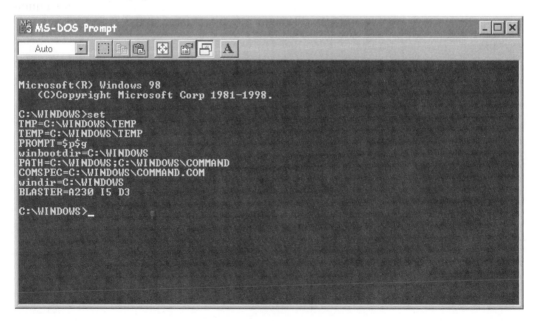

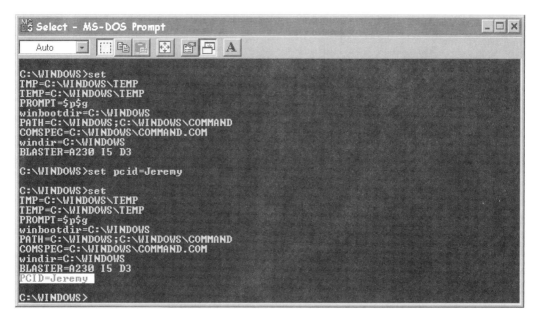

Figure 9–6
Environment space modification from SET command.

your current directory is displayed in the prompt; the $G puts a "greater than" symbol (>) after the path so it does not run into the cursor. There are a number of different prompt parameters you can set, as shown in Table 9–3.

Table 9–3 Prompt Command Special Characters

$Character	Output
A	The & Character
B	The | Character
C	The (Character
D	Date
E	The ESC Key (For invoking ANSI.SYS)
F	The) Character
G	The > Character
H	Back Space, Deletes Character Left of Cursor
L	The < Character

593

Table 9-3   Prompt Command Special Characters (Continued)

$Character	Output
N	Designates Current Drive
P	Designates Path
Q	The = Character
S	Space
T	Time
V	DOS Version
_	(Underscore) Move Cursor to The Next Line

Additionally, you can type in PROMPT followed by anything and it will display that as the prompt. Try it out; type "prompt Turn the page please." In order to create fancier prompts, the ANSI.SYS device driver must be loaded and its special escape sequences used to change the prompt.

LH C:\DOS\MSCDEX.EXE /D:MSCD001 /M:10

This line loads the CD-ROM interface service MSCDEX (Microsoft CD-ROM extension). Your CONFIG.SYS file must have a DEVICE or DEVICE-HIGH command that loads a CDROM device driver.

This driver should come with the CD-ROM, or you can usually get it off the Internet from the CD-ROM drive manufacturer's Web site. Windows 98/Me startup disks have several CD-ROM device drivers, as shown in Figure 9–7. The ASP????.SYS, BT?????.SYS, FLAHPT.SYS and OAKCDROM.SYS are the CD-ROM drivers. The OAKCDROM.SYS is the most commonly used CD-ROM driver for EIDE CD-ROM drives. In the DEVICE line, there should also be a /D:drivername parameter. This parameter is referenced in the MSCDEX line of the AUTOEXEC.BAT. Until this line is executed, the CD-ROM does not function.

The LH at the beginning of the line is an internal DOS command, which stands for "load high." This command tells DOS to load MSCDEX driver into the UMA if there is enough space for it. If there is not, then DOS automatically loads MSCDEX into conventional memory.

Some flags and switches used by the MSCDEX.EXE are:

/D:MSCD001—Identifies the CD-ROM device driver. The driver flag MSCD001 must match the parameter specified by the /D switch in the CONFIG.SYS file.

/M:10—Sets the number of sector buffers to be used by MSCDEX. This may increase CD-ROM performance.

/L:letter—Assigns a drive letter to the first CD-ROM drive. If there is more than one CD-ROM drive, DOS assigns additional CD-ROM drive letters from available drive letters.

/S—Shares the CD-ROM drives on a Windows for Workgroups LAN.

The AUTOEXEC.BAT executes each line in order, meaning means that if you want your disk-caching program to work with your CD-ROM, you must make sure that the line that loads the disk cache program is after the line with MSCDEX.

C:\DOS\SMARTDRV.EXE

C:\DOS\SMARTDRV.EXE runs the DOS disk-caching program SMART-DRV. This program, when loaded, uses a portion of your extended memory for a disk cache. This can increase both the write and read performance of your

Figure 9–7
SMARTDRV Windows launch time in seconds vs. RAM size.

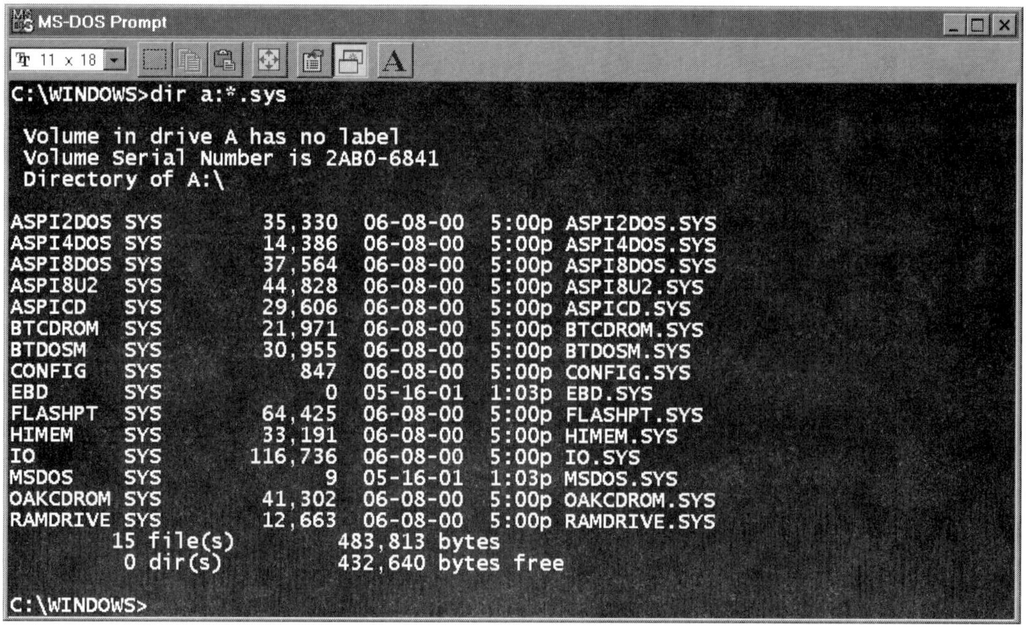

```
MS-DOS Prompt                                                      _ □ ×

Tr 11 x 18 ▾    □ 🗐 🗐 🗗 🗗 🗗  A

C:\WINDOWS>dir a:*.sys

 Volume in drive A has no label
 Volume Serial Number is 2AB0-6841
 Directory of A:\

ASPI2DOS SYS        35,330  06-08-00  5:00p ASPI2DOS.SYS
ASPI4DOS SYS        14,386  06-08-00  5:00p ASPI4DOS.SYS
ASPI8DOS SYS        37,564  06-08-00  5:00p ASPI8DOS.SYS
ASPI8U2  SYS        44,828  06-08-00  5:00p ASPI8U2.SYS
ASPICD   SYS        29,606  06-08-00  5:00p ASPICD.SYS
BTCDROM  SYS        21,971  06-08-00  5:00p BTCDROM.SYS
BTDOSM   SYS        30,955  06-08-00  5:00p BTDOSM.SYS
CONFIG   SYS           847  06-08-00  5:00p CONFIG.SYS
EBD      SYS             0  05-16-01  1:03p EBD.SYS
FLASHPT  SYS        64,425  06-08-00  5:00p FLASHPT.SYS
HIMEM    SYS        33,191  06-08-00  5:00p HIMEM.SYS
IO       SYS       116,736  06-08-00  5:00p IO.SYS
MSDOS    SYS             9  05-16-01  1:03p MSDOS.SYS
OAKCDROM SYS        41,302  06-08-00  5:00p OAKCDROM.SYS
RAMDRIVE SYS        12,663  06-08-00  5:00p RAMDRIVE.SYS
        15 file(s)        483,813 bytes
         0 dir(s)         432,640 bytes free

C:\WINDOWS>
```

fixed disk drives and CD-ROM drives. This line does not have the LH in front of it. The reason for this is that SMARTDRV does not require the LH command to load itself in the UMAs because SMARTDRV is designed to load itself there by default. Like using the LH command, SMARTDRV loads into conventional memory if the UMA is already full. SMARTDRV disk performance depends on the amount of RAM installed in the PC. Figure 9–7 illustrates how optimal performance is achieved with 2 MB of RAM assigned to SMARTDRV.

SMARTDRV can be loaded in both CONFIG.SYS and AUTOEXEC.BAT. When it is loaded in CONFIG.SYS, it enables the doublebuffering operation required for compatibility with some fixed disk controllers. This compatibility ensures proper addressing of sector data on the drive. No real caching is performed in this case. When SMARTDRV is run from AUTOEXEC.BAT, it sets up the disk cache. SMARTDRV can be run from AUTOEXEC.BAT alone without the double_buffering enabled. However, if your PC's disk controller requires double_buffering and it is not enabled, you run the risk of trashing data stored on the fixed disk drive.

LH C:\DOS\DOSKEY

This last command line in the AUTOEXEC.BAT file is one that is not essential. DOSKEY is a DOS TSR (Terminate-and-Stay-Resident) program (external DOS command) that adds additional functionality to your keyboard. Like MSCDEX, you can load this external DOS command into the upper memory blocks by using the LH command before it.

MODE

Mode is a DOS command that sometimes appears in the AUTOEXEC.BAT file. It is used to speed up the keyboard typematic repetition rate, and to set up printing on serial ports rather than on parallel ports. The command for speeding up the keyboard the most is:

```
MODE CON: Rate=30 Delay=1
```

This sets the typematic rate at 30 characters per second and the start delay to 1 second.

ANSI.SYS

ANSI.SYS is device driver software that adds additional keyboard and screen control features to DOS. These features match the specifications created by ANSI. A few old DOS programs required these extended features, but they are generally not required by software today. Some of the screen display features are identified in the prompt command above.

HIMEM.SYS

HIMEM.SYS is one of the two programs used by DOS to manage PC memory. Of the two programs, it is the essential memory manager. Although loading DOS on your PC does not require HIMEM.SYS, using Windows and other DOS applications needing extended memory requires that HIMEM.SYS be loaded.

HIMEM.SYS controls the memory above 1,024 KB in your computer. This memory manager provides access to two areas of memory in your computer. The first area is the XMS and the second is the HIMEM area, which is the first 64 KB of memory above 1,024 KB. As we discuss later in Chapter 13, HIMEM is a key memory management program because all memory above 1,024 KB is basically managed by HIMEM.SYS.

The HIMEM area and EMS are created from XMS. When the following statement in the CONFIG.SYS file accompanies HIMEM, DOS loads a large portion of itself into the HIMEM area.

```
DOS=HIGH
```

HIMEM.SYS also manages the rest of your memory from 1,088 KB to your maximum amount of XMS. Windows 3.x can run on systems that use only extended memory and the HIMEM area.

EMM386.EXE

EMM386.EXE is the second of the DOS memory managers. Its job is to provide access to UMAs, which are divided into upper memory blocks (UMBs), and to emulate EMS in XMS. EMS was required for some older DOS and Windows 3.x programs. If you do not need EMS, the EMM386.EXE memory manager also provides access to the UMBs when using the following line in the CONFIG.SYS.

```
DOS=UMB
```

UMBs permit DOS to load device drivers and other software into the UMA. This can provide more conventional memory for use by DOS programs. The DOS programs that use the largest amounts of conventional memory are typically game programs. It is possible to configure EMM386 to function without creating any EMS in XMS. This is done using the switch setting NOEMS when you put the DEVICE line in the CONFIG.SYS file for EMM386.EXE.

Study Break: Examining CONFIG.SYS and AUTOEXEC.BAT

Examine the CONFIG.SYS and AUTOEXEC.BAT file on your PC.

1. Open a DOS Window on your PC. Enter DIR CONFIG.* /S at the C:\ root directory. This should list any old and current copies of CONFIG.SYS. If there is no CONFIG.SYS, try using CONFIG.DOS or another CONFIG file.
2. EDIT the CONFIG file by entering EDIT CONFIG.SYS. This should launch the DOS editor and load CONFIG.SYS into it.
3. Open a second DOS window. Now identify the commands used in CONFIG.SYS and, in the second DOS window, enter HELP followed by the command name. For example, HELP LASTDRIVE. Follow the help menu to understand the options set for the command.
4. Perform the same procedure using AUTOEXEC.BAT in place of CONFIG.SYS.
5. Are there any commands that have options that look helpful? Try this one. In a DOS Window enter PROMPT $p $g. Does the prompt change? Try PROMPT $D $p $g. What happens? Try also PROMPT $D $T $p $g. What happens?

This exercise illustrates some of the CONFIG.SYS and AUTOEXEC.BAT file command options.

Summary

This chapter has covered the DOS operating system fundamentals. The three main sections in this chapter focused on functions, components, and key system files used in this operating system. The first section, on DOS functions, provided a detailed view of file, disk, and PC system and application management topics. The next section provided a brief introduction to DOS components, which led directly to the final section that covered important DOS system files and their purpose and use. Separate discussions on each significant file provided detail on the function of the file and its characteristics.

Chapter Review Questions

1. *How is CONFIG.SYS used?*

    A. It loads DOS.
    B. It loads MSCDEX.EXE.
    C. It matches PC hardware to DOS.
    D. It loads .SYS files.

Answer: C, it matches PC hardware to DOS. The CONFIG.SYS file does not load DOS but helps DOS load device driver programs that match PC hardware to DOS. MSCDEX.EXE is loaded in AUTOEXEC.BAT. CONFIG.SYS does load .SYS files but it does other DOS configuring functions as well.

2. *How is AUTOEXEC.BAT used?*

    A. It starts TSR and other programs frequently used by PC operators.
    B. It loads and starts DOS.
    C. It starts EMM386.EXE.
    D. It manages the HIMEM area.

Answer: A., it starts TSR and other programs frequently used by PC operators. DOS is loaded using the hardware BIOS, IO.SYS, CONFIG.SYS, and AUTOEXEC.BAT. EMM386.EXE is started by CONFIG.SYS. HIMEM is managed by the HIMEM.SYS program loaded by CONFIG.SYS.

3. *What commands are not in CONFIG.SYS?*

    A. Device=
    B. Devicehigh=
    C. Files=
    D. SET

Answer: D, SET. CONFIG.SYS contains Device=, Devicehigh=, or Files= commands, but no DOS prompt commands like SET.

4. *When a command is entered at the DOS prompt, what program starts processing it?*

    A. IO.SYS
    B. COMMAND.COM
    C. MSCDEX.EXE
    D. HIMEM.SYS

Answer: B, COMMAND.COM. IO.SYS loads DOS and handles IO operations. In Windows DOS, DOS itself is IO.SYS. MSCDEX.EXE is the CD-ROM DOS interface program. HIMEM.SYS manages the HIMEM and XMS memory.

5. *What command formats a disk drive and makes it bootable?*

    A. SYS
    B. FORMAT /B
    C. FORMAT
    D. FORMAT A: /S

Answer: D, FORMAT. A: /S formats the A: drive and makes it bootable. SYS transfers the operating system to the target drive. There is no FORMAT /B and FORMAT alone does not make a drive bootable.

6. *How is DRIVER.SYS used in a CONFIG.SYS file?*

    A. To install more than two floppy drives
    B. To permit more drivers to follow
    C. Both A and B
    D. None of the Above

Answer: D, none of the above. DRIVER.SYS was used to modify floppy diskette configuration parameters.

7. *What is the drive letter of the second DOS partition?*

    A. C:
    B. D:
    C. E:
    D. F:

Answer: B, D:. The first DOS partition is assigned the drive letter C; the next partition is assigned the drive letter D.

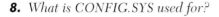

8. *What is CONFIG.SYS used for?*

    A. It loads DOS.

    B. It loads SMARTDRV.EXE.

    C. Loads hardware drivers and memory management programs. Configures DOS to the PC hardware.

    D. It loads DOS parameters.

Answer: C, loads hardware drivers and memory management programs. Configures DOS to the PC hardware. The CONFIG.SYS file does not load DOS but helps DOS load device driver programs that match PC hardware to DOS. SMARTDRV.EXE is loaded in AUTOEXEC.BAT. CONFIG.SYS does load DOS parameters but it does load other DOS driver programs (.SYS) as well.

9. *What is AUTOEXEC.BAT used for?*

    A. It loads MSCDEX

    B. Loads added software, e.g., DOSKEY to custom configure DOS operation.

    C. It sets DOS operating parameters using the SET command

    D. All of the Above

    E. None of the Above

Answer: D, all of the Above. AUTOEXEC.BAT loads MSCDEX and added software, e.g., DOSKEY to custom configure DOS operation. It also sets DOS operating parameters using the SET command.

10. *What commands are not found in CONFIG.SYS?*

    A. DEVICE=, DEVICEHIGH=, SMARTDRV.EXE

    B. FILES=, LASTDRIVE=, HIMEM.SYS

    C. MODE, DOSKEY, MSCDEX

    D. EMM386.EXE, SHARE.EXE, BUFFERS=

Answer: C, MODE, DOSKEY, MSCDEX CONFIG.SYS uses DEVICE= and DEVICEHIGH= to load hardware device drivers. SMARTDRIVE.EXE, HIMEM.SYS and EMM386.EXE are programs loaded by CONFIG.SYS to configure disk caching and to manage PC memory. FILES=, LASTDRIVE=, BUFFERS= are used in CONFIG.SYS to set DOS operating parameters.

11. *Commands typed at the DOS prompt are acted on by what?*

    A. COMMAND.COM

    B. IO.SYS

    C. MSDOS.SYS

    D. HIMEM.SYS

Answer: A, COMMAND.COM. IO.SYS loads DOS and handles IO operations (in Windwos 95/98/ME IO.SYS is DOS), MSDOS.SYS is DOS which schedules programs for execution to perform the commands processed by COMMAND.COM. HIMEM.SYS manages PC memory.

12. *What command formats a drive and installs DOS?*

    A. FDISK
    B. FORMAT
    C. FORMAT /D
    D. FORMAT /B
    E. FORMAT /S

Answer: E, FORMAT /S FDISK partitions disks. Format alone does not install DOS. There is no /D or /B parameters for FORMAT.

13. *MSDOS boots in which sequence?*

    A. IO.SYS, MSDOS.SYS, COMMAND.COM, CONFIG.SYS, AUTOEXEC.BAT
    B. MSDOS.SYS, IO.SYS, COMMAND.COM, CONFIG.SYS, AUTOEXEC.BAT
    C. COMMAND.COM, IO.SYS, MSDOS.SYS, CONFIG.SYS, AUTOEXEC.BAT
    D. IO.SYS, MSDOS.SYS, CONFIG.SYS, COMMAND.COM, AUTOEXEC.BAT

Answer: D, IO.SYS, MSDOS.SYS, CONFIG.SYS, COMMAND.COM, AUTOEXEC.BAT IO.SYS first loads and proceeds to load the remaining programs and files needed to start DOS. MSDOS is the DOS scheduling program and the second file to load. Next CONFIG.SYS is used to load device driver programs, then COMMAND.COM is loaded and in turn processes the commands in AUTOEXEC.BAT.

14. *Which of these does each FAT entry use?*

    A. Cluster
    B. Sector
    C. Byte
    D. Track
    E. Allocation Unit

Answer: E, allocation unit, or A, Cluster. Although every disk is divided into sectors, the FAT combines sectors into allocation units, which it manages. A Byte is 8-bits or a single piece of information on the disk. Tracks are the areas on the disk that contain the sectors.

15. *Which command removes a directory and all of its contents?*

    A. RMDIR
    B. RD
    C. DEL
    D. DELTREE

Answer: D, DELTREE. DEL only deletes files in the current directory. RD and RMDIR remove empty directories.

16. *What is the size limit of a DOS primary or extended partition logical drive?*

    A. 4 GB
    B. 1GB
    C. 504 MB
    D. 2 GB

Answer: D, 2 GB. Both 504 MB and 1 GB are too small, and 4 GB is too large.

17. *Which files are placed on a fixed disk drive by running the FORMAT /S command in DOS 6.22?*

    A. IO.SYS, MSDOS.SYS, and COMMAND.COM
    B. IO.DOS, MSDOS.DOS, and COMMAND.COM
    C. COMMAND.COM, AUTOEXEC.BAT, and CONFIG.SYS
    D. MSDOS.SYS, CONFIG.SYS, and COMMAND.COM

Answer: A, IO.SYS, MSDOS.SYS, and COMMAND.COM. There is no IO.DOS or MSDOS.DOS. AUTOEXEC.BAT and CONFIG.SYS are not mandatory files for DOS to boot, while IO.SYS, MSDOS.SYS and COMMAND.COM must be on the disk for DOS to boot.

18. *Memory above 1 megabyte is what?*

    A. High memory
    B. Expanded memory
    C. Upper memory
    D. Base memory
    E. Extended memory

Answer: E, extended memory. XMS is best, but B, expanded memory, is also correct. There is no base memory. High memory could be the HIMEM area but there is not high memory per se. Upper memory is between 640 KB and 1 MB.

19. *The clusters that make up a single file on a fixed disk drive are called what?*

        A. A chain
        B. A fragment
        C. A sector
        D. A track

Answer: A, a chain. A file may be fragmented but there are no fragments. Sectors are the first level division of the bytes stored on the disk, and tracks are the areas of the disk where sectors reside.

Chapter 10

WINDOWS 3.X ARCHITECTURE

Chapter Syllabus

- Windows 3.x Functions

- Windows 3.x Components

- Windows 3.x Key System Files

Windows 3.x is no longer part of the objectives of the A+ exam. However, the concepts developed and implemented in Windows 3.x are found throughout Windows 95/98/Me and Windows NT/2000. Consequently, the concepts and terminology presented in this chapter may help answer a question or two on the A+ exam. This chapter also explains how Windows evolved from DOS to Windows 3.x to Windows Me. It helps explain why Windows 2000 and Windows NT are different from Windows 95/98/Me.

Windows 3.x is an operating system that utilizes many of the DOS components. It augments DOS by adding an easy-to-use GUI and a multitasking kernel (KRNL) that provides the ability to use more than one application at the same time and supports virtual memory operation. This chapter examines the functions, components, and key system files of Windows 3.x. To understand how Windows 3.x and DOS work together, you first need to examine a typical PC that has both Windows 3.x and DOS installed. Windows 3.x modifies DOS to provide:

- A GUI
- Access to XMS and EMS for applications
- Virtual memory for applications machines
- Cooperative multitasking that permits (to a limited extent) multiple functions running simultaneously on the same PC

The popularity of Windows 3.x lies in its ability to make a graceful transition from the DOS command line to the Windows 3.x graphical environment. Furthermore, Windows 3.x standardizes to some extent the interface for all users. Consequently, once you have used one Windows 3.x application, it is easy to learn another.

The basic structure of Windows 3.x is:

- The GUI supporting the display, keyboard, and mouse
- The Windows' API and its Windows 3.x extensions
- The dynamic link libraries (DLLs)
- The kernel that modifies DOS
- The memory managers

Windows 3.x rests on a foundation created by DOS. The key to successful Windows 3.x operation is to configure DOS optimally. In this case, optimally means reliable operation with Windows 3.x, rather than maximizing the amount of conventional PC memory (we discuss this in more detail later).

One last note—the DOS configuration commands go hand-in-hand with Windows 3.x because Windows 3.x relies on DOS components to perform some functions. Thus, understanding the functions, components, and key files of DOS is also essential for Windows 3.x troubleshooting.

Windows 3.x Functions

Since Windows 3.x is an operating system that uses DOS components and provides a GUI, DOS is not used to manage the same functions examined in the Chapter 9. Windows 3.x can perform, for example, disk caching, when 32-bit disk access and file access are activated.

Windows-specific applications perform file, application, and print management. For example, the Windows 3.x file manager (WINFILE) performs file management tasks, while the program manager (PROGMAN) manages applications.

These applications then communicate with the appropriate DOS component or, in some cases, with the hardware, after being passed through Windows 3.x components. Just like DOS, Windows 3.x does not understand the word FORMAT but the Windows 3.x file manager talks with BIOS to perform the FORMAT function. Or, in a DOS window, FORMAT communicates with BIOS via Windows. Windows 3.x also has multiple components performing similar translations for Windows. For example, Windows 3.x WRITE must send data to a printer. In this case, just as the file manager talks with BIOS, WRITE communicates with BIOS to send data to the printer.

Figure 10–1 illustrates this GUI/operating system breakdown. The diagram shows the interaction of DOS and Windows 3.x components.

Windows 3.x manages the system resources for application programs. The GUI comprises USER.EXE and GDI.EXE. They in turn use driver programs for the display (VGA.DRV), the keyboard (KEYBOARD.DRV), and the mouse (MOUSE.DRV). The GUI uses a data area that is 64 K (referred to technically as a heap, like a heap of data, or a heap of garbage—oftentimes with Windows 3.x one seems exactly like the other). When you measure your available resources (click on help and then click on "about program manager"), this is one of the parameters measured.

Below the GUI are the applications with their dynamic link libraries (DLLs) tailoring them to the Windows 3.x environment and thus to the PC hardware components.

DOS and the Windows 3.x kernel coordinate activities in the system. They use special programs to manage RAM (HIMEM and EMM386), disk access (SMARTDRV), printers (HPPCL.DRV for HP LaserJet and compatibles), and the network (VNETWARE.386). IPX and NETx are still required, along with Windows 3.x VNETWARE.386, to have the workstation access the network through Windows.

To make Windows 3.x work effectively with your PC, you need to know the key program players. Those players are the DOS memory management programs, the disk cache programs, and the network programs. Novell's programs are IPX, NETx, VNETWARE.386, and VIPX.386. The remaining programs are important for understanding Windows, but are less directly involved in making it work. Making Windows 3.x perform reliably requires knowledge of Windows 3.x operating structure and, in particular, its memory management structure.

DOS driver programs are used by Windows 3.x to control the hardware directly, just as they do for DOS. The Windows 3.x kernel (KRNL) provides the scheduling and cooperative multi-tasking capabilities. Other Windows 3.x

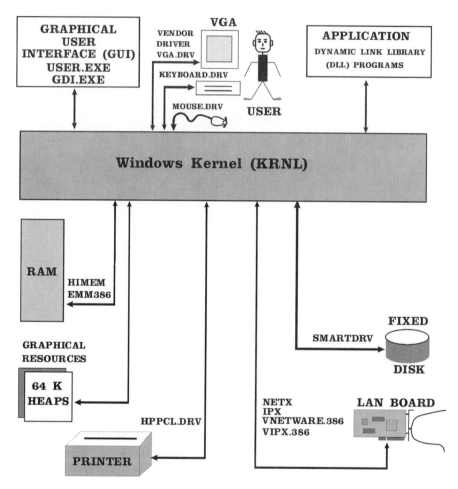

Figure 10–1
Windows 3.x architecture.

components provide the GUI (GDI.EXE and USER.EXE) and implement Windows 3.x applications (the application dynamic link libraries—DLL and EXE program components). They run through the kernel and the DOS drivers to provide the fancy VGA displays for the PC user.

Let's examine the Windows 3.x applications that provide the management functions.

Managing Applications

Windows 3.x is designed to handle 16-bit applications. Under Windows 3.0, applications were designed to run in a 16 MB address spaceso they could run on 80286 CPU chip systems. The 80286 and many of the 80386 SX CPU chips could only address a maximum of 16 MB. There was little need for Windows 3.x to be capable of working with more RAM.

This address space is implemented using virtual memory. In Windows 3.1, this address space was increased to the 4 GB address space used by both Windows 95/98/Me and Windows NT. Most Pentium CPU chips are capable of addressing 4 GB of RAM, maximum. Hence, just as Windows 3.x is limited to 16 MB, Windows 95/98/Me and NT address 4 GB of memory, but Windows 2000 may address 64 GB RAM. Such large memory address spaces are rarely fully used.

Any unused virtual memory is a combination of XMS and swapfile storage on the PC's fixed disk drive. Windows 3.x supports and manages virtual memory access for all applications.

This is a necessity, not simply a nicety, because many systems running Windows 3.x had small amounts of RAM (2 or 4 M). Simply starting Windows 3.x on a PC requires about 1.5 MB disk space for swapping, even if it is a 16 MB RAM system.

Windows 3.x substitutes disk space for RAM for both programs and data. See Figure 10–2.

When Windows 3.x started, its 1.5 MB disk space was for program swapping to the disk drive, and not for data. There may be lots of space used for temporary data swapping, depending on the software you are running. There are TIFF (*.TIF) files that contain high-resolution scanned graphic images which can easily be about 1 MB alone. Try placing a few of those images on a single desktop publishing page and see how Windows 3.x slows to a crawl on that page.

When Windows 3.x runs out of space in any of the disk areas it uses, bad things happen. Consequently, picking a good strategy for providing Windows 3.x with ample disk swapping space is important for reliable and effective operation.

The options for Windows 3.x disk space files are a temporary swapfile, a permanent swapfile, or no swapfile. Running with 64 MB RAM or more? Try the no swapfile option for fun. It could speed up Windows 3.x because there is less of a need for Windows 3.x to swap data to disk. To set this up, select the Windows 3.1x control panel, then 386 enhanced mode, then virtual memory and change. The drop-down panel permits changing the swapfile type and specifying its size.

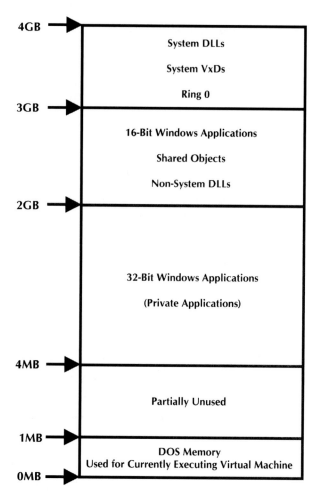

Figure 10–2
Windows 3.x memory
usage.

Temporary Swapfile

The temporary swapfile that grows and shrinks as determined by available disk space is WIN386.SWP. It appears when you start Windows 3.x and is removed by Windows 3.x upon exiting. To see it, open a Windows 3.x DOS box and perform DIR on C:\WINDOWS. A better way to handle program swapping for Windows 3.x is to use a permanent swapfile.

Permanent Swapfiles

Windows 3.x can use a permanent swapfile for program storage. This file is named:

```
386SPART PAR 12288000 1-21-92 5:48p HSA
```

The 386SPART.PAR file is located in the root directory of the drive you specify when it is created. The drive must be one of the physical disk drives on your system. Network and RAM disk drives cannot be used for 386SPART.PAR. This file must be placed in contiguous locations on the disk drive. When you create a permanent swapfile, defragment your disk drive with DOS 6.0-6.2 DEFRAG, Norton's SPEEDISK, or PCTOOLS compress.

To create a permanent swapfile in Windows 3.0:

1. Click on the Windows 3.x file menu selection.
2. Run SWAPFILE. This only works when Windows 3.x is in real operating mode.

To start Windows 3.x in real mode, type WIN /R.
To create a Windows 3.1 swapfile:

1. Use the control panel 386 enhanced menu selection.
2. Select Change Virtual Machine Settings.
3. Create a permanent swapfile that is about 4 MB to 8 MB (when possible).

It was once rumored that only a small permanent swapfile is required for Windows. We tried operating with a 1 MB swapfile, but discovered that this degraded Windows 3.x performance. Heavy Windows 3.x users may require a larger swapfile.

Data Swapping

The data swapping area is specified in the SET C:\TEMP statement in the AUTOEXEC.BAT file. It should point at a disk drive (volume) that has plenty of free space. Windows 3.x applications that run out of data space usually give the unrecoverable application error or general protection fault messages or other equally bad responses to the user.

As an exercise, go into the 386 enhanced section of the control panel. From the 386 enhanced section, click on the Virtual Memory button and review the different virtual memory settings.

Applications Architecture

DOS applications, in contrast to Windows 3.x applications, are designed to operate in conventional memory (the lower 640 KB). As a result, the Windows 3.x application architecture created both a Windows 3.x system virtual machine (which we refer to as a Windows 3.x virtual machine) and DOS virtual machines.

Figure 10–3 shows the Windows 3.x application architecture with the Windows 3.x virtual machine (Windows 3.x system virtual machine). The Windows 3.x system virtual machine (or Windows 3.x virtual machine) ran all the Windows 3.x 16-bit applications, performing cooperative multi-tasking between them. The problem here is that when one Windows 3.x application crashed, this typically crashed the Windows 3.x system virtual machine as well. DOS applications run in separate DOS virtual machines, not in a single virtual machine. So when a DOS application crashed, it was less likely to crash all of Windows 3.x because it was more isolated from the other Windows 3.x applications.

With the release of Windows 3.1x, the operation of the Windows 3.x system virtual machine (or Windows 3.x virtual machine) was altered to make it more resilient. This alteration had Windows 3.x watch the applications more carefully to spot potential memory conflicts. When they were spotted, Windows 3.x issued a general protection fault, hopefully permitting the PC user to shut down the offending application without killing the entire Windows 3.x system virtual machine. While not foolproof, this did improve Windows 3.x reliability.

Figure 10–3
Windows 3.x application architecture.

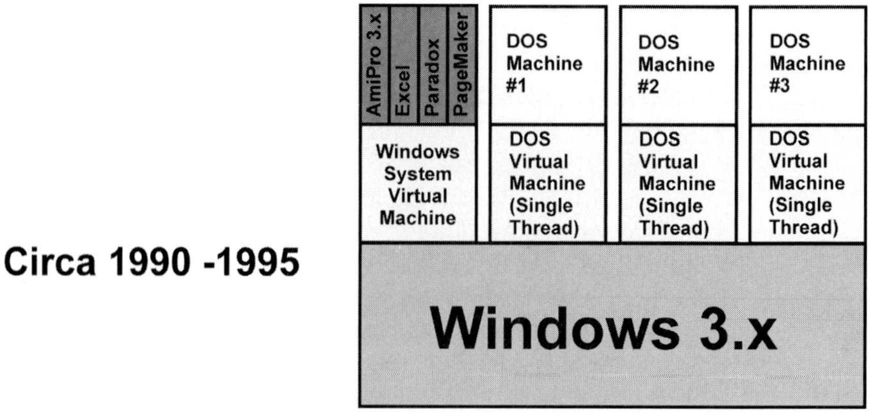

The main user interface for Windows 3.x is the desktop. The desktop is the area that encompasses the entire screen. Applications icons reside in this area. The default interface for the desktop is the program manager. The program manager assigns each application executable (EXE) an icon to provide a standardized user interface. These icons are then organized into program groups.

Figure 10–4 shows the program manager with program groups and application icons. The program manager is not the heart of the GUI but rather the user interface into the GUI. It is specified by the shell= statement in the [boot] section of the SYSTEM.INI file.

You can substitute other programs in this line and have them start as the user interface to Windows. For example, try using WINFILE.EXE, the executable file for the file manager under Windows. In this case, when you start Windows, the file manager becomes your user interface.

Just as the program manager is not the heart of Windows, icons used to represent programs are only markers of actual executable programs. When you double-click on an icon, it tells Windows 3.x to load and run the executable file, much like DOS does when you type the name of the executable at the command prompt. The icon properties are shown in Figure 10–5. To see how this works, go to the icon for the file manager and select it by single-clicking on the icon. Now simply hit the Alt + Enter keys to view the icon properties. Alternatively, after clicking on the icon, you can go to the file menu and select

Figure 10–4
Program manager Groups and Icons.

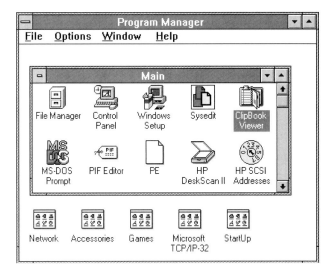

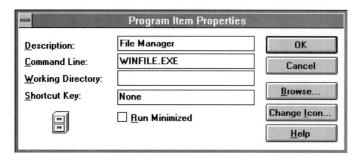

Figure 10–5
File manager icon properties.

properties. You should see a window that pops up that allows you to edit information about the program.

The file properties can be changed to point to a different location for the program using the browse button; the icon representing the program can also be changed by selecting the change icon button. Other properties are available to specify a working directory or a shortcut key for the program, or to run the program minimized. Running a program minimized makes it appear as a small icon on the Windows 3.1 desktop; when it is launched, it does not jump up in a window or full screen. Assigning a shortcut key provides a means to launch the program without using the mouse. In this instance, a key combination can be used to run the program.

Managing Disks and PC Components

Disk management under Windows 3.x is performed using the DOS FDISK program. FORMAT is incorporated into the Windows 3.x file manager, but it is largely DOS dependent. Similarly, other PC components are managed using the driver programs that were run under DOS and that used the PC's ROM BIOS.

Windows 3.x began to move away from such DOS dependency with the implementation of 32-bit disk access and 32-bit file access with Windows 3.1x versions.

These drivers were some of the first to bypass the DOS BIOS structure. It is important to understand the evolution of disk management software under both DOS and Windows 3.x because they lay the foundation for the disk configuration, management, and diagnostic software used by Windows 95/98/Me and Windows NT/2000 PC's today. Knowing what role DOS plays and how Windows 3.x has changed that role gives us a good understanding of which disk configuration, management, and diagnostics tools to employ. For example, most disks are configured using DOS because it provides direct access to the physical hardware. Some SCSI disks may be low-level formatted and tested using ROM software on the SCSI controller card. DOS has limitations in the functions and capacities with which it can work. For large disks, it can be used to set up the initial partitions, but may not be used to build very large partitions or SCSI RAID sets. Using BIOS or special disk driver software helps us understand the role SCSI adapter card ROM software plays in configuring and accessing attached fixed disks and the appearance of that disk drive to the Windows 3.x software running on the PC.

Windows 3.x 32-bit disk access functions

Thirty-two bit disk access is provided by Windows 3.1x for nonSCSI disk drives and specially designed SCSI disk controllers (one old DTC SCSI controller supported 32-bit disk access). Thirty-two bit disk and file access is initiated by selecting 386 enhanced selection in the control panel. Change to virtual machine settings to see the 32-bit disk and file access options as shown in Figure 10–6.

Figure 10–6
Thirty-two bit disk and file access selection.

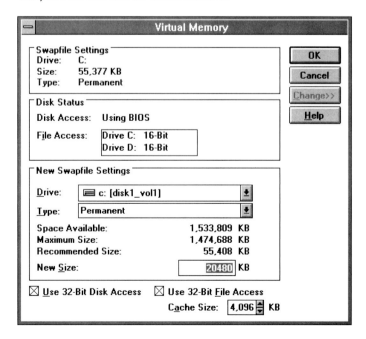

There are two 32-bit functions:

1. 32-bit disk access available in Windows 3.1 and Windows for Workgroups 3.10 and 3.11
2. 32-bit file access available in Windows for Workgroups 3.11

Let's look at 32-bit disk access first.

32-bit Disk Access (Fast Disk)

Thirty-two bit disk access was developed to speed up disk access over that provided by the PC BIOS. Some PC BIOSs perform fixed disk I/O better than others. Windows 3.x uses 32-bit disk access, also known as fast disk, to offset lackluster BIOS performance.

Fast disk loads a set of virtual device drivers into RAM that enhance PC BIOS by intercepting the interrupt 13H calls to the hard disk controller and redirecting them to either the 32-bit interface with the hard disk controller or the system BIOS, whichever is most efficient. Even though Windows 3.x runs in protected mode, it still switches back to real mode for DOS programs, or to communicate to DOS and the system BIOS. This switching is time consuming and, when bypassed, potentially speeds up our PC. This is great for tech-heads but most people do not even sense the increase in speed provided by 32-bit disk and file access. For example, if a DOS program running in real mode needs to read from a file, under Windows 3.x it must first issue an interrupt 21H in real mode. This gets trapped and switched to protected mode so that the 386 enhanced virtual devices can interpret it. If none of the devices claim the interrupt 21H call, then it is sent on to DOS in real mode. DOS processes the call and eventually issues an interrupt 13H that in turn is trapped and switched to protected mode where the virtual devices evaluate it. If this second interrupt is not claimed, it is passed to the BIOS and then to the fixed disk controller. As you can see, there is unnecessary switching performed.

Figure 10–7 illustrates fixed disk interrupt processing without 32-bit disk access. The virtual devices that are used by Windows 3.x to enable 32-bit disk access are listed in the SYSTEM.INI file's [386 Enhanced] section. The Western Digital Controller Statement was required for 32-bit disk access to work. The SYSTEM.INI [ENH] section statement was:

```
device=*wdctrl
```

This set up Windows 3.x communication with WD 1003-compatible fixed disk controllers and was required in most cases for 32-bit disk and file access to work. Note that the asterisk in front of wdctrl denotes that it is an internal

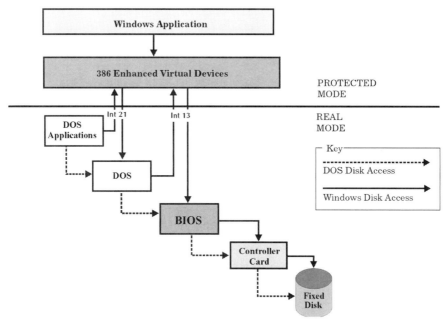

Figure 10–7
Fixed disk access using PC BIOS.

component of Windows 3.x and not an external device driver. Other related SYSTEM.INI file statements are:

```
; 32BitDiskAccess=OFF <= original win31
32BitDiskAccess=ON
; OverlappedIO=off <= original win31
OverlappedIO=ON
PageBuffers=16
;Specifies the number of 4 Kb page buffers Windows
;uses to store asynchronous read write pages
;when 32BitDiskAccess is activated. Default=4
```

Also, SCSI disk controllers do not support 32-bit disk access without special drivers. We have used an AMI SCSI disk controller that supported 32-bit disk access.

Windows 3.x with 32-bit Disk Access Switched On

When fast disk (32-bit disk access) is turned on, things work differently, as shown in Figure 10–8.

Windows 3.x now processes the interrupt 13H in protected mode instead of sending it back to real mode and the BIOS. Fast disk is then communicating with the controller without a switch, saving the time wasted every time a switch was made. Additionally, fast disk supports overlapped I/O allowing multiple requests to be made to the disk. All requests get queued so that when one request finishes, the next one is serviced immediately. Paging to and from the Window's swapfile also occurs in the background with overlapped I/O.

To activate Windows 3.x 32-bit functions, you must change the virtual memory settings through the control panel. Changing virtual memory settings opens a control window shown in Figure 10–9. At the bottom of the virtual memory control window is a box that activates 32-bit disk and file access.

The 32-bit disk access feature appeared first. It minimized switching between real mode and protected mode operation by the PC's CPU chip, and thus accelerated disk input/output operations. The 32-bit disk access was based on compatibility with Western Digital fixed disk controllers. It used several Windows 3.x internal drivers including *Int13 (trapped interrupt 13), *PageFile (performed virtual memory paging), *BlockDev (the core 32-bit

Figure 10–8
PC with 32-bit access enabled.

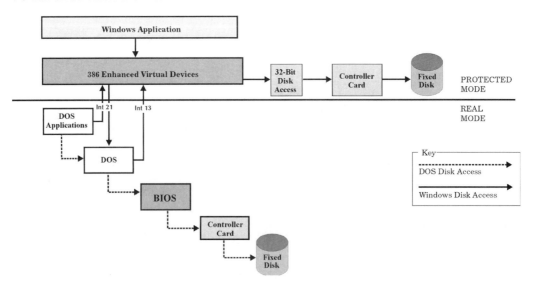

disk management component creating and managing fixed disk drive service requests), and *wdctrl (the component talking to standard Western Digital disk drive controllers).

The 32-bit file access reduces switching between real and protected mode in the same way 32-bit disk access does. Thirty-two bit file access performs these functions for interrupt 21 calls, implemented by the VFAT.386 and IFS-MGR.386 device drivers that, like BIOS routines, control reading and writing data to the fixed disk drive. VFAT.386 and IFSMGR.386 operate in protected mode, while the BIOS routines are relegated to real mode. Thirty-two bit file access is more than just intercepting interrupt 21 calls; it also performs disk caching. The VCACHE.386 component performs fixed cache functions equivalent to SMARTDRV.EXE while running in protected mode.

Blocking 32-bit Disk Access

Sometimes Windows 3.x does not enable 32-bit disk access, as illustrated in Figure 10–9.

Figure 10–9
Thirty-two bit disk access disabled.

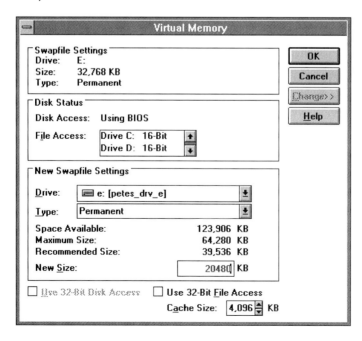

This happens when the disk controller is incompatible with fast disk. The Window's virtual device that lets fast disk communicate with your controller is *wdctrl. This virtual device works with any controller that is Western Digital 1003 compatible (IBM AT used this type of controller). As long as Windows 3.x senses during installation that there is a WD 1003-compatible controller, it adds the needed virtual devices for fast disk. Does that mean that if your controller is not WD 1003 compatible, you cannot have 32-bit disk access? No. If Microsoft limited fast disk to those controllers that are WD 1003 compatible, that would limit their market. As we said, Windows 3.x comes with just one virtual device for talking to disk controller cards, but manufacturers of disk controllers may provide a virtual device driver for their specific controller that supports fast disk. In general, most IDE drives work with the Windows 3.x virtual device for the WD 1003.

If you have checked to see if you have the ability to use fast disk, you may notice that the ability is there but it is still disabled by Windows. This is because Windows 3.x cannot assume that you are working on a desktop PC instead of a laptop PC. Some laptop PCs come with power saving features that will shut down a disk (stop it from spinning) to conserve the batteries. Sometimes this power-saving feature may not recognize that 32-bit disk access is actually using the interrupt 13H to access the disk (they only look for it to come from the BIOS). If this happens, the disk may stop spinning in the middle of a disk write, causing the loss of data or its corruption. We recommend that you refrain from using fast disk on laptop and notebook PCs, or at least turn off the power-saving features, if possible.

32-bit File Access

Window's 3.1x 32-bit disk access improves disk performance under Windows, but Windows for Workgroups 3.11 provides the added capability of 32-bit file access. These features are both implemented in Windows 95/98/Me, as well as in Windows NT/2000.

Figure 10–10 enables you to surmise how 32-bit file access improves upon 32-bit disk access.

Thirty-two bit disk access improves performance by processing the interrupt 13H in protected mode instead of switching it to real mode to be handled by the BIOS. It also allows overlapped I/O. Although it stops the interrupt 13H switching to real mode, it still sends the interrupt 21H to DOS. This involves switching from protected mode to real mode, and wastes time. When 32-bit file access is turned on, the virtual device VFAT.386 now handles interrupt 21H in protected mode directly. When loaded, VFAT.386 inventories the physical hard drives of your system and assigns itself to those supporting 32-bit disk access, or those that have a real mode mapper for the drive.

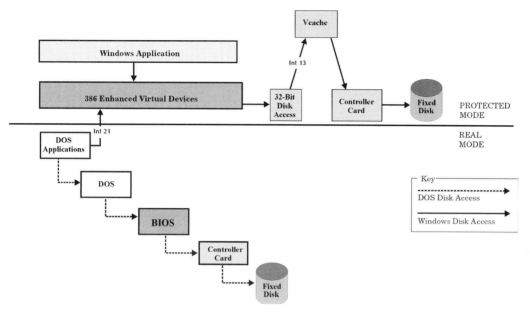

Figure 10–10
Windows 3.1x 32-bit file and disk access operation enabled.

Some disk drives do not support protected mode 32-bit disk access. They can still use 32-bit file access when 32-disk access is disabled because Windows 3.x provides a 32-bit protected-mode-compatible interface via the real mode mapper component. This Windows 3.x component is RMM.D32. It is not loaded directly but is loaded by the VXLDR.386 Windows 3.x component as required to provide a compatible 32-bit protected mode disk access interface for VFAT.386.

That means when 32-bit disk access is not used, then 32-bit file access does not activate. Drive controllers not supported by the Windows 3.x *wdctrl device driver may be supported by one from the controller manufacturer.

When you cannot use 32-bit disk access, you can use 32-bit file access but you sacrifice peak performance. See Figure 10–11. Thirty-two-bit file access still works because Windows for Workgroups comes with a real mode mapper that services protected mode I/O's from the VFAT.386. The file that does this is RMM.D32, found in your system subdirectory. This file is not specifically loaded from any of the .INI files; instead, it is used if you have the following device lines in your SYSTEM.INI [386] Enhanced section:

```
device=ios.386
device=vxdldr.386
```

621

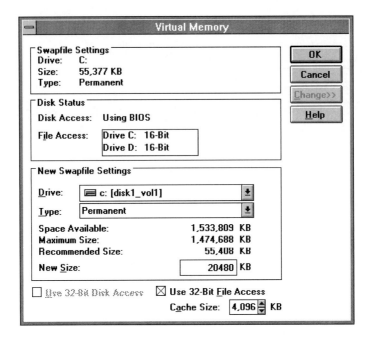

Figure 10–11
Thirty-two-bit file access enabled and 32-bit disk access disabled.

These lines are not added until 32-bit file access is turned on for the first time and the system either detects that 32-bit disk access is disabled, or there is a compressed disk. Compressed disks cannot use 32-bit disk access.

Managing Files

Windows 3.x provides file management capabilities that improve on those offered by DOS. The improvements are to make managing files easier for users. They utilize the GUI interface and an object model to view, copy, delete, and launch programs manipulating the files. The Windows 3.x file manager implements these file management capabilities. Of course, files could still be manipulated using the old DOS commands. However, Windows 3.x file manager gives less sophisticated users a mechanism to work with their files easily.

The file manager opened separate windows within the file manager program for each disk drive it was working on. This is shown in Figure 10–12 with separate windows open for drive C: a local drive, and drive N: a network drive.

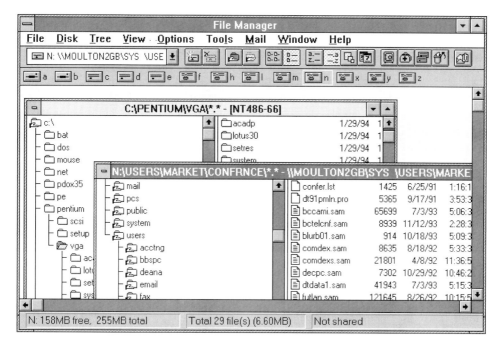

Figure 10–12
Windows 3.x file manager.

Object-oriented file management means the user can select a file and, holding down the right mouse button, drag the file to the desired location and drop it. Windows 3.x then copies or moves the file. The file drag and drop can be more precisely controlled using the SHIFT and CTRL keys to move and copy the file respectively.

```
SHIFT = move the file
CTRL = copy the file
```

Furthermore, Windows 3.x allows data files to be associated with particular applications. The Windows 3.x file manager can launch programs associated with specific file types. This association is performed using the file name extension. Hence, TXT extensions are associated with the Windows 3.x notepad application. Double-clicking on those files would launch notepad and load the file contents into it for editing. Similarly, other common application programs have file associations built into Windows 3.x. Users can also create new file extension types and associate those with specific applications.

Printing

Windows 3.x also manages printers and printing. It provides the driver programs for printers so that any application could use any printer installed under Windows. This removes most hardware dependencies from Windows 3.x application programs; the applications focus on the application functions and not on the hardware installed in the PC. Since it was impossible for Windows 3.x to include drivers for every piece of hardware in the standard operating system, manufacturers of special hardware began to provide drivers for the Windows 3.x environment, despite the fact that they didn't need to. This simplified application development and made Windows 3.x operation more reliable.

Figure 10–13 illustrates Windows' printer setup.

Figure 10–13
Windows 3.x printer setup.

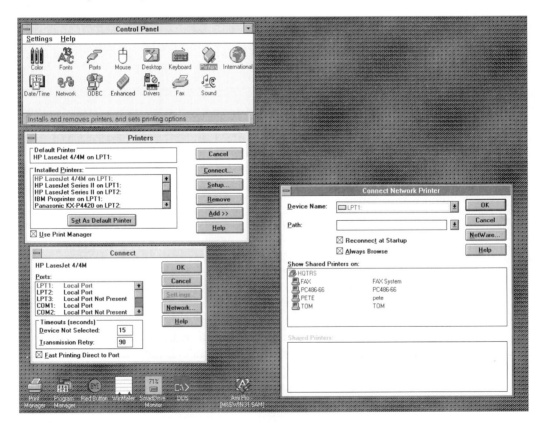

Windows 3.x implemented print spooling. Unlike DOS applications, Windows 3.x applications did not print directly to the printer, but rather to the Windows 3.x print spooling program.Printing under Windows 3.1x is different from printing under DOS. Windows 3.1x prints all images and text in a document as graphics images; most printers implement either HP Page Composition Language HPPCL or PostScript page description language to print graphical printouts from text or other files. Graphical printout permits font scaling as opposed to printing fonts as specific bit patterns. The Windows 3.x printer drivers get data from the application in a specific printer command format. They in turn translate it into HPPCL or PostScript commands recognized by the printer, and pass the translated information (the graphics printout) to the printer. However, if Windows 3.x were to wait during this translation process while the printer printed chunks of data and then requested more data, printing any document would occupy Windows 3.x and bore the user for inordinate periods of time. Consequently, Windows 3.x translates printing into the graphical command language output and stores it on disk in a print spooling queue. The print manager then sends the graphical image from the print queue on disk to the printer as controlled by the printer. Passing the graphical image to the printer uses fewer PC resources (CPU cycles) than translating and passing at the same time. Consequently, the print manager can send the data to the printer as a background task while the PC user continues his or her work.

One of the most troublesome areas with Windows 3.x is printers. They seldom print what we expect, and can be insanely slow. In Windows, printer drivers and some DLL programs control printers. The printer driver programs for HP LaserJet 4 printers are:

```
HPPCL   DRV 152,192 11-01-93 3:11a
HPPCL5A DRV 428,672 03-10-92 3:10a
HPPCL5E DRV 399,888 11-01-93 3:11a
HPPCL5E1 DLL 75,468 11-01-93 3:11a
HPPCL5E2 DLL 58,672 11-01-93 3:11a
HPPCL5E3 DLL 100,001 11-01-93 3:11a
HPPCL5E4 DLL 24,576 11-01-93 3:11a
```

Windows 3.x interfaces to printers through driver programs, meaning that any application running on Windows 3.x can access the printer attached to the PC and use its full functionality (more or less). Printing problems between PCs can include differences in printer set up, installed fonts, and kinds of printers themselves. When Windows 3.x translates the text and images into a printer graphics language for printing, it makes the translation using the graphical font definitions installed with Windows 3.x on the PC. When a document is created on a PC that has different graphical font definitions than the

PC printing a document, the PC printing the document must use the graphical font definitions it has to print the document. Since these are not exactly the same as those on the original PC where the document was created, the printout looks different—i.e., the page breaks and paragraph layouts hit at different points than expected. This difficulty is avoided by imbedding the font definitions in the document created so that Windows 3.x can use them to perform the printing. Desktop application programs would provide the option to embed the fonts when saving or printing a document.

Configuring Printers in Windows 3.x

Printer installation and configuration is performed using the Windows 3.x control panel, as shown in Figure 10–14.

Bit-mapped and TrueType Fonts are both installed using the fonts selection in the control panel, as shown in Figure 10–15. With Windows 3.1x, Adobe Type Manager fonts were installed and managed by a separate Adobe Type Manager program. TrueType fonts that appeared in earnest in Windows 3.11 have effectively replaced all these for most PC-based desktop-publishing applications use. Since many of the early fonts were bit-mapped images of the characters, and the bitmap files differed from font vendor to font vendor, special software—for instance, the Adobe Type Manager—was needed to transfer the fonts into any document using them. The special program would help Windows 3.x create a graphical image while printing a document.

One basic printer problem that impacts HP LaserJet 4 printers is the memory specification; it is very easy to get memory overflow errors with a LaserJet

Figure 10–14
Control panel printer configuration.

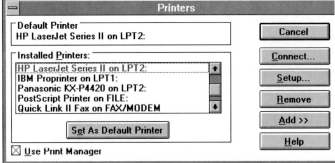

4 printer. When documents were translated into graphical images, they were much larger than the memory in the printer could hold. A single print page requires about 1.5 MB of RAM in the printer to print. Furthermore, the printers did not respond to Windows to make it aware of the memory they had available to store the printing image. Consequently, when Windows 3.x printed, it had to estimate the amount of data to transmit before stopping to permit the printer to print the image. The amount of data to send was a guess on Windows 3.x's part that was determined by the printer memory entered in the Windows 3.1x control panel printer configuration box; Figure 10–15 illustrates this.

If the memory installed in the printer was incorrectly specified, or other problems caused the printer to miss graphical commands, a memory overflow message ensued and the printout turned to junk. Such an event was painfully evident by an error message on the printer's operator control display panel or by the pile of paper containing garbage characters in the printer's output paper bin.

When printing high-resolution graphics and pictures, the Windows 3.1x printers required as much memory as you can afford to install. HP recommended 6 MB, but 10 MB or more was better. In spite of the Windows 3.x settings for the LaserJet 4, we still had memory overruns with less than 6 MB of memory.

One solution to memory-overrun situations was to install the printer as a LaserJet II printer with 2 MB of RAM. This older printer driver seemed to manage printing and memory very well.

Figure 10–15
Windows 3.x control panel printer configuration menu.

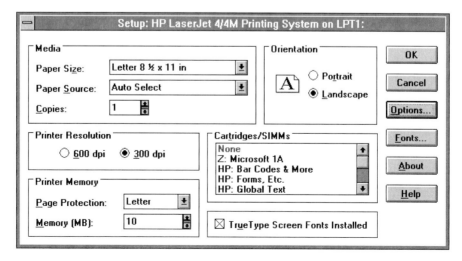

HP LaserJet 4 Setup Options

The HP LaserJet 4 menu permits selecting the amount of memory installed in the printer, the printing resolution (300 or 600 dots per inch), and the page protection mode. The best resolution we as humans can differentiate without magnifying glasses is 600 DPI. We can tell that shading in an image is not uniform, but we cannot pick out the dots. When printing a document to be copied by a xerographic copier, it is best to print the image at 300 DPI and let the graphics be coarse images. This produces dotted printed images that the copier can focus in on and produce a consistent printed image. Refer to Chapter 6 for more information.

The page protection feature reserves printer memory for complex text or graphics. With page protection, a printer can create an entire page image in its memory before printing it. Setting page protection helps prevent printer memory overrun errors.

Sometimes the memory overflows regardless of how the resolution and page protection features are set. This happened to us with 6 MB or less of printer memory. One solution to this problem was to set up the HP LaserJet 4 printer as an HP LaserJet Series II printer.

How Windows 3.x Uses Printers

Windows 3.x uses printers in a different manner from DOS. When printing in DOS, text characters are sent to the printer for printing. In order to print graphics, DOS employs a graphics program (GRAPHICS.COM) to produce bit-mapped output for the printer.

Windows 3.x treats printers as graphics devices and sends output to them in graphics mode. The print driver for the printer under Windows 3.x converts the application program's printer output into a graphics image for printing, similar to what graphics.COM does for DOS. It may shift to text mode for some printing, but because Windows regards all printers are graphics devices, it tries to print to them in the highest graphics resolution permitted. One printer setup option is to print TrueType fonts as graphics. When we set this option, Windows 3.x printed a test page in 24 to 26 seconds, as opposed to 30 to 31 seconds when it was not set. The implication is that switching Windows 3.x to text mode for printing slows Windows 3.x down.

Printer Drivers

A printer driver is a program that controls a printer. Whenever a document is printed, the printer driver assumes control and feeds data with the correct printing control commands to the printer. Windows 3.x comes with a variety of printer drivers for the common printers. They must be installed before a printer can be used. Updated drivers can usually be downloaded from a printer manufacturer's Web site.

To take maximum advantage of a printer's features, the printer drivers should be installed under Windows. If these drivers are not available, or if they cause serious printing problems, most Windows 3.x PCs have HP LaserJet printer drivers that can be used as a general driver for most printers. Because many printers implement HP graphics language, they in effect emulate HP LaserJet printers. The text or generic printer driver is useful for sending text data quickly to any printer.

Fax drivers are used to create data for transmission by fax modems. Postscript drivers are used to generate output for text-to-slide production. Because PostScript is used to produce high quality printed documents, installing PostScript drivers permits PC users to view documents as though they were printed on a PostScript printer. Using the print preview function in any application makes Windows 3.x display the page as it would appear if printed on a PostScript printer.

Both of these drivers produce files that are then transmitted to other devices that print the desired copy.

Fonts and Font Managers

One troublesome aspect of printing is fonts. Frequently, font reproduction can vary from printer to printer, in ways that are not always predictable. There are also both display and printer fonts.

Display fonts were used by Windows 3.x to produce screen images and menus. With Windows 3.0, a limited number of screen fonts were provided; these were fonts comprised of bit maps for different display resolutions like EGA and VGA. Printers used printer fonts for printing. The trick with Windows 3.x was to match the display fonts to the printer fonts so that the documents represented on the display screen matched the printout. This became simpler with Windows 3.1 because TrueType fonts were introduced. When applications use TrueType fonts, the same font could be used for both the display and the printer. Fonts can also be classified as bit-mapped or scalable.

Bit-mapped fonts use specific bit images of the characters to create the display or printout. Scalable fonts describe to the display or printer how to construct the character and what size to make it. This means that a document using TrueType scalable fonts can be changed to any size, and the fonts would scale up and down smoothly with a document on the display screen. With Windows 3.1, bit-mapped fonts have all but disappeared.

The remaining bit-mapped fonts are the standard Windows 3.x menu display fonts; Courier, Fixedsys, Modem, MS Serif, MS-DOS CP 437, Small Fonts, Symbol, System, and Terminal. Some of these fonts come with bit maps for 8514, VGA, and CGA displays. When viewing fonts in the control panel under fonts, the display icons show TT for TrueType and A for bit-mapped fonts. These standard Windows 3.x menu display fonts are retained for backwards compatibility with previous versions of Windows.

Scalable printer fonts are TrueType and Adobe Type Manager (ATM) fonts. TrueType font processing is built directly into Windows, while ATM font processing requires that the ATM driver program be added to Windows. Both font management programs have their merits and more fonts than any Windows 3.x user could ever hope to employ in a document. Since the support for TrueType fonts was built into Windows 3.x (and thus does not require special driver software), TrueType fonts are used by most Windows 3.x systems today.

Installing too many fonts can consume lots of disk space and reduce your GUI data heap capacity. Under Windows 3.x, TrueType fonts are installed in the WINDOWS\SYSTEM directory. ATM fonts are installed wherever specified.All fonts display and print depending upon the printer's capability and display resolution. Smaller fonts cannot be accurately displayed on a VGA resolution (640 by 480) display. Larger fonts can also appear to have jagged edges. "Hinting" is the name of the technique employed to improve the typeface display as a type font by your PC. For example, say a typeface character does not match perfectly with the dots on your display or printer. Hinting determines which dots are activated to produce the typeface or font.

The most common problem encountered with fonts is that users install far too many fonts, more than they could ever possibly need. For example, on our systems there are over 400 fonts installed and we use about 50 of them, tops. When Windows 3.1 systems support many fonts, it ran the risk of reducing the system resource heaps to low levels that would crash Windows 3.x when many different fonts were used in documents. These fonts had to be loaded into the graphical resource heaps for Windows 3.1 when they were used. We found that when printing the graphical resource heaps, under Windows 3.1, would drop to zero much to our surprise. We were able to observe this because we monitored the resource heaps as we printed. This sometimes causes our PC to crash. A normal PC user would just see the PC crashing and have no idea why. The simple solution would be to just install the fonts that were required.

Using the Control Panel

The Windows 3.x control panel provides access to several set up and tuning features. Significant among these is access to the 386 Enhanced Mode operation that can alter the multitasking and virtual memory options of Windows 3.x.

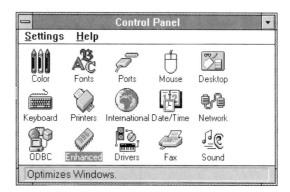

Figure 10–16
Windows for Workgroups
control panel.

The features in the Windows 3.x control panel vary depending upon the version of Windows. Windows for Workgroups has more and slightly different features than does normal Windows. The control panel in Figure 10–16 is from a Windows for Workgroups PC.

Color changes the screen colors, and Fonts installs different fonts (as discussed earlier, TrueType fonts are the easiest to install). The mouse, desktop and keyboard options alter the look and feel of Windows 3.x to suit the PC user's preferences, and the ontrol panel options are used to add printer driver programs, printer fonts, configure printers, and share and attach to network printers (Windows for Workgroups). Date and time settings modify the date and time, while International changes the display representation of the date and time. The network selection permits configuring network boards and protocols. Open Data Base Connectivity (ODBC) provides Windows 3.x SQL database access to Dbase, FoxPro, MS Access and Paradox database applications. The 386 enhanced selection controls time slicing, swapfiles, and disk access. It is one means of tuning Windows. Multimedia and sound card driver programs are installed using the drivers selection. If a speaker driver is installed, the sound selection can assign sounds to different operator actions, such as starting and closing Windows. With Windows for Workgroups, you have a fax option for your email that is installed and managed using the FAX control panel selection.

Study Break: Fonts

Let's examine the fonts installed on your system. This exercise works similarly for Windows 3.1 as well as Windows 95, Windows 98, and Windows Me.

1. Start up Windows and open the control panel.
2. Find the fonts icon and click on it. The fonts installed in Windows should appear. They are most likely displayed as icons.
3. Go to the menu and select view and then list fonts by similarity. The fonts should be listed with a notation of whether they are similar or not similar to other fonts.
4. Under view, be sure the status bar is checked. It should be displayed at the bottom of the fonts window. The status bar should display the total number of fonts installed. How many fonts are installed on the PC?
5. When viewing the fonts, display how many of the fonts are not similar. One might think that Windows just doesn't know whether they are similar or not similar.

The goal of this exercise is to give you a better understanding of the fonts typically installed on a user PC.

Windows 3.x Components

Windows 3.x components are:

- Driver programs, interfacing PC hardware to Windows 3.x software
- DLLs, implementing application programs
- The kernel, providing all the system control and scheduling functions
- GUI, consisting of GDI.EXE and USER.EXE
- Resource heaps, storing graphics information for GUI
- INI files, controlling starting Windows 3.x and applications programs.

Some of these components are configured and manipulated using the control panel icons, while other components are the core components of Windows 3.x and not directly manipulated by the control panel icons. Let's look at these briefly.

Driver Programs

Driver programs are required to interface Windows 3.x to the PC hardware. Windows 3.x or the hardware component manufacturer can provide the requisite driver programs. Driver programs intrinsically know how to transfer data between the PC's RAM and the specific hardware component. They are written to work with specific IRQs, input/output ports, and memory ranges. They buffer requests, queue them for processing and perform other detailed tasks that support the PC hardware. Standard driver programs are provided for the mouse, the keyboard, and the display.

Memory Management and Disk Caching

The HIMEM and EMM386.EXE programs perform Windows 3.x memory management. The HIMEM program enables the use of XMS and creates the HIMEM area from it. EMM386.EXE creates EMS and turns other XMS into the UMA, dividing it into UMBs. The DOS SMARTDRV provides the disk cache driver for Windows 3.x. Only with Windows 3.11 are there 32-bit disk and file access drivers that largely replace the SMARTDRV disk cache.

Local Area Network Drivers

LAN driver programs are required for NICs produced by hardware manufacturers. Under Windows 3.x, the hardware manufacturer typically provided the LAN card driver programs. They were not provided as standard drivers with Windows 3.x, but this has changed with Windows 95/98/Me. Many LAN NIC card drivers are provided with Windows 95/98/Me and Windows 2000. Once installed, the NIC card drivers must be bound (linked) to the protocols that communicate between PCs across the LAN.

Generally, the hardware manufacturers provide driver software for Windows 3.x, Windows NT, and Novell NetWare, in addition to other operating systems. The NetWare software for a 3Com Ethernet board is LSL.COM, 3C509.EXE, IPXODI.COM and then the Windows 3.x or NetWare VLM programs. These drivers are loaded and configured in DOS prior to running Windows 3.x.

Novell NetWare dominated the DOS LAN marketplace. Because of this domination, most DOS and Windows PCs used the Novell software for LAN communications. With Windows 95/98/Me networks, the LAN environment has changed. LANs use TCP/IP protocols and Microsoft's software more frequently than they use Novell's.

Dynamic Link Libraries

Dynamic link libraries are either DLL or EXE file types. They implement specific functions or tasks for applications. For example, a spell-checking function in a desktop publishing program is performed by a single DLL.

The EXE programs that run under DOS and produce the error message "This program requires Windows to execute" are DLL programs that rely on the Windows 3.x GUI for many of their display and operator interface functions. They are not to be confused with the EXE programs commonly used in DOS. This means that DLLs have both a DLL and an EXE extension.

"Dynamic" means something that happens on the fly while Windows 3.x is running. "link" indicates an address or start point of another program, and "library" means that there are many of DLLs employed to accomplish specific tasks under Windows. The EXE programs are DLLs that usually launch an application program. They rely on other DLLs that are loaded and unloaded in Windows 3.x memory as required to perform the application program's functions. Windows 3.x itself and applications that run under Windows 3.x rely on many DLLs. Most DLLs are common to many programs and Windows. They are stored in the \windows and \windows\system folders. Application programs store common DLLs in those folders as well, and store other DLLs in the folder into which they install.

The Kernel

The kernel performs the most important core functions of an operating system. It schedules and coordinates execution of applications and of input/output operations. Windows 95/98/Me, Windows NT/2000, OS/2, and other operating systems have kernels; Windows 3.x also comes with its own kernels, as shown in Table 10–1. The standard mode kernel was provided with Windows 3.0 to permit it to run on 286 CPU chip PCs.

Table 10–1 Windows 3.x Kernels and Operating Modes

Kernel Program	Size	Date Time	Windows Mode
KRNL286.EXE (Windows 3.0)	71,730	03-10-92 3:10a	Standard mode
KRNL386.EXE (Windows 3.1, 3.11)	75,490	03-10-92 3:10a	386 enhanced mode and real mode

The 386 kernel operated in both real and 386 enhanced mode. Real mode was required to provide compatibility for older driver programs that would only operate with the PCs BIOS. With Windows 3.1x, the applications migrated to operating and 386 enhanced mode to take advantage of the virtual memory space and the faster 386 enhanced mode display and disk driver programs.

Windows 3.x kernels interface between DOS and DOS memory managers to provide access to the PC's XMS for Windows 3.x.

GDI.EXE and USER.EXE

Windows 3.x GUI is created at system startup. The actual interface is a combination of two programs, GDI.EXE and USER.EXE. GDI.EXE is the Windows 3.x graphical display interface manager and USER.EXE is the Windows 3.x input manager. These programs together are responsible for managing all the Windows 3.x created systemwide and for drawing items on your screen. To display the system resources, select Help and then About from the program manager. Figure 10–17 illustrates free graphical resources in the Windows 3.x display.

Both of these programs use data areas called the graphical resource heaps to manage these items. The graphical resource heaps are approximately 64 KB

Figure 10–17
Program manager showing free graphical resources in Windows 3.x.

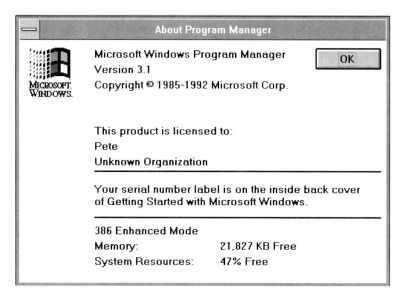

in size and operate in real mode, regardless of what operating mode was selected at startup. Why so small a size for such a large task? Windows 3.x does this because calling objects from a known area 64 KB in size is faster than doing the same across large regions of memory.

When you start Windows, your graphical resource area is about 80 to 85 percent free. It never gets much higher because some graphical resources are used by the Windows 3.x desktop and the program manager. Each additional window you create in your shell or in an application takes approximately 2 percent or more of the available resources. You can view the resources your PC is using by choosing Help followed by About in program manager. This displays the free resource percentage down at the bottom of the screen. When your resources fall below the 15 percent mark, you are unable to open additional windows, regardless of the total amount of RAM your machine has installed. Additionally, a program like print manager, when loaded, may only need 2 percent of your resources; when it comes time to print, however, it may require 20 to as much as 50 percent of your resources. Running out of resources is a surefire way to make Windows 3.x slow way down.

When you display Help and About in program manager, Windows 3.x shows the resources available in the graphical heap with the least resources. Typically the USER.EXE heap runs out of resources first.

Resource Heaps

To view the Windows 3.x resource heaps go to Help and then About in the program manager. HA.EXE is a program that continually monitors your heaps while you open and close Windows 3.x applications.

Figure 1–18 provides more detail on the use of the resource heaps than does the Windows 3.x control panel display. When you run out of space in your resource heaps, there is not much to do but shut down Windows 3.x and restart to correct the problem. This means that detailed information about the resource heaps is interesting, but not that helpful in solving problems. Because they do tell you when your resources are exhausted or near exhaustion (putting Windows 3.x at risk of crashing), a PC user is able to avert a crash by shutting down Windows.

Figure 10–18
Heap Alert detailed display.

Study Break: Windows Graphical Resources

This exercise examines the Windows graphical resources and how to monitor them.

1. Get a Windows 95, 98 or Me PC. Open the control panel and click on System.
2. Click on the performance tab and look for system resources. What percentages are free? This represents the heap with the fewest resources. When the number is low, the PC is in danger of crashing.
3. Use the Windows Explorer and open the Windows directory. Find the program RSRCMTR.EXE. Double-click on it to launch it. What resources does it display as available? Do they match with what you saw under the control panel display?

The resource monitor program, RSRCMTR.EXE, permits us to continuously view the available graphical resources. By placing it in the Windows\start menu\programs\startup folder, the resource meter can be launched when Windows starts. Its icon then appears in the SYSTRAY, providing a continuous monitoring of all available graphical resources.

Key Windows 3.x System Files

Installing Windows 3.x is as simple as running the setup program. However, making it run reliably and quickly is not so simple. Let's examine key Windows 3.x components in a PC to see precisely how they impact performance and operation. Later we examine these files in detail to discover the results produced by different parameter values.

Several files play a key role in Windows 3.x operation. These files are:

- INI files—These are the program initialization files. They tell Windows 3.x and its applications how to configure themselves for operation under Windows. There are two key files for Windows 3.x alone: the WIN.INI, equivalent to the DOS AUTOEXEC.BAT file, and the SYSTEM.INI file, equivalent to the DOS CONFIG.SYS file. Generally, the SYSTEM.INI file configures Windows 3.x with the PC's hardware, while WIN.INI sets up the desktop display and applications under Windows. INI files are most often text files that can be edited with any editor program. Its operation is altered once Windows 3.x is edited and restarted. See Figure 10–19.

Figure 10–19
Some Windows 3.1x INI files.

```
Volume in drive C is EISA50MHZ_2
 Volume Serial Number is 1B3B-08D1
 Directory of C:\WIN
123W         INI   4454       02-08-93 11:51a
ALDUS        INI    671       02-08-93 11:05a
AMIDLGIC     INI     77       09-23-91  1:48p
AMIDRAW      INI    246       01-30-93  4:23a
AMIDW        INI   8283       06-18-92 10:56a
AMIEQN       INI    898       06-03-92  2:47p
AMIFONT      INI    301       01-30-93  4:18a
AMIIMAGE     INI    447       04-09-91  8:26a
AMILABEL     INI  10014       06-19-92  9:52a
AMIOW        INI  23822       12-17-91 12:05p
AMIPRO       INI   6463       02-09-93  3:40p
AMIVISD      INI   4958       02-08-93 11:37a
ATM          INI   6455       02-09-93  3:22p <= sets up Adobe Type Manager
CONTROL      INI   4253       02-09-93  7:19p <= sets up Windows Desktop
CORELCHT     INI   1797       02-08-93 11:45a
DOSAPP       INI   1144       02-09-93  7:00p <= sets up DOS Applications
EXCEL        INI     52       02-08-93 11:38a
PROGMAN      INI    217       02-08-93 10:46a<= sets up Program Manager
SYSTEM       INI   3914       02-09-93  6:36p <= sets up hardware
WIN          INI  14669       02-09-93  7:22p <= sets up Windows programs
WINFILE      INI    150       02-08-93 10:43a
WPM          INI    184       02-09-93  7:10p
SOL          INI     33       02-09-93  6:46p <= sets up Solitaire Game
    28 file(s)   95326 bytes
       11606016 bytes free
```

- GRP files—Group files describe the program groups displayed by Windows.

- DLL files—These files are the application programs designed to work specifically in the Windows 3.x graphical environment. DLL files are found in application subdirectories and in the Windows\system directory.

- SCR files—SCR files are the screen saver displays used by Windows. They reside in the Windows 3.x directory.

- DRV and SYS files—These are the hardware driver programs used by Windows 3.x to communicate with the PC's hardware. They reside in the Windows\system directory.

- INF files—INF files are used by setup to configure Windows. Altering them changes the setup process.

- EXE files—Windows 3.x programs are implemented as EXE files. These are not the same as DOS executable files because they need the Windows 3.x GUI environment operating to be executed. All Windows 3.x programs are EXE files except for one, which is a COM file. The WIN.COM program is the key Windows 3.x COM file.

- WAV files—These files are the sound files for Windows. They can be used by the speaker driver program (available from the Microsoft forum on Compuserve) to produce various sounds on your PC's speaker.

- BMP files—BMP files are large bit-mapped graphics used for various displays. Because of their large size, it is not good to use those graphics.

- PIF files—These files are used to start DOS applications under Windows. It is not necessary to start all DOS applications using PIF files, but when special control of the DOS application is needed, the PIF files provide that control. PIF files are not used to start Windows 3.x applications.

- ICO and LIB files—Windows 3.x icons are described in these files. The icons are either individual icons or libraries of icons. Once an icon is chosen for an application under program manager, the ICO and LIB file are no longer needed. However, if there is any change to the relationship between the Windows 3.x icon under program manager, the program usually makes you reinstall the icon.

- COM files—There are very few COM files in Windows 3.x today. The most important file, and the one that we're all familiar with, is the one that launches Windows, WIN.COM.

- FON, FOT, and TTF files—FON and TTF files are files that describe Windows fonts. The FON files are for bit-mapped fonts and the TTF

639

files describe TrueType fonts. Both files are typically found in the Windows\system folder.

- HLP files—HLP files provide the help menu displays for Windows. They comprise the electronic instruction manual that comes with Windows.

- 386 files—The 386 files are drivers and Windows 3.x components that are not built into Windows. They support network connectivity, 32-bit disk and file access, and other Windows 3.x features.

Windows 3.x uses other file types for specialized functions; most play a minor role compared to the INI files. If the INI files are not set up properly, or if another file (for instance, a font file) specified in an INI file is not found by Windows 3.x at startup, bad things happen. Understanding the INI files is important for fixing Windows 3.x problems without needlessly rerunning SETUP.

INI Files

Much like DOS uses certain files to configure itself (CONFIG.SYS and AUTOEXEC.BAT), Windows 3.x uses several specific files to configure itself during startup. The two files are the SYSTEM.INI and WIN.INI. The SYSTEM.INI file determines how the PC hardware interacts with Windows. It is also a key file for making Windows 3.x operate properly in 386 enhanced mode.

Both SYSTEM.INI and WIN.INI are used by Windows 95/98/Me and Windows 2000 to preserve compatibility with Windows 16-bit (Windows 3.x) applications. For example, Corel Draw 5.0 is one application program that uses settings in the WIN.INI file under Windows 95/98/Me and Windows 2000.

We look at WIN.INI first.

WIN.INI

The WIN.INI file controls how your Windows 3.x applications operate with Windows. One function of the WIN and other INI files is to provide the mechanism for Windows 3.x to remember where you last retrieved a text file versus an AmiPro file, etc. INI files are constantly altered by Windows. When Windows 3.0 was first introduced, all application INI statements went into the WIN.INI file. Today, many applications maintain their own set of INI files in the Windows 3.x subdirectory and elsewhere. These two INI files are the precursors to the registry file used in Windows 95/98/Me and Windows NT/2000.

One problem with the WIN.INI file is that statements always get placed there, but none ever seem to be removed. Cleaning up a WIN.INI file can be a chore; the easiest way to do it is to start with a simple WIN.INI file, then add back the program statements from the "dirty" WIN.INI file for each Windows application installed. If statements are missed, the applications typically do not start and give a brief error message.

There are many sections to the WIN.INI file. Some standard Windows sections are identified below. They include:

[Windows]—contains Windows look-and-feel information and is changed using the control panel.

[Desktop]—describes desktop look and is changed using the control panel.

[Extensions]—associates files with applications.

[intl]—sets Windows up for international operation.

[ports]—identifies the ports available to Windows, for example, COM and printer ports.

[FontSubstitutes]—identifies fonts that can be substituted for other fonts.

[TrueType]—tells Windows whether TrueType fonts are turned on for all applications.

[Sounds]—causes sounds to be made for certain Windows events.

[mci extensions]—identifies multimedia file types.

[Compatibility]—ensures applications display properly.

[winsetup]—identifies the path to which Windows was installed.

[fonts]—identifies installed fonts for Windows.

[embedding]—describes how applications interact with Windows.

[colors]—sets up the Windows colors. This is controlled through the control panel.

[Windows Help]—tells Windows where to display the Help screen.

[MRU_Files]—tells Windows where to find specific files. This is similar to the path statement.

[spooler]—records print spooler setup information.

[PrinterPorts]—tells Windows the printer port configurations.

[devices]—associates printer descriptions with printer ports for Windows.

Each section is identified in the file by brackets. Within the sections are the commands that Windows 3.x and application programs use to configure themselves to operate on this particular Windows 3.x PC. Some sections are changed using the Windows 3.x control panel. The application program may change others or they may just be references that the application program uses.

[Panasonic KX-P4420,LPT2]

[Network]

[HPPCL,LPT2]

[WINFAX]

[AnyFax]

[WfxPbLinks]

[PSPLUS]

Other sections like the ones above may also be included in the file. These depend on the options installed in Windows 3.x and the applications installed on a PC.

Understanding WIN.INI

Let's examine a WIN.INI file. This first statement loads the programs that you want to run every time Windows 3.x is started. The NWPOPUP.EXE program is for Novell Networks. Other commonly used programs can be loaded with the load statement as well.

```
[windows]
load=nwpopup.exe resgauge.exe d:\aftrdark\ad.exe redbtn.exe
```

If you want to jump into an application when Windows starts, place the file name after the RUN= line.

```
run=
```

These are standard WIN.INI file statements. They permit Windows to beep in specific circumstances. The NullPort statement identifies to Windows that all ports are assigned to physical devices.

```
Beep=yes
NullPort=None
```

The statements that follow identify the driver program for printer port 1.

The first line is a comment, as indicated by the semicolon (;) preceding the text. Normal device and other WIN.INI commands are statements that appear on a single line with an equal sign following them. They are disabled by placing a semicolon (;) at the beginning of the line.

```
;default printer specification from Control Panel is below.
Spooler=no
device=Panasonic KX-P4420,HPPCL,LPT1:
```

The next statements set up some of the GUI parameters. These parameters are typically changed using programs found in the Windows 3.x control panel. For example, the colors and desktop configuration can be changed using control panel applets.

```
BorderWidth=3
KeyboardSpeed=31
CursorBlinkRate=200
DoubleClickSpeed=820
MouseThreshold1=4
MouseThreshold2=6
MouseSpeed=2
```

This statement specifies the program extensions that are executable.

```
Programs=com exe bat pif
```

These statements control programs.

```
Documents=
DeviceNotSelectedTimeout=15
TransmissionRetryTimeout=45
```

This statement specifies a swap disk if it is different from the Windows 3.x default drive.

```
swapdisk=
```

The CoolSwitch an addes parameter for Windows 3.1 determines whether you can Alt-Esc or Ctrl-Esc from applications. The control panel programs control the other parameters.

```
CoolSwitch=1
ScreenSaveActive=0
ScreenSaveTimeOut=120
KeyboardDelay=0
DosPrint=no
NetWarn=0
```

Slower displays (like LCD displays on laptops) use this mouse trails setting. The mouse trail setting delays removal of the mouse pointer image as the mouse is moved around the screen, making it appear as though its leaving trails. On displays with slow refresh rates, the mouse trail helps the user to locate the mouse when it is moved rapidly.

```
MouseTrails=7
```

This next settings are responsible for our desktop display parameters. These can also be modified using the "Display" dialog found in the control panel program group. The grid granularity sets up a spacing grid that Windows 3.x uses to create the desktop.

```
[Desktop]
Pattern=0 68 166 29 168 68 34 17
Wallpaper=(None)
TileWallpaper=1
GridGranularity=0
IconSpacing=60
```

This section goes on and on, identifying file extensions associated with any application we have launched from Windows. It covers both DOS and Windows 3.x applications.

```
[Extensions]
smm=C:\AMIPRO\amipro.exe ^.smm
sam=C:\AMIPRO\amipro.exe ^.sam
doc=winword.exe ^.doc
cal=calendar.exe ^.cal
crd=cardfile.exe ^.crd
trm=terminal.exe ^.trm
txt=C:\PE\GOPEB.BAT ^.TXT
pcx=pbrush.exe ^.pcx
bmp=pbrush.exe ^.bmp
rec=recorder.exe ^.rec
LZH=LH.BAT ^.LZH
. . . . . . . . . . . . . . . .
cdr=D:\WINAPPS\COREL\CORELDRW\coreldrw.exe ^.cdr
```

The country settings for the PC are specified below. The country setting controls the default settings for time and date, along with other standard defaults specific to the country, such as typical currency symbols. This section just grows and grows with seemingly no end as well.

```
[intl]
sCountry=United States
iCountry=1
iDate=0
iTime=0
iTLZero=0
iCurrency=0
iCurrDigits=2
iNegCurr-0
iLzero=1
iDigits=2
iMeasure=1
s1159=AM
s2359=PM
sCurrency=$
sThousand=,
sDecimal=.
sDate=/
sTime=:
sList=,
sShortDate=M/d/yy
sLongDate=dddd, MMMM dd, yyyy
```

The following codes specify the display colors we have chosen. Changing these numbers can have some wild results. Try PUNK for a unique color combination. These settings can be changed once Windows 3.x is active using the display dialog in the control panel program group.

```
[colors]
Background=105 128 0
AppWorkspace=255 255 128
Window=255 255 255
WindowText=0 0 0
Menu=255 255 255
MenuText=0 0 0
ActiveTitle=64 128 128
InactiveTitle=128 255 255
TitleText=255 255 255
ActiveBorder=255 128 64
```

645

```
InactiveBorder=255 128 128
WindowFrame=0 0 0
Scrollbar=129 129 129
```

Here the PC's physical ports are identified—that is, assigned a number. The LPT port lines assigned printer port number 1 to LPT1 and printer port number two to LPT2. Nothing follows the LPT port assignments because there are no setup parameters that Windows 3.x controls for them. In contrast, when Windows 3.x assigns a number to a COM port, it also specifies the speed and character layout. The EPT designation stands for enhanced parallel port.

```
[ports]
; A line with [filename].PRN followed by an equal sign causes
; [filename] to appear in the control panel's Printer Configuration dialog
; box. A printer connected to [filename] directs its output into this
; file.
LPT1:=
LPT2:=
LPT3:=
COM1:=9600,n,8,1
COM2:=9600,n,8,1
COM3:=9600,n,8,1
COM4:=9600,n,8,1
EPT:=
FILE:=
LPT1.OS2=
LPT2.OS2=
```

This specifies where Windows 3.x Help box appears. Move yours around and then exit, saving changes to see what range of movement is permitted here.

```
[Windows Help]
Xl=609
Yu=163
Xr=945
Yd=579
Maximized=1
```

This section begins the display and printer font identification to Windows. These are standard Windows 3.x display and printing fonts.

```
[fonts]
Modern (Plotter)=MODERN.FON
Roman (Plotter)=ROMAN.FON
Script (Plotter)=SCRIPT.FON
MS Sans Serif 8,10,12,14,18,24 (8514/a res)=SSERIFF.FON
MS Serif 8,10,12,14,18,24 (8514/a res)=SERIFF.FON
Small Fonts (8514/a res)=SMALLF.FON
```

Use Windows 3.x TrueType fonts as identified below. These are the fonts loaded by the Windows 3.x GUI and used to produce documents and screen displays.

```
Arial (TrueType)=ARIAL.FOT
Arial Italic (TrueType)=ARIALI.FOT
Courier New (TrueType)=COUR.FOT
Courier New Italic (TrueType)=COURI.FOT
WingDings (TrueType)=WINGDING.FOT
Motor (True Type)=C:\WIN\SYSTEM\motorn.fot
................
Timpani Bold Italic (True Type)=C:\WIN\SYSTEM\timpanit.fot
TimpaniHeavy Italic (True Type)=C:\WIN\SYSTEM\timpnihi.fot
ZurichCalligraphic Italic (True Type)=C:\WIN\SYSTEM\zurichi.fot
Lincoln (True Type)=C:\WIN\SYSTEM\lincolnn.fot
```

The TrueType section specifies whether TrueType fonts should be used only in applications or whether Windows 3.x can use both TrueType and bit-mapped fonts.

```
[TrueType]
TTEnable=1
TTOnly=0
```

Now WIN.INI specifies font descriptions that are assigned to the printer ports. These make it possible for all Windows 3.x applications to print with the same fonts.

Below is the weird [wt4gpi8s56bz] Windows 3.1 specification for printer fonts. This is sometimes found on Windows 3.x PCs with desktop publishing applications installed. It helps Windows 3.x match the screen display to the printed output.

```
[wt4gpi8s56bz]
```

The operating parameters for the printers and printing programs installed on our PC are:

```
[HP LaserJet Series II,LPT1:,LPT2:,LPT3]
Memory=4491
Number of Cartridges=1
Cartridge 1=30
[HPPCL,LPT1]
duplex=0
prtcaps=32896
paperind=5
winver=310
sfdlstyle=16
numcart=1
cartindex1=
[HPPCL5A,LPT1]
prtcaps2=3
```

Printer specifications are often required for special programs, such as send/receive fax modem programs. The font specifications for the WINFAX program are below.

```
[WINFAX]
Fax Path=d:\appsw\winfax\data\
Fax Device=Class1
modem=*F2
Paper Format=Letter (8.5 x 11 inches)
Orientation=Portrait
Dial Prefix=
Resolution=Standard
Retries=0
Call Progress=Yes
CSID=MCO—Remote
Sender=Pete Moulton
Header Left=The Moulton Company
Header Center=Building User Knowledge, Since 1980
Header Right=FAX # 410 988-9861
Max Tx Rate=9600
Retry Time=60
Dial Control=Busy
Volume=Med
Speaker Mode=Connect
Dial Mode=Tone
```

Network printer assignments are specified in the WIN.INI file, as shown below.

```
[Network]
LPT2:=MOULTON676/PANASONIC
LPT2-OPTIONS=8,1,8,30,0,,PETE
```

Other printer assignments are also specified in the WIN.INI file, as shown below.

```
[PrinterPorts]
PCL / HP LaserJet=HPPCL,LPT1:,15,45,LPT2:,15,45
Canon LBP-8II=LBP8II,None,15,45
Epson 9 pin=EPSON9,None,15,45
IBM Graphics=IBMGRX,None,15,45
IBM Proprinters=PROPRINT,None,15,45
PostScript Printer=PSCRIPT,FILE:,15,45
```

This covers the major printer specifications. Next come setup and operating parameter specifications for the XTALK communications program.

```
[XTALK]
ModemCom1Name=Hayes V9600
ModemCom1Prefix=ATDT
ModemCom1Suffix=^M
ModemCom1Setup=ATS0=1^M
ModemCom1Init=^M~ATV1E0X4^M~AT&M4&B1&Y2&C1&D2^M
ModemCom1Hangup=~~+++~~ATH0^M
ModemCom1Ok=OK^M^J
ModemCom1Error=ERROR^M^J
ModemCom1Connect=CONNECT^M^J
ModemCom1Speed=CONNECT %^M^J
ModemCom1Dial=TONE^M^J
ModemCom1Ring=RING^M^J
ModemCom1NoDial=NO DIAL^M^J
ModemCom1Busy=BUSY^M^J
ModemCom1Carrier=NO CARRIER^M^J
Maximized=0
DirXwp=D:\WINAPPS\XTKWIN\PHONE
DirXws=D:\WINAPPS\XTKWIN\SCRIPTS
DirFil=D:\
Editor=c:\pe\PE2.exe
Startup=e
```

```
Backups=1
Secret=0
Paste=1
OutNumber=
WatchDial=1
CustomPrefix=ATX0DT
CustomSuffix=^M
CustomSetup=ATS0=1^M
CustomInit=^M~ATV1E0X0^M
CustomHangup=~~+++~~ATH0^M
CustomOk=OK^M^J
CustomError=ERROR^M^J
CustomConnect=CONNECT^M^J
CustomSpeed=CONNECT %^M^J
CustomDial=TONE^M^J
CustomRing=RING^M^J
CustomNoDial=NO DIAL^M^J
CustomBusy=BUSY^M^J
CustomCarrier=NO CARRIER^M^J
CustomChange=0
ModemCom1Change=1
Comm=16384
LdNumber=1 619 755-2019
ModemCom1ARQ=CONNECT %/REL^M^J
```

Several applications are now set up in the WIN.INI file. For example, the following WIN.INI statement sets up the clock display format, which is in analog or digital format.

```
[Clock]
iFormat=0
```

The following lines specify the solitaire game parameters.

```
[Solitaire]
Back=11
Options=67
```

Windows 3.x comes with a simple terminal program. It is pointed at COM1 with the following WIN.INI statement.

```
[Terminal]
Port=COM1
```

The Windows 3.x calculator can be set to a normal or scientific calculator, which can do different types of scientific calculations. This statement determines how the scientific calculator is set up.

```
[SciCalc]
layout=0
[Paintbrush]
width=552
height=144
clear=COLOR
```

The above entries are associated with the Windows 3.x utilities and games we use.

There were about five pages of other program parameter specifications that we just removed to reduce the amount of redundant data we examine. We stopped here because it looks like Corel Draw wins the award for the shortest program specification. It uses only two lines:

```
[CorelDraw]
Dir=D:\WINAPPS\COREL\CORELDRW
```

This finishes our quick tour of the WIN.INI file. Next let's see what can be done with it.

As an exercise, use Windows WRITE to open the WININI.WRI found in the C:\WINDOWS subdirectory, which gives the Windows documentation of special WIN.INI file parameters. The best way to understand the Windows 3.1x INI files is to work with them on a Windows 3.1 PC. If that is not available, you might be able to find information in the Microsoft knowledge base at the Microsoft web site, although this is kind of like searching for a needle lost on the moon.

SYSTEM.INI

In this next section we examine SYSTEM.INI; we also present some changes we can make in it, and their impact on Windows.

The SYSTEM.INI loads and configures Windows for your hardware and software. Every time you add something new to your PC that is used through Windows, this file is updated. This, like any text file, can be edited and viewed though most text editors. A word of caution before you make changes—some lines can have a drastic effect on Windows. Some lines can even stop Windows 3.x from running. For the most part you do not edit this file through a text editor; instead, you rely on the Windows 3.x control panel or the Windows 3.x setup program to make the modifications. In this section, we look closely at the important sections of the SYSTEM.INI file and provide you with additional hints that may improve Windows 3.x performance. The parameter settings (lines) you see here are some of the more common settings. However, your PC may contain different ones because it has a different configuration. Some of the entries you see are ones that must be added and are rarely used.

To begin viewing, select the RUN command from the file menu and execute SYSEDIT. SYSEDIT is probably the best way to view the SYSTEM.INI file. It only views and edits the seven most important files for Windows, which are:

```
AUTOEXEC.BAT
CONFIG.SYS
SYSTEM.INI
WIN.INI
PROTOCOL.INI
MSMAIL.INI
SCHDPLUS.INI
```

These files establish the operating environment for Windows 3.x as it boots. They establish the memory configuration, the desktop interface, the LAN operation, and the operation of key Windows 3.x programs such as Microsoft Mail and the scheduler program.

SYSTEM.INI File Sections

Sections in the SYSTEM.INI file, like the [boot] section, [386enhanced] section (containing device= lines), and the [keyboard] section, have parameter settings assigned automatically, based on choices that were made at the time Windows 3.x was installed. These settings are not cast in stone, but changing some of them could cause Windows 3.x to function incorrectly. The key SYSTEM.INI sections are:

[**boot**]—This section of the SYSTEM.INI file lists all the Windows modules and drivers needed for Windows 3.x to configure itself every time it starts. These files are typically found in the \windows\system folder or directory. Unless otherwise noted, all the following lines are essential. Changing or disabling any of them could prevent Windows 3.x from starting. If Windows 3.x does not boot, try using the /b parameter to create BOOTLOG.TXT. Remember: be careful about changes you make. If by accident you hit a key and make a change you cannot find, then close the file and answer "no" when prompted to save.

[boot description]—provides the descriptions displayed by the SETUP.EXE program for display, keyboard, network, and so on. These are the current choices for the basic hardware configuration options.

[drivers]—other names for drivers are included here.

[keyboard]—provides special keyboard settings for different PC keyboards, for example, 84-key v.s 101-key v.s 104-key. The entries in this section are required. Unlike other sections in the SYSTEM.INI file, these lines have no defaults.

[mci]—lists multimedia drivers installed.

[386ENH]—the 386 enhanced mode operation section. This sets up operating parameters for the operation of Windows 3.x in the 386 enhanced mode. It controls multitasking operation, swapfiles, networking operation, and the virtual machine device drivers that are loaded to activate the Windows 3.x virtual machine.

[standard]—This section controls Windows 3.x in standard mode operation. It is seldom used because the real power of Windows 3.x comes from operating in 386 enhanced mode.

[NonWindowsApp]—controls the DOS virtual machines. The DOS virtual machine behavior can be changed here. However, this is typically left empty so that the default values are used.

[NETWARE]—When NetWare LAN software is used with Windows, this section configures that software.

Not all sections appear in every SYSTEM.INI file. Some sections are always present in every SYSTEM.INI file, like the [386ENH], the [boot], and the [boot description] sections.

Selected SYSTEM.INI File Parameters

There are many SYSTEM.INI file parameters. The file we examine here contains the typical parameters placed in the system INI file by SETUP. Some additional parameters may be there as well, but there are many more SYSTEM.INI parameters that can be used in the file. These other parameters are rarely used.

Let's now tour the SYSTEM.INI file, looking at some of the parameters in turn from top to bottom. The file used in these notes is not in the identical sequence as other SYSTEM.INI files encountered because it was set up by hand to demonstrate the SYSTEM.INI file parameters. The parameters in this file cover those in most other SYSTEM.INI files. Follow along by opening your SYSTEM.INI file on your machine using the Windows Notepad.

The SYSTEM.INI file parameters are as follows:

```
[boot]
```

The [boot] section parameters are:

```
shell=progman.exe
```

shell=filename—tells Windows 3.x what shell it is going to use. Setup assumes the program manager shell PROGMAN.EXE. The program manager that displays the Windows 3.x Icon menus is run by this SYSTEM.INI file command. The shell could also be set to the Windows 3.x file manager, WINFILE.EXE.

```
network.drv=nctware.drv
```

network.drv=filename— names the Windows 3.x network (Winnet) driver you will use. The Windows for Workgroups default is wfwnet.drv, and Novell is netware.drv. These were the principal drivers used in Windows 3.1, although some PCs were configured to work with Banyan Vines networks.

The netware.drv statement is required for using Windows 3.x on NetWare. Different drivers are required for other network software, such as IBM's OS/2 LAN server software which uses NETBIOS.

```
language.dll=
```

language.dll=filename—tells Windows 3.x which language DLL to use for language-specific functions, enabling Windows 3.x to appear in French, Italian, German, etc. This line is changed using the international control panel icon or by rerunning setup. The default is blank (none), in which case Windows 3.x uses the built-in English (U.S.) library.

```
sound.drv=mmsound.drv
```

sound.drv=filename—indicates the name of the system sound driver you are using. You can change this yourself by editing the SYSTEM.INI. These statements control the PC's speaker and communications ports. Under Windows 3.11, the sound driver is a multimedia sound driver; the original Windows 3.1 sound driver specification line was:

```
sound.drv=sound.drv)
comm.drv=comm.drv
```

This is the communications driver specification for your serial communications port.

```
;386grabber=vgadib.3gr
;286grabber=vgacolor.2gr
;display.drv=svga256.drv
```

The lines above specify SVGA display drivers. The semicolon (;) at the beginning of the line is the comment character, so it disables the SVGA drivers.

The grabber and display driver statements control the Windows 3.x displays. To change display types, change those statements.

386grabber=filename—assigns the grabber for Windows. Grabbers make a DOS application visible when you run it in Windows 386 enhanced mode. This item is changed when you change display driver settings.

286grabber=filename—same as above, only it is used when Windows 3.x runs in standard mode as opposed to 386 enhanced.

display.drv=filename—your Windows 3.x display driver. It determines what resolution and how many colors Windows 3.x uses. Make sure your monitor and card support this driver. This is changed through setup in the main group or from DOS setup. The default is blank (none). The most common is VGA.DRV, the Windows 3.x standard 640x480 VGA display driver.

```
386grabber=vga.3gr
286grabber=vgacolor.2gr
display.drv=vga.drv
```

The above statements set up the standard VGA display drivers for the Windows 3.x standard VGA. Other special display driver programs for a specific manufacturer's VGA board being used in a PC are installed by changing the 386grabber, 286grabber, and display.drv lines. There is a fourth line in the 386 enhanced section that must also be changed for specific manufacturer's VGA boards.

```
fonts.fon=vgasys.fon
fixedfon.fon=vgafix.fon
oemfonts.fon=vgaoem.fon
```

These three statements set up the PC's menu fonts.

oemfonts.fon=filename—This font specification defines the font for your display settings. The OEM character set is changed running setup under DOS. The default is blank (none). For higher resolutions or larger display fonts, use the 8514 series of fonts.

fixedfont.fon=filename—the fixed font used by Windows 2.x applications. This is changed when you change your display settings.

fonts.fon=filename—This font is used as the proportionally spaced system font. This item is also changed through the display settings in setup. The default is blank (none).

Substituting different font statements here can make the display characters larger or smaller because these are bit-mapped fonts. When 8514 fonts are used on a VGA screen, the letters contain more dots so they appear larger on the VGA display. If the CGA fonts are used, the display characters would appear smaller.

The character size varies because for a given display there are only a fixed number of dots—there are more dots for an 8514 than for a CGA. The 8514 fonts have more dots in each character to maintain the same relative physical readable size when it appears on the 8514 display with 1,024 by 768 dots. When the 8514 fonts are used with a VGA display, they produce larger visible characters because each character has more dots. VGA fonts have fewer dots because the total VGA dots are only 640 by 480 dots.

```
mouse.drv=filename
```

This statement specifies which mouse driver you will use. This setting is changed through the Windows 3.x setup. The Microsoft mouse driver is specified by the command:

```
mouse.drv=mouse.drv
```

Other mouse drivers are listed below. They include the Mouse Systems mouse drivers for the PS/2 mouse port as well as those for the serial ports COM1 AND COM2.

```
; mouse.drv=msmouse1.drv
: mouse.drv=mscmouse.drv
; Mouse Systems driver for COM1
; mouse.drv=msmouse2.drv
; mouse.drv=mscbc3.drv
; Mouse Systems driver for COM2
keyboard.drv=keyboard.drv
```

This is your keyboard driver, as selected during setup. To change this parameter, use setup in the main group.

```
[keyboard]
subtype=
subtype=#—This helps the keyboard driver discern special
features of a particular keyboard. To change this setting,
go through the Windows 3.x setup.

;type=3
;Type 3 is for 84 key AT keyboard.
type=4
;Type 4 is for 101 key AT keyboard.
```

These statements specify the type of keyboard used by Windows. A 101-key keyboard is specified as Type 4 and an 84-key keyboard is specified as Type 3. If a 101-key keyboard is identified as a Type 3 keyboard, some keys fail to operate.

type=#—This section uses a value to specify the keyboard type. In the absence of a type, the keyboard driver (KEYBOARD.DRV) selects the type. The chart below lists the different keyboard types. Changes are made through the Windows 3.x setup in the main group.

Number	Type
1	83 Key IBM PC XT Compatible
2	Olivetti 102 Key
3	84-86 Key IBM PC AT Compatible
4	101-102 Key IBM Compatible

```
oemansi.bin=
```

oemansi.bin=filename—for PCs using other than code page 437, this specifies the code page translations for US OEM/ANSI. Changes are made in the DOS setup under Code Page.

```
keyboard.dll=
```

Keyboard.dll=filename—This DLL defines keyboard layouts for nonUS keyboards. If you use any keyboard other than IBM PC, XT, AT, AT&T 301/302, or Olivetti 83-key, then you must have an entry on this line. Changes are made through the Windows 3.x setup in the main group.

```
;Required for Adobe Type Manager SEE also line AFTER fonts
system.drv=atmsys.drv
;Required for Adobe Type Manager SEE also line BEFORE fonts
atm.system.drv=system.drv
```

In this example, the ATM is being used. It requires substituting ATM-SYS.DRV for the SYSTEM.DRV. ATM fonts and Windows 3.x TrueType fonts can be used at the same time without any difficulties.

To remove ATM, just revert to the original line:

```
;system.drv=system.drv
```

The system.drv=filename tells Windows 3.x what your system hardware driver will be. To change this, run the Windows 3.x setup from DOS and select a new system.

```
taskman.exe=filename
```

The taskman.exe=filename describes which task-switching application you will use when you use CTRL + ESC. To change this you must edit the SYSTEM.INI file itself. The default is Taskman.exe. This statement only appears when a different task manager is used.

drivers=filename—describes installable drivers or aliases of installable drivers that load when Windows 3.x starts. Installable drivers are DLL files. The drivers also may have parameters that are defined with their alias in the [drivers] section of the SYSTEM.INI file. You will probably not change this setting, as the installation program of the specific software you install usually makes changes.

CachedFileHandles=#—sets the number of EXE and DLLs that stay open. Like disk cache, Windows 3.x keeps the recently used EXE and DLL files in memory instead of closing them. When they are used again, Windows 3.x performance is increased because it accesses them from memory rather than from the fixed disk. The parameter can be 2 to 12 file handles. The default is 12.

CacheFilesHandles can cause a problem when running Windows 3.x off a server if the network setup limits the number of concurrent open files on the server. When the server setting is less than 12, lower Windows' CacheFileHandles. Changes are made using SYSEDIT.

```
SCRNSAVE.EXE=(None)
```

Windows 3.1 incorporates screen savers. These are disabled by default as specified by the SCRNSAVE.EXE= (None) line.

```
[boot.description]

nework.drv=NetWare Device Driver for Windows v1.03

language.dll=English (American)

;keyboard.typ=All AT type keyboards (84-86 keys)
keyboard.typ=Enhanced 101 or 102 key US and non-US keyboards

; mouse.drv=Microsoft, or IBM PS/2
mouse.drv=Mouse Systems (or VisiOn) connected to COM2

display.drv=Super VGA (1024x768, 256 colors, small fonts)

;aspect=100,96,96

;display.drv=VGA

system.drv=MS-DOS or PC-DOS System
```

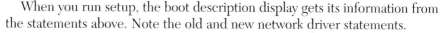

When you run setup, the boot description display gets its information from the statements above. Note the old and new network driver statements.

`[386ENH]`

The 386 enhanced section of the SYSTEM.INI file contains special hardware setup parameters that make the PC either operate or fail with Windows. These parameters and their influence on the PC are shown below. This section contains 386 enhanced mode-operating parameters and virtual device driver program specifications, and has the settings for 32-bit disk access, virtual memory, Windows 3.x scheduling priorities, and the Windows 3.x virtual device drivers. The virtual drivers in this section are loaded from the many device statements. They can be actual files like "device=vpmtd.386," or as a "*" with a name like "device=*vpd." The files that end with the ".386" extension are actual files found in the \windows\system folder or directory, whereas the names with the "*" are built in virtual devices to the WIN386.EXE kernel.

If you find this confusing, think of it as the difference between internal and external commands in DOS. There are approximately 144 possible entries in this section, not to mention the numerous "device=" entries. The average SYSTEM.INI file will contain from 30 to 40 of these lines. In this section, we look at a good portion of the possible lines found here, but not all lines appear in every SYSTEM.INI file.

Probably the most confusing section in the SYSTEM.INI file is the [386ENH] section because every time new software or hardware is added to a Windows 3.x PC, lines are also added to the [386ENH] section. To discover what happened, copies of the SYSTEM.INI file before and after the hardware/software changes were compared.

When problems occur after installing something, the changes causing the problem can often be located in this section. For example, when installing a new fax/modem and WinfaxPro from Delrina, we were warned about speed mismatches between different class fax machines. Furthermore, we were offered an opportunity to have the setup compensate for this. After installation, we could not send a fax. All faxes sent were garbled. Several days later, after trying everything short of reinstallation, we noticed a line in the [386ENH] section: COM2FIFO=1. This added line caused a speed mismatch. By changing the line value to 0 (disabling value), we overcame the fax problem. The solution took several days because we did not notice the change in the [386ENH] section.

To solve these problems and understand the [386ENH] section, we applied the philosophy of line-by-line organization to the [386ENH] section. This approach separates the "device=" statements and groups them together alphabetically. It then groups the remaining lines alphabetically. Now any time a line is added to the [386ENH] section, it is easily found because it is either in a wrong group or out of alphabetical order. Even without organizing the file, a before-and-after comparison is effective in determining what has been changed in the file.

Organization is a good tool to help troubleshoot problems. To organize, you must know what you are organizing. In the fax example, part of the problem was we did not know the impact of any of the lines. In that case, how were we to be sure which line caused a specific problem without knowing what each line did?

`AllEMSLocked=on/off`

Turning this on keeps all EMS contents from being swapped to the swap-file, even the DOS applications. This setting supersedes any PIF settings, and should be used if you are using a disk cache in expanded memory. This entry must be in the SYSTEM.INI file. The default value is off.

`AllXMSLocked=on/off`

This entry probably is not used, and it is better set it to off. It keeps Windows 3.x from swapping information from the XMS to the swapfile, over-riding PIF settings. This parameter must be manually added.

`AllVMsExclusive=on/off`

This entry forces all programs to run exclusively in full screen mode. Again, it overrides PIF settings. Try using this if you have any TSR or old network software that is incompatible with Windows. This line is manually added and is defaulted to off.

`AutoRestoreScreen=on/off`

This command tells Windows 3.x who restores DOS applications screens when multi-tasking, the application or Windows. If the setting is on, then Windows 3.x is responsible. It stores the application's screen information in memory until it is restored. The advantage to this is that Windows 3.x restores the screen faster than the application. The disadvantage is that the screen is stored in XMS, reducing available memory for other applications. If the entry is off, the application is responsible for the screen, which reduces performance but does not use additional RAM. The default is on. You must add this line to the SYSTEM.INI file.

```
MaxBPs=1024
;Maximum Break Points—memory allocation for interrupts under Windows
```

The Max Point Breaks operating reduces Windows General Protection Faults. If you set this to 1,024, randomly occurring GPFs are supposed to be reduced.

```
SystemROMBreakPoint=FALSE
```

Windows 3.x does not need the SystemROMBreakPoint=FALSE operating parameter set. QEMM and 386 MAX required setting this parameter, which specifies whether Windows 3.x should use ROM address space between F000:0000 and 1 MB for a break point. Windows in 386 enhanced mode normally searches this space to find a special instruction that is used as a system break point. If this address space contains something other than permanently available ROM, you should disable this setting.

```
EMMExclude=a000-afff
;x=a000-afff This is the VGA Graphics swap range.

EMMExclude=b800-bfff
;x=B800-BFFF This is the VGA Text swap range.

EMMExclude=c000-C7FF
;x=C000-C7FF This is the VGA ROM range.

EMMExclude=c800-cbff
;x=c800-cbff This is the SCSI controller ROM range.

EMMExclude=f000-ffff
;x=f000-ffff This is the system ROM range.
```

The EMMExclude parameter may cure some Windows 3.x problems. Commonly, it is not required because Windows 3.x chooses settings from a standard set and from those in the CONFIG.SYS file. In most cases, choosing the default settings for these parameters gives the best Windows 3.x performance.

EMMExclude specifies a range of memory that Windows 3.x will not scan to find unused address space. This has the side effect of turning off the RAM and ROM search code for the range. The range (two paragraph values separated by a hyphen) must be between A000 and EFFF. This scanning can interfere with some adapters that use the same memory area. The starting value is rounded down and the ending value is rounded up to a multiple of 16K. For example, you could set EMMExclude=C800-CFFF to prevent Windows 3.x from scanning the addresses C800:0000 through CFFF:000F. You can specify more than one range by including more than one EMMExclude line. The EMMExclude lines are generally not necessary for Windows' proper operation, because Windows 3.x uses the memory specifications in the CONFIG.SYS file to set up the memory exclusions. The EMMExclude lines would only be used in extraordinary situations where application programs in some way corrupted Windows 3.x memory setup.

```
ebios=*ebios
```

Ebios=filename indicates the extended BIOS being used by Windows 3.x in the 386 enhanced mode. To change this, you must edit the SYSTEM.INI file. The default is whatever Windows 3.x has set up during installation. This SYSTEM.INI parameter would only be changed if its special PC hardware required it. Normally it is left at the Windows 3.x internal setting, that is, with an asterisk preceding ebios.

```
keyboard=*vkd
mouse=*vmd
```

The =*vkd and =*vmd statements specify using the standard internal Windows 3.x driver programs and DLLs for keyboard and mouse.

The network drivers for NetWare are specified here.

```
network=*vnetbios, vnetware.386, vipx.386
```

Other specifications for VGA display drivers for a Super VGA board are above. These lines must be changed along with the other VGA lines to change display types. display=filename indicates the selected display device that will be used by Windows. To change this, run setup in DOS.

```
;Set for VGA Version 3.0
;display=VDDVGA30.386
;Set for SVGA
;display=vddsvga.386
;Set For Std VGA
display=*vddvga
```

Device=filename specifies the virtual device drivers used by Windows 3.x in 386 enhanced mode. These commands are typically grouped in one area in the 386 enhanced section of the SYSTEM.INI file.

```
device=filename
```

Other commands used in place of "device=" are:

```
transport=
```

specifies the network protocols

```
display=
```

specifies special display drivers

```
ebios=
```

specifies any extended BIOS that is installed

```
secondnet=
```

specifies the second networking protocol when two networking protocols are installed

```
mouse=
```

specifies a special mouse driver program

```
keyboard=
```

specifies the keyboard driver. The *vkd is a standard Windows 3.x internal keyboard driver.

```
network=
```

specifies the type of network support installed. This is most often support for NetWare and the Microsoft Windows 3.x network.

The values are file names with the 386 extension on them, or a name that begins with an asterisk (*). Windows 3.x sets these lines during the initial setup or whenever you install new applications that require unique commands.

Windows 3.x adds lines based on your PC hardware. For Windows 3.1, the following is set:

```
device=vtdapi.386
device=*vpicd
device=*vtd
device=*reboot
device=*vsd
device=*v86mmgr
device=*pageswap
device=*dosmgr
device=*vmpoll
device=*wshell
device=*vhd<=set by Windows 3.0
device=*vpd
device=*parity
device=*biosxlat
device=*vcd
device=*vmcpd
device=*combuff
device=*cdpscsi
local=CON
```

The SYSTEM.INI specification local=con tells Windows 3.x that the console is the keyboard attached to the PC.

```
device=*blockdev
```

These lines described are the key SYSTEM.INI specifications for setting up 32-bit disk access and 32-bit file access. They coordinate I/O between block and 32-bit disk access devices. A disk controller card (typically IDE) that is Western digital 1003 MFM controller compatible adds the blockdev line to your [386ENH] section, permitting 32-bit disk access. This line may be deleted if 32-bit file access is enabled.

> device=*wdctrl—used to communicate with WD 1003-compatible fixed disk controllers.
>
> device=*INT13—emulates and traps INT13h calls
>
> device=*pagefile—handles the virtual memory paging

```
; 32BitDiskAccess=OFF <=original win31
32BitDiskAccess=ON
```

32bitDiskAccess=on/off—When a PC is capable of supporting 32-bit disk access, this line controls it. The default setting is off. The virtual memory settings in the 386 enhanced section of the control panel activate it. When PCs do not support this feature, the line is absent. As an exercise, go to the 32-bit disk access section and see if your PC qualifies. When set on, humans see no perceptible difference in disk performance. Generally SCSI disk controllers do not support 32-bit disk access without special drivers. We have an AMI SCSI disk controller that supports 32-bit disk access.

```
; OverlappedIO=off <=original win31
```

OverlappedIO=ON—The overlapped I/O specification allows several read and write requests to be issued to the disk before the first request is finished, which can speed up disk operations. Unfortunately, but not surprisingly, most humans do not notice a speedup.

PageBuffers=16—This statement specifies the number of 4 Kb page buffers Windows 3.x uses to store asynchronous read/write pages when 32BitDiskAccess is activated. The default value is 4. Increasing the value here could improve Windows 3.x performance, typically when a system has lots of RAM. Again, most humans would not notice a speed increase. We have increased speed and thought everything really ran faster. It probably seemed to run faster because we knew we had made the change.

DOSPromptExitInstruc=no—DOSPromptExitInstruct=on/off (or yes/no) —This turns on or off the annoying Windows 3.1x message displayed when a

DOS Window is opened. Leave this unchanged for new Windows 3.x users or they may think they exited Windows. The default setting is Yes. If enabled, when you start the MS-DOS prompt, a message box appears with instructions on how to exit and switch away from the MS-DOS prompt. If you do not want to see the message, disable this setting. by adding the DOSPromptExitInstruct line to the SYSTEM.INI file. The default is on.

`PermSwapDOSDrive=D`

PermSwapSizeK=16000—These SYSTEM.INI controls set up the permanent swapfile. They are changed using the Windows 3.x control panel and selecting the 386 enhanced icon, then virtual memory settings.

`LocalReboot=off—`

The default setting is On. This LocalReboot parameter specifies whether you can press Ctrl + Alt + Del to quit applications that cause an unrecoverable error in 386 enhanced mode without restarting Windows. If this setting is enabled, you can quit the applications. If this setting is disabled, pressing Ctrl + Alt + Del normally restarts the PC.

`COM#(1-4)AutoAssign=#/sec—`

This line sets a contention value to the available COM ports. The number controls port sharing between applications. At least one application is a DOS application. If the number is –1, you get a message asking which application is going to control the port. A 0 value means any application can use the port. The seconds value assigns an amount of time after one application stops using the port before another can assume control. This line is set through the 386 enhanced dialog in the control panel. The default seconds is 2 and can be as high as 1000.

;COMBoostTime=<milliseconds>—sets the amount of time in milliseconds that Windows 3.x allows a virtual machine to process a COM interrupt. This is helpful if you are seeing characters lost on your screen by communications programs. It is easy to see lost characters because text appears garbled as it is received. You must add this line yourself. The default number is 2.

COM#(1-4)Base=address—sets the base port for the serial ports in your computer. To change these, go to the Advanced button on the ports control panel window. Check device documentation for potential conflicts.

COM#(1-4)Irq=#—sets the IRQ for the device used at a particular serial port. Check device documentation to avoid any conflicts. If a conflict arises, try setting the value to –1 to disable input on that IRQ. The defaults for the ports are shown below. Any changes can be made from the Advanced button on the ports control panel window.

```
; device=*vhd <= set by Windows 3.0 but removed for Windows 3.1
; device=*vpd <= set by Windows 3.0 but removed for Windows 3.1
device=*PAGEFILE<=set by Windows 3.1
device=*vfd<=set by Windows 3.1
```

These statements were used by Windows 3.1:

```
[NonWindowsApp]
localtsrs=dosedit,ced
CommandEnvSize=2000
```

The non-Windows application section of the SYSTEM.INI file is used to control DOS sessions. DOS applications are passed information by these statements. The local terminate-and-stay-resident line specifies the TSR programs loaded for the DOS sessions. The environment space size specifies the amount of memory to set aside for the DOS environment space.

```
MinTimeslice=20
WinTimeslice=300,100
WinExclusive=0
```

These statements specify how the CPU's time is distributed among the different Windows 3.x virtual machines or active Windows. Processors with slow clock speeds (6 MHz to 16 MHz) should probably use the Windows 3.x default of 20 Ms as the minimum time slice. Faster CPUs, such as 50 MHz, could set the minimum time slice to 5 Ms. At 50 MHz, each millisecond permits the CPU to execute (conservatively) about 5,000 computer instructions (50,000,000/1,000/10 clock cycles per instruction). Five milliseconds permits each virtual machine to execute about 25,000 instructions before releasing the CPU to another virtual machine. At 500 MHz, this increases to 250,000 instructions. The best strategy here is to leave the minimum time slice set as specified by Windows. We have experimented with large and small values for the minimum time slice only to find that both large and small values made Windows 3.x operation erratic. Windows 3.x would either become very jerky or very slow, depending on whether the value is set very large or very small.

```
CGA80WOA.FON=CGA80WOA.FON
```

CGA80WOA.FON=filename—The display font used when DOS-based applications use the 80 columns and 25 or fewer screen lines. To change this, run setup and change the code page or display setting. The default is blank (none).

```
CGA40WOA.FON=CGA40WOA.FON
```

CGA40WOA.FON=filename—The same as above, however this is for the 40-column, 25-or-fewer lines screen.

```
EGA80WOA.FON=EGA80WOA.FON
```

EGA80WOA.FON=filename—The same as the CGA80WOA.FON, however this is for 80 columns with 25 or more line screens.

```
EGA40WOA.FON=EGA40WOA.FON
```

EGA40WOA.FON=filename—This is the same as the CGA40WOA.FON; however this is for 40 columns with 25 or more line screens.

FileSysChange=off—Additional NetWare parameters include the SYSTEM.INI line disabling, alerting Windows 3.x every time a file is manipulated by an application. The default value is "on" because, on a single-user PC, there are programs manipulating the files. In contrast, when a PC is networked, many programs can work with files simultaneously.

NetHeapSize=32—specifies the network heap or buffer area size. The default is 12 or 8. This is the size (in kilobytes) of the buffers that Windows in 386 enhanced mode allocates in conventional memory for transferring data over a network. All values are rounded up to the nearest 4K. Using Netware increases that value.

;PagingDrive=e:—These parameters are used to control the temporary program paging space on a fixed disk drive. The PagingDrive default value is "none." It specifies the disk drive where Windows in 386 enhanced mode allocates a temporary swapfile (WIN386.SWP). This setting is ignored if you have a permanent swapfile. If you don't have a permanent swapfile and no drive is specified or the specified drive does not exist, Windows 3.1x attempts to put your temporary swapfile on the drive containing your SYSTEM.INI file. If the specified drive is full, paging is disabled.

;swapdisk=c:\win386.swp—This sets the location of the temporary program swapfile (WIN386.SWP).

;MinUserDiskSpace=4096—This specifies disk space to leave free when creating a temporary program swapfile.

;MaxPagingFileSize=4096—This specifies disk space to leave free when creating a temporary program swapfile.

```
;TimerCriticalSection=10
;TimerCriticalSection=10000
;Typical Network Setting is 10000
;Default: 0
```

The above commands instruct Windows 3.x how to behave in a special section of software designed to handle timer-critical functions. This timer-critical section of software is entered as part of all timer-interrupt code in Windows 3.1x. The parameters specify a time-out period (in milliseconds); specifying a positive value ensures that only one virtual machine at a time receives timer interrupts. Some networks and other global memory-resident software may fail unless this setting is used. Using these parameters slows down performance and can make the system sluggish or seem to stop for short periods of time. This parameter is sometimes used for special network settings, including special settings for NetWare.

```
[NETWARE]
```

The NetWare section is set up when NetWare is installed on a Windows 3.x PC. It contains the last of the special NetWare parameter settings.

```
RestoreDrives=false
```

Normally, when you exit Windows, all of your drive mappings are restored to the way they were before you started Windows, and all changes you made inside Windows 3.x are lost. If you set the RestoreDrives value to false, the mappings you made inside Windows 3.x remain when you exit Windows.

```
NWShareHandles=false
```

Normally, each virtual machine you start from Windows 3.x has its own set of drive mappings, and changes you make in one virtual machine do not affect another. If you set the NWShareHandles value to true, drive mappings become global, and changes made in one virtual machine affect all other applications. The NWShareHandles setting permits you to look at new network drives in different Windows 3.x while the nonactive Windows 3.x remain at the drive locations you had originally left them.

Changing the SYSTEM.INI file under Windows 3.x can have disastrous results if the driver programs specified are not resident in the WINDOWS\SYSTEM subdirectory of your PC. Missing display drivers or fonts cause Windows 3.x to unceremoniously dump you out to DOS instantly. Other settings may result in strange error messages or PC lockups when Windows 3.x is running.

Windows 3.1 References to Multimedia Drivers

Multimedia drivers are installed and configured using the control panel.

```
;multimedia drivers
[mci]
```

Multimedia drivers reference the media control interface (MCI) SYSTEM.INI file section.

```
CDAudio=mcicda.drv
Sequencer=mciseq.drv
WaveAudio=mciwave.drv
[drivers]
midimapper=midimap.drv
Wave1=speaker.drv
timer=timer.drv
 [speaker.drv]
CPU Speed=48
Volume=500
Version=774
Enhanced=1
Max seconds=3
Leave interrupts enabled=0
```

This is the [speaker.drv] speaker driver section for using WAV files with the PC's speaker. This matches with the Wave1=speaker.drv above line.

Altering the SYSTEM.INI file changes Windows. Before making any changes to the file, please copy it to SYSTEMIN.001. This backup copy is to ensure that you can return to the current Windows 3.x setup without reinstalling Windows.

Whenever you change the contents of any INI file, you should make a copy of the file before altering it.

We have completed our examination of WIN.INI and SYSTEM.INI files. It is now time to look at the remaining files that comprise Windows 3.1. Some of these files are just programs while others are a combination of a program and an INI file.

USER.EXE

The USER.EXE program in Windows 3.x is one of the GUI programs. It manages Windows 3.x inputs and keeps track of all the windows created by applications on the PC. The Windows 3.11 USER.EXE file is:

```
USER EXE 264,096 05-02-97 10:07a
```

The USER.EXE program is a DLL used by the Windows 3.x system virtual machine. To perform its Windows 3.x management function, it uses a 64 KB data segment (data heap) in real mode memory. This real mode data segment is faster to access than some data segment elsewhere in memory. Such speed is needed to keep Windows 3.x actively moving for the PC user.

GDI.EXE

The Graphical Device Interface program, or GDI.EXE, is also a Windows 3.x system DLL that manages the Windows 3.x graphic display interface. It works in conjunction with the USER.EXE program, managing the Windows 3.x by managing all the drawing objects on the screen; drawing objects are color palettes and fonts. The Windows 3.11 GDI.EXE file is:

```
GDI EXE  220,800      11-01-93 4:11a
```

It is found in the \windows\system directory along with the USER.EXE program.

WIN.COM

WIN.COM is the program that launches Windows 3.x. It is located in the C:\Windows directory. During installation, a command line reference is placed in the AUTOEXEC.BAT file, which causes WIN.COM to run and launch Windows. The WIN.COM program is:

```
WIN COM  50,904           08-15-95 10:44a
```

WIN.COM has several options to modify Windows 3.x operation. The options can be viewed at any time by typing WIN.COM /? These options include:

- WIN [/B] [/N] [/D:[C][F][S][V][X]]
- /B—creates a file, BOOTLOG.TXT, that records system messages generated during system startup (boot).
- /N—causes Windows 3.x not to load network drivers.
- /D:—used in combination with one or more of the following switches for troubleshooting when Windows 3.x does not start correctly.
- C—turns off 32-bit file access.
- F—turns off 32-bit disk access. Equivalent to SYSTEM.INI file setting: 32BitDiskAccess=FALSE.
- S—specifies that Windows 3.x should not use ROM address space between F000:0000 and 1 MB for a break point. Equivalent to

SYSTEM.INI file setting: SystemROMBreakPoint=FALSE.

- V—specifies that the ROM routine will handle interrupts from the hard disk controller. Equivalent to SYSTEM.INI file setting: VirtualHDIRQ=FALSE.

- X—excludes all of the adapter area from the range of memory that Windows 3.x scans to find unused space. Equivalent to SYSTEM.INI file setting: EMMExclude=A000-FFFF.

The Windows 3.0 WIN.COM had different options for loading Windows 3.x in real mode, standard mode, or 386 enhanced mode. See the kernel section earlier in this chapter for a brief explanation of these modes.

With Windows 3.1 and 3.11, these options changed to become more troubleshooting tools, as we see above.

PROGMAN.EXE and PROGMAN.INI

PROGMAN.EXE is the primary user interface or shell program under Windows 3.x. When you exit PROGMAN.EXE, you exit Windows 3.x because it is the shell program. The program manager (PROGMAN.EXE) launches the application programs. They are identified as icons in several groups. These files are:

```
PROGMAN  INI         297     05-12-99 1:38p
PROGMAN  EXE     115,312     11-01-93 4:11a
```

In Windows 3.x, groups organize the different programs we use by containing their icons. In addition, we applied some custom settings to program manager to help us organize the groups and applications, such as automatically saving settings on exiting. To keep track of all these different settings and groups, program manager records them in a file called PROGMAN.INI. Just like the WIN.INI and the SYSTEM.INI files, the PROGMAN.INI file is only a text file. The easiest way to view this file is through the text editor NOTEPAD. The following is an example of a typical PROGMAN.INI and a description of what each line does:

```
[Settings]
Window=68 48 580 384 1
SaveSettings=0
AutoArrange=0
[Groups]
```

```
Group1=C:\WINDOWS\MAIN.GRP
Group2=C:\WINDOWS\ACCESSOR.GRP
Group4=C:\WINDOWS\CLOSE-UP.GRP
Group3=C:\WINDOWS\README.GRP
Group5=C:\WINDOWS\APPLICAT.GRP
Group6=C:\WINDOWS\LOTUSAPP.GRP
Group7=C:\WINDOWS\MICROSOF.GRP
Group8=C:\WINDOWS\DOSUTIL.GRP
Group9=C:\WINDOWS\WINUTIL.GRP
Group10=C:\WINDOWS\SETUP.GRP
Group11=C:\WINDOWS\WPW51US.GRP
```

The first section is [Settings], which is for controlling where program manager is located and any automatic settings that have been enabled or disabled.

The WINDOWS– parameter is for describing the location and the size of the program manager window. This parameter means:

Window=68 48 580 384 1

68 is the horizontal distance from the upper left corner of display screen.

48 is the vertical distance from the upper left corner of the display.

580 is the horizontal width of the window.

384 is the vertical height of the window.

1 specifies if the window is represented as an icon or a window.

This setting is updated every time you exit Windows 3.x with the save settings feature enabled. The measurement values are done in pixels.

```
SaveSettings=0
```

The SaveSettings= line enables or disables the Save Settings feature. A "0" is enabled while a "1" is disabled.

```
AutoArrange=0
```

The AutoArrange= line enables the Auto Arrange feature. This allows Windows 3.x to arrange the icons so they fit optimally in the program manager. A "1" indicates enabled while a "0" represents disabled.

```
[Groups]
Group1=C:\WINDOWS\MAIN.GRP
Group2=C:\WINDOWS\ACCESSOR.GRP
Group4=C:\WINDOWS\CLOSE-UP.GRP
Group3=C:\WINDOWS\README.GRP
Group5=C:\WINDOWS\APPLICAT.GRP
Group6=C:\WINDOWS\LOTUSAPP.GRP
Group7=C:\WINDOWS\MICROSOF.GRP
Group8=C:\WINDOWS\DOSUTIL.GRP
```

```
Group9=C:\WINDOWS\WINUTIL.GRP
Group10=C:\WINDOWS\SETUP.GRP
Group11=C:\WINDOWS\WPW51US.GRP
```

Finally, the [Groups] section tells program manager where it can find the GRP file for the different groups it manages. This section is updated every time you create a new item or group, or delete an item or group.

KRNLxxx.EXE

For Windows 3.11 there is only a 386 enhanced mode kernel program provided. It is:

```
KRNL386 EXE       76,400       11-01-93 4:11a
```

This program is the heart of Windows 3.x. Kernel programs are also found in UNIX and Windows 95/98/Me/NT/2000. The Windows 3.x KRNL386.EXE performs scheduling functions for all Windows 3.x activities. It implements cooperative multitasking, based on the time slicing specified in the SYSTEM.INI file.

When initially released, Windows 3.0 provided a real mode kernel program and an enhanced mode kernel program. As Windows 3.x evolved, the real mode kernel became unnecessary and only the enhanced mode kernel was provided. In Windows 95/98/Me, the enhanced mode kernel now supports preemptive multitasking. The cooperative multitasking, like real mode operation, has become unnecessary. The Windows 3.x KRNL386.EXE is loaded into memory during the boot process. It replaces the DOS MSDOS.SYS scheduling program. Hence, Windows 3.x is really an operating system in itself, separate (mostly) from DOS. It only relies on DOS for memory management and disk drive input/output functions.

PIF files

Windows 3.x uses program interface files (PIF) to provide backward compatibility to older DOS programs. The standard PIF files that come with Windows 3.1x are:

```
DOSPRMPT        PIF     545     01-03-94 2:55a
DEFAULT         PIF     545     01-03-94 2:55a
```

These files control the launching of the DOS program specifying the DOS virtual machine operating properties for the program. For example, multitasking of DOS and Windows 3.x applications is set at a default time-slice combination or altered by using the PIF files for the DOS application. To enable multitasking, the Background box must be marked in the PIF. See Figure 10–20.

The "detect idle time" box under the advanced options should also be marked. The numbers determine processing cycle allocation between DOS and Windows 3.x tasks. This permits the DOS virtual machines to multitask under Windows 3.x.

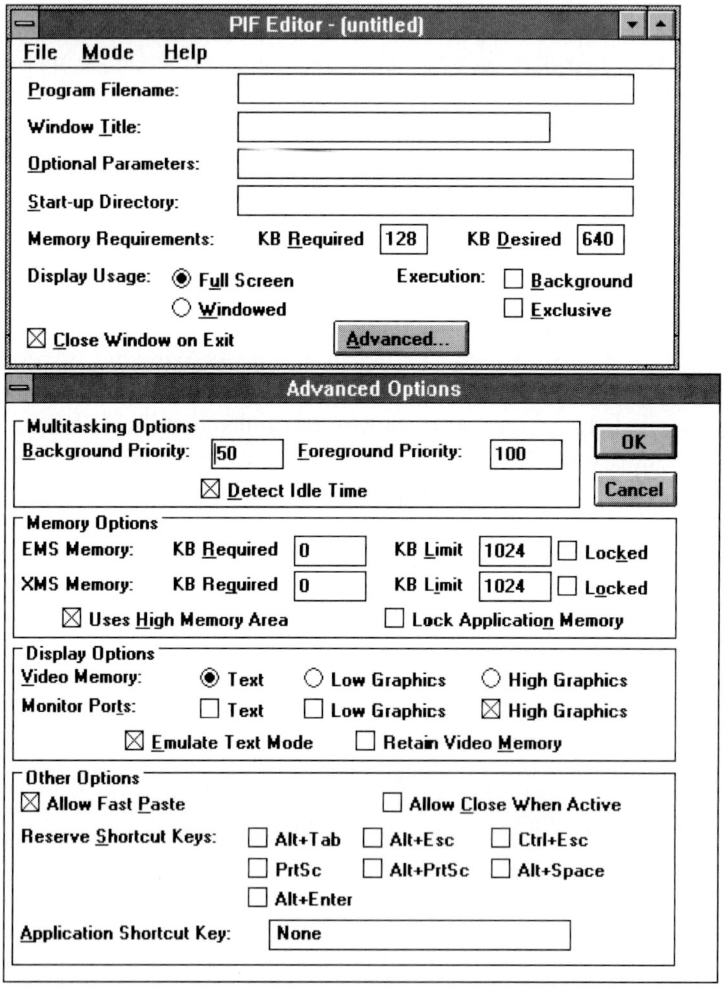

Figure 10–20
PIF file options.

PIF file capabilities are built into Windows 95/98/Me/NT/2000 DOS program shortcuts. Altering the properties of the shortcut in Windows 95/98/Me/NT/2000 changes them.

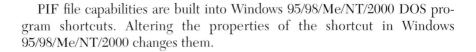

Study Break: Windows Documentation

This exercise examines the Windows 3.1 SYSTEM.INI documentation.

1. Get a Windows 3.1 PC or get a copy of the Windows 3.1.WRI files.
2. Open the SYSINI.WRI documentation found in the C:\WINDOWS directory using WRITE.EXE or WORDPAD.EXE.
3. Use your "find" feature to locate MaxBPs.
4. Browse the rest of the file.

The goal of this example was to illustrate the electronic documentation that is available with Windows on the SYSTEM.INI and WIN.INI files.

Summary

This chapter closely examined Windows 3.1x. It looked at the overall functions and architecture of Windows 3.1x and identified Windows 3.1x components. Each component was examined in some detail, in addition to the key Windows 3.1x system files. The overall goal of the chapter was to provide a better understanding of Windows 3.1x and how it lays the foundation for the current Windows 95/98/Me and Windows 2000 operating environments. There are some underlying similarities between the Windows 3.1x operating environment and Windows 95/98/Me/2000 operating environments, but overall, they are really quite different in their design and implementation.

Chapter Review Questions

1. *When running Windows 3.1, how can you view the resources available?*

A. You cannot
B. Go to help
C. Select Control Panel, then System
D. Select Help, then About

Answer: D, select Help, then About. You can determine the resources under Windows 3.x but not by going to Help or the Control Panel.

2. *What is the function of WIN.INI?*

A. To start Windows File Manager
B. It configures Windows for a specific user and loads programs frequently used.
C. To load 32-bit disk access
D. Configure the control panel
E. None of the Above

Answer: B, it configures Windows for a specific user and loads programs frequently used. WIN.INI does not start the file manager or 32-bit disk access. The control panel is not configured by WIN.INI.

3. *What is the function of SYSTEM.INI?*

A. To start Windows File Manager
B. It configures Windows for a specific user and loads programs frequently used.
C. To load 32-bit disk access
D. It configures Windows to PC hardware.
E. None of the Above

Answer: D, it configures Windows to PC hardware. While SYSTEM.INI may load 32-bit disk access, that is not its only function. It does not configure Windows 3.x File Manager or configure Windows 3.x for a specific user.

4. *What loads MOUSE.SYS?*

A. AUTOEXEC.BAT
B. CONFIG.SYS
C. WIN.INI
D. SYSTEM.INI

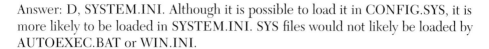

Answer: D, SYSTEM.INI. Although it is possible to load it in CONFIG.SYS, it is more likely to be loaded in SYSTEM.INI. SYS files would not likely be loaded by AUTOEXEC.BAT or WIN.INI.

5. *What processing mode and CPU is not supported in Windows 3.1?*

    A. 286—real mode

    B. 8080—real mode

    C. 8086/88—standard more

    D. 286—standard mode

Answer: D, 286—standard mode. The processor removed was the Intel 80286 chip and the mode was Windows standard mode of operation. Real mode operation is performed by the chip and used in Windows 95/98/Me today.

6. *Windows 3.1 displays available resources when you do what?*

    A. Start Windows

    B. Open Help/About Program Manager or Help/About Control Panel

    C. Select Control Panel, then System

    D. None of the above

Answer: B, open Help/About Program Manager or Help/About Control Panel. Starting Windows restores the resources but does not necessarily display them. Selecting Control Panel, then System in Windows 98/Me/2000 displays information about Windows and the CPU chip but not about resources.

7. *How should you save your Windows 3.1 groups before upgrading?*

    A. You Cannot

    B. Open Help/About Program Manager

    C. Backup the .GRP files

    D. None of the above

Answer: C, back up the .GRP files. Groups are stored in GRP files which can be backed up.

8. *You start to defrag the system of a DOS/Win3.x computer. Rather than running DEFRAG, the message "incorrect DOS version" is displayed. What has happened?*

    A. A bootable disk was left in the floppy drive containing a different DOS version

    B. The SYS command was accidentally run on the drive

    C. Both of the above

    D. Neither of the above

Answer: C, both of the above.

9. *Which character(s) at the front of a line in an INI file make it a comment?*

    A. Colon
    B. Semicolon
    C. REM
    D. Quotation marks surrounding the line

Answer: B, semicolon. Colons designate disk drives, e.g., C:, and REM statements are used in AUTOEXEC.BAT. Quotation marks surround information to be displayed in BASIC and elsewhere.

10. *What is the Windows tool for viewing and manually editing INI files, AUTOEXEC.BAT, and CONFIG.SYS?*

    A. File manager
    B. SYSVIEW
    C. REGEDIT
    D. SYSEDIT

Answer: D, SYSEDIT. The File Manager views the contents of disks, there is no SYSVIEW and REGEDIT is used in Windows 95/98/Me/NT/2000 to edit the registry files.

11. *A new software package from a CD needs to be installed in twenty Win3.x machines. However, when installing it on any of the systems, you get a variation of the access denied error and the setup program terminates. Why won't the new software install?*

    A. The CD is defective and should be replaced by the manufacturer
    B. Someone set EditLevel=5 in the PROGMAN.INI files for this department
    C. The systems do not have enough free hard disk space
    D. The new software is incompatible with your version of Windows

Answer: B, someone set EditLevel=5. Defective CD's would cause CD read errors, insufficient fixed disk space would cause an out of fixed disk space error, and incompatible software most often causes General Protection Faults.

12. *If Windows 3.x setup hangs during the installation, what might resolve the problem?*

    A. Reboot and run a:\setup /I
    B. Reboot, run a:\setup, and choose "safe recovery" when prompted
    C. Call Microsoft for a replacement diskette
    D. Comment out any unnecessary lines in AUTOEXEC.BAT and CONFIG.SYS

Answer: A, Reboot and run a:\setup. /I Editing AUTOEXEC.BAT and CONFIG.SYS are as about as productive as a call to Microsoft.

13. *Windows 3.x file associations are stored in what file?*

    A. The SYSTEM.INI file
    B. The OLE.INI file
    C. The WIN.INI file
    D. The WINASSOC.INI file

Answer: A, the SYSTEM.INI file. There is no WINASSOC.INI file, or as I recall any OLE.INI file. The WIN.INI file customizes the Windows 3.x PC for the specific user.

14. *The Windows 3.1 INI files are all what?*

    A. Binary files edited with SYSEDIT
    B. Hidden and read-only files
    C. Text files that can be edited with NOTEPAD
    D. Stored in the root directory of the disk drive

Answer: C, text files that can be edited with NOTEPAD. They are not binary files or marked as hidden or read-only as are the Windows 95/98/Me/NT/2000 Registry files.

15. *What is the best way for average users to modify their system settings?*

    A. Edit the registry and make the needed changes
    B. Use the control panel dialogs to make the needed changes
    C. Run SYSEDIT and make the needed changes to SYSTEM.INI and WIN.INI
    D. A and C

Answer: B, use the control panel dialogs to make the needed changes Registry editing is not good for average users, and changing SYSTEM.INI and WIN.INI can cause bad things to happen with Windows 3.x. The average user is much safer sticking with the control panel dialog boxes.

Chapter 11

WINDOWS 95/98/ME AND WINDOWS 2000 ARCHITECTURE

Chapter Syllabus

- Windows 3.x versus Windows 9x

- Windows 95/98/Me Functions

- Windows 95/98/Me Components

- Windows 95/98/Me Key System Files

Windows 3.x versus Windows 9x

Windows 95/98/Me is significantly different from Windows 3.x. A complete exploration of the differences between these various versions of Windows is well beyond the scope of this book, but a brief overview of the differences and similarities between Windows 3.x and Windows 95/98/Me is provided here to facilitate a better understanding of the evolution of PC software and to help understand the troubleshooting differences between Windows 95/98/Me and

Windows 3.x. First, some general introductions: Windows Me is just about the same as Windows 98, but Windows 98 is in general better than Windows 95. Windows 98 and Windows 98 SE are significant improvements on Windows 95, and Windows Me is a minor update to Windows 98 SE. Although there are plenty of improvements, the two systems seem quite the same, regardless. Windows 95/98/Me improved on Windows 3.x in several general areas including:

Improved user interface—There are many changes and improvements made to the GUI for Windows 95/98/Me, making it easier for all users. These improvements included above others the task bar, Windows Explorer, and an improved desktop interface.

Plug-and-play (or plug-and-pray) installation—Plug-and-play makes it less necessary to flip switches and set jumpers. This was a major start on future PCs, which will all be configurable through the software.

Integrated networking software—All the networking software you could possibly use is built into Windows 95/98/Me. This includes TCP/IP software as well as Novell's SPX/IPX software.

Better operating environment—Pre-emptive multi-tasking makes Windows 95/98/Me more bulletproof. It also offers better handling of Windows 3.x applications and improved Windows 95/98/Me 32-bit applications.

While Windows 95/98/Me preserves some of the same overall structures of Windows 3.x, underneath they are really quite different operating systems. Windows 3.x relied on DOS programs for memory and disk management functions, whereas Windows 95/98/Me has replaced them with 32-bit protected mode programs that are designed to better support the Windows multi-tasking environment. Windows 95/98/Me is truly a 32-bit operating system in that it takes full advantage of the capabilities of today's CPU chips.

Furthermore, Windows 95/98/Me has increased the level of network functionality incorporated into the operating system. This functionality can be seen in the TCP/IP protocol modules that allow Windows to easily integrate with the Internet and various intranets. Support for LANs and ATM communications are now incorporated into Windows.

The design of Windows 95/98/Me is aimed at making technical support less necessary. We have had some Windows PCs run for months on end without being restarted. (The rule here is to keep them focused on a narrow set of tasks.) Windows 2000 is designed to be even more reliable than Windows 95/98/Me in order to reduce support time and costs.

From an A+ viewpoint, it is important to understand the commonalities and differences between DOS, Windows 3.x, and Windows 95/98/Me. The commonalities mean that the troubleshooting procedures that are employed on Windows 3.x systems generally work the same way in Windows 95/98/Me systems. To recover from a general protection fault, CTRL+ALT+DEL is hit. See Figure 11–1.

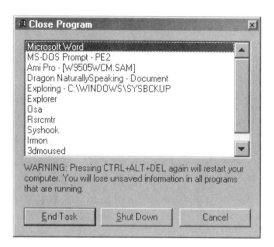

Figure 11-1
Windows 98 task manager.

This key combination starts Windows 98/Me's task manager program, giving you the options of closing the offending application, other applications running under Windows, or restarting Windows. The options are similar for Windows 3.x. However, Windows 3.x is not nearly as flexible.

The differences mean that there are other areas that require new troubleshooting procedures, for example, installing hardware options with Windows 95/98/Me plug-and-play. Some hardware configurations require that you remove boards and then restart Windows for proper installation of the plug-and-play features. We had a laptop with a SCSI PCMCIA (PC CARD) interface that had to be installed using the remove-then-restart-and-reinstall procedure. Windows 98/Me and Windows 2000 are much better at installing plug-and-play devices.

New networking features mean that, in future A+ certification tests, networking questions and configuration are becoming more prevalent. These questions were almost nonexistent in the older A+ certification tests. Furthermore, the movement to USB peripherals that is occurring now mitigates the need for knowledge of the RS-232 serial port details, which have appeared on earlier tests.

More details on Windows 95/98/Me troubleshooting are covered in Chapter 15. Included in this chapter are:

1. Special boot options for troubleshooting—for instance, hold the left shift key or F5 key while booting.

2. The task manager; CTRL-ALT-DEL activates the task manager to remove misbehaving programs.

3. Control panel tools, for instance, the system selection.

4. Configuring and managing virtual memory and disk cache.
5. Windows 98/Me utilities such as the system monitor and the resource meter.

There were three versions of Windows 95: the original release, the OSR2 or B version, and the final release, the C version. The OSR2 or B version of Windows 95 implemented FAT 32 bit, and the C version provided software support for the USB. Windows 98 has also had numerous updates. Most of these updates have had to do with improved Internet security. One major improvement is the release of the Internet Explorer 5, or IE5. Windows 98/Me/2000 updates and patches are available through the Internet. Windows 98/Me/2000 incorporate an update button which, when activated, connects to the Microsoft Windows 98/Me/2000 updates site. At this site, Windows 98/Me/2000 patches and drivers can be downloaded to upgrade the version of Windows installed on a PC. Windows 98/Me also provides utilities for making backups, utilities for cleaning up fixed disk drives, and maintenance wizards. These help the PC user perform routine maintenance tasks that keep their PC operating properly. Windows 98/Me incorporates an active desktop feature. This feature permits receiving information directly from the Internet. The user tailors the information received from the Internet via the active desktop to suit their specific needs.

Knowing and understanding the evolution of DOS and Windows software helps troubleshoot PC problems, regardless of the operating environment being used.

Study Break: Desktop Settings

The Windows 95/98/Me display settings can be changed easily from the desktop. This exercise shows how the display settings are changed from the desktop. It is similar to changing the settings using the control panel, but quicker.

1. On a Windows 95/98/Me PC, shut down all active programs.
2. Move the mouse pointer to the desktop.
3. Right-click on the mouse. Select properties. The Windows display properties box should appear.
4. Select Cargo Net pattern and change wallpaper to none. Fancy wallpaper requires more resources than simple patterns.

5. Select screen saver and change to simple flying Windows or flying through space. These screen savers require fewer CPU cycles than the Open GL screen savers. They are not things of beauty but they work just fine. Newer flat panel monitors should be powered down when not in use rather than having a screen saver program run because their backlighting dims as they are run over time. Use the power management settings to turn off the monitor when the system is inactive.

6. Select apply. The Windows display should change.

You can restore the settings to their original values. This exercise was to illustrate how easily these settings can be changed from the desktop and which settings reduce the load on the PC.

Windows 95/98/Me is designed to provide more reliable operation and to reduce support costs through such features as true "plug-and-play" device integration. It changes the user interface to make it easier for novice users to adapt. The famous design quote from Microsoft was that Windows 95 was designed so that your grandmother could easily use it; this was in many ways accomplished. The "plug-and-play" capabilities, however, still proved to be a support headache. As Windows 95 evolved to Windows Me and Windows 2000, the "plug-and-play" problems have largely disappeared. Windows 95/98/Me provides a 32-bit operating system architecture and is no longer dependent on DOS components for its implementation.

Windows 95/98/Me is still launched using a Windows 95/98/Me DOS. This DOS performs the basic functions needed to load the Windows programs. It can also be controlled by CONFIG.SYS and AUTOEXEC.BAT for backwards compatibility to earlier DOS and Windows applications. The big step with Windows 95/98/Me is that networking functionality is now built into the Windows operating environment. This means that DOS driver and higher-level programs are not required to network PCs with Windows NT/2000 and Novell servers.

Windows 95/98/Me also adds some support functions to make management and administration of multiple PCs easier. These functions are additional centralized security for network operations, the ability to edit and alter system policies (configurations), separate user hardware profiles to permit multiple users to operate a single PC, and remote administration and backup facilities. There are three versions of Windows 95: Release 950a (the original Windows 95), OEM Service Release 2 (950b adding the 32-bit FAT capability), and 950c, which incorporated USB support into Windows 95. Windows 98 incorporated all these features and finally fixed most of the "plug-and-play" problems.

Windows releases are:

Version Designation	Description	Release Date
Win 95 Gold	Original Windows 95 (version 4.00.950)	July 11, 1995
Win 95 a	Service Pack 1 update (version 4.00.950 a)	December 31, 1995
Win 95 b	OSR 2.0 (version 4.00.950 b)	August 24, 1996
Win 95 b	OSR 2.1 (version 4.00.950 b)	August 27, 1997
Win 95 c	OSR 2.5 (version 4.00.950 c)	November 18, 1997
Win 98	Original Windows 98 (version 4.10.1998)	May 11, 1998
Win 98 SE	Windows 98 Special Edition (version 4.10.2222)	April 23, 1999
Win Me	Windows Millennium Edition (version 4.90.3000)	June 8, 2000
Win 9x	All versions of Windows 95, Windows 98, and Windows Me	

Windows 95/98/Me Functions

The functions performed by Windows 95/98/Me are similar to those performed by Windows 3.x. However, the functions are performed by new 32-bit software components. Windows 95/98/Me still uses a KRNL386.EXE and USER.EXE and GDI.EXE programs, similar to the old Windows 3.x. However, these programs have been rewritten to provide more robust and reliable operation. Furthermore, some new functional areas are added to Windows. Windows 95/98/Me manages disk drives and files, PC components, applications, files, networking, and printing with added functionality.

For example, Windows 95/98/Me and Windows 2000 use the Explorer program in place of the Windows 3.x file manager program. The Explorer program provides the same functions as the file manager program, but it does so through a "folders" panel that works with multiple disk drives using drop-down tree-structured navigation. In contrast, Windows 3.x file manager opens separate panels for each disk drive. File manipulation and navigation with the Windows 95/98/Me Explorer is much easier for the PC user. Similarly, Windows 95/98/Me provides control of the PC using the control panel.

Windows 3.x also has control panel functions, but they are not nearly as comprehensive as those for Windows 95/98/Me. Furthermore, in Windows 3.x, the networking functions rely on DOS and add-in programs. In particular, TCP/IP networking was an additional modification to Windows 3.11. Windows 95/98/Me has all the networking software built in. These are just some of the examples of the added functionality of Windows 95/98/Me versus the original functionality of Windows 3.x.

Managing Disks and Files

Windows 95/98/Me uses the Windows 95/98/Me DOS program FDISK to configure the fixed disk. With the first release of Windows 95 (950a), little was changed from Windows 3.x beyond the total migration to 32-bit disk and file managers that were started with Windows 3.11. There were cosmetic changes, however, that provided a new look to the system.

See Figure 11–2. Real mode drivers were included for backwards compatibility with older Windows devices. These real mode drivers are 16-bit Windows software.

Figure 11–2
Windows 98 system properties.

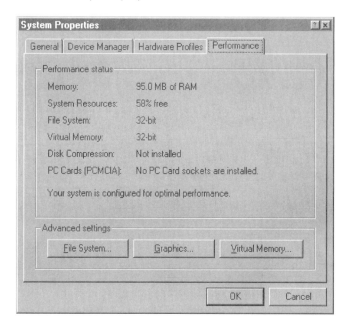

With the Windows 950b release, known as OEM Service Release 2, came the long-awaited 32-bit FAT, which expanded single disk partition size beyond the 2 GB limit imposed by the 16-bit FAT. Unfortunately, the 32-bit FAT feature could only be implemented by destroying all the data on the fixed disk drive when using FDISK to convert from FAT 16 to FAT 32. Once the conversion to FAT 32 was accomplished, there was no way to return to a FAT 16 structure without again using FDISK to destroy all the data on the disk drive. With Windows 98, there is a utility program that converts from a FAT 16 to a FAT 32 structure without destroying data on the disk drive. In this instance, a disk is not required to move from FAT 16 to FAT 32. However, to revert back to FAT 16, FDISK must be used, which destroys all data on the disk drive. Windows 98/Me and Windows 2000 all work with FAT 32.

Windows 95 also changed file management operations by supporting long file names. The file names were no longer limited to the DOS 8.3 file naming convention. Longer file names means that users can give their files more meaningful, complete names. The price you pay for this luxury is that all the older DOS and Windows programs still operate with the DOS 8.3 formats. When they encounter a long file name it is automatically truncated to fit into the 8.3 DOS file name structure. If files are referenced and not copied to different folders, the long file names remain generally intact.

Managing PC Components

The big change in managing PC components is the implementation of "plug-and-play" component installation. Thus, with special BIOS and specially designed peripheral interface cards, installation of components did not require users to set switches and jumpers on the hardware cards. Windows automatically sorted out I/O port and IRQ assignments during the installation and boot process. The most immediate impact here was on laptop installation with PCM-CIA card bus controllers. Windows made installation workable with these systems. Laptop components were a nightmare to install under Windows 3.x. Windows 98 and the earlier availability of the PCI have made "plug-and-play" installation much more reliable and predictable. Windows 2000 is better at plug-and-play installation than Windows 98. Changes in both Windows and PC hardware make it possible to incorporate more devices into a basic PC system.

Managing Applications

Windows application management became more reliable because the 32-bit applications created for Windows 98/Me now ran in the Windows system virtual machine, but in their separate address space. Windows 16-bit applications still run in a shared address space, making them less reliable.

Figure 11–3 is an extension of the Windows 3.x applications architecture that makes Windows 95/98/Me more reliable for Windows 32-bit applications.

From an operating point of view, Windows 16-bit and Windows 32-bit applications seem to be similar. One major difference between them however is that the 16-bit allocations only modify entries in the WIN.INI and the SYSTEM.INI files, while Windows 95/98/Me primarily modifies the Registry files and not the WIN.INI and SYSTEM.INI files. Also, the Windows 16-bit applications are typically smaller, and thus install much more quickly than do the Windows 32-bit applications. Windows 16-bit applications are less reliable than Windows 32-bit applications because they share a single Windows virtual machine. Windows 32-bit applications all run in their own separate virtual machines. Therefore, a problem with one Windows 32-bit application should not impact other Windows 32-bit applications. Unfortunately, this is not always true.

Windows then presented the Windows 2000 operating system, which is based on Windows NT. Although Windows NT 4.01 was released prior to Windows 98, it is an entirely different and much more robust design than Windows 98. Windows Me was released as the final version of the Windows 95/98/Me software product. Future Windows products will be built around the foundation laid by Windows NT and developed by Windows 2000. Windows NT evolved from the Microsoft joint development with IBM of OS-2. Windows NT/2000 was designed to be an entirely different operating envi-

Figure 11–3
Windows 95/98/Me applications architecture.

689

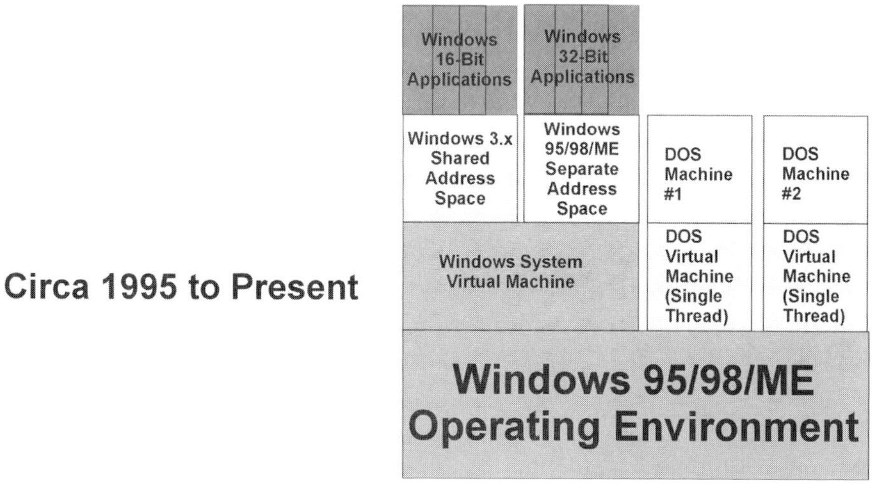

ronment from Windows 95/98/Me. There was no concern in the original design of Windows NT for backward compatibility with previous versions of Windows. Windows NT did not rely on DOS for loading and configuring disk drives. Windows NT/2000 also changes the application architecture so that Windows 32-bit applications run in their own address space, working directly with the Windows NT/2000 operating environment. Furthermore, Windows NT/2000 can be configured so that Windows 16-bit applications can run in a common Windows virtual machine or in their own Windows virtual machine. Windows 2000 makes more accommodations to run Windows 95/98/Me applications than did Windows NT, and also has the drivers and the plug-and-play capabilities that Windows NT lacked; see Figure 11–4.

The significance of this is that applications run so they do not crash Windows NT/2000. In Windows NT/2000, an application itself can crash, but it is less likely. Furthermore, if an application crashes, it is less likely to crash Windows NT/2000. With this said, we have had Windows 2000 come abruptly to a halt, freezing the display screen on more than a few occasions. This was not caused by application program problems, but rather by incorrect or mismatched display driver programs.

It is important to understand how Windows has evolved to make applications support more reliable and better performing, helping us understand what the next enhancements to Windows 2000 may be. Of course, the Windows operating environments underneath the applications architecture are also more reliable as we move from Windows 3.x to Windows 95/98/Me to Windows NT/2000. One design goal of Windows 2000 was to dramatically

Figure 11–4
Windows NT/2000 applications architecture.

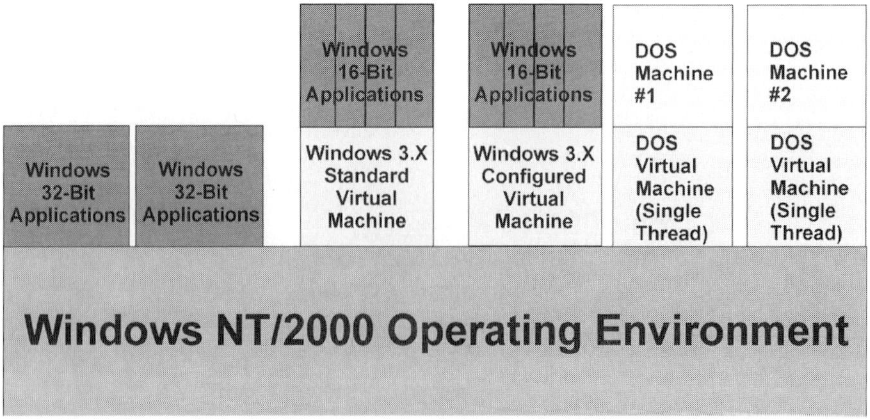

reduce the software down time that users experienced with Windows 3.x and Windows 95/98/Me.

Windows NT was originally designed to be an entirely new operating system that supported client/server networking. It was not primarily aimed at supporting applications software that ran under DOS or Windows; such software support was an ancillary capability of Windows NT. Hence, not all DOS and Windows programs would run under NT. Windows NT server provided all the functionality required for setting up a server in a client/server networking environment. Windows NT workstation was designed to provide a secure client for a client/server network. Windows 2000 Professional continues to replace Windows NT Workstation as the secure client software.

The Windows NT Network Operating System (NOS) was created from scratch in the late 80s and sold to the public in 1993 as Windows NT Advanced Server Version 3.1. As a server, it was designed to run 32-bit applications designed for Windows NT and those DOS and Windows applications that behaved well in a Windows NT environment. Windows 95 was more complex than Windows NT because it tried to be compatible with a much wider range of DOS and Windows applications, as well as a wider range of PC hardware and software. Windows 2000 and Windows XP were the next step in NT evolution; they enhanced the range of hardware components that Windows 2000 works with by incorporating Windows 95/98/Me "plug-and-play" capabilities. As applications evolve in step with Windows 95/98/Me and Windows NT/2000, these operating environments will support a greater variety of them. The biggest improvements will be in the area of networking. Both Windows 95/98/Me and Windows NT/2000 incorporate networking capabilities, but these abilities are expanding to provide enhanced Internet and intranet features that make full use of high speed connectivity and the multimedia capabilities of future PCs.

Managing Printing

Printing is managed using two components: a universal printer driver and a minidriver. The printer driver is common to all printing.

It interprets the printing languages used by the applications programs. Some such page description languages are HP PCL and Adobe's PostScript. The minidrivers handle detailed printer-specific operations; they are the detailed printer hardware drivers and usually come from the printer manufacturer as part of the printer installation instructions and programs, or they can often be loaded from the Windows 95/98/Me/NT/2000 installation CD. This gives all versions of Windows the ability to use a wide range of printers from many manufacturers.

The minidrivers are found on both Windows 98/Me and Windows NT/2000 systems. They are used as required and not always memory resident; they adapt specific hardware functions to Windows; and they support multiple function interfaces, such as those found in audio hardware and multifunction networking adapters in laptops.

Networking

Networking is a new capability built into Windows 95/98/Me and NT/2000 that was not previously found in the 3.x or earlier versions of the operating systems. Windows provides not only the driver programs for a wide variety of NICs, but it also standardizes the PC's interface to TCP/IP networks, including the Internet. This standardized TCP/IP interface is the current Windows Sockets 2.0 API, sometimes referred to as WINSOCK32 because 32-bit DLLs (WSOCK32.DLL and WS2_32.DLL) support the API.

Such standardization has resulted in a move away from the dominant DOS networking protocols, NetWare Sequenced Packet Exchange/Internet Packet Exchange (SPX/IPX), and onto the more universal TCP/IP protocols. Chapter 16, "Windows Networking," provides more information on the various Windows protocols.

Windows 95/98/Me has several security levels aimed at supporting networking features. There is a share level of security aimed at supporting peer-to-peer networking configurations. In this case, the user specifies a password for every resource that they share on the network. User-level security is aimed at larger client-server network configurations. Here, users are validated by a password on a central server. That validation determines their access to network resources—disk drives and printers. More detail on peer-to-peer versus client/server networking appears in Chapter 16. Basic LAN installation and WAN operations were discussed in Chapter 8, "LANs and Communications."

Windows 95/98/Me supports both NetWare protocols and TCP/IP protocols over a variety of network interfaces, including LAN and dial-up connections. This interface support is expanding with Windows 98/Me/2000 to include new high-speed networking technologies like ATM for both LAN and WAN connections. The central thrust here is to provide high-speed connectivity locally as well as to the Internet. This will be a key area for A+ maintenance activities and troubleshooting in future PC systems.

Administrative Functions

Windows 95/98/Me incorporates some central management facilities that permit a single support person to centrally manage Windows PC clients. These central support mechanisms control Windows system policies (configurations). A system policy editor lets an administrator define rights and restrictions to specific resources for individual users and computers. They also support establishment of default configurations for all users.

Windows can be set up from central servers. (This is a good idea, but not necessarily recommended for all user installations. Central management is good for facilities with large numbers of Windows PCs.) Custom setup scripts control the setup process. These scripts consistently configure Windows on all PCs with a set of custom default options. Users then can modify this configuration to suit their individual needs, which are stored in a user profile for that specific user. Is also possible with Windows NT servers to configure profiles that roam from PC to PC when the user logs on to a specific PC. While this sounds very helpful, roaming user profiles must be precisely configured to work properly.

Study Break: Windows 95/98/Me User Profiles

In this exercise, we set up the user profile on a Windows 95/98/Me PC. This will customize the PC for that specific user and permit other users to work on that PC with specific user profiles as well.

1. Open the control panel.
2. Highlight the users icon and double-click.
3. Follow the users wizard to set up a single user configuration on this PC. Either create copies of the current items and their content or create new items to save this space to set up yourself as a user on this PC.
4. Click the finish button to complete the user setup.
5. Repeat the process for a new user, but this time choose the opposite configuration of what you originally used in Step 3.

This exercise illustrates the procedure for customizing Windows 95/98/Me PCs for individual users.

Windows 95/98/Me Components

The architecture components of Windows 95/98/Me include device drivers, a virtual machine manager, an installable file system manager, a configuration manager, the registry, the Windows core operating system and a 32-bit shell. These components are implemented primarily in DLLs and EXE programs. There are also other types of supporting files including driver programs (DRV, SYS, VxD, and more), registry files (DAT), initialization files (INI) for backward compatibility, and more.

Device Drivers

The Windows 3.x device drivers were device-specific and complex to develop. Windows 95 changed that by implementing a two-tiered structure in which common functions were placed in a universal driver while specific hardware interfacing was performed by minidrivers. The universal driver performed most of the functions for a specific class of device, such as a modem, a LAN NIC, or a printer. The minidriver contains specific interfacing instructions needed to operate a single manufacturer's hardware.

The universal drivers are implemented in VxD software modules under Windows 95/98/Me. These VxD programs are 32-bit protected-mode driver software that more than one application can use at any given time.

Figure 11–5 shows some of the Windows Me VxDs installed on a Windows Me PC. These are typically installed in the \windows\system folder. Minidrivers are .?PD installation modules. Once installed, they become .?PD modules, as shown in Figure 11–6.

The figure also shows printer port drivers (PPD) and asynchronous port drivers (APD). In the figure, those modules in the \win98 folder are the installation files, and the installed files are in the \windows\system and \windows\system\iosubsys folders. These device drivers are installed when new hardware components are added to the PC. The hardware component manufacturer provides special device drivers which are stored in the \windows\system\iosubsys folder and loaded by the I/O supervisor.

Virtual Machine Manager

The virtual machine manager provides the resources needed by each application and process that run under Windows 95/98/Me. It creates virtual

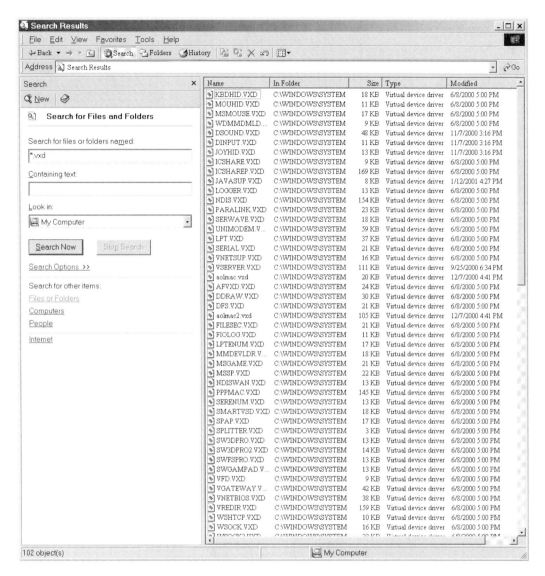

Figure 11–5
Windows Me virtual device drivers—VxDs.

machines which are imaginary PC's created by software in RAM that run PC applications. There are separate virtual machines for each DOS application and a system virtual machine to run the Windows applications. Windows applications share the same virtual machine, and 16-bit applications share the same

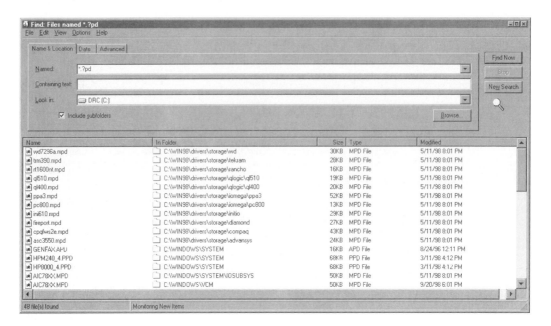

Figure 11–6
Windows 98 driver modules.

address space and 32-bit applications use an individual address space. To provide a migration path from Windows 3.x to Windows 95/98/Me, Windows 95/98/Me provides a single system virtual machine for the Windows 16-bit applications. Since Windows 32-bit applications do not run on Windows 3.x, they were designed to run in their own virtual machine under Windows 95/98/Me. Furthermore, allocating individual address space for 32-bit applications makes those applications less likely to corrupt the address space used by other applications. Because they operate in their own virtual machine and their address space is not shared with other applications, 32-bit applications run more reliably than 16-bit applications.

The virtual machines manager performs process scheduling and memory paging functions for all applications. It also provides MS-DOS support to DOS applications, requiring exclusive access to PC resources. The virtual machine manager implements pre-emptive multi-tasking operations.

Installable File System

The installable file system supports multiple file systems. In Windows 95 it supported long file names, 32-bit file allocation table (VFAT), 32-bit CD-ROM file system (VCDFS), and a redirector for network file operations. Windows 98 adds a 32-bit universal disk format (UDF) file system driver for writing to CD/RW drives. The IFSMGR.VxD arbitrates access to the different file system components. A block I/O subsystem handles the physical input/output operations. This was expanded to include support for 32-bit physical FAT in Windows 95 OEM Service Release 2 (950 B and 950 C versions of Windows 95) and in Windows 98. The 32-bit FAT (VFAT) driver provides significant improvement over Windows 3.x 32-bit disk and file access because it is re-entrant and multithreaded. Windows Me and Windows 2000 both support 32-bit FAT.

Each 32-bit application running under Windows 95/98/Me is a process, and each process is comprised of at least a single thread of executing code. Thus a thread is a piece of executing code which follows a process path to produce useable results. Threads can obtain a slice of time from the operating system and run concurrently with other threads. Re-entrant programs permit multiple threads to safely execute concurrently, and a single thread can safely re-enter the program as a result of a recursive process. When an operating system can work on multiple threads concurrently, it offers better performance than an operating system that cannot.

Windows Core Operating System

The Windows core operating system is composed of USER.EXE, GDI.EXE, and the kernel, each consisting of a 16-bit and a companion 32-bit DLL. These DLLs together provide services for applications.

The 16-bit DLLs retain compatibility with earlier Windows applications and are also used where they provide equivalent functionality to 32-bit code without degrading performance while lowering memory usage. The USER.EXE program provides window and menu management services. It accepts user input. The GDI.EXE module manages graphics, deals with fonts, printing, spooling, and other graphics functions. The kernel performs the scheduling, synchronization, memory management, input/output, and console operations, among others.

Windows 95/98/Me 32-Bit Shell

The Windows shell is based on the Windows Explorer program. The shell provides desktop tools like the start menu, the network neighborhood, my computer, the recycle bin and the briefcase. The shell provides common controls including dialog boxes, tree views, Web views and list views to all Windows applications. The user profile determines the look of the Windows desktop for that specific user, and Windows Explorer uses parameters to create the Windows desktop. For example, the Windows desktop programs are contained in the windows\desktop folder. Similarly, the Windows start menu programs are contained in the \Windows start menu\programs folder. The Windows Explorer program can also be run on its own to act as a general mechanism for formatting disks, copying files, and launching application programs.

DLLs

Windows 95/98/Me, Windows NT/2000 and Windows applications are implemented using DLLs, as is Windows 3.x. Windows 95/98/Me and Windows NT/2000 DLLs can be 32-bit, re-entrant, and multithreaded. This translates into smoother multi-tasking in a Windows 95/98/Me or a Windows NT/2000 environment. Windows 95/98/Me/NT/2000 DLLs, similar to Windows 3.x DLLs, are separate executable programs loaded by other programs to perform specific tasks.

EXEs

Similar to Windows 3.x, EXE files are executable programs. They are a type of DLL that is typically used to initiate or launch an application. Several Windows applets—small specific function programs—are EXE files alone. For example, solitaire is SOL.EXE; paintbrush is PBRUSH.EXE; and notepad is NOTEPAD.EXE.

The Registry

The registry files are the main Windows 95/98/Me and Windows NT/20000 control structures. They control Windows startup, shutdown, and the loading and execution of applications. The registries began with REG.DAT in Windows 3.1, which held the file extension associations and the OLE server applications.

Because the Windows INI files are text files of limited size, users easily change them. However, because they have a linear structure, they are insufficient to provide the control mechanisms required by Windows 95/98/Me/NT/2000. In contrast, the registry files are not text files and consequently require a special REGEDIT program to alter them. Furthermore, the registries are broken down into hives that each have a hierarchical structure of keys and values. Registries are not limited to size; they provide a single source for configuring PC hardware application device drivers, and more. They can be configured using standard control panel tools; they can be remotely administered; and they provide network-independent functions, permitting examination of configuration data and setting system configuration information on remote networked PCs.

The Windows 95/98/Me registry is now more than a single file. It is comprised of the following files:

- SYSTEM.DAT. This file is used to define an individual PC configuration and the applications installed on that PC. These items include plug-and-play hardware, I/O, IRQs, and DMAs.

- USER.DAT. This file is used to define the user's preferences for the desktop and the applications.

These files are typically stored on the PC in the \windows folder. For a specific user's configuration to be present regardless of the machine they log on to, USER.DAT must be on a server. All registry files are read-only, system, hidden files stored in a binary format.

For the most part, these registries are inaccessible to the common user. It is possible for users to run REGEDIT, but system administrators could block access to REGEDIT and thus block users from altering the registries.

PC support personnel can, however, view the registries using the REGEDIT program, which is in the Windows folder or directory on the C drive. When REGEDIT is run, it loads the contents of both SYSTEM.DAT and USER.DAT into memory.

Figure 11–7 shows a REGEDIT view of the combined SYSTEM.DAT and USER.DAT registries for both Windows 95 and Windows 2000.

REGEDIT displays a hierarchical structure of the registries. Many changes for Windows are frequently made in the *HKEY_LOCAL_MACHINE\software\microsoft\windows* registry key.

In Figure 11–8, below the computer you see the root key names that start with an "HKEY" (Hive Keys) prefix that corresponds to the set of key values in the Win32 API.

An API consists of programs, protocols, and tools for building software applications, and makes it easier to develop applications by providing building

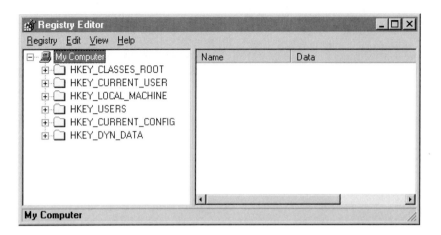

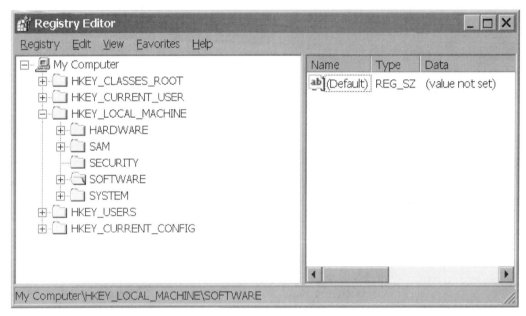

Figure 11-7
Windows 95 (top) and Windows 2000 (bottom) REGEDIT registry view.

blocks. Windows, like most operating environments, provides an API for 32-bit applications—the Win 32 API. APIs are ultimately good for users because all programs using a common API have similar interfaces. This similarity and consistency helps users learn new programs.

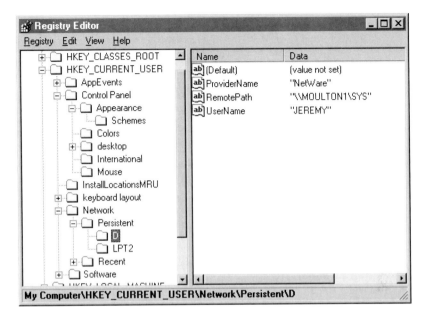

Figure 11–8
Windows 95 HKEY hierarchical structure.

The following list defines the "HKEY" list.

- HKEY_CLASES_ROOT—registers the file type name, based on its extension, of each application that uses the file. Entries are created when an application is installed. The more difficult program information to monitor is in CLSID entries. These perform detailed application control functions, like recording the installation date in a binary form to track license expirations. This is stored in the file SYSTEM.DAT.

- HKEY_CURRENT_USER—registers the information about the specific user currently logged into this Windows 95 PC. It contains the user's logon ID and password, as well as other information. The information is copied from the common HKEY_USER stored in USER.DAT.

- HKEY_LOCAL_MACHINE—registers the hardware and software data for the local PC. Most application program information resides here. HKEY_LOCAL_MACHINE is stored in the SYSTEM.DAT file.

- HKEY_USERS—registers a list of all users of this PC and their corresponding passwords. This is an accessible root key via a remote computer system and is stored in USER.DAT.

- HKEY_CURRENT_CONFIG—registers the current user's desktop and keeps track of the most recently used documents.

- HKEY_DYN_DATA—registers the data used to update the system monitor display. This information is not stored in the registry files but rather is created and exists while the PC is running.

The "HKEYS" structure is shown in Figure 11–8. You expand each key by clicking on the plus sign next to the key. This is similar in structure to the Windows NT registry, but they are not identical.

The registry path to the network reveals the network drive mapping for this local computer. In the left panel under network, and then in "Persistent," is the letter D (highlighted in Figure 11–8). The right panel lists the remote path with its data value of *Moulton1\SYS*.

Registry entries can be edited, but be very cautious; an incorrect value can possibly disable Windows 95/98/Me/NT/2000. The only way to recover may be reinstallation of Windows 95/98/Me/NT/2000.

The ERU.EXE program available for Microsoft and sold as part of the Windows 95 Plus package is excellent for backing up the registry. ERU makes copies of all key Windows files, including USER.DAT and SYSTEM.DAT, when the backup files are stored in a fixed disk folder. Before editing the registry and installing new software, run ERU and store the backup, selecting the other directory option. By placing numbered subfolders under the ERU folder, you can make an audit trail of changes to the PC's registry. This audit trail permits you to return to any previous operating state with Windows 95/98/Me. Several errors that would have normally have necessitated a reinstall of Windows were recovered by restoring the registries from audit trails.

The "Windows Protection Fault" boot message is a registry-setting problem. By moving the SYSTEM.DAT registry from an identical PC, we were able to boot a PC displaying the "Windows Protection Fault" message.

Editing the registry changes the location of the Windows installation files. The registry key *HKEY_LOCAL_MACHINE\Software\Microsoft\Windows \CurrentVersion\Setup* contains entries for CommandLine and for SourcePath. Changing these lines can change the location from which Windows seeks the installation files. The registry key *HKEY_CURRENT_ USER\InstallLocationsMRU* may also influence this. When Windows installation files reside on the fixed disk, it is sometimes convenient to change this registry entry to point at those installation files. Therefore, when the Windows configuration is altered, Windows automatically finds the files on fixed disk rather than requesting insertion of a CD in the CD-ROM drive.

Study Break: Searching the Registry

In this exercise, we search the Windows registry to find a specific key value. The REGEDIT program is our primary tool for doing this.

1. Click on the Windows start button, then select run.
2. Enter REGEDIT, then click OK. This launches the REGEDIT program and loads the registries.
3. Select edit from the menu at the top, and then select find. Alternatively, holding down the control key and tapping the F key can enter the find function.
4. In the entry panel, enter InstallLocations. Click on "find next." After a while, InstallLocationsMRU should be highlighted under HKEY_ current_user.
5. Review the values and the MRUList order.
6. Check each value to see that it exists. Use Windows Explorer to find the appropriate folder on the disk drive identified. If the value doesn't exist, delete the value. Be sure to remove the entry from the MRUList as well.
7. Click on the registry menu item, then export registry file.
8. Export the registry file to "my documents" as TEST.REG.
9. Exit the REGEDIT program.
10. Use the Windows Explorer to locate TEST.REG under "my documents." What size is TEST.REG? If it is about 1K in size, that means you have only exported the InstallLocationsMRU key. If it is much larger than 1K, you have exported more than the single key.
11. Open WordPad. Go to C:\My Documents and drag and drop TEST.REG into WordPad. TEST.REG must be dropped on the WordPad menu bar for it to open the file as a text file. Once opened in WordPad, you should be able to view a text version of the key that was just modified. If necessary, search the text file for InstallLocationsMRU.

The goal of this exercise is to practice searching the registry, altering registry keys and values, and exporting registry keys.

Windows 95/98/Me Key System Files

Windows 95/98/Me has the same files used to implement Windows 3.x. While these files perform similar functions, they are not equivalent. These files and their roles are examined briefly here.

SETUP.EXE

SETUP.EXE is the file that starts Windows 95/98/Me installation. When a Windows PC becomes corrupted, reinstalling Windows can fix a multitude of problems. Users cause problems on Windows PCs by installing lots of software, shutting off the PC without gracefully exiting Windows, and trying unsuccessfully to recover from normal Windows errors. Running SETUP can fix these problems.

To reinitialize the registries and recover from hardware problems, Windows reinstallation can be done right over an existing Windows installation. This preserves the software settings for Windows while fixing basic registry errors. More serious software corruption problems that cannot be fixed by uninstalling and reinstalling the offending software require a clean Windows installation. This requires you to remove the existing Windows installation and reinstall it and all the software applications from scratch. To shorten this procedure, PC support functions often make a disk image of their standard Windows installation and use it to replace all files on the PC's fixed disk.

Remember: prior to performing this type of uninstall/reinstall activity, it's always wise to make a full backup of your system in the case that something goes wrong during the process!

Figure 11–9 illustrates how SETUP can be run during a reinstallation process. Windows installation is discussed more in Chapter 14, "Software Installation, Configuration and Upgrade."

IO.SYS

The IO.SYS file is a hidden, read-only system file in the root directory of the bootable fixed disk drive. IO.SYS controls input/output operations for the PC. It is the first file loaded after the cold boot loader routing is loaded from the fixed disk master boot record.

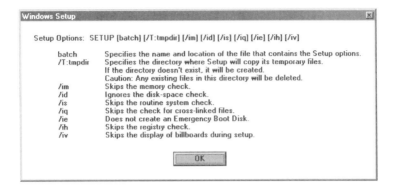

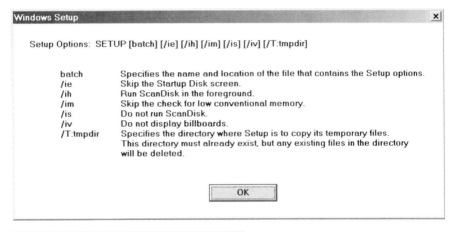

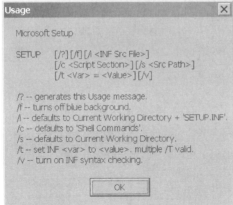

Figure 11-9

Windows 95 (top), Windows 98/Me (center) and Windows 2000 (bottom) SETUP options.

Windows replaces the DOS IO.SYS with a Windows 95/98/Me IO.SYS file. This file has key booting parameters set into it. Hence, many CONFIG.SYS parameters are not required. The Windows 95/98/Me IO.SYS file automatically loads HIMEM.SYS, IFSHLP.SYS, SETVER.EXE, and the disk compression programs (DRVSPACE and DBLSPACE) when they are present on the PC's fixed disk. Standard CONFIG.SYS settings are also applied during the booting process.

These settings and their default values are:

- DOS=HIGH—loads DOS into the HIMEM area.
- HIMEM.SYS—loads HIMEM to access XMS and load DOS into the HIMEM area.
- IFSHLP.SYS— loads the 32-bit installable file system manager.
- SETVER.EXE—provides compatibility for MS-DOS programs requiring earlier versions of DOS.
- FILES=60—not required by Windows but provided for compatibility with older software.
- LASTDRIVE=z—not required by Windows but provided for compatibility with older software.
- BUFFERS=30—not required by Windows but provided for compatibility with software using IO.SYS calls.
- STACKS=9,256—not required by Windows but provided for compatibility with older software.
- SHELL=COMMAND.COM—specifies the command interpreter with the /p switch set to indicate that it is loaded permanently and should not be unloaded.
- FCBS=4—This is only required by older programs.

Entries placed in the CONFIG.SYS file override the standard IO.SYS parameter settings. If you use applications requiring EMS, the EMM386.EXE must be loaded using CONFIG.SYS because it is not by default loaded by the Windows 95/98/Me IO.SYS. Some CONFIG.SYS guidelines for operation with Windows 95/98/Me are:

- Do not use the fixed disk cache provided by SMARTDRV. Windows 95/98/Me has built-in disk caching and double buffering.
- Remove mouse driver programs because Windows 95/98/Me has built-in mouse drivers.
- Remove the settings for files, buffers, stacks, and lastdrive because Windows 95/98/Me sets proper default values for them.

MSDOS.SYS

MSDOS.SYS performs program and file management for DOS. It is also a hidden, read-only system file in the root directory of the bootable disk drive.

Like IO.SYS, Windows also replaces MSDOS.SYS with a Windows 95/98/Me MSDOS.SYS file. This is now a text file specifying paths used to locate Windows files like the registry. See Figure 11–10.

A PC can be set up to dual boot into Windows 3.x and Windows 95/98/Me. To dual boot, install Windows 3.x in c:\Windows and install Windows 95/98/Me in a different directory, say c:\win95. Then BootMulti=1 is added to the MSDOS.SYS file.

Figure 11–10
Windows 98 MSDOS.SYS.

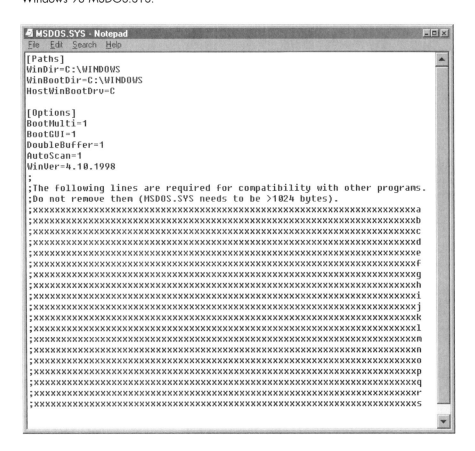

The MSDOS.SYS file can be modified using NOTEPAD to specify additional Windows boot options (see Tables 11–1 and 11–2).

Table 11–1 [Paths] Section Parameters

Parameter	Description
HostWinBootDrv=c	Boot drive root directory location.
WinBootDir=	Pointer to the Windows startup files. Typically c:\windows.
WinDir=	Location of the Windows directory.

Table 11–2 [Options] Section Parameters

Parameter	Description
AutoScan=1	Runs SCANDISK on restart.
BootDelay=2	Delays booting 2 seconds.
BootFailSafe=0	Enables safe mode startup.
BootGUI=1	Starts the GUI. The same as Windows 3.x WIN.COM start.
BootKeys=1	Enables modifying startup using F5, F6, and F8 keys. Shift+F5 bypasses all boot files and starts Windows in Safe Mode. Shift+F6 bypasses boot files and starts Windows in Safe Mode with network support (not supported with Windows 98—it is the same as Shift+F5). Shift+F8 permits line by line examination of CONFIG.SYS and AUTOEXEC.BAT during startup, then places PC in safe mode.
BootMenu=0	Controls display of Windows 98 startup menu.
BootMenuDefault=#	Sets the menu item on the Windows startup menu. A value 3 is for standalone PC configurations and a value 4 is for networked PCs.
BootMenuDelay=30	Sets the number of seconds to display the Windows Startup menu.
BootMulti=0	A setting of 1 permits booting MS-DOS by pressing F4 or F8.
BootWarn=1	Provides safe mode start warning.
BootWin=1	Sets Windows 98 as the default operating system.
DblSpace=1	Loads DBLspace.bin.
DoubleBuffer=0	Enables double buffering required by some SCSI fixed disk controllers.

Table 11-2   [Options] Section Parameters (Continued)

Parameter	Description
DrvSpace1	Loads DRVspace.bin
LoadTop=1	Loads COMMAND.COM and DRVSPACE.BN at the top of conventional memory.
Logo=1	Displays animated logo.
Network=0	Supposed to start safe mode with networking support. No longer supported in Windows 98.

COMMAND.COM and AUTOEXEC.BAT

COMMAND.COM is also installed in the root directory of the bootable fixed disk. It has normal file attributes. COMMAND.COM is used to process the DOS commands in the AUTOEXEC.BAT file.

IO.SYS performs some AUTOEXEC.BAT commands. Consequently, including a "net start" command and a "set path" command in AUTOEXEC.BAT for COMMAND.COM execution is now unnecessary.

Windows 95/98/Me also sets the environment space of the PC to:

```
tmp=c:\windows\temp
temp=c:\windows\temp
prompt=$p$g
path=c:\windows;c:\windows\command
comspec=c:\windows\command\command.com
```

Environment space commands in AUTOEXEC.BAT are now unnecessary as well. However, if the environment space must be set differently from the standard Windows 95/98/Me settings, then commands in the AUTOEXEC.BAT file are used to make the desired modifications.

When changing an AUTOEXEC.BAT file for Windows 95/98, follow these suggestions:

1. Reference only the Windows 95/98/Me folder in your path AUTOEXEC.BAT statement and no other versions of Windows.
2. Start paths with *c:\windows; c:\windows\command.com*.
3. Retain the previous MS-DOS directory in the path.

4. Do not run SMARTDRV or other disk cache programs—Windows provides the necessary disk caching.

5. Do not load mouse support programs—Windows provides mouse support.

6. Commands to connect to network servers can be dumped. If necessary, run a batch file from the Windows startup directory to perform this task.

7. During installation, unnecessary statements are removed from AUTOEXEC.BAT by the Windows installation program. The only real programs run from AUTOEXEC.BAT are virus scanners and simple terminate-and-stay-resident programs like DOSKEY.

REGEDIT.EXE

As we saw earlier, REGEDIT provides the ability to examine and change registry entries directly. It loads both the SYSTEM.DAT and USER.DAT into memory for editing and displays them as a single registry. REGEDIT.EXE also permits exporting the entire registry or specific registry keys and subkeys as text files. These files are labeled with a REG extension. These REG files can then be used later to alter the registry.

REGEDIT is in the *windows* folder. It can be launched by double-clicking on the icon or by going to the Windows Start, Run selection and entering REGEDIT.

SYSTEM.DAT

SYSTEM.DAT is a registry file. It is the largest registry file and controls Windows during the startup process. It contains hardware and computer-specific settings. The control panel device manager displays in the hardware profiles and these parameters.

SYSTEM.DAT is stored in the \\windows folder or directory. It is possible to have it reside elsewhere, but not advisable. Windows 95 makes a backup copy of the SYSTEM.DAT file as SYSTEM.DA0. Windows 98/Me makes several backup copies of the registry files using the SCANREG program. The Windows 95 and Windows 98 backup copies of the registry help recover from some problems, but our experience suggests that they are only effective when you do not really need them to be effective. It is better to use ERU registry backups stored on the fixed disk to recover from Windows registry errors. Our most effective backup approach is to use a separate utility like Norton's GHOST to create a binary image of a good, working Windows partition with all the application software properly installed. This image can then quickly replace a corrupted Windows partition, restoring the PC's software to pristine working condition.

Because the registry is reasonably complex and difficult for most people to understand, and because installed software typically makes multiple changes to the registry, it is easiest to keep copies of the entire registry to fix Windows problems rather than to seek the individual registry changes that would correct the Windows malfunction. I have spent many hours searching the registry to correct a Windows problem to no avail. In contrast, replacing the registry from an ERU backup has saved me several times.

USER.DAT

The USER.DAT registry file holds user-specific parameters that implement user profiles. Such information covers screen colors, patterns, screen savers, and the like. Similar to the SYSTEM.DAT file, the USER.DAT file resides in the \windows directory. Windows 95 also makes a backup file, USER.DA0, maintained there as well. Both files are read-only, hidden, and system files. Windows 98/Me makes a backup using the SCANREG program.

These Windows 98/Me Registry backups are stored in the *\windows\sys-bckup* directory as rb000.cab, rb001.cab, rb002.cab, rb003.cab and rb004.cab, as shown in Figure 11–11.

Figure 11–11
rb004.cab contents.

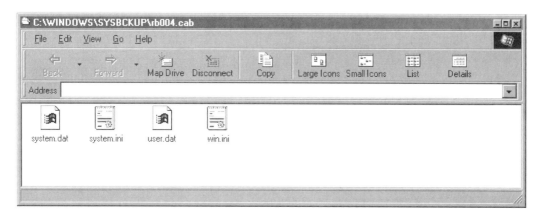

They contain copies of both SYSTEM.DAT and USER.DAT.

In addition, they store the WIN.INI and SYSTEM.INI files. The CAB files can be opened using the Windows 98/Me Explorer or using WINZIP.

WIN.COM

WIN.COM launches Windows 95/98/Me in the same way it launches Windows 3.x, and can also launch Windows from the command prompt. This can be helpful when trying to isolate an error condition.

During the Windows startup, WIN.COM determines if Windows was shut down properly by examining the FAT. When it detects an improper shutdown, WIN.COM runs SCANDISK to check the drive for errors.

The WIN.COM troubleshooting options modifying Windows startup include the following:

```
WIN [/D:[F][M][S][V][X]]
```

- /D—Used for troubleshooting when Windows does not start correctly.
- :F—Turns off 32-bit disk access. Equivalent to SYSTEM.INI file setting: 32BitDiskAccess=FALSE.
- :M—Enables safe mode.This is automatically enabled during safe start (function key F5).
- :N—Enables safe mode with networking.This is automatically enabled during safe start (function key F6).
- :S—Specifies that Windows should not use ROM address space between F000:0000 and 1 MB for a break point. Equivalent to SYSTEM.INI file setting: SystemROMBreakPoint=FALSE.
- :V—Specifies that the ROM routine will handle interrupts from the hard disk controller. Equivalent to SYSTEM.INI file setting: VirtualHDIRQ=FALSE.
- :X—Excludes all of the adapter area from the range of memory that Windows scans to find unused space. Equivalent to SYSTEM.INI file setting: EMMExclude=A000-FFFF.

WIN.COM also participates in the Windows shutdown process. It uses the FAT entry to signal that Windows shut down properly after writing the VFAT to disk successfully.

Study Break: Saving Registry Files

This exercise saves copies of the SYSTEM.DAT and USER.DAT files to the root directory of the C drive as SYSTEM.00 and USER.00, SYSTEM.01, and USER.01, etc. The sequential numbering creates an audit trail of registry files, permitting the PC to be recovered to a previous operating state. This is an effective method of backing up Windows 95/98/Me configurations. It can be used in place of the emergency recovery utility (ERU) program to back up Windows configurations.

1. Create the following BAKREG.BAT file:

```
attrib c:\windows\system.da? -r -h -s
attrib c:\windows\user.da? -r -h -s
copy c:\windows\system.dat c:\system.%1
copy c:\windows\user.dat c:\user.%1
attrib c:\windows\system.da? +r +h +s
attrib c:\windows\user.da? +r +h +s
```

This batch file can be run in an MS-DOS window under Windows 95/98/Me to create backup copies of the SYSTEM.DAT and USER.DAT files.

2. Once the file is created as BAKREG.BAT, open a DOS window and run the batch file by entering:

```
BAKREG 00
```

This causes the batch file to copy the SYSTEM.DAT and USER.DAT into the root directory of the C drive as SYSTEM.00 and USER.00.

The goal of this exercise is to provide a simple technique for backing up the registry. The batch file permits you to make backup copies of the registry files and permits you to keep them in a numeric sequence starting with 00, then 01, etc.

Summary

This chapter explored the differences between Windows 3.x and Windows 9x. We discussed a variety of Windows 95/98/Me functions, including file and disk management, networking, and more. Windows 95/98/Me components were identified and described, and Windows 95/98/Me key system files were examined. Throughout the chapter, Windows NT/2000 was generally contrasted to Windows 95/98/Me in order to provide an overall perspective on the evolution of Windows from Windows 3.x to Windows 2000.

Chapter Review Questions

1. *The Windows 95 memory organization uses what?*

    A. Conventional, upper, extended memory
    B. Used and free memory
    C. Heaps
    D. Blocks

Answer: C, heaps. Conventional memory, upper memory and extended memory are also used by DOS and Windows 3.x. Unused and free memory is in every computer system. Blocks are wooden things. There are also UMBs used by DOS and Windows 3.x

2. *Windows 95 and Windows NT Workstation support the following protocols except:*

    A. NetBEUI
    B. IPX/SPX
    C. TCP/IP
    D. DLCC

Answer: D, DLCC. There is no DLCC, only DLC protocol.

3. *The registry in Windows 95 is organized into:*

    A. Keys
    B. Hives
    C. Values
    D. Trees

Answer: A, keys. While the registry is structured into several major hives forming a tree structure, and the keys have values, the central registry elements are keys.

4. *A Windows 95 and NT 4.0 utility managing the fixed disk drive is called what?*

    A. File manager
    B. Program manager
    C. Control panel
    D. Explorer

Answer: D, Explorer. The file manager is a Windows 3.x program for managing disk drives. Similarly, the program manager is also a Windows 3.x program for organizing the programs run under Windows 3.x. The control panel does not directly manage the fixed disk drives.

5. *To determine if specific hardware is supported by Windows NT, check the:*

    A. HAL
    B. HCL
    C. HSL
    D. RFC

Answer: B, HCL (Hardware Compatibility List). HAL is the Windows NT/2000 Hardware Adaptation Layer software matching Windows NT/2000 to the PC hardware. RFC is a request for comments used for development of Internet and other communications specifications. HSL could stand for High-speed Local, but we are not sure about that.

6. *Assuming user level access control security is disabled on a PC computer, what must be done after installing file and print sharing under Windows 95 to allow users access to the computer?*

    A. No further configuration is necessary
    B. Specify access permission for each individual user or group who uses the computer
    C. Share a folder through Explorer or my computer
    D. Reboot the computer

Answer: C, share a folder through Explorer or my computer. Further configuration is needed because disks and printers are not automatically shared on a network. When sharing a disk or printer under share level access control, the sharing process configures the security level of the shared resource (read-only, full) and the password needed to access that resource. User level access control uses domain users and groups to control access to the PC disk and printer resources. Rebooting the computer does not automatically share disk and printer resources.

7. *The Windows 3.x REG.DAT file size exceeding 65,000 bytes can indicate what?*

    A. A corrupted Windows 3.x registry
    B. A faulty Windows installation
    C. A virus
    D. Nothing—REG.DAT grows as new applications are installed

Answer: A, a corrupted Windows 3.x registry, because its size should be less than 64 Kb. Windows 95/98/Me/NT/2000 have much larger registries.

8. *In Windows NT/2000, what is used to recover from a failed boot?*

    A. DOS boot disk
    B. Last known good configuration
    C. Both B and C
    D. None of the above

Answer: B, last known good configuration. A DOS boot disk most likely would do little because the Windows NT/2000 disk drives could be using NTFS instead of FAT 16 or FAT 32.

9. *What loads the Windows NT operating system?*

    A. NTLDR
    B. MBR
    C. NTOSKRNL.EXE
    D. MBA

Answer: B, MBR (Master Boot Record). While NTLDR does load the NT operating system, all operating systems are loaded starting with the MBR on the fixed disk drive.

10. *Windows 95 supports the following NICs except:*

    A. Token ring
    B. Ethernet
    C. ARCnet
    D. JetDirect

Answer: D, JetDirect. All are NICs except JetDirect.

11. *Where does Win95 set up record hardware detection information?*

    A. In DETLOG.TXT
    B. In DETLOG.LOG
    C. In SETUPLOG.TXT
    D. In DETCRASH.LOG

Answer: A, in DETLOG.TXT. There is no DETCRASH.LOG and no DETLOG.LOG. SETUPLOG.TXT records the Windows software boot and installation process and BOOTLOG.TXT follows the Windows boot process. DETLOG.TXT records hardware detection information.

12. *A new Windows application is installed and runs fine. However, when opening Word, which was previously installed, a general protection fault is generated, and Word terminates. After reinstalling Word, it still refuses to run. What is a probable cause?*

    A. The new application overwrote key DLL files related to Word.
    B. The Word installation files have become corrupted, and you need new installation media.
    C. Run REGEDIT to reregister Word in the registry.
    D. The new application used too much RAM and not enough is left to run Word.

Answer: A, the new application overwrote key DLL files related to Word. Usually, any general protection fault is caused by software conflicts and not a lack of RAM. Running REGEDIT will not fix a general protection fault problem. Since Word was not installed, its installation files have not likely become corrupted. However, a new application may use a DLL common to both it and Word, which was replaced during its installation causing the general protection fault.

13. *A Windows 95 machine generates errors while printing. A check of the resources reveals the GDI resources at 60 percent. After rebooting and opening only the program to print from, the GDI resources are at 75 percent. What steps could increase your resources?*

    A. Install more RAM
    B. Upgrade your video card
    C. Lower your video resolution and color palette
    D. All of the above

Answer: C, Lower your video resolution and color palette. Adding RAM does not increase Windows resources. Changing video cards may fix the problem but it requires buying a new card. Lowering video resolution and the number of colors are a low cost, better approach for solving the problem.

14. *The Win95 Registry is comprised of which two files?*

    A. SYSTEM.DAT and USER.DAT
    B. SYSTEM.REG and USER.RET
    C. SYSTEM.INI and WIN.INI
    D. REG.DAT and SETUP.REG

Answer: A, SYSTEM.DAT and USER.DAT. There are not RET files. The INI files are used by Windows 3.x and are not registry files. DAT and REG files are not blended to create the registry, so the only remaining answer is SYSTEM.DAT and USER.DAT.

15. *A new video card is installed and configured. When the PC is rebooted, Windows 95 hangs on the logo screen. What troubleshooting steps should resolve the problem?*

    A. Boot the computer in safe mode and change the video driver to VGA.
    B. Boot "step-by-step confirmation" and don't load anything that isn't necessary for the system to boot.
    C. Boot "Command Prompt Only" and comment any unnecessary lines from AUTOEXEC.BAT and CONFIG.SYS.
    D. Reinstall Windows.

Answer: A, boot the computer in safe mode and change the video driver to VGA. Reinstalling will not necessarily help because the same hardware and driver programs would be installed. The programs affecting Windows video are not loaded in AUTOEXEC.BAT and CONFIG.SYS and both are not needed to boot Windows. How could you tell using "step-by-step" confirmation what to load or not load? It would take many reboots to test each and every "step-by-step" combination. Generally, incorrect video drivers cause Windows to hang, so using safe mode and standard VGA drivers are likely to get Windows started. To solve the problem, get new video drivers from the manufacturer off the Internet. Use DRIVERSHQ.COM to easily find them.

16. *Windows 95 plug-and-play BIOS enables what?*

    A. The devices that are not plug-and-play first
    B. The plug-and-play devices first
    C. The devices only after CONFIG.SYS is read
    D. An automatic virus scan

Answer: A, the devices that are not plug-and-play first. The BIOS runs before any virus scan or any CONFIG.SYS files are loaded. The devices that are plug-and-play get whatever resources remain after the resources are assigned to the legacy (non-plug-and-play) devices.

17. *What is the best way for an average user to modify PC system settings?*

    A. Edit the registry to make the necessary changes
    B. Use control panel applets to make the necessary changes
    C. Run Sysedit to make the necessary changes to SYSTEM.INI and WIN.INI
    D. A and C

Answer: B, use control panel applets to make the necessary changes. An average user modifying the registry is not good. An average user modifying WIN.INI and SYSTEM.INI is also not good. The best approach is to use the control panel so that Windows Wizards and menus guide their modifications.

18. *Two primary utilities for maintaining/optimizing hard drives in DOS and Win95 are:*

    A. SCANDISK and BACKUP
    B. DEFRAG and BACKUP
    C. SCANDISK and DEFRAG
    D. SCANDISK and FDISK

Answer: C, SCANDISK and DEFRAG. The clue here is maintaining and optimizing. Neither Backup nor FDISK optimize, and so the only remaining option is SCANDISK and DEFRAG.

19. *A dual boot system with Win95 and Win3.11 locks up during a Windows 95 boot when it tries to load a particular device driver from CONFIG.SYS. It boots to Win3.11. To correct the problem preventing Win95 from booting, you edit c:\CONFIG.SYS but cannot find the device driver reference. Why?*

    A. Win95 automatically deleted the line that prevented the system from booting.
    B. The device file doesn't load from CONFIG.SYS; it loads from AUTOEXEC.BAT.
    C. The Win95 CONFIG.SYS is currently CONFIG.W95.
    D. The Win95 CONFIG.SYS is currently CONFIG.W40.

Answer: D, The Win95 CONFIG.SYS is currently CONFIG.W40. Windows does rename the CONFIG.SYS and AUTOEXEC.BAT files to .W40 files. Sometimes the names may be different, so check all CONFIG. Files.

20. *What is the maximum number of entries in a hard disk's root directory in DOS 6.22 and Win95?*

    A. 512 entries
    B. 150 entries
    C. 1000 entries
    D. There is no limit to the number of entries in any directory.

Answer: A, 512 entries. Fixed disk root directories have a limited number of entries. Only subdirectories are (theoretically) unlimited in size. The limit is 512 entries.

21. *Why won't an OS/2 application run on an NT machine?*

    A. The application accesses the hard drive directly

    B. Some OS/2 applications are not compatible with NT

    C. OS/2 applications can only be run on OS/2 machines

    D. OS/2 applications must access the hardware directly

Answer: B, some OS/2 applications are not compatible with NT. While OS-2 and NT were both developed by Microsoft, they are more like distant cousins rather than siblings. Direct access to the fixed disk drive would cause an application not to run under NT, but direct fixed disk access is not permitted by OS2 as well. Some OS2 applications can run under NT.

22. *Which Windows environments can use 4 GB memory address space in the PC?*

    A. Windows 3.x

    B. Windows 95

    C. Windows NT

    D. B and C

Answer: D, B and C. Only Windows 3.x uses less than 4 GB of address space. Windows 2000 can use 64 GB address space.

23. *Windows 95/98/Me file associations are stored in:*

    A. The registry

    B. The OLE.INI file

    C. The WIN.INI file

    D. The WINASSOC.INI file

Answer: A, the registry. There is no WINASSOC.INI or OLE.INI files. The WIN.INI file is used for backward compatibility for some Windows applications, but not to store file associations.

24. *In order to dual boot, Win3.x is installed in c:\windows and Win95 is installed in a directory called c:\win95. What additional step must you take to enable the system to dual boot?*

    A. Add BootWin=2 to the MSDOS.SYS file

    B. Add BootMenu=1 to the MSDOS.SYS file

    C. Add BootMulti=1 to the MSDOS.SYS file

    D. Add BootDual=1 to the MSDOS.SYS file

Answer: C, Add BootMulti=1 to the MSDOS.SYS file. There is no BootWin, BootMenu, or BootDual setting in MSDOS.SYS.

25. *For Windows NT to allow a remote PC to dial in, what must be installed and running?*

    A. The PPP protocol service
    B. The IPX/SPX protocol service
    C. The RAS service
    D. The Mac service

Answer: C, the RAS (Remote Access Server) service. PPP protocol is used to dial out to the Internet, IPX/SPX is used to connect to Novell servers, and the Mac service would connect with Apple Macintosh computers.

Chapter 12

DISK NAVIGATION PROCEDURES AND MANAGEMENT

Chapter Syllabus

- File System Basics

- DOS File Operations

- Windows File Operations

- Disk Management Procedures

- Disk Management Utilities

All computer programs and data are in files stored on the PC's disk drives. PC users often misunderstand good data management practices and procedures, and do not think of using the DOS or Windows disk utilities on a periodic basis to maintain the integrity of the data stored on their fixed disk drive. Their first encounter with DOS and Windows fixed disk utility programs is usually when they are desperately attempting to recover data from a corrupted fixed disk drive. Therefore, a critical skill for PC troubleshooting and maintenance is the ability to effectively use DOS and Windows disk and file maintenance utility programs. Also, an understanding of how to organize data and manage files on a PC's disk drives can be helpful in educating PC users and helping them avoid corrupting the data and programs stored on their PC's fixed disk drive. Navigating up and down the hierarchy of directories and subdirectories, as well as copying, deleting, moving, displaying, and loading files are essential skills for managing data on PC fixed disk drives.

File System Basics

Files have specific characteristics. These characteristics cover what they contain, their name, and their attributes. When we work with files, understanding the implications of these characteristics helps with the file management process. For example, understanding whether a file is a text or binary file helps us when we wish to view the contents of the file. If a file is binary, we need a special filter or software to represent the contents in a meaningful way.

Binary vs. Text Files

Files usually contain either text or binary information. Text information is comprised of the 96 printable ASCII characters plus some simple control characters, like Carriage Return (Cr) and Line Feed (LF). Text files in DOS and Windows end with the SUB character, which is created by striking F6 or by holding down the Ctrl key and striking the Z character (displayed as ^z).

- To create a text file from a PC keyboard, use the command COPY CON filename.TXT.
- Type the text you want in the file.
- Finally, hit Ctrl+Z or F6.
- The PC should display "1 file(s) copied."

ASCII—American (national) Standard Code for Information Interchange—has seven bits of information and a parity bit, which enables it to represent 128 unique alphanumeric, punctuation, and control characters. This is referred to as 7-bit ASCII. An 8-bit version of the ASCII code is used to represent international characters and symbols. The 8-bit version of ASCII does not have a parity bit. PCs use a special 8-bit version of ASCII, called IBM PC-8, to represent special graphics and foreign alphabet symbols.

Use the steps above to create a text file. Creating text files using just the keyboard is an important troubleshooting skill. There are times when you have only DOS and its ability to run batch files to perform file management miracles. Creating a series of simple batch files using the COPY CON command saves the day in those situations.

The MSDOS.SYS file created by Windows 95/98/Me is a text file, while the MSDOS.SYS file for DOS is a binary file containing program object code. If we try to display it, we get no meaningful output. See a notepad view of a text and binary file in Figure 12–1. The binary displays strange characters because any pattern of zeros and ones can occupy each byte of the file. Binary files use all 256 patterns of zeros and ones to represent information in the bytes contained in the file. Text files, in contrast, use a limited set of patterns, which is somewhat less than the 128 patterns of zeros and ones specified by the ASCII code. This is because text files contain only a few of the 16 control characters defined by the ASCII code. The SUB character, the Cr character and the LF character are some of the ASCII code control characters.

There are few pure text files—most files have some special formatting. HTML or HTM files are text files that incorporate descriptive markup that is recognized by web browser software. The web browser interprets the markup to translate the text file into a fancy website display.

In Figure 12–2, the browser and the notepad program are viewing the same file. The browser interprets the markup in the file to produce the web page display. The source files for programs are text files. Executable programs are binary files, as are graphic images and sound files. The registries are binary files that require REGEDIT to display. Text files include special control files, such as AUTOEXEC.BAT, CONFIG.SYS, INI files (WIN.INI and SYSTEM.INI), TXT files, HTM files, and others. Email messages were largely text files until more sophisticated email programs permitted embedded images and other features. Today, email is a mix of text and binary files.

File Naming Conventions

Files have names similar to our names. These filenames are assigned in a standard format just like common names; they use a first and last name. Files have a filename and an extension which permit certain characters. Common names and filenames do not usually use punctuation characters. Two file naming conventions are used today: the original DOS 8.3 format and Windows 3.1 long filenames. Let's examine them in more detail.

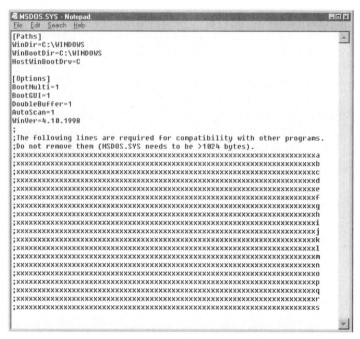

Figure 12-1

Windows 98 MSDOS.SYS text and MSDOS.SYS binary file.

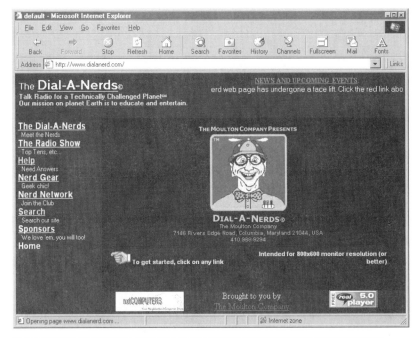

Figure 12–2

Browser and HTML text view of web page.

The 8.3 Format

The DOS 8.3 filenames use up to eight characters for a filename and up to three characters for an extension, with a period as a separator. This made them 11 characters total length, not including the separator. These characters,

```
" / \ [ ] : * < > | + ; , ?
```

cannot be used in DOS filenames. Space characters are also not permitted in DOS filenames. The period is only used as a DOS file name separator character. Characters that can be used in filenames include:

```
$ % ` - @ ~ ` ! ( ) ^ # & _
```

A DOS 8.3 filename example could be filename.ext. (Filename is exactly 8 characters long and ext is exactly 3 characters long, so it exactly matches the DOS 8.3 filename format.) The name identified the contents of the file for a PC user. The extension was used to identify the file type or formatting. DOC extensions were formatted in an MS Word format, while HTM files in an HTML format were used by web browsers.

Long Filenames

Long filenames were implemented in Windows 95 and Windows NT. The MAC and OS/2 PCs also use long filenames. Support for both long and short filenames is available under Windows 95/98/Me and Windows NT/2000, as well as translation for those applications that do not support long filenames. Windows had to supply this support because all applications initially run under Windows 95 were older Windows 3.x applications incapable of using long filenames.

The Windows 95/98/Me long file naming convention rules are:

• Long filenames can contain up to 255 characters.
• Valid characters are the same but Windows 95 can use the added characters: + , ; [ ].
• Spaces within names are ignored.
• Lowercase characters are preserved in long filenames.
• A complete path specification for a long filename can be 260 characters.

As you can see, this allows you to describe the file you are using in great detail. You can even stick with file extensions, but they can be longer than 3 characters. See Figure 12–3.

When long filenames are viewed or manipulated by programs that can only

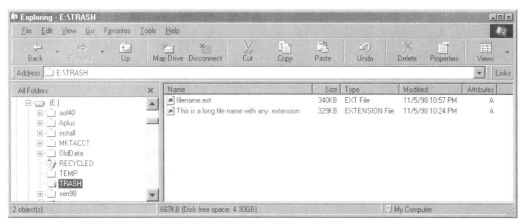

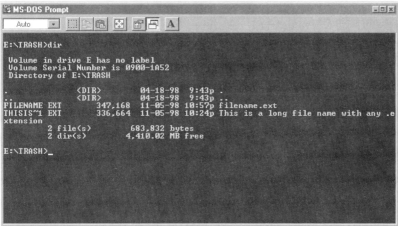

Figure 12-3
Long filenames displayed by Explorer and DIR.

work with short filenames, the long filenames are truncated at the sixth character, and a ~1, etc., is substituted as a place holder for the long name characters that are missing. Sometimes the long filename is not disturbed, and other times the truncated name replaces the long filename. If older DOS programs copy files with long filenames, the long filename is commonly replaced by the truncated name. If the file is not copied, the filename is not replaced.

In reality, files named very descriptively without regard to extension can be very difficult for the user to locate on a disk drive because it can be difficult to figure out which characters to search for. It is much easier to seek a file with only 11 characters in the name than it is to search for one with 65 characters like "This is the name of the file that I just created for this example.txt".

Long filenames are implemented in the directory. A directory entry consists of several components. The filename field is 11 bytes in size because of the old DOS 8.3 rule, making the total filename length 11 bytes. The other fields store the additional important file information, which are called attributes.

Microsoft discovered they could add a volume attribute in the file attribute field, which is 1 byte in size. Next, Microsoft developed a special volume-locking API. All changes to a directory entry with the volume attribute had to be processed by the special API. This now meant that no entries would change without Windows 95/98/Me knowing about it, even when using older utilities. Additionally, this gave Windows 95/98/Me total control over all disk entries.

A long filename essentially consists of a short filename plus additional directory entries to allow for the extra characters of the long name. All directory entries in the FAT are 32 bytes in size. A long name requires a directory entry in excess of 256 bytes. Changing the directory entry size would wreak havoc on PC programs. So instead of increasing the size of the entry, Microsoft instead assigned multiple directory entries to a single long filename. Since a directory entry is only 32 characters, when several entries are used Windows must have a way to keep track of the directory entries for a single file. It does this by modifying the directory entries.

To create the long filenames, Windows 95/98/Me modifies what is stored in the additional directory entries. The information stored there does not have to conform to the structure as seen in the top of Figure 12–3. If it did, then Windows 95/98/Me would use far too many directory entries. Instead it uses a large portion of the directory entry for the filename itself. Windows 95/98/Me uses some bytes to track related entries. In fact, it must have a way to associate the long filename with its short filename. If the association is lost, the file can become corrupt because all long filenames must have a short filename. Figure 12–4 shows a directory entry for a long filename and a classification entry.

A long filename directory entry starts with a sequence number used by Windows 95/98/Me to track the entry and modifications made to the entry. The attribute field lists the attributes for the file. The type defines what kind of directory entry it is, a component of the filename or a classification entry. Lastly, a checksum created from the short name entry of the file is included. This creates a directory entry with a name field of 26 bytes out of the 32 total bytes for the directory entry. This is far better than the 11-byte name field in DOS 8.3 format directory entry.

A long filename must have a short filename associated with it to be used by DOS applications. Windows generates a unique short filename for each long

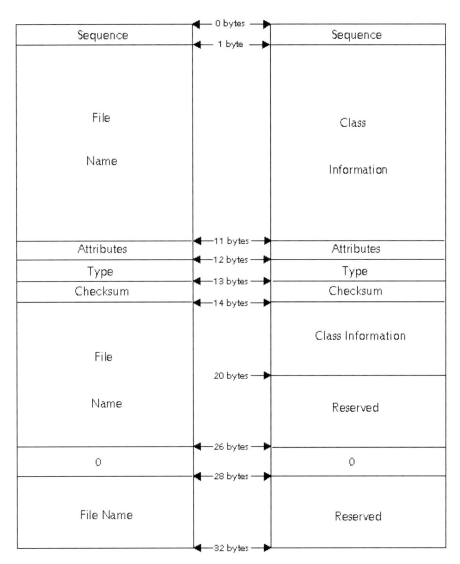

Figure 12–4
Long filename directory entry structure.

filename. The rules followed by Windows 95/98/Me to create a unique short filename for a long filename are:

- As a long name is created, Windows 95/98/Me creates the linked short name.

731

- If your long name is really a short name, it must be unique within the directory where it resides. No other short name can be exactly like it in that directory. Filenames are not case sensitive. FILENAME.TXT and filename.txt are the same file as far as Windows and DOS are concerned.

- When creating the short filename, Windows 95/98/Me tries several valid truncations to create the unique short name.

- If you create a short name (using the old DOS API), then the long name is the same. If the long name conflicts, then the short name cannot be created.

Using long filenames as far as DOS is concerned is no problem. Windows 95 extended the DOS INT21h interface to accommodate the use of long filenames by DOS. This software allows Windows and DOS programs to manipulate files using the short filenames.

File Attributes

File attributes control access to the file by determining whether the file is visible and accessible to the PC users. DOS supports archive, read-only, system, hidden, directory, and volume attributes. The directory and volume attributes are not file attributes per se. They are used by the operating system and are not manipulated by the user. The attributes are stored as bits in the attribute byte for each file in the directory.

Read-Only

Read-only files are generally programs and special parameter files that should not be moved or changed in any way. This attribute is used to prevent users from accidentally erasing or corrupting the files. Among others, the registry files are marked with read-only file attributes. The Windows system programs read from and write to this file. Hence, the read-only file attribute prevents only naive users from changing the file. DEFRAG, which is discussed later in this chapter, typically does not move read-only files.

System

The system attribute denotes a file that is used by the operating system. Deleting system files could cause the system to crash or misbehave.

732

Hidden

The hidden attribute makes the file invisible to the normal directory, the Windows file manager, Explorer programs, and other DOS commands. The goal here is to keep important files from being moved or deleted from the PC's disk drives. Hiding files can also reduce directory clutter for the user. For example, many programs store data and program files in the same folder. Marking the program files as hidden would prevent them from being deleted and leave a folder displaying only the data files.

Archive

The archive attribute is to help backup programs determine if a file has been altered since the last backup. Every time a file is updated, the archive attribute is set. Backup programs reset the archive attribute when they make a backup copy of the file. Better backups are made simply using the date and time stamp information available in the directory entry for the file.

Changing File Attributes

File attributes can be viewed and changed in DOS using the ATTRIB command and in Windows using the file manager or Explorer.

The DOS external ATTRIB command options are listed in Table 12–1.

```
ATTRIB [+R | -R] [+A | -A] [+S | -S] [+H | -H] [[drive:][path]filename] [/S]
```

Table 12–1   ATTRIB File Attributes and Attribute Modifiers

Option	Description
+	Sets an attribute.
-	Clears an attribute.
R	Read-only file attribute.
A	Archive file attribute.
S	System file attribute.
H	Hidden file attribute.
/S	Processes files in all directories in the specified path.

Similarly, Windows Explorer can display and set file attributes. The Windows 95/98/Me Explorer View ➤ Folder Option ➤ View ➤ Advanced Settings has a box for showing file attributes in a detailed view. See Figure 12–5.

Directory and volume attributes are not set using the ATTRIB command.

Explorer File Attributes Setting

If the Explorer detailed view option is set, the file attributes are displayed in the right panel along with other file details. Selecting a file and choosing File ➤ Properties provides a menu panel that permits selection of the read-only, system, hidden, and archive file properties. See Figure 12–6.

Figure 12–5
Explorer file attributes setting.

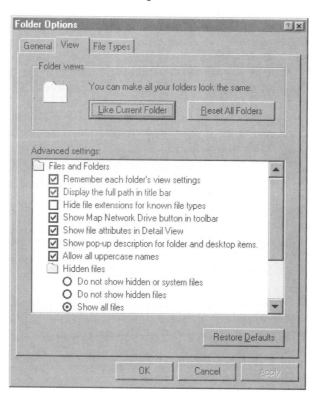

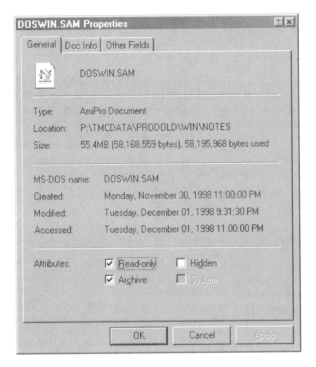

Figure 12-6
Changing file properties.

Study Break: File Attributes

In this exercise we use the ATTRIB command to see the impact of file attributes. We first set them and then use the directory command or Windows Explorer to view the files.

1. Open a DOS window. Enter SET DIRCMD=/Ogn. This sets the directory command to sort out the files in order with subdirectories first and then alphabetically by name when it creates the directory list display.

2. Change to the root directory of the C drive. Enter the command DIR AUTO*.* to display all AUTOEXEC files that reside there. There should be several variations of the AUTOEXEC files that are the remnants of application software installations.

3. Use the ATTRIB command to set the hidden attribute on these files. The command would be:

```
ATTRIB AUTO*.* +H
```

This sets the hidden attribute on those AUTOEXEC files.

4. Again, enter the command DIR AUTO*.* to display all AUTOEXEC files. Because the hidden attribute is set on the files, no files should be listed in the directory display.

5. View the root directory with Windows Explorer. Generally, the AUTOEXEC files would not also be displayed there because the hidden attribute is set.

6. Next enter SET DIRCMD=/Ogn /A. This sets the directory command to view all files. Similarly, in Windows Explorer, select view from the top menu, then folder options. Select view again, then show all files. This sets Windows Explorer to display all the files. Apply the change by clicking OK.

7. Now view the root directory of the C drive. If the AUTOEXEC files are not visible, tap the F5 key to refresh the display.

8. Again enter the command DIR AUTO*.* to display all AUTOEXEC files. Note that this time the AUTOEXEC files are displayed because the directory command has been instructed by the /A option to display all files. To check the settings of the directory command, enter SET. This causes DOS to display the environment space. In the environment space listing should be a line DIRCMD=/Ogn /A.

9. Use the ATTRIB command to view the file attributes. The command would be:

```
ATTRIB AUTO*.*
```

10. Finally, use the ATTRIB command to return the AUTOEXEC files to their normal status. The command would be:

```
ATTRIB AUTO*.* -H
```

This exercise illustrates the use of file attributes to hide files, the ATTRIB command used under DOS to set the file attributes, and settings for both the directory command and Windows Explorer that permit listing files in the directory display regardless of their attribute settings.

DOS File Operations

DOS provides several basic functions:

- Starts programs. (This is called launching programs under Windows.) In this case, the programs are .COM, .EXE, or .BAT files stored on the disk drive.
- Provides support programs for managing files on both your floppy and fixed disk drives. This includes file maintenance functions such as copying, deleting, and renaming files.
- Provides commands that perform system functions. The DOS TIME command and the DOS DATE command display and change the PC's clock time and date respectively.

Some DOS commands are focused on file operations. COPY, DEL, MOVE, RENAME, ATTRIB and EDIT are examples of file manipulation commands. The EDIT command permits editing of text and batch files. Help with DOS commands is available at the DOS prompt by entering HELP. This causes DOS to display its online documentation.

Editing TXT and BAT Files

Editing text (TXT) and batch (BAT) files can be either easy or tough depending on using the Edit command or the Copy Con command. DOS 6.x had an EDIT command that launched the DOS text editor, as shown in Figure 12–7. This program was originally part of the QBASIC provided with DOS 6.x. The DOS text editor makes editing text and batch files easy. It works with a mouse or with keyboard shortcuts. Table 12–2 lists and describes the DOS text editor.

Table 12–2   DOS Editing Commands

Function	Action
Select Text	Highlight text using the mouse or by depressing the Shift key while changing the cursor position with the arrow keys
Copy Text	Press Ctrl + Ins while the text is selected
Cut Text	Press Shift + Del
Delete Text	Press Del key while text is selected
Search	Requires menu selection operation, but a search can be continued using the F3 key. Search and Replace (Change) functionality was also present.

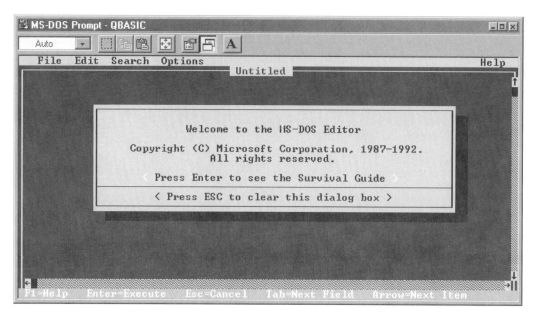

Figure 12-7
MS-DOS text editor program.

Alternatively, text files could be created with the COPY CON command, which copied the keyboard keystrokes to a file specified by COPY CON. Text files could be displayed using the TYPE command and then combined using the COPY command. Files were concatenated by:

```
COPY file1.txt+file2.txt file3.txt
```

In this case, file3.txt contained the contents of file1.txt and file2.txt.

Earlier versions of DOS provided a crude text file editing capability with the EDLIN (line editor) program. This made editing files very difficult. Although EDLIN was no great editor, it was better than some of the other line editing programs that came with other operating systems.

Launching Programs

To launch a program in DOS, you must type the program name in at the keyboard and strike Enter. When starting programs, DOS looks at what has been typed on the keyboard. It checks it to see if it is an internal command, like DIR. If not, it checks the file extension to determine if it is EXE, COM, or BAT. Since the extension is not likely to be entered, DOS searches the current diskette or fixed disk directory for the filename. Once it finds the file, DOS checks its extension. When the file cannot be found in the current directory, DOS then searches a path previously entered into the PC for the file. When the file cannot be found, DOS displays for the user:

```
C:\ >dumb
Bad command or file name
```

The path is searched for BAT, COM, and EXE files. Other files are ignored in the search.

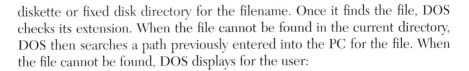

Study Break: Path Operations

This exercise illustrates how the path statement works. It requires using the Windows ATTRIB command and MODE command programs.

1. Make a directory on the C drive called test. The command is:

    ```
    MD C:\test
    ```

    Change to that directory.
2. Copy from C:\windows\command the ATTRIB.EXE and the MODE.COM commands to the C:\test directory.
3. Rename these files to A.EXE and A.COM.
4. Now create a batch file with the name A.BAT. To create the batch file enter the following commands:

    ```
    COPY CON A.BAT ENTER
    REM This is the batch file.
    Hit Ctrl Z (or F6), then Enter.
    ```

5. Three files should now reside in the test directory. These files are A.BAT, A.COM, and A.EXE. Reset the path so that it applies only to the test directory, using the following commands.

    ```
    CD C:\
    PATH>OP.BAT
    PATH=C:\TEST
    ```

6. Once the path has been reset, we are ready to begin our test of the path command. Enter A and strike the Enter key. The DOS win-

dow should display the results of the MODE.COM command since it was renamed A.COM.

7. Enter A.EXE and strike the Enter key. The DOS window should now display the results of the ATTRIB.EXE command, since it has been renamed A.EXE.

8. Finally enter A.BAT and strike the Enter key. The DOS window should now display the results of the A.BAT that was created.

9. Delete A.COM from the test directory. Enter A and strike the enter key. The DOS window should now display the results of the ATTRIB.EXE command since EXE files take precedence over BAT files and since ATTRIB.EXE was renamed A.EXE.

10. Reset the path by entering OP. This executes a batch file that stored the original path and restores the path to its original settings.

This exercise illustrates the operation of the PATH command. It shows that the PATH command searches first for COM files, then EXE files, and finally BAT files.

Windows File Operations

Windows can perform file operations using DOS commands and using the GUI. The file management features of Windows changed between Windows 3.x and Windows 95/98/Me. Windows NT 3.5x behaves like Windows 3.x and Windows NT/2000 behaves similarly to Windows 95/98/Me when performing file operation functions.

All versions of Windows associate data files with applications using the file extension. Standard associations for common application programs are built into Windows, which also has the ability to make new file associations.Creating file associations differs with the operating system. With DOS, the application programs themselves determined file associations. DOS would merely provide a path to the data files using the DOS APPEND command.

With Windows 3.1x, file associations were created using the file manager. Clicking on File in the file manager menu yielded a drop-down menu containing "Associate". This menu item permitted associating files extensions with different specific programs. Clicking on the menu item would bring up an associate panel permitting the entry of the file extension. By typing in the extension of a standard file, the program associated with it would appear in a panel below. Those files not associated with a specific program could, using their extension and the browse function, be assigned a program association. This was a rather simplistic process.

Windows 95/98/Me and Windows NT/2000 manage file associations similarly. With both Windows 95/98/Me and Windows NT/2000 this can be accomplished using the Explorer program. Windows 95/98/Me provides alternative paths to the file associations panel. Using Explorer, open View on the menu bar, then Options. This brings up the view box that permits managing file types. Click on the file types tab to see a listing of the file types and their programs. It can be difficult to manage the file associations with Windows 95/98/Me and Windows NT/2000 because the file extension cannot be entered directly to identify the programs associated with it. In this case, scrolling through the list of file extensions while watching the panel to identify the file extension can reset the association, but this is an awkward and time-consuming process. Alternatively, in Windows 98/Me/2000 you may reset the associations using the Explorer. Selecting the file and then clicking with the right mouse button can reset the association. This causes a menu to pop up that has an "Open With" selection that in turn permits you to choose a program from the panel shown in Figure 12–8. By selecting the "Always use this program to open these files" option, the file association is reset.

Figure 12–8
Resetting File Associations in Windows 98/Me/2000.

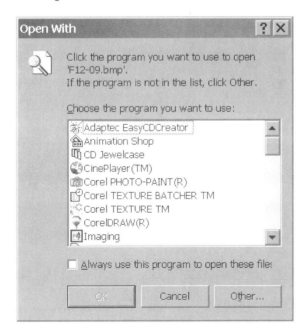

Fortunately, most file associations are set by the applications as they are installed in Windows. Unfortunately, some applications change the file associations that you desire. In this event, you must search through these file associations to find the extension you wish to associate with a program and then reassign it.

The file associations permit Windows users to double-click on the data file to launch the associated application and to load the data file contents into the application's working memory.

Windows 3.x File Manager

Windows 3.x uses the Windows file manager (WINFILE.EXE) to perform file management operations. See Figure 12–9. The Windows 3.x file manager program represents disk drives and other storage devices, such as tape drives, as

Figure 12–9
WINFILE program.

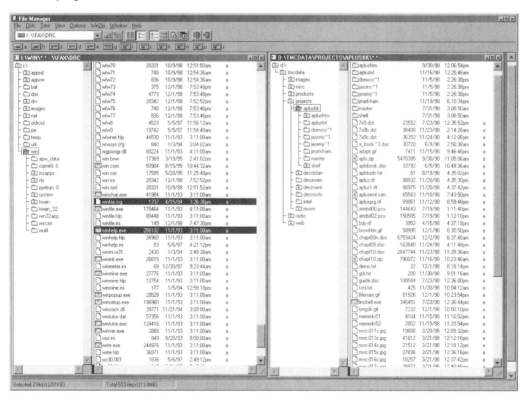

separate Windows within the file manager program. It displays all physical disk drives and all network disk drives mapped to disk drive letters in the top menu area. A path entry box permits direct selection of physical drives and mapped drives not displayed. Icons support quick changes in the disk drive file content views, for instance, sorting in alphabetical and reverse alphabetical order.

The file manager menu items include the following standard selections:

- FILE
- DISK
- TREE
- VIEW
- OPTIONS
- WINDOW
- HELP

FILE operations include selections for opening files, moving files, copying files, renaming files, and setting file properties. The file selection also supports running programs, changing associations, creating directories, searching for specific files, and using wild card characters to select specific files for display; i.e., *.* (all files) or *.EXE (EXE files only).

The DISK menu selection permits copying diskettes, labeling disk volumes, formatting disks, installing the bootable system files on disks, and connecting/disconnecting network drives.

TREE operations expand and collapse the hierarchical directory structure and display which directories (or folders) can be expanded and collapsed. Selecting the "indicate expandable branches option" causes the file manager program to place "+" symbols into those folders that have subfolders.

The VIEW menu changes the display and sorting options for each disk drive Window. It also permits changing between a simultaneous directory tree and directory contents view of the disk drive or a view of the directories or contents alone. The By File Type selection permits filtering of the files displayed. This option also allows the file manager to display all hidden and system files.

A few users prefer the old Windows file manager to the newer Windows Explorer. The Windows 3.x file manager runs in Windows 98, provided that the SCONFIG.DLL is accessible to Windows 98, so that those users preferring it can run it under Windows 95/98. However, it is really better to learn the Windows 95/98/Me/2000 Explorer program.

743

Searching for Files

The file manager can search for files using the search option which is found under the File menu selection. See Figure 12–10.

It opens a search option box that permits specifying the type of file for which to search. The DOS DIR wild card characters are used to specify the file types. This search is equivalent to the DIR filespec /S command. Once the search is started, it displays the results in a new box. Files can be deleted from this box or dragged and dropped to move or copy them. This is easier than using DOS commands.

Drag-and-Drop Operations

The Windows GUI supports drag-and-drop file operations. Using the mouse pointer and the left mouse button, files can be selected and then dragged from one file manager disk drive window and dropped into the desired directory (folder) in another disk drive window. When this drag-and-drop operation goes between two disk drives, the file is copied. If the drag-and-drop operation is on the same disk drive, the file is moved.

To more precisely control copying and moving of files, the Shift and Ctrl keys are used in conjunction with dragging and dropping file icons. Shift causes the file to be moved when dragged and dropped, and Ctrl makes the drag-and-drop operation copy the file. These keys are held while dragging and dropping the file. Alternatively, you can use the right mouse button along with the copy/cut/paste options.

Editing TXT Files

Windows comes with NOTEPAD and WRITE applets that allow you to edit text files. NOTEPAD is strictly an ASCII text file editor that can handle files up to

Figure 12–10
WINFILE search option.

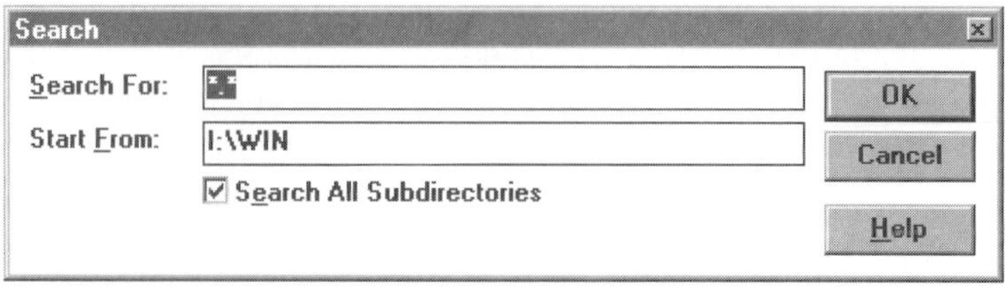

744

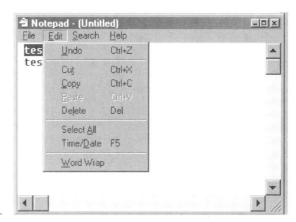

Figure 12-11
NOTEPAD editing commands.

64 KB in size. It provides minimal editing features and no text formatting. NOTEPAD has the same basic features as the DOS EDIT program. It supports simple text searching, but has no replace feature. The newer version found in NT/2000 and Windows 98/Me has a search option and a replace feature.

Cutting, copying, and pasting selections are supported with the mouse and with the DOS EDIT keyboard commands. NOTEPAD cuts highlighted text with Ctrl+X, copies selected text with Ctrl+C, and pastes selected text with Ctrl+V or Shift+Ins. The Ctrl+Z keystroke combination undoes the last edit function. These keystroke shortcuts are used in Windows 98/Me/2000 editing programs as well. See Figure 12–11.

The Windows WRITE applet provides similar text editing capabilities, and can work with files larger than 64 KB in size. WRITE provides simple word processing capabilities over and above the simple text editing of NOTEPAD. With WRITE, images can be inserted in the documents created. Its word processing capabilities permit specifying fonts and font sizes, paragraph formatting, and rudimentary page layout features, including simple headers and footers. The most important feature of WRITE from an A+ point of view is the ability to work with files larger than 64 KB.

Windows WRITE has the ability to handle a limited number of file formats. The Windows 98/Me version, called WordPad, is the most flexible. WordPad accepts Word documents (DOC), WRITE files (WRI), Rich Text Format files (RTF), and text files (TXT).

Launching Programs

The strategy Windows 3.x used for launching programs was to first start the program, and then load the data into the program. This was an extension of the

DOS model of launching programs. In the case of DOS, the program had to be started first because there was no mechanism to link the data files to the application program. Windows 3.x changed that model by implementing file associations.

Windows 3.x supports launching programs in several different ways, including:

- Double-clicking on the program manager (PROGMAN) shell icons. This is the DOS model of starting the application, then loading the data.

- Running the program from the file manager (WINFILE) File—Run menu selection. This is another incarnation of the DOS model.

- Finding the data file with the file manager, then double-clicking on the desired data file. This implements the Windows file association model of launching the program. Here the program associated with the data file is launched and the data file used to launch it is loaded into the program's working memory.

Windows 3.x was the first step in implementing an object model of managing files and programs. The object model focus is not the traditional load the program and then load the data, but rather is on using data objects to dictate the work performed.

Windows 95/98/Me Overview

Windows has several new features. Most important of these are the desktop, the taskbar, and Explorer. Additionally, Windows 95/98/Me does most of its hardware configuration using the control panel.

The Desktop

When viewing Windows 95 for the first time, the desktop may appear shockingly different than the Windows 3.x desktop. In Windows 3.x, the desktop's primary job was to display a minimized program's icon. The Windows 95/98/Me desktop is similar to the Windows 3.x desktop, but it incorporates more functionality. The Windows Me desktop uses different icons than the Windows 98 desktop, but its functionality is essentially the same.

Because Windows 95/98/Me/2000 are object-oriented systems, the desktop creates a look and feel on your PC screen like the look and feel of your real desk. In the same way that you place items on your desk, like a telephone or a bunch of papers, you can place items used on your computer on the Windows 95/98/Me/2000 desktop regardless of whether they are files or programs. To activate an object, you simply double-click on the appropriate icon. When you minimize a program, it goes to the taskbar, leaving the desktop less cluttered. See Figure 12–12.

Windows 98/Me/2000 Explorer and Microsoft's Internet Explorer combine local and web-based information sources into the Windows desktop. The desktop support makes it possible to customize the desktop, launch programs, switch between files, and keep up with changing national and international news by integrating the Internet and the World Wide Web into the desktop. The Active Desktop interface allows you to place changing information from web pages on the desktop. For example, continually updated TV news broadcasts could be placed on the desktop, making you immediately aware of breaking news. The desktop can be customized by adding active content items, such as news, weather, sports, or stock reports. The Active Desktop interface is automatically turned on when web style is chosen for the desktop. Otherwise,

Figure 12–12
The Windows 95 desktop.

activate the Active Desktop by right-clicking on the desktop and pointing to Active Desktop. Be sure to set View as Web Page as well. Turn off the Active Desktop interface by clicking the Start button, pointing to Settings, pointing to Active Desktop, and then clicking View as Web Page to reset the Web Page View to off.

We typically disable Active Desktop to make Windows operate more reliably. This is because problems connecting to remote resources across LANs and the Internet tend to lock or stall Windows when those resources are no longer available to Windows.

Down the left side of the desktop are the standard Windows 95 objects. The taskbar and its menus are at the bottom. The desktop itself is the remainder of the screen. Data and program objects may be placed on the desktop. When this is done they are placed in a *c:\windows\desktop* folder. The standard objects do not appear in the folder because they are created by registry entries.

The Taskbar

A highlight of the new desktop is the taskbar. It provides functions similar to the Windows 3.x program manager. The taskbar is a tool that allows users to quickly start applications and switch between applications. The taskbar provides both a task list and program manager functionality. See Figure 12–13.

Two main components of the taskbar are the bar itself and the Start button. The bar is responsible for holding and displaying the minimized applications. To activate one, simply point to the item on the bar and single-click. Once clicked on, the application expands to full screen or a portion thereof. The minimized taskbar items act like buttons; an active application button appears depressed. The taskbar is always present wherever you are using Windows so when you want to switch applications, simply point to the application on the taskbar and click. Program icons are no longer hidden from view. The downside to this design is cluttering the taskbar with many open programs.

The Start button launches applications like the Windows 3.x Program Manager. It provides a menu list of applications. Clicking the Start button gives a selection menu, and pointing to one of the menu items and pausing produces additional menu lists. This continues until you reach a program that can be launched by a single click.

On the far right side of the taskbar is a box that contains a system clock, and, when a sound card is installed, a volume control icon. Using these, the date and time can be adjusted along with the sound card speaker volume.

The taskbar and Start menu can be configured using the Settings option which is accessed from the drop-down menu that is displayed by clicking on the start button. Clicking on settings immediately brings up the taskbar properties panel. This permits selection of all the taskbar display options, including

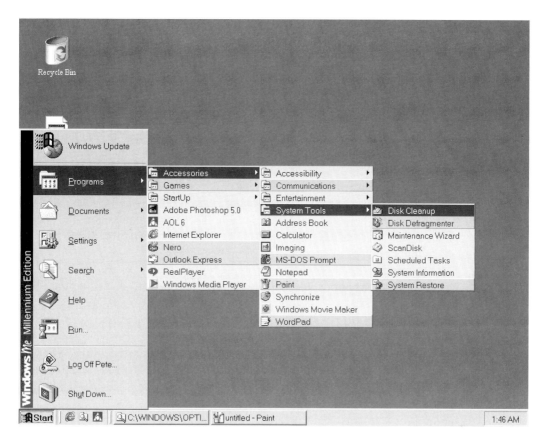

Figure 12-13
Windows Me taskbar and Start button menus.

always on top, auto hide, show small icons, and show clock. The start menu programs tab permits changing the programs as they appear from the start menu. The advanced option opens to start menu folder, showing programs listed underneath it. This folder can also be accessed using the Windows Explorer. It resides in the Windows folder. Rearranging the shortcuts and folders under the start menu\programs folder changes the way the programs appear in the start menu. Toolbars can be added to the taskbar by pointing at the taskbar with the mouse pointer and clicking on the right mouse button. A panel appears with toolbars listed at the top. In this way, different toolbars can be activated and deactivated at the user's discretion.

Exploring

The object model orientation found in Windows 3.x was further enhanced by the Windows 95/98/Me/2000 implementation of Explorer. Explorer replaces the Windows 3.x file manager. However, Explorer has more controls and operating capabilities built into it than did file manager. The Explorer model has menus to launch programs and perform system functions. In some ways, the Explorer is similar to the file manager. For example, the left side of the Explorer displays a hierarchical tree of your system resources. This includes the folders (directories) present on your disk drives. These resources have been expanded to include network connections and your desktop. The tree starts at the top with your desktop, followed by your PC disk, and the directory trees below them. The right side displays the contents of the selected item on the left side, similar to file manager displaying the directory contents in its right pane, as shown in Figure 12–14.

The primary focus of Explorer is on the data files on the disk drive; it extends the associations and object-oriented approach to managing data that Windows 3.x began. To understand the evolution from Windows 3.x to Windows 95/98/Me/2000, we need to examine the operation of Windows 95/98/Me/2000.

The Explorer covers the Windows 3.x file manager functions. Network drive mappings (connections) can be established, you can view directory lists,

Figure 12–14
Windows 2000 Explorer.

in different formats, and you can search for something on your drive. There are some differences: directories are called folders, there are many more icons used to identify items quicker, and you can even create shortcuts for your applications (similar to aliases with the MAC System 7).

One significant difference between the Windows 3.x file manager and Explorer is that the file manager made a separate window for each disk drive within file manager. Explorer creates a hierarchy showing all system resources and disk drives within a single Explorer window. File management is performed within this single window. It is possible to run several copies of Explorer. Each copy functions independently of the other copies. Furthermore, files can be manipulated between copies of Explorer. For example, a file can be dragged from one copy of Explorer and dropped onto a folder on another copy of Explorer, causing the file to be copied into the folder it was dropped on. The copy of Explorer that the file was dropped into performs the copy operation and the Explorer that dropped the file is now free to perform other file management tasks. In contrast, with the file manager only a single file manager copy could be run at any given time. When it was busy performing file manipulation tasks, no other file management could be performed.

Novice users adapt more easily to object-oriented operation than experienced Windows 3.x users. MAC users find the Windows object-oriented desktop a lot like the desktop of a MAC. However, Windows is a bit more politically correct because it uses a recycle bin rather than the Macintosh trash can.

Searching for Files

Like the 3.x file manager, Explorer provides a file search capability which is accessible from the tools menu selection of the Explorer or launched by Ctrl+F (Ctrl + Find). A dialog window guides you through the search process. The search is performed using DOS wild card characters or using date/time or size parameters from the dialog windows.

The search results appear in a dialog window extension. This extension can be sorted by any of the file characteristics displayed, for instance, name, size, or date/time. Clicking on the file characteristic in the title bar causes the files to be sorted in ascending order for that characteristic. Clicking again causes them to be sorted in descending order. The objects found through the search function can be dragged and dropped, deleted, and otherwise manipulated using the Windows 95/98/Me/2000 Explorer capabilities.

Drag-and-Drop Operations

Similarly to Windows 3.x, Windows 95/98/Me/2000 supports drag-and-drop file operations. The same controls and keys apply to Windows 98/Me/2000 Explorer drag-and-drop operations as they do to Windows 3.x. Dragging and dropping between two drives copies files, and dragging and dropping on the same drive moves the files or creates a shortcut to the file. The Ctrl and Shift keys force the drag-and-drop operation to copy the file or to move the file, respectively. Drag-and-drop operations work on folders as well as individual files.

Editing TXT Files

Windows 95/98/Me/2000 have a NOTEPAD text editor program equivalent to the NOTEPAD program provided with Windows 3.x. It has equivalent features to the Windows 3.x NOTEPAD, except that fonts can be changed in the data being edited. NOTEPAD is designed to edit simple BAT and other text files.

Windows 95/98/Me/2000 also has WordPad for word processing. Similar to WRITE, it can handle large files, change fonts, insert pictures, and search and replace text. Unlike WRITE, WordPad does not have the ability to work with simple document headers and footers separate from the main document.

Launching Programs

Similar to Windows 3.x, programs are launched in Windows 95/98/Me/2000 using the Start button menus and double-clicking on the desired program icon. This is equivalent to the DOS "launch the program first, then load the data" operating model. Double-clicking on the data associated with the program also launches the program and loads the data into the application's working memory. This is Window's object-oriented program launching.

Additionally, Windows 95/98/Me/2000 all permit dragging the data file over to the application program icon and dropping it into the program. This is the Windows model, which uses the data to launch the program without associating it with the program. Here, BMP files may be associated with the PAINT program, but they could be dragged and dropped into the Microsoft Photo Editor program, launching it and loading the BMP file into its working memory. In this case, the Microsoft Photo Editor would be used to work on the BMP image. There are some limitations here. Launching the WordPad program with a BMP file has WordPad open the BMP image as a binary file rather than inserting it as an image in some document being created. Similar results are seen with Microsoft Word.

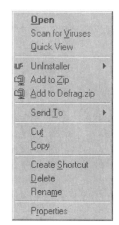

Figure 12-15
Object options menu.

Finally, programs can be launched from shortcut icons. Create shortcuts by pointing to a program file (an EXE file), then clicking the right mouse button. A file options menu window appears that contains a selection "Create Shortcut." Selecting this creates a shortcut file to that application (or data object). See Figure 12–15.

The shortcut object can be placed anywhere. Double-clicking on the shortcut icon launches an application. This can be a data file shortcut or a program file shortcut icon.

Study Break: Creating Shortcuts

This exercise creates shortcuts to some Windows programs on the desktop.

1. Open Windows Explorer. Select the Windows folder and sort the files by type.
2. The EXE files should appear somewhere near the top of the file panel on the right of the Explorer display. Find the WRITE.EXE file. Click on the file and drag it to the desktop. This should create a shortcut to the WRITE.EXE program.
3. Locate the "send to" folder under Windows. Drag the WRITE.EXE shortcut to the "send to" folder. This should move the new shortcut from the desktop into the "send to" folder.
4. Find a TXT file. Click on the file to highlight it, then right-click to

bring up the file options menu. Highlight "send to" and then WRITE.EXE. This should cause the WRITE program to launch and open the file.

This exercise has illustrated the simplest way to create a shortcut to an EXE program. There are also other ways to create shortcuts to programs. The exercise also showed how to use such a shortcut to make convenient opening text files with the WRITE.EXE program.

Disk Management Procedures

Disk management procedures consist of preparing the disk for use and maintaining the disk once it is in operation. To prepare a disk for use, it must be partitioned, formatted, and made bootable. To maintain a disk drive, it must be checked for errors and defragmented.

Partitioning

Partitioning a disk drive is done using FDISK. FDISK is menu-driven and generally straightforward to use. The major issue is whether 16-bit or 32-bit FAT is used for the partition table. The FAT system installed on a fixed disk is largely determined by the software release today. Older Windows 95 systems most often use the 16-bit FAT. All new Windows 98/Me systems employ 32-bit FAT. Windows NT systems use 16-bit FAT or NTFS partitions. Windows 2000 systems may use 16-bit FAT, 32-bit FAT or NTFS. There are a few exceptions. The 32-bit FAT does not work with disk drives that are less than 500 MB, for example.

The FAT system determines the partitioning strategy for the fixed disk drive. The larger the total drive capacity is, the larger the allocation unit size becomes. Large allocation units make for inefficient disk capacity utilization. This is illustrated in the exercise below.

FAT 16 vs. FAT 32

The major difference between using FAT 16 versus FAT 32 is in how efficiently data is stored on large fixed disks. The smaller an allocation unit size is, the more efficient the storage. It is not uncommon to increase effective disk capacity by as much as 100 MB for a 4 GB fixed disk drive just by reducing the allocation unit size from 32 KB to 8 KB.

Cluster or allocation unit sizes for various size disk drives are listed in Table 12–3.

This suggests the following partitioning strategies:

• For 16-bit FAT drives that are 2 GB in size, make two 1 GB partitions. On larger drives, use 2 GB partitions, keeping the last partition as a swap and temporary storage area.

• For 32-bit FAT drives that are up to 8 GB in size, use multiple partitions to organize your data, because a smaller partition size does not improve disk utilization efficiency.

• For drives with greater than 8 GB capacity, create 8 GB partitions to use the drive space most efficiently.

Large capacity drives are so prevalent now that storage efficiency is much less of an issue. So with drives over 32 GB, do not worry much about storage efficiency with 32-bit FAT. We use 32-bit FAT on drives of 60 to 80 GB with just a single large partition.

Table 12–3   Allocation Unit Sizing

Drive Capacity	16-bit FAT Allocation Unit Size	32-bit FAT Allocation Unit Size
Less than 256 MB	4 KB or 8 sectors	Not supported
256 MB to 511 MB	8 KB or 16 sectors	Not supported
512 MB to 1023 MB	16 KB or 32 sectors	4 KB or 8 sectors
1024 MB to 2 GB	32 KB or 64 sectors	4 KB or 8 sectors
2 GB to 8 GB	Not supported	4 KB or 8 sectors
8 GB to 16 GB	Not supported	8 KB or 16 sectors
16 GB to 32 GB	Not supported	16 KB or 32 sectors
32 GB and up	Not supported	32 KB or 64 sectors

Primary and Extended DOS Partitions

FDISK breaks up a fixed disk into primary and extended DOS partitions. With 16-bit FAT, the maximum partition size is 2 GB. The primary DOS partition cannot exceed this size. Drives larger than 2 GB must have an extended DOS partition with logical drives assigned to it. Drives of 2 GB or less are also permitted to have both a primary and an extended DOS partition. With older Windows 3.x systems on smaller disk drives, it was a good strategy to set the primary partition size at 256 MB, install only Windows on it with the swap files, and make an extended partition of the remaining drive space. The extended partition would contain the program and data files.

With 32-bit FAT, large drives can be partitioned with a single primary DOS partition for Windows 98/Me DOS. MS-DOS does not recognize 32-bit FAT partitions, and neither does Windows NT. Hence, with MS-DOS you're limited to using 16-bit FAT partitions. With Windows NT you can also use 16-bit FAT partitions or you can use NTFS partitions. Windows 2000 works with 32-bit FAT partitions, 16-bit FAT partitions, and NTFS partitions.

Logical Drives

A logical drive is a subdivision of the extended DOS partition. It is limited to 2 GB in size for 16-bit FAT systems. Logical drives must be assigned using FDISK to make the extended DOS partition useable.

Active Partitions

The active partition is the bootable partition. When FDISK creates a primary partition, it does not necessarily make it active. If the bootable partition is not set active, the PC does not boot. Whenever a PC does not boot from the fixed disk, you can run FDISK and verify that the primary DOS partition has been set active.

Non-DOS Partitions

FDISK can find non-DOS partitions. These can be created by other operating systems like Windows NT/2000 using the NT File System (NTFS) and NetWare. Newer versions of FDISK can often remove these partitions, but not create them.

File Allocation Tables and the Directory

Files on the disk are accessed using the directory and the FAT, which are illustrated in Figures 12–16, 12–17, and 12–18.

Figure 12–16 illustrates a relationship between the directory and the FAT. The directory entry contains the basic information describing the file stored on

Figure 12–16
Directory entry and FAT relationship.

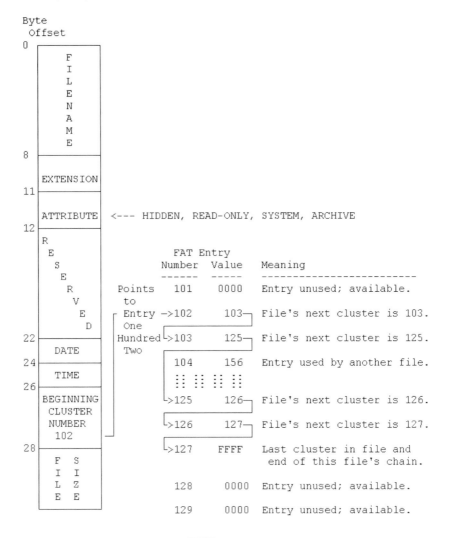

a fixed disk drive. It is linked to the FAT using a beginning cluster or allocation unit number. This number points to a single entry in the file allocation table. That entry number contains the entry number of the next allocation unit in the chain of allocation units that contain the data in the file. In Figure 12–16, the directory entry points to FAT entry 102, which contains a number 103 that points to the next allocation unit in the chain. That entry 103 contains a number 125. So far the file is stored in allocation unit numbers 102, 103, and 125. FAT entry 125 points to entry 126. Entry 126 points to entry 127. Entry 127 is the final entry in the chain of allocation units storing the data in the file because it contains all ones. When DOS or Windows retrieves this file, it would first go to the directory entry, then read the data from allocation units 102, 103, 125, 126, and 127. These allocation units form a chain in the FAT where the data in the file are stored. Figures 12–17 and 12–18 show an additional illustration of this process. These figures were taken from directory entries and FAT entries on a real disk drive using the DOS version of Norton Utilities.

When data is stored on a fixed disk, it is stored in chains that are one cluster right after another. However, as files are modified, they grow and shrink. To save them, DOS needs additional clusters or allocation units. It cannot get them exactly following the original clusters so it just grabs the next available cluster to place at the end of the chain. This means that the chains become broken into chunks called blocks. "Noncontiguous blocks" means that DOS has the file stored in allocation units or clusters that are not next to each other on the

Figure 12–17
Fixed disk directory (Norton Utilities).

Name	.Ext	Size	Date	Time		Cluster	Arc	R/O	Sys	Hid	Dir	Vol
Sector 129												
IO	SYS	33430	4-09-91	5:00	am	2	Arc	R/O	Sys	Hid		
MSDOS	SYS	37394	4-09-91	5:00	am	19	Arc	R/O	Sys	Hid		
PETE486P	1	0	9-12-91	11:28	pm	0	Arc					Vol
BAT		0	9-12-91	11:38	pm	62					Dir	
DISKFIX		0	11-23-91	7:05	am	1583					Dir	
DOS50		0	9-12-91	11:38	pm	63					Dir	
NOVELL		0	9-12-91	11:38	pm	73					Dir	
PCKWIK		0	9-12-91	11:38	pm	1585					Dir	
PDOX35		0	9-12-91	11:38	pm	70					Dir	
PE		0	9-12-91	11:38	pm	71					Dir	
QEMM		0	11-27-91	3:21	pm	72					Dir	
TEMP		0	11-27-91	3:17	pm	74					Dir	
UTIL		0	9-12-91	11:39	pm	75					Dir	
WINDOWS		0	12-09-91	9:02	pm	988					Dir	
124	BAT	51	12-16-91	4:40	pm	356	Arc					
386SPART	PAR	12288000	1-20-92	2:39	am	8145	Arc		Sys	Hid		
Sector 130												
64	BAT	48	12-12-91	7:18	am	561	Arc					
80		48	12-12-91	5:55	pm	562	Arc					

758

```
Object   Edit    Link    View    Info    Tools   Quit                F1-Help
   Sector 1
      - -       - -        3       4       5       6       7       8
        9       10       11      12      13      14      15      16
       17       18    <EOF>      20      21      22      23      24
       25       26       27      28      29      30      31      32
       33       34       35      36      37   <EOF>      39      40
       41       42       43      44      45      46      47      48
       49       50       51      52      53      54      55      56
       57       58       59      60      61   <EOF>   <EOF>      64
    <EOF>        0        0       0       0       0   <EOF>   <EOF>
    <EOF>    <EOF>    <EOF>      76   <EOF>   <EOF>   <EOF>      80
       81       82       83      84      85      86      87      88
       89       90       91      92      93      94      95      96
       97       98       99     100     101     102     103     104
      105      106      107     108     109     110     111     112
      113      114      115     116     117     118     119     120
      121      122      123     124     125     126     127     128
      129      130      131     132     133     134     135     136
      137      138      139     140     141     142     143     144
      145      146      147     148     149     150     151     152
      153      154    <EOF>     156     157     158     159     160
    FAT (1st Copy)                                        Sector 1
    C:\IO.SYS                                       Cluster 2, hex 2
    Press ALT or F10 to select menus                   Disk Editor
```

Figure 12-18
DOS 16-bit fixed disk file allocation table (Norton Utilities).

disk. Such day-to-day operations lead to fragmenting files stored on the disk. To retrieve these files, Windows must move the disk read/write heads all over the disk drive, slowing overall system performance. Defragmenting the drive reduces this activity and speeds up the PC. Badly fragmented disk drives exhibit excessive disk activity. The same is true of PCs with insufficient RAM. Figure 12–17 illustrates the contents of a DOS directory entry. Figure 12–18 displays the first sector of a 16-bit FAT.

Using these diagrams we can see how IO.SYS is stored on this fixed disk. The IO.SYS directory entry points to the first entry in the FAT, that is, address 2. FAT addresses 0 and 1 contain the boot record and partition table information. They are represented by "--" in Figure 12–18. The first address after 0 and 1 is 2. The contents of that address point to FAT entry address 3 that contains 4. We follow this chain in the diagram until it reaches address 18, which contains the End Of File (EOF) byte. The next file MSDOS.SYS begins with FAT entry 19. FAT entry 19 points to address 20, and so on.

Understanding basic directory and FAT operation is important fixed disk troubleshooting knowledge. This structure is generally carried forward into 32-bit FAT systems, although 32-bit FAT system details are not as simple as illustrated here.

Virtual File Allocation Table (VFAT)

VFAT is an extension to the FAT files system introduced with Windows 95. It is essentially the Windows 95/98Me file system. It is not a type of FAT, but rather software that reads and writes data to the disk drive. It uses the 32-bit protected mode or the 16-bit real mode driver programs to read and write data to the disks. VFAT is the equivalent of Windows 3.1 32-bit file access software.

VFAT is implemented in IFSHLP.SYS in Windows 95/98/Me. It processes read and write requests for the PC's local fixed disk. VFAT 32-bit file access operates in protected mode and supports threading. This improves disk performance significantly in Windows 95/98/Me over Windows 3.1, which employed 16-bit real mode software to work with the FAT. VFAT was first introduced as 32-bit file access under Windows 3.11. Under Windows 95/98/Me, VFAT handles long filenames. These names can be up to 255 characters long and may contain more than one period. Both long filenames and DOS 8.3 filenames are supported by VFAT using aliases. Every long filename has an alias entry associated with it that conforms to the DOS 8.3 filename rules. In this manner, Windows 95/98/Me VFAT supports older MS-DOS and Windows 3.1x programs.

Formatting

The last phase in preparing a disk drive for use is to format it and install an operating system. For most PCs, this means installing a bootable version of DOS or Windows 95/98/Me. The FORMAT.EXE program performs these functions. Floppy disks can also be formatted from within the Window GUI, but generally fixed disk setup uses only DOS.

The FORMAT program builds the directory and the FAT depending on the partitioning performed. FORMAT /S causes the operating system on the DOS prompt drive to be installed as well. Initial formatting performs a surface verification to assure that the disk drive is useable. If it finds bad spots on the disk, it marks them as bad so they are not used to store data.

Because the disk drive hardware today performs error correction, there should be no bad spots on a new fixed disk drive. Sometimes areas of a fixed disk become corrupted. Simply formatting the drive does not usually restore these areas. If, however, the surface is wiped by writing all zeros on the drive surface, and then reformatted, the bad areas may be restored to full operation.

FORMAT.EXE has the options shown below, which are further listed and explained in Table 12–4.

```
FORMAT drive: [/V[:label]] [/Q] [/F:size] [/B | /S] [/C]
FORMAT drive: [/V[:label]] [/Q] [/T:tracks /N:sectors] [/B | /S] [/C]
FORMAT drive: [/V[:label]] [/Q] [/1] [/4] [/B | /S] [/C]
FORMAT drive: [/Q] [/1] [/4] [/8] [/B | /S] [/C]
```

Similar options are provided with the Windows GUI floppy format function.

Table 12–4   Format Command Options

Option	Description
/V[:label]	Specifies the volume label.
/Q	Performs a quick format.
/F:size	Specifies the size of the floppy disk to format (such as 160, 180, 320, 360, 720, 1.2, 1.44, 2.88).
/B	Allocates space on the formatted disk for system files.
/S	Copies system files to the formatted disk.
/T:tracks	Specifies the number of tracks per disk side.
/N:sectors	Specifies the number of sectors per track.
/1	Formats a single side of a floppy disk.
/4	Formats a 5.25-inch 360K floppy disk in a high-density drive.
/8	Formats eight sectors per track.
/C	Tests clusters that are currently marked "bad."

Repairing

The SCANDISK program is the principal repair tool for disk drives. It verifies the directory and file structure. When SCANDISK is started, it presents a panel that permits selecting the physical and logical disk drives for scanning, the type of scan to perform (standard or thorough), and automatic error correction. When selecting the drives for scanning, they can be individually highlighted or highlighted together for scanning by SCANDISK. In this manner, all disk drives can be scanned. When several drives are selected for scanning, the PC user manually signals the completion of scanning on each selected drive so that SCANDISK can move on to the next drive selected. For further details on SCANDISK, see the section entitled Disk Management Utilities later in this chapter.

Defragmenting

Defragmenting the disk drive to improve PC performance is done using the DEFRAG program. Defragmenting is the process of rearranging the clusters that contain the file data so they are accessed with minimal head movement on the fixed disk. To us, this looks like placing the clusters for a file in ascending numeric sequence. For the disk drive, this is not strictly true. Clusters in the same cylinder on a disk drive are accessed without moving the disk drive's read/write heads. Hence, clusters in the same cylinder are accessed equally fast.

More details on the DEFRAG program are covered in the section entitled Disk Management Utilities later in this chapter.

Study Break: Disk Allocation Units

This exercise illustrates how files are stored in allocation units on the fixed disk drive.

1. Do a directory command. Record the free space on your fixed disk.
2. Create a file called T using:

```
COPY CON T
T Cr
Ctrl Z
```

3. Perform the directory command again. What is the size of the file T? It should be one or two characters.
4. How much free space is left on your disk? From the amount of free space before making the file, subtract the amount of free space after making the file to determine the allocation unit or cluster size for this specific PC system.

The result of this exercise should illustrate that a file of a single character consumes an entire allocation unit of disk space. This means that, depending upon the allocation unit size, disk space could be wasted by storing lots of small files on the fixed disk drive. Hence, fixed disk drive space is used more effectively by using ZIP to compress many small files into a single large file.

Disk Management Utilities

A key function of primarily DOS software is disk management. DOS utilities are used to partition disk drives, format them, and make them bootable. Once data and software are installed on a disk drive, other DOS and Windows utilities check the disk and file structure for errors and organize the files on the disk drive for optimal performance.

There are four basic disk management functions:

- Partitioning a disk and creating the master boot record.
- Formatting the drive to create the directory structure and install the bootable operating system.
- Checking the disk drive file structure and data files for errors and, if errors are found, examining the physical disk surface for bad areas.
- Organizing the files and data on the disk for optimal performance.

DOS and Windows utility programs perform these functions.

FDISK

FDISK is the DOS or Windows 98/Me DOS utility that is used to partition a fixed drive and create the master boot record. The master boot record contains a cold boot loader program and descriptive information on the capacity and layout of the fixed disk drive. It is essential for booting DOS or Windows from the fixed disk drive and for enabling DOS and Windows to read and write information from the fixed disk drive. FDISK is not used on floppy drives, and is run prior to formatting a drive and making it bootable with DOS.

FDISK can also be employed as a diagnostic program to verify that a disk drive and its companion disk controller card are functioning properly. When there are malfunctions, FDISK reports that the controller is bad or that it cannot read the fixed disk.

FDISK is run from the DOS prompt. It is menu-driven, with the menu selections made in a fixed sequence controlled by FDISK. This means that a drive must have an extended partition specified before logical drives can be assigned.

When a disk is prepared with a single partition, that partition is the primary partition. Each disk drive may have a primary partition. DOS and Windows assign drive letters to the primary partitions first and then to the extended partitions. The second partition on a fixed disk drive is the extended partition. It is also possible to create an extended DOS partition on a second disk drive. The extended partition is subdivided into logical drives. These logical drives are assigned drive letters after the primary partitions have been assigned their drive letters. Only primary partitions are bootable. To be bootable they must be marked as active partitions.

The hierarchy of fixed disk partitions is:

- Primary DOS partition marked active on boot drive—C
- Primary DOS partition on second drive—D
- Extended DOS partition on the active boot drive
- Extended DOS partition on the second fixed disk drive

The Windows 98/Me FDISK program supports 32-bit FAT. This means that it can view a single large drive as one partition. Earlier versions of FDISK worked with 16-bit FAT. They were practically limited to maximum partition and logical drive sizes of 2 GB. At the 2 GB size, the allocation units were assigned 64 sectors, making them highly inefficient for storing small files. At that allocation unit size, a file of one character (or byte) would use 32 KB of disk storage space. When Windows 98/Me FDISK is run, the message below determines whether 32-bit or 16-bit FAT is used. The differences between FAT 16 and FAT 32 were covered in the section entitled Disk Management Procedures earlier in this chapter.

```
Do you wish to enable large disk support (Y/N).......? [Y]
```

The "Y" response implements 32-bit FAT operation.

This version of Windows includes improved support for large disks, resulting in more efficient use of disk space on large drives, and allowing disks over 2 GB to be formatted as a single drive.

If you enable large disk support and create any new drives on this disk, you are not able to access the new drive(s) using other operating systems, including some versions of Windows 95 and Windows NT, as well as earlier versions of Windows and MS-DOS. In addition, disk utilities that were not designed explicitly for the FAT32 file system are not able to work with this disk. If you need to access this disk with other operating systems or older disk utilities, do not enable large disk support. At this time, large disk support works only with Windows 95 OSR2 and Windows 98/Me/2000 PCs. When these PCs are networked, there are no problems transferring files across the network to other PCs without large disk support (32-bit FAT). If a PC is going to be used to support Windows 95 and Windows NT, the 32-bit FAT should not be used because Windows NT cannot access it.

The main FDISK menu begins with creating a primary DOS partition or logical drive. This is the first step in preparing a disk drive for use, as it creates the partition table and the FAT. To be bootable, a drive must be set as active. Deleting a partition kills all the data in that partition. Once deleted, data in a partition is not recoverable unless special procedures and software are used. Displaying partition information causes FDISK to read the drive. This is the diagnostic capability of FDISK.

```
                Microsoft Windows 98
             Fixed Disk Setup Program
          (C)Copyright Microsoft Corp. 1983-1998


             FDISK Options


Current fixed disk drive: 1

Choose one of the following:

1. Create DOS partition or Logical DOS Drive
2. Set active partition
3. Delete partition or Logical DOS Drive
4. Display partition information
5. Change current fixed disk drive


Enter choice: [1]


Press Esc to exit FDISK
```

When you select option 4, display partition information, FDISK produces a partition information display that identifies the partitions and can display the logical drive information for the selected disk drive.

```
             Display Partition Information

Current fixed disk drive: 1

Partition   Status      Type   Volume  Label   Mbytes  System   Usage
  C: 1      A PRI DOS   DRC    3004    FAT32   38%
     2      EXT DOS            5005            62%

Total disk space is 8009 Mbytes (1 Mbyte = 1048576 bytes)

The Extended DOS Partition contains Logical DOS Drives.
Do you want to display the logical drive information (Y/N)......?[Y]

Press Esc to return to FDISK Options
```

FDISK tries to create partitions that use the entire fixed disk drive capacity, which is expressed in Kbytes or Mbytes with K = 1,024 bytes. Therefore, drives sometimes appear to have a smaller capacity than advertised. Drives can be subdivided into smaller partitions, as the 8 GB drive above is divided into a 3 GB and a 5 GB partition. The bootable partition has been assigned a logical drive letter C and has been set active. The Windows 95/98/Me FDISK performs a surface verification to assure that the fixed disk drive is readable where the system files and FAT are to be stored.

Creating an extended DOS partition is similar to creating the primary DOS partition. The main difference is that the menu items selected are for the extended DOS partition, and the extended DOS partition must be subdivided into logical drives. When the extended DOS partition is created, FDISK asks whether the entire extended DOS partition should be assigned to a single logical drive. This is similar to the question that FDISK asks when creating the primary DOS partition—do you wish to use the entire disk for a primary DOS partition? If more than one logical drive is created, then disk space must be allocated to each logical drive. Once this is complete, FDISK assigns drive letters to the logical drives.

FORMAT

FORMAT sets up the allocation units and builds the disk drive directory and FAT. In spite of the FORMAT command warning that it deletes files from the disk drive, FORMAT does not really delete data from the disk drive. On a new disk drive, FORMAT establishes the allocation units. On an older disk drive, FORMAT uses the allocation units previously created. In both cases, FORMAT recreates the directory and FAT. On older disk drives, FORMAT attempts to store away the old directory and FAT in the event that the old data needs to be recovered from the fixed disk drive. When it cannot save this information, FORMAT issues a warning message stating that the data on a drive will be unrecoverable.

The new Windows 95/98/Me format verifies the drive in the process of laying out the allocation units, creating the FAT and creating the disk drive directory. FORMAT is run after FDISK partitions the drive.

FORMAT does not rewrite the directory and FAT tables until it has completed its disk verification. If FORMAT is stopped prior to completion, old disk information remains intact. Disk verification does not destroy the data on the disk; FORMAT leaves the data untouched and only creates a new directory and FAT.

The DOS 6.2x UNFORMAT command uses the saved directory and FAT data to restore a fixed disk to its original operating state as long as nothing has been written on the disk since the format operation. FORMAT is used to prepare floppy diskettes for use. Floppy disks are not partitioned prior to formatting.

Floppy disk formatting can be performed from the "My Computer" object on the desktop. Open my computer and click on the diskette drive icon, then right-click for an options menu and choose Format. Floppy diskette formatting can be quick or full (which performs a surface test). The system files can also be transferred alone. This is equivalent to the DOS SYS command. Fixed disk formatting is done from DOS.

The FORMAT command line options are shown in Table 12–4. One particular option, the /C option, should be avoided because it attempts to reuse clusters. Sometimes reused clusters are really bad, and data is lost when stored in them. Because of the risk of losing data stored in those clusters, it is much better to leave any suspect clusters marked bad than it is to attempt to rejuvenate them.

SCANDISK

SCANDISK is a disk analysis and repair program for fixed disks, floppy diskettes, RAM drives and memory card drives. The Windows 98/Me SCANDISK works with 32-bit FAT drives. Other versions work with compressed drives. SCANDISK tests the FAT, long filenames, the file structure, the directory tree, the drive surface, and Windows Compressed drives for errors. SCANDISK automatically repairs the errors it finds or it permits operator input to determine how errors are resolved. It also scans individual disk drives or all the disks.

The program uses a second copy of the FAT to fix cross-linked files and lost file fragments. A file is a chain of allocation units tied to a directory entry that contains the data in a file. Cross-linked files have the chain of allocations units, described in the FAT, pointing to different locations at some point in the chain. One FAT believes the file is comprised of allocation units that are different from the allocation units assigned to the file in the other FAT. SCANDISK resolves these cross-link references by comparing both FATs. File fragments are allocation unit chains that do not match the file size reported in the directory. Other fragments are chains of allocation units not tied to a directory entry. SCANDISK fixes these problems by adjusting the directory size information and by creating directory entries (for example, FILE0000.CHK, FILE0001.CHK) for the lost chains of allocation units.

Windows comes with SCANDISK.EXE that runs from the DOS prompt and SCANDISKW.EXE that runs under Windows. Both SCANDISK programs work with long filenames, an improvement upon earlier versions of the DOS SCANDISK. SCANDISK's advanced scanning options are illustrated in Figure 12–19.

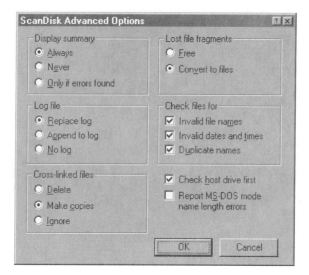

Figure 12–19
SCANDISK advanced options.

These advanced options customize SCANDISK operation to an individual user's needs. The default-advanced options are all the selected options, except checking files for invalid dates and times and duplicate names.

Windows and Windows applications use temporary files as scratch storage areas. These files are kept open by the application. As a result, shutting off the PC without exiting Windows gracefully creates directory errors, which SCAN-DISK fixes. It uses the two copies of the FAT to resolve cross-linked file errors and converts lost file chains with no directory entries into FILE00nn.CHK files.

SCANDISK advanced options are capable of performing a nondestructive surface test of the disk drive. This means when bad areas are encountered, SCANDISK recovers the information by rereading the bad areas and moving the recovered data to a different area on the disk. If SCANDISK recovers the data, it usually turns out well. The nondestructive surface test makes SCAN-DISK require a long time to complete its testing of a fixed disk drive. Large and slow fixed disks can require hours to completely test. Windows 95/98/Me can be set up to perform SCANDISK maintenance automatically. By default it is scheduled to run at night on a weekly basis.

There are two versions of SCANDISK: a Windows graphical utility and a DOS implementation. The Windows SCANDISK works with long filenames while the DOS version does not. The Windows SCANDISK provides additional controls under an advanced options selection. These controls change the summary display, logging, and file correction options. The file correction options permit files cross-linked on the same allocation unit to be deleted, ignored, or preferably copied to new directory entries. Similarly, file correction options permit lost file fragments to be converted to files or to be freed, recovering the disk space for future use. SCANDISK can also be set up to check files for invalid filenames, invalid date and time stamps, and duplicate names.

The FAT System and Directories

To understand the evolution of the FAT system, we need to return to the first PC fixed disks. With the introduction of the IBM PC-XT in 1983, DOS was designed to work with fixed disks. The first XT fixed disk was 10 MB. This quickly increased to 30 MB with the release of the IBM PC-AT in 1985. DOS had built into it a fixed disk addressing capability, the FAT that limited the total disk size to 32 MB. There was a limit of 16 KB entries in the fixed disk space address table. Each entry could address one allocation unit or cluster consisting of four 512 character sectors. Therefore, each FAT entry represented 2 KB characters of disk space, or a total of 2 KB by 16 K or 32 MB total disk space. DOS 4.0, 5.0, and 6.x permit the allocation unit (or cluster sizes) to be larger than 4 sectors. In this manner more than 32 MB total disk capacity can be addressed by DOS using the 16 K entry FAT (but not as efficiently as when 4 sectors are used). With Windows 95 OSR2, a 32-bit FAT was introduced which changed the effective maximum disk drive capacity that could be handled by Windows to 2 terabytes (TB).

DOS used a 12-bit FAT to manage files on floppy drives and logical drives smaller than 16 MB. The 16-bit FAT was first introduced in DOS 3.0.

In order for files to be placed on the fixed disk drive, they needed to be organized. DOS provided tree-structured directories. Tree-structured directories are so named because they look like an inverted tree with branches springing out from the root of the tree. In the case of the DOS directory structure, the root directory is at the top and subdirectories are below it. In Windows 95/98/Me/NT/2000, the directories are called folders.

Each fixed disk subdirectory or folder acts like a disk drive itself. When you move to that subdirectory by entering CD and the subdirectory name, it looks like the entire fixed disk only contains the files in that subdirectory. So why not put all files in the root directory? The root directory has a limited number of entries. It can contain only 512 files on 16-bit FAT fixed disks, 65,535 files on 32-bit FAT fixed disks, and, on floppy diskettes, only 64 or 128 files. Subdirectories are not limited in the number of files they contain because subdirectory entries are files themselves. A comparison of file systems is given in Table 12–5.

Table 12–5 PC File Systems

PC File System	FAT-16 DOS	FAT-32 Windows 95/98/Me/2000	HPFS OS/2	NTFS Windows NT/2000
Maximum Size	2 GB	2 TB (TeraBytes)	4 GB	16 EB (ExaBytes or 16K TeraBytes)
Filename Size	8	255	254	254
Extension Size	3	3 or more	3	3 or more
Security Features	None	None	Limited when used with LAN server software	Subdirectory and file access limitations
International Language Support	None	Unicode character encoding standard	None	Unicode character encoding standard
Crash Recovery	SCANDISK Transaction Tracking	SCANDISK Transaction Tracking	CHKDSK (OS/2 Program)	CHKDSK (NT Program) Built-in recovery features
Extended Attributes	Hidden, read-only, system and archive	Hidden, read-only, system and archive	Yes Shareable, write-protected, etc.	Yes Shareable, write-protected, etc.

FAT and the DIR command

Since DOS cannot address each of the 512-byte sectors on a disk individually, it must group them to work with fixed disks of varying capacity. DOS can address 65,525 or 268,435,445 clusters or allocation units in its FAT. If each allocation unit were one sector in size, DOS could address 32 MB using a 16-bit FAT. Consequently, for large fixed disk drives, DOS must cluster together sectors into larger allocation units. The largest allocation unit size is 32 KB or 64 sectors.

The DIR command displays four pieces of information:

- Filename (up to eight characters)
- Extension (up to three characters)
- Size in bytes (characters)
- Date and time when created or last modified

This information is contained in the directory entry for the file along with additional information instructing DOS how to gather the sectors (which clusters it should read) off the fixed disk to form the file. The directory entry points to a beginning cluster number in the FAT which in turn points to the next cluster number that is simply a numeric position in the FAT table. This points to the next cluster number, and so on until we reach a FAT entry signaling the end of the file. These FAT entries form a chain of clusters that comprise the file. This chain is associated with a directory entry through the first FAT number contained in the file's directory entry. Figure 12–16 earlier in this chapter illustrates how the DOS directory and the FAT work together.

The boot record information is the first data stored on a fixed disk. It is stored in fixed length entries on all disks regardless of the FAT or directory structure. The boot record and the partition table are created by FDISK. FORMAT sets up the directory and FAT. It then places IO.SYS as the first DOS file on the drive and MSDOS.SYS as the second.

CHKDSK and CHKDSK Messages

The CHKDSK DOS utility program identifies and resolves conflicts between the directory and the FAT. On Windows systems, SCANDISK provides this functionality and more.

When CHKDSK *.* /V is run, a typical PC response could be:

```
Directory A:\
  A:\ARC520.COM
  A:\BWVID.ARC
  A:\CDISK.ARC
  A:\CORETEST.ARC
  A:\DIPSET.ARC
  A:\DISKPARK.ARC
  A:\DSKMON.ARC
  A:\DSKWATCH.COM
  A:\EQUIPCFG.COM
  A:\ERRCODES.ARC
  A:\FASTCOPY.ARC

Errors found, F parameter not specified.
Corrections will not be written to disk.
```

This indicates that there are conflicts between the directory and the FAT. Since we have not yet used the /F parameter, DOS does not resolve these conflicts; it only displays where they are on this fixed disk. If CHKDSK is run with the /F parameter, it corrects the discrepancies between the FAT and the directory. When this is done, some data on the fixed disk is lost.

```
A:\FASTCOPY.ARC
Allocation error, size adjusted.
No chain for this entry, size will be set to 0.
  A:\HDAT.ARC
  A:\HDTABL.ARC
  A:\HDTEST.ARC
  A:\INFO.ARC
  A:\LAND.ARC
  A:\LPT2DSK.ARC
  A:\MEMSET.COM
  A:\MEMSET.DOC
  A:\MIPS.ARC
  A:\NMI.ARC
  A:\PDIAGS.ARC
  A:\READTHIS.1ST
  A:\SPEED.ARC
  A:\TESTMEM.COM

29 lost clusters found in 7 chains.
Convert lost chains to files (Y/N)? n
 29696 bytes disk space
    would be freed.
```

This means that several chains of clusters discovered in the FAT have no corresponding directory entry. These chains are converted to files when CHKDSK /F is run. Similarly, SCANDISK converts such lost chains to files. The files are placed in the root directory with the name FILE0000.CHK, FILE0001.CHK, etc. The FILE00xx.CHK files may contain salvageable data. Following is more bad news. Three files share the same cluster. These files are cross-linked. What can be true here? Only one file is good and the remaining two are bad. Can you tell which one is good? There is no real way to determine the good file.

```
A:\FASTCOPY.ARC
 Is cross-linked on cluster 255
A:\HDAT.ARC
 Is cross-linked on cluster 255
A:\MIPS.ARC
 Is cross-linked on cluster 255

 362496 bytes total disk space
```

```
319488 bytes in 25 user files
13312 bytes available on disk

720896 bytes total memory
165008 bytes free

A:\FASTCOPY.ARC
  Contains 2 noncontiguous blocks.
A:\HDAT.ARC
  Contains 2 noncontiguous blocks.
```

Finally, at the end of the CHKDSK output, we see the innocuous message that our files are resident in noncontiguous clusters. This might mean that we are having reduced performance from our fixed disk drive. This problem pales in comparison to the preceding problems.

Whenever a Windows program exits due to an unrecoverable application error, temporary data storage files on a fixed disk often leave cluster chains with no corresponding directory entry. These chains with no directory entry eventually congest the disk, leaving no space for additional files. It is a good policy to once a week or more perform a SCANDISK test on each fixed disk drive or partition on Windows PCs. When any lost chains are found, they should be converted to files and then erased from the fixed disk.

DEFRAG

The DEFRAG program defragments files on disk drives. As described earlier in this chapter, defragmenting involves rearranging the clusters that contain the file data so they are accessed with minimal head movement on the fixed disk.DEFRAG has few options. When launched it provides options to select the disk drive to be defragmented and a button to change the settings. The settings that can be changed are: (1) having DEFRAG optimize the program file arrangement so that applications launch more quickly, and (2) checking the disk surface for errors. These can be set to run either one time or every time that DEFRAG is launched.

When the option to rearrange program files is selected, DEFRAG works with a log file to see which programs are launched most often. It then locates these programs in the order they are accessed, making them load faster. DEFRAG starts by presenting an option to select the drive to defragment. One selection is all fixed disk drives. It also provides a settings button that permits configuring DEFRAG to make the programs start faster and to check the surface for errors. Figure 12–20 illustrates these selections.

DEFRAG displays the defragmentation progress in a small and more detailed window. The defragmentation progress identifies the clusters to be optimized as belonging at the beginning, middle, or end of the disk drive, as shown in Figure 12–21.

Hidden, read-only, and system files that cannot be moved are identified in the defragmentation progress detailed window. When a drive is defragmented and other programs are actively changing data on the drive, DEFRAG restarts every time it detects a change to the stored data. This can cause defragmentation to require hours of time. Consequently, it is best to close all programs

Figure 12–20
Windows 95/98/Me Defrag options show these selections.

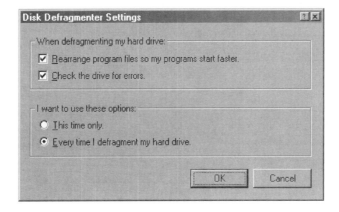

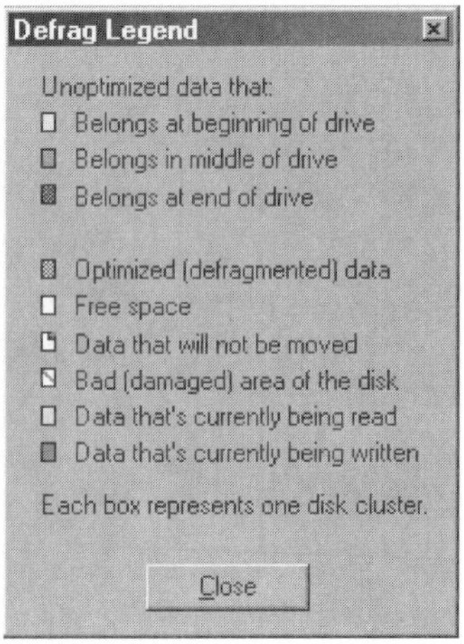

Figure 12–21
Windows 95/98/Me DEFRAG detailed
display legend

except DEFRAG when defragmenting a drive. This means disabling the screen saver and other power management features that run in the background.

As with SCANDISK, Windows 95/98/Me can be set up to perform DEFRAG maintenance automatically. Its default is to run at night once a week but on a different night than SCANDISK runs.

When running DEFRAG in Windows 95/98/Me, it is best to disable virus scanning because the added CPU load and disk activity from virus scanning software prevents DEFRAG from completing its work. When virus scanning software is running, DEFRAG tends to either hang at 10 percent complete or takes days to finish. Windows NT does not have a DEFRAG program, but Windows 2000 comes with one.

SYS

SYS installs the system files on a fixed disk or on a diskette. It can be used to recover from some nonbootable disk problems. SYS can be run from a fixed disk directory while the DOS command prompt is pointing at a floppy diskette drive containing the IO.SYS and MSDOS.SYS files.

Using a DOS 6.x bootable diskette to make a Windows 95/98 fixed disk bootable is not recommended because the MSDOS.SYS file on the Windows fixed disk is different. The DOS MSDOS.SYS file is a binary program, while the Windows 95/98/Me MSDOS.SYS is a text file instructing Windows how to initialize.

Study Break: CHKDSK

This exercise illustrates the CHKDSK program and functions it performs.

1. Run CHKDSK C:*.* /V. What error messages appeared?
2. Did the warning message saying that SCANDISK is better than CHKDSK appear?
3. Were there any lost clusters or allocation units not assigned to directory entries? When programs that use temporary files are exited abnormally, the temporary files are left as lost clusters or allocation units on the fixed disk drive. Therefore, this is a common CHKDSK error message.
4. Were there any cross-linked clusters or allocation units? At one time, this error was sometimes found with fixed disk drives.

However, newer drives are much more reliable than the older drives and it is highly unusual to find this error.

5. Was the total memory size reported as 655,360 bytes? If the number was lower, scan the system immediately for viruses.

Of these error messages, the memory size message remains the most useful today because SCANDISK performs the functionality of CHKDSK more effectively. Under Windows NT there is no SCANDISK program; it uses a special CHKDSK program to verify drive integrity and fix errors.

Summary

This chapter has described the DOS and Windows fixed disk file and data management operations. It covered setting up fixed disk drives as well as the use of both DOS and Windows utility programs that manage data on a PC's fixed disk drives. PCs are moving to a Windows-only operating environment, which is very focused on networked PCs, meaning that the A+ testing objectives will shift to those types of PCs. DOS is not, however, any less important, because it continues to be the number one tool for setting up, maintaining, and troubleshooting PC fixed disk drives. Because DOS permits direct access to the PC's hardware, it continues to be the platform that runs PC diagnostics and prepares the PC for installation of Windows 95/98/Me and Windows NT/2000. The basic fixed disk drive diagnostics are typically run using DOS. This chapter has described basic DOS and Windows file system concepts, DOS file management and disk maintenance utilities, and Windows file management and disk maintenance utilities. It illustrated the most commonly used DOS and Windows disk utility programs.

Chapter Review Questions

1. *The number of boot records per hard drive is what?*

    A. One boot record per drive
    B. One boot record per partition
    C. One boot record for each primary partition; no boot record for extended partitions
    D. None, the boot record is stored in the BIOS, not the hard drive

Answer: B, one boot record per partition. One boot record per drive, one boot record for a primary partition, and no boot records for an extended partition say the exact same thing, so they are incorrect. The BIOS does not store boot records.

2. *When installing Windows on a compressed drive, where is the swap file placed?*

    A. In the root directory of the compressed drive
    B. In the same directory into which Windows is installed
    C. On the uncompressed host drive
    D. Windows decides on the optimal place for the swap file

Answer: C, on the uncompressed host drive. The compressed drive is a single file on the uncompressed drive so the swap file needs to be on the real uncompressed drive. Answers A and B say the same thing. Windows decides nothing.

3. *Disk thrashing refers to what?*

    A. A fixed disk drive has many bad sectors and has to map data around them
    B. A fixed disk drive is failing and making excessive noise
    C. The system RAM is full most of the time, resulting in excessive paging
    D. The hard drive is too fragmented to effectively manage file I/O

Answer: C, the system RAM is full most of the time, resulting in excessive paging. Thrashing is swapping data excessively between RAM and the disk drive. Bad sectors do not cause thrashing, nor does a failing fixed disk drive. Fragmenting just slows down the fixed disk drive and does not cause thrashing.

4. *What does FAT stand for?*

    A. File Allotment Table
    B. File Allocation Table
    C. File Assignment Table
    D. File Allocation-unit Table

Answer: B, File Allocation Table. There is no allotment, assignment, or allocation unit table. Allocation units are how the sectors on a disk drive are arranged to store the files of data on the drive.

5. *The FAT entries are:*

    A. Disk sectors
    B. Numbers
    C. Random
    D. Allocation units

Answer: B, numbers. The FAT entries do not represent sectors but allocation units. They are not the allocation units themselves and are not random. The FAT entries are just numbers.

6. *Which program corrects disk directory and FAT problems?*

    A. FORMAT
    B. FDISK
    C. CHKDSK
    D. XCOPY

Answer: C, CHKDSK. FORMAT sets up the directories and the FAT, FDISK partitions a drive, and XCOPY copies files.

7. *Which program is used to partition a Windows fixed disk drive?*

    A. FORMAT
    B. FDISK
    C. CHKDSK
    D. EXPLORER

Answer: B, FDISK. FORMAT sets up the directories and the FAT, CHKDSK checks the disk for errors, and EXPLORER manages files and folders.

8. *What does SCANDSK do that CHKDSK does not do?*

    A. Checks the directory structure
    B. Checks the FAT
    C. Corrects directory and FAT problems
    D. Fixes bad data files

Answer: D, fixes bad data files. While both check the directory structure and the FAT and correct directory and FAT problems, SCANDSK recovers bad data files as well.

9. *What is the difference between the DOS and Windows SCANDISK program?*

    A. Windows SCANDISK only runs in a DOS window
    B. Windows SCANDISK works with long filenames
    C. Windows SCANDISK can be launched using the mouse
    D. Windows uses SDISK and DOS uses SCANDISK

Answer: B, Windows SCANDISK works with long filenames. SCANDISK does not run in a DOS window and can be run from the RUN prompt in addition to being launched with a mouse. There is no SDISK.

10. *Lost chains are commonly caused by what?*

    A. Exiting Windows
    B. Power outages
    C. Abnormal termination of Windows
    D. Abnormal termination of Windows applications

Answer: D. Abnormal termination of Windows applications is best, but answer C, abnormal termination of Windows is also a good answer. Exiting Windows properly should cause no problems and power outages may or may not shut down a PC causing abnormal Windows termination.

11. *VCACHE is:*

    A. An internal fixed disk manager in Windows 3.11 and Windows 95
    B. A fixed disk program in Windows 98 that manages disk cache
    C. A virtual cache manager program
    D. An EXE program

Answer: A, an internal fixed disk manager in Windows 3.11 and Windows 95. VCACHE is not found beyond Windows 95.

12. *What does large disk support do?*

    A. Permits MS-DOS to operate with drives over 2 GB
    B. Works with Windows NT to set up NTFS
    C. Permits Windows 95 to use 4 GB partitions
    D. Permits Windows 98 to use disk drives over 2 GB as one partition

Answer: D, permits Windows 98 to use disk drives over 2 GB as one partition. MS-DOS does not support large disk drives. Only Windows 95 B, Windows 98, and Windows Me DOS support large disk drives using (FAT 32). Windows NT does not support FAT 32, and neither do all Windows 95 systems.

13. *Which operating system can convert to 32-bit FAT without using FDISK?*

> A. Windows NT
> B. Windows 95 OSR2
> C. Windows 98
> D. Windows 3.1x

Answer: C, Windows 98. Windows NT and Windows 3.x do not use FAT 32, and Windows 95 OSR2 does not have a conversion program.

14. *A PC could operate with FAT-16 and FAT-32 partitions.*

> A. FALSE
> B. TRUE

Answer: B, TRUE. Any Windows 98/Me/2000 PC could use either FAT 16 or FAT 32.

15. *FAT-16 stores data more efficiently than FAT-32.*

> A. FALSE
> B. TRUE

Answer: A, FALSE. FAT-32 uses large disk drives more efficiently than FAT-16.

16. *Which is the most used fixed disk utility?*

> A. FORMAT
> B. FDISK
> C. CHKDSK
> D. SCANDISK

Answer: D. SCANDISK is best, but answer C, CHKDSK is okay as well. FORMAT and FDISK are used once to set up a disk drive, so CHKDSK and SCANDSK are the best answers.

Chapter 13

DOS AND
MEMORY MANAGEMENT

Chapter Syllabus

- Types of Memory

- Memory Conflicts and Their Resolution

- PC DOS Memory Setup

Windows 95 resolved many memory management conflicts, and Windows 98/Me/2000 resolves most all memory management conflicts, making memory management with them a low priority issue. However, a good understanding of PC memory basics helps solve software problems. Even though Windows 95/98/Me/2000 applications have the memory they need, older DOS and Windows 3.1 applications still function as though they were in a memory-limited PC. Furthermore, memory resource conflicts by hardware in the UMAs still pose difficult problems for Windows 95 systems, but have been largely resolved in Windows 98/Me/2000. Resolving hardware conflicts for upper memory is based on a good understanding of how DOS uses memory in PCs because that is where it all started. Windows 95/98/Me/NT/2000 requires that there be no hardware conflicts for upper memory blocks (UMB)

781

addresses. This chapter examines DOS/Windows 3.1x memory management and Windows 95/98/Me memory usage.

To describe the basics of memory management in the PC, we must begin with how the PC chips look at memory and how this translates into DOS and then Windows memory management. From an A+ testing viewpoint, the key information concerns programs that permit you to configure PC memory using DOS and the memory layout. As older PC software products fade into oblivion, knowledge of the techniques for configuring PC memory using DOS has become much less important. However, the types of memory and the lay-out of memory remain the foundation for future PC systems.

Memory in the PC is used in a variety of ways. We most often think of it as a storage place for the executable program code and the data that the program is operating on. However, memory addresses have other functions as well. For example, some memory addresses are assigned to contain ROM programs from the system BIOS and the VGA adapter. These ROM programs perform the basic input/output operations for the PC. Other areas are assigned to heaps. Windows uses heaps as storage areas for different program parameters such as color palettes, fonts, and other graphical information. Finally, memory is used as a buffer for swapping data between different memory areas and different hardware components. Generally pages of memory (pages vary in size depending upon the operation being performed) are swapped to the device from the page memory area and vice versa. These buffer areas are sometimes called paging areas or page frames. With these concepts in mind, let's examine the memory areas used by DOS in the PC.

Types of Memory

The CPU chips used to build the PC largely determined the types of memory in PCs. The early PCs were based upon Intel 8088 and 8086 CPU chips that could address only 1,024 K of RAM. This led to the famous Bill Gates quote stating that 640 K of RAM would be all the memory anyone would ever need in a PC. IBM designated the remaining 384 KB of RAM as a reserved memory area, but it in fact had several uses. The system ROM, display text swapping, and display ROM were assigned to that memory area.

DOS memory management began to change with the introduction of the IBM PC AT using the Intel 80286 chip, which was capable of addressing RAM beyond the 1,024 K range. To preserve backward compatibility with the older DOS PC systems, the original memory layout continued to be used. The 80286 chips operated in real mode and in protected mode. Real mode emulated the 8088 chips, while protected mode permitted utilizing up to 16 MB of random access memory. This 16 MB limit was imposed on DOS and Windows software until the introduction of Windows 95.

Windows 95 took advantage of the 80386 chip technology, the next CPU chip technology produced by Intel. It is basically used by all 80386, 80486, and Pentium CPU chips today, and can address 4 GB of RAM. Although no PCs are built with this much RAM, the addressing capability is used with virtual memory so that applications developers can utilize a very large flat address space when building their windows 95/98/Me/NT/2000 programs.

The new 64-bit chip, the Intel Itanium chip (code named Merced), will drive the next step in PC memory management. This chip is capable of addressing 16 terabytes of RAM.

CPU chip developments precede software developments. This statement remains largely true today, although the development of CPU capabilities requires some measure of collaboration with software developers that will utilize CPU capabilities. As a result of CPU hardware preceding software, the CPU chips have built-in capabilities that enable software to avoid potential memory conflicts. The earliest and simplest of these capabilities was the protected mode operation of the 80286 chips. In this operating mode, the chip protected software components from using the same memory areas. It provided software with basic capabilities for detecting when programs tried to utilize the same RAM locations. Virtually all CPU chips provide similar and more sophisticated capabilities today.

As CPU chips evolved, so did other parts of the PC. The display capabilities increased and most PCs became multimedia devices incorporating CD-ROM and sound capabilities. Modern and future PCs include IEEE1394 video input as well. The PC system that I'm using to write this book is a multimedia PC with sound and video capabilities. It has two flat panel monitors, web camera, and USB microphone input. I'm using these capabilities to run speech-to-text software, permitting me to dictate this material directly into the PC. Such PC component developments have also impacted memory management.

Memory management concerns have evolved from the early days of DOS, where the major objective was to provide as much of the basic 640 K of RAM as possible for PC application programs. With Windows today this is less of a concern. The more important issue from a PC support perspective is ensuring that there are no hardware memory conflicts within the PC. This translates into careful configuration of the UMB area within the PC. Figure 13–1 identifies the different types of PC memory.

Conventional -- (REAL Mode)

HIMEM -- (REAL Mode)

UPPER MEMORY BLOCKS (UMB) -- (REAL Mode)

EXTENDED -- XMS

EXPANDED - EMS

Figure 13–1
PC memory types.

There are five basic areas of PC memory:

- Conventional memory—the lower 640 K DOS and game users have grown to know and love.
- XMS memory—provided by any 286, 386, 486, and Pentium CPU chips in PCs having physically over 1 million characters (1,024 K) of memory installed.
- HIMEM—created by an addressing anomaly in the Intel chips. It is the first 64 K of extended memory space that is above the 1 million character (1,024 K) boundary. HIMEM can be accessed in real operating mode.
- UMBs —blocks of memory in the reserved memory area not used for the display memory swapping area, ROMs, the expanded memory page swapping area, or LAN buffer areas.
- EMS memory—can be in any PC, provided the PC has hardware and software drivers that support EMS. Old 8088 CPU chip PCs with a special EMS board and driver software could access more than 640 K of memory. In 386 and above, a PC's EMS is created from XMS using only special software.

Figure 13–2 illustrates the PC memory areas. On the left-hand side of the diagram, the first megabyte of memory and the HIMEM area are shown. Hexadecimal addresses for each of the significant memory areas are listed on the right-hand side of the memory areas. The equivalent K addresses are shown on the left-hand side of the diagram. Therefore, the HIMEM area is

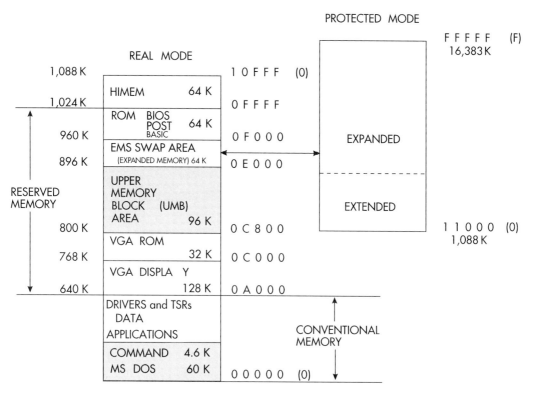

Figure 13–2
PC memory map.

from 1,024 K to 1,088 K. This corresponds to the hexadecimal addresses of 0 FF FF and 1 0F FF. The left box covers conventional memory, the reserved memory area (or UMA), and the HIMEM area. The XMS and EMS memory areas appear at the side of the first megabyte of memory to help illustrate EMS swapping. The diagram illustrates a maximum memory of 16 MB, which is equivalent to 16,383 K.

Conventional

Intel's 8086 and 8088 chips access conventional memory directly. The 80286, 80386, 80486, and Pentium chips access conventional memory when operating in real mode. In DOS-based PC systems, all the work activity was performed using conventional memory. This memory area started from address 0

K to 640 K or, in hexadecimal notation, from address 0000 to address 0A00. In real mode, Intel chips work with this memory in 64 K chunks. There are 10 chunks, or memory segments, making up the 640 K of conventional memory. Almost all DOS programs operated exclusively in this area.

DOS is a very important diagnostic tool; because it performs one task at a time, it is a relatively safe tool to use for resolving a variety of PC hardware problems. Furthermore, DOS diagnostic programs directly manipulate PC hardware. This capability is prohibited or greatly restricted in a Windows environment. The major drawback of using DOS and DOS-based diagnostic tools is that they operate in 640 K of RAM, which usually means limited data manipulation capabilities, especially when it comes to large fixed disks.

The lower address range in conventional memory contains the interrupt handling routines for DOS. Consequently, not all of the 640 K of conventional memory can be used to run DOS programs. The same areas are used by Windows to interrupt handling routines.

The study break "Understanding Memory Addresses" presents some detailed information on how the same memory addresses are represented in different documentation.

Study Break: Understanding Memory Addresses

Memory addresses can be difficult to follow and understand. They can be expressed in kilobytes or in hexadecimal notation.

In K or KB notation, a kilobyte is 1024 bytes. This is different from a kilo being 1000, as we most often think. This means that 640 K of RAM is equivalent to exactly 655,360 bytes of RAM. The DOS memory management programs report available RAM in both K notation and as thousands of bytes. Generally the thousands of bytes notation is displayed inside parentheses.

Hexadecimal notation can be more difficult to understand and interpret. Hexadecimal representation of numeric values ranges from 0 to F. F represents a number 15 in decimal notation. Later in this chapter, we have some memory address calculators that use hexadecimal representation of RAM and permit you to identify readily where various hardware components occupy UMB addresses.

When installing hardware for DOS, 4 hexadecimal digits typically represented UMB hexadecimal addresses. This means that the starting address of conventional memory was 0000. The ending address of conventional memory was 09FF. Thus the beginning UMB address was 0A00 and the HIMEM beginning address was 1000.

This four-digit representation only described the upper four hexadecimal digits of the memory address. Programmers would have to deal with addresses that added a fifth hexadecimal digit to the address, so that they viewed addresses as 0A00 (0).

Extended Memory (XMS)

When PCs have over 1 MB of RAM installed, they have XMS. XMS is supported by any 286, 386, 486, and Pentium CPU chips. CPU chips in protected operating mode address XMS, and real mode operation does not access XMS. Real mode operation accesses only the real mode memory (the first 1MB and HIMEM).

The XMS memory is the memory from which the remaining types of memory are derived. Think of them as merely special assignments for areas of XMS memory. Furthermore, other types of memory in the PC are also implemented using XMS memory. For example, shadow RAM—a hardware memory implementation—maps ROM into XMS RAM. This is done to speed up input/output operations on older PCs. In a Windows 95/98/Me/NT/2000 environment, shadow RAM is not required because input/output operations are implemented using 32-bit driver programs in RAM. In Windows systems, ROM is only used during the initial system setup process and is then bypassed in favor of the 32-bit RAM resident input/output driver programs.

In Windows systems, application programs are run in XMS memory. DOS does not have the ability to manipulate XMS memory without running the HIMEM.SYS device driver program. As we shall see, HIMEM.SYS is the DOS and Windows 3.x program that controls XMS memory. This changes with Windows 95/98/Me/NT/2000. Note that Windows NT still employs a HIMEM.SYS to access the HIMEM memory area.

Windows limited the useable capacity of XMS. Windows 3.x could not utilize XMS over 16 MB of RAM. This restriction was due to the amount of XMS that could be addressed by the Intel 80286 CPU chip. This restriction does not exist with Windows 95/98/Me/NT/2000. These Windows environments are capable of addressing the full 4 GB of memory supported by Intel Pentium chips. Although most current PCs have 64 MB to 256 MB of RAM installed,

Windows creates virtual memory which it addresses using a 4 GB flat address space model.

High Memory (HIMEM)

HIMEM was created to take advantage of an addressing anomaly in Intel chips. When CPU chips address memory and they go beyond their designed memory boundary, the memory addresses typically wrapped around to the lowest address. For example, if an upper memory address limit was 1000 and a program tried to address location 1001, the resultant address would be 001. However, in Intel chips this did not happen for the first 64,000 addresses after the million-character boundary. It meant that the first 64 K over the one-million-character boundary was addressable by the CPU chip in real mode. This 64 K is the HIMEM area.

HIMEM is a special type of XMS. It is accessed using a driver program in real operating mode which permits placing DOS components in HIMEM, in addition to managing all XMS. Not all the HIMEM 64 K can be used because the HIMEM driver program consumes some of the memory. Since Windows PCs are generally using over 64 MB of RAM, the use of the HIMEM area is much less critical than it was with DOS and Windows 3.x.

Upper Memory Blocks (UMBs)

UMBs are blocks of memory in the reserved memory area not used for the display memory swapping area, ROMs, the XMS page swapping area, or PC expansion card or LAN card buffer areas. UMBs in the reserved memory area are accessible using DOS's EMM386 program in real operating mode. Pragmatically, there is about 96 K of RAM available into which memory-resident and hardware driver programs may fit. The remainder of the UMBs are used by ROMs, display buffers, etc.

Figure 13–3 illustrates the UMB address assignments for an Adaptec SCSI controller card. The challenge with DOS memory management was to place as many driver programs as possible into the UMB area. This was sometimes not possible because driver programs and other terminate-and-stay-resident programs required more memory to load than to run. In some cases, a 5 K program would require 32 K to load and 5 K to operate. If the 32 K were not available in the UMBs, the program would be loaded into conventional memory. It is also possible to run application programs in the UMBs. This is not generally practical because of the limited amount of memory available in the UMB

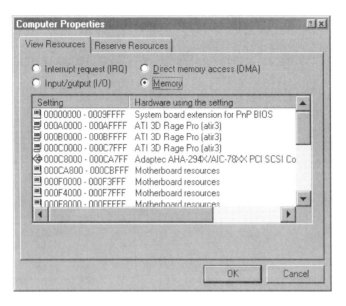

Figure 13–3
Windows 98 memory assignments.

area. Only very small DOS programs that used very little memory could operate there. Typically, programs that worked in conventional memory could not utilize UMB memory and vice versa. The DOS 6.2x SMARTDRV was the only program we saw capable of installing itself in conventional memory and then spilling over into the UMB area.

The UMB address assignments can be viewed using the Microsoft diagnostic program (MSD). It displays the memory assignments using a 4-digit hexadecimal format or the kilobyte format. Each row display represents 16 K of memory with each placeholder representing 1 K of UMB RAM. MSD displays the typical system ROM, video ROM, and video paging address ranges. It may also sense address ranges used by LAN NICs and other adapter cards, provided that the driver software for these cards has been loaded. There are versions of MSD for DOS and Windows. MSD does not always query the physical hardware to determine which address ranges are in use. Sometimes it just guesses, based on what the typical standard PC hardware address assignments are. Just as in the case where your doctor says we need to open you up for open heart surgery tomorrow, the first thought that should jump into your mind when viewing output from MSD is that you need a second opinion. An MSD memory map display appears in Figure 13–4.

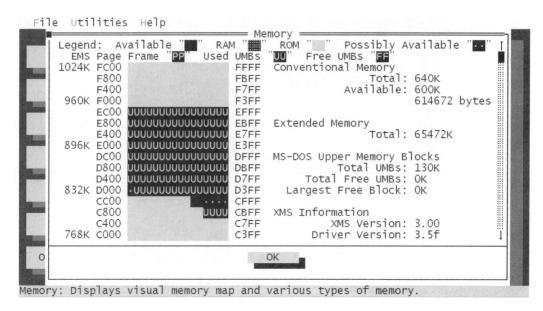

Figure 13–4
MSD program examining the UMA.

In the figure, we see the memory display from the 1 MB boundary down to the C000 address or the 768K boundary. MSD permits viewing all the UMA from the 640 K boundary to the 1,024 K boundary. The display does not permit viewing it all at one time, so the screen must be scrolled to view the portion of memory not visible. Each line represents 16 K of memory with each letter equivalent to a 1-K block of memory. The F000 to FFFF range contains the system ROM. The D000 to EFFF range is unused and available to store programs. The other memory areas are occupied by ROM, are used by the VGA display, or are potentially available for storing programs. Since the other free memory areas are not contiguous, their ability to act as program storage areas is limited.

ROM Assignments

In the UMB area, standard ROM assignments are for the system ROM and the video ROM. The system ROM provides the BIOS software that controls the PC. This includes POST routines used once during the boot process to determine the functioning PC hardware in addition to the BIOS routines used by DOS for basic input/output activities. The highest 64 K memory segment in the UMB address range is typically where system ROM resides. This is the memory segment F000–FFFF. Some PCs required a larger system ROM area; the most notable of these was the IBM PS/2.

Video ROM occupies 32 K in the UMB C000–C7FF address range. This ROM controls operation of the PC graphics card. Other adapter cards also have ROM in the UMB address range, like SCSI disk controller cards and LAN NIC cards. SCSI disk controllers often use the C800–CBFF address range for their ROM. Adaptec SCSI controllers have their SCSI-select software in ROM on the controller card. This software is used to diagnose and configure SCSI drives attached to that card. The SCSI ROM software can do low-level formatting, perform service verification, and provide adapter card setup and configuration routines. Similarly, LAN NIC cards place their ROM in the C or D UMB address segments.

In DOS-based systems, ROM address assignments were configured manually. In Windows systems, this is done more automatically, unless an adapter card requires a manual configuration to set the proper ROM address range in the UMBs. Regardless of how the ROM address configuration is performed, address conflicts cause system failures.

Video Usage

Video cards also use UMB address ranges to page swap data between the PC's RAM and the RAM resident on the video display adapter. The display we see is produced from the RAM on the video display adapter. It contains the image viewed on the PC's monitor. To update the image, the PC must swap that RAM with the RAM the PC uses for data manipulation. This swapping is done through the video RAM address ranges in the UMBs. Video adapters use the A address segment to swap graphics information between the video card memory and the working RAM in the PC. They also employ 32 K of the B address segment to perform text swapping between the display adapter card and the working RAM in the PC. The address range used was C800–CFFF. The lower part of the C address segment (C000–C7FF) was used for video swapping by monochrome display adapters. Today, this memory area is largely available for use. Because Windows 95/98/Me/NT/2000 do not need to squeeze extra memory out of the UMB area, it is much less important than it was in DOS and Windows 3x.

Expanded Memory (EMS)

Accountants caused EMS; in the first PCs, its major application was spreadsheets. When accountants saw the capabilities of spreadsheets to perform sophisticated financial analysis, they quickly created spreadsheets that gobbled up all available PC memory. The dominant spreadsheet program was Lotus 1-2-3. Sensing an opportunity to make more money, Lotus, Intel, and Microsoft collaborated on an EMS specification. As a result, any PC, provided it has special hardware and the appropriate software drivers, can support EMS. Old 8088 CPU chip PCs with special EMS boards and driver software could access more than 640 K of memory. EMS support came at a cost: Pages of memory had to be swapped between the conventional RAM and the EMS board in 8088 PCs. This swapping required the E UMB address segment to act as a paging area.

In 386, 486, and Pentium chip PCs, EMS is created from XMS using only special software. In DOS and Windows 3x, the EMM386.EXE program creates EMS in addition to providing access to the UMBs. EMS is divided into pages similar to sectors on a disk drive. The pages are moved as required into the conventional memory where the chip in real mode manipulates the data. Once finished, the page is swapped back to the EMS. This emulates the EMS operation that would be performed by an 8088 CPU chip PC. Since 386, 486, and Pentium chip PCs can address XMS directly, there is no need to perform the swapping. With these systems and Windows, it is possible to emulate EMS without actually performing any swapping between the XMS and the conventional memory areas.

Sometimes DOS also needed EMS as a generalized scheme to manage some of the memory in 386, 486, and Pentium chip PCs. Page swapping was performed, but this provided a scheme for DOS to effectively fit all types of programs and data into its EMS. The EMS emulation is performed using protected operating mode, HIMEM to manage HIMEM and the XMS, and EMM386 to make XMS emulate EMS.

Shadow ROM

Shadow ROM was implemented in almost all PC hardware. It is designed to speed up overall PC input/output operations by copying the contents of ROM into RAM; because ROM is 15 times slower than RAM, copying the ROM routines into RAM speeds up the PC. Furthermore, since the ROM routines are used continuously, the speed increase provided by shadow RAM can be measured. From a practical point of view, only the geekiest PC users would notice the increase in speed achieved by using shadow ROM. Windows 95/98/Me/NT/2000 all bypass BIOS and use I/O driver programs that run in RAM so that shadow RAM does not really speed them up.

Virtual Memory

Windows PCs use virtual memory. Because it is impractical and costly to install huge amounts of RAM in a PC, Windows PCs make the disk drive appear to be RAM. They create a swap file on the disk drive that then becomes part of the 4 GB CPU address space. Application program components are continually moved between this fixed disk swap area and RAM while Windows is running. The virtual memory swap files vary in size depending on the amount of physical RAM installed in the PC. It is possible in Windows 3x and in Windows 95/98/Me to set aside a permanent swap file area on the fixed disk. However, the default Windows 95/98/Me installation sets up a temporary swap file which works fine for almost all Windows PCs. A permanent swap file is a potential cure for an out-of-memory error message from Windows 95/98/Me. A general virtual memory layout of Windows 95/98/Me is shown in Figure 13–5.

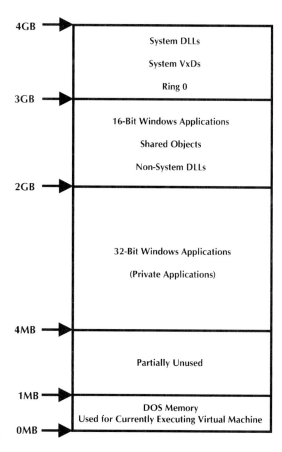

Figure 13–5
Windows virtual memory layout.

CONFIG.SYS Memory Control Statements

The DOS CONFIG.SYS file is the principal control mechanism for memory management under DOS and Windows 3x. Because Windows 95 and Windows 98/Me/2000 have memory management built in, they do not require a CONFIG.SYS file to perform memory management functions. If a CONFIG.SYS file is used with Windows 95/98/Me/2000, it is usually to provide backward compatibility with older DOS and Windows 3x programs.

The CONFIG.SYS file loads the XMS and HIMEM memory management program, HIMEM.SYS. It also loads the EMS and UMB memory management program, EMM386.EXE. The statements that act like keys to the UMAs and HIMEM areas are also present in the CONFIG.SYS file. The statement DOS=HIGH, UMB opens these areas for use. A typical CONFIG.SYS file basic memory control commands are shown here.

```
DEVICE = C:\WINDOWS\HIMEM.SYS
DEVICE = C:\WINDOWS\EMM386.EXE noems i=e800-efff
DOS = HIGH
DOS = UMB
SHELL = c:\dos\command.com c:\dos\ /e:2048 /p
BUFFERS = 16
FILES = 64
STACKS = 0,0
LASTDRIVE = z
```

In the CONFIG.SYS file above, the first line loads the XMS manager HIMEM.SYS. The second line loads the EMM386.EXE program to control the UMA and set up EMS when requested. In this case, the NOEMS parameter specifies that EMS not be used. The I=E800-EFFF parameter specifies including the E800–EFFF range in the UMBs. The DOS=HIGH and the DOS=UMB lines unlock both a HIMEM area and the UMBs for use by DOS.

Study Break: HIMEM.SYS and EMM386.EXE

This exercise shows the impact of Windows 98 DOS HIMEM.SYS and EMM386.EXE.

1. Create a bootable Windows 98 or Windows Me diskette. Opening a DOS window and entering the command FORMAT A: /S accom-

plishes this. From the Windows directory, copy HIMEM.SYS and EMM386.EXE to this diskette. From the Windows\command folder, copy DOS.COM, EDIT.COM, MEM.EXE, and SMART-DRV.EXE to the diskette.

2. Use the edit program to create an AUTOEXEC.BAT file with the following line: LH DOSKEY.

3. Shut down Windows 98/Me, place the diskette in the PC's floppy disk drive, and reboot into Windows 98/Me DOS from the diskette. (Be sure the CMOS setup is set to boot from a diskette drive first and then from the fixed disk drive.)

4. Once the PC is booted, run the MEM program to view the memory configuration. In this case, about 202 K of conventional memory should be used to contain DOS. XMS should be available for use by Windows. If the MEM /D /P command is used, it should show that DOSKEY is loaded into the PC's conventional memory.

5. Using the edit program, create a CONFIG.SYS file that contains the statements DEVICE=HIMEM.SYS and DOS=HIGH. Now reboot the PC. This time the MEM program should show about 139 K of conventional memory used for DOS.

6. Using the edit program, add to the CONFIG.SYS file the statements DEVICE=EMM386.EXE and DOS=UMB. Now reboot the PC and rerun the MEM program. This time, only about 60 K of conventional memory is used for DOS. In all cases, the DOSKEY program still loads into conventional memory.

7. Using the edit program, change the CONFIG.SYS file by removing the statements DEVICE=HIMEM.SYS and DOS=HIGH or by turning them into remarks using REM at the beginning of each line. Now reboot the PC. What error messages do you see?

This exercise illustrates the impact of HIMEM SYS and EMM386.EXE on memory for Windows 98/Me DOS. This exercise could also be performed with DOS 6.22. With DOS 6.2, however, the DOSKEY program is loaded into the UMBs, making the resulting available conventional memory larger. Also, the process could be repeated with SMART-DRV.EXE included in the AUTOEXEC BAT file. The last and most important point here is that the results of changes in CONFIG.SYS and AUTOEXEC.BAT vary from DOS version to DOS version. If you have lots of PCs to support with a particular version of DOS, then perform an exercise with those PCs to see what memory configurations and errors are caused by the changes you make.

Memory Conflicts and Their Resolution

Memory conflicts cause several types of problems in PCs, the most common of which is insufficient RAM. This problem most often manifests itself on DOS PCs running games. When DOS games are run on Windows PCs, similar problems can occur. Is also possible to have Windows programs run out of memory. There are different types of memory being used with Windows. Some of it is your everyday working RAM, while other parts of memory are heaps used to store graphics information. If any of these memory areas is exhausted, bad things usually happen to Windows. So it is not enough to focus on just having sufficient RAM to run programs, but rather one must look at the entire PC system and how the memory is used to ensure that programs operate without failure.

DOS versus Windows Memory Conflicts

Windows memory conflicts are generally different from those of DOS, which runs one application program at a time. It does some primitive multi-tasking between terminate-and-stay-resident (TSR) programs and application programs. As a result, it is possible to have memory usage conflicts. But this is a rare event.

DOS memory conflicts are resolved or prevented by careful loading of device drivers and TSR programs. Some EMM386.EXE configurations simply do not work with some PCs' BIOS. In this case, you cannot use the advanced capabilities of EMM386.EXE and the DOS memory configuration program, MEMMAKER, to maximize available conventional memory. More conservative configurations are required for the PC to operate properly.

Memory usage conflicts are much more common with Windows. In the original Windows 3.0, such memory errors produced "unrecoverable application errors" (UAEs). When Windows 3.1 was released, Microsoft vowed to eliminate UAEs, which they accomplished by renaming the unrecoverable application errors as "general protection faults" (GPFs). A general protection fault error is displayed by Windows when it detects that more than one application program is requesting the same area of RAM. Windows then displays the GPF message, permitting you to shut down the offending programs before they crash Windows. Other Windows memory errors are signaled by "illegal operation" messages. Basically, all Windows error messages are caused by some memory conflict between programs running under Windows. So regardless of what error messages are called, they are all in some way caused by memory errors and thus are memory error messages. Memory conflict errors have been greatly reduced with Windows 2000.

General Protection Faults and Illegal Operation Errors

The single most common symptom of memory conflict problems used to be a general protection fault between the core Windows 95 programs—the kernel, the explorer, and the control panel programs. A typical general protection fault error message is illustrated in Figure 13–6.

There are six general Windows 95/98/Me problem sources for general protection faults and illegal operation errors. These sources are:

- Hardware failures—Bad video drivers, misconfigured I/O cards, failed disk, overheated CPU, memory signal errors, and more.
- Resource starvation—Software needs RAM, cannot get it, and stops.
- Memory violations—Software needs RAM, cannot have it, steals it, causes page fault, then Windows shuts it down.
- Poor error handling—Software seeks file, file not found, doesn't know what to do, quits.

Figure 13–6
GPF error message.

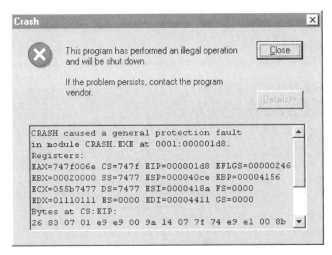

- Racing hardware—A PC waits for printer response, while printer waits for PC response.

- Infinite loops—Software runs and runs and finds nothing.

Windows 95/98/Me can also have memory problems when the GDI.EXE and the USER.EXE data heaps are exhausted. Both USER.EXE and GDI.EXE are key Windows programs. The USR.EXE program receives input from the user and provides window and menu management functions. The GDI.EXE program handles graphics, manages fonts, supports printing, and other graphics functions.

Heaps are areas of memory that get allocated to satisfy different application memory requests. Windows has both local heaps and global heaps. A local heap is contained within an application's address space, while global heaps reside in the areas belonging to the system. Changes in a local heap as requested by an application require adjustments to the application's memory space. Global changes affect the shared system memory pool.

With Windows 3.x, software conflicts often caused the entire Windows environment to crash. Sixteen-bit Windows application programs sharing the same Windows virtual machine cause this (Windows virtual machines were discussed in Chapter 11). Basically, a Windows virtual machine is an imaginary PC that an application exclusively controls or shares with other applications.

In other words, all 16-bit applications ran in one single Windows virtual machine. This was changed in Windows 95/98/Me/2000. Similar to Windows 3x, Windows 95/98/Me/2000 run DOS applications in separate virtual machines and run 16-bit Windows 3x applications in a single Windows 3x virtual machine. However, Windows 95/98/Me/2000 32-bit applications now run in separate virtual machines. Each 32-bit application has its own virtual machine, separate from the other 32-bit applications. If a single 32-bit application misbehaves, its virtual machine can be killed off. The remaining 32-bit applications would still be running in their own individual virtual machines. Because each 32-bit application works within its own virtual machine, software conflicts are reduced and Windows 95/98/Me/2000 reliability is increased.

Resolving Windows Problems

There are several ways to resolve Windows problems. Most often, resolving Windows problems requires reinstalling the offending software. In many cases, it can require reinstallation of Windows itself. While there may be a simple single parameter change in the software that can resolve the problem, this single change is not easy to identify. As a result, the quickest and easiest way to resolve problems with Windows software is reinstallation of the Windows software.

For example, Windows 95 would sometimes attempt to start, but instead it would freeze before the desktop was set up. Windows stopped and left you suspended with a blank desktop displaying its background pattern or wallpaper and a moving mouse pointer. However, there was nothing to select with the mouse.

In this case, restarting the PC at the command prompt and running SCAN-DISK to fix the directory and file structure on the disk drive solved the problem. In the process, SCANDISK (DOS) often would report directories corrupted and create several DIR000xx files. If this did not resolve the problem, then the solution was to "burn the field" and reinstall Windows 95. Reinstallation places a fresh copy of Windows 95 over the corrupted copy. The cause of this problem was a mismatch between the PC's system ROMs and the Windows 95 SCSI disk drivers.

Minor problems are evidenced by innocuous symptoms. These can be as simple as an application program locking up under Windows 95/98/Me or the warning icon displayed for installed hardware options. In most cases, reinstallation of the offending hardware or software cures the error message.

Display drivers seemed to be the most critical component of Windows 2000. Bad display drivers would cause our Windows 2000 system to inexplicably reboot. Other times, application programs would crash or memory errors would occur. Replacing the display drivers with the Windows certified drivers fixed these problems.

Software problems can freeze Windows 95/98/Me. Because of the preemptive multi-tasking, the PC is most likely not totally frozen. The Ctrl-Alt-Del warm reboot keys jump you to the Windows 95/98/Me/2000 task manager window. The Windows 95/98/Me and the Windows 2000 task manager windows are shown in Figure 13–7.

This usually permits you to kill off offending programs or to shut down the PC. When loading and operating too many programs on Windows 95/98/Me causes software conflicts, simply restart Windows to cure the problem. If a problem persists with a specific program, uninstalling and reinstalling that software program may correct the problem. Such procedures generally work fine, but there is no absolute guarantee.

When Windows itself has become corrupted, then a complete reinstallation is often the solution. Sometimes the registry misdirects Windows (the Windows control structure that controls loading Windows and application software components). The registry is discussed in Chapter 11.

A common example of this is a Windows general memory protection error. A faulty registry setting generates this error message. Unfortunately, the registry cannot be fixed because Windows refuses to start and displays the general memory protection error message. A reinstallation of Windows corrects this registry problem. It is also possible (but not recommended) to copy a good

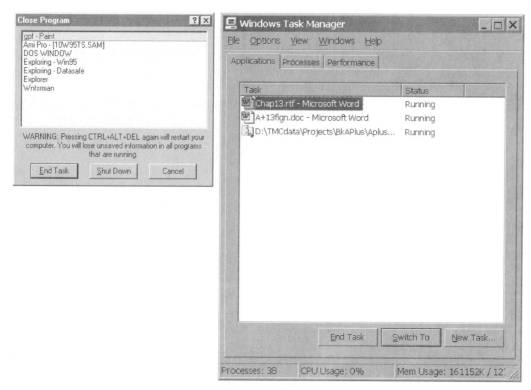

Figure 13–7
Windows 95/98/Me(left) and Windows 2000 (right) task manager windows.

registry that is exactly matched to the PC's hardware and software configuration over the old corrupted registry. If the PC's hardware and software configuration do not match, then copying registries can cause more work straightening out the configuration with the copied registry than reinstalling Windows from scratch.

Using the control panel to delete the hardware component before restarting Windows 95/98/Me can often clear up hardware problems. This can require some tricky footwork if the hardware malfunction locks the PC. In this case, Windows must be started in safe mode with a limited set of hardware drivers. You can force Windows to enter safe mode by holding down the shift key during the Windows restart process.

Figure 13–8 shows the safe mode warning display. When this happens, Windows defaults to the lowest resolution VGA display operation. The control panel functions can be used to remove or change the properties assigned to hardware components.

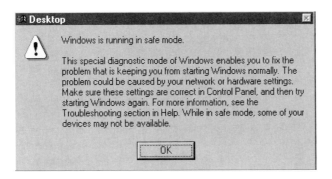

Figure 13–8
Windows safe mode notification message.

To change or configure the PC hardware, enter the control panel and select the system icon. Next, click on the device manager tab. This reveals a hierarchical list of devices starting with CD-ROM and ending with system devices.

The device manager under the Windows control panel uses several different icons to indicate the status of the device. For example, when a device has been disabled in a hardware profile, a red "X" appears over the device. Devices that have potential problems may display a yellow triangular warning sign with a "!" in the middle. Generally, any device displaying a warning signal has potential configuration problems.

Clicking on a device entry reveals the devices installed in the PC under that entry. For example, clicking on ports (COM & LPT) typically reveals entries for communications and printer ports. Clicking on the entry for the printer port highlights it, permitting us to then select properties from the menu below the entry window. When the properties menu item is selected, we then see a tab for resources, allowing us to manually set the port hardware parameters (IRQ, port address, and DMA channel) for the printer port as shown by Figure 13–9.

The panel on the left shows a printer port that is properly installed. When Windows detects hardware conflicts, it displays a panel like the one on the right. This panel is requesting that the configuration be set manually to resolve the resource conflicts that Windows has encountered. The manual configuration panel would be displayed if the PC is booted in Windows safe mode.

When the set configuration manual selection is clicked on, a new panel appears, permitting us to specify automatic configuration or to manually configure hardware for the card. For example, configuring an SCSI card would require setting interrupt request, input/output port range, and memory ranges for SCSI ROM. If this SCSI card was an older ISA bus card, the settings

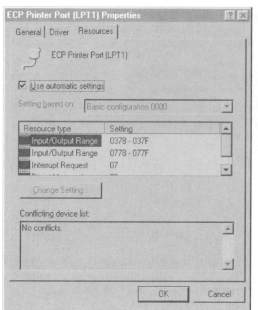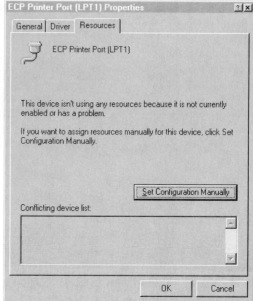

Figure 13-9

Setting manual configuration in safe mode.

selected for Windows would need to match the settings selected by the jumpers and switches on the SCSI card exactly. Figure 13–10 shows settings for an Adaptec SCSI card.

As each resource type is selected, conflicts with resource allocations of all the devices are identified to assist in selecting a resource configuration that has no conflicts. Windows 95/98/Me does not necessarily identify all conflicts in this manner. There are some conflicts that are not readily apparent from the display. In this case, even though no conflicts are indicated, the device fails to work properly with the resource settings specified. To resolve such problems, one keeps selecting new resources for the device until the device begins to work because the hidden conflict is resolved. Such hidden conflicts are most often memory range conflicts, although some have been input/output port conflicts.

There are a couple of system tools that Windows provides to help improve the PC's performance and identify depleted resources. These tools are the system monitor and the system resource meter.

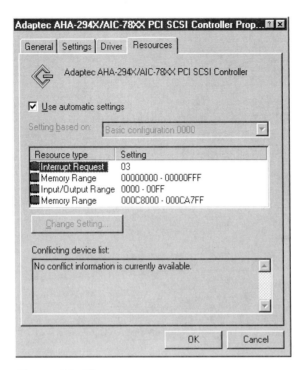

Figure 13–10
Adaptec SCSI controller properties.

System Monitor

Windows 95/98/Me has a system monitor program that can display activity of the PC's CPU, disk, and network components.

Figure 13–11 shows a typical system monitor display. While the system monitor provides an interesting display, the usefulness of this monitoring program is somewhat limited. Since Windows automatically sets many of the operating parameters for the CPU, disk, and network, there is little tuning left to the PC user. This means that even if we were to configure the system monitor program to provide information that indicated disk-caching problems, we would not likely be able to modify Windows disk cache operation to improve performance. The system monitor in some circumstances can help us improve the PC's performance. When the PC is slow, we use a system monitor to identify whether it is CPU bound, has problems with disk caching, or is I/O bound. By setting up the system monitor to track CPU utilization, disk cache activity, and I/O operations, we may be able to identify the type of performance constraint.

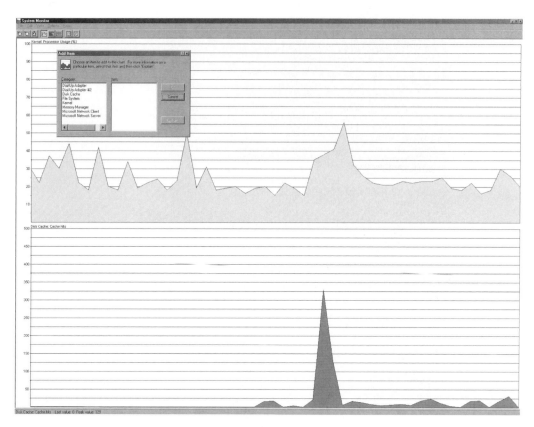

Figure 13–11
System monitor display.

However, a more useful Windows 95/98/Me diagnostic tool is the system resource meter.

System Resource Meter

The system resource meter monitors consumption of the system resource heaps. It provides a taskbar icon display of resource utilization that uses green to indicate that sufficient resources are available to run Windows programs. The icon changes to yellow and then to red as the system resources are exhausted. Figure 13–12 shows the more detailed system resource meter percent free display of the system, USER, and GDI memory heaps.

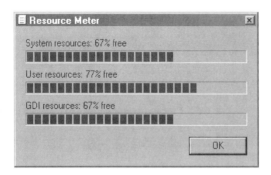

Figure 13-12
System resource meter detailed display.

By double-clicking on the taskbar icon for the system resource meter, a more detailed display appears. This display shows the current utilization of each of the key windows resource heaps. The system resource meter diagnostic program has been provided with Windows 3.x and Windows 95/98/Me.

Generally, to launch new Windows application programs, the resource meter should indicate that all heaps have at least 60 percent free resources available. These resources are consumed by Windows applications as they use fonts and other graphics objects. Printing also consumes huge amounts of space from the system resource heaps. Sometimes Windows programs do not return the resources to the heaps when they are closed. Consequently, when lots of programs are used and then shut down, after a period of time, Windows itself must be shut down and restarted to clean up the memory and restore the resources to the resource heaps.

MEMMAKER

MEMMAKER is the DOS program used to automatically configure the PC's RAM for Windows use. MEMMAKER was delivered with DOS 6.x. MEMMAKER optimizes the PC memory by moving memory-resident programs and hardware device drivers into the UMBs. The goal here was to free conventional memory for Windows 3.x use. MEMMAKER is not required for Windows 95/98/Me/NT/2000. Figure 13–13 illustrates CONFIG.SYS file commands modified by MEMMAKER.

Figure 13–13 focuses on the EMM386.EXE command line in CONFIG.SYS. In each case, the NOEMS parameter specifies that no EMS should be set aside. The X= commands are used to exclude UMAs. The ROM=

805

DEVICE = C:\DOS\EMM386.EXE NOEMS x=b000-b7ff ROM=c000-c7ff x=d800-dfff ROM=f000-ffff

An EMM386.EXE configuration using no Expanded Memory and excluding VGA and System ROM areas.

DEVICE = C:\DOS\EMM386.EXE NOEMS HIGHSCAN ROM=c000-c7ff ROM=f000-ffff

An EMM386.EXE configuration using no Expanded Memory that scans upper memory aggressively and excludes VGA and System ROM areas.

DEVICE = C:\DOS\EMM386.EXE NOEMS ROM=c000-c7ff ROM=d800-dfff ROM=f000-ffff WIN=D500-D7FF WIN=D200-D4FF

An EMM386.EXE configuration using no Expanded Memory that excludes VGA and System ROM areas and is optimized for Windows use.

Figure 13–13
MEMMAKER-modified CONFIG.SYS EMM386.EXE commands.

commands identify UMAs occupied by ROMs. The C000–C7FF range is used by the VGA adapter ROM. The F000–FFFF memory range is used by system ROM. The HIGHSCAN command releases ROM memory areas that are used only once during the boot process and reuses them as UMBs to store device driver software. The WIN= command assigns an UMA for Windows 3.x use exclusively. A brief explanation of each EMM386.EXE command line appears below it in the figure.

MEMMAKER automatically cycles through a series of menus to determine how to configure the PC RAM. It performs a loading process based upon the sequence in which the device drivers and programs are loaded in CONFIG.SYS and AUTOEXEC.BAT. Sometimes MEMMAKER's results can be improved by changing the sequence or order that the device drivers and the AUTOEXEC.BAT programs are loaded in.

MEMMAKER uses the space bar to change menu selections. This is not what is done typically with most other programs. After MEMMAKER is started, it permits you to select express or custom setup. In the custom setup, MEMMAKER first asks you if you have any programs that need EMS. Next, the advanced options permit you to specify selecting drivers and TSR programs to include in optimization, or to select them all. We encountered some SCSI adapter drivers that could not be configured using MEMMAKER. The remaining advanced options, as shown in Figure 13–14, cover scanning upper memory aggressively, optimizing memory for use with Windows, using the monochrome display swapping area (B000–B7FF) to contain programs, keeping current memory exclusions and inclusions, and moving the extended BIOS data area from conventional to upper memory. Once these selections are complete, MEMMAKER checks to see if Windows is installed on the PC. It then optimizes the device drivers loaded by CONFIG.SYS and the programs loaded by AUTOEXEC.BAT. This process requires reboot of the PC, permit-

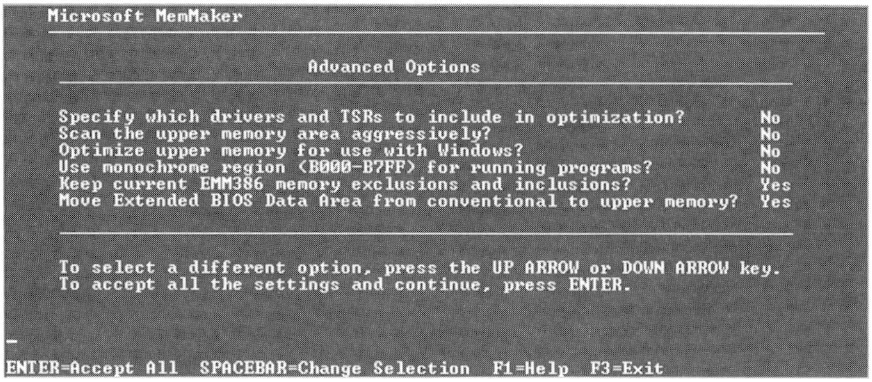

```
Microsoft MemMaker

                        Advanced Options

  Specify which drivers and TSRs to include in optimization?    No
  Scan the upper memory area aggressively?                      No
  Optimize upper memory for use with Windows?                   No
  Use monochrome region (B000-B7FF) for running programs?       No
  Keep current EMM386 memory exclusions and inclusions?         Yes
  Move Extended BIOS Data Area from conventional to upper memory? Yes



  To select a different option, press the UP ARROW or DOWN ARROW key.
  To accept all the settings and continue, press ENTER.


ENTER=Accept All  SPACEBAR=Change Selection  F1=Help  F3=Exit
```

Figure 13–14
MEMMAKER advanced options.

ting MEMMAKER to observe how the programs are loaded and the amount of memory they require. It then determines which UMB regions can be used to load and then run the device driver or program.

Figure 13–15 shows a single memory region, Region 1, in the UMA. Regions are assigned numeric values—for instance, 1, 2, 3. The resulting CONFIG.SYS and DOS statements specify the region into which the device driver or program is to be loaded. The memory configurations produced by MEMMAKER were very good. Occasionally, Windows 3.x would not run properly, usually when the upper memory was scanned aggressively using the HIGHSCAN option.

Figure 13–15
MEMMAKER region assignment.

```
Free Conventional Memory:
  Segment           Total
  -------     ------------------
   00B38              80    (0K)
   00BBE           1to76    (0K)
   011C6          88,992   (87K)
   02780         493,472  (482K)
  Total Free: 582,720  (569K)

Free Upper Memory:
  Region   Largest Free      Total Free       Total Size
  ------   -------------    -------------     -------------
     1     17,504  (17K)    17,600  (17K)    174,976 (171K)
```

In this case, it appeared as though scanning the memory aggressively by itself produced the problem. Removing the HIGHSCAN option from the EMM386.EXE command line permitted the PC to run Windows 3.x properly. This problem was readily recognized because Windows 3.1x would just lock when Windows was started. When Windows locks, a memory conflict is usually the source of the problem.

HIMEM.SYS

HIMEM.SYS is the device driver that controls HIMEM and XMS memory. HIMEM has some parameters that modify its operation. In almost all cases, these parameters are rarely used. The HIMEM parameters include the /M: parameter, which designates machine type. This may overcome some operating difficulties with different types of PCs. Defined machine types are shown in Figure 13–16.

Figure 13–16

HIMEM machine type parameters.

```
Number      Name              Computer type
-------------------------------------------------------------
   1        AT              ; IBM AT or 100% compatible.
   1        JDR             ; JDR 386/33
   1        COMPUADD        ; COMPUADD 386 systems   or /m:8
   2        PS-2            ; IBM PS/2
   2        DATAMEDIA       ; Datamedia 386/486
   2        UNISYS          ; UNISYS PowerPort
   3        PTLCascade      ; Phoenix Cascade BIOS
   4        HPVectra        ; HP Vectra (A & A+)
   5        ATT6300plus     ; AT&T 6300 Plus
   6        ACER1100        ; Acer 1100
   7        Toshiba         ; Toshiba 5100, 1600 & 1200XE
   8        Wyse            ; Wyse 12.5 Mhz 286
   8        Hitachi         ; Hitachi HL500C
   8        Intel           ; Intel 301z or 302
   8        Phoenix         ; Phoenix BIOS   or /m:1
12,13,14    IBM-PC          ; Other IBM  PC machines.
  16        Bull            ; Bull Micral 60
```

Other HIMEM parameters include:

```
REM /a20control:[on|off]
```

Determines whether HIMEM.SYS controls the A20 line. The default is on. When on is specified, control is assumed only if A20 was off when loaded. The A20 line is a hardware interrupt line that activates the software for accessing the high memory area (HMA). The HMA is the first 64 KB above the 1 MB memory address boundary. With HIMEM controlling the A20 line, software operation should be more reliable and predictable.

```
REM /int15=xxx
```

Allocates XMS to the Interrupt 15h interface. Interrupt 15h extends the original PC ROM BIOS to include a way for software to find out how much conventional plus extended RAM is installed in the PC. Programs use this BIOS extension to discover how much XMS the PC has. The programs then redirect Interrupt 15h to them and then report <xxx>K less memory available to other programs. This effectively allocates <xxx>K of XMS from the top of the PC's RAM. In this manner a program allocates its own XMS from the top of the PC's memory pool. The default is zero bytes. Older DOS applications sometimes use the interrupt 15h interface to allocate XMS instead of using the XMS (eXtended Memory Specification) method provided by HIMEM. When such applications are encountered, manually setting the xxx value to 64 KB larger than the XMS required by the application provides enough memory for them.

```
REM /shadowram:[on|off]
```

Specifies whether HIMEM.SYS should switch off shadow RAM. When there is less than 2 MB of RAM, the default is off; with more than 2 MB, the default is on.

```
REM /cpuclock:[on|off]
```

Determines if HIMEM changes CPU clock speed. When clock speed slows upon loading HIMEM, try on. Selecting on slows HIMEM.SYS and other programs using XMS. Default is off.

SMARTDRV

SMARTDRV.EXE is the Microsoft disk-caching program. A caching program works on the 80/20 rule of computers. There are always 80/20 rules, like the IRS 80/20 rule—they get 80 and you get 20. The 80/20 computer rule goes something like this—80 percent of the times you need new data, it is in the next memory location after the data you just used. So if the PC were to read a lot of data off the fixed disk into RAM, it is very likely the data the PC needs next is in RAM and not on the slower fixed disk.

SMARTDRV caches data transfers to or from the PC's fixed disk. SMART-DRV works in XMS or in the UMA. It is one of the few programs that will split itself between XMS and the UMA. SMARTDRV requires 2 MB of RAM for optimal operation. However, drive performance improvements are realized using as little as 256 K of RAM.

Depending on the amount of installed RAM in older PCs, SMARTDRV would adjust its memory size. Table 13–1 gives the SMARTDRV cache size for several different XMS memory sizes. This is a moot point today because most PCs come with more than 16 MB of RAM. Further, cache size would vary depending on whether Windows was being run or whether the PC was operating on DOS alone. Typical SMARTDRV configurations are:

Table 13–1   XMS Size vs. SMARTDRV Cache Allocation

XMS Size	DOS Cache Size	Windows Cache Size
1 to 2 MB	1 MB	256 K
2 to 4 MB	1 MB	512 K
4 to 6 MB	2 MB	1 MB
over 6 MB	2 MB	2 MB—Optimal for SMARTDRV

The Device=c:\dos\SMARTDRV.EXE /double_buffer is entered in the CONFIG.SYS file to install double buffering for SCSI disk drives. The double_buffer SMARTDRV option is required to prevent some SCSI and other disk drive controllers from trashing the data they store on the fixed disk drive. It slightly diminishes (about a 4 percent reduction) the PC's disk performance. Double buffering correctly translates data addresses used by SCSI and other disk controllers to the correct physical allocation unit (groups of sectors) addresses.

To determine whether double_buffer is required, first install double buffering with SMARTDRV, then run SMARTDRV /S at the DOS prompt. If double buffering is not required, the buffering column states "no". When double buffering may be required, SMARTDRV displays a "-". A "yes" indicates that double buffering should be used. SMARTDRV status displays illustrating double buffering requirements are shown in Figure 13–17 and 13–18.

In Figure 13–17, the buffering status for fixed disk drives C and D as well as the CD-ROM drive E is displayed as "no". This means that double buffering is not required for these drives. Figure 13–18 displays a different result. For drives C and D, the "yes" status indicates that double buffering is required

```
Microsoft SMARTDrive Disk Cache version 5.0
Copyright 1991,1993 Microsoft Corp.
      Room for    2,048 elements of   8,192 bytes each
There have been    24,535 cache hits    and    2,208 cache misses
Cache size:  16,777,216 bytes
Cache size while running Windows:  16,777,216 bytes
             Disk Caching Status
drive    read cache    write cache    buffering
-------------------------------------------
  A:        yes           no           no
  B:        yes           no           no
  C:        yes           yes          no <== Not Required
  D:        yes           yes          no <== Not Required
  E:        yes           yes          no <== Not Required
Write behind data will be committed before command prompt returns.
For help, type "SMARTDRV /?"
```

Figure 13–17
Double buffering not required.

Figure 13–18
Double buffering required.

```
Microsoft SMARTDrive Disk Cache version 5.0
Copyright 1991,1993 Microsoft Corp.
      Room for    2,048 elements of   8,192 bytes each
There have been    24,535 cache hits    and    2,208
cache misses
Cache size:  16,777,216 bytes
Cache size while running Windows:  16,777,216 bytes
             Disk Caching Status
drive    read cache    write cache  buffering
-------------------------------------------
  A:        yes           no           no
  B:        yes           no           no
  C:        yes           yes          yes <== Required
  D:        yes           yes          yes <== Required
  E:        yes           yes          -   <== Possibly
Required
Write behind data will be committed before command
prompt returns.
For help, type "SMARTDRV /?".
```

for these drives. The "-" status display for the E (CD-ROM) drive indicates that double buffering may be required for that drive. However, since it is a CD-ROM drive, data cannot be corrupted on the drive so for this drive, double buffering is optional.

EMM386.EXE and UMBs

EMM386.EXE is the EMS manager program that makes XMS look like XMS. EMM386 is also the program that manages access to the UMBs. There are several options for EMM386. The most commonly used parameter options are:

- AUTO—Automatically provides type of memory program requests, extended or expanded.
- RAM—Provides access to both expanded and the UMBs.
- X= 0x000-0y000—Exclude this memory range from use. Most often required when LAN boards are used.
- m9—Set the EMS page frame in the 0E000 to 0EFFF memory segment. Other choices might be

```
m1  = C000      m8  = DC00
m2  = C400      m9  = E000
m3  = C800      m10 = 8000
m4  = CC00      m11 = 8400
m5  = D000      m12 = 8800
m6  = D400      m13 = 8C00
m7  = D800      m14 = 9000
```

- NOHI—causes EMM386.EXE to load into conventional memory
- /Frame=—Sets the page frame location. /Frame=NONE runs EMS without the page frame using 64 K. Memory pages and frames are described at the beginning of this chapter.
- DOS=HIGH, UMB—This causes DOS and other programs to be loaded first into HIMEM and then into the UMBs.

The memory address calculator in Figure 13–19 can be used to determine the locations of ROM and RAM buffer areas used in a PC's conventional memory, UMBs, and HIMEM areas. Intel 286, 386, 486, and Pentium chips access these areas when operating in real mode. In protected and other operating modes, the 286, 386, 486, and Pentium chips address XMS, and with special software, EMS areas.

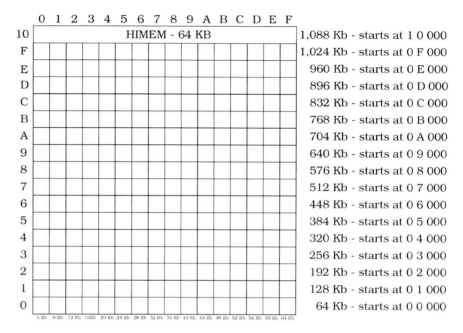

Each verticle increment is 64 Kb of memory starting from address 00000 represented by 0. The upper 640 Kb boundary 0A000 is represented by A.

Each horizontal increment or box is 4 Kb. Thus the VGA ROM that is 32 Kb in size uses addresses from 0C000 to 0C800.

Figure 13-19
Blank memory address calculator.

To locate a specific memory address, for instance, CC00, divide the address into two halves, CC and 00. Use the left half (CC) to locate first row C then column C. Next, use the right half, 00, to locate the side of the cell. The left side is 00 and the right side is FF. This approach is used in both Figure 13–19 and Figure 13–20 to locate areas in the UMBs that are used for hardware ROM and hardware memory paging.

The memory address calculator in Figure 13–20 has had the conventional, VGA display, EMS page frame, system BIOS ROM, VGA ROM (video BIOS), and HIMEM areas identified. CMOS is located in the conventional memory area.

The page frame area is set by software, so it may be moved from the E000 memory segment to any other contiguous (unbroken stretch) of free memory. This shows about 64KB + 32KB or 96 KB of free UMBs available for holding hardware device drivers and other memory-resident programs.

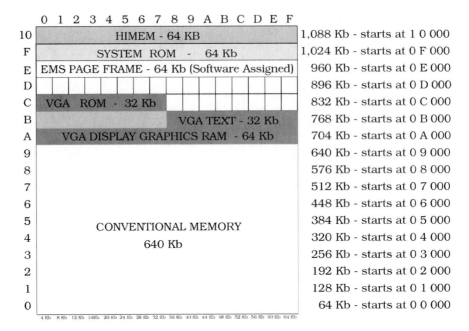

Each verticle increment is 64 Kb of memory starting from address 00000 represented by 0. The upper 640 Kb boundary 0A000 is represented by A.

Each horizontal increment or box is 4 Kb. Thus the VGA ROM that is 32 Kb in size uses addresses from 0C000 to 0C800 as illustrated above.

Figure 13–20
Memory address calculator.

Study Break: Understanding UMBs

This exercise uses the memory address calculators to locate areas of memory commonly used by VGA adapters, system ROM, and LAN cards.

1. Use the blank memory address calculator in Figure 13–19 to locate the address range C000–C7FF. This is a typical address range used by the VGA adapter ROM. Split C000 into C0 and 00. Use C0 to identify the C row and the 0 column. The 00 address is on the left-hand side of the C0 block. Similarly, split the C7FF address into its C7 and FF components. Again, C identifies the row and 7 identifies the column. The FF address is on the right-hand side of the C7 block. In Figure 13–20, this address range is highlighted as the VGA ROM address range. It is 32 K in size.

2. Repeat the process to locate the address range from 0000 to 90FF. This is the address range labeled conventional memory in Figure 13–20.

3. Use the same process once again to locate the address range from F000 to FFFF. In Figure 13–20, this address range is labeled the system ROM address range.

4. Run MSD and use the memory option to verify the VGA ROM address range and system ROM address range in your PC.

The purpose of this exercise was to familiarize you with the HMA hardware ROM address assignments typical of most PCs.

PC DOS Memory Setup

As a final look at PC memory setup under DOS, we go step by step and configure PC RAM to illustrate the impact of each program on the memory configuration process. Although this exercise is not particularly important for meeting the A+ exam objectives, it provides detailed insight into the operation of PC memory and the areas of memory used by PC hardware today.

Memory management under DOS is similar for almost all versions. DOS 6.x provides the MEMMAKER program to automatically configure a PC's RAM. It gives more precise control for loading programs into UMBs. Finally, it provides an understandable MEM program, which lets you view your PC's RAM more accurately.

The bad news is that when DOS 6.x data compression and virus protection are used, you end up with significantly less memory. The DOS 6.x memory tests shown start with no memory usage and then add in driver programs to show the impact on free memory caused by changes in the CONFIG.SYS and AUTOEXEC.BAT files. We start with DOS 6.x in conventional memory. DOS loads DOUBLESPACE automatically in the event that disk compression is desired. We start with no AUTOEXEC.BAT and CONFIG.SYS files, making DOS use its default values. Total conventional memory available at this time is 534 KB. Figure 13–21 was created using the DOS MEM program after the PC was rebooted into DOS with no AUTOEXEC.BAT and CONFIG.SYS files.

```
Memory: ───────────────────────────────────────────────────────────
Modules using memory below 1 Mb:
Name            Total      =   Conventional   +   Upper Memory
--------    ------------       ------------       ------------

MSDOS          58397   (57K)      58397   (57K)        0    (0K)
DBLSPACE       44944   (44K)      44944   (44K)        0    (0K)
COMMAND         4992    (5K)       4992    (5K)        0    (0K)
Free          546944  (534K)     546944  (534K)        0    (0K)


Memory Summary:

Type of Memory       Total     =     Used     +    Free
----------------  ------------     ------------    ------------

Conventional        655360 (640K)    108416 (106K)   46944   (534K)
Upper                    0   (0K)         0   (0K)       0    (0K)
Adapter RAM/ROM     393216 (384K)    393216 (384K)       0    (0K)
Extended (XMS)     3145728(3072K)   3145728(3072K)       0    (0K)
----------------  ------------     ------------    ------------
Total memory      4194304(4096K)   3647360(3562K)  546944(534K)

Total under 1Mb    655360 (640K)    108416 (106K) 546944   (534K)
Largest executable program size                   546928   (534K)
Largest free upper memory block                        0    (0K)


Environment Space: ───────────────────────────────────────────────
PATH=C:\DOS
PROMPT=$P$G
COMSPEC=C:\COMMAND.COM
```

Figure 13-21
DOS memory configuration without CONFIG.SYS and AUTOEXEC.BAT.

The first step is to add a Path statement and some set statements to the AUTOEXEC.BAT file. There are no changes to CONFIG.SYS.

The DOS defaults for files and buffers are added to the CONFIG.SYS file. When the defaults are hit exactly, no reductions or increases are made to conventional memory. See Figure 13–22.

In the MEM program output above, the largest executable program size remains the same from our initial configuration. We can see that the programs using memory are MSDOS, the DBLSPACE disk cache program, and COMMAND.COM. The resulting environment space variables are:

```
Environment Space: _____
COMSPEC=C:\COMMAND.COM
PROMPT=$p $g
```

```
PATH=C:\;C:\DOS;C:\WIN;C:\QEMM;C:\NETW;
TEMP=d:\temp
TMP=d:\temp
```

The HIMEM program is run with the DOS=HIGH to unlock the HIMEM area. DOS uses HIMEM only when it is unlocked by the DOS=HIGH command. Next, we use the CONFIG.SYS file below and reboot our PC. In our new CONFIG.SYS, a REM statement stops DOS from loading into the high memory area (HMA).

Figure 13–22
DOS memory configuration with CONFIG.SYS and AUTOEXEC.BAT default values.

```
AUTOEXEC.BAT:─────────────────────────────────────────
prompt $p $g
path c:\;c:\dos;c:\win;c:\qemm;c:\netw;
set temp=d:\temp
set tmp=d:\temp


CONFIG.SYS: ──────────────────────────────────────────
files=8
buffers=15
break=on
Lastdrive=Z
stacks=9,128
Fcbs=1,10


Memory: ──────────────────────────────────────────────
Modules using memory below 1 Mb:
Name           Total        =   Conventional    +   Upper Memory
--------     -------------       -------------       -------------
MSDOS          58397   (57K)      58397   (57K)         0    (0K)
DBLSPACE       44944   (44K)      44944   (44K)         0    (0K)
COMMAND         4992    (5K)       4992    (5K)         0    (0K)
Free          546880  (534K)     546880  (534K)         0    (0K)
Memory Summary:
Type of Memory       Total     =     Used      +   Free
--------------     -----------       -----------     -----------
Conventional       655360 (640K)    108480 (106K) 546880   (534K)
Upper                   0   (0K)         0   (0K)      0     (0K)
Adapter RAM/ROM    393216 (384K)    393216 (384K)      0     (0K)
Extended (XMS)    3145728(3072K)   3145728(3072K)      0     (0K)
--------------     -----------       -----------     -----------
Total memory      4194304(4096K)   3647424(3562K) 546880   (534K)
Total under 1 Mb  655360 (640K)    108480 (106K) 546880   (534K)
Largest executable program size       546784   (534K)
Largest free upper memory block            0     (0K)
```

```
CONFIG.SYS: _____
device=HIMEM.SYS
REM DOS=HIGH
files=8
buffers=15
break=on
Lastdrive=Z
stacks=9,128
Fcbs=1,10
```

The MEM program results also show that 64 KB of XMS are being used. This 64 KB is the HIMEM area. Once HIMEM is run to utilize the XMS, MEM shows the 64 KB HIMEM area is being used regardless of whether it is occupied by programs or not. In our example, we lose 4 KB of conventional memory because it is needed to run HIMEM. This reduces the available conventional memory to 530 KB. See Figure 13–23.

Figure 13–23

DOS memory configuration with CONFIG.SYS loading HIMEM.SYS.

```
Modules using memory below 1 Mb:
  Name          Total       =   Conventional    +   Upper Memory
  --------   ----------------     ----------------    -------------
  MSDOS       58413   (57K)       58413   (57K)        0   (0K)
  HIMEM        3792    (4K)        3792    (4K)        0   (0K)
  DBLSPACE    44944   (44K)       44944   (44K)        0   (0K)
  COMMAND      4992    (5K)        4992    (5K)        0   (0K)
  Free       543088  (530K)      543088  (530K)        0   (0K)

Memory Summary:

  Type of Memory      Total      =    Used     +    Free
  ---------------   -------------     -------------  -------------
  Conventional      655360 (640K)   112272 (110K) 543088   (530K)
  Upper                  0   (0K)        0   (0K)      0     (0K)
  Adapter RAM/ROM   393216 (384K)   393216 (384K)      0     (0K)
  Extended (XMS)    3145728(3072K)        65536  (64K)3080192  (3008K)
  ---------------   -------------     -------------  -------------
  Total memory      4194304(4096K)   571024 (558K)3623280  (3538K)

  Total under 1 Mb 655360 (640K)   112272 (110K) 543088   (530K)

  Largest executable program size          542992   (530K)
  Largest free upper memory block               0     (0K)
  The high memory area is available.
```

Next, the HIMEM area is unlocked by the DOS=HIGH command. Notice that the REM preceding the device = HIMEM.SYS statement has been removed. This activates the DOS=HIGH line in the CONFIG.SYS file.

```
CONFIG.SYS: _____
device=HIMEM.SYS
DOS=HIGH
files=8
buffers=15
break=on
Lastdrive=Z
stacks=9,128
Fcbs=1,10
```

In this case, we gain conventional memory because DOS components have been moved to the HMA and we pick up an additional 50 KB of conventional memory (increasing conventional memory to 580 KB) as a result. See Figure 13–24.

Figure 13–24

DOS memory configuration with DOS=HIGH activated.

```
Modules using memory below 1 Mb:
   Name            Total       =   Conventional   +   Upper Memory
   --------    ---------------     ---------------     -------------

   MSDOS           13277  (13K)       13277  (13K)         0   (0K)
   HIMEM            1168   (1K)        1168   (1K)         0   (0K)
   DBLSPACE        44224  (43K)       44224  (43K)         0   (0K)
   COMMAND          2992   (3K)        2992   (3K)         0   (0K)
   Free           593568 (580K)      593568 (580K)         0   (0K)

Memory Summary:

   Type of Memory      Total      =     Used     +    Free
   --------------  -------------      -------------   -------------

   Conventional    655360 (640K)       61792  (60K) 593568   (580K)
   Upper                0   (0K)           0   (0K)      0    (0K)
   Adapter RAM/ROM 393216 (384K)      393216 (384K)      0    (0K)
   Extended (XMS)  3145728(3072K)      65536  (64K)3080192  (3008K)
   --------------  -------------      -------------   -------------
   Total memory    4194304(4096K)     520544 (508K)3673760  (3588K)

   Total under 1 Mb 655360 (640K)      61792  (60K) 593568   (580K)

   Largest executable program size           593472   (580K)
   Largest free upper memory block                 0   (0K)
   MS-DOS is resident in the high memory area.
```

Next, EMM386.EXE is run to access the UMBs and EMS, if required. Our CONFIG.SYS file has been modified to include the EMM386.EXE and DOS=UMB commands that configure and enable the UMBs.

```
CONFIG.SYS: _____
device=HIMEM.SYS
DOS=HIGH
Device=EMM386.EXE
DOS=UMB
files=8
buffers=15
break=on
lastdrive=Z
stacks=9,128
fcbs=1,10
```

Notice we have less conventional RAM, but have gained 91 KB of upper memory. See Figure 13–25.

At this point, several more steps were taken to configure the DOS memory. The SHELL command increased the DOS environment space to 2,000 characters. This reduced conventional memory by 1,744 characters (2000–256 bytes = 1744) because 256 bytes are already allocated to the environment space. The upper memory remained unchanged.

The DEVICE=ANSI.SYS was added to the CONFIG.SYS file. This reduced conventional memory by about 4 KB. The upper memory remained unchanged.

Next, the DEVICEHIGH= was added to the CONFIG.SYS file for both DBLSPACE and ANSI.SYS to restore the conventional memory. This resulted in about 618 KB of conventional memory and 44 KB remaining in upper memory.

The files were increased to 64 and the buffers to 32. The file increase reduced conventional memory to about 615 KB, with 44 KB remaining in upper memory.

The SMARTDRV program automatically loaded high. However, DOSKEY loaded into conventional memory. This reduced conventional memory to about 611 KB, with 17 KB remaining in upper memory.

Next, the DOSKEY program was loaded high using the LH command. This reduced conventional memory to about 604 KB, with 24 KB remaining in upper memory. Because SMARTDRV was loaded into both conventional

```
Modules using memory below 1 Mb:
   Name            Total      =    Conventional    +   Upper Memory
   --------    ----------------    ----------------    --------------

   MSDOS          13293  (13K)       13293  (13K)          0    (0K)
   HIMEM           1168   (1K)        1168   (1K)          0    (0K)
   EMM386          3120   (3K)        3120   (3K)          0    (0K)
   DBLSPACE       44224  (43K)       44224  (43K)          0    (0K)
   COMMAND         2992   (3K)        2992   (3K)          0    (0K)
   Free          683712 (668K)      590432 (577K)      93280   (91K)

Memory Summary:

   Type of Memory       Total      =     Used      +    Free
   ----------------  -------------     -------------    -------------

   Conventional       655360 (640K)     64928  (63K) 590432   (577K)
   Upper               93280  (91K)         0   (0K)  93280    (91K)
   Adapter RAM/ROM    393216 (384K)    393216 (384K)      0     (0K)
   Extended (XMS)*   3052448 2981K)     496544485K)    25559 (2496K)
   ----------------  -------------     -------------    -------------

   Total memory      4194304(4096K)    954688 (932K)3239616  (3164K)


   Total under 1 Mb  748640 (731K)     64928  (63K) 683712   (668K)


   Total Expanded (EMS)                 3473408 (3392K)
   Free Expanded (EMS)*                 2801664 (2736K)


   * EMM386 is using XMS memory to simulate EMS memory as needed.
     Free EMS memory may change as free XMS memory changes.


   Largest executable program size          590336  (577K)
   Largest free upper memory block           93280   (91K)
   MS-DOS is resident in the high memory area.
```

Figure 13-25

DOS memory configuration with EMM386 and UMBs enabled.

memory and upper memory, less conventional memory is left than if DOSKEY had been loaded directly into conventional memory. However, by loading DOSKEY as the last program, conventional memory is restored to 615 KB and upper memory is reduced to 13 KB. The rule is to load large programs first and small programs last to provide DOS the best opportunity to fit all programs into the UMAs. Loading DOSKEY last increased our available conventional memory in this example.

Finally, the NOEMS command was added to the EMM386.EXE line. Conventional memory remained at 615 KB, but because an EMS page frame is no longer needed, upper memory increased to 77 KB. The final AUTOEXEC.BAT and CONFIG.SYS files in our example are shown below.

```
AUTOEXEC.BAT: _____
prompt $p $g
path c:\;c:\dos;c:\win;
set temp=d:\temp
set tmp=d:\temp
c:\dos\smartdrv.exe
Loadhigh c:\dos\doskey

CONFIG.SYS: _____
device=c:\dos\himem.sys
device=c:\dos\emm386.exe noems x=a000-c7ff
dos=high,umb
shell=c:\dos\command.com c:\dos /e:2000 /p /f
devicehigh=c:\dos\dblspace.sys
devicehigh=c:\dos\ansi.sys
files=64
buffers=32
break=on
lastdrive=z
stacks=9,128
fcbs=1,10
```

The final memory configuration resulting from all these changes is shown in Figure 13–26. Note that DBLSPACE, ANSI.SYS, SMARTDRV, and DOSKEY are all loaded into upper memory. Only HIMEM, EMM386, and COM-MAND.COM are loaded into conventional memory. The largest executable program size is 615 KB.

Simple CONFIG.SYS and AUTOEXEC.BAT files are shown in Listings 13–1 and 13–2. These files provide adequate conventional memory and should work for almost all DOS and Windows 3.x configurations, except those demanding the absolute maximum amount of free conventional memory.

With DOS PCs, the easiest way to configure memory is to use the MEM-MAKER program. It automatically configures DOS to provide maximum conventional RAM for DOS applications. Further, its resulting configurations run reliably and predictably. However, the one rule identified above also applies to PCs using MEMMAKER to configure their conventional memory; load the bigger programs first and the smaller programs last. We have seen configurations where rearranging the device driver and terminate-and-stay-resident program loading order increased conventional memory significantly.

```
Modules using memory below 1 Mb:
    Name            Total         =    Conventional   +   Upper Memory
    --------     ----------------      ----------------     ------------
    MSDOS        16749    (16K)        16749    (16K)         0    (0K)
    HIMEM         1168     (1K)         1168     (1K)         0    (0K)
    EMM386        3120     (3K)         3120     (3K)         0    (0K)
    COMMAND       4736     (5K)         4736     (5K)         0    (0K)
    DBLSPACE     44256    (43K)            0    (0K)      44256   (43K)
    ANSI          4256     (4K)            0    (0K)       4256    (4K)
    SMARTDRV     27280    (27K)            0    (0K)      27280   (27K)
    DOSKEY        4144     (4K)            0    (0K)       4144    (4K)
    Free        708352   (692K)       629440   (615K)     78912   (77K)


Memory Summary:

    Type of Memory       Total      =      Used      +     Free
    ----------------  ------------      ------------     --------------
    Conventional       655360 (640K)        25920  (25K) 629440    (615K)
    Upper              158848 (155K)        79936  (78K)  78912     (77K)
    Adapter RAM/ROM    393216 (384K)       393216 (384K)      0      (0K)
    Extended (XMS)    2986880(2917K)      1270656(1241K)1716224   (1676K)
    ----------------  ------------      ------------     --------------
    Total memory      4194304(4096K)      1769728(1728K)2424576   (2368K)

    Total under 1 Mb 814208 (795K)       105856 (103K) 708352     (692K)


    Largest executable program size         629344    (615K)
    Largest free upper memory block          78704     (77K)
    MS-DOS is resident in the high memory area.
```

Figure 13-26
Final DOS memory configuration.

Listing 13-1   CONFIG.SYS

```
Device=c:\dos\HIMEM.SYS
DOS=HIGH
Device=c:\dos\EMM386.EXE NOEMS
DOS=UMB
Files=64
Buffers=10
Lastdrive=Z
shell=c:\dos\command.com /E:2048 /P
stacks=0,0
FCBS=1,0
```

823

Listing 13-2   AUTOEXEC.BAT

```
SET TEMP=C:\TEMP
SET TMP=C:\TEMP
SET DIRCMD=/Ogn /A
verify on
prompt $p $g
path c:\;c:\dos;c:\windows;......
c:\dos\mode con rate=32 delay=1
LH c:\mouse\mouse
LH c:\dos\doskey
```

These simple CONFIG.SYS and AUTOEXEC.BAT files configure PC RAM in a fashion that works on almost all PCs running DOS and Windows 3.x. If problems occur with these configurations, removing the EMM386.EXE device driver from CONFIG.SYS usually resolves the problems.

Study Break: DOS Memory Layout

Use the MEM command to view the conventional and high memory configuration in your PC.

1. Open a DOS window. Enter MEM to view the memory layout summary. How much conventional memory is available?
2. Enter MEM /D /P to view the conventional memory configuration in detail. What are the very first things resident in the lowest memory locations? These are the interrupt routines or pointers (vectors) to the interrupt handling software routines (components).
3. What comes next? Device drivers for standard I/O devices are loaded.
4. The next memory locations in conventional memory should contain HIMEM, EMM386, and DBLBUFF. With Windows 98/Me DOS, double buffering is automatically loaded.
5. Next you should see MSDOS, some environment storage space, terminate-and-stay-resident programs, and finally the MEM program itself.

6. How many upper memory regions do you have? On our machine it is two, with the second and largest region containing system data and space reserved for buffers, FCBs, and stacks.

The purpose of this exercise was to illustrate the layout of conventional memory in a PC as viewed by the DOS MEM program.

Summary

This chapter described the basics of PC memory management. We began with how PC chips look at memory and then discussed how DOS and Windows perform memory management.

Windows makes knowing how DOS manages memory a low-priority issue. However, a good understanding of PC memory configuration basics helps solve software problems. Memory resource conflicts by hardware in the UMAs continue to present difficult problems for Windows 95 systems. Such problems are greatly diminished on Windows 2000 systems and somewhat diminished on Windows 98/Me/NT systems.

Memory management for DOS is a much less critical issue than it was years ago, since most systems use Windows 95/98/Me/NT/2000. However, the issue with DOS memory configuration is less one of maximizing conventional RAM and more one of configuring the memory for trouble-free DOS and Windows operation. Since most diagnostic tools rely on DOS and since Windows still must have UMB hardware conflicts resolved, knowing the DOS memory configurations can be helpful troubleshooting knowledge.

Chapter Review Questions

1. *What is EMM386.EXE used for?*

    A. Manage UMA (UMBs) and create EMS
    B. Create HIMEM
    C. Use conventional memory
    D. None of the above

Answer: A, manage upper memory area (UMBs) and create EMS. HIMEM is created by HIMEM.SYS and conventional memory is used during real mode operations by Pentium chips.

2. *Where does extended memory start?*

> A. 0 K
> B. 640 K
> C. 1088 K
> D. 1024 K

Answer: D, 1024 K. The start of all RAM is at 0 K, the UMBs begin at 640 K, and the end of the HIMEM area is at 1088 K.

3. *Where is "HMA" located?*

> A. 0K to 64 K
> B. 1024 K to 1088 K
> C. 640 K to 1024 K
> D. FFFFFF0 to FFFFFFF

Answer: B, 1024 K to 1088 K. The 0 to 64 K area is in conventional memory, 640 K to 1024 K are the location of the UMBs, and FFFFFF0 to FFFFFFF is way out there in memory.

4. *What commands are used in CONFIG.SYS?*

> A. ECHO
> B. PAUSE
> C. DEVICE
> D. DEVICEHIGH

Answer: C. DEVICE and D. DEVICEHIGH. ECHO and PAUSE are used in AUTOEXEC.BAT.

5. *What command in DOS do you use to enable use of EMS?*

> A. EMM386.EXE
> B. EXPAND.EXE
> C. EXPANDED.COM

Answer: A, EMM386.EXE. There are no EXPAND.EXE or EXPANDED.EXE commands.

6. *Where does the HMA always start and how large is it?*

> A. At 1024 K for 64 K
> B. Immediately after 640 K for 64 K
> C. At FFFF h (65,535) for 64 K

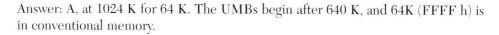

Answer: A, at 1024 K for 64 K. The UMBs begin after 640 K, and 64K (FFFF h) is in conventional memory.

7. *Which area of memory is most often used for BIOS programs?*

    A. Conventional memory
    B. Upper memory
    C. Extended memory
    D. Shadow memory

Answer: B, upper memory. The PC BIOS ROM is often set at 960 K to 1024K in the UMA. It is not in the conventional memory (under 640 K) or in XMS (over 1024 K). BIOS can be copied into Shadow RAM, which may then be set up in XMS memory; however, this is a PC setup option and not the standard BIOS memory location.

8. *What does MEMMAKER do?*

    A. Offers you an automated way to manage upper and extended memory
    B. Edits your CONFIG.SYS and AUTOEXEC.BAT files
    C. Optimizes memory
    D. All of the above

Answer: D, all of the above. MEMMAKER is a comprehensive memory management program that automates memory management functions, and edits the DOS CONFIG.SYS and AUOTEXEC.BAT files to optimize memory use under DOS.

9. *TSRs are usually device drivers loaded from:*

    A. The CONFIG.SYS file
    B. The AUTOEXEC.BAT file
    C. The COMMAND.COM file
    D. The Windows system directory

Answer: A, the CONFIG.SYS file. Terminate-and-Stay-Resident (TSR) device drivers are loaded from CONFIG.SYS. Some TSR programs like DOSKEY are loaded from AUTOEXEC.BAT, but they are not device drivers. COMMAND.COM and the Windows\SYSTEM directory (folder) do not load device drivers.

10. *How much memory is base (conventional) memory?*

    A. 320K
    B. 640K
    C. 1024K
    D. 384K

Answer: B, 640 K. Conventional memory size is 640 KB. The maximum UMA is 384 KB. The 384 KB and 640 KB are equal to 1024 KB and 320 KB is 384 KB less 64 KB.

11. *Swapping RAM contents to the fixed disk drive is called what?*

    A. Caching
    B. Interleaving
    C. DRAM
    D. Memory paging

Answer: D, memory paging. Caching is used to match a slower memory type to a faster memory type – disk cache matches disk memory to RAM. Separating RAM into banks that operate independently with the CPU speeds up RAM operation and is called interleaving. DRAM is Dynamic Random Access Memory, a RAM technology.

12. *Every PC with more than 1 MB of RAM does not necessarily have what type of memory?*

    A. XMS
    B. EMS
    C. Conventional
    D. HMA

Answer: B, EMS. Every PC with more than 1 MB of RAM has the 640 KB of conventional RAM, the HMA and XMS. Installing special software creates EMS. Consequently, PCs do not necessarily have EMS. Windows 95/98/.NT/2000 applications do not use EMS.

13. *Do system ROMs ever use more than 64 K?*

    A. Yes
    B. No

Answer: B, no. Only the PS-2 had ROMs greater than 64 KB.

14. *How much memory is typically used for VGA ROM?*

    A. 32K
    B. 64K
    C. 96K
    D. 128K

Answer: A, 32K. The VGA ROM typically uses one half a 64 KB UMB memory segment, or 32 KB.

Chapter 14

Software Installation, Configuration, and Upgrade

Chapter Syllabus

- Operating System Installation Procedures

- Software Upgrades

- Booting Procedures

- Loading and Adding Device Drivers

- Windows Configuration

- Launching Windows Applications

This chapter covers installing DOS, Windows 3.x, Windows 95/98/Me and Windows 2000. It describes the process of upgrading from DOS to Windows 3.x and also to Windows 95/98/Me, and examines booting the PC and launching applications. Installation and configuration of DOS and Windows 3.x are not objectives of the current A+ exam, but they help explain what goes on behind the scenes with Windows 98/Me and Windows 2000. The configuration steps that were performed by the PC user under Windows 3.x are done automatically under Windows 98/Me/2000. Understanding some details from earlier versions of Windows helps us understand what is happening automatically with the most current Windows versions. Many of the file names for functions in Windows 3.x are similar to the file names for the same functions under Windows 98/Me/2000.

When it comes to software installation, the best procedure is to install from scratch, that is, install with only the software that will be used on the PC. Trying to upgrade and preserve software configuration settings is a noble objective that can be achieved, but it is more practical to install from scratch and results in the most reliable and best performing system. Table 14–1 presents typical installation requirements for several operating environments.In addition to these requirements, Windows 98 optionally uses a CD-ROM drive. The minimum Windows 98 display adapter is a 16 color VGA (640 by 480) adapter. Windows Me and Windows 2000 both use a CD-ROM that is 8X (Me) or 12X (Windows 2000 or W2K) or a DVD drive of equivalent speed. They both use a VGA or better adapter. An SVGA that supports 256 colors or an XGA display supporting 256 colors and 1024 by 768 resolution is better for both Windows Me and Windows 2000.

The minimum hardware requirements for each operating system specified by Microsoft permits the operating system to run, but it cannot do much more without beating the disk drive to death or having programs run out of memory. For example, we encountered a Compaq PC running Windows 95 with 8 MB RAM using a 1 GB disk drive. This was the most stressed out Compaq PC we had ever seen. It was constantly swapping data to the disk drive. Any operation required it to swap data from RAM to the disk drive. All screen updates required disk data swapping. Consequently, even the simplest of operations took several seconds as the PC wrote and read the display data from the disk drive. It could only effectively run the Windows accessory programs and AOL software. For proper operation, more memory was required and a bigger disk drive was in order.

Table 14-1 Operating System Hardware Requirements

Operating System	CPU Chip Required (Range)	RAM Required (Typical)	Fixed Disk Used (Typical)
DOS	8088 (8088 to Pentium)	640 KB and up	Used about 6.48 MB disk space for DOS 6.22 (Fixed disk size of 30 MB to 100 MB was OK for DOS alone)
Windows 3.x	80286 for standard mode 80386 for 386 enhanced mode (80386 to Pentium)	3 MB (Most systems ran fine with 16 MB of RAM but you could use up to 64 MB)	Required 15 MB disk space (100 MB to 1GB)
Windows 95	80386 DX 20 MHz (A Pentium is needed for effective operation, Pentium 133 to Pentium 4 and AMD K7)	4 MB minimum 8 MB recommended 16 MB for Pentium-based PCs (32 MB to 128 MB Systems with 40 MB of RAM ran OK)	20 MB normal 10 MB compact installation 40 MB minimum disk size (1 GB to typically 2 GB or 4GB)
Windows 98	80486 DX 66 MHz (A Pentium is needed for effective operation, Pentium 200 to Pentium 4 and AMD K7)	16 MB minimum (32 MB and more Systems with 64 MB to 128 MB of RAM ran fine)	120 MB disk space minimum (355 MB can be used for new install 2 GB to typically 4 GB or 8 GB)

Table 14-1 Operating System Hardware Requirements (Continued)

Operating System	CPU Chip Required (Range)	RAM Required (Typical)	Fixed Disk Used (Typical)
Windows Me	Pentium 150 *(A 300 to 400 MHz Pentium is needed for multimedia and video editing, Pentium 300 to Pentium 4 and AMD K7)*	32 MB minimum *(64 MB and more)*	480 MB *(8 GB and up)*
Windows NT	Pentium class *(A 200 MHz Pentium is adequate for disk and printer sharing, Pentium 200 to Pentium 4 and AMD K7)*	12 MB minimum and 16 MB recommended *(But if you believe this I have a bridge in Brooklyn to sell. 64 MB and up—the more the better)*	110–120 MB minimum *(2 GB and up—about 4 GB to 16 GB was used for NT Workstation. NTFS can support terabytes.)*
Windows 2000 and Windows XP	Pentium 133 *(A 300 MHz Pentium II is recommended. Pentium II 300 to Pentium 4 and AMD K7. Can support multiple CPUs.)*	64 MB and up—the more the better *(typically 128 MB to 512 MB or more)*	2 GB with 650 MB free space *(8 GB and up—about 8 GB to 80 GB is used for Windows 2000 Professional. NTFS can support terabytes)*

Operating System Installation Procedures

DOS is the starting point for installing virtually all software operating environments. Because DOS permits direct interaction with the fixed disk drive, it is used to partition and format the disk. Generally, those partitions prepared by DOS can be translated into other formats during the operating system installation process. For example, Windows NT translates DOS FAT partitions into NTFS partitions during installation of Windows NT. Windows NT can translate DOS partitions into NTFS partitions using the Windows NT CONVERT utility program. CONVERT.EXE is an NT program that is used during NT setup to convert FAT partitions to NTFS. When NT is installed, the initial partition is always FAT, so NT installation must go through a FAT-to-NTFS conversion for all NTFS partitions. CONVERT.EXE can also be run from a DOS Window after the NT system has been installed. In most cases, Windows can be upgraded by installing a newer version over an older version. This can work well and preserve the configuration from the older version. However, it is wiser to work from a clean disk. Record the key configuration information and backup before doing any upgrades to the operating system. Remove the older version of Windows and the applications by reformatting the hard drive. Install the upgraded version of Windows and reinstall the necessary applications and data. A comparison of FAT-12, FAT-16, FAT-32 and NTFS is given in Table 14–2.

Table 14–2 FATs and NTFS

Partition Type	Operating System Support	Maximum Partition Size	Security	Redundant Array of Independent Disks (RAID)	Drives Supported
FAT-12	DOS Win95/98 DOS Windows 95 a Windows 95 b Windows 98 Windows NT 3.5x Windows NT 4.0 Windows 2000 Windows XP	16 MB with 4KB allocation unit size	None	No	Old IDE

833

Table 14–2 FATs and NTFS (Continued)

Partition Type	Operating System Support	Maximum Partition Size	Security	Redundant Array of Independent Disks (RAID)	Drives Supported
FAT-16	DOS Win95/98 DOS Windows 95 a Windows 95 b Windows 98 Windows NT 3.5x Windows NT 4.0 Windows 2000 Windows XP	2 GB with 32 KB allocation unit size	None	Hardware controller	Smaller IDE SCSI
FAT-32	Win98 DOS WinMe DOS Windows 95 b Windows 98 Windows Me Windows 2000 Windows XP	28-bit FAT 256 M entries 512 MB with 4 KB allocation unit size to 2 terabytes with 32 KB allocation unit size *(I think)* *(I run a 75 MB fixed disk using FAT 32 under Windows 2000 with a 16 KB allocation unit size)*	None	Hardware controller	Large IDE SCSI
NTFS	Windows NT Windows 2000 Windows XP	2 terabytes but higher sizes are possible	Cannot be accessed by DOS Provides disk and file security features for networking	NT software and hardware controller	Huge IDE SCSI

Convert FAT partition to NTFS partitions by using the convert utility provided with Windows NT. The FAT to NTFS partition conversion is performed with the command:

```
CONVERT x:/FS:NTFS[/V]
x:—specifies the drive to convert to NTFS.
/FS:NTFS—specifies to convert the volume to NTFS.
/V—specifies that CONVERT runs in verbose mode.
```

Windows 2000 CONVERT will convert FAT32 to NTFS but Windows NT CONVERT will not. The conversion is one way; you cannot convert back to FAT.

Once the boot process is finished, the PC is running the file system software, and the BIOS is bypassed, the partition size can be much larger. The maximum partition size for BIOS is 1,204 cylinders × 256 heads × 64 sectors per track, giving 7.8 GB maximum capacity. These limits are the maximums that a PC's BIOS can use because of hardware limitations in the number of bits assigned to the disk addressing function, as was explained at the beginning of the chapter.

Suggested partitioning strategies for different size drives are shown in Table 14–3.

Table 14–3 Partitioning strategies

Drive Size	FAT-16	FAT-32	NTFS
2 GB	C—Boot—1 GB D—Data—1 GB	C—Boot—1 GB D—Data—1 GB	C—Boot—FAT-16—1 GB (reduced security) D—Data—NTFS—1 GB
4 GB	C—Boot—2 GB D—Data—2 GB	C—Boot—1 GB D—Data –3 GB	C—Boot—FAT-16—1 GB (reduced security) D—Data—NTFS—3 GB
8 GB	Use FAT-32	C—Boot—2 to 4 GB D—Data—4 GB E—Install—2 GB (optional)	C—Boot—FAT-16 or 32—2 GB (reduced security) D—Data—NTFS—4 GB E—Install—NTFS—2 GB (optional)

Table 14–3 Partitioning strategies (Continued)

Drive Size	FAT-16	FAT-32	NTFS
10 GB and up	Use FAT-32	C—Boot—20% of drive capacity up to 12 GB D—Data—40% of drive capacity or 50% of remaining capacity E—Data—40% of drive capacity or 50% of remaining capacity	C—Boot—Fat-32—20% of drive capacity up to 12 GB (reduced security) D—Data—40% of drive capacity or 50% of remaining capacity E—Data—40% of drive capacity or 50% of remaining capacity

These strategies are based on the file system and how the PC is used. Generally, the bigger the partition with the smaller the allocation unit, the more efficiently the disk drive space is utilized, as illustrated in Figure 14-1.

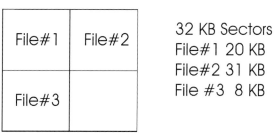

32 KB Sectors
File#1 20 KB
File#2 31 KB
File #3 8 KB

Case 1 -- Storing the three files consumes three quarters of the disk capacity.

8 KB Sectors
File#1 20 KB
File#2 31 KB
File #3 8 KB

Figure 14–1
Allocation unit size vs. storage efficiency.

Case 2 -- Storing the three files consumes one half of the disk capacity.

However, Windows 95/98/Me must boot using a DOS partition. Windows NT/2000/XP can boot from either an NTFS partition or a FAT partition. If NT/2000/XP is booted from a FAT partition, the security for the PC is reduced because operating system files and data files on that drive are generally accessible from DOS.

A bootable partition of 2 to 12 GB should be sufficient to hold the operating system, the operating system installation files, and some applications software. The second partition should be used to store all active data. Isolating the data from the software makes for easy backup and recovery in the event of failure, permits reinstallation of the disk software installation without losing data, and easily preserves critical data when software is upgraded.

Having a third partition is useful for making backups (although it is on the same physical disk, having a separate partition backup can be extremely useful) and holding application software installation files. The third partition contains either backups of key data and program files or device drivers and other installation programs for Windows. This is not the active data, but a backup copy of the active data. For example, it can be handy to use a program like GHOST to make a complete binary copy of the boot drive C: on the third drive. If the boot partition ever gets corrupted, this copy can be used to quickly recover it. With disk drive capacity increasing at a dizzying rate and prices for IDE drives remaining low, a third partition backup disk is an effective insurance policy to solve software problems.

Some PCs use partition-duplicating software GHOST to duplicate the data or the boot partition on a third backup partition. In the event of software failure or Windows becoming corrupted during software installation, the duplicate partition is loaded over the corrupted partition.

With Windows 95/98/Me, the registry often becomes corrupted, causing Windows to crash, operate poorly, or not boot at all (the ugly Windows protection error). Microsoft provides a simple utility ERU.EXE (the Emergency Recovery Utility) that backs up the registry and all key files that configure Windows 95/98/Me. This utility can be found at the Microsoft web site by searching for ERU. Using ERU, the key files can be backed up to a folder on the fixed disk drive (like drive C or E or a ZIP or JAZ drive.) Backing them up on a floppy drive does not save the most important file, SYSTEM.DAT, so it is not an effective alternative. See Figure 14–2. These backup files require several MB of storage space. When the drive is accessible from DOS, the ERD.EXE program created by ERU.EXE is used to restore the snapshot backup of the PC's key configuration files. ERU cannot be used to resurrect the registry from corruption problems occurring with Window NT/2000. A good strategy with Windows 95/98/Me is to periodically perform these backups using a third partition, like a drive E. In this fashion, if the primary partition is deleted or reformatted, the key Windows configuration files have not

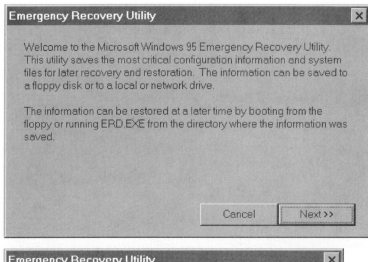

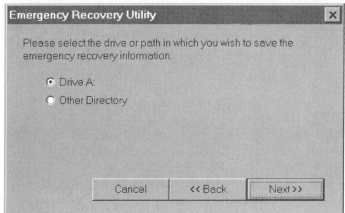

Figure 14–2
ERU utility Windows.

been destroyed. If an audit trail of these files is maintained in numbered folders (for example, 001,002, and 003), they can easily consume 20 to 100 MB of disk space. It is best to keep these key file ERU backups in a backup partition.

NT has a built-in emergency repair disk utility called RDISK.EXE. The RDISK.EXE utility program builds a bootable emergency repair disk for Windows NT, which contains setup programs that restore the Windows NT registry and repair corrupted Windows NT files. Windows 2000 has a backup utility that backs up files and creates emergency repair diskettes, as shown in Figure 14–3 .

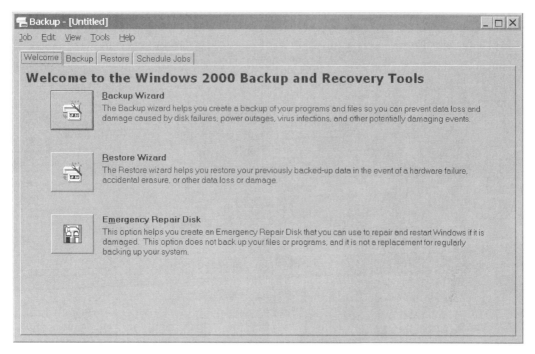

Figure 14–3
Windows 2000 backup utility.

Once you have prepared the disk, the next step is to partition it. The next section covers the procedure for partitioning fixed disks.

Partitioning a Fixed Disk

The second step in software installation is to partition the fixed disk. Partitioning erases all data on the disk. This is not a problem with new disk drives, but partitioning an older disk with existing data erases the data from the disk so that it is unrecoverable.

Several years ago, new disk drives needed to be low-level formatted before partitioning could take place. The low-level format wrote zeros or ones across the entire disk surface and tested it for flaws. Today this process has been performed at the factory for all IDE drives and SCSI drives. Furthermore, IDE drives, because they perform sector and cylinder translations, can be damaged if a low-level format is attempted.

```
Your computer has a disk larger than 512 MB. This version of Windows
includes improved support for large disks, resulting in more efficient
use of disk space on large drives, and allowing disks over 2 GB to be
formatted as a single drive.

IMPORTANT: If you enable large disk support and create any new drives on this
disk, you will not be able to access the new drive(s) using other operating
systems, including some versions of Windows 95 and Windows NT, as well as
earlier versions of Windows and MS-DOS. In addition, disk utilities that
were not designed explicitly for the FAT32 file system will not be able
to work with this disk. If you need to access this disk with other operating
systems or older disk utilities, do not enable large drive support.

Do you wish to enable large disk support (Y/N)...........? [Y]
```

Figure 14–4
FDISK file system selection.

When FDISK is run, the first screen determines the DOS and Windows files system used. See Figure 14–4.

Answering "Y," the default setting, to the large disk support installs FAT-32. An "N" for no installs FAT-16. FAT-32 should work with older BIOS. In this case, the disk drive capacity may be limited because of Cylinder-Head-Sector (CHS) addressing due to the BIOS's inability to provide Logical Block Addressing (LBA)-mode addressing. The next screen is used to partition the drive and examine the partitions. FDISK works with multiple disk drives. Selecting additional drives is performed using selection 5 on the FDISK main menu. See Figure 14–5.

The fixed disk main menu is used to:

- Create a DOS partition or logical drive.
- Set the partition as active.
- Delete partitions or logical DOS drives.
- Display partition information.
- Change to a second fixed disk drive.

Fixed disk setup proceeds by creating a DOS partition or logical drive. Option 1 permits creation of a primary DOS partition or an extended DOS partition. Logical drives are then defined in the extended DOS partition. The primary DOS partition is used as the boot partition and should be set to active. The extended DOS partition is then used to set up the remaining drive space. The logical drive designations subdivide the extended DOS partition.

Disk partitions are specified in MB. Sometimes disk vendors specify disk capacities in their absolute number of bytes, using 1,000 bytes. This can be

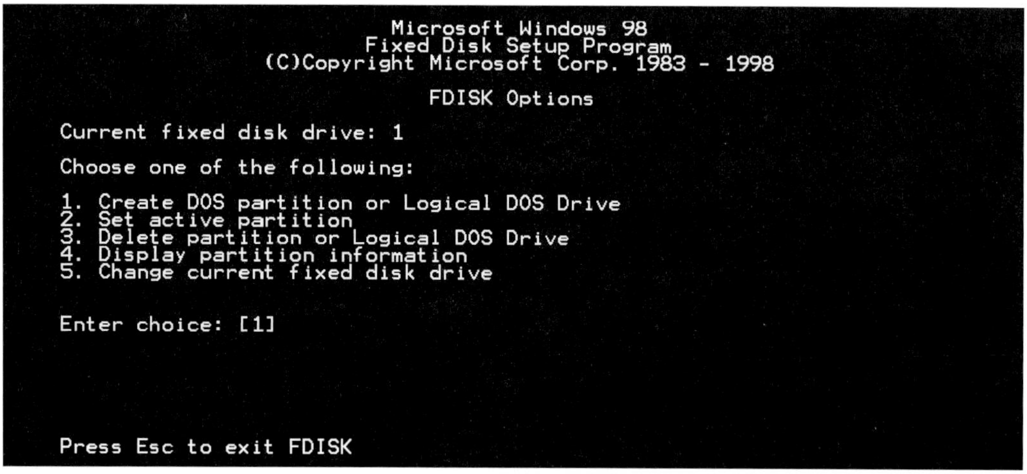

```
                      Microsoft Windows 98
                   Fixed Disk Setup Program
               (C)Copyright Microsoft Corp. 1983 - 1998

                        FDISK Options

  Current fixed disk drive: 1

  Choose one of the following:

  1. Create DOS partition or Logical DOS Drive
  2. Set active partition
  3. Delete partition or Logical DOS Drive
  4. Display partition information
  5. Change current fixed disk drive

  Enter choice: [1]




  Press Esc to exit FDISK
```

Figure 14–5
FDISK main menu.

confusing because the actual drive sizes in MB are slightly smaller, since they are defined in 1,024 byte increments. FDISK always reports partition sizes in 1,024 byte increments or true megabytes so they may seem smaller than the advertised disk capacity. FDISK accepts capacity specifications in megabyte sizes (e.g., 10) or as a percentage (e.g., 20%). When partitioning large drives, it is easiest to use percentages to specify partition capacities.

Once primary and extended DOS partitions have been defined and the logical drives assigned, it is time to set the bootable partition as active. Menu selection number 2 in the FDISK main menu sets the active partition. An "A" in the status entry for that partition designates the active partition.

The delete partition or logical drive menu item is used to remove logical drives or partitions. When they are removed, all data in those partitions or logical drives is lost and cannot be recovered. This option is used to reconfigure the partitions and thus the logical drive letter on a PC. Most PCs do not have their partitions reconfigured.

The display partition information provides a summary display of the partitions defined on the disk drive and permits viewing the logical drive assignments. See Figure 14–6.

The FDISK display partition information shows the primary drive disk letter assignment, active status, size in MB, and the file system used on the disk. The extended DOS partition and its size is also identified. When there are multiple disk drives installed in the PC, the change current fixed disk drive option permits us to partition the second, third, or fourth drive in the PC.

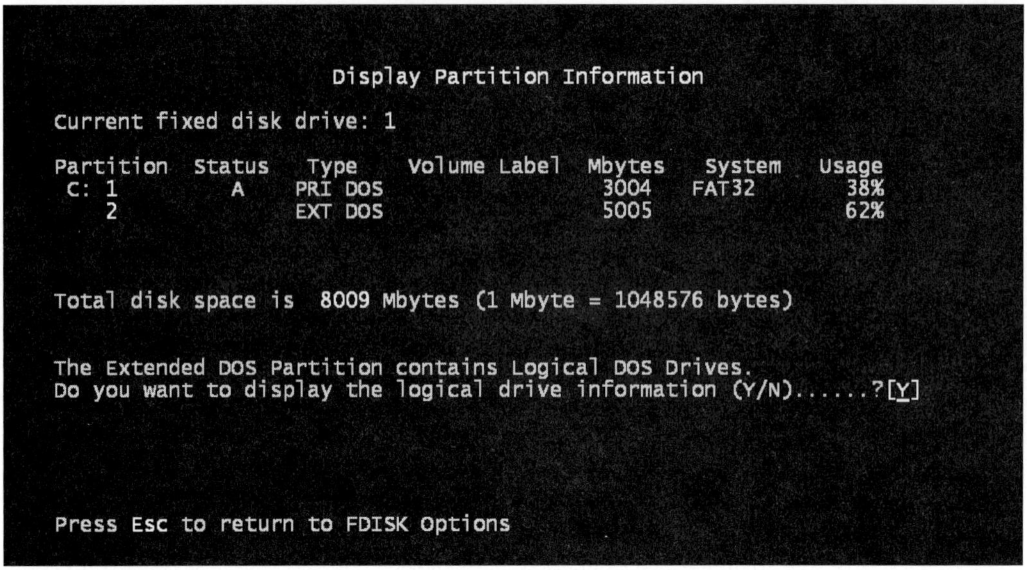

```
                    Display Partition Information
Current fixed disk drive: 1

Partition  Status   Type   Volume Label   Mbytes   System   Usage
   C: 1      A     PRI DOS                  3004    FAT32     38%
      2            EXT DOS                  5005              62%


Total disk space is  8009 Mbytes (1 Mbyte = 1048576 bytes)


The Extended DOS Partition contains Logical DOS Drives.
Do you want to display the logical drive information (Y/N)......?[Y]




Press Esc to return to FDISK Options
```

Figure 14-6
FDISK partition information display.

Selecting this option also provides a convenient overview display of the disk drive capacities and partitions created for all the disk drives in the PC.

FDISK can be run at any time. Running FDISK in a DOS window under Windows 95/98/Me and striking Alt PrintScreen captured these images. FDISK is also an effective disk diagnostic tool. When FDISK cannot read the disk drive, it displays an error message indicating that it cannot read the fixed disk. In the event of a fixed disk controller failure, FDISK displays a different message, indicating that the fixed disk controller has failed.Once the disk has been partitioned, the next step in operating system installation is to format the fixed disk drive partitions.

Formatting a Bootable Disk

Formatting a bootable fixed or floppy disk in DOS or Windows 95/98/Me can be performed using the DOS utility FORMAT.COM. See Figure 14–7.

To make the formatted disk drive bootable, use the FORMAT /S option. The /S option causes FORMAT to install the operating system files on both fixed disk drives and floppy diskettes. FORMAT.COM automatically installs the following files in the root directory of the formatted disk drive:

```
COMMAND COM 93,880 14-14-98 4:59p COMMAND.COM
DRVSPACE BIN 68,871 05-11-98 8:01p DRVSPACE.BIN
IO SYS   222,390 05-11-98 8:01p IO.SYS
MSDOS SYS    9 05-11-98 8:01p MSDOS.SYS
```

While the filenames are the same for both DOS and Windows 95/98/Me FORMAT programs, the files themselves are quite different. The plain FORMAT /S command does not install memory management programs.

The DRVSPACE.BIN program is used for disk compression and can usually be deleted to provide added space on floppy diskette drives. There are no CONFIG.SYS and AUTOEXEC.BAT files created.

Performing a DOS installation using a SETUP.EXE program provides a complete installation of DOS on the fixed disk.

Similarly, installing Windows 95/98Me on a bootable fixed disk would provide a more complete installation by including additional files for booting into Windows 95/98/Me. Both FDISK and FORMAT can be used to prepare fixed disk drives for Windows NT/2000/XP installation. If FAT partitions are going to be used, the FDISK and FORMAT programs can be used to set up very large drives with FAT-32.

When NTFS is used, Windows NT, Windows 2000, and Windows XP have a disk manager program that partitions and formats drives with FAT or NTFS.

Figure 14–7
FORMAT command options.

```
C:\>

C:\>format /?
Formats a disk for use with MS-DOS.

FORMAT drive: [/V[:label]] [/Q] [/F:size] [/B | /S] [/C]
FORMAT drive: [/V[:label]] [/Q] [/T:tracks /N:sectors] [/B | /S] [/C]
FORMAT drive: [/V[:label]] [/Q] [/1] [/4] [/B | /S] [/C]
FORMAT drive: [/Q] [/1] [/4] [/8] [/B | /S] [/C]

  /V[:label]   Specifies the volume label.
  /Q           Performs a quick format.
  /F:size      Specifies the size of the floppy disk to format (such
               as 160, 180, 320, 360, 720, 1.2, 1.44, 2.88).
  /B           Allocates space on the formatted disk for system files.
  /S           Copies system files to the formatted disk.
  /T:tracks    Specifies the number of tracks per disk side.
  /N:sectors   Specifies the number of sectors per track.
  /1           Formats a single side of a floppy disk.
  /4           Formats a 5.25-inch 360K floppy disk in a high-density drive.
  /8           Formats eight sectors per track.
  /C           Tests clusters that are currently marked "bad."
```

In Windows 2000/XP the disk manager is entered using the Windows Help and searching for disk. Alternatively, you may, with administrative privileges, open COMPMGMT.MSC with the Windows 2000/XP Explorer, and go directly to the local Computer Management Console to run the disk management software. See Figure 14–8 for Windows 2000 disk manager.

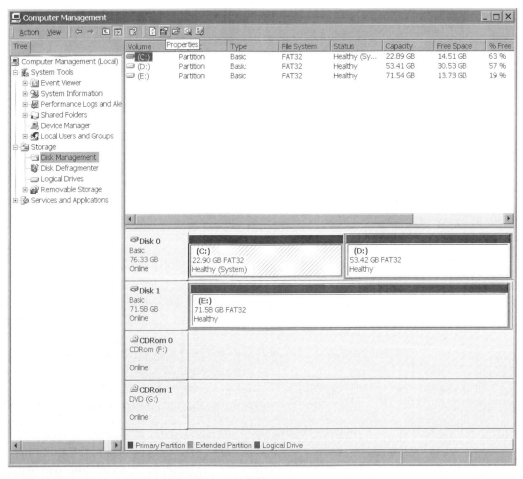

Figure 14–8
Windows 2000 COMPMGMT.MSC disk manager.

DOS Installation

After the fixed disk has been partitioned and formatted, the next step in the operating system installation process is installing DOS. DOS 6.22, the last DOS version before Windows 95 DOS (DOS 7.0) and Windows 98/Me DOS, is installed using a SETUP.EXE program. This SETUP.EXE program creates an uninstall diskette as well as installing DOS 6.x. It examines your system to determine previously installed versions of DOS, the display type, and the directory in which to install the new DOS. See Figure 14–9. This setup program used standardized keys for navigation. As seen in the figure, the F1 key displays help information, the F3 key exits setup, Enter selects the menu choice, and arrow keys are used to move from menu item to menu item.

The SETUP.EXE program then proceeds to copy the DOS files to the designated subdirectory, completing the DOS installation. This installation process does not necessarily optimize memory utilization under DOS. When DOS is installed over a previous version of DOS, the AUTOEXEC.BAT and CONFIG.SYS file settings are preserved. Otherwise, minimal AUTOEXEC.BAT and CONFIG.SYS files are created and saved.

Figure 14–9
MS-DOS 6.22 setup.

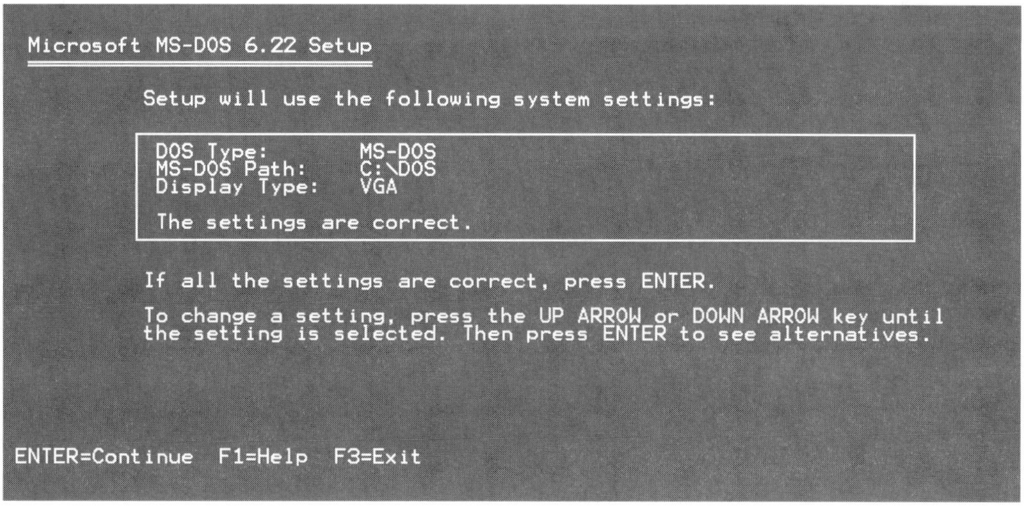

```
Microsoft MS-DOS 6.22 Setup

        Setup will use the following system settings:

       ┌─────────────────────────────────────────────────────┐
       │ DOS Type:        MS-DOS                              │
       │ MS-DOS Path:     C:\DOS                              │
       │ Display Type:    VGA                                 │
       │                                                     │
       │ The settings are correct.                           │
       └─────────────────────────────────────────────────────┘

        If all the settings are correct, press ENTER.

        To change a setting, press the UP ARROW or DOWN ARROW key until
        the setting is selected. Then press ENTER to see alternatives.




 ENTER=Continue  F1=Help  F3=Exit
```

Memory Configuration

Initial DOS memory configuration is performed using MEMMAKER.EXE. After the basic DOS 6.x and higher installation is complete and the hardware driver and DOS TSR programs are configured to run under DOS, run MEM-MAKER to perform the memory configuration. This program examines the PC and observes the programs loading during the boot process to determine the optimal memory configuration. It then creates CONFIG.SYS and AUTOEXEC.BAT files that properly load the memory resident and driver programs into HIMEM and the UMA. See Figure 14–10.

Both the DOS installation program (SETUP) and MEMMAKER are menu-driven and easy to run. DOS must be installed and the memory optimized prior to the installation of Windows 3.x. Once these solutions steps are complete, it is time to install Windows 3.x.

Windows 3.x Installation

The optimal strategy for installing virtually all versions of Windows is to copy the Windows installation files to a directory on the fixed disk. Then Windows is installed from those files copied into that installation directory on the fixed disk. In this man-

Figure 14–10
MEMMAKER advanced options.

```
Microsoft MemMaker

                         Advanced Options

    Specify which drivers and TSRs to include in optimization?     No
    Scan the upper memory area aggressively?                       No
    Optimize upper memory for use with Windows?                    No
    Use monochrome region (B000-B7FF) for running programs?        No
    Keep current EMM386 memory exclusions and inclusions?          Yes
    Move Extended BIOS Data Area from conventional to upper memory? Yes


    To select a different option, press the UP ARROW or DOWN ARROW key.
    To accept all the settings and continue, press ENTER.



ENTER=Accept All   SPACEBAR=Change Selection   F1=Help   F3=Exit
```

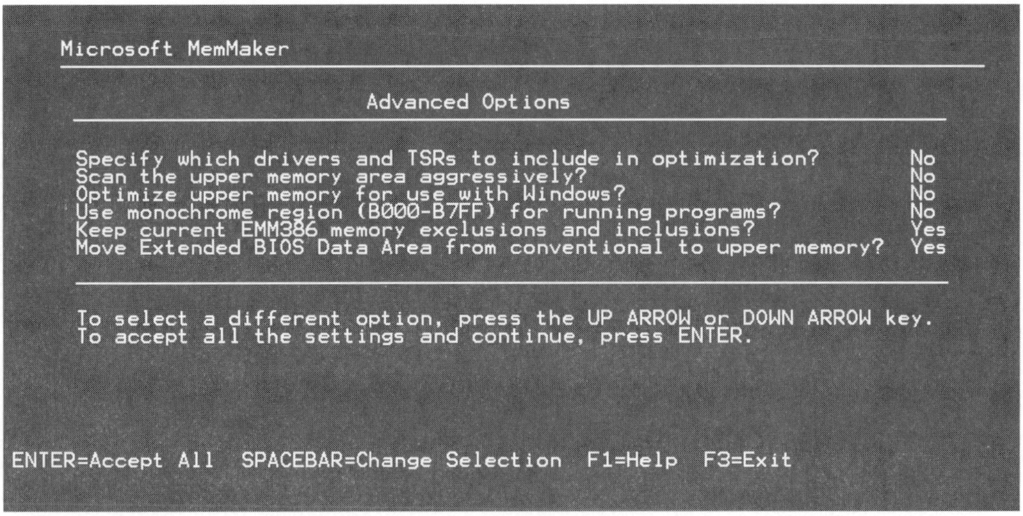

ner, whenever the Windows files are required to upgrade or reconfigure Windows, they are readily available. If Windows is installed from a CD-ROM, upgrades and reconfigurations to Windows require that CD-ROM to be readily available.

Windows 3.x is installed using the SETUP.EXE program found on the first disk of the Windows 3.x installation diskettes. This program has several command line options that are easily viewed by entering SETUP /?, as shown in Figure 14–11.

Figure 14–11
SETUP command line options.

```
Sets up Windows for Workgroups 3.11 on your system.
setup  [/N]  [/I]  [/O:file]  [/S:path]  [/B]  [/T]  [/C]
[/A]
       [/H:file] [/F]

 /N         - Sets up a shared copy of Windows for
              Workgroups from a network server.

 /I         - Ignores hardware detection. During Setup,
              the user will need to check accuracy of
              settings on the System Information screen,
              and possibly make corrections.

 /O:file  - Specifies the SETUP.INF file.

 /S:path  - Specifies a path to the setup disk(s).

 /B         - Allows use of a monochrome monitor with a
              color graphics card.

 /T         - Searches the drive for memory-resident
              (TSR) programs and notifies you about
              certain programs. For information about
              using specific programs with Setup or
              Windows for Workgroups, see SETUP.TXT.

 /C         - Turns off the search for memory-resident
              (TSR) programs.

 /A         - Administrative setup. Places Windows for
              Workgroups on a network server. Setup
              Expands and copies all files on every disk
              to a given directory, and marks them
              read-only.

 /H:file  - Batch mode setup. Sets up Windows for
              Workgroups with little or no user
              interaction. "File" is the name of the
              system settings file that contains user's
              configuration settings. If "file" is
              not in the directory from which Windows
              for Workgroups is being set up, the path
              must be included.

 /F         - Forces network card detection.
```

These options permit customization of the Windows 3.x installation process. Similar to the DOS SETUP.EXE program, Windows 3.x SETUP.EXE uses the F1 key to display help information, the F3 key to exit setup, Enter to select the menu choice, and arrow keys to move from menu item to menu item.

Setup provides both express and custom installation options. The express setup option will automatically configure the mouse, keyboard, and language options. When a network is present and detected, SETUP.EXE will configure it if it can determine the NIC hardware configuration. AUTOEXEC.BAT and CONFIG.SYS files are also configured. SETUP.EXE then proceeds to install the Windows 3.x files into a C:\Windows directory. See Figure 14–12.

Other express setup functions include searching all drives for available disk space when the disk space on drive C is not enough to hold the Windows installation files. Setup can also perform a partial installation of Windows if the disk space is insufficient for a full installation. When upgrading from a previous version of Windows, express setup duplicates the current printer installations. It also determines which applications are on the desktop and creates icons for specific standard programs.

In performing a custom setup, SETUP.EXE examines the PC's hardware configuration and reports that configuration to the person installing Windows 3.x. Once the configuration is identified and properly detected by the installation program, SETUP.EXE proceeds to copy the Windows 3.x program files onto the fixed disk. Once this is complete, Windows restarts. The remaining installation is performed using the Windows setup program. See Figure 14–13.

Figure 14–12
Windows 3.x setup.

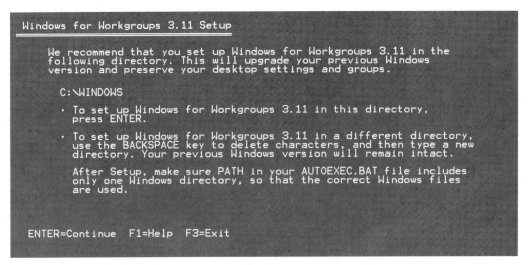

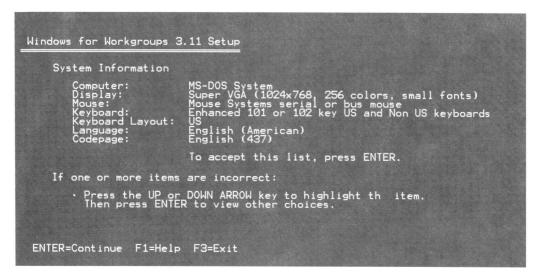

Figure 14–13
Windows 3.x hardware detection.

The Windows 3.x setup program can be used at any time to change the hardware configuration. It can be run from the DOS prompt, or launched through the Windows 3.x control panel using the Windows setup icon.

When Windows setup is launched using the control panel, the display in Figure 14–14 appears. The initial panel identifies the display, keyboard, mouse, and network settings for the installed version of Windows 3.x. Changes are made to the Windows 3.x configuration using drop-down menus. The options menu allows you to change the system settings that control the display, keyboard, and mouse configuration; change the network settings; set up applications; and add or remove Windows 3.x installed software components.

Figure 14–14
Windows 3.x control panel setup.

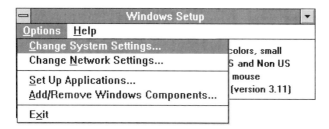

During installation, the Windows setup program performs three functions: setting up Windows components, setting up printers, and setting up applications already installed on the fixed disk. Setting up Windows components involves copying the system files, the accessory programs, the game programs, screen savers, and the wallpaper and sound files on the hard disk. Windows setup also permits customization of the Windows installation. You can select for copying individual files, groups of files, or all the files in one area. See Figure 14–15.

For a specific set of components like accessories, Windows permits selecting individual programs, such as the calculator, or selecting all accessory components. See Figure 14–16.

During the setup process, Windows provides the option to set the size and type of the virtual memory swap file. A permanent or temporary swap file can be selected. A permit swap file requires contiguous free disk space equal to the size of the swap file. Creating a permanent swap file creates two files, the swap file, 386SPART.PAR, and a control file, SPART.PAR. These files guarantee availability of a specific size of virtual memory. With a temporary swap file, there is no guarantee of specific available virtual memory because the contigu-

Figure 14–15
Choosing Windows 3.x components.

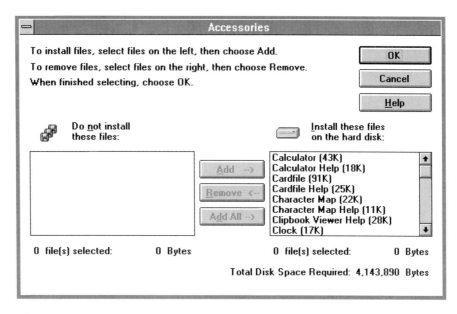

Figure 14–16
Selecting accessory components.

ous free disk space needed to store the swap file may diminish as the disk drive is used and becomes fragmented. The Windows 2000 swap file is called PAGE-FILE.SYS. See Figure 14–17 for Windows 3.x permanent swap file setup.

The best installation strategy is to set a permanent swap file, guaranteeing a specific amount of virtual memory is always the available to Windows. Windows 3.x automatically recommends an optimal swap file size based on the available contiguous free disk space and the PC's installed RAM, as well as specifies the maximum swap file size for the permanent swap file. Often the optimal and maximum sizes are the same. We prefer to set the swap file size at the maximum size automatically recommended by Windows 3.x.

It is also possible to set a permanent swap file with Windows 98/Me using the virtual memory settings. Selecting the Windows 98/Me Control Panel ➤ System ➤ Performance ➤ Virtual Memory and specifying your own virtual memory settings that are about 3 times bigger than the PC's RAM can fix the swap file size. This is like setting up a permanent swap file in Windows 3.x. Once you set the Windows 3.x swap file and specify what programs are to be installed, the selected Windows 3.x components are then copied to the fixed disk.

Printers can also be installed during initial setup or after Windows 3.x has been rebooted. The correct printer drivers should be installed for correctly

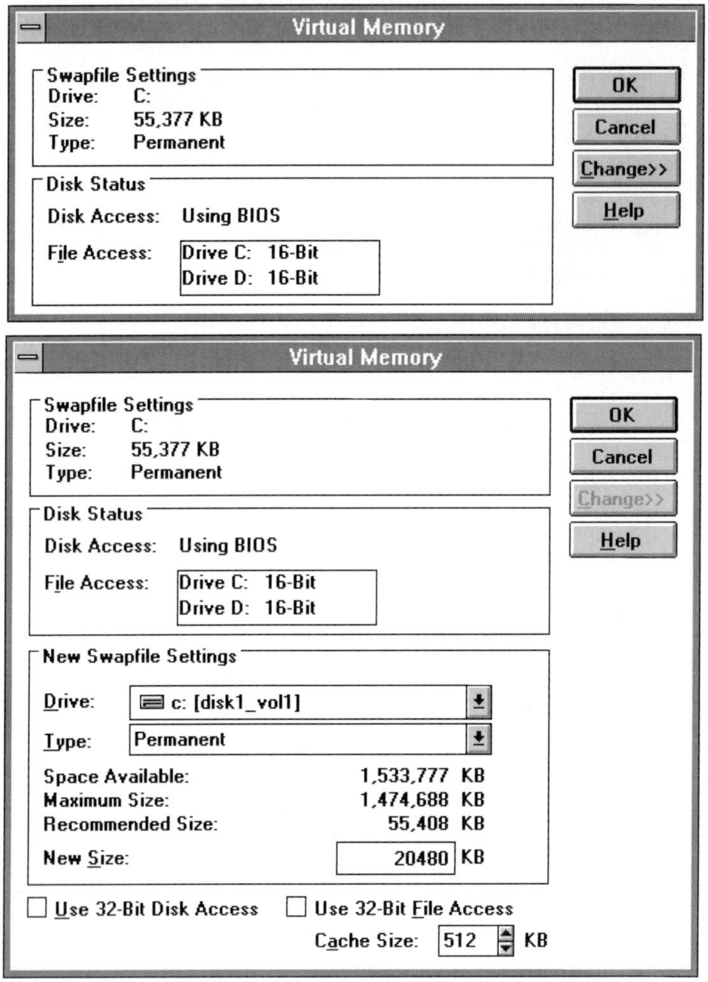

Figure 14-17

Virtual memory swap file setup.

attached parallel port printers and network printers that the computer uses. Installing a printer requires selecting the specific printer driver software from the list of available printers presented by Windows or using the printer drivers that are supplied by the printer manufacturer. See Figure 14–18.

Once a printer is selected, the driver programs are installed. When a printer is installed, it is set to use LPT1 as the default printer port. Windows automatically selects the first printer as the default printer for this PC, unless you

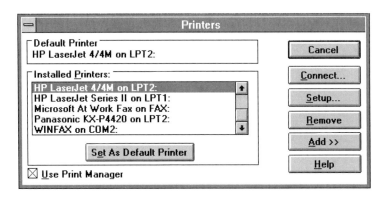

Figure 14–18
Windows printer setup.

have a network printer.In the last parts of the Windows 3.x installation process, Windows 3.x scans the fixed disks for applications, sets them up with icons in a program group, and gives the installer the option of installing the applications it discovers. Windows 3.x creates the standard program groups for the control panel, accessory programs, network programs, and more. It also creates the necessary CONFIG.SYS, AUTOEXEC.BAT, SYSTEM.INI, and WIN.INI files.

Directory Layout

The Windows 3.x programs are stored on the fixed disk in a Windows directory. This directory contains EXE, INI, DLL, BMP, RLE, FON/FOT/TTF, and HLP files.

- EXE files are the Windows 3.x applets and other programs that launch applications software under Windows.
- INI files are initialization files that hold configuration parameters for Windows programs and Windows applications programs. These parameters describe how the program will look while running under Windows.
- DLLs are the dynamic link library files implementing the application and Windows programs that run under Windows.
- BMPs are bit-mapped graphics used for icons and other Windows images.
- RLEs are compressed image files that contain the Windows start up display and other images.

- FON/FOT/TTF files are the files that describe the bit-mapped (FON) or TrueType fonts (FOT/TTF).

- HLP files contain the Windows help display information.

The accessory and game programs are EXE files residing in the Windows directory. The system directory is under the Windows directory, which also stores DLL

Figure 14–19

Windows 3.x directory layout.

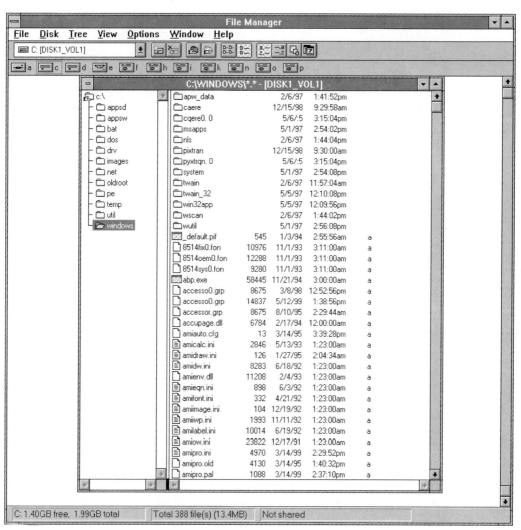

files. A good strategy with Windows 3.x is to place all the DLL files in the system directory even if the application install programs don't put them there. This avoids duplication of DLL files and the software errors that may result from such duplication. The system directory also contains driver programs (DRV) that control the PC hardware. Standard system applications are stored in other directories under the Windows directory or elsewhere as desired. See Figure 14–19. However, most third-party applications are not installed under the Windows directory, but are usually installed in default locations specified by the application vendor.

Driver Programs

The Windows 3.x driver programs include the standard display mouse and keyboard drivers as well as multimedia sound drivers, speaker drivers, communications drivers, and more. The Windows 3.x driver programs from a typical Windows 3.x installation are shown in Table 14–4.

Table 14–4 Windows 3.x driver programs

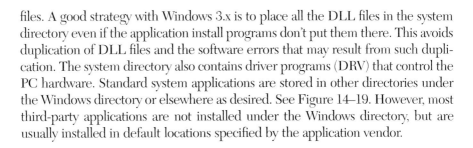

Display

VGA	DRV	73,200	11-01-93	3:11a
8514	DRV	92,032	11-01-93	3:11a
SUPERVGA	DRV	73,504	11-01-93	3:11a
SVGA256	DRV	117,440	11-01-93	4:11a
VGAMONO	DRV	45,616	05-01-90	3:00a
HVGA1280	DRV	82,384	04-21-92	3:13p
HVGA960	DRV	82,384	04-21-92	2:14p
STLTH32	DRV	157,616	03-15-94	12:42p
STLTH32B	DRV	102,480	03-15-94	12:43p
STLTH32H	DRV	140,096	03-15-94	12:42p
STLTH32T	DRV	163,392	03-15-94	12:43p

System

SPEAKER	DRV	7,088	05-28-92	4:44p
SOUND	DRV	3,440	11-01-93	3:11a
SYSTEM	DRV	2,304	11-01-93	4:11a
TIMER	DRV	4,192	11-01-93	4:11a
COMM	DRV	5,968	11-01-93	4:11a
KEYBOARD	DRV	7,568	11-01-93	4:11a
MSRLE	DRV	11,776	11-19-93	12:00a

MultiMedia Sound

MCIAVI	DRV	72,192	03-03-94	12:00a
MCICDA	DRV	13,824	11-01-93	4:11a
MCICMV50	DRV	86,816	05-26-94	12:00a
MCIMIXER	DRV	10,240	06-08-92	1:30a
MCIQTW	DRV	39,888	06-18-93	12:00a
MCISEQ	DRV	25,264	11-01-93	3:11a
MCIWAVE	DRV	28,160	11-01-93	3:11a
MIDIMAP	DRV	52,784	11-01-93	3:11a
MMSOUND	DRV	3,440	11-01-93	4:11a
ICCVID	DRV	58,880	11-19-93	12:00a

Mouse

MOUSE	DRV	10,672	11-01-93	3:11a
LMOUSE	DRV	12,928	11-01-93	3:11a
MSC3BC2	DRV	4,832	11-01-93	3:11a
MSCMOUSE	DRV	4,960	11-01-93	4:11a
MSMOUSE1	DRV	2,176	14-31-90	3:00a
MSMOUSE2	DRV	2,176	14-31-90	3:00a

Network

WFWNET	DRV	308,864	11-01-93	4:11a
NETWARE	DRV	165,632	14-24-94	2:29p

Printer

HPPCL	DRV	152,192	11-01-93	3:11a
HPPCL5A	DRV	428,672	03-14-92	3:10a
HPPCL5E	DRV	399,888	11-01-93	3:11a
PROPRINT	DRV	8,288	11-01-93	3:11a
PSCRIPT	DRV	314,576	11-01-93	4:11a

Fax Drivers

WINFAX	DRV	28,000	04-15-93	12:00a
EFAXDRV	DRV	11,776	11-01-93	3:11a
ENVOYDRV	DRV	182,352	06-24-94	12:00a
QLFXDRVR	DRV	18,741	02-16-93	1:32p
WFXCOMM	DRV	9,488	04-01-93	12:00a
WSP48024	DRV	123,920	07-14-92	4:47p
WSPDPBF	DRV	111,824	07-14-92	12:56p
WSPDPSF	DRV	109,376	07-14-92	12:55p

The table shows the standard Windows 3.x display drivers: VGA.DRV, 8514.DRV, SUPERVGA.DRV, SVGA256.DRV, and VGAMONO.DRV. The VGA card manufacturer provides the other display drivers for the specific VGA card installed in the PC if the standard drivers don't work. The standard Windows 3.x system drivers are SPEAKER.DRV, SOUND.DRV, the SYSTEM.DRV, TIMER.DRV, KEYBOARD.DRV and MSRLE.DRV. The MSRLE.DRV is a driver program that works with run length encoded (RLE) files, which contain compressed images. The RLE files used by Windows 3.x are wallpaper bitmaps. Windows 3.x generally installs a single mouse driver. On this PC, all Windows 3.x mouse drivers are installed to illustrate all possible mouse driver programs, because most PCs have some mouse different from an MS mouse. The most common and universal driver is the Logitech mouse driver. This is also true of Windows today. These drivers cover Microsoft mice, Logitech mice, and Mouse Systems mice. Hewlett-Packard laser printer drivers are also installed. This PC was set up with fax software, so there are special fax drivers to add as well.

These driver programs reside in the C:\WINDOWS\SYSTEM directory. GRP files describe the Windows 3.x program groups. These files can be created and modified using the Windows 3.x program manager. The registry concept was first used in Windows 3.x. There is a single REG.DAT file that is the Windows 3.x registry. It can be viewed using the command REGEDIT /V. This Registry stores information on applications running under Windows 3.x to support dynamic data exchange between applications. It is not central to Windows itself.

Windows 3.x installation is menu-driven. Running the Windows 3.x SETUP.EXE program on a DOS 6.2x PC with memory configured to use XMS starts the Windows 3.x installation process. The installation process creates a Windows directory, copies key files into that directory, and configures Windows INI flies. It can also scan for existing applications and install them automatically into program groups. At that point, the basic Windows 3.x installation is complete.

Windows 95/98/Me Installation

Setup for Windows 95/98/Me can be performed from within Windows or from the DOS command prompt. In both cases, setup is completed using a Windows setup program and an installation wizard. A wizard is a program that leads the PC user step-by-step through a procedure, providing explanations of each step along the way. These explanations are provided in dialogue boxes with buttons indicating the next step. See Figure 14–20.

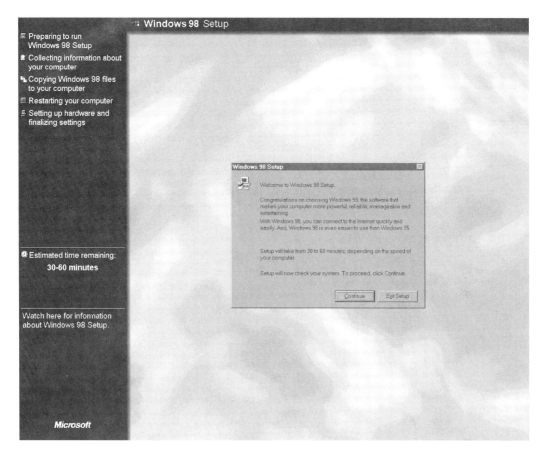

Figure 14–20
Windows 98 setup dialog box.

Similar to Windows 3.x and DOS, Windows 95/98/Me is installed using a Windows 95/98/Me SETUP.EXE program.

There are several versions of Windows 95, two versions of Windows 98, and Windows Me. The Windows 95 versions are the original release of Windows (950 or revision A), operating system release 2 (OSR2 or revision B), and the final revision C. Windows 98 has an original release and the Windows 98 SE (special edition), which is similar to Windows 95 OSR2. Each revision had slightly different features and capabilities. For example, Windows 95 revision A did not support the 32-bit FAT, while revisions B and C did. Furthermore, revision C supported the USB bus.

The original version of Windows 95 could be installed using either floppy diskettes or a CD-ROM. The floppies were provided because not all PCs had a

CD-ROM drive installed. There were about 19 floppy diskettes required to install Windows 95, as opposed to a single CD-ROM. However, in order to install all the CD-ROM files, a working CD-ROM drive was required under DOS. The Windows 95 startup disk did not support the CD-ROM drive, but the Windows 98 startup disk does, making installation from a CD-ROM very easy.

Because DOS and Windows 3.x did not automatically support a CD-ROM drive, original equipment manufacturers (OEM) generally copied the Windows 95/98/Me installation files to the fixed disk in a folder called \windows\options\cabs. They then installed Windows 95/98/Me from this fixed disk directory.

The Windows 95/98/Me installation files consist predominantly of CAB files, several EXE files like SETUP.EXE and SCANDISK.EXE, and other supporting TXT, BIN, and INF files. The CAB, or cabinet, files contain the Windows 95/98/Me software and configuration files. These CAB files are special compressed files created to contain the Windows 95/98/Me software. The Windows 98 startup diskette has a CAB file created on it that contains diagnostic and other software needed to fix a corrupted Windows 98 installation.

Running Setup

The SETUP.EXE program for Windows 98 and Windows Me have command line options shown in Figure 14–21 similar to the command line options for Windows 3.1 x SETUP.EXE. The SETUP.EXE program for Windows 95 is slightly different from the SETUP.EXE program for Windows 98. Similarly, Windows 98 SETUP.EXE options are slightly different from those of Windows Me. The Windows 95 setup program has /C, /iL, and /in options that are not provided by the Windows 98 setup program. The /C option causes the SMARTDRV disk cache program not to be loaded, the /iL option loads a Logitech mouse driver in place of the Microsoft mouse driver, and finally the /in option runs setup without performing the network setup. Windows 98 has three options that Windows 95 setup does not have: /ie, which bypasses the emergency diskette creation; /ih, which skips the registry check; and /iv, which bypasses the Windows displays seen during the setup process. The Windows Me options are in the bottom panel of Figure 14–21. Windows Me does not provide the /id and /iq options available with Windows 98 that permit ignoring the disk space check and checking for cross linked files. The Windows 95/98/Me SETUP.EXE program runs a Real Mode SCANDISK check, copies the files needed to run the Windows setup program, and then launches Windows setup.

```
Setup Options: SETUP [/C] [/iL] [batch] [/T:tmp] [/im] [/id] [/is] [/iq] [/in]
   /C          Instructs Setup not to load the SmartDrive disk cache.
   /iL         Loads the Logitech mouse driver instead of the Microsoft
               mouse driver. Use this option if you have a Logitech
               Series C mouse.
   [batch]     Specifies the name and location of the file that contains
               Setup options.
   /T:tmp      Specifies the directory where Setup will copy its temporary
               files. If the directory doesn't exist, it will be created.
               WARNING: Any existing files in this directory will be deleted.
   /im         Skips the memory check.
   /id         Skips the disk-space check.
   /is         Doesn't run ScanDisk.
   /iq         Skips the check for cross-linked files.
   /in         Runs Setup without the Network Setup module.
Note: The /a and /n options are no longer valid. Use NETSETUP.EXE instead.
```

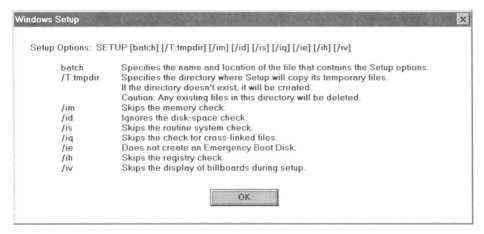

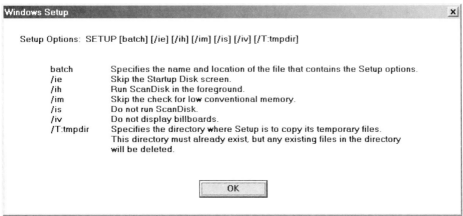

Figure 14–21
SETUP.EXE command display comparison.

Windows 98/Me installation steps are:

1. Prepare to run Windows Setup. See Figure 14–22.
2. Collect information on the PC.
3. Copy Windows files to the PC.
4. Restart the PC.
5. Set up the hardware and finalize settings.

When Windows sets up and runs the Windows SETUP.EXE program, it soon displays the Windows end user license agreement (EULA) dialog box as part of the process of collecting information on your PC. See Figure 14–23.

Figure 14–22
Windows Me preparing to run Windows setup.

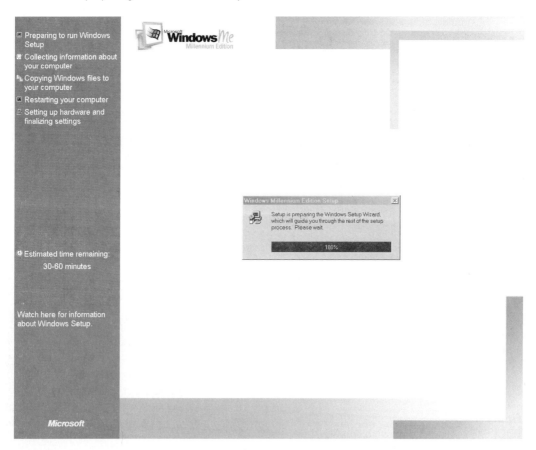

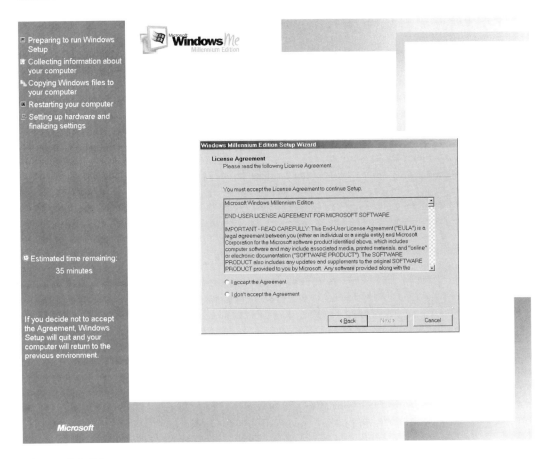

Figure 14–23
Windows Me EULA dialog box.

It then creates a setup log file, identifies where Windows is to be installed, creates a temporary installation directory, and runs the installation wizard program.

The wizard program gathers information about your computer. Windows setup reviews the license agreement, asks the user to enter the product key code, asks the user to select or specify the directory into which to install Windows and then prepares this directory, as shown in Figure 14–24.

Next, the Windows 95/98 setup program, through the Windows setup wizard, permits the installer to select typical, portable, compact, or custom setup. These options pre-select certain groups of files to install or not install, depending on the PC's available disk space. These options can be viewed as Microsoft recommendations for different types of computers. In all cases, the installer can cus-

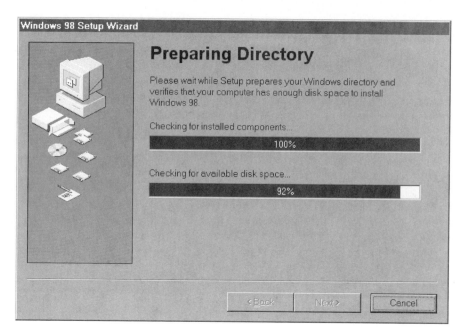

Figure 14–24
Windows directory preparation.

tomize the Windows 95/98 installation as though the custom setup were selected. Further Windows components can always be added after the initial installation is completed using the control panel and add/remove programs. See Figure 14–25. For that type of PC operation, Microsoft uses these installation options only to pre-select specific Windows software components, as it deems best.

Windows setup requests the user to enter name and company information. The user can also specify at different times in the Windows 95 and Windows 98 installation process the Windows components to install. As shown in Figure 14–26, the Windows accessories are listed, permitting them to be individually selected for installation. When selected, the amount of disk space required is displayed. The selection box also displays the amount of disk space required by setup and the amount of disk space available to install Windows.

Upon entry of the username and company information, Windows 95 and 98/Me vary slightly in the installation process. Windows 95 analyzes your computer at this point, as shown in Figure 14–27.

After the analysis is complete, Windows 95 setup moves to selecting Windows software components depending on the setup option (typical, portable, compact, or custom setup) selected. Windows 95 completes network component selection

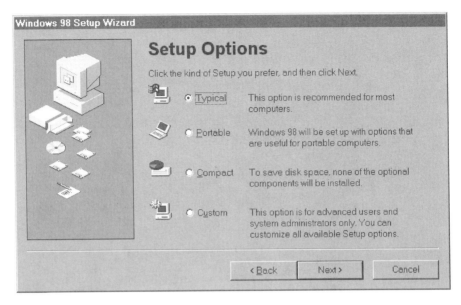

Figure 14–25
Windows95/98 setup options.

Figure 14–26
Accessory component selections.

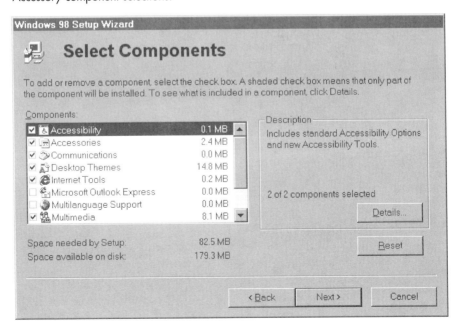

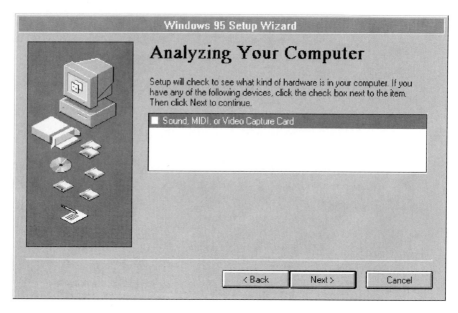

Figure 14–27
Windows 95 PC analysis.

and then enters the computer identification information. Upon completion, a startup diskette is created based on user input. Then Windows 95 setup copies the requisite Windows files to the fixed disk. Once Windows setup has copied the necessary files to the fixed disk, the PC is restarted.

In contrast, Windows 98 moves directly to selecting Windows software components, depending on the setup option (typical, portable, compact, or custom setup) selected. Then Windows 98 performs the PC analysis done earlier in the sequence by Windows 95. The Windows 98 hardware analysis performed at this time is more accurate than the hardware analysis performed by Windows 95 because only Windows 98 software programs are running.

The final step, installing the plug-and-play hardware and finalizing the Windows settings, is performed during the Windows boot process. Windows displays the message "Getting ready to start Windows 98 for the first time." In this final stage, Windows setup configures the control panel, the start menu, Windows help files, MS-DOS program settings, the applications to start automatically, the date and time settings, and the final system configuration.

Windows installation can be performed on a new system or on an existing Windows system. When performed on an existing Windows system, the installation process does not change the application software settings. It does, however, redo the hardware installation settings. Often, reinstalling Windows over

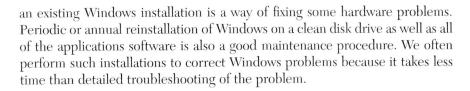
an existing Windows installation is a way of fixing some hardware problems. Periodic or annual reinstallation of Windows on a clean disk drive as well as all of the applications software is also a good maintenance procedure. We often perform such installations to correct Windows problems because it takes less time than detailed troubleshooting of the problem.

Directory (Folder) Layout

Windows 95/98/Me directory or folder layout is different from Windows 3.x directory layout. In both cases, Windows by default installs itself in a C:\Windows directory or folder. See Figure 14–28.

At the root directory level, Windows 95/98/Me adds some other important folders. These folders are the "program files" folder, the "recycled" folder, the "my documents" folder and the "multimedia files" folder. Of these new folders, the most used (aside from the Windows folder) and thus most important are the program files folder and the recycled folder. Application programs are generally installed in the program files folder by default. Data erased from the fixed disk is placed in the recycled folder so that it may be retrieved later if it was removed by mistake. The recycled folder must be periodically emptied. Windows provides a menu option for emptying the recycle bin and clearing the recycled folder.

Under the C:\Windows folder there are some additional folders specific to Windows 95/98/Me. As with Windows 3.x, there is the system subdirectory or folder that holds DLL, EXE, DRV, HLP, and other files. There are also important subdirectories under the system subdirectory. One key subdirectory is the IOSYS subdirectory that contains the VxD and MPD (MIDI port driver) files.

Another key folder is the Start Menu folder, which establishes the structure for the start menu, the application, and Windows components that are installed on the PC. The start menu structure itself is in a programs folder under the Start Menu folder. See Figure 14–29. In the programs folder is a startup folder (or subdirectory). Items placed in the startup folder are launched automatically during the Windows boot process. Not all programs that start automatically are launched using the startup folder. Some programs are launched automatically from entries in the Windows 95/98/Me registry. Details on the registry are provided in Chapter 11.

Changing or rearranging the folders under the programs subdirectory changes and rearranges the start menu items.

The desktop folder contains the items visible on the desktop. As things are added to or removed from the desktop, the contents of this folder (or subdirectory) change. Other folders are related to Internet software, i.e., the cookies folder, the downloaded program files folder, the history folder,

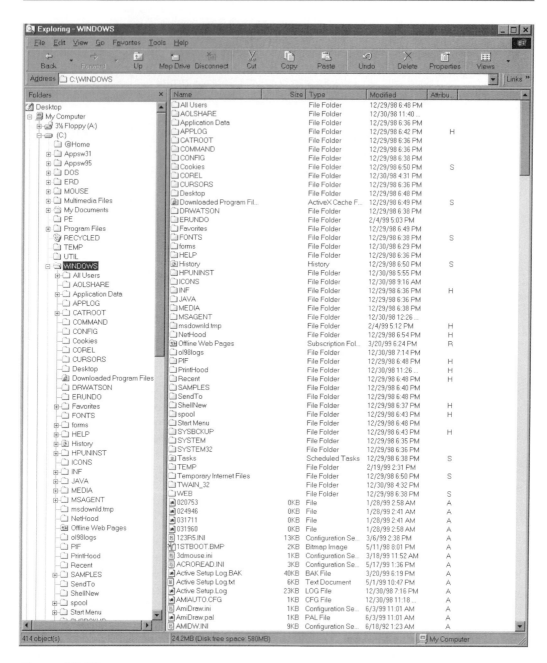

Figure 14–28
Windows directory layout.

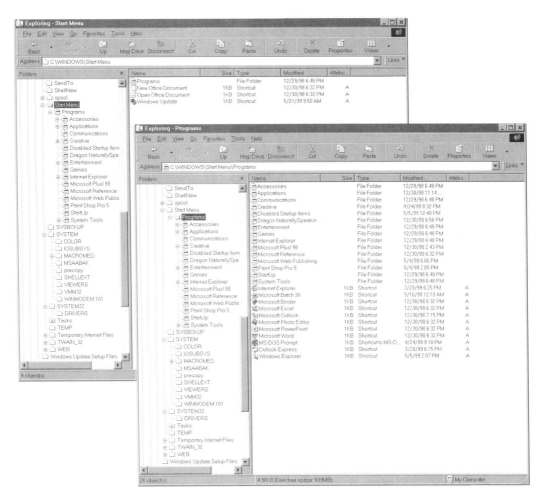

Figure 14–29
Windows Start Menu folder.

MSdownld.TMP folder (sometimes found on a PC when Windows has been upgraded using the Internet update option), and the temporary Internet files folder among others. The fonts used by Windows 95/98/Me are stored in the fonts folder in the Windows folder.

The operation and look of Windows is controlled by the contents of special file folders in the Windows folder and in the root directory. We will examine a few of the key folders here.

867

Driver Programs—DOS Mode vs. 32 bit

Both 32-bit Windows driver programs and 16-bit DOS mode compatible driver programs work with Windows 95/98/Me. Windows 32-bit driver programs provide the best PC performance because they operate correctly with the hardware and do not rely on ROM BIOS. If possible, the Windows 32-bit driver programs should always be used. This can be checked using the Windows control panel, selecting system, and then the performance tab. See Figure 14–30. This displays whether the 32-bit driver programs or the 16-bit driver programs are being used for the file system and the virtual memory. These are equivalent to the Windows 3.x 32-bit disk and 32-bit file access drivers.

Figure 14–30
Windows 32-bit driver programs.

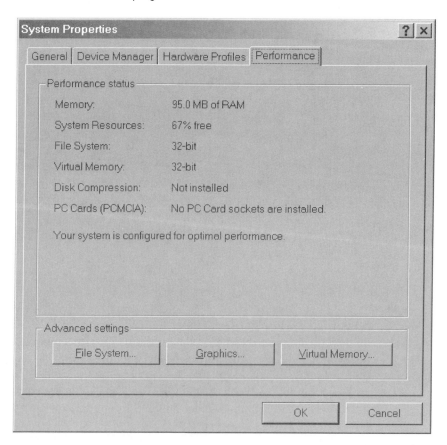

When 16-bit driver programs are installed, the performance tab displays a message stating 16-bit driver programs are used for MS-DOS compatibility. In this case, the DOS drivers in the CONFIG.SYS and AUTOEXEC.BAT file for the CD-ROM may be installed. Removing the CONFIG.SYS and AUTOEXEC.BAT drivers should normally cause Windows to install the proper 32-bit Windows drivers. The Windows 32-bit drivers are the VxD files found in the IOSYS folder.

Plug-and-Play Components

Windows 95/98/Me provides for plug-and-play hardware component installation. This plug-and-play hardware component installation is dependent on the PC's BIOS as well as the hardware component itself. Both must be designed to work with the Windows plug-and-play software, which works more effectively in Windows 98, Windows Me, and Windows 2000 than in Windows 95. Part of the increased effectiveness results from how the plug-and-play process is performed during Windows installation. Remember, Windows 98/Me performs the final plug-and-play analysis after the system is rebooted. This means that only Windows 98/Me software components are running while the plug-and-play installation process is being completed. As a result, Windows 98/Me makes fewer mistakes in configuring hardware plug-and-play components. The plug-and-play hardware installation can be run at any time using the control panel to select Install New Hardware. See Figure 14–31.

Windows plug-and-play installation is a function of the Windows software and the PC's BIOS. They work together to permit Windows to identify all plug-and-play hardware components installed in the PC and to properly configure their IRQs, I/O addresses, and memory regions. Generally, all PCI bus components are plug-and-play, as are some specially designed ISA bus components. Components with hardware jumper settings are generally not plug-and-play devices.

An alternative way to make Windows 95/98/Me perform plug-and-play hardware installation is to actually remove the hardware driver from Windows 95/98/Me. This is done by opening the control panel, selecting system, selecting device manager, opening the device, and removing the device from the Windows configuration. This approach works well with multimedia devices, communications ports, network adapters, modems, and some display adapters.

It is not a good idea to remove disk drives from the Windows configuration in this manner because once the disk drive is removed, Windows cannot write the registry information to the disk drive. The registry was discussed earlier in Chapter 11. After a disk drive is removed, Windows believes it has no disk drive to write to. This can cause Windows to lock (abruptly halt operation).

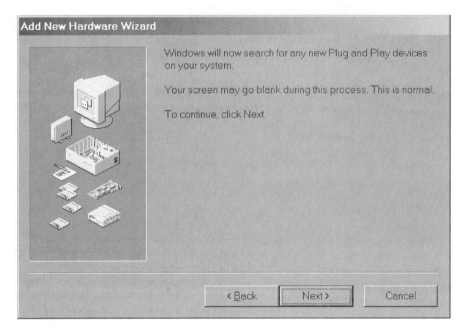

Figure 14–31
Windows plug-and-play hardware configuration.

Another way to force hardware reinstallation is to set up a new hardware profile. Forcing hardware reinstallation can sometimes resolve Windows plug-and-play installation problems. This is done using the hardware profiles tab.

The current profile "original configuration" is copied to a new hardware profile name. Windows is then restarted. During the restart process, Windows asks which profile to use to start Windows. Three choices are given: (1) original configuration, (2) new configuration, and (3) none of the above. Selecting none of the above causes Windows to perform the plug-and-play hardware installation for all devices. This sometimes resolves plug-and-play hardware problems, but there is of course no guarantee that it will.

Study Break: Hardware Profiles

This study break deals with Windows 95/98/Me hardware profiles, their implementation, management, and helpfulness in the troubleshooting process. We will create a new hardware profile, reboot Windows to see what this does to the Windows reboot process, and then remove the profile.

Using a Windows 95, Windows 98 or a Windows Me PC, open the control panel, then select system and hardware profiles. This should display a panel showing the "original configuration" hardware profile.

Select copy and enter the title "current" in the "To" box. Click OK. Now two configurations should appear in the configuration box. One should be current and one should be the original configuration.

Click OK. Shut down and restart Windows; you should now be presented with a menu option to select between current, original configuration, or none of the above as the hardware profile in which Windows is started. Select current as the hardware configuration in which to start Windows.

After Windows is running, open the control panel and select the system icon. Double-click to open system properties, then select device manager. Pick the ports icon and expand it by clicking on the "+." Select a communications port, preferably COM2. Open properties and check disable in this hardware profile. Click OK. This should return you to the device manager screen where the communications port COM2 is displayed with a red X, indicating it has been disabled.

Restart Windows and now select original configuration as the hardware profile for Windows. Once Windows is running, open the control panel and select the system icon. Double-click to open system properties, then select device manager. Expand the communications port icon as before. In this case the COM2 port should not be disabled because it was disabled only in the "current" hardware profile.

Open hardware profiles again. Select "original configuration" and attempt to delete it. Because it is in use, Windows should prevent you from deleting this configuration. Next delete the "current" configuration. Since this configuration is not in use, it can be deleted.

Restart Windows at this point. Now no hardware configuration profile needs to be selected because we have returned Windows to its original configuration.

The goal of this exercise was to illustrate how Windows works with different hardware profiles. If we had selected "none of the above" during our reboot process, Windows would perform a complete hardware analysis to reconfigure the plug-and-play hardware in the PC.

Windows NT/2000/XP Installation

Windows 2000/XP implements plug-and-play hardware installation like Windows 95/98/Me, but Windows NT does not. This means that hardware drivers and standardized disk drives were very important for Windows NT to install and run properly. The range of hardware components supported by NT was narrow compared to those supported by Windows 95/98/Me and by Windows 2000/XP. Neither Windows NT nor Windows 2000/XP uses the same hardware driver programs, as do Windows 95/98/Me. Generally, most hardware manufacturers make Windows 9x drivers for Windows 95/98/Me and Windows NT as well as Windows 2000/XP drivers. These may be separate driver programs for each operating system.

Although Windows 2000/XP installation is similar to Windows 98/Me installation, there are some significant added steps and considerations in Windows NT/2000/XP installation. Generally, the basic hardware install uses a Wizard that follows a procedure very similar to that used by the Windows 98/Me installation Wizard. However, extra care must be made to use Windows NT/2000/XP compatible hardware. You must choose whether to use FAT or NTFS, and the added security of Windows NT/2000/XP requires an administrator to set up an administrative password, a user account, and password on the Windows NT/2000/XP PC.

Before installing Windows 2000/XP or Windows NT, be sure that the key PC hardware components including MLB, CPU, display adapter, disk drive controller, and disk drive are compatible. In the support folder on the Windows 2000 installation CD is the hardware compatibility list (HCL.TXT file) that lists all hardware tested with Windows 2000/XP. Hardware compatibility lists for all Windows products are available on Microsoft's web site at:

`http://www.microsoft.com/hcl/`

This site lists the latest Windows compatible hardware. Additional drivers and compatibility information would also be available at the hardware manufacturer's web site. The best authority on hardware compatibility would be Microsoft. Incompatible hardware components cause Windows NT/2000/XP installation to rudely fail (the significant word here is rudely). Windows XP has more plug-and-play hardware device drivers than does Windows 2000 or Windows NT.

The MLB, display, and disk controller BIOS should be the latest updated version of the BIOS. Windows 2000/XP depends on these BIOS for the plug-and-play and power management features to work properly. A failure of the plug-and-play installation causes abrupt Windows 2000 installation failures. Windows 2000 had just completed installation only to reboot from the power off state because the PC we installed it on did not have the latest display BIOS and companion Windows 2000 driver programs.

We always believe a fresh install is the best policy. Windows 2000/XP is set up to upgrade readily from previous versions of Windows. However, little extra time is required for a fresh install of Windows 2000 and the applications commonly used on the PC, and a fresh install has a much greater assurance that problems do not unexpectedly crop up from some remnant of a previous Windows installation.

Windows NT/2000/XP is installed from the I386 folder that resides on a fixed disk drive, CD-ROM, or network drive. The Windows install CD-ROM can create Windows NT, Windows 2000, or Windows XP setup diskettes using the MAKEBOOT.EXE. The MAKEBOOT command for Windows 2000 does this:

```
E:\BOOTDISK>makeboot /?
****************************************************
This program creates the Setup boot disks
for Microsoft Windows 2000.
To create these disks, you need to provide 4 blank,
formatted, high-density disks.
```

Although these disks can be created, we like installing Windows 2000/XP using a Windows 98/Me startup diskette. This diskette can be used to prepare a fixed disk drive, copy the I386 folder to the drive, and run the WINNT.EXE setup program that installs Windows XP, Windows 2000, or Windows NT.

The WINNT.EXE options are:

```
WINNT [/s[:sourcepath]] [/t[:tempdrive]]
     [/u[:answer file]] [/udf:id[,UDF_file]]
     [/r:folder] [/r[x]:folder] [/e:command] [/a]
```

1. /s[:sourcepath]
    Specifies the location of the Windows 2000 installation files. The location must be specified as a full path of the form x:[path] or \servershare[path].

2. /t[:tempdrive]
    Setup places temporary files on the specified drive and installs Windows 2000/XP on that drive. When a location is not specified, Setup attempts to locate a drive for you.

3. /u[:answer file]
   Performs an unattended Setup using an answer file (requires /s).
   The answer file provides answers to the prompts that the user nor-
   mally responds to during Setup.

4. /udf:id[,UDF_file]
   Setup uses an identifier (id) to specify how a Uniqueness Database
   File (UDF) modifies an answer file (see /u).The /udf parameter
   overrides values in the answer file, and the identifier determines
   which values in the UDF file are used.

5. /r[:folder]
   Specifies an optional folder to be installed that remains after Setup
   finishes.

6. /rx[:folder]
   Specifies an optional folder to be copied that is deleted after Setup
   finishes.

7. /e
   Specifies a command that is executed at the end of GUI-mode
   Setup.

8. /a
   Enables accessibility options.

Windows NT/2000/XP can be set up from within Windows by using
WINNT32.EXE. WINNT32.EXE sets up or upgrades Windows 2000/XP and
can be run from a Windows 95, Windows 98, Windows Me or Windows NT
command prompt. Its options are:

```
WINNT32 [/s:sourcepath] [/tempdrive:drive_letter]
[/unattend[num]:[answer_file]] [/copydir:folder_name]
[/copysource:folder_name] [/cmd:command_line]
[/debug[level]:[filename]] [/udf:id[,UDF_file]]
[/syspart:drive_letter] [/checkupgradeonly]
[/cmdcons]
[/m:folder_name] [/makelocalsource] [/noreboot]
```

1. /s:sourcepath
   Specifies the location of the Windows 2000/XP I386 folder installation files. Specify multiple /s sources to simultaneously copy files
   from multiple servers, When multiple /s switches are used, the first
   specified server must be available or Setup fails.

2. /tempdrive:drive_letter
   Setup places temporary files on the specified partition and installs Windows 2000/XP in that partition.

3. /unattend
   Upgrades previous versions of Windows 2000, Windows NT 3.51–4.0, Windows Me, Windows 98, or Windows 95 in unattended Setup mode. All user settings are taken from the previous installation, so no user intervention is required during Setup. Using the /unattend switch to automate Setup requires reading and accepting the End User License Agreement (EULA) for Windows 2000.

4. /unattend[num]:[answer_file]
   Performs a fresh installation in unattended Setup mode. The answer file provides Setup with custom specifications. Num is the number of seconds between the time that Setup finishes copying the files and when it restarts the PC. Num is used on any computer running Windows NT or Windows 2000. Answer_file is the name of the answer file.

5. /copydir:folder_name
   Creates an additional folder within the folder where the Windows 2000 files are installed. When a source folder contains a folder called Private_drivers that has modifications for a specific site, type /copydir:Private_drivers so that Setup copies that folder to the installed Windows 2000 folder. The new folder location would be C:\Winnt\Private_drivers. Use /copydir to create as many additional folders as needed.

6. /copysource:folder_name
   Creates a temporary additional folder within the folder where the Windows 2000 files are installed. When a source folder contains a folder called Private_drivers that has modifications just for specific site, type /copysource:Private_drivers so that Setup copies that folder to the installed Windows 2000 folder and uses its files during Setup. The temporary folder location would be C:\Winnt\Private_drivers. Unlike folders that /copydir creates, /copysource folders are deleted after Setup completes.

7. /cmd:command_line
   Causes Setup to execute a specific command before the last Setup phase. This occurs after the computer has restarted twice and after Setup has collected needed configuration information, but before Setup is complete.

8. /debug[level]:[filename]

   Creates a debug log at the level specified. The default log file is
   C:\%Windir%\Winnt32.log. The default debug level is set to 2.
   The debug log levels are: 0-severe errors, 1-errors, 2-warnings, 3-
   information, and 4-detailed information for debugging. Each level
   includes all levels below it.

9. /udf:id[,UDB_file]

   Sets up an identifier (id) that Setup uses to specify how a
   Uniqueness Database (UDB) file modifies an answer file (See the
   /unattend entry). The UDB overrides data in the answer file. The
   identifier determines which values in the UDB file are used.

10. /syspart:drive_letter

    Specifies that Setup can copy startup files to a hard disk, and mark
    the disk as active. The disk can then be installed in another PC.
    When that computer starts, the next Setup phase automatically
    begins. The /tempdrive parameter must always be used with the
    /syspart parameter. The /syspart switch for Winnt32.exe only runs
    from computers that already have Windows NT 3.51, Windows
    NT 4.0, or Windows 2000 installed on it. It cannot be run from
    Windows 9x computers.

11. /checkupgradeonly

    Checks the computer for upgrade compatibility with
    Windows 2000. For Windows 95 or Windows 98 upgrades, Setup
    creates a report named Upgrade.txt in the Windows installation
    folder. For Windows NT 3.51 or 4.0 upgrades, it saves the report
    to the Winnt32.log in the installation folder.

12. /cmdcons

    This adds a Recovery Console option to the operating system
    selection screen. The Recovery Console option repairs a failed
    installation. It is only used post-Setup.

13. /m:folder_name

    Specifies copying files from an alternate location. Setup looks in
    the alternate location first and if files are present, uses them
    instead of the files from the default location.

14. /makelocalsource

    Setup copies all installation source files to the local hard disk.
    When /makelocalsource is used while installing from a CD, instal-
    lation files are provided from the local fixed disk if the CD is not
    available later in the installation.

15. /noreboot

    Setup does not restart the computer after the file copy phase of WINNT32 is completed so that other commands can be executed.

Once the WINNT or WINNT32 programs are run, the setup Wizard steps automatically through the installation process prompting for user input as needed. The Windows setup program prompts for the file system to use. At that point you can delete any existing partitions and create new partitions as desired. DoubleSpace or DriveSpace compressed drives should be converted to uncompressed drives before installing Windows NT/2000/XP. Dual boot PCs must use a FAT partition for Windows 9.x but Windows NT/2000/XP PCs can use NTFS alone. If a PC boots into Windows 9.x or DOS, Windows NT/2000/XP automatically makes it into a dual boot PC.

After selecting a file system, the disk is tested and the installation files are copied to the fixed disk drive. The PC then reboots to continue setup using a Windows 2000 GUI. The PC is inspected and device drivers are installed for the hardware found. Setup continues with a Wizard that gets user input to verify the installation key, set up regional date and time settings, enter user and company names, set a computer name and an administrative password (write this down), and collect network workgroup or domain identification and settings. After all the information is collected, Windows 2000 offers to install additional operating system components like the Internet Information Server (IIS). This phase is concluded by setting up the start menu, creating and configuring registry entries for selected components, saving the settings, and removing the temporary files used during installation. Windows 2000 is once again restarted.

At this point the basic Windows 2000 installation is complete. Now a user account must be set up in addition to the administrator account. During the reboot process, a logon dialog box requests that you strike CTRL-ALT-DEL. Next, a username and password are requested to logon to the PC. This creates a basic user account, but blocks that user from administering the PC. Logging on as the administrator using the proper password permits user accounts to be created with full administrative privileges. Once the user information is completed, Windows 2000 setup is virtually finished, save for some added network configuration. The final step in Windows XP installation is registering Windows XP online. This bonds XP to the specific PC on which it is installed.

Software Upgrades

With DOS and Windows software products, upgrading from previous versions to newer versions is a planned migration path. Upgrade and new installation procedures are both designed into the newer versions of Windows. The goal of upgrade procedures is to preserve the existing application software installation. This saves time by not requiring all application software to be reinstalled when upgrading from one version of software to another. There are typically two drawbacks to the upgrade process. Generally when upgrading from one version of software to the next version of software, the newer software requires significantly increased hardware capabilities. These capabilities may not be installed on the existing PC. This is particularly true of free capacity on the fixed disk drive. Newer versions of software tend to require significantly increased storage capacities. For example, Windows 3.x could be installed on a 512MB disk drive. Upgrading to Windows 98 could require as much as 355MB of disk space. As a result, the upgrade may not be possible in this instance.

The second problem comes from the installed software itself. If the system has a bad software blend—that is, it does not run properly and crashes frequently—then installing an upgrade on top of a bad software installation can easily make things worse. The best strategy in this case is to start fresh by reformatting the fixed disk, then installing Windows and the application software to be used on the PC.

Upgrades preserve the existing Windows software configuration. When an existing Windows software configuration is operating reliably, then preserving that configuration is a good upgrade strategy. If, however, the existing software configuration is not reliable and solid, then a fresh configuration that removes the existing Windows installation is most likely the better strategy. In all cases, when upgrading a Windows configuration does not go smoothly for whatever reason, a fresh installation usually resolves the problems encountered.

Users should consider upgrading to new releases of Windows whenever they become available. Generally, a new release operates more reliably and predictably than older Windows versions. For example, when Windows 95 was first released, it was more reliable than Windows 3.x. Similarly, the first release of Windows 98 was an improvement in reliability over that of Windows 95. While features also evolved to more user-friendly levels with each release of the Windows operating system, reliability is a more important factor in the move to upgrade from one version of Windows to another. The major drawback to upgrading is that some systems are operating reliably and predictably as configured with earlier versions of Windows. The maxim, "When it ain't broke, don't upgrade it" applies to those PCs reliably running earlier versions of Windows. Some of our PCs ran Windows 3.x and Windows 95 for months without being restarted. They encountered no problems during these periods, and there was no need to rush to upgrade them. In contrast, several PCs that were always running newer Windows applications operated less reliably with older, earlier versions of Windows than with newer versions of Windows. In general, Windows 95 is more reliable than Windows 3.x, Windows 98 is more reliable

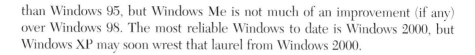

than Windows 95, but Windows Me is not much of an improvement (if any) over Windows 98. The most reliable Windows to date is Windows 2000, but Windows XP may soon wrest that laurel from Windows 2000.

System Requirements

As a minimum to run Windows 95, an 80386 DX 20 MHz processor is required; to run Windows 98, an 80486 DX 66 MHz processor is needed, as shown in Table 14–5. Windows NT requires resources similar to Windows 98 for a minimum system configuration. Windows 3.x requires the fewest resources. Minimum installation requirements are a 386 SX CPU chip with 3 MB of RAM and 15 MB of disk space. Minimum hardware requirements for Windows 95/98/Me, Windows 3.x, and Windows NT/2000 are given in Table 14–1. Table 14–5 presents Windows 95, Windows 98, and Windows 2000 upgrade requirements.

Table 14–5   Windows 95/98 Minimum Upgrade Requirements

Operating System	Minimum CPU Required	Minimum Required RAM	Minimum Fixed Disk Capacity
Windows 95	80386 DX 20 MHz	4 MB minimum 8 MB recommended	20 MB normal 10 MB compact installation
Windows 98	80486 DX 66 MHz	16 MB minimum 32 MB and more	120 MB disk space minimum 355 MB can be used for new install
Windows 2000	Pentium 133 MHz (but a Pentium III 300 MHz or faster is recommended)	64 MB minimum 128 MB and up recommended	2 GB with 650 MB free minimum 8 GB and up recommended

No need to worry today about meeting the minimum CPU chip requirements, because 386 SX CPU chips are no longer manufactured. Actually, when it comes right down to it, the only new CPU chips you can effectively purchase today are Pentium-class CPU chips that run at a minimum of 400 MHz. Thus, the minimum CPU requirement is met for all Windows operating systems. Most systems are produced with 64 MB or 128 MB of RAM so that minimum requirements are also fulfilled,

In all cases a 400 MHz or higher Pentium II class CPU chip or equivalent is a more realistic alternative. The recommended RAM is 8 MB for Windows 95 and 16 MB for Windows 98/Me. About 64 MB of RAM provides effective performance in both cases. RAM size of 128 MB to 256 MB is better.

The second big upgrade component is the disk drive capacity. Since the smallest disk drives are 20 GB or greater, disk space is no longer an upgrade issue. Windows specifies the required capacity in MB of free disk space needed to install Windows. Upgrading DOS to Windows 95 may require 30 MB of free disk space. A Windows 95 system should have a 2 GB fixed disk with 512 MB of free capacity to run Windows 95 most effectively. Disk drive capacity for a Windows 98 upgrade varies from 120 MB to 295 MB when moving up from Windows 3.x and Windows 95. A 32-bit FAT new installation requires less free fixed disk space. In this instance, Microsoft recommends 140 MB to 255 MB. A new 16-bit FAT installation of Windows 98 can consume as much as 355 MB of free fixed disk space. This is because the 32-bit FAT stores data more efficiently by using smaller allocation units than the 16-bit FAT. A client installation from across a network requires 175 MB to 225 MB of free disk space for Windows 98 because the network and installation software must run in the PC while Windows 98 is being installed. Obviously, disk drive capacities in excess of 20 GB meet all of these upgrade requirements.

Upgrading also requires at least a VGA or Super VGA adapter with sufficient memory for 16-color displays. More effective use of the PC is with a 1,024 by 768 VGA display with 256 colors. This should be on a 15-inch to 19-inch monitor. A display with 24-bit color (16 million colors) or 32-bit color provides a better display for graphics and images. Most AGP graphics cards have 4 MB to 32 MB of RAM so that they can support resolutions for up to 1,600 by 1,200 with 24-bit or 32-bit color. Getting the correct graphics drivers is more of an issue than meeting the Windows display requirements.

In each case, upgrading to Windows requires a mouse (using keyboard shortcuts for mouse movements really stinks) and a CD-ROM (the faster the better). Windows 98 also recommends having at least a 28.8 KBPS modem. The modem is needed to permit upgrades to Windows 98 from the Internet. A 28.8 KBPS modem permits upgrades across the Internet, but a 56 KBPS modem is better. However, upgrades and maintenance of Windows from the Internet at these speeds requires hours of time. With the size of upgrade files increasing, a cable modem or a DSL connection supporting down link speeds of over 400 Kbps is absolutely best for Internet upgrades. The process is reduced to minutes with a high-speed cable modem or DSL connection. See Figure 14–32.

The Windows 98 Internet upgrade is used to upgrade Windows 98 software components, not to perform upgrades from one version of Windows to another. Windows 95 cannot be upgraded to Windows 98 via the Internet.

Figure 14–32
Windows 98 Internet upgrade.

General Upgrade Procedure

The upgrade procedure starts by running the SETUP.EXE program. This program guides you through the Windows setup process. There are different ways

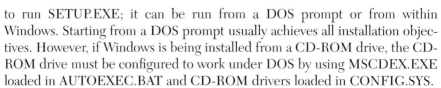

to run SETUP.EXE; it can be run from a DOS prompt or from within Windows. Starting from a DOS prompt usually achieves all installation objectives. However, if Windows is being installed from a CD-ROM drive, the CD-ROM drive must be configured to work under DOS by using MSCDEX.EXE loaded in AUTOEXEC.BAT and CD-ROM drivers loaded in CONFIG.SYS.

The easiest way to get a bootable DOS diskette that has drivers for most CD-ROM drives is to create a Windows 98/Me startup diskette using the control panel—add/remove programs—startup disk menu selection.

Use any old Windows 98/Me PC to create a Windows 98/Me startup diskette, as shown in Figure 14–33. This diskette boots into DOS and has CD-ROM drivers for SCSI and IDE CD-ROM drives. This diskette can be used to install both Windows 98/Me and Windows 95 despite its status as a Windows 98/Me startup diskette.

Figure 14–33
Windows 98 startup diskette creation.

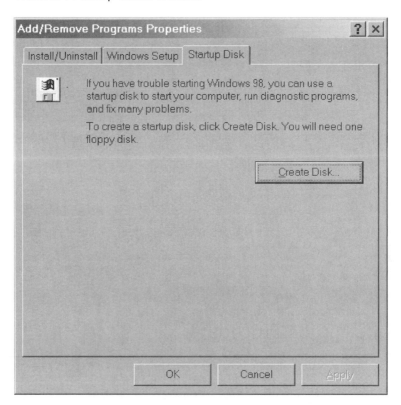

After booting from the DOS prompt, change to the Windows 95 or Windows 98 setup directory (generally it is d:\win98, where "d" represents the drive letter of your computer's CD-ROM drive) on the CD-ROM and run SETUP.EXE. SETUP.EXE is used as an installation program for almost all software today. It was initially used as an installation program with DOS 6.x, and has been used with Windows 3.x, Windows 95, and Windows 98. Windows NT, Windows XP, and Windows 2000 use WINNT.EXE or WINNT32.EXE to perform its installation.

DOS to Windows 95/98/Me

A DOS-to-Windows upgrade can be difficult because DOS PCs have very few hardware resources. Installing DOS itself requires about six or seven megabytes of free disk space. In contrast, Windows 3.x requires only 15 MB of disk space, while Windows 98 can need 120 MB to 355 MB of free disk space. The most difficult part of upgrading from DOS to Windows is finding the required memory and free fixed disk space resources on a DOS system.

Because DOS PCs have minimal resources compared to Windows PCs, it is best to think of an upgrade from DOS as an initial install of Windows 95/98. The install is accomplished by booting into DOS with the proper CD-ROM drivers so that the CD-ROM drive works, then running SETUP.EXE from the Windows install directory on the CD-ROM drive. Alternatively, the install files can be copied to the fixed disk (provided there is sufficient space to hold the install files and to install the Windows upgrade) and then Windows can be installed from the files copied to the fixed disk.

Windows 3.x to Windows 95/98/Me

There are several scenarios for upgrading to Windows 95 and 98 from Windows 3.x.

Upgrading to Windows 95

When upgrading to Windows 95 from Windows 3.x, the preferred approach is to run SETUP.EXE from within Windows 3.x. Windows finds the existing Windows 3.x installation and proceeds to install Windows 95 in the same directory. During this process, the WIN.INI, SYSTEM.INI, and PROTOCOL.INI files are used to create the new Windows 95 equivalent files. Also, file associations and application and network settings are transferred from the existing Windows 3.x configuration to the upgraded Windows 95 installation. Finally,

Windows 95 converts the Windows 3.x program groups into directories used to create the Windows 95 start menu.

Because Windows 95/98/Me expects to be installed in a \Windows directory, upgrading Windows 3.x installed in a \Win directory to Windows 95/98/Me can become difficult when Windows 95/98/Me is upgraded using the \Win directory of Windows 3.x. Such an upgrade prohibits Windows 95/98/Me from being installed in a \Windows directory, in which case it would be installed in the \Win directory. As a result, Windows 95/98/Me would encounter complications when it was looking for its installed components in a \Windows directory.

Upgrading to Windows 95 and installing it into a new directory (a directory different from the existing Windows 3.x directory) preserves the old Windows 3.x installation. Application program settings are not moved to Windows 95 in this case. Special setup steps are needed to enable a dual-boot—that is, the ability to boot the PC into either Windows 3.x or Windows 95. The basic steps required to set up a dual-boot Windows 3.x and Windows 95 PC are to install Windows 95 in a separate directory from the Windows 3.x files and to set the BootMulti=1 entry in the Windows 95 MSDOS.SYS file. Dual-boot systems are rare and only required if there is software that only runs on the older operating system, Windows 3.x.

Upgrading to Windows 98/Me

Upgrading to Windows 98/Me from DOS or from Windows 3.x is a significant step compared to upgrading to Windows 98/Me from Windows 95, or upgrading to Windows 95 from DOS or Windows 3.x. There are several different strategies.

Upgrading from DOS is like setting up a new installation. SETUP.EXE is run and the Wizard is followed to install Windows 98/Me. It is critical that you have the necessary PC hardware resources. The PC hardware resource most lacking for a Windows-95-to-Windows-98 upgrade is likely to be free space on the fixed disk drive unless a new disk drive is purchased for the upgrade (new 20 GB drives are about $60). When upgrading from Windows 3.x, the preferred approach is to run SETUP.EXE from within Windows 3.x. Windows 98/Me copies most of the information it needs to upgrade Windows 3.x to Windows 98/Me from the existing Windows 3.x installation. The current configuration and installed programs are migrated into Windows 98/Me during upgrade installation. There can be a problem with this approach when real-mode driver and interface programs are used like the real mode drivers for Novell NetWare. If SETUP.EXE is run while such real mode programs are operating, SETUP stops and won't continue. You are also likely to get an error message that in a general sense identifies the conflicting software that prevents

SETUP from completing the installation. Simply remove the real mode driver programs before running SETUP.EXE, but be sure to note any network configuration information first. Windows 98/Me provides all the needed LAN drivers and software for peer-to-peer networking and client/server networking with Novell NetWare.

Upgrading to Windows 98/Me from Windows 95 is similar to upgrading to Windows 95 from Windows 3.x. Windows 98/Me can be installed in the same directory as Windows 95, or a new directory. Running SETUP.EXE from within Windows 95 installs Windows 98/Me in the existing Windows 95 directory and preserves the computer name, network settings, start menu programs, installed applications, and more. This upgrade procedure requires the least amount of user interaction. Similar to upgrading from Windows 3.x to Windows 95, the current configuration and application settings are migrated into the Windows 98/Me during upgrade installation. A limitation here is that the Windows 98/Me directory cannot be changed to a different directory from the Windows 95 directory. To have a clean installation of Windows 98/Me, change the directory into which Windows 98/Me is installed and install Windows 98/Me from DOS. This installation strategy option permits changing the installation directory for Windows 98/Me, selecting setup options, entering user information, identifying the computer on the network, and changing the computer settings—for instance, the language support. Booting the PC into DOS using a floppy, exiting Windows 95 to DOS, or using the F5 key to bypass the Windows 95 and DOS startup files can do this. (See booting discussion that follows.) Once at the DOS prompt, change to the Windows 98/Me setup disk directory (or to the directory containing the Windows 98 CAB files and the SETUP.EXE program—generally, it is a \win98 or a \win9x folder) and run the SETUP.EXE program. Installing Windows 98/Me into a new directory is more work because the user and network information must be re-specified to Windows 98, and applications and other special driver programs may need to be installed. Installing Windows 98/Me into a new directory provides a more reliable Windows 98/Me installation overall.

When upgrading from Windows 95 to Windows 98/Me, the Windows 95 settings and configuration are preserved to the greatest extent when Windows 98/Me is installed from within Windows 95. To install a clean configuration of Windows 98/Me, the Windows 98/Me installation is performed from DOS as opposed to from within Windows 95.

When problems are encountered during setup of Windows 95/98, they are usually caused by anti-virus software, third-party utilities, third-party hardware driver programs, and DOS real-time programs. During Windows 95/98/Me installation, the setup program may provide a general warning about conflicting software, but it is not likely to identify the specific software conflicts. As a general rule it is best to not run any other software aside from the Windows

95/98/Me SETUP.EXE program. To ensure smooth installation, anti-virus software, third-party utilities, special hardware driver programs, and DOS real-time programs should be disabled. Returning Windows 3.x and Windows 95 to a standard operating state (that is, VGA mode with no special Video, LAN, communications, and other drivers) using only Microsoft Windows drivers is a good strategy to follow when upgrading to Windows 98/Me.

Special drivers and utility software designed to operate with Windows 3.x and Windows 95 can cause problems because during Windows 98/Me installation, older DLLs, VxDs, DRV and other Windows programs used by these special devices can be retained. Since they may not be updated to newer Windows 98/Me versions, the old drivers may or may not work properly with Windows 98/Me. For example, when installing Windows 98/Me, if the PC enters safe mode operation there is a good likelihood that the display drivers do not work with Windows 98/Me. To correct such problems, the most current hardware drivers and utilities should be obtained from the Internet web site of the manufacturer and installed. The latest driver and utility software is often needed for Windows 98/Me to run reliably. Leaving old driver and other software on a PC provides a fertile environment for a bad software mix to develop, causing Windows 98/Me to crash or run miserably.

We cannot emphasize enough that when upgrading software, the proper driver programs that match the release of the operating system should be used. They should be Windows certified drivers for best results. Beta release drivers, although more current than certified drivers, contain many unpleasant surprises and should be avoided. Display drivers can cause severe problems during upgrade. It is often easiest to replace a display board rather than trying to use a display controller with bad drivers. Troubleshooting driver program problems wastes huge amounts of time because the errors they cause in no way seem related to the bad display driver programs. We have had printing errors caused by bad display drivers. Replacing the display controller with a Windows supported (as noted by the HCL) display controller fixed the problem.

Upgrading to Windows 2000

Upgrading to Windows 2000 from Windows 98/Me has some added considerations. Meeting the hardware requirements is relatively easy with the CPU chips, RAM and fixed disk drives used in PCs today. It is important to use a VGA controller and a NIC that is Windows 2000 certified and has the Windows 2000 certified driver software. Special disk drive controllers installed on the MLB and old MLBs should have their BIOS upgraded to the ACPI and latest plug-and-play standard. Special driver programs are sometimes needed for VIA chip set and similar MLBs. Any Windows 2000 drivers should be obtained from the Internet from the hardware manufacturer's web site prior to starting the Windows 2000 upgrade. CD-ROMs, floppy drives, and mice that are ATA IDE, standard floppy interface and Microsoft or Logitech compatibles respectively generally work just fine with Windows 2000.

When upgrading to Windows 2000, use the WINNT32 /checkupgradeonly command to determine any potential problems with the upgrade. A \windows\UPGRADE.TXT file is created specifically for the PC tested. Resolve any outstanding problems by upgrading the PCs hardware or software. Uninstall noncompliant software and get Windows 2000 versions of it.

Perform the upgrade to Windows 2000. If problems are encountered, check the \winnt folder for logs created during setup. These logs can be viewed with NOTEPAD. They are:

1. SETUPact.log is a setup action log that lists chronologically every step setup performs. Errors are also listed which help to identify unloaded device drivers or uncopied installation files.

2. SETUPapi.log lists the device classes such as 1394 Interface, battery, and CDROM installed. It identifies successful installation as installation with no errors.

3. SETUPerr.log records setup errors.

4. SETUPlog.txt records and lists setup events. This log is somewhat less useful because it contains too much detail on the Windows 2000 setup process, including messages like "unable to find" that may or may not indicate setup errors.

Figure 14–34 shows the set up log files and the contents of SETUPact and SETUPapi. Use the logs to identify Windows 2000 setup problems. Remove noncritical hardware components to resolve problems if needed. Sound cards, DVD decoders, SCSI controllers and other hardware components not essential to Windows 2000 operation can be removed and then added later. The key components needed are MLB, RAM, Video controller, IDE disk controller, mouse, keyboard, and perhaps a LAN NIC.

The Windows upgrade process is becoming easier because there are less hardware resource restrictions, plug-and-play hardware and software is greatly improved, and there is a greater variety of hardware and software products made specifically for Windows 9x, Windows 2000, and Windows XP.

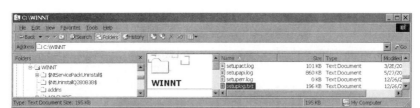

Figure 14–34
Set up log files and their contents.

Study Break: Finding Windows CAB Files

In this exercise we will look for the Windows CAB installation files on our fixed disk drive.

Go to a Windows 95 or Windows 98/Me PC.

Open Windows Explorer, select tools from the menu bar, point to find, then click on files and folders. This should open up the search window, permitting us to search for files on the fixed disk drives.

Under the name and location tab in the named panel, enter *.CAB. Click on find now. This causes explorer to search for the CAB files on the drive specified by the "Look In:" panel. The specified drive should be the C disk drive.

If no CAB files are located, then Windows 95/98/Me was most likely installed directly from a CD-ROM drive. When CAB files are located, note the folder where they reside. This is most often the \windows\options\cabs folder (directory).

Make a note of the date on the CAB files. This date can be used to determine the version of Windows installed on the PC. Check with the Windows release dates listed in Chapter 11.

The goal of this exercise was to familiarize you with where Windows installation files can be located.

Booting Procedures

Booting procedures for DOS, Windows 3.x, and Windows 95/98/Me are similar. With Windows, though, the procedure involves different components. There is both a cold boot and a warm boot process. The cold boot process starts from a power off and on cycle—physically turning the computer off and then on again—or a hard PC reset. In this case, the contents of RAM are lost and the PC starts with a fresh memory configuration. To remove a virus program from memory, a cold boot is needed. A warm boot is initiated by the Ctrl-Alt-Del keystroke sequence, which does not clear memory. Virus programs can intercept the Ctrl-Alt-Del keystroke sequence before Windows processes it. This gives the virus programs an opportunity to hide themselves and survive a PC reboot. Windows 95/98/Me uses Ctrl-Alt-Del to perform other functions, like loading the task manager program to kill off unresponsive Windows tasks.

All PC boot processes use the real mode BIOS routines. They perform the POST of the PC's hardware, which mostly checks for the presence of several key devices, including the display controller, the keyboard, the floppy diskettes, and the fixed disk drive. On newer PCs, a CD-ROM drive is also sometimes detected (for booting), but if not present, an error is not reported. The system RAM is tested to determine if it matches the RAM parameter stored in the CMOS setup parameter memory. The BIOS boot process displays on the monitor the results of its testing and any PC ROM and special device ROM messages. Generally, the last BIOS POST message displays what was discovered about the PC, including CPU chip and clock speed, floppy disk drives and capacities, fixed disk drive and capacity, the presence and configuration of LPT and COM ports, and the total amount of RAM detected. The process causes the PC to sometimes beep twice, indicating all is well so far. Different series of beeps without the Windows screens appearing generally indicate hardware malfunctions during the boot process. The other boot options, including the function keys, are covered later in this chapter.

Booting DOS

DOS boots using BIOS, IO.SYS, MSDOS.SYS, and COMMAND.COM. The BIOS performs the cold boot loading process in real mode. It runs a cold boot loader program that first determines the boot device. When it is a floppy diskette, the BIOS loads a cold boot loader program from the first diskette sector, the DOS boot record. If there is no floppy DOS boot record (DBR), BIOS displays "Nonsystem disk or disk error. Replace and strike any key when ready." The nonbootable floppy can be replaced by a bootable floppy and the process continued.

When the boot device is a fixed disk, the BIOS loads a cold boot loader found in the master boot record (MBR) of the fixed disk. A CD-ROM boot is similar, with a cold boot loader loading from a CD-ROM boot record. The cold boot loader program in the master boot record determines the fixed disk's partition configuration from data it stores. It locates the active bootable partition (usually drive C) and then loads IO.SYS from the active partition on the fixed disk.

If IO.SYS cannot be found, the error "Missing Operating System" is displayed. Other DOS boot errors are described in Chapter 2, "PC Installation and Upgrade." The "Missing Operating System" error can sometimes be fixed by using the DOS commands FDISK /MBR and SYS C:\. FDISK /MBR rewrites the master boot record while SYS C: reinstalls the system boot files on the drive C (hopefully the bootable) partition. This is why a bootable-diskette-troubleshooting tool should contain both the FDISK and SYS programs as described in the Chapter 3 study break exercise, "Creating a Bootable Diskette." FDISK is also discussed in Chapter 3, "Troubleshooting and Problem Resolution" and Chapter 12, "Disk Navigation Procedures and Management."

Next, IO.SYS is loaded to complete the boot process, and loads the remaining programs. It loads MSDOS.SYS and then processes the DEVICE= commands, the FILES=, and other commands in CONFIG.SYS. The DEVICE= commands load real mode hardware device drivers for special hardware installed in the PC, and the FILES= and other commands configure the PC's environment space and memory allocation for parameters and buffers. IO.SYS usually completes the commands in CONFIG.SYS from top to bottom of the file, but this is not always the case. Some commands (for instance, DOS=HIGH and DOS=UMB) are processed first, regardless of where they appear in the file.

IO.SYS passes control to COMMAND.COM, which is installed in the root directory of the bootable partition. A SHELL= statement can redirect the loading of COMMAND.COM from another directory. When COM-

MAND.COM does not match the DOS IO.SYS and MSDOS.SYS files, an "Invalid command.com" message is displayed.

Once loaded, COMMAND.COM processes the commands from AUTOEXEC.BAT. These commands load the programs that complete the DOS configuration. Some programs like SMARTDRV and DOSKEY perform special functions. Other commands like SET configure the environment space used to store DOS parameters used by application programs. A good SET command is SET DOSCMD=/Ogn /A. This causes the DIR command to display all files (/A) in alphabetical order with subdirectories first (/Ogn).

Required DOS Boot Files

The files needed for DOS to boot are:

1.   IO.SYS

2.   MSDOS.SYS

3.   COMMAND.COM

In some cases, the CONFIG.SYS file is needed to load HIMEM.SYS (DEVICE=HIMEM.SYS) and set DOS=HIGH because without them there is not enough memory to run the desired programs. When installing Windows, it is also good to have an AUTOEXEC.BAT file that loads SMARTDRV.EXE, the disk cache program. The SDMARTDRV disk cache program speeds up Windows installation by a factor of 14.

Creating a DOS Bootable Diskette

Using the FORMAT command creates a bootable DOS diskette. The command is:

```
FORMAT A: /S
```

or

```
FORMAT C: /S
```

to format a fixed disk drive.

The /S option causes the system files to be installed on the floppy. Other format options are described in Chapter 12. This works for DOS, Windows 3.x, and Windows 95/98/Me as well. Formatting in DOS is better than in Windows because it deals more directly with the diskette drive hardware through BIOS. Windows does a fine job as well, but it has less direct hardware control.

Also installed with the current DOS and Windows versions is DRV-

SPACE.BIN. DRVSPACE is only needed if there is a compressed disk that must be accessed. Often it is desirable to remove DRVSPACE from a bootable floppy to make room for other more important diagnostic and utility programs. IO.SYS, MSDOS.SYS, and DRVSPACE.BIN are all system, read-only, hidden files. To remove DRVSPACE, the system, read-only, and hidden file attributes must be removed so it can be deleted from the diskette. Changing file attributes is described in Chapter 12.

The DOS SYS command makes an empty formatted diskette into a bootable diskette. It transfers the system files from a bootable partition or diskette to the target drives. The command is:

SYS A: or SYS C:

This command works with DOS, Windows 3.x in a DOS window, and Windows 95/98/Me in a DOS window. The interesting thing with Windows 95/98/Me is that the bootable floppy produced uses only IO.SYS and COMMAND.COM to perform the DOS functions. The MSDOS.SYS file is merely a placeholder. It contains the text FORMAT if the bootable diskette was produced by the FORMAT program and SYS if the bootable diskette was produced using the SYS program.

The DOS booting process is followed for DOS, Windows 3.x, and Windows 95/98/Me. However, for all versions of Windows, the DOS booting process is just the beginning of the overall boot process. The Windows 95/98/Me DOS uses only IO.SYS and COMMAND.COM to provide the DOS functions. MSDOS.SYS has become more a placeholder and parameter file for Windows 95/98/Me DOS.

Bypassing Startup Files

The DOS CONFIG.SYS and AUTOEXEC.BAT files can be bypassed during the boot process by using the F5 and F8 keys. When the PC displays the message "Starting MS-DOS…" or "Starting Windows 98…" striking the F5 key bypasses both CONFIG.SYS and AUTOEXEC.BAT files and loads DOS. This boots the PC without any special driver programs or configuration options. During the boot, DOS displays "MS-DOS is bypassing your CONFIG.SYS and AUTOEXEC.BAT files" or "Windows 98/Me is bypassing your CONFIG.SYS and AUTOEXEC.BAT files".

The disk compression software DBLSPACE is still loaded into memory for Windows 98/Me and cannot be bypassed (not loaded). It means that about 197 KB is used to load Windows 98/Me DOS versus 62 KB for DOS 6.x.

The Windows 3.x Boot Process

This section covers the Windows 3.x boot process. Since Windows 3.x rides on top of DOS 6.x, the initial boot process is the same for both. The difference is that the Windows boot process starts Windows after DOS is loaded and configured. Running the WIN.COM program launches Windows. The same is also true for Windows 98/Me, but WIN.COM launches automatically and is not launched from the AUTOEXEC.BAT file.

WIN.COM loads Windows 3.x in 386 enhanced mode. It first loads extended memory support and the WIN386.EXE. The WIN386.EXE then loads the virtual machine manager (VMM) and all virtual device drivers (VxDs) listed in the SYSTEM.INI file. The network support virtual device driver (VNTE-SUP.386) starts the network VxDs including the NetBEUI protocol (VNB.386), the NETBIOS interface (VNETBIOS.386), the network redirector (VREDIR.386) and the WORKGRP.SYS device driver. The appropriate software linkages or bindings are made by VNETSUP.386. The VREDIR.386 starts the workstation service.

WIN386.EXE loads the 386 enhanced mode kernel program (KRNL386.EXE). KRNL386.EXE loads the Windows drivers (*.DRV) listed in the SYSTEM.INI file, the GDI.EXE (graphics device interface), the USER.EXE, the supporting files (like fonts files), and the network driver (the Windows for Workgroups WFWNET.DRV program).

The server service (VSERVER.386) is started and the device shares are enabled. The network device data exchange application (NETDDE.EXE) is loaded in addition to the ClipBook server application (CLIPSRV.EXE). Then the WFWNET.DRV program handles the network logon and the network connections are restored. Finally, KRNLx86.EXE starts the Windows shell program (PROGMAN.EXE) or the shell identified in the Windows SYSTEM.INI file SHELL= [boot] section statement.

The Windows 95/98/Me Boot Process

Windows 95, Windows 98, and Windows Me boot similarly to DOS and Windows 3.x with some exceptions. The BIOS boot phase is designed to boot using a plug-and-play BIOS. Plug-and-play and non-plug-and-play ISA bus cards are set up by a plug-and-play BIOS using NVRAM or CMOS RAM) information. The nonvolatile random access memory enables the cards and devices built into the MLB, maps their ROMs into memory addresses, and assigns I/O port, DMA channel, and IRQs to the cards. The BIOS then programs all cards before POST. Otherwise the cards are disabled to eliminate conflicts.

Windows then determines the current configuration from the hardware profile. Since most PCs use only a single hardware profile, this setup does not display any visible messages. Multiple hardware profiles can be set up using the control panel. See Figure 14–35.

When more than a single profile is used, a select profile message is displayed. The message states:

Windows cannot determine what configuration your computer is in.

Select one of the following:

```
1. Original configuration
2. New configuration
3. None of the above
Enter your choice:
```

Once the choice is selected, the boot process continues. The CONFIG.SYS and AUTOEXEC.BAT files are processed next. Although not required by Windows 95/98/Me, they provide a mechanism to ensure backward compati-

Figure 14–35
Hardware profile setup.

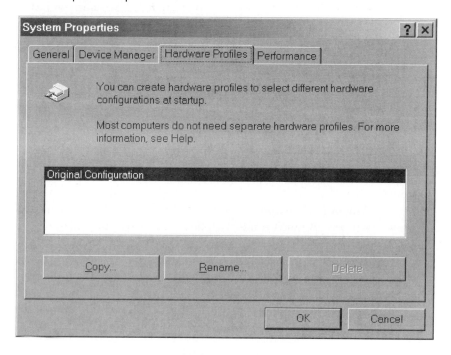

bility for DOS and Windows 3.x applications. For example, they set up the DOS windows with paths and load TSR programs like DOSKEY.EXE.

Windows now moves on to initializing the static virtual device drivers (VxDs) in the same way Windows 3.x does when starting in 386 enhanced mode. The Windows 95/98/Me virtual machine manager (VMM32.VXD) includes a real-mode loader, a virtual machine manager, and common static VxDs. There are also dynamically loaded VxDs that are supported as well. Dynamic VxDs are loaded only when needed by Windows. The static VxDs were specified in the [386ENH] section of the SYSTEM.INI file. They are built into VMM32.VxD for Windows 95/98/Me or specified in the registry and the SYSTEM.INI file. Devices specified in SYSTEM.INI take precedence over devices specified in the registry.

Dynamically loaded device drivers for the network and other hardware components are loaded by a device loader (for example, *IOS. for SCSI adapter miniport drivers). When they are needed, the device loader loads and initializes these dynamic drivers in a very specific load sequence.

Upon completion of the static VxD initialization, WIN.COM has loaded and checked the core Windows 95/98/Me components, VMM32.VXD has created virtual machines and loaded the static VxDs, and the VxDs specified by SYSTEM.INI have been loaded. Next, the CPU chip is switched to protected-mode operation to load the KERNEL32.DLL and the KRNL386.EXE. The KRNL386.EXE loads more Windows device drivers. Then GDI.EXE and GDI32.EXE as well as USER.EXE and USER32.EXE are loaded. The fonts are then loaded, the WIN.INI values are checked and the EXPLORER.EXE shell and desktop components are loaded. Finally, Windows displays the logon screen, requesting the username and password.

Required Files for Booting Windows 95/98/Me

Some key parameter and program files and their role in the Windows 95/98/Me booting process are:

1. IO.SYS—a real-mode Windows 98/Me operating system equivalent to DOS. IO.SYS has default drivers built into it that are loaded. They are HIMEM.SYS, IFSHLP.SYS (Installable File System help), SETVER.EXE, and DBLSPACE.BIN.

2. MSDOS.SYS—a text file that contains loading parameters for Windows and provides compatibility with programs requiring a MSDOS.SYS file.

3. COMMAND.COM—the DOS command prompt interpreter containing the internal DOS commands, for instance, DEL and COPY.

4. CONFIG.SYS and AUTOEXEC.BAT—text files used to load special 16-bit device drivers and to set up DOS window operation. These are not absolutely needed for Windows to boot.

5. WIN.INI and SYSTEM.INI used to load drivers and other programs to assist with maintaining compatibility with Windows 3.x application software. Sometimes Windows TSR applications are launched from WIN.INI using the LOAD= or RUN= statements in it.

6. PROTOCOL.INI—a text file that sets up the network protocols and binds (links) them to the installed LAN card drivers.

7. The Windows 95/98/Me Registry—The SYSTEM.DAT and USER.DAT provide additional loading instructions for configuring Windows and for loading Windows 95/98/Me TSR programs like virus scanning programs.

The Microsoft Emergency Recovery Utility (ERU) program as a way to recover from Windows failures saves these key files. When Windows 98/Me blew up on Bill Gates at a pre-release press conference, the ERU program and the key Windows 98/Me boot files created by ERU restored the PC to operating status in a minute. The ERU program was discussed in detail earlier in this chapter.

The 32-bit virtual machine manager (VMM32) program takes control from IO.SYS and continues the loading process, calling the Windows programs that are needed. Windows also loads programs or program shortcuts in the C:\windows\start menu\programs\startup directory during the boot process. See Figure 14–36. Programs loaded here often appear in the Windows 95/98/Me SYSTRAY section of the taskbar.

Windows TSR programs can be loaded from CONFIG.SYS and AUTOEXEC.BAT, from the Windows registry, from the WIN.INI file, and from the startup directory. Of these, the registry is the most difficult to troubleshoot.

Windows 95/98/Me also renames some original DOS files to preserve them and to permit Windows to substitute new files it needs in their place. As a reminder, the renamed files are:

1. AUTOEXEC.BAT renamed AUTOEXEC.DOS

2. CONFIG.SYS renamed CONFIG.DOS

3. COMMAND.COM renamed COMMAND.DOS

4. IO.SYS renamed IO.DOS

5. MSDOS.SYS renamed MSDOS.DOS

6. MODE.COM renamed MODE_DOS.COM

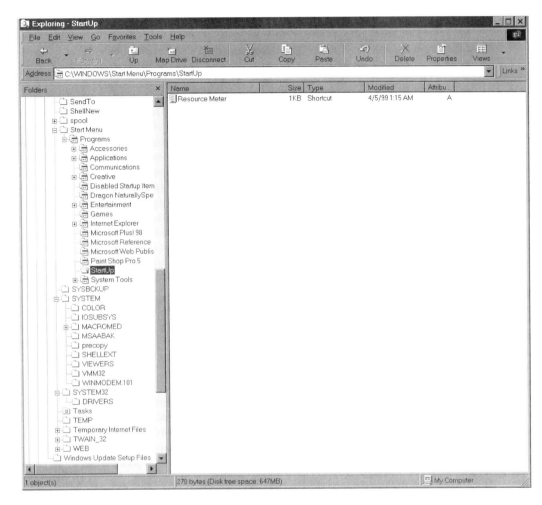

Figure 14–36
Startup programs.

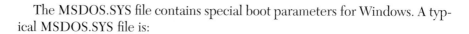

The MSDOS.SYS file contains special boot parameters for Windows. A typical MSDOS.SYS file is:

```
[Paths]
WinDir=C:\WINDOWS
WinBootDir=C:\WINDOWS
HostWinBootDrv=C

[Options]
BootMulti=1
BootGUI=1
DoubleBuffer=1
AutoScan=1
WinVer=4.14.1998
;
;The following lines are required for compatibility with other programs.
;Do not remove them (MSDOS.SYS needs to be >1024 bytes).
;xxxxxxxxxxxxxxxxxxxxxxxxxxxxxxxxxxxxxxxxxxxxxxxxxxxxxxxxxxxxxxxxa
;xxxxxxxxxxxxxxxxxxxxxxxxxxxxxxxxxxxxxxxxxxxxxxxxxxxxxxxxxxxxxxxxb
;xxxxxxxxxxxxxxxxxxxxxxxxxxxxxxxxxxxxxxxxxxxxxxxxxxxxxxxxxxxxxxxxc
;xxxxxxxxxxxxxxxxxxxxxxxxxxxxxxxxxxxxxxxxxxxxxxxxxxxxxxxxxxxxxxxxd
;xxxxxxxxxxxxxxxxxxxxxxxxxxxxxxxxxxxxxxxxxxxxxxxxxxxxxxxxxxxxxxxxe
;xxxxxxxxxxxxxxxxxxxxxxxxxxxxxxxxxxxxxxxxxxxxxxxxxxxxxxxxxxxxxxxxf
;xxxxxxxxxxxxxxxxxxxxxxxxxxxxxxxxxxxxxxxxxxxxxxxxxxxxxxxxxxxxxxxxg
;xxxxxxxxxxxxxxxxxxxxxxxxxxxxxxxxxxxxxxxxxxxxxxxxxxxxxxxxxxxxxxxxh
;xxxxxxxxxxxxxxxxxxxxxxxxxxxxxxxxxxxxxxxxxxxxxxxxxxxxxxxxxxxxxxxxi
;xxxxxxxxxxxxxxxxxxxxxxxxxxxxxxxxxxxxxxxxxxxxxxxxxxxxxxxxxxxxxxxxj
;xxxxxxxxxxxxxxxxxxxxxxxxxxxxxxxxxxxxxxxxxxxxxxxxxxxxxxxxxxxxxxxxk
;xxxxxxxxxxxxxxxxxxxxxxxxxxxxxxxxxxxxxxxxxxxxxxxxxxxxxxxxxxxxxxxxl
;xxxxxxxxxxxxxxxxxxxxxxxxxxxxxxxxxxxxxxxxxxxxxxxxxxxxxxxxxxxxxxxxm
;xxxxxxxxxxxxxxxxxxxxxxxxxxxxxxxxxxxxxxxxxxxxxxxxxxxxxxxxxxxxxxxxn
;xxxxxxxxxxxxxxxxxxxxxxxxxxxxxxxxxxxxxxxxxxxxxxxxxxxxxxxxxxxxxxxxo
;xxxxxxxxxxxxxxxxxxxxxxxxxxxxxxxxxxxxxxxxxxxxxxxxxxxxxxxxxxxxxxxxp
;xxxxxxxxxxxxxxxxxxxxxxxxxxxxxxxxxxxxxxxxxxxxxxxxxxxxxxxxxxxxxxxxq
;xxxxxxxxxxxxxxxxxxxxxxxxxxxxxxxxxxxxxxxxxxxxxxxxxxxxxxxxxxxxxxxxr
;xxxxxxxxxxxxxxxxxxxxxxxxxxxxxxxxxxxxxxxxxxxxxxxxxxxxxxxxxxxxxxxxs
Network=0
```

Table 14–6 shows the MSDOS.SYS file parameter options and their purpose.

Table 14–6   MSDOS.SYS File Parameters

Parameter	Description
WinDir=C:\WINDOWS	Specifies the directory where Windows is installed and run from.
WinBootDir=C:\WINDOWS	Specifies where the Windows startup files can be found.
HostWinBootDrv=C	Specifies the Windows boot drive containing the root directory.
BootMulti=1	Enables booting two operating systems. A value of 1 permits starting MS-DOS by pressing F4 or starting with the startup menu by pressing F8.
BootGUI=1	Starts Windows automatically, like placing a WIN statement in an AUTOEXEC.BAT file.
DoubleBuffer=1	Loads the double-buffer driver needed by some SCSI disk controllers.
AutoScan=1	Runs SCANDISK automatically when the PC is abruptly restarted.
WinVer=4.14.1998	Identifies the version of Windows installed.
Bootdelay=#	Delays the boot process for # seconds.
BootFailSafe=	Starts system in safe mode. Default is 0, causing Windows to start normally.
BootKeys=	Enables (default) or disables the F5, F6 and F8 key functions during Windows startup.
BootMenu=	Displays the startup menu.
BootMenuDefault=#	Picks the Windows startup menu default item. The default is 3 for Windows with no networking and 4 for Windows with networking installed.
BootMenuDelay=#	Delays startup # seconds when boot menu is used.
BootWarn=	Displays safe mode startup warning.
BootWin=	Sets Windows as the default operating system.
LoadTop=	Loads COMMAND.COM or DRVSPACE.BIN into the top of the 640 K real mode memory. Default value is 1, loading the programs into that top memory area.
Logo=	Controls display of the Windows logo while booting. Default value is 1 to display the logo.
Network=	Controls safe mode network operation. This should be disabled with Windows 98 by setting value to 0.

Similar to the controls in MSDOS.SYS, WIN.COM also has parameters that can be used to control the Windows boot process. The WIN.COM parameters are displayed by running WIN.COM /?. WIN.COM command syntax is:

```
WIN [/D:[F][M][S][V][X]]
```

The parameters are:

/D—Troubleshoots when Windows does not start correctly.

:F—Turns off 32-bit disk access. Equivalent to SYSTEM.INI file setting 32BitDiskAccess=FALSE.

:M—Enables safe mode. This is automatically enabled during safe start (F5).

:N—Enables safe mode with networking. This is automatically enabled during safe start (F6).

:S—Specifies that Windows should not use ROM address space between F000:0000 and 1 MB for a break point. Equivalent to SYSTEM.INI file setting: SystemROMBreakPoint=FALSE.

:V—Specifies that the ROM routine will handle interrupts from the hard disk controller. Equivalent to SYSTEM.INI file setting VirtualHDIRQ=FALSE.

:X—Excludes all of the adapter area from the range of memory that Windows scans to find unused space. Equivalent to SYSTEM.INI file setting EMMExclude=A000-FFFF.

The bootlog.txt file keeps a record of the events during the boot process. See Figure 14–37.

The status of the Windows components and drivers loaded and initialized is recorded in the bootlog.txt file. Both loading successes and failures are logged. Finding which drivers or Windows components failed to load properly during the boot process can facilitate troubleshooting a Windows installation. The event entries cover errors, failures, load success, initialization success, load failures, system initialization, device initialization, dynamic device loading and initialization, and current status.

Figure 14–37
Bootlog.txt contents.

The Windows 95/98/Me Bootable Diskette Diagnostic Tool

A bootable diskette for Windows 95/98/Me can be created by using the FOR-MAT /S command in a DOS window or by formatting a diskette using the Windows Explorer. Alternatively, the Windows 98/Me startup diskette can be readily modified to make a bootable diskette that boots a PC with CD-ROM support. The difference between the DOS window format and the Windows Explorer format is that the MSDOS.SYS file produced by the DOS format contains ";FORMAT" while the MSDOS.SYS file produced by Windows Explorer is an empty file (0 bytes). See Figure 14–38. A bootable floppy is created when the copy system files option is checked.

A quick or full format can be performed. The full format verifies the diskette, while the quick format only rewrites the boot record, FAT, and directory areas on the diskette. See Figure 14–39. The copy system files only option

Figure 14–38
Explorer FORMAT window.

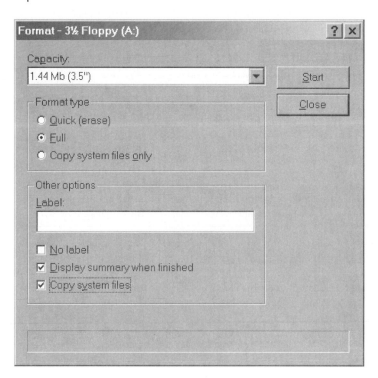

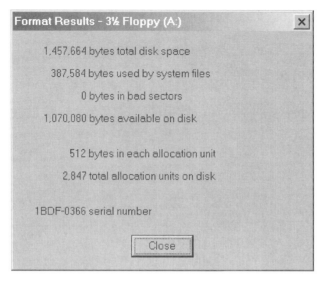

Figure 14–39
Explorer FORMAT report.

is equivalent to DOS's SYS command installation. It can be used to turn a previously formatted diskette into a bootable diskette. The procedure here is the same for both Windows 95 and Windows 98/Me.

The DOS format program is more dependent on the BIOS for operating with the diskettes and has more direct control. A 32-bit Windows program performs the explorer formatting, which means that sometimes the DOS formatting works better than the Windows Explorer formatting.

Creating a Windows startup diskette also creates a bootable diskette. The startup diskette contains more than just DOS files. The Windows 98/Me startup diskette has CD-ROM drivers and other software installed on it that assist in troubleshooting Windows or in installing Windows.

Windows 95/98/Me Function Key Boot Impacts or Bypassing Startup Files

During Windows startup, the startup files can be bypassed using the following keys:

F5—bypasses all startup files and enters safe mode operation directly.
    Booting can take quite some time because the disk cache programs
    are not installed during the Windows safe mode startup.

F6—bypasses the startup files and enters safe mode operation with minimal network support.

F8—enters the Windows startup menu, permitting startup from the following menu options:

Normal

Logged (\BOOTLOG.TXT)

Safe mode

Step-by-step confirmation

Command prompt only

Safe mode command prompt only

The default selection is 1, normal operation boot. Combining the Shift key and the F5 key (Shift+F5) causes Windows to boot to the command prompt. Entering WIN to launch the WIN.COM program then runs Windows. Combining the Shift key and the F8 key (Shift+F8) causes Windows to start in the Windows startup menu and perform step-by-step confirmation of the driver programs loaded during the boot process for the menu item selected. Some of the confirmations for booting Windows normally are:

Load DoubleSpace driver—disk cache and compression

Process the system registry

Create a startup log file (BOOTLOG.TXT)

Process the startup device drivers (CONFIG.SYS)

List the lines in CONFIG.SYS

Process the startup command file (AUTOEXEC.BAT)

List the lines in AUTOEXEC.BAT

WIN—starts Windows

Load all Windows drivers

Install special drivers

Override standard CONFIGMG—configuration manager

Override standard NTKERN—kernel program

Override standard VCOMM—communications

Override standard VDD—virtual device driver

Override standard VMCPD—virtual machine CPD

Override standard VMM—virtual machine manager

Override standard VMOUSE—virtual mouse driver

Override standard VTDAPI—virtual TD application program interface

vnetsup.vxd—virtual network support

ndis.vxd—network device interface specification driver

ndis2sup.vxd—network device interface specification 2 support

JAVASUP.VXD—JAVA support

netbios.vxd—NETBIOS interface

ndiswan.vxd—net device interface specification wide area networks

vredir.vxd—virtual redirector

fs.vxd

LMOUSE.VXD—Logitech mouse driver

vserver.vxd—virtual server

ASPIENUM.VXD—SCSI bus ASPI enumerator

C:\windows\system\vrtwd.386

C:\windows\system\vfixd.vxd—virtual fixed disk

filesec.vxd—file security

mssp.vxd

C:\windows\system\VSHINIT.VXD—virtual shell initialization

vwavsyn.386—virtual wave synthesizer

This is a typical listing of the confirmations requested when booting with the Shift+F8 key. Shift+F5 causes Windows to boot without loading the DoubleSpace driver that performs both disk compression and disk cache functions. Booting using the Ctrl key alone makes Windows display the startup menu. The Shift key alone starts Windows in safe mode. The Esc key, if hit during boot up, removes the Windows animated logo screen and displays the commands being performed during the startup process.

Booting to Safe Mode

Booting Windows into safe mode with minimal drivers is performed from the Windows Startup menu by selecting safe mode, or by holding down the Ctrl key during the boot process. Booting into safe mode bypasses the real-mode configuration and loads a standard driver protected-mode configuration. The core drivers support VGA display, IDE fixed disk, mouse, and keyboard. When safe mode starts and there are other problems preventing Windows from normal startup, the conflict preventing normal startup could be in hardware settings, real-mode configuration problems, program and driver incompatibilities, or damage to the registry. Safe mode is a diagnostic tool to resolve conflicts that prevent Windows from starting normally.

The most common reason for booting to safe mode is that Windows video drivers are incorrect or do not match. When a safe mode boot happens, check for video driver updates or change video controllers first to save time resolving the problem.

Booting to DOS vs. the MS-DOS Command

Prompt in Windows

A PC can be booted from a floppy diskette directly into Windows DOS, or it can boot into Windows 95/98/Me and then exit to the DOS prompt. Booting from a floppy diskette into Windows DOS loads the real-mode operating system. IO.SYS starts and loads HIMEM.SYS to provide access to XMS memory and sets DOS=high. It then loads the 32-bit installable file system manager (IFSHLP.SYS). The SERVER.EXE program that provides compatibility for older DOS programs requesting a specific DOS version is loaded and the FILES=60 is set to establish a working set of file handles. Other configuration commands set are lastdrive=z, buffers=30, stacks=9,256, fcbs=4 and shell=command.com. These settings are standard settings for a Windows environment. Some settings are larger than those used in a DOS environment: for instance, DOS sets the stacks at 9,128. Placing settings into a CONFIG.SYS file can override the standard Windows IO.SYS settings.

The Windows DOS in real mode connects to the PC components using the PC's BIOS. This means that Windows DOS is important for running PC hardware diagnostics that must directly control the hardware components.

Booting into Windows 95/98/Me permits using a DOS Window to emulate DOS operation with Windows running in protected mode. Windows is using its 32-bit protected-mode drivers to access hardware components. The 32-bit Windows protected-mode drivers can prevent some diagnostic programs from running properly. Specifically, real-mode diagnostics often cause Windows error messages stating that the program tried to access hardware resources directly and was prevented from doing so by Windows.

The Windows NT/2000/XP Boot Process

Windows NT, Windows 2000, and Windows XP differ from the Windows 98/Me boot process. They do not use DOS components to start Windows NT/2000/XP. The Windows 2000 boot process is: Power on start and hardware POST are executed. This is the hardware dependent portion common to starting all PC operating systems. Windows 2000/XP requires a plug-and-play BIOS to properly configure the PCs plug-and-play hardware. BIOS startup and OS detection is also common to all PCs. In this stage, the BIOS loader programs search for the loadable operating system as directed by the CMOS or NVRAM setup parameters. The floppy disk, fixed disk, CD_ROM, or network are usually searched for a bootable operating system.

Windows 2000/XP bootstrap loading is performed, allowing multiple operating systems to be loaded. Windows NT and Windows 2000/XP do not need to reside on the primary partition of the first or active fixed disk drive. The key Windows 2000/XP files required to load Windows 2000/XP are:

1. NTLDR
2. BOOT.INI
3. NTDETECT.COM
4. CDLDR

Other files present for dual boot or multiple-boot systems are:

5. BOOTSEC.DAT

Systems with large SCSI or EIDE drives may also have:

6. NTBOOTDD.SYS

Other files that are not necessarily needed but may be located elsewhere are:

7. HYBERFILL.SYS
8. NTOSKRNL.EXE
9. HAL.DLL
10. SYSTEM.KEY

NTLDR presents the multi-boot option and loads the operating system selected. When Windows 2000/XP is selected, the CPU is placed into 32-bit flat memory addressing operating mode, the NTFS or FAT file system is identified, and BOOT.INI is examined to determine the operating systems available. See Figure 14–40. At this point the user is also presented an option: "For troubleshooting and advanced startup options for Windows 2000/XP, press F8". This enters the alternative boot up selections where the user is permitted to boot:

1. Safe Mode
2. Safe Mode with Networking
3. Safe Mode with Command Prompt
4. Enable Boot Logging
5. Enable VGA Mode
6. Last Known Good Configuration
7. Directory Services Restore Mode (Windows 2000 domain controllers only)
8. Debugging Mode
9. Boot Normally
10. Return to OS Choices Menu

When Windows 2000/XP continues to boot normally, NTDETECT.COM performs hardware detection providing the computer ID, fixed disk adapter type, video controller, keyboard, mouse, serial ports, parallel port, and floppy disk drive type. The user is then offered to select alternative hardware profiles if they were established for this PC. Next NTLDR loads the Windows 2000 kernel (NTOSKRNL.EXE) and the hardware abstraction layer (HAL.DLL) into RAM. The NTOSKRNL.EXE then looks at the configuration and collects information on the PC's network connections and user logons. The kernel then starts the services that have been configured to load automatically. The hardware registry settings are confirmed and initialized. Finally, the user logon screen is displayed on the PC's monitor.

The user must strike CTRL+ALT+DEL to logon to the Windows 2000 PC and the network to which it is attached. The final step is to load the user profile and other settings that customize Windows 2000 to that user.

Figure 14–40
Windows 2000 BOOT.INI file.

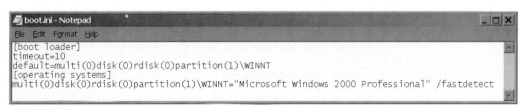

Study Break: Boot Errors

The purpose of this exercise is to determine what errors occur during the boot process when specific software programs are missing from a PC.

Go to a Windows 95/98/Me PC. Make a fresh startup diskette.

Change to the *Windows* directory and rename the WIN.COM program WINCOM.

Reboot the PC to see what happens. What error messages are displayed?

Use the startup diskette to reboot the system into Windows DOS. Change to the \\Windows directory and rename the WINCOM program back to WIN.COM. Next rename CONFIG.SYS to CONFIG and AUTOEXEC.BAT to AUTOEXEC.

Reboot the PC again and see what happens. Generally, Windows should boot normally. DOS TSR programs like DOSKEY cannot be run, but otherwise the PC should function properly.

Rename CONFIG to CONFIG.SYS and AUTOEXEC to AUTOEXEC.BAT. Now rename MSDOS.SYS to MSDOS. Again, reboot the PC to determine the impact of this file missing during the boot process.

Use the startup disk if necessary to return MSDOS to MSDOS.SYS.

The purpose of this exercise was to illustrate the impact of missing files on the Windows 95/98/Me boot process.

Loading and Adding Device Drivers

Device drivers are programs that interface directly with PC hardware components, such as printers, CD-ROMs, specialized boards and so forth. They are the programs that directly interact with the PC hardware. Device drivers can be loaded for DOS and Windows. Manufacturers of the devices themselves frequently provide these drivers.

Device Drivers and DOS

DOS device drivers are loaded using statements in the CONFIG.SYS file. The DEVICE= and DEVICEHIGH= statements load the device driver specified into lower memory or into the UMA. The most common device drivers loaded are the memory managers (device=HIMEM.SYS and device=EMM386.EXE) and the CD-ROM driver programs. Device drivers are added to or modified in CONFIG.SYS manually by special device installation programs or by MEMMAKER.

Device Drivers and Windows 3.x

Windows 3.x adds device drivers on top of those loaded by DOS. It specifies added device driver programs in the SYSTEM.INI file with DEVICE= statements. Some statements load standard drivers like "device=*vfd", which specifies the standard floppy disk driver. The * denotes a standard driver. In contrast "device=vcache.386" loads an enhanced device driver for managing cache memory.

Device drivers are added to or modified in SYSTEM.INI, the Windows 3.x setup program, or by special device installation programs. It is possible to manipulate the device drivers manually with a simple text-editing program like NOTEPAD.EXE. This, however, is not the recommended approach to managing device drivers for Windows 3.x.

Device Drivers and Windows 95/98/Me

Windows 95/98/Me can use CONFIG.SYS and SYSTEM.INI to install device drivers, but more often device drivers are specified in the registry. The Windows 95/98/Me device drivers are installed during Windows setup by the plug-and-play device installation, by special device installation programs, or using the system utility in the Windows control panel. Windows 95, Windows 98/Me, and Windows 2000 all have similar device driver installation procedures. Windows 95, Windows 98/Me, and Windows 2000/XP come with device drivers for most standard PC hardware components. Windows 98/Me and Windows 2000/XP come with a very wide variety of device drivers. However, components often require added device drivers to perform to their full potential.

Special Hardware Device Drivers

Many hardware components need the latest Windows certified or special device drivers to activate all their features and capabilities. Windows 98/Me has device drivers built in for the components listed in Figure 14–41. Windows 2000/XP also comes with many built-in device drivers.

Figure 14–41
Windows 98/Me built-in device drivers.

However, when a device needs newer or updated drivers, these can be installed by entering the control panel, selecting add new hardware, letting Windows search for plug-and-play devices, then selecting the device category from the list that finally appears. Once the category is selected, a more detailed list of manufacturers appears. Each manufacturer has their components and the built-in Windows drivers listed. New special drivers can now be added by selecting the "Have Disk" option. See Figure 14–42.

To update drivers, the control panel's system icon can be used to select the component and open its properties. The device driver for that specific component can be updated in the properties window. This is helpful when installing new device drivers for a specific Windows component. This installation approach also provides a "Have Disk" option.

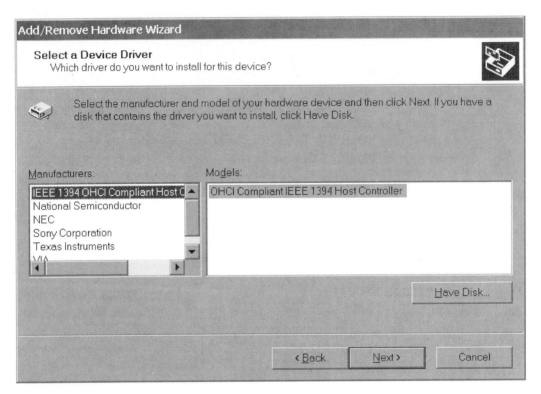

Figure 14–42
Windows 2000 hardware Wizard.

The "Have Disk" option prompts for insertion of a manufacturer's installation diskette into drive A. The files can be resident anywhere because browsing for the files is supported. See Figure 14–43.

Windows goes to the installation diskette and searches for an INF file that describes how to install the PC component. The INF files provide the Windows SETUP program with detailed information on how to install drivers for a specific hardware and software component. They specify which software files are to be copied into which specific directories. The INF files contain the registry updates needed to complete the installation. The component manufacturer provides INF files to guide the SETUP program during installation of the specific hardware component.

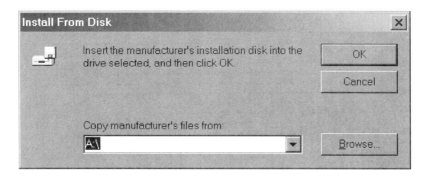

Figure 14–43
Manufacturer installation disk window.

A typical INF file is listed is as follows:

```
; Setup file for Kensington Scroll Mouse minidriver
; Copyright (C) 1993-1997, All rights reserved.
[Version]
Signature="$CHICAGO$"
Class=Mouse
Provider=%Provider%
ClassGUID={4D36E96F-E325-11CE-BFC1-08002BE10318}
[DestinationDirs]
DefaultDestDir = 11   ; LDID_SYS
Serial.Copy = 11
PS2.Copy = 11
mouclass_CopyFiles = 12   ;DIRID_DRIVERS
Ser_CopyFiles = 12
PS2_CopyFiles = 12
PMouse_CopyFiles = 11
[SourceDisksNames]
91=%PMouseDisk%,,1
[SourceDisksFiles]
ksmcplx.dll=91
ksmoused.exe=91
ksmousep.vxd=91
.

.
NTuninst.EXE=91
; Manufacturer Sections
; ─────────────────────
```

```
[Manufacturer]
%Mfg%=Mfg
[Mfg]
%PS2.Desc%=PS2_Inst,*PNP0F13,*PNP0F0E,*PNP0F12,*PNP0F0B,*PNP0F03,*PNP0F
19
%Se-
rial.Desc%=Ser_Inst,SERENUM\PEL0002,*PNP0F0C,*PNP0F01,*PNP0F08,*PNP0F0A
,*PNP0F0F
[ClassInstall]
AddReg=MouseReg
[MouseReg]
HKR,,,0,"Mouse"
HKR,,Installer,0,SetupX.Dll, Mouse_ClassInstaller
HKR,,Icon,0,-2
; ─────────────────────
; Install sections
; ─────────────────────
;──────── Serial Mouse Win95 ────-
[Ser_Inst]
DelReg=Prev.DelReg
Ad-
dReg=Serial.AddReg,3DMouse.AddReg,3DMouse.AddUninstallReg,3DMouse.AddUn
installReg.95
CopyFiles=Serial.Copy,3DMouse.Copy
UpdateInis=Serial.Ini
[Serial.AddReg]
HKR,,DevLoader,,*vmouse
HKR,,MouseDriver,,ksmouses.vxd
HKR,,MouseType,0,Serial
HKR,,NoSetupUI,0,1
HKR,,ProviderName,,%Provider%
HKR,,DriverVersion,,%DriverVersion%
[Serial.Copy]
ksmouses.vxd
[Serial.Ini]
system.ini,boot.description,,"mouse.drv="%Serial.Desc%
system.ini,boot,,"mouse.drv=mouse.drv"
system.ini,386Enh,,"mouse=*vmouse"
;──────── PS2 Mouse Win95 ────-
[PS2_Inst]
.
.
HKLM,"Software\Microsoft\Windows\CurrentVersion\Uninstall\3DMouse\Delet
eFiles",ksmousep.vxd,0,"%SYS_DIR%"
```

```
HKLM,"Software\Microsoft\Windows\CurrentVersion\Uninstall\3DMouse\Delet
eFiles",ksmouses.vxd,0,"%SYS_DIR%"
HKLM,"Software\Microsoft\Windows\CurrentVersion\Uninstall\3DMouse\Resto
reDriver\"%Provider%,%PS2.Desc%,0,"Standard PS/2 Mouse"
HKLM,"Software\Microsoft\Windows\CurrentVersion\Uninstall\3DMouse\Resto
reDriver\"%Provider%,%Serial.Desc%,0,"Standard Serial Mouse"
HKLM,"Software\Microsoft\Windows\CurrentVersion\Uninstall\3DMouse\Delet
eKey","Software\PEL\3DMouse",0,HKEY_CURRENT_USER
HKLM,"Software\Microsoft\Windows\CurrentVersion\Uninstall\3DMouse\Delet
eKey","Enum\Root\PEL0002",0,""
[3DMouse.AddUninstallReg.NT]
HKLM,"Software\Microsoft\Windows\CurrentVersion\Uninstall\3DMouse\Delet
eFiles",ksmi8042.sys,0,"%SYS32_DIR%"
.

.
ksuninst.exe,NTUninst.EXE
; ————————————————
; User-visible Strings
[Strings]
Provider = "Kensington"
MouseClassName = "Mouse"
DriverVersion = "1.36"
ProductName = "Kensington Scroll Mouse"
; Mfg Names
Mfg="Kensington"
; Disk Names
.

.
; Description of device also controlled by a shared driver
PS2_Inst.SharedDriverMsg = "Keyboard Port"
```

The INF file copies the new EXE, DRV, DLL and other software components to the system to install the special PC hardware component. It makes the necessary registry changes to load these software drivers and components when Windows is restarted.

Special hardware drivers can be updated or installed using the system selection in the control panel. Opening system and selecting device manager shows a list of the hardware devices installed in the PC. See Figure 14–44.

Under each item arethe devices installed in that category. As shown in Figure 14–44, this PC has an ATI 3D Rage Pro installed. By opening display adapters, you can see a list of the specific hardware installed. Opening properties for the specific hardware component provides information on its configuration and the driver programs used by Windows. The properties window displays general properties, the driver program, and the resources used by the

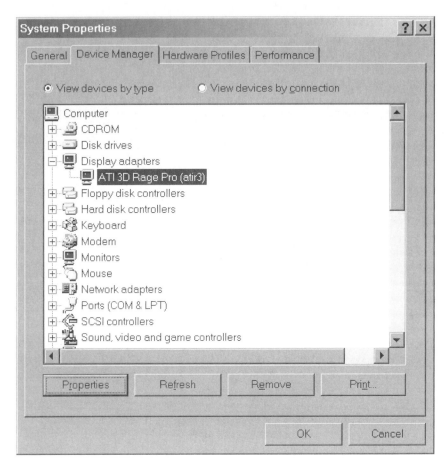

Figure 14–44
Hardware list.

hardware component, as shown in Figure 14–45. When the driver tab is selected, the update driver button appears. This button can be used to update or install special drivers for that specific hardware component. Similar to the "Have Disk" installation, Windows will search for a diskette or browse for a directory containing an INF file that installs the drivers for the selected hardware component.

Special hardware drivers are installed in both Windows 95 and 98/Me and Windows 2000/XP using these approaches. Even with standard driver support, the full features of a specific hardware component are not utilized unless special driver software for that component is installed. USB devices are a classic example. Although communication can be established with the device, it is not

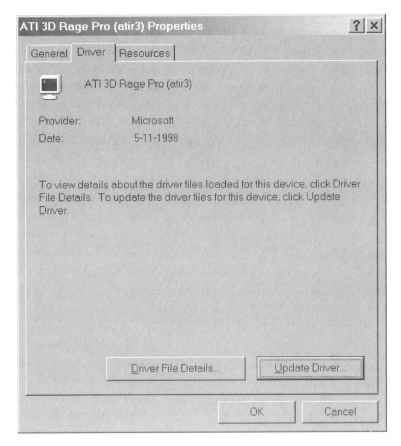

Figure 14–45
Hardware properties.

often integrated into the Windows installation effectively until special driver software is installed.

Plug-and-Play Drivers

Plug-and-play drivers can be installed using the control panel to select the "Add New Hardware" option, which causes Windows to perform its plug-and-play hardware scan in an attempt to spot new plug-and-play hardware components. See Figure 14–46. A full discussion of plug-and-play and its functionality is covered earlier in this chapter.

917

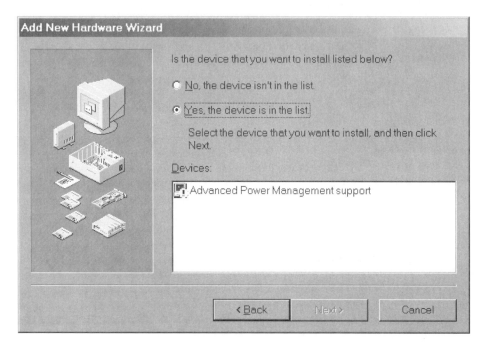

Figure 14–46
Entering plug-and-play scan.

Study Break: INF Files

The purpose of this exercise is to illustrate the use of INF files during PC hardware component installation.

Go to a Windows 95/98/Me PC. Identify a hardware component that has special drivers like a display controller, sound board, or mouse.

Find the driver diskette with those special drivers. If a diskette cannot be found, locate the vendor's web site and find the latest driver files for the component.

Copy or set up the drivers in a \INSTALL\device_name folder.

Copy the (or one of the) INF file(s) found to file_name.OLD to preserve a copy of the original file.

Edit the INF file using NOTEPAD or WordPad (WRITE.EXE). Locate individual sections in the file. A section is identified by [SECTION_NAME]. What sections are there? Can you find [version], [SourceDisksNames], [SourceDisksFiles], [Manufacturer], [UninstHlp], [INFFiles], [INFOther], [SysFiles], [IniFiles], and [Strings] sections?

Delete the INF file and try updating the component's drivers using the control panel–system–device manager. Select the specific hardware component for this driver diskette, then open the driver tab and use update drivers. Does it find the drivers on the diskette or in the fixed disk folder you created?

Use the backup copy of the INF file to restore the INF file. Repeat the process above to determine if the device drivers for the hardware component are found.

This exercise demonstrated the role that INF files play in installing and configuring Windows.

Windows Configuration

Every Windows PC has specific Windows applets, hardware components, and application programs installed that comprise the Windows configuration for that specific PC. Changing the Windows configuration is accomplished using the control panel and the "Add Hardware" and "Add/remove Programs" options. We have just examined the "Add Hardware" selection. Windows components and applications are changed using the "Add/remove Software" selection identified in Figure 14–47.

The "Add/remove Programs" selection permits application programs to be removed, Windows components to be added or removed, or a startup diskette to be created.

Figure 14–47
Configuration change icons.

Add New Hardware

Add/Remove
Programs

Changing Installed Options

Once "Add/remove Programs" is selected, the properties window appears, as shown in Figure 14–48. The first tab, install/uninstall, permits software to be removed from the PC. Application software installation is not typically performed from this menu but rather by a setup program provided by the software

Figure 14–48
Add/remove program properties.

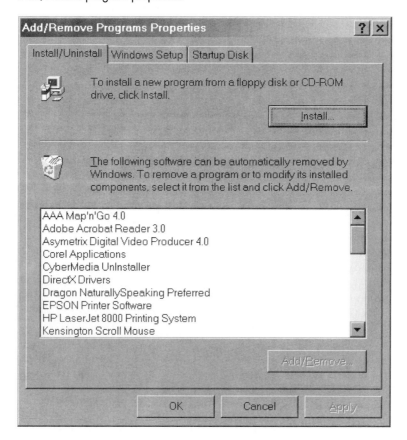

manufacturer. Uninstalling software using the "uninstall" option depends upon a DEISL1.ISU, DEISL2.ISU, DEISL3.ISU, … DEISLn.ISU or other .ISU files specifically tailored to uninstall an application. Windows creates this file during installation. These are binary files that cannot be readily edited. If the specific file cannot be found, then Windows cannot uninstall the application.

When this happens, the best alternative is probably to use third-party uninstall software to remove the program. Otherwise, you can reinstall and then immediately uninstall the software to remove the entries. Unfortunately, with Microsoft software it seems that the uninstall process still leaves some entries in the registry and some program files on the fixed disk. The only absolute way to uninstall such programs is to have the third-party uninstaller software observe the installation process to record every installation change and to assure that every registry entry and program has been removed.

Clicking on the Windows setup option displays the Windows components that have been configured for the PC. See Figure 14–49. Checking or unchecking the boxes causes Windows to install or uninstall the components.

Sometimes this is used to add or change the mix of desktop themes or to add other components, like disk compression, or the Windows 98/Me FAT-16 to FAT-32 conversion program. When more disk space is needed or when program interaction is causing Windows to crash, the add/remove programs selection is used to remove unnecessary and potentially troublesome Windows components.

The Windows components may be installed individually or as an entire group identified in the Windows setup properties window.

Installing and Configuring Printers

Printer installation under Windows 95/98/Me is an easy process. It is described in the Chapter 6 study break exercise, "Setting Up A Printer" and reviewed here. Windows NT/2000/XP installation is similar to the Windows 95/98/Me installation. For DOS-based PCs, the application program was configured to operate with specific printers. For example, Lotus 1-2-3 under DOS used special SET files to configure display and printer options for the DOS-based Lotus 1-2-3 program. Windows 3.x changed this by providing the first printer setup for all applications. Windows 95/98/Me and Windows NT/2000/XP use printer setup wizards that guide you through the installation process, reducing the chance of making mistakes. Installing printers and the printer installation wizard is activated through the control panel printers icon or through the "My Computer" printers icon. See Figure 14–50.

Double-clicking on the icon allows access to installed printers and the "Add Printer" icon. Each printer in the windows represents a printer and a queue

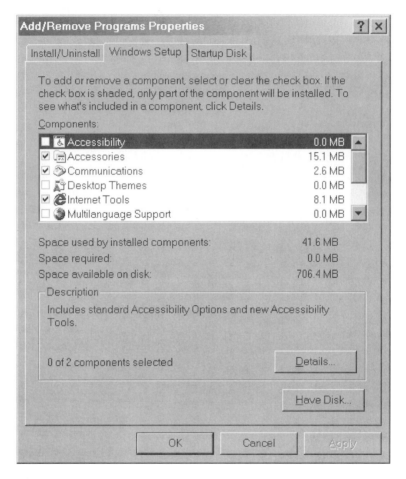

Figure 14-49
Windows component setup.

Figure 14-50
Printers icon.

for holding data for printout. Opening a printer displays the print queue and manages the print jobs. Opening the "Add Printer" icon starts the "Add Printer" Wizard. See Figure 14–51.

922

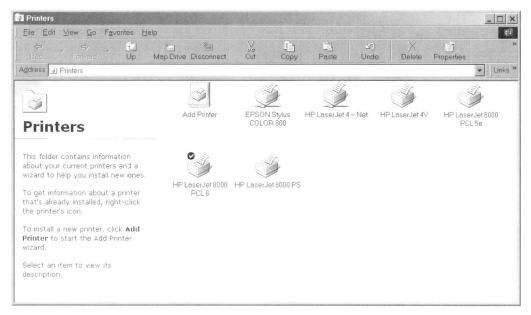

Figure 14-51
Printers window.

Once the printers Wizard is started, it steps through the printer installation process. First it asks whether it is a local or network printer, then it lists built-in drivers for printers by manufacturer.

The printer to be installed is selected from this list. When a manufacturer or printer is not on the list, the "Have Disk" button can install the special driver software for that printer. See Figure 14-52.

After you have selected the printer from the list, then Wizard queries on which port is the printer installed if you indicated it is to be a local printer.

The port options for local printers are COM1, COM2, COM3, File or LPT1. The Wizard then asks for a printer name and finally offers to print a test page. This completes the printer installation and the new printer now appears as an icon in the printers window.

Sometimes printers cannot be matched exactly, and the software controls vary from printer to printer. HP LaserJet printers are a classic example. When it is necessary to operate a new HP LaserJet printer and the driver software is not available for it, choosing LaserJet II drivers often installs the printer and permits it to act effectively. This is because newer LaserJet printers are designed to be backward compatible with older LaserJet printers. The new printers have features that the older software cannot utilize. They can perform all the basic printing functions using the older driver software.

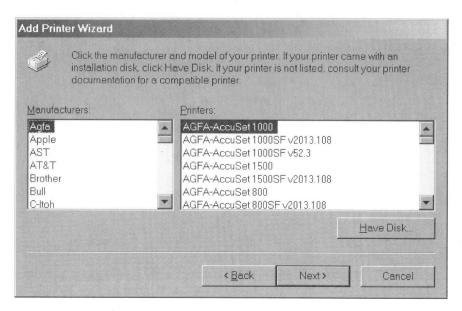

Figure 14–52
Printer selection list.

Network printers are as easily installed as local printers. The difference between a network installation and a local printer installation is that network is specified during the installation process and not local printer. The network is then browsed for the specific printer queue that is appropriately shared. Once found, this is captured and assigned to the printer. Now the printing is redirected across the network to the network printer.

Some network printers are directly network attached. Their installation is most easily performed using the installation disk or CD-ROM provided by the printer manufacturer. This installation may require configuring the printer using a web browser to assure that the printer's IP address matches the IP addresses of the network. See Figure 14–53. Such configurations are easily made following the menu options displayed on the web browser.

Sharing a printer is equally easy. A locally configured printer can be shared on any PC that is network attached by sharing the printer on the network. The printer is shared with a local password or as part of a domain with domain-administered security.

When a network-defined printer is not connected or powered on, Windows sends an error message to the user trying to print and queues the data sent for printing. Once the printer is returned to service, Windows sends the data in the queue to the printer for printing.

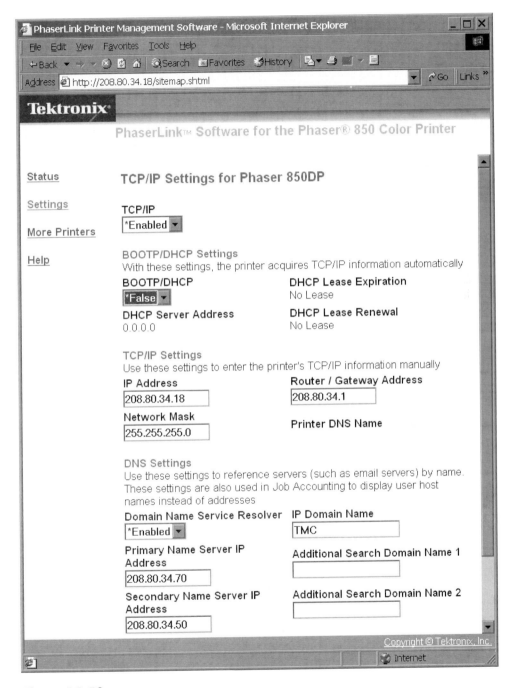

Figure 14–53
Web browser printer configuration.

Study Break: Printer Operation

The purpose of this exercise is to illustrate printer operation under Windows.

Go to a Windows 95/98/Me PC that has a local printer. Open NOTEPAD and use it to edit a single page text file.

Print the file to the local printer. The page should print OK.

Now power off the printer and attempt to reprint the file. What error message does Windows display?

Shut down the PC and restart. Does Windows display any startup warnings?

Power the printer back on. Does the page print OK?

The purpose of this exercise is to illustrate how Windows behaves when the printer is powered down or generally not available to print. The same steps can be performed using a network printer.

Launching Windows Applications

Windows applications can be launched in several different ways. This section briefly discusses the ways in which Windows applications can be started, including the start menu, file associations, shortcuts, and running the program.

The most common way is to use the start menu similar to the Windows 3.x program manager. The start menu lists the programs installed on the PC in groupings established by the *C:\windows\start menu\programs* directory structure. Double-clicking on the application icon or shortcut launches the application.

File associations can also start applications. Every file type is associated with an application. When the user double-clicks on the data file, Windows launches the application and loads the data into it. For example, JPG image files on our PCs are associated with the Microsoft photo editor. Double-clicking on an image file launches the Microsoft photo editor and loads the JPG image into it. Often, installing new software changes the file associations that were previously used on a PC. This greatly dismays the PC user. With Windows, selecting the file, clicking the right mouse button, selecting "Open with", and selecting the desired application program can quickly restore these associations. Be sure this is done with the "Always use this program to open these files" box checked. This procedure restores the previous program associations or creates new ones. See Figure 14–54.

Another way to run Windows programs is to create desktop shortcuts. A shortcut is an icon that points to the EXE file launching the application. Double-clicking on the shortcut icon launches the application. These shortcuts can be placed on the desktop or in the quick launch toolbar, and are activated by a single click in the quick launch toolbar.

The final way to launch programs is to use the Windows run function. Open the start menu and select run to bring up the run window, as shown in Figure 14–55.

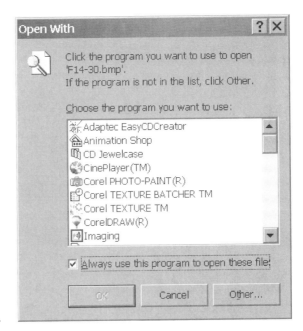

Figure 14–54
Open with ... panel.

Figure 14–55
Run window.

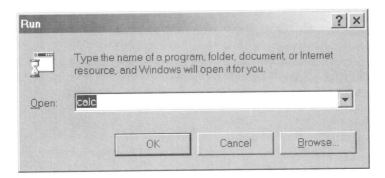

Entering the name of the program and selecting OK launches the program. Some common program names are SOL for solitaire, CALC for the calculator, COMMAND for the DOS prompt and REGEDIT for the registry editor.

Study Break: Windows Run Function

This exercise demonstrates the run function.

Go to a Windows 95/98/Me PC and click on the start button. Select run and enter NOTEPAD. Click on OK to launch the NOTEPAD program.

Repeat the same sequence of steps to run COMMAND to open a DOS Window.

Repeat the same sequence of steps to run SOL, the Windows solitaire game.

Click on the start button and select run again. This time use the down-arrow to the right of the entry panel to drop down the list of programs previously run. This should show NOTEPAD, COMMAND, and SOL in reverse chronological order (the most recently run program should be at the top of the list).

Click on the Browse button and select WRITE.EXE or WORDPAD.EXE. This should launch WordPad.

This exercise illustrated that the run function can be used to launch both Windows and DOS programs, and that it remembers the programs recently run.

Summary

This chapter has examined the procedures and technical aspects of installing DOS and Windows. It identified the differences between Windows 3.x, Windows 95/98/Me and Windows 2000 installation and listed the requirements for upgrading to newer versions of Windows. These requirements are much less significant because newer PC hardware easily exceeds the minimal hardware requirements for upgrading to newer versions of Windows. The key upgrade consideration is hardware compatibility and availability of Windows certified hardware driver programs. This is particularly true of the key hardware components: MLB, disk controller, video adapter, and NIC. The boot procedures and startup process were described, including special startup options for DOS and Windows. These presented the basic procedures for beginning to troubleshoot Windows installation problems. Finally, configuring device drivers and Windows software components were discussed, along with procedures for launching Windows software.

Chapter Review Questions

1. *What disk is used to COLD boot a PC?*

    A. Setup disk
    B. System disk
    C. Diagnostic disk
    D. Program disk

Answer: B, system disk. While operating system setup diskettes can boot a PC, application program and hardware component setup diskettes do not boot a PC. Diagnostic and program diskettes may also boot a PC, but some diagnostic programs and other programs are so large that they make it impossible to boot the PC from the diagnostic or program diskette.

2. *IFS means:*

    A. Installable file system
    B. Installable fixed-disk system
    C. Inflatable file system
    D. Independent file system

Answer: A, installable file system. Nothing is inflatable or independent when it comes to file systems. There are only file systems, no fixed disk systems.

3. *What program is used to install 32-bit FAT?*

    A. FORMAT
    B. EXPLORER
    C. FDISK
    D. SCANDISK

Answer: C, FDISK. The 32-bit FAT is a partitioning decision. Consequently, FORMAT formats a drive that has the 32-bit FAT partition on it, SCANDISK examines the partition and file structure and corrects errors it finds, and EXPLORER helps manage files on disks with a 32-bit FAT.

4. *The Windows program used to begin Windows installation is:*

    A. FORMAT
    B. INSTALL
    C. AUTOEXEC.INF
    D. SETUP

Answer: D, SETUP. FORMAT formats a drive or prepares it to receive Windows installation files. INSTALL is used with some software as an installation program, but rarely (if ever) with Microsoft produced software. AUTOEXEC.INF is not a file used to start anything. AUTORUN.INF is a startup file for CD-ROMs that may lead to the Windows SETUP program. AUTOEXEC.BAT starts programs in DOS.

5. *Windows is typically installed in which directory?*

    A. WIN
    B. Windows
    C. System
    D. Windows\options\cabs
    E. Program Files
    F. WIN\SYSTEM

Answer: B, Windows. Windows 95/98/Me is installed in a Windows folder by default and Windows NT/2000 is installed in a WINNT folder. There is no standard folder called WIN. The System folder contains some key Windows files, but not all of them. System is found under the Windows folder. Windows\options\cabs is the typical location for the Windows installation files. The Program Files folder contains the application program installation files but not Windows files. If there is no "WIN\SYSTEM" folder created by Windows during installation.

6. *Installing Windows 98 requires what?*

    A. 16 MB RAM
    B. 486 25 MHz CPU
    C. 8 GB fixed disk
    D. 8 MB VGA card

Answer: A, 16 MB RAM. 8 MB RAM is the minimum for Windows 95, but 16 MB is minimum for Windows 98. The VGA card has more RAM than required, and the fixed disk size well exceeds the minimum required for Windows 98. While Windows 98 is designed to run (rather slowly, I might add) on a 486 chip PC (and fortunately

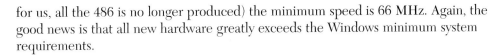

for us, all the 486 is no longer produced) the minimum speed is 66 MHz. Again, the good news is that all new hardware greatly exceeds the Windows minimum system requirements.

7. *Windows boot problems often result from device conflicts where?*

    A. The fixed disk
    B. The registry and plug-and-play components
    C. DOS
    D. SCSI devices and the registry

Answer: B, the registry and plug-and-play components. EIDE fixed disk drives cause few Windows problems, in addition to SCSI devices. Most Windows boot problems do not happen while DOS is starting the PC, but rather when control is handed to Windows.

8. *Windows must be installed from a CD-ROM drive.*

    A. TRUE
    B. FALSE

Answer: B, FALSE. The fastest way to install Windows is to use SMARTDRV and copy the Windows installation files to a fixed disk, then install from the fixed disk. Windows can be installed from a fixed disk, a network, or a CD-ROM drive.

9. *CD-ROM drives are not bootable.*

    A. TRUE
    B. FALSE

Answer: B, FALSE. Depending upon the PC's BIOS and the CD_ROM used, CD-ROMs can be used to boot a PC and install software directly.

10. *Which files are required for DOS to boot?*

    A. MSDOS.SYS, CONFIG.SYS and COMMAND.COM
    B. IO.SYS, MSDOS.SYS, CONFIG.SYS and COMMAND.COM
    C. IO.SYS MSDOS.SYS, and COMMAND.COM
    D. MSDOS.SYS, AUTOEXEC.BAT and COMMAND.COM

Answer: C, IO.SYS, MSDOS.SYS, and COMMAND.COM. CONFIG.SYS and AUTOEXEC.BAT are optional but not required.

11. *Which file is the Windows 95/98/Me real mode operating system?*

    A. MSDOS.SYS
    B. CONFIG.SYS
    C. COMMAND.COM
    D. WIN.COM
    E. None of the above

Answer: E, none of the above. Windows 95/98/Me do not operate in real mode. Only Windows 3.x provided real mode for 80286 chip systems.

12. *Holding the F5 key during Windows boot acts like what other key?*

    A. F8
    B. Ctrl
    C. F6
    D. Shift

Answer: D, Shift. Holding down the Shift key causes Windows 98 to bypass the startup files just like holding down the F5 key and boot into safe mode. Holding down the CTRL key boots into the Windows startup menu. F6 boots into safe mode with minimal network support. F8 boots to the Windows startup menu providing the NORMAL, LOGGED, SAFE MODE, Step-by-Step CONFIRMATION, COMMAND PROMPT ONLY, or SAFE MODE COMMAND PROMPT ONLY boot options.

13. *Holding the Ctrl key boots Windows into what?*

    A. Safe mode
    B. MS-DOS
    C. The Windows startup menu
    D. Step-by-step confirmation

Answer: C, the Windows startup menu. Safe mode is entered when Shift or F5 is held down. MS-DOS is entered when Shift+F5 is held down. Holding down F8 enters the Windows startup menu. Step-by-step confirmation is entered directly by holding down Shift+F8.

14. *A cold boot is performed by:*

    A. Hitting Ctrl-Alt-Del
    B. Powering off the monitor
    C. Hitting the reset button
    D. Exiting Windows
    E. Booting from a floppy disk in drive A:

Answer: C, hitting the reset button. Hitting CTRL+ALT+DEL opens the task manger. Powering off the monitor only causes the display to be off and does not reboot the PC. Sometimes powering off the PC causes a cold boot, but with ATX style MLBs this is not a guarantee. During a warm or cold boot, the PC can boot from a floppy disk drive.

15. *Application programs are launched in Windows:*

    A. From the run window
    B. By double-clicking on the data
    C. By double-clicking on a desktop shortcut
    D. By clicking on a quick launch shortcut
    E. All of the above
    F. None of the above

Answer: E, all of the above. Opening Start, then "Run", and entering the name of the program in the run panel launches the application program. Windows associates data files with an application program so double-clicking on the data launches the program. Double-clicking on a desktop shortcut or clicking on a quick launch short-cut also launches applications programs.

16. *PCs can boot from:*

    A. The fixed disk
    B. The floppy disk
    C. The CD-ROM
    D. A network
    E. All of the above

Answer: E, all of the above. A PC usually boots from the floppy disk first and then the fixed disk drive. Depending upon the BIOS and the PC components, the PC could also boot from a CD-ROM or from the network.

17. *Device drivers can be installed in Windows using what?*

    A. The control panel ➤ add new hardware
    B. Installing the plug-and-play component in the PC
    C. The control panel ➤ system ➤ device manager ➤ selecting the device and then properties and update driver
    D. Running manufacturer-supplied installation software
    E. All of the above
    F. None of the above

Answer: E, all of the above. Device drivers are installed in a variety of ways, including the add new hardware selection under the control panel, selecting control panel–system–device manager–the device–properties and then update driver, or running manufacturer-supplied installation software. Plug-and-play hardware drivers are installed when a device is first plugged into the PC and the PC is booted.

Chapter 15

DOS AND WINDOWS SOFTWARE PROBLEM DIAGNOSIS AND RESOLUTION

Chapter Syllabus

- Common Software Error Messages

- Resolving Frequent Software Problems

- DOS and Windows Utilities

- Viruses and Virus Protection

This chapter covers identifying and resolving software problems in both DOS and Windows environments. Common error messages and their resolution are presented. Although DOS and Windows error messages vary from one version of DOS and Windows to another, the error messages identify common software problems. We discuss DOS and Windows maintenance and problem resolution utilities and explore their use in preventing and resolving software problems. Finally, there is a discussion of virus detection and virus removal.

Common Software Error Messages

The software error messages for DOS and Windows are quite different, although they sometimes stem from common problems. Generally, both DOS and Windows errors are caused by memory conflicts, inadequate memory, or incorrect versions of software. A bad mix (or blend) of Windows software (mixing old and new virtual device drivers (VxDs), DLLs, and driver programs) causes the worst type of error, resulting in the "blue screen of death." In this instance, the quickest and most effective solution is to reinstall Windows with the latest Microsoft certified hardware drivers. Reinstalling Windows is what most people dread, but it is a faster and more reliable route to solving software conflicts than trying to find the misbehaving software components. We have spent eight to ten hours seeking bad software and trying unsuccessfully to remove it from Windows in a vain attempt to solve software conflict problems. If we had updated hardware drivers and reinstalled Windows, we would have been operating reliably in about two hours.

In contrast, when problems can be directly attributed to specific hardware components, they may be easily corrected. Most often correcting such hardware errors only requires installing the latest hardware driver programs that are readily available from the hardware manufacturer off the Internet. A good source for hardware driver web site references is www.DRIVERSHQ.COM.

Safe Mode

Safe mode is a special Windows diagnostic mode that is used primarily to resolve hardware driver conflicts in Windows. A Windows PC is quite often thrown into safe mode during the boot process when there are problems with the basic hardware driver programs required for Windows to run. These conflicts most often involve the PC's video or display drivers. Otherwise, safe mode is entered using the F5 or F8 keys as described in Chapter 11, "Windows 95/98/Me and Windows 2000 Architecture" and Chapter 14, "Software Installation, Configuration, and Upgrade." The basic hardware drivers are display, EIDE fixed disk, SCSI disk (if a SCSI disk drive is the boot drive), and sometimes LAN card drivers (particularly if they interfere with the display drivers). See Figure 15–1. The C:\BOOTLOG.TXT file can be examined to determine which drivers are in conflict. A quick test is to remove the network adapter and reboot.

It is difficult to tell whether safe mode is needed or not, and Windows sometimes thinks that it should enter safe mode when it should not. However, when

Figure 15–1
Safe mode warning message.

Windows was running successfully with the current PC hardware configuration and safe mode suddenly pops up, there is a good chance it can be ignored. In this case, rebooting and selecting normal mode resolves the problem.

In safe mode, Windows does not provide detailed information for any adapter card settings because it has detected a hardware conflict that prevents the plug-and-play components from completing the resource assignments. See Figure 15–2. The problem resolution strategy from a Windows plug-and-play software perspective is to have the user select specific settings for the conflicting hardware, such as a network card, and then reboot. The hope is that the specific selected settings resolve the Windows plug-and-play software conflict. The Windows plug-and-play software operation should properly complete configuring the PC hardware. This sometimes does not work and results in a continuous cycle of Windows rebooting into safe mode. To break out of the continuous safe mode reboot cycle, the user typically selects specific con-

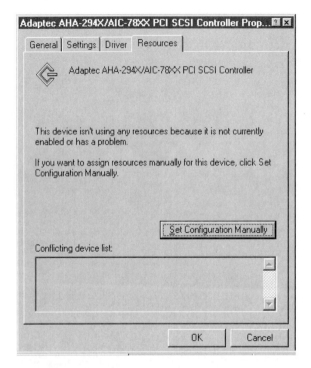

Figure 15–2
Safe mode properties box.

figurations for several components. These configurations can often develop new conflicts that toss the PC back into the continuous safe mode reboot cycle. The ultimate resolution may be to use different hardware components or to find better drivers for the hardware components installed.

The most effective hardware troubleshooting technique is to focus on the display, the MLB, the EIDE fixed disk, and the network adapter. Since the PC should boot properly without a network adapter, remove it and get the PC to boot normally. This action may require adding special display, upgrading MLB BIOS and drivers, and adding fixed disk controller driver programs. Other components are ancillary to Windows booting normally (like sound boards and video camera inputs) and can be removed or ignored. CD and DVD drives use the EIDE interface and usually do not interfere with booting any more than any EIDE fixed disk drive. Zip and Jaz drives may use an SCSI interface, and should probably be removed. Once the PC boots normally with the display and EIDE fixed disk, the other peripherals can then be added one at a time to help the plug-and-play boot software sort out the hardware component assignments. Before adding new components, the IRQ, I/O port, and reserved RAM address settings that work for the display and the EIDE fixed disk should be recorded. The settings can be documented using the Windows control panel—system—device manager selections and then selecting print.

If the PC blows up into safe mode when a new component is added, we can determine that it is the culprit. If this is the case, its configuration must be set manually or better driver programs are required so Windows detects no conflicts.

In safe mode, a standard set of drivers is used for the keyboard, mouse, fixed disk and display. These standard drivers treat the display as a 640 by 480 VGA display, which causes high-resolution display desktop configurations to display at low resolution so that only part of the desktop is visible, making the display less understandable. See Figure 15–3. If Windows works in safe mode, then basic drivers make it boot. Finding and changing the conflicting driver software or related hardware component configuration should permit Windows to boot in normal

Figure 15–3
Safe mode VGA display.

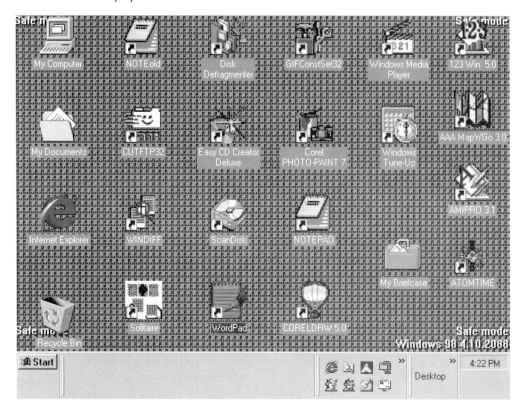

mode. Booting into safe mode signals that there is most likely some conflict with the video or display drivers. Using an older, Windows certified video controller could resolve such safe mode problems until better video drivers are found.

Driver programs are easily updated using the control panel—system—device manager. Making these selections produces a panel that lists all devices. Nonfunctioning devices are typically identified by a red "X" or a yellow "!" warning symbol. Click on the specific device, then the driver tab, for Windows to open a wizard that updates drivers. The new driver program can be loaded from the fixed disk, a floppy diskette, or a CD.

Sometimes Windows indicates no conflicts when in fact there are. There is no outward sign that there is a problem except that the device simply refuses to work.

In this instance, changing an I/O address or a memory address range can make all the difference in the world. Hardware conflicts in Windows are not easy to resolve. Safe mode is a tool to help resolve the most severe hardware conflicts. It is not foolproof. Changing hardware component settings and drivers one component at a time is an effective strategy for using safe mode to resolve severe hardware component conflicts.

The first component to attack when resolving such hardware conflicts is any unusual adapter or component, the LAN card, then the VGA card. Removing all unusual adapters gets the PC back to a basic configuration and sets the foundation for step-by-step troubleshooting. Sometimes disabling USB interfaces is required to return to a basic PC configuration. USB interfaces are disabled using the hardware BIOS (or CMOS) setup. Fixed disk hardware is the most critical for Windows to run and generally works OK when safe mode is entered, except for when Windows is booted from a floppy; this is because the fixed disk cannot boot Windows. If entering "WIN" while the DOS prompt points to the C:\windows directory to launch Windows, Windows may not recognize any of the fixed disks. Making the fixed disk bootable directly into Windows would correct this. Making a fixed disk bootable using a Windows bootable floppy requires that the floppy contain the SYS.COM program. This program is found in the \windows\command folder. When SYS.COM is on a bootable floppy or a readable fixed disk drive, performing the command SYS C: from the bootable floppy diskette drive A causes SYS.COM to transfer the operating system from A to C.

Other hardware component and driver conflicts are generally resolved in normal mode. Windows can boot with other conflicts and the control panel can be used to adjust and resolve hardware component IRQ, I/O port, and memory address conflicts.

Because Windows NT and Windows 2000 work with a more Windows certified base of PC hardware components, fewer "crash upon boot" problems occur. Our experience has been that NT has problems with disk drive controllers; this causes an immediate blue screen of death that tells you nothing usable. Windows 2000 had display driver problems causing the equivalent of a power off reboot time after time. These problems were resolved by using an EIDE disk controller for Windows NT and by striking F8 during the Windows 2000 boot process to get to VGA or Safe Mode and loading the Microsoft certified display drivers. Other Windows 2000 boot problems were caused because the latest MLB ACPI (Advanced Control and Power Interface) and plug-and-play BIOS were not available. A simple BIOS flash to upgrade the BIOS solves this problem.

Incorrect DOS Version

DOS programs are linked to a specific version of DOS. Their features and functions were designed to work with other DOS programs of that specific DOS version. For example, the DOS SHARE.EXE program for DOS 4.x had features in it that were required for using large fixed disk drives. The DOS 5.x and DOS 6.x versions of SHARE.EXE had a different set of features. Running older DOS programs with newer DOS versions could cause some software compatibility problems. Microsoft set up DOS to recognize the specific DOS version with which a DOS program is to work. If the program is started with a different version of DOS, the program stops and displays the message:

```
C:\>chkdsk
Incorrect DOS version
```

This problem is prevented by placing a DEVICE=SETVER.EXE command in the CONFIG.SYS file; this command loads a version table. Windows 3.1 requires SETVER to prevent conflicts. Sometimes the version table must be modified for a specific DOS program by running SETVER to update the version table for that program.

The SETVER.EXE program to update the version table for CHKDSK above is run by:

```
C:\>setver chkdsk.exe 5.00
```

The SETVER.EXE program would enter the CHKDSK program version 5.00 information in a version table which, when queried by the DOS program, would return the DOS version information expected by the DOS program. The SETVER.EXE program function is built into Windows 95/98/Me IO.SYS.

The correct DOS version is only needed for DOS external commands and not for DOS application programs. For example the DOS 5.0 external commands CHKDSK, DISKCOPY, and MODE may require SETVER to run under DOS 6.22, while application programs like the old IBM Personal Editor program

941

(PE2.EXE) or the DOS version of Lotus 1-2-3 do not require SETVER. The DOS EDIT.COM also runs with other versions of DOS without requiring SETVER because it is more like an application program than an external DOS command.

DOS programs using extended memory would not run with DOS 2.x because it was not supported. If they were started with DOS 2.x, they would not display an "Incorrect DOS version" message, but would display a memory error message instead.

Running older DOS programs in a Windows 2000 command prompt Window produces "Incorrect DOS version" messages. See Figure 15–4.

Missing Operating System

When a DOS or Windows bootable disk has no operating system files (IO.SYS, MSDOS.SYS, and COMMAND.COM) to load, the BIOS displays a "missing operating system" or a "non-System disk or disk error" message. This error message may vary depending on the BIOS of the PC. This scenario often occurs

Figure 15–4
Windows 2000 Incorrect DOS version.

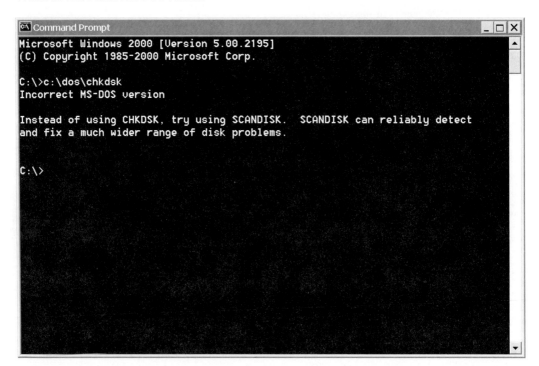

when you have inadvertently left a data disk in the floppy drive. Floppy disks are usually replaced or removed; hit the space bar to continue the booting process.

When this error message is displayed while attempting to boot from a fixed disk, it means that the disk is often partitioned properly, formatted properly, and viewable to the PC and DOS, but the MBR loader program cannot find the DOS files needed to boot. In some cases, there can be serious damage to the fixed disk as well, making it unrecoverable. When a fixed disk is damaged, this message is displayed when BIOS or the MBR loader goes to load DOS and finds a corrupted IO.SYS file.

To tell the difference between a seriously corrupted fixed disk and a fixed disk that is OK but does not boot, boot the PC into DOS using a bootable floppy disk containing SCANDISK.EXE and running SCANDISK.EXE. If SCANDISK.EXE runs OK, the fixed disk is good and the operating system needs to be reinstalled. When SCANDISK reports errors, your problems are more serious.

When SCANDISK runs on a damaged disk it displays error messages as it encounters problems. SCANDISK tries to recover the data and correct the errors as best it can, but severely damaged fixed disks are not recoverable. Minor damage to a fixed disk can be repaired with SCANDISK. If it is repaired, it should probably be replaced because there is a risk that the disk may have more serious errors in the near future.

When SCANDISK.EXE runs okay and the "no operating system found" error message is displayed, the disk and often the data on it can be recovered using FDISK and SYS. The SYS.COM DOS program installs the operating system on a formatted disk drive. When the IO.SYS and MSDOS.SYS files cannot be found, SYS C: executed from a bootable floppy in drive A reinstalls those programs and makes the drive bootable. In the event this does not succeed, FDISK /MBR rewrites the master boot record without losing any data on the fixed disk drive. Performing SYS C: from a bootable floppy in drive A should make the drive bootable. If the boot sector of the drive is physically damaged, this procedure does not work. FDISK would then display an error message like "cannot write to fixed disk."

```
Error in CONFIG.SYS Line xx
```

When DOS or Windows 95/98Me DOS boots a PC, the CONFIG.SYS file may be used to match the PC hardware to DOS as discussed in Chapter 9, "DOS Architecture." Sometimes there can be command errors in the CONFIG.SYS file. If CONFIG.SYS has commands it does not recognize, it displays a message:

```
Unrecognized command in CONFIG.SYS
Error in CONFIG.SYS line xx
```

This indicates that the CONFIG.SYS file has a command line error, which can be fixed by editing the CONFIG.SYS file and changing the specific line to a recognized command.

In the example above, we created the erroneous command "devices=" to produce the error message. When we changed it to "device=," the PC stopped displaying the error message. This error message is displayed when CONFIG.SYS commands are not recognized by IO.SYS. Correcting the command in CONFIG.SYS resolves the errors. Some errors to look for in CONFIG.SYS are common typing errors like entering DEVICE= as DEVCIE=, missing "=" signs, incorrect driver specifications, and incomplete program names like DEVICE=SMARTDRV as opposed to DEVICE=SMARTDRV.EXE.

Bad or Missing COMMAND.COM

Sometimes the COMMAND.COM program as described in Chapter 9 cannot be found, or it is not matched with the version of DOS being used. In this instance, DOS displays the error messages:

```
Invalid COMMAND.COM
Enter correct name of Command Interpreter
(eg, C:\COMMAND.COM)
>>
```

or a

```
Bad or Missing COMMAND.COM
```

DOS cannot find a valid COMMAND.COM or any COMMAND.COM to load into memory and permit further interaction with commands typed in by the PC user. To resolve this problem, find a valid COMMAND.COM that matches the DOS version being used and place it in the root directory of the boot disk drive. With later versions of DOS and Windows DOS, pointing Windows to the COMMAND.COM in the Windows directory as shown below returns DOS to command line operation. Entering "c:\windows\command.com" when prompted points to COMMAND.COM.

```
Invalid COMMAND.COM
Enter correct name of Command Interpreter
(eg, C:\COMMAND.COM)
>>c:\windows\command.com
C:\WINDOWS>
```

This returns DOS 6.xx and Windows DOS to normal operation. Earlier versions of DOS would simply stop running if the COMMAND.COM program were not found. DOS finds the command processor program in either a default location, like the root directory or c:\windows\command, in a location specified by the "SET COMSPEC = c:\dos" DOS command in the AUTOEXEC.BAT file, or by a SHELL=C:\dos\command.com in the CONFIG.SYS file. The set and SHELL commands add the COMMAND.COM location to the DOS environment space.

Bad or Missing HIMEM.SYS

When HIMEM.SYS is referenced in the CONFIG.SYS file but cannot be found during the DOS boot process, the message:

```
Starting MS-DOS...
Bad or missing C:\HIMEM.SYS
```

is displayed. If HIMEM.SYS is corrupted, the system typically locks after the "Starting MS-DOS" message is displayed, necessitating a system reboot that bypasses (using the F5 key) the CONFIG.SYS and AUTOEXEC.BAT startup files. The problem is then resolved by simply placing the correct HIMEM.SYS file in the directory specified in CONFIG.SYS. HIMEM.SYS is provided with both DOS and Windows. To get a good HIMEM.SYS file, check the c:\windows folder, the C:\Windows\Options\Cabs folder, or the original Windows installation CD on a Windows 95/98 PC. A good copy can often be found in these locations.

Missing HIMEM.SYS

Some DOS programs require access to extended memory, and Windows must have extended memory available to run. HIMEM.SYS controls access to both extended memory and the HIMEM area. If HIMEM.SYS is not loaded and a program requests access to extended memory, the error message below indicating that extended memory is not present and that HIMEM.SYS is not loaded is displayed.

```
C:\ >win
Missing HIMEM.SYS;
```

Make sure that the file is in your Windows directory and that its location is correctly specified in your CONFIG.SYS file.

Attempting to run Windows 3.1x without HIMEM.SYS loaded generated this error message. To fix this problem, add the following lines to CONFIG.SYS:

```
Device=c:\HIMEM.SYS
DOS=HIGH
```

The HIMEM.SYS program resides in the root directory of the bootable drive C. With Windows 95/98, the HIMEM.SYS function is loaded by IO.SYS and does not need to be loaded in the CONFIG.SYS file. Windows 95/98 can also require the HIMEM.SYS program. When booted from the recovery diskette without HIMEM.SYS and the extended memory accessed by RAMDrive, Windows 98/Me displays these messages:

```
RAMDrive: Extended Memory Manager not present.
Warning: the high memory area (HMA) is not available.
Additional low memory (below 640K) will be used instead.
To fix this problem add to CONFIG.SYS the lines:
Device=a:\HIMEM.SYS
DOS=HIGH
```

HIMEM.SYS program is installed on the Windows bootable floppy diskette in drive A.

Swap File Error Messages

Swap files are used by Windows to store display images, program code, and other RAM contents on the disk as opposed to in RAM. The swap file creates the Windows virtual memory. In Windows 98/Me/NT/2000 this is a dynamic (temporary) virtual memory swap file that grows and shrinks depending upon the demands placed on the PC. In Windows 3.1x, it could be a temporary or a permanent swap file. The permanent swap file was preferred with Windows 3.1x because it guaranteed that a specific amount of disk space would be set aside for virtual (or paging) memory. The Windows 3.11 permanent swap file was set up using the control panel ➤ 386 enhanced mode ➤ virtual memory selections. (Windows 3.0 used the SWAPFILE program run in real mode to create the swap file.) Windows supports changing from the default temporary swap file to a fixed permanent swap file. See Figure 15–5.

Once established, the swap file settings created SYSTEM.INI entries and SPART.PAR and 386SPART.PAR files on the fixed disk. The 386SPART.PAR file was the actual swap file. The SPART.PAR file in the Windows directory was the control file that pointed to the 386SPART.PAR file.

Sometimes the SYSTEM.INI entries would be changed or the swap file would not match the SPART.PAR and SYSTEM.INI entries. In this event, Windows 3.11 displayed the blue screen "corrupt swap file" warning message, as shown in Figure 15–6. The corrupt swap file warning is only for permanent swap files, because temporary ones are created fresh whenever Windows 3.11 is launched. Although the corrupt swap file message seems alarming because it fills the entire PC display screen, is not a critical error message.

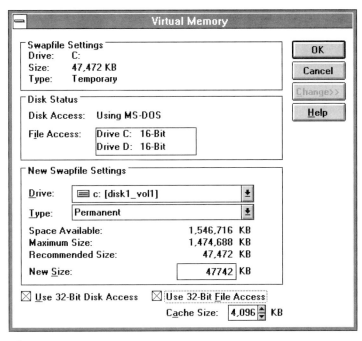

Figure 15–5
Windows 3.1x swap file setup.

Figure 15–6
Swap file warning.

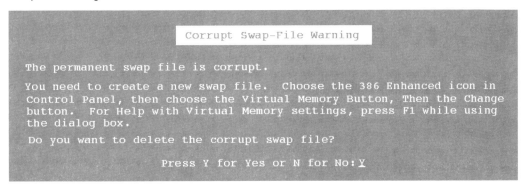

Deleting the corrupt swap file and setting its length to zero as instructed by Windows are the first steps in resolving the problem. Windows performs this process for you when you answer "yes" to the remove the corrupt swap file message query. See Figure 15–7. Once Windows 3.11 has created a new permanent swap file, Windows needs to be shut down and restarted for the new swap file to be used. This is not a reboot from DOS, only a Windows 3.11 shutdown and restart.

Setting up a permanent swap file using the virtual memory settings would then reestablish the permanent swap file. Windows 3.11 recommends a swap file size automatically, but a rule of thumb is to set a swap file at about two to three times the size of the PC's installed RAM. For example, a 64 MB RAM PC should have a 128 MB to 192 MB swap file. The final step is to restart Windows 3.1x to complete the corrective procedure.

Windows 95, Windows98/Me, and Windows NT/2000 use a dynamic swap file that Microsoft touts as a cross between a permanent and a temporary swap file. In reality, using the PC's "let me specify my own virtual memory settings" menu option permits Windows 95/98/Me to use the equivalent of a permanent swap file. See Figure 15–8.

Setting a permanent swap file in Windows 98/Me in this fashion can resolve some memory problems with Windows 95/98/Me. In any case, Windows 95/98/Me and Windows NT/2000 do not display the corrupt swap file message.

The major advantage to letting Windows set a default swap file is that it automatically sets a swap file size that lets almost all PCs deliver speedy and flawless performance for most users. Setting your own swap file can help if you are a power user experiencing memory problems with the programs that you run. In that case, a permanent swap file may make your PC run more reliably, but a human being would not notice any performance differences between Windows automatic settings and a manually set swap file. There is one swap

Figure 15–7
Setting swap file length to zero.

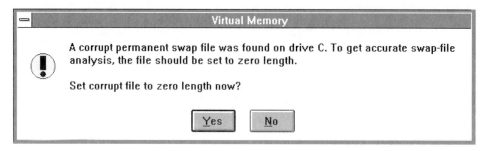

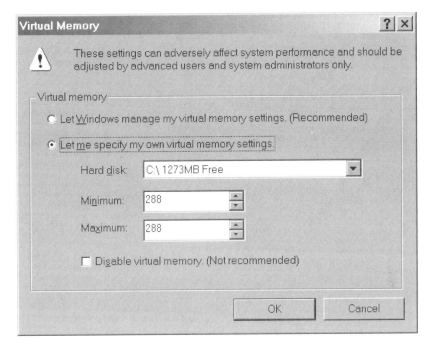

Figure 15-8
Windows 98 permanent swap file setup.

file that Windows uses. It is possible in multiple disk systems to set this swap file on any disk drive. Normally, Windows sets it on the bootable Windows drive C. We set ours on our backup drive E.

Specifying a very large swap file is not really better than a smaller one, and may in some ways degrade performance. When data is swapped to disk, Windows must manage that swap file. Smaller swap files have smaller data structures to process than larger swap files. Hence, a large swap file may actually degrade performance rather than improve it. The primary focus of a permanent swap file is not so much performance, but rather making Windows 95/98/Me perform more predictably when a large variety of programs are run.

Cannot Find a Device File Needed to Run Windows

Sometimes with Windows 3.1x and Windows 95/98/Me/NT/2000, DLLs and other files referenced in the SYSTEM.INI file and in the registry are removed from the hard drive and thereby from the system.

When Windows is started and does not find these files on the disk drive, Windows 3.1x displays the following message:

```
Cannot find a device file that may be needed to run Windows.
Make sure that the PATH line in your AUTOEXEC.BAT file
points to the directory that contains the file and that it
exists on your hard disk. If the file does not exist, try
running Setup to install it or remove any references to it
from your SYSTEM.INI file.
vnetware.386
Press a key to continue
```

Windows 95/98 displays:

```
Cannot find a device file that may be needed to run Windows
or a Windows application.
The windows registry or SYSTEM.INI file refers to this
device file, but the device file no longer exists.
If you deleted this file on purpose, try uninstalling the
associated application using its uninstall or setup
program.
If you still want to use the application associated with
this device file, try reinstalling that application to
replace the missing file.
Dummy.386
Press a key to continue
```

The file identified in the error message is the source of the problem. With Windows 3.1x, it is referenced in the SYSTEM.INI file; in Windows 95/98/Me/NT/2000, the reference is usually found in the registry.

These error messages are resolved by replacing the missing file to the c:\Windows\System directory or by removing references to it from the SYSTEM.INI file or the registry. To remove registry references, run REG-EDIT and use the search function to locate all references to the missing file. See Figure 15–9.

The registry keys are then removed to stop the error message from appearing.

Figure 15–9
Searching the Windows registry.

Study Break: Windows 98 HIMEM

This study break exercise examines how Windows 98/Me DOS behaves when HIMEM.SYS is not loaded.

Go to a Windows 98/Me PC and create a startup diskette. Copy DOSKEY.EXE and MEM.EXE to the startup diskette root directory.

951

Using the DOS EDIT program or Windows Notepad, edit the CONFIG.SYS file and REM out the DEVICE=HIMEM.SYS /testmem:off line in the [NOCD] section. The lines should read as follows upon completion:

[NOCD]

REM device=himem.sys /testmem:off

Shut down windows and reboot the PC using the startup diskette. When requested, boot into NOCD and start the computer without CD-ROM support.

What error messages does Windows 98/Me DOS display? Do you get the RAMDrive: and Warning: messages previously identified in this chapter?

Run the MEM program. Does it display XMS as available? How much XMS is free? There should be none free.

Run LH DOSKEY. Does DOSKEY load? It should. Where does MEM show it loading? It should load into conventional memory.

Repeat these exercises when booting into CD, and start the computer with CD-ROM support. Now HIMEM.SYS is properly loaded. The results should show that XMS is available. DOSKEY still loads into conventional RAM because EMM386.EXE is needed to activate the UMBs.

This exercise illustrates that when booted from a floppy diskette, Windows 98/Me DOS still requires HIMEM.SYS and EMM386.EXE to make XMS and UMBs available to applications.

Resolving Frequent Software Problems

There are several common Windows problems that cause Windows to request operator termination of the application program. Generally they result in Windows 3.1x and sometimes Windows 95/98/Me displaying a blue screen (of death) warning message. Such warning messages indicate that Windows has detected a potential conflict between programs running in Windows. If these programs continue to run it will corrupt memory or cause some other conflict that will cause Windows to crash. To prevent such a crash, Windows issues blue screen-warning messages permitting the user to shut down one of the offending applications. Windows then continues (most times) to run, allowing the user to perform a normal shutdown and restart. See Figure 15–10.

Both Windows 3.1x and Windows 95/98/Me perform similarly here, although Windows 95/98/Me provides better error recovery and diagnostic tools. Blue screen messages appear because of general protection faults, illegal operations, missing diskettes or CD-ROMs, and invalid directories. Active applications programs may also produce blue screen messages, and Windows software components themselves occasionally generate blue screen messages.

Such blue screen errors are much less frequent with Windows NT and rarely (if ever) happen with Windows 2000 because the fundamental design of these operating systems provides better memory and PC resource management resulting in fewer conflicts. Windows 2000 goes a step further by monitoring applications and seeking outdated or corrupted DLL programs. These programs are replaced to provide more reliable and predictable applications.

Application Program Errors

Application programs writing into RAM used by other applications cause illegal operation errors. If two programs placed code in the same memory locations, the instructions would be corrupted, making Windows unstable and ready to crash. Windows 3.1x and Windows 95/98/Me perform similarly, but

Figure 15–10
Windows 3.1x blue screen warning.

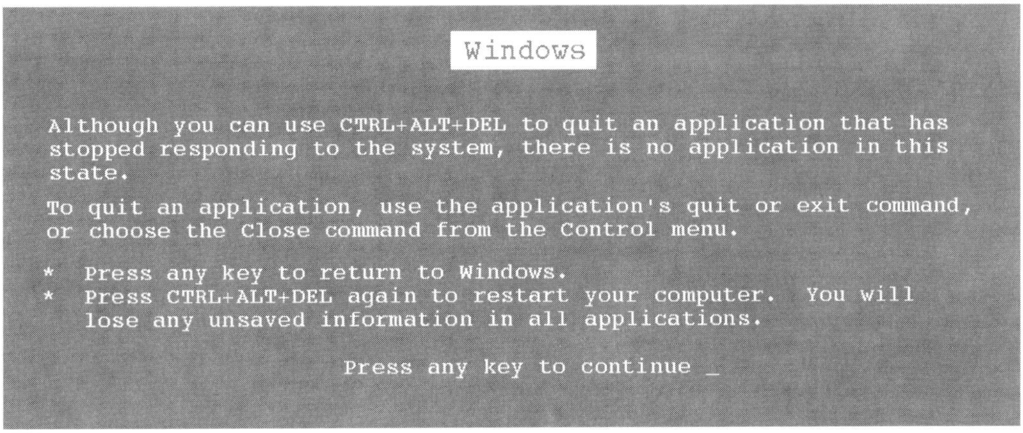

```
                              Windows

Although you can use CTRL+ALT+DEL to quit an application that has
stopped responding to the system, there is no application in this
state.

To quit an application, use the application's quit or exit command,
or choose the Close command from the Control menu.

*  Press any key to return to Windows.
*  Press CTRL+ALT+DEL again to restart your computer.  You will
   lose any unsaved information in all applications.


              Press any key to continue _
```

there are variations in response with Windows 95/98/Me for older 16-bit applications and newer 32-bit applications. Windows 2000 and Windows NT behave differently; Windows NT, Windows 2000, and Windows XP errant applications are shut down and little else is affected. Of course, all data resident in RAM and not saved to the fixed disk is lost.

When a 16-bit application performs an illegal operation, Windows displays a "General Protection Fault" error message. See Figure 15–11.

Ignoring the error causes Windows to not execute the instruction that caused the error. This usually just leaves the program in an endless loop and forces the user to close the application, and all data in RAM is lost. Unless the

Figure 15–11
Windows 98 16-bit error message.

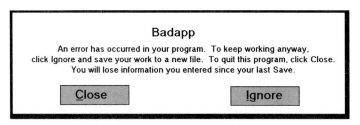

Figure 15–12
Windows 98 general protection fault error box.

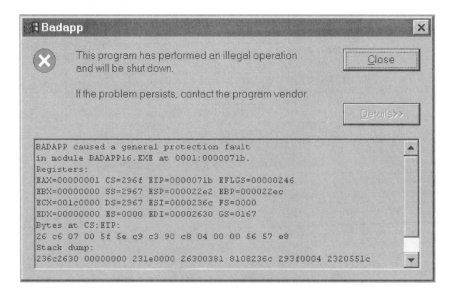

data was previously saved to disk, the user has no way to preserve the data. When the 16-bit application is executed, Windows 95/98/Me displays the close application box and identifies the error as a general protection fault. See Figure 15–12.

For 32-bit Windows applications, the initial application error screen is not displayed. Windows identifies the error as an invalid page fault. See Figure 15–13.

With 32-bit applications, there is no option to ignore and attempt to continue. The application must be closed and the data in RAM lost. With all memory conflict errors, it is best to immediately shut down Windows and then restart. Once memory becomes messed up, Windows does not do a particularly good job of cleaning up the memory allocations so that opening new programs are then more likely to generate additional illegal operation errors.

To troubleshoot illegal operation errors, the following steps are suggested.

Check the application to ensure it was not written for an earlier version of Windows. Applications written for earlier versions of Windows may have incompatibilities with Windows 95/98/Me and Windows 2000 that could result in operation errors. We have found that Windows 2000 handles older applications more predictably than Windows 98/Me.

Check system resources by going to the program manager help menu display and make sure they are sufficient. Windows 3.x needs more than 60 percent free resources to launch new applications. Remember, the resource level

Figure 15–13
Windows 98 invalid page fault message.

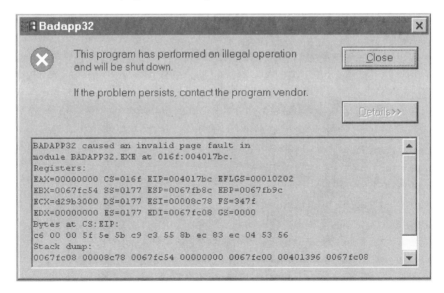

reported is that of the heap with the fewest resources. This means that the other heaps have more than 60 percent resources available. Sometimes applications running in the background use more resources than is evident. When resources are low, close all unnecessary applications. Windows 98/Me are better at managing resources, but they suffer from the same resource limitations as Windows 3.x. Windows NT/2000/XP does not use resource assignments like Windows 98/Me and consequently does not suffer lack of resource problems.

In Windows 98/Me systems with continually low resources, reinstalling the offending application software sometimes corrects the problem. Perhaps a file or a part of the program (a DLL) has become corrupt.

Run SCANDISK or CHKDSK to test the fixed disk drives. When there are lost allocation units, it could cause Windows applications to blow up or indicate a more serious fixed disk problem. Perhaps there are errors in FAT table entries hampering an application's ability to locate some data or code. The SCANDISK automatically fixes FAT and disk errors. The CHKDSK /F command corrects or fixes those errors as well.

Remove the existing WIN.INI and restart Windows. Before doing this, make sure to save or rename the WIN.INI file so that it can be restored. This ensures that the error was not caused by any corrupted fonts, print drivers, or software loaded from the "Run=" or the "Load=" commands If this works, then put a (;) in front of the "Load=" and the "Run=" to prevent any software from loading. Rename the WIN.INI file to restore it.

In the [386ENH] section of SYSTEM.INI file, add MaxBPs=1024. This changes the memory allocation boundary for break points, which can reduce illegal operation errors.Call the manufacturer of the problem software to determine if there is a free fix or patch to correct the problem.

System Freezing or Application Programs Hang

Application programs that get very busy cannot respond to user input. This is a common error with communications programs, which include programs using modem, LAN and USB devices. When a modem loses carrier with another modem, or when a mapped drive on a local network or PC is shut down, programs using these communications links can hang. The Microsoft Internet Explorer is the program that fails to respond most often on our PCs. This happens because communications links fail and become broken.

Sometimes the timeout period expires and the PC begins responding again. Other times the hanging program never regains control from the communications software components. In this event, the hourglass pointer is displayed whenever the mouse is pointed at the application, as shown in Figure 15–14.

Communications problems are not the only source of hung applications. Disk drive errors and problems can also cause an application to hang when data is written to the disk drive. Because Windows devotes much of its attention to waiting for the disk operation to complete before proceeding, it can appear locked. Furthermore, reading corrupted files from a disk drive often causes Windows to develop memory conflicts, producing illegal operation errors. Additional description and discussion of these errors preceded this section in this chapter.

When a program hangs, The Ctrl-Alt-Del keys are struck to bring up the task manager program. See Figure 15–15.

Figure 15–14
Hung application.

Figure 15–15
Windows task manager.

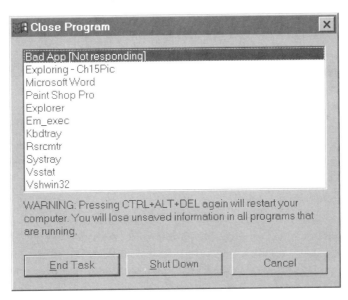

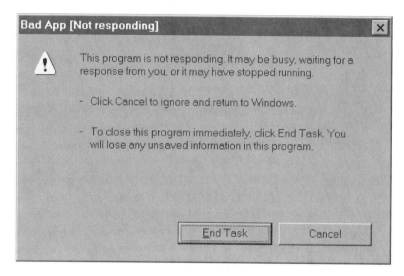

Figure 15–16
End task display box.

The task manager program labels the hung program as "Not Responding." Highlighting it and clicking on the end task button clears the application not responding. In this event, all data in RAM is lost. Windows does provide a second chance to continue waiting for the application to finish its I/O activities in the event that the data in RAM is critical to the user. See Figure 15–16.

The cancel button returns to Windows without closing the application, while the end task button closes the application but does not close Windows.

Low Resources

Windows 95/98/Me user and graphics resources can run low; when this happens, applications fail to respond and Windows 95/98/Me can crash. Other unpleasant things can happen as well. However, the resource meter can monitor the resources to prevent Windows resources from running low.

The resource meter in Windows 95/98/Me is the program RSRCMTR.EXE found in the c:\windows folder (directory). Placing a shortcut to this program in the c:\windows\start menu\programs\startup causes it to be launched each time Windows boots. It then places an icon in the SYSTRAY, which has a green (good), yellow (dangerous), and red (red is dead) bar display of the available Windows resources. The SYSTRAY icon appears in the upper left hand corner of Figure 15–17.

When the resources hit about 30 percent, the resource meter flashes a warning message. We cannot show the warning message because Windows 98 did not see fit to permit us to recover from our low-resource warning message and continue working on this chapter. However, we were able to capture the resulting crash message, as shown in Figure 15–18. The PC is waiting for the close program dialog box to appear. It cannot be displayed because there are not enough graphic resources to create it. Consequently, the PC waits and waits and does nothing. A forced reboot is most often the only recourse.

Figure 15–17
Windows 98 resource meter display.

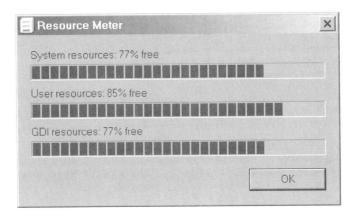

Figure 15–18
Windows low resource crash message.

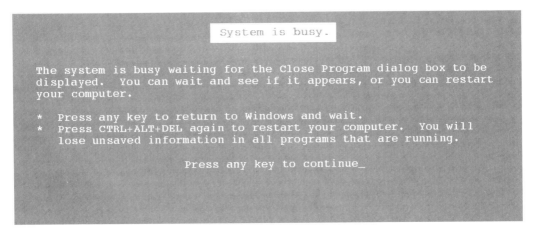

When this message appears, Windows is going down. With low resources, selecting the press any key to return to Windows 95/98/Me and wait produces a blank screen, because Windows95/98/Me has no resources to create or rewrite the display.

When Windows 95/98/Me resources are low, the best resolution of the problem is to immediately close all applications and restart. This cleans up Windows memory and restores the resources to their initial operating levels. Because Windows 95/98/Me resources are automatically controlled by Windows and cannot be increased, the only solution to low resource problems is to run fewer applications simultaneously and to immediately shut down applications when resources hit critically low levels.

Missing Floppy or CD-ROM

Once an application program is started, it may require data stored on a floppy or CD-ROM. In the event that the floppy drive diskette or the CD-ROM drive's CD is removed, Windows displays the missing floppy diskette or missing CD error message.

Pointing the Windows Explorer at the floppy drive that contains no diskette causes floppy drive errors. See Figure 15–19.

The floppy drive error is easily resolved by either putting a floppy diskette in the drive or by pointing the Windows Explorer at a fixed disk drive.

Perhaps more common is the CD-ROM error message, because many applications reference data on CD-ROMs. See Figure 15–20.

Again, inserting a CD easily rectifies this error. If the problem persists, the CD-ROM lens may be dirty or the CD itself may be dirty or unreadable. A lens-cleaning CD will brush the lens and remove dirt that prevents it from reading CDs. Cleaning the CD can sometimes fix the problem of a nonreadable CD. Reading another CD in the CD-ROM drive easily tests this. When several CDs are unreadable and the lens has been cleaned, then the drive itself may be bad and need replacement.

Figure 15–19
Floppy drive error message.

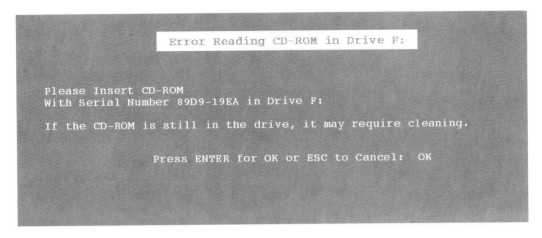

Figure 15–20
Missing CD error message.

Invalid Working Directory

Programs often reference data or DLLs on the fixed or removable disks. These references can be lost or corrupted. In this event, the PC can issue error messages indicating an invalid working directory. See Figure 15–21.

If the directory and its contents have been removed, replacing the missing directory is required to fully correct this error. When the directory is moved to a place that Windows does not expect, updating the directory pointer to the new directory location is all that is generally needed to fix the problem. Pointing to the correct working directory is done using the properties option for the program or its representative shortcut icon. See Figure 15–22.

Figure 15–21
Invalid working directory error message.

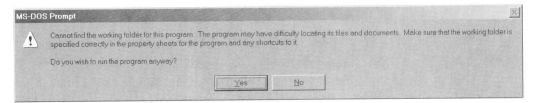

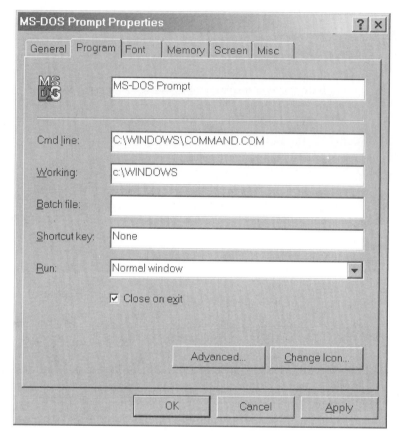

Figure 15–22
Program shortcut properties.

Changing the working directory is performed by selecting the program tab and then entering the correct working directory in the Working entry section. Applying the changes immediately alters the program's working directory and permits testing to ensure that the working directory change fixed the problem. The OK selection also immediately changes the working directory, but in addition exits the properties box. If the change is not correct, the properties box would need to be reopened to again to adjust the working directory.

Critical Hardware Errors, or the "Option will not function" Message

Critical hardware errors prevent Windows from starting or force it to start in safe mode. Other hardware errors can cause applications to fail or functions to simply not work. Soundboards and other PC peripheral components often behave in this fashion. Sometimes, the application or Windows issues error messages indicating that the option is not functioning. More often, they just stop working. In any event these errors are due to a PC peripheral hardware component and Windows mismatch. The most likely scenario is that the hardware drivers do not match Windows or they are not the latest drivers (supporting the full hardware component capabilities) required by Windows or the application. Updating the drivers and checking for hardware conflicts are the approaches used to resolve these types of errors.

To resolve these problems, first identify the malfunctioning hardware. The Windows control panel ➤ system ➤ device manager should display the malfunctioning devices with a red "X" indicating that they are not functioning. In Windows 2000/XP, the device manager is accessed through the control panel ➤ system ➤ hardware then device manager. The next step is to find the latest software drivers for the component on the Internet. Go to the component manufacturer's web site and find technical support and software drivers. Use DRIVERSHQ.COM to locate the site. Download the drivers and place them in an install directory (folder) on the PC's fixed disk.

Next, using the Windows control panel ➤ system ➤ device manager (or in Windows 2000/XP, control panel ➤ system ➤ hardware ➤ device manager), try selecting the device and the install new drivers option, or just uninstall the malfunctioning device so that Windows automatically reinstalls it when it restarts. Laptop PCMCIA and card bus cards run Windows completely without the card plugged into the card slot. Once Windows is operating completely, plug in the PCMCIA cards one at a time for Windows to attempt to install the driver software. Once the proper drivers are installed, the misconfiguration should be resolved. In the event this does not resolve the problem, consider using an alternative product. Hardware is relatively cheap compared to the cost of the hours it may take to resolve the simplest of PC misconfiguration problems.

Application Does Not Load or Start

Application programs can fail to launch. This is often caused by an application shortcut failing to point correctly to the application. When a missing application is launched, Windows immediately permits searching for the missing application to fix the problem. See Figure 15–23.

When the application is searched for and not found, Windows displays the missing application error message, as shown in Figure 15–24.

Searching for the application and then pointing the shortcut to the application's location on the fixed disk drive can solve the missing application problem. This is performed using the properties selection for the shortcut to the application. The target entry area for the shortcut icon must point to the directory and the application. When this happens, the missing application error is resolved. See Figure 15–25.

The properties box allows browsing for the target application. The find target option is not an automatic search. It permits the PC user to manually view the disk directories until the application is located. A more effective approach to locating a missing application is to use the explorer search function, which is activated through the explorer menus or by striking Ctrl-F (F equals Find). The missing file can then be automatically located on the disk drives using wild card character searches. For example, you could search for any program using the first four letters of the program name—msinfo32.exe could be found using

Figure 15–23
Searching for the application.

Figure 15–24
Missing application error message.

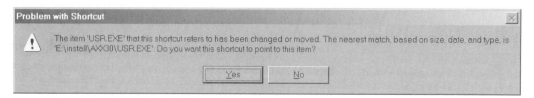

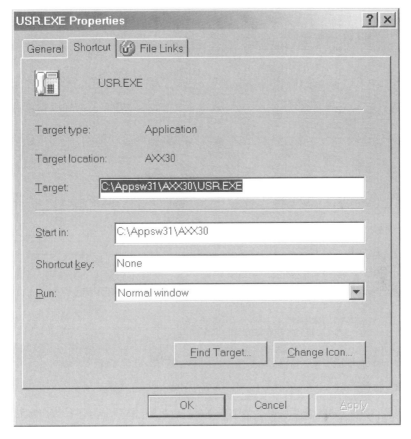

Figure 15-25
Shortcut target.

msin*.exe. Windows finds this file and MSINF16H.EXE when drive C is searched in this fashion. Once located, the shortcut target can be easily and accurately updated. The shortcut properties box identifies the file name of the missing or moved application.

Cannot Log onto Network

Most PCs are connected to some type of network, making network problems a common occurrence. They have three sources: PC hardware, PC software, or the network itself. When a PC expects to work on a network, first have the user log onto the network servers or peer-to-peer PC sharing resources. There are two network logon options: logging on and restoring network connections, or logging on quickly to the network and only restoring network connections when they are used or accessed by the PC user. See Figure 15–26.

The quick logon option permits the PC to run faster because the network drive mappings do not require validation when the "restore network connections" option is selected. In either event, the user is logged onto the network during the boot process unless there is a network problem that prevents logon. When the user cannot log on to the network, Windows displays a logon error message, as shown in Figure 15–27.

This error can be caused by a failure to find peer-to-peer connections while trying to restore them, or by not being able to log on to a Windows NT domain. In both cases, the PC cannot find the logon PC or server. With peer-to-peer

Figure 15–26
Network logon options.

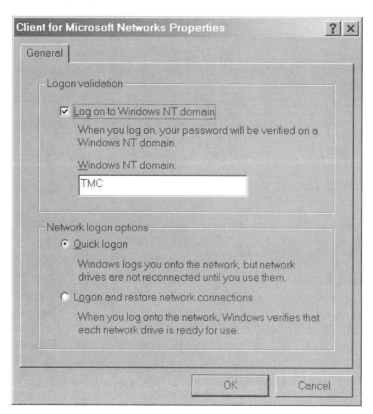

Figure 15–27
Network logon error message.

networks, the network cabling could be faulty or the target peer-to-peer PC could be turned off or be (if it is a laptop) removed from the network. In a Windows NT domain, the domain controller server (the primary domain controller, or PDC) could be down. In large Windows NT domain networks, there are backup domain controllers (BDC) that take control of the network in the event that the primary domain controller (PDC) fails or is taken off the network. This means that failing to connect to the network domain controller in a large network is more likely caused by a cabling problem than a faulty server.

"Failing to connect" error messages indicate that network servers and resources are not available for use. However, the user's PC can be used with the data and programs resident on its fixed disk drives. Once the network connection is repaired, the PC can be logged onto the network, normally correcting the problem. Windows NT/2000 experience similar performance and network problems when they map to network drives. Windows NT/2000 network logon typically requires certification by a network security provider, like a Windows NT PDC. While Windows NT/2000 network operation can use disk drive mappings, it is best not to map drives, because Windows NT/2000 performance degrades when they are not available.

Study Break: System Resource Meter

This study break exercise examines installing and using the system resource meter to monitor system resources. It builds on the Chapter 10 study break, "Windows Graphical Resources."

Go to a Windows 98/Me PC and install a shortcut to the system resource meter in the startup folder.

Use explorer to open the Windows folder and find the file RSR-CMTR.EXE. Right click on it and select create shortcut. A shortcut is immediately created as the last file in \windows and is highlighted.

Right click and select cut to cut the shortcut from \Windows. Then select the \windows\program files\programs\startup folder, right click and select paste to place the shortcut in that folder

Restarting Windows should load the resource meter and produce a warning message. Disable the warning message, or else it will appear each time Windows is restarted.

Point to the resource meter icon in the SYSTRAY. What resources are available in system, user, and GDI heaps? Double-click to see a graphic display of the available resources.

Open several application programs and see the resources decrease. How many programs can be opened before a low resource warning is issued?

If no warning is issued, use MS Word to print a complex document containing lots of graphics. Does this diminish resources to the warning point?

The purpose of this exercise was to illustrate how to make the resource meter a continuous resource-monitoring tool. We also demonstrated how system resources are consumed and the impact of printing on system resources.

DOS and Windows Utilities

The primary software diagnostic tools are DOS and Windows utility programs. These programs provide a variety of diagnostic and problem resolution capabilities for both hardware and software. Both DOS and Windows tools are used to resolve software problems for Windows 95/98/Me/NT/2000.

FDISK.EXE—Fixed Disk

The FIDSK program is the fixed disk partitioning utility. It is used to set up the PC's fixed disk drives and also functions effectively as a fixed disk diagnostic program that detects fixed disk hardware problems. When FDISK is run, it should quickly enter its main menu, as shown in Figure 15–28.

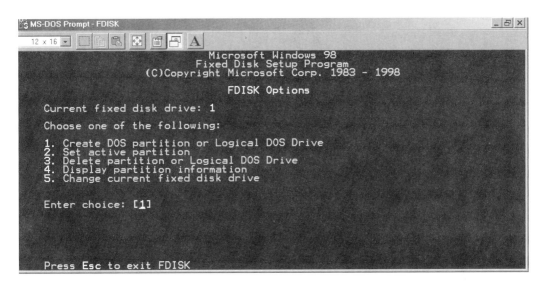

Figure 15-28
FDISK main menu.

When there are fixed disk problems. FDISK displays messages indicating that it cannot read the fixed disk drive, or that the disk drive controller is bad. These messages are displayed when there is a fixed disk hardware failure. The cannot read fixed disk drive error indication works regardless of the partitioning (FAT or NTFS) of the fixed disk drive.

FDISK can also repair the MBR. The command FDISK /MBR rewrites the master boot record on the fixed disk. In rare instances, this can remove some viruses from the boot sector of the fixed disk drive. It can also help restore an operating system to the fixed disk.

SCANDISK—Scan Disk Files and Directories

SCANDISK is a fixed disk FAT and directory diagnostic program primarily. It can also test the surface integrity of the fixed disk. See Figure 15-29. With Windows NT/2000, the CHKDSK program is used in lieu of SCANDISK.

Whenever Windows is shut down abruptly and does not have a chance to gracefully close applications and write the last registry entries to the fixed disk, Windows forces SCANDISK to run during the reboot process. This is to find and fix any corruption to the FAT and the files on the disk drive. In the hundreds of times it has run after we have shut down Windows abruptly by pulling

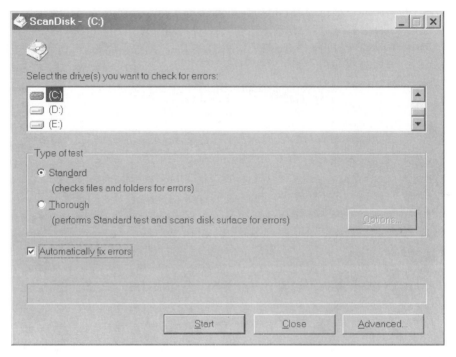

Figure 15–29
SCANDISK menu selections.

the plug, SCANDISK has never found a problem with the FAT or the files. That may be because we have always waited for the disk activity light on the front of the PC to indicate there is no further disk drive activity.

SCANDISK can scan individual drives or all drives. The standard check option only examines the directory structure, the files stored on the fixed disk, and FAT for errors. The thorough check also tests the disk surface for errors. When a bad spot is found, it attempts to recover the data by reading it several times and then to move the data in that spot to a safe area of the disk. For SCANDISK to fix errors the "Automatically fix errors" option needs to be selected.

DEFRAG.EXE—Fixed Disk Defragment

The DEFRAG program reorganizes the data on a fixed disk drive or on all fixed disk drives so that the allocation units for each file are stored next to each other. See Figure 15–30. This permits the fixed disk to retrieve the file data

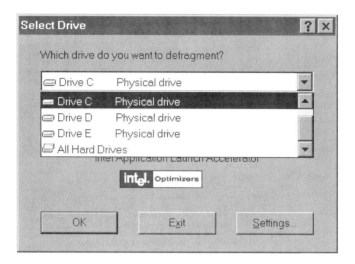

Figure 15–30
DEFRAG drive selection.

without moving the read/write heads of the fixed disk drive, thus speeding up file access. The DEFRAG program is different for DOS, Windows 95/98/Me and Windows 2000/XP but it performs the same disk defragmenting task.

The Windows 98/Me DEFRAG program moves frequently used program files to the outside tracks of the fixed disk to speed up access to those programs and their software components. See Figure 15–31. The goal is to minimize the fixed disk's read/write head movement, thus speeding up access to data stored on the fixed disk.

DEFRAG can also be used as a diagnostic program. While defragmenting a fixed disk, DEFRAG typically reads and writes all the files on the fixed disk. This is a test of the data integrity and the fixed disk itself. While not a thorough disk surface test like the SCANDISK advanced option performs, it is nonetheless an effective test of the disk drive, and does improve performance once complete. DEFRAG does not come with Windows NT, but a special version is provided with Windows 2000/XP.

When DEFRAG runs, it displays progress towards completion in a compact or detailed display. The compact progress display box is shown in Figure 15–32.

When running DEFRAG, it is best to close all other active programs except DEFRAG, otherwise it takes a long time to scan the bootable drive (usually C:) containing the Windows files because Windows updates the registry and other areas as DEFRAG runs. Whenever Windows performs an update, DEFRAG restarts from the beginning of the drive, and such restarts consume

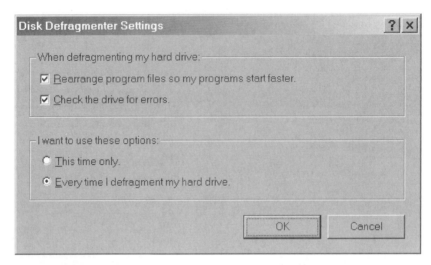

Figure 15–31
DEFRAG options.

Figure 15–32
DEFRAG compact progress display.

lots of time. Often when Windows is first installed, the Windows task scheduler program is set up to run DEFRAG every night. This is fine, but sometimes DEFRAG can hang because of the programs active in the PC necessitating a forced reboot. We believe that it is best to manually run DEFRAG about once each week.

MEM.EXE—Memory Check Program

MEM displays the current memory configuration of the PC. It provides summary and detailed displays of memory contents, as shown in Figure 15–33.

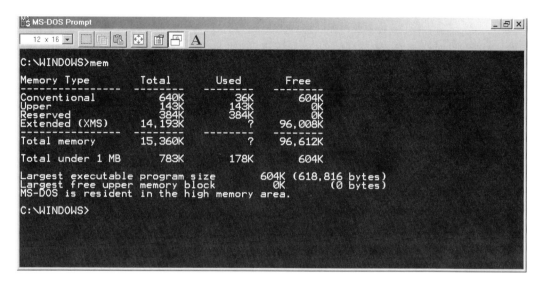

Figure 15–33
MEM summary report.

The detailed displays only cover the programs resident in real mode memory (the first megabyte of RAM). The MEM program does not display the programs resident in XMS. This program is most useful in troubleshooting DOS and Windows 3.1x memory problems, and is not all that helpful with Windows 95/98/Me and Windows NT/2000/XP. MEM helps with troubleshooting by displaying those programs loaded into the UMBs and the regions that they are broken into. The size of each region is also displayed, which permits re-arranging program loading to achieve the maximum amount of conventional RAM for DOS applications. MEMMAKER configures memory optimally for a given program loading order as determined by CONFIG.SYS and AUTOEXEC.BAT, but does not change program load order so it cannot provide the maximum amount of available RAM.

ATTRIB.EXE—Change Attributes

ATTRIB is not a diagnostic program per se. It changes the attributes of files. The DOS and Windows file attributes that ATTRIB can change are archive (A), hidden (H), read-only (R), and system (S). This is helpful in performing some troubleshooting and diagnostic procedures because some key system files (for instance, the registry files) are marked as hidden, read-only, and system. See Figure 15–34.

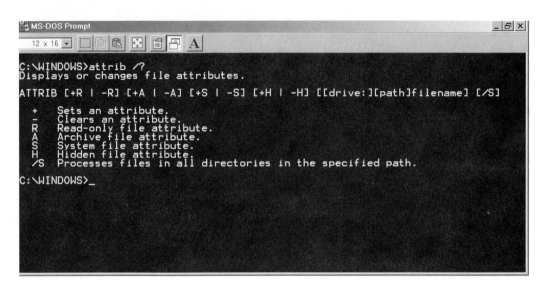

Figure 15–34
ATTRIB command options.

ATTRIB is used to set files to a viewable, read/write status permitting replacement and editing of Windows control files. ATTRIB provides an /S option, permitting execution in a directory and its subdirectories. This is sometimes helpful when deleting data from the fixed disk because the Windows explorer does not delete read-only, hidden or system files. Furthermore, the Windows explorer permits changing file attributes, but requires continual manual effort to complete attribute changes for subdirectories. ATTRIB with the /S option is more automatic and much faster at this task. ATTRIB also displays all the files on the fixed disk drive regardless of their attributes.

EXTRACT.EXE—Cabinet File Extraction Tool

The EXTRACT program works with the Windows cabinet (CAB) installation files. This is helpful when Windows just needs a single missing DLL or DRV file to correct a problem. See Figure 15–35.

The /D option permits EXTRACT to display the contents of an individual cabinet file. When combined with the "| MORE" pipe to display 24 lines per screen, the cabinet (CAB) files can be searched to find the missing Windows driver or software component.

Figure 15-35
EXTRACT command options.

For example, the WD.VXD file could be located in the Windows 98 cabinet files by the following command:

```
extract base4.cab wd.vxd /a /d |more
```

Use this EXTRACT to search through all the Windows 98 CAB files starting with base4.cab and display:

```
Microsoft (R) Cabinet Extraction Tool—Version (16) 1.00.603.0
(08/14/97)
Copyright (c) Microsoft Corp 1994-1997. All rights reserved.
 Cabinet base4.cab
 Cabinet BASE5.CAB
 Cabinet BASE6.CAB
05-11-1998 8:01:00p A—  18,329 wd.vxd
 Cabinet NET7.CAB.
```

EXTRACT's /E command line option would extract the file from its location in base6.cab.

CAB files can also be viewed and updated using the latest version of the WINZIP.EXE program. This third-party application integrates itself with Windows to handle many types of compressed library and archive files.

EXPAND.EXE—File Expansion Tool

The EXPAND program expands individual installation software component files. Software installation files for Windows 3.1x were individually compressed as opposed to being compressed as groups in cabinet (CAB) files. The individually compressed files had extensions with the last character being the underscore character; for example, EXE files were compressed as EX_ and DLL files were compressed as DL_ files. The EXPAND program expands these individually compressed files. See Figure 15–36.

The EXPAND program, like the EXTRACT program, is used to replace or update Windows drivers and software components.

EDIT.COM—The Microsoft Text Editor Program

EDIT is the DOS-based text editor program. In DOS mode, it permits editing of text files like CONFIG.SYS, AUTOEXEC.BAT, SYSTEM.INI, WIN.INI, and *.REG. See Figure 15–37. Windows provides equivalent text editing for the Notepad program.

EDIT and Notepad are not diagnostic tools but rather programs that permit changing DOS and Windows configuration files. The text versions of the

Figure 15–36
EXPAND command options.

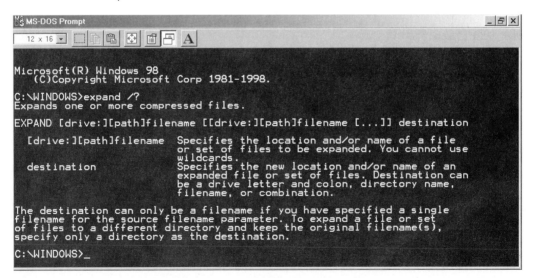

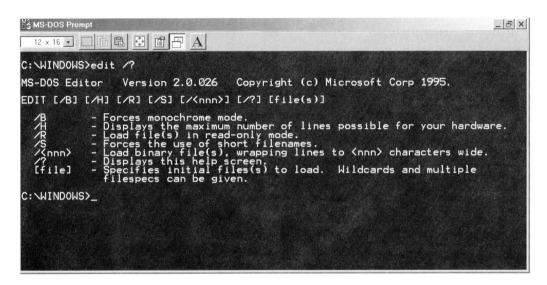

Figure 15–37
EDIT Command options.

registry (*.REG) and Windows installation control files (*.INF) are text files that can be edited using EDIT or Notepad. EDIT is particularly useful, as are all the DOS diagnostics, because they operate in DOS mode, where Windows does not lock its key operating and configuration control files.

SYSEDIT.EXE—System Configuration Editor

SYSEDIT is a Windows program that opens all text Windows control files at one time. When launched, it opens PROTOCOL.INI, SYSTEM.INI, WIN.INI, CONFIG.SYS, and AUTOEXEC.BAT. See Figure 15–38. It provides the same capabilities as Notepad, but differs in that it opens up all key text Windows control and configuration files at the same time.

SYSEDIT, like Notepad and EDIT, cannot edit binary files, such as the registry SYSTEM.DAT and USER.DAT files.

MSD.EXE—Microsoft Diagnostics Program

The MSD program is a diagnostic program helpful in verifying PC hardware. It displays information on the computer CPU chip and BIOS, RAM software and hardware assignments for real-mode UMBs, display information, disk drives,

977

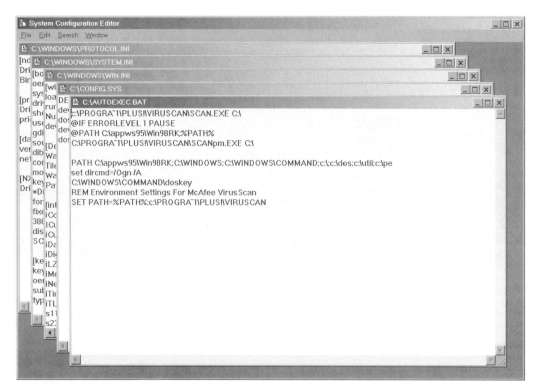

Figure 15–38
SYSEDIT.

communications, printer ports, and more. See Figure 15–39. Once a PC is booted, MSD can be run in either Windows or DOS mode.

The easiest way to run MSD is to open a DOS window and type in MSD. The PC jumps to a full screen display as MSD is launched. It can be returned to a Windows display by using Alt+Enter. Using the start menu run option launches MSD in the same fashion.

The primary use of MSD as a diagnostic tool is to report the PC hardware configuration as determined by DOS during the boot process. This can assist in troubleshooting some configuration problems such as communication port conflicts. An interesting feature is the disk drive option that reports the total disk space and free disk space for each drive letter it finds. Both local and network drives are scanned and reported. Being a DOS-based program, the maximum drive space is reported as 2 GB, which makes this total drive space information less useful. Free drive space is reported accurately. This can be very useful in troubleshooting application program problems. Often problems

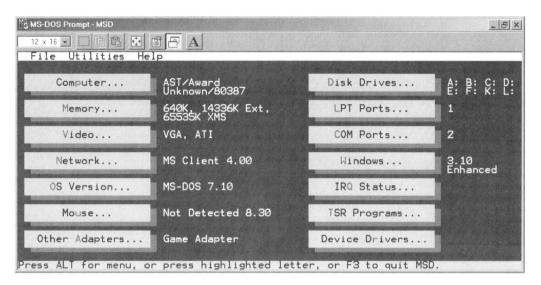

Figure 15–39
MSD menu options.

are caused by insufficient free space on fixed disk drives. PC users typically think that fixed disk space is unlimited (as indeed it seems on a new PC) when it is not. After using the PC for a year or so, the disk can become very full, causing a variety of Windows problems. The MSD disk drive report could help quickly identify which drives were very full and help resolve problems caused by insufficient fixed disk space.

The Device Manager

In Windows 95, Windows 98, and Windows Me, the device manager is found under control panel—system—device manager; in Windows 2000 the device manager is found under control panel—system—hardware—device manager. The device manager controls the PC hardware installed under Windows and identifies the hardware in device categories; the individual devices are then installed in each category. See Figure 15–40. In the figure, the device manager points to the general category of display adapters and shows the specific display adapter installed, a RAGE PRO TURBO AGP adapter.

The device manager can display the properties of hardware components. These properties include the IRQ setting, the I/O port address, and the mem-

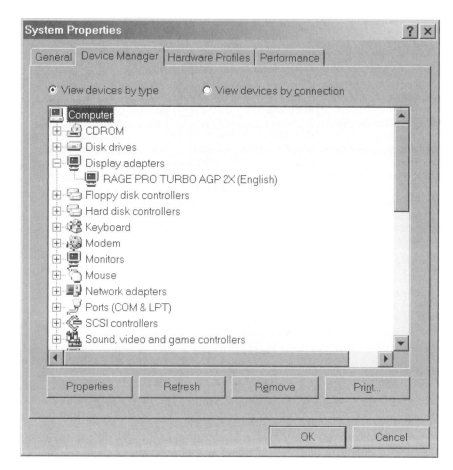

Figure 15–40
Windows device manager.

ory areas used. The properties can be set automatically using Windows plug-and-play capabilities or they can be set manually to bypass hardware conflicts.

When the computer entry is selected, the PC's IRQ, I/O port, DMA channel and memory ranges used by the PC's hardware components are displayed. This is helpful in resolving PC hardware conflicts. The control panel—system—device manager is used to uninstall software for the PC's hardware components. The process of uninstalling hardware device drivers and then reinstalling them sometimes resolves Windows hardware problems.

MSINFO32.EXE—MS System Information

The Microsoft System Information program (MSINFO32.EXE) is the Windows equivalent of the MSD program, and provides more information on the PC than does MSD. The only drawback is that it runs in Windows 98/Me and Windows 2000. The MSINFO32 program displays information on both hardware and Windows software components. See Figure 15–41.

Somewhat similar to MSD, MSINFO32 displays overall system information, hardware resource assignments, and data on multimedia and network hardware components and on the Windows software environment. More

Figure 15–41
MSINFO32 program.

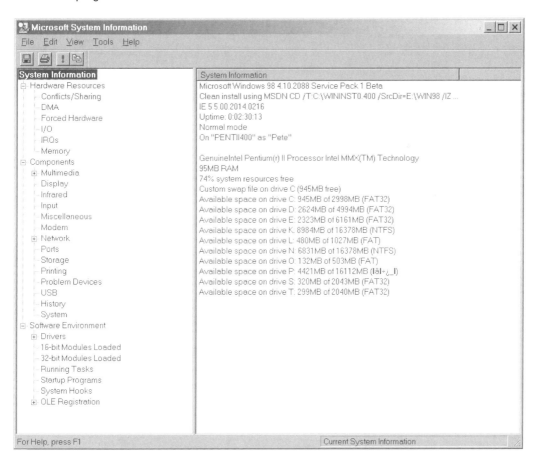

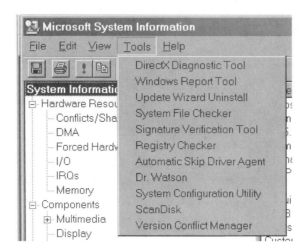

Figure 15–42
MSINFO32 tools menu.

importantly, under the tools menu option, it provides a set of tools to test and verify Windows hardware and software, as shown in Figure 15–42.

Some of the MS system information software tools are helpful in preventing and resolving Windows problems. A short discussion of each is presented here.

DirectX Diagnostic Tool (98/Me/2000)

DirectX software plays an integral role in Windows 98 desktop and Internet operations. DirectX comprises DirectX drivers and other display, sound, music, and input driver programs. The DirectX Diagnostic tool verifies that these files are installed, are the correct versions, and are operating properly.

The easiest way to launch the DirectX Diagnostic tool is from the MSINFO32.EXE tools menu selection. Once launched, it provides an introductory display with several tabs. The DirectX files and drivers tabs present the results of a DirectX diagnostic tool verification process. In most cases, no problems are found. The display, sound, and music tabs also verify the supporting DirectX software. In addition, they permit testing of the PC hardware for proper functioning with the installed DirectX software. The DirectX diagnostic tool provides mainly a verification of the DirectX software installed on the PC.

SIGVERIF.EXE—Signature Verification Tool (98/Me/2000)

This application scans the PC's fixed disks for both files that are signed and unsigned. A file signature identifies:

1. The version of the file—V3
2. The file serial number—twenty hexadecimal digits
3. The signature algorithm—md5RSA
4. The issuer—generally Microsoft Windows Hardware Compatibility Publisher
5. The validity dates—from 3/01/1998 3:00 AM to 2/15/00 3:00 AM
6. The Public Key—RSA (2,048 bits)
7. Enhanced Key usage
8. Authority Key Identifier—certificate issuer is generally Microsoft Corporation
9. A Thumbprint algorithm—sha1
10. A Thumbprint—forty hexadecimal digits

For unsigned files, the properties can be displayed, which may assist in verifying driver and software component compatibility with Windows. A signed file has a copyright notification in it; there are few Windows files today that are signed files. One signed file is WINIPCFG.EXE, and the signature is by Microsoft Windows Hardware Compatibility Publishing. This could be used to check for legal compliance with copyright laws. When a signed program was found on a system where the software was not legally installed, that could identify a potential copyright violation.

SFC.EXE—System File Checker (98/Me)

The system file checker verifies the integrity of the PC's system files. It determines which files are altered and then prompts to restore the original copy of the file from its installation location (generally a CAB file). When files are known to be good, the verification information for the files can be updated from those originally recorded for the system file checker application. When Windows performs poorly, this application may find Windows components that are the source of the problem.

SCANREG.EXE—Registry Checker (98/Me)

The registry checker program checks the Windows registry for obvious errors and attempts to repair them. This is not a registry-cleaning program; it only detects errors and tries to correct them. Other non-Microsoft programs like Uninstaller provide more thorough registry cleaning and verification functions. SCANREG also backs up the registry files, providing a mechanism for recovering them from a corrupted registry. We prefer the ERU.EXE program for making backup copies of the key Windows startup files.

The SCANREG.EXE program that comes with Windows 98 is run automatically each time Windows 98 is started. It can also be used when installing new hardware and software components to provide registry backups in the event that the installations do not go as smoothly as expected. It would be run prior to the installation on a good working PC, and immediately after the installation to back up a successful installation.

MSCONFIG.EXE—MS System Configuration Utility (98/Me)

The MS system configuration utility provides a menu selection control of Windows startup. It lets the user mark off the files and functions performed during the Windows boot process. In this manner, individual functions and programs can be bypassed to assist in troubleshooting the Windows booting process. See Figure 15–43. Unchecking an item bypasses it during the Windows boot process.

The Windows system configuration utility controls entries in the CONFIG.SYS, AUTOEXEC.BAT, SYSTEM.INI, and WIN.INI files, as well as the Windows startup process.

VCMUI.EXE—Version Conflict Manager (98/Me)

When new software is installed or old software updated, the version conflict manager registers software components that conflict with other installed software. Such conflicting software versions are a potential source of Windows problems. Restoring original or updated versions of software components that eliminate conflicts can make Windows more reliable. On our PCs, no conflicting software versions have been identified.

Windows 2000/XP System Information Utility Tools

Windows 2000 has the Signature Verification Tool and the Direct X Diagnostic Tool, in addition to some different tools than provided with Windows 98/Me.

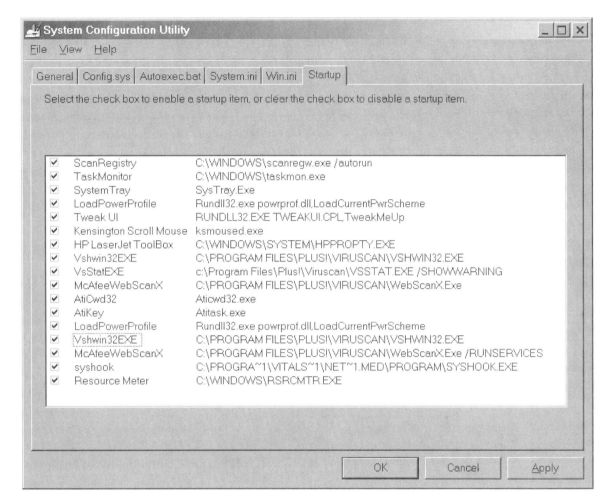

Figure 15–43
System configuration utility Windows control.

These include the disk clean-up tool (CLEANMGR.EXE), the Dr. Watson error logging tool, the hardware installation wizard, the network connections configuration tool, a backup tool that can backup and restore system files and data, an uninstall tool, and a Windows report tool that reports problems to Microsoft. These are similar to programs provided with Windows 98/Me (e.g., CLEANMGR.EXE). Some of these tools can be more helpful than others. The backup and restore utility can really help restore lost files; in contrast, reporting problems to Microsoft takes really low priority in most of our lives.

ERU.EXE—Emergency Recovery Utility

The Emergency Recovery Utility (ERU.EXE) program is a powerful error recovery tool when used to make an audit trail of the key Windows 95/98/Me files (it does not work with Windows 2000/XP). We use ERU to create backup copies of all the key Windows files on the fixed disk in sequenced subdirectories to form such an audit trail. When copying files to a fixed disk directory, ERU backs up all the critical files. If a backup is made to a floppy diskette, the SYSTEM.DAT registry file is not backed up. When Windows startup problems occur, the SYSTEM.DAT file is the most common source. So floppy backups make ERU much less effective than the fixed disk backups. The key files copied are:

1. AUTOEXEC.B_T   — the AUTOEXEC.BAT file
2. COMMAND.C_M   — the COMMAND.COM
3. CONFIG.S_S   — the CONFIG.SYS file
4. ERD.EXE   — the DOS program that restores the files
5. ERD.INF   — the ERD.EXE control file
6. MSDOS.S_S   — the MSDOS.SYS file
7. PROTOCOL.I_I   — the PROTOCOL.INI file
8. SYSTEM.D_T   — the SYSTEM.DAT registry file
9. SYSTEM.I_I   — the SYSTEM.INI file
10. USER.D_T   — the USER.DAT registry file
11. WIN.I_I   — the WIN.INI file

The beauty of ERU is that it is a DOS program. When Windows 95/98/Me doesn't start even in safe mode, booting into DOS can run the ERD.EXE program. One Windows error that prevents Windows from starting up is a Windows protection fault error. When this error occurs, Windows cannot start up. An entry in the SYSTEM.DAT file is the cause of the problem. In this case, ERD can then restore a good version of the key files (including SYSTEM.DAT), permitting Windows to start up normally. By running ERU after each application program is installed, an audit trail of the PC's configuration is preserved. This permits returning to a previously good configuration when subsequent configurations will not start up.

One improvement in Windows Me is that the ERU utility function was included as a control panel applet that tracks and restores system file backups as check points made at specific dates and times. Accessing this control panel applet makes it easy to save or restore these date- and time-stamped system checkpoints from within Windows Me.

Tweak User Interface—Tweak UI

The Tweak User Interface (UI) program is a control panel addition available from Microsoft. It was first offered on the Windows 95 Plus! pack CD. It can be found at the Microsoft web site by searching for Tweak UI. It works on Windows 95, Windows 98, Windows Me and Windows 2000, and can adjust the Windows user interface by customizing the desktop, menu speed, window animation, the Internet Explorer, and more. Once installed, a Tweak UI icon appears in the control panel. Double-clicking enters the main Tweak UI menu box, as shown in Figure 15–44.

Figure 15–44
Tweak UI box.

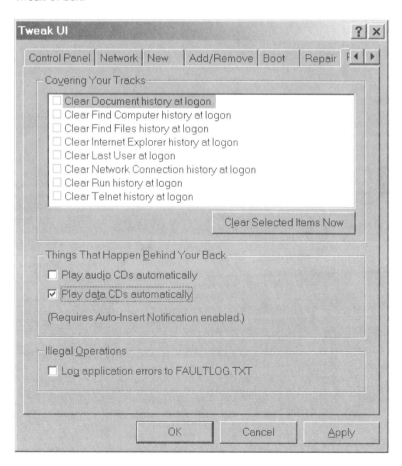

Tweak UI provides options for automatically clearing data cached or temporarily stored on the fixed disk for the Internet Explorer and more. It also facilitates rebuilding the desktop icons while running Windows. Tweak UI is a general tool for customizing the Windows user interface.

MKCOMPAT.EXE—Make Compatible Utility

MKCOMPAT.EXE is a Windows utility targeted at resolving problems between Windows 95/98/Me and older Windows 3.x application programs. It makes Windows 95/98/Me behave more like Windows 3.x for those programs in an effort to prevent software errors. The MKCOMPAT is run and pointed to a specific program file on the command line. Depending on the program referenced, MKCOMPAT returns an option selection box. See Figure 15–45.

This box provides options that make Windows behave like Windows 3.x by not spooling print out to enhanced metafile formats, providing more stack space, misrepresenting the Windows version number and the printer device mode size, and providing Windows 3.x style controls. These adjustments can resolve some application program compatibility problems.

Figure 15–45
MKCOMPAT menu box.

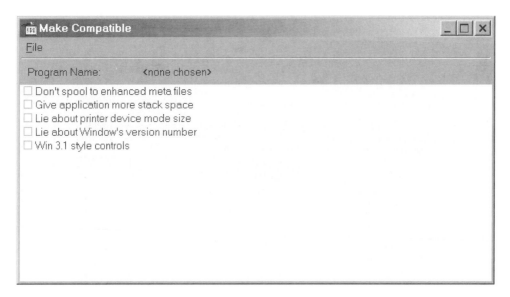

Study Break: Windows 98/Me MSINFO32.EXE

This study break exercise examines the PC using the Windows 98/Me MSINFO32.Exe diagnostic and configuration reporting tool.

Go to a Windows 98/Me PC, hit the start button and select run. Enter MSINFO32 and click OK.

Review the system information MSINFO32 reports. Are there any problem devices? This is under the components section.

Open the tools menu item. Run the DirectX diagnostic tool. What tests can you run? Sound and video tests probably run, but unless there is a joystick, those diagnostics won't run.

Run the system file checker. Does it find any out-of-date files? Are these files really corrupt? They may be, but they are not necessarily corrupted; but the verification information does not match the system file checker database.

Run the automatic skip driver agent. Are any problems reported? Our PC here says that Windows had a problem getting statically allocated resource information (…hmmm … work to do).

Run the system configuration utility. Are there any startup entries that are loaded twice? Disable the duplicates and restart.

Run the version conflict manager. Does it report problems?

The purpose of this exercise was to illustrate the Windows 98 diagnostic and configuration reporting tools.

Viruses and Virus Protection

Virus writers are prolific. What we mean here is that there are plenty of 20—30-year old males that slave away for hours on their PC to create a virus like the Michelangelo virus, the Melissaworm, or the I Love You worm. Another common image is that virus writers are young pranksters to whom creating and propagating viruses is a hobby that helps them keep their coding skills fresh. Our perception here is that they are just common criminals like anyone that holds up a bank.

Some viruses have become widespread enough to gain a footnote in computer history (in addition to a nice jail cell, as was the reward of the writer of the Melissa virus). Viruses and the need to protect against them are inevitable realities in today's world of PCs.McAfee reports the top ten viruses at their web site. This is a sort of advertising for their products and also helpful to the general PC-owning public. Their site is:

```
http://www.mcafee.com/anti-virus/
```

In the early and middle 1980s, computer viruses didn't exist. Universities were responsible for the first viruses created because they researched the concept of a virus and created the first crude virus programs in the process. In 1987, viruses showed up at universities around the world, including the three most commonly visible viruses: Stoned, Cascade, and Friday the 13th.

Actually, we did get the FORM virus on one of our PCs from a nonbootable floppy diskette given to us by a company in Chicago. When we rebooted the PC in our hotel room at the Chicago Hilton, something did not seem quite right. So we immediately powered off the PC and scanned for viruses. Luckily, we caught the FORM virus before it could infect anything. The FORM virus was an early boot sector-infecting virus that was the parent of some of the better-known viruses identified below.

Viruses versus Trojan Horse/Worm programs

There are several types of programs, and each exhibits a different modus operandi for infecting user PCs. The most prolific programs labeled generally as virus programs are not really virus programs at all, but Trojan horse/worm programs that are distributed via Microsoft email products. A true virus program gains entry to the PC by riding on software or disks in an unobtrusive fashion. In contrast, Trojan horse/worm programs are sent most typically as Microsoft Outlook email attachments transmitted across the Internet. The Trojan horse/worm program pretends to do something good while masking its real destructive intent and activity from the PC user. Once the PC is infected, viruses spread themselves to other PCs by copying their code to the boot sectors or program files of other diskettes, thus riding along on these disks to other PCs. Trojan horse/worm programs use the PCs Microsoft Outlook email to send themselves as email attachments on to other unsuspecting PC users.

Virus Programs

The major characteristic of a virus program is that it is written to intentionally load and run in a PC without a user's knowledge. Viruses attach to files or boot sectors by copying their code into EXE, COM, and other files or into the boot sector. They then disguise this event to hide it from the PC user and virus scanning programs. A virus thus hides itself by making itself part of other program files. Viruses replicate themselves by this copying process to continue spreading to other PCs. Some viruses do little but replicate. In contrast, other viruses can cause serious damage to a PC's disk files or can significantly slow PC and application program performance.

Viruses can:

1. Remain memory-resident—A very common virus characteristic is that the virus loads like a TSR program, remaining in memory where it can easily replicate by attaching itself to programs or copying itself into boot sectors.

2. Be non-memory-resident—Much less common are viruses that do not remain in memory after the virus host program is closed. They only infect files while the application program is running.

All viruses have a triggering mechanism. This is some action a virus performs that is set off by a date, a particular keystroke sequence, or a Windows or DOS function. Very often the action is a simple message displayed by the PC; sometimes the action is a serious destruction of the data and programs on the fixed disk drive.

Groups tracking virus infections classify viruses as "in the wild" when they cause an infection outside the laboratory. Viruses in the laboratory that have never roamed the real world are referred to as "in the zoo."

Trojan Horse/Worm Programs

In contrast to viruses, worm programs do not attach to other programs in the PC to disguise themselves. They may rename themselves and use other strategies to remain hidden, but they are separate standalone programs. They spread most often today as separate email attachments that are Microsoft Word DOC files or EXE files. Once opened or executed, they infect the PC and propagate themselves by automatically sending more email messages.

One EXE file is the HAPPY99.EXE program. This EXE file is not a virus but rather a worm, received through email and newsgroup postings. If the person receiving the program named HAPPY99.EXE in the email or article attachment executes it, it opens a window entitled "Happy New Year 1999!!" showing a fireworks display. This disguised the program that was copying itself as SKA.EXE and that was extracting an SKA.DLL into WINDOWS\SYSTEM directory. It modifies WSOCK32.DLL in WINDOWS\SYSTEM directory and copies the original WSOCK32.DLL into WSOCK32.SKA. The WSOCK32.DLL modification allows the worm routine to run when an Internet connection is made. When the PC is online, the modified WINSOCK32.DLL code loads the worm's SKA.DLL. The SKA.DLL in turn creates a new email or a new article with uuencoded HAPPY99.EXE inserted into the email or article. The email was reportedly sent to the first fifty names in the PC user's email address file or the article was posted, thus replicating the worm program in its entirety.

Similar to worm programs, a Trojan horse program is a complete program that does not hide but rather appears to provide a desirable feature to the PC user. Unlike worm programs, Trojan horse programs do not generally attach and replicate themselves; they just act when some trigger event launches them. Newer variations of Trojan horse programs do replicate and distribute themselves via Microsoft Outlook email.

A Worm program that became well known is zipped_files.exe or EXPLORE.EXE that uses MAPI commands and Microsoft Outlook/Microsoft Exchange to email itself as an attachment to this message:

Hi (A friend's or business associate's name)

I received your email and I shall send you a reply ASAP.

Till then, take a look at the attached zipped docs.

Bye or Sincerely (the friend's or business associate's name)

The attachment is zipped_files.exe which, when executed, copies EXPLORE.EXE to the Windows directory of the PC and modifies WIN.INI to run EXPLORE.EXE. Then EXPLORE.EXE mails itself to other PCs by replying to unread messages in the Microsoft Outlook/Microsoft Exchange Inbox of the infected PC. Additionally, this worm program searches networked drives mapped to that PC and networked machines for Windows installations. Once a mapped drive or accessible networked PC is found, this worm program copies EXPLORE.EXE to the remote PC's Windows directory, then modifies the WIN.INI file to run EXPLORE.EXE. EXPLORE.EXE is a true worm program. In addition to propagating itself, EXPLORE.EXE destroys specific files as designated by the file extension on fixed disk drives, on mapped network drives, and on accessible network machines. EXPLORE.EXE monitors the PC's email Inbox for new messages and uses them to send itself to those

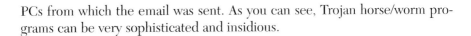

PCs from which the email was sent. As you can see, Trojan horse/worm programs can be very sophisticated and insidious.

Boot-Sector-Infecting Viruses

The Michelangelo virus was a boot-sector-infecting virus that became widespread in the early 1990s. Like many boot-sector-infecting viruses, Michelangelo becomes memory resident by loading from a diskette or fixed disk boot sector. It then infects the boot sectors of floppy diskettes accessed by the system or all the fixed disk drives. The Michelangelo virus resides at the top of system memory but below the 640 K DOS boundary. CHKDSK could be used to detect the Michelangelo virus because it would report fewer than 655,360 bytes of total conventional memory in the PC. Similar boot-sector-infecting viruses could also be detected in this fashion.

What made the Michelangelo virus become widespread is that it remained dormant until March 6th each year (Michelangelo's birthday). On that date, the virus would destroy data on the PC's fixed disk and on diskettes. There was no indication of the virus until one hapless PC user's date hit March 6th and their disk drive data was destroyed.

Since boot-sector-infecting viruses are passed from PC to PC using diskettes, it is relatively easy to prevent infection and to clean the viruses from infected PCs.

Program-Infecting Viruses

Program-infecting viruses originally infected .COM, and .EXE files. Today they may infect .OVL, .DRV, .SYS, or .BIN files, or any program file in the PC used by DOS or Windows. They replicate by attaching themselves to other program files. This means that they can travel as program attachments to email. Some program-infecting viruses can be:

1. Stealth viruses—These viruses hide from detection and cleaning by redirecting disk reads to avoid detection or by altering disk directory data to hide the host program size increase caused by the bytes added by the virus.

2. Encrypting viruses—These viruses hide by transforming their code into encrypted symbols. These viruses must at some point decode to execute and spread. At that time, the encrypting virus can be detected.

3. Polymorphic viruses—These viruses mutate by changing code segments to look different from one infection to another. This is the most challenging virus to detect.

Depending on the sophistication of the virus-disguising technique, they may be very difficult to detect. All viruses must decode to continue infecting other files and PCs.

Macro Viruses

Macro viruses are similar to Trojan horse/worm programs that use the macro commands (which are like any other programming language) implemented in spreadsheet or desktop publishing software to infect and distribute viruses to new systems. The Melissa and the I Love You viruses were macro viruses that used Visual BASIC programming because Visual BASIC is supported by most Microsoft products. Melissa was initially distributed as an attachment to an email message that was posted to a newsgroup server. The original message contained a listing of sex sites. When the attachment was opened, the Melissa macro virus executed and disabled the Microsoft macro virus warning. It then sent itself as an email message to addresses listed in the PC's Microsoft Outlook email list. The damage done here was not to individual PCs but rather to corporate email servers, which became overloaded with heavy email volumes generated by the spreading virus.

Visual BASIC, because of its widespread implementation in Microsoft products, is used as one of the programming languages for macro viruses. Microsoft Word files have macros attached that can carry such viruses. However, any popular program (for instance, a Microsoft program) that implements macros can be used to distribute a virus with its macro commands.

Some of the current worm programs do not write themselves to disk at all but rather remain memory resident in Windows NT and Windows 2000 servers. They are spread by attacking TCP "well known" Port 80 that services HTTP requests. The first of these was the Code Red worm. These worms create a buffer overflow, which then permits a worm's software code to run in at System level. The worm software is embedded in a Window's software GET request. Once it executes the Windows NT or Windows 2000 system is infected with the worm program that then has its pleasure with the Windows NT or Windows 2000 system and uses it to spread to other Windows systems.

Combination macro, boot sector, and program-infecting viruses may combine all distribution mechanisms to widely distribute the next alarming virus.

Sources of Viruses

The most likely means of virus distribution today is the Internet. The viruses can be posted as email or document attachments that infect the PC when opened. The key here is that the document must be opened so that the macro virus (the infecting program) infects the PC. When the file is a program attachment (.EXE file, .COM file, etc.), it must be run to infect the PC. Such virus infections can be received as email or can be downloaded from newsgroup or other software distribution sites.

Several simple precautions can prevent Internet-distributed viruses from infecting your PC and your network. These precautions are:

1. Do not open email attachments unless you know who sent them and you expect them to be a very specific file.

2. Do not download programs from newsgroups. Newsgroup postings were how Melissa and other email viruses were first distributed.

3. Use a more proprietary email program. While Microsoft Outlook and Exchange Server are dynamite products, they are currently the primary means for distributing viruses. Maybe use MS Outlook and Exchange server for internal email and something else for external email.

4. Check McAfee or Symantec virus-reporting sites daily for information on new harmful viruses.

5. Run virus-scanning software that checks Internet mail as well as program files for known viruses. Keep your virus data files current (they are updated monthly).

These are some precautions for preventing email infection, but other precautions must be observed for diskette-borne viruses. Most people think that the common source of viruses is disks shared by PC users. While viruses are spread in this fashion, most PC users today are cognizant enough to employ virus-scanning software on their PC that make virus transmission from user to user quite uncommon. PC service personnel can easily distribute a virus from user to user because the diagnostic software diskettes they use are in many different PCs. Service personnel must take special precautions to ensure that they do not distribute viruses inadvertently while servicing their users. Setting diagnostic disks to read-only status is a simple precaution and is quite effective in preventing virus distribution.

Detecting Viruses

There are many ways to spot virus activity before the virus damages a PC's data and program files. Some common virus symptoms are:

1. Programs suddenly requiring more time to launch

2. Programs failing to run

3. Changing program sizes

4. File date or time stamps changing or not matching that of other files

5. Fixed disks continually running out of free space

6. Continual Windows 32-bit illegal operation errors

7. Fixed disk drive activity light flashing continually when nothing is being done

8. Bad sectors appearing on floppy diskettes

9. Booting from drive A, preventing access to the fixed disk drive

10. Many files or strange files appearing on the PC's fixed disk drive

11. Weird sounds coming from the PC and keyboard

12. The PC desktop behaving strangely with letters or icons moving

13. The PC not retaining CMOS settings even when the battery is fresh

Employing memory-resident virus scanning and detection software like that from McAfee or Norton AntiVirus by Symantec is the best means of detecting and preventing the spread of viruses.

CHKDSK Quick Check

Memory-resident viruses often reduce the conventional memory size as reported by CHKDSK; it can therefore provide a quick check for virus infection every time it is run. Viruses have been detected on several occasions in our PC troubleshooting seminars using CHKDSK. When CHKDSK is run, it reports the total amount of conventional memory. This total should be 655,360 bytes, as shown in Figure 15–46.

When the total bytes free figure is less than 655,360, a memory-resident virus may be the cause. It is possible for some SCSI controllers to cause CHKDSK to report less conventional memory without a virus infection being present.

Virus Scanning Programs

The best defense against viruses is a memory-resident virus scanning and detection program, of which there are many on the market. It is a good idea to have both DOS and Windows virus-scanning software. When troubleshooting any PC, first booting into DOS, run SCANDISK, and then run a virus-scanning program before doing anything else. Both McAfee and Symantec virus-scanning programs create DOS bootable disks that check for virus infection. FPROT is another DOS-based virus-scanning program. All these pro-

Figure 15–46
CHKDSK report.

grams can be downloaded from sites on the Internet or from AOL. The latest virus scanning programs run as an online application from the McAfee Web site. See Figure 15–47.

Clean systems should have a Windows virus scanning and detection program installed. Windows 98 comes with virus scanning software from McAfee with several months of virus signature updates (these can also be downloaded monthly from the McAfee web site). They keep the virus scanning software up to date with the binary patterns (virus signatures) that identify the presence of viruses in any file. See Figure 15–48.

The memory resident V-shield program searches each program as it executes on the PC for viruses. It also scans email for macro viruses, scans files downloaded into the PC for viruses, and filters Internet JAVA and ActiveX applications for virus infections. Downloaded files can be of particular concern because they may be compressed programs containing viruses, or documents containing macro viruses. Because they are compressed, the virus scanning software does not see the virus signature unless the file is decompressed and scanned.

Virus Removal Procedure

The first thing to do when dealing with a virus is to clean the PC of viruses. To clear the viruses or determine that there are none in a PC:

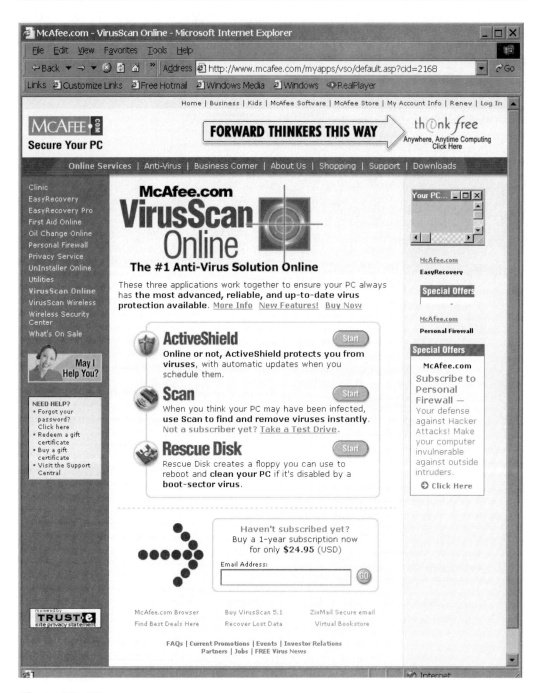

Figure 15–47
McAfee Online virus scan.

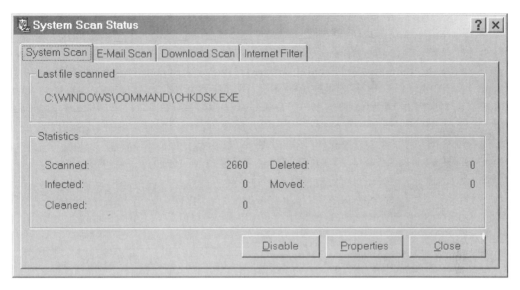

Figure 15–48
McAfee V-shield control panel.

1. Boot the PC from a virus-free DOS diskette that has the virus-cleaning software on it. Be sure the diskette is set to write-protected and that the CMOS of the PC points to booting from the floppy diskette in drive A:. Viruses can set the CMOS to boot from C: and cause the PC to become infected again, so be sure that the CMOS setup boots the PC from drive A:.

2. Booting must be performed from a powered off or cold boot start. The Ctrl-Alt-Del warm boot does not clear viruses from memory; they merely infect the boot diskette unless it is set to a write-protected state.

3. As for the software, get the latest Symantec, FPROT, AVP, or McAfee anti-virus software that runs from a DOS boot diskette. This should be available from the web or from a local store.

4. Once the PC is booted, run the virus scanning and removal software to clean the virus infection from the PC.

A bootable diskette cannot be created using an infected PC, only on a virus-free PC. Get a clean boot diskette from any non-infected Windows 98 PC. Computer retail stores often perform virus removal, so a PC can be taken there if necessary.

FPROT and other virus-removing software can be downloaded from the Internet or from AOL. In AOL, use the keyword virus, then go to the software libraries to find virus removal software.

If there is a clean boot diskette and the virus is a boot-sector-infecting virus, it may be removed by using FDISK. To remove boot sector viruses, fix the master boot record by using a clean DOS bootable diskette and running FDISK /MBR. It is far more effective to use the latest virus scanning and removal software.

Study Break: Virus Scanning

This study break exercise scans a PC for viruses.

Go to a Windows PC and install any popular virus scanning software. Get the trial version off the web sites or from AOL.

Create the DOS bootable diskette with the virus scanning software installed on it.

Make this diskette read-only by opening the hole in the upper left corner of the diskette.

Using this diskette, scan several office PCs by powering them off, then booting using the virus scanning diskette. Find any viruses?

The purpose of this exercise was to illustrate how to check for viruses using virus-scanning software installed on a diskette.

Summary

This chapter has examined common DOS and Windows software error messages and their cause. Steps to resolve the errors causing the common error messages were covered. Furthermore, other frequent Windows software problems were identified. Resolution of those software problems was presented. DOS and Windows diagnostic programs, problem prevention programs, and troubleshooting utilities were identified. Effective use of these programs was presented. The chapter concluded with a discussion of viruses, virus protection, and virus removal.

Chapter Review Questions

1. *GPF stands for what?*

    A. General program fault
    B. A type of Windows software error
    C. General processing format
    D. Gross program fault

Answer: B, a type of Windows software error. There are no program or processing faults. GPF is General Protection Fault.

2. *When a disk drive activity light is suddenly on continuously, what could cause the problem?*

    A. The diskette is upside down.
    B. The PC has halted.
    C. The PC is infected with a program-infecting virus.
    D. An illegal operation error has occurred.

Answer: C, The PC is infected with a program-infecting virus. Diskettes do not fit in upside down. When the disk activity light is on the PC is not necessarily halted or frozen. Illegal operations cause error messages to be displayed.

3. *To fix a frozen PC, you should:*

    A. Immediately power off the PC
    B. Run CHKDSK
    C. Exit Windows to the DOS prompt
    D. Hit Ctrl-Alt-Del to start the task manager and use it to stop the unresponsive application

Answer: D, hit Ctrl-Alt-Del to start the task manager and use it to stop the unresponsive application. Powering off resets a frozen PC, but this may cause more problems. Exiting Windows to the command prompt is not likely to be possible from a frozen PC. Running CHKDSK may not be possible and does nothing but check the disk drive for errors. Evoking the task manager and stopping the unresponsive application can return control of the PC and permit closing other programs and shutting it down.

4. *What maximum conventional memory should CHKDSK report?*

      A. 655,360 bytes
      B. 640K
      C. 1,024K
      D. 1,048,576 bytes

Answer: A, 655,360 bytes. Conventional memory is 640 KB or 655,360 bytes as reported by CHKDSK.

5. *What PC diagnostic program repairs fixed disk problems?*

      A. MSD
      B. CHKDSK /R
      C. SCANDISK
      D. MSINFO32

Answer: C, SCANDISK. CHKDSK /F does some fixed disk repair but it is not as thorough as SCANDISK. MSINFO32 and MSD report information on the PC but do not fix problems.

6. *Fixed disk hardware problems are identified using:*

      A. MSD
      B. The registry scanner
      C. FDISK
      D. CHKDSK

Answer: C, FDISK. When the fixed disk does not work, FDISK reports that it "cannot read from the fixed disk drive." CHKDSK only works after the PC boots and the fixed disk drive works. MSD and the registry scanner do not test the fixed disk drive.

7. *An illegal operation error is an invalid page fault.*

      A. TRUE
      B. FALSE

Answer: A, TRUE. An illegal operation error is a memory conflict error, like an invalid page fault.

8. *Viruses infect disk boot records, .COM programs, or .DOC files.*

      A. TRUE
      B. FALSE

Answer: A, TRUE. A virus may infect any or all of these.

9. *Windows startup problems dump Windows into what?*

    A. Virus scanning mode
    B. Normal diagnostic mode
    C. Safe mode
    D. None of the above

Answer: C, safe mode. There is not a Windows virus scanning mode, or a normal diagnostic mode. There is normal mode and safe mode.

10. *A "permanent swap file is corrupt" message means what?*

    A. Windows 98 has crashed
    B. The registry is corrupted
    C. Windows 3.1x cannot find the permanent swap file it expects
    D. None of the above

Answer: C, Windows 3.1x cannot find the permanent swap file it expects. This is not a serious error. Swap file errors have nothing to do with the registry and are not displayed for Windows 98.

11. *A missing operating system error is corrected by:*

    A. Running FDISK
    B. Reinstalling the application program
    C. Performing the SYS C: command from a bootable floppy
    D. All of the above

Answer: C, performing the SYS C: command from a bootable floppy. FDISK partitions the fixed disk but does not restore the operating system. Reinstalling an application has nothing to do with restoring the operating system.

12. *Viruses are always memory resident programs.*

    A. TRUE
    B. FALSE

Answer: B, FALSE. Some viruses may reside in files or email attachments. Although they need to run in memory to do their damage, they are not always memory resident.

13. *Virus programs can:*

    A. Destroy data
    B. Replicate themselves
    C. Hide as part of other programs
    D. Be attached to email
    E. All of the above
    F. None of the above

Answer: E, all of the above. Virus programs can destroy data, make copies of themselves to infect other files and computers, hide in other programs, and be attached to email.

14. *Stealth viruses:*

    A. Sometimes redirect disk drive writes to hide
    B. Misreport directory information to hide
    C. Are not memory-resident
    D. Are boot-sector-infecting viruses

Answer: B, misreport directory information to hide. Many viruses misdirect disk drive writes to hide and are not memory resident. Stealth viruses misreport directory information to hide.

15. *SCANDISK does not:*

    A. Fix disk FAT errors
    B. Scan the disk surface to detect hardware faults
    C. Help detect viruses
    D. Correct errors in the disk directory structure

Answer: C, help detect viruses. SCANDISK tests the FAT for errors, and scans the disk surface to detect hardware faults. SCANDISK does not detect viruses.

16. *ERU is what?*

    A. The Emergency Recycle Utility
    B. A program that backs up the fixed disk drive
    C. The Emergency Reuse Utility
    D. A program that backs up key Windows files including the registry
    E. None of the above

Answer: D, a program that backs up key Windows files including the registry. There are no reuse or recycle utilities. MSBACKUP or Windows 2000 backup (NTBACK-UP) make backup copies of fixed disk drive files and directories. ERU backs up the registry and key Windows files.

17. *What disk is used to COLD boot a PC?*

    A. Setup diskette
    B. System disk
    C. Diagnostic diskette
    D. Program diskette

Answer: B, system disk. Setup diskettes, diagnostic diskettes, and program diskettes may boot a PC but there is no guarantee. System diskettes always boot a PC.

Chapter 16

WINDOWS NETWORKING

Chapter Syllabus

- LAN Networking Functions

- LAN Types and Cards

- Configuring for Internet Access

This chapter examines networking with DOS and Windows. It presents an overview of LAN and Internet networking using Windows software. Networking is a key PC application; most PCs are used at one time or another to connect to the Internet, and it is the most frequently mentioned reason for purchasing a PC. LANs are an essential part of any business environment. They facilitate the sharing of information, collaboration on work, and email, making work activities more productive than they ever were in the past. Everyone handles the same amount of paper that they did five and ten years ago, but the amount of information assimilated, analyzed, and disseminated by any worker has grown to 10,000 times what it was just a few years ago. Networking facilitated this ten thousand-fold increase in information handling.

PC networking with Windows is focused in LANs and the Internet. LANs provide high-speed connections for sharing data and multimedia information. The Internet provides access to current information on any topic and a means to publish information on your special interests for anyone to find. Let's examine LAN and Internet networking using Windows software.

LAN Networking Functions

Windows 95/98/Me/NT/2000/XP provides all the required driver programs and network software to build a LAN. Two types of LANs are supported with the Windows software: peer-to-peer and client-server. Most LANs use both peer-to-peer software and client-server software. Peer-to-peer are simple LANs that permit all PCs to share their disk drives and printers with other networked computers. Security in peer-to-peer LANs is not foolproof. Client-server LANs have central servers that provide better overall security and network management capabilities. Both types of LANs provide disk and print sharing capabilities, meaning they permit access to their attached printers and their disk drives from other PCs attached to the LAN. Peer-to-peer LANs are administered at each PC sharing resources on the LAN, while client-server LANs are administered centrally at special primary domain controller (PDC) servers.

Disk Sharing

One of the reasons for having a LAN is that it allows a PC to share disk resources. Disk sharing occurs when a disk drive on a PC is shared with other users, or when a server has a shared disk resource for all authorized users, as in a client-server LAN.

Disk sharing does not mean that the entire disk is available for use; in fact, in most instances a very specific area of the disk is shared. Windows 95/98/Me support sharing disks and folders on fixed disk drives and Windows NT/2000/XP using NTFS support sharing folders and files. This is to help organize the people using a shared resource and provide some level of security. Having access to a disk or a server disk leaves a PC open to an attack from unscrupulous employees.

Depending on the type of LAN (peer-to-peer or client-server), there are different access controls. Peer-to-peer can only make a disk or directory read-only, full access, and full access password protected. With a client-server LAN, access at the user or group level can be set. This fine-tunes access by providing more access to those who need it and less to those who do not.

With Windows NT/2000/XP, there are other types of sharing that go beyond the common storage of a fixed disk. Windows NT/2000/XP can also combine free space on several disks into what appears to be a single logical unit called a *volume set*. Additionally, Windows NT/2000/XP creates logical units that are combinations of several disks, striping the data evenly across each. This is called a *stripe set* or *RAID set*. Each of these units may then be shared out to the network users or populace.

File Sharing

File sharing is a lot like disk sharing, except it is focused on a file. File sharing in definition may be very broad. For example, if access to a directory is allowed on a PC in a peer-to-peer network, users on the network are allowed to access those files. The access to the files may be read-only, but they do have access and thus it is considered file sharing. If using a Windows NT/2000/XP client-server network, in most cases, access permissions can be set individually for each file in the shared directory. File sharing is tricky to master. With a small network (five to ten users), file sharing and setting permissions is not too difficult. In these types of networks, users tend to be liberal with permissions because they can yell down the hall to see if someone is currently using a shared file. However, in a large network environment, users from all over a facility or the world may be using the shared file, and yelling down the hall does not accomplish much in this case except annoying your neighbors. So in larger networks, complex and carefully planned file sharing is necessary.

Print Sharing

Print sharing is the sharing of a print resource such as a printer or a document center device across the network. This print resource can be attached to any network PC, to a server on a network, or as a node on the network if it has its own NIC and IP address. The advantages are obvious—a good quality printer can be purchased and shared with everyone on the network instead of buying a printer for each person.

Sharing a printer is easy, but there can be some problems. The most common pitfall is that the correct software drivers are required on the PC in order to print to a printer across the network. This means that in most cases the driver software must be installed as if a new printer is being installed. If a Windows NT/2000/XP server is used for print sharing, then that server can load the drivers that the client PC needs for printing. What happens in this case is that when a PC goes to print, that PC downloads the driver from the Windows NT/2000/XP print server and installs it temporarily on the client PC to perform the print job.

Windows 95/98/Me and NT/2000/XP also allow setting printers out on a network as nodes. There are special jet direct drivers for HP printers that can be loaded on a Windows PC that allow administration and control of printers as though they were directly attached to a client PC.

Print sharing also can have an effect on the machine it is installed on. In order to handle the multiple requests made on the printer, the machine that the printer is attached to must allow some of its resources to be used in support of printing and have adequate disk space to hold a print queue. This can slow down the machine the printer is attached to when there are heavy printing loads.

Study Break: Identifying Peer-to-Peer and Client-Server LANs

This study break exercise determines what type of LAN you have using Windows 95/98/Me.

Use a Windows 98/Me PC attached to a LAN. Open the network neighborhood desktop icon. Windows should search for network PCs and should list some PCs and the entire network icon for a peer-to-peer network.

Double-click on entire network. This should open a window with some network names. These names are for workgroups of PCs or domains.

Double-click on the icons you can see. If the list of computers in the first screen pops up, it is the workgroup to which your PC belongs. The PC names displayed are PCs belonging to a peer-to-peer workgroup.

If a "domain is not accessible" error message says domain resources are unavailable, try the icon at least three more times. Sometimes it takes a while before Windows can find the information for the domain.

Once the domain information is found, Windows will display a list of the domain servers. These are PCs acting as servers in a client-server network.

Double-click on each PC identified to see what disk drives are shared and accessible.

Close all windows and right-click on the network neighborhood icon, then select the access control tab. What type of access control is set?

Share level access control is used for peer-to-peer networks while user level access control can be used for both client-server and peer-to-peer networks. Click on the cancel button.

This exercise illustrated how to determine the network configuration of a Windows 95/98/Me PC. It showed some of the setup options for both peer-to-peer and client-server networks.

LAN Types and Cards

Windows supports many different LAN types. In Chapter 8, "LANs and Communications," two network types were identified, Ethernet and Token Ring. These are the most common LAN boards used, but there are other network types that are supported as well.

By providing Windows with the ability to support multiple LAN types, Microsoft has an edge in the LAN market. Windows 95/98/Me is positioned to become the universal client, and is able to be used as a workstation operating system on any type of network. Windows NT/2000/XP server does the same thing in an attempt to become the universal server.

Part and parcel of this are the software protocols that are used and how the systems interact with others on the network. This section focuses on the NICs and examines the different types of cards that are supported. Each card's capabilities are also described.

Ethernet

Ethernet protocol and technology networks are the most common and widely installed networks. Created in the 1960s, Ethernet has used basically the same protocol since its inception. Ethernet protocols have been used in both *broadband* (analog transmission) and *baseband* (digital transmission) communications media. LAN transmission speeds for Ethernet-protocol-based LANs have varied as well, from 1 Mbps to 10 Gbps with typical speeds being 10 Mbps, 100 Mbps and 1 Gbps. This makes it very useful for many organizations.

True Ethernet is a standardized technology. The IEEE 802 committee sets standards for how Ethernet products operate. These standards include transmission speed specifications. For example, normal Ethernet communicates up to 10 Mbps, fast Ethernet communicates at speeds of 100 Mbps, and Gigabit Ethernet operates at speeds of 1 Gbps.

The standard also sets what data communications protocol the Ethernet PC board or NIC uses. Ethernet cards employ CSMA/CD, or *Carrier Sense Multiple Access with Collision Detection* protocol, to transfer data between one card and another across the LAN.

On Ethernet, any device can try to send data at any time. Each device, before it transmits, senses whether the line is idle and therefore available to be used. If the line is idle, the device begins to transmit its first frame. This works great except it is possible to have two devices sense idle on the line and transmit at the same time. If another device has tried to send at the same time, a collision occurs and the frames are discarded. To remove the potential for a second collision, each device then waits a random amount of time and retries until its transmission is sent successfully.

This protocol is only used with Ethernet cards, meaning that an Ethernet board cannot talk to any machines on a token ring network unless a protocol translation device is employed, since the token ring network uses a different protocol.

In order for the Ethernet card to access the network, the operating system of the machine must have the appropriate driver software installed. Windows 95/98/Me comes with almost all the driver support needed for any Ethernet card. If the correct drivers are not available before installing any NIC, go to the manufacturer's web site and download the driver. These drivers are usually in a zipped file containing the driver and an installation INF file to tell Windows plug-and-play software components how to configure the operating system and operating system registry settings during the install.

Windows 95 and 98 support approximately 76 different manufacturers' NICs. Windows Me, Windows 2000, and Windows XP no doubt support more. Each of these manufacturers has an average of about four different models of Ethernet cards. In other words, Windows supports a huge number of Ethernet cards, more than would be practical to list here. A complete list of the supported cards can be found on Microsoft's web site.

Some more notable cards supported are LinkSys and 3Com cards. These are very popular and in some cases are hardware designed into PC motherboards. Another popular board type was the NE2000 compatible board. This is found under the Novell/Anthem manufacturer listing when adding a NIC. This driver was significant in that it is a very universal driver, able to work on many Ethernet cards as an alternative driver to the one that comes specifically with the NIC. Most Ethernet NICs sold are certified to work with Windows so the NE2000 standard has diminished significantly in importance. See Figure 16-1.

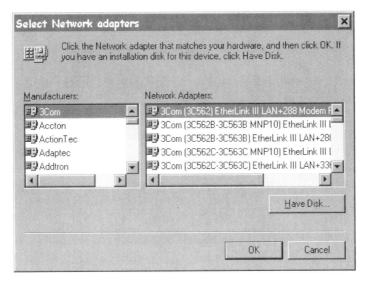

Figure 16–1
Windows Ethernet NIC support.

Token Ring

Token Ring networks are the second most popular networks in use today. The design and implementation is newer than Ethernet, and the data communications protocol is more sophisticated than Ethernet. Despite these characteristics, sales and usage is less than Ethernet due to the cost of equipment required.

Like Ethernet, the IEEE standardizes Token Ring technology. The 802.5 standard is the Token Ring standard. The largest developer and implementer of Token Ring networks is IBM with their IBM Token Ring network. Other technologies use token-passing protocols, although differently. Fiber Distributed Data Interface (FDDI) is an example of an older LAN technology using token-passing ring protocols similar in some ways to, but also different from, IBM token ring products. The IBM Token Ring uses a single ring and ring-repairing hubs, while FDDI employed dual counter rotating rings to provide similar ring self-healing capabilities.

Like today's Ethernet networks, Token Ring networks use baseband transmission. On a Token Ring network, all workstations are connected in a true ring (a star-wired topology) and a token-passing scheme similar to polling each terminal is used to prevent collision between two workstations that want to send messages at the same time (two PCs cannot transmit at the same time). In order to ensure there are no conflicts, empty information frames are continuously circulated on the ring. When a node wishes to transmit, it inserts a token in an empty frame (this is simply a change of a single bit in the frame from a 0 to a 1) and then puts the rest of the information including a destination identifier in the frame. Each successive node then views the frame. If the node recognizes that it is the destination for the message, it copies the message from the frame and changes the acknowledgement bits at the end of the frame to 1s. When the frame gets back to the sender, it changes the token to 0, meaning the frame is available to be used by another PC on the ring. The 1s in the acknowledgement bits at the end of the frame designate the message as copied and received. The node removes the message and the acknowledgement bits from the frame. The frame continues to circulate, ready to be taken by a node when it has a message to send.

Although Token Ring networks run at lower speeds than do new Ethernet networks and the Token Ring technology is moving into a smaller niche market, Token Ring drivers are supported by Windows 95/98/Me/2000. See Figure 16–2.

Asynchronous Transfer Mode (ATM)

Asynchronous Transfer Mode (ATM) is a new communications network technology for WANs and LANs that is being used predominantly by large organizations

Figure 16–2
Windows token ring NIC support.

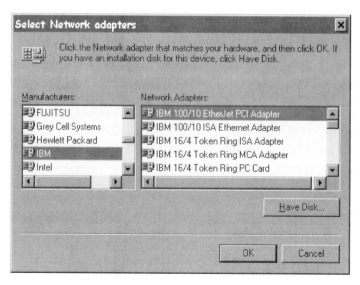

to combine voice, data, and video communication on the same communications network. In order to do this, high data rates are needed (25Mbps, 155Mbps, or greater) as well as the ability to rapidly switch traffic across virtual channels. Data, in and of itself, does not require huge bandwidth because it arrives in bursts. Voice and video, on the other hand, are very sensitive to timing and also hog a constant bandwidth. For that reason, to combine voice, video and data traffic, a technology that can dynamically handle all these types of traffic flows is needed. ATM promises to solve such networking problems.

ATM accomplishes the task of transmitting multiple types of transmissions by implementing a dedicated-connection switching technology to organize digital data into 53-byte cells or packets and transmitting them over a medium using digital signal technology. Each cell is processed asynchronously relative to other related cells and is queued before being multiplexed over the line.

This technology is mostly thought of as a wide area technology; however, it is being used more and more as both a local and wide area technology. The high-speed switching makes it ideal in very large/high data throughput LANs. Windows 98/Me does come with support for Adaptec and other ATM cards. Previous Windows versions would require the driver to be provided by the manufacturer of the card. See Figure 16–3.

Figure 16–3
Windows ATM NIC support.

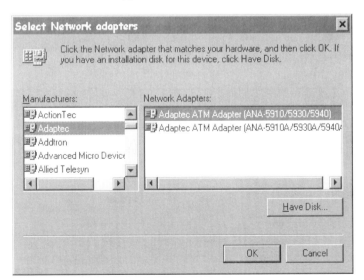

ARCnet

ARCnet is an obsolete network type that is only mentioned here to provide a historic context for Windows networking. It enjoyed popularity at one time because of its low cost. Although cheaper in its time than Ethernet and the Token Ring (nothing was more expensive than Token Ring NICs), ARCnet never gathered enough of a following to claim any dominance in the LAN market place.

ARCnet was a LAN technology from the Datapoint Corporation, the originator of the local area network. ARCnet used a token-bus scheme for managing line sharing among the various devices connected on the LAN. The server continuously circulates empty message frames on a bus (the wire that attaches to every device). When a device wants to send a message, it inserts a token into an empty frame and then inserts a message. When the destination device reads the message, it resets the token for reuse by the other devices. The technology was effective in moderate traffic since all devices are afforded the same opportunity to use the shared network.

ARCnet can use coaxial or fiber optic cable with lengths up to 2,000 feet per segment and a total network span of 20,000 feet. ARCnet's bandwidth or information flow capacity is from 2.5 MBPS to 20 MBPS. See Figure 16–4.

Figure 16–4
Windows ARCnet NIC support.

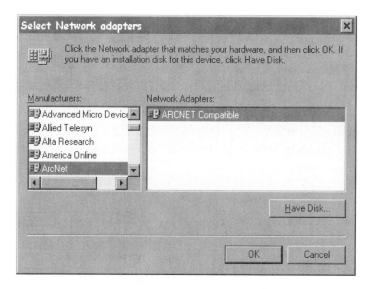

Study Break: NIC Cards

This exercise examines the LAN NIC cards installed in a Windows 95/98/Me PC. It also illustrates the types of NIC cards that Windows 98/Me supports.

1. Use a Windows 98/Me PC attached to a LAN. Right-click on the network neighborhood icon and select properties. Windows 95/98/Me should display a list of the client software, networking adapters (including LAN NICs), protocols (protocol stacks), and services installed. What type of NIC card is installed in this PC?
2. Double-click on the LAN NIC card. Does it use enhanced mode 32-bit drivers? Generally the NIC cards should use 32-bit drivers.
3. Click on bindings. What protocols is the NIC card bound to? Click on cancel to return to the network panel.
4. Click on add. Select adapter and click add again. After Windows builds a driver information base, scroll through the list of drivers. In Windows 98/Me, which manufacturers offer ATM drivers? There are at least Adaptec, Digital, Efficient Networks, and Olicom. Which type of network has the most support? Ethernet should. Which has the least? Our guess is ARCNet.

The goal of this exercise was to illustrate which NIC cards are widely used in PC networks.

Configuring for Internet Access

One of the most important aspects of networking PCs today is enabling them to connect to the Internet. Since Windows 3.11, TCP/IP has become a part of the Windows interface; this transport protocol and its configuration are critical for connecting to the Internet.

There are two main ways to connect to the Internet using Windows: through an ISP or through a dial-up connection via modem, or an internal LAN to the Internet. Each ISP provides the TCP/IP setup and configuration parameters needed for Windows, while the internal LAN involves careful configuration of the TCP/IP protocol bound to your PC's NIC card. The LAN administrator usually provides these settings for the specific PC.

Dial-Up Configuration

Dial-up networking is the process of using a modem to connect to and participate on a network. It is most commonly used today as a way to connect to the Internet, but can also be used to connect remotely to an office network.

Dial-up networking is an installable component under Windows 95/98/Me. Most machines have Windows dial-up networking software components installed when they arrive from the manufacturer. If by some chance a PC does not, then Windows dial-up networking components can easily be installed from the add/remove programs feature in the control panel. See Figure 16–5.

Once the software components are added, you can begin configuring a dial-up networking connection. Multiple connections can be set up if there are several different connection sites used. To start the process, go to the start menu button on the taskbar, follow the menus from program files to accessories and then to communications, where dial-up networking is now visible. Selecting it displays the screen shown in Figure 16–6.

Figure 16–5
Windows dial-up networking software support.

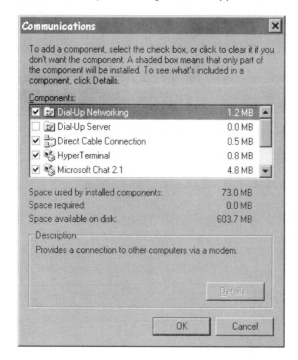

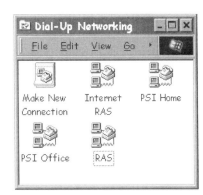

Figure 16–6
Dial-up networking box.

This window contains all the current dial-up networking configurations as well as the Make New Connection wizard. If no connections have been set up, start by double-clicking on the wizard to create a new connection.

Once the wizard is activated, setup is very easy. It asks you to name the connection—for instance, "My ISP". Doing that identifies each connection uniquely when there is more than one. On the same screen it asks for the device that is used to make the connection. Usually, since most machines contain a single modem, this is the only device. Last, it asks for the number to dial. Once the phone number is provided, the dial-up networking phone configuration is complete. A complete networking configuration requires a phone configuration and a network configuration.

To configure the networking side of a new connection, find it in the dial-up networking screen and click the right mouse button while pointing at it. A small pop-up menu appears. Choose properties and the box in Figure 16–7 appears.

This box configures all the network parameters that are required for a dial-up connection. Several tabs in this box are configured. In most cases, changes to the server type are all that is required. The dial-up networking configuration includes:

- **General**—The first tab, general, is used to configure the phone number as well as the modem. Modem settings may include things like memory buffering size, use of terminal screens for logging in, and adding any additional modem strings.

- **Server type**—Server type is used to configure the type of server connection used. Additionally, with the connection different types of logon encryption or security features can be set. A transport protocol is also chosen. If choosing TCP/IP, then there are additional settings to configure with parameters provided by the ISP. Generally with

TCP/IP settings, a fixed IP address is not set and a server-assigned IP address is used. Often the ISP has a specific name server. The name server or DNS provides the PC information that supports navigating from Internet site to Internet site.

- **Scripting**—Scripting is used to turn off any type of automated process or batch process during logon. This can be used for logon processes that require the user to input information.

- **Multi-link**—Multi-linking is a function whereby the PC can link more than one phone line and modem together in a communication. This requires that the site which the PC is connecting to can provide multi-link connections.

In almost all cases, the items under the tabs other than server types are accepted as defaults. Under the server tab there are a number of important choices to make. First, choose the connection type of the server this machine dials into. There are four choices: NRN (NetWare Connect), PPP (Point to

Figure 16–7
Dial-up network configuration box.

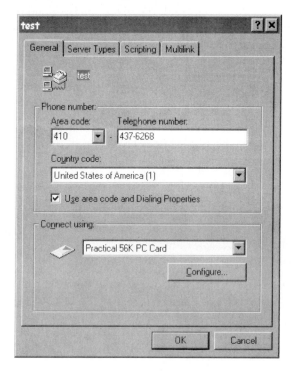

Point Protocol), SLIP (Serial Line Interface Protocol, used with UNIX servers), and Windows for Workgroups. The PPP connection type is the most often used; it can use all the different transport protocols (TCP/IP, IPX/SPX, NetBEUI).

Both IPX/SPX and NetBEUI require no special setup with dial-up networking. TCP/IP however, requires some configuration information. This information is obtained from the dial-up ISP. There are a few basic things needed for TCP/IP to work properly. These are:

- First, know whether or not the logon server assigns an IP address to the PC or if there is a pre-assigned address that must be input to the PC as a fixed IP address. Most dial-up providers use server-assigned IP addressing. If this is the case, the configuration job is easy. When configuring dial-up networking for a specific location, the properties ➤ server types ➤ TCP/IP settings may be left at the default settings when dial-up providers assign IP addresses. If not, then the ISP must provide an IP address and the "specify IP address" must be set with the exact IP address assigned by the dial-up service provider.

- Second, know the name server address assignment. Like the IP address, the dial-up server can assign the name server address. If not, a name server address that is provided by the dial-up ISP must be entered into Windows. For dial-up networking to configure a name server address, the properties ➤ server types ➤ TCP/IP settings are used. Similar to the IP address assignments, the name server address settings may be left at the default setting "server assigned name server address" when the dial-up provider's server assigns the name server addresses. Otherwise, the exact name server IP address must be specified using the "specify name server address selection." Entering the information requires clicking on the radio button and then entering the 4-number (for example, 208.80.68.10) IP address. The addresses use the numbers between 0 and 255 for each separate address number. Specifying these addresses correctly is crucial for being able to get onto the Internet.

For example, if a PC does not have a DNS assigned, domain lookup errors are displayed when the web browser is used and you may not be able to browse the web at all. If the dial-up service is connected to an office network, not having a WINS server defined prevents finding any of the other servers or peer-to-peer networked PCs on the LAN. See Figure 16–8. Other TCP/IP networking configuration settings are also discussed in Chapter 8 in the study break exercise "Viewing Windows 98 Network Configuration."

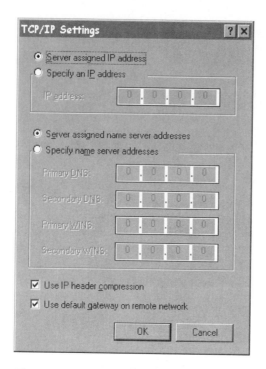

Figure 16–8
Dial-up TCP/IP configuration.

TCP/IP

If the connection to a network is not dial-up, the TCP/IP settings must be configured for the PC's NIC card. When a transport protocol is loaded on a PC, the protocol is bound (linked) automatically to all of the network adapters that are currently installed. Each separate adapter then has to be configured separately for TCP/IP to work properly. Each adapter must have unique TCP/IP settings that identify it on the TCP/IP network. Conflicting IP addresses cause conflicting devices to remove themselves from the LAN. See Figure 16–9.

If TCP/IP is not loaded on a Windows 95/98/Me PC, then this protocol must be added to the PC's current setup. To add it, simply open the Windows 95/98/Me network control panel item from within the control panel. When the network controls appear, select the add button, select protocols, and the TCP/IP protocol found under the Microsoft list of protocols. This adds and binds TCP/IP to all the adapters the Windows 95/98/Me PC uses for net-

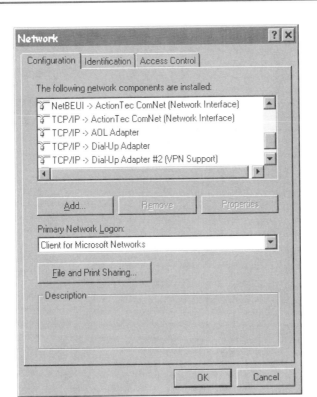

Figure 16–9
TCP/IP NIC configuration.

working. A similar procedure is used for adding the TCP/IP protocol to Windows 2000. See Figure 16–10.

To configure the TCP/IP settings for a specific adapter, simply select the TCP/IP binding from the list for that adapter and select the properties button. This brings up a TCP/IP properties box as shown in Figure 16–11.

There are several tabs in this configuration window. Only a few are really necessary, so do not become overwhelmed. Most selections remain as default selections. The LAN administrator usually assigns the information on your network needed to complete the PC's network configuration. Before we look at the primary items, let's look at what each tab is used for:

- **IP Address**—This is where a specific IP address is assigned to a PC. LAN administrators generally provide specific IP address assignments. If a specific IP address is not assigned, the network provides the PC an IP address from a DHCP logon server, using the Dynamic Host

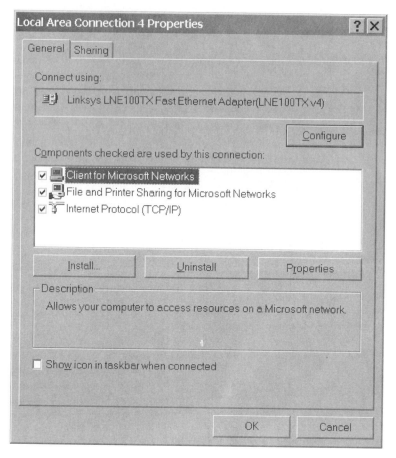

Figure 16–10
Windows 2000 LAN configuration.

Configuration Protocol (DHCP). The DHCP server is set up and managed by the network administrators. If the PC is on a Windows NT/2000 network, then a Windows NT/2000 server is very likely running DHCP. If the LAN has a Windows NT/2000 server using DHCP, then IP address configuration is easy. The DHCP server automatically sets up all the required fields in this configuration screen.

• **WINS Configuration**—The WINS is a server on a LAN that dynamically translates NETBIOS names into TCP/IP addresses. NETBIOS names identify the shared resources of the network. As an example, we have a drive we share called DRC. If a PC looks at a TCP/IP

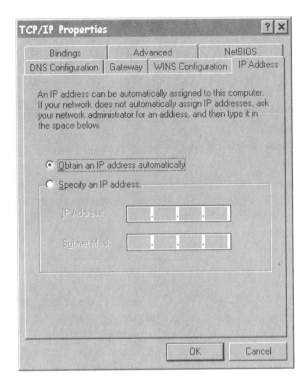

Figure 16–11
TCP/IP properties box.

address for a share named DRC, it has a hard time finding it unless
another machine tells it where to look. That is where WINS comes in.
If a Windows NT/2000/XP server is using DHCP, then this can be
automatically assigned, but if not, the TCP/IP address of the WINS
server must be provided and set as a parameter in the Windows
TCP/IP configuration.

• **Gateway**—The gateway or default gateway is the router that allows
communications outside a LAN. This can be a router internally to
other segments of the network, or a router out to the Internet.
Without a router, a PC is restricted to communicating on a single logical network segment and not on an internetwork of logical network
segments. We use a LinkSys cable modem/DSL router switch to connect all the computers on our internal network to the Internet.
Gateway IP addresses are low number IP addresses on a network like
nnn.nnn.nnn.1, nnn.nnn.nnn.2, and nnn.nnn.nnn.3.

1025

- **DNS Configuration**—DNS is a service that resolves domain names like dialanerd.com to a TCP/IP address. This, like the WINS server, can be assigned through the DHCP server. If a DNS server is not assigned, then the IP address of a DNS service must be entered in Windows. This is crucial for using an office intranet or the Internet. Without a DNS server, an Internet name like dialanerd.com is meaningless.

- **Bindings**—Bindings show the services and client types that the protocol is using. This should be bound to all client types and services automatically.

- **Advanced**—Advanced settings permit viewing any advanced setting selected. Additionally, TCP/IP can be selected to be the default protocol for this adapter. This makes TCP/IP the first protocol bound to the adapter, which can result in a minor increase in network performance for that specific PC.

- **NetBIOS**—This setting allows NetBIOS to piggyback itself across the TCP/IP protocol. This makes NetBIOS calls across TCP/IP possible.

Of all these parameter settings, the IP address and the default gateway settings are the most important. However, do not neglect to find out whether or not a DNS or a WINS server address is needed and available. In any large organization, the network system administrator usually has the detailed information required. When signing up with an ISP, they provide the necessary DNS and IP address setup information.

On our network, we prefer to use DHCP to set this up for the PC clients. We find it easier to input information once into the DHCP server and have it set this up for each machine as they log on. The Network administrator must set up the DHCP server before it can be used to automatically assign IP addresses. Some typical problems with DHCP servers are:

1. Placing standard network IP addresses in the scope (range of address numbers—208.80.68.0 to 208.80.68.255) of addresses administered by the DHCP server. For example, the 208.80.68.0 address designates the subnetwork and must not be included in the DHCP scope; or, if included, it must be identified as a pre-assigned address. This problem is fixed by identifying the standard network-assigned IP addresses as unavailable for dynamic DHCP assignment.

2. If the network, the servers and other special function PCs having fixed IP addresses are not properly identified and designated in the DHCP scope, the DHCP server thinks that it can use those

addresses for dynamic assignment. This causes conflicts in IP addresses on the network. This problem is fixed by identifying all servers and their fixed IP addresses as not available for dynamic DHCP assignment.

3. Having more PCs on a network than available IP addresses in the DHCP address range (scope). Shortening the IP address lease period may solve this problem. When a DHCP address is assigned to a PC at logon, it is leased from the DHCP server for a predetermined time. Making this time an hour can potentially free up IP addressees for reuse by other active PCs.

4. Having the DHCP server down when PCs are starting and attempting to log on to the network. Since the DHCP server is down, no IP addresses can be assigned and error-warning messages are issued the PCs as they logon to the network. The PCs may attempt to use old DHCP assigned addresses to communicate; whereas this may work, some PCs will be locked out of the network until the DHCP server is operational. These difficulties can be resolved by making the DHCP server very reliable or installing the NETBEUI nonroutable protocol stack on the networked PCs as well as TCP/IP. With the NETBEUI protocol stack installed, the networked PCs can perform some network communications, although the entire network's resources may not be available to them.

These are some potential problems and solutions using DHCP servers. The network administration personnel at the DHCP server implement most solutions.

The World Wide Web (WWW)

The World Wide Web is a standardized way of representing information in text and graphics linked together on computers. The World Wide Web is implemented by software running in computers connected to the Internet. The Internet is the planet-wide communications network using TCP/IP that interconnects WWW and other computers for the purpose of exchanging data, image, voice, and video information. The World Wide Web uses HTML and the HTTP to send information from WWW servers to client PCs running web browser software for display across TCP/IP-based networks.

The information is referenced through hyperlinks to other documents on the Web. The hyperlinks employ URLs to identify and connect to other computers on the Web. Special programs, called "browsers," such as Microsoft's Internet Explorer and Netscape's Navigator, are used to access the information on the Web.

Prior to the World Wide Web, information on the Internet was presented primarily in ASCII text. Such text information was searched using ARCHIE and VERONICA software. Some was set up in an indexed, more searchable form. One such form was called GOPHER space. However, the free form hypertext links of the World Wide Web have now become the dominant form for presenting information on the Internet.

Universal Resource Locators (URLs)

A URL is the text string that identifies the location of information (web pages) on the Internet. A typical URL is:

```
http://www.dialanerd.com.
```

Note that this URL jumps immediately to the Dial-A-Nerd web page. Use URLs to go directly to any information displayed on the Internet. Generally, web-browsing software jumps to the INDEX.HTML file at each web site.

HyperText Markup Language (HTML)

HTML is the ASCII text codes that are used by web browsing software to translate the plain text files with the embedded HTML markup into the interesting text and graphics displays presented on our client PCs.

An HTML view of text is shown in Figure 16–12.

HyperText Transfer Protocol (HTTP)

HTTP is the communications language used between Internet web servers and clients to exchange web page information. It makes it possible to reference or link to other pages of information on the Internet.

File Transfer Protocol (FTP)

File Transfer Protocol transfers text and binary files across the Internet. There are special standalone FTP programs and FTP software built into web browsers that make it easy to download software from across the Internet.

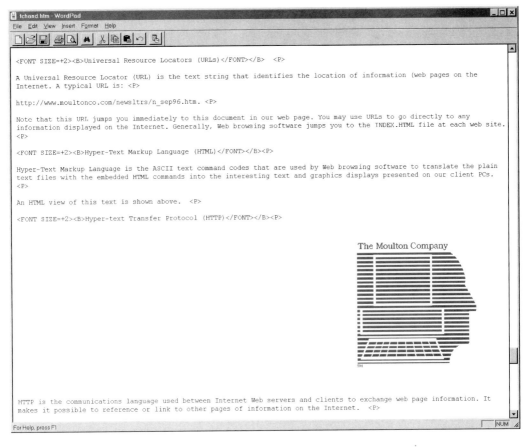

Figure 16–12
Raw HTML.

Domain Names (Web Site Designations)

Domain names are text representations of registered Internet IP addresses. For each domain, there is a specific registered IP address. Domain name servers (DNS) translate the text domain name into a routable IP address. Routers in the Internet to direct traffic between the PC client and the server supporting the domain name, then use the IP address. That server provides access to the domain's web site files.

A domain server is a PC system that runs a UNIX or a Windows NT operating system. Its disk drives house the files for the web sites that are for one

1029

domain or are part of a larger domain. For example, we have two domains running on one Internet domain server. They are MOULTONCO.COM and DIALANERD.COM. Each domain has a specific IP address. The moultonco.com IP address is 209.8.195.52, and the dialanerd.com IP address is 209.8.195.51. The kickoff file for each domain is index.html. This is the same as the kickoff file for any web site. When someone on the Internet accesses the index.html file using a web browser, the website-opening page is displayed on his or her web browser. (At one time they were routed to the MDConnect.net ISP's Windows NT or UNIX domain server from the MAE-East NAP through a feeder network.) The web browser software and the index.html files make our domain sites part of the World Wide Web (WWW). Web browser software does not present the detailed commands used to produce the web page displays; it only presents the web page display. A web site is comprised of linked HTML files on the server assigned to a domain name that has a registered (official) Internet IP address.

Domain names have extensions depending upon their use. Some current extensions are:

1. .GOV for government
2. .NET for network providers
3. .MIL for military organizations
4. .EDU for educational organizations and universities
5. .ORG for nonprofit organizations
6. .COM for commercial enterprises

New domain extensions have been planned for a while, but the U.S. Government has caused a delay in their release. Some of the planned high-level domain name extensions are:

1. .firm
2. .info
3. .shop
4. .arts
5. .rec
6. .nom
7. .web

These proposed new domain name extensions are to better identify the type of enterprise behind the domain.

Domain names make it easy for people to find web sites. It is much easier for us to identify and remember moultonco.com than it is to identify and remember 209.8.195.52. To assure that each domain name correlates with a single domain and IP address, domain names must be unique. No organization can share the same domain name.

This has produced some legal issues for people registering domain names that are commercial trademark names. In one case, the YAHOO-2000 name case, the person who originally registered the name was forced legally to give it up because YAHOO had established YAHOO as a trademark.

Internet Service Providers (ISPs)

An ISP is an organization offering access to the Internet for a fee. They may be a feeder network provider reselling high speed Internet access to smaller ISPs. The smaller ISPs in turn sell Internet access to individual Internet users. We purchase Internet access from MDconnect.net and AOL, which both offer access to the Internet. AOL provides nationwide service while Mdconnect.net is local to Baltimore, Maryland. Our web site information resides on MDconnect.net's Internet server.

In the Internet food chain, an Internet user sits at his office PC and connects through a dial-up line using a modem to his local ISP. Telephone company switching equipment routes his call to the ISP's server. Alternatively, a higher-speed cable modem or DSL connection may be used to connect to the local ISP. These connections differ from dial-up connections in that they are higher speed and continuously connected (24 hours a day 7 days a week). At the server, the web browser finds the files that comprise the web site. The Internet is literally thousands and thousands of these information pages located on ISP Server disk drives accessible to anyone connected to the Internet.

Email

A major application of networking and the Internet is email. Internet electronic mail is messages sent between systems, including PCs, connected to the Internet. Mail servers and gateways are used to deliver the mail to the addressed PCs.

Email today can contain text messages, binary images or pictures, or binary file attachments, such as programs and other data. Email has several different origins. There was:

1. Host-based
2. PC LAN-based
3. Internet-based, including:
   a. BITnet
   b. ARPAnet
   c. CompuServe
   d. MCI Mail

Early host-based email systems were PROFS and ALL-IN-ONE software packages that ran on IBM and DEC mainframe computers. PC LAN-based packages are Lotus Notes mail, cc:Mail, Word Perfect Office, and Microsoft mail, which run on PC LANs. Internet mail systems were supported by several types of mail software systems that ran on different mainframes, each with a specific audience, but interconnected in such a way that they form a cohesive mail system for all connected computers. For example, BITnet (Because It's Time net) provides email support for the academic community. ARPAnet (Advanced Research Projects Agency in the Department of Defense) is email for organizations performing Federal Government research and other work. MCI mail is a commercial service aimed at businesses.

In 1985 our early email experiences were with MCI mail and DEC. One time we were developing seminar notes for an Advanced Data Communications seminar with DEC. MCI mail was just starting and they laser printed their messages with four-hour delivery to the destination. We thought that it would make an impression and show that we were using the latest technology if we sent the new course notes to DEC via MCI mail. It cost only $0.33 per page to print the pages on their laser printers. Our notes were only about 300 pages, or about $100 to print the notes. The surcharge for four-hour delivery was only $25, (After spending the $100, what is an additional $25 for four hour delivery!) So we sent the notes via MCI mail. This meant that we needed to format the pages to 53 lines per page, and to make the drawings with "-", "=", and "+" characters. Once complete, we transmitted the notes at 1,200 BPS to MCI Mail.

Whenever employing new technology for the first time it is difficult to understand its practical limits. For example, we requested instant four-hour delivery, but it required more than four hours' transmission time to send the data to MCI mail. Also, there was no error correction, so every error required that we stop transmission and restart at a point prior to the error.

Once the message was received in its entirety by MCI mail, we rechecked the destination address by requesting it be played back (or so we believed) because it is bad to send a $125 message to an incorrect address. Nothing came back, so we reentered the destination address and requested another playback. Again nothing. The procedure was repeated with identical results, so we carefully entered the correct address and quickly sent the message before it was accidentally dropped into the electronic bit bucket. Then we played back the message that had been sent only to discover that we had transmitted four identical messages and spent $500!

When something like this happens, you quickly attempt to correct the mistake. We did so by immediately contacting MCI mail. They tried to cancel the message only to discover that it had overloaded their system (it wasn't designed to handle 300 page messages) and had to be purged. Consequently, we were not charged the $500.

Today virtually all ISPs provide email as part of Internet service. To set up a PC to use email, an email program like Microsoft Outlook (fondly called Microsoft LookOut by its users) is used. Outlook must be installed on the user's PC. Once installed, it is pointed to an email server such as a Microsoft Exchange server, which acts as the post office for email. Mail sent to the user is stored on it until the users log into the server and retrieve their email. Outlook manages the receipt and display of the messages. PCs that are used on AOL need no special software beyond the proprietary AOL software. Email is built into the standard AOL software, and uses AOL servers as the email post office.

There is no payment for email other than the fees paid for normal Internet access. Some Internet email services provide fee service with the proviso that the subscribers are subject to on-screen advertising while they send and retrieve email. Furthermore, email message formats are standardized to the point that any email system can exchange email with any other email system worldwide.

Study Break: HTML Documents

This exercise illustrates the formatting and display of HTML documents using Microsoft's Internet Explorer.

1. Use a Windows 98/Me PC attached to the Internet. Open Internet Explorer and open the http://www.moultonco.com/ web page.
2. Select view source. This shows the HTML tags added to text that creates the web page display on the browser. Similar commands are used in Netscape to edit web page source code. Sometimes the edit source command opens Microsoft Word. In that case you would need to view the HTML source to see the HTML tags added to the text.

3. Return to the IE menus and select view–Internet options (for IE4) or tools–Internet options (for IE5). This opens the setup and controls for the Internet Explorer. Select connections and view the dial-up and LAN connections for IE.

4. Click on LAN settings. If the PC connects to the Internet through a LAN, this shows whether a proxy server is used to route the network traffic to the Internet. A proxy server is a special server that represents a LAN to the Internet as a typically single IP address. It filters packets and routes them to the appropriate connected LAN that is browsing the World Wide Web.

5. Click on cancel, then on the security tab. What security level is set? The default for Windows in general is medium security for Internet access.

The goal of this exercise is to illustrate HTML code for web pages and to show some of the Microsoft Internet Explorer settings for connecting to the Internet using a LAN. There are similar settings for Netscape, but different menu selections are used to access them. We use IE as our example here; it is likely found on most Windows 95/98/Me PCs, whether it is used to access the Internet or not.

Summary

This chapter examined types and functions of LANs. Windows software supports both disk sharing and printer sharing for peer-to-peer and client-server network types. NIC driver software is provided with Windows for Ethernet, token ring and obsolete ARCnet cards. Newer ATM cards also have software support provided by Windows. The dominant NICs are likely to be Ethernet and ATM because they operate at high speeds and can handle newer voice and video data streams. Finally, the chapter discusses configuring PC and Windows for Internet access. This involves setting up Windows TCP/IP software for dial-up network and LAN Internet access.

Chapter Review Questions

1. *LAN stands for:*

    A. Limited Area Network
    B. Locally Arranged Network
    C. Limited Access Network
    D. Local Area Network

Answer: D, Local Area Network. There is no limited or arranged in any LAN.

2. *LANs can be what?*

    A. Peer-to-peer or client-server
    B. ARCnet
    C. Ethernet
    D. Token Ring
    E. Asynchronous Transfer Mode
    F. All of the above

Answer: F, all of the above. LAN software is client/server or peer-to-peer. There are obsolete ARCnet cards as well as Token Ring, Ethernet and ATM NICs.

3. *The oldest LAN technology is what?*

    A. Ethernet
    B. ATM
    C. Token Ring
    D. FDDI

Answer: A, Ethernet. Ethernet was first used in the early 1980s. The Token Ring first came out in 1987.

4. *Which LAN technologies are most likely to prevail in the next millennium?*

    A. Ethernet and ATM
    B. Ethernet and token ring
    C. ARCnet and token ring
    D. FDDI and token ring

Answer: A, Ethernet and ATM. ARCnet is obsolete and the Token Ring and FDDI are both either niche market LANs or quickly becoming obsolete. ATM is the principal competitor to Ethernet.

5. *What Windows software is needed for Internet access?*

    A. Special display drivers
    B. Communications software
    C. TCP/IP software components
    D. Dial-up networking software

Answer: C, TCP/IP software components. Display drivers are not needed to access communications and the Internet. Communications software and dial-up networking software are too general an answer. While they may be used to access the Internet, they are not necessarily required. TCP/IP software components however are a must for accessing the Internet.

6. *TCP means what?*

    A. Transmission Control Properties
    B. Transfer Control Protocol
    C. Transmission Centric Protocol
    D. Transmission Control Protocol

Answer: D, Transmission Control Protocol. Since we have three transmissions, transmission is a good guess for the first word. Centric and properties do not describe anything having to do with communications, leaving Transmission Control Protocol.

7. *CSMA/CD means what?*

    A. Collision Sense Multiple Access with Carrier Detection
    B. Carrier Sense Multiple Access with Common Detection
    C. Carrier Sense Multiple Account with Carrier Detection
    D. Carrier Sense Multiple Access with Collision Detection

Answer: D, Carrier Sense Multiple Access with Collision Detection. Three answers involving the phrase Carrier Sense makes that a good first choice. There are no multiple accounts or common detection in communications, leaving Carrier Sense Multiple Access with Collision Detection.

8. *Which network uses CSMA/CD?*

    A. Token Ring
    B. Ethernet
    C. ATM
    D. ARCnet
    E. FDDI

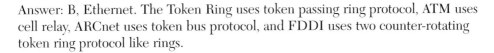

Answer: B, Ethernet. The Token Ring uses token passing ring protocol, ATM uses cell relay, ARCnet uses token bus protocol, and FDDI uses two counter-rotating token ring protocol like rings.

9. *Ethernet and Token Ring are:*

    A. Networking software
    B. Windows components
    C. NICs
    D. Wide area networking technologies

Answer: C, NICs. Ethernet and Token Ring are not networking software or Windows components (also software). They are LAN technologies implemented in NICs.

10. *Modems support:*

    A. LANs
    B. Voice communications
    C. Dial-up communications
    D. Access to AOL only

Answer: C, dial-up communications. A modem is a telephone for a computer supporting all dials up communications including access to AOL. Modems do not communicate across LANS or perform voice communications like a telephone.

11. *An ISP _____ .*

    A. Hosts web sites
    B. Provides email services
    C. Connects dial-up users to the Internet
    D. All of the above
    E. None of the above

Answer: D, all of the above. ISPs host web sites, provide email services, and connect dial-up users to the Internet. AOL provides these services so, in this sense, AOL is an ISP.

12. *HTTP means what?*

    A. HyperText Transmission Protocol
    B. HyperText Transfer Procedure
    C. Hyperlink-Text Transfer Protocol
    D. HyperText Transfer Protocol

Answer: D, HyperText Transfer Protocol. HyperText is in three answers so it is a good choice for the first part, similarly protocol is a good choice for the last term, and there is no procedure. HyperText Transfer Protocol is therefore the best answer choice.

13. *HTML is used to:*

      A. Transfer data across the Internet
      B. Install Windows Internet software
      C. Build web browsers
      D. Format web site files
      E. None of the above

Answer: D, format web site files. HTTP transfers the data, software installation is performed using installation Wizards, and building web browsers is done by creating software but not by HTML

14. *A URL is what?*

      A. A list of Web sites
      B. Used by TCP/IP
      C. A link to another web site
      D. Unique Resource Location

Answer: C, a link to another web site. A URL is no list, but there could be a list of URLs. TCP/IP does not directly use URLs, but Web browser software uses the URLs along with DNS servers to locate Web pages. While a URL is unique and specifies a location, it is a Universal Resource Locator.

15. *Domains can have* _____ .

      A. .COM and .GOV name extensions
      B. Unique IP addresses
      C. HTML files
      D. All of the above
      E. None of the above

Answer: D, all of the above. Some domains are .COM and .GOV along with .EDU and other extensions. Domains also have unique IP addresses, and use HTML files.

16. *Servers are:*

    A. Devices that route data
    B. PCs connecting LANs to the Internet
    C. Web site browsers
    D. Network diagnostic computers
    E. All of the above
    F. None of the above

Answer: F, none of the above. Servers do not route data or connect LANs to the Internet; routers and gateways perform those tasks. Servers are not web site browsers, but they can host a web site. Servers are not necessarily network diagnostic computers.

Chapter 17

CUSTOMER SATISFACTION

Chapter Syllabus

- Communicating with the Customer

- Understanding Customer Problem Descriptions

- Communicating at the Appropriate Technical Level

- Establishing Customer Rapport

- Professional Conduct

- Responding to and Closing Service Calls

- Handling Customer Complaints

- Empathy for Customer Problems

Although customer service is an important part of PC support, the objectives of the A+ exam have now focused more on the technical issues of PC support rather than on customer service. Consequently, when studying for the exam, it is more important to study the materials in the technical chapters; however, this in no way diminishes the importance of PC support personnel to empathetic and mannerly customer service. The good, hard-earned reputation of many an employer is quickly erased by rude, unmannerly, and arrogant PC support personnel. Practicing customer service techniques and manners is an important part of being an excellent PC support person. PC support personnel never know the latest technical information about any PC because it incessantly and rapidly changes. However, practicing customer service and satisfaction techniques and finding the solution to a customer's problem offsets any lack of technical knowledge.

This chapter deals with customer service and satisfaction issues. It covers personal interactions, professional conduct, projecting confidence and winning credibility, and keeping a perspective and sense of humor when solving customer problems. Getting reliable information from the customer and PC user is a key step in troubleshooting and resolving PC problems. Understanding customer needs and perspectives is also crucial when providing PC support. See Figure 17–1. When a customer's PC is not working properly, it often means that your customer cannot perform assigned tasks and productivity suffers.

Figure 17–1
Typical customer with PC problem.

Communicating with the Customer

Simply fixing a PC problem does not necessarily solve the customer's problem. For example, suppose a business owner had a problem with the FAX software on his Windows machine. A service person got the software to start and then placed it in the Windows\Programs\Startup folder so that it was launched each time the PC was started. This was not helpful to the customer; he only needed it on the desktop so that it could be reliably launched when he needed to fax. The customer spent a full day trying to figure out how to stop the fax from automatically launching when the PC was powered on. Having the fax software act reliably when he needed it to was vital to his international trade business. He lived or died by being able to fax to suppliers and customers. The service technician never understood the importance of faxing to the customer, and as a result misconfigured the fax software on the PC.

There are two primary forms of customer communication; face-to-face and telephone communications. Another form of customer communication is solving problems via email, as we have done as part of our broadcasts on radio and TV. However, solving problems via email is very difficult; because you never get all the facts or see the actual PC, there is a lot of reading between the lines. Answers usually start people down the path that reveals how to solve the problem, but may not directly correct the problem itself. Let's examine the other forms of customer communications.

Face-to-Face

The ability to communicate effectively with customers face to face is essential to solving problems efficiently. Accurate, complete information from the customer saves a great deal of time and makes each service call more productive. Factors that are unique in face-to-face communications are:

1. **Appearance**—The first impression that customers receive from service personnel is visual. A neat, well-groomed, professional appearance inspires confidence and helps to alleviate anxiety. Wrinkled clothes or scuffed shoes are not the mark of a competent professional.

2. **Demeanor**—Act calm. Customers will almost always be upset. To get clear and accurate information, they must be relaxed. Slow down the rate of your speech and speak at a lower, relaxed pitch. If a customer does not follow suit, ask them to slow down.

1043

3. **Eye contact**—Look at customers and maintain eye contact. This assures them you are listening and are just as concerned as they are with the problem. When customers have problems, they want undivided attention. This gives them confidence that their problem will be solved.

4. **Take notes**—It is impossible to remember every detail that a customer describes. Taking notes ensures that every bit of information available is at your disposal and reassures the customer that you are listening and understanding what they say.

5. **Explain everything**—Teaching the customer what happened and why prevents reoccurrence of the same problem. It also builds confidence in your solution and helps uncover additional troubleshooting information.

Following these five steps can greatly improve customer communications and help find the root cause of most PC problems.

Telephone Communications

Telephone communications are plagued by unique problems that are caused by being unable to physically see the customer and the customer's PC. Furthermore, the customer cannot see you, so the confidence-building visual demeanor cannot be conveyed. However, utilizing a few simple techniques can create an image of professionalism and competence. These techniques are:

1. **Project a professional image**—Speak clearly and distinctly. Observe the rules of proper grammar and express questions or comments in complete sentences. Avoid technical jargon, slang words, or phrases. Speak in descriptive terms and, if possible, analogies that are clearly understood rather than vague phrases or technical acronyms that may be misinterpreted. NEVER EAT OR DRINK WHILE SPEAKING WITH A CUSTOMER. Always be polite and smile when on the phone because a smile has a surprising effect on any presentation.

2. **Demeanor**—Remain calm, just as with a face-to-face conversation. The customer must be relaxed if you are going to get clear and accurate information. As with face-to-face communication, slow down the rate of speech and speak at a lower, relaxed pitch. When a customer does not follow suit, ask them to slow down.

3. **Clarify and confirm**—Frequently summarize what has been heard and ask the customer to confirm that they have been understood correctly. This step reassures customers that someone is listening and interested in their problem. This also ensures that any information received has not been misinterpreted.

4. **Take notes**—Take accurate and complete notes to preserve all the important details that have been expressed by the customer. Calling a customer back for clarification makes a service representative look much less knowledgeable and helpful.

5. **Explain everything**—As with face-to-face contact, explaining to a customer what happened and why prevents a problem from reoccurring. Explaining how and why a problem occurred helps uncover additional troubleshooting information and builds confidence in the problem solution.

Since telephone conversations cannot always directly fix PC hardware malfunctions, documenting the symptoms and verifying failures is critical to service personnel following up the call. Missing the root cause of the problem because you did not explore all symptoms with the customer on the telephone often results in a follow-up repair call by the field personnel. Following these five techniques improves customer telephone information and symptom gathering. Acting highly knowledgeable as opposed to being very interested in discovering new information can limit the effectiveness of telephone communications. The primary goal here is to discover all the symptoms and describe them accurately. Only then can the problem be solved.

Study Break: Communicating with the Customer

List three ways that you personally can improve your skills.

1. Think over your interaction with a PC user in the last month. What could you have done differently to make them feel less stressed?
2. What could you have done to cause them to laugh without making them feel they were the object of ridicule?

The goal here is to think of better ways to interact with the customer.

Understanding Customer Problem Descriptions

All service calls, whether in person or by telephone, start with a verbal description of the problem provided by a customer. This initial conversation provides valuable information if time is taken to understand the customer's description of the problem and symptoms.

The key technique to understanding your customer is active listening. Active listening is a technique which encourages your customer to "tell you all about it" while you guide the description in the most productive direction through the use of questions. (In psychology, this is called reflecting the other person's statements.) The following are the guidelines for active listening:

1. **Do not assume**—Many technicians instantly begin to diagnose a problem based on the limited description that is given when the service call is dispatched. They often fail to listen to added details given by customers. Listen objectively to the customer and then determine the best course of action to resolve or further diagnose the problem based on the facts.

2. **Don't interrupt**—Allow the customer to describe the problem completely without interruption. Most customers forget important details and become confused when repeatedly stopped to answer questions. Customers also appreciate courtesy. Courtesy and patience in handling customer communications increases their confidence in the technician's ability to help them solve their PC problem.

3. **Clarify with questions**—After hearing the complete problem description, ask questions to clarify the problem description or to verify your hypothesis as to the root source of the problem. These questions should require a yes or no or specifically detailed answer and should directly relate to the description. For example, if the customer says that a PC is running slowly, a question to ask is, "Does it run slow all day or only at just some specific times?" If the slowdown only occurs during peak activity on a network or the Internet, the problem could be excessive network traffic and have nothing to do with the PC hardware or software components. Ask, "Did you attempt this?" Or, "Did you try to…?"

4. **Summarize and confirm**—After you have completed questioning a customer, summarize the problem and obtain confirmation from

the customer that you have all of the details. It is very important that the customer confirms the understanding of the problem. If there is any discrepancy between the understanding and the customer description, repeat Step 3, clarify with questions. Ask, "Why is this important to them?" or "What is important to them?"

Active listening is a technique for extracting the maximum amount of information from the customer during the troubleshooting process. When performed properly, active listening helps to clarify what exactly is important to the customer and at the same time provides the essential clues to solving the problem.

Verbal and Nonverbal Cues

Being observant and attending to both verbal and nonverbal cues helps identify key troubleshooting information. People often provide valuable facts without even knowing that they are doing it. For example, if the user is running Windows 95 but keeps referring to the Explorer function as the file manager, he or she may be a new Windows 95 user who has not been properly trained on Windows 95. The problem may be operator error due to inadequate training. A great deal of time could be wasted investigating a hardware or system problem that doesn't exist.

Nonverbal cues can also be helpful. Problems that are caused by faulty hardware and not software glitches are indicated by overloaded power outlets; a lack of a surge protectors; poor ventilation; coffee stains on carpets or desks; lots of loose paper clips; excessive dust; dry conditions and wool carpets; and filled ash trays.

Helping with Problem Identification

Helping with problem identification is based upon postulating tests that verify problem symptoms and hypothesized solutions. Based on customer descriptions, suggest simple tests that can verify the problem description or solution. Does the difficulty happen repeatedly under the same set of circumstances or is it more intermittent? What patterns can you spot and verify? Which general area is the problem in—hardware, software, or network? Explain the "why" of each question to the customer to encourage them to further describe what happened and what changed in their system prior to this specific problem arising. One helpful thing to do is have the user walk you through the process, show you what causes the error, what steps are taken, and how the problem manifests itself.

Study Break: Understanding Customer Problem Descriptions

List three ways that you personally can improve your ability to zero in on PC problems when talking with a user.

1. Describe the symptoms of a typical customer problem to a friend or another student and see if they can identify the problem.
2. Do you think that your customers are better able to describe problems than you?

The goal here is to think of better ways to identify problems as described by customers.

Communicating at the Appropriate Technical Level

Customers are usually anxious to help by answering questions and giving a description of the problem. It is important, however, to recognize the level of technical knowledge and savvy of the customer. Asking questions that are beyond the capability of the customer to understand because they contain technical jargon wastes time, and embarrasses and angers customers. Communicating at a mismatched technical level can often provide inaccurate information that hinders problem resolution. If the contact is not capable of answering specific questions (e.g., the PC configuration description and installed options), use PC diagnostic tools to gain new insight into the problem, request assistance from another person, or perhaps contact the technical support person originally responding to the call.

When you find the appropriate contact, involve them in the process and be sure to recognize their knowledge and contribution to the solution. People, especially technical personnel, want to know that their knowledge is respected and appreciated. They are much more willing to assist resolving a PC problem if they receive credit for their efforts.

Study Break: Communicating at the Appropriate Technical Level

A customer is complaining of extremely slow performance and prolonged pauses in the operation of their PC.

1. List three questions you would ask the nontechnical user to try and diagnose the cause of the problem.
2. List three questions you would ask the support manager to try and diagnose the cause of the problem.

The goal here is to understand the difference in the way technical and non-technical people communicate.

Establishing Customer Rapport

Many people have an incorrect understanding of the concept of customer rapport and assume that they should become friends with their clients. Good customer rapport is established when a working relationship is developed which allows for the efficient delivery of service satisfying the needs of both the customer and the provider. Always remember that a relationship with a customer is based on their need for services and that nothing should interfere with the efficient resolution of their problems.

Ways to encourage good customer rapport include:

1. Learn the name and title of all contacts.
2. Determine the standards of service that a customer expects and then meet those standards.
3. Keep all promises.
4. Do not make promises contingent upon factors outside of your immediate control.
5. Keep customer contacts and other involved parties informed.
6. Periodically ask the customer if they are happy with the service and how the service might be made better.

Following these simple guidelines keeps customers and other parties involved in the service effort happy.

Study Break: Establishing Customer Rapport

Describe what you plan to do to establish good customer rapport.

1. What would you do to learn the name and title of all contacts?
2. What would you do to determine the standards of service?
3. What would you do to keep promises?
4. What would you do to not make promises contingent upon factors outside of your immediate control?
5. What would you do to keep customers informed?
6. How would you check on customer satisfaction?

The goal here is to explicitly identify tangible things that can be done to establish customer rapport.

Professional Conduct

Professional conduct is always associated with the best organizations in any industry. IBM set the standard for service in the data processing marketplace by insisting on professional conduct by everyone in the organization. This lesson was learned by H. Ross Perot when he founded and developed EDS to be the premier service organization in the U.S. During his tenure at EDS, all EDS employees worked in suits. This action set a standard for professional service and support conduct throughout the industry.

The following actions help set up recognition of the service person as a true professional.

1. Put your customer's interest first—A self-serving act may be profitable in the short term; however, an honest concern for the welfare of the client establishes and maintains a long and mutually rewarding relationship.

2. Maintain a neat appearance—Clothing should be neat and clean, shoes polished or brushed, and personal hygiene maintained. Clothes make the PC service person. Many companies have dispensed with neckties as part of the dress code for their service engineers and technicians; however, all clothing should be appropriate for a business environment.

1050

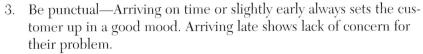

3. Be punctual—Arriving on time or slightly early always sets the customer up in a good mood. Arriving late shows lack of concern for their problem.

4. Be honest—State facts clearly and concisely and never exaggerate the good or bad aspects of a situation.

5. Respect your customer's time—Focus on the task at hand and do not spend excessive amounts of time socializing with customers or customer contacts; everyone has work to do, so do not waste their time and yours.

6. Never flirt with or make suggestive comments to customers or their employees.

7. Focus on the job at hand—Do not become involved in internal company politics or personal matters outside of the responsibilities as a service provider.

These actions can become habits. When they do, the service personnel practicing them look highly competent and professional.

Punctuality

Always be on time. Excessive lateness, or failing to arrive as promised, undoes all of the goodwill accumulated. When you know there will be a delayed arrival, call the customer and advise them of the arrival status. The customer can then decide whether to work with the late arrival or to reschedule the service call.

Late arrival without extraordinary circumstances implies that the customer's problem is unimportant. It may be less important to the service personnel, but it is critical to the customer because their business depends on PCs working properly.

Avoiding Conflicts

Computers are a critical component of almost all business operations. Any interruption of service is considered a major problem. It is inevitable that situations will escalate to a point of producing some conflict between the service person and the client. Many of these conflicts can be avoided if two rules are observed: (1) Stick to the facts, and (2) The customer has the final word (the "customer is always right" rule).

A clear understanding of all the facts is most important when there is a potential conflict. Most of us are good at getting details; however, in this situation, summarizing and confirming the customer's problem must be followed. If everyone can agree on the problem, it becomes much easier to agree on the solution. If there is a disagreement regarding the problem description, go back and revisit the questions and clarify the details before again trying to reach agreement on the problem description.

If a conflict remains after agreeing on the problem, it is probably due to a disagreement regarding the solution. All options should be explained completely to the customer, along with their implications. If it is appropriate, recommend a solution. But the customer determines the course of action. Their first choice may not be the technician's recommendation, but the customer makes the final decision. If the customer insists on a course of action that is inappropriate or impossible to deliver, explain the reasons why their wishes cannot be fulfilled. When the customer's wishes cannot be met, escalate the matter to management.

It is an unfortunate fact of life that "they cannot all be won." However, professional conduct is possible even in the worst conflicts. Always maintain a professional demeanor and never offend the customer. Clearly state the facts and offer the best possible solution. Never get caught up in emotional arguments or personal attacks. Finally, never agree to any detail or solution that is not correct, workable, and in the best interest of the customer. A customer may be unhappy with the turn of events, but they always in the long-term respect integrity and professionalism. Long-term respect is usually enough to earn a second or third chance when the next problem occurs.

Study Break: Professional Conduct

Describe the last encounter you had with a service technician or sales person who acted professionally.

1. Would you deal with them again?
2. How could you act more like them?
3. What did they do that made them seem professional?

The goal here is to determine what makes a service person appear professional.

Responding to and Closing Service Calls

When responding to a call, observe the following steps:

1. Determine the urgency of the situation if the dispatcher does not automatically volunteer that information.
2. Contact the customer in a timely fashion and advise them of the assignment to their call. Tell them when they should expect arrival at their site.
3. Be on time. Make sure that arrival at the site is within the time committed to the customer.
4. Upon arrival at the site, go directly to the contact and confirm the nature of the problem.

After you have identified the problem and implemented the repair, you should close out the call as follows:

1. Thoroughly test all repairs to make sure that the problem has been resolved.
2. Advise the customer of the successful completion of the call and explain the steps that were taken.
3. Obtain confirmation from the customer that the problem has been fixed and they are satisfied.
4. Call dispatch and advise them of the time of completion and your status.
5. If the problem cannot be resolved, advise the customer that further effort is required. Give them a clear description of why the problem cannot be fixed now and let them know when someone will return to complete the repair.

Study Break: Responding to and Closing Service Calls

List three mistakes that could be made when responding to a service call.

1. How could these mistakes be averted?
2. How could these mistakes be corrected?
3. Who is responsible for correcting the mistakes?
4. Who pays for correcting the mistakes?

The goal here is to determine how to avert and correct common mistakes.

Handling Customer Complaints

The process required for effective resolution of customer complaints may be summed up in five steps: maintain a professional demeanor, listen and empathize, clarify, repeat and confirm, and present a solution. Let's examine these steps in detail:

1.   Maintain a professional demeanor—Your customer is already upset; it is your job to instill confidence by speaking calmly and letting your customer know that they have your full attention by maintaining eye contact.

2.   Listen and empathize—Allow the customer to explain the problem their way and at their pace. It may be tedious to listen to nonessential details; however, an interruption may cause the customer to forget important information that you need. Frequently reassure the customer that their problem is important to you and empathize with them and the difficulties that they have encountered.

3.   Clarify—Ask specific questions to clarify details of the information that you are being given. Try to pick an appropriate time to ask clarification questions so as not to interrupt the customer. Take notes, as you cannot be expected to remember everything without writing it down.

4.   Repeat and confirm—Finally, summarize the facts as they have been told to you and solicit confirmation from the customer that you have an accurate understanding of their complaint.

5. Present a solution—Outline a plan of action that resolves the problem to the satisfaction of your customer. As always, make sure the customer verifies that they will be satisfied with your solution when it is implemented.

Handling complaints without anger goes a long way to building a long-term customer relationship. Remember, we all make mistakes. It is always the best policy to immediately admit the mistake, take responsibility for what was done and then determine a solution to rectify the problem that satisfies the customer within the limits of the business environment.

Study Break: Handling Customer Complaints

Describe the way you were treated the last time you filed a customer complaint.

1. Were you pleased with the outcome?
2. How could the person you talked to have done a better job?

The purpose of this exercise is to illustrate how to handle customer complaints.

Empathy for Customer Problems

When customers have a problem, they can often feel responsible in some way or that no one else is having such difficulties. It is important to let the customer know that their problem is understood and that their frustration is recognized. The customer now has a partner in finding a solution. One way to show empathy is to recount similar circumstances in which you were involved and how the problem was resolved or fixed. Expressing the frustration and other emotions involved in the troubleshooting and problem resolution process may help with customer empathy.

Be empathetic when a customer feels that they have caused the problem or are incapable of understanding the technical complexities of the situation. Assure them that computers and LANs are complex and that you have undergone extensive training to be able to provide support. Assure the customer that their contribution is important and that both of you are in this together.

Sense of Urgency

When a customer's system is down, their only desire is to have the problem solved and the system functional as quickly as possible. It is essential to demonstrate an understanding of their priorities and let the customer know that their urgency is shared. Demonstrate concern in the following ways:

1. Respond to the call quickly.
2. Be on time.
3. Get right to the point; do not waste time with idle conversation or funny comments.
4. Do not make jokes about the seriousness of the situation.
5. Keep the customer contact informed of progress as the problem is being solved.
6. Reassure the contact that everything possible is being done.
7. Where appropriate, request assistance to speed up the diagnosis and solution implementation.

Not every problem is an emergency, but solving a problem and moving on builds customer confidence and respect for the service personnel as technical professionals.

Flexibility

Rigidly following company policies when working on customer problems can result in conflicts. These conflicts can easily escalate into something that can be more costly than bending the rules to quickly solve a customer problem.

For example, customer-induced problems (such as not knowing that you have to turn on the power switch on the surge protector) are chargeable under the warranty period. Taking five minutes to educate the customer and waiving the charges of the call can assure you of a satisfied and loyal customer. On the other hand, repeated customer-induced errors cannot be forgiven due to the cost of this support.

Company policies are guidelines for conduct that should be followed when they make sense. However, they are written by managers that are probably not working and may not ever have worked in the field with customers. A customer never wants to hear the word "no." Bending rules to solve a problem that saves both the customer and the service organization money always makes more sense than following the rules exactly.

Study Break: Empathy for Customer Problems

List three ways to demonstrate empathy for the customer's problem.

1. How do these ways help the customer feel that you are empathetic?
2. How can this help solve the customer's problem?

The purpose of this exercise is to examine ways to be empathetic with a customer.

Summary

The service engineer or technician is the most important person in the relationship between the service organization and the customer. Their actions and words form the image of the service organization and are the only criteria that the customer has to assess the value of the service provided.

For example, accurately documenting service calls and keeping accurate records reassure the customer that you are providing them with the best possible support. This attention to detail and focus on the customer will make you a partner rather than a vendor. The professional technician that is perceived as honest, knowledgeable, and willing to put the customer first is always a valuable asset to any organization.

Chapter Review Questions

1. *Which of the following factors are part of good telephone communications?*

    A. Speaking clearly
    B. Frequently summarizing what you have been told
    C. Taking notes
    D. All of the above

Answer: D, all of the above.

2. *Active listening is a key technique for understanding customer problem descriptions. Which of the following best describes active listening?*

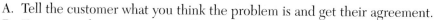

A. Tell the customer what you think the problem is and get their agreement.
B. Encourage the customer to "tell you all about it" while you guide the description in the most productive direction through the use of questions.
C. Ask closed-ended or descriptive questions.
D. Frequently summarize the description and get confirmation from the customer.

Answer: B, encourage the customer to "tell you all about it" while you guide the description in the most productive direction through the use of questions.

3. *An example of a verbal cue is what?*

A. Learning the contact's name and title.
B. The customer states that their PC is running slow.
C. Remain calm and speak at a slower speed.
D. The customer refers to Windows Explorer as the file manager.

Answer: D, the customer refers to Windows Explorer as the file manager.

4. *Which of the following statements regarding avoiding conflicts is false?*

A. All conflicts can be resolved to everyone's satisfaction.
B. Getting agreement on the nature of the problem can help avoid conflicts.
C. An unresolved disagreement does not always result in a lost customer.
D. There may be more than one solution to a problem.

Answer: A, all conflicts can be resolved to everyone's satisfaction.

5. *An example of a non-verbal cue is what?*

A. The computer fails to power up.
B. There are stains on the desk from spilled coffee.
C. The customer states that the fan in the PC is not running.
D. The problem is the result of a power failure.

Answer: B, there are stains on the desk from spilled coffee.

6. *Which of the following statements describe professional conduct?*

A. Maintain a neat appearance.
B. Be punctual.
C. Never flirt with, or make sexually suggestive comments to, your customer or their employees.
D. All of the above.

Answer: D, all of the above.

7. *Good customer rapport can best be described as:*

    A. The customer is always right.

    B. A good technician is the customer's best friend.

    C. A working relationship allowing efficient delivery of services that satisfies the needs of both the customer and the provider.

    D. A happy customer.

Answer: C, a working relationship allowing efficient delivery of services that satisfies the needs of both the customer and the provider.

8. *Which of the following is not one of the five steps for handling customer complaints?*

    A. Escalate the problem.

    B. Maintain a professional demeanor.

    C. Listen and empathize.

    D. Clarify.

    E. Repeat and confirm.

    F. Present a solution.

Answer: A, escalate the problem.

9. *Which of the following is not part of the process for understanding customer problem descriptions?*

    A. Do not assume.

    B. Do not interrupt.

    C. Clarify with questions.

    D. Present a solution.

Answer: D, present a solution.

10. *Why should you communicate at the appropriate technical level?*

    A. You may waste your time.

    B. You may embarrass or anger your customer.

    C. To avoid obtaining inaccurate information.

    D. All of the above.

Answer: D, all of the above.

Chapter 18

PC TALES

Chapter Syllabus

- Tools in a Pinch
- PC Repair Tales

If you have read this far, it is time to have some fun. This chapter concludes the book with some tales of what you can do to act like the TV hero MacGyver in a pinch and become a PC hero. You know the kind of tales we are referring to, the ones field engineers tell after they have had several beers around the campfire, burning a 286 PC. We will now look at PC tools in a pinch and some what-happens-when tales. You have gotten this far, so let's have some fun!

Tools in a Pinch

You are at a cocktail party and attacked by the host and asked to fix their home PC. You have no tools. When you are naked (without tools), what kind of tools can be employed to fix PCs in a pinch? Certainly Swiss Army knives are effective, but somewhat cumbersome PC repair tools! The multifunction pliers in a single unit tool works as well. However, we have from time to time found it necessary to use whatever was at hand to perform PC troubleshooting and repair tasks.

Our personal favorite tool is a Sears magnetic screwdriver—either the ratchet or nonratchet model works fine. They have multiple tips (or bits) that work on flat, cross-point, or Torx bolts. Once in a seminar we were asked if our Sears magnetic screwdriver caused any problems with the PC. We said no, it never had. And just to really drive home the concept we waved it across a running PC CPU chip and MLB components like a magic fairy wand. The PC continued to run. Next we waved it across the fixed disk drive. The PC continued to run as before. We entered the command DIR C: only to have the PC display "Sector not found." Oops! Since the metal casing around the disk drive was aluminum, it permitted the magnetic flux from the screwdriver to corrupt the data on the fixed disk drive.

Electric screwdrivers are also considered a gift from heaven because they make PC disassembly and reassembly much quicker and easier. Some other tools we have used are:

- Superglue
- Chewing gum
- Flashlight bulb and wire
- Old LEDs
- Lamp
- AM radio
- Finger—heat sensor
- Nose
- Floor
- Paper clips
- Other PC components

Superglue is good for repairing broken plastic parts in rental PCs. It holds them just long enough for the rental technicians to complete testing with the diagnostic programs. Once the plastic component is touched for a second time, it breaks again. By that time the equipment has been returned to the rental facility and no one can pinpoint where it was broken. Superglue is great for fixing broken MLB memory mounts and leaving no hint that they were ever broken.

Chewing gum is an excellent tool for repairing broken SIMM, DIMM, or RIMM mounts. It is flexible and moulds to just about any shape. When dry, it is harder than iron. Although the concept of memory held in place by chewing gum is somewhat gross, it works.

Most PC voltages are low voltages—3-volts, 5-volts, or 12-volts. Dangerous voltages are only inside the power supply. An effective tester for the presence of electrical power is a **flashlight bulb** soldered to two wires. This is used as a probe to test for the presence of low-voltage DC power. It can be used to test power supply output (5 volt and 12 volt) and other low-voltage power sources.

Similarly, an old **light-emitting diode (LED)** can also act as a voltage tester. LEDs only light up when current flows in one direction. This means that in order to perform a thorough test, the connecting wires must be tested by connecting contact A to contact B and then by connecting B to contact A.

Any old **lamp** can also verify that a PC is plugged into a live wall socket. There have been some occasions where a PC would not power on because the wall socket was dead, not the PC. It is always good to start troubleshooting by verifying that a facility has electrical power. It is most embarrassing to discover that lack of power is the source of a PC failure.

AM radios are good tools for finding high RF fields. When tuned to the bottom or top of the AM frequency band, they should make no noise because there are no stations broadcasting in those frequencies. Moving the AM radio close to a monitor, PC or any other electrical device causes it to emit from its speaker white noise static. Any place the radio produces white noise static has a high RF field that could cause the PC to malfunction.

An ancillary benefit of using the AM radio is that it makes for great nerd party entertainment. Just open the case on any PC. Power off the PC and place the AM radio on top of or next to the CPU chip. Next power up the PC and listen to the sounds the radio makes as the POST tests memory and loads the OS from the disk drives. You can almost tell just by listening what the PC is doing. OK, so this is a real nerdy party joke.

The **index finger** is also a good diagnostic tool. Generally, bad or failed components are shorted out internally and generate a lot of heat. By feeling the components on a board, the bad components or a bad board can be spotted. When one component is much hotter than the other components (chips), it indicates a failed component.

The **nose** can also be used to locate failed components. Burnt components have a cooked polyvinyl chloride smell. Just think of it as "the smell" because it is very distinctive and unforgettable. Components having "the smell" are likely failed components. They are easy to locate when you follow your nose.

A student once brought his luggable Compaq PC (an 8086 chip unit) to a seminar class to work on some exercises at night. When he checked in to the flight (on a crop duster plane) he asked the US Air people whether he should carry on his PC or check it as baggage. They of course (being helpful airline people) advised him to check it. When he was settled in the hotel the night before the seminar, he powered on the PC only to discover nothing happened. Soon he smelled "the smell" and knew something was drastically wrong. He was so panicked that he removed the outside plastic case from the Compaq using his bare hands (a feat of super human strength). Of course once the plastic was off, he could go no further without tools to open the metal chassis.

We disassembled the PC after the seminar was over and discovered that a memory expansion board had popped up in its connector and shorted the edge connector 5-volt power lead directly to the ground lead. This shut down the PC. It also heated up the circuit connection (or run) on the memory board, so much so that the gold plating melted off and the copper forming the connection lifted off the fiberglass. Once the memory board was removed from the PC, it worked just fine. If we had had super glue to reattach the copper edge connection to the fiberglass board, we could have probably fixed it as well.

The **floor** can sometimes be used to fix disk drives, which sometimes have their heads land on the disk surface and stick there. They stick to the surface with such force that the disk drive motor cannot rotate the disk. We have had this happen to at least four IDE drives. The solution is to hit the disk drives with a severe physical jolt.

We tried hitting them with a screwdriver handle without success. We then dropped them two feet to the floor. Our success rate was not outstanding; one drive was fixed and several others were destroyed (of course, they were not working anyway). The one that was repaired reported in a SCANDISK surface scan that a bad spot had developed on the surface of the disk drive. No kidding!

Paper clips are excellent gender menders for female-to-female connectors. They can also be used to create test plugs for COM port interfaces. A connection from pin 20 Data Terminal Ready (DTR) to pin 5 Clear to Send (CTS) changes the status of the port from disabled to enabled. Paper clips can also be used to eject stuck floppies and CDs, and can also substitute for a cable in a pinch. Once we had bid to set up the communications for a $10 million government contract. This involved PCs, terminals, and multiplexing equipment connected using RS-232 cables. To assure the RS-232 connections were made exactly so that the devices would communicate, we performed a pilot test, which involved going to a government facility one morning around 11:00 A.M. when we had to fly from Baltimore airport at 6:00 P.M. We brought all the RS-232 test equipment we could carry; cables, breakout boxes, modems, switch boxes, etc. At the site, we set up for the test with the multiplexing equipment, a terminal, an A-B switch, and a modem. The government personnel were all excited to see the new equipment they would soon work with in action.

We made all the needed connections to perform the test except one between the terminal and the A-B switch. When we went to make this final connection, we found that we needed to connect two 25-pin female RS-232 connectors. So two words came instantly to mind ... not the two words that pilots say just before they crash their plane, but rather Radio Shack.

Radio Shack has gender menders and other RS-232 components that can solve almost any RS-232 connection problem. But there was no way that we would be able to leave the facility, find a Radio Shack, get some stuff, return, perform the tests, and catch our plane at BWI at 6:00 P.M. So the next natural thought was ... you guessed it ... paper clips. We were given paper clips that we promptly straightened out and stuck between the two female connectors. However, the test still did not work. We noticed that some paper clips were touching other paper clips, creating undesired connections. So insulation was needed. We thought paper would do and requested some. A pad of yellow paper was produced which we immediately tore into strips and placed between the paper clips.

Just envision what these poor government workers are saying now. Another low bid job. We appeared to be just like the person in Central Park NYC that was observed crumpling up paper and flattening the paper out again. When asked by a passerby what they were doing, the reply was keeping away tigers and elephants. When the passerby informed them that there were no loose tigers or elephants around, they replied "Effective, isn't it?"

In spite of our effort to insulate with the paper, the test still did not work. So the next step was to disassemble the terminal and examine the inside for any glitches or deliberate traps set by the previous contractor. We powered off and disassembled the terminal only to find no obvious problems. At this point we believed that we had failed with our paper clips. So we reassembled the terminal and were about to pack up our equipment and reschedule the test, when we noticed that **it worked**! We asked ourselves later "What did we do to make it work?" After some intensive reflection we remembered that when the terminal was disassembled and reassembled it had been powered off. Powering the terminal off reset the RS-232 configuration and permitted our paper clip cable to work. Always remember when troubleshooting that the best starting point for any test is from the powered off position.

Other and old **PC components** act as the best test equipment. The old boards that seem useless can effectively help diagnose a variety of problems. Old video boards can as a temporary fix replace nonfunctioning boards to pinpoint a video problem. External modems with lights act as COM port testers. Old Adaptec SCSI controllers with their CTRL-A SCSI select ROM utility make excellent SCSI bus and drive testers. Just remember that anything can act as a tool for testing and repairing PCs.

PC Repair Tales, or What Happens When...?

We treat most PCs with respect, but there have been those few occasions when frustration outweighed common sense and we have treated a PC badly. Liquids and magnets bring to mind some stories.

PCs and Liquids

In our first PC repair seminars (back in the days when Apple outsold IBM) we were lecturing on PC maintenance for the American Management Association. One of the students, Leo, 65 and owner of a foundry, was very excited because he had something to contribute to the lecture. We called on him for his contribution. He related that about once a month on Friday night he would remove all the boards from his PC system (an 8-bit rack-mount computer, at that) and carry them home. At home he would run a sink full of the hottest water he could stand and put in some Woolite. Next he washed off all his boards.

About that time we were thinking, "Oh, this was a good idea."

But he continued to report that he then placed the boards into a 200-degree oven to heat and dry them. Then, on Monday morning, he placed the cleaned boards back into the PC. He had been repeating this process for some time. Of the steps above, heating the boards to 200 degrees is definitely not recommended. Any dry air will dry out wet components sufficiently.

He started this process because the foundry air was full of dust that contained metallic particles. Eventually the build-up of metallic particle dust on the PC's circuit boards shorted out the electrical connections and caused the PC to fail. By cleaning the boards periodically, the failures were averted. However, he could have used some safer cleaning solution designed for electronics as opposed to washing the boards.

When should boards in a PC be washed? When the PC has been in a flood.

At a training conference we did a PC troubleshooting presentation. In the presentation, the plan was to disassemble and then reassemble a PC to illustrate how easy PC repair could be performed. The sacrificial PC in this case was a new IBM PS/2. It was not a 1987 PS/2 but a non-MCA (Micro Channel Architecture) version. Unfortunately for us, in order to disassemble this PS/2, a bolt holding the floppy disk drive had to be removed, and the stubborn bolt would not come loose. It was as though IBM knew and had super-glued the bolt to the chassis. Being trainers, the attendees were not tolerant of presentation miscues. Soon eggs, tomatoes and other vegetables were flying from the audience up to the speaker's platform. There was no disassembling the PC so we removed the RAM SIMMs and used them for swizzle sticks in a glass of water. We were so frustrated at that point that we used both ends of the SIMM to make sure it was thoroughly wet. We then returned the SIMMs to the PS/2, powered it on and **it worked**!

Similar to our first TV appearance—we wanted to make a splash so we used the PC on a block of wood in the basement, as shown in Figure 18–1.

It is always good to have a block of wood PC in the basement just in case. At any rate, the TV shot setup was to have us washing a PC board off in the basement bathroom sink, place the wet board into the block of wood brand PC, then power it on to show that it worked OK. We ran a test prior to the show using the video board only to discover that the wet board produced no video. It required several hours of drying before the display again operated properly. We then used a serial port board that worked just fine. The TV shot went as planned.

For this revision of the book, we upgraded the block of wood PC from the original 486 MLB with an accelerator chip to a true Pentium CPU PC. It still runs Windows 3.1 and is connected to both Novell Netware and Windows NT servers. See Figure 18–2.

Figure 18–1
Block of wood PC.

Figure 18-2
Block of wood PC upgraded to true Pentium CPU.

PCs and Magnets

Our other favorite PC abuser is a magnet. This can result in all kinds of fun things. Try placing a powerful magnet in the center of a high-resolution monitor. It makes all kinds of strange colors and patterns (yes, they do eventually return to normal operation). Several degaussing procedures may be needed to return the display to normal.

Bad Power

It is often possible to misconnect the power connections into a PC. On at least one occasion we have switched the MLB P8 and P9 connectors. The operating rule there is that the black (ground) wires go side by side. This just caused the PC not to work. Fortunately nothing was damaged or rendered inoperable. We have on other occasions misconnected power to the MLB and haven't caused any damage yet.

In almost all instances, the PC just would not start. There was no display. Once we misconnected the power connector on a 3.5-inch floppy drive. Just a single pin to the right or left and the 5-volt power is connected directly to the PC ground. This caused the PC to not start when a second before it had started. We kept turning it on and then off, attempting to find the source of the problem. When nothing could be found, we just turned it on and left it on until ... smoke came out the top. The power supply did not have an automatic overload feature so it just kept providing power and heating up the power cable to the floppy drive. When the cable reached the correct temperature, the insulation began to smoke and catch fire. We then found the problem.

Impact

There are many tales we can relate about PCs and physical shock. One customer told us he had a PC that fell off the back of a truck. We thought that this PC may have been delivered at night by friends one does not mention to the police, but it really had been dropped off the back of a truck. The chassis of this Panasonic 386 SX PC was all dented. When we opened it up to see if we could make it run, we found the disk drive had some rails along the outside that were bow legged (like a cowboy that has ridden a horse for a month straight). When the PC was powered on, strange noises came from the disk drive and DOS did not see it. So we replaced it and the PC worked. Of course the case was dented beyond belief. There was no chance of someone stealing it because it was such an ugly computer.

PCs and X-Rays

The one question that most travelers have is, do I pass my machine through the x-ray machine or do I endure the strip search at the airport? For years, back in the early '80s when portable PCs were luggable Compaq suitcases, we passed our PC around x-rays. Of course, those bulky Compaq PCs would not have fit through most x-ray machines anyway. This lasted until the Compaq III machines. Then in one seminar we met a student that carried information around on removable fixed disk drives (for security purposes) and always passed them through the x-ray machine. So we thought, why not? and haven't been strip-searched since. The x-ray machines have never caused a problem with any of our PCs. Many airports, including San Francisco International in the heart of the Silicon Valley, now ask you to turn on your computer even if you send it through the x-ray. This is an interesting problem as the emissions from the drive belt motors on the x-ray machines can actually do potentially more harm than the x-rays themselves.

Study Break: Mission Accomplished

If you have arrived at this point, you definitely have earned a reward. This goal of this exercise is to have some fun and exchange a tale or two.

1. The tale: A digital field service engineer in the '60s assigned to servicing the first PDP-11 computers got a call from a university research lab to repair their PDP-11. The field service engineer arrived at the university lab around lunchtime, so no one was there. He found what appeared to be the PDP-11 and ran a memory diagnostic. Unknown to him at the time was that the lab was performing behavior research on animals. The PDP-11 computer he tested was attached to electrodes installed in a monkey's brain. Needless to say the monkey's brain did not pass the memory diagnostic, nor did the monkey for that matter. This is certainly a sick but true tale.
2. Do you have any fun PC stories? We would like to hear them. Send them along to *help@dialanerd.com* along with your snail mail address. In exchange we will send you an official DialANerd pocket protector.

The goal of this exercise is to have some fun and reward those dedicated readers who have read this far.

Summary

This chapter finally allowed us to have some fun. It listed the "unofficial tools" you need for a PC repair kit and looked at some PC repair tales describing what happens when... If you have read this far, we hope you enjoyed the tales: remember, the truth is always better than fiction.

Chapter Review Questions

1. *X-ray machines:*

     A. Destroy data on PC disk drives
     B. Erase diskettes
     C. Have no impact on PCs
     D. Destroy PC CPU chips

   Answer: C, have no impact on PCs. We used to avoid them and endure the airport strip search, but no more. For the last ten years our PCs have passed through x-ray machines in every major airport.

2. *When would you use water to clean a PC?*

     A. When it gets dusty
     B. When the power is turned off
     C. When it has been in a flood
     D. Once a month

   Answer: C, when it has been in a flood. You may certainly use water to clean a PC at any time, but there are much better cleaning techniques and solvents than water. However, if the PC is already wet and full of mud, then why not use water to clean it? Come to think of it, a power washer would probably get it really clean.

INDEX

E

T

V

W